NHS Law and Practice

Available as an eBook at www.lag.org.uk

LAG eBook

The purpose of Legal Action Group is to promote equal access to justice for all members of society who are socially, economically or otherwise disadvantaged. To this end, it seeks to improve law and practice, the administration of justice and legal services.

NHS Law and Practice

David Lock QC and Hannah Gibbs

with Samantha Broadfoot QC, Fiona Scolding QC, Andrew Byass, Richard Clarke, Ben Fullbrook, Alistair Mills and James Neill of Landmark Chambers

Legal Action Group
2018

This edition published in Great Britain 2018
by LAG Education and Service Trust Limited
National Pro Bono Centre, 48 Chancery Lane, London WC2A 1JF
www.lag.org.uk

British Library Cataloguing in Publication Data
a CIP catalogue record for this book is available from the British Library.

This book has been produced using Forest Stewardship Council (FSC) certified paper. The wood used to produce FSC certified products with a 'Mixed Sources' label comes from FSC certified well-managed forests, controlled sources and/or recycled material.

FSC www.fsc.org MIX Paper from responsible sources FSC® C020438

print ISBN 978 1 912273 06 5
ebook ISBN 978 1 912273 07 2

Typeset by Refinecatch Limited, Bungay, Suffolk
Printed by Hobbs the Printers, Totton, Hampshire

With love and thanks to Bernie, Becky, Ant, Pippa, Joe, Julie, Mike, Edward and Sheila.

Foreword

by Sir James Munby, President of the Family Division

Yet again we are immensely indebted to the Legal Action Group. Its latest publication – I hesitate to use the word Handbook for such a necessarily lengthy volume – more than lives up to the well-deserved reputation of its various eminent predecessors.

Even more are we indebted to David Lock QC and Hannah Gibbs and the impressive team they have gathered around them for the enormous labour that must have gone into the preparation of *NHS Law and Practice*. It is truly a ground-breaking book. Although our shelves groan under the ever-growing weight of the ever-increasing number of books on medical law and related topics, there has until now been nothing remotely comparable to this book or focusing on the very important topics with which *NHS Law and Practice* is concerned. And never has the need for such a book been greater than today.

This is a book which will be invaluable to the legal practitioner or judge, whether they be experienced or not in this particular area of the law. Not least it will be invaluable in providing the definitive answer, together with the relevant 'chapter and verse', for those embroiled in one of those many areas of legal endeavour where understanding the role of the NHS may be crucial even if it arises as a more or less peripheral issue. And I suspect that this book will be an invaluable companion and guide for many within the NHS.

No-one, within or outside the NHS, who needs to understand the legal structures and frameworks within which the NHS operates can afford to be without *NHS Law and Practice*.

That the book is so long and the treatment so detailed is no criticism of the authors – far from it – but rather the inevitable reflection of the vast complexity of a topic to which they have brought great understanding and exemplary clarity.

James Munby
2 May 2018

Preface

The NHS is perhaps the most important public service provided by the British state. It may also be the most loved public service, and politicians mess with the NHS at their peril. However, there is no such thing as 'the NHS'. The National Health Service comprises a complex network of commissioners of NHS services, providers of services to NHS patients and regulators. The secretary of state sits at the apex of the NHS pyramid, even though he or she now has substantial limitations on his or her ability to influence the day to day functioning of NHS services. Those limitations exist in law but do not prevent the secretary of state having considerable influence on how the NHS operates.

Today, particularly after the Health and Social Care Act 2012, the NHS operates (or ought to operate) as a complex, regulated 'managed market'. Our aim in writing this book has been to attempt to set out the rules under which the NHS managed market is required by law to operate and, in particular, how patients can enforce their rights to the treatment they have a legal right to access.

It is astonishing, in one sense, that there is no existing textbook to explain how the legal rules of the NHS operate. There is no single text which tried to explain how a series of public bodies should spend over £120 billion per year of public money. However, very soon after we started grappling with the myriad of different statutory schemes, we came to understand why no-one had completed a book on the law of the NHS. The rules which bind NHS commissioners and providers of NHS services are not easily accessible and, in parts, are of such Byzantine complexity that they are impenetrable even for specialist lawyers. By way of example, the secretary of state is entitled to issue directions to some NHS bodies but there is no published list of the directions that are in force at any time.

We seriously wonder how either the Department of Health and Social Care or NHS England could possibly expect NHS managers and patients to be able to navigate their way around one of the most complex legal frameworks we have ever come across. Indeed, such are the complexities that it is not uncommon for guidance to NHS bodies to recommend that NHS staff work in ways that are clearly contrary to their legal duties. Ensuring that public bodies comply with their legal obligations ought to be treated as a matter of considerable importance for all public bodies, including NHS organisations. This book will, we hope, act as a guide through the NHS maze but we cannot, for example, pretend that the Responsible Commissioner rules are either straightforward or coherent.

There is one thing about which we can be totally confident. Our first attempt at describing the law of the NHS will contain both errors and omissions. We take full responsibility for both, but ask our readers to bear with us. Please take the time to contact us to point out any errors or omissions. We will make every effort to correct them in later editions.

We would like to thank Lord Justice Munby for his kind and supportive words in the foreword. We particularly value his endorsement because he has taken a strong interest in medical law throughout his long and distinguished career both as a barrister and as a judge and has crafted so much of the jurisprudence that underpins the legal reasoning we attempt to describe in this book.

Any book like this is a collective effort. As editors, we would like to express huge thanks to our colleagues at Landmark Chambers who have applied their expertise in writing chapters. We are indebted to Sam Broadfoot QC, Fiona Scolding QC, Alistair Mills, Richard Clarke, James Neill, Andrew Byass and Ben Fullbrook. We state where chapters have been written by our colleagues, all other chapters are written by David and Hannah.

We would also like to thank our clerks who have supported us in ways that only barristers understand. We are grateful to Jay Fullilove, Neil Perry, Ben Connor, Richard Bolton, Matt Dowdall, and, in David's case, Andy Bisbey. Each of you has helped us more times than we care to remember. We value your experience, wisdom, patience, good humour and constant attention to detail.

There are many people who have read chapters in draft, provided input and comment and ensured that errors are removed and misunderstandings are resolved or have provided helpful comments on early versions of the text. We are also grateful to solicitors who have instructed us over the years, opponents and judges, all of whom have focused our minds on the complexities of the law of the NHS and helped us to improve our understanding as to how the rules operate. The NHS is such a strange world that some, particularly senior people who work for NHS bodies, who have provided valuable assistance to us feel they have to remain nameless for fear that they will be associated with anything we have written which is critical of the Department or NHS England. They know who they are and we are grateful to each of them. Those who can be named include Professor Emily Jackson, Professor Chris Newdick, Ben Troke, Jill Mason, Jill Weston, Simon Taylor, Jane Williams, Richard Stein, Rosa Curling, Zoë Leventhal, Merry Varney, Jenni Richards QC, Eleanor Grey QC, Oliver Wright, Andrea James, David Blundell, Steve Knafler QC, Stephen Pearson, Nageena Khalique QC, James Maurici QC, Helen Holmes, Adit and Archie Jain and many, many more.

A book does not come together without an editor and we have had the pleasure of working with one of the best. Many thanks to Esther Pilger and the team at LAG for allowing us to breach every deadline we ever signed up to, and never requiring us to seek relief from sanctions.

Finally, we have to extend thanks to our families. Writing a 1000-page book has taken up too much family time over the last five years. David is indebted to Dr Bernie Gregory for her constant support, forever patiently putting him right on medical terminology and always keeping his feet firmly on the ground. His children Becky, Anthony and Pippa will be grateful to know that 'the book' is finally not taking up family time (until the next edition comes around).

'The book' likely has a similar resonance for Hannah's family and the myriad of others who have supported her. Many a day has been spent getting lost down the rabbit hole of NHS publications and guidance (and they are numerous!). As a very junior barrister, this was always going to be an ambitious project to take on, but it was made possible by the unfaltering support, guidance and, particularly, patience of David, from whom she has learnt so much during the course of writing and in general. She would also like to thank those who have mentored and supported her, including Nathalie Lieven QC, Camilla Lamont, Rob Walton, Galina Ward, Carine Patry, Sasha Blackmore and Richard Bolton. Finally, she thanks Joe (to whom she has an IOU in proof reading), Julie, Mike, Sheila and Edward, and bitterly regrets that her grandfather, Michael, who would have been so proud, is not here to see this.

David Lock QC and Hannah Gibbs
Landmark Chambers
London
April 2018

Authors

David Lock QC was called to the Bar in 1985 and made a QC in 2011. He has appeared in the Supreme Court, the Court of Appeal, the High Court, the county court, the Court of Protection, has drafted parliamentary bills and has advised individuals, companies and government bodies in a variety of international jurisdictions. Since becoming a QC in 2011, David has appeared in a series of high profile administrative and public law cases, acting for public bodies and against them. He has been in many of the leading cases concerning the law of the NHS in recent years. He was on the panel of Treasury counsel before taking silk. He is a recognised specialist in healthcare law and is one of the authors of the leading practitioners' book in the area, *Principles of Medical Law* (Grubb, Laing and McHale eds, OUP) and joint editor (along with David Blundell) of the leading journal *Judicial Review*. In his diverse career David has served as a local councillor, member of parliament, government minister and has chaired national and regional government bodies. He is a member of the BMA ethics committee and a Visiting Professor of Law at the London School of Economics. Outside of the law, David is married to Bernie, who is a GP. They regularly take time out of their careers to cycle the world and maintain the cycling blog www.decade2australia.org.

Hannah Gibbs is a barrister at Landmark Chambers with a varied public law practice, acting for clients in the Supreme Court, the Court of Appeal, High Court, the county court and various tribunals, including the First-tier Tribunal (SEND). She acts for individuals, public bodies and private clients in a broad range of public law matters. These include healthcare and the NHS, social care, education, disability discrimination, public services ombudsmen, local government, planning and environmental, immigration and asylum, unlawful detention, and social security. Hannah has a particular expertise in the law of the NHS. She regularly advises on health law-related issues, particularly in the context of controversial service reconfigurations. Hannah also teaches medical law at the London School of Economics, examining the legal framework within which health services are provided, and exploring some of the complex ethical dilemmas that arise in areas such as organ donation, abortion, assisted dying, fertility treatment and genome editing.

Samantha Broadfoot QC is a barrister at Landmark Chambers and wrote the chapter on NHS regulation. She is a public law specialist, with a wide ranging public law practice. She has extensive experience of cases involving regulators, whether as a result of acting for them, against them or simply acting for clients in front of them. In the healthcare sector specifically, and most recently, she acted for the campaign group in the December 2017 *Horton Hospital* challenge, and prior to that she had acted for the secretary of state in a series of cases involving the regulation of fertility treatment. She has acted for the CQC in relation to the regulation of residential care homes. Samantha is also a Recorder, sitting as a part-time judge in Woolwich Crown Court.

Fiona Scolding QC specialises in education, social and healthcare work for a range of individuals, charities, local and central government and private providers. She is particularly interested in cases concerning those with learning disabilities, and those who are looked after by the local authority (whether as children or formerly looked after children). Fiona co-authored the chapter on NHS provider trusts.

Andrew Byass practices in several public law areas, and has a broad depth of experience including from when working as a senior public law solicitor for the Government Legal Department prior to joining Landmark Chambers. Since switching to the self-employed bar, Andrew has continued to build on his public law experience, representing both claimants and defendants in a range of tribunals and courts. His public law experience includes advising on a range of matters relating to healthcare law, including the vires and legality of actions of NHS bodies, NHS continuing healthcare, primary care contracts, and procurement and contracting issues. Andrew also has particular experience dealing with equality issues and matters relating to the impact of decision-making on private and family life rights, including the rights of children. Andrew wrote the chapter on community dental services.

Richard Clarke is a barrister at Landmark Chambers specialising in public, planning and property law. Richard advises on a broad range of public law issues, acting for individuals, campaign organisations, local authorities and central government. Richard is a member of the Attorney General's C panel of counsel. Prior to independent practice, Richard worked as a barrister for the Government Legal Department. He is the author of the chapter on the powers and duties of clinical commissioning groups.

Ben Fullbrook is a barrister practising in public, planning, environmental and property law at Landmark Chambers. He co-authored the chapter on GP practice management with Hannah Gibbs. Ben has appeared for clients in the magistrates' court, county court, High Court, and various First-tier and Upper Tribunal. Ben's recent clients have included individual claimants and defendants, developers, environmental groups, landlords, tenants, local authorities and government departments. Prior to joining Landmark Chambers, Ben worked for five years as a civil service fast-streamer at the Ministry of Defence. His work spanned various aspects of defence and security policy and included liaison with foreign governments, dealing with public law challenges and the application of international human rights law.

Alistair Mills is a barrister at Landmark Chambers, where he practises in public law, and planning and environmental law. He contributed the chapter on public health. Alistair has a wide range of interest in public law matters, and is on the Attorney General's C panel of counsel. His experience includes social security (EU and domestic), immigration, healthcare, judicial reviews of planning decisions and environmental matters. He accepts instructions from central and local government, regulators, private individuals, and companies. He has appeared in the Court of Appeal (both led and unled), as well as in the High Court and the Upper Tribunal. He is an External College Lecturer in Law at Magdalene College, Cambridge, where he provides supervisions in administrative law. He is the assistant editor of the journal *Judicial Review*, and has published widely. He was awarded Oxford University's Eldon Law scholarship in 2011.

James Neill was called to the Bar in 2006. He practises in all areas of domestic public law and has particular expertise in public procurement litigation (both within the healthcare sector and more generally). He practises from Landmark Chambers where he is the joint head of the Public Procurement Group and a member of the Healthcare Group. Prior to joining Landmark Chambers in 2016 he worked as an associate in the corporate litigation team at Allen & Overy LLP for five years focussing on commercial judicial review disputes. He is a member of the Procurement Lawyers Association and the Administrative Law Bar Association. James wrote the chapter on procurement in the NHS.

Contents

Table of cases

R (National Association of Health Stores) v Secretary of State for Health [2005] EWCA Civ 154, (2005) *Times*, March 9	3.40
R (Newman) v Parliamentary and Health Service Commissioner [2017] EWHC 3336 (TCC)	20.52, 20.65
R (QSRC Ltd) v NHS Commissioning Board (NHS England) [2015] EWHC 3752 (Admin), (2016) 148 BMLR 77	21.99, 21.146
R (Rapp) v Parliamentary and Health Service Ombudsman [2015] EWHC 1344 (Admin), [2015] ELR 439	20.57
R (Reffell) v Hammersmith Hospitals NHS Trust 2000 WL 1274140, unreported, 26 July	15.123
R (Rogers) v Swindon NHS Primary Care Trust [2006] EWCA Civ 392, [2006] 1 WLR 2649, (2006) 9 CCLR 451, [2006] Lloyd's Rep Med 364, (2006) 89 BMLR 211, (2006) 103(17) LSG 23, (2006) 156 NLJ 720, (2006) 150 SJLB 575, (2006) *Independent*, April 25; *Reversing* [2006] EWHC 171 (Admin), (2006) 88 BMLR 177	3.58, 7.9
R (Rose) v Thanet Clinical Commissioning Group [2014] EWHC 1182 (Admin), (2014) 138 BMLR 101, [2014] ACD 120	2.56–2.58, 7.11, 9.24, 12.84
R (Royal Brompton and Harefield NHS Foundation Trust) v Joint Committee of Primary Care Trusts [2012] EWCA Civ 472, (2012) 126 BMLR 134, (2012) 109(18) LSG 20; *Reversing* [2011] EWHC 2986 (Admin), [2012] ACD 31	17.44, 17.45–17.47
R (S) v Dudley Primary Care Trust [2009] EWHC 1780 (Admin)	14.159, 14.160, 14.162, 16.194
R (S) v Knowsley NHS Primary Care Trust [2006] EWHC 26 (Admin), [2006] Lloyd's Rep Med 123, [2006] ACD 60 (2006) *Times*, February 2	4.102, 4.106, 4.107
R (S (a child)) v NHS England [2016] EWHC 1395 (Admin), (2016) 19 CCLR 336, [2016] Med LR 329, (2017) 154 BMLR 114, [2016] ACD 103	9.9, 9.103, 9.105, 13.36
R (St Helens BC) v Manchester Primary Care Trust [2008] EWCA Civ 931, [2009] PTSR 105, (2008) 11 CCLR 774, [2009] PIQR P4, (2008) *Times*, October 6	16.107, 16.173
R (Sim) v Parole Board for England and Wales [2003] EWCA Civ 1845, [2004] QB 1288, [2004] 2 WLR 1170, [2004] HRLR 15, [2004] Prison LR 44, (2004) 101(5) LSG 29, (2004) 148 SJLB 60, (2004 *Times*, January 2	4.109
R (Simpson) v Police Medical Appeal Board [2012] EWHC 808 (Admin)	12.70, 13.54
R (Smith) v East Kent Hospital NHS Trust [2002] EWHC 2640 (Admin), (2003) 6 CCLR 251	17.102, 17.103
R (Stirling) v Haringey LBC [2013] EWCA Civ 116, [2013] PTSR 1285, [2013] BLGR 251, (2013) 157(9) SJLB 31	17.103
R (Sunderland City Council) v South Tyneside Council [2012] EWCA Civ 1232, [2013] 1 All ER 394, [2013] PTSR 549, [2013] BLGR 51, (2012) 15 CCLR 701, [2012] MHLR 404	15.24
R (Supportways Community Services Ltd) v Hampshire CC [2006] EWCA Civ 1035, [2006] BLGR 836, (2006) 9 CCLR 484	11.97
R (T) v Haringey LBC [2005] EWHC 2235 (Admin), (2006) 9 CCLR 58	16.211
R (The Pharmaceutical Services Negotiating Committee) v Secretary of State for Health [2017] EWHC 1147 (Admin), [2017] PTSR 1451	2.45, 3.22–3.24, 3.27, 3.28, 4.15, 4.59, 8.20, 9.41

Table of statutes

Table of statutory instruments

National Health Service Commissioning Board and Clinical Commissioning Groups (Responsibilities and Standing Rules) Regulations (RSR Regs/2012 Regulations) 2012 SI No 2996 *continued*	
Pt 5	10.12, 12.69, 12.72, 16.198
Pt 6	16.2, 16.36, 16.46, 16.54, 16.140
Pt 6A	14.7
Pt 8	12.18, 12.28, 12.37, 12.44, 12.45, 12.50, 12.59, 12.65, 12.77, 12.80
Pt 9	21.111
reg 2	9.35, 10.9, 10.10, 10.11, 12.21, 12.22, 12.44, 12.68, 13.20, 13.128
reg 2(2)(a)–(c)	13.143
reg 3	13.17, 13.19
reg 4(1)	13.78, 13.79, 13.83
reg 4(2)–(4)	13.78
reg 4(2)	13.77, 13.82
reg 4(2)(c)	13.82
reg 4(4)	13.77, 13.80
reg 5	5.59, 9.24, 13.22, 13.24, 13.25
reg 6	13.16
reg 7	13.21, 13.22, 16.54
reg 7(1)(a)	13.21
reg 7(1)(b)	13.21
reg 7(2)(b)	13.21
reg 7(3)	13.21
reg 7(6)(b)	13.21
reg 7(7)(b)	13.21
reg 7(8)	13.21
reg 8	13.22
reg 9	13.22
reg 10	13.23, 16.54
reg 10(1)	13.23
reg 10(2)	12.44, 13.23
reg 11	6.61, 13.34, 13.39
reg 12	13.45
reg 13	13.45
reg 13(1)	13.45
reg 16	10.12, 10.13, 12.72
reg 16(1)	12.72
reg 16(1)(a)	12.72
reg 16(1)(b)	12.72
reg 16(1B)	10.12
reg 16(4)	12.72
reg 17	10.13, 12.74, 21.103
reg 17(1)	10.13
reg 17(1)(a)	10.13
reg 17(1)(b)	10.13
reg 17(4)	10.13, 10.16, 12.73
reg 20	16.48, 16.136
reg 20(2)	16.54
reg 21	16.64, 16.142

Table of European and international legislation

Table of guidance

Department of Health and Social Care

Table of abbreviations

A&E	Accident & Emergency
ACO	accountable care organisation
APMS	Alternative Provider Medical Services
APPG	All Party Parliamentary Group
AQP	any qualified provider
BDA	British Dental Association
BMA	British Medical Association
CCA 2004	Civil Contingencies Act 2004
CCG	clinical commissioning group
CCG IAF	clinical commissioning group improvement and assessment framework manual .
CCG Regs 2012	National Health Service (Clinical Commissioning Groups) Regulations 2012 SI No 1631
CCGDR Regs 2013	National Health Service (Clinical Commissioning Groups – Disapplication of Responsibility) Regulations 2013 SI No 350
CEDR	Centre for Effective Dispute Resolution
CFO	chief finance officer
CHAI	Commission for Healthcare Audit and Inspection
CHC	Continuing Healthcare
CJEU	Court of Justice of the European Union
CJIA 2008	Criminal Justice and Immigration Act 2008
CMA	Competition and Markets Authority
COV Regs 2015	National Health Service (Charges to Overseas Visitors) Regulations 2015 SI No 238
CPD	continuing professional development
CQC	Care Quality Commission
CQC Assessments Regs 2018	Care Quality Commission (Reviews and Performance Assessments) Regulations 2018 SI No 54
CRG	Clinical Reference Group
CSCA	Commission for Social Care Inspection
DHSC	Department of Health and Social Care
DMBC	decision-making business case
DNACPR	do not attempt cardio-pulmonary resuscitation
DP Regs 2013	National Health Service (Direct Payments) Regulations 2013 SI No 1617
DPA 1998	Data Protection Act 1998
DWP	Department for Work and Pensions
eFI	electronic Frailty Index
EHIC	European Health Insurance Card
EIA	equality impact assessment
FD	Finance Director
FGM	female genital mutilation
FHSAU	Family Health Services Appeal Unit
FT	foundation trust

FTAC	Fixated Threat Assessment Centre
GC	General Condition
GDS	General Dental Services
GDSC Regs 2005	National Health Service (General Dental Services Contracts) Regulations 2005 SI No 3361
GMC	General Medical Council
GMS	General Medical Services
GMS SFE	General Medical Services Statement of Financial Entitlements Directions
GMS Regs 2015	National Health Service (General Medical Services Contracts) Regulations 2015 SI No 1862
GP	general practitioner
GPC	BMA General Practitioners Committee
HA 2009	Health Act 2009
HCHS	hospital and community health service
HCPC	Health and Care Professions Council
HEE	Health Education England
HFEA	Human Fertilisation and Embryology Authority
HMA 1988	Health and Medicines Act 1988
HOSC	Health Overview and Scrutiny Committee
HRG	Healthcare Resource Group
HSCA 1993	Health Service Commissioners Act 1993
HSCA 2001	Health and Social Care Act 2001
HSCA 2008	Health and Social Care Act 2008
HSCA 2012	Health and Social Care Act 2012
HSC(CHS)A 2003	Health and Social Care (Community Health and Standards) Act 2003
HSG	Health Service Guidance
HTA	Human Tissue Authority
HWB	health and wellbeing board
IA 2014	Immigration Act 2014
IAA 1999	Immigration and Asylum Act 1999
IFR	individual funding request
IHS	immigration health charge / immigration health surcharge
IRP	Independent Reconfiguration Panel
ITT	invitation to tender
IVF	in-vitro fertilisation
JCPCT	Joint Committee Primary Care Trust
JHWS	Joint Health and Wellbeing Strategy
JLaR	Joint Licensing and Regulation
JSNA	Joint Strategic Needs Assessment;
LGPIHA 2007	Local Government and Public Involvement in Health Act 2007
LHB	Local Health Board
Licencing Exemption Regs 2013	National Health Service (Licence Exemptions, etc) Regulations (Licence Exemption Regs) 2013 SI No 2677
LMC	Local Medical Committee
MCA 2005	Mental Capacity Act 2005
MFF	Market Forces Factor
MHA 1983	Mental Health Act 1983
MHAC	Mental Health Act Commission
MP	member of parliament
MPS	Medical Protection Society
MSHTU	Modern Slavery Human Trafficking Unit
NGO	non-governmental organisation
NHS Act 1948	National Health Service Act 1948

NHS Act 1977	National Health Service Act 1977
NHS Act 2006	National Health Service Act 2006
NHS BSA	NHS Business Services Agency
NHS England	The National Health Service Commissioning Board
NHS Procurement Regs 2013	National Health Service (Procurement, Patient Choice and Competition) (No 2) Regulations 2013 SI No 500
NHSCCA 1990	National Health Service and Community Care Act 1990
NHSI	NHS Improvement
NHSLA	NHS Litigation Authority
NHSOF	National Health Service Outcomes Framework
NHS(PC)A 1997	National Health Service (Primary Care) Act 1997
NHS(W)A 2006	National Health Service (Wales) Act 2006
NHST(MP) Regs 1990	National Health Service Trusts (Membership and Procedure) Regulations 1990
NICE	National Institute for Health and Care Excellence
NICE Regs 2013	National Institute for Health and Care Excellence (Constitution and Functions) and the Health and Social Care Information Centre (Functions) Regulations 2013
NMC	Nursing and Midwifery Council
NRLS	National Reporting and Learning System
NRM	National Referral Mechanism
OJEU	Official Journal of the European Union
OGSCR	Service Change and Reconfiguration
OOH	out of hours
OVM	Overseas Visitors Manager
PALS	Patient Advice and Liaison Service
PAYE	Pay As You Earn
PbR	Payment by Results
PB(AM)A 1960	Public Bodies (Admission to Meetings) Act 1960
PC Regs 2015	Public Contracts Regulations 2015 SI No 102
PCBC	pre-consultation business case
PCR	patient charge revenue
PCT	primary care trust
PCT Regs 2002	National Health Service (Functions of Strategic Health Authorities and Primary Care Trusts and Administration Arrangements) (England) Regulations 2002
PDS	Personal Dental Services
PDSA Regs 2005	National Health Service (Personal Dental Services Agreements) Regulations 2005 SI No 3373
PGM	*Primary medical care – policy and guidance manual* (NHS England)
PHA 1984	Public Health (Control of Disease) Act 1984
PHB	personal health budget
PHE	Public Health England
PIN	Prior Information Notice
PL Regs 2004	National Health Service (Performers Lists) Regulations 2004 SI No 585
PLE Regs 2013	National Health Service (Performers Lists) (England) Regulations 2013 SI No 335
PMS	Personal Medical Services
PMS Regs 2004	National Health Service (Personal Medical Services Agreements) Regulations 2004 SI No 627

PMS Regs 2015	National Health Service (Personal Medical Services Agreements) Regulations 2015 SI No 1879
PMS Transitional Order 2004	General Medical Services and Personal Medical Services Transitional and Consequential Provisions Order 2004 SI No 865
PPG	Patient Participation Group
PPI	patient and public involvement
PSED	public sector equality duty
PSHO	Parliamentary and Health Service Ombudsman
QOF	Quality and Outcomes Framework
R&D	research and development
RAS	Resource Allocation System
Regulated Activities Regs	Health and Social Care Act 2008 (Regulated Activities) Regulations 2014 SI No 2936
RSR Regs 2012	National Health Service Commissioning Board and Clinical Commissioning Groups (Responsibilities and Standing Rules) Regulations 2012 SI No 2996
SC	Special Condition v
SEAP	support, empower, advocate, promote
SEN	special educational needs
SFA	statement of fees and allowances
SFE	statement of financial entitlements
SFE Directions	General Medical Services Statement of Financial Entitlement Directions
SHA	special health authority
SLHT	South London Healthcare NHS Trust
SOC	Strategic Outline Case
STI	sexually transmitted infection
STP	sustainability and transformation partnership
SUS	Secondary Uses Service
TAG	Technology Appraisal Guidance
TAR	Technology Appraisal Recommendations
TDA	Trust Development Authority
TPP	total purchasing pilot scheme
TSA	trust special administrator
UDA	units of dental activity
UIT	User Independent Trust
UKVI	Home Office Visas and Immigration
UNCAT	United Nations Convention against Torture and other Cruel, Inhuman or Degrading Treatment or Punishment
UOA	units of orthodontic activity
WHO	World Health Organization

Part 1
Introduction to the NHS

CHAPTER 1

An introduction to the legal structures of the NHS

Introduction

1.1 The former Chancellor Nigel Lawson famously said that 'The NHS is the closest thing the English have to a religion'. That quotation accurately described the intense levels of support for the NHS among the British public. The intensely 'political' nature of the NHS is shown by the fact that funding and promises about improved delivery of NHS services are key issues in every General Election campaign. However, the strength of the commitment that staff, patients and the public have to the NHS is often matched by anger and frustration about the way that NHS decisions are made when, as regrettably happens, the services that the public receive are less than they feel they have a right to expect. Clinicians give advice and take decisions about options available to millions of individual patients in the NHS on a daily basis. Those decisions are mainly driven by clinical issues – what is the correct diagnosis, what are the right treatment options and what drugs should be prescribed to assist the patient. However, all NHS clinical decisions are taken within a legal framework which explains what treatment decisions are open to NHS clinicians and what options are not available to them.

1.2 The purpose of this book is to attempt to explain the legal structures of the NHS and how decisions are made in areas other than the treatment choices open to a clinician and a patient. The legal structures of the NHS govern how clinicians are employed, the options open to them, the ways in which patients can be referred for treatment and how funds flow from the Department of Health and Social Care (DHSC) to meet the costs of providing NHS services. If everything goes right in the general practitioner's (GP's) consulting room or on the operating table, the structures behind the delivery of those services are rarely important. However, if things go wrong or if a clinician cannot offer a patient the most clinically effective treatment, the decision-making structures that lie behind the treatment offered to individual patients comes under intense scrutiny.

1.3 Although the public see 'the NHS' as a single entity, that is not the case. The NHS operates through networks of different organisations. Some of these are public bodies, but many are commercial 'for profit' organisations whose business is the delivery of NHS services in exchange for contract monies paid by NHS commissioners. Collectively, more than 1.7 million people work in organisations that deliver NHS services. Of those, just under half are clinically qualified (including 39,780 GPs), 370,327 nurses, 18,687 ambulance staff and 105,711 hospital and community health service medical and dental staff. If the NHS were a single employer (which it is not), only the Chinese People's Liberation Army, the Walmart supermarket chain and Indian Railways directly employ more people.

1.4 The creation of the NHS was a political decision which emerged from the Beveridge Report, officially titled the *Report of the Inter-Departmental Committee on Social Insurance and Allied Services*. The original budget for the NHS was £437 million (roughly £15 billion at today's values) and the politicians and civil servants confidently predicted that the budget would be able to be reduced as the health of the nation improved. The health of the nation has undoubtedly improved since 1948, when average life expectancy was 66 years for men and

77 for women. In 2012–2014, a man in the UK aged 66 had an average further 17.4 years of life remaining and a woman had an average further 20.9 years of life. In 1948, infant mortality was 34 deaths per thousand births, whereas, as of 2014, it is just five. Hence, the 1948 predictions of a healthier nation with the NHS were right (although the NHS has only been one factor in increased health outcomes – reductions in smoking rates probably have had far more impact). However, the prediction that this would lead to a reduced requirement for NHS spending was perhaps 'optimistic'.

1.5 The overall budget for the NHS continues to be a matter of intense political debate, but the numbers are staggering. The NHS budget[1] in 2014/15 was £118.3 billion – that is £118,300 million. That is just short of £2,000 per person in the UK. The budget grew to £121.9 billion in 2015/16 and to £122.6 billion in 2016/17. The King's Fund helpfully summarises budget position as follows:

> Planned spending for the Department of Health in England is approximately £123.7 billion in 2017/18 (at 2017/18 prices).
>
> In the 2015 Spending Review the government announced that funding for the Department of Health would increase to £133.1 billion (or £126.5 billion at 2017/18 prices after adjusting for inflation) by 2020/21. The increase in health spending between 2015/16 and 2020/21 is less than the government has claimed, mainly because ministers have chosen to highlight the funding provided to NHS England only, rather than the Department of Health's total budget.
>
> Though NHS funding is continuing to grow, the rate of growth is slowing considerably compared to historical trends. The Department of Health budget will grow by 1.1 per cent in real terms between 2009/10 and 2020/21. This is far below the long-term average increases in health spending of approximately 4 per cent a year (in real terms) since the NHS was established.
>
> Looking ahead, between 2017/18 and 2019/20 the Department of Health budget will increase by just 0.6 per cent on average each year in real terms. This will place increasing pressure on the NHS, as demand for services is continuing to grow.

1.6 However, the legal structures within which the NHS operates are largely unclear – both to those who work in the NHS and those who work outside. There are huge public protests against any perceived 'privatisation' of the NHS, but those protesting appear to fail to realise that the NHS has always delivered a large part of its services through doctors in primary care who ran 'for profit' businesses which contracted into the NHS rather than being NHS employees. It is perhaps inevitable that an organisation which is as complex as the NHS would have a hugely complex set of interlocking legal relationships which govern the rights and obligations of those working in the NHS.

1.7 The NHS took legal form under the National Health Service Act (NHS Act) 1946.[2] That Act of Parliament was amended on numerous occasions.

1 These are figures from the Department of Health Annual Report, helpfully summarised in a report from the King's Fund at www.kingsfund.org.uk/projects/nhs-in-a-nutshell/nhs-budget.

2 There are numerous academic works on the history of the NHS but the outline details are at www.nhs.uk/NHSEngland/thenhs/nhshistory/Pages/the-nhs%20history.aspx.

All of the changes to the legal structures of the NHS were brought together in the National Health Service Act 1977. Numerous further changes followed, particularly the creation of the 'purchaser/provider' split for the NHS and the creation of semi-autonomous hospital trusts as a result of the National Health Service and Community Care Act (NHSCCA) 1990, which came into effect in 1993. By 2006 there had been so many changes to the National Health Service Act 1977 that a new consolidated Act of Parliament was needed. The new Act was – predictably – called the National Health Service Act (NHS Act) 2006.

1.8 Today the legal structure of the NHS is substantially governed by the present version of the NHS Act 2006. However, the NHS Act 2006 has been amended on many occasions since it was passed in 2006. The present version of the NHS Act 2006 includes many amendments which were made by the Health and Social Care Act (HSCA) 2012, which made very substantial changes to the structure of the NHS. In addition, many of the sections of the NHS Act 2006 permit the Secretary of State for Health and Social Care to make regulations which, once made, affect the legal obligations of NHS bodies.

1.9 There is also a wide range of other Acts of Parliament and other sources of law, including European Union (EU) law, which impacts on the NHS. Hence, for example, procurement in the NHS is governed by the general rules on procurement within the Public Contracts Regulations 2006 as well as specialist regulations for the procurement of NHS medical services known as the National Health Service (Procurement, Patient Choice and Competition) (No 2) Regulations 2013.[3]

The division between commissioners and providers in the NHS

1.10 At the start of his judgment in *Keep Wythenshawe Special Ltd v NHS Central Manchester CCG and others*[4] Dove J helpfully explained that:

> As a consequence of successive legislative reforms, the provision of healthcare under the auspices of the National Health Service ('NHS') in England is a complex web of organisations with separate roles to play in the provision of services to patients . . .

1.11 The separation of commissioners and providers has been the policy of successive governments, starting with Rt Hon Ken Clarke who was secretary of state between 1988 and 1990 and steered the NHSCCA 1990 through parliament. The 1990 Act created the first NHS trusts and thus started the divide between those bodies which have a duty to arrange services and those whose duty it was to treat patients.

1.12 Successive governments have maintained the separation between the NHS organisations that plan how resources should be allocated and what care should be commissioned for NHS patients on the one hand, and those organisations that deliver care to patients on the other. This was

3 SI No 500.

4 [2016] EWHC 17 (Admin), (2016) 19 CCLR 19.

originally known as the 'purchaser/provider split' with some NHS organisations acting as 'purchasers' and others as 'providers'.

1.13 The terminology used by the present government and laid down in the HSCA 2012 (and by previous governments) is that there should be a divide between 'commissioners' and 'providers'. Whether this model remains appropriate for today's NHS is a subject of active debate, particularly given the creation of the 'sustainability and transformation partnerships' (STPs) which are the latest attempt to make the NHS operate in a more efficient manner. STPs are entirely non-statutory and hence their decisions have no direct legal effect.

1.14 Once NHS commissioners have decided what services they wish to commission, they enter into 'arrangements' with NHS bodies and a range of other organisations and individuals who agree to deliver those services to NHS patients who have a need of that service. These 'arrangements' can be either:

a) a legal contract, normally in the form of an NHS Standard Contract, which defines the way in which the services are to be provided; or
b) an 'NHS contract' which is a non-legally binding service level agreement which can only be enforced through the NHS's own dispute resolution processes.

1.15 Chapter 10 below describes the processes involved in NHS contracting and how the NHS's dispute resolution processes operates. However, for now it is sufficient to note that these contracts are usually structured using the 'Payment by Results' (PbR) processes set out in the national tariff. PbR arrangements operate 'call-off' arrangements under which a provider of NHS services earns the right to a defined fee when the provider delivers a service to an NHS patient. While an NHS provider can arrange for its clinicians to deliver any type of medical care to patients that its clinicians are willing to provide, an NHS provider will only be paid for delivering those services that are set out in the commissioning contract. Hence, in practice, NHS providers are only willing to provide care to NHS patients which is within the scope of the relevant commissioning contract.

Does the NHS have a duty to provide a comprehensive healthcare system?

1.16 One of the myths circulating in the NHS, and frequently perpetuated by politicians who are either supporting or attacking those currently running the NHS, is that the NHS has a duty to provide a comprehensive health service. The correct legal position is more nuanced. Section 1 of the NHS Act 2006 provides that the secretary of state has a duty to 'continue the promotion' of a comprehensive health service. NHS England is also under this legal duty but it is not imposed on either the local commissioners of NHS services, namely clinical commissioning groups (CCGs), or on any providers of NHS services.

1.17 CCGs and NHS England do not have a legal duty to provide services which, added together, amount to a comprehensive health service. The primary legal duties on CCGs and NHS England is imposed by section 3(1) of the NHS Act 2006, namely to 'arrange for the provision' of a wide range of health services 'to such extent as it considers necessary to meet the reasonable requirements of the persons for whom it has responsibility'. NHS England has like duties, and also has duties to put in place primary care, dental and pharmacy services. However, none of the obligations to set up specific services require the cumulative effect of the services to add up to a comprehensive health service for patients.

1.18 There is an important distinction in law between the duty on the secretary of state to *promote* (or continue the promotion of) a comprehensive health service and a duty to *provide* a comprehensive health service. The statutory duty to promote a comprehensive health service has limited overall legal effect because the combination of budgetary, staffing and other resource pressures on the NHS mean that a truly comprehensive health service will never, in fact, be provided. The supply of publicly funded health services, largely free at the point of use, means that NHS doctors can do more for patients and that, in turn means that there is more demand for health services. The NHS cannot ever provide a truly comprehensive health service (in the same way as no publicly funded health services anywhere in the world can be comprehensive). However, the statutory duty exists to remind the secretary of state that his or her duty is to ensure the NHS should be as comprehensive as budgets and other resources permit. The Court of Appeal considered the conundrum of a legal duty which can never be fulfilled in *R v North and East Devon Health Authority ex p Coughlan*,[5] where the court said:

> 24. The first qualification placed on the duty contained in section 3 makes it clear that there is scope for the Secretary of State to exercise a degree of judgment as to the circumstances in which he will provide the services, including nursing services referred to in the section. He does not automatically have to meet all nursing requirements. In certain circumstances he can exercise his judgment and legitimately decline to provide nursing services. He need not provide nursing services if he does not consider they are reasonably required or necessary to meet a reasonable requirement.
>
> 25. When exercising his judgment he has to bear in mind the comprehensive service which he is under a duty to promote as set out in section 1. However, as long as he pays due regard to that duty, the fact that the service will not be comprehensive does not mean that he is necessarily contravening either section 1 or section 3. The truth is that, while he has the duty to continue to promote a comprehensive free health service and he must never, in making a decision under section 3, disregard that duty, a comprehensive health service may never, for human, financial and other resource reasons, be achievable. Recent history has demonstrated that the pace of developments as to what is possible by way of medical treatment, coupled with the ever increasing expectations of the public, mean that the resources of the NHS are and are likely to continue, at least in the foreseeable future, to be insufficient to meet demand'

1.19 The duties on commissioners under section 3(1) of the NHS Act 2006 impose legal obligations on commissioners to make arrangements for services that can be accessed by patients that wish to do so. However, these

5 [2001] QB 213, (1999) 2 CCLR 285.

duties do not create private law legal duties owed to individual patients. The secretary of state has no general private law[6] duty of care to members of the public as potential patients and neither do NHS commissioning bodies. The legal duties under the NHS are fulfilled if health and social care services are made available to potential patients to meet what the NHS commissioners consider to be their 'reasonable requirements'. Thus the NHS Act 2006 does not impose legal duties on NHS bodies to provide healthcare to individual patients (save possibly in the case of patients who are sectioned under the Mental Health Act 1983). The role of NHS commissioners and providers is to put services in place so they are accessible, if the public wish to avail themselves of those services.

The NHS triple lock: patient, treating clinician and NHS commissioner

1.20 There is a triple lock operating in the NHS. A patient will only secure NHS-funded treatment if the patient, the relevant treating clinician and the relevant NHS commissioner all concur that medical treatment is clinically appropriate for a particular patient. The NHS commissioner defines the broad categories of medical treatment that it is prepared to support and then leaves the selection of appropriate patients to clinicians to decide, using parameters defined by the commissioners. However, no NHS-funded treatment will be provided unless all three of the patient, the treating clinician and the NHS commissioner have agreed that NHS-funded treatment will be given.

1.21 One reason why the NHS Act 2006 imposes no direct legal duty on doctors to treat patients is that, ordinarily, no one who has the legal capacity to make his or her own decisions to receive or refuse treatment is under any legal obligation to consult a doctor or attend a hospital. Save in unusual situations, such as compulsory mental health treatment, patients have the right to take their own decisions about receiving medical treatment. However ill a patient is, the patient has the absolute right to refuse to accept medical treatment. Whether an individual patient with capacity wishes to access such services or not is a matter for that individual, not for doctors or the individual's relatives. Save in the case of a detained mental health patient, we all have the right to refuse medical treatment. In *Re T (adult: refusal of treatment)*[7] Lord Donaldson MR said:

> An adult patient who, like Miss T., suffers from no mental incapacity has an absolute right to choose whether to consent to medical treatment, to refuse it or to choose one rather than another of the treatments being offered . . . This right of choice is not limited to decisions which others might regard as sensible. It exists notwithstanding that the reasons for making the choice are rational, irrational, unknown or even non-existent: see *Sidaway v Board of Governors of the Bethlem Royal Hospital and the Maudsley Hospital* [1985] AC 871, 904–905.

6 Ie a legal duty which can be the subject of a private law action for damages if it is alleged to have been breached.

7 [1992] 3 WLR 782.

1.22 Thus the UK state, acting through the NHS, cannot have a duty to provide medical care unless a patient requests it. While this absolute right of a patient to make his or her own decisions is confined to patients with capacity, a person is not to be treated as unable to make a decision merely because he or she makes a decision that is unwise. It is important in this regard to recall the words of Peter Jackson J in *Heart of England NHS Foundation Trust v JB*:[8]

> The temptation to base a judgment of a person's capacity upon whether they seem to have made a good or bad decision, and in particular on whether they have accepted or rejected medical advice, is absolutely to be avoided. That would be to put the cart before the horse or, expressed another way, to allow the tail of welfare to wag the dog of capacity. Any tendency in this direction risks infringing the rights of that group of persons who, though vulnerable, are capable of making their own decisions. Many who suffer from mental illness are well able to make decisions about their medical treatment, and it is important not to make unjustified assumptions to the contrary.

1.23 However, where a patient decides that his or her medical condition should be treated by a clinician, patients do not have a legal right to demand a specific form of medical treatment. Medical treatment within the NHS is not based on a consumer relationship – a patient cannot 'purchase' any item off the shelf and demand that it is provided to him or her. The doctor or nurse has a duty to consider what medical treatment is clinically appropriate for a patient and is fully entitled not to offer to provide medical treatment which the doctor or nurse considers is not clinically indicated by the patient's presenting condition. Thus, in *Re R (a minor) (wardship: consent to treatment)*[9] Lord Donaldson said:

> However consent by itself creates no obligation to treat. It is merely a key which unlocks a door.

1.24 Thus consent gives the doctor the legal right to treat a patient but imposes no legal duty on the doctor to do so. However, a doctor has a duty of care to the patient and that will usually lead the doctor to having a duty to provide advice to a patient to define the appropriate treatment options for the patient and, once the patient has made the choice among those options, a duty to provide the treatment selected by the patient. However, where a doctor is working within the NHS, the treatment options that a doctor is able to offer to a patient may be circumscribed by decisions made by an NHS commissioner.

1.25 Each NHS commissioning organisation is required to work within a defined, limited annual budget. This means that NHS cannot offer unlimited care to any patient or guarantee that patients will have access to NHS funds to support any medical care which might be clinically effective for that patient. NHS bodies have a duty to break even financially and so are not only entitled to ration care but have a legal duty to do so in a rational way. This can lead NHS commissioning organisations to take the decision not to make a clinically appropriate treatment available to a patient, even though both the patient and the treating doctor have reached the view that

8 [2014] EWHC 342 (COP) at [7].
9 [1992] Fam 11.

the patient should have the treatment: see for example *R (Condliff) v North Staffordshire Primary Care Trust.*[10]

1.26 Hence, in practice, NHS-funded treatment is only provided where all three of the patient, the treating doctor and the relevant NHS commissioner approves the treatment.

The role of the different public bodies within the NHS

1.27 The NHS is composed of a large number of public bodies, all of which have different functions and on occasions overlapping responsibilities. Making sense of the legal systems operating in the NHS requires an understanding of the roles and responsibilities of the different public bodies operating within the NHS and how they interact with private sector providers who contract to deliver services to NHS patients.

1.28 NHS bodies can broadly be divided into four types, namely:

1) overarching national NHS bodies;
2) commissioners of NHS services;
3) providers of NHS services; and
4) regulators of NHS services, namely public bodies which supervise the performance of those individuals and public bodies who commission or provide NHS services and body that oversee the performance of NHS bodies.

1.29 Some NHS bodies perform more than one function. Hence, for example, NHS England is both a commissioner and a regulator.

The secretary of state

1.30 The secretary of state sits at the apex of the NHS. The secretary of state is a cabinet minister and a member of parliament (MP), usually an elected MP. The present occupant of the office is Rt Hon Jeremy Hunt MP. The secretary of state has overall political responsibility for the NHS and plays a key strategic role, particularly by setting the Annual Mandate for NHS England. However, the legal duties directly owed by the secretary of state to NHS patients have been substantially diminished by the HSCA 2012.

1.31 Section 1 of the NHS Act 2006 provides:

> (1) The Secretary of State must continue the promotion in England of a comprehensive health service designed to secure improvement–
>
> (a) in the physical and mental health of the people of England, and
> (b) in the prevention, diagnosis and treatment of physical and mental illness.
>
> (2) For that purpose, the Secretary of State must exercise the functions conferred by this Act so as to secure that services are provided in accordance with this Act.
>
> (3) The Secretary of State retains ministerial responsibility to Parliament for the provision of the health service in England.

10 [2011] EWCA Civ 910, (2011) 14 CCLR 656.

1.32 The secretary of state has a duty to 'promote' a comprehensive health service under this section. In order to achieve this vision of a comprehensive health service, CCGs and NHS England have a duty to provide a range of services to meet the reasonable requirements of patients for services, as well as making arrangements to provide primary care, dental and pharmaceutical services.

1.33 There were fierce debates about the role of the secretary of state during the passage of the Health and Social Care Bill which led to the 2012 Act. The then secretary of state, Andrew Lansley, saw the role of the secretary of state to set the strategic framework but to be detached from any duty to implement those decisions. However, that meant that no one was accountable in parliament for decisions taken within the NHS. A compromise is reflected in section 1(3) of the 2012 Act which provides that

> The Secretary of State retains ministerial responsibility to Parliament for the provision of the health service in England.

1.34 Thus, as has always been the case, the minister is required to take responsibility in parliament and in the media for decisions to close hospitals, for breaches of waiting list targets and anything else that goes wrong right across the NHS.

1.35 The secretary of state has a range of procedural duties which govern the way in which he or she is required to discharge his or her functions, set out in sections 1A–1G of the NHS Act 2006, including the duty to exercise his or her functions with regard to the need to reduce inequalities.

Commissioners of NHS services

1.36 The term 'commissioning' is not defined in the NHS Act 2006. The NHS England website describes 'commissioning' as follows:[11]

> At its simplest, commissioning is the process of planning, agreeing and monitoring services. However, securing services is much more complicated than securing goods and the diversity and intricacy of the services delivered by the NHS is unparalleled. Commissioning is not one action but many, ranging from the health-needs assessment for a population, through the clinically based design of patient pathways, to service specification and contract negotiation or procurement, with continuous quality assessment. There is no single geography across which all services should be commissioned: some local services can be designed and secured for a population of a few thousand, while for rare disorders, services need to be considered and secured nationally.

1.37 This definition suggests that 'commissioning' NHS services is a continuing activity for NHS commissioners. Within the overall commissioning process, specific decisions may have to be made, such as closing down or reconfiguring a particular NHS service. When that happens, an NHS commissioner will enter into a particularly intense period of decision-making regarding the defined service. However, as the above definition explains, the overall commissioning duties of NHS commissioners are

11 See www.england.nhs.uk/commissioning/.

continuous and work on commissioning matters continue at all times and exist outside of any specific processes set up for service areas.

1.38 The commissioning process for every clinical commissioning group works on an annual cycle which is, at least in part, is defined by the NHS commissioners' annual plan which ought to set out its commissioning intentions. The main commissioners in the NHS are:

1) *NHS England*: NHS England was created by the HSCA 2012. It licences and, to a limited extent, performance manages, CCGs. However, NHS England is also a commissioner of a wide range of specialist NHS services, including prison health services, medical services for the armed forces and a wide range of specialised and tertiary acute services. NHS England commissions services for patients with rare conditions and also commissions primary care medical and dental services. This means that all GP practice contracts are made between NHS England and the local GP provider. Detailed arrangements for NHS England are set out in Schedule 1 to the HSCA 2012.
2) *CCGs*: These are local corporate public bodies created by the HSCA 2012. The members of a CCG are the local general practices in the CCG area who hold NHS commissioning contracts with NHS England. CCGs substantially replaced primary care trusts (PCTs) by taking on the commissioning of a range of acute and community NHS services (other than primary care, dental care and specialist services) for the patients for which the CCG has responsibility. The CCG has a constitution and a board, which is partly elected by the local GPs, and partly consists of other stakeholders in the local NHS. Detailed arrangements for CCGs are set out in Schedule 2 to the HSCA 2012.
3) *Local social services authorities*: The HSCA 2012 transferred responsibility for public health commissioning from PCTs to the local authorities. In practice this means that commissioning public health services is the responsibility of unitary local authorities or, in a case where there are two tiers of local authority, the county council.

1.39 The division of commissioning responsibility between NHS England, CCGs and local authorities is largely set out in the NHS Act 2006 and the National Health Service Commissioning Board and Clinical Commissioning Groups (Responsibilities and Standing Rules) Regulations 2012[12] ('the RSR Regs 2012'). The division between the services defined in section 3(1) of the NHS Act 2006 that are commissioned by NHS England and those that are commissioned by CCGs is described in chapter 4 below. NHS England also has a duty to commission the following services:

- primary care medical services (see Part 4 of NHS Act 2006);
- primary care dental services (see Part 5 of the NHS Act 2006);
- ophthalmic services (see Part 6 of the NHS Act 2006); and
- community pharmaceutical services (see Part 7 of the NHS Act 2006).

1.40 Included within the overall responsibilities of NHS England is the duty to commission 'specialist services': see Schedule 4 to the RSR Regs 2012. The budget for specialised services has grown substantially in recent years

12 SI No 2996.

and is now is in the region of £15.6 billion and so constitutes about 13 per cent of the overall NHS budget. It has grown from ten per cent of the overall budget between 2012 and 2014. The list of 152 specialist areas (as at April 2018) has been amended on various occasions since the list was published in 2012, and looks set for further amendment. Some descriptions of services which are commissioned by NHS England are fairly generic such as 'Specialist surgery for children and young people'. However, further details are set out in the *Manual for specialised commissioning* published by NHS England.

1.41 Local authorities only had a limited role in the NHS until the HSCA 2012. However that Act transferred public health functions from primary care trusts to the local authority which had social services functions. This is a county council in areas where there are two tiers of local authorities or unitary authorities in those areas just having a single local authority. Local authorities are required to work jointly with the secretary of state to appoint a 'Director of Public Health' (see section 73A of the NHS Act 2006).

1.42 The primary duties of local authorities are expressed widely in section 2B of the NHS Act 2006 as follows:

> Each local authority must take such steps as it considers appropriate for improving the health of the people in its area.

1.43 These are, of course, open-ended obligations which are severely restricted by the budgets available to local authorities. They include health prevention services, sexual health services and a host of other areas where timely intervention can reduce the need for later acute services. A useful guide to discharging public health functions has been prepared by the King's Fund.[13]

1.44 The main commissioning duties of CCGs are set out in section 3(1) of the NHS Act 2006 which provides as follows:

> (1) A clinical commissioning group must arrange for the provision of the following to such extent as it considers necessary to meet the reasonable requirements of the persons for whom it has responsibility–
> (a) hospital accommodation,
> (b) other accommodation for the purpose of any service provided under this Act,
> (c) medical, dental, ophthalmic, nursing and ambulance services,
> (d) such other services or facilities for the care of pregnant women, women who are breastfeeding and young children as the group considers are appropriate as part of the health service,
> (e) such other services or facilities for the prevention of illness, the care of persons suffering from illness and the after-care of persons who have suffered from illness as the group considers are appropriate as part of the health service,
> (f) such other services or facilities as are required for the diagnosis and treatment of illness.

1.45 Section 3(1E) provides that the duty in subsection (1) does not apply in relation to a service or facility if the board has a duty to arrange for its

13 www.kingsfund.org.uk/sites/default/files/field/field_publication_file/improving-the-publics-health-kingsfund-dec13.pdf.

provision. There can therefore be no 'overlap' between the services NHS England is obliged to commission and those which are the responsibility of local CCGs. Thus CCGs only have commissioning responsibility for the above services to the extent that these are not the commissioning responsibility of NHS England.

Providers of NHS services

1.46 The main providers of NHS services are:

a) *GP practices*: Almost all GP practices are private-sector businesses which contract with NHS England to provide primary care services to NHS patients across one or more practice areas. A GP practice can be owned by a single GP, a partnership of GPs, a partnership consisting of GPs and other approved persons or by a medical company.
b) *Dental practices*: Almost all NHS dental practices are private-sector businesses which contract with NHS England to provide primary care services to NHS patients across one or more practice areas. Largely similar restrictions on ownership apply to dentists as apply to GP practices.
c) *NHS trusts*: These are NHS bodies created under Chapter 3 of Part 2 of the NHS Act 2006. NHS trusts enter into acute services contracts with CCGs to provide a wide range of community, mental health and hospital services to patients. The plan of the government was that all NHS trusts should become NHS foundation trusts or be taken over by an NHS foundation trust by 2016. The secretary of state has the power to issue directions to an NHS trust under section 8 of the NHS Act 2006 which, if lawfully made, imposes specific legal obligations on NHS trusts to do things or provide services, or to cease to do something or cease to provide a service as specified in the direction.
d) *NHS foundation trusts*: These are public benefit corporations under Chapter 5 of Part 2 of the NHS Act 2006. NHS foundation trusts have members and governors, as well as a board of directors. NHS foundation trusts are accountable to a regulator, known as Monitor and are accountable to their members. The secretary of state has no power to issue directions to an NHS foundation trust.
e) *Special health authorities*: These are NHS bodies that perform particular specialist functions within the NHS, such as NHS Blood and Transplant which co-ordinates the supply of blood and organ transplantation services for the NHS.

Regulators of NHS services

1.47 The main bodies that regulate the performance of services by NHS bodies and have an interest in the way that NHS bodies are managed are as follows:

a) *Care Quality Commission (CQC)*: The CQC is the statutory body with responsibility for ensuring that hospitals, care homes, dental and GP surgeries, and all other care services in England provide people with safe, effective, compassionate and high-quality care, and to encourage them to make improvements. The CQC inspects and reports on all providers of social and health care in England, covering both the state and private sectors.

b) *Monitor*: Monitor was previously known as the Independent Regulator for NHS Foundation Trusts. However, its role was changed by Part 3 of the HSCA 2012. Its new role is to 'protect and promote the interests of patients' by attempting to ensure that the whole health sector works for their benefit. It was set up as, in effect, the competition regulator for the health market and so now has interests which extend far beyond NHS foundation trusts. It exercises a range of powers granted by parliament, which include setting and enforcing a framework of rules for providers and commissioners, implemented in part through licences issued to NHS-funded providers.

c) *Trust Development Authority (TDA)*: The TDA provides support to NHS trusts in a similar way to Monitor; it oversees and works with NHS foundation trusts. In operational terms (but not in legal terms), the TDA and Monitor have now been amalgamated in a single organisation known as 'NHS Improvement'. However, these two organisations continue to be separate legal entities.

d) *NHS England*: NHS England has a limited regulatory function in respect of CCGs. It licences CCGs and can step in if a CCG is not performing properly.

e) *Healthwatch*: Healthwatch is the latest in a long line of public bodies which are designed to feed the voice of the patient into the NHS. Previous bodies include Community Health Councils and PALS. Healthwatch England is a new public body set up by the HSCA 2012 to act as a national champion of patients' interests. There are now 152 local healthwatch groups who are supposed to champion the interests of patients in their local NHS. It is too early to tell whether local healthwatch groups are likely to have any real impact on local service delivery.

f) *Health overview and scrutiny committees*: These are committees made up of members of the local social services authority. Their role is to 'review and scrutinise' any matter relating to the planning, provision and operation of the health service in its area: see Part 4 of the Local Authority (Public Health, Health and Wellbeing Boards and Health Scrutiny) Regulations 2013.[14] The committee must be consulted about any 'substantial development of the health service in the area of a local authority' and, if they consider that the development is not 'in the interests of the health service in its area', it can refer the decision to the secretary of state, who then becomes the final decision-maker.

g) *Health and wellbeing boards*: These boards are intended to operate as a forum where key leaders from the health and care system work together to improve the health and wellbeing of their local population and reduce health inequalities, in particular by facilitating better working between health and social care services. Health and wellbeing board

14 SI No 218.

members ought to collaborate to understand their local community's needs, agree priorities and encourage commissioners to work in a more joined-up way. As a result, patients and the public should experience more joined-up services from the NHS and local councils in the future.

1.48 It is difficult, if not impossible, to argue that the NHS is set up in a coherent or entirely logical way. The arrangements have as much to do with politics as with good governance. However, the above system is designed to ensure a system of checks and balances, with the patient supposedly at the centre of all decision-making. Whether that happens in practice is, of course, a matter of considerable debate. Within the complex legal system operating in the NHS, clinicians undertake a variety of different functions and, depending on which function they are undertaking, will have different legal obligations. For example, a GP wears a large number of legal 'hats' depending on which function the GP is undertaking. An individual GP can be:

- a doctor who owes duties in tort (ie in negligence) to the patients of that individual doctor;
- a partner in a GP practice with legal duties to his or her partners under the deed of partnership;
- an employer of other clinical and non-clinical staff with a variety of contractual and statutory duties to his or her employees;
- part of a CCG and thus someone who takes commissioning decisions. These are administrative decisions which are taken within the scope of the public law duties of the CCG;
- a professional who has regulatory obligations to the General Medical Council (GMC);
- a person whose duties can attract the attentions of the police and the criminal justice system.

1.49 A clinician who works in hospitals has some but not all of the above legal duties. He or she (and the NHS trust or NHS foundation trust that employs the clinician) has private law duties to patients and is a regulated professional. However, unlike his or her colleagues in primary care, the clinician will be a direct employee of an NHS body rather than a self-employed professional or an employee of a primary care organisation.

1.50 In order to provide a description of the legal rights and obligations of a clinician in any individual situation, it is necessary to identify the legal function or functions the clinician is undertaking because, depending on what 'hat' the clinician is wearing, the legal responsibilities will vary. However, different types of legal obligation are engaged in any situation faced by a practising doctor, nurse or other NHS employee. It is not enough to ask if a proposed act is 'lawful' or not. The word 'lawful' is used and misused in common parlance, and can have a wide variety of meanings depending on the type of legal obligation involved. It is thus necessary to identify the type of legal obligation engaged in any particular set of facts and in particular to identify the consequences for that individual of any breach of that legal duty.

The different meanings of 'law' and legal obligations in the NHS

Types of legal obligations

1.51 The different types of legal obligations which arise for a clinician or anyone working in the NHS can, in general terms, be summarised as follows:

a) *Criminal law obligations*: Criminal law statutes and the common law define criminal offences which apply to everyone in defined circumstances. If a clinician acts in breach of those duties, then he or she may be prosecuted for breach of the criminal law in the same way as any other citizen. Hence, for example, a GP who assists a person to commit suicide may face prosecution in the Crown Court under section 2 of the Suicide Act 1961. The outcome of a prosecution for the breach of the criminal law is a punishment imposed by the criminal courts, which can vary from a sentence of imprisonment to a fine depending on the circumstances.

b) *Contractual law obligations*: Clinicians that are employed by an NHS body should have a contract of employment. That contract sets out contractual rights and duties on both sides.

   GPs tend either to be employees of a GP practice, principals in that practice or self-employed locums. In each situation, the GP will be party to one or more contracts which define contractual rights and duties on both sides. If a GP is a party to a partnership deed, the GP can acquire legal duties under this deed. This can give rise a wide range of legally binding obligations.[15] GP practices will hold a contract with NHS England[16] which defines their obligations and set out the duties of NHS England to make payments to the practice. Patients who are treated by a GP privately will have a contractual relationship with the GP. Employees of a GP practice are owed duties under their contracts of employment and, on a smaller scale, a GP may be a party to a contract to lease a photocopier. Each of these contracts gives rise to private law legal obligations. Contractual rights can be enforced by the GP or by another party against the GP in the civil courts (namely the County Court or the High Court). If a breach of contract is proved, the remedies available include damages and/or injunctions.

c) *Non-contractual private law legal obligations*: There is no contract between an NHS clinician and his or her NHS patients. However, where a clinician is treating patients, the clinician owes a legal 'duty of care' to his or her patients for treatment which is given or omitted to be given. Other legal duties include the duty to maintain the confidentiality of patient-related information held by the clinician. These

15 A 'contract' for these purposes is an agreement of sufficient certainty of terms concluded between two or more parties who intend to create legal relations supported by adequate consideration and where there is no other legal objection to the creation of enforceable legal obligations between the parties.

16 NHS England is the operating name for the National Health Service Commissioning Board. For details see www.england.nhs.uk/.

are private law duties which are owed because of the relationship between a clinician and his or her patients. It is the nature of the relationship which gives rise to the duty of care owed by the clinician to the patient for medical treatment and to maintain confidentiality. Any allegations of breach of this duty would be an allegation that the clinician has committed a civil wrong, which can give rise to a claim for damages. Such claims are tried in the civil courts if not otherwise resolved.

GPs who are not direct NHS employees are professionally required to be insured against such claims, usually with the Medical Protection Society or the Medical Defence Union.

d) *Information governance duties*: NHS bodies, including GP practices, hold vast quantities of personal data relating to their patients and others. Both NHS bodies and GP practices have to be registered 'data controllers' under the Data Protection Act 1998. Medical information relating to patients is defined as being sensitive personal data under the Data Protection Act 1998. As a result, NHS bodies have a series of complex legal duties concerned with the handling of personal data. Any complaint that they have breached such duties can result in a compliant to the Information Commissioner's Office.

In addition, NHS bodies are 'public bodies' within the Freedom of Information Act 2000. They thus have disclosure duties under that Act, although these duties do not apply to personal data which is covered exclusively by the Data Protection Act 1998. Any complaint that an NHS body (including a GP practice) has breached its duties under the Freedom of Information Act 2000 can also result in a compliant to the Information Commissioner's Office.

e) *Professional regulatory obligations*: In order to be lawfully entitled to deliver primary care medical services to patients, virtually all clinicians working in the NHS are required to be included on the list of the statutory regulator which is relevant to their professional group. Doctors must be on the list maintained by the General Medical Council (GMC), and nurses are regulated by the Nursing and Midwifery Council (NMC). The purpose of the GMC is to protect, promote and maintain the health and safety of the public by ensuring proper standards in the practice of medicine. Breaches of the GMC Code of Conduct will not necessarily amount to a breach of any other legal obligation owed by the doctor to his or her patient or indeed to anyone else, but may do so. A breach of the Code of Conduct may result in the GMC taking regulatory action against the doctor to seek removal from the Medical List or the imposition of conditions on the doctor's continuing inclusion on the list.

f) *Performers list obligations*: In addition to the regulatory role of the GMC, regulations require that every primary care professional (including GPs) delivering services to NHS patients (as opposed to treating patients privately) is included on a performers list maintained by NHS England. NHS England is entitled to seek the removal of a primary care professional from the Performers List in a variety of circumstances, including where NHS England conclude that it would be 'prejudicial to the efficiency of the services which those included in that performers list perform' to maintain the primary care professional on the Performers List or that the practitioner is 'unsuitable to be included in that performers list'.

g) *Statutory duties*: A huge variety of Acts of Parliament or regulations made under Acts of Parliament impose legal obligations on doctors working in the NHS including GPs. These are known as 'statutory duties'. There are, for example, statutory duties arising out the Health and Safety at Work etc Act 1974 which require GP practices to make their premises reasonably safe for visitors and those who work there. The Employment Rights Act 1996 imposes duties on employers to protect staff and prohibits NHS bodies from unfairly dismissing staff. The Equality Act 2010 imposes a range of duties on everyone providing public services not to discriminate when undertaking public functions. The obligation to pay a wide variety of taxes is all set out in statutes and enforced by HMRC.

   All these statutes create legal obligations and then provide a variety of mechanisms for determining whether there has been a breach of the statutory duty. Breach of statutory duty can result in a criminal case (as with health and safety breaches), a case before a tribunal (such as with employment rights that are heard before an Employment Tribunal) or may result in a civil claim for damages. Hence, by way of a further example, section 5B of the Female Genital Mutilation Act 2003 imposes a duty on healthcare professionals to make a report of any act of FGM that comes to their knowledge. Breach of that duty is an 'unlawful' act but the statute does not provide for any penalty. Nonetheless, a clinician who breached that legal duty could expect to face professional discipline charges.

h) *Public law obligations*: Lastly, there are specific legal obligations that are owed by public bodies. CCGs, NHS trusts and NHS foundation trusts are clearly public bodies as a result of the statutory duties imposed on them by the NHS Act 2006. A GP practice can also be treated as a public body for some purposes. CCGs are public bodies with a wide variety of public law duties, breach of which can result in action in the administrative court. Public bodies have a range of specific legal obligations, both at common law and under a huge variety of statutory schemes.

   Different public law obligations are enforced in different ways. For example, breaches of the duties under Freedom of Information Act 2000 are enforced by the Information Commissioner and on appeal to the First-tier Tribunal (Information Rights). If there is no other enforcement mechanism laid down in legislation, breaches of public law duties are enforced by way of applications for judicial review in the High Court.

How do these multiple legal duties work out in practice for a NHS clinicians and managerial staff?

1.52 A single act or sequence of events involving an NHS clinician or a staff member may engage more than one of the above legal duties. Hence, to take an extreme example, it may be alleged that a GP has delivered seriously substandard care to a patient who has subsequently died as a result of the failure of the care provided by the GP. Such a GP may find himself or herself having to meet the following legal problems:

- The GP may be prosecuted for breach of the criminal law, probably for the offence of manslaughter. If such a criminal case were to be brought, it will be tried in the Crown Court.
- The actions of the GP may be alleged to be a breach of the contract the GP holds with NHS England (such as a General Medical Services Contract). That may entitle NHS England to impose contract sanctions or even terminate the GMS contract.
- The actions of the GP may leave him or her in breach of his or her duties to his or her partners, and may lead to expulsion from the medical partnership.
- The GP will have breached his or her duties to the patient, and thus the patient's executors or administrators may sue the GP for damages. That claim would be brought in the civil courts. The GP may be able to rely on his or her professional indemnity insurance (provided for example by the MDU or MPS) to meet any damages.
- The GMC may take action to remove the GP from the Medical List by bringing the GP before a Fitness to Practise Panel.
- The GP may also face action from NHS England to remove him or her from the Performers List.

1.53 Each of the above legal consequences will involve different legal considerations even though they arise from the same set of primary facts.

1.54 A hospital doctor who was in a similar situation would face a slightly different set of legal issues, namely:

- The hospital doctor may be prosecuted for breach of the criminal law, probably for the offence of manslaughter. If such a criminal case were to be brought, it will be tried in the Crown Court.
- The actions of the hospital doctor may be alleged to be a breach of his or her employment contract with his or her employing trust. That may entitle the trust to suspend and eventually dismiss the doctor.
- The hospital doctor will have breached his or her duties to the patient and thus the patient's executors or administrators may sue the employing trust and possibly also the doctor for damages. That claim would be brought in the civil courts. The NHS Litigation Authority will become involved as the in-house 'insurer' for NHS trusts.
- The GMC may take action to remove the hospital doctor from the Medical List by bringing the doctor before a Fitness to Practise Panel.

1.55 In each case the doctor will have to work closely with the lawyers he or she has appointed (and possibly more than one set of lawyers) to protect his or her position. Some aspects of this legal work will be covered by professional indemnity insurance in the case of a GP, or the NHS Litigation Authority for a hospital doctor. However, in assessing and understanding the legal options and risks for the doctor, it will be essential to understand the particular legal framework within which the doctor is working, and the legal principles that apply to that particular legal action.

1.56 This book seeks to look in detail at the legal obligations that arise within the NHS and the legal rights and duties of various players within the NHS system in a variety of different situations. However, it is important that anyone working in the NHS or who advises NHS employees recognise that legal problems rarely exist in individual silos. The same set of primary facts can give rise to multiple legal issues, with NHS clinicians wearing different 'hats'. Individual chapters of this book are able to point out some occasions where there are likely to be multiple legal effects, but it would be impossible to predict every situation where one set of facts or allegations will give rise to multiple legal issues.

1.57 There are limitations to the extent to which a general guide can assist in a particular set of circumstances. If the text of this book is insufficient to assist in starting to address relevant questions, readers would be well advised to seek expert legal advice in relation to the particular facts of a case, building on the initial guidance obtained from this book.

CHAPTER 2

The purpose and effect of the NHS Constitution

Introduction

2.1 It is rare for a day to go by without one newspaper or another commenting that an NHS body is breaching the NHS Constitution. Such comments are particularly prevalent in the context of some of the more controversial health issues, notably referral to treatment, A&E waiting times or access to certain medical treatments or drugs. Journalists regularly pray in aid on patients' rights in the Constitution, such as the 'right to access certain services commissioned by NHS bodies within maximum waiting times'.[1]

2.2 The NHS Constitution, while certainly well-intentioned in its aims, is a widely misunderstood, underused, and in a sense misleading document. For those who are aware of this document (and the evidence suggests that there is still a woeful percentage of patients and, more worryingly, staff who do not know that it exists[2]), its exact legal status, as well as the source and applicability of the legal rights and responsibilities set out in it, can be obscure. Moreover, while the NHS Constitution seeks to simplify and explain existing legal rights and scenarios for the benefit of patients and staff, at times it over-simplifies the underlying web of inter-connecting rules, regulations and statutory obligations that the various NHS bodies are subject to.[3]

2.3 The purpose of this chapter is to explain exactly what the NHS Constitution is, what legal status it has, and how legal practitioners, patients and those working in the NHS may seek to use or rely on it.

What is the NHS Constitution?

2.4 The NHS Constitution is a document published by the Secretary of State for Health and Social Care that applies to the NHS in England. The secretary of state is required to publish an NHS Constitution as a result of section 1 of Chapter 1 of Part 1 of the Health Act 2009. The most recent version of the Constitution was published on 27 July 2015.

2.5 The NHS Constitution was developed as part of the NHS Next Stage Review led by Lord Darzi and was first published on 21 January 2009. The key legislation that underpins the NHS Constitution, Chapter 1 of Part 1 of the Health Act 2009, was brought into force almost a year later on 19 January 2010. The NHS Constitution was the result of extensive consultation and engagement with key stakeholders. The underlying purpose for creating the NHS Constitution was to bring about cultural change in the NHS; to move away from the idea of rival interests or a transactional relationship between staff and patients.[4]

1 The NHS Constitution is available in PDF form here: www.gov.uk/government/uploads/system/uploads/attachment_data/file/480482/NHS_Constitution_WEB.pdf.

2 See Chapter 2 of the latest *Report on the effect of the NHS constitution*, which suggests that public awareness of the NHS Constitution is at 24% and staff awareness is at 69%: www.gov.uk/government/uploads/system/uploads/attachment_data/file/440171/2904073_Report_on_the_NHS_Accessible_v0.1.pdf.

3 For an exposition of how one scenario in healthcare could engender multiple legal consequences and liabilities, please see 'An introduction to the legal structures of the NHS', para 1.52.

4 See the parliamentary debate here: https://publications.parliament.uk/pa/cm200809/cmpublic/health/090616/am/90616s06.htm.

2.6 The NHS Constitution describes itself as follows:

> The NHS is founded on a common set of principles and values that bind together the communities and people it serves – patients and public – and the staff who work for it.
>
> This Constitution establishes the principles and values of the NHS in England. It sets out rights to which patients, public and staff are entitled, and pledges which the NHS is committed to achieve, together with responsibilities, which the public, patients and staff owe to one another to ensure that the NHS operates fairly and effectively.
>
> The Secretary of State for Health, all NHS bodies, private and voluntary sector providers supplying NHS services, and local authorities in the exercise of their public health functions are required by law to take account of this Constitution in their decisions and actions.
>
> References in this document to the NHS and NHS services include local authority public health services, but references to NHS bodies do not include local authorities. Where there are differences of detail these are explained in the Handbook to the Constitution.

2.7 The NHS Constitution can be described as a 'framework' document for the NHS. In four chapters it sets outs:

- the principles that guide the NHS;
- the values of the NHS;
- the rights of patients and members of the public using the NHS;
- pledges the NHS makes to its patients;
- patients' responsibilities;
- the rights of NHS staff;
- pledges the NHS makes to its staff; and
- staff responsibilities.

2.8 It is accompanied by *The Handbook to the NHS Constitution* ('the Handbook'), the most recent version of which was also published on 27 July 2015.[5] The Handbook is designed to provide an explanation or rationale for everything contained within the Constitution.

2.9 The Constitution states:

> The Constitution will be renewed every 10 years, with the involvement of the public, patients and staff. It is accompanied by the Handbook to the NHS Constitution, to be renewed at least every three years, setting out current guidance on the rights, pledges, duties and responsibilities established by the Constitution. These requirements for renewal are legally binding. They guarantee that the principles and values which underpin the NHS are subject to regular review and recommitment; and that any government which seeks to alter the principles or values of the NHS, or the rights, pledges, duties and responsibilities set out in this Constitution, will have to engage in a full and transparent debate with the public, patients and staff.

2.10 It is important to note at the outset that the NHS Constitution is *not* legally enforceable per se. Rather, the NHS Constitution is best described as a declaratory document. The intention behind the creation of the document was that it would bring together and set out, in an easy-to-understand

5 The Handbook is available in PDF form here: www.gov.uk/government/uploads/system/uploads/attachment_data/file/474450/NHS_Constitution_Handbook_v2.pdf.

format, a combination of law, aspirations for the NHS and public commitments, as well as lay down the broad principles of the NHS. The NHS Constitution merely declares what the pre-existing law affecting the NHS is. It does not, and was not intended to, make law or create new rights or obligations.

2.11 This does not mean, however, that the NHS Constitution has no legal teeth. The Secretary of State for Health and Social Care, all NHS bodies, private and voluntary sector providers supplying NHS services, and local authorities in the exercise of their public health functions are required by law to 'have regard to' the NHS Constitution in their decisions and actions. There are also additional duties on NHS England and CCGS to promote the NHS Constitution and to promote awareness of it. The nature of these duties will be explored in this chapter.

2.12 When the Labour government introduced the NHS Constitution, it did not want the document to create any additional litigation for an already stretched NHS. As we will see in this chapter, that has broadly been the journey the NHS Constitution has taken. To the present day, there have been very few cases to even reference it, and still the legal duties and the framework that underpin the NHS Constitution have not been a source of much dispute.

What does the NHS Constitution contain?

NHS principles

2.13 The first chapter of the NHS Constitution is entitled 'Principles that guide the NHS'. This section contains seven key principles, which are intended to 'guide the NHS in all it does'. These principles are the foundation of the NHS Constitution and can only be amended pursuant to regulations. The seven principles are as follows:

1) The NHS provides a comprehensive service,[6] available to all.
2) Access to NHS services is based on clinical need, not an individual's ability to pay.
3) The NHS aspires to the highest standards of excellence and professionalism.
4) The patient will be at the heart of everything the NHS does.
5) The NHS works across organisational boundaries and in partnership with other organisations in the interest of patients, local communities and the wider population.
6) The NHS is committed to providing best value for taxpayers' money and the most effective, fair and sustainable use of finite resources.
7) The NHS is accountable to the public, communities and patients that it serves.[7]

6 The NHS does not in reality provide a comprehensive health service. The secretary of state and NHS England have a duty to promote a comprehensive health service but, as the Court of Appeal recognised in *R v North and East Devon Health Authority ex p Coughlan* [2001] QB 213, (1999) 2 CCLR 285, demand for NHS services will always outstrip resources, and a comprehensive health service may never in fact be provided.

7 The accompanying text gives further guidance on the principles.

NHS values

2.14 The second chapter of the Constitution contains the 'NHS values', which are expressed to 'provide common ground for co-operation to achieve shared aspirations, at all levels of the NHS'. They are as follows:

- Working together for patients.
- Respect and dignity.
- Commitment to quality of care.
- Compassion.
- Improving lives.
- Everyone counts.[8]

2.15 Neither the principles nor the values have any direct legal consequence in and of themselves, although it is clear that they are largely influenced by the legal framework that the NHS operates within.

Patient rights

2.16 Chapter 3a of the Constitution is entitled, 'Patients and the public – your rights and NHS pledges to you'. This part of the NHS Constitution is arguably the most widely known. The introductory paragraphs state:

> Everyone who uses the NHS should understand what legal rights they have. For this reason, important legal rights are summarised in this Constitution and explained in more detail in the Handbook to the NHS Constitution, which also explains what you can do if you think you have not received what is rightfully yours. This summary does not alter your legal rights.
>
> The Constitution also contains pledges that the NHS is committed to achieve. Pledges go above and beyond legal rights. This means that pledges are not legally binding but represent a commitment by the NHS to provide comprehensive high quality services.

2.17 The chapter sets out a long list of legal 'rights' of NHS patients, and pledges or public commitments, pertaining to various areas including:

- access to health services;
- quality of care and environment;
- nationally approved treatments, drugs and programmes;
- respect, consent and confidentiality;
- informed choice;
- involvement in your healthcare and in the NHS; and
- complaint and redress.

2.18 It is beyond the scope of this chapter to analyse every single one of the 'rights' set out in the Constitution, but some of the more frequently quoted rights are:

> You have the right to receive NHS services free of charge, apart from certain limited exceptions sanctioned by Parliament.
>
> . . .
>
> You have the right to drugs and treatments that have been recommended by NICE for use in the NHS, if your doctor says they are clinically appropriate for you.

8 The accompanying text provides guidance as to the meaning of the values.

> . . .
>
> You have the right to access certain services commissioned by NHS bodies within maximum waiting times, or for the NHS to take all reasonable steps to offer you a range of suitable alternative providers if this is not possible. The waiting times are described in the Handbook to the NHS Constitution.

2.19 The word 'rights' in this context is to some extent a misnomer. Many of the rights in the Constitution are more accurately analysed as summations of multiple legal obligations, which stem from a range of legal sources. These sources include public law duties, the law of negligence, the criminal law, and various regulations. It is therefore advisable that one goes to the Handbook to the Constitution to better understand the rights. The Handbook sets out for each right: i) what it means for patients and ii) what the source(s) of the right is or are.

2.20 For example, the NHS Constitution includes a:

> right to expect NHS bodies to monitor, and make efforts to improve continuously, the quality of healthcare they commission or provide. This includes improvements to the safety, effectiveness and experience of services.

This is not a recognised legal right. As the Handbook sets out, this right derives from a number of disparate sources:

- Under National Health Service Act (NHS Act) 2006 s13D, NHS England is under a duty to exercise its functions effectively, efficiently and economically.
- Under NHS Act 2006 s13E, NHS England is under a duty as to the improvement in quality of services provided to individuals.
- Under NHS Act 2006 s14S, clinical commissioning groups (CCGs) are under a duty to assist and support NHS England in discharging its duty under section 13E so far as relating to securing continuous improvement in quality of primary medical services.
- Under NHS Act 2006 s14R, CCGs are under a similar duty to NHS England as to improvement in quality of services provided to individuals.
- Under NHS Act 2006 s1A, the secretary of state is likewise under a similar duty as to improvement in quality of services provided to individuals.
- In discharging these duties (under section 1A, and under section 13E), the secretary of state and NHS England must have regard to any quality standards prepared by NICE under Health and Social Care Act (HSCA) 2012 s234.
- The law of negligence imposes a duty of care on providers of healthcare. This is a duty to take reasonable care and skill in the provision of treatment or other healthcare. For a health professional, what constitutes 'reasonable care and skill' will be determined by reference to professional practice. In the case of an NHS body or private organisation, it must take reasonable care to ensure a safe system of healthcare – using appropriately qualified and experienced staff.
- Individual health professionals are also governed by the standards set under the professional regulatory regime that applies to their profession.
- Under the HSCA 2008 persons who carry on regulated activities in England, including NHS, private and voluntary providers, have to register with the Care Quality Commission (CQC) and meet a set of essential requirements of safety and quality.
- This right is also based on the new 'fundamental standards', which set out the required level of quality and safety providers must meet fit and proper

persons employed as set out in Health and Social Care Act 2008 (Regulated Activities) Regulations 2014[9] regs 12 and 19. The CQC's role is to improve care by regulating and inspecting services. The CQC ensures that only persons carrying out the regulated activity who have made a legal declaration that they meet the essential fundamental standards are allowed to provide care. The CQC actively works as part of the wider system to detect and address failing organisations, sharing its findings with other regulators, including Monitor, and the commissioners of services.

2.21 The 'fundamental standards' in the Health and Social Care Act 2008 (Regulated Activities) Regulations 2014 form the basis of several of the rights in the NHS Constitution.[10] The CQC is able to take enforcement action against providers that do not meet these standards. Failure to meet the fundamental standards can, in some circumstances, have consequences under the criminal law. For example, reg 12 provides for the fundamental standard relating to safe care and treatment and is one of the sources of the right set out above. The 2014 Regulations prescribe that a registered person commits an offence if the they fail to comply with the requirements of the regulation and such failure results in:

(a) avoidable harm (whether of a physical or psychological nature) to a service user,
(b) a service user being exposed to a significant risk of such harm occurring, or
(c) in a case of theft, misuse or misappropriation of money or property, any loss by a service user of the money or property concerned.

2.22 The CQC may prosecute such providers. The 2014 Regulations provide for different levels of penalties and methods of enforcement.

2.23 What this brief analysis of just one of the rights in the Constitution demonstrates is as follows – although expressed as a 'right', it will invariably not be possible for a person who feels that his or her care has fallen short to go to court and cite his or her 'right to expect NHS bodies to monitor, and make efforts to improve continuously, the quality of healthcare they commission or provide'. Moreover, where an individual may be able to claim in a negligence action that an NHS provider has not taken reasonable care or skill in the provision of the individual's treatment or care, it is only the CQC that can enforce the fundamental standards. Thus the first step for every person seeking to rely on a right in the Constitution should be to go to the Handbook. To better understand the source(s) of that right, it would also be wise to seek legal advice, since one factual scenario may involve a multitude of legal obligations and liabilities.

Patient responsibilities

2.24 Chapter 3b of the Constitution is entitled, 'Patients and the public – your responsibilities'. The introductory paragraph states, 'The NHS belongs to all of us. There are things that we can all do for ourselves and for one another to help it work effectively, and to ensure resources are used responsibly'. Patients are asked to do the following things:

9 SI No 2936.

10 Other examples are the 'right to be protected from abuse and neglect, and care and treatment that is degrading' and the 'right to receive suitable and nutritious food and hydration to sustain good health and wellbeing'.

> Please recognise that you can make a significant contribution to your own, and your family's, good health and wellbeing, and take personal responsibility for it.
>
> Please register with a GP practice – the main point of access to NHS care as commissioned by NHS bodies.
>
> Please treat NHS staff and other patients with respect and recognise that violence, or the causing of nuisance or disturbance on NHS premises, could result in prosecution. You should recognise that abusive and violent behaviour could result in you being refused access to NHS services.
>
> Please provide accurate information about your health, condition and status.
>
> Please keep appointments, or cancel within reasonable time. Receiving treatment within the maximum waiting times may be compromised unless you do.
>
> Please follow the course of treatment which you have agreed, and talk to your clinician if you find this difficult.
>
> Please participate in important public health programmes such as vaccination.
>
> Please ensure that those closest to you are aware of your wishes about organ donation.
>
> Please give feedback – both positive and negative – about your experiences and the treatment and care you have received, including any adverse reactions you may have had. You can often provide feedback anonymously and giving feedback will not affect adversely your care or how you are treated. If a family member or someone you are a carer for is a patient and unable to provide feedback, you are encouraged to give feedback about their experiences on their behalf. Feedback will help to improve NHS services for all.

2.25 Except where the Constitution makes clear that violence towards staff and other patients, or causing a nuisance or disturbance on NHS premises, could have criminal consequences, it is doubtful whether a failure by a patient to comply with any of the 'responsibilities' imposed in this section could have legal consequences for him or her. In reality, this section of the Constitution reflects the modern aspiration for a more collaborative relationship between clinicians and the NHS with patients. In a period where the NHS is increasingly pressed for resources, it encourages patients to take more responsibility for their health needs.

Staff rights

2.26 Chapter 4a of the Constitution is entitled 'Staff – your rights and NHS pledges to you'. It is outside the scope of this book to analyse the vast employment and discrimination law framework relevant to staff working in the NHS. These rights are set out not in the Constitution itself but in the Handbook. However, the Constitution makes clear that:

> These rights are there to help ensure that staff:
>
> - have a good working environment with flexible working opportunities, consistent with the needs of patients and with the way that people live their lives;
> - have a fair pay and contract framework;
> - can be involved and represented in the workplace;

- have healthy and safe working conditions and an environment free from harassment, bullying or violence;
- are treated fairly, equally and free from discrimination;
- can in certain circumstances take a complaint about their employer to an Employment Tribunal; and
- can raise any concern with their employer, whether it is about safety, malpractice or other risk, in the public interest.

2.27 Like chapter 3a of the Constitution concerning patients' rights, chapter 4a also makes a number of pledges or public commitments to staff in relation to their employment conditions and working environment.

Staff responsibilities

2.28 Finally, chapter 4b of the Constitution is entitled 'Staff – your responsibilities'. Unlike chapter 3b concerning patient responsibilities, this section does summarise the legal duties on staff within the NHS. Again the sources of these responsibilities are diverse. They include: the Employment Rights Act 1996, the Health and Safety at Work etc Act 1974, the Equality Act 2010, the Human Rights Act 1998 and the Data Protection Act 1998, just to name a few. Chapter 4b also includes 'expectations that reflect how staff should play their part in ensuring the success of the NHS and delivering high quality care'.

The secretary of state's procedural duties concerning the NHS Constitution

2.29 The Health Act (HA) 2009 referred to the NHS Constitution which had been published in January 2009 and required the secretary of state to ensure that the NHS continued to have an NHS Constitution, as well as a Handbook to support the NHS Constitution. While it listed the NHS bodies which were required to have regard to the NHS Constitution, curiously the secretary of state was not originally required to have regard to the NHS Constitution when discharging his or her functions as secretary of state. The secretary of state only came under a duty to have regard to the NHS Constitution under the HSCA 2012.

2.30 Section 1 of the HA 2009 gives legal status to the NHS Constitution and the Handbook:

> (1) In this Chapter the 'NHS Constitution' means–
> (a) the document entitled 'The NHS Constitution' published by the Secretary of State on 21 January 2009, or
> (b) any revised version of that document published under section 3 or 4.
> (2) In this Chapter the 'Handbook' means–
> (a) the document entitled 'The Handbook to the NHS Constitution' published by the Secretary of State on 21 January 2009, or
> (b) any revised version of that document published under section 5.

2.31 Section 2 of the HA 2009 creates a duty for a defined list of NHS bodies and providers of NHS services to 'have regard' to the NHS Constitution. This duty is discussed fully in the following section.

2.32 Section 3 of the HA 2009 relates to the availability and review of the NHS Constitution. It creates a duty on the secretary of state to review the NHS Constitution every ten years and sets out consultation requirements in the event of such a review. It also prohibits amendment of the seven 'guiding principles' in the NHS Constitution (defined in subsection (7)) without the making of regulations. It provides as follows:

(1) The Secretary of State must ensure that the NHS Constitution continues to be available to patients, staff and members of the public.
(2) At least once in any period of 10 years the Secretary of State must carry out a review of the NHS Constitution (referred to in this Chapter as a '10 year review').
(3) The following must be consulted about the NHS Constitution on a 10 year review–
(a) patients and bodies or other persons representing patients,
(b) staff and bodies or other persons representing staff,
(c) carers,
[. . .]
(e) members of the public,
(f) the bodies and persons listed in section 2(2), (4) and (5), and
(g) such other persons as the Secretary of State considers appropriate.
(4) The first 10 year review must be completed not later than 5 July 2018.
(5) The guiding principles may not be revised as a result of a 10 year review, except in accordance with regulations made by the Secretary of State setting out the revision to be made.
(6) The Secretary of State must publish the NHS Constitution after any revision made as a result of a 10 year review.'

2.33 Section 4 of the HA 2009 relates to the secretary of state's powers to make revisions to the NHS Constitution other than a ten-year review. It contains similar provisions to section 3 regarding consultation requirements and the guiding principles. It provides as follows:

(1) This section applies to any revision of the NHS Constitution made other than as a result of a 10 year review (including any such revision which revises the guiding principles).
(2) Before any revision the Secretary of State must undertake appropriate consultation about the proposed revision.
(3) The persons consulted must include such patients, staff, members of the public and other persons as appear to the Secretary of State to be affected by the proposed revision.
(4) The guiding principles may not be revised, except in accordance with regulations made by the Secretary of State setting out the revision to be made.
(5) The Secretary of State must publish the NHS Constitution after any revision.

2.34 Section 5 of the HA 2009 relates to the availability, review and revision of the Handbook. Unlike the NHS Constitution, it creates an obligation to review the Handbook every three years. This reflects the fact that the Handbook contains the legal sources of much of the information in the NHS Constitution. The underlying framework regularly changes, meaning the Handbook requires fairly frequent revision. The latest Handbook was published on 27 July 2015. Section 5 of the HA 2009 provides as follows:

(1) The Secretary of State must ensure that the Handbook continues to be available to patients, staff and members of the public.

(2) At least once in any period of 3 years the Secretary of State must carry out a review of the Handbook.
(3) The first review must be completed not later than 5 July 2012.
(4) The Secretary of State must publish the Handbook after any revision (whether made as a result of a review under this section or otherwise).

2.35 Section 6 of the HA 2009 imposes a duty on the secretary of state to publish a report every three years on the effect of the NHS Constitution. It provides as follows:

(1) The Secretary of State must publish a report every 3 years on how the NHS Constitution has affected patients, staff, carers and members of the public, since the last report was produced under this subsection.
(2) The first report must be published not later than 5 July 2012.
(3) The Secretary of State must lay before Parliament a copy of each report under subsection (1).

2.36 The most recent report, published on 1 July 2015, makes fairly woeful reading in terms of patient awareness of the NHS Constitution.[11] However, the report is more positive about staff awareness and attitude towards the NHS Constitution. The Executive Summary states:

> It is clear that patients and NHS staff believe it is important that the NHS has a Constitution; and indeed, there is evidence that the higher the awareness, the greater the support. Yet public awareness of the NHS Constitution remains low, and has even dropped since the 2012 research, from 27% to 24%. There remains little evidence that patients are using the NHS Constitution as a means of exercising their rights.
>
> Staff awareness of the NHS Constitution is significantly higher than the first report in 2012, rising from 54% to 69%. Furthermore there is a statistically significant increase in the understanding of the NHS Constitution amongst staff. Increasingly, NHS staff feel that the NHS Constitution is beneficial to patients, particularly in allowing them to understand their entitlements. Finally, 81% NHS staff believe that it is important that the NHS has a Constitution.

2.37 Finally, section 7 of the HA 2009 creates a power for the secretary of state to make regulations pursuant to section 3 or 4.

The duty to have regard to the NHS Constitution

2.38 Section 2 of the HA 2009 imposes a duty on a number of bodies 'to have regard to the NHS Constitution' in performing their health service functions. It provides:

(1) Each of the bodies listed in subsection (2) must, in performing its health service functions, have regard to the NHS Constitution.
(2) The bodies are–

. . .

(c) National Health Service trusts;
(ca) the National Health Service Commissioning Board;
(cb) clinical commissioning groups;

11 The report is available here: www.gov.uk/government/uploads/system/uploads/attachment_data/file/440171/2904073_Report_on_the_NHS_Accessible_v0.1.pdf.

(cc) local authorities (within the meaning of section 2B of the National Health Service Act 2006);
(d) Special Health Authorities;
(da) the National Institute for Health and Care Excellence;
(db) the Health and Social Care Information Centre;
(e) NHS foundation trusts;
(f) Monitor;
(g) the Care Quality Commission;
(h) Health Education England.

2.39 Subsection (3) provides that 'in subsection (1) a "health service function" means any function under an enactment which is a function concerned with, or connected to, the provision, commissioning or regulation of health services'. Subsection (7) provides for the purposes of Chapter 1 of the HA 2009 that '"health services" means health services provided in England for the purposes of the health service continued under section 1(1) of the National Health Service Act 2006'.

2.40 As well as the NHS bodies listed in section 2(2) of the HA 2009, any person (for example, a private provider or voluntary organisation) who provides health services under a contract, agreement or other arrangement, or any person who makes arrangements under a subcontract for another person to provide or assist in providing those services, or any person who is providing or assisting in providing health services under a subcontract, must also have regard to the NHS Constitution. The duty is therefore far-reaching and applies to any provider who holds a contract with an NHS commissioner or who operates as a subcontractor to an NHS provider. Subsections (4)–(6) provide:

(4) Each person who–
(za) provides health services under arrangements made by the National Health Service Commissioning Board or a clinical commissioning group under or by virtue of section 3, 3A, 3B or 4 of, or Schedule 1 to, the National Health Service Act 2006,
(a) provides health services under a contract, agreement or arrangements made under or by virtue of an enactment listed in subsection (6),
(b) provides or assists in providing health services under arrangements under section 12(1) of the National Health Service Act 2006, or
(c) provides health services under arrangements made by a local authority for the purposes of its functions under or by virtue of section 2B or 6C(1) of, or Schedule 1 to, that Act,
must, in doing so, have regard to the NHS Constitution.
(5) Each person who–
(a) in pursuance of a contract, agreement or arrangements as mentioned in subsection (4)(za), (a), (b) or (c), makes arrangements ('sub-contracting arrangements') for another person to provide or assist in providing health services, or
(b) provides or assists in providing health services under sub-contracting arrangements,
must, in doing so, have regard to the NHS Constitution.
(6) The enactments referred to in subsection (4)(a) are the following provisions of the National Health Service Act 2006–
(a) section 83(2)(b) (arrangements made by PCTs for provision of primary medical services);

(b) section 84(1) (general medical services contracts);
(c) section 92 (other arrangements for the provision of primary medical services);
(d) section 100(1) (general dental services contracts);
(e) section 107(1) (other arrangements for the provision of primary dental services);
(f) section 117(1) (general ophthalmic services contracts);
(g) section 126(1) (pharmaceutical services);
(h) section 127(1) (additional pharmaceutical services);
(i) Schedule 12 (local pharmaceutical services schemes).

2.41 The secretary of state was conspicuously absent from the list of bodies subject to the duty under section 2 of the HA 2009. The secretary of state was made subject to the same duty to have regard to the NHS Constitution when section 1B was inserted into the NHS Act 2006 by the HSCA 2012. Section 1B of the NHS Act 2006 provides:

(1) In exercising functions in relation to the health service, the Secretary of State must have regard to the NHS Constitution.
(2) In this Act, 'NHS Constitution' has the same meaning as in Chapter 1 of Part 1 of the Health Act 2009 (see section 1 of that Act).

2.42 The legal effect of the NHS Constitution thus stems predominantly from this 'have regard' duty. However, a duty to 'have regard' to the NHS Constitution is not a duty to 'comply' with it. It will not necessarily be unlawful in and of itself for the secretary of state or one of the bodies subject to the section 2 duty to act in a way that contravenes or breaches the NHS Constitution. The 'have regard' duty is a duty which bites on the procedure used by an NHS body for making decisions. Any NHS body which is subject to the duty must have understood and very carefully considered the relevant provisions of the NHS Constitution whenever it is making decisions or exercising NHS functions. However, a decision-maker who properly considers the NHS Constitution could nonetheless depart from the rights set out in the NHS Constitution if there are good and justifiable reasons to do so.

2.43 The duty to have regard to the NHS Constitution was aptly characterised by Green J in *R (Justice for Health Ltd) v Secretary of State for Health*[12] as a 'target duty'. Having referred to a number of the general duties on the secretary of state under section 1 of the NHS Act 2006,[13] he said:

> 88. The duties referred to above are loosely termed 'target duties' because although cast in mandatory terms they lay down broad objectives to be achieved and impose upon the Minister the obligation to act in a way which is eg 'designed to achieve' or 'secure' the objective (section 1(1)) or to act 'with a view to securing' the objective (section 1A(1)) or to 'have regard to' the objective (section 1B(1)). They are target duties in the sense that (a) they do not specify a particular or precisely defined end result as opposed to a broad aim or object and (b) their mandatory nature is diluted by the fact that they do not compel the achievement of that end result instead requiring the Secretary of State only to factor those objectives into consideration.

12 [2016] EWHC 2338 (Admin). A challenge by a group of junior doctors to the manner in which a new set of terms and conditions of employment were to be rolled out across the NHS (the junior doctors' contract).

13 On which see chapter 3 on the powers and duties of the secretary of state.

2.44 The claimants had relied on the section 1B duty on the secretary of state to the effect that he should have had regard to chapter 4a of the NHS Constitution, which sets out the rights of and commitments to staff. It followed that the secretary of state was to have regard to such employment-related matters when seeking to achieve his target duties and exercise his statutory powers and functions relevant to the new junior doctors' contract. While, as is increasingly common, the judge included the 'have regard' duty in part of the judgment setting out the general legal framework to the dispute, nothing in the case turned on the section 1B duty.

2.45 The nature of a 'have regard' duty was also considered by Collins J in *R (The Pharmaceutical Services Negotiating Committee) v Secretary of State for Health*[14] in the context of the duty on the secretary of state under section 1C of the NHS Act 2006 to 'have regard to the need to reduce inequalities between the people of England with respect to the benefits that they can obtain from the health service'.[15] Considering whether there was any substantive difference between a duty to 'have regard' and one to 'have due regard', he said:

> . . . I am equally wholly unpersuaded that there is in reality any material difference between the obligations to have regard and to have due regard. Merely to have regard in the sense that the existence of the statutory requirements is recognised is never likely to suffice, albeit much will turn on the nature of the matters to which regard must be had. In section 1C it is a specific need to reduce inequalities so that the defendant is obliged to show that that need is recognised and that what is proposed does not in his view at the very least cause an increase in such inequalities.

2.46 The Court of Appeal also considered the secretary of state's duty under section 1B of the NHS Act 2006 to have regard to the NHS Constitution in *R (Tracey) v Cambridge University Hospitals NHS Foundation Trust.*[16] The claimant argued that the secretary of state's failure to issue a national 'do not attempt cardio-pulmonary resuscitation' (DNACPR) policy, was not only a violation of Article 8 of the European Convention on Human Rights (ECHR) but constituted a breach of the duty under section 1B of the NHS Act 2006. The claimant relied on the part of the NHS Constitution that said:

> You have the right to be involved in discussions and decisions about your health and care, including your end of life care, and to be given information to enable you to do this. Where appropriate this right includes your family and carers.

Instead of issuing such a national policy, the Department of Health had in a Health Service Circular published in 2000 commended a joint statement from the British Medical Association, Resuscitation Council (UK) and the Royal College of Nursing *Decisions relating to cardiopulmonary resuscitation* (1999), as an appropriate basis for trusts to form their own local resuscitation policies.

2.47 Dismissing the claimant's argument, Lord Dyson MR said:

> 83. I cannot accept the submission that the Secretary of State is in breach of section 1B(1) of the 2006 Act in failing to issue a national DNACPR policy.

14 [2017] EWHC 1147 (Admin).

15 On which see chapter 3 on the powers and duties of the secretary of state. This case is due to be heard in the Court of Appeal in 2018.

16 [2014] EWCA Civ 822.

The obligation is to 'have regard' to the constitution. The constitution does not prescribe the means by which its objective of patient involvement is to be achieved. The decision to commend the joint statement was sufficient to discharge the statutory obligation.

2.48 In practice, how can those subject to the 'have regard' duty comply with it? Put broadly, decision-makers should ensure that their decision-making process, including a consideration of the relevant part of the NHS Constitution and any reasons for acting in a way contrary to the NHS Constitution, is clearly recorded. It would be advisable, although it is not a statutory requirement, for any decision-maker to also consider the Handbook, which gives important background and detail to the information and guidance set out in the NHS Constitution. Further possible steps include:

- having a regular item on the agenda of board meetings to consider how the body is performing against the NHS Constitution;
- assessing existing policies and activities such as annual reports, or staff or patient surveys, to ensure that they are in line with the NHS Constitution;
- looking for opportunities to build the NHS Constitution into any policy making; and
- checking against the NHS Constitution before publishing any new policy or document of the body.

Additional duties on NHS England, clinical commissioning groups and other NHS bodies in relation to the NHS Constitution

2.49 In addition to the 'have regard' duty under section 2 of the HA 2009, some NHS bodies are under additional duties in relation to the NHS Constitution.

2.50 Under section 13C of the NHS Act 2006, NHS England is under a duty as to the promotion of the NHS Constitution. Section 13C is a dual-pronged duty and provides:

> (1) The Board[17] must, in the exercise of its functions–
> (a) act with a view to securing that health services are provided in a way which promotes the NHS Constitution, and
> (b) promote awareness of the NHS Constitution among patients, staff and members of the public.

2.51 CCGs are subject to an identical duty under section 14P of the NHS Act 2006, which provides:

> (1) Each clinical commissioning group must, in the exercise of its functions–
> (a) act with a view to securing that health services are provided in a way which promotes the NHS Constitution, and
> (b) promote awareness of the NHS Constitution among patients, staff and members of the public.

2.52 Additionally, under section 99(4) of the Care Act 2014, Health Education England (HEE) is required to 'exercise its functions with a view to securing that education and training for healthcare workers is provided

17 'The Board' refers to NHS England.

in a way which promotes the NHS Constitution'. HEE is an executive non-departmental public body responsible for education, training and workforce development in the health sector.

2.53 As NHS England, CCGs and HEE are already subject to the HA 2009 s2 'have regard' duty, it is difficult to envisage circumstances in which the above sections impose additional obligations on them. The wording of the first limb of the NHS Act 2006 ss13C and 14P duties, and of the Care Act 2014 s99(4) duty, appears weak. Like the section 2 'have regard' duty, they can be categorised as 'target duties'. The statutory obligation is not to ensure that health services (or education and training) are provided in a way that complies with the NHS Constitution, nor even that they are provided in a way that promotes the NHS Constitution. The duty is to 'act with a view to securing' the latter, so it is one further step removed.

2.54 The explanatory notes to the Health and Social Care Bill are equally vague:

> 183. Duty to promote NHS Constitution. New section 13C places a duty on the NHS Commissioning Board to promote and raise awareness of the NHS Constitution when exercising its functions. This is in addition to the duty on the NHS Commissioning Board under the Health Act 2009 (as amended by paragraph 167 of Schedule 5) to 'have regard' to the NHS Constitution. The new duty means that when exercising all of its functions, the Board has to act with a view to securing that health services are provided in a way that promotes the NHS Constitution, is required to promote awareness of the NHS Constitution among patients, staff and members of the public. This means that not only must the Board act in accordance with the NHS Constitution but it should also ensure that people are made aware of their rights under it and that they contribute as far as possible to the advancement of its principles, rights, responsibilities and values, through its own actions and through facilitating the actions of stakeholders, partners and providers.[18]

2.55 Given the weak nature of the promotion duties, it is doubtful that a court would be able to hold that a CCG or NHS England was in breach if it at least attempted to comply with the NHS Constitution in the exercise of its functions. This does not mean, however, that the promotion duties have been entirely insignificant in litigation against NHS bodies. If one can identify a trend from the very few reported cases in which they are cited, it is that the duties to promote the NHS Constitution are being relied on as a sort of reinforcing factor by claimants in the context of claims based on breaches of more specific public law duties. For example, Green J in *National Aids Trust v NHS England*[19] at first instance cited NHS England's duty under section 13C of the NHS Act 2006. He did so to support his conclusion that NHS England had misdirected itself in law when it concluded that it had no power to commission PrEP, an antiretroviral drug to be used on a preventative basis for those at high risk of contracting AIDS, on the basis that this was a 'public health function' to be carried out by the secretary of state or local authorities. At the heart of the case was the question about whose budget the cost of PrEP medication was to be paid from (the budget of NHS

18 These notes refer to the Health and Social Care Bill as brought from the House of Commons on 8 September 2011, HL Bill 92.

19 [2016] EWHC 2005 (Admin), (2016) 19 CCLR 459.

England or that of local authorities). Green J referred to the section 13C duty as a 'reinforcing factor' and 'purposive consideration' from the NHS Act 2006 that supported his conclusion.[20] He said:

> d) Under section 13C NHSA 2006 NHS England has a duty to act 'with a view to securing that health services are provided in a way which promotes the NHS Constitution' which includes, at principle 1, that the service is 'designed to improve, prevent, diagnose and treat both physical and mental health conditions' and involves a 'duty to promote equality through the services it provides'. The Mandate (see paragraph [11] above) is to the same effect.[21]

2.56 The NHS Act 2006 s14P duty on CCGs was also referred to by the court as a reinforcing factor in construing the nature of the defendant's public law duties in the case of *R (Rose) v Thanet CCG*.[22] This case was challenge to the defendant's refusal of the claimant's Individual Funding Request (IFR) for oocyte cryopreservation (ie freezing of her eggs) before she had chemotherapy and treatment for her severe form of Crohn's disease, which would likely make her infertile. The claimant argued that the fact that the National Institute for Health and Care Excellence (NICE) had made a 'strong' recommendation that oocyte cryopreservation should be offered to those in like cases to her was a relevant consideration bearing on the CCG's public law obligation, reflected in the NHS Constitution, to make rational decisions following a proper evaluation of the evidence. She relied on the following rights as set out in the NHS Constitution:

> **Nationally approved treatments, drugs and programmes:**
>
> You have the right to drugs and treatments that have been recommended by the National Institute for Health and Care Excellence ('NICE') for use in the NHS, if your doctor says they are clinically appropriate for you.
>
> You have the right to expect local decisions on funding of other drugs and treatments to be made rationally following a proper consideration of the evidence. If the local NHS decides not to fund a drug or treatment you and your doctor feel would be right for you, they will explain that decision to you.

2.57 The recommendation in question was a recommendation made under regulation 5 of the National Institute for Health and Care Excellence (Constitution and Functions) and the Health and Social Care Information Centre (Functions) Regulations 2013[23] ('the NICE Regulations'). This was not a 'technology appraisal recommendation' or 'highly specialised technology appraisal recommendation', which CCGs must comply with in accordance with the statutory scheme. General recommendations under regulation 5 are akin to advice or guidance.

2.58 In construing the exact nature of the defendant's public law duty to make a lawful funding decision, Jay J relied on the quoted passage in the

20 At para 80.

21 It should be noted that, while upholding his order, the Court of Appeal did not support Green J's analysis of section 1H of the NHS Act 2006, in the context of which he called the section 13C duty a 'reinforcing factor' (see Longmore LJ at paras 28–33, [2016] EWCA Civ 1100, (2017) 20 CCLR 30). Green J's reference to section 13C, however, was not expressly disapproved.

22 [2014] EWHC 1182 (Admin).

23 SI No 259.

NHS Constitution as a 'reinforcing factor' in his conclusion that NICE recommendations under regulation 5 have the status of public law relevant considerations.[24] The judge also referred to the NHS Constitution, stating that, 'in the present case the CCG's obligation under the NHS Constitution is to make rational funding decisions grounded on a proper appraisal of the evidence base'.[25]

2.59 However, it is a principle of statutory construction that every section of an Act of Parliament must be given a meaning. Hence the sections in the HSCA 2012 must be construed in a way that adds to the legal duties on CCGs, NHS England and HEE over and above their duties under the HA 2009, even if it is difficult to envisage the precise circumstances where that difference will lead to a different legal obligation on an NHS body.

2.60 Arguably the second limb of the duties under NHSA 2006 ss13C and 14P has greater legal force. The duty is a direct duty to 'promote awareness of the NHS Constitution among patients, staff and members of the public'. It is plain to see why a duty to ensure awareness of the Constitution would place a near impossible burden on NHS England and CCGs. However, the wording of this duty is stronger than that of the first limb. It is suggested that NHS England and CCGs might comply with this duty by, for example:

- ensuring that the Constitution is available on their website or in paper or other formats on request;
- ensuring that those with whom they 'make arrangements' to provide NHS services do the same;
- monitoring whether those patients and staff for whom they are responsible are aware of the Constitution; and
- ensuring that the objective of increasing awareness of the Constitution is built into their decision-making and policy creation wherever possible.

2.61 Of course, CCGs and NHS England should also be aware of their duties under section 149 of the Equality Act 2010 (the 'public sector equality duty') and ensure that they can provide copies of the Constitution in audio format, large-type format, braille, and foreign languages, for example.

Conclusion

2.62 In practice, the NHS Constitution has not made great legal shockwaves, and was never intended to do so; it is a declaratory document. It is increasingly used, though, by judges in the context of purposive constructions of NHS bodies' statutory and public law duties. Arguably the real strength of the Constitution is not legal but practical – it provides in an easy-to-understand format a summary of relevant obligations owed by NHS commissioners and providers. This document may arm a patient or member of NHS staff with information in the face of a dispute or problem with a patient's care. If, however, patients and (less so) staff continue to be unaware that it exists, as the latest report on the effect of the Constitution suggests, its potential as a useful tool for patients and staff will remain unfulfilled.

24 See para 23.
25 At para 91.

Part 2
The roles and responsibilities of NHS bodies

CHAPTER 3

The powers and duties of the secretary of state

Introduction

3.1 The Secretary of State for Health and Social Care sits at the pinnacle of the NHS with ultimate political responsibility for the performance of NHS. However, the secretary of state is not a healthcare professional and may not have any NHS management experience. He or she will be a hugely experienced politician leading a public service where the personal is political. Thus the NHS needs the political skills of an astute secretary of state just as the secretary of state needs the technical and professional guidance of all those who advise him and her. In recent years, secretaries of state have tended to remain in post over a number of years and have learned the complexities of the NHS while discharging the complex functions of the office. They have also (in almost all cases and regardless of party) developed a steely commitment to the NHS throughout their time in office, albeit that may not always be apparent to those operating outside the Whitehall machine.

3.2 The Secretary of State for Health and Social Care has a very wide range of powers and duties as a result of a variety of Acts of Parliament and subordinate legislation. This chapter lists the main functions undertaken by the secretary of state but it is not a comprehensive list of every function undertaken by the secretary of state (which would require a separate book). Hence, for example, the secretary of state has a substantial role in relation to the prices that the NHS pays for medicines under section 260 of the National Health Service Act (NHS Act) 2006 (as recently changed by the Health Service Medical Supplies (Costs) Act 2017 which has not yet been implemented). The details of this complex statutory scheme to control drug prices are a specialist area of law and are hence beyond a description of the general powers of the secretary of state.

3.3 The NHS Act 2006, as substantially amended by the Health and Social Care Act (HSCA) 2012, removed significant parts of the operational duties owed by the secretary of state and replaced these duties with an overall strategic role for the ministers. Hence, for example, the duty of the secretary of state to commission services for patients in section 3 of the NHS Act 2006 was replaced with the commissioning duties being owed by a combination of clinical commissioning groups (CCGs) and the National Health Service Commissioning Board (which operates under the name of 'NHS England'). This technical legal change attracted considerable (and possibly misguided) criticism, but it did not involve any substantial change in practice. Under previous arrangements, the secretary of state had delegated performance of his duty to commission services for patients to local NHS commissioners for many years[1] and challenges to the exercise of that decision-making functions were made against the local NHS commissioners and not the secretary of state. However, the political controversy about the perceived abandonment of the secretary of state's direct respons-

1 Prior to the HSCA 2012 this delegation was under the National Health Service (Functions of Strategic Health Authorities and Primary Care Trusts and Administration Arrangements) (England) Regulations 2002 SI No 2375 (as amended).

ibility for providing services to patients led to a new section 1(3) of the NHS Act 2006, which provides:

> The Secretary of State retains ministerial responsibility to Parliament for the provision of the health service in England.

It follows that the secretary of state is *politically* responsible for the NHS to parliament even though operational responsibility sits with NHS England, the CCGs and the various organisations (both NHS bodies and others) that provide services to patients.

3.4 The primary duty on the secretary of state lies in section 1 of the NHS Act 2006 which provides that the secretary of state has a duty to 'continue the promotion of' a comprehensive health service. Section 1 provides:

> (1) The Secretary of State must continue the promotion in England of a comprehensive health service designed to secure improvement–
> (a) in the physical and mental health of the people of England, and
> (b) in the prevention, diagnosis and treatment of physical and mental illness.

3.5 Section 1H imposes a like duty on the National Health Service Commissioning Board (ie NHS England) as follows:

> (1) There is to be a body corporate known as the National Health Service Commissioning Board ('the Board').
> (2) The Board is subject to the duty under section 1(1) concurrently with the Secretary of State except in relation to the part of the health service that is provided in pursuance of the public health functions of the Secretary of State or local authorities.
> (3) For the purpose of discharging that duty, the Board–
> (a) has the function of arranging for the provision of services for the purposes of the health service in England in accordance with this Act, and
> (b) must exercise the functions conferred on it by this Act in relation to clinical commissioning groups so as to secure that services are provided for those purposes in accordance with this Act.

Thus, the duty to promote a comprehensive health service is imposed on both the secretary of state and NHS England.

3.6 There is an important distinction in law between the duty on the secretary of state to *promote* a comprehensive health service and a duty to *provide* a comprehensive health service.[2] It follows that while the secretary of state and NHS England must have this duty in mind at all times, neither the secretary of state nor NHS England will be in breach of the duty if the NHS fails to deliver a comprehensive health service. Indeed, as the budget for NHS services is limited and the demand for NHS services will expand as services are provided and thus is practically infinite, it seems inevitable that, in practice, the secretary of state will never be in a position to ensure that the NHS provides a comprehensive health service.

2 Please see para 1.18 above for more detail on the difference between a duty to *promote* a comprehensive healthcare service and a duty to *provide* a comprehensive healthcare service.

The secretary of state's mandate to NHS England

3.7 Section 13A of the NHS Act 2006, as introduced by the HSCA 2012, formalised the relationship between the Secretary of State for Health and Social Care and NHS England (which is referred to in legislation as 'the Board'). It provides:

> **13A Mandate to Board**
> (1) Before the start of each financial year, the Secretary of State must publish and lay before Parliament a document to be known as 'the mandate'.
> (2) The Secretary of State must specify in the mandate–
> (a) the objectives that the Secretary of State considers the Board should seek to achieve in the exercise of its functions during that financial year and such subsequent financial years as the Secretary of State considers appropriate, and
> (b) any requirements that the Secretary of State considers it necessary to impose on the Board for the purpose of ensuring that it achieves those objectives.
> (3) The Secretary of State must also specify in the mandate the amounts that the Secretary of State has decided to specify in relation to the financial year for the purposes of section 223D(2) and (3) (limits on capital and revenue resource use).
> (4) The Secretary of State may specify in the mandate any proposals that the Secretary of State has as to the amounts that the Secretary of State will specify in relation to subsequent financial years for the purposes of section 223D(2) and (3).
> (5) The Secretary of State may also specify in the mandate the matters by reference to which the Secretary of State proposes to assess the Board's performance in relation to the first financial year to which the mandate relates.
> (6) The Secretary of State may not specify in the mandate an objective or requirement about the exercise of the Board's functions in relation to only one clinical commissioning group.
> (7) The Board must–
> (a) seek to achieve the objectives specified in the mandate, and
> (b) comply with any requirements so specified.
> (8) Before specifying any objectives or requirements in the mandate, the Secretary of State must consult–
> (a) the Board,
> (b) the Healthwatch England committee of the Care Quality Commission, and
> (c) such other persons as the Secretary of State considers appropriate.
> (9) Requirements included in the mandate have effect only if regulations so provide.

3.8 There are supplemental provisions in section 13B which provide:

> **13B The mandate: supplemental provision**
> (1) The Secretary of State must keep the Board's performance in achieving any objectives or requirements specified in the mandate under review.
> (2) If the Secretary of State varies the amount specified for the purposes of section 223D(2) or (3), the Secretary of State must revise the mandate accordingly.
> (3) The Secretary of State may make any other revision to the mandate only if–

(a) the Board agrees to the revision,
(b) a parliamentary general election takes place, or
(c) the Secretary of State considers that there are exceptional circumstances that make the revision necessary.

(4) Revisions to the mandate which consist of adding, omitting or modifying requirements have effect only if regulations so provide.

(5) If the Secretary of State revises the mandate, the Secretary of State must–
(a) publish the mandate (as so revised), and
(b) lay it before Parliament, together with an explanation of the reasons for making the revision.

3.9 The requirement on the secretary of state to issue NHS England with a mandate was introduced by the HSCA 2012. It replaced the *NHS operating framework* which was a Department of Health and Social Care (DHSC) framework document which was issued each year in the years prior to the implementation of the HSCA 2012. The *NHS operating framework* sought to set out the secretary of state's broad priorities for the NHS in each financial year, albeit it was issued in the name of the Chief Executive of the NHS (not the Permanent Secretary at the DHSC). The last *NHS operating framework* was issued in November 2011 for the financial year 2012/13[3] and was described as follows:

> This document outlines the business and planning arrangements for the NHS in 2012/13. It describes the national priorities, system levers and enablers needed for NHS organisations to maintain and improve the quality of services provided, while delivering transformational change and maintaining financial stability.

3.10 *The Government's mandate to NHS England for 2017–18*[4] set a number of objectives that the secretary of state required NHS England to seek to achieve, namely:

- Through better commissioning, improve local and national health outcomes, and reduce health inequalities.
- To help create the safest, highest quality health and care service.
- To balance the NHS budget and improve efficiency and productivity.
- To lead a step change in the NHS in preventing ill health and supporting people to live healthier lives.
- To maintain and improve performance against core standards.
- To improve out-of-hospital care.
- To support research, innovation and growth.

3.11 Section 13A(7) of the NHS Act 2006 requires NHS England to 'seek to achieve' these objectives. However, as it is a target duty, NHS England will not necessarily act unlawfully if the objectives are not achieved or are only partly achieved, provided NHS England is striving to achieve the objectives set out in the mandate. There will probably be no breach of the legal duties created by the mandate if the NHS fails to live within its budget, provided it can shows that it 'seeks' to do so. Nonetheless, the mandate does create a substantial level of expectation and thus NHS England may

3 See www.gov.uk/government/uploads/system/uploads/attachment_data/file/216590/dh_131428.pdf.

4 See www.gov.uk/government/uploads/system/uploads/attachment_data/file/601188/NHS_Mandate_2017-18_A.pdf.

be acting unlawfully if it did not allocate resources appropriately with a view to seeking to achieve the terms of the mandate.

The general duties on the secretary of state in Part 1 of the NHS Act 2006

3.12 There are procedural duties imposed on the Secretary of State for Health and Social Care in Part 1 of the NHS Act 2006, which were largely introduced as a result of the HSCA 2012. The precise meaning and effect of these duties is unclear because their scope has not been explored in High Court judgments. However, these procedural duties are likely to become increasingly important as the secretary of state is called upon to make contentious decisions.

3.13 The first duty imposed on the secretary of state by section 1A is to discharge his or her functions with a view to securing continuous improvement in the quality of NHS services and, in particular, the outcomes for NHS patients. It provides as follows:

> (1) The Secretary of State must exercise the functions of the Secretary of State in relation to the health service with a view to securing continuous improvement in the quality of services provided to individuals for or in connection with–
> (a) the prevention, diagnosis or treatment of illness, or
> (b) the protection or improvement of public health.
> (2) In discharging the duty under subsection (1) the Secretary of State must, in particular, act with a view to securing continuous improvement in the outcomes that are achieved from the provision of the services.
> (3) The outcomes relevant for the purposes of subsection (2) include, in particular, outcomes which show–
> (a) the effectiveness of the services,
> (b) the safety of the services, and
> (c) the quality of the experience undergone by patients.
> (4) In discharging the duty under subsection (1), the Secretary of State must have regard to the quality standards prepared by NICE [National Institute for Health and Care Excellence] under section 234 of the Health and Social Care Act 2012.

3.14 This is a duty to 'act with a view to' achieving continuous improvements in services and outcomes. That formulation probably gives the secretary of state a wide area of discretionary decision-making, provided he or she remains focused on the objective of improving services and outcomes for NHS patients. The question as to whether the secretary of state has acted in breach of this duty when making a particular decision or issuing a specific direction would depend upon a precise analysis of the decision-making process. However, at a minimum, officials advising the secretary of state would be required to draw this legal duty to the attention of the secretary of state and to explain the basis upon which he or she could make the decision in compliance with the duty. If there is no reference to the duty in the documents showing the decision-making process, there may be a case that the decision is unlawful because the secretary of state has not exercised his or her functions in order to achieve the statutory objective.

3.15 The importance of the duty on the secretary of state to 'act with a view to' achieving continuous improvements in services and outcomes is reflected in section 247D of the NHS Act 2006 which provides that the secretary of state must publish an annual report about the NHS which contains the secretary of state's assessment of the effectiveness of his or her discharge of the duties under section 1A. It provides:

> (1) The Secretary of State must publish an annual report on the performance of the health service in England.
> (2) The report must include the Secretary of State's assessment of the effectiveness of the discharge of the duties under sections 1A and 1C.
> (3) The Secretary of State must lay any report prepared under this section before Parliament.

Thus the secretary of state's annual report (which in practice is included as part of the *Department of Health annual report and accounts*) needs to report specifically on compliance with the section 1A duty.

3.16 Section 1B of the NHS Act 2006 imposes a duty on the secretary of state to have regard to the NHS Constitution. It provides:

> (1) In exercising functions in relation to the health service, the Secretary of State must have regard to the NHS Constitution.
> (2) In this Act, 'NHS Constitution' has the same meaning as in Chapter 1 of Part 1 of the Health Act 2009 (see section 1 of that Act).

3.17 The meaning and legal effect of the NHS Constitution is explored in chapter 2 above. It is only necessary for present purposes to note that the secretary of state was originally omitted from the list of NHS bodies that were obliged to have regard to the constitution in the Health Act 1999. However, this omission was remedied by section 3 of the HSCA 2012 which introduced section 1B into the NHS Act 2006.

3.18 Section 1C of the NHS Act 2006 contains a duty on the secretary of state to exercise his or her functions so as to reduce health inequalities. It provides:

> In exercising functions in relation to the health service, the Secretary of State must have regard to the need to reduce inequalities between the people of England with respect to the benefits that they can obtain from the health service.

3.19 This is a deceptively simple but potentially far-reaching provision. The duty is concerned with inequalities between people 'with respect to the benefits that they can obtain from the health service'. The background is that the NHS provides universal services which can be accessed by anybody, but the decision to access an NHS service is a decision by the patient alone. Aside from very special cases, such as mental health or infectious diseases, there is no duty on any NHS body to *provide* medical care to anyone. The NHS has a duty to *offer* medical services. The patient decides whether, how and when to access services. So a patient who suffers pain or symptoms of a condition has the ability to go to the pharmacist or the GP to seek treatment, or could decide not to do so.

3.20 There is a wealth of evidence of persistent inequality in the health of people in the UK, and this is partly related to the way in which NHS services are accessed. This evidence was summarised in the *Acheson report*[5] published in 1998. The conclusion is that universal services open to all do not, of themselves, deliver equal benefits. Hence the assumption behind the wording of section 1C appears to be that making services available on a universal basis – of itself – does not deliver equal benefits to people.

3.21 Thus, when determining whether the duty has been complied with, the statutory starting point must be to see whether the decision maker has understood that there is existing unequal access to the benefits of NHS services, and has then asked himself what steps could be taken to *reduce* that inequality of benefit. The wording of section 1C refers to the 'need' to 'reduce' the inequalities that presently exist with respect to the benefits that people can obtain from the health service (ie the NHS). 'Need' and 'reduce' are both strong words, implying an added level of urgency to achieving the objective (but falling short of an absolute requirement to do so). Accordingly, a duty to have regard to the 'need to reduce' X is a stronger duty than a duty just to 'have regard' to X. By way of contrast, the secretary of state must have regard to the NHS Constitution under section 1B but not the 'need to ensure compliance with the NHS Constitution', which would be a stronger form of duty.

3.22 These duties were the subject of a decision by the High Court *in R (The Pharmaceutical Services Negotiating Committee) v Secretary of State for Health* (The *NPA* case).[6] The secretary of state had argued that a 'have regard' duty was a lesser form of duty to the 'have due regard' duty under section 149 of the Equality Act 2010 (about which there has been considerable litigation[7]). The submission was rejected by the judge, who said:

> But I am equally wholly unpersuaded that there is in reality any material difference between the obligations to have regard and to have due regard. Merely to have regard in the sense that the existence of the statutory requirements is recognised is never likely to suffice, albeit much will turn on the nature of the matters to which regard must be had. In section 1C it is a specific need to reduce inequalities so that the defendant is obliged to show that that need is recognised and that what is proposed does not in his view at the very least cause an increase in such inequalities. All that 'due' adds in my view is a specific recognition that the effect of the decision on the specified matters must be properly taken into account. It could indeed be argued that 'due' does not strengthen but rather weakens in that it recognises that there may be circumstances in which regard is not needed. But it seems to me in any event that the argument was a barren one having regard to the nature of the obligation in section 1C.

3.23 The judge did not accept that there was a breach of the section 1C duty. He said:

> Cuts of the nature required will inevitably produce some hardships for individual pharmacies and for some who make use of them. But that cannot mean that in times of the need for some retrenchment no cuts can be made. The Department has, as the material now disclosed shows, given detailed and careful consideration to the way in which the cuts can be made. I do not

5 See www.gov.uk/government/uploads/system/uploads/attachment_data/file/265503/ih.pdf.

6 [2017] EWHC 1147 (Admin).

7 See part 4 below.

> doubt that some criticism is properly made in that it is possible to think that different means might have been better. But that is not for this court, since it is only if unreasonableness is established that it is proper to intervene.

3.24 The criticism can be made that the judge did not grapple with the nature and effect of the duty, and applied a *Wednesbury* test when this was not the relevant test to determine compliance with the statutory scheme.[8] The case has been granted permission to go to the Court of Appeal and is due to be heard in May 2018.

3.25 The wording of the duty suggests that the key factor to which the secretary of state is obliged to have regard is the need to *reduce* inequalities with respect to the *benefits* that different people can obtain from health services. This appears to involve:

a) a recognition that it is inevitable that a service which is provided generally to the population, as part of the health service, will be accessed by people in an unequal way; and
b) a recognition that there is a need to reduce the inequality of benefits between different groups of people notwithstanding the provision of universally available NHS services.

3.26 Hence, the secretary of state must consider how his functions could be exercised with the aim of reducing this inequality of benefit. There are groups of people who get less benefit from universally provided services than those who are more comfortable about accessing health services. These groups include:

- those whose first language is not English;
- the learning disabled who have physical health problems;
- those with poor education;
- other identifiable groups, such as travellers.

All of these groups may well not get equal benefit from NHS services for a variety of reasons. There are a myriad of such groups, but a common theme is that they are disproportionately represented in deprived communities.

3.27 The section 1C duty is thus not just about ensuring that deprived communities have adequate health services, although that would be an essential part of delivering on the duty. It is primarily a duty to have regard to the need to design health services in a way that tackles the existing inequality benefit that a variety of groups of people – in practice – get from services that are available to all.

3.28 The section 1C duty must be part of the secretary of state's annual report. The 2015/16 annual report contained the following assessment:

> 236. The government's vision is for measurable and sustained reductions in health inequalities where more people can enjoy good health throughout life, wherever they live or whatever their social position. The need to reduce health inequalities across society has been highlighted as part of delivering the Shared Delivery Plan. This aim is also reflected in the NHS Constitution, the 2016–17 mandate to NHS England and is a key part of Public Health England's remit for 2016–17.

8 The author is leading counsel for the claimant, so his views may reflect submissions made in this case and to be made on appeal rather than the decision of the judge.

> . . .
>
> 239. Across the set of indicators, the data show a mixed picture on inequalities. For the overarching inequalities indicator in the PHOF [Public Health Outcomes Framework] in 2012–14 the gap in life expectancy at birth between the most and least deprived areas, as measured by the Slope Index of Inequality 38, was 9.2 years for males and 7.0 years for females. The gaps in healthy life expectancy at birth were wider: 19.0 years for males and 20.2 years for females. There has been little change in the life expectancy gaps since 2002–04, or in the healthy life expectancy gaps since 2009–11 (the earliest data available).
>
> 240. For the NHSOF [National Health Service Outcomes Framework] health inequalities assessed indicators, inequalities by deprivation continued to narrow between 2013 and 2014 for cardiovascular disease (CVD) mortality and infant mortality. The gap in CVD death rates (ages under 75) between the most and least deprived areas narrowed by 3% between 2013 and 2014. The infant mortality inequalities gap has more than halved since 2003. Inequalities by ethnicity also narrowed in 2014 for health-related quality of life for people with long term conditions.
>
> 241. However, inequalities by deprivation widened in 2014 for emergency admissions for acute conditions not usually requiring an admission, continuing a longer term widening trend. Inequalities also widened in 2014 for satisfaction with GP services and making a GP appointment, a worsening in the trend which had been flat over recent years. Satisfaction decreased across all deprivation deciles, but decreases were larger in more deprived areas, and inequalities by ethnicity and sexual orientation also widened. Inequalities by deprivation in life expectancy at 75 have also been widening (but data is not yet available to assess progress since 2013).
>
> 242. Other NHSOF inequalities indicators show little change in inequalities over recent years (for example cancer mortality and adult potential years of life lost due to causes considered amenable to healthcare).
>
> 243. The Government is keenly aware that reducing health inequalities is very challenging with complex drivers, many of which are outside health system control. The Secretary of State's assessment of how well his duty to have regard to the need to reduce health inequalities between the people of England has been discharged in 2015–16 is that there has been reasonably good progress. However there is still more to do, in particular to support effective action across all communities and to strengthen the evidence and knowledge of what works.

If the above analysis is correct, the secretary of state appears to have misinterpreted the focus of the duty by looking at health inequalities more widely rather than the inequality of benefit that NHS patients secure from universally available services. These issues may be explored further by the Court of Appeal when the *NPA* case[9] comes to court in May 2018.

3.29 Section 1D of the NHS Act 2006 imposes a duty on the secretary of state to promote the autonomy of NHS commissioning and provider bodies. It provides:

> (1) In exercising functions in relation to the health service, the Secretary of State must have regard to the desirability of securing, so far as consistent with the interests of the health service–

9 See para 3.22 above.

(a) that any other person exercising functions in relation to the health service or providing services for its purposes is free to exercise those functions or provide those services in the manner that it considers most appropriate, and
(b) that unnecessary burdens are not imposed on any such person.

(2) If, in the case of any exercise of functions, the Secretary of State considers that there is a conflict between the matters mentioned in subsection (1) and the discharge by the Secretary of State of the duties under section 1, the Secretary of State must give priority to the duties under that section.

3.30 The origin of this duty appears to have been the follow-up document to the white paper *Equity and Excellence: liberating the NHS* which was published in July 2010. This said:[10]

> The Government's reforms will liberate professionals and providers from top-down control. This is the only way to secure the quality, innovation and productivity needed to improve outcomes. We will give responsibility for commissioning and budgets to groups of GP practices; and providers will be freed from government control to shape their services around the needs and choices of patients. Greater autonomy will be matched by increased accountability to patients and democratic legitimacy, with a transparent regime of economic regulation and quality inspection to hold providers to account for the results they deliver.

3.31 This policy was followed by *Liberating the NHS: legislative framework and next steps 1* in December 2010. This stated that the bill, then in a preparatory stage, would:

> . . . enshrine the principle of autonomy at the heart of the NHS [by] maximising the autonomy of individual commissioners and providers and minimising the obligations placed upon them, in a way that is consistent with the effective operation of a comprehensive health service.

3.32 The explanatory notes to the bill explained the purpose of clause 4 of the HSCA 2012, which introduced section 1D into the NHS Act 2006, as follows:

> **The origin of Clause 4 – The Secretary of State's duty as to promoting autonomy**
> 74. This clause seeks to establish an overarching principle that the Secretary of State should act with a view to promoting autonomy in the health service. It identifies two constituent elements of autonomy: freedom for bodies/persons in the health service (such as commissioning consortia or Monitor) to exercise their functions in a manner they consider most appropriate (1C(a)), and not imposing unnecessary burdens from those bodies/persons (1C(b)). The clause requires the Secretary of State to act with a view to securing these aspects of autonomy in exercising his functions in relation to the health service, so far as is consistent with the interests of the health service.
>
> 75. This duty would therefore require the Secretary of State, when considering whether to place requirements on the NHS, to make a judgement as to whether these were in the interests of the health service. If challenged, the Secretary of State would have to be able to justify why these requirements were necessary.
>
> 76. The duty covers the arm's length body sector and commissioners and providers of NHS services. Although the Secretary of State would not have

10 At para 4.1.

the same direct relationship with providers of NHS services as he currently has with NHS trusts, he would still have certain functions which impact on providers. For example, he would be able to require certain terms to be included in contracts entered into by the NHS Commissioning Board and consortia for the provision of NHS services by virtue of regulations made under clause 16.

3.33 The duty does not appear to have been the subject of any judicial observations. However, the dominant thinking at the time of the HSCA 2012 was that efficiency and effectiveness would be promoted by setting the NHS up as a properly functioning market, with clear legal separations between commissioners and providers and a variety of private and public sector suppliers competing for the right to deliver NHS services. Thus complying with competition law was seen as a central part of the way the NHS was required to operate. The section 1D duty to respect the autonomy of providers was part of this thinking. Its aim appears to have been to encourage the NHS to allow providers to deliver NHS services in innovative ways as opposed to forcing providers to deliver services according to well established patterns of activity.

3.34 The wording of the duty, namely that the secretary of state must have 'regard to the desirability of securing so far as consistent with the interests of the health service'. is a very weak form of words and it is difficult to envisage any circumstances in which a court would be able to hold that a secretary of state, acting rationally, could be held to act in breach of this duty. However, the rigidity of the recently published sustainability and transformation partnership (STP) processes may well be hard to equate with performance of this duty because the frameworks operating tend to uniformity of service provision rather than encouraging diversity.

3.35 Section 1E of the NHS Act 2006 contains a duty on the secretary of state to promote research which is relevant to the NHS. It provides:

> In exercising functions in relation to the health service, the Secretary of State must promote–
> (a) research on matters relevant to the health service, and
> (b) the use in the health service of evidence obtained from research.

This is more than a 'have regard' duty, but is only a duty of promotion rather than a hard duty of provision. Nonetheless, the duty requires the secretary of state to ensure that an appropriate amount of the NHS budget is allocated for appropriate research and that procedures are in place to ensure that the product of research is used in the NHS.

3.36 Section 1F of the NHS Act 2006 imposes a duty on the secretary of state in relation to education and training. It provides:

> (1) The Secretary of State must exercise the functions of the Secretary of State under any relevant enactment so as to secure that there is an effective system for the planning and delivery of education and training to persons who are employed, or who are considering becoming employed, in an activity which involves or is connected with the provision of services as part of the health service in England.
> (2) Any arrangements made with a person under this Act for the provision of services as part of that health service must include arrangements for securing that the person co-operates with the Secretary of State and Health Education England in the discharge of the duty under

subsection (1) (or, where a Special Health Authority is discharging that duty by virtue of a direction under section 7, with the Special Health Authority).

(3) In subsection (1), 'relevant enactment' means–
  (a) section 63 of the Health Services and Public Health Act 1968,
  (b) this Act,
  (c) the Health and Social Care Act 2008,
  (d) the Health Act 2009, and
  (e) the Health and Social Care Act 2012.

This is a stronger form of wording than some of the other duties in this Part of the Act. It requires the secretary of state to 'secure that there is an effective system for the planning and delivery of education and training' for staff working in the health service. In practice, medical training is delivered through Health Education England (HEE) but the secretary of state is required to have regard to the need to ensure that systems operate to deliver appropriate training for all staff across the NHS.

3.37 Section 1G of the NHS Act 2006 required the secretary of state to lay a report before parliament:

> . . . on the treatment of NHS health care providers as respects any matter, including taxation, which might affect their ability to provide health care services for the purposes of the NHS or the reward available to them for doing so.

This report may have been laid[11] as required but it does not appear to have been referred to in any published document by the NHS at any later date.

3.38 The secretary of state has a duty to keep the performance of NHS bodies under review and has the power to include his or her assessment of their performance in his or her annual report to parliament. This power is under section 247C of the NHS Act 2006, which provides:

(1) The Secretary of State must keep under review the effectiveness of the exercise by the bodies mentioned in subsection (2) of functions in relation to the health service in England.

(2) The bodies mentioned in this subsection are–
  (a) the Board;
  (b) Monitor;
  (c) the Care Quality Commission and its Healthwatch England committee;
  (d) the National Institute for Health and Care Excellence;
  (e) the Health and Social Care Information Centre;
  (ea) Health Education England;
  (f) Special Health Authorities.

(3) The Secretary of State may include in an annual report under section 247D the Secretary of State's views on the effectiveness of the exercise by the bodies mentioned in subsection (2) of functions in relation to the health service.

Thus the secretary of state has a duty to review the effectiveness of the NHS bodies in relation to the health service in England, but a discretion about whether to report on the outcomes of his or her review in his or her annual report.

11 It does not appear to feature as part of any internet search and has not, as far as the authors are aware, been referred to in any other NHS document.

The public sector equality duty

3.39 The secretary of state is bound by the public sector equality duty (PSED) imposed by section 149 of the Equality Act 2010 and by the non-discrimination duties set out in that Act. Section 149 provides:

> (1) A public authority must, in the exercise of its functions, have due regard to the need to–
> (a) eliminate discrimination, harassment, victimisation and any other conduct that is prohibited by or under this Act;
> (b) advance equality of opportunity between persons who share a relevant protected characteristic and persons who do not share it;
> (c) foster good relations between persons who share a relevant protected characteristic and persons who do not share it.
>
> (2) A person who is not a public authority but who exercises public functions must, in the exercise of those functions, have due regard to the matters mentioned in subsection (1).
>
> (3) Having due regard to the need to advance equality of opportunity between persons who share a relevant protected characteristic and persons who do not share it involves having due regard, in particular, to the need to–
> (a) remove or minimise disadvantages suffered by persons who share a relevant protected characteristic that are connected to that characteristic;
> (b) take steps to meet the needs of persons who share a relevant protected characteristic that are different from the needs of persons who do not share it;
> (c) encourage persons who share a relevant protected characteristic to participate in public life or in any other activity in which participation by such persons is disproportionately low.
>
> (4) The steps involved in meeting the needs of disabled persons that are different from the needs of persons who are not disabled include, in particular, steps to take account of disabled persons' disabilities.
>
> (5) Having due regard to the need to foster good relations between persons who share a relevant protected characteristic and persons who do not share it involves having due regard, in particular, to the need to–
> (a) tackle prejudice, and
> (b) promote understanding.
>
> (6) Compliance with the duties in this section may involve treating some persons more favourably than others; but that is not to be taken as permitting conduct that would otherwise be prohibited by or under this Act.
>
> (7) The relevant protected characteristics are–
> - age;
> - disability;
> - gender reassignment;
> - pregnancy and maternity;
> - race;
> - religion or belief;
> - sex;
> - sexual orientation.
>
> (8) A reference to conduct that is prohibited by or under this Act includes a reference to–
> (a) a breach of an equality clause or rule;
> (b) a breach of a non-discrimination rule.
>
> (9) Schedule 18 (exceptions) has effect.

3.40 A summary of the case-law on the PSED was set out by McCombe LJ in *R (Bracking) v Secretary of State for Work and Pensions:*[12]

> (1) As stated by Arden LJ in *R (Elias) v Secretary of State for Defence* [2006] 1 WLR 3213, para 274, equality duties are an integral and important part of the mechanisms for ensuring the fulfilment of the aims of anti-discrimination legislation.
>
> (2) An important evidential element in the demonstration of the discharge of the duty is the recording of the steps taken by the decision-maker in seeking to meet the statutory requirements: *R (BAPIO Action Ltd) v Secretary of State for the Home Department* [2007] EWHC 199 (QB) (Stanley Burnton J).
>
> (3) The relevant duty is upon the minister or other decision-maker personally. What matters is what he or she took into account and what he or she knew. Thus, the minister or decision-maker cannot be taken to know what his or her officials know or what may have been in the minds of officials in proffering their advice: *R (National Association of Health Stores) v Department of Health* [2005] EWCA Civ 154 at [26] and [27] per Sedley LJ.
>
> (4) A minister must assess the risk and extent of any adverse impact and the ways in which such risk may be eliminated before the adoption of a proposed policy and not merely as a 'rearguard action', following a concluded decision: per Moses LJ, sitting as a judge of the Administrative Court, in *R (Kaur) v Ealing London Borough Council* [2008] EWHC 2062 (Admin) at [23] and [24].
>
> (5) These and other points were reviewed by Aikens LJ, giving the judgment of the Divisional Court, in *R (Brown) v Secretary of State for Work and Pensions* [2009] PTSR 1506, as follows:
>
> i) the public authority decision-maker must be aware of the duty to have 'due regard' to the relevant matters;
> ii) the duty must be fulfilled before and at the time when a particular policy is being considered;
> iii) the duty must be 'exercised in substance, with rigour, and with an open mind'. It is not a question of 'ticking boxes'; while there is no duty to make express reference to the regard paid to the relevant duty, reference to it and to the relevant criteria reduces the scope for argument;
> iv) the duty is non-delegable; and
> v) is a continuing one.
> vi) It is good practice for a decision-maker to keep records demonstrating consideration of the duty.
>
> (6) '[General] regard to issues of equality is not the same as having specific regard, by way of conscious approach to the statutory criteria': per Davis J (as he then was) in *R (Meany) v Harlow District Council* [2009] EWHC 559 (Admin) at [84], approved in this court in *R (Bailey) v Brent London Borough Council* [2012] LGR 530, paras 74–75.
>
> (7) Officials reporting to or advising ministers/other public authority decision-makers, on matters material to the discharge of the duty, must not merely tell the minister/decision-maker what he/she wants to hear but they have to be 'rigorous in both inquiring and reporting to them': *R (Domb) v Hammersmith and Fulham London Borough Council* [2009] LGR 843, para 79, per Sedley LJ.

12 [2013] EWCA Civ 1345, (2013) 16 CCLR 479 at [26].

(8) Finally, and with respect, it is I think, helpful to recall passages from the judgment of Elias LJ in *R (Hurley) v Secretary of State for Business, Innovation and Skills* [2012] HRLR 374 (Divisional Court) as follows:

(i) at paragraphs [77]–[78]:

'[77] Contrary to a submission advanced by Ms Mountfield, I do not accept that this means that it is for the court to determine whether appropriate weight has been given to the duty. Provided the court is satisfied that there has been a rigorous consideration of the duty, so that there is a proper appreciation of the potential impact of the decision on equality objectives and the desirability of promoting them, then as Dyson LJ in *Baker v Secretary of State for Communities and Local Government (Equality and Human Rights Commission intervening)* [2009] PTSR 809, para 34 made clear, it is for the decision-maker to decide how much weight should be given to the various factors informing the decision.

[78] The concept of 'due regard' requires the court to ensure that there has been a proper and conscientious focus on the statutory criteria, but if that is done, the court cannot interfere with the decision simply because it would have given greater weight to the equality implications of the decision than did the decision-maker. In short, the decision-maker must be clear precisely what the equality implications are when he puts them in the balance, and he must recognise the desirability of achieving them, but ultimately it is for him to decide what weight they should be given in the light of all relevant factors. If Ms Mountfield's submissions on this point were correct, it would allow unelected judges to review on substantive merits grounds almost all aspects of public decision making.'

(ii) At paragraphs [89]–[90]:

'[89] It is also alleged that the PSED in this case involves a duty of inquiry. The submission is that the combination of the principles in *Secretary of State for Education and Science v Tameside Metropolitan Borough Council* [1977] AC 1014 and the duty of due regard under the statute requires public authorities to be properly informed before taking a decision. If the relevant material is not available, there will be a duty to acquire it and this will frequently mean than some further consultation with appropriate groups is required. Ms Mountfield referred to the following passage from the judgment of Aikens LJ in Brown (para 85):

'the public authority concerned will, in our view, have to have due regard to the *need* to take steps to gather relevant information in order that it can properly take steps to take into account disabled persons' disabilities in the context of the particular function under consideration.'

[90] I respectfully agree . . .'

3.41 The importance of compliance with the PSED has very recently been re-emphasised by the Supreme Court. Per Lord Toulson, with whom Lord Neuberger, Lord Mance, Lord Sumption and Lord Hughes agreed, in *R (Carmichael) v Secretary of State for Work and Pensions*:[13]

67. As Lord Dyson MR said, the PSED is a duty on the part of a public authority to follow a form of due process, that is, an obligation to have due regard to the need to eliminate discrimination, and advance equality of opportunity, between those with and without a relevant protected characteristic . . .

13 [2016] UKSC 58, (2017) 20 CCLR 103.

> 68. . . . it was not sufficient for a decision-maker to have a vague awareness of his legal duties. Rather, he must have a focused awareness of the duties under section 149 of the Equality Act and, in a disability case, their potential impact on people with disabilities.

3.42 A challenge to the rules for charging overseas visitors succeeded on the grounds that the Secretary of State had failed to have regard to the PSED in *R (Cushnie) v Secretary of State for Health.*[14] The court held the secretary of state had acted unlawfully for failing properly to consider the impact of the National Health Service (Charges to Overseas Visitors) Regulations 2011[15] on overseas visitors who had a disability. Singh J said:[16]

> The purpose of the duty is to make sure that public authorities do not inadvertently overlook the impact of their decisions on relevant groups, because too often in the past they were overlooked.

3.43 While this duty is wide-ranging in theory, its impact may have been considerably reduced by the decision of the Court of Appeal in *Secretary of State for Communities and Local Government v West Berkshire District Council and another*[17] which has, in effect, sanctioned public bodies undertaking equality impact assessments after a decision has been taken and thus validating them ex post facto.

The secretary of state's powers and duties to make regulations

3.44 The NHS Act 2006 and other statutes governing the operation of the NHS frequently provide a power for the secretary of state to make regulations. This power is often subject to a prior duty of consultation with a representative body and with such other persons as the secretary of state considers fit. Hence, by way of example, the secretary of state has the power to make regulations about direct payments: see section 12(1) of the NHS Act 2006.[18]

3.45 Where the secretary of state has power to make regulations, the regulation must be laid before parliament for 40 days once it is made. A regulation will be either subject to a positive or negative resolution power – namely, it either requires a positive resolution of both Houses of Parliament to affirm the regulations or will have effect unless a resolution of both Houses of Parliament objects to the regulations. However, the regulations have legal effect on the date when they are made, not at the expiry of the 40-day period: see the Statutory Instruments Act 1946.

3.46 An important example of the secretary of state's regulation-making powers is under section 251 of the NHS Act 2006, which gives the secretary of state wide powers to make regulations about the extent to which NHS bodies can use patient data, including without obtaining the informed and explicit consent from patients to use data about their health conditions. It provides:

14 [2014] EWHC 3626 (Admin).

15 SI No 1556.

16 See para 115.

17 [2016] EWCA Civ 441.

18 Please see chapter 14 for details as to how the regulations operate to bring a system of direct payments into force.

(1) The Secretary of State may by regulations make such provision for and in connection with requiring or regulating the processing of prescribed patient information for medical purposes as he considers necessary or expedient–
   (a) in the interests of improving patient care, or
   (b) in the public interest.

(2) Regulations under subsection (1) may, in particular, make provision–
   (a) for requiring prescribed communications of any nature which contain patient information to be disclosed by health service bodies or relevant social care bodies in prescribed circumstances–
      (i) to the person to whom the information relates,
      (ii) (where it relates to more than one person) to the person to whom it principally relates, or
      (iii) to a prescribed person on behalf of any such person as is mentioned in sub-paragraph (i) or (ii),

   in such manner as may be prescribed,
   (b) for requiring or authorising the disclosure or other processing of prescribed patient information to or by persons of any prescribed description subject to compliance with any prescribed conditions (including conditions requiring prescribed undertakings to be obtained from such persons as to the processing of such information),
   (c) for securing that, where prescribed patient information is processed by a person in accordance with the regulations, anything done by him in so processing the information must be taken to be lawfully done despite any obligation of confidence owed by him in respect of it,
   (d) for creating offences punishable on summary conviction by a fine not exceeding level 5 on the standard scale or such other level as is prescribed or for creating other procedures for enforcing any provisions of the regulations.

(3) Subsections (1) and (2) are subject to subsections (4) to (7).

(4) Regulations under subsection (1) may not make provision requiring the processing of confidential patient information for any purpose if it would be reasonably practicable to achieve that purpose otherwise than pursuant to such regulations, having regard to the cost of and the technology available for achieving that purpose.

(5) Where regulations under subsection (1) make provision requiring the processing of prescribed confidential patient information, the Secretary of State–
   (a) must, at any time within the period of one month beginning on each anniversary of the making of such regulations, consider whether any such provision could be included in regulations made at that time without contravening subsection (4), and
   (b) if he determines that any such provision could not be so included, must make further regulations varying or revoking the regulations made under subsection (1) to such extent as he considers necessary in order for the regulations to comply with that subsection.

(6) Regulations under subsection (1) may not make provision for requiring the processing of confidential patient information solely or principally for the purpose of determining the care and treatment to be given to particular individuals.

(7) Regulations under this section may not make provision for or in connection with the processing of prescribed patient information in a manner inconsistent with any provision made by or under the Data Protection Act 1998.

(8) Subsection (7) does not affect the operation of provisions made under subsection (2)(c).

(9) Before making any regulations under this section the Secretary of State must, to such extent as he considers appropriate in the light of the requirements of section 252, consult such bodies appearing to him to represent the interests of those likely to be affected by the regulations as he considers appropriate.

(10) In this section 'patient information' means–

(a) information (however recorded) which relates to the physical or mental health or condition of an individual, to the diagnosis of his condition or to his care or treatment, and

(b) information (however recorded) which is to any extent derived, directly or indirectly, from such information,

whether or not the identity of the individual in question is ascertainable from the information.

(11) For the purposes of this section, patient information is 'confidential patient information' where–

(a) the identity of the individual in question is ascertainable–

(i) from that information, or

(ii) from that information and other information which is in the possession of, or is likely to come into the possession of, the person processing that information, and

(b) that information was obtained or generated by a person who, in the circumstances, owed an obligation of confidence to that individual.

(12) In this section 'medical purposes' means the purposes of any of–

(a) preventative medicine, medical diagnosis, medical research, the provision of care and treatment and the management of health and social care services, and

(b) informing individuals about their physical or mental health or condition, the diagnosis of their condition or their care and treatment.

(12A) In this section–

'care' includes local authority social care,

'local authority social care' means–

(a) social care provided or arranged for by a local authority, and

(b) any other social care all or part of the cost of which is paid for with funds provided by a local authority,

'patient' includes an individual who needs or receives local authority social care or whose need for such care is being assessed by a local authority,

'social care' includes all forms of personal care and other practical assistance provided for individuals who are in need of such care or assistance by reason of age, illness, disability, pregnancy, childbirth, dependence on alcohol or drugs or other similar circumstances.

(13) In this section–

'health service body' means any body (including a government department) or person engaged in the provision of the health service that is prescribed, or of a description prescribed, for the purposes of this definition,

'processing', in relation to information, means the use, disclosure or obtaining of the information or the doing of such other things in relation to it as may be prescribed for the purposes of this definition,

'relevant social care body' means–

(a) a local authority, or

(b) any other body or person engaged in the provision of local authority social care.

3.47 The use of these powers is hugely controversial because of the tensions between the free-flow of information being available to clinicians and researchers to assist patients (both individually and generally) and the strongly expressed desire of many people to protect the confidentiality of information about their health and not to allow that confidential information to be used without their consent. The secretary of state has made the Health Service (Control of Patient Information) Regulations 2002.[19] Regulation 3 provides powers for the NHS to process patient information relating to communicable diseases without the consent of the patient. Use of data can also be justified as part of clinical audit: see paragraph 5 of the Schedule to these Regulations. However the recent problems of 'care.data'[20] (which was abandoned in July 2016) shows that this is an area where there are acute sensitivities, and thus the powers are used sparingly.

The secretary of state's power to issue directions

3.48 A direction is an order issued by the secretary of state[21] which creates a public law duty on the person named in the order to do the thing which is referred to within the direction or to refrain from doing a specific thing referred to in the direction. A direction can set a level of remuneration for those providing a specified type of NHS services, require an NHS commissioner to exercise its powers in a certain way or require a named individual to be removed from a post within an NHS organisation. There are two types of directions within the scheme of NHS law, namely:

1) directions to NHS bodies or others which are subject to a general direction making power; and
2) directions governing a specific function or payment scheme.

General direction making powers

3.49 Until the implementation of the HSCA 2012, all NHS bodies other than NHS foundation trusts were capable of being the subject of general directions issued by the secretary of state. This general direction making power was contained in section 8 of the NHS Act 2006, which, when passed, provided:

19 SI No 1438.

20 There are many articles on the problems of NHS Digital and the use of patient data, but for a summary see: www.theguardian.com/technology/2016/jul/06/nhs-to-scrap-single-database-of-patients-medical-details. The essential debate in the care.data saga was the extent to which NHS bodies were entitled to assume that patients gave implied consent to data about their clinical conditions being shared with other NHS clinicians and/or used for other internal NHS purposes (such as working out how much one NHS body should be charged for delivering clinical services). Concerns about sharing of data with commercial organisations and the inaccurate assumptions about the extent of implied patient consent was widely reported in the media and eventually caused the whole scheme to be abandoned.

21 Or another public body such as NHS England which is authorised by statute to issue the direction.

> (1) The Secretary of State may give directions to any of the bodies mentioned in subsection (2) about its exercise of any functions.
> (2) The bodies are–
> (a) Strategic Health Authorities,
> (b) Primary Care Trusts,
> (c) NHS trusts, and
> (d) Special Health Authorities.
> (3) Nothing in provision made by or under this or any other Act affects the generality of subsection (1).

3.50 The general power to make directions to require any NHS body to do something (or refrain from doing something) gave the secretary of state (or in practice civil servants working for the Department of Health and Social Care) the ability to intervene in virtually any part of the NHS. In practice, the existence of the power meant that directions rarely needed to be issued to force a chief executive to step down when there was a perceived fault (such as the infamous incident where the Bedford Hospitals chief executive stepped down after being criticised by the then secretary of state for permitting dead bodies to be stored in the hospital's chapel of rest). However, the ability to issue directions came to be seen in Whitehall as a burden on the secretary of state. If the secretary of state had the ability to intervene to correct something, it was entirely legitimate for MPs or the media to call on the secretary of state to exercise that power by intervening. The cry 'something must be done' is often made in the NHS when things do not work out as well as anyone hopes, and a general power for the secretary of state to issue directions often meant that the 'something' had to be done directly by the secretary of state.

3.51 A decision was taken that the secretary of state should not have the ability to issue directions to NHS foundation trusts when this new form of 'independent' NHS body was created by the Health and Social Care (Community Health and Standards) Act 2003. That policy was substantially extended by the HSCA 2012, which created CCGs in place of primary care trusts (PCTs) as the local NHS commissioners. CCGs were subject to oversight by NHS England, but could not be made the subject of directions issued by the secretary of state. The present form of section 8 of the NHS Act 2006 thus reads as follows:

> (1) The Secretary of State may give directions to any of the bodies mentioned in subsection (2) about its exercise of any functions.
> (2) The bodies are–
> (a) . . .
> (b) . . .
> (c) NHS trusts, and
> (d) Special Health Authorities.
> (3) Nothing in provision made by or under this or any other Act affects the generality of subsection (1).

3.52 The original scheme of the HSCA 2012 was that all NHS trusts should either become NHS foundation trusts by April 2016 or be taken over by an NHS foundation trust by that date. The HSCA 2012 accordingly contained power for all of the legislative provisions relating to NHS trusts, including the power to issue directions, to be repealed: see Schedule 14 to the HSCA 2012. The growing financial crisis in the NHS, as shown by the spiralling deficits for NHS provider trusts since 2014, and the reversion to central control of NHS bodies, with the effective abandonment of the concept of the managed NHS market, as shown by the interventions by NHS England and NHS Improvement in a majority of NHS bodies (partly based on concerns arising from poor financial performance) has meant that the policy of forcing all NHS trusts to become NHS foundation trusts has not been a priority. Accordingly, NHS trusts continue in existence and continue to be subject to the secretary of state's direction-making powers.

3.53 The remaining category of NHS bodies who can be the subject of directions is special health authorities. Prior to 2006 there was a long list of such bodies but there are now only three – namely, NHS Blood and Transplant; the NHS Business Services Agency; and the NHS Litigation Authority.

Powers to make directions governing a specific function or payment scheme

3.54 The secretary of state retains the right to make directions about specified matters under a number of different provisions within the NHS Act 2006. This direction making power gives the secretary of state a considerable ability to influence how the NHS functions and to set priorities for spending.

3.55 By way of example, the secretary of state has the right to make directions which define the payments to general practitioner (GP) practices working under General Medical Services (GMS) contracts: see NHS Act 2006 s87(1). The secretary of state has used that power to set a complex set of directions which define how much GMS GP practices should be paid for providing services to NHS patients, namely the GMS Statement of Financial Entitlements (SFE) Directions,[22] first created in 2013. Changes to these directions are negotiated on an annual basis between NHS employers, which is part of the NHS Confederation.[23] The changes are published annually and then, from time to time, the changes are consolidated into a new set of directions. Hence, the present GMS SFE directions constitute the 2013 set of directions[24] as amended by directions made

22 See www.gov.uk/government/publications/nhs-primary-medical-services-directions-2013.

23 'NHS employers' was described as follows by Green J in the recent junior doctors judicial review challenge: *R (Justice for Health Ltd) v The Secretary of State for Health* [2016] EWHC 2338 (Admin):

> The NHS Confederation is a charity and company limited by guarantee that acts as a membership organisation for entities that commission and provide NHS services. Its members include: acute trusts, ambulance trusts, community health service providers, foundation trusts, mental health providers, clinical commissioning groups, and some independent and voluntary healthcare organisations. It is right to observe that there are some employers who are not represented by the NHS Confederation. One component of its membership comprises a network that represents trusts in England on employment and workforce issues. This is known as 'NHS Employers'. Detailed evidence on behalf of the NHS Confederation was given by Mr Daniel Mortimer, the Chief Executive of NHS Employers. As observed this body is part of the NHS Confederation and has no separate legal personality or status. It is therefore the individual members of NHS Employers that employ junior doctors and who will in due course introduce the new contracts either (i) when doctors join the NHS for the first time, or (ii) transfer to a new post within the NHS as part of their training, with effect from 5 October 2016.

24 See www.gov.uk/government/uploads/system/uploads/attachment_data/file/233366/gen_med_servs_statement_financial_entitlements_directions_2013_acc.pdf.

between 2014 and 2017.[25] There is also a separate set of directions which define the way in which GMS GP practices are remunerated for providing appropriate premises, namely the NHS (General Medical Services – Premises Costs) Directions 2013.[26]

3.56 The secretary of state also has the right to make numerous other types of specific directions, including, for example, to set the remuneration paid to pharmacists under the Drug Tariff: see NHS Act 2006 s127(3).

The power of the secretary of state to issue guidance

3.57 There is no specific power in the NHS Act 2006 to permit the secretary of state to issue guidance. However, the secretary of state has a general power in section 2 of the NHS Act 2006[27] as follows:

> The Secretary of State, the Board or a clinical commissioning group may do anything which is calculated to facilitate, or is conducive or incidental to, the discharge of any function conferred on that person by this Act.

3.58 In *R (Rogers) v Swindon NHS Primary Care Trust and another*[28] Bean J said:

> The origin of the power to issue guidance is to be found in the general enabling powers of section 2.

3.59 The effect of guidance given by the secretary of state has been considered in a number of cases. In *R v North Derbyshire Health Authority ex p Fisher*[29] Dyson J (as he then was) was concerned with strong statements made by the secretary of state in favour of the use of Interferon for patients suffering from the relapsing/remitting form of multiple sclerosis. He said:[30]

> The difference between a policy which provides mere guidance, and one in which the health authority is obliged to implement is critical. Policy which is in the form of guidance can be expressed in strong terms and yet fall short of amounting to directions. There is no reference in the Circular to the word 'directions', and read as a whole there is no indication that the Circular is intended to trigger the statutory duty of compliance to be found in section 13(1) of the 1977 Act.[31] The Circular includes words such as 'asks', 'suggested', 'taking into account'. It does not include the word 'shall' or any of the other badges of mandatory requirement.

3.60 Hence, an NHS body is not under any absolute duty to act in accordance with guidance made by the secretary of state, however strongly that guid-

25 These are listed at www.gov.uk/government/publications/nhs-primary-medical-services-directions-2013.

26 See www.gov.uk/government/uploads/system/uploads/attachment_data/file/184017/NHS__General_Medical_Services_-_Premises_Costs__Directions_2013.pdf.

27 As amended by the HSCA 2012. Section 2(1) of the NHS Act 2006, as originally passed, read: '(1)The Secretary of State may (a) provide such services as he considers appropriate for the purpose of discharging any duty imposed on him by this Act, and (b) do anything else which is calculated to facilitate, or is conducive or incidental to, the discharge of such a duty'.

28 [2006] EWHC 171 (Admin) at para 52.

29 [1997] EWHC Admin 675, (1997–98) 1 CCLR 150.

30 At para 10.

31 The part of the NHS Act 1977 covering the power of the secretary of state to issue directions.

ance is expressed. However the judge then expressed the effect of guidance as follows:[32]

> If the Circular provided no more than guidance, albeit in strong terms, then the only duty placed upon health authorities was to take it into account in the discharge of their functions. They would be susceptible to challenge only on *Wednesbury* principles if they failed to consider the Circular, or they misconstrued or misapplied it whether deliberately or negligently: see *Grandsden & Co Ltd and another v Secretary of State and Another* (1985) 54 P&CR 86, 93–94.

3.61 Hence an NHS body acts unlawfully if it:

a) fails to consider guidance issued by the secretary of state;
b) misconstrues it (ie reads it but misunderstands what the NHS body is required to consider doing); or
c) disapplies it (ie reads and understands it but applies it in a way that the secretary of state did not intend).

3.62 However, even if the NHS body properly considers the guidance, understands its meaning and does not misapply it, an NHS body is only entitled to depart from guidance if it has a good reason to do so. This was expressed by Dyson J where he said:[33]

> They were not obliged to follow the policy, but if they decided to depart from it, they had to give clear reasons for so doing, and those reasons would have been susceptible to a *Wednesbury* challenge.

3.63 In the *Fisher* case, the health authority were somewhat unclear as to why they had refused to implement the guidance by making Interferon available to NHS patients in accordance with the secretary of state's guidance. However, a substantial factor was that the local clinicians disagreed with the secretary of state's assessment that the drug had been sufficiently tested to prove that it was clinically effective. The judge appears to have considered that it was not open to the local health authority to form a different view on clinical effectiveness to the secretary of state. He said:[34]

> The respondents failed to implement any aspect of national policy, principally because they disagreed with it altogether. They now seek to argue that at least they acted consistently with that policy, although for the reasons that I have given that is plainly not the case. Accordingly, they do not seek to justify their policy as a rational exception to the national policy. That is hardly surprising, since I expect that the situation in which the respondent found themselves when the Circular was issued was not materially different from that faced by most other health authorities. The respondents did not take the Circular into account and decide exceptionally not to follow it. They decided to disregard it altogether throughout 1996, because they were opposed to it. That is something which in my judgment they were not entitled to do.

3.64 This part of the judgment needs to be treated with some caution as the observations appear to have been grounded in the explanations or lack of explanations advanced on behalf of the health authority. Local NHS commissioners are the decision-makers as to which treatments should be

32 At para 11.
33 At para 54.
34 At para 56.

funded for the patients for whom they have commissioning responsibility and are under a duty to use their resources in an effective manner. If local clinicians reach a rational view that a drug or other treatment is not either clinically effective or a cost-effective use of NHS resources, they probably have the right to decline to follow NHS guidance: see *R (Condliff) v North Staffordshire Primary Care Trust*.[35] A local prioritisation decision not to follow the National Institute for Health and Care Excellence (NICE) guidelines on bariatric surgery for resources reasons was upheld in both the High Court and the Court of Appeal.

The role of the secretary of state in the trust failure regime

3.65 The Health Act (HA) 2009 grappled with the problem as to what action should be taken where there was a wholesale failure by an NHS body. This is a problem that has vexed the NHS for many years – what should the centre do if an NHS body fails. The scheme under the HA 2009 involved the appointment of a trust special administrator (TSA) by the secretary of state.

3.66 This power was used by the secretary of state to appoint a TSA to take over South London Healthcare NHS Trust (SLHT): see the South London Healthcare National Health Service Trust (Appointment of Trust Special Administrator) Order 2012.[36]

3.67 Unfortunately part of the TSA's proposed remedy for the woes of SLHT, which was losing about £1 million per week at that stage, was to require major changes at the neighbouring Lewisham Hospital. However, Lewisham Hospital was not run by SLHT but by a different trust. The secretary of state accepted the TSA's recommendation, but his decision was challenged in a judicial review. Both the High Court and the Court of Appeal sided with the objectors and so that part of the plan was quashed: see *Trust Special Administrator Appointed to South London Healthcare NHS Trust and another v Lewisham LBC and another*.[37] The High Court and the Court of Appeal determined that NHS trusts were separate legal entities and the powers of the TSA in relation to SLHT did not extend to either the TSA or the secretary of state, in reliance on a report produced by the TSA, making decisions which affected Lewisham Hospital, which was run by a wholly different NHS trust.[38]

3.68 The HSCA 2012 removed the powers to appoint a TSA from the secretary of state and provided that they be exercised by Monitor. They have only been used once, namely in the case of Mid-Staffordshire NHS Foundation Trust following the well-publicised quality problems at Stafford Hospital. Those problems were laid bare in the comprehensive report by Robert Francis QC.[39] However, the consequent TSA process

35 [2011] EWHC 872 (Admin) and [2011] EWCA Civ 910.

36 SI No 1806.

37 [2013] EWCA Civ 1409.

38 This restriction on the powers of the TSA was subsequently amended by the Care Act 2014. However, the new powers have not yet been used.

39 See http://webarchive.nationalarchives.gov.uk/20130104234315/http://www.dh.gov.uk/en/Publicationsandstatistics/Publications/PublicationsPolicyAndGuidance/DH_113018.

proved to be an astonishingly expensive and legally cumbersome way of dealing with management failure at a provider trust.

3.69 It thus seems far more likely that the NHS will return to the traditional way of dealing with provider failure, namely by using a mixture of powers and influence to change management, remove a chair (often with Monitor exercising powers to do so under the HSCA 2012) or to require an effective take-over of a failing trust by a nearby successfully operating trust. It thus seems highly unlikely that the trust failure regime in the NHS Act 2006 (as amended by the HSCA 2012) will be used in the foreseeable future.

NHS Act 2006 Sch 1 powers and duties

3.70 Schedule 1 to the NHS Act 2006 contains a series of powers and duties on the secretary of state covering a number of ancillary matters relating to the operation of the NHS. Hence, for example, para 7C provides:

> The Secretary of State must for the purposes of the health service make arrangements for–
> (a) collecting, screening, analysing, processing and supplying blood or other tissues,
> (b) preparing blood components and reagents, and
> (c) facilitating tissue and organ transplantation.

NHS Blood and Transplant, which is a special health authority, performs these tasks for the wider NHS.

3.71 Schedule 1 also contains a specific power on the secretary of state to make arrangements for contraceptive services. Paragraph 8 provides:

> The Secretary of State must arrange, to such extent as he considers necessary to meet all reasonable requirements, for–
> (a) the giving of advice on contraception,
> (b) the medical examination of persons seeking advice on contraception,
> (c) the treatment of such persons, and
> (d) the supply of contraceptive substances and appliances.

3.72 The secretary of state also has wide powers to fund research under Schedule 1. Paragraph 13 provides:

> (1) The Secretary of State, the Board or a clinical commissioning group may conduct, commission or assist the conduct of research into–
> (a) any matters relating to the causation, prevention, diagnosis or treatment of illness, and
> (b) any such other matters connected with any service provided under this Act as the Secretary of State, the Board or the clinical commissioning group (as the case may be) considers appropriate.
> (2) A local authority may conduct, commission or assist the conduct of research for any purpose connected with the exercise of its functions in relation to the health service.
> (3) The Secretary of State, the Board, a clinical commissioning group or a local authority may for any purpose connected with the exercise of its functions in relation to the health service–
> (a) obtain and analyse data or other information;
> (b) obtain advice from persons with appropriate professional expertise.

(4) The power under sub-paragraph (1) or (2) to assist any person to conduct research includes power to do so by providing financial assistance or making the services of any person or other resources available.

3.73 The references to the secretary of state in many of the other parts of Schedule 1 in the original form of the NHS Act 2006 were replaced by references to other NHS bodies by the HSCA 2012, as part of the general policy of moving the role of the secretary of state away from an operational role to a strategic role.

The emergency powers of the secretary of state

3.74 Section 253 of the NHS Act 2006 contains extremely wide emergency powers which are available to the secretary of state to deal with any emergency in the NHS. It provides:

(1) The Secretary of State may give directions under this section if he considers that by reason of an emergency it is appropriate to do so.

(1A) A direction under this section may be given to–

(a) an NHS body other than a Local Health Board;

(b) the National Institute for Health and Care Excellence;

(c) the Health and Social Care Information Centre;

(d) any body or person, other than an NHS body, providing services in pursuance of arrangements made–

(i) by the Secretary of State under section 12,

(ii) by the Board or a clinical commissioning group under section 3, 3A, 3B or 4 or Schedule 1,

(iii) by a local authority for the purpose of the exercise of its functions under or by virtue of section 2B or 6C(1) or Schedule 1, or

(iv) by the Board, a clinical commissioning group or a local authority by virtue of section 7A.

(2) In relation to a body within subsection (1A)(a) to (c), the powers conferred by this section may be exercised–

(a) to give directions to the body about the exercise of any of its functions;

(b) to direct the body to cease to exercise any of its functions for a specified period;

(c) to direct the body to exercise any of its functions concurrently with another body or person for a specified period;

(d) to direct the body to exercise any function conferred on another body or person under or by virtue of this Act for a specified period (whether to the exclusion of, or concurrently with, that body or person).

(2A) In relation to a body or person within subsection (1A)(d), the powers conferred by this section may be exercised–

(a) to give directions to the body or person about the provision of any services that it provides in pursuance of arrangements mentioned in subsection (1A)(d);

(b) to direct the body or person to cease to provide any of those services for a specified period;

(c) to direct the body or person to provide other services for the purposes of the health service for a specified period.

(2B) The Secretary of State may direct the Board to exercise the functions of the Secretary of State under this section.

(2C) The Secretary of State may give directions to the Board about its exercise of any functions that are the subject of a direction under subsection (2B).
(2D) In this section, 'specified' means specified in the direction.
(3) The powers conferred on the Secretary of State by this section are in addition to any other powers exercisable by him.

3.75 The bodies to whom directions can be given in an emergency include any NHS body. The term 'NHS body' is defined in section 275 of the NHS Act 2006 as follows:

'NHS body' means–
(a) the Board,
(b) a clinical commissioning group,
(c) a Special Health Authority,
(d) an NHS trust,
(e) an NHS foundation trust, and
(f) a Local Health Board.

3.76 However, the secretary of state cannot use emergency powers to direct a 'Local Health Board' (LHB), because the LHBs fall within the scope of the Government of Wales: see section 253(1A)(a).

3.77 The powers to give directions in an emergency situation also extend to any commercial or voluntary sector provider who delivers NHS services under contract with NHS England or a CCG. Thus any contractor who supplies NHS services could be subject to a legal duty to act in accordance with directions made by the secretary of state. It is unclear precisely how this could work if, for example, a contractor was required to expend money to comply with the directions without being provided with a proper level of remuneration.

CHAPTER 4

The powers and duties of NHS England

Introduction

4.1 The National Health Service Commissioning Board was created by the Health and Social Care Act (HSCA) 2012 to take over many of the functions that were previously undertaken by the Department of Health and Social Care (DHSC), to take over some functions previously undertaken by primary care trusts (PCTs), to act as a commissioner for specialised services and to act as a quasi-regulator of clinical commissioning groups (CCGs). The National Health Service Commissioning Board decided to refer to itself as 'NHS England', but the change of name does not imply any change in function.

4.2 NHS England has assumed a much larger role in the running of the NHS in England than it was allocated by the HSCA 2012. Its website[1] says:

> NHS England leads the National Health Service (NHS) in England. We set the priorities and direction of the NHS and encourage and inform the national debate to improve health and care.
>
> We want everyone to have greater control of their health and their well-being, and to be supported to live longer, healthier lives by high quality health and care services that are compassionate, inclusive and constantly-improving.
>
> NHS England shares out more than £100 billion in funds and holds organisations to account for spending this money effectively for patients and efficiently for the tax payer.
>
> A lot of the work we do involves the commissioning of health care services in England. We commission the contracts for GPs, pharmacists, and dentists and we support local health services that are led by groups of GPs called Clinical Commissioning Groups (CCGs). CCGs plan and pay for local services such as hospitals and ambulance services.
>
> We have devised a strategic vision for the NHS, along with our partners in health, called the Five Year Forward View. And now, with our partners, we are delivering that vision.
>
> This vision shows that we are getting serious about prevention, identifying and delivering improvements in health care, redesigning the NHS so it continues to meet the needs of patients, ensuring the NHS is financially sustainable and engaging the public in this whole process.
>
> We strongly believe in health and high quality care for all, now and for future generations.

4.3 That broad statement gives a general idea of the range of the powers and duties imposed on NHS England. However, it uses its position as the conduit of money for other parts of the NHS to impose considerable influence on how other, supposedly independent, NHS bodies are required to operate.

4.4 This chapter explains the legal structures within which NHS England is required to operate and the overarching legal duties on NHS England. It first looks at the range of functions carried out by NHS England, and then considers the overarching duties which are engaged when NHS England discharges any of its functions. Finally, it looks at a series of areas where NHS England has legal obligations.

1 See www.england.nhs.uk/about/about-nhs-england/.

Structure and composition of NHS England

4.5 NHS England operates at a series of levels. It is headed by a board, which has both executive and non-executive members.[2] It discharges its functions with national teams, regional teams and area teams. The NHS England website states that it has five regional teams, but only four such teams are listed on the website.[3] This is because the former 'South' regional team has now been divided into the South East and South West regional teams. Each region has a series of 'area teams' who report into the regional teams.

4.6 NHS England has a co-extensive duty with the Secretary of State for Health and Social Care to continue the promotion in England of a comprehensive health service designed to secure improvement a) in the physical and mental health of the people of England and b) in the prevention, diagnosis and treatment of physical and mental illness. The nature and effect of this duty is considered in chapter 3 on the powers and duties of the secretary of state.

4.7 Paragraph 1 of Schedule A1 to the NHS Act 2006 defines the status of NHS England as follows:

> (1) The Board is not to be regarded as a servant or agent of the Crown, or as enjoying any status, privilege or immunity of the Crown.
> (2) The Board's property is not to be regarded as property of, or property held on behalf of, the Crown.

4.8 It follows that NHS England is a company, albeit one which is not registered at Companies House or required to comply with the provisions of the Companies Act 2006. Nonetheless, in the unlikely event that NHS England failed to pay its debts as they fell due, a winding up petition could be presented against it as an 'unregistered company' under section 222 of the Insolvency Act 1986.

4.9 The composition of the board of NHS England is set out in para 2 of Schedule 1A to the NHS Act 2006, which provides:

> (1) The Board is to consist of–
> (a) a chair appointed by the Secretary of State,
> (b) at least five other members so appointed, and
> (c) the chief executive and other members appointed in accordance with paragraph 3.
> (2) In this Schedule–
> (a) references to non-executive members of the Board are references to the members appointed in accordance with sub-paragraph (1)(a) and (b), and
> (b) references to executive members of the Board are references to the other members.
> (3) The number of executive members must be less than the number of non-executive members.

2 See www.england.nhs.uk/about/board/members/. At the time of writing, the Chair of NHS England is Sir Malcolm Grant and the Chief Executive of NHS England is Simon Stevens.

3 See www.england.nhs.uk/about/regional-area-teams/.

4.10 The role of the chief executive and the other executive members is governed by para 3 of Schedule A1 to the NHS Act 2006, which provides:

(1) The chief executive and the other executive members of the Board are to be appointed by the non-executive members.
(2) A person may not be appointed as chief executive without the consent of the Secretary of State.
(3) The chief executive and the other executive members are to be employees of the Board.
(4) The first chief executive of the Board is to be appointed by the Secretary of State.

4.11 The role and functions of non-executive members is set out in para 4 of the Schedule. It provides:

(1) A person holds and vacates office as a non-executive member of the Board in accordance with that person's terms of appointment.
(2) A person may at any time resign from office as a non-executive member by giving notice to the Secretary of State.
(3) The Secretary of State may at any time remove a person from office as a non-executive member on any of the following grounds–
(a) incapacity,
(b) misbehaviour, or
(c) failure to carry out his or her duties as a non-executive member.
(4) The Secretary of State may suspend a person from office as a non-executive member if it appears to the Secretary of State that there are or may be grounds to remove that person from office under sub-paragraph (3).
(5) A person may not be appointed as a non-executive member for a period of more than four years.
(6) A person who ceases to be a non-executive member is eligible for re-appointment'

4.12 Suspension of non-executive members is governed by para 5 of the Schedule, and their payment is governed by para 6. The remaining parts of the Schedule give NHS England general powers to engage staff on whatever terms it considers fit (paras 8 and 9), operate through committees (para 10) and for its business to be discharged in any way it considers appropriate (para 13). The remaining paragraphs of the Schedule deal with the duty on NHS England to prepare annual accounts and for NHS England to have its own seal.

The duties of NHS England

4.13 The HSCA 2012 imposed a series of specific procedural duties on NHS England. These were introduced as new sections to the NHS Act 2006.

4.14 This part will consider the general duties of NHS England. However, special mention is needed for two significant duties, namely the duty to tackle health inequalities and the duty to secure patient and public involvement. Those duties are sufficiently significant that they merit a separate section below.

The general duties of NHS England

Introduction

4.15 The general duties cover a wide range of different factors. These duties which are engaged on every occasion that NHS England undertakes any function. The wording is slightly different for each of the duties, the subject matters are different and some may push decision-making in different directions. However, taken together, they impose substantial procedural requirements which must be fulfilled whenever NHS England take decisions. The duties are to 'have regard' to certain factors or 'exercise its functions with a view to' achieving defined objectives. These are procedural duties which require specific factors to be taken into account by NHS England when discharging all of its functions. There is an analogy with the public sector equality duty (PSED) which places a duty on public bodies, including NHS England, to have 'due regard' to specific factors when making decisions. In *R (The Pharmaceutical Services Negotiating Committee and another) v Secretary of State for Health*[4] Collins J decided that a duty to 'have regard' was just as significant and placed a similar level of duty on a public body as a duty to have 'due regard'.[5]

4.16 Each of the procedural duties on NHS England sets up legal obligations which are concerned with the way in which decisions are undertaken. They do not require NHS England to make specific decisions (such as commissioning a specific service), but are concerned with ensuring that NHS England takes into account defined factors when making decisions. It is difficult to describe precisely what each of these duties means in practice in any particular circumstances because the relevance of each factor will depend on the circumstances of each commissioning decision. However, if the duties operate in a way which is similar to the PSED, the general guidance given by Aitkens LJ in *R (Brown) v Secretary of State for Work and Pensions*[6] becomes relevant. The judge gave the following guidance about how a public body was expected to act in order to demonstrate compliance with the PSED:

a) Decision-makers within NHS England (or acting on behalf of NHS England) must be made aware of each of the above duties. A decision-maker is likely to be in difficulties in asserting that he or she has complied with their legal obligations in making decisions if those who have made the decisions were not aware of each one of the legal duties engaged by the relevant decision.
b) The mind of the decision-maker must be focused on each of the relevant duties at some relevant point during the decision-making processes. Decision-makers must have a 'conscious approach and state of mind'

4 [2017] EWHC 1147 (Admin).

5 This case is the subject of an appeal by the claimants to the Court of Appeal which is due to be heard in May 2018. It is possible that the Court of Appeal may reconsider this point when the appeal is heard. However, despite the fact that the secretary of state argued that the duty on a public body which was required to 'have regard' to factors was a lower duty than a duty of 'due regard', there is no respondents notice from the secretary of state seeking to re-open that issue on appeal.

6 [2008] EWHC 3158 (Admin).

which is focused upon the legal obligation when they are taking decisions.

c) Each legal duty must be exercised in substance, with rigour and with an open mind.
d) The duties are non-delegable duties.
e) The duties are continuing duties throughout the decision-making process.
f) It is good practice for those exercising public functions in public authorities to keep an adequate record showing that they had actually considered their duties and pondered relevant questions. Proper record-keeping encourages transparency and will discipline those carrying out the relevant function.

4.17 In practice, NHS England could prove compliance with these duties by carrying out the equivalent of an 'equality impact assessment' (EIA) for every significant decision, but expanding the EIA to cover the discharge of the specific procedural duties imposed on NHS England (as listed below). That would be possible for significant decisions, but it would be very difficult (if not impossible) for NHS England to show that it has complied with every single procedural duty when taking every single decision. A certain measure of common sense must thus be used to ensure that NHS England can demonstrate that, at some level, every decision has been guided by a decision-making process that has properly taken each of the duties listed below into account.

The duty to promote the NHS Constitution

4.18 Section 13C of the NHS Act 2006 provides a duty to promote the NHS Constitution. It states:

> (1) The Board must, in the exercise of its functions–
> (a) act with a view to securing that health services are provided in a way which promotes the NHS Constitution, and
> (b) promote awareness of the NHS Constitution among patients, staff and members of the public.
> (2) In this section, 'patients' and 'staff' have the same meaning as in Chapter 1 of Part 1 of the Health Act 2009 (see section 3(7) of that Act).

4.19 The duty is in two parts, but both apply to everything that NHS England does – it is engaged whenever NHS England is exercising its functions. Section 13C(1)(a) provides that NHS England has a specific duty to act with a view to securing that health services are provided in a way which promotes the NHS Constitution; and section 13C(1)(b) provides that NHS England must 'promote awareness of the NHS Constitution'. The full meaning of this duty is explained in chapter 2 on the NHS Constitution.

The duty to exercise functions effectively, efficiently and economically

4.20 Section 13D of the NHS Act 2006 provides:

> The Board must exercise its functions effectively, efficiently and economically.

4.21 This is the same duty as imposed on CCGs. The duty is a 'procedural' duty because it governs the way (ie the procedure) by which NHS England takes decisions, as opposed to defining the type of decision that NHS England is required to make. NHS England has a wide area of discretion in deciding what decisions to take in discharge of these duties but it is possible to envisage circumstances in which a court would hold that NHS England has acted unlawfully because it failed to act effectively, efficiently or economically. Thus, for example, a gross delay by NHS England in taking a decision or issuing promised guidance might be a breach of the duty to act efficiently. However, the section 13D duty is likely to be more useful to NHS England as a defence against taking an unpopular decision (ie an unpopular but necessary decision which can be argued to be necessary to ensure the NHS is delivered in a way which is effective, efficient and/or economical).

4.22 It may be difficult for challengers to demonstrate that NHS England is acting unlawfully unless the considerations that led NHS England to take a decision are clearly the antithesis of this decision. However, this duty would be highly relevant if, for example, NHS England bowed to pressure from politicians to take a decision that was clearly unjustified (and thus could not be said to be consistent with its duty to act in a way that was effective, efficient and/or economical).

The duty to secure continuous improvement in the quality of NHS services

4.23 Section 13E of the NHS Act 2006 imposes a duty on NHS England to strive to secure continuous improvement in the quality of NHS services. It provides:

(1) The Board must exercise its functions with a view to securing continuous improvement in the quality of services provided to individuals for or in connection with–
  (a) the prevention, diagnosis or treatment of illness, or
  (b) the protection or improvement of public health.

(2) In discharging its duty under subsection (1), the Board must, in particular, act with a view to securing continuous improvement in the outcomes that are achieved from the provision of the services.

(3) The outcomes relevant for the purposes of subsection (2) include, in particular, outcomes which show–
  (a) the effectiveness of the services,
  (b) the safety of the services, and
  (c) the quality of the experience undergone by patients.

(4) In discharging its duty under subsection (1), the Board must have regard to–
  (a) any document published by the Secretary of State for the purposes of this section, and
  (b) the quality standards prepared by NICE under section 234 of the Health and Social Care Act 2012.

4.24 Section 13D(1) requires NHS England to exercise its functions with a view to securing continuous improvement in the quality of services provided to NHS patients. This duty includes, but is not limited to, the services commissioned by NHS England. It also applies to the exercise of all of NHS England's powers. Hence, NHS England is required to have a consistent focus on the quality of services provided to NHS patients across the variety of providers where it has a measure of influence. This can involve direct influence (where a service is commissioned by NHS England) or indirect influence (as a result of its intervention powers with CCGs).

4.25 The duty is likely to come under sharp focus if NHS England permits any relaxation in quality standards in order to respond to the financial pressures on the NHS. Any de facto relaxation of quality standards to meet the exigencies of a financial or staffing crisis will need to be taken with a clear regard to the duty to improve standards. While it is not impossible for a lawful decision to be taken to reduce quality standards (to save money) while having regard to the duty under section 13E, it would present considerable challenges. It would be important to see what considerations were in the mind of the decision-maker at the time that the decision was taken, and to demonstrate that the duty to improve quality standards was carefully considered as part of the decision-making process.

The duty to promote autonomy

4.26 Section 13F is of the NHS Act 2006 is one of the less straightforward duties imposed on NHS England:

> (1) In exercising its functions, the Board must have regard to the desirability of securing, so far as consistent with the interests of the health service–
> (a) that any other person exercising functions in relation to the health service or providing services for its purposes is free to exercise those functions or provide those services in the manner it considers most appropriate, and
> (b) that unnecessary burdens are not imposed on any such person.
> (2) If, in the case of any exercise of functions, the Board considers that there is a conflict between the matters mentioned in subsection (1) and the discharge by the Board of its duties under sections 1(1) and 1H(3)(b), the Board must give priority to those duties.

4.27 The thinking behind this duty was the political philosophy which dominated the agenda that led to the HSCA 2012, namely that the NHS should, as much as possible, operate as a managed market with competition between providers to secure contracts from commissioners. The duty was aimed at preventing commissioners from stifling innovation by providers which could lead to greater efficiency for the NHS. The 'market' was supposed to lead to a brave new world which would reward innovation in the delivery of health services, and this duty was supposed to ensure that NHS England did not stifle that innovation. It is, however, a weakly worded duty and the author is not aware that it has ever been referred to in any case brought before the High Court.

The duty to promote patient involvement

4.28 Section 13H of the NHS Act 2006 provides:

> The Board must, in the exercise of its functions, promote the involvement of patients, and their carers and representatives (if any), in decisions which relate to–
> (a) the prevention or diagnosis of illness in the patients, or
> (b) their care or treatment.

4.29 The duty to involve patients in their own care is the subject of statutory guidance called *Involving people in their own health and care: Statutory guidance for clinical commissioning groups and NHS England.*[7] This guidance explains the purpose of the duty as follows:[8]

> **Personalised care and support planning**
>
> Personalised care and support planning is a systematic way of ensuring that individuals living with one or more long term condition are supported through proactive conversations, with their clinician or health and care professionals. These conversations should focus on what matters most to that individual (their personal goals) and the support they need to manage their health and wellbeing. It should be a process of sharing information, identifying medical and non-medical support needs, discussing options, contingency planning, setting goals, documenting the discussion (often in the form of a care plan) and monitoring progress through regular review.

4.30 The guidance then explains what CCGs and NHS England should do in practice to give effect to the duty. The guidance sets out ten elements of the discharge of the duty with links to numerous further online resources as follows:

1. **Support patients, carers and representatives**
   - Inform individuals and provide information they can understand about their right to be involved in and make choices about their care.
   - Engage with individuals to learn how involved they are in their care and how they feel they could become more involved.
   - Make it easier for patients to access information about their health.
   - Make use of existing insight – national surveys and local feedback or research – to understand the views, experiences and preferences of broader communities or individual groups as a context for understanding how this links to what an individual wants and needs. Further information on sources of insight and feedback, such as the GP Patient Survey, and their use in commissioning is available on the NHS England website.
   - Require providers to take measures such as those set out above.
2. **Publicise and promote personal health budgets**
   - Publish the local personal health budget offer, setting out where personal health budgets are offered or will be offered and how to get more information.
   - Inform people in receipt of continuing healthcare, or children in receipt of continuing care, of their legal right to have a personal health budget.
3. **Publicise and promote the choices available to patients**
   - Publicise and promote awareness of information about the health service providers that people can choose for an elective referral.
   - Publicise details and promote awareness of where such information can be found.
4. **Commission for involvement**
   - Introduce requirements and incentives in relation to individual involvement in contracts, service specifications and tenders.

7 See www.england.nhs.uk/wp-content/uploads/2017/04/ppp-involving-people-health-care-guidance.pdf.

8 At p7.

- Consider the need for individual involvement in all aspects of service commissioning, including prevention, diagnosis, care planning, treatment and care management.
- Engage with healthcare providers and professionals to understand what challenges and opportunities they face in involving individuals in their care.
- Co-produce services and pathways with patients, carers and the public to better understand what challenges and opportunities they face in becoming more involved and to create more effective health services.

5. **Promote and publicise the involvement of individuals**
   - Promote the importance of involving people in their own health and care in conversations with staff, providers and the general public.
   - Publicise how people can be involved in their own health and care and share good practice.
   - Publicise individuals' right to be involved in and make choices about their care.
6. **Assure themselves that providers are involving people in their own health and care to an acceptable standard**
   - Do providers systematically identify and engage with people with long term conditions or disabilities who would benefit from more personalised support, including the offer of integrated personal commissioning or a personal health budget?
     This could be through a variety of means, including the use of the Patient Activation Measure (PAM) which identifies individuals according to their level of skills, knowledge and confidence in managing their own health and wellbeing.
   - Do providers systematically provide personalised care and support planning for people living with long term conditions or disabilities who would benefit from:
   - a more personalised approach to their care and support
   - and/or more support to develop the knowledge, skills and confidence to manage their health and wellbeing?
   - Do providers give people access to their own health records?
   - Do providers ensure their clinicians and care professionals systematically share decisions across all care pathways?
   - Are providers following the Accessible Information Standard? All organisations that provide NHS care or adult social care are legally required to follow the standard.
   - Are the needs of carers being considered? NHS England has produced commissioning for carers principles.
   - Are providers aware of the Information Standard? Do they use information from organisations that are members of the Information Standard and are they tailoring information provision to an individual's level of health literacy?
   - Are providers offering meaningful choice to patients when it comes to the provision of care or support services?
   - Are providers providing and promoting online patient facing services that support shared decision making, encourage understanding and empower people to make best use of health services?
7. **Use and promote tools and resources**

The personalised care and support planning tool by 'Think Local Act Personal' is for health and care leaders, commissioners, planners, clinicians and practitioners.[9]

9 See www.thinklocalactpersonal.org.uk/personalised-care-and-support-planning-tool/.

NHS England has resources available including a personalised care and support planning handbook[10] and support materials to promote online services.

NHS England has developed a resource pack[11] for commissioners – Embedding shared decision-making.[12]

A curated collection of health literacy resources[13] is available online.

8. Assure themselves that they are commissioning services that match the needs and preferences of their population

- The need to commission services that address what people are saying matters to them and to change/decommission those services that do not.
- The need for supported self care approaches, for example:
  - Commissioning the right mix of generic and condition specific self-management education programmes (face to face or online) to match the needs of their population. Realising the Value has a range of resources on self-management education.[14]
  - Commissioning health coaching for people living with long term conditions who have low levels of knowledge, skills and confidence to manage their health and wellbeing. Realising the Value[15] has relevant tools and resources for commissioners and Health Education England (HEE) has developed a good practice project on health coaching in the east of England.
  - Commissioning peer support and group activities as a core service offer. Realising the Value's At the heart of health report explores the value of people and communities, in support of the NHS Five Year Forward View.
- The need to utilise local community assets, such as local organisations, groups, activities and resources, in their commissioning to provide a breadth of services that address a variety of health and care needs, such as through social prescribing. For example:
  - Provision of a dedicated contact for individuals and communities such as link workers or local area coordinators.
  - Working closely with their local authority, local voluntary, community and social enterprise (VCSE) sector and faith organisations and signposting people to relevant services.
- The need to systematically identify, support and involve carers as described in the Commitment to Carers.

9. Implement a workforce strategy to support health and care professionals to involve people in their own health and care

Involving individuals in managing their health and wellbeing relies on a changed relationship between individuals and professionals. Key to achieving this is ensuring that all those working in health and care have person-centred and community-centred skills, competencies, values and behaviours.

10 See www.england.nhs.uk/wp-content/uploads/2016/04/core-info-care-support-planning-1.pdf.

11 See www.england.nhs.uk/patient-online/support/.

12 See www.england.nhs.uk/ourwork/pe/sdm/capita/res-pck/.

13 See www.healthliteracy.org.uk/index.php?option=com_content&view=article&id=299&Itemid=183.

14 See www.nesta.org.uk/self-management-education.

15 See www.nesta.org.uk/realising-value-resource-centre.

In addition, it means understanding which staff roles would benefit from training in specific approaches that promote the involvement of individuals in their own health and care through:

- personalised care and support planning
- shared decision making
- health coaching
- other forms of partnership working, for example through care coordinator, link worker and health and care navigator roles.

CCGs and NHS England may need to invest in training in these approaches based on HEE's person-centred core skills education and training framework. There are also useful toolkits to help develop a person-centred workforce, such as the Royal College of General Practitioners' Collaborative Care and Support Planning Toolkit[16] and HEE's health coaching quality framework[17].

10. Advance equality and reduce health inequalities

Creating the conditions for involving people in their health and wellbeing means proactively reaching out to those who experience the greatest health needs, those who face barriers to access and participation, and those groups protected under the Equality Act 2010. An equality and health inequality analysis can help to identify those groups.

For NHS England staff further information about completing an analysis is available on the intranet. Both NHS England and CCGs can access the NHS England Equality and Health Inequalities Hub[18] for more information and resources.

Opportunities should be created to ensure fair and equitable access to person-centred care regardless of a person's cultural, linguistic, religious background, communication and accessibility needs. Particular attention should be paid to the needs of those people who are most excluded from traditional services; for example, the homeless, sex workers, recent migrants and Travellers. A holistic approach should be taken which recognises people's lived experience and the range of barriers they experience, rather than tick box approaches to addressing barriers. Conversations between professionals and individuals should be based on principles of mutual respect and listening, understanding and acting on different experiences and perspectives. They should also pay particular regard to people's level of health literacy[19] which may be a significant barrier to effective involvement in care.

CCGs and NHS England should connect with existing patient, service user and VCSE organisations to reach into, and learn from, diverse communities.

Auditing and monitoring person-centred care planning for people from equalities protected groups supports staff to manage and improve performance in reaching these groups and helps to reduce health inequalities through improved commissioning and accountability. CCGs and NHS England are required to respond to the Public Sector Equality Duty of the Equality Act 2010. Without effective involvement of individuals in their own care, CCGs and NHS England will not be able to respond to the duty

16 See www.rcgp.org.uk/clinical-and-research/toolkits/collaborative-care-and-support-planning-toolkit.aspx.

17 See www.hee.nhs.uk/sites/default/files/documents/HEE_HealthCoaching_QualityFramework.pdf.

18 See www.england.nhs.uk/about/equality/equality-hub/.

19 See www.healthliteracy.org.uk/.

> in a meaningful way. Staff should use the Equality Delivery System[20] for the NHS (EDS2), a tool to help deliver better outcomes for people and communities and better working environments, which are personalised.
>
> All organisations that provide NHS care or adult social care are required to follow the Accessible Information Standard[21], including NHS Trusts and Foundation Trusts, and GP practices. This standard aims to ensure that people who have a disability, impairment or sensory loss are provided with information that they can easily read or understand with support, so they can communicate effectively with services. CCGs and NHS England should have regard to these duties when managing contracts with providers. NHS England has produced Involving people in their own health and care equality and health inequalities – full analysis and associated resources, in relation to this guidance'

4.31 This guidance sets a very high standard for patient involvement. It appears to be written with considerable academic input, and to require considerable investment of time and resources by NHS England staff to make sure that these standards are met in practice. NHS England staff have a duty to consider the guidance when making decisions and may act unlawfully if they either do not understand the guidance or make decisions which depart from the guidance without having good reasons to do so.

4.32 There is a considerable link between this duty and both patient choice rights and personal budgets. Further details concerning those areas are set out in the individual chapters on those topics.

The duty to enable patients to exercise choices

4.33 Section 13I of the NHS Act 2006 provides:

> The Board must, in the exercise of its functions, act with a view to enabling patients to make choices with respect to aspects of health services provided to them.

This duty is explained in detail in chapter 12 on patient choice rights.

The duty to obtain appropriate advice

4.34 Section 13J of the NHS Act 2006 provides:

> The Board must obtain advice appropriate for enabling it effectively to discharge its functions from persons who (taken together) have a broad range of professional expertise in–
> (a) the prevention, diagnosis or treatment of illness, and
> (b) the protection or improvement of public health.

4.35 This is a duty to obtain advice from professionals who have expertise in two areas, namely a) the prevention, diagnosis or treatment of illness, and b) the protection or improvement of public health. The first part of the legal duty requires NHS England to seek disease-specific advice before, for example, commissioning specialist services. NHS England discharges this duty through Clinical Reference Groups (CRGs) who provide disease-specific advice as part of the specialist commissioning functions.

20 See www.england.nhs.uk/about/equality/equality-hub/eds/.
21 See www.england.nhs.uk/ourwork/accessibleinfo/.

4.36 The second part requires NHS England to seek advice on the wider impacts of its decision-making on public health. There is repeated emphasis in the HSCA 2012 about the need for the NHS to move from being a service which copes with the consequences of diseases to a service that promotes the health of the population. This is seen in the above duty, but also in the general duty on the secretary of state and NHS England under section 1(1). Public health services have often competed unsuccessfully for funds, coming well behind disease specific health services in the NHS's priorities. Decision making may well be driven by the immediate consequences of underfunding in A&E or cancer services, whereas public health funding delivers greater benefits over a longer timescale. While the structure of legal duties in the HSCA 2012 is designed to promote public health as an important objective, the duties may well not have been crafted with sufficient precision to enable successful challenges against resource allocation decisions which leave public health underfunded.

The duty to promote innovation

4.37 Section 13K of the NHS Act 2006 provides:

(1) The Board must, in the exercise of its functions, promote innovation in the provision of health services (including innovation in the arrangements made for their provision).
(2) The Board may make payments as prizes to promote innovation in the provision of health services.
(3) A prize may relate to–
  (a) work at any stage of innovation (including research);
  (b) work done at any time (including work before the commencement of section 23 of the Health and Social Care Act 2012).

4.38 This duty covers some of the same area as the duty to promote provider autonomy under section 13F. There is a specific power (but not a duty) to award prizes for innovation.

The duty to promote research

4.39 Section 13L of the NHS Act 2006 provides:

The Board must, in the exercise of its functions, promote–
  (a) research on matters relevant to the health service, and
  (b) the use in the health service of evidence obtained from research.

4.40 The NHS has always been involved in research to find new and better ways to treat patients. For many hospital consultants, research is an essential part of their professional lives and career progression. The NHS is also involved in research which it does not directly fund. Funding to support clinical research is provided by pharmaceutical companies, universities, charities and a variety of other sources. Often the NHS support for research involves providing access to a combination of NHS staff and patients who take part in clinical trials. In April 2017, NHS England published a research strategy which sets out the various ways it will support research as part of the discharge of this duty.[22]

22 See www.england.nhs.uk/wp-content/uploads/2017/04/nhse-research-plan.pdf.

The duty to promote education and training

4.41 Section 13M of the NHS Act 2006 provides:

> The Board must, in exercising its functions, have regard to the need to promote education and training for the persons mentioned in section 1F(1) so as to assist the Secretary of State and Health Education England[23] in the discharge of the duty under that section.

4.42 The 'persons mentioned in section 1F(1)' are 'persons who are employed, or who are considering becoming employed, in an activity which involves or is connected with the provision of services as part of the health service in England'. This duty thus ensures that NHS England maintains a focus on working with Health Education England.

The duty to promote integration

4.43 Section 13N of the NHS Act 2006 provides:

> (1) The Board must exercise its functions with a view to securing that health services are provided in an integrated way where it considers that this would–
> (a) improve the quality of those services (including the outcomes that are achieved from their provision),
> (b) reduce inequalities between persons with respect to their ability to access those services, or
> (c) reduce inequalities between persons with respect to the outcomes achieved for them by the provision of those services.
>
> (2) The Board must exercise its functions with a view to securing that the provision of health services is integrated with the provision of health-related services or social care services where it considers that this would–
> (a) improve the quality of the health services (including the outcomes that are achieved from the provision of those services),
> (b) reduce inequalities between persons with respect to their ability to access those services, or
> (c) reduce inequalities between persons with respect to the outcomes achieved for them by the provision of those services.
>
> (3) The Board must encourage clinical commissioning groups to enter into arrangements with local authorities in pursuance of regulations under section 75 where it considers that this would secure–
> (a) that health services are provided in an integrated way and that this would have any of the effects mentioned in subsection (1)(a) to (c), or
> (b) that the provision of health services is integrated with the provision of health-related services or social care services and that this would have any of the effects mentioned in subsection (2)(a) to (c).
>
> (4) In this section–
> 'health-related services' means services that may have an effect on the health of individuals but are not health services or social care services;
> 'social care services' means services that are provided in pursuance of the social services functions of local authorities (within the meaning of the Local Authority Social Services Act 1970 or for the purposes of the Social Services and Well-being (Wales) Act 2014).

23 The words 'and Health Education England' in square brackets inserted by the Care Act 2014 s97(4)(b).

(5) For the purposes of this section, the provision of housing accommodation is a health-related service.[24]

4.44 The problem of 'joining up' services both within the NHS and between the NHS and social care systems has been a perennial problem for governments since the separate systems of health and social care were created by the post-WWII Labour government in the National Health Service Act 1946 and the National Assistance Act 1948. The NHS has clear divisions between primary, community and acute care, with different NHS organisations delivering different parts of the care pathway for an individual patient. Thus providing NHS services in an 'integrated' way has always been a huge practical problem for NHS commissioners. The difficulties are even greater in attempts to integrate health and social care services because of the two key differences between NHS and social care services, namely:

a) NHS services are run by NHS bodies whereas social care services are run by local authorities; and
b) NHS services are generally free at the point of delivery whereas social services are means tested benefits.

4.45 Section 13N seeks to impose procedural duties to promote integration both within the NHS and between NHS and social care services. The practical delivery of integration and in particular the operation and development of 'section 75' agreements is beyond the scope of this chapter. However, for details see the NHS Bodies and Local Authorities Partnership Arrangements Regulations 2000[25] (as amended) which set out the rules for joint working between NHS bodies and local authority bodies.

Section 13O: the duty to have regard to impact on services in certain areas

4.46 The NHS Act 2006 is concerned with the management of the NHS in England. National health services in Wales, Scotland and Northern Ireland are devolved matters and are accordingly within the powers of the Scottish and Welsh governments and the Northern Ireland Assembly. However patients will access the health services that are most appropriate for their particular condition, regardless as to whether those NHS services are located in England, Scotland or Wales. Section 13O requires NHS England to consider the extent to which decisions it makes will impact on those living close to the borders of Scotland and Wales. It provides:

(1) In making commissioning decisions, the Board must have regard to the likely impact of those decisions on the provision of health services to persons who reside in an area of Wales or Scotland that is close to the border with England.
(2) In this section, 'commissioning decisions', in relation to the Board, means decisions about the carrying out of its functions in arranging for the provision of health services.

24 Section 13N(5) was introduced by the Care Act 2014 and, at the time of writing, this provision has yet to be brought into force.
25 SI No 617.

4.47 This is a procedural duty which requires NHS England to 'have regard' to the likely impact of those decisions on the provision of health services to persons who reside in an area of Wales or Scotland that is close to the border with England and, by implication, may wish to access NHS services that are located in England. NHS England is, of course, not limited to commissioning services from providers that are physically located in England. It could use its powers to commission services from providers that are located in Wales or Scotland if, in a particular case, this was the most appropriate provider.

Section 13P: The duty as respects variation in provision of health services

4.48 This is a provision which was intended to ensure that NHS England manages providers in the NHS 'managed market' properly. The section reads as follows:

> The Board must not exercise its functions for the purpose of causing a variation in the proportion of services provided as part of the health service that is provided by persons of a particular description if that description is by reference to–
> (a) whether the persons in question are in the public or (as the case may be) private sector, or
> (b) some other aspect of their status

4.49 This is a substantive duty, not just a procedural duty. It imposes a legal bar on NHS England exercising its functions for the purpose of causing a variation in the proportion of services which are provided either by public bodies or by private sector providers. It also prevents policies that are designed to limit providers by reference to some other aspect of their status. The clear intention of the clause is to prevent NHS England having a policy which has the purpose of discriminating in favour of or against providers of NHS services that are not public bodies. It does not mandate equality of treatment between public and private sector suppliers, but has a narrower focus, namely preventing any decision which purposively discriminates in favour of or against a group of providers. Hence, for example, it would be unlawful for NHS England to have a policy of only commissioning a type of specialist services from NHS foundation trusts, because being a foundation trust is a 'status' and is thus outlawed by section 13P(b). It is unclear how far the concept of 'status' extends and whether the word is to be interpreted as broadly as the concept of status under Article 14 of the European Convention on Human Rights (ECHR).

Section 13R: The duty to establish systems to hold information on safety of services provided by the health service

4.50 Section 13R imposes a duty on NHS England to establish and operate systems for collecting and analysing patient safety information within the NHS. It provides:

> (1) The Board must establish and operate systems for collecting and analysing information relating to the safety of the services provided by the health service.
> (2) The Board must make information collected by virtue of subsection (1), and any other information obtained by analysing it, available to such persons as the Board considers appropriate.

(3) The Board may impose charges, calculated on such basis as it considers appropriate, in respect of information made available by it under subsection (2).
(4) The Board must give advice and guidance, to such persons as it considers appropriate, for the purpose of maintaining and improving the safety of the services provided by the health service.
(5) The Board must monitor the effectiveness of the advice and guidance given by it under subsection (4).
(6) A clinical commissioning group must have regard to any advice or guidance given to it under subsection (4).
(7) The Board may arrange for any other person (including another NHS body) to exercise any of the Board's functions under this section.
(8) Arrangements made under subsection (7) do not affect the liability of the Board for the exercise of any of its functions.

4.51 The National Reporting and Learning System (NRLS) is a central database of patient safety incident reports which was set up in 2003. Over four million incident reports have been submitted to the system and all information submitted is, to an extent, analysed to identify hazards, risks and opportunities with the aim of continuously improve the safety of patient care. On 1 April 2016 the statutory patient safety functions previously delivered by NHS England transferred with the national patient safety team to NHS Improvement in exercise of the powers under section 13R(7).[26]

Section 13S: Guidance in relation to processing of information

4.52 Section 13S of the NHS Act 2006 imposes specific duties on the board to publish guidance on the practices to be followed by NHS bodies in relation to patient and other information. It provides:

(1) The Board must publish guidance for registered persons on the practice to be followed by them in relation to the processing of–
  (a) patient information, and
  (b) any other information obtained or generated in the course of the provision of the health service.
(2) Registered persons who carry on an activity which involves, or is connected with, the provision of health care must have regard to any guidance published under this section.
(3) In this section, 'patient information', 'processing' and 'registered person' have the same meaning as in section 20A of the Health and Social Care Act 2008.

4.53 Numerous individual pieces of guidance have been issued by or on behalf of NHS England explaining how information should be reported. It is beyond the scope of this book to describe every piece of guidance.

The two significant duties of NHS England

The duty to reduce inequalities

4.54 The HSCA 2012 introduced specific duties on the secretary of state, NHS England and CCGs to tackle health inequalities. The nature and effect of these far-ranging duties have yet to be worked out in case-law but, in due

26 See www.nrls.npsa.nhs.uk/patient-safety-data/.

course, their effect is likely to be as far-ranging as the PSED under the Equality Act 2010.

4.55 The duty on NHS England to tackle health inequalities is in section 13G of the NHS Act 2006, which provides:

> The Board must, in the exercise of its functions, have regard to the need to–
> (a) reduce inequalities between patients with respect to their ability to access health services, and
> (b) reduce inequalities between patients with respect to the outcomes achieved for them by the provision of health services.

4.56 There is a wealth of evidence of persistent inequality in the health of people in the UK. This is partly related to the way in which NHS services are accessed, but the majority of the factors leading to inequalities in health are unrelated to the NHS. The extent of health inequalities was summarised in the *Acheson Report*[27] published back in 1998. The clear conclusion of that report was that universal services open to all do not, of themselves, deliver equal benefits. Hence the assumption behind the wording of the duty on the secretary of state under section 1C and the parallel duties on both NHS England under section 13G and CCGs under section 14T appears to be that making NHS services available on a universal basis – of itself – will not deliver equal benefits for all patients.

4.57 The steps that NHS England are required to take to reduce health inequalities are more specific than those on the secretary of state. However, readers are referred to the relevant part of chapter 3 on the powers and duties of the secretary of state concerning health inequalities for an introduction to this subject.[28]

4.58 In December 2015 NHS England published guidance to assist decision-makers within NHS England and CCGs (who have a like duty) discharge this duty, namely *Guidance for NHS commissioners on equality and health inequalities legal duties*. The introduction sets out the background for this duty as follows:

> Avoidable health inequalities are – by definition – unfair and socially unjust. A person's chance of enjoying good health and a longer life is determined by the social and economic conditions in which they are born, grow, work, live and age. These conditions also affect the way in which people look after their own health and use services throughout their life. Addressing such avoidable inequalities and moving towards a fairer distribution of good health requires a life course approach and action to be taken across the whole of society.
>
> The NHS Five Year Forward View sets out the need to address the health and wellbeing gap, preventing any further widening of health inequalities. To do so requires a move towards greater investment in health and health care where the level of deprivation is higher.
>
> The World Health Organisation (WHO) defines health inequalities as 'differences in health status or in the distribution of health determinants between different population groups'. There is clear evidence that reducing health inequalities improves life expectancy and reduces disability across

27 See www.gov.uk/government/uploads/system/uploads/attachment_data/file/265503/ih.pdf.

28 See paras 3.18–3.28.

the social gradient. Tackling health inequalities is therefore core to improving access to services, health outcomes, improving the quality of services and the experiences of people. It is also core to the NHS Constitution and the values and purpose of the NHS.

The NHS Constitution states that the NHS has a duty to '. . . pay particular attention to groups or sections of society where improvements in health and life expectancy are not keeping pace with the rest of the population'. This is reflected in the National Health Service Act 2006 (as amended by the Health and Social Care Act 2012), which introduced for the first time legal duties.

4.59 The guidance suggests that a 'have regard' duty is to be interpreted in the same way as the 'have due regard' PSED under section 149 of the Equality Act 2010.[29] That approach was later supported by the decision of Mr Justice Collins in *R (The Pharmaceutical Services Negotiating Committee and another) v Secretary of State for Health*.[30]

4.60 This is a procedural duty in two parts: a) the first is a duty to have regard to the need to reduce inequalities between patients with respect to their ability to access health services; and b) the second is to have regard to the need to reduce inequalities between patients with respect to the outcomes achieved for them by the provision of health services. The first part of the duty is primarily about NHS England exercising its powers to commission services (and influence the way CCGs commission services) in a way that acknowledges that different people access health services in different ways, and seeks to meet the challenge of making those services more accessible to those who have greater levels of health inequality. The second part involves a focus on securing better outcomes for those who suffer health inequalities.

4.61 The guidance sets out the practical effects of the legal duty as follows:

5.3.2 What do the duties mean in practice?

To be compliant with the legislation, CCGs and NHS England should consistently have regard to the need to reduce inequalities when exercising their functions. This is likely to require considering:

- the impact on inequalities as part of all decision making processes, and keeping a record of such processes;
- which dimensions of inequality are relevant to their work, and taking account of how inequalities could be reduced;
- strategically the potential impact on health inequalities and the application of the duty to their functions.

An internal analysis template document is available to help NHS England staff consider the implications of their work on equality and addressing health inequalities. This aims to help ensure that the action they are taking has the best chance of achieving improvements in the health outcomes and the experiences of people; reducing health inequalities; advancing equality of opportunity; whilst capturing the evidence of doing so.

This approach should support NHS England in meeting its separate legal duties on equality and health inequalities. Section one of the document contains the equality analysis and section two the health inequalities analysis.

29 At para 5.2.3.

30 [2017] EWHC 1147 (Admin). Contrary to the arguments of the secretary of state in that case. For details see the chapter on the secretary of state's powers and duties at para 3.11.

If a CCG would like a copy of this NHS England analysis template document please contact england.eandhi@nhs.net.

Other issues that CCGs and NHS England may consider include:

- How local communities' experiences of the NHS influences future action?
- Has action been taken to ensure all staff are aware of the duties?
- Is there clear accountability at a sufficiently senior level?
- Is there clear communication to ensure the duties are being applied?
- Is the approach being taken evidence-based?
- Are inequalities in access and outcomes being routinely monitored?
- Have records and evidence of compliance with the duty been kept?

Using The Equality Delivery System – EDS2 is also likely to support organisations to deliver on aspects of their health inequalities work'

4.62 Further guidance about the impact of the duty on NHS England is set out as follows:

5.3.7 NHS England

NHS England has a duty to have regard to the need to reduce inequalities between patients in access to services commissioned through its direct commissioning functions. This may involve:

- Identifying health inequalities, evaluating how such inequalities might impact on people's ability to access services, and commissioning for all of the population and all needs.
- Identifying evidence of what has previously worked in reducing inequalities in access to services and evaluating notable practice.

NHS England may also consider whether:

- services are universal and should reach all members of society, which may be achieved by explicitly targeting specific population groups;
- services are commissioned on the basis of need, which may be achieved by ensuring the quantity and quality of services in deprived areas is adequate.

NHS England also has a duty to have regard to the need to reduce inequalities between patients in outcomes from services commissioned through its direct commissioning functions. This involves:

- Effective monitoring and evaluation that identifies health inequalities and to support action to overcome inappropriate variations in outcomes for all people.
- Looking at how the outcome is distributed across society by area of deprivation and by different groups, rather than focusing on average outcomes for all people.
- Considering how services can be commissioned to reduce inequalities and prevent undesirable outcomes. For example, targeting life-style factors in health and compliance with treatment, and developing key provider indicators with health inequality outcomes.

Many changes to address health inequalities will have a long-term impact on health outcomes, so their effectiveness may not be visible on an annual reporting basis. This should not detract from implementing such changes, if they are based upon robust evidence supporting the reduction in health inequalities'

4.63 However, as with so many aspects of decision-making involving NHS England, the problems do not arise primarily with the adoption of compliant policies (albeit such policies were not adopted until several years after NHS started functioning) but with decision-makers who either do not understand the nature or effect of the duties on NHS England to tackle health inequalities or fail to record any steps taken in compliance with these policies when making significant decisions. That is an area of considerable legal risk for NHS England and constitutes an opportunity for those seeking to challenge the legality of NHS England decisions.

The public and patient involvement duties of NHS England (section 13Q)

Overview

4.64 Debate about how to ensure that the public have a right to have their voices heard in decisions made by NHS commissioners and providers has been a perennial issue in the NHS. NHS decisions are, in practice, dominated by the interests of suppliers of NHS services and the budgetary concerns of the commissioners. The NHS has long recognised that commissioning decisions should not just be matters agreed after discussions between commissioners and providers, but should be determined with patient voices being at the heart of the decision making process. However, achieving this in practice has proved hugely difficult for NHS managers, particularly in a time of austerity where unpopular decisions have to be made between competing priorities, which can lead to popular local services being sacrificed for more efficient and effective services at a regional level.

4.65 There have been specific statutory obligations on NHS commissioners to involve patients and the public in commissioning decisions for NHS services (known as 'patient and public involvement' (PPI) arrangements) since (at least) section 11 of the Health and Social Care Act (HSCA) 2001.[31] The present relevant statutory provision relating to NHS England is now in section 13Q of the NHS Act 2006, which is set out below and has echoes of section 11 of the HSCA 2001. However, the senior management of the NHS has repeatedly recognised that the NHS has been poor at properly involving patients and the public in decision-making processes within the NHS.

4.66 In 2008 the then NHS chief executive emphasised that the NHS needed to improve its engagement with patients. Sir David Nicholson, said (in a forward to guidance on a previous version of the statutory duty to involve patients):[32]

> The NHS needs to be much better at involving all stakeholders. This includes patients and their representatives, carers, members of the public,

31 Section 11 of the HSCA 2001 provided: '(1) It is the duty of every body to which this section applies to make arrangements with a view to securing, as respects health services for which it is responsible, that persons to whom those services are being or may be provided are, directly or through representatives, involved in and consulted on – (a) the planning of the provision of those services, (b) the development and consideration of proposals for changes in the way those services are provided, and (c) decisions to be made by that body affecting the operation of those services'.

32 See http://webarchive.nationalarchivesection gov.uk/20130107105354/http://www.dh.gov.uk/prod_consum_dh/groups/dh_digitalassets/@dh/@en/documents/digitalasset/dh_089785.pdf

clinicians, staff and political leaders, and it needs to become more open and transparent about why it is proposing changes, what it is proposing to change and what it believes the benefits will be for the people who use the services.

Whether change is on the scale of a major service reconfiguration or how a particular service operates, the NHS must get better at explaining why change is needed. It must make sure that people who use or may use local health services are actively involved in the planning of services, and the development and consideration of proposals for changes that impact on the provision of services and decision-making.

4.67 The need to involve patients in commissioning decision-making is not merely important to discharge the legal duties on NHS commissioners. Patient involvement feeds a patient perspective into the decision-making process and thus assists NHS commissioners to ensure that NHS patients receive services they can access and are arranged in a way that is appropriate for patients. Patient involvement also affects the quality of care received by NHS patients. The Francis Report into the failings at Mid-Staffordshire Hospitals NHS Foundation Trust emphasised the problems that the NHS experiences when patients and NHS management became disengaged. A report by the King's Fund[33] explained the core findings as follows:

Within this kind of culture, leaders become detached from those on the front line and from the consequences of their decisions – a trend discernible from the Department of Health downwards. As Francis notes: 'DH [DOH] officials are at times too remote from the reality of the impact of the service they oversee on patients. This led to the board and senior managers prioritising and explicitly rewarding the achievement of financial targets while overlooking patient safety and basic care standards – to such an extent that frontline staff began to see finance and targets as ends in themselves. The result, in Francis's words, is 'a culture focused on doing the system's business – not that of the patients'.

4.68 The need for openness and transparency in commissioning decision is also highlighted in the NHS Constitution which provides:[34]

You have the right to be involved, directly or through representatives,[35] in the planning of healthcare services commissioned by NHS bodies, the development and consideration of proposals for changes in the way those services are provided, and in decisions to be made affecting the operation of those services.

4.69 The specific PPI duties imposed by parliament on NHS England are now contained in section 13Q of the NHS Act 2006, which provides:

33 See www.kingsfund.org.uk/sites/files/kf/field/field_publication_file/patient-centred-leadership-rediscovering-our-purpose-may13.pdf.

34 See www.nhsection uk/choiceintheNHS/Rightsandpledges/NHSConstitution/Documents/2013/the-nhs-constitution-for-england-2013.pdf at pp6–7. The legal effect of the NHS Constitution is set out in the Health act 2009.

35 This wording appears to be taken from section 242 of the NHS Act 2006 and was written before the HSCA 2012. The duties on NHS England under section 13Q are more extensive because NHS England is required to involve patients directly. The option of working 'through representatives' is omitted from the wording of PPI duty on NHS England under section 13Q. See further below.

Public involvement and consultation by the Board

(1) This section applies in relation to any health services which are, or are to be, provided pursuant to arrangements made by the Board in the exercise of its functions ('commissioning arrangements').

(2) The Board must make arrangements to secure that individuals to whom the services are being or may be provided are involved (whether by being consulted or provided with information or in other ways)–

(a) in the planning of the commissioning arrangements by the Board,

(b) in the development and consideration of proposals by the Board for changes in the commissioning arrangements where the implementation of the proposals would have an impact on the manner in which the services are delivered to the individuals or the range of health services available to them, and

(c) in decisions of the Board affecting the operation of the commissioning arrangements where the implementation of the decisions would (if made) have such an impact.

(3) The reference in subsection (2)(b) to the delivery of services is a reference to their delivery at the point when they are received by users.

(4) This section does not require the Board to make arrangements in relation to matters to which a trust special administrator's report or draft report under section 65F or 65I relates before the Secretary of State makes a decision under section 65K(1), is satisfied as mentioned in section 65KB(1) or 65KD(1) or makes a decision under section 65KD(9) (as the case may be).

4.70 The Board has responsibility for a wide range of NHS commissioning arrangements including primary medical care, primary dental care, primary pharmaceutical services, NHS services in prisons and secure environments, specialised services and for armed forces personnel.[36] Accordingly, the section 13Q duty is engaged in a very wide range of commissioning functions.

What does a duty to 'make arrangements' mean in practice?

4.71 The words 'arrange' and 'arrangements' are used on numerous occasions throughout the NHS Act 2006. A duty to 'make arrangements' refers to a public law duty on an NHS body to have a specific agreement or process in order to discharge a specific function. The duty under section 13Q thus requires NHS England to identify a specific process, normally by adopting a policy, which defines precisely how the patients who receive primary care services can become involved in NHS England's decision-making. In order to be lawful, the policy must explain how NHS England commits itself to giving patients the opportunity for their voice to be heard when it is making relevant decisions about services that it is commissioning.

4.72 CCGs are under the same PPI duties as NHS England as a result of section 14Z2 of the NHS Act 2006. Section 14Z2(4) gives power to NHS England to publish guidance about how CCGs should perform their PPI duties. In September 2013, NHS England exercised this power to publish guidance, which is directed both to itself and to CCGs as to how NHS commissioners ought to put arrangements in place to ensure that patients are properly involved in all relevant aspects of commissioning, called

36 Full details are set out in chapter 13 on the responsible commissioner.

Transforming participation in health and care: The NHS belongs to us all.[37] The guidance starts with the following statement of principle:

> The NHS is a cherished national institution. Its founding principle is to provide healthcare which is free at the point of delivery, to anyone who needs it, regardless of their circumstances. The NHS must be more responsive to the needs and wishes of the public, all of whom will use its services at some point in their lives.
>
> NHS England will ensure that public, patient and carer voices are at the centre of our healthcare services, from planning to delivery. Every level of our commissioning system will be informed by insightful methods of listening to those who use and care about our services.

4.73 The guidance then provides practical recommendations as to what CCGs and NHS England should do in order to involve patients in all relevant aspects of its commissioning decision making. The then National Director of Patients and Information at the Board, Mr Tim Kelsey, is quoted in the guidance saying:

> We must put the citizen and patient voice absolutely at the heart of every decision we take in purchasing, commissioning and providing services.

4.74 The guidance then provides details about how CCGs and NHS England should engage with patients throughout the commissioning cycle. It provides:

> Evidence suggests that engaging and involving communities in the planning, design and delivery of health and care services can lead to more joined-up, co-ordinated and efficient services that are more responsive to local community needs. Public participation can also help to build partnerships with communities and identify areas for service improvement. NHS England will work with partners to identify any further evidence and disseminate it widely'
>
> . . .
>
> Insight gathered from the public helps to improve services and outcomes as well as potentially helping to spot failures. Listening to and using the voice of patients and the public were never more forcefully presented than in the Francis report.

4.75 The guidance outlines ten areas where NHS England should act to develop PPI arrangements, namely:

- involve the public in governance;
- explain public involvement in commissioning plans/business plan;
- demonstrate public involvement in annual reports;
- promote and publicise public involvement;
- assess, plan and take action to involve;
- feed back and evaluate;
- implement assurance and improvement systems;
- advance equality and reduce health inequalities;
- provide support for effective involvement;
- hold providers to account.

4.76 Section 13Q came into force on 27 March 2012. However, notwithstanding the provisions of section 13Q, NHS England failed to adopt any arrangements for patient involvement in primary care commissioning

37 See www.england.nhs.uk/wp-content/uploads/2013/09/trans-part-hc-guid1.pdf.

until November 2015. In 2014 NHS England faced judicial review proceedings challenging its lack of any PPI arrangements. It admitted the breach of its public law legal obligations, and a declaration was made by Mr Justice Popplewell that it was acting unlawfully.[38]

4.77 It took NHS England another 12 months before it published a document which it stated to be its 'arrangements' for ensuring that patients and the public were able to be involved in its commissioning decisions, namely the NHS England *Statement of arrangements and guidance on patient and public participation in commissioning.*[39] Unfortunately, the arrangements document is so general that it is nearly impossible to understand what NHS England commits itself to doing in particular circumstances. The arrangements document appears to have gone through several internal iterations and gives the appearance of being primarily designed to ensure that NHS England's existing practices were not open to challenge by anyone who was complaining about a lack of patient involvement prior to decisions being taken as opposed to clarifying precisely how NHS England would involve patients in decision-making. Thus the arrangements document appears to attempt to be more concerned to give the green light to management practices which involved a lack of patient involvement as opposed to securing greater levels of patient involvement in decision-making. That may be explained by the fact that the arrangements document was created against a background of further pressure on NHS England to correct the legal errors demonstrated in the *Curry* case.

4.78 The arrangements document states:[40]

> The section 13Q duty is aimed at ensuring that NHS England acts fairly in making plans, proposals and decisions in relation to the health services it commissions, where there may be an impact on services. The duty requires NHS England to make arrangements for public involvement in commissioning.
>
> Public involvement in commissioning is about offering people ways to voice their needs and wishes, and to influence plans, proposals and decisions about their NHS services. Patients and the public can often identify innovative, effective and efficient ways of designing and delivering services if given the opportunity to provide meaningful and constructive input.

4.79 This passage appears to misunderstand the underlying purpose of the section 13Q duty. The duty is not primarily about ensuring that NHS England acts 'fairly'. It is about ensuring that the patient voice is heard loudly and clearly at all stages of the commissioning process so that commissioners are fully sighted on patient perspectives before decisions are made. That requirement is not primarily about 'fairness' but about ensuring that decisions are taken with a full understanding of the patient's perspective on the impact of the decisions.

4.80 The section 13Q duty is engaged in the 'planning of the commissioning arrangements by the Board', whether these will have any impact on the

38 See *R (Curry) v NHS Commissioning Board* in CO/4386/2014: Decision of 18 November 2014.

39 See www.engage.england.nhs.uk/survey/strengthening-ppp/supporting_documents/ppppolicystatement.pdf-1.

40 At para 1.2.

way patients or not. The arrangements document properly recognises this, saying:[41]

> NHS England is required to always have arrangements in place to involve the public in the planning of its commissioning arrangements, regardless of what the impact upon services such plans would have if they were implemented.

4.81 In contrast, NHS England only has a duty to involve patients and the public in the development and consideration of proposals by NHS England for changes in its commissioning arrangements 'where the implementation of the proposals would have an impact on the manner in which the services are delivered to the individuals or the range of health services available to them'. Thus a decision to change from provider A to provider B that is working at the same location and providing exactly the same services does not require patient involvement unless the identity of the individual clinicians is relevant to patients. In *Smith v North Eastern Derbyshire Primary Care Trust and another*[42] Collins J considered the scope of the duty under section 11 of the HSCA 2001[43] in connection with plans to make changes at a general practitioner (GP) practice. He said:

> 18. Virtually any decision by the PCT in connection with the provision of health services or the manner in which they are delivered is capable of falling within s11(1)(c). However, there is, I think, force in the submission of Mr Herberg that the purpose behind s11 is to ensure that patients' views are obtained where decisions may make a material change to the services being or to be provided or may materially affect patients.
>
> 19. Thus I accept that a change of personnel or of contractual terms or of the form of a contract may not of themselves be covered by s11. But the background is highly relevant. The need to replace a failed service should mean that the reasons for the failure are addressed and that may well, as was the case here, lead to a need to consider whether any different arrangements to deal with any problems which have manifested themselves are required. Thus public input may assist the PCT and will certainly help to allay concerns.
>
> 20. I have no doubt that the circumstances of this case did give rise to the s11 duty. It can be said that any case where services have failed and must be replaced will amount to reprovision of those services. That merely underlines the point that the label 'reprovision' does not give the answer in favour of the defendant and the Secretary of State. For the reasons I have indicated, a failure is often likely to require a consideration of its causes and so whether changes are indeed needed.

4.82 Thus, as in so many areas of public law, context is everything in deciding whether the duty is engaged.[44] In contrast to the approach advocated by Collins J, the arrangements document suggests that public involvement would not be necessary in either of the following cases:[45]

41 At p12.

42 [2006] EWHC 1338 (Admin).

43 See footnote 24 above.

44 As Lord Stein famously said in *R (Daly) v Secretary of State for the Home Department* [2001] 2 AC 532.

45 At p13.

> The retirement of a GP from a practice may mean that patients with a preferred choice of doctor will need to be seen by a different GP. However, this would not typically affect the range of services or the manner of their delivery, in which case public involvement is unlikely to be required.
>
> The termination of a GP contract and the award of a new contract to a provider, with no change in the specification of such a contract, would not ordinarily be expected to result in changes to the way that services are delivered to patients or the range of services available. In such circumstances there may be no legal requirement to involve the public.

4.83 The first paragraph may be right, but the second is clearly wrong. Patients who have a long-standing personal relationship with a well-known GP, are entitled to say that a change of GP will have an 'impact on the manner in which the services are delivered to' them even if the terms of the contract with NHS England remain unaltered. A new GP service will be bound to impose some changes to the way that a GP practice runs. There may be more or fewer appointments. There may be more or less specialised clinics. The way in which every GP handles home visits varies. Further, it is hard to see why patients should not be entitled to have a say in who should become their family doctor. Thus the arrangements document appears erroneous because it suggests that a PPI duty only arises where there are differences in the contractual arrangements between a provider of NHS services and NHS England, as opposed to focusing on whether changes in arrangements result in patients receiving NHS services in a way that patients would consider amounted to differences in the services they experience.

What does NHS England have to do to satisfy the duty where it is engaged?

4.84 The wording of the duty makes it clear that full '*Gunning*'[46] compliant consultation is not necessary in every case. The arrangements document properly recognises this, saying:[47]

> The Act is not prescriptive about what constitutes involvement, however it explicitly states that people may be involved 'by being consulted, or by being given information, or in other ways.' Engagement, consultation, participation and patient voice are all phrases that can be used to describe different types of involvement activity. It is therefore clear that consultation and involvement are not mutually exclusive – rather, consultation is one of many possible types of public involvement that NHS England can carry out to discharge its duty under section 13Q.

4.85 The persons who have to have the chance to become involved in the PPI exercise are 'individuals to whom the services are being or may be provided'. NHS England thus has to offer everyone who is presently using the relevant service or may wish to use the service to have their say before any changes are made to the commissioning of a service. There is a clear difference in this aspect of the wording between the section 14Z2 duty and

46 The principles which had to be developed for a fair consultation were set out by counsel for the claimant, Stephen Sedley in *R v Brent LBC ex p Gunning* (1985) 84 LGR 168 and approved in *R (Moseley) v London Haringey LBC* [2014] UKSC 56. They are explained at para 17.76 below.

47 At p15.

the wording of the section 242 duty.[48] The latter duty explicitly allows engagement to be carried on by way of 'representatives' of patients. This was always somewhat problematic because there is often no formal system for appointing patient 'representatives' and thus NHS bodies could discharge the duty by confining their engagement to very limited groups of patients who were unlikely to raise any problems with the proposed changes. The ability of the NHS commissioner to discharge its duty by identifying self-selected patient 'representatives' is omitted from the wording of the section 14Z2 duty. Unfortunately, this difference in wording has not been appreciated by those who drafted the arrangements document, since it states:[49]

> While the duty on NHS England is to make arrangements to involve individuals to whom the services are being or may be provided, case law has established that in some cases public involvement can take place via representatives. For example, a policy or review group with appropriate expertise and representatives of those affected may be sufficient where direct public involvement is not practicable. Where involvement takes place via representatives, NHS England should try to ensure that they offer a fair representation of the views of those for whom they speak, rather than a narrower or different interest.

4.86 It is correct that case-law such as *Smith* concerning the discharge of the duty under section 242 of the NHS Act 2006 provided that public involvement could take place via representatives, because that was what section 242 allowed. That is not part of the wording of the section 14Z2 duty.

When should involvement take place?

4.87 The wording of the duty makes it clear that the public have the right to be involved in decision-making throughout the commissioning cycle, from the planning of commissioning arrangements, through the development and consideration of proposals for changes in commissioning arrangements and in decisions of affecting the operation of the commissioning arrangements. It is not a 'one-off' chance to become involved, but a right to have a patient voice at the table throughout the commissioning process. However, the arrangements document seeks to depart from the wording of the statutory duty by limiting patient involvement to a single stage of the process. It says:[50]

> The timing of public involvement is again a matter of broad discretion for NHS England. However, involvement, when it does take place, should meet the requirements of fairness set out above in order to be meaningful.
>
> Involvement should not typically be a stand-alone exercise (e.g. a formal consultation open for 12 weeks). It will generally be part of an ongoing dialogue or take place in stages. A phased approach can often maximise involvement Commissioners should consider who will be involved, when and how this will take place, and the purpose of engagement. It is good practice to provide regular communications throughout and have a documented engagement plan.

48 The PPI duty on NHS provides under NHS Act 2006 s242.

49 At para 17.

50 At p18.

> The public does not necessarily need to be involved at the earliest possible opportunity. If involvement takes place too early there may be insufficient information for the public to consider. It will sometimes be appropriate to first develop a proposal, shortlist of options, a preferred option or even a decision in principle. However, involvement should never be left to the last minute.

4.88 This passage misunderstands the continuing duty on NHS England to involve patients at all stages of the commissioning cycle. It also appears inconsistent with the (correct) statements that the public should also be involved in planning of commissioning arrangements.

Urgent changes based on patient safety

4.89 There is a widespread misunderstanding in the NHS that patient involvement is not necessary where changes to services are needed for patient safety reasons. This argument was advanced by an NHS body in *R (Morris) v Trafford Healthcare NHS Trust*[51] and was rejected by the judge. Mr Justice Hodge said:

> 61. I accept that the consultants were concerned about workload and about the apparent practice of referring patients who fall outside the rehabilitative group to AGH. But there is a duty on the Trust to consult. The position could have been stabilised by properly restricting the patients referred from Trafford General Hospital to Altrincham General Hospital to those for whom services could be provided. The difficulty of providing medical cover was real but had been present for some months before 7th March 2006. The position could have been contained in my judgment while a short period was allowed so that proper consultation over the closure could take place.
>
> 62. The section 11 duty to consult is of high importance. The public expect to be involved in decisions by healthcare bodies, particularly when the issues involved are contentious as they clearly were with AGH. I do not accept that the need to close the wards at Altrincham General Hospital was so urgent that it was right that no public consultation should take place. There ought to have been consultation under section 11 about the closure of the wards in so important a local provision as Altrincham General Hospital. In those circumstances I regard the decision to close the wards as unlawful and will quash it.

4.90 The arrangements document steers a line between the judgment in *Morris* and the generally accepted wisdom that patient involvement can be avoided wherever a decision is urgent or is labelled as being for 'patient safety' reasons. It says:[52]

> **3.6 What if a decision needs to be taken urgently?**
>
> In an urgent situation, it may be necessary to balance the duty to make arrangements for public involvement in a decision with the public interest in maintaining continuity of care and protecting the health, safety or welfare of patients or staff.
>
> It will only be reasonable to justify carrying out a limited or no public involvement exercise on grounds of urgency when the lack of time was genuinely caused by an urgent development or where there is a genuine

51 [2006] EWHC 2334 (Admin), (2006) 9 CCLR 648.

52 At p21.

risk to the health, safety or welfare of patients or staff. It does not permit NHS England to leave public involvement until the last moment without enough time to carry out a fair and proportionate exercise, when the public could and should have been involved earlier or to a greater extent.

4.91 This part of the arrangements document is unobjectionable as far as it goes. However, it does not say that NHS managers cannot allow a crisis to develop in order to permit a situation where changes can be forced through quickly without public involvement. It also fails to say that, even if public involvement around urgent changes is not practicable, that does not remove the need for full public involvement in any long term future arrangements which are put in place beyond an immediate emergency.

4.92 NHS England has a wide range of different areas of commissioning responsibility. It has well-developed patient involvement procedures for its specialised commissioning functions. These are properly noted in the arrangements document, which says:[53]

> Within **specialised commissioning** patients and carers are involved at almost every level of governance, including on panels for Individual Funding Requests and the Cancer Drugs Fund. A range of stakeholders including patient and the public representatives (both individuals and from the voluntary sector) are involved directly in policy development through the various Clinical Reference Groups.
>
> We hold regular stakeholder engagement sessions to inform our work and when appropriate have undertaken formal public consultations around different work areas which are publicised widely to relevant groups and key voluntary sector partners. Registered stakeholders are kept informed of our work via the Specialised Commissioning Bulletin, the NHS England website or through targeted communications.
>
> Additionally, we have the Patient and Public Participation Assurance Group (PPVAG). The PPVAG maintains oversight of the implementation of the participation model, ensures there is appropriate patient and public participation in decision making and reviews and advises on patient and public participation processes.

4.93 NHS England has published a *Framework for patient and public participation in primary care commissioning.*[54] This sets out the ways in which NHS England commits itself to involve patients in primary care commissioning. It contains a helpful summary which describes the headlines of participation as follows:

> **Summary of key points and actions for primary care commissioners:**
>
> - Primary care services are required by the whole population; not everyone is registered with a GP and the needs of under-represented and 'seldom heard' groups need particular consideration in respect of primary care. More than any other part of the NHS, primary care has the potential to reduce health inequalities in the population.
> - Patient and public participation is an essential component of commissioning, and should be considered at all stages of the commissioning cycle (planning, buying and monitoring health and care services).

53 At p26.

54 See www.england.nhs.uk/commissioning/wp-content/uploads/sites/12/2016/03/framwrk-public-partcptn-prim-care.pdf.

- NHS England and Clinical Commissioning Groups need to work in partnership with other commissioners and providers to make primary care services joined up and effective for patients and the public.
- Consider the need for – and best approach – to participation depending on the situation, the population in question, and existing sources of information and insight; these sources may be national, regional or local.
- Keep good records of your approach to participation including how you have assessed the legal duty to involve the public in commissioning. NHS England commissioners are required to document their assessment of whether Section 13Q (the legal duty to involve the public in commissioning) applies using the standard form available on the NHS England intranet.
- Plan for participation – including identifying benefits (with measures of impact where appropriate) and costing participation activity; participation plans need to be factored in to overall business planning and programme planning.
- Involve people early on, not as an afterthought.
- Involve people in ways that are appropriate to their needs and preferences, and provide them with the necessary information, resources and support to enable them to participate.
- Work with partners in involving people, including other commissioners, providers, Patient Participation Group (PPG) networks, Healthwatch, and the voluntary and community sector.
- Feed back to those you have involved about the impact of their participation. Explain how their participation has influenced commissioning, and if not, why not.
- Document and report on participation activities and impact for assurance and quality improvement purposes, publicising and celebrating success and sharing learning'

4.94 The document is particularly focused on those groups in society who are hardest to reach. It explains:[55]

> There are groups who face specific barriers to participation in primary care commissioning, and whose specific needs must be taken into account. Examples of these groups are children and young people, carers, and patients and service users with disabilities and long-term conditions. There are also groups that experience poorer access to primary care and poorer health outcomes, eg insecurely housed people, Gypsy Traveller groups, refugees, asylum-seekers, migrants, sex workers, and people with mental health problems, learning disabilities, low health literacy, and drug and alcohol problems. This includes people who may not be registered with GP practices or 'visible' in the primary care system.

The document then sets out the ways in which these 'hard to reach' groups will be given the opportunity to become involved in primary care commissioning.

4.95 There is a clear relationship between compliance with the duty to secure patient involvement in commissioning decisions and the duty on NHS England to tackle health inequalities. This document shows that there are senior managers within NHS England who are focused on the issues and are driving policies designed to assist in improving the existing state of health inequalities. The document explains the

55 At p8.

linkage between PPI duties and the duty to tackle health inequalities as follows:[56]

> **7 Equality and health inequalities analysis**
>
> NHS England has completed an equality and health inequalities analysis of patient and public participation in its work which can be found on the NHS England website. Several themes in relation to primary care commissioning were highlighted during co-production and wider engagement on this framework.
>
> - It is important that commissioners use a flexible range of methods to hear and engage with potentially excluded groups, or there is a risk that participation will reinforce inequalities in access to primary care services and health outcomes. For example, some methods such as digital engagement may exclude certain groups that do not have access to technology, and enable others who might find it hard to attend a face to face meeting. Some practical approaches are outlined in section 4.
> - Planning involvement proactively (including identifying resources and support, and working with partners) helps commissioners to reach people with protected characteristics and those that experience health inequalities. A planned approach will maximise involvement from different groups and reduce the risk that participation activities will engage the same groups and individuals. This should include budgets to support accessible engagement.
> - Activities should be planned and adapted to ensure equitable access to public participation opportunities regardless of a person's cultural, linguistic, religious background, communication and accessibility needs.
> - Commissioners are required to support the Accessible Information Standard. This mandatory standard aims to make sure that disabled people have access to information that they can understand and any communication support they might need. External stakeholders have highlighted the importance of ensuring that opportunities for people to participate in primary care commissioning are accessible to people with communication support needs.
> - Commissioners should connect with existing patient, service user and voluntary sector organisations to reach and develop relationships with diverse communities, and especially with people whose voices can be harder to hear.
> - Auditing and monitoring participation of equalities protected groups, eg in events and formal governance roles, supports commissioners to manage and improve performance in involving a more reflective range of people.
> - Engagement on the framework has uncovered examples of good practice in inclusive participation in primary care, for example for people with learning disabilities. These are being shared through this framework and other channels such as training and online resources.

4.96 There is a substantial challenge for NHS England and the CCGs with whom it works as 'co-commissioners' of primary care in putting these principles into practice. In particular, procurement processes for primary care services have tended to follow a set 'procurement' model without building in anything but a token element of patient involvement. Equally decisions

56 At p21.

about the approval of a change of GP practice location or closing a GP practice which is perceived to be failing tend to be delivered within the contractual or regulatory framework, without giving patients an active say in decision-making. Such an approach leaves NHS England open to challenge.

4.97 In January 2017, NHS England published a set of arrangement for securing patient and public involvement in prisons and other secure environments, called the *Framework for patient and public participation in health and justice commissioning*.[57] This contained the following summary of the actions that should be taken:

Summary of key points and actions for health and justice commissioners:

- Patient and public participation is an essential component of commissioning, and should be considered at all stages of the commissioning cycle (planning, buying and monitoring health and care services).
- Consider the need for – and best approach to – participation depending on the situation, the population in question, and existing sources of information and insight; these sources may be national, regional or local.
- People using health and justice services may face specific barriers to engagement. Involve people in ways that are appropriate to their needs and preferences, and provide them with the necessary information, resources and support to enable them to participate.
- Work with partners to involve people, including other commissioners, providers, service user and carer networks, Healthwatch, and the voluntary and community sector.
- Plan for participation – including identifying benefits (with measures of impact where appropriate) and costing participation activity; participation plans need to be factored in to overall business planning and programme planning.
- Involve people early on in the process, not as an afterthought.
- Feed back to those you have involved about the impact of their participation. Explain how their participation has influenced commissioning, and if not, why not.
- Keep good records of your approach to participation including how you have assessed the legal duty to involve the public in commissioning. NHS England commissioners are required to document their assessment of whether Section 13Q (the legal duty to involve the public in commissioning) applies using the standard form available on the NHS England intranet.
- Document and report on participation activities and impact, for assurance and quality improvement purposes, publicising and celebrating success and sharing learning.
- NHS England needs to work in partnership with other commissioners and providers to make health and justice services joined up and effective for service users'

4.98 This document recognises the challenges of engaging prisoners in issues about NHS services. However, it has developed some impressive 'core principles' – the document provides:[58]

- People in prison have a right to be involved in their healthcare and have a say in shaping and improving the healthcare services that they receive.

57 See www.england.nhs.uk/wp-content/uploads/2017/01/hlth-justice-frmwrk.pdf.

58 At pp29 and 30.

- People with recent experience of being in prison can also provide a different perspective of what worked and what didn't with the benefit of hindsight.
- The unique population, culture, regime and range of providers (including healthcare providers) in each prison must be considered when planning engagement with the patient population.
- There can be a barrier of mistrust to engagement that exists between people in prison, especially those who have been in prison on multiple occasions, and people who represent authority such as prison or healthcare staff. Participation activities should take this into consideration.
- The power dynamics of the prison setting mean that people in prison can be less likely to get involved as a result of the potential consequences. Principles such as independence and confidentiality are therefore especially important.
- Participation activities should aim to involve a representative sample of the prison population. Participation activities can attract those who are more articulate and more compliant. While it is important that these people are involved, they do not always reflect the wider population.
- Families, carers and friends of people in prison should also be consulted with and engaged in this process – please see the section on involving family members and carers.

4.99 These are arrangements which, if followed in practice, will comply with NHS England's statutory duties. Any challenge is likely to be focused on the extent to which those who are commissioning NHS services in secure environments are aware of the arrangements document and have complied with its terms.

4.100 There is a huge range of attitudes among NHS managers – from those who see the full involvement of patients as essential to the effective discharge of commissioning functions, through to those who seem to believe that patients do not understand what is good for them and patient involvement only 'gets in the way' of proper management of the NHS. The policies adopted by NHS England make it clear that any 'tick-box' approach to patient involvement is unacceptable, and that patients should have a real say in how commissioning decisions are made. The existence of 'arrangements' documents sets up a series of legitimate expectations that NHS England will discharge its functions in accordance with the policies. Hence any NHS England commissioning decision-making process which failed to comply with the relevant PPI arrangements document may be struck down by the court on an application for judicial review. Given the entrenched practices of some NHS managers who, at best, only give token consideration to patient involvement in NHS decision-making, delivering real involvement in practice may be considerably more challenging than producing policies which comply with the primary statutory duty. The documents explain the need for NHS England to replace the traditional commissioner/provider discussions which take place in advance of commissioning decisions with a meaningful commissioner/provider/patient set of discussions. There is evidence that this is happening in some areas of NHS England's commissioning, such as specialised services. There is precious little evidence that it is working in other areas.

NHS England's performer list management functions

4.101 Doctors, nurses and other medical professionals working for NHS trusts are employees of the trust. The NHS can thus expect an employing trust to monitor the professionalism and integrity of its employees and ensure that they are delivering a competent standard of care to patients, are acting honestly and are not engaging in abusive behaviour. Primary care professionals (that is, doctors working in general practice) are not generally employees of NHS bodies. GP and dental practices operate as private sector businesses which contract with the NHS. This means that the primary care professional can be a self-employed contractor (or sub-contractor), a partner or shareholder in the contracting business or an employee of the contracting business. While there are governance measures that could be deployed through the contract and primary care professionals could be referred to their own governing bodies,[59] the government decided it needed to have a system for registering and regulating primary care performers.[60]

4.102 In *R (S) v Knowsley NHS Primary Care Trust*,[61] the judge reported the frustrations of the secretary of state at the previous system as follows:

> It was submitted on behalf of the Secretary of State that under the regime before the Regulations were introduced the procedure for stopping unsatisfactory doctors from working in the NHS was so labyrinthine and expensive as to deter health authorities from using it.

Section 179 of the Health and Social Care (Community Health and Standards) Act 2003 created a new section 28X of the NHS Act 1977.[62] Sections 179(1) and (2) provided:

> (1) Regulations may provide that a health care professional of a prescribed description may not perform any primary medical service for which a Primary Care Trust or Local Health Board is responsible unless he is included in a list maintained under the regulations by a Primary Care Trust or Local Health Board.
>
> (2) Regulations may provide that a health care professional of a prescribed description may not perform any primary dental service for which a Primary Care Trust or Local Health Board is responsible unless he is included in a list maintained under the regulations by a Primary Care Trust or Local Health Board.

4.103 The system under the 2003 Act thus only applied to primary medical care and primary dental care professionals. The regulations made under this section were the National Health Service (Performers Lists) Regulations (PL Regs) 2004.[63] The PL Regs 2004 provided for each PCT to maintain a 'medical performers list'. Thus, from 1 April 2004, a GP was not entitled

59 Such as the General Medical Council in respect of doctors.

60 The immediate trigger for this appears to have been the reports which followed the case of the GP, Dr Howard Shipman, who murdered a large number of his patients. The report identified that there was no effective system for raising concerns about a self-employed GP apart from a referral to the GMC, which was not seen as an effective route for the NHS because, among other matters, it was not within NHS control.

61 [2006] EWHC 26 (Admin).

62 The NHS Act 1977 was the consolidating NHS Act in place in 2003.

63 SI No 585.

to work within NHS primary medical care unless he or she had his or her name included in a PCT performers list. Inclusion on the list gave a right to work but did not amount to a 'possession' held by the doctor within Article 1 of Protocol 1 of the ECHR: see *R (Malik) v Waltham Forest NHS Primary Care Trust and another*.[64]

4.104 The PL Regs 2004 described the processes that could be followed if a PCT had concerns about the performance standards of a GP. Guidance was issued to assist PCTs in delivering their duties under the PL Regs 2004. PCTs were required to undertake three completely separate functions under the PL Regs 2004, namely:

a) *investigating* a cause of concern about a GP or dentist;
b) *presenting* a case against a GP or dentist before a fair tribunal; and
c) *adjudicating* on the case.

4.105 The final decision could only be made after the adjudication panel had made findings which resolved any conflict about facts. Once the facts were resolved, the adjudication panel needed to decide what, if any, sanction was merited. The PCT also had the power to suspend the performer while a disciplinary process was continuing. Many PCTs had considerable difficulties with the governance challenges of running a fair process when the same organisation was 'investigator, prosecutor and judge'.

4.106 The PCT panels that made final decisions were required to act in a quasi-judicial manner when discharging these functions because a decision to remove a GP from the performers list effectively prevented the GP from being able to carry on his or her profession. Accordingly it was essential that a fair process was followed by PCTs before any decision was taken. In *R (S) v Knowsley NHS Primary Care Trust*[65] Toulson J decided that PCTs had a legal duty to act fairly throughout any list management process and that any breach of that duty was potentially challengeable by way of judicial review.

4.107 The Department of Health and Social Care made an initial attempt through its guidance to prevent list management hearings turning into 'mini-trials' with legal representation on both sides. However, in *R (S) v Knowsley NHS Primary Care Trust* the court did not accept that this was likely to be consistent with the duty of fairness. Toulson J said:

> As to legal representation, the statement in paragraph 31.7 of the DOH Advice that there will be no right to legal representation on the part of either the PCT or the doctor is true in the sense that the Regulations do not give the doctor a general right of legal representation, but is liable to be understood as it was by Dr Fraser in her letter dated 19 September 2005 on behalf of the Northumberland PCT, when she wrote that 'the DOH guidance does not permit legal representation'. That is going too far. It may be that in many cases legal representation would be unnecessary, but the question in each case must be whether the doctor can reasonably be expected to represent himself or whether legal representation is necessary in order to enable him to be able properly to present his case. I do not see that this can be a matter of presumption but must depend on the circumstances, including particularly the complexity of the allegations and the evidence.

64 [2007] EWCA Civ 265.
65 [2006] EWHC 26 (Admin).

4.108 Hence, a doctor is entitled to legal representation in any case where 'the complexity of the allegations and the evidence' means that 'legal representation is necessary in order to enable him to be able properly to present his case'. Given the serious professional consequences for the doctor, it is difficult to envisage a situation in which that test will not be met.

4.109 The High Court considered what approach should be taken where there is a conflict of factual evidence which goes to the heart of the case against the doctor. In *Emmanuel v South Gloucestershire Primary Care Trust and another*[66] the court was concerned with a case where a GP was alleged to have had a sexual relationship with a patient. The GP's defence was that the sexual relationship only started after the patient had transferred to another practice. The patient was not called to give evidence at the panel hearing or at the appeal stage. The doctor's appeal was allowed. HHJ David Pearl, sitting as a Deputy High Court Judge, adopted the approach identified by the Court of Appeal in *Secretary of State for the Home Department v Sim and Parole Board*[67] in saying that where:

> . . . the evidence in question is so fundamental to the decision that fairness requires that the offender be given the opportunity to test it by cross-examination before it is taken into account at all. As so often, what is or is not fair will depend on the circumstances of the case.

It follows that the duty of fairness was breached because the PCT panel (and the appeal panel) did not call the witness and have her evidence tested by cross-examination. That case also sat until 7.45pm. Counsel for the doctor criticised the panel, and the judge tended to agree. He said:

> Good practice surely demands that Tribunals and indeed Courts should not place themselves in a situation where their sitting hours become so unreasonable that it can no longer be stated with any certainty that the conduct of proceedings is fair.

4.110 Section 28X of the NHS Act 1977 became section 91 of the NHS Act 2006 (in relation to healthcare professionals providing primary care medical services) and section 106 of the NHS Act 2006 (in relation to healthcare professionals providing primary care dental services). Section 123 of the NHS Act 2006 introduced a performers list for healthcare professionals providing primary ophthalmic services, and section 146 provided a like provision for healthcare professionals providing local pharmaceutical services.

4.111 Responsibility for managing the medical, dental and ophthalmic lists transferred from PCTs to NHS England on 1 April 2013, when NHS England came into existence and PCTs ceased to exist. The key difference between the performers list system being operated by NHS England and local PCTs is that NHS England operates a single primary care medical list, a single list for community dental services and a single list for ophthalmic services. Thus the practice of GPs moving from one list to another to avoid disciplinary actions ought to have come to an end.

4.112 At the same time, a new set of regulations came into force to govern the exercise of performers list powers, namely the National Health Service

66 [2009] EWHC 3260 (Admin).

67 [2003] EWCA Civ 1845.

(Performers Lists) (England) Regulations (PLE Regs) 2013.[68] The provisions relating to pharmaceutical performers under section 146 are due to be repealed by the HSCA 2012. However, that provision has not yet been brought into effect. Nonetheless, there are no current regulations that provide for a listing for individual pharmacists performing NHS functions or which permit an individual pharmacist to be suspended or removed from a performers list. Concerns about the performance of NHS pharmacists are managed through the pharmaceutical list system under the National Health Service (Pharmaceutical and Local Pharmaceutical Services) Regulations 2013.[69] This list includes a pharmacy business (under a named pharmacist) for NHS community pharmacies as opposed to a list of individual pharmacists working at that pharmacy.

4.113 Regulation 3 of the PLE Regs 2013 provides:

> (1) The Board is to prepare, maintain and publish, in accordance with this Part as modified or supplemented by the relevant Part–
> (a) a medical performers list;
> (b) a dental performers list; and
> (c) an ophthalmic performers list
> (2) The performers lists must be made available by the Board for public inspection.

4.114 NHS England thus maintains three separate lists for healthcare professionals working in the three different areas. NHS England has issued guidance explaining how it proposes to exercise its performers list powers – namely the *Framework for managing performer concerns.*[70] The guidance explains the structures that NHS England has set up to try to act fairly in cases where NHS England is investigator, prosecutor and judge. It explains:[71]

> NHS England has established performers lists decision panels (PLDPs) and performance advisory groups (PAGs) within area teams in order to support its responsibility in managing performance of primary care performers. The PAG's role is investigative and advisory; the role of the PLDP is to make decisions under the performers lists regulations.
>
> The PAG considers all complaints or concerns that are reported about a named clinician and can determine that an initial investigation is to be carried out. If action is considered to be necessary under the performers lists regulations, the case is referred to a PLDP. In cases where there is a conflict of interest or a perception of bias, an alternative PLDP shall be convened to consider the case.

4.115 The key paragraph in the guidance which explains the approach that NHS England is supposed to take is as follows:[72]

> NHS England has an overriding obligation to take account of all information provided to it. Where this information gives rise to concerns relating to an individual performer's conduct, performance or health the area team will take appropriate action to safeguard patients and the performer involved.

68 See SI No 335. These regulations have been amended on a number of occasions since they were first made.

69 SI No 349.

70 See www.england.nhs.uk/wp-content/uploads/2014/08/Performer-list-frmwrk.pdf.

71 At para 4.

72 At para 8.

In this event the area team will assess against the NHS England risk matrix and, taking into account all other available clinical governance information, identify the nature of the concern and take a decision on immediate next steps.

The responsible officer/medical director is responsible for ensuring that the following key actions are taken:

1. Clarify what has happened and the nature of the problem or concern.
2. Seek appropriate advice from the regulator and external advisers, for example in the case of medical and dental performers, the National Clinical Assessment Service (NCAS).
3. Consider if any immediate steps to protect patient safety such as restriction of practice or suspension are required, including considering if a request should be made to NCAS to issue a HPAN notice.
4. If appropriate, ensure the performer is informed about the complaint or concern.
5. Consider if the case can be progressed by mutual agreement with the performer.
6. If a formal approach is required, appoint a case investigator and agree terms of reference.
7. Convene a PAG/PLDP to consider the case and decide on next steps.
8. Ensure accurate actions and decisions are recorded contemporaneously in the performer's file.

Where the regulator notifies NHS England of any actions or conditions the PLDP will consider the implications in relation to the performer's fitness for purpose and consider if further action is required.

In line with the performers lists regulations 12(6) where NHS England considers it necessary to do so for the protection of patients or members of the public or is otherwise in the public interest, it may determine that a suspension is to have immediate effect. NHS England has nominated responsible officers/ medical directors with the power to order an immediate suspension following discussion with one other director. This decision must be reviewed by two members of the PLDP who have not been previously involved in the decision to suspend, within two working days beginning on the day the decision was made. The case must then be considered by the PLDP in accordance with the regulations.

All cases will be managed in line with the terms of reference of the PAG and PLDP (Annexes 2 and 3).

4.116 These procedures are used to decide which healthcare professionals should be admitted to the performers lists, who should be suspended from them and who should be removed from the lists. This is a very considerable power but, if used carefully and in accordance with the guidance, it will be exercised lawfully.

NHS England's annual business plan and annual report

Annual business plan

4.117 Section 13T of the NHS Act 2006 imposes an obligation on the Board to publish a business plan setting out how it proposes to exercise its functions in the coming year and the following year. It provides:

(1) Before the start of each financial year, the Board must publish a business plan setting out how it proposes to exercise its functions in that year and each of the next two financial years.
(2) The business plan must, in particular, explain how the Board proposes to discharge its duties under–
(a) sections 13E, 13G and 13Q, and
(b) sections 223C to 223E.
(3) The business plan must, in particular, explain how the Board proposes to achieve the objectives, and comply with the requirements, specified in the mandate for the first financial year to which the plan relates.
(4) The Board may revise the plan.
(5) The Board must publish any revised plan.

4.118 The 'financial year' for the NHS runs from 1 April through to 31 March of the following year. It thus does not quite mirror the tax year, which runs from 6 April through to 5 April of the following year.

4.119 The business plan is required to explain how NHS England proposes to discharge certain specific duties, namely:

a) the duty to secure continuous improvement in the quality of services (section 13E);
b) the duty to have regard to the need to reduce inequalities (section 13G);
c) the duty to involve the public in its decision-making (section 13Q);
s) the financial duties of the Board (sections 223C–223E).

4.120 The business plan for 2017/18 is a mere eight pages, which may be insufficient to discharge its statutory duties.[73] It is an annex to the larger document, *Next steps on the NHS five year forward view*,[74] which sets out the service development plans NHS England has developed for the NHS. This document clearly sets out the central challenges for the NHS, as follows:

The NHS in 2017 confronts five paradoxes:

- We're getting healthier, but we're using the NHS more. Life expectancy has been rising by five hours a day, but the need for modern NHS care continues to grow. Demand for health care is highly geared to our growing and aging population. It costs three times more to look after a seventy five year old and five times more to look after an eighty year old than a thirty year old. Yet today, there are half a million more people aged over 75 than there were in 2010. And there will be 2 million more in ten years' time. Demand is also heavily impacted by rising public expectations for convenient and personal care, the effectiveness of prevention and public health, and availability of social care. Even more significant is the steady expansion of new treatments and cures, of which the public are often unaware.
- The quality of NHS care is demonstrably improving, but we're becoming far more transparent about care gaps and mistakes. Outcomes of care for most major conditions are dramatically better than three or five or ten years ago. Annual cancer survival rates are up. Heart attack and stroke deaths have tumbled. But greater transparency and rising expectations mean greater awareness of care gaps and variation. And although they are substantially lower than they were a decade ago, waiting times have been edging up.

73 See www.england.nhs.uk/wp-content/uploads/2017/03/nhse-funding-resource-supporting-fyfv.pdf.

74 See www.england.nhs.uk/wp-content/uploads/2017/03/NEXT-STEPS-ON-THE-NHS-FIVE-YEAR-FORWARD-VIEW.pdf.

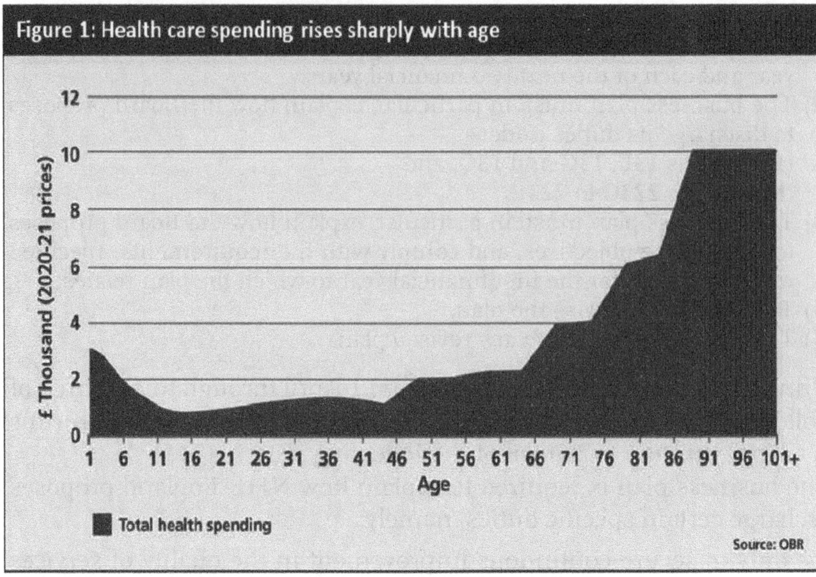

Figure 1: Healthcare spending rises sharply with age

- Staff numbers are up, but staff are under greater pressure. Over the two years from November 2014, there has been an increase of around 8000 more doctors and nurses working in the NHS5 but there are still gaps in some professions and specialties. Frontline NHS staff say their experience at work continues to improve, with this year's annual staff survey scores at a five year high. Yet only 52% of staff are satisfied with the opportunities for flexible working and 15% have experienced physical violence from patients, relatives or members of the public.
- The public are highly satisfied with the NHS, but concerned for its future. Perhaps surprisingly, newly published independent data spanning three decades shows that public satisfaction with the NHS is higher than in all but three of the past 30 years. And it reveals public satisfaction with hospital inpatients is at its highest for more than two decades. As a result The King's Fund says that 'In 2016 the NHS remained popular with the public, far more so than it was 10 or 20 years ago'. Looking internationally, 69% of the public in this country say they get good healthcare, compared with 57% in France and 59% in Germany, and only 47% in 22 other nations. But a higher proportion of our public are worried about the future of the NHS'.
- There is now an underlying consensus about how care needs to change to 'future proof' the NHS, but the ability to do so risks being overtaken by what CQC has called today's 'burning platform'. That's why in Autumn 2014, in the wake of several years of contentious political and legislative debate, the NHS nationally came together – to chart for the first time its own direction for the years ahead'.

4.121 The claim that there is consensus about how the NHS should be developed is, perhaps, more a statement of hope rather than a statement of reality. As an organisation, NHS England could be fairly criticised for not recognising alternative views. This approach is reflected in the following part of the business plan:

> The NHS Five Year Forward View crystallised a consensus about why and how the NHS should change. It described three improvement

opportunities: a health gap, a quality gap, and a financial sustainability gap. It proposed a series of measures to bring about the 'triple integration' of primary and specialist hospital care, of physical and mental health services, and of health and social care. And it argued that while much of this lay within the power of the NHS itself to bring about, it was also dependent on well-functioning social care, extra capital investment, transformation funding to support double running costs, and activism on prevention and public health.

4.122 Nonetheless, NHS England is seeking to plot a strategic direction for the development of the NHS, as summarised in its business plan.

Annual report

4.123 NHS England is under a statutory duty to produce an annual report. This duty is set out in section 13U of the NHS Act 2006, which provides:

> (1) As soon as practicable after the end of each financial year, the Board must publish an annual report on how it has exercised its functions during the year.
> (2) The annual report must, in particular, contain an assessment of–
> (a) the extent to which it met any objectives or requirements specified in the mandate for that year,
> (b) the extent to which it gave effect to the proposals for that year in its business plan, and
> (c) how effectively it discharged its duties under sections 13E, 13G and 13Q.
> (3) The Board must–
> (a) lay the annual report before Parliament, and
> (b) once it has done so, send a copy of it to the Secretary of State.
> (4) The Secretary of State must, having considered the annual report, set out in a letter to the Board the Secretary of State's assessment of the Board's performance of its functions in the financial year in question.
> (5) The letter must, in particular, contain the Secretary of State's assessment of the matters mentioned in subsection (2)(a) to (c).
> (6) The Secretary of State must–
> (a) publish the letter to the Board, and
> (b) lay it before Parliament.

4.124 The NHS England annual report is published each year in accordance with this duty.[75] Specific sections of the report are required to show how effectively NHS England discharged its duties to secure continuous improvement in the quality of services (section 13E), to have regard to the need to reduce inequalities (section 13G) and to involve the public in its decision-making (section 13Q), as well as giving an overall assessment concerning the effective discharge of the business plan.

4.125 One interesting aspect of the statutory scheme is the requirement on the Secretary of State for Health and Social Care to provide a response containing his or her assessment of NHS England's performance. This assessment is inevitably somewhat anodyne because the secretary of state is politically responsible for NHS England's performance. Accordingly, the language used in the assessment is negotiated carefully between DHSC officials and staff

75 See www.england.nhs.uk/wp-content/uploads/2017/07/Annual-Report-Full_201617.pdf for the 2016/17 report.

working for NHS England. An example of this is the assessment of the extent to which NHS England has complied with its duties around health inequalities. The data shows that health inequalities are worsening, although the primary causes are, arguably, outside the control of the NHS. The language used by the secretary of state in assessing performance of this duty in 2016/17 carefully avoids any reference to the objective data, saying:

> My assessment of your organisation's progress against its duty to have regard to the need to reduce health inequalities is that reasonable progress has been made across the reporting period in embedding processes but more still needs to be done to reduce inequalities in access, outcomes and experience, as shown by the available data.

This approach is perhaps inevitable given the political sensitivities around the NHS.

NHS England's additional powers

4.126 Sections 13V–13Y of the NHS Act 2006 provide a series of discrete additional powers to augment the general power of competence given by section 2 of the NHS Act 2006. Section 2 provides:

> The Secretary of State, the Board or a clinical commissioning group may do anything which is calculated to facilitate, or is conducive or incidental to, the discharge of any function conferred on that person by this Act.

4.127 This general power is extended by sections 13V–13Y which provide:

> **13V Establishment of pooled funds**
> (1) The Board and one or more clinical commissioning groups may establish and maintain a pooled fund.
> (2) A pooled fund is a fund–
> (a) which is made up of contributions by the bodies which established it, and
> (b) out of which payments may be made, with the agreement of those bodies, towards expenditure incurred in the discharge of any of their commissioning functions.
> (3) In this section, 'commissioning functions' means functions in arranging for the provision of services as part of the health service.
>
> **13W Board's power to generate income, etc**
> (1) The Board has power to do anything specified in section 7(2) of the Health and Medicines Act 1988 (provision of goods, services, etc) for the purpose of making additional income available for improving the health service.
> (2) The Board may exercise a power conferred by subsection (1) only to the extent that its exercise does not to any significant extent interfere with the performance by the Board of its functions.
>
> **13X Power to make grants etc**
> (1) The Board may make payments by way of grant or loan to a voluntary organisation which provides or arranges for the provision of services which are similar to the services in respect of which the Board has functions.
> (2) The payments may be made subject to such terms and conditions as the Board considers appropriate.

13Y Board's incidental powers: further provision
The power conferred on the Board by section 2 includes, in particular, power to–
(a) enter into agreements,
(b) acquire and dispose of property, and
(c) accept gifts (including property to be held on trust for the purposes of the Board).

4.128 The income generation power under section 7(2) of the Health and Medicines Act 1988 is a series of specific powers which can be used to generate income in a wide range of circumstances.

4.129 Section 13Z enables NHS England to discharge its functions jointly with other NHS bodies. It provides:

(1) This section applies to functions exercisable by the Board under or by virtue of this Act or any prescribed provision of any other Act.
(2) The Board may arrange for any such function to be exercised by or jointly with–
(a) a Special Health Authority,
(b) a clinical commissioning group, or
(c) such other body as may be prescribed.
(3) Regulations may provide that the power in subsection (2) does not apply in relation to a function of a prescribed description.
(4) Where any functions are (by virtue of subsection (2)) exercisable jointly by the Board and another body, they may be exercised by a joint committee of the Board and the other body.
(5) Arrangements under this section may be on such terms and conditions (including terms as to payment) as may be agreed between the Board and the other party to the arrangements.
(6) Arrangements made under this section do not affect the liability of the Board for the exercise of any of its functions.
(7) This section is subject to sections 13ZA and 13ZB in the case of arrangements that are devolved arrangements (within the meaning of section 13ZA).

Section 13Z(7) was added as a result of the Cities and Local Government Devolution Act 2016 to facilitate devolution of powers by NHS England to metropolitan authorities who then take a strategic approach to the delivery of NHS and social care services.

4.130 Section 13ZA makes further provisions about the devolution of functions by NHS England. Sections 13ZA and 13ZB provide:

13ZA Section 13Z: further provision in relation to devolved arrangements
(1) This section applies to arrangements under section 13Z(2) for one or more functions of the Board to be exercised in relation to a particular area by or jointly with a relevant prescribed body ('devolved arrangements').
(2) 'Relevant prescribed body' means a body prescribed under section 13Z(2)(c) that is either–
(a) a combined authority whose area includes the whole or part of the area to which the arrangements relate, or
(b) a local authority (within the meaning of section 2B) whose area includes the whole or part of that area.
(3) The power of the Board under section 13Z(2) to enter into devolved arrangements in relation to any functions includes power to arrange for such functions to be exercised in relation to the area to which the arrangements relate–

(a) by the relevant prescribed body jointly with one or more other eligible bodies;
(b) jointly with the Board, the relevant prescribed body and one or more other eligible bodies.

(4) A body is an 'eligible body' if it–
(a) falls within paragraph (a), (b) or (c) of section 13Z(2), and
(b) exercises functions in relation to the area to which the arrangements relate.

(5) Where, by virtue of subsection (3), the Board enters into devolved arrangements with a relevant prescribed body and one or more eligible bodies, at least one of those eligible bodies must be a clinical commissioning group.

(6) Where, by virtue of subsection (3), one or more eligible bodies are a party to devolved arrangements, the power under section 13Z(4) to establish a joint committee includes a power to establish a joint committee of which one or more of the eligible bodies are members.

(7) But the members of a joint committee established under section 13Z(4) by virtue of subsection (6) must include–
(a) the relevant prescribed body;
(b) at least one clinical commissioning group with whom a function is exercised jointly under the devolved arrangements;
(c) if under the devolved arrangements a function is exercisable jointly with the Board, the Board.

(8) The terms and conditions on which devolved arrangements are made may include terms authorising a joint committee established by virtue of subsection (6) to establish and maintain a pooled fund.

(9) A pooled fund is a fund–
(a) which is made up of payments received from the Board under the devolved arrangements in accordance with terms of payment agreed under section 13Z(5), and
(b) out of which payments may be made towards expenditure incurred in the discharge of any of the functions in relation to which the devolved arrangements are made.

13ZB Section 13Z: arrangements in relation to the function under section 3B(1)(d)

(1) This section applies to arrangements under section 13Z(2) that are or include arrangements in relation to the exercise of a relevant commissioning function.

(2) 'Relevant commissioning function' means a function of the Board under section 3B(1)(d) of arranging for the provision of services or facilities in respect of a particular area ('the commissioning area').

(3) The power to enter into the arrangements under section 13Z is subject to the following provisions of this section.

(4) The arrangements must provide for the relevant commissioning function to be exercisable by at least one relevant prescribed body jointly with–
(a) one or more eligible bodies, or
(b) the Board and one or more eligible bodies,
(and the arrangements are, accordingly, devolved arrangements to which section 13ZA applies).

(5) At least one of the eligible bodies mentioned in subsection (4) must be a clinical commissioning group.

(6) The Board may enter into the arrangements in relation to the provision of a service or facility in the commissioning area only if it considers it appropriate to do so having regard to–

(a) the impact on the provision of the service or facility in the commissioning area;
(b) the impact on the provision of the service or facility in other areas;
(c) the number of persons in the commissioning area to whom the service or facility is provided;
(d) the number of persons who are able to provide the service or facility;
(e) the cost of providing the service or facility;
(f) the financial implications for the relevant prescribed body, and for other bodies, with whom the arrangements are made.

(7) Regulations may provide for this section not to apply to arrangements so far as relating to a relevant commissioning function of a prescribed description.
(8) In this section, 'eligible body' and 'relevant prescribed body' have the same meaning as in section 13ZA.

4.131 No regulations have yet been made under section 13Z(3). These powers have been used to devolve responsibilities in Manchester. It remains to be seen how successful these arrangements are in improving joined up working between NHS and social care organisations.

4.132 Section 13Z1 contains a reserve power to enable the secretary of state to make regulations to impose additional functions on NHS England that are connected to an existing function. It provides:

13Z1 Power to confer additional functions on the Board

(1) Regulations may provide that the Board is to have such additional functions in relation to the health service as may be specified in the regulations.
(2) A function may be specified in regulations under subsection (1) only if the function is connected to another function of the Board.

4.133 This power was used to make the National Health Service Commissioning Board (Additional Functions) Regulations 2017.[76] These regulations impose additional functions on NHS England to include and manage framework agreements for the supply of drugs, medicines or other products needed for the NHS. This power allows NHS England to negotiate framework agreements primarily with pharmaceutical companies to secure discounts for the NHS so as to pave the way for pharmaceutical drugs and other medical devices being used within the NHS. Regulation 4 provides:

4 Power to conclude and manage framework agreements

(1) The Board may conclude and manage framework agreements to facilitate the purchase and supply of a service, drug, medicine or other substance or product to which paragraph (2) applies.
(2) This paragraph applies to a service, drug, medicine or other substance or product that is to be provided as part of the health service for–
(a) the purposes of preventing, diagnosing, monitoring or treating a physical or mental illness;
(b) the purposes of providing care to an individual; or
(c) a purpose related to any matter mentioned in sub-paragraph (a) or (b).

76 SI No 212.

(3) In this regulation–
   (a) 'framework agreement' means an agreement between the Board and one (or more than one) economic operator (within the meaning of regulation 2 (definitions) of the Public Contracts Regulations 2015), the purpose of which is to establish the terms governing contracts to be entered into during a given period, in particular with regard to price and, where appropriate, the quantity envisaged; and
   (b) 'other substance or product' includes–
      (i) medical supplies within the meaning of section 260(5) of the 2006 Act;
      (ii) a medical device within the meaning of regulation 2 (interpretation) of the Medical Devices Regulations 2002; and
      (iii) a human blood component.

4.134 Section 13Z2 provides for powers to enable the secretary of state to intervene if NHS England fails to discharge any functions.

4.135 Section 13Z3 contains wide powers by NHS England to disclose information, even if (in some cases) there is a common law power which would otherwise make disclosure unlawful. The section provides:

13Z3Permitted disclosures of information

(1) The Board may disclose information obtained by it in the exercise of its functions if–
   (a) the information has previously been lawfully disclosed to the public,
   (b) the disclosure is made under or pursuant to regulations under section 113 or 114 of the Health and Social Care (Community Health and Standards) Act 2003 (complaints about health care or social services),
   (c) the disclosure is made in accordance with any enactment or court order,
   (d) the disclosure is necessary or expedient for the purposes of protecting the welfare of any individual,
   (e) the disclosure is made to any person in circumstances where it is necessary or expedient for the person to have the information for the purpose of exercising functions of that person under any enactment,
   (f) the disclosure is made for the purpose of facilitating the exercise of any of the Board's functions,
   (g) the disclosure is made in connection with the investigation of a criminal offence (whether or not in the United Kingdom), or
   (h) the disclosure is made for the purpose of criminal proceedings (whether or not in the United Kingdom).
(2) Paragraphs (a) to (c) and (h) of subsection (1) have effect notwithstanding any rule of common law which would otherwise prohibit or restrict the disclosure'

It is unclear whether the specific provisions substantially add to the common law powers of NHS England to disclose information in appropriate circumstances. However, they provide a legal basis for disclosing personal data and for the purposes of the Data Protection Act 1998. Any disclosure of personal data would nonetheless have to satisfy the remaining conditions under that Act in order to be compliant with the provisions of the data protection regime.

NHS England's financial duties

4.136 Section 24 of the HSCA 2012 introduced sections 223B–223F of the NHS Act 2006 in order to provide a financial framework for NHS England. Further powers were given to the secretary of state by the Care Act 2014, which brought section 223B(6)–(8) into effect. The present version of the financial provisions are as follows:

> **223B Funding of the Board**
>
> (1) The Secretary of State must pay to the Board in respect of each financial year sums not exceeding the amount allotted for that year by the Secretary of State towards meeting the expenditure of the Board which is attributable to the performance by it of its functions in that year.
>
> (2) An amount is allotted to the Board for a financial year under this section when the Board is notified in writing by the Secretary of State that the amount is allotted to it for that year.
>
> (3) The Secretary of State may make a new allotment under this section increasing or reducing the allotment previously so made only if–
> (a) the Board agrees to the change,
> (b) a parliamentary general election takes place, or
> (c) the Secretary of State considers that there are exceptional circumstances that make a new allotment necessary.
>
> (4) The Secretary of State may give directions to the Board with respect to the payment of sums by it to the Secretary of State in respect of charges or other sums referable to the valuation or disposal of assets.
>
> (5) Sums falling to be paid to the Board under this section are payable subject to such conditions as to records, certificates or otherwise as the Secretary of State may determine.
>
> (6) Where the mandate specifies objectives relating to service integration, the requirements that may be specified under section 13A(2)(b) include such requirements relating to the use by the Board of an amount of the sums paid to it under this section as the Secretary of State considers it necessary or expedient to impose.
>
> (7) The amount referred to in subsection (6)–
> (a) is to be determined in such manner as the Secretary of State considers appropriate, and
> (b) must be specified in the mandate.
>
> (8) The reference in subsection (6) to service integration is a reference to the integration of the provision of health services with the provision of health-related services or social care services, as referred to in sections 13N and 14Z1.
>
> **223BC Financial duties of the Board: expenditure**
>
> (1) The Board must ensure that total health expenditure in respect of each financial year does not exceed the aggregate of–
> (a) the amount allotted to the Board for that year under section 223B,
> (b) any sums received by the Board or clinical commissioning groups in that year under any provision of this Act (other than sums received by the Board under section 223B or by clinical commissioning groups under section 223G), and
> (c) any sums received by the Board or clinical commissioning groups in that year otherwise than under this Act for the purpose of enabling it or them to defray such expenditure.

(2) In this section, 'total health expenditure', in relation to a financial year, means–
  (a) expenditure which is attributable to the performance by the Board of its functions in that year, other than sums paid by it under section 223G, and
  (b) expenditure which is attributable to the performance by clinical commissioning groups of their functions in that year.
(3) The Secretary of State may by directions determine whether expenditure by the Board or a clinical commissioning group which is of a description specified in the directions must, or must not, be treated for the purposes of this section as part of total health expenditure.
(4) The Secretary of State may by directions determine the extent to which, and the circumstances in which, sums received by the Board or a clinical commissioning group under section 223B or (as the case may be) 223G but not yet spent must be treated for the purposes of this section as part of total health expenditure, and to which financial year's expenditure they must be attributed.
(5) The Secretary of State may by directions require the Board to use banking facilities specified in the directions for any purposes so specified.

223D Financial duties of the Board: controls on total resource use

(1) In this Chapter–
  'total capital resource use', in relation to a financial year, means the use of capital resources in that year by the Board and clinical commissioning groups (taken together);
  'total revenue resource use', in relation to a financial year, means the use of revenue resources in that year by the Board and clinical commissioning groups (taken together).
(2) The Board must ensure that total capital resource use in a financial year does not exceed the amount specified by the Secretary of State.
(3) The Board must ensure that total revenue resource use in a financial year does not exceed the amount specified by the Secretary of State.
(4) The Secretary of State may give directions, in relation to a financial year, specifying descriptions of resources which must, or must not, be treated as capital resources or revenue resources for the purposes of this Chapter.
(5) The Secretary of State may give directions, in relation to a financial year, specifying uses of capital resources or revenue resources which must not be taken into account for the purposes of this Chapter.
(6) The Secretary of State may give directions, in relation to a financial year, specifying uses of capital resources or revenue resources which must be taken into account for the purposes of this section.
(7) The amount specified for the purposes of subsection (2) or (3) may be varied only if–
  (a) the Board agrees to the change,
  (b) a parliamentary general election takes place, or
  (c) the Secretary of State considers that there are exceptional circumstances which make the variation necessary.
(8) Any reference in this Chapter to the use of capital resources or revenue resources is a reference to their expenditure, consumption or reduction in value.

223E Financial duties of the Board: additional controls on resource use

(1) The Secretary of State may direct the Board to ensure that total capital resource use in a financial year which is attributable to matters specified in the direction does not exceed an amount so specified.

(2) The Secretary of State may direct the Board to ensure that total revenue resource use in a financial year which is attributable to matters specified in the direction does not exceed an amount so specified.

(3) The Secretary of State may direct the Board to ensure–

(a) that total revenue resource use in a financial year which is attributable to such prescribed matters relating to administration as are specified in the direction does not exceed an amount so specified;

(b) that the Board's use of revenue resources in a financial year which is attributable to such prescribed matters relating to administration as are specified in the direction does not exceed an amount so specified.

(4) The Secretary of State may give directions, in relation to a financial year, specifying uses of capital resources or revenue resources which must, or must not, be taken into account for the purposes of subsection (1) or (as the case may be) subsection (2) or (3).

(5) The Secretary of State may not give a direction under subsection (1) or (2) unless the direction is for the purpose of complying with a limit imposed by the Treasury.

223F Power to establish contingency fund

(1) The Board may use a proportion of the sums paid to it under section 223B to establish a contingency fund.

(2) The Board may make a payment out of the fund where the payment is necessary in order to enable–

(a) the Board to discharge any of its commissioning functions, or

(b) a clinical commissioning group to discharge any of its functions.

(3) The Board must publish guidance as to how it proposes to exercise its powers to make payments out of the contingency fund.

(4) In this section, 'commissioning functions' means functions in arranging for the provision of services as part of the health service'

4.137 Section 223BC contains the essential duty of NHS England to conduct its functions so that its expenditure does not exceed its income. However, that control total includes sums that NHS England receives and allocates to CCGs.

NHS England's powers as a regulator of clinical commissioning groups

4.138 NHS England has a series of specific duties in relation to CCGs, but does not have any statutory powers to oversee the day-to-day performance of CCGs. Despite the absence of any formal powers, in practice many CCGs have surrendered the operational independence that was given to them by the HSCA 2012, and operate as if NHS England had 'performance management' functions over them similar to those that were previously exercised by Strategic Health Authorities. Accordingly, the statutory scheme envisaged by those who framed the HSCA 2012, which made NHS England an arms-length strategic body and gave considerable operational freedom to CCGs, has not been achieved in practice.

4.139 NHS England has powers related to the formation and functioning of CCGs under section 14A of the NHS Act 2006. Applications for the establishment of a CCG must be made to NHS England, and then determined by NHS England: see sections 14B and 14C. The establishment of a CCG follows a decision by NHS England: see section 14D.

4.140 NHS England has the right to approve variations to a CCG constitution: see section 14E and Part 9 of the National Health Service (Clinical Commissioning Groups) Regulations 2012.[77] The procedure to be followed by NHS England when it receives such an application is set out at Part 10 of these regulations.

4.141 NHS England also has power to vary the specified area of a CCG or to add or remove members from the group: see section 14F. It also has a decision-making role in applications for mergers or dissolutions of CCGs, with the necessary powers to make transfer orders consequent upon any merger or dissolution: see sections 14G–14K.

4.142 Section 14Z8 gives NHS England the power to issue guidance CCGs concerned the exercise of their commissioning functions, and, where such statutory guidance has been issued, CCGs are required to 'have regard' to that guidance.

4.143 Section 14Z16 of the NHS Act 2006 provides that NHS England is required to conduct an annual assessment of the performance of each CCG. It provides:

> (1) The Board must conduct a performance assessment of each clinical commissioning group in respect of each financial year.
> (2) A performance assessment is an assessment of how well the clinical commissioning group has discharged its functions during that year.
> (3) The assessment must, in particular, include an assessment of how well the group has discharged its duties under–
> (a) sections 14R, 14T, 14W and 14Z2,
> (b) sections 223H to 223J, and
> (c) section 116B(1) of the Local Government and Public Involvement in Health Act 2007 (duty to have regard to assessments and strategies).
> (4) In conducting a performance assessment, the Board must consult each relevant Health and Wellbeing Board as to its views on the clinical commissioning group's contribution to the delivery of any joint health and wellbeing strategy to which the group was required to have regard under section 116B(1)(b) of that Act of 2007.
> (5) The Board must, in particular, have regard to–
> (a) any document published by the Secretary of State for the purposes of this section, and
> (b) any guidance published under section 14Z8.
> (6) The Board must publish a report in respect of each financial year containing a summary of the results of each performance assessment conducted by the Board in respect of that year.

4.144 NHS England has published an assessment and improvement framework[78] which is used to conduct the annual assessments. However, it is not required to publish the full assessments and only publishes a brief summary, with a ranking for each CCG.

77 SI No 1631.

78 See www.england.nhs.uk/wp-content/uploads/2017/11/ccg-improvement-and-assessment-framework-2017-18.pdf.

4.145 Sections 14Z21 and 14Z22 provide for NHS England intervene in the management of CCGs in tightly defined circumstances. These sections provide:

14Z21 Power to give directions, dissolve clinical commissioning groups etc

(1) This section applies if the Board is satisfied that–
   (a) a clinical commissioning group is failing or has failed to discharge any of its functions, or
   (b) there is a significant risk that a clinical commissioning group will fail to do so.

(2) The Board may direct the clinical commissioning group to discharge such of those functions, and in such manner and within such period or periods, as may be specified in the direction.

(3) The Board may direct–
   (a) the clinical commissioning group, or
   (b) the accountable officer of the group,
   to cease to perform any functions for such period or periods as may be specified in the direction.

(4) The Board may–
   (a) terminate the appointment of the clinical commissioning group's accountable officer, and
   (b) appoint another person to be its accountable officer.

(5) Paragraph 12(4) of Schedule 1A does not apply to an appointment under subsection (4)(b).

(6) The Board may vary the constitution of the clinical commissioning group, including doing so by–
   (a) varying its area,
   (b) adding any person who is a provider of primary medical services to the list of members, or
   (c) removing any person from that list.

(7) The Board may dissolve the clinical commissioning group.

(8) Where a direction is given under subsection (3) the Board may–
   (a) exercise any of the functions that are the subject of the direction on behalf of the clinical commissioning group or (as the case may be) the accountable officer;
   (b) direct another clinical commissioning group or (as the case may be) the accountable officer of another clinical commissioning group to perform any of those functions on behalf of the group or (as the case may be) the accountable officer, in such manner and within such period or periods as may be specified in the directions.

(9) A clinical commissioning group to which a direction is given under subsection (3) must–
   (a) where the Board exercises a function of the group under subsection (8)(a), co-operate with the Board, and
   (b) where a direction is given under subsection (8)(b) to another clinical commissioning group or to the accountable officer of another clinical commissioning group, co-operate with the other group or (as the case may be) the accountable officer.

(10) Before exercising the power conferred by subsection (8)(b) the Board must consult the clinical commissioning group to which it is proposing to give the direction.

(11) Where the Board exercises a power conferred by subsection (6) or (7), the Board may make a property transfer scheme or a staff transfer scheme.

(12) In subsection (11), 'property transfer scheme' and 'staff transfer scheme' have the same meaning as in section 14I.

(13) Part 3 of Schedule 1A applies in relation to a property transfer scheme or a staff transfer scheme under subsection (11) as it applies in relation to a property transfer scheme or (as the case may be) a staff transfer scheme under section 14I(1).

(14) For the purposes of this section–

(a) a failure to discharge a function includes a failure to discharge it properly, and

(b) a failure to discharge a function properly includes a failure to discharge it consistently with what the Board considers to be the interests of the health service.

14Z22 Procedural requirements in connection with certain powers

(1) Before exercising the power to dissolve a clinical commissioning group under section 14Z21(7) the Board must consult the following persons–

(a) the clinical commissioning group,

(b) relevant local authorities, and

(c) any other persons the Board considers it appropriate to consult.

(2) For that purpose, the Board must provide those persons with a statement–

(a) explaining that it is proposing to exercise the power, and

(b) giving its reasons for doing so.

(3) After consulting those persons (and before exercising the power), the Board must publish a report containing its response to the consultation.

(4) If the Board decides to exercise the power, the report must, in particular, explain its reasons for doing so.

(5) Regulations may make provision as to the procedure to be followed by the Board before the exercise of the powers conferred by sections 14Z18, 14Z19 and 14Z21.

(6) The Board must publish guidance as to how it proposes to exercise the powers conferred by those sections.

(7) For the purposes of subsection (1) a local authority is a relevant local authority if its area coincides with, or includes the whole or any part of, the area of the clinical commissioning group'

4.146 NHS England published the *CCG improvement and assessment framework manual* (CCG IAF)[79] which sets out the procedures that NHS England will follow prior to the exercise of intervention powers. This manual sets out 60 indicators which NHS England will track. One of the following threshold criteria have to be met before NHS England is entitled to exercise these intervention powers: NHS England is satisfied that:

a) a CCG is failing to discharge its functions; or

b) has failed to discharge any of its functions; or

c) that there is a significant risk that a CCG will fail to discharge any of its functions.

4.147 Once NHS England has the right to exercise these powers, it is entitled to give directions to a CCG to remedy the perceived failing. This can include a direction for the removal of accountable officer. These powers are regularly used formally or informally NHS England.

79 See www.england.nhs.uk/wp-content/uploads/2017/11/ccg-iaf-methodology-manual.pdf.

A possible merger between NHS England and NHS Improvement

4.148 Close working between NHS England and NHS Improvement (which is itself a merger of a number of NHS regulatory and patient safety bodies) is becoming a fact of life in the NHS. However the legal structures created by the HSCA 2012 require NHS England and NHS Improvement to carry out distinctly different roles. Hence, for example, Monitor (now part of NHS Improvement) is required to fix the prices under the National Tariff. A key part of that process is co-operation between NHS England, acting on behalf of commissioners, and Monitor, which is supposed to act on behalf of the wider NHS health economy. It is difficult to see how a legal merger between bodies that are required to operate independently could be successfully achieved.

4.149 Further, Monitor is the NHS's competition regulator. That means it oversees the functions discharged by both commissioners and providers so as to ensure that the NHS managed market operating lawfully. It is therefore difficult to see how that function could be properly discharged if Monitor and the NHS's largest commissioner, namely NHS England, were part of the same organisation.

4.150 Accordingly, there would be very substantial legal obstacles to any formal merger between NHS Improvement and NHS England. Further, closer working together between these two organisations may well give rise to substantial legal risks for both NHS England and NHS Improvement.

CHAPTER 5

The powers and duties of clinical commissioning groups[1]

1 By Richard Clarke.

Introduction

5.1 Clinical commissioning groups (CCGs) are statutory NHS bodies responsible for the planning and commissioning of healthcare services for their local area.

5.2 CCGs were created by the Health and Social Care Act (HSCA) 2012, by means of amendments to the National Health Service (NHS) Act 2006, and replaced primary care trusts (PCTs) on 1 April 2013. There are 207 CCGs in England which collectively are responsible for approximately two-thirds of the NHS budget (£73.6 billion in 2017/18).[2]

5.3 Local NHS general practitioner (GP) practices form the membership of CCGs. CCGs are led by an elected governing body made up of GPs, other clinicians and lay members. The core function of CCGs is to assess the health needs of their local population, decide upon priorities and then commission a range of health and social care services on behalf of the local population from providers including hospitals, clinics and community health providers. CCGs are also increasingly commissioning primary care services on behalf of NHS England.

Legal foundation and governance of CCGs

Creation of CCGs

5.4 In order to understand the powers and duties and CCGs it is first necessary to have an understanding of their legal foundations and governance arrangements. CCGs are statutory bodies, created by section 10 of the HSCA 2012, which inserted section 1I into the NHS Act 2006. This provides:

> (1) There are to be bodies corporate known as clinical commissioning groups established in accordance with Chapter A2 of Part 2.
> (2) Each clinical commissioning group has the function of arranging for the provision of services for the purposes of the health service in England in accordance with this Act.

5.5 Part 2 of Chapter A2 of the NHS Act 2006, at sections 14A through to 14Z24, together with Schedule 1A, makes detailed provision for the creation and governance of CCGs and imposes a series procedural and substantive legal duties on CCGs.

5.6 An application to establish a CCG must be made to NHS England.[3] Applications may be made by any two or more persons each of whom is or wishes to be a provider of NHS primary care serves and wishes to be a member of the clinical commissioning group.[4] Applications must also comply with the requirements of section 14B(3), which provides that an application must be accompanied by:

2 Estimates taken from www.nhscc.org/ccgs/ and www.nhs.uk/NHSEngland/thenhs/about/Pages/nhsstructure.aspx.

3 Section 14B(1).

4 Section 14B(2)

a) a copy of the proposed constitution of the CCG;
b) the name of the person whom the group wishes NHS England to appoint as its accountable officer;[5] and
c) such other information as NHS England specifies.
Section 14B(3)(c) empowers NHS England to publish a document specifying the further information required under this section.

5.7 NHS England must grant an application where it is satisfied that the conditions listed in section 14C(2) are met. Requirements include the CCGs constitution complying with the requirements of Part 1 of Schedule 1A,[6] each member specified in the constitution being a provider of primary medical services (ie GP practices, dentists and pharmacists) on the date the CCG is established[7] and appropriate arrangements having been made to ensure the CCG will be able to discharge its functions.

5.8 Approval of the application establishes the CCG, on the terms of the constitution submitted as part of the application.[8] Section 14E provides a mechanism by which CCGs can apply to NHS England to vary their constitutions. NHS England may vary the constitution of a CCG itself, without an application, where the requirements of section 14F are satisfied, which include adding/removing a provider of primary care services to the constitution where 1) the CCG consents or 2) where NHS England considers the variation necessary to discharge any of its own duties under section 14A.

5.9 The NHS Act 2006 also makes provision for the merger of CCGs,[9] their dissolution[10] and the transfer of CCG property and staff connected with any variation, dissolution or merger.[11]

Constitution of CCGs

5.10 Paragraph 1 of Part 1, Schedule 1A to the NHS Act 2006 mandates that CCGs must have a constitution. The constitution must specify:

a) The name of the CCG, its members and area.[12]
b) The arrangements made by the CCG for the discharge of its functions, including determining the terms and conditions of its employees[13] and the procedure the CCG will follow in making decisions, including arrangements made by the CCG to ensure transparency in its decision-making.[14] These arrangements must secure effective participation by each member of the CCG in the exercise of the group's functions.[15]

5 As to which see Sch 1A para 12.
6 Section 14C(2)(a).
7 Section 14C(2)(b).
8 Section 14D.
9 Section 14G.
10 Section 14H.
11 Section 14I together with Sch 1A Part 3.
12 Sch 1A Part 1 para 2.
13 Sch 1A Part 1 para 3.
14 Sch 1A Part 1 para 4.
15 Sch 1A Part 1 para 6.

The arrangements may include provision for the functions of the CCG to be exercised on its behalf by any of its members or employees, its governing body or a committee/subcommittee of the CCG.[16]

c) The arrangements made by the CCG to discharge its duties in section 14O of the NHS Act 2006 (which concerns managing potential conflicts of interest).
d) The arrangements made by the CCG for the discharge of the functions of its governing body,[17] which must include provision for the appointment of an audit committee and remuneration committee of the governing body. Arrangements may also include provision for any functions of the governing body to be exercised on its behalf by a committee or subcommittee of the governing body, a member of the governing body, a member of the CCG who is an individual but not a member of the governing body, or an individual of a description specified in the constitution.
e) The procedure to be followed by the governing body in making decisions, including the arrangements made by the CCG to ensure transparency about the decisions of the governing body and the manner in which they are made. This must include provision for meetings of governing bodies to be open to the public except where the CCG considers it would not be in the public interest to permit members of the public to attend a meeting or part of a meeting.[18]

5.11 These requirements are non-exhaustive and the constitution can make further provision as to other matters.[19]

5.12 Section 14J requires CCGs to publish their constitutions, including any variations made under section 14E or 14F. Section 14K empowers NHS England to publish guidance as to:

a) the making of applications under section 14B to establish a CCG, including guidance on the form, content and publication of the CCG's proposed constitution;
b) the making of an application under section 14E (variation of a CCG's constitution), 14G (merger of CCGs) or 14H (dissolution of CCGs);
c) the publication of a CCG's constitution under section 14J.

5.13 At the time of writing, this guidance is contained in the NHS England document *Procedures for CCGs to apply for constitution change merger or dissolution* (November 2016).[20]

Governing body of CCGs

5.14 CCGs are required to have a governing body.[21] Section 14L(2) explains that:

16 Sch 1A Part 1 para 3(3).
17 Sch 1A Part 1 para 7.
18 Sch 1A Part 1 para 8.
19 Sch 1A Part 1 para 9.
20 All of NHS England's guidance for CCGs is available at www.england.nhs.uk/resources/resources-for-ccgs/.
21 Section 14L(1).

(2) The main function of the governing body is to ensure that the group has made appropriate arrangements for ensuring that it complies with–
(a) its obligations under section 14Q, and
(b) such generally accepted principles of good governance as are relevant to it.

5.15 Section 14Q provides that each CCG 'must exerciser its functions effectively, efficiently and economically'. The main function of governing body is therefore to ensure that the CCG has made appropriate arrangements to meet these objectives. Section 14L(3) adds that the governing body also has:

a) the function of determining the remuneration, fees and allowances payable to the employees of the CCG or to other persons providing services to it ('remuneration function');
b) the function of determining the allowances payable under a pension scheme established under para 11(4) of Schedule 1A (which authorises CCGs to establish and administer a pension scheme) ('allowances function');
c) such other functions 'connected with the exercise of its main functions' as may be specified in the CCGs constitution or in regulations.

5.16 NHS England may publish guidance for governing bodies on the exercise of the remuneration and allowances functions.[22] Section 14L(6) provides that regulations may make provision requiring governing bodies to publish prescribed information relating to determinations made as part of their remuneration and allowances functions. This is currently done by reg 16 of the National Health Service (Clinical Commissioning Group) Regulations (CCG Regs) 2012[23] which states that:

(1) A CCG's governing body must publish papers considered at meetings of its governing body, except where the governing body considers that it would not be in the public interest to do so in relation to a particular paper or part of a paper.
(2) Subject to paragraphs (3) and (4), a CCG's governing body must publish the following information relating to determinations made under subsection (3)(a) and (b) of section 14L of the 2006 Act (which relates to remuneration, fees and allowances, including allowances payable under certain pension schemes)–
(a) in relation to each senior employee of the CCG, any determination of the employee's salary or of any travelling and other allowances payable to the employee, including any allowances payable under a pension scheme established under paragraph 11(4) of Schedule 1A to the 2006 Act;
(b) any recommendation of the remuneration committee in relation to any such determination.
(3) Information as to the determination of a senior employee's salary need specify only a band of £5,000 into which the salary determined falls.
(4) The governing body must not publish any information referred to in paragraph (2) if the governing body considers that it would not be in the public interest to publish it.

22 Section 14L(7). Again, guidance is available at www.england.nhs.uk/resources/resources-for-ccgs/, and is currently contained in the document titled *Clinical commissioning groups: Remuneration guidance for chief officers (where the senior manager also undertakes the accountable officer role) and chief finance officers.*

23 SI No 1631.

(5) In paragraph (2)(a), 'senior employee' means an employee who has authority over or responsibility for directing or controlling the exercise of the CCG's functions.'

5.17 By section 14L(5), regulations may also make provision requiring a CCG to obtain the approval of its governing body before exercising any of the functions specified in the regulations, though none are currently in force.

5.18 By section 14L(4), membership of the governing body is restricted to:

a) a member of the CCG who is an individual;
b) an individual appointed by virtue of regulations made under section 14N(2);
c) an individual of a description specified in the constitution of the group.

5.19 The governing body of a CCG is required to have an audit committee and a remuneration committee.[24] By section 14M(2) the audit committee has:

(a) such functions in relation to the financial duties of the clinical commissioning group as the governing body considers appropriate for the purpose of assisting it in discharging its function under section 14L(2), and
(b) such other functions connected with the governing body's function under section 14L(2) as may be specified in the group's constitution or by regulations.

5.20 By section 14M(3), the remuneration committee has:

(a) the function of making recommendations to the governing body as to the discharge of its functions under section 14L(3)(a) and (b),[25] and
(b) such other functions connected with the governing body's function under section 14L(2) as may be specified in the group's constitution or by regulations.

5.21 Much of the detail as to the membership and functioning of governing bodies is left to regulations made under section 14N, currently the CCG Regs 2012.

5.22 By reg 11 of the CCG Regs 2012, a CCGs governing body must:

a) have at least six members (including its chair and deputy chair);
b) include the accountable officer;
c) include at least one of each of the following:
   i) an employee of the CCG who has a professional qualification in accountancy and the expertise or experience to lead the financial management of the CCG (and who is to be designated as the CCG's chief finance officer (CFO));[26]
   ii) a registered nurse;[27]

24 Section 14M(1).
25 The remuneration and allowances functions.
26 Reg 11(3)(a).
27 Reg 11(3)(b), other than a nurse who falls within reg 12(1). A nurse (or secondary care specialist) will fall within reg 12(1) if they are an employee or member (including shareholder) of, or a partner in a) a provider of primary medical services for the purposes of Chapter A2 of Part 2 of the NHS Act 2006 or b) a body which provides any relevant service to a person for whom the CCG has responsibility. For the definition of relevant service, see reg 12(2).

iii) an individual who is a secondary care specialist;[28]
iv) a lay person who is qualified for membership by virtue of reg 12(3). Regulation 12(3) requires the lay person to have qualifications, expertise or experience such as to enable them to express informed views about financial management and audit matters;[29]
v) a layperson qualified for membership by virtue of reg 12(4).[30] Regulation 12(4) requires the layperson to have knowledge about the area specified in the CCG's constitution such as to enable the person to express informed views about the discharge of the CCG's functions.

5.23 Individuals of the descriptions set out in Schedule 4 to the CCG Regs 2012 are not laypersons for these purposes[31] (which includes the employees of local authorities and various public bodies involved in the healthcare system). Individuals of the descriptions set out in Schedule 5 are disqualified from membership of a CCG's governing body.[32]

5.24 The governing body must have a chair and deputy chair.[33] Persons falling within reg 13(2) are disqualified from being the chair of the governing body, including the CCG's accountable officer and any person who falls within reg 11(3)(a), (b), (c) or (d).

5.25 The audit committee of a CCG's governing body must also have a chair, which must be a lay person who has qualifications, expertise or experience such as to enable the person to express informed views about financial management and audit matters.[34] The chair of the CCG's governing body and the CFO are disqualified from membership of a CCGs audit committee.[35]

5.26 The remuneration committee must also have a chair, and all members of the governing body other than the lay members are disqualified from being the chair.[36]

5.27 Regulation 16 makes provision for transparency in the way a governing body fulfils its functions, requiring that a CCG's governing body:

a) must publish papers considered at meetings of its governing body, except where the governing body considers that it would not be in the public interest to do so in relation to a particular paper or part of a paper;

28 Reg 11(3)(c)) and who meets the conditions specified in reg 11(6) of the CCG Regs 2012, other than a person who falls within reg 12(1).

29 Reg 11(3)(d).

30 Reg 11(3)(e).

31 See the list in Schedule 4, which includes employees of local authorities, the DHSC, the CQC, Monitor, an NHS foundation trust or other NHS body other than a CCG.

32 See the list in Schedule 5, which includes members of parliament and local authorities (paras 1–2); persons with recent criminal convictions (para 4); bankrupts (para 5); struck off healthcare professional (para 7); disqualified company directions (para 8); removed charity trustees (para 9); dismissed employees of various healthcare bodies (para 6) and Individuals who by arrangement with the CCG provide it with a service in order to support the CCG to discharge its commissioning functions (or an employee or shareholder of a body which does so) (para 3).

33 Reg 13(1).

34 Reg 14(2).

35 Reg 14(3).

36 Reg 15.

b) must publish information relating to determinations made under its remuneration and allowances functions, unless in the governing body's view it is not in the public interest to do so. The information which must be published is:
   i) in relation to each senior employee[37] of the CCG, any determination of the employee's salary (within a band of £5,000) or of any travelling and other allowances payable to the employee, including any allowances payable under a pension scheme;
   ii) any recommendation of the remuneration committee in relation to any such determination.

5.28 Further provision is made by Part 2 of Schedule 1A to the NHS Act 2006. In particular:

a) CCGs must have an accountable officer, who is appointed by NHS England as opposed to being appointed by the members of the CCG itself.[38]
b) A CCG may appoint such persons to be employees of the group as it considers appropriate[39] and must:
   i) pay its employees remunerations and travelling and other allowances in accordance with the determinations made by its governing body under section 14L(3)(a);[40]
   ii) employ them on such terms and conditions as it may determine.[41]
c) CCGs may:
   i) pay members of the governing body such remuneration and travelling and other allowances as it considers appropriate;
   ii) make arrangements for providing pensions, allowances and gratuities to members of its governing body, including the establishment of a pension scheme,[42] but not for members of the governing body who are 1) members or employees of the CCG or 2) members or employees of a body that is a member of the CCG.[43]
d) A CCG may pay such travelling and other allowances as it considers appropriate to:
   i) members of the CCG who are individuals;
   ii) individuals authorised to act on behalf of a member of the CCG;
   iii) members of any committee or sub-committee of the CCG or its governing body.[44]
e) CCGs may enter into 'externally financed development agreements'.[45] These are agreements certified as such in writing by the Secretary of

37 Defined as 'an employee who has authority over or responsibility for directing or controlling the exercise of the CCG's functions': reg 16(5).
38 Sch 1A Part 2 para 12.
39 Sch 1A Part 2 para 11(1).
40 Sch 1A Part 2 para 11(2)(a).
41 Sch 1A Part 2 para 11(2)(b).
42 Sch 1A Part 2 para 13.
43 Sch 1A Part 2 para 13(6).
44 Sch 1A Part 2 para 14.
45 Sch 1A Part 2 para 16(1).

State for Health and Social Care.[46] The secretary of state may certify an agreement as such if:

i) in the secretary of state's opinion the purpose or main purpose of the agreement is the provision of services or facilities in connection with the discharge by a clinical commissioning group of any of its functions; and
ii) a person proposes to make a loan to, or provide any other form of finance for, another party in connection with the agreement.[47]

f) However, by Schedule 1A Part 2 para 16(6), 'the fact that an agreement made by a clinical commissioning group has not been certified under this paragraph does not affect its validity'. It is arguable that this saving provision weakens the effectiveness of the requirement for the secretary of state to certify externally financed development agreements, albeit a deliberate failure to obtain certification would likely be me misconduct and subject to sanctions other than the agreement being invalid.
g) A CCG must keep proper accounts and records in relation to its accounts, and must preparing annual accounts. The annual accounts must be audited and the audited accounts sent to NHS England.[48]
h) NHS England may direct CCGs to provide it with such information relating to its accounts and expenditure as NHS England requires. CCGs are under a statutory duty to comply with any such direction.[49]
i) The secretary of state may direct CCGs to provide NHS England with such information as the secretary of state considers it necessary to have for the purposes of the secretary of state's functions in relation to the health service.[50] This power must be 'exercised in the same way in relation to each CCG'.[51] It thus appears that this restriction prevents the secretary of state making ad hoc directions for information against individual CCGs. NHS England must pass any information obtained under this power onto the secretary of state.[52] Again, CCGs are under a statutory duty to comply with any such direction.[53]

General power of CCGs

5.29 Section 2 of the NHS Act 2006 provides:

> The Secretary of State, the Board or a clinical commissioning group may do anything which is calculated to facilitate, or is conducive or incidental to, the discharge of any function conferred on that person by this Act.

5.30 Section 2 is a broad power for a CCG to take any steps needed to support the discharge of its functions. It mirrors the provision made for local

46 Sch 1A Part 2 para 16(2).
47 Sch 1A Part 2 para 16(3).
48 Sch 1A Part 2 para 17.
49 Sch 1A Part 2 para 18.
50 Sch 1A Part 2 para 19.
51 Sch 1A Part 2 para 19(3).
52 Sch 1A Part 2 para 19(4).
53 Sch 1A Part 2 para 19(2).

authorities in section 111 of the Local Government Act 1972.[54] However, CCGs are statutory bodies whose powers are limited to the discharge of their specific functions. Hence, unlike local authorities, they do not benefit from the general power of competence available to local authorities in section 1 of the Localism Act 2011.

5.31 For the section 2 power to be engaged, the CCG must be able to identify the function in the NHS Act 2006 which the specific act of the CCG is said to 'facilitate, be conducive or incidental to' in order to give the CCG competence to undertake the act. Whilst these are broad concepts, the limits of the powers granted by section 2 were considered by the Court of Appeal in *R (National Aids Trust) v National Health Service Commissioning Board (NHS England)*.[55] In that case, the issue arose of whether the defendant had the power to commission pre-exposure prophylaxis ('PrEP'), an anti-retroviral drug used on a preventative basis for those at high risk of becoming infected with HIV. The Court of Appeal decided that PrEP did not fall under the 'public health functions' exception in section 1H(2) of the NHS Act 2006 but nonetheless the defendant had the power to commission it under section 3B(1) of the NHS Act 2006 and reg 11 and para 17 of Schedule 4 to the CCG Regs 2012[56] because treatment for a condition included treatment which prevented a patient acquiring the condition.

5.32 The Court of Appeal also went on to consider, obiter, whether the commissioning of PrEP could fall within NHS England's section 2 power. Lord Justice Longmore, with who Lord Justice King agreed,[57] considered that:

> 42. On any view NHS England has the function of commissioning treatment for those infected with HIV. It thus has the power to do precisely that. The question is, therefore, whether the discharge of that function is facilitated by commissioning treatment which prevents the onset of HIV and avoids the expenditure of treating those with full-blown HIV. To my mind the only answer to that question is 'Yes'.
>
> 43. If NHS England has the function of commissioning treatment for HIV, the discharge of that function will be greatly helped by reducing the numbers of persons infected with HIV. If, therefore, there is an available medical treatment for reducing those numbers, section 2 of the Act authorises the commissioning of that treatment because it makes it easier and less expensive for the primary function of providing services to those infected with HIV to be discharged.
>
> 44. One can alternatively ask whether commissioning such treatment is conducive to the discharge of the primary function of providing services to HIV infected patients. Again the answer must be yes, since the number of

54 For an example where a local authority was held to have exceeded the scope of s111, see *McCarthy & Stone (Developments) Ltd v Richmond upon Thames LBC* [1992] 2 AC 48. There the House of Lords held that while the provision of pre-application advice to an applicant for planning permission was incidental to a local authorities functions under the Town and Country Planning Act 1990 (pp52–53), *charging* for that advice was 'at best, incidental to the incidental and not incidental to the discharge of the functions' and therefore unlawful (p75).

55 [2016] EWCA Civ 1100, (2017) 20 CCLR 30.

56 For more details on implications arising from this case, please see chapter 6 on public health.

57 See [70].

HIV infected patients will reduce and their treatment will overall be less expensive for the health service in general and NHS England in particular.

5.33 Lord Justice Underhill declined to decide whether section 2 was broad enough to include commissioning PrEP though cautioned he was 'not sure' that he would be 'prepared to give section 2 of the 2006 Act as expansive an effect as [LJ Longmore] does'.[58]

5.34 NHS Act 2006 Sch 1A Part 2 para 20 confirms that the section 2 power includes the power to:

a) enter into agreements;
b) acquire and dispose of property; and
c) accept gifts (including property to be held on trust for the purposes of the clinical commissioning group).

CCG duty to commission services

5.35 The core function commissioning function of CCGs is contained in section 3 of the NHS Act 2006:

(1) A clinical commissioning group must arrange for the provision of the following to such extent as it considers necessary to meet the reasonable requirements of the persons for whom it has responsibility –
  (a) hospital accommodation,
  (b) other accommodation for the purpose of any service provided under this Act,
  (c) medical, dental, ophthalmic, nursing and ambulance services,
  (d) such other services or facilities for the care of pregnant women, women who are breastfeeding and young children as the group considers are appropriate as part of the health service,
  (e) such other services or facilities for the prevention of illness, the care of persons suffering from illness and the after-care of persons who have suffered from illness [as the group considers are appropriate as part of the health service,
  (f) such other services or facilities as are required for the diagnosis and treatment of illness.

(1A) For the purposes of this section, a clinical commissioning group has responsibility for–
  (a) persons who are provided with primary medical services by a member of the group, and
  (b) persons who usually reside in the group's area and are not provided with primary medical services by a member of any clinical commissioning group.

(1B) Regulations may provide that for the purposes of this section a clinical commissioning group also has responsibility (whether generally or in relation to a prescribed service or facility) for persons who–
  (a) were provided with primary medical services by a person who is or was a member of the group, or
  (b) have a prescribed connection with the group's area.

(1C) The power conferred by subsection (1B)(b) must be exercised so as to provide that, in relation to the provision of services or facilities for

58 See [58].

emergency care, a clinical commissioning group has responsibility for every person present in its area.

(1D) Regulations may provide that subsection (1A) does not apply–

(a) in relation to persons of a prescribed description (which may include a description framed by reference to the primary medical services with which the persons are provided);

(b) in prescribed circumstances.

(1E) The duty in subsection (1) does not apply in relation to a service or facility if the Board has a duty to arrange for its provision.

(1F) In exercising its functions under this section and section 3A, a clinical commissioning group must act consistently with–

(a) the discharge by the Secretary of State and the Board of their duty under section 1(1) (duty to promote a comprehensive health service), and

(b) the objectives and requirements for the time being specified in the mandate published under section 13A'

5.36 In *R (JF, by her litigation friend RW) v NHS Sheffield Clinical Commissioning Group*,[59] it was common ground, and accepted by the judge, that:

a) the section 3 duty is not 'an absolute duty to provide the health services' and a CCG is 'entitled to have regard to the resources available to it';

b) although the section 3 duty may require the assessment of individual cases, 'there is no individually enforceable entitlement to a particular level of care from the NHS';

c) it is in theory possible that circumstances could arise where the services a CCG had commissioned from hospitals would be inadequate for the reasonable requirements of a person for whom the CCG has responsibility. In those circumstances the section 3 duty would require that the CCG commission additional services to meet that person's reasonable needs;

d) CCGs are public law bodies susceptible to public law challenges on the grounds of *Wednesbury* unreasonableness.

5.37 The section 3 duty is supplemented by the power in section 3A to commission 'certain health' services:

(1) Each clinical commissioning group may arrange for the provision of such services or facilities as it considers appropriate for the purposes of the health service that relate to securing improvement–

(a) in the physical and mental health of the persons for whom it has responsibility, or

(b) in the prevention, diagnosis and treatment of illness in those persons.

(2) A clinical commissioning group may not arrange for the provision of a service or facility under subsection (1) if the Board has a duty to arrange for its provision by virtue of section 3B or 4.[60]

59 [2014] EWHC 1345 (Admin).

60 Section 3B ('Secretary of State's power to require Board to commission services') provides that regulations may require NHS England to arrange, to such extent as it considers necessary to meet all reasonable requirements, for the provision as part of the health service of: a) dental services of a prescribed description; b) services or facilities for members of the armed forces or their families; c) services or facilities for persons who are detained in a prison or in other accommodation of a prescribed description; and d) such other services or facilities as may be prescribed. Section 4 requires NHS England to arrange for the provision of hospital accommodation and services for persons who are liable to be detained under the Mental Health Act 1983 and in the opinion of the secretary of state require treatment under conditions of high security on account of their dangerous, violent or criminal propensities.

(3) Subsections (1A), (1B) and (1D) of section 3 apply for the purposes of this section as they apply for the purposes of that section.

5.38 Persons 'to whom a CCG has responsibility' are set out in section 3(1A) and in the CCG Regs 2012. Please see chapter 13 on the responsible commissioner for a full description of the persons and services for which each CCG has commissioning responsibility.

5.39 Additional commissioning provision is made by Schedule 1 to the NHS Act 2006.[61] Paragraph 9(1) (provision of vehicles for disabled persons) provides that a CCG:

> ... may make arrangements for the provision of vehicles (including wheelchairs) for persons for whom the group has responsibility and who appear to it to have a physical impairment which has a substantial and long-term adverse effect on their ability to carry out normal day-to-day activities.

5.40 This is a deliberately broad power, reflecting the range of vehicles that disabled persons may require and the range of health conditions which may give rise to a need for a vehicle. Although para 9 does not, in terms, require that the physical impairment has an adverse impact upon the person's mobility, this will usually be the case where a person's ability to carry out normal day-to-day activities is substantially impaired. 'Vehicle' is not defined, other than the confirmation in para 9 that it includes wheelchairs.

5.41 Paragraph 10 authorises CCGs to make arrangements and pay grants to disabled persons for the purpose of adapting, maintaining, running storing and insuring a vehicle:

> (1) Sub-paragraphs (2) and (3) apply in respect of–
> (a) a vehicle provided in pursuance of arrangements made under paragraph 9, and
> (b) a vehicle belonging to a person mentioned in that paragraph.
> (2) The clinical commissioning group may make arrangements for–
> (a) the adaptation of the vehicle to make it suitable for the circumstances of the person in question,
> (b) the maintenance and repair of the vehicle,
> (c) the taking out of insurance policies relating to the vehicle and the payment of any duty with which the vehicle is chargeable under the Vehicle Excise and Registration Act 1994,
> (d) the provision of a structure in which the vehicle may be kept, and the provision of all material and the execution of all works necessary to erect the structure.
> (3) A clinical commissioning group may make payments by way of grant towards costs incurred by a person mentioned in paragraph 9 in respect of any matter mentioned in sub-paragraph (4) in relation to the vehicle.
> (4) The matters are–
> (a) the taking of action referred to in sub-paragraph (2),
> (b) the purchase of fuel for the purposes of the vehicle, so far as the cost of the purchase is attributable to duties of excise payable in respect of the fuel, and
> (c) the taking of instruction in the driving of the vehicle.

61 By section 5: 'Schedule 1 makes further provision about the provision of services for the purposes of the health service in England'.

(5) The powers under sub-paragraph (2) and sub-paragraph (3) may be exercised on such terms and subject to such conditions as the clinical commissioning group may determine.

5.42 Paragraph 13(1) empowers CCGs to conduct, commission and assist in the conduct of research into any matters relating to the causation, prevention, diagnosis or treatment of illness. Paragraph 13(2) provides that a CCG may 'for any purpose connected with the exercise of its functions in relation to the health service':

a) obtain and analyse data or other information;
b) obtain advice from persons with appropriate professional expertise.

5.43 Paragraph 13(4) confirms that para 13(1) and (2) powers to assist any person to conduct research includes power to do so by providing financial assistance or making the services of any person or other resources available.

Primary care co-commissioning between NHS England and CCGs

5.44 Increasingly, CCGs are becoming involved in the co-commissioning of primary care services despites the conflicts of interest that have the potential to arise wherever a CCG is commissioning services from one of its own members. The move towards primary care co-commissioning was set out in the NHS *Five year forward view*.[62] According to NHS England, 'it gives Clinical Commissioning Groups (CCGs) an opportunity to take on greater responsibility for general practice commissioning' and was 'introduced to support the development of integrated out-of-hospital services, based around the needs of local people'.[63] However, it may be more accurate to say that NHS England recognised that the abolition of PCTs resulted in the removal of locally based primary care commissioning; and that attempting to commission these services by Local Area Teams from NHS England was not a great success, and thus it has been restored as a local commissioning function.

5.45 The aim of primary care co-commissioning is stated by NHS England to be superior joined up care, with:

a) improved access to primary care and wider out-of-hospital services, with more services available closer to home;
b) high quality out-of-hospital care;
c) improved health outcomes and reduced health inequalities;
d) a better patient experience through more joined up services.

5.46 In 2014/15, NHS England invited CCGs to take on greater responsibility for general practice commissioning through one of three models:

a) *Greater involvement* – an invitation to CCGs to work more closely with their local NHS England teams in decisions about primary care services.
b) *Joint commissioning* – where one or more CCGs jointly commissions general practice services with NHS England through a joint committee.

62 October 2014. See www.england.nhs.uk/wp-content/uploads/2014/10/5yfv-web.pdf.
63 See www.england.nhs.uk/commissioning/pc-co-comms/pc-comms/.

c) *Delegated commissioning* – where CCGs take on full responsibility for the commissioning of general practice services.

5.47 According to NHS England, as of 1 April 2017, 197 of the 207 CCGs have some form of co-commissioning agreement with NHS England.[64] The obvious risk with the co-commissioning of primary care is that CCGs, the membership of which consists of providers of primary care, will be commissioning services mainly from their own members and thus will have substantial challenges to manage the attendant risks of conflicts of interest. This issue is addressed below.

Duties governing how CCGs are required to discharge their functions

5.48 Sections 14P to 14Z24 of the NHS Act 2006, supplemented by the National Health Service Commissioning Board and Clinical Commissioning Groups (Responsibilities and Standing Rules) Regulations (RSR Regs) 2012,[65] makes further detailed provision for the way in which CCGs must discharge their functions. The sections can be broadly grouped into the following areas:

a) the production of commissioning plans and associated obligations in the RSR Regs 2012;
b) procedural obligations when CCGs exercise their functions;
c) duties as to patient involvement in their decision-making processes;
d) transparency in decision making and scrutiny of CCG performance;
e) CCG duties relating to NHS England;
f) powers and duties relating to joint working;
g) financial provision; and
f) disclosure of information.

5.49 These provisions are interpreted in accordance with the definitions in section 14Z24. In particular, any reference to the functions of a clinical commissioning group is taken to includes a reference to the functions of the secretary of state that are exercisable by the group by virtue of arrangements made under the provisions listed in section 14Z24(2).

Production of commissioning plans

5.50 The commissioning process is set out in detail in chapter 9. Section 14Z11(1) of the NHS Act 2006 requires CCGs, before the start of each financial year, to prepare a plan setting out how it proposes to exercise its functions in that period. By section 14Z11(3) the plan must, in particular, explain how the group proposes to discharge its duties under:

a) sections 14R (securing continuous improvement in the quality of services), 14T (duty to have regard to the need to reduce inequalities

64 See www.england.nhs.uk/commissioning/pc-co-comms/pc-comms/.
65 SI No 2996.

between patients in access to health services) and 14Z2 (patient involvement); and

b) sections 223H to 223J (which impose duties in relation complying with spending limits set by NHS England to ensure that CCGs do not exceed their budgets).

5.51 The CCG must publish the plan[66] and give a copy to NHS England by the date it specifies in a direction.[67] A copy must also be given to each health and wellbeing board (HWB) whose area coincides with, or includes the whole or any part of the area of the CCG.[68]

5.52 Published CCG commissioning plans may be revised under section 14Z12(1). If the revision is, in the CCG's view, 'significant', then the CCG must publish the revised plan and supply copies to NHS England and the relevant HWBs.[69] If the plan is revised in any other way, the CCG must publish a document setting out the changes made to the plan and supply a copy to NHS England and the relevant HWBs.[70]

5.53 Section 14Z13(1)–(2) requires CCGs when preparing a commissioning plan, or revising one in a way which it considers to be significant, to consult with individuals to whom it has responsibility under section 3. This is a specific consultation duty and not just a duty to 'involve' local people in decision-making. Thus the full *Gunning* requirements must be satisfied in the consultation process. The CCG must also involve each relevant HWB in preparing or revising the plan[71] which, in particular, requires that the CCG:[72]

a) give each relevant HWB a draft of the plan or (as the case may be) the plan as revised; and

b) consult each such HWB on whether the draft takes proper account of each joint health and wellbeing strategy published by it which relates to the period (or any part of the period) to which the plan relates. The HWBs may provide the CCG with an opinion on whether the plan does so.[73]

5.54 The published commissioning plan must include[74] a summary of the views expressed by individuals consulted on the plan and an explanation of how the group took account of those views, as well as a statement of the final opinion of each relevant Health and Wellbeing Board consulted on the plan.

5.55 NHS England may publish guidance for CCGs on the discharge of their functions under sections 14Z11, 14Z12 and 14Z13,[75] and CCGs are under a statutory duty to 'have regard' to any such guidance.[76]

66 Section 14Z11(4).
67 Section 14Z11(5).
68 Section 14Z11(6) and (9).
69 Section 14Z12(2).
70 Section 14Z12(3).
71 Section 14Z13(3).
72 Section 14Z13(4).
73 Section 14Z14.
74 Section 14Z13(8).
75 Section 14Z11(7).
76 Section 14Z11(8).

National Health Service Commissioning Board and Clinical Commissioning Groups (Responsibilities and Standing Rules) Regulations 2012

5.56 Regulations 34–36 of the RSR Regs 2012 impose a series of duties on NHS commissioning bodies, including CCGs (which are a 'relevant body' for these purposes), governing the way in which commissioning decisions are taken:

> **34 Duty of a relevant body in respect of the funding and commissioning of drugs and other treatments**
> (1) A relevant body must have in place arrangements for making decisions and adopting policies on whether a particular health care intervention is to be made available for persons for whom the relevant body has responsibility.
> (2) Arrangements under paragraph (1) must–
> (a) ensure that the relevant body complies with relevant NICE recommendations; and
> (b) include arrangements for the determination of any request for the funding of a health care intervention for a person, where there is no relevant NICE recommendation and the relevant body's general policy is not to fund that intervention.
>
> **35 Duty to give reasons for decisions**
> (1) A relevant body must–
> (a) publish on its website a written statement of its reasons for any general policy it has on whether a particular healthcare intervention is to be made available for persons for whom it has responsibility; or
> (b) where it has not published such a statement, provide a written statement of the reasons for any such policy when any person makes a written request for such a statement.
> (2) Where a relevant body–
> (a) makes a decision to refuse a request for the funding of a health care intervention for a person; and
> (b) its general policy is not to fund that intervention,
> the relevant body must provide that person with the reasons for that decision in writing.
>
> **36 Duty to provide written information**
> Each relevant body must compile information in writing describing the arrangements it has made pursuant to the requirements in regulation 34 and must ensure that that information is–
> (a) published on the website of the relevant body; and
> (b) available to inspect at the head or main office of the relevant body.

5.57 These regulations summarise good commissioning practice arising out of the Department of Health and Social Care's (DHSC's) 'world class commissioning' programme, which was subsequently abandoned by the DHSC. They recognise that most commissioning decisions are taken under commissioning policies that are adopted by local commissioners. Hence, for example, the CCG will carefully consider which cancer drugs provide clinically effective and cost effective treatment for different cancers and how many cycles of IVF should be funded for women seeking fertility treatment. These decisions reflect relative priorities and must be informed by the joint strategic health needs assessment.[77] In each case the regulations require the policy to explain the reasons that some treatments will be funded and others will not generally attract NHS funding. The CCG planning cycle will need to estimate the number of patients expected to be funded under each policy and the likely annual costs to the CCG of adopting this particular policy.

5.58 There will always be patients whose needs are outside the range of commissioning policies adopted by a CCG because, for example, the presenting condition is so rare that the CCG has no policy governing access to treatment for such patients. There will be other patients who seek treatment on an exceptional basis which is not normally funded because, for example, the patient cannot tolerate the usually funded treatment. Regulation 34(2)(b) requires the CCG to have a decision-making process which explains how it will decide whether funding should be provided in such cases. These are usually known as 'individual funding arrangement' (IFA) policies.

5.59 The effects of these regulations were partially summarised by Mr Justice Jay *in R (Rose) v Thanet Clinical Commissioning Group*[78] as follows:

> 26. In my judgment, and insofar as is relevant to this case, there are three express regulatory obligations on the CCG and two implied ones. The express obligations are (i) to have in place arrangements and general policies for deciding whether to make available for persons particular health care interventions, (ii) to provide or make available its reasons for any general policy not to fund a particular intervention, and (iii) to include within its decision-making framework arrangements for dealing with specific requests by a person for funding in circumstances where there is no NICE-driven duty to make available the intervention at issue and the CCG's general policy is not to fund. Put in these terms it may be seen that express obligation (iii) is addressed to the determination of exceptional cases. It is to be noted that Regulation 34(1) refers to 'persons' and Regulation 34(2) to 'a person', underlining the distinction between general policies and special cases.
>
> 27. As for the CCG's implied obligations imposed by force of public law and/or the true construction of the regulatory scheme, the first is that the duty to have regard to NICE recommendations made under Regulation 5 must bear on the formulation of its general policies (see (i) above) rather than its exceptional policies (see (ii)). This flows from the structure of the regulatory scheme but I will be amplifying this point subsequently. The second implied obligation, and it flows from the first, is that the duty to give reasons for any general policy not to fund a particular intervention must encompass the giving of a reasoned explanation of why a NICE recommendation made under Regulation 5 is not being followed.

77 See chapter 9 on commissioning. In summary, a joint strategic needs assessment must be carried out by the HWB on behalf of the CCGs operating in a local authority and the local authority: see section 116(1) of the Local Government and Public Involvement in Health Act 2007. CCGs are required, working through the HWB, on an annual basis to work with the local authority to carry out an assessment of all of the actual and potential needs in the local authority area for NHS or social care services.

78 [2014] EWHC 1182 (Admin).

5.60 Taken together, sections 3 and 14Z11 of the NHS Act 2006, together with regs 34–36 of the RSR Regs 2012, sets out a framework under which:

a) CCGs must have an annual commissioning plan.
b) The annual commissioning plan needs to include or reference the individual policies adopted by the CCG. These policies set out agreed care pathways and define clinical criteria which set out which patients are entitled to NHS-funded healthcare for each medical condition. Once a policy has been agreed, patients are entitled to expect that the CCG will routinely agree to fund the medical treatment set out in the for policy patients who fulfil the stated clinical criteria. CCGs have a duty to publicise their commissioning policies on their website. Thus, for example, patients are entitled to know what approach a CCG takes to funding IVF treatment.
c) Patients whose clinical criteria are outside the scope of a policy will not be routinely funded for NHS care, even if the medical treatment has the potential to benefit an individual patient. However, there is always the possibility of the CCG making an individual decision to depart from its own policy. All CCGs are required to have policies which explain how they will take decisions when asked to provide funding outside their normal policies. These are usually known as IFA policies. Where a patient is seeking funding for a treatment for a condition for which the CCG has a policy, the essential question is whether the CCG should provide this patient with NHS funding to support a medical treatment even though the other patients with the same clinical presentation are being denied funding for the same treatment. This is, of course, a controversial issue, and CCGs will need to formulate such policies with great care to avoid legal challenges by other patients denied the same treatment.

5.61 Both section 3 of the NHS Act 2006 and the RSR Regs 2012 place CCGs under the legal duty to 'make arrangements'. This form of words is used in many other places in the NHS Act 2006 and in other legislation which imposes statutory duties on public bodies. The nature of the duty to make arrangements gives a considerable amount of discretion to CCGs. Subject to other legal constraints CCGs are able to decide for themselves what decision-making processes they should adopt. However, once the CCG has put its 'arrangements' in place, the public body comes under a public law legal duty to follow its own procedures when making commissioning decisions.

5.62 Some guidance about the meaning of a duty to make 'arrangements' was given by Underhill LJ in the first instance decision of *R (Nash) v Barnet LBC (Capita plc)*. The judge said:[79]

> ... the reference to 'making arrangements' would make it clear that the duty was concerned with intentions rather than outcome. It may also be that the draftsman wanted to emphasise the need to build the fulfilment of the best value duty into authorities' plans and procedures. Or perhaps it is just circumlocution. But, whatever the explanation, the important point for present purposes is what the arrangements are aimed at, namely securing improvements in the way in which authorities perform their functions.

79 [2013] EWHC 1067 (Admin) at para 70.

5.63 Regulation 36 of the RSR Regs 2012 provides that the CCG must publicise the arrangements it has made on its website. It is, arguably, unlawful for a CCG or NHS England to make commissioning decisions in accordance with procedures which are not publicised.

Obligations on CCGs in exercising their functions

5.64 CCGs are under a number of further statutory duties in exercising their functions. When exercising its functions, a CCG must:

a) act with a view to securing that health services are provided in a way which promotes the NHS Constitution;[80]
b) promote awareness of the NHS Constitution among patients, staff and members of the public;[81]
c) exercise its functions effectively, efficiently and economically;[82]
d) act with a view to securing continuous improvement in the quality of services provided to individuals for or in connection with the prevention, diagnosis or treatment of illness,[83] and in particular must act with a view to securing continuous improvement in outcomes that are achieved from the provision of the services;[84]
e) have regard to the need to i) reduce inequalities between patients with respect to their ability to access health services, and ii) reduce inequalities between patients with respect to the outcomes achieved for them by the provision of health services;[85]
f) act with a view to enabling patients to make choices with respect to aspects of health services provided to them[86] (ie support patient choice);
g) obtain advice appropriate for enabling it effectively to discharge its functions from persons who (taken together) have a broad range of professional expertise in i) the prevention, diagnosis or treatment of illness, and ii) the protection or improvement of public health; and have regard to any guidance published by NHS England on complying with this duty;[87]
h) promote innovation in the provision of health services (including innovation in the arrangements made for their provision);[88]
i) promote research on matters relevant to the health service and the use in the health service of evidence obtained from research;[89]

80 Section 14P(1)(a).
81 Section 14P(1)(b).
82 Section 14Q.
83 Section 14R(1).
84 Section 14R(2). Outcomes include outcomes which show the effectiveness of the services, their safety and quality of the experience undergone by the patients (section 14R(3)(a)–(c)). In discharging this duty regard must be had to any guidance published under section 14Z8.
85 Section 14T.
86 Section 14V.
87 Section 14W(1) and (3). NHS England may publish guidance to CCGs on the s14W(1) duty by virtue of s14W(2).
88 Section 14X.
89 Section 14Y.

j) have regard to the need to promote education and training for employees and future employees of the health service;[90]

k) act with a view to securing that health services are provided in an integrated way where it considers that this would:
   i) improve the quality of those services (including the outcomes that are achieved from their provision;
   ii) reduce inequalities between persons with respect to their ability to access those services, or
   iii) reduce inequalities between persons with respect to the outcomes achieved for them by the provision of those services;[91]

l) act with a view to securing that the provision of health services is integrated with the provision of health-related services or social care services where it considers that this would:
   i) improve the quality of the health services (including the outcomes that are achieved from the provision of those services);
   ii) reduce inequalities between persons with respect to their ability to access those services; or
   iii) reduce inequalities between persons with respect to the outcomes achieved for them by the provision of those services.[92]

5.65 As can be seen, there is significant variation in the context, wording and formulation of the duties to which CCGs are subject. Not all of the duties will be relevant to each decision taken by a CCG. It is difficult to describe in the abstract precisely what each of these duties requires, as much will depend on the particular circumstances.

5.66 As a general point, many (though not all) of the duties are procedural rather than substantive: the CCG must 'have regard' to certain factors or 'act with a view' to achieving specified objectives. These are procedural duties which require specific factors to be taken into account, or specific objectives to be targeted by a CCG when discharging its functions, rather than obligations to actually achieve a particular outcome. They do not impose obligations on a CCG to make specific commissioning decisions (such as continuing to commission a particular service).

5.67 Given the number and scope of the duties, common sense is needed when determining whether a CCG can demonstrate that, at some level, every decision has been guided by a decision-making process that has properly taken each of the above duties into account. Not every duty will be relevant to every decision.

5.68 Even those duties which are substantive rather than procedural (for example, the duty on CCGs to promote innovation in the provision of health services) involves the exercise of specialist judgment as to how it is achieved, against which a court will only interfere if the duty has been overlooked when taking a decision to which it was relevant, or the judgments reached are *Wednesbury* unreasonable. NHS England is under a similar set of procedural duties. Readers are referred to the section of chapter 4 on NHS England for a discussion on the meaning and effect of these duties.

90 Section 14Z.
91 Section 14Z1(1).
92 Section 14Z1(2).

Patient and public involvement

5.69 Section 14U of the NHS Act 2006 requires CCGs, in the exercise of their functions, to 'promote the involvement of patients, and their carers and representatives (if any), in decisions which relate to the prevention or diagnosis of illness in the patients, or their care or treatment'. NHS England has published guidance for CCGs on the discharge of this duty,[93] and CCGs are under a statutory duty to have regard to that guidance.[94] NHS England currently provide an 'involvement hub' with a range of resources on patient involvement.[95] Current statutory guidance is contained in *Involving people in their own health and care: Statutory guidance for clinical commissioning groups and NHS England*.[96]

5.70 Public involvement is secured through the public law legal duty on CCGs to act in accordance with their own policies. This once a CCG has adopted a patient and public involvement (PPI) policy in order to comply with the requirements of section 14Z2 of the NHS Act 2006, patients and members of the public can hold the CCG to account by requiring its decision-making processes to be conducted with the involvement of patients, as set out in the policy. The section applies in relation to any health services which are, or are to be, provided pursuant to arrangements made by a clinical commissioning group in the exercise of its functions ('commissioning arrangements'). The CCG must:

> (2) . . . make arrangements to secure that individuals to whom the services are being or may be provided are involved (whether by being consulted or provided with information or in other ways)–
> (a) in the planning of the commissioning arrangements by the group,
> (b) in the development and consideration of proposals by the group for changes in the commissioning arrangements where the implementation of the proposals would have an impact on the manner in which the services are delivered to the individuals or the range of health services available to them, and
> (c) in decisions of the group affecting the operation of the commissioning arrangements where the implementation of the decisions would (if made) have such an impact.
> (3) The clinical commissioning group must include in its constitution–
> (a) a description of the arrangements made by it under subsection (2), and
> (b) a statement of the principles which it will follow in implementing those arrangements.

5.71 The duty is broadly framed, leaving an element of discretion with the CCG on how best to comply with it both generally and for a particular set of changes (consultation, provision of information or some other way), provided the method used is in accordance with the policy. NHS England has published guidance for CCGs on the discharge of their functions under section 14Z2,[97] and a CCG must have regard to the current or any

93 Section 14U(2).
94 Section 14U(3).
95 See www.england.nhs.uk/participation/.
96 See www.england.nhs.uk/wp-content/uploads/2017/04/ppp-involving-people-health-care-guidance.pdf.
97 Section 14Z2(4).

adapted form of such guidance.[98] The current statutory guidance is *Patient and public participation in commissioning health and care: Statutory guidance for clinical commissioning groups and NHS England.*[99]

Transparency in decision-making and scrutiny of CCG performance

5.72 As set out above, the meetings of the governing bodies of CCGs should be open to the public and key CCG documents on which decisions should be based, including their constitutions and commissioning plans, have to be published.

5.73 Section 14Z15(1) further requires CCGs, in each financial year other than their first financial year, to prepare an annual report on how it has discharged its functions in the previous financial year. The annual report must, in particular:

a) explain how the CCG has discharged its duties under sections 14R, 14T and 14Z2; and
b) review the extent to which the group has contributed to the delivery of any joint health and wellbeing strategy to which it was required to have regard under section 116B(1)(b) of the Local Government and Public Involvement in Health Act 2007.[100] In preparing the review, the CCG must consult each relevant HWB.[101]

5.74 NHS England may give directions to CCGs as to the form and content of an annual report.[102] CCGs must supply a copy of their annual report to NHS England before the date specified by NHS England in a direction, and must publish the annual report and hold a meeting for the purpose of presenting the report to members of the public.[103]

5.75 NHS England is required by section 14Z16(1) of the NHS Act 2006 to conduct a performance assessment of each CCG in respect of each financial year, being an assessment of 'how well the clinical commissioning group has discharged its functions during that year'.[104] As part of the assessment, NHS England must consult each HWB as to its views on the CCG's contribution to the delivery of any joint health and wellbeing strategy.[105] NHS England must publish a report in respect of each financial year, containing a summary of the results of each performance assessment conducted by it in respect of that year.[106] The framing of this provision is slightly unusual because NHS England has a duty to conduct an assessment but has no duty to publish the full assessment, or even to provide a copy to the CCG or any HWB. It would seem good practice for

98 Section 14Z2(5).
99 See www.england.nhs.uk/wp-content/uploads/2017/05/patient-and-public-participation-guidance.pdf.
100Section 14Z15(2).
101 Section 14Z15(3).
102 Section 14Z15(4).
103 Section 14Z15(5)–(6).
104 Section 14Z16(2).
105 Section 14Z16(4).
106 Section 14Z16(6).

NHS England to do so. In any event, the full assessment would almost certainly be a document that would be required to be disclosed under any freedom of information (FOI) request.

5.76 Where NHS England has reason to believe a CCG might have failed, might be failing or might fail to discharge any of its functions[107] the powers in 14Z18 and 14Z19 apply. Where section 14Z18(1) applies, NHS England may:

> ... require a person mentioned in subsection (2) to provide to [NHS England] any information, documents, records or other items that [NHS England] considers it necessary or expedient to have for the purposes of any of its functions in relation to the clinical commissioning group.
>
> Subsection (2) includes CCGs and 'any member or employee of the group who has possession or control of the item in question'. Section 14Z18(3) places the CCG/employee under a statutory duty to comply with the request under section 14Z18(1).

5.77 Where section 14Z19(1) applies, NHS England may:

> ... require the clinical commissioning group to provide it with an explanation of any matter which relates to the exercise by the group of any of its functions, including an explanation of how the group is proposing to exercise any of its functions.

NHS England may require the explanation to be given orally at such time and place as NHS England specifies, or in writing,[108] and the CCG must comply.[109]

5.78 By s14Z21, where NHS England is satisfied that a CCG is failing or has failed to discharge any of its functions,[110] or there is a significant risk that a CCG will fail to do so, it may direct the CCG or the accountable officer for the group 'to cease to perform any functions for such period or periods as may be specified in the direction'. NHS England may also:

a) terminate the appointment of the CCG's accountable officer and appoint another person to be its accountable officer;[111]
b) vary the constitution of the CCG;[112]
c) dissolve the CCG;[113]
d) exercise the functions of the CCG which are the subject of a direction, or direct another CCG to exercise those functions.[114] The CCG is under a statutory duty to co-operate with NHS England / the CCG which takes over those functions.[115]

107 Section 14Z17.
108 Section 14Z19(2).
109 Section 14Z19(3).
110 A failure to discharge a function includes a failure to discharge it properly, and a failure to discharge a function properly includes a failure to discharge it consistently with what NHS England considers to be the interests of the health service (section 14Z21(14)).
111 Section 14Z21(4).
112 Section 14Z21(6).
113 Section 14Z21(7).
114 Section 14Z21(8).
115 Section 14Z21(9).

5.79 Section 14Z22 imposes procedural requirements on NHS England before it can dissolve a CCG under section 14Z21(7). NHS England must:

a) consult the CCG and relevant local authorities, providing them with a statement explaining that is proposes to dissolve the CCG and its reasons for doing so;
b) after the consultation, publish a report containing its response to the consultation, including the reasons for dissolving the CCG, if NHS England decides to do so.

5.80 There are no specific procedural requirements that NHS England must follow before it exercises any of the other powers. The fact that there are specific procedural requirements for the exercise of one of these powers, namely the dissolution of the CCG, suggests that it is unlikely that there are any other procedural steps that NHS England has to take before, for example, issuing directions to a CCG. However, these are only default powers and thus NHS England is only entitled to exercise them if it is satisfied (after reasonable inquiry) that the CCG has defaulted or is likely to default.

CCG duties relating to NHS England

5.81 CCGs are under a statutory duty to 'assist and support' NHS England in discharging its duty under section 13E of the NHS Act 2006 to secure continuous improvement in the quality of primary medical services.[116] Given that the members of the CCG are GP practices that are all providing primary medical services, this duty places an obligation on CCGs to focus on ensuring that their members are continuing to improve the services that they provide to NHS patients. However, a CCG is highly unlikely to be in breach of this duty simply by the fact that an individual GP practice which was a member of the CCG failed to deliver services of an acceptable standard. The CCG may be in legal difficulties if it attempted to support the member practice's low standards as opposed to seeking continuous improvement in those services.

5.82 NHS England is under a statutory duty to publish guidance for CCGs on the discharge of their commissioning functions, and CCGs are under a corresponding statutory duty to have regard to that guidance.[117] The current guidance is contained in a number of different NHS England documents, including passages within NHS England's: *Managing conflicts of interest: revised statutory guidance for CCGs 2017*[118] (which is considered below).

5.83 Where NHS England provides assistance or support to a CCG under section 14Z10, subject to terms or conditions, the CCG is under a statutory duty to comply with those terms and conditions.[119]

116 Section 14S.

117 Section 14Z8.

118 See www.england.nhs.uk/wp-content/uploads/2017/06/revised-ccg-coi-guidance-jul–17.pdf.

119 Section 14Z10(5).

Powers and duties relating to joint working

5.84 Section 14Z3(1)–(2) empowers CCGs to make arrangements for the functions of the CCGs to being exercised jointly, or for one CCG to exercise the functions of another CCG on its behalf. Where functions are exercised jointly, they may be exercised by a joint committee of the CCGs.[120] Under such arrangements, a CCG may:

a) make payments to another CCG;[121]
b) make the services of its employees or other resources available to another CCG;[122]
c) establish and maintain a pooled fund.[123]

5.85 A CCG may also arrange for any of its commissioning functions to be exercised jointly with a combined authority, including functions being exercised on behalf of another CCG, or functions exercised by CCGs jointly under section 14Z3 of the NHS Act 2006.[124] Where any commissioning functions of a CCG (or CCGs) are exercised jointly with a combined authority under subsection (1) or (2), they may be exercised by a joint committee of the group (or groups) and the authority.[125] Arrangements under this section may be on such terms and conditions (including terms as to payment) as may be agreed between the CCG (or CCGs) and the combined authority.[126]

5.86 By section 14Z9(1) of the NHS Act 2006, NHS England may at the request of a CCG, exercise on its behalf any of its functions under section 3 or 3A, and any other functions of the CCG which are related to those functions. NHS England and the CCG may also make arrangements for the functions of the CCG to be exercised jointly with NHS England[127] and, where this occurs, the functions may be exercised by a joint committee of NHS England and the CCG.[128] Arrangements made by the CCG under this section 'may be on such terms and conditions (including terms as to payment) as may be agreed between the Board and the clinical commissioning group'.[129]

Financial provision

5.87 Section 14Z5(1) of the NHS Act 2006 provides that CCGs have the power to do anything 'specified in section 7(2)(a), (b) and (e)–(h) of the Health and Medicines Act 1988 (provision of goods etc) for the purpose of making additional income available for improving the health service', subject to the limitation in subsection (2) that the power may only be exercised to the

120 Section 14Z3(2A).
121 Section 14Z3(3)(a).
122 Section 14Z3(3)(b).
123 Section 14Z3(4)-(5).
124 Section 14Z23(1)(b) and (2).
125 Section 14Z23(4).
126 Section 14Z23(5).
127 Section 14Z9(1A).
128 Section 14Z9(1B).
129 Section 14Z9(3).

extent that 'its exercise does not to any significant extent interfere with the performance by the group of its functions'. The section 7(2) powers conferred on CCGs are:

> (a) to acquire, produce, manufacture and supply goods;
> (b) to acquire land by agreement and manage and deal with land;
> . . .
> (e) to provide instruction for any person;
> (f) to develop and exploit ideas and exploit intellectual property;
> (g) to do anything whatsoever which appears to [the CCG] to be calculated to facilitate, or to be conducive or incidental to, the exercise of any power conferred by this subsection; and
> (h) to make such charge as [the CCG] considers appropriate for anything that [the CCG] does in the exercise of any such power and to calculate any such charge on any basis that [the CCG] considers to be the appropriate commercial basis.'

5.88 By section 14Z6, CCGs may 'make payments by way of grant or loan to a voluntary organisation which provides or arranges for the provision of services which are similar to the services in respect of which the group has functions', which may be made 'subject to such terms and conditions as the group considers appropriate'. While this is an express power, CCGs should be careful about the use of such powers where a grant could be seen as a contract for services, and thus procurement rules may arise in relation to the proposed arrangement.

5.89 Under section 14Z7(1) NHS England may publish a document specifying the circumstances in which a clinical commissioning group is liable to make a payment to a person in respect of services provided by that person in pursuance of arrangements made by another clinical commissioning group in the discharge of its commissioning functions, and how the amount of any such payment is to be determined. As far as our researches have established, no such document has yet been published. Section 14Z7(2) requires CCGs to make payments in accordance with any document published under subsection (1). Where the requirement to make payments under subsection (2) arises, no other CCG is liable to make the payment and 'any obligation of another clinical commissioning group to make the payment ceases to have effect'.[130] Sums payable by virtue of subsection (2) may be recovered summarily as a civil debt (without prejudice to any other method of recovery).[131]

Disclosure of information

5.90 By the nature of their functions, CCGs will be in the possession of a substantial volume of confidential and sensitive personal data. CCGs are 'data controllers', and thus have all the usual duties of a data controller under the Data Protection Act 1998 in respect of personal data. The circumstances in which the NHS Act 2006 permits a CCG to disclose information generally obtained in the exercise of its functions (which may

130 Section 14Z7(3)–(4).
131 Section 14Z7(5).

or may not include personal data relating to any individual) are specified by section 14Z23(1). Information may be disclosed if:

(a) the information has previously been lawfully disclosed to the public,
(b) the disclosure is made under or pursuant to regulations under section 113 or 114 of the Health and Social Care (Community Health and Standards) Act 2003 (complaints about health care or social services),
(c) the disclosure is made in accordance with any enactment or court order,
(d) the disclosure is necessary or expedient for the purposes of protecting the welfare of any individual,
(e) the disclosure is made to any person in circumstances where it is necessary or expedient for the person to have the information for the purpose of exercising functions of that person under any enactment,
(f) the disclosure is made for the purpose of facilitating the exercise of any of the clinical commissioning group's functions,
(g) the disclosure is made in connection with the investigation of a criminal offence (whether or not in the United Kingdom), or
(h) the disclosure is made for the purpose of criminal proceedings (whether or not in the United Kingdom).

5.91 Further, by section 14Z23(2), paras (1)(a)–(c) and (h) have effect notwithstanding any rule of common law which would otherwise prohibit or restrict the disclosure. The rules under the Data Protection Act 1998 are not rules of common law but obligations which originate in a European Union Treaty. Accordingly, while the NHS Act 2006 gives CCGs certain powers to publish data, if any of that data amounts to personal data, the decision to publish that information also needs to be justified under the Data Protection Act 1998.

Public sector equality duty

5.92 CCGs established under section 14D of the NHS Act 2006 are listed in Schedule 19 to the Equality Act 2010 as being amongst those public bodies subject to the section 149 public sector equality duty (PSED). In exercising their functions, by section 149(1) CCGs must therefore have 'due regard' to the need to:

(a) eliminate discrimination, harassment, victimisation and any other conduct that is prohibited by or under this Act;
(b) advance equality of opportunity between persons who share a relevant protected characteristic and persons who do not share it;
(c) foster good relations between persons who share a relevant protected characteristic and persons who do not share it.

5.93 The protected characteristics for this purpose are:[132] age; disability; gender reassignment; pregnancy and maternity; race; religion or belief; sex; and sexual orientation.

5.94 The requirements of the PSED are considered in detail in the context of the secretary of state at paras 3.39–3.43. The same principles apply in the context of decision-making by CCGs.

132 See Equality Act 2010 s149(7).

Managing conflicts of interest

5.95 CCGs are public bodies whose members are all individuals or businesses which receive remuneration from the NHS. The actions of members of a CCG, both while acting on behalf of the CCG and when acting to promote the interests of GP practices, affect the finances of other NHS bodies and the finances of their own practices. Hence managing conflicts of interests in a transparent and effective manner was always going to be a difficult task for CCGs. That task has become significantly more difficult in an era where CCGs are involved in making decisions about primary care commissioning, since they are, in effect, making decisions that affect the financial interests of their own members. The effective management of potential conflicts of interest is thus of considerable importance because decisions which are made without the conflicts being recognised and properly managed are potentially open to legal challenge.

5.96 Section 14O of the NHS Act 2006 requires that:

(1) Each clinical commissioning group must maintain one or more registers of the interest of–
  (a) the members of the group,
  (b) the members of its governing body,
  (c) the members of its committees or sub-committees or of committees or sub-committees of its governing body, and
  (d) its employees.

(2) Each clinical commissioning group must publish the registers maintained under subsection (1) or make arrangements to ensure that members of the public have access to the registers on request.

(3) Each clinical commissioning group must make arrangements to ensure–
  (a) that a person mentioned in subsection (1) declares any conflict or potential conflict of interest that the person has in relation to a decision to be made in the exercise of the commissioning functions of the group,
  (b) that any such declaration is made as soon as practicable after the person becomes aware of the conflict or potential conflict and, in any event, within 28 days, and
  (c) that any such declaration is included in the registers maintained under subsection (1).

(4) Each clinical commissioning group must make arrangements for managing conflicts and potential conflicts of interest in such a way as to ensure that they do not, and do not appear to, affect the integrity of the group's decision-making processes.

(5) The Board must publish guidance for clinical commissioning groups on the discharge of their functions under this section.

(6) Each clinical commissioning group must have regard to guidance published under subsection (5).

(7) For the purposes of this section, the commissioning functions of a clinical commissioning group are the functions of the group in arranging for the provision of services as part of the health service.'

5.97 These measures are supplemented by the requirements set out above to ensure transparent decision-making by CCGs, such as the publication of their commissioning policies and the meetings of their governing bodies being held in public.

5.98 Detailed guidance is provided in NHS England's *Managing conflicts of interest: Revised statutory guidance for CCGs 2017.*[133] The guidance defines a conflict of interest as :

> . . . a set of circumstances by which a reasonable person would consider that an individual's ability to apply judgement or act, in the context of delivering, commissioning, or assuring taxpayer funded health and care services is, or could be, impaired or influenced by another interest they hold.[134]

The guidance continues that a conflict of interest might be actual or potential, and that 'the perception of an interest can be as damaging as an actual conflict of interest'.[135] Further, 'a benefit may arise from the making of a gain or the avoidance of a loss'.[136] The guidance continues that:

> 15. Conflicts of interest can arise in many situations, environments and forms of commissioning, with an increased risk in primary care commissioning, out-of-hours commissioning and involvement with integrated care organisations and new care models, as CCG staff may here find themselves in a position of being both commissioner and provider of services. Conflicts of interest can arise throughout the whole commissioning cycle from needs assessment, to procurement exercises, to contract monitoring.

5.99 The wide scope for potential conflicts of interests can be seen from the four types of interests specified (paragraph 16) as being relevant:

> i. **Financial interests:** This is where an individual may get direct financial benefits from the consequences of a commissioning decision. This could, for example, include being:
>
> - A director, including a non-executive director, or senior employee in a private company or public limited company or other organisation which is doing, or which is likely, or possibly seeking to do, business with health or social care organisations. This includes involvement with a potential provider of a new care model;
> - A shareholder (or similar ownership interests), a partner or owner of a private or not-for-profit company, business, partnership or consultancy which is doing, or which is likely, or possibly seeking to do, business with health or social care organisations;
> - A management consultant for a provider; or
> - A provider of clinical private practice.
>
> This could also include an individual being:
>
> - In employment outside of the CCG (see paragraph 79–81);
> - In receipt of secondary income;
> - In receipt of a grant from a provider;
> - In receipt of any payments (for example honoraria, one-off payments, day allowances or travel or subsistence) from a provider;
> - In receipt of research funding, including grants that may be received by the individual or any organisation in which they have an interest or role; and
> - Having a pension that is funded by a provider (where the value of this might be affected by the success or failure of the provider).

133 See www.england.nhs.uk/wp-content/uploads/2017/06/revised-ccg-coi-guidance-jul–17.pdf.

134 Paragraph 12.

135 Paragraph 14.

136 Paragraph 16.

ii. **Non-financial professional interests:** This is where an individual may obtain a non-financial professional benefit from the consequences of a commissioning decision, such as increasing their professional reputation or status or promoting their professional career. This may, for example, include situations where the individual is:

- An advocate for a particular group of patients;
- A GP with special interests e.g., in dermatology, acupuncture etc.;
- An active member of a particular specialist professional body (although routine GP membership of the Royal College of General Practitioners (RCGP), British Medical Association (BMA) or a medical defence organisation would not usually by itself amount to an interest which needed to be declared);
- An advisor for the Care Quality Commission (CQC) or the National Institute for Health and Care Excellence (NICE);
- Engaged in a research role;
- The development and holding of patents and other intellectual property rights which allow staff to protect something that they create, preventing unauthorised use of products or the copying of protected ideas; or
- GPs and practice managers, who are members of the governing body or committees of the CCG, should declare details of their roles and responsibilities held within their GP practices.

iii. **Non-financial personal interests:** This is where an individual may benefit personally in ways which are not directly linked to their professional career and do not give rise to a direct financial benefit. This could include, for example, where the individual is:

- A voluntary sector champion for a provider;
- A volunteer for a provider;
- A member of a voluntary sector board or has any other position of authority in or connection with a voluntary sector organisation;
- Suffering from a particular condition requiring individually funded treatment;
- A member of a lobby or pressure group with an interest in health and care.

iv. **Indirect interests:** This is where an individual has a close association with an individual who has a financial interest, a non-financial professional interest or a non-financial personal interest in a commissioning decision (as those categories are described above) for example, a:

- Spouse / partner;
- Close family member or relative e.g., parent, grandparent, child, grandchild or sibling;
- Close friend or associate; or
- Business partner.

A declaration of interest for a 'business partner' in a GP partnership should include all relevant collective interests of the partnership, and all interests of their fellow GP partners (which could be done by cross referring to the separate declarations made by those GP partners, rather than by repeating the same information verbatim).

Whether an interest held by another person gives rise to a conflict of interest will depend upon the nature of the relationship between that person and the individual, and the role of the individual within the CCG.

17. CCGs should provide clear guidance to their employees, members and governing body and committee members on what might constitute a conflict of interest, providing examples of situations that may arise.

5.100 The guidance rightly emphasises that these examples 'are not exhaustive and a common-sense approach should be adopted'. Further, the:

> . . . CCG should exercise discretion on a case by case basis . . . in deciding whether any other role, relationship or interest may impair or otherwise influence the individual's judgement or actions in their role within the CCG. If so, this should be declared and appropriately managed.[137]

5.101 Paragraphs 19–30 of the guidance set out the general principles for the management of conflicts of interest. The guidance emphasises[138] that CCG should observe:

a) The 7 principles of public life, namely:
   i) **Selflessness** – Holders of public office should act solely in terms of the public interest. They should not do so in order to gain financial or other benefits for themselves, their family or their friends;
   ii) **Integrity** – Holders of public office should not place themselves under any financial or other obligation to outside individuals or organisations that might seek to influence them in the performance of their official duties;
   iii) **Objectivity** – In carrying out public business, including making public appointments, awarding contracts, or recommending individuals for rewards and benefits, holders of public office should make choices on merit;
   iv) **Accountability** – Holders of public office are accountable for their decisions and actions to the public and must submit themselves to whatever scrutiny is appropriate to their office;
   v) **Openness** – Holders of public office should be as open as possible about all the decisions and actions they take. They should give reasons for their decisions and restrict information only when the wider public interest clearly demands;
   vi) **Honesty** – Holders of public office have a duty to declare any private interests relating to their public duties and to take steps to resolve any conflicts arising in a way that protects the public interest;
   vii) **Leadership** – Holders of public office should promote and support these principles by leadership and example.

b) The Good Governance Standards for Public Services (2004), Office for Public Management (OPM) and Chartered Institute of Public Finance and Accountancy (CIPFA);[139]

c) The seven key principles of the NHS Constitution, namely that;
   i) The NHS provides a comprehensive service available to all;
   ii) Access to NHS services is based on clinical need, not an individual's ability to pay;
   iii) The NHS aspires to the highest standards of excellence and professionalism;
   iv) The NHS aspires to put patients at the heart of everything it does;
   v) The NHS works across organisational boundaries and in partnership with other organisations in the interest of patients, local communities and the wider population;

137 Paragraph 18.

138 Paragraph 20.

139 *The Good Governance Standards for Public Services*, 2004, OPM and CIPFA, see www.opm.co.uk/wp-content/uploads/2014/01/Good-Governance-Standard-for-Public-Services.pdf.

vi) The NHS is committed to providing best value for taxpayers' money and the most effective, fair and sustainable use of finite resources;
vii) The NHS is accountable to the public, communities and patients that it serves;

d) The requirements of the Equality Act 2010;
e) The UK Corporate Governance Code;[140]
f) Standards for members of NHS boards and CCG governing bodies in England.[141]

5.102 Useful guidance for CCGs is provided by paras 22–23, which recommends that:

22 . . . to support the management of conflicts of interest, CCGs should:

- **Do business appropriately**: Conflicts of interest become much easier to identify, avoid and/or manage when the processes for needs assessments, consultation mechanisms, commissioning strategies and procurement procedures are right from the outset, because the rationale for all decision making will be clear and transparent and should withstand scrutiny;
- **Be proactive, not reactive:** Commissioners should seek to identify and minimise the risk of conflicts of interest at the earliest possible opportunity;
- **Be balanced, sensible and proportionate**: Rules should be clear and robust but not overly prescriptive or restrictive. They should ensure that decision-making is transparent and fair whilst not being overly constraining, complex or cumbersome;
- **Be transparent:** Document clearly the approach and decisions taken at every stage in the commissioning cycle so that a clear audit trail is evident;
- Create an **environment and culture** where individuals feel supported and confident in declaring relevant information and raising any concerns.

23. In addition to the above, CCGs need to bear in mind:

- A perception of wrongdoing, impaired judgement or undue influence can be as detrimental as any of them actually occurring;
- If in doubt, it is better to assume the existence of a conflict of interest and manage it appropriately rather than ignore it;
- For a conflict of interest to exist, financial gain is not necessary.'

5.103 The guidance continues to make detailed further provision and recommendations for specific situations and topics, including:

a) gifts and hospitality (paras 31–63);
b) outside employment (paras 79–81);
c) managing conflicts of interest at meetings (paras 82–92);
d) primary care commissioning committees and subcommittees (paras 93–104);
e) procurement and awarding grants (paras 118–130);
f) internal audit (paras 142–144);
g) raising concerns and reporting breaches (paras 145–155).

140 *UK Corporate governance code*, see www.frc.org.uk/Our-Work/Codes-Standards/Corporategovernance/UK-Corporate-Governance-Code.aspx.

141 *Standards for members of NHS boards and CCG governing bodies in England*, see www.professionalstandards.org.uk/publications/detail/standards-for-members-of-nhs-boards-andclinical-commissioning-group-governing-bodies-in-england.

5.104 In practice, to manage conflicts of interest it will important for CCGs to have clear conflict of interest polices, a register of potential conflicts of interest and open, transparent and properly recorded decision making, together with robust auditing and well-established systems for the raising of concerns and reporting of breaches. As set out above, each CCG's arrangements for complying with the section 140 duties must be set out in its constitution.

CHAPTER 6

Public health[1]

1 By Alistair Mills. I am grateful for comments from Dr Susanna Mills and David Lock QC on a previous draft. Any errors, of course, remain my own.

> True security is based on people's welfare – on a thriving economy, on strong public health and education programmes, and on fundamental respect for our common humanity.
>
> *Ban Ki-Moon, UN Secretary-General*[2]

Introduction

6.1 This chapter will seek to answer the following questions:

- What is public health?
- Who are the different actors in the public health process?
- What are the powers and duties of the actors in the public health sector?
- What duties are there in relation to cooperation concerning public health?
- What charges may be made for public health services?
- What is the impact of the Healthy Start Scheme and Welfare Food (Amendment) Regulations 2005?[3]
- What are the powers under the Public Health (Control of Disease) Act 1984?
- What impact does European Union (EU) law have upon public health?

What is public health?

6.2 A number of different definitions or approaches to the concept of public health have been provided. Public health is not defined in legislation relating to the National Health Service (NHS), and the answer to the question is made more complicated by the fact that 'public health' has been given a wide range of meanings over time:[4] in Victorian legislation, it related to matters so diverse that they would in the 21st century be dealt with by the planning regime,[5] regulation of water companies,[6] or employment protection.[7] While these matters are capable of having an impact upon public health in the modern sense, they are beyond the scope of this chapter.

6.3 In *R (National Aids Trust) v National Health Service Commissioning Board (NHS England)*,[8] Longmore LJ described certain legislative provisions as 'refer[ring] to a number of services which would typically fall

2 UN Secretary-General's message to Peace Memorial Ceremony, 6 August 2013, www.un.org/sg/en/content/sg/statement/2013–08–06/secretary-generals-message-peace-memorial-ceremony-delivered-ms.

3 SI No 3262.

4 The phrase can still be used to mean 'environmental hygiene': *Cross on local government law*, Bailey (ed) (Sweet & Maxwell), para 19–01.

5 Public Health (Buildings in Streets) Act 1888 s3 (prohibition on bringing buildings forward in urban areas).

6 Public Health Act 1875 s55 ('pure and wholesome water').

7 Public Health (Fruit Pickers Lodgings) Act 1882 s2 (the power of local authorities to secure decent lodging and accommodation of persons engaged in hop-picking within their area to extend to those picking fruit and vegetables).

8 [2016] EWCA Civ 1100, (2017) 20 CCLR 30.

within the description "public health" '.[9] These provisions concern the medical inspection of school pupils, weighing and measuring of children, and powers in relation to research.[10] Longmore LJ considered that the fact that health services are preventative does not necessarily make them part of public health functions. Neither did the fact that services constituted treatments mean that they were not part of public health functions.[11] In the same case the judge said:[12] 'The distinction between public health functions and non-public health functions must be sought in some distinction other than that between prevention and cure'. It might be thought that this says where the dividing line should not be placed but says little about where it should lie.

6.4 Sir Donald Acheson provided the following, still widely accepted, definition of 'public health' in his landmark report *Public Health in England*:[13]

> . . . the science and art of preventing disease, prolonging life, and promoting health through the organised efforts of society.

6.5 An editorial in the *Journal of public health* provided the following guidance (subject to heavy caveat):[14]

> . . . if you know that somebody benefits but you can't say who – and particularly if the recipients are asymptomatic – then it is probably public health.

6.6 The Faculty of Public Health states that public health concerns groups of people rather than individuals, and is concerned with 'the bigger picture'.[15]

6.7 The UK Public Health Association notes the different definitions of public health used by different organisations.[16] It considers that public health is an 'approach'. The focus is upon society as opposed to being focused on individual patients. It includes prevention of illness and disease, as well as promoting health and well-being.

6.8 The UK Public Health Association identifies three main priorities for public health:[17]

1) health inequalities;
2) sustainable development;
3) anti-health forces.

6.9 Not all of these three priorities will be met by the NHS. The Secretary of State for Health and Social Care has a specific target duty concerning seeking to reduce health inequalities.[18] The quest for sustainable development is largely pursued through the planning system, and is the watchword of the *National*

9 At para 15.
10 NHS Act 2006 Sch 1 paras 1–7B and 13, considered in further detail below.
11 *National Aids Trust*, para 33.
12 At para 33.
13 Stationery Office, 1988.
14 Eugene Milne, 'What is public health?' (2016) 38(4) *Journal of Public Health* 633, 634.
15 See www.fph.org.uk/uploads/about_us_leaflet_2007.pdf.
16 See www.ukpha.org.uk/about-us/index.html.
17 See www.ukpha.org.uk/about-us/index.html.
18 NHS Act 2006 s1C.

Planning Policy Framework,[19] which is the responsibility of the Secretary of State for Communities and Local Government. Anti-health forces are likely to be within the purview of the Secretary of State for Health and Social Care, although other state institutions play a key role (such as the police and social services who work to prevent injuries from domestic violence).[20]

Who are the different actors in the public health process?

6.10 A number of different bodies have a role to play in the process of maintaining and promoting public health. The main legal powers and duties are held by:

- local authorities;
- the Secretary of State for Health and Social Care;
- NHS England.[21]

Local authorities

6.11 The reforms brought about by the Health and Social Care Act (HSCA) 2012 restored the local authorities to their position as providers of public health services. This had been the position prior to 1948 and, to some extent, had reflected practice between 1948 and 2013 in areas such as the control of infectious diseases where local authorities continued to play a key role. A 'local authority' for the purposes of the legislation means:[22]

(a) a county council in England;
(b) a district council in England, other than a council for a district in a county for which there is a county council;
(c) a London borough council;
(d) the Council of the Isles of Scilly;
(e) the Common Council of the City of London.

6.12 Local authorities are required, acting jointly with the secretary of state, to appoint a Director of Public Health, who has responsibility for public health functions.[23] The appointment is terminable by the local authority, having consulted the secretary of state.[24] The secretary of state has the power to direct the local authority to review a director's performance, and investigate any failings, and consider taking certain steps, as well as reporting to the secretary of state on action taken in relation to the direction.[25]

19 See www.gov.uk/guidance/national-planning-policy-framework; for judicial decisions interpreting the *National Planning Policy Framework*, see www.landmarkchambers.co.uk/nppf.

20 See, for instance, the guidance on the packaging of tobacco products at www.gov.uk/government/publications/packaging-of-tobacco-products.

21 NHS England's role in what may be broadly conceived as public health was considered in *R (National Aids Trust) v National Health Service Commissioning Board (NHS England)* [2016] EWCA Civ 1100, (2017) 20 CCLR 30.

22 NHS Act 2006 s2B(5).

23 NHS Act 2006 s73A(1).

24 NHS Act 2006 s73A(5), (6).

25 NHS Act 2006 s73A(4).

6.13 The responsibilities of directors of public health prescribed by the secretary of state under section 73A(1)(f) of the National Health Service Act (NHS Act) 2006 are set out at regulation 14 of the NHS Bodies and Local Authorities (Partnership Arrangements, Care Trusts, Public Health and Local Healthwatch) Regulations (Partnership Arrangements Regs) 2012:[26]

(a) any of the [local] authority's functions arising from it being an authority which must be consulted pursuant to section 5(3)(bb) (statement of licensing policy) of the Licensing Act 2003;

(b) any of the authority's functions arising from it being a responsible authority, by virtue of sections 13(4)(bb) (authorised persons and responsible authorities), 69(4)(bb) (authorised persons and responsible authorities) or 172B(4)(da) (procedural requirements for early morning alcohol restriction order) of the Licensing Act 2003, for the purposes of the following sections of that Act–

  (i) sections 18, 35 and 41B (representations by a responsible authority in relation to applications for, or to vary, premises licences);
  (ii) section 31 (representations by a responsible authority in relation to determination of application for provisional statement);
  (iii) sections 51, 52 and 53 (applications and representations by a responsible authority for and in relation to a review of premises licences);
  (iv) section 53C (representations by a responsible authority in relation to summary reviews of premises licences);
  (v) sections 72, 85 and 86B (representations by a responsible authority in relation to applications concerning club premises certificates);
  (vi) sections 87, 88 and 89 (applications and representations by a responsible authority for and in relation to a review of club premises certificates);
  (vii) section 96 (powers of a responsible authority in relation to inspection of club premises);
  (viii) section 167 (representations by a responsible authority in relation to review of premises licence following closure order);
  (ix) section 172B (representations by a responsible authority in relation to early morning alcohol restriction orders).

(c) any of the authority's functions arising from its duty to provide, or arrange the provision of, healthy start vitamins under regulation 8A of the Healthy Start Scheme and Welfare Food (Amendment) Regulations 2005.

Secretary of State

6.14 The secretary of state has his or her own powers in relation to public health, set out further below. The secretary of state may arrange for other bodies to carry out his or her public health functions, namely:[27]

- NHS England;
- a clinical commissioning group (CCG);

26 SI No 3094. These functions are functions in the exercise of which a local authority must have regard to documents of the secretary of state produced for that purpose: reg 15; NHS Act 2006 s73B(2)(e).

27 NHS Act 2006 s7A.

- a local authority (as defined above);
- a combined authority.[28]

6.15 Section 13E of the NHS Act 2006 imposes public health responsibilities upon NHS England, which are considered further below. However, section 1H(2) of the NHS Act 2006 otherwise excludes NHS England from concurrent provision of public health services with the secretary of state (except when delegated by the secretary of state under section 7A).

6.16 Public Health England is a very significant body, employing around 5,500 staff (full-time equivalent). It performs a role in the provision of information, advocacy and providing specialist public health services.[29] Its strict legal role in its own right is limited, but will frequently discharge the secretary of state's public health duties.[30]

6.17 CCGs have some part to play: they must 'take appropriate steps for securing that [they are] properly prepared for dealing with a relevant emergency'.[31]

6.18 The Faculty of Public Health is an association of public health professionals. The Faculty provides examinations, accreditation and continuing professional development (CPD) in the field of public health, and is the main training and standard-setting body.[32] The Faculty was one of the bodies which agreed to Annex B to *Protecting the health of the local population.*[33]

The powers and duties of the actors in public health

Local authorities

Public Health (Control of Disease) Act 1984

6.19 Local authorities have specific powers under the Public Health (Control of Disease) Act 1984 (PHA 1984). These are considered in a separate section below dealing with that legislation.

28 'Combined authority' is defined in section 175 as meaning 'a combined authority established under section 103 of the Local Democracy, Economic Development and Construction Act 2009'.

29 See www.gov.uk/government/organisations/public-health-england/about.

30 *Protecting the health of the local population*, Public Health England and Local Government Association, May 2013, available online at www.gov.uk/government/uploads/system/uploads/attachment_data/file/199773/Health_Protection_in_Local_Authorities_Final.pdf.

31 NHS Act 2006 s252A(1).

32 See www.fph.org.uk/about_us and http://www.fph.org.uk/uploads/about_us_leaflet_2007.pdf.

33 *Protecting the health of the local population: the new health protection duty of local authorities under the Local Authorities (Public Health Functions and Entry to Premises by Local Healthwatch Representatives) Regulations 2013*, p10.

Primary duty

6.20 Local authorities have a general and wide discretion to expend money and take actions to discharge their overall duties concerning public health.[34] The primary duty is under section 2B of the NHS Act 2006 which requires local authorities to 'take such steps as [they] consider appropriate for improving the health of the people in [their] area'.[35] This is a target duty which gives a large amount of discretion to local authorities to decide how to perform their duties. However, as seen below, there are a number of specific public health interventions that must be carried out on a universal basis.

6.21 The steps which may be taken to comply with the section 2B duty include:[36]

(a) providing information and advice;
(b) providing service or facilities designed to promote healthy living (whether by helping individuals to address behaviour that is detrimental to health or in any other way);
(c) providing services or facilities for the prevention, diagnosis or treatment of illness;
(d) providing financial incentives to encourage individuals to adopt healthier lifestyles;
(e) providing assistance (including financial assistance) to help individuals to minimise any risks to health arising from their accommodation or environment;
(f) providing or participating in the provision of training for persons working or seeking to work in the field of health improvement;
(g) making available the services of any person or any facilities.

6.22 In exercising a range of public health functions, local authorities must have regard to any document published by the secretary of state for that purpose.[37]

6.23 Guidance issued by the secretary of state has sought to deal with the difficult question of when the socially beneficial functions which have been carried out by local authorities for many years come within the scope of health improvement services:[38]

> 1.17 Local authorities have always provided services that can have a bearing – sometimes a significant one – on the health of the local population. Currently they include social care, leisure, housing, planning refuse collection and many more. It does not follow that such services now have the purpose of improving health in terms of the 2012 Act. Social care is still social care, not health improvement. Local authority-run sports facilities

34 'The range of activity that local authorities might decide to engage in under their new health improvement duty is wide and goes beyond health services for individuals.' *Guidance: Local authority charging for public health activity*, 1.6 available online at www.gov.uk/government/publications/guidance-for-local-authority-charging-on-public-health-activity--2.

35 NHS Act 2006 s2B(1).

36 NHS Act 2006 s2B(3).

37 NHS Act 2006 s73B.

38 *Guidance: Local authority charging for public health activity*, 1.17–1.18, available online at www.gov.uk/government/publications/guidance-for-local-authority-charging-on-public-health-activity--2.

> may have the incidental benefit of improving health for some of those who use them but they can continue to be a leisure service – except when a local authority arranges access to them for certain individuals specifically to improve their health. Where a service has a number of purposes, local authorities should consider the primary purpose – if health improvement is only an incidental effect or ancillary purpose, the service should continue to be carried out under other local authority powers.
>
> 1.18 If, on the other hand, a local authority was providing a service under pre-existing powers that does have health improvement as its primary purpose (smoking cessation, for example) and continues to provide that service from April 2013, then it must do so under its new duty in section 2B and will no longer be able to charge for it (except in the limited circumstances described above).

6.24 It is notable that the secretary of state's view is that functions which had been provided by local authorities prior to the entry into force of the HSCA 2012 may be subsumed within the general duty in section 2B of the NHS Act 2006. Hence, for example, the general provision of local authority sports facilities delivers public health benefits but it not a public health service. However, an exercise class provided as part of rehabilitation for those recovering from a specific medical condition would be a public health measure (and so must be provided free of charge subject to the charging regime discussed below).

Students

6.25 Schedule 1 to the NHS Act 2006 includes a duty upon local authorities to provide for medical inspection and medical treatment of pupils in attendance at schools maintained by that local authority.[39] The governing body of a foundation, voluntary or foundation special school must make available to a local authority appropriate accommodation to assist it in making provision in relation to pupils at the school in question.[40] A local authority has a discretion in relation to the provision of inspection or treatment of students at a further education college maintained by the authority, or child or young person who is receiving primary or secondary education otherwise than at a school.[41] In relation to the further education college, the inspection or treatment may occur only with the consent of the governors of the institution.[42]

6.26 Where an educational establishment within its area is not maintained by the local authority, it may provide for medical inspection or treatment of junior or senior pupils in attendance, with the arrangement of the proprietor of the establishment.[43] The arrangement may involve payment of the local authority by the proprietor.[44]

6.27 Local authorities have specific powers in relation to schools under the PHA 1984, considered further below.

39 NHS Act 2006 Sch 1 para 1.
40 NHS Act 2006 Sch 1 para 5.
41 NHS Act 2006 Sch 1 para 2(1).
42 NHS Act 2006 Sch 1 para 4.
43 NHS Act 2006 Sch 1 para 2(2).
44 NHS Act 2006 Sch 1 para 3.

Undertaking public health functions of the secretary of state

6.28 Regulations may also require a local authority to undertake the public health functions of the secretary of state.[45] The Local Authorities (Public Health Functions and Entry to Premises by Local Healthwatch Representatives) Regulations (Public Health Functions Regs) 2013[46] sets out a number of public health duties upon local authorities:

- weighing and measuring children;
- health check assessment;
- universal health visitor reviews of pregnant women and infants;
- sexual health services;
- public health advice services;
- advice to other public bodies.

Weighing and measuring children

6.29 A local authority is under a duty, so far as is reasonably practicable, to provide for the weighing and measuring of children registered in a school in that local authority's area at the age of 4–5 and 10–11.[47]

Health check assessment

6.30 The duty is slightly different in relation to health check assessments: a local authority shall 'provide, or shall make arrangements to secure the provision of', health checks. Health checks are to be offered to 'eligible persons' in a local authority's area. Eligible persons are those who are aged 40–74. An eligible person shall be offered such a health check once in every 'relevant period'. A relevant period is essentially a period of five years.[48] A local authority is to act with the aim of increasing the percentage of eligible persons within its area participating in health checks.[49] Certain people are not eligible people:[50]

- those who have been diagnosed with particular conditions (including coronary heart disease, diabetes, hypertension and stroke);
- those who are being prescribed statins for the purpose of lowering cholesterol;
- those who, via some form of NHS health check, have been assessed as having a twenty percent or higher risk of having a 'cardiovascular event' during the following ten years.

6.31 Regulation 5 of the Public Health Functions Regs 2013 sets out various details of the health checks to be carried out:

(a) people between 65 and 74 are to be given information to raise awareness of dementia, and the availability of memory services;
(b) certain information which must be recorded is prescribed (including age, smoking status, body mass index, blood pressure, physical activity

45 NHS Act 2006 s6C.
46 SI No 351.
47 Public Health Functions Regs 2013 reg 3.
48 Public Health Functions Regs 2013 reg 4(4).
49 Public Health Functions Regs 2013 reg 4(6).
50 Public Health Functions Regs 2013 reg 4(5).

levels, and family history of coronary heart disease of parent or sibling when under 60 years), AUDIT[51] score of alcohol consumption);

(c) various pieces of information are to be communicated to the person who has undergone the health test (their BMI, cholesterol level, blood pressure, cardiovascular risk score, and AUDIT score);

(d) if the information is not carried out by the individual's general practitioner (GP), the information should be forwarded to his or her GP;

(e) the assessment must be carried out by a healthcare professional.[52]

6.32 Local authorities have a *discretion* as to whether to provide for the weighing of junior pupils in maintained schools; (by arrangement with the proprietor), in non-maintained schools in the local authority's area; (by arrangement with the proprietor) at registered early years providers.[53] The detail of the personal information to be disclosed is set out in Part 3 of the Local Authority (Public Health, Health and Wellbeing Boards and Health Scrutiny) Regulations (Local Authority Regs) 2013. Regulation 11 sets out conditions for weighing and measuring under Schedule 1 to the NHS Act:

> (2) The conditions are–
> (a) the child to be weighed and measured is able and willing to stand unaided on scales and under a height measure;
> (b) a parent of the child has not withdrawn the child from participation in the weighing and measuring exercise;
> (c) the weighing and measuring exercise is conducted in a room or screened area where information on the measurements is secure and cannot be seen or heard by anyone who is not assisting in the conduct of the exercise or overseeing it; and
> (d) the arrangements for the weighing and measuring exercise are managed on behalf of the local authority by a registered medical practitioner, a registered nurse or a registered dietitian.

6.33 A local authority must take steps such that parents are given a reasonable opportunity to withdraw their child from participation in the exercise, and if a child has been withdrawn, then they are not weighed or measured.[54] Information may be processed, so that it can be transferred to a parent of the child in question, with advisory material relating to the weight of children.[55] Information gathered must be provided to the Health and Social Care Information Centre, established under section 252 of the HSCA 2012.[56]

Universal health visitor reviews of pregnant women and infants

6.34 The secretary of state has published a policy guidance paper entitled *The healthy child programme.*[57] This sets out a programme for reviews,

51 *The Alcohol Use Disorders Identification Test, Guidelines for Use in Primary Care,* Babor et al (2nd edn), WHO/MSD//MSB/01.6a, World Health Organisation, 2001. Available online at www.who.int/substance_abuse/publications/audit/en/.

52 As defined in section 25(3) of the National Health Service Reform and Health Care Professions Act 2002.

53 NHS Act 2006 Sch 1 para 7A.

54 Local Authority Regs 2013 reg 12.

55 Local Authority Regs 2013 reg 14.

56 Local Authority Regs 2013 reg 15.

57 Available online at www.gov.uk/government/publications/healthy-child-programme-pregnancy-and-the-first–5-years-of-life.

screening tests, immunisations, health promotion guidance and support for pregnant women, infants and their families. Local authorities are under a duty to provide, or to make arrangements for the provision of, universal health visitor reviews.[58] Universal health visitor reviews are assessments and reviews of the eligible person's health and development. These must be provided once in each of the following periods:[59]

- a woman who is more than 28 weeks pregnant;
- a child who is aged between one day and two weeks;
- a child who is aged between six and eight weeks;
- a child who is aged between nine and 15 months; or
- a child who is aged between 24 months and 30 months.

6.35 Universal health visitor reviews are to be carried out by a health visitor (a registered nurse or midwife who is also registered as a Specialist Community Public Health Nurse or Health Visitor), a healthcare professional trained in child health and development, a nursery nurse, or where an individual has links with a family nurse partnership, a family nurse.[60] There is however, doubt as to whether regs 5A and 5B remain in force.

Sexual health services

6.36 Each local authority shall provide, or shall make arrangements to secure the provision of, sexual health services in its area. This is to be achieved in two ways: 1) by making arrangements for contraceptive services; and 2) by exercising functions for preventing the spread of sexually transmitted infections, for treating, testing and caring for people with such infections, and for notifying sexual partners of people with such infections.[61]

6.37 These sexual health services are to be 'open access', meaning that they are 'available for the benefit of all people present in the local authority's area', which in practice means that the services can be accessed by individuals without being referred to the service by a GP (unlike other NHS elective services).[62] The contraceptive services are to include advice on, and reasonable access to, a broad range of contraceptive substances and appliances, as well as advice on preventing unintended pregnancy.[63] However, the local authority does not have to offer services in relation to sterilisation or vasectomy, other than preliminary advice on the availability of those procedures.[64] The duty under regulation 6 does not extend to treating or caring for those infected with HIV.[65]

Public health advice services

6.38 A local authority is to provide a public health advice service to any CCG whose area falls wholly or partly within that authority's area.[66] Such a

58 Public Health Functions Regs 2013 reg 5A(1).
59 Public Health Functions Regs 2013 reg 5A(2).
60 Public Health Functions Regs 2013 reg 5B.
61 Public Health Functions Regs 2013 reg 6.
62 Public Health Functions Regs 2013 reg 6(2).
63 Public Health Functions Regs 2013 reg 6(3).
64 Public Health Functions Regs 2013 reg 6(4).
65 Public Health Functions Regs 2013 reg 6(5).
66 Public Health Functions Regs 2013 reg 7.

service consists of the provision 'of such information and advice to a clinical commissioning group as the local authority considers necessary or appropriate, with a view to protecting and improving the health of the people in the authority's area'.[67] In deciding what matters to cover in the advice, the local authority shall have regard to the needs of people in its area. The decision is to be by agreement between the local authority and the CCGs; if there is no agreement, the range of services is decided by the local authority alone.[68]

Advice to other public bodies

6.39 A local authority is responsible for providing information or advice to a range of 'responsible persons' and 'relevant bodies' so that the responsible person or relevant body may prepare or participate in appropriate 'local health protection arrangements'. The secretary of state has said '[t]he Department of Health does not expect local authorities to produce a single all-encompassing "health protection plan" for an area, but rather to promote preparation of effective health protection arrangements by local organisations, operating in their areas'.[69] There is a list of responsible bodies,[70] which includes the relevant head of the police and fire service. There is no list of relevant bodies, such bodies instead being defined as 'a body whose activities, in the opinion of the local authority, have a significant effect upon, or whose activities may be significantly affected by a threat to, the health of individuals in the local authority's area'.[71] The regulations provide an indicative list, including school governing bodies, providers of social care services, voluntary organisations, registered charities, and businesses.

6.40 'Local health protection arrangements' are defined as 'arrangements made for the purpose of protecting individuals in the area of the authority from events or occurrences which threaten, or are liable to threaten, their health'.[72] They may in particular include arrangements to deal with infectious disease, environmental hazards and contamination, and extreme weather events. They may also include arrangements for epidemiological surveillance, for environmental hazard monitoring, for coordinating incident management with another local authority, and for stockpiling medicines and medical supplies.[73]

Dental public health functions

6.41 The dental public health functions of local authorities in England are set out in regulation 17 of the Partnership Arrangements Regs 2012:

> (1) Each local authority shall have the following functions in relation to dental public health in England.

67 Public Health Functions Regs 2013 reg 7(2).
68 Public Health Functions Regs 2013 reg 7(5).
69 *Protecting the health of the local population*, p6.
70 Public Health Functions Regs 2013 reg 8(3).
71 Public Health Functions Regs 2013 reg 8(3).
72 Public Health Functions Regs 2013 reg 8(4).
73 Public Health Functions Regs 2013 reg 8(4).

(2) A local authority shall provide, or shall make arrangements to secure the provision of, the following within its area–
  (a) to the extent that the authority considers appropriate for improving the health of the people in its area, oral health promotion programmes;
  (b) oral health surveys[74] to facilitate–
    (i) the assessment and monitoring of oral health needs,
    (ii) the planning and evaluation of oral health promotion programmes,[75]
    (iii) the planning and evaluation of the arrangements for provision of dental services as part of the health service, and
    (iv) where there are water fluoridation programmes[76] affecting the authority's area, the monitoring and reporting of the effect of water fluoridation programmes.

(3) The local authority shall participate in any oral health survey conducted or commissioned by the Secretary of State under paragraph 13(1) of Schedule 1 to the 2006 Act (powers in relation to research etc) so far as that survey is conducted within the authority's area.

Research

6.42 Local authorities have the power to 'conduct, commission or assist' research for 'any purpose connected with the exercise of its functions in relation to the health service'.[77]

Emergencies

6.43 Local authorities, as Category 1 responders, have duties to assess the risk of emergencies, to plan for emergencies, to publish plans in relation to emergencies and to maintain arrangements to warn the public, and to provide information and advice to the public, if an emergency is likely to occur or has occurred, pursuant to section 2 of the Civil Contingencies Act (CCA) 2004. Under section 5 of the CCA 2004 ministers of the Crown may by order require local authorities to perform their functions of the purpose of preventing the occurrence of an emergency, reducing, controlling or mitigating the effects of an emergency, or taking other action in connection with an emergency. In urgent cases, a minister may make directions under section 7.

Complaints about the public health functions of local authorities

6.44 Detailed provision regarding complaints about the public health functions of local authorities is set out at regulations 19–33 of the Partnership

74 Defined in reg 16 of the Partnership Arrangements Regs 2012 as 'survey[s] to establish the prevalence and incidence of disease or abnormality of the oral cavity'.

75 Defined in reg 16 of the Partnership Arrangements Regs 2012 as 'health promotion and disease prevention programme[s] the underlying purpose of which is to educate and support members of the public about ways in which they may improve their oral health'.

76 Defined in reg 16 of the Partnership Arrangements Regs 2012 as fluoridation arrangements made under section 87(1) (fluoridation of water supplies at request of relevant authorities) of the Water Industry Act 1991.

77 NHS Act 2006 Sch 1 para 13.

Arrangements Regs 2012. Local authorities are required to make arrangements for the handling and consideration of complaints, which must be such as to ensure that:[78]

> (2) The arrangements for dealing with complaints must be such as to ensure that–
> (a) complaints are dealt with efficiently;
> (b) complaints are properly investigated;
> (c) complainants are treated with respect and courtesy;
> (d) complainants receive, so far as is reasonably practical–
> (i) assistance to enable them to understand the procedure in relation to complaints, or
> (ii) advice on where they may obtain such assistance;
> (e) complainants receive a timely and appropriate response;
> (f) complainants are told the outcome of the investigation of their complaint; and
> (g) action is taken if necessary in the light of the outcome of a complaint.

6.45 Information regarding the arrangements for complaints, and how further information about those arrangements may be obtained, must be publicised.[79]

6.46 Local authorities are required to designate a responsible person (for ensuring compliance with the arrangements), and a complaints manager (to be responsible for managing the procedures for handling and considering complaints in accordance with arrangements made under the regulations.[80] The responsible person is to be the local authority's chief executive or other person designated as the authority's head of paid service.[81] The complaints manager can be the same person, but need not (and indeed not even be an employee of the local authority).[82]

6.47 Unless there is good reason, and it remains possible to investigate the complaint effectively and fairly, a complaint must be accepted for an investigation if it is made more than twelve months after the date on which the matter the subject of the complaint occurred or (if later), the date on which the matter came to the notice of the complainant.[83] However, the complaint need not be made in writing: it can be made orally or electronically.[84] If the investigation of the response does not give rise to a conclusion within six months (or other period agreed with the complainant), the authority must notify the complainant in writing, explaining the reason for the delay in responding to the complaint.[85]

6.48 A local authority must maintain a monitoring record including records of each complaint received about the delivery of public health services, the subject-matter and outcome of each complaint, and whether the report of the outcome was sent to the complainant within the response period.[86]

78 Partnership Arrangements Regs 2012 reg 21.
79 Partnership Arrangements Regs 2012 reg 31.
80 Partnership Arrangements Regs 2012 reg 22(1).
81 Partnership Arrangements Regs 2012 reg 22(4).
82 Partnership Arrangements Regs 2012 reg 22(5).
83 Partnership Arrangements Regs 2012 reg 27.
84 Partnership Arrangements Regs 2012 reg 28(1).
85 Partnership Arrangements Regs 2012 reg 29(4).
86 Partnership Arrangements Regs 2012 reg 32.

There is an obligation on local authorities to prepare annual reports in relation to complaints.[87]

Secretary of State

6.49 Section 2A of the NHS Act 2006 provides:

> (1) The Secretary of State must take such steps as the Secretary of State considers appropriate for the purpose of protecting the public in England from disease or other dangers to health.
> (2) The steps that may be taken under subsection (1) include–
> (a) the conduct of research or such other steps as the Secretary of State considers appropriate for advancing knowledge and understanding;
> (b) providing microbiological or other technical services (whether in laboratories or otherwise);
> (c) providing vaccination, immunisation or screening services;
> (d) providing other services or facilities for the prevention, diagnosis or treatment of illness;
> (e) providing training;
> (f) providing information and advice;
> (g) making available the services of any person or any facilities.
> (3) Subsection (4) applies in relation to any function under this section which relates to–
> (a) the protection of the public from ionising or non-ionising radiation, and
> (b) a matter in respect of which a relevant body has a function.
> (4) In exercising the function, the Secretary of State must–
> (a) consult the relevant body; and
> (b) have regard to its policies.
> (5) For the purposes of subsections (3) and (4), each of the following is a relevant body–
> (a) the Health and Safety Executive;
> (b) the Office for Nuclear Regulation.

6.50 Paragraph 7C of Schedule 1 to the NHS Act 2006 provides:

> The Secretary of State must for the purposes of the health service make arrangements for–
> (a) collecting, screening, analysis, processing and supplying blood or other tissues,
> (b) preparing blood components and reagents, and
> (c) facilitating tissue and organ transplantation.

6.51 The secretary of state has a duty to make arrangement 'to such extent as he considers necessary to meet all reasonable requirements' for giving advice on contraception, the medical examination of persons seeking advice on contraception, the treatment of such persons, and the supply of contraceptive substances and appliances.[88] This is the same wording as is used for the CCG duty to provide acute services under section 3 of the NHS Act 2006. Accordingly the court's interpretation that this wording gives a wide discretion afforded to the decision maker will apply to the discharge of this duty.

87 Partnership Arrangements Regs 2012 reg 33.
88 NHS Act 2006 Sch 1 para 8.

6.52 Schedule 1 para 12 to the NHS Act 2006 provides the power for the secretary of state to carry on such activities as in his or her opinion can conveniently be carried on in conjunction with a microbiological service. Charges may be made for services or materials supplied.

6.53 The secretary of state (as well as NHS England, and CCGs) is given the power to 'conduct, commission or assist' research into 'any matters relating to the causation, prevention, diagnosis or treatment of illness', and any such other matters connected with any service under the Act as the body thinks fit.[89]

6.54 The secretary of state is under an obligation to make arrangements to deliver vaccination programmes pursuant to recommendations made by the Joint Committee on Vaccination and Immunisation where the recommendation:[90]

(i) relates to new provision for vaccination under a national vaccination programme or to changes to existing provision under such a programme;
(ii) is made by the Joint Committee on Vaccination and Immunisation (not merely by a subcommittee);
(iii) is in response to a question referred to the Joint Committee by the Secretary of State;
(iv) is based on an assessment which demonstrates cost-effectiveness; and
(v) does not relate to vaccination in respect of travel or occupational health.

6.55 The duty on the secretary of state comes to an end where the Joint Committee withdraws its recommendation.[91] There is an unresolved legal issue about the extent to which vaccination and immunisation programmes can offer NHS services to individuals selected on the basis of a protected characteristic under the Equality Act 2010 (such as sex, age, race of a particular disability). In order to make the most effective use of resources, vaccination and immunisation programmes are targeted at those who are most likely to benefit from the programme. However, to the extent that such targeting is defined by relation to a patient's sex (or some other another protected characteristic) there appears to be a strong argument that the denial of the opportunity for other patients to have access to the service may constitute direct discrimination in the provision of public services. If the targeting constitutes indirect discrimination on the grounds of a protected characteristic, a case may be made that the discrimination is justified. However if targeting constitutes direct discrimination, a justification defence will not apply.

6.56 The secretary of state has particular duties imposed upon him in relation to emergency powers. Section 253 of the NHS Act 2006 provides:

(1) The Secretary of State may give directions under this section if he considers that by reason of an emergency it is appropriate to do so.
(1A) A direction under this section may be given to–
(a) an NHS body other than a Local Health Board;
(b) the National Institute for Health and Care Excellence;
(c) the Health and Social Care Information Centre;
(d) any body or person, other than an NHS body, providing services in pursuance of arrangements made–

89 NHS Act 2006 Sch 1 para 13.
90 Health Protection (Vaccination) Regulations 2009 SI No 38 regs 1–2.
91 Health Protection (Vaccination) Regulations 2009 reg 2(4).

(i) by the Secretary of State under section 12,
(ii) by the Board or a clinical commissioning group under section 3, 3A, 3B or 4 or Schedule 1,
(iii) by a local authority for the purpose of the exercise of its functions under or by virtue of section 2B or 6C(1) or Schedule 1, or
(iv) by the Board, a clinical commissioning group or a local authority by virtue of section 7A.

(2) In relation to a body within subsection (1A)(a) to (c), the powers conferred by this section may be exercised–
(a) to give directions to the body about the exercise of any of its functions;
(b) to direct the body to cease to exercise any of its functions for a specified period;
(c) to direct the body to exercise any of its functions concurrently with another body or person for a specified period;
(d) to direct the body to exercise any function conferred on another body or person under or by virtue of this Act for a specified period (whether to the exclusion of, or concurrently with, that body or person).

(2A) In relation to a body or person within subsection (1A)(d), the powers conferred by this section may be exercised–
(a) to give directions to the body or person about the provision of any services that it provides in pursuance of arrangements mentioned in subsection (1A)(d);
(b) to direct the body or person to cease to provide any of those services for a specified period;
(c) to direct the body or person to provide other services for the purposes of the health service for a specified period.

(2B) The Secretary of State may direct the Board to exercise the functions of the Secretary of State under this section.

(2C) The Secretary of State may give directions to the Board about its exercise of any functions that are the subject of a direction under subsection (2B).

(2D) In this section, '*specified*' means specified in the direction.

(3) The powers conferred on the Secretary of State by this section are in addition to any other powers exercisable by him.

6.57 Public Health England has a responsibility for specialist health protection response, including the response to incidents and outbreaks, to be exercised through Public Health England Centres.[92]

6.58 The secretary of state, as a Category 1 responder for the purposes of section 2A of the NHS Act 2006, has duties to assess the risk of emergencies, to plan for emergencies, to publish plans in relation to emergencies and to maintain arrangements to warn the public, and to provide information and advice to the public, if an emergency is likely to occur or has occurred, pursuant to section 2 of the CCA 2004. Under section 5 of the CCA 2004 ministers of the Crown may by order the secretary of state to perform their functions of the purpose of preventing the occurrence of an emergency, reducing, controlling or mitigating the effects of an emergency, or taking other action in connection with an emergency. In urgent cases, a minister may make directions under section 7.

92 *Protecting the health of the local population*, p2.

NHS England

6.59 Section 1H of the NHS Act 2006 provides:

(1) There is to be a body corporate known as the National Health Service Commissioning Board ('the Board').
(2) The Board is subject to the duty under section 1(1) concurrently with the Secretary of State except in relation to that part of the health service that is provided in pursuance of the public health functions of the Secretary of State or local authorities.
(3) For the purpose of discharging that duty, the Board–
  (a) has the function of arranging for the provision of services for the purposes of the health service in England in accordance with this Act, and
  (b) must exercise the functions conferred on it by this Act in relation to clinical commissioning groups so as to secure that services are provided for those purposes in accordance with this Act.
(4) Schedule A1 makes further provision about the Board.
(5) In this Act–
  (a) any reference to the public health functions of the Secretary of State is a reference to the functions of the Secretary of State under sections 2A and 2B and paragraphs 7C, 8 and 12 of Schedule 1, and
  (b) any reference to the public health functions of local authorities is a reference to the functions of local authorities under sections 2B and 111 and paragraphs 1 to 7B and 13 of Schedule 1.

6.60 Section 13E of the NHS Act 2006 provides:

(1) The Board must exercise its functions with a view to securing continuous improvement in the quality of services provided to individuals for or in connection with–
  (a) the prevention, diagnosis or treatment of illness, or
  (b) the protection or improvement of public health.
(2) In discharging its duty under subsection (1), the Board must, in particular, act with a view to securing continuous improvement in the outcomes that are achieved from the provision of the services.
(3) The outcomes relevant for the purposes of subsection (2) include, in particular, outcomes which show–
  (a) the effectiveness of the services,
  (b) the safety of the services, and
  (c) the quality of the experience undergone by patients.
(4) In discharging its duty under subsection (1), the Board must have regard to–
  (a) any document published by the Secretary of State for the purposes of this section, and
  (b) the quality standards prepared by NICE under section 234 of the Health and Social Care Act 2012.

6.61 The extent of NHS England's powers (and duties) came to a head in the case of *R (National Aids Trust) v National Health Service Commissioning Board*.[93] Services for patients with HIV are 'specified services' under regulation 11 of and Schedule 4 to the National Health Service Commissioning Board and Clinical Commissioning Groups (Responsibilities and Standing

93 [2016] EWCA Civ 1100, (2017) 20 CCLR 30.

Rules) Regulations 2012,[94] and thus NHS England was the responsible commissioner for any such services.[95]

6.62 NHS England argued that, despite the wording of section 13E, it did not have the power to fund a drug for patients who were at risk but had not yet contracted HIV. The Court of Appeal agreed that NHS England did not have general public health functions but disagreed that the proposed treatment fell within the scope of 'public health' under the NHS Act (despite the fact that the recipients of the drug had not contracted HIV) as opposed to treatment for individual patients. Longmore LJ, giving the leading judgment, held that NHS England had commissioning responsibility for HIV services. He held that treatment for HIV included treatment designed to prevent a patient contracting HIV.

6.63 Underhill LJ held:[96] 'Parliament did indeed intend to exclude NHS England from any responsibility in the field of public health, subject to the particular power given to the secretary of state by section 7A of the Act, under which he may arrange for it to exercise any of his public health functions'. Underhill LJ considered it unlikely that different bodies would be entrusted with substantially identical functions. The prophylactic effect of PrEP forms a 'seamless continuum with its provision for those who have just been exposed to HIV infection (ie PEP)'.[97] Hence, perhaps reluctantly, he agreed that a drug to prevent a patient contracting HIV constituted treatment for HIV. While there is a strong argument that the court reached the right decision on the facts of the PreP case, the judgments leave a considerable amount of uncertainty as to what measures would fall within the scope of a local authority's public health duty and which fall on NHS England or CCGs.

6.64 NHS England is under a duty to obtain 'advice appropriate for enabling it effectively to discharge its functions from persons who (taken together) have a broad range of professional expertise in . . . the protection or improvement of public health'.[98] This includes the advice of local authorities.[99]

6.65 NHS England has particular responsibilities in relation to preparation for emergencies. Section 252A of the NHS Act 2006 (which also imposes duties upon providers) states:

> (1) The Board and each clinical commissioning group must take appropriate steps for securing that it is properly prepared for dealing with a relevant emergency.
> (2) The Board must take such steps as it considers appropriate for securing that each clinical commissioning group is properly prepared for dealing with a relevant emergency.
> (3) The steps taken by the Board under subsection (2) must include monitoring compliance by each clinical commissioning group with its duty under subsection (1).

94 SI No 2996.

95 See chapter 13 for a description of the division between services commissioned by CCGs and services commissioned by NHS England.

96 At para 50.

97 At para 55.

98 NHS Act 2006 s13J.

99 *Protecting the health of the local population*, p6.

(4) The Board must take such steps as it considers appropriate for securing that each relevant service provider is properly prepared for dealing with a relevant emergency.

(5) The steps taken by the Board under subsection (4) must include monitoring compliance by the service provider with any requirements imposed on it by its service arrangements for the purpose of securing that it is properly prepared for dealing with a relevant emergency.

(6) The Board may take such steps as it considers appropriate for facilitating a co-ordinated response to an emergency by the clinical commissioning groups and relevant service providers for which it is a relevant emergency.

(7) The Board may arrange for any body or person to exercise any functions of the Board under subsections (2) to (6).

(8) Where the Board makes arrangements with another body or person under subsection (7) it may also arrange for that other body or person to exercise any functions that the Board has, by virtue of being a Category 1 responder, under Part 1 of the Civil Contingencies Act 2004.

(9) A relevant service provider must appoint an individual to be responsible for–

(a) securing that the provider is properly prepared for dealing with a relevant emergency,

(b) securing that the provider complies with any requirements mentioned in subsection (5), and

(c) providing the Board with such information as it may require for the purpose of discharging its functions under this section.

(10) In this section–

'relevant emergency'–

(a) in relation to the Board or a clinical commissioning group, means any emergency which might affect the Board or the group (whether by increasing the need for the services that it may arrange or in any other way);

(b) in relation to a relevant service provider, means any emergency which might affect the provider (whether by increasing the need for the services that it may provide or in any other way);

'relevant service provider' means any body or person providing services in pursuance of service arrangements;

'service arrangements', in relation to a relevant service provider, means arrangements made by the Board or a clinical commissioning group under or by virtue of section 3, 3A, 3B, 4 or 7A or Schedule 1.

6.66 NHS England, as a Category 1 responder, has a duty to assess the risk of emergencies, to plan for emergencies, to publish plans in relation to emergencies and to maintain arrangements to warn the public, and to provide information and advice to the public, if an emergency is likely to occur or has occurred, pursuant to section 2 of the CCA 2004. Under section 5 of the CCA 2004 ministers of the Crown may by order require NHS England to perform its functions of the purpose of preventing the occurrence of an emergency, reducing, controlling or mitigating the effects of an emergency, or taking other action in connection with an emergency. In urgent cases, a minister may make directions under section 7. NHS England has a detailed *Emergency preparedness, resilience and response for the NHS* available online.[100]

100 See www.england.nhs.uk/ourwork/eprr/.

Co-operation in relation to public health functions

6.67 Sir Ivor Jennings famously said that parliament's sovereignty extends so far as to permit it to prohibit a Frenchman from smoking on the streets of Paris (the prohibition forming part of English law, the practical issue being enforcement of it).[101] Similar issues arise regarding duties of co-operation which are imposed on a variety of NHS bodies around the delivery of public health issues.

6.68 Section 247B of the NHS Act 2006 imposes co-operation duties which give vires to NHS bodies but, in practice, are probably unenforceable, at least in some cases. It provides:

> (1) This section applies to any body or other person that exercises functions similar to those of the Secretary of State under section 2A (whether or not in relation to the United Kingdom).
> (2) The Secretary of State must co-operate with the body or other person in the exercise by it of those functions.
> (3) If the Secretary of State acts under subsection (2) at the request of the body or other person, the Secretary of State may impose charges in respect of any costs incurred by the Secretary of State in doing so.
> (4) The body or other person must co-operate with the Secretary of State in the exercise by the Secretary of State of functions under section 2A.
> (5) If the body or other person acts under subsection (4) at the request of the Secretary of State, it may impose charges in respect of any costs incurred by it in doing so.

6.69 Section 271 of the NHS Act 2006 imposes a territorial limit upon the exercise of ministerial functions. However, this limit is expressly excluded from applying to section 247B (section 271(3)(da)).

6.70 The upshot is that bodies exercising public functions in relation to territories other than the UK may be required by UK law to co-operate with the secretary of state, and may be subjected to charges if the body requests cooperation by the secretary of state. How this is to work in practice remains to be seen.

Charging for local authority functions

6.71 Local authorities have a wide general power to charge for their public health functions when:[102]

a) providing information and advice;
b) providing service or facilities designed to promote healthy living (whether by helping individuals to address behaviour that is detrimental to health or in any other way);
c) providing or participating in the provision of training for persons working or seeking to work in the field of health improvement;
d) making available the services of any person or any facilities.

101 *The law and the constitution* (University of London Press, 5th edn, 1959), p170, cited in 'The conceptual foundations of parliamentary sovereignty: reconsidering Jennings and Wade', Michael Gordon [2009] PL 519, 523.

102 Public Health Functions Regs 2013 reg 9.

6.72 The secretary of state has issued guidance in relation to charging in respect of public health functions: *Guidance for local authority charging on public health activity*.[103] The guidance provides two circumstances where local authorities may decide to charge:[104]

- where the activity relates to an organisation, not an individual – private companies, academic institutions, etc; and
- where the activity relates to an individual, but is not for the purposes of improving that individual's health – training an individual to provide public health advice, for example. The regulations provide specifically that an individual cannot be charged for any service or facility provided to them, or any other step take [sic] in relation to them, if that service, facility or other step is for the purpose of improving their health.

6.73 However, the power to charge in respect of public health functions only applies where the person who would be charged has requested or agreed the provision of those functions.[105] Additionally, '[n]o charges may be recovered from an individual in respect of the provision of a service or facility to that individual, or the taking of any other step in relation to that individual, for the purpose of improving the individual's health'.[106]

6.74 There can be no charge for a function which the local authority is required to take under Part 2 of the Public Health Functions Regs 2013.[107] This excludes the power to charge from the following functions:[108]

- dental public health functions under regulations under section 111 of the NHS Act 2006;
- arranging the weighing and measuring of children at school under para 7A of Schedule 1 to the NHS Act 2006;
- provision of contraceptive services under the secretary of state's duty under para 8 of the Schedule 1 to the NHS Act (which local authorities must exercise under regulation [6] of the Public Health Functions Regs 2013); and
- provision of information and advice with a view to promoting local health protection arrangements (local authorities must provide such information in exercise of the secretary of state's duty under section 2A of the NHS Act 2006, as required by the Public Health Functions Regs 2013).

6.75 The guidance indicates that charges should not be applied so as to make a profit, but they may be calculated so as to cover the costs of the local authority.[109]

103 Available online at www.gov.uk/government/publications/guidance-for-local-authority-charging-on-public-health-activity--2.

104 At para 1.6.

105 Public Health Functions Regs 2013 reg 9(3).

106 Public Health Functions Regs 2013 reg 9(4).

107 Public Health Functions Regs 2013 reg 9(5).

108 *Guidance*, para. 1.11.

109 *Guidance*, para. 1.12.

Healthy Start Scheme and Welfare Food (Amendment) Regulations 2005

6.76 The Healthy Start Scheme and Welfare Food (Amendment) Regulations 2005 provide for a scheme for food and vitamin vouchers to be made available for pregnant women and infants in low-income families. The scheme was originally piloted within four postcode districts before being rolled out nationally.[110] The food that can be provided under the scheme is milk (being liquid cow's milk, but not including milk where chemicals, vitamins, flavours or colours have been added or removed); infant formula (which must satisfy by itself the nutritional requirements of the infants for whom it is intended); and fresh or frozen[111] fruit or vegetables (to which no fat, salt, sugar, flavouring or any other ingredients have been added).[112] Claims are to be made to the secretary of state.[113]

Public Health (Control of Disease) Act 1984

6.77 The PHA 1984 provides for the power for the secretary of state to make regulations in relation to a number of matters. Regulations made under the Act include:

- Health Protection (Vaccination) Regulations 2009;[114]
- Health Protection (Local Authority Powers) Regulations 2010;[115]
- Health Protection (Part 2A Orders) Regulations 2010;[116]
- Health Protection (Notification) Regulations 2010;[117]
- amendments to regulations concerning public health and ships and aircraft.

6.78 The Chartered Institute of Environmental Health website contains a *Health protection regulations 2010 toolkit* (dated June 2011, revisions made October 2015).[118]

6.79 The Health Protection Agency (now Public Health England) and the Department of Health and Social Care, in consultation with the Chartered

110 The amendment being made by reg 4 of the Healthy Start Scheme and Welfare Food (Amendment No 2) Regulations 2006 SI No 2818, which came into force on 27 November 2006.

111 The additional to allow frozen fruit and vegetables was introduced by the Healthy Start Scheme and Welfare Food (Amendment) Regulations 2011 SI No 426 reg 2, which came into force on 6 April 2011.

112 Healthy Start Scheme and Welfare Food (Amendment) Regulations 2005 Sch 3.

113 Healthy Start Scheme and Welfare Food (Amendment) Regulations 2005 reg 4.

114 SI No 38.

115 SI No 657.

116 SI No 658.

117 SI No 659.

118 See www.cieh.org/policy/health-protection-regulations-toolkit.html. The *Toolkit* is headed Public Health England, Lewes District Council, and Chartered Institute of Environmental Health. It states that it was produced 'through partnership working between Environmental Health at Lewes District Council, and the Surrey and Sussex Health Protection Unit of the Health Protection Agency (now Public Health England South East)' (p2).

Institute of Environmental Health, published *Health protection legislation (England) guidance 2010* in March 2010. It pre-dates the HSCA 2012, and is not available on the main www.gov.uk site, but is available on the webarchive site.[119] It should therefore be treated with more care. The revised version of the *Toolkit* was produced more recently.

Part 2A Orders

6.80 The Health and Social Care Act 2008 introduced Part 2A into the PHA 1984. This includes a power to make orders which constitute health measures to be taken in relation to persons, things and premises. The *Health protection legislation (England) guidance 2010* ('the *Guidance*') states that the 'health protection powers are for use where voluntary cooperation to avert a health risk cannot be secured and where other methods of control are ineffective, unsuitable or disproportionate to the risk involved'.[120] They should be viewed as a 'last resort'.[121] The *Toolkit* contains a flowchart, a checklist, draft letters, a draft notice of intention and a draft order.[122] The powers require an application of the principle of proportionality, and should follow risk assessment.[123] The *Guidance* suggests considering risk of transmission, impact of transmission, necessity, proportionality and context.[124]

6.81 Section 45G of the PHA 1984 provides:

(1) A justice of the peace may make an order under subsection (2) in relation to a person ('P') if the justice is satisfied that–
  (a) P is or may be infected or contaminated,
  (b) the infection or contamination is one which presents or could present significant harm to human health,
  (c) there is a risk that P might infect or contaminate others, and
  (d) it is necessary to make the order in order to remove or reduce that risk.

(2) The order may impose on or in relation to P one or more of the following restrictions or requirements–
  (a) that P submit to medical examination;
  (b) that P be removed to a hospital or other suitable establishment;
  (c) that P be detained in a hospital or other suitable establishment;
  (d) that P be kept in isolation or quarantine;
  (e) that P be disinfected or decontaminated;
  (f) that P wear protective clothing;
  (g) that P provide information or answer questions about P's health or other circumstances;
  (h) that P's health be monitored and the results reported;
  (i) that P attend training or advice sessions on how to reduce the risk of infecting or contaminating others;
  (j) that P be subject to restrictions on where P goes or with whom P has contact;
  (k) that P abstain from working or trading.

119 See http://webarchive.nationalarchives.gov.uk/20130105041349/http://www.dh.gov.uk/en/Publicationsandstatistics/Publications/PublicationsPolicyAndGuidance/DH_114510.

120 Executive Summary, p8.

121 At 7.4.3, p46.

122 At pp42–47.

123 At 7.4.2–3, pp45–46.

124 At 7.5, p47.

(3) A justice of the peace may make an order under subsection (4) in relation to a person ('P') if the justice is satisfied that–
   (a) P is or may be infected or contaminated,
   (b) the infection or contamination is one which presents or could present significant harm to human health,
   (c) there is a risk that a related party might infect or contaminate others, and
   (d) it is necessary to make the order in order to remove or reduce that risk.

(4) The order may impose on or in relation to P a requirement that P provide information or answer questions about P's health or other circumstances (including, in particular, information or questions about the identity of a related party).

(5) 'Related party' means–
   (a) a person who has or may have infected or contaminated P, or
   (b) a person whom P has or may have infected or contaminated.

(6) An order under this section may also order a person with parental responsibility (within the meaning of the Children Act 1989) for P to secure that P submits to or complies with the restrictions or requirements imposed by the order.

(7) The appropriate Minister must by regulations make provision about the evidence that must be available to a justice of the peace before the justice can be satisfied as mentioned in subsection (1) or (3).

(8) Any reference in this section to a person who is infected or contaminated includes a reference to a person who carries the source of an infection or contamination, and any reference to infecting or contaminating others includes a reference to passing that source to others.

6.82 Section 45K(2) of the PHA 1984 provides:

> A Part 2A order may include, in addition to the restrictions or requirements mentioned in the provision under which it is made, such other restrictions or requirements as the justice considers necessary for the purpose of reducing or removing the risk in question.

6.83 The *Guidance* states (after summarising the powers at subsection 45G(2)):[125]

> A JP [justice of the peace] may impose any of the above restrictions or requirements, or more than one if needed. The JP may also impose further restrictions or requirements not listed above, if needed for the same health protection purpose. Any such restriction or requirement should complement the one(s) imposed under the list above, and must not be more restrictive or onerous for the person concerned than those listed (which are indicative of the maximum limits of the respective restrictions or requirements which may be imposed). For example, if a Part 2A Order requires that a person be detained in hospital to avert a risk to others, the order cannot additionally require that the person accept treatment.

6.84 The treating clinician should usually be involved, and an application should be pursued against the advice of the treating clinician in only exceptional circumstances.[126]

125 *Health protection legislation (England) guidance 2010*, 10.1, p79.

126 *Health protection legislation (England) guidance 2010*, 10.1.2, p80.

6.85 If an order requires a person to be detained or kept in isolation or quarantine at a place, and the person leaves the place contrary to the requirement in the order, then (during the period that the requirement is in force), a constable may take the person into custody and return the person to that place.[127] However, it is significant that the *Guidance* indicates that, despite section 45K(2), the justice of the peace (ie a magistrate) does not have the power to require the infected person to submit to treatment for the condition.[128] Thus a person can be isolated and offered appropriate treatment (and kept in isolation until the risk of infection is reduced) but cannot be required to accept any medication which is offered.

6.86 Orders under Part 2A are known as Part 2A Orders.[129] Certain evidence which must be provided in relation to an application under section 45G(1) or (3) is set out in regulation 4 of the Health Protection (Part 2A Orders) Regulations 2010:

> (2) That evidence is–
> (a) a report which gives details (insofar as known and relevant), or gives reasons for the omission of details, of–
> (i) the signs and symptoms of the infection or contamination in the person (P) who is the subject of the application,
> (ii) P's diagnosis,
> (iii) the outcome of clinical or laboratory tests, and
> (iv) P's recent contacts with, or proximity to, a source or sources of infection or contamination;
> (b) a summary of the characteristics and effects of the infection or contamination which P has or may have which includes an explanation of–
> (i) the mechanism by which the infection or contamination spreads,
> (ii) how easily the infection or contamination spreads amongst humans, and
> (iii) the impact of the infection or contamination on human health (by reference to pain, disability and the likelihood of death);
> (c) in relation to applications seeking an order under section 45G(2), an assessment of the risk to human health that P presents, including a description of any acts or omissions, or anticipated acts or omissions, of P which affect that risk;
> (d) in relation to applications seeking an order under section 45G(4), an assessment of the risk to human health that the related party presents, including any acts or omissions, or anticipated acts or omissions, of the related party which affect that risk;
> (e) in relation to applications seeking an order under section 45G(2), an assessment of the options available to deal with the risk that P presents; and
> (f) in relation to applications seeking an order under section 45G(4), an assessment of the options available to deal with the risk that the related party presents.

6.87 Regulation 4 further provides that a report under para 2(a) must include the details mentioned in at least one of paras 2(a)(i)–(iv); the evidence

127 Section 45O(5)–(6).
128 This is stressed in the Executive Summary, p9.
129 Section 45K(1).

must be given by persons suitably qualified to give the evidence, and the evidence may be given orally or in writing.

6.88 Regulation 8 stipulates that, where an order has been made in relation to a person, the local authority must take all reasonable steps to ensure that the person who is the subject of the order understands the effect of the order, the reason it has been made, the power under which it has been made and the person's right to apply for a variation or revocation of the order, and the relevant support services available to the person, and how to access them. These steps must be taken as soon as reasonably practicable after the order is made.

6.89 Once an order has been made, the local authority which made the application for the Part 2A order must have regard to the impact of the order on the welfare of the person subject to the order, and his or her dependants, for the duration of the order.[130] The *Guidance* provides a flow-chart in relation to section 45G applications.[131]

6.90 Legislative provision concerning infected things has considerable pedigree.[132] Section 45H makes provision for seizure, quarantine, disinfection, cremation, destruction etc of a 'thing' which is thought may be infected or contaminated. A 'thing' includes human tissue, a dead body or human remains, animals, and plant material.[133] It also provides a power for the owner of a thing to provide information about a thing. Section 45I provides a like power in relation to premises.[134] The *Toolkit* provides flowcharts, checklists, draft letters, draft notices of intention and draft orders,[135] with particular documentation in relation to dead bodies.

6.91 Orders under sections 45G, 45H and 45I can be made in relation to groups of persons, things or premises.[136] The issue of a Part 2A order is authority for those to whom it is addressed to do the things necessary to give effect to the order.[137]

6.92 The local authority must give notice to specified persons, set out in regulation 3 of the Health Protection (Part 2A Orders) Regulations 2010, when applying for a Part 2A Order. There is no specific timescale for giving notice in the legislation, but this should be done as soon as practicable.[138] However, notice need not be given where the person subject to an order, in the reasonable view of the local authority, is likely to abscond or otherwise take steps to undermine the order applied for.[139] It is also not necessary to give notice to a person with parental responsibility for a child,

130 Health Protection (Part 2A Orders) Regulations 2010 reg 9.

131 *Health protection legislation (England) guidance 2010*, p86.

132 It features in Old Testament law: Leviticus 13:47ff and has been the subject of a series of specific laws over the centuries.

133 Section 45T(5).

134 Which also features in the Old Testament: Leviticus 14:33ff. As with s45I(2)(d), Old Testament law provided that contamination of premises could lead to their demolition: Leviticus 14:45.

135 At pp48–65.

136 Section 45J.

137 Section 45K(8).

138 *Health protection legislation (England) guidance 2010*, 9.3, p72.

139 Reg 3(8).

where exceptional circumstances exist such that notifying such a person would not be in the child's best interests.[140]

6.93 Part 2A orders may order the payment of compensation or expenses.[141] Where an order is made under section 45H or 45I, the local authority may impose a charge upon the owner or person with custody or control of a thing subject to an order under section 45H, or the owner or occupier of the premises subject to an order under section 45I. The amount of the charge must not exceed the actual costs (including staff costs) to the local authority in taking measures in relation to the thing or premises pursuant to the order, and must be reasonable in all the circumstances.[142] Questions may arise regarding the phrase 'pursuant to the order': one reading of this could be that costs can arise pursuant to an order only once the order has been made. However, such costs will not be quantifiable in the order itself. This reading would also exclude costs incurred in investigating the need for an order. The *Guidance* states:[143]

> A JP can require payment of compensation or expenses in connection with the measures specified in a Part 2A Order. For example, a local authority could be required to pay compensation to a person who incurs financial loss as a result of an order.
>
> However, the JP cannot assign liability for the costs of carrying out the measures in the Part 2A Order. (Note that this does not affect the JP's ability to apportion the costs of the proceedings.) In some cases, where the local authority needs to take action as a result of a Part 2A Order, the authority may make a charge.

6.94 An application under Part 2A need not be heard in open court.[144]

6.95 The requirements for service of notices are set out at section 60 of the PHA 1984. This provides that service can be effected by:

> (a) by delivering it to that person, or
> (b) in the case of a coroner or the proper officer of a local authority, by leaving it or sending it in a prepaid letter addressed to him, at either his residence or his office, and, in the case of any other officer of a local authority, by leaving it, or sending it in a prepaid letter addressed to him, at his office, or
> (c) in the case of any other person, by leaving it, or sending it in a prepaid letter addressed to him, at his usual or last known residence, or
> (d) in the case of an incorporated company or body, by delivering it to their secretary or clerk at their registered or principal office, or by sending it in a prepaid letter addressed to him at that office, or
> (e) in the case of a document to be given to or served on a person as being the owner of any premises by virtue of the fact that he receives the rack-rent of the premises as agent for another, or would so receive it if the premises were let at a rackrent, by leaving it, or sending it in a prepaid letter addressed to him, at his place of business, or

140 Reg 3(9). The *Health protection legislation (England) guidance 2010*, 9.3, p73 suggests that this may arise when the issue concerns the sexual health of the child.

141 Section 45K(7).

142 Health Protection (Part 2A Orders) Regulations 2010 reg 7.

143 *Health protection legislation (England) guidance 2010*, 9.1.1, p70.

144 Health and Social Care Act 2008 (Commencement No 15, Consequential Amendments and Transitional and Savings Provisions) Order 2010 SI No 708 art 10.

(f) in the case of a document to be given to or served on the owner or the occupier of any premises, if it is not practicable after reasonable inquiry to ascertain the name and address of the person to or on whom it should be given or served, or if the premises are unoccupied, by addressing it to the person concerned by the description of 'owner' or 'occupier' of the premises (naming them) to which it relates, and delivering it to some person on the premises, or, if there is no person on the premises to whom it can be delivered, by affixing it, or a copy of it, to some conspicuous part of the premises.

6.96 A justice of the peace may vary or revoke a Part 2A order made under section 45G of the PHA 1984 on the application of:[145]

- a local authority;
- an authority with the function of executing or enforcing the order in question;
- the person in hospital or quarantine;
- the hospitalised/quarantined person's husband, wife or civil partner;
- someone living with the hospitalised/quarantined person as a husband, wife or civil partner;
- a person holding power of attorney.[146]

6.97 A justice of the peace may vary or revoke a Part 2A order made under section 45H on application by the owner of the thing, or the person with custody or control of the thing, or any person required to provide information or answer questions.[147] Likewise, a justice of the peace may vary or revoke a Part 2A order made under section 45I on application by the owner of the premises, or the occupier of the premises, or any person required to provide information or answer questions.[148] However, where a Part 2A order is varied or revoked, that does not invalidate anything done under the order prior to the variation or revocation.[149]

6.98 Part 2A orders must be for a specified period, but this period can be extended.[150] However, such an order cannot authorise keeping a person in hospital or in quarantine for a period of more than 28 days.[151] The period of any extension may not exceed 28 days.[152] Where the order is varied to impose a new restriction or requirement, the period of that restriction or requirement must not exceed 28 days beginning with the day of variation of the order.[153]

6.99 A person who fails without reasonable excuse to comply with a restriction or requirement imposed by or under a Part 2A order, or wilfully obstructs anyone acting in the execution of a Part 2A order, commits an offence, which is punishable by a fine.[154] If infection or contamination

145 Section 45M.
146 Health Protection (Part 2A Orders) Regulations 2010 reg 6(2).
147 Section 45M(7), (9).
148 Section 45M(8)–(9).
149 Section 45M(10).
150 Section 45L(1)–(2).
151 Section 45L(3).
152 Health Protection (Part 2A Orders) Regulations 2010 reg 5(3).
153 Health Protection (Part 2A Orders) Regulations 2010 reg 5(4).
154 Section 45O(1)–(2).

spreads as a result, then the court may order that the person take or pay for remedial action.[155]

6.100 Every time a local authority makes a Part 2A application, it must provide a written report to the chief executive of Public Health England, including the name of the local authority, contact details of a responsible officer, a copy of the Part 2A application (with details enabling the identification of the person subject to the application redacted), a copy of the order (again with identifying details redacted), and a reason for the Part 2A order not being made, if it is not made.[156] The email address for making such a report is Part2AOrder@phe.gov.uk.[157] Public Health England states that it 'tracks the use of Part 2A orders', but does not act upon individual orders.[158] The *Toolkit* provides a draft email report to Public Health England.[159] The time period for providing the report is short: as soon as practicable after determination of the application, and no later than ten days beginning with the day of determination of the application.[160] There is a similar duty to report variations or revocations (but only when these are granted; there is no need to report unsuccessful applications for variations or revocations).[161]

6.101 Sections 61–62 of the PHA 1984 provide for rights of entry. A proper officer can enter as of right only if 24 hours' notice has been given. A warrant is required to enter a dwelling.

6.102 Local authorities have powers connected to Part 2A under the Health Protection (Local Authority Powers) Regulations 2010: on the request of owners or persons with custody or control of a thing, they may disinfect or decontaminate (or case to be disinfected or decontaminated) the thing. The local authority may charge for doing so, but the charge must not exceed the costs of doing so. A charge can be imposed only where the owner or person with custody or control of the thing was made aware of the charge in advance, and agrees to pay it. Where the request is made by a person with custody or control, the local authority may take steps only if reasonably satisfied that the financial value of the thing will not be reduced as a consequence of the disinfection or decontamination.[162] Equivalent powers apply in relation to disinfection of premises on request of the owner or tenant of the premises.[163] The *Toolkit* provides flowcharts, checklists and draft letters.[164]

155 Section 45O(3).
156 Health Protection (Part 2A Orders) Regulations 2010 reg 10(1)–(2).
157 See www.gov.uk/government/organisations/public-health-england/about/our-governance.
158 See www.gov.uk/government/organisations/public-health-england/about/our-governance.
159 At p66.
160 Health Protection (Part 2A Orders) Regulations 2010 reg 10(3).
161 Health Protection (Part 2A Orders) Regulations 2010 reg 11.
162 Health Protection (Local Authority Powers) Regulations 2010 regs 4–5.
163 Health Protection (Local Authority Powers) Regulations 2010 regs 6–7.
164 At pp23–28.

Other powers of local authorities under the Public Health (Control of Disease) Act 1984

Children and school

6.103 Where a local authority is satisfied that a child[165] is or may be infected or contaminated, such as to potentially pose a significant risk to human health, there is a risk of infection or contamination of others, it is necessary to keep the child away from school[166] in order to reduce or remove the risk, and doing so it proportionate, then the local authority may serve notice on the child's parent requiring the parent to keep the child away from school. The headteacher of the school must be informed as soon as reasonably practicable. The maximum period for the notice is 28 days, but consecutive notices may be served. A local authority may vary or revoke a notice. The child's parents may request a review. The local authority must review the notice on the first request, but has discretion thereafter. Failure to comply with a notice is an offence which gives rise to the payment of a fine.[167] A flowchart, checklist, draft notice and drafts of various letters are available on the *Toolkit*.[168]

6.104 Where a local authority is satisfied that a person who is or has recently been on the school's premises is or may be infected or contaminated, such as to potentially pose a significant risk to human health, there is a risk of infection or contamination of pupils at the school, and it is necessary for the local authority to have a list of names, addresses and contact telephone numbers for all the pupils of the school (or a group of pupils which the local authority specifies), then it may serve a notice on the headteacher of the school, requiring provision of the list. Failure without reasonable excuse to comply with the notice constitutes an offence. [169] A flowchart, checklist, draft notice and draft of a letter to a head teacher are available on the *Toolkit*.[170] The *Guidance* states the following regarding the location of exposure:[171]

> This power cannot be used to require the provision of contact details of children if the potential exposure did not occur on the school's premises. If the potential exposure occurred off the school premises, but those who may have been exposed subsequently returned to the school premises thereby potentially infecting or contaminating other pupils, then this power could be used to obtain the contact details of relevant pupils.
>
> If a local authority needs contact details for school pupils who may have been exposed to a health risk while off the school's premises, and the headteacher refuses to provide them, the local authority could make a

165 A child is a person *under* 18 Health Protection (Local Authority Powers) Regulations 2010 reg 2(14); it therefore does not include 18-year-olds.

166 *Health protection legislation (England) guidance 2010* makes it clear at 8.4, p51 that the power can be used only in relation to school (not, for instance, scout group, Sunday school etc).

167 Health Protection (Local Authority Powers) Regulations 2010 reg 2.

168 At pp10–18.

169 Health Protection (Local Authority Powers) Regulations 2010 reg 3.

170 At pp19–22.

171 *Health protection legislation (England) guidance 2010*, 8.5, p55.

formal request using the power to request cooperation for health protection purposes, or if necessary apply to a JP for a Part 2A Order.

Requests for co-operation

6.105 A local authority has power to serve notice on a person or group of persons, to request that they do, or refrain from doing, anything for the purpose of preventing, protecting against, controlling or providing a public health response to the incidence or spread of infection or contamination which presents or could present significant harm to human health. Such a notice must provide contact details for an officer of the local authority who is able to discuss the notice. The local authority may offer compensation or expenses in connection with the request.[172] The *Toolkit* contains flowcharts, a checklist, a draft notice, and draft letters.[173] The *Guidance* suggests that a formal request may be made as a precursor to an application for a Part 2A Order if the request is not granted,[174] although it is not a necessary precursor, especially if the situation is urgent.[175]

Restriction of contact with, access to, or relocation of, dead bodies

6.106 A local authority has powers to restrict contact with a dead body,[176] prohibit a person from entering a room in which a dead body is located,[177] and relocate a dead body,[178] when satisfied that a dead body is or may be infected or contaminated and may infect or contaminate people, and that this would be a proportionate response. Failure to comply with these provisions is a criminal offence. The *Toolkit* contains flowcharts, a checklist, draft notices and a draft letter.[179]

Notification duties

6.107 The Health Protection (Notification) Regulations 2010 impose duties upon registered medical practitioners to notify the proper officer of a local authority[180] of suspected disease, infection or contamination in patients or corpses, where he or she considers that the infection or contamination presents or could present (or may have done while the dead person was alive) significant harm to human health.[181] The registered medical practitioner should not wait for laboratory confirmation in order to notify.[182] The list of diseases which *must* be notified is not exclusive: other infections or

172 Health Protection (Local Authority Powers) Regulations 2010 reg 8.
173 At pp29–35.
174 *Health protection legislation (England) guidance 2010*, 8.7, p63.
175 *Health protection legislation (England) guidance 2010*, 9.1, p69.
176 Health Protection (Local Authority Powers) Regulations 2010 reg 9.
177 Health Protection (Local Authority Powers) Regulations 2010 reg 10.
178 Health Protection (Local Authority Powers) Regulations 2010 reg 11.
179 At pp37–40.
180 This is apparently usually a consultant in communicable disease control or health protection, although this may be a senior environmental health practitioner: *Health protection legislation (England) guidance 2010*, 5.1, p39.
181 Regulations 2–3.
182 *Health protection legislation (England) guidance 2010*, pp.7, 14.

contaminations which, in the view of the registered medical practitioner, present or could present significant harm to human health must be notified.[183] The *Guidance* suggests that regulated healthcare professionals who are not registered medical practitioners (such as registered nurses) who suspects the patient to have a notifiable disease, infection or contamination, then they have a duty of care to initiate a referral to a registered medical practitioner.[184] Notification must be in writing within three days, but if the case is urgent, then notification must be provided orally as soon as reasonably practicable.[185] Where the proper officer has received such notification, he or she must inform Public Health England, the proper officer of the local authority in whose area the person usual resides, or the proper officer of the port health authority or local authority if the person has recently disembarked,[186] and the officer considers disclosure appropriate.[187] The deadline for notification is three days beginning with the day of notification, although if the case is urgent, then disclosure must be made orally as soon as reasonably practicable.[188]

6.108 There is a similar duty upon diagnostic laboratories to notify Public Health England where the laboratory identifies a causative agent[189] in a human sample.[190] The time period for notifying is seven days, unless the case is urgent.[191] In the case of the duty upon diagnostic laboratories, failure to comply without reasonable excuse is an offence which can result in the imposition of a fine upon the corporate body operating the laboratory or (if there is none), the directory of the laboratory.[192] It is not sufficient to say that the case has already been notified by a registered medical practitioner.[193] The *Guidance* states that, where samples are sent from one laboratory to another (reference laboratory or sub-commissioned laboratory), then the legal responsibility for notification lies with the first laboratory.[194] To the extent that this means that the second laboratory is not bound to notify, the basis for this in the Regulations is unclear. On notification to Public Health England, Public Health England may

183 Health Protection (Notification) Regulations 2010 reg 2; guidance is provided by the *Health protection legislation (England) guidance 2010*, 3.2, p15.

184 *Health protection legislation (England) guidance 2010*, 3.10, p24.

185 Guidance on urgency is provided by the *Health protection legislation (England) guidance 2010*, 3.7.1, p21. Additionally, an indication as to whether the reporting of specific conditions is likely to be urgent is at pp25–27.

186 *The health protection regulations 2010 toolkit* includes at p7 a 'Proper officer checklist for disclosure of information to Port Health Authority/Local Authority for the port'.

187 Health Protection (Notification) Regulations 2010 reg 6.

188 Guidance on urgency is provided by the *Health protection legislation (England) guidance 2010*, 5.4, pp39–40.

189 Listed in Schedule 2 to the Regulations.

190 Health Protection (Notification) Regulations 2010 reg 4.

191 Guidance on urgency is provided by *Health protection legislation (England) guidance 2010*, 4.3.1, pp29–30. Additionally, an indication as to whether the reporting of specific notifiable organisms is likely to be urgent is at pp35–38.

192 Health Protection (Notification) Regulations 2010 reg 4(9)–(10).

193 *Health protection legislation (England) guidance 2010*, 4.3.3, p31.

194 *Health protection legislation (England) guidance 2010*, 4.4, p33.

seek further information.[195] The *Toolkit* contains a flowchart for local communication routes.[196] The *Guidance* provides another flowchart for the notification process.[197]

Public Health (Aircraft) Regulations 1979 and Public Health (Ships) Regulations 1979

6.109 These regulations contain provisions concerning the prevention of infection or disease spreading from aircraft or ships. The detail of these regulations is beyond the scope of this book.

Public health and European Union law

6.110 Powers are conferred on the EU by virtue of Article 168 of the Treaty on the Functioning of the EU. Union powers are to complement actions of member states, and to encourage co-operation between member states. The European Parliament and Council are to adopt measures in relation to:

- high standards of quality and safety for organs and substances of human origin, blood and blood derivatives (although member states may take more stringent protective measures);
- veterinary and phytosanitary fields to protect public health;
- high standards of quality and safety for medicinal products and devices for medical use.

6.111 Article 168(5) states:

> The European Parliament and the Council, acting in accordance with the ordinary legislative procedure and after consulting the Economic and Social Committee and the Committee of the Regions, may also adopt incentive measures designed to protect and improve human health and in particular to combat the major cross-border health scourges, measures concerning monitoring, early warning of and combating serious cross-border threats to health, and measures which have as their direct objective the protection of public health regarding tobacco and the abuse of alcohol, excluding any harmonisation of the laws and regulations of the Member States.

6.112 However, the actions of EU institutions are to have in mind the responsibilities of member states (Article 168(7)):

> Union action shall respect the responsibilities of the Member States for the definition of their health policy and for the organisation and delivery of health services and medical care. The responsibilities of the Member States shall include the management of health services and medical care and the allocation of the resources assigned to them. The measures referred to in paragraph 4(a) [i.e. concerning organs and blood] shall not affect national provisions on the donation or medical use of organs and blood.

195 Health Protection (Notification) Regulations 2010 reg 5.
196 At p8.
197 At p20.

6.113 EU law can also be used to seek to undermine measures which are introduced with the purpose of improving public health. The minimum price per unit of alcohol, proposed by the Scottish Government, was challenged by the Scotch Whisky Association on grounds that it was a disproportionate interference on the free movement of goods under EU law. This challenge was rejected by the Supreme Court,[198] after a reference to the Court of Justice of the European Union.[199]

198 *Scotch Whisky Association v Lord Advocate* [2017] UKSC 76, 2017 SLT 1261.
199 Case C-333/14 *Scotch Whisky Association v Lord Advocate* [2016] 1 WLR 2283.

CHAPTER 7

NHS provider trusts[1]

continued

1 By David Lock QC, Fiona Scolding QC and Hannah Gibbs.

Introduction

7.1 The separation of NHS bodies that commissioned care and NHS bodies that delivered care to patients formally started with the implementation of Part 1 of the National Health Service and Community Care Act (NHSCCA) 1990. This Act created a new species of NHS body, namely the 'NHS trust'. It also introduced the idea of an NHS contract to govern relationships between the then commissioners of NHS services, regional and district health authorities, and the new 'trusts'. The Secretary of State for Health at the time was Rt Hon Kenneth Clarke MP. He explained the thinking behind the creation of NHS trusts as follows:

> I was convinced that, instead of one body – the health authority – being responsible for both providing health care and purchasing it, the patient should be supported by his clinical advisers, mainly GPs, who would purchase contracts with NHS hospitals and other providers, based on their judgement of what would produce the best likely outcome for the patient and value for money for the taxpayer. Hospitals and other providers would bid for the contractual right to deliver services to a particular set of patients with a particular set of conditions. Purchasers would aim to obtain the maximum number of patient services that finite resources could provide.
>
> The key principles were competition and choice, with the aim of better outcomes for the patient being the fundamental issue in deciding where resources were directed. These principles formed the basis for the 'internal market' and have, in my opinion, been at the root of every successful development of the NHS since I introduced them.[2]

7.2 It is not necessary for the purposes of this book to examine whether Mr Clarke is right or wrong in his perception that the internal market has been the success that he claims it has been. However, the Conservative governments between 1990 and 1993 created the internal market structure of the NHS and, with modifications, that has remained in place ever since.

7.3 The second major milestone in the creation of NHS provider trusts was the Health and Social Care (Community Health and Standards) Act (HSC(CHS)A) 2003, which was passed by a Labour government with Rt Hon Alan Milburn as Secretary of State for Health. This created a new form of NHS trust, namely the NHS foundation trust (FT). These bodies were intended to be more detached from both government and commissioners, to bring commercial acumen to the NHS and deliver both cutting edge care for NHS patients and commercial health services (which would then subsidise the delivery of NHS care). They were hugely controversial at the time (and have not been adopted as a model in either Scotland or Wales).

7.4 Following the HSC(CHS)A 2003 there are three types of public body which provide NHS services to patients, namely:

a) NHS trusts;
b) care trusts; and
c) NHS FTs.

2 From chapter 12 of Kenneth Clarke's autobiography, *A Kind of Blue* (2016).

7.5 NHS trusts and NHS FTs primarily deliver NHS services. In contrast, care trusts deliver both NHS and social care services. Care trusts are created out of NHS trusts as a result of the powers under section 77 of the National Health Service Act (NHS Act) 2006 and regulations made under that section. The differences between NHS trusts and care trusts are considered below.

7.6 The Health and Social Care Act (HSCA) 2012 passed legislation to repeal all of the provisions relating to NHS trusts, in anticipation that all NHS trusts would become NHS FTs by April 2016, or its activities would be subsumed by a local and the better performing NHS FT. The programme of transferring NHS trusts into NHS FTs has largely been abandoned as a political priority. It thus looks highly unlikely that these parts of the HSCA 2012 will be implemented in the short or medium term. This chapter will first look at the law relating to NHS trusts, then consider the operation of care trusts, will look to see how the structures are different for NHS FTs, and finally will consider some of the legal issues arising for both NHS trusts and NHS FTs.

The legal duty on NHS bodies to have regard to official guidance

7.7 Section 2 of the NHS Act 2006 provides a wide power for the Secretary of State for Health and Social Care to 'do anything which is calculated to facilitate, or is conducive or incidental to, the discharge of any function conferred on that person by this Act'. This has been interpreted as including the power to issue Guidance to NHS bodies on the discharge of their functions: see *R (Whapples) v Birmingham CrossCity Clinical Commissioning Group and another.*[3]

7.8 In contrast to the position with clinical commissioning groups (CCGs) (as a result of section 14Z8 of the NHS Act 2006), there is no wording in the NHS Act 2006 which imposes a statutory duty on trusts to have regard to official NHS guidance or to act in accordance with such guidance. However, once official guidance has been issued, trusts have a legal duty to consider the guidance and to act in accordance with its terms unless the trust has a good reason to depart from the guidance. The extent of this duty was explained by Dyson J in *R v North Derbyshire Health Authority ex p Fisher*[4] as follows:

> If the circular provided no more than guidance, albeit in strong terms, then the only duty placed upon health authorities was to take it into account in the discharge of their functions. They would be susceptible to challenge only on *Wednesbury* principles if they failed to consider the circular, or if they misconstrued or misapplied it whether deliberately or negligently: see *EC Gransden & Co Ltd v Secretary of State* (1987) 54 P&CR 86 at 93–4. If the circular gave directions, then the health authorities would have an absolute duty to comply. I agree that it is important that the court should be slow to

3 [2015] EWCA Civ 435, (2015) 18 CCLR 300.
4 [1997] EWHC Admin 675, (1997–98) 1 CCLR 150.

> construe a document as a direction in the absence of clear words that that is what it is intended to be. The language of the circular is very far from clearly demonstrating an intention to give directions. It is, of course, important to examine substance rather than form. The substance here is to be found in the language of the circular.

7.9 Just as directions need to be in a set form, so there is a certain formality that needs to be present before a document issued by the Department of Health and Social Care (DHSC) can give rise to the legal duties identified above. Hence, by way of example, in *R (Rogers) v Swindon NHS Primary Care Trust and another*[5] the secretary of state had made a speech saying the NHS was making Herceptin available to breast cancer patients, had issued a press release about this and the department had referred to both in a weekly bulletin to NHS and local authority chief executives and directors of social services. Despite the very strong encouragement that the language of these documents gave to NHS commissioning bodies to fund the cancer drug, Herceptin, and despite this barrage of documents coming from the top of the NHS, the Court of Appeal noted:

> It is also common ground that neither the press release of 5 October nor the speech of 25 October amounted to guidance, still less to a direction. The full text of the speech was not distributed to the PCT and other trusts. Like the judge, we were referred to evidence which the Secretary of State gave to the House of Commons Select Committee on Health on 6 December 2005, which was very much on the lines of her 25 October 2005 speech. Again, it is common ground that what she said then cannot constitute guidance, let alone a direction.

7.10 Hence the working rule should be that a document issued by the secretary of state is not guidance unless it states that it is guidance.

Guidance issued by other bodies

7.11 There are a huge number of national and international organisations that publish information about the best ways to deliver healthcare. These range from NICE[6] through to Royal Colleges and All-Party Parliamentary Groups (where the documents are often, in effect, written by lobbying groups who 'support' such committees with a view to advancing their agenda). Trusts and other NHS bodies have a *Fisher* duty to have regard to NICE Guidance (see *R (Rose) v Thanet Clinical Commissioning Group*[7]) but have no legal duty to consider guidance issued by bodies outside the NHS, however eminent that body may appear to be. There is nothing unlawful in carefully considering and acting in accordance with guidance issued by, for example, a Royal College, but a trust has no legal duty to do so and generally will not be acting unlawfully if it takes a decision without having had regard to such guidance.

5 [2006] EWCA Civ 392, (2006) 9 CCLR 451.

6 The National Institute for Health and Social Care Excellence.

7 [2014] EWHC 1182 (Admin).

NHS bodies and directions

7.12 A key distinction between NHS trusts and NHS FTs is that the secretary of state retains ultimate control over the functioning and decision making in an NHS trust as a result of his ability to give directions. The direction-making power is set out in section 9 of the NHS Act 2006, which provides:

> (1) The Secretary of State may give directions to any of the bodies mentioned in subsection (2) about its exercise of any functions.
> (2) The bodies are–
> ...
> (c) NHS trusts, and
> (d) Special Health Authorities.
> (3) Nothing in provision made by or under this or any other Act affects the generality of subsection (1).

7.13 A direction can be given to NHS trusts generally or can be directed towards a particular NHS trust (or a defined group of trusts). Once made, the trust comes under a public law statutory duty to act in accordance with the terms of the direction. Accordingly, unless the trust considers that the direction is unlawful (because, for example, it breaches the human rights of patients), the trust has no lawful choice apart from acting in accordance with the terms of the direction.

7.14 Directions are formal written statements which make it clear that a trust must act in a particular manner. The secretary of state also has the right to issue guidance to NHS trusts and, on occasion, it can be difficult to determine from the wording used in ministerial statements whether the secretary of state was intending to issue a direction or was issuing 'firm' guidance. This issue arose in *R v North Derbyshire Health Authority ex p Fisher*[8] where a patient argued that a ministerial circular amounted to a direction. The secretary of state disagreed and, through counsel,[9] explained how to distinguish between firm guidance and a ministerial direction. The judge, who accepted the submission, recorded it as follows:

> For the Secretary of State, Mr Elvin, whose submissions are adopted by Mr Seys Llewellyn, submits that it is clear on the face of the Circular that its function is to provide guidance to help authorities which they should take into account in the discharge of their functions, and not to impose mandatory requirements which are they are absolutely obliged to follow. If it is the intention of the Secretary of State to give directions which attract a statutory duty of compliance, then he should make it clear that this is what he is doing. The difference between a policy which provides mere guidance, and one in which the health authority is obliged to implement is critical. Policy which is in the form of guidance can be expressed in strong terms and yet fall short of amounting to directions. There is no reference in the Circular to the word 'directions', and read as a whole there is no indication that the Circular is intended to trigger the statutory duty of compliance to be found in section 13(1) of the 1977 Act. The Circular includes words such as 'asks', 'suggested', 'taking into account'. It does not include the word 'shall' or any of the other badges of mandatory requirement'.

8 [1997] EWHC Admin 675, (1997–98) 1 CCLR 150.

9 Mr David Elvin, now Mr David Elvin QC of Landmark Chambers.

7.15 Thus a document which is produced by either the Department of Health and Social Care or by NHS Improvement should not be treated as being a direction under section 9 unless it says clearly that it is a direction.

7.16 It is implicit in the power to issue directions to a trust that the secretary of state also has the power to rescind a direction. Once a direction is rescinded, a trust is no longer under a statutory duty to act in accordance with its terms. Unfortunately, as far as the authors are aware, there is no definite list of current directions affecting NHS trusts and so it is not possible easily to determine whether an NHS trust is or is not still subject to a direction which may have been made by a previous government. However, the working assumption must be that once a direction is made, it continues to have effect (notwithstanding a change of government) unless either:

a) it is expressly rescinded; or
b) the government adopts a policy or issues guidance which is plainly inconsistent with the direction having continuing effect.

The role of NHS Improvement

7.17 The NHS Trust Development Authority (TDA) was set up by the government as a Special Health Authority as part of the changes to the NHS arising out of the HSCA 2012, with the twin aims of regulating NHS trusts (largely in the same way that Monitor regulated NHS FTs) and managing the processes to enable NHS trusts to become NHS FTs or to merge (or be acquired by) an NHS FT. That latter aim has largely been side-lined in recent years and the TDA has now de facto merged with Monitor (and other NHS organisations) to become NHS Improvement (NHSI). However, as a matter of law, the TDA still exists and NHSI appears to be an administrative vehicle through which the TDA operates.

7.18 The TDA describes[10] its role as follows:

> **NHS Trust Development Authority**
> The NHS Trust Development Authority is here to provide support, oversight and governance for all NHS Trusts on their journey to delivering what patients want; high quality services today, secure for tomorrow.
>
> The range of services provided by NHS Trusts covers the entire spectrum of healthcare, from acute hospitals to ambulance services through to mental health and community providers; the size of organisation varies from very small providers through to some of the largest organisations in the NHS, and therefore each Trust has a set of unique challenges.
>
> Due to this variation, we recognise that there is not going to be a 'one size fits all' solution to the challenges Trusts face. Our goal is first and foremost to help each and every NHS Trust to improve the services they provide for their patients.

7.19 The HSCA 2012 introduced a requirement for every provider of NHS services to be licensed and regulated by Monitor. However, NHS trusts are

10 See http://webarchive.nationalarchives.gov.uk/20161104155633/https://improvement.nhs.uk/about-us/who-we-are/.

(at least at present) exempted from being licensed: see reg 4 of the National Health Service (Licence Exemptions, etc) Regulations 2013.[11] It follows that the regulation undertaken by the TDA (part of NHSI) is not pursuant to a statutory regime.

7.20 In 2016, following the administrative merger of the TDA and Monitor into NHSI, the secretary of state issued the following directions[12] which set out the role the TDA (as part of NHSI) was required to fulfil. The relevant parts of the Directions are as follows:

> **Functions relating to improvement in the health service**
>
> 2(1) The Secretary of State directs the Authority to work collaboratively with Monitor under a single leadership and operating model, including supporting work, to ensure improvement in quality of care, patient safety and financial sustainability across the health service.
>
> (2) The Secretary of State directs the Authority to take such steps as it considers necessary and appropriate to assist and support persons providing services as part of the health service to ensure continuous improvement in the quality of the provision of such health services and their financial sustainability.
>
> **Functions of the Authority relating to designing methods, developing and publishing guidance**
>
> 3(1) The Secretary of State directs the Authority to take such steps as it considers necessary and appropriate, to design methods to be used by the Authority and develop and publish guidance as the Authority considers necessary, in connection with the Authority–
>
> (a) making appointments of the chair and non-executive directors of English NHS trusts, special trustees and trustees for English NHS trusts and NHS foundation trusts;
>
> (b) overseeing, developing and supporting English NHS trusts including in relation to clinical quality, governance and management of risk in English NHS trusts, compliance by English NHS trusts with relevant standards, and the progress of English NHS trusts as set out in direction 6(b)(i)(cc); and
>
> (c) working collaboratively with Monitor to oversee, develop and support providers of health services with the objective of continuing the improvement in the quality of such services.
>
> (2) The reference in paragraph (1) to developing and publishing guidance in relation to sub-paragraphs (a) and (b) is to be read as guidance to English NHS trusts, special trustees and trustees for English NHS trusts and NHS foundation trusts'

7.21 The directions also provided that the role of appointing individuals to chair NHS trusts and to be non-executive directors was to be undertaken by the TDA (ie by NHSI) on behalf of the secretary of state.

7.22 Perhaps the most controversial role played by the TDA is to designate a trust as requiring 'special measures'. The NHSI website explains:

> Special measures apply when NHS trusts and foundation trusts have serious problems and there are concerns that the existing leadership cannot make the necessary improvements without support.

11 SI No 2677.

12 See www.gov.uk/government/uploads/system/uploads/attachment_data/file/511610/Directions_2016.pdf.

They consist of a set of interventions designed to remedy problems within a reasonable timeframe. Trusts may be placed in special measures as a result of serious failures in quality of care and/or serious financial problems.

Special measures for quality reasons: guidance for trusts
This guidance, jointly produced by the Care Quality Commission (CQC) and NHS Improvement, describes how special measures work for quality reasons. It explains:

- why trusts are placed in special measures for quality reasons
- the process for entering special measures
- what will happen to trusts during special measures and how long special measures are intended to last
- the roles and responsibilities of key organisations involved
- when and how trusts will exit special measures, including the relationship between quality and financial performance
- if and how a trust can re-enter special measures.

7.23 There are broadly two areas where NHSI commences the 'special measures' processes, namely a) financial and governance issues and b) clinical outcome quality issues. However, these are rarely entirely separate types of intervention, because trusts which are in financial or governance difficulties also tend to be those which face clinical challenges. The 'special measures' regime is a purely administrative regime as opposed to a series of steps which have been defined in legislation (because NHS trusts are outside of the licensing scheme). Despite being administrative NHS trusts are, in practice, required to co-operate with NHSI and the special measures regime because the secretary of state's powers of direction lie behind all of the actions taken by NHSI.

7.24 The role played by NHSI in relation to NHS trusts is largely non-statutory. In contrast, the role by NHSI in relation to NHS FTs is governed by a statutory scheme. It is thus considered in the chapter on Monitor/NHSI.

NHS trusts

7.25 NHS trusts are public bodies whose powers and duties are set out in a combination of Part 3 and Schedules 4 and 5 to the NHS Act 2006. Part 3 consists of sections 25–27, which provide as follows:

NHS trusts
25(1) The Secretary of State may by order establish bodies, called National Health Service trusts ('NHS trusts'), to provide goods and services for the purposes of the health service.
(2) An order under subsection (1) is referred to in this Act as 'an NHS trust order'.
(3) No NHS trust order may be made until after the completion of such consultation as may be prescribed.
(4) Schedule 4 makes further provision about NHS trusts.

General duty of NHS trusts
26 An NHS trust must exercise its functions effectively, efficiently and economically.

Financial provisions relating to NHS trusts
27 Schedule 5 makes provision about the financing of NHS trusts.

7.26 Thus, NHS trusts are created by an order made by the secretary of state. Once created, they have the primary purpose of providing 'goods and services for the purpose of the health service'. The 'health service' means the National Health Service, as governed by the NHS Act 2006.

The statutory provisions about the powers and duties of NHS trusts

7.27 Schedules 4 and 5 to the NHS Act 2006 provide the details of the powers of NHS trusts and set out the way in which NHS trusts are required to function. Paragraphs 1 and 2 of Schedule 4 set out the legal status of an NHS trust. They provide:

1 Each NHS trust is a body corporate.
2(1) An NHS trust must not be regarded as the servant or agent of the Crown or as enjoying any status, immunity or privilege of the Crown.
(2) An NHS trust's property must not be regarded as property of, or property held on behalf of, the Crown.

7.28 It follows that NHS trusts are 'bodies corporate' albeit that they are not companies that are required to be registered at Companies House under the Companies Act 2006. As an unregistered company, an NHS trust could potentially face a winding up petition if it failed to pays its debts: see section 222 of the Insolvency Act 1986.

7.29 Paragraph 2 of Schedule 4 to the NHS Act 2006 provides that a trust is not to be treated a part of the Crown, and thus a trust is a self-governing body which holds its own property and is entitled to make its own decisions, after following its own decision-making processes. Thus, other government bodies only have such powers over a trust as are set out in statutory schemes. However, as NHS trusts are not part of the Crown, the Secretary of State does not have a general power to take over decision-making other than by issuing formal directions under section 8 of the NHS Act 2006 or by exercising formal emergency intervention powers. It also means that neither the National Health Service Commissioning Board (NHS England) nor NHSI can dictate how NHS trusts should operate, save for the limited statutory powers given to those bodies to intervene in how NHS trusts operate. It may well be that, in practice, these legal constraints are more a matter of legal theory than day to day reality. For examples, see the contrasting approaches where this point was taken that the secretary of state could not make decisions for a trust in *R (Lewisham LBC and another) v Secretary of State for Health and others*[13] and *Gibb v Maidstone and Tunbridge Wells NHS Trust*[14] where it was assumed (wrongly and unlawfully) that the Department of Health and Social Care could dictate decisions to an NHS trust which then had to follow them. In the latter case, the courts deprecated in strong terms offering up the dismissal of senior leaders to placate press or political pressure where that leader was not personally at fault for

13 [2013] EWHC 2381 (Admin).
14 [2010] EWCA Civ 678.

the problems at the trust. Sedley LJ said the decision to terminate the Chief Executive's position was a:

> . . . sacrifice on the altar of public relations a senior official who had done nothing wrong.

7.30 Section 26 imposes a statutory duty on NHS trusts to 'exercise its functions effectively, efficiently and economically'. The same obligation is placed on both CCGs and NHS England. However, this duty was treated as having very little, if any, legal effect by the Court of Appeal in *Gibb v Maidstone and Tunbridge Wells NHS Trust*.

The trust board

7.31 The requirement for an NHS trust to have a board of directors is set out at para 3 of Schedule 4 to the NHS Act 2006, which provides:

> **Board of directors**
> **3**(1) Each NHS trust has a board of directors consisting of–
> (a) a chairman appointed by the Secretary of State, and
> (b) executive and non-executive directors.
> (2) Sub-paragraph (1)(b) is subject to paragraph 7(2).
> (3) An executive director is a director who is an employee of the NHS trust, and a non-executive director is a director who is not an employee of the NHS trust.
> (4) Sub-paragraph (3) is subject to any provision made by regulations under paragraph 4(1)(d).
>
> **Regulations**
> 4(1) The Secretary of State may by regulations make provision with respect to–
> (a) the qualifications for and the tenure of office of the chairman and directors of an NHS trust (including the circumstances in which they cease to hold, or may be removed from, office or may be suspended from performing the functions of the office),
> (b) the persons by whom the directors and any of the officers must be appointed and the manner of their appointment,
> (c) the maximum and minimum numbers of the directors,
> (d) the circumstances in which a person who is not an employee of the NHS trust is nevertheless, on appointment as a director, to be regarded as an executive rather than a non-executive director,
> (e) the proceedings of the NHS trust (including the validation of proceedings in the event of a vacancy or defect in appointment), and
> (f) the appointment, constitution and exercise of functions by committees and sub-committees of the NHS trust (whether or not consisting of or including any members of the board).
> (2) Regulations under sub-paragraph (1) may, in particular, make provision to deal with cases where the post of any officer of an NHS trust is held jointly by two or more persons or where the functions of such an officer are in any other way performed by more than one person'

7.32 Regulations have been made under para 4, namely the National Health Service Trusts (Membership and Procedure) Regulations (NHST(MP) Regs) 1990.[15] The NHST(MP) Regs 1990 came into force on 9 November

15 SI No 2024.

1990, and have been amended on various occasions since to reflect changes in NHS legislation – references here are to the version of the regulations in force on 1 April 2018. Regulation 3 of the NHST(MP) Regs 1990 provides for the number of directors as follows:

(1) Subject to paragraphs (3) to (6) and regulation 9B(2), the maximum number of directors of an NHS trust shall be twelve, excluding the Chairman.

(2) Subject to paragraphs (3) to (6), an NHS trust shall have no more than seven non-executive directors (excluding the Chairman), and no more than five executive directors.

(3) In the case of an approved mental health NHS trust–
   (a) the maximum number of directors of the NHS trust shall be fourteen, excluding the chairman, and
   (b) the NHS trust shall have no more than seven non-executive directors (excluding the chairman) and no more than seven executive directors.

(4) In the case of a Care Trust–
   (a) the maximum number of directors shall be fourteen, excluding the Chairman; and
   (b) the number of executive directors shall not exceed 7 and nor shall it exceed the number of non-executive directors.

(5) Paragraphs (1) and (2) shall not apply to an NHS trust that became an NHS trust by virtue of an order made under section 52D(1) of the 2006 Act (de-authorisation) during any period specified in relation to that trust under section 52D(5) of that Act.

(6) Paragraphs (1) and (2) shall not apply to an NHS trust that became an NHS trust by virtue of an order under section 65E(1) of the 2006 Act (NHS foundation trusts: de-authorisation and appointment of trust special administrator) until the date an order made in respect of that trust under section 65L(4) of that Act (trusts coming out of administration) comes into force.

7.33 Thus, an NHS trust can have up to 12 directors plus the chair,[16] with a maximum number of five employee executive directors and a maximum of seven non-executive directors (who cannot be employees of the trust). There is no minimum number of directors provided for within the regulations, and no specific requirement that the number of non-executives should equal or exceed the executive directors (although that would be good practice).

7.34 Regulation 4 of the NHST(MP) Regs1990 provides that non-executive directors of an NHS trust must be appointed by the secretary of state (although in practice this function is undertaken by the NHSI on behalf of the secretary of state[17]). It provides:

(1) Subject to regulation 4(5), the non-executive directors of an NHS trust shall be appointed by the Secretary of State.

(2) The executive directors of an NHS trust shall be appointed by the relevant committee.

16 The regulations refer to the chairman of the trust but in the text we will use the gender neutral phrase 'chair'. They mean the same thing, but it seems more respectful to the significant number of talented and effective women who chair (and have chaired) trust boards.

17 The directions requiring NHS Improvement to undertake this function are at www.gov.uk/government/uploads/system/uploads/attachment_data/file/511610/Directions_2016.pdf.

7.35 Regulation 11 of the NHST(MP) Regs 1990 defines the persons who are ineligible to be appointed to be directors of an NHS trust. It provides for persons who hold offices which are incompatible with being an NHS trust director and a series of persons whose past conduct disqualifies them from holding such an office. It provides:

(1) Subject to regulation 12 a person shall be disqualified for appointment as the chairman or non-executive director of an NHS trust if–
  (a) he has within the preceding five years been convicted in the United Kingdom, the Channel Islands or the Isle of Man of any offence and has had passed on him a sentence of imprisonment (whether suspended or not) for a period of not less than three months without the option of a fine; or
  (b) he is the subject of a bankruptcy restrictions order [or an interim bankruptcy restrictions order, or a debt relief restrictions order or interim debt relief restrictions order under Schedule 4ZB to the Insolvency Act 1986; or
  (c) he has been dismissed, otherwise than by reason of redundancy, from any paid employment with a health service body; or
  (d) he is a person whose tenure of office as the chairman, a member, a director or a governor of a health service body other than a clinical commissioning group has been terminated on the grounds–
    (i) that it was not in the interests of the health service body or of the health service that he should continue to hold the office,
    (ii) of non-attendance at meetings,
    (iii) of non-disclosure of a pecuniary interest, or
    (iv) of misbehaviour, misconduct or failure to carry out his duties;
  (da) he is a person who has been removed from office as the chair or a member of the governing body of a clinical commissioning group;
  (e) he is a chairman, member, director or employee of a health service body other than a clinical commissioning group or an NHS foundation trust; or
  (ea) he is a person who is the chair or a member of the governing body of a clinical commissioning group, or an employee of such a group;
  (ee) he is a chairman, director or employee of an NHS foundation trust; or
  (f) he–
    (i) . . .
    (ii) performs or provides primary dental services, primary medical services or primary ophthalmic services under the National Health Service Act 2006,
    (iii) is a partner in a partnership that, or a legal and beneficial owner of shares in a company that, or a director of a body corporate that provides primary dental services, primary medical services or primary ophthalmic services,
    (iv) is an employee of any of those; or
  (g) . . .
  (h) he has had his name removed, by a direction under section 46 of the National Health Service Act 1977, from any list prepared under Part II of that Act and has not subsequently had his name included in such a list or a list prepared pursuant to section 28X of that Act; or
  (i) he is the chairman or another member of Monitor.

(1A) In the case of a Care Trust, in addition to the circumstances set out in paragraph (1), a person shall be disqualified for appointment as the chairman or non-executive director if he has been dismissed, otherwise than by reason of redundancy, from any paid employment with a local authority.

(2) For the purposes of paragraph (1)(a) the date of conviction shall be deemed to be the date on which the ordinary period allowed for making an appeal or application with respect to the conviction expires, or if such an appeal or application is made, the date on which the appeal or application is finally disposed of or abandoned or fails by reason of it not being prosecuted.

(3) For the purposes of paragraph (1)(c), a person shall not be treated as having been in paid employment by reason only of having been–
  (a) in the case of an NHS foundation trust, the chairman, a governor or a non-executive director of the trust;
  (b) in the case of a clinical commissioning group, the chair or a member of the governing body of the group; or
  (c) in the case of any other health service body, the chairman, a member or a director of the health service body in question.

(4) A person shall not be disqualified by–
  (a) paragraph (1)(e) from being the chairman of an NHS trust where that person is a chairman or non-executive director of another NHS trust;
  (b) paragraph (1)(e) from being a non-executive director of an NHS trust where that person is a chairman, non-executive director, executive director or employee of another NHS trust;
  (c) pa ragraph (1)(ee) from being the chairman of an NHS trust where that person is a chairman or a non-executive director of an NHS foundation trust;
  (d) paragraph (1)(ee) from being a non-executive director of an NHS trust where that person is a chairman, director or employee of an NHS foundation trust;
  (e) paragraph (1)(f)(ii) to (iv) from being a non-executive director of an NHS trust where that person–
    (i) performs or provides primary dental services, primary medical services or primary ophthalmic services under the 2006 Act;
    (ii) is a partner in a partnership that, or a legal and beneficial owner of shares in a company that, or a director of a body corporate that provides primary dental services, primary medical services or primary ophthalmic services; or
    (iii) is an employee of any of those providers, partners or bodies referred to in paragraph (i) or (ii); or
  (f) paragraph (1)(e) or (ee) from being a non-executive director of an NHS trust referred to in paragraph 5(1)(d) of Schedule 4 to the 2006 Act by reason of that person's employment with a health service body.

(5) A person shall not be disqualified by paragraph (1)(e) from being the non-executive director of an NHS trust by reason of being a chairman or non-officer member of

. .

(c) the National Health Service Litigation Authority,

. . .

(h) the NHS Blood and Transplant (Gwaed a Thrawsblaniadau'r GIG)],

(6) A person shall not be disqualified by paragraph (1)(e) from being the chairman or a non-executive director of an NHS trust during the period between the date on which it is established and its operational date by virtue of being–

(a) the chairman or a non-executive director of another NHS trust; or
(b) the chairman or a non-officer member of the Ashworth Hospital Authority, the Broadmoor Hospital Authority or the Rampton Hospital Authority.

7.36 There is a limited discretionary power in reg 12 of the NHST(MP) Regs 1990 for the secretary of state to lift a disqualification after two years in limited cases.

7.37 Regulation 4 of the NHST(MP) Regs 1990 makes provision for the key roles of chief officer of the trust (often called the chief executive), chief finance officer (CFO) (often called the finance director (FD)), medical director and chief nurse as well as specific roles in secure mental health trusts and care trusts. It provides:

(1) The executive directors of an NHS trust shall include–
(a) the chief officer of the trust;
(b) the chief finance officer of the trust;
(c) except in the case of a trust mentioned in paragraph (2) a medical or dental practitioner and a nurse or midwife registered on the register maintained by the Nursing and Midwifery Council under article 5 of the Nursing and Midwifery Order 2001.
(2) Paragraph 1(c) shall not apply in the case of a trust–
(a) which does not provide services directly to patients; or
(b) whose principal function is to provide ambulance or patient transport services.
(3) The executive directors of an approved mental health NHS trust shall include, in addition to those directors specified in paragraph (1), a chief officer with responsibility for high security psychiatric services.
(4) The executive directors of a Care Trust shall include, in addition to those directors specified in paragraph (1), a person with experience of the health-related functions of local authorities.
(5) The non-executive directors of a Care Trust shall include at least one member of each relevant local authority, appointed by the Secretary of State following nomination by that authority.

7.38 Regulation 17 of the NHST(MP) Regs 1990 requires the trust to form a committee of the chair and the non-executive directors for the purposes of appointing a chief officer. It provides:

17 Committee for appointing chief officer as director
An NHS trust shall appoint a committee whose members shall be the chairman and non-executive directors of the trust whose function will be to appoint the chief officer as a director of the trust [and in the case of a Care Trust the non-executive directors must include a person mentioned in regulation 4(5).

Regulation 18 of the NHST(MP) Regs 1990 then provides that the Chief Officer will join this committee when it comes to appointing other executive directors.

7.39 Paragraph 3(3) of Schedule 4 to the NHS Act 2006 provides that an executive director should be an employee of the trust. However, there is an exception to this in reg 5 of the NHST(MP) Regs 1990 to cover situations where a person is seconded to the trust or works for the trust under arrangement with another employer, such as a university. It provides:

A person who is not an employee of an NHS trust but–
(a) holds a post in a university with a medical or dental school, and also works for the trust; or
(b) is seconded from his employers to work for the trust; or
(c) is a person mentioned in regulation 4(4)
is nevertheless, on appointment as a director, to be regarded as an executive rather than a non-executive director of the trust.

7.40 Regulation 6 of the NHST(MP) Regs 1990 allows for job-sharing arrangements between two or more persons for the role where an executive director is required. It provides:

Where more than one person is appointed jointly to a post in an NHS trust which qualifies the holder for executive directorship or in relation to which an executive director is to be appointed, those persons shall become or be appointed an executive director jointly, and shall count for the purposes of regulation 2 as one person.

7.41 The period of tenure of directors is set out in reg 7 of the NHST(MP) Regs 1990. It provides:

(1) Subject to paragraphs (1A) and (3) and regulation 9, the chairman and non-executive directors of an NHS trust shall be appointed for such period not exceeding four years as the Secretary of State may specify on making the appointment.
(1A) A non-executive director of a Care Trust who is a person mentioned in regulation 4(5) shall be appointed for a period not exceeding his remaining term of office as a member of the local authority.
(2) Subject to paragraph (3) and regulation 8, the tenure of office of executive directors, other than the chief officer and chief finance officer, shall be for such period as the [relevant committee] may specify on making the appointment.
(3) Paragraphs (1) and (2) shall not apply to a person who became a chairman or director of an NHS trust by virtue of paragraph 4(3) of Schedule 8A to the 2006 Act (de-authorised foundation trusts: board of directors).

7.42 Thus a chair and non-executive can be appointed for up to four years, but there are no term limits. Thus there is no specific restriction which prevents a person being re-appointed at the end of a first or repeated term of office. This is confirmed in reg 11 of the NHST(MP) Regs 1990. However, there are restrictions on the appointment.

7.43 The tenure and suspension of executive directors is covered in reg 8 of the NHST(MP) Regs 1990, which provides:

(1) Subject to paragraphs (2) to (4) and regulation 7(2), an executive director of an NHS trust shall hold office–
(a) if he is not the chief officer or the chief finance officer, for as long as he holds a post in the trust;
(b) if he is the chief officer or the chief finance officer, for as long as he holds that post in the trust.
(2) Subject to paragraph (2A), if the relevant committee is of the opinion that it is not in the interests of the NHS trust that an executive director of an NHS trust other than the chief officer or chief finance officer should continue to hold office as director the relevant committee shall forthwith terminate his tenure of office.
(2A) In the case of a Care Trust, the relevant committee shall not terminate the tenure of office of a director under paragraph (2) unless it has consulted each relevant local authority.

(3) If an executive director of an NHS trust is suspended from his post in the trust he shall be suspended from performing his functions as director for the period of his suspension.

(4) An executive director other than the chief officer or chief finance officer of an NHS trust may resign his office at any time during the period for which he was appointed by giving notice in writing to the relevant committee.

7.44 These provisions mean that the an executive director (other than the chief officer or CFO) can resign as a Board director at any time on giving notice and will cease to be a director even if that person remains employed in a particular position at the trust. There is no provision to allow the chief officer or CFO to remain in their post and yet resign as a board director. However, if the chief officer or CFO ceases to hold that position in the trust, that person automatically ceases to be a member of the board. In contrast, any other executive director will remain as a director for as long as that person is an employee of the trust (in any position), even if they cease to hold the position which led them to be appointed to be director.

7.45 For directors other than the chief officer or CFO, the 'relevant committee' has the power to remove an executive as a director of the trust at any time if it is of the opinion that it is not in the interests of the NHS trust that this executive director should continue to hold office as director. The 'relevant committee' is the committee that appoints non-executives and must constitute the chair, the non-executive directors and the chief officer: see regs 2 and 18 of the NHST(MP) Regs 1990.

7.46 There is no express provision for the removal of the chief officer or CFO from the board of a trust, but anyone holding a directorship must hold that position as an employee of the trust. The trust may therefore take the decision to remove a chief officer or CFO from his or her post and, if the decision is legally effective, the chief officer or CFO will automatically cease to be a director of the trust. There have been a series of cases where pressure on an NHS trust has led to a perceived need to remove the chief executive even though there was no question of the chief executive having breached their contract (or even been a substandard performer). The rationale appeared to be that media and public pressure that someone is required to be sacked when there is a scandal at the trust. The removal of a chief executive in such circumstances can lead to huge legal complications because HM Treasury guidance is firmly against the approval of significant pay-offs. The position may be further complicated by the decision of the Supreme Court in *Societe Generale, London Branch v Geys*[18] where the court decided that an employment contract could not be unilaterally terminated by an employer. Thus, possibly depending on the terms of a contract, a trust which attempted to summarily dismiss a chief executive or CFO who was not in breach of contract and refused to accept the attempt to dismiss him or her. In such a case, the individual would remain as a member of the board. However, reg 8(3) of the NHST(MP) Regs 1990 provides that any executive director (including a chief executive or CFO) who is suspended from their post shall be suspended from being a director. Thus, as long as the trust suspended a chief executive or CFO, that person could not continue to function as a director.

18 [2012] UKSC 63.

7.47 Chairs and non-executive directors have the right to resign their office at any time by giving notice to the secretary of state (although in practice notice is sent to NHSI which handles these matters for the secretary of state). The power to remove chairs and non-executive directors lies with the secretary of state and not the trust itself. These provisions are set out in reg 9 of the NHST(MP) Regs 1990, which provides:

> (1) The chairman or a non-executive director of an NHS trust may resign his office at any time during the period for which he was appointed by giving notice in writing to the Secretary of State.
>
> (2) Where during his period of directorship a non-executive director of a trust is appointed chairman of the trust, his tenure of office as non-executive director shall terminate when his appointment as chairman takes effect.
>
> (3) Subject to paragraph (8), if the Secretary of State is of the opinion that it is not in the interests of the health service for a person appointed as a chairman or non-executive director of an NHS trust to continue to hold that office, the Secretary of State may forthwith terminate that person's tenure of office.
>
> (4) Subject to paragraph (8), if a chairman or non-executive director of an NHS trust has not attended a meeting of the trust for a period of three months the Secretary of State shall forthwith terminate his tenure of office unless the Secretary of State is satisfied that–
>
> (a) the absence was due to a reasonable cause; and
>
> (b) the chairman or non-executive director will be able to attend meetings of the trust within such period as the Secretary of State considers reasonable.
>
> (5) Where a person has been appointed the chairman or non-executive director of an NHS trust–
>
> (a) if he becomes disqualified for appointment under regulation 11 the Secretary of State shall forthwith notify him in writing of such disqualification; or
>
> (b) if it comes to the notice of the Secretary of State that at the time of that person's appointment he was so disqualified, he shall forthwith declare that the person was not duly appointed and so notify him in writing,
>
> and upon receipt of any such notification, his tenure of office, if any, shall be terminated and he shall cease to act as chairman or non-executive director.
>
> (6) Subject to paragraph (8), if it appears to the Secretary of State that the chairman or non-executive director of an NHS trust has failed to comply with regulation 20 (disclosure etc on account of pecuniary interest) he may forthwith terminate that person's tenure of office.
>
> (7) Where a person appointed as a non-executive director pursuant to paragraph 3(1)(*d*) of Schedule 2 to the Act ceases to hold a post in the university in question the Secretary of State shall terminate his appointment as non-executive director.
>
> (8) In the case of a Care Trust the Secretary of State shall not terminate the tenure of office of a chairman or non-executive director under paragraph (3), (4) or (6) unless he has consulted each relevant local authority.
>
> (9) Where a relevant local authority notifies the Secretary of State in writing that they no longer wish a relevant director to continue as a director of the Care Trust the Secretary of State shall forthwith terminate the tenure of office of that director.

(10) In paragraph (9), a relevant director means a director nominated by the authority in accordance with regulation 4(5).

(11) If the chairman or a non-executive director of a Care Trust who is a member of a local authority is suspended from being a member of that authority by virtue of a decision of a case tribunal made under section 79 of the Local Government Act 2000 he shall be suspended from performing his functions as a member of the Care Trust for the period of the suspension.

7.48 Most of these provisions are self-explanatory. They give the secretary of state a wide discretion to remove any person as a director. NHSI has published a policy[19] on how (on behalf of the secretary of state) these powers will be used. It explains the circumstances in which NHSI may reach the view that a person should be removed. This provides:

7. Chairs and NEDs can also be removed from office if it is not in the interests of the health service that they continue in office. Matters which may indicate that this criteria has been met include if:

- the office holder is found to be an unfit person as set out in the Health and Social Care Act 2008 (Regulated Activities) Regulations 2014;
- an appraisal or sequence of appraisals are unsatisfactory;
- the office holder no longer enjoys the confidence of the board chair, other board members, the public or local community, or NHSI in a substantial way. It is recognised, however, that there are times when decisions are taken which may initially prove unpopular with some sections of the local community. Other factors such as whether the office holder is pursuing agreed board or national policy, and whether the situation has arisen as a result of the office holder's personal handling of the situation will be taken into consideration when considering this condition;
- a chair fails to ensure that the board monitors the performance of the organisation in an effective way;
- the office holder fails to meet agreed annual objectives or deliver work against pre-agreed targets, or their performance falls significantly short of expected levels over a sustained period;
- there is a breakdown in essential relationships, e.g. between the office holder and the chair, the chief executive, or NHSI, or between the office holder and other members of the board. In such circumstances, the views of other board members will be considered to establish an understanding of the position;
- the office holder fails to demonstrate the personal behaviours, values, technical competence and business practices outlined in 'The standards for members of NHS boards and clinical commissioning group governing bodies in England' produced by the Professional Standards Authority;
- the office holder fails to demonstrate the standards of selflessness, integrity, objectivity, accountability, openness, honesty and leadership set out in the Seven Principles of Public Life;
- the office holder fails to comply with the letter and / or principle of the Trust's internal policies and procedures, insofar as they are applicable to the appointee's role;
- an investigation into allegations of wrong doing results in a finding against the office holder;
- a capability or other board effectiveness review indicates that the appointee is not making a full contribution to the board; and

19 See https://improvement.nhs.uk/uploads/documents/20170419_Termination-and-suspension_V2.pdf.

- a chair has reviewed the contribution of the Trust's NEDs and identified performance issues and/or skills gaps and believes the continuation in office of the appointee is not in the best interests of the organisation.

8. This list is not intended to be exhaustive or definitive and each case will be considered on its merits, taking account of all relevant factors.

7.49 Referrals to NHSI suggesting a director should be removed are investigated by the Provider Leadership Committee within NHSI. The policy sets out the approach which will be taken. If a final decision has to be made to remove a director, the decision will be made by the NHSI board after considering a recommendation from the NHSI Termination of Appointment Panel. The affected director will be invited to attend and present his or her case before the panel. This is a fairly complex procedure which, if followed to the letter, will ensure that any decision is taken in accordance with the human rights of the director.

7.50 Regulations 9A–9D of the NHST (MP) Regs 1990 give the secretary of state power to suspend chairs and non-executive directors and make a series of consequential provisions for the management of the trust's business while a chair or director is suspended, including allowing the vice-chair to act up as chair while the chair is suspended. The NHSI policy explains how NHSI will exercise the power to suspend chairs and non-executive directors on behalf of the secretary of state.

Appointment of vice-chairs

7.51 Regulation 13 of the NHST(MP) Regs 1990 gives a power (but not a duty) for a trust to appoint a vice-chair. It provides:

(1) For the purpose of enabling the proceedings of the trust to be conducted in the absence of the chairman, the directors of an NHS trust may appoint a non-executive director from amongst them to be vice-chairman for such a period, not exceeding the remainder of his term as non-executive director of the trust, as they may specify on appointing him.

(2) Any non-executive director so elected may at any time resign from the office of vice-chairman by giving notice in writing to the chairman and the directors of the trust may thereupon appoint another non-executive director as vice-chairman in accordance with paragraph (1).

(3) This regulation does not apply in relation to any NHS trust to which regulation 9C applies.

7.52 The reference to reg 9C is a reference to the situation where the secretary of state suspends the chair, in which case the existing vice-chair does not automatically take over but a vice-chair falls to be appointed by the secretary of state (who could be the director holding the position of vice-chair). The powers of the vice-chair are set out in reg 14 of the NHST(MP) Regs 1990, which provides:

Where the chairman of an NHS trust has died or has otherwise ceased to hold office or where he has been unable to perform his duties as chairman owing to illness, absence from England and Wales[, suspension under regulation 9A] or any other cause, references to the chairman in the Schedule to these Regulations shall, so long as there is no chairman able to perform his duties, be taken to include references to the vice-chairman.

Trust committees

7.53 Regulation 15 allows an NHS trust to appoint committees of the trust board which may (or may not) contain members of the board for all purposes other than the appointment of the chief officer or other executive directors. This is a wide power and allows for a committee to consist of persons who are neither employees nor directors of the trust and to take decisions on behalf of the trust. It provides:

> (1) Subject to regulations 17 and 18 an NHS trust or a trust special administrator may appoint committees of the trust consisting wholly or partly of directors of the trust or wholly of persons who are not directors of the trust.
>
> (2) A committee appointed under this regulation may appoint sub-committees consisting wholly or partly of members of the committee (whether or not they include the directors of the trust) or wholly of persons who are not members of the committee (whether or not they include directors of the trust).

7.54 Regulation 16 of the NHST(MP) Regs 1990 gives power for the board of the trust to delegate decision-making authority on behalf of the trust to a trust committee which has been appointed in accordance with reg 15. It provides:

> **16 Arrangements for the exercise of functions**
>
> Subject to regulations 17 and 18 an NHS trust or a trust special administrator may make arrangements for the exercise, on behalf of the trust, of any of the trust's functions by a committee or sub-committee appointed by virtue of regulation 15 subject to such restrictions and conditions as the trust or administrator thinks fit.

Standing orders for NHS trusts

7.55 Regulation 19 of the NHST(MP) Regs 1990 provides that, save where a trust special administrator has been appointed, an NHS trust is required to conduct its meetings and take decisions in accordance with:

a) the terms of the NHST(MP) Regs 1990;
b) the terms of the Schedule to the NHST(MP) Regs 1990 (which provided for some procedural rules); and
c) its own standing orders.

7.56 The full text of reg 19 is as follows:

> (1) Subject to paragraph (1A), the meetings and proceedings of an NHS trust shall be conducted in accordance with the rules set out in the Schedule to these Regulations and with Standing Orders made under paragraph (2).
>
> (1A) Paragraph (1) and the Schedule shall not apply where a trust special administrator has been appointed.
>
> (2) Subject to those rules and to regulation 20 an NHS trust shall make and may vary or revoke, or a trust special administrator may make, vary or revoke, Standing Orders for the regulation of the trust's proceedings and business and provision may be made in such Standing Orders for the suspension of them.
>
> (3) An NHS trust or a trust special administrator may make, vary and revoke Standing Orders relating to the quorum, proceedings and place

of meetings of a committee or sub-committee but, subject to paragraphs (17), (18) and regulation 20 and to any such Standing Orders, the quorum, proceedings and place of meeting shall be such as the committee or sub-committee may determine.

(4) The proceedings of an NHS trust shall not be invalidated by any vacancy in its membership or by any defect in a director's appointment.

7.57 The Schedule to the NHST(MP) Regs 1990 provides as follows:

1 The first meeting of an NHS trust shall be held on such day and at such place as may be fixed by the chairman and he shall be responsible for convening the meeting.

2 (1) The chairman may call a meeting of the NHS trust at any time.

(2) If the chairman refuses to call a meeting after a requisition for that purpose, signed by at least one third of the whole number of directors, has been presented to him or if, without so refusing, the chairman does not call a meeting within seven days after such requisition has been presented to him, such one third or more members shall forthwith call a meeting.

(3) Before each meeting of an NHS trust, a notice of the meeting, specifying the business proposed to be transacted at it and signed by the chairman, or by an officer of the trust authorised by the chairman to sign on his behalf, shall be delivered to every director or sent by post to the usual place of residence of such director so as to be available to him at least three clear days before the meeting.

(4) Lack of service of the notice on any director shall not affect the validity of a meeting.

(5) In the case of a meeting called by directors in default of the chairman, the notice shall be signed by those directors and no business shall be transacted at the meeting other than that specified in the notice.

3 (1) At any meeting of an NHS trust the chairman, if present, shall preside.

(2) If the chairman and vice-chairman (if any) are absent such non-executive director as the directors present shall choose shall preside.

(3) Every question at a meeting shall be determined by a majority of the votes of the directors present voting on the question and, in the case of any equality of votes, the person presiding shall have a second casting vote.

(4) The names of the directors present at the meeting shall be recorded.

(5) No business shall be transacted at a meeting of an NHS trust which is not a Care Trust unless one third of the whole number of directors are present including on or after the operational date at least one executive director and one non-executive director.

(5A) No business shall be transacted at a meeting of a Care Trust unless one third of the whole number of directors are present including, on or after the operational date of the trust, one executive and two non-executive directors one of which non-executive directors shall be a director mentioned in regulation 4(5).

(6) The minutes of the proceedings of a meeting shall be drawn up and submitted for agreement at the next ensuing meeting where they will be signed by the person presiding at it.

4 Where a post of executive director is shared by more than one person in pursuance of regulation 6–

(a) both persons shall be entitled to attend meetings of the NHS trust;

(b) either of those persons shall be eligible to vote in the case of agreement between them;

(c) in the case of disagreement between them no vote shall be cast;
(d) the presence of either or both of those persons shall count as one person for the purpose of paragraph 3(5) of this Schedule.

7.58 The rules set out in reg 19 of the NHST(MP) Regs 1990 and the Schedule to those regulations appear to provide for good governance practice.

The duty to hold meetings of the trust in public

7.59 The Schedule to the Public Bodies (Admission to Meetings) Act (PB(AM)A) 1960 provides that NHS trusts are public bodies to whom the PB(AM)A 1960 applies. It follows that directors of an NHS trust are required to comply with the public access provisions in the PB(AM)A 1960. Section 1 of the PB(AM)A 1960 provides:

(1) Subject to subsection (2) below, any meeting of a . . . body exercising public functions, being a body to which this Act applies, shall be open to the public.
(2) A body may, by resolution, exclude the public from a meeting (whether during the whole or part of the proceedings) whenever publicity would be prejudicial to the public interest by reason of the confidential nature of the business to be transacted or for other special reasons stated in the resolution and arising from the nature of that business or of the proceedings; and where such a resolution is passed, this Act shall not require the meeting to be open to the public during proceedings to which the resolution applies.
(3) A body may under subsection (2) above treat the need to receive or consider recommendations or advice from sources other than members, committees or sub-committees of the body as a special reason why publicity would be prejudicial to the public interest, without regard to the subject or purport of the recommendations or advice; but the making by this subsection of express provision for that case shall not be taken to restrict the generality of subsection (2) above in relation to other cases (including in particular cases where the report of a committee or sub-committee of the body is of a confidential nature).
(3A) Where the public are excluded from a meeting of a relevant local government body under subsection (2), the body may also prevent any person from reporting on the meeting using methods–
(a) which can be used without that person's presence at the meeting, and
(b) which enable persons not present at the meeting to see or hear the proceedings at the meeting as it takes place or later.
(4) Where a meeting of a body is required by this Act to be open to the public during the proceedings or any part of them, the following provisions shall apply, that is to say,–
(a) public notice of the time and place of the meeting shall be given by posting it at the offices of the body (or, if the body has no offices, then in some central and conspicuous place in the area with which it is concerned) three clear days at least before the meeting or, if the meeting is convened at shorter notice, then at the time it is convened;
(b) there shall, on request and on payment of postage or other necessary charge for transmission, be supplied for the benefit of any

newspaper a copy of the agenda for the meeting as supplied to members of the body (but excluding, if thought fit, any item during which the meeting is likely not to be open to the public), together with such further statements or particulars, if any, as are necessary to indicate the nature of the items included or, if thought fit in the case of any item, with copies of any reports or other documents supplied to members of the body in connection with the item;

(c) while the meeting is open to the public, the body shall not have power to exclude members of the public from the meeting and duly accredited representatives of newspapers attending for the purpose of reporting the proceedings for those newspapers shall, so far as practicable, be afforded reasonable facilities for taking their report and, unless the meeting is held in premises not belonging to the body or not on the telephone, for telephoning the report at their own expense;

(d) in the case of a meeting of a relevant local government body, while the meeting is open to the public any person attending is to be permitted to report on the meeting.

(4A) Subsection (4)(d) does not require a relevant local government body to permit oral reporting or oral commentary on a meeting as it takes place if the person reporting or providing the commentary is present at the meeting.

(5) Where a meeting of a body is required by this Act to be open to the public during the proceedings or any part of them, and there is supplied to a member of the public attending the meeting, or in pursuance of paragraph (*b*) of subsection (4) above there is supplied for the benefit of a newspaper, any such copy of the agenda as is mentioned in that paragraph, with or without further statements or particulars for the purpose of indicating the nature of any item included in the agenda, the publication thereby of any defamatory matter contained in the agenda or in the further statements or particulars shall be privileged, unless the publication is proved to be made with malice.

(6) When a body to which this Act applies resolves itself into committee, the proceedings in committee shall for the purposes of this Act be treated as forming part of the proceedings of the body at the meeting.

(7) Any reference in this section to a newspaper shall apply also to a news agency which systematically carries on the business of selling and supplying reports or information to newspapers, and to any organisation which is systematically engaged in collecting news for sound or television broadcasts or for programme services (within the meaning of the Broadcasting Act 1990) other than sound or television broadcasting services or, in the case of a relevant local government body, for use in electronic or any other format to provide news to the public by means of the internet; but, subject to subsection (4)(d), nothing in this section shall require a body to permit the taking of photographs of any proceedings, or the use of any means to enable persons not present to see or hear any proceedings (whether at the time or later), or the making of any oral report on any proceedings as they take place.

(8) The provisions of this section shall be without prejudice to any power of exclusion to suppress or prevent disorderly conduct or other misbehaviour at a meeting.

(9) In this Act–
'relevant local government body' means–
(a) the Council of the Isles of Scilly;
(b) a parish council; or
(c) a parish meeting of a parish which does not have a separate parish council;

'reporting' means–
(a) filming, photographing or making an audio recording of proceedings at a meeting;
(b) using any other means for enabling persons not present to see or hear proceedings at a meeting as it takes place or later; or
(c) reporting or providing commentary on proceedings at a meeting, orally or in writing, so that the report or commentary is available as the meeting takes place or later to persons not present'

7.60 The effect of this section is that NHS trust board meetings are required to be held in public unless the comparatively narrow 'public interest' exemption under section 1(2) is engaged. The requires the trust to pass a resolution to the effect that the directors have formed the view that publicity would be prejudicial to the public interest by reason of the confidential nature of the business to be transacted or for other special reasons stated in the resolution and arising from the nature of that business or of the proceedings. The confidentiality must be inherent in the nature of the matters being discussed rather than simply being a matter which the trust would prefer not to come into the public domain at that stage. If the reason is a 'special reason' for holding a meeting in private session, the reason needs to be stated in the resolution.

7.61 A combination of the wording of sections 1(6) and 2 of the PB(AM)A 1960 suggests that the rules about holding meetings in public only apply to meetings of a committee of the board of an NHS trust (ie where the committee consists of all of the members of the board). In other cases, the provisions of the PB(AM)A 1960 do not appear to be engaged where a board committee of an NHS trust holds a meeting.

7.62 Where a board meeting is held in public, advance notice must be given to the public of the meeting and the agenda must be provided to the media (but not necessarily the full papers). There are also provisions about providing facilities to allow reporting of the meeting and to permit the trust to expel anyone from the meeting who commits an act of disorderly conduct or other misbehaviour. The rules do not require the trust to permit the meeting to be broadcast, or for photographs to be taken in the meeting.

7.63 These provisions are potentially important because decisions made at a meeting to which the public have been denied access could be the subject of a challenge by way of judicial review. Section 1A of the PB(AM)A 1960 provides:

(1) Any person who attends a meeting of a relevant local government body for the purpose of reporting on the meeting may use any communication method, including the internet, to publish, post or otherwise share the results of the person's reporting activities.
(2) Publication and dissemination may take place at the time of the meeting or occur after the meeting.

7.64 This means that trusts cannot prohibit members of the public from tweeting or sending emails expressing their views during a meeting (or afterwards). It is an interesting question as to whether these provisions could prevent a journalist from recording the words used at a meeting in order to ensure that he or she had an accurate record of the meeting. The wording of sections 1 and 2 are not entirely clear but this appears to be permissible because of the definition provisions in section 1(9).

Pecuniary interests of NHS trust directors

7.65 Regulation 20 of the NHST(MP) Regs 1990 covers the requirement of the trust to have a policy providing for directors to disclose pecuniary interests. It provides:

> (1) Subject to the following provisions of this regulation, if a director of an NHS trust has any pecuniary interest, direct or indirect, in any contract, proposed contract or other matter and is present at a meeting of the trust at which the contract or other matter is the subject of consideration, he shall at the meeting and as soon as practicable after its commencement disclose the fact and shall not take part in the consideration and discussion of the contract or other matter or vote on any question with respect to it.
>
> (2) The Secretary of State may, subject to such conditions as he may think fit to impose, remove any disability imposed by this regulation, in any case in which it appears to him in the interests of the health service that the disability shall be removed.
>
> (3) An NHS trust may, by Standing Orders made under regulation 19 provide for the exclusion of a director from a meeting of the trust while any contract, proposed contract, or other matter in which he has a pecuniary interest, direct or indirect, is under consideration.
>
> (4) Any remuneration, compensation or allowances payable to a director by virtue of paragraph 9 of Schedule 2 to the Act shall not be treated as a pecuniary interest for the purpose of this regulation.
>
> (5) Subject to paragraphs (2) and (6), a director shall be treated for the purposes of this regulation as having indirectly a pecuniary interest in a contract, proposed contract or other matter if–
>
> (a) he, or a nominee of his, is a director of a company or other body, not being a public body, with which the contract was made or is proposed to be made or which has a direct pecuniary interest in the other matter under consideration; or
>
> (b) he is a partner of, or is in the employment of, a person with whom the contract was made or is proposed to be made or who has a direct pecuniary interest in the other matter under consideration and, in the case of married persons living together, the interest of one spouse shall be deemed for the purpose of this regulation to be also an interest of the other.
>
> (6) A director shall not be treated as having a pecuniary interest in any contract, proposed contract or other matter by reason only–
>
> (a) of his membership of a company or other body if he has no beneficial interest in any securities of that company or other body;
>
> (b) of an interest in any company, body or person with which he is connected as mentioned in paragraph (5) which is so remote or insignificant that it cannot reasonably be regarded as likely to influence a director in the consideration or discussion of or in voting on, any question with respect to that contract or matter.

(7) Where a director–
(a) has an indirect pecuniary interest in a contract or other matter by reason only of a beneficial interest in securities of a company or other body; and
(b) the total nominal value of those securities does not exceed £5,000 or one hundredth of the total nominal value of the issued share capital of the company or body, whichever is the less; and
(c) if the share capital is of more than one class, the total nominal value of shares of any one class in which he has the beneficial interest does not exceed one hundredth of the total issued share capital of that class,

this regulation shall not prohibit him from taking part in consideration or discussion of the contract or other matter or from voting on any question in respect to it without prejudice however to his duty to disclose his interest.

(8) This regulation applies to a committee or sub-committee of an NHS trust as it applies to the trust and applies to any member of any such committee or sub-committee (whether or not he is also a director of the trust) as it applies to a director of the trust.

7.66 This regulation only applies to pecuniary interests which may cause a conflict of interest on the part of the director. It does not cover non-pecuniary interests. These rules provide that a director is required to disclose any material pecuniary interest in any contract or matter being considered by the trust. Having disclosed the pecuniary interest, the regulation requires the director to remain silent during the board discussion of the item and not to vote on any resolution relating to the matter (ie he shall not take part in the consideration and discussion of the contract or other matter or vote on any question with respect to it). However, the regulation does not require the director to absent himself from the meeting, although the standing orders can require exclusion from the meeting.

7.67 The secretary of state is entitled to decide to waive the right of a director to take part in trust decision despite a pecuniary interest where he judges that it is 'in the interests of the health service that the disability shall be removed'. The regulation provides that remuneration from the trust for an office or employment does not constitute a relevant pecuniary interest and has rules about which prevent a director being excluded for other de-minimis interests.

Standing orders and schemes of delegation

7.68 NHS trusts are required by the NHST(MP) Regs 1990 to have standing orders, but the precise rules set out in the standing orders are matters for the board of individual trusts. The Department of Health and Social Care published *Model standing orders* for NHS trusts in 2006,[20] including recommended schemes of delegation of decision-making. No new form of standing orders appears to have been published since then and most NHS trust standing orders and schemes of delegation follow the 2006 model.

20 See http://webarchive.nationalarchives.gov.uk/20080817162914/http://www.dh.gov.uk/en/Publicationsandstatistics/Publications/PublicationsPolicyAndGuidance/DH_4132059.

Remuneration for chairs and non-executive directors

7.69 Paragraph 11 of Schedule 4 to the NHS Act 2006 provides that the secretary of state is required to fix the level of remuneration for chairs and non-executives of NHS trusts. It provides:

(1) An NHS trust must pay–
  (a) to the chairman and any non-executive director of the NHS trust remuneration of an amount determined by the Secretary of State, not exceeding such amount as may be approved by the Treasury,
  (b) to the chairman and any non-executive director of the NHS trust such travelling and other allowances as may be determined by the Secretary of State with the approval of the Treasury,
  (c) to any member of a committee or sub-committee of the NHS trust who is not also a director such travelling and other allowances as may be so determined.
(2) If an NHS trust so determines in the case of a person who is or has been a chairman of the NHS trust, the NHS trust must pay such pension, allowances or gratuities to or in respect of him as may be determined by the Secretary of State with the approval of the Treasury.
(3) Different determinations may be made under sub-paragraph (1) or sub-paragraph (2) in relation to different cases or descriptions of cases.

7.70 Thus the level of remuneration for both chairs and non-executives can be different between different trusts. This reflects the markedly different levels of responsibilities between different types of trust. Members of trust committees cannot be paid remuneration but can be paid travelling and other expenses, as set by the secretary of state.

The duty for NHS trusts to produce an annual report

7.71 Paragraphs 12 and 13 of Schedule 4 to the NHS Act 2006 provide that each NHS trust is required to produce and publish an annual report in a form prescribed by the secretary of state and to provide such other information to the secretary of state as may be requested. The paragraphs provide:

Reports and other information

12 (1) For each accounting year an NHS trust must prepare and send to the Secretary of State an annual report in such form as may be determined by the Secretary of State.
(2) At such time or times as may be prescribed, an NHS trust must hold a public meeting at which must be presented–
  (a) its audited accounts and annual report, and
  (b) any report on the accounts made pursuant to [paragraph 1 of Schedule 7 to the Local Audit and Accountability Act 2014.
(2A) In the case of NHS Direct National Health Service Trust the reference to a report under paragraph 1 of Schedule 7 to the Local Audit and Accountability Act 2014 has effect as a reference to a report under paragraph 6(2) of Schedule 15 to this Act.
(3) In such circumstances and at such time or times as may be prescribed, an NHS trust must hold a public meeting at which such documents as may be prescribed must be presented.

13 An NHS trust must furnish to the Secretary of State such reports, returns and other information, including information as to its forward planning, as, and in such form as, he may require.

7.72 In practice, the secretary of state requires NHS trusts to provide a huge amount of data on their activities to a range of NHS bodies, including NHSI. There is no express limitation in the wording of para 13 on the types of information that can be requested or the frequency of the requests. There is also no provision entitling an NHS trust to charge the secretary of state (or any other NHS body to whom it is directed to provide information by the secretary of state) for the costs of complying with this obligation.

The powers of NHS trusts

7.73 Paragraphs 14–27 of Schedule 4 to the NHS Act 2006 provide that NHS trusts have a number of general and specific powers. The secretary of state has a general power by order to create new powers for NHS trusts under para 22 (although this power does not appear to have been used to create any new powers for NHS trusts at present). The following paragraphs consider the nature and effect of each of these powers.

7.74 Paragraph 14 provides a general power of competence for an NHS trust. It provides:

> (1) An NHS trust may do anything which appears to it to be necessary or expedient for the purposes of or in connection with its functions.
> (2) In particular it may–
> (a) acquire and dispose of property,
> (b) enter into contracts, and
> (c) accept gifts of property (including property to be held on trust, either for the general or any specific purposes of the NHS trust or for any purposes relating to the health service).
> (3) The reference in sub-paragraph (2)(c) to specific purposes of the NHS trust includes a reference to the purposes of a specific hospital or other establishment or facility at or from which services are provided by the NHS trust.

7.75 NHS trusts are creatures of statute and are, accordingly, only able lawfully to act in a manner which is intra vires their powers. Hence an NHS trust has no power to take steps or expend money for purposes which are unconnected to its primary purpose, namely 'to provide goods and services for the purposes of the health service': see section 25(1) of the NHS Act 2006. However, NHS trusts are provided with wide discretionary powers to decide how their wish to run their organisations in order to deliver on that primary purpose. An NHS trust will be acting intra vires if it does anything or expends money which it considers necessary or expedient in pursuit of this purpose.

7.76 The decision as to whether a particular course of action or decision is one which is necessary or expedient in pursuit of the trust's purpose is a discretionary matter for the directors to decide. Provide they reach a view that is not irrational, it is irrelevant whether any other trust would have reached that view or whether a court would have made that decision: see *R v Greater London Council ex p Burgess*.[21]

21 [1978] ICR 991.

7.77 The discretionary decision-making of the directors is subject to the limitation that the trust should not take decisions which could be characterised as being 'irrationally generous'. The Court of Appeal explained in *Gibb v Maidstone and Tunbridge Wells NHS Trust*[22] that:

> This is a term of art, since the reference to irrationality is to unreasonableness in the *Wednesbury* ([1948] 1 KB 223) sense – a decision so unreasonable that no reasonable decision-maker could have arrived at it.

The test of irrationality introduces a high threshold and thus gives the directors a large measure of discretion to decide how to exercise their powers in order to deliver on the trust's purposes.

7.78 The decision-making powers of the trust and the trust's resources must be deployed for the purposes of the trust and not for purposes which have no connection to the discharge of the trust's functions. It is beyond the scope of this chapter to provide a detailed guide to the law relating to the manner in which public bodies should act and when their decisions are intra vires (within their powers) or unlawful for being ultra vires (ie beyond their powers). NHS trusts should are recommended to seek specialist advice on the facts of a particular case if a question of vires arises.

NHS contracts

7.79 Paragraph 15 of Schedule 4 to the NHS Act 2006 permits NHS trusts to enter into 'NHS contracts'. It provides:

> In addition to carrying out its other functions, an NHS trust may, as the provider, enter into NHS contracts.

7.80 The law relating to NHS contracts is explained at chapter 10 on contracting. NHS trusts (unlike NHS FTs) do not have power to enter into legally binding contracts with NHS commissioners because section 9(5) of the NHS Act 2006 provides that any such arrangement 'must not be regarded for any purpose as giving rise to contractual rights or liabilities'. Accordingly, any form of contract or agreement between an NHS trust and a CCG or NHS England can only take effect as an NHS contract.

Research and training

7.81 Paragraphs 16 and 17 of Schedule 4 to the NHS Act 2006 give power to NHS trusts to undertake or commission research and to provide training for both its own staff and anyone else who is delivering NHS services. They provide:

> **Research**
> 16. An NHS trust may undertake and commission research and make available staff and provide facilities for research by other persons.
>
> **Training**
> 17. An NHS trust may–

22 [2010] EWCA Civ 678.

(a) provide training for persons employed or likely to be employed by the NHS trust or otherwise in the provision of services under this Act, and
(b) make facilities and staff available in connection with training by a university or any other body providing training in connection with the health service.

Both these powers are permissive and thus impose no obligation on an NHS Trust to become involved in either research or training. However both research and staff training are core functions of virtually all NHS organisations.

Joint decision-making

7.82 Paragraph 18 of Schedule 4 to the NHS Act 2006 provides a wide power for NHS trusts to enter into arrangements with other public bodies and private individuals for joint working and joint decision-making. It provides:

> **Joint exercise of functions**
> An NHS trust may enter into arrangements for the carrying out, on such terms as the NHS trust considers appropriate, of any of its functions jointly with any . . . Special Health Authority, Local Health Board or other NHS trust, or any other body or individual'

7.83 The wide wording suggests that an NHS trust is entitled to enter into joint working arrangements with any other public body or with a company or with an individual person (ie a real person as opposed to a corporate person) for the discharge of its functions. It follows that joint working arrangements between NHS trusts and CCGs or local authorities are potentially intra vires, provided the directors of the trust consider that such working arrangements are necessary or expedient in order to assist in the discharge of the trust's purpose.

The provision of private medical care and other commercial activities

7.84 NHS trusts have always had wide powers to provide private medical services, which used to be called 'pay beds'. The power is now in para 19 of Schedule 4 to the NHS Act 2006. This provides:

> (1) According to the nature of its functions, an NHS trust may make accommodation or services available for patients who give undertakings (or for whom undertakings are given) to pay any charges imposed by the NHS trust in respect of the accommodation or services.
> (2) An NHS trust may exercise the power conferred by sub-paragraph (1) only–
> (a) to the extent that its exercise does not to any significant extent interfere with the performance by the NHS trust of its functions or of its obligations under NHS contracts, and
> (b) in circumstances specified in directions under section 8, with the Secretary of State's consent.

7.85 Given the huge controversy that emerged about the ability of NHS FTs to undertake private patient work, there has been remarkably little comment on the longstanding ability of NHS trusts to treat private patients. As far as the authors are aware, there are no directions in force concerning the exercise of these powers. Thus, for all practical purposes, para 19(2)(b) is not relevant.

7.86 Paragraph 19(1) is only concerned with the ability of trusts to charge for accommodation or services which it makes available for patients. In broad terms, this covers two types of patients, namely:

a) patients who are receiving NHS-funded care and agree to pay for additional services which are not usually provided to NHS patients, such as a private room or access to telephone or internet services. It can also include granting access to medical treatment which is not made available to NHS-funded patients, such as expensive cancer drugs which a CCG is refusing to fund; and
b) private patients who are receiving medical care which has not been commissioned by an NHS commissioner and are paying for the whole of their care (whether it is care that would be funded by an NHS commissioner or not).

7.87 In 2006 the Department of Health and Social Care issued best practice guidance[23] to NHS trusts on the exercise of income generation powers, including the exercise of these powers ('the 2006 guidance'). This guidance[24] was mainly concerned with income generation under arrangements that did not involve services to patients (which are considered below), but provided:

> **Amenity Beds**
> 30.19 Income generation powers allow NHS bodies to provide patients with a separate room with extra facilities such as a television and telephone. The person is still an NHS patient but has chosen to pay for these additional facilities.
>
> **Charges for Certain Patient Services**
> 30.20 If an item or service is considered to be an integral part of a patient's treatment by their clinician then a charge should not be made. However NHS bodies can charge for certain patient services that are considered to be additional treatments over and above the normal service provision. There is no blanket policy to cover this and each case should be considered in the light of the patient's clinical need.

7.88 The question about how privately funded care could be provided to NHS patients alongside NHS care was the subject of further guidance: *Guidance on NHS patients who wish to pay for additional private care*.[25] That guidance was particularly concerned to provide a framework for patients to seek to purchase extra drugs which were not available as part of NHS funded care as part of their treatment, even if a poorer patient in the next bed with the same condition could not gain access to the same treatment. The guidance was prepared by Professor Mike Richards, who also had a leading role in delivering NHS cancer services. Given the interests of the author, it was

23 See http://webarchive.nationalarchives.gov.uk/20130124072327/http://www.dh.gov.uk/prod_consum_dh/groups/dh_digitalassets/@dh/@en/documents/digitalasset/dh_4130668.pdf.

24 This was guidance issued prior to the substantial changes to the NHS caused by the HSCA 2012 and so part of it is out of date. However, it never appears to have been formally withdrawn and is still a source of useful guidance.

25 See www.gov.uk/government/uploads/system/uploads/attachment_data/file/404423/patients-add-priv-care.pdf. This is current guidance.

unsurprising that the guidance favoured the ability for NHS patients to purchase additional medical services (such as cancer drugs) that were not part of NHS-funded care. However, it sought to ensure that, as far as possible, this would be delivered in a way that was fair to the patient and the trust, and that no other NHS patient would be prejudiced if such additional care was provided.

7.89 A summary of the guidance provided as follows:

- NHS organisations should not withdraw NHS care simply because a patient chooses to buy additional private care.
- Any additional private care must be delivered separately from NHS care.
- The NHS must never charge for NHS care (except where there is specific legislation in place to allow charges) and the NHS should never subsidise private care.
- The NHS should continue to provide free of charge all care that the patient would have been entitled to had he or she not chosen to have additional private care.
- NHS trusts and FTs should have clear policies in place, in line with these principles, to ensure effective implementation of this guidance in their organisations. This includes protocols for working with other NHS or private providers where the NHS trust or FT has chosen not to provide additional private care.

7.90 While the guidance recommended that any private treatment should be delivered separately from NHS care, it also recognised that, in practice, it may not always be possible to separate the care that a patient is paying for from NHS-funded care.

Other income generation activities by NHS trusts

7.91 The general power in para 14 of Schedule 4 to the NHS Act 2006 could include an NHS trust engaging in commercial activities to raise money or provide services for remuneration in order to assist the trust in funding services for patients. However, specific powers are given for trusts to engage in income generation activities in para 20 of Schedule 4, which provides:

> **Additional income**
>
> **20** (1) For the purpose of making additional income available in order better to perform its functions, an NHS trust has the powers specified in section 7(2) of the Health and Medicines Act 1988 (extension of powers of Secretary of State for financing the health service).
>
> (2) The power conferred by sub-paragraph (1) may be exercised only–
>
> (a) to the extent that its exercise does not to any significant extent interfere with the performance by the NHS trust of its functions or of its obligations under NHS contracts, and
>
> (b) in circumstances specified in directions under section 8, with the consent of the Secretary of State.

7.92 The meaning of this paragraph is not entirely clear, but it is suggested that it gives NHS trusts power to enter into any of the types of income generation schemes specified in section 7(2) of the Health and Medicines Act (HMA) 1988, provided the purpose of the scheme is to generate additional income in order to enable the trust better to perform its functions of providing NHS services. However, the secretary of state has the right to issue directions to require NHS trusts to seek consent from the secretary of state before they are lawfully entitled to enter into any particular type of income generation scheme defined in the directions.

7.93 Section 7(2) of the HMA 1988 has been amended on a number of occasions since it was initially passed. The current version of section 7 reads as follows:

> (1) In order to make more income available for improving the health service (as defined in the National Health Service Act 2006 or the National Health Service (Scotland) Act 1978), the Secretary of State shall have the powers specified in subsection (2) below; but for the avoidance of doubt it is hereby declared that nothing in this section authorises him or any body to which he gives directions under subsection (3) below to disregard any enactment or rule of law or to override any person's contractual or proprietary rights.
>
> (2) The powers mentioned in subsection (1) above are powers (exercisable outside as well as within Great Britain)–
> (a) to acquire, produce, manufacture and supply goods;
> (b) to acquire land by agreement and manage and deal with land;
> (c) to supply accommodation to any person;
> (d) to supply services to any person and to provide new services;
> (e) to provide instruction for any person;
> (f) to develop and exploit ideas and exploit intellectual property;
> (g) to do anything whatsoever which appears to him to be calculated to facilitate, or to be conducive or incidental to, the exercise of any power conferred by this subsection; and
> (h) to make such charge as he considers appropriate for anything that he does in the exercise of any such power to calculate any such charge on any basis that he considers to be the appropriate commercial basis.
>
> . . .
>
> (6) The Secretary of State shall exercise the powers specified in subsection (2)(c) and (d) above only if and to the extent that he is satisfied that anything which he proposes to do in the exercise of those powers does not fall within section 65 of the National Health Service Act 1977 or section 57 of the National Health Service (Scotland) Act 1978.
>
> (7) The Secretary of State shall exercise the powers specified in subsection (2)(f) above only after consulting (to the extent that it appears to him to be practical) any person who appears to him to have an interest through his own previous research in the ideas or intellectual property in question as to whether he should exercise them and, if so, as to any financial arrangements.
>
> (7A) The power specified in paragraph (g) of subsection (2) above includes power for the Secretary of State–
> (a) to form, or participate in the forming of, companies,
> (b) to invest in companies (whether by acquiring assets, securities or rights or otherwise), and
> (c) to provide loans and guarantees and make other kinds of financial provision to or in respect of companies,
> where it appears to him that to do so is calculated to facilitate, or to be conducive or incidental to, the exercise of any power conferred by that subsection.
>
> (7B) In subsection (7A) above 'companies' means companies as defined in section 1(1) of the Companies Act 2006; and that subsection is without prejudice to–

(a) the generality of paragraph (g) of subsection (2) above, and
(b) any powers of the Secretary of State exercisable otherwise than by virtue of this section.

. . .

(7D) In subsection (7C) above 'companies' means companies as defined in section 1(1) of the Companies Act 2006; and that subsection is without prejudice to the generality of subsection (2) above.

(8) The Secretary of State shall exercise the powers specified in subsection (2) above only if and to the extent that he is satisfied that anything which he proposes to do–
(a) will not to a significant extent interfere with the performance by him of any duty imposed on him by the National Health Service Act 2006 or the National Health Service (Scotland) Act 1978; and
(b) will not to a significant extent operate to the disadvantage of persons seeking or afforded admission or access to accommodation or services at hospitals vested in the Secretary of State for the purposes of his functions under either of those Acts (whether as resident or non-resident patients) otherwise than under section 65 of the National Health Service Act 1977 or section 57 of the National Health Service (Scotland) Act 1978.

(8A) The references in subsection (6) and subsection (8) to section 65 of the National Health Service Act 1977 are references to that section prior to its repeal by the National Health Service (Consequential Provisions) Act 2006 . . .

7.94 The reference to section 65 of the National Health Service Act (NHS Act) 1977 is a reference to the relevant section in the NHS Act 1977 which allowed the secretary of state to set up schemes for private patients in NHS hospitals. This is now covered by para 19 of Schedule 4 to the NHS Act 2006, which is described above.

7.95 Section 7(2) of the HMA 1988 thus gives NHS trusts the power to enter into a wide range of commercial activities for the purpose of generating additional revenue for the trust and thus assisting the trust in meeting the cost of delivering NHS services. This is the power which trusts use to charge fees for car parking, which is a subject of political controversy from time to time. The 2006 guidance explains:[26]

> Income generation powers enable NHS bodies (abiding by specific rules) to raise additional income from marketing any spare capacity resulting from a non-core function, or from exploiting intellectual property rights, to raise additional income for health services.

7.96 There is a specific power in section 7(7A) of the HMA 1988 to create companies for the purpose of carrying income generation activities. In 2002 the secretary of state issued directions relating to the exercise of powers under section 7(2) and section 7(7A) of the HMA 1988.[27] Assuming these directions remain in force, the relevant parts of the directions provide:

26 At para 30.3.

27 There is no published list of all directions made by the secretary of state and so finding out what directions have been published, which have been rescinded or remain in force is far from straightforward to find out. The 2002 directions are in Part 2, Appendix 5 of: http://webarchive.nationalarchives.gov.uk/20120503225438/http://www.dh.gov.uk/prod_consum_dh/groups/dh_digitalassets/@dh/@en/documents/digitalasset/dh_4077307.pdf. Thanks must go to Tim Winn of Mills & Reeve for assistance here.

2 (1) The Secretary of State directs that, save as otherwise allowed by him, a relevant body shall not exercise any of the powers in subsection (7A) of section 7 of the 1988 Act in connection with the exercise of any of the powers in subsection (2) of that section, unless it has submitted to the Secretary of State a proposal, and the other information and documents specified in the Schedule to these Directions and the Secretary of State has notified the body that he considers that the proposal–

(a) satisfies the tests specified in section 7(8) of the 1988 Act;

. . .

(c) where the body is a National Health Service trust, satisfies the criteria specified in section 5(9) of the 1990 Act; and

(d) represents an appropriate exercise of the powers in subsection (7A) by the body, having regard in particular to the matters specified in sub-paragraph (2) below.

(2) The matters referred to are–

(a) the financial risks for the health service and the financial benefits for the health service (in terms of greater income for improving the health service) which appear to him to be associated with the proposal;

(b) where the proposal concerns the exercise of the powers in subsection (7A) in connection with the powers in subsection (2)(f) (ideas and intellectual property), the conditions on which the ideas or intellectual property may be made available to bodies established in countries outside England and Wales being bodies that are concerned with the delivery of health care in those countries, following the exercise of the powers in subsection (7A); and

(c) where the proposal concerns the exercise of the powers in subsection (7A) in connection with the powers in subsection (2)(f) (ideas and intellectual property), the conditions on which the ideas or intellectual property may be made available for the purposes of the health service, following the exercise of the powers in subsection (7A).

Conditions applying to the exercise of the powers in section 7(2) and (7A)

3 The Secretary of State directs that a relevant body which exercises any of the powers in subsection (7A) of section 7 shall, subject to any enactment, rule of law or any person's contractual or proprietary rights–

(a) save where otherwise allowed by the Secretary of State, and subject to sub-paragraph (b), exercise the powers in subsection (7A), and any powers in subsection (2) in connection with which the powers in subsection (7A) are exercised, in accordance with the proposal which has been the subject of a notification by the Secretary of State as referred to in paragraph 2(1) including the documents referred to in paragraph (a)(vii) and (viii) of the Schedule to this Order, but otherwise excluding any documents attached to the proposal;

(b) exercise the powers in subsection (7A) in accordance with any restrictions laid down by the Secretary of State at any time (being restrictions which do not have retrospective effect) relating to –

(i) the amount of money or other property which the body may provide in connection with investment in the company, including any restrictions as to the amount which may be provided within a particular period or periods of time; and

(ii) the amount which may be provided to or in respect of the company by way of loans, guarantees or other financial provision, including any restrictions as to the amount which may be provided within a particular period or periods of time; and

(c) in exercising the powers in subsection (7A), and any powers in subsection (2) in connection with which the powers in subsection (7A) are exercised, have regard to any relevant guidance issued by the Secretary of State.

Information concerning the exercise of the powers in section 7(2) and (7A)

4 The Secretary of State directs that, where the Secretary of State has notified a relevant body as referred to in paragraph 2(1), the relevant body shall supply the Secretary of State with such information in its possession, or to which it is entitled, concerning –

(a) the exercise by it of any of the powers in section 7(7A) of the 1988 Act, and of any of the powers in section 7(2) of the 1988 Act in connection with which the powers in section 7(7A) are exercised; and

(b) the activities of the company connected with the exercise of those powers,

as the Secretary of State may request at any time.

7.97 These directions are self-explanatory. They require NHS trusts to seek and obtain the consent of the secretary of state if they propose to use the powers in section 7(7A) of the HMA 1988 to form, or participate in the forming of, companies, to invest in companies (whether by acquiring assets, securities or rights or otherwise), and to provide loans and guarantees and make other kinds of financial provision to or in respect of companies, as part of an income generation scheme. If consent is given subject to conditions, the directions require the trust to comply with the conditions.

Providing services outside England and Wales

7.98 Paragraph 21 of Schedule 4 to the NHS Act 2006 permits an NHS trust to arrange for accommodation and services to be provided to NHS patients outside of England and Wales. Thus it would be intra vires for an NHS trust to set up a facility to treat English NHS patients in Scotland, another EU country or even outside the EU entirely.

Powers of NHS trusts to enter into externally financed development agreements

7.99 Paragraph 23 of Schedule 4 to the NHS Act 200 gives NHS trusts specific powers to enter into externally financed development agreements. It provides:

(1) The powers of an NHS trust include power to enter into externally financed development agreements.

(2) For the purposes of this paragraph, an agreement is an externally financed development agreement if it is certified as such in writing by the Secretary of State.

(3) The Secretary of State may give a certificate under this paragraph if–

(a) in his opinion the purpose or main purpose of the agreement is the provision of facilities or services in connection with the discharge by the NHS trust of any of its functions, and

(b) a person proposes to make a loan to, or provide any other form of finance for, another party in connection with the agreement.

(4) If an NHS trust enters into an externally financed development agreement it may also, in connection with that agreement, enter into an agreement with a person who falls within sub-paragraph (3)(b) in relation to the externally financed development agreement.

(5) 'Another party' means any party to the agreement other than the NHS trust.

(6) The fact that an agreement made by an NHS trust has not been certified under this paragraph does not affect its validity'

7.100 This is the power used by NHS trusts to enter into public-private partnerships. However, these are wide powers and could include development agreements with other public bodies, such as a local authority.

The delivery of primary medical and dental care by NHS trusts

7.101 NHS trusts were originally set up to run NHS hospitals. They have expanded over the years into running a wide range of NHS acute and community services for patients who have both physical health and mental health needs. However, NHS trusts have rarely become involved in delivering primary care medical or dental services. Nonetheless, paragraph 24 of Schedule 4 to the NHS Act 2006 provides that it *intra vires* for an NHS trust to take on a Personal Medical Services (PMS) contract to deliver primary care services to NHS patients or a Personal Dental Services (PDS) contract to deliver primary dental services. It provides:

> An NHS trust may provide services under an agreement made under section 92 (primary medical services) or section 107 (primary dental services) and may do so as a member of a qualifying body (within the meaning given by section 93 or section 108).

7.102 It follows that NHS England (which is the commissioner of these services, albeit that they are partially now delegated to CCGs) is entitled to enter into a PMS or PDS contract with an NHS trust under which the trust agrees to deliver primary care medical and dental services. There are relatively few examples of such arrangements but, where they operate, the trust employs general practitioner doctors, dentists and other care staff to deliver primary care services.

The employment of staff by NHS trusts

7.103 Paragraph 25 of Schedule 4 to the NHS Act 2006 give an NHS trust power to employ staff on any terms that it considers appropriate. In practice, the vast majority of trust staff are engaged on standard terms which have been negotiated on behalf of trust employers by NHS employers (which is part of the NHS Confederation, the trade body representing NHS providers). This paragraph provides:

(1) An NHS trust may employ such staff as it considers appropriate.

(2) An NHS trust may–

(a) pay its staff such remuneration and allowances, and

(b) employ them on such other terms and conditions,
as it considers appropriate.

(3) An NHS trust must–
(a) in exercising its powers under sub-paragraph (2), and
(b) otherwise in connection with the employment of its staff,
act in accordance with regulations and any directions given by the Secretary of State.

(4) Before making any regulations under sub-paragraph (3), the Secretary of State must consult such bodies as he may recognise as representing persons who, in his opinion, are likely to be affected by the regulations.

7.104 There are no relevant regulations and no directions which are known to the authors. The issue as to whether, given the power for each NHS employer to enter into their own terms of employment, it was intra vires for the secretary of state to push for national terms of employment was considered by Green J in *R (Justice for Health Ltd) v The Secretary of State for Health.*[28] The judge decided that there was nothing incompatible between individual NHS trusts having the power to engage staff on any terms they considered and NHS employers generally (with the secretary of state) devising national terms and conditions that they recommended should be adopted by all NHS trusts.

7.105 Paragraph 26 provides that NHS trusts have the power to arrange for the provision of pensions to their employees as follows:

(1) An NHS trust may, for or in respect of such of its employees as it may determine, make arrangements for providing pensions, allowances or gratuities.

(2) Such arrangements may include the establishment and administration, by the NHS trust or otherwise, of one or more pension schemes.

(3) The reference in sub-paragraph (1) to pensions, allowances or gratuities to or in respect of employees of an NHS trust includes a reference to pensions, allowances or gratuities by way of compensation to or in respect of any of the NHS trust's employees who suffer loss of office or employment or loss or diminution of emoluments.

(4) This paragraph does not affect the generality of paragraphs 14 and 25.

7.106 In practice, NHS trusts use this power to make contributions on behalf of employees to the NHS pension scheme which is operated under the National Health Service Pension Scheme Regulations 1995[29] (as amended). However, NHS trusts are not obliged to work within the NHS pension scheme and could, at least in theory, operate their own pension schemes or contract with a commercial pension scheme.

Compulsory purchase powers

7.107 Paragraph 27 of Schedule 4 to the NHS Act 2006 gives the secretary of state the power to make an order to enable a trust compulsorily to purchase land. It provides:

28 [2016] EWHC 2338 (Admin).

29 SI No 300.

(1) An NHS trust may be authorised to purchase land compulsorily for the purposes of its functions by means of an order made by the NHS trust and confirmed by the Secretary of State.
(2) Subject to sub-paragraph (3), the Acquisition of Land Act 1981 applies to the compulsory purchase of land under this paragraph.
(3) No order may be made by an NHS trust under Part 2 of the Acquisition of Land Act 1981 with respect to any land unless the proposal to acquire the land compulsorily–
  (a) has been submitted to the Secretary of State in such form and together with such information as he may require, and
  (b) has been approved by him.

7.108 It is beyond the scope of this book to give a detailed account of the exercise of compulsory purchase powers. Trusts that seek to make use of these powers should seek specialist legal advice.

Dissolution of NHS trusts

7.109 The arrangements for the dissolution of NHS trusts are set out in paras 28–31 of Schedule 4 of the NHS Act 2006. These provide:

28 (1) The Secretary of State may by order dissolve an NHS trust.
(2) An order under this paragraph may be made–
  (a) on the application of the NHS trust concerned, or
  (b) if the Secretary of State considers it appropriate in the interests of the health service.
(3) Except where it appears to the Secretary of State necessary to make an order under this paragraph as a matter of urgency [or where the order is made following the publication of a final report under section 65I(3)], no such order may be made until after the completion of such consultation as may be prescribed.

29 (1) If an NHS trust is dissolved under paragraph 28, the Secretary of State may by order transfer, or provide for the transfer, to himself or an NHS body of such of the property and liabilities of the NHS trust which is dissolved as in his opinion is appropriate; and any such order may include provisions corresponding to those of paragraph 9.
(2) The liabilities which may be transferred by virtue of sub-paragraph (1) to an NHS body include criminal liabilities.
(3) An order under this paragraph may make provision in connection with the transfer of staff employed by or for the purposes of the NHS trust which is dissolved; and such an order may include provisions corresponding to those of paragraph 8, including provision for the making of a scheme by such . . . Special Health Authority, Local Health Board or other body as may be specified in the order.
(4) No order may be made under this paragraph until after completion of such consultation as may be prescribed.

30 (1) If an NHS trust is dissolved under paragraph 28, the Secretary of State or such other NHS trust, . . . Special Health Authority or Local Health Board as he may direct must undertake the responsibility for the continued payment of any such pension, allowances or gratuities as, by virtue of paragraph 11(2) or paragraph 26, would otherwise have been the responsibility of the NHS trust which has been dissolved.
(2) Sub-paragraph (1) does not affect the generality of paragraph 29.

31 Subject to section 56AA, an NHS trust may not be dissolved or wound up except in accordance with paragraph 28 or section 57.

7.110 These are rarely used powers and accordingly no commentary is provided concerning their effect. There are also miscellaneous powers in paras 32–34 of Schedule 4 and limited definitions of terms used in the Schedule.

The financial powers and duties of NHS trusts

7.111 NHS trusts are unlike many other public bodies in that they do not generally receive funds from the government to enable them to discharge their duties. Trusts are (at least in theory) supposed to operate with one main income stream, namely the sums payable to them under NHS contracts. NHS trusts have a huge variety of other sources of income (from car parking through private patients to research grants), all of which are used to meet the costs of delivering NHS services to patients. Schedule 5 to the NHS Act 2006 sets out the essential financial framework under which trusts have to operate. This is supplemented by a vast body of guidance, notably in the Department of Health and Social Care's *Group accounting manual*. It is beyond the scope of this book to provide a detailed analysis of all of the guidance, but the following is a guide to the main provisions within Schedule 5.

7.112 Paragraph 1 provides for the trust to have an 'originating capital' and for the Treasury to set a charge for the trust to pay an annual capital charge to reflect the capital provided to the trust. This is, in effect, an interest payment to reflect the fact that the trust started life with a substantial injection of public capital. The secretary of state can make 'loans' to a trust (as to which see below) or can provide additional amounts of capital which are then added to the originating capital and attract capital charges. Paragraph 7 of Schedule 5 also permits the secretary of state to provide capital to an NHS trust which is neither a loan nor is added to the trust's capital on which capital charges have to be paid.

7.113 The primary revenue duty of an NHS trust is set out in para 2 of Schedule 5, which provides:

Financial obligations of NHS trusts

(1) Each NHS trust must ensure that its revenue is not less than sufficient, taking one financial year with another, to meet outgoings properly chargeable to revenue account.

(2) Each NHS trust must achieve such financial objectives as may from time to time be set by the Secretary of State with the consent of the Treasury and as are applicable to it.

(3) Any such objectives may be made applicable to NHS trusts generally, or to a particular NHS trust or to NHS trusts of a particular description.

7.114 The primary financial duty on every trust is thus, taking one financial year with another, to ensure that it at least breaks even on its revenue account. A trust which made a surplus would deliver on this duty. A trust will not be in breach of this legal duty if, in a particular financial year, it operates at a loss. The legal duty requires the trust to operate on a financially stable basis over a series of years.

7.115 The borrowing powers of a trust are set out in paras 3–6 of Schedule 5 to the NHS Act 2006, which provide:

Borrowing

3 (1) For the purpose of its functions an NHS trust may borrow (both temporarily, by way of overdraft, and longer term) from the Secretary of State or from any other person.

(2) Sub-paragraph (1) is subject to any direction given by the Secretary of State under section 8, to the provisions of this paragraph and to any limit imposed under this Schedule.

(3) An NHS trust may not mortgage or charge any of its assets or in any other way use any of its assets as security for a loan.

(4) The Secretary of State must determine the terms of any loan made by him to an NHS trust (including terms as to the payment of interest, if any).

Guarantees of borrowing

4 (1) The Secretary of State may guarantee, in such manner and on such conditions as, with the approval of the Treasury, he considers appropriate, the repayments of the principal of, and the payment of interest on, any sums which an NHS trust borrows from a person other than the Secretary of State.

(2) Immediately after a guarantee is given under this paragraph, the Secretary of State must lay a statement of the guarantee before each House of Parliament.

(3) Where any sum is issued for fulfilling a guarantee so given, the Secretary of State must lay before each House of Parliament a statement relating to that sum as soon as possible after the end of each financial year beginning with that in which the sum is issued and ending with that in which all liability in respect of the principal of the sum and in respect of interest on it is finally discharged.

(4) If any sums are issued in fulfilment of a guarantee given under this paragraph, the NHS trust concerned must make to the Secretary of State, at such times and in such manner as the Secretary of State may from time to time direct–

(a) payments of such amounts as the Secretary of State with the consent of the Treasury so directs in or towards repayment of the sums so issued, and

(b) payments of interest, at such rates as the Secretary of State with the consent of the Treasury so directs, on what is outstanding for the time being in respect of sums so issued.

Limits on indebtedness

5 The aggregate of all sums borrowed by NHS trusts which are required to provide or manage services at or from hospitals or other establishments or facilities which are situated in England must not exceed £5,000 million or such other sum not exceeding £10,000 million as may be specified by order made by the Secretary of State with the consent of the Treasury'

7.116 These provisions allow a trust to borrow money from the secretary of state or from another commercial borrower. Hence, it is lawful for a trust to run an unsecured overdraft with its bankers or obtain an unsecured commercial loan.

Surplus funds

7.117 There have been occasions in the past[30] where NHS trusts have built up large cash surpluses. Paragraph 8 of Schedule 5 to the NHS Act 2006 permits the secretary of state to be able to require the money to be paid back to the 'Consolidated Fund', which in effect means that it is handed back to the Treasury. It provides:

> If it appears to the Secretary of State that any sum held by an NHS trust otherwise than as trustee is surplus to its foreseeable requirements, the trust must, if the Secretary of State with the approval of the Treasury and after consultation with the trust so directs, pay that sum into the Consolidated Fund.

Investment powers

7.118 Paragraphs 9 and 10 of Schedule 5 to the NHS Act 2006 provide for trusts to have power to make investments as follows:

> **Investment**
> **9** (1) An NHS trust has power to invest money held by it in any investments, including investments which do not produce income, specified in directions under section 8.
> (2) Sub-paragraph (1) does not apply in relation to money held by an NHS trust as trustee.
> **10** Any direction under section 8 with respect to–
> (a) the power conferred on an NHS trust by paragraph 3, or
> (b) the maximum amount which an NHS trust may invest in any investments or class of investments,
>
> may be given only with the consent of the Treasury.

Annual accounts for an NHS trust

7.119 There are detailed provisions in Schedule 15 to the NHS Act 2006 which provide that NHS trusts 'must keep proper accounts and proper records in relation to the accounts'. The NHS trust must prepare annual accounts and these must be audited in accordance with the Local Audit and Accountability Act 2014.

Care trusts

7.120 Care trusts are a type of NHS trust or NHS FT that delivers social care services (under agreements with one or more local authorities) as well as NHS services. Section 77 of the NHS Act 2006 describes the legal regime under which care trusts must operate. Care trusts were first introduced by the 'NHS Plan' in 2000, where they were described as follows:

> Care Trusts will be able to commission and deliver primary and community healthcare as well as social care for older people and other client groups. Social services would be delivered under delegated authority from local

30 However, this is possibly unlikely in the present NHS financial climate.

councils. Care Trusts will usually be established where there is a joint agreement at local level that this model offers the best way to deliver better care services.

7.121 Care trusts thus represented one attempt to amalgamate the delivery of NHS and social care services. This amalgamation was always inherently difficult because the vast majority of NHS services are free to patients at the point of delivery whereas social care services are means tested and thus the local authority has a duty to impose charges for the delivery of the services. There are not many care trusts in England now, but some have been successful in providing a greater level of 'joined-up' services between health and social care than services delivered by different public bodies.

7.122 Care trusts offer a differing range of services. Their focus is typically on areas where 'joined up' local authority and NHS working may be particularly effective and provide better outcomes for patients, such as mental health (both in-patient and community services) and services for older people or those with learning disabilities. Other services might include sexual health services, community dental services, children's services and community nursing services, for example.

7.123 The ability for NHS bodies, including NHS trusts and FTs (as well as CCGs) to work with local authorities as part of a care trust is underpinned by section 75 of the NHS Act 2006. Section 75 provides for arrangements between local authorities and NHS bodies, such as pooled fund arrangements, the ability for NHS bodies to deliver prescribed health-related functions of the local authorities and for local authorities to deliver prescribed functions of NHS bodies.

7.124 This ability to work together and undertake each other's functions, is only permitted under section 75(1) 'if the arrangements are likely to lead to an improvement in the way in which those functions are exercised'.

7.125 Section 75(8) defines 'health-related functions of the local authorities' as follows:

> 'health-related functions', in relation to a local authority, means functions of the authority which, in the opinion of the Secretary of State–
> (a) have an effect on the health of any individuals,
> (b) have an effect on, or are affected by, any functions of NHS bodies, or
> (c) are connected with any functions of NHS bodies'

7.126 A fuller description of health-related functions of the local authorities is provided in the NHS Bodies and Local Authorities Partnership Arrangements Regulations 2000.[31] The functions include many social services functions, local housing authority functions, waste collection functions and environmental health services functions.

7.127 Section 75(3) of the NHS Act 2006 provides for regulations to be made to make provision:

> (a) as to the cases in which NHS bodies and local authorities may enter into prescribed arrangements,

31 SI No 617.

(b) as to the conditions which must be satisfied in relation to prescribed arrangements (including conditions in relation to consultation),
(c) for or in connection with requiring the consent of the Secretary of State to the operation of prescribed arrangements (including provision in relation to applications for consent, the approval or refusal of such applications and the variation or withdrawal of approval),
(d) in relation to the duration of prescribed arrangements,
(e) for or in connection with the variation or termination of prescribed arrangements,
(f) as to the responsibility for, and the operation and management of, prescribed arrangements,
(g) as to the sharing of information between NHS bodies and local authorities.

The NHS Bodies and Local Authorities (Partnership Arrangements, Care Trusts, Public Health and Local Healthwatch) Regulations 2012[32] have been made under this section.

7.128 Section 75(5) also provides that arrangements under section 75 do not affect the liability of either NHS bodies or local authorities for any of their functions, nor does the fact that the NHS body may be exercising what are local authority functions mean that there is any change to the power or duty to recover charges for those services.

7.129 Section 77 of the NHS Act 2006 provides for a care trust to be designated by a NHS body and a local authority in order to become a vehicle by which NHS services and health-related functions of the local authorities are delivered by a single organisation. It provides:

(1) Where–
  (a) . . . an NHS trust or a clinical commissioning group or an NHS foundation trust is, or will be, a party to any existing or proposed LA delegation arrangements, . . .
  (b) the body and the local authority concerned consider that designation of the body as a Care Trust would be likely to promote the effective exercise by the body of prescribed health-related functions of the local authority (in accordance with the arrangements) in conjunction with prescribed NHS functions of the body, and
  (c) the requirements in subsection (1A) are satisfied,

  the body and the local authority may jointly designate the body as a Care Trust.
(1A) The body and the local authority must, before designating the body as a Care Trust under this section–
  (a) publish in the prescribed form and manner–
    (i) the reasons why they consider that the proposed designation would be likely to have the result mentioned in subsection (1)(b), and
    (ii) information about the proposed governance arrangements of the Care Trust, and
  (b) consult on the proposed designation in accordance with regulations.
(1B) Where a body has been designated as a Care Trust under this section, the body and the local authority must notify prescribed persons of the designation.
(2) . . .

32 SI No 3094.

(3) . . .

(4) A body designated as a Care Trust under this section may (in addition to exercising health-related functions of the local authority as mentioned in subsection (1)(b)) exercise such prescribed health-related functions of the local authority as are agreed in relation to persons in any area so agreed, even though it does not exercise any NHS functions in relation to persons in that area; and 'agreed' means agreed by the body and the local authority.

(5) Where a body is designated as a Care Trust under this section, the body and the local authority may jointly revoke that designation.

(5A) Before revoking a designation as a Care Trust under this section, the body and the local authority must consult on the proposed revocation of the designation in accordance with regulations.

(5B) Where the designation of a body as a Care Trust under this section has been revoked, the body and the local authority must notify prescribed persons of the revocation.

(5C) Regulations under subsection (1A)(b) or (5A) may include provision requiring a body and a local authority to publish prescribed information following a consultation.

(5D) Where a duty is imposed by or by virtue of this section on a body and a local authority, they may make arrangements for the function to be discharged–

(a) by both of them acting jointly,
(b) by each of them acting separately, or
(c) by one of them acting on behalf of both of them.

(6) . . .

(7) . . .

(8) Regulations may make such incidental, supplementary or consequential provision (including provision amending, repealing or revoking enactments) as the Secretary of State considers expedient in connection with the preceding provisions of this section.

(9) Regulations under subsection (8) may, in particular, make provision–

(a) . . .
(b) . . .
(c) . . .
(d) for supplementing or modifying, in connection with the operation of subsection (4), any provision made by regulations under section 75.

(10) The designation of a body as a Care Trust under this section does not affect any of the functions, rights or liabilities of that body in its capacity as . . . NHS trust or clinical commissioning group or NHS foundation trust.

(11) In connection with the exercise by a body so designated of any relevant social services functions of a local authority in England under LA delegation arrangements–

(a) section 7 of the Local Authority Social Services Act 1970 (c 42) (authorities to exercise social services functions under guidance), and
(b) section 7A of that Act (directions as to exercise of such functions),

apply to the body as if it were a local authority within the meaning of that Act.

(11A) In connection with the exercise by a body so designated of any relevant social services functions under LA delegation arrangements, sections 145 to 149 of the Social Services and Well-being

(Wales) Act 2014 (codes on the exercise of social services functions) apply to the body as if it were a local authority within the meaning of that Act.

(12) In this section–

'health-related functions' has the meaning given by section 75(8),

'LA delegation arrangements' means arrangements falling within section 75(2)(b), whether or not made in conjunction with any pooled fund arrangements,

'NHS functions' means functions exercisable by . . . NHS trust [or clinical commissioning group or NHS foundation trust] in its capacity as such,

'pooled fund arrangements' means arrangements falling within section 75(2)(a),

'relevant social services functions' means–

(a) in relation to a local authority in England, health-related functions which are social services functions within the meaning of the Local Authority Social Services Act 1970;

(b) in relation to a local authority in Wales, health-related functions which are social services functions within the meaning of the Social Services and Well-being (Wales) Act 2014.

7.130 Section 77 of the NHS Act 2006 provides that when the relevant NHS body (which may be a trust or FT) and the relevant local authority, consider that the designation of the NHS body as a care trust would promote the effective exercise of the body of the prescribed health functions of the local authority, they can jointly designate the body as a care trust. Before doing so, there are requirements that the bodies must publish their reasons and information about the proposed governance arrangements of the care trust, and consult on that information.

7.131 Section 77(4) gives the care trust a power to exercise health functions of the local authority in relation to persons in any area agreed between the local authority and the NHS body. The care trust may therefore operate in a wider area than the trust's area if the local authority's area is wider.

7.132 Section 77(5) gives the NHS body and the local authority the power to jointly revoke the designation of care trust, although again there are consultation requirements.

7.133 Section 77(11) provides that sections 7 and 7A of the Local Authority Social Services Act 1970, concerning secretary of state guidance and directions, apply to the care trust as if it were a local authority within the meaning of that Act in relation to any relevant social services function of the local authority it exercises.

7.134 The requirements of the NHST(MP) Regs 1990 concerning such matters as the appointment and functions of chairs and directors are varied in relation to care trusts, because of the fact that they carry out both NHS and local authority functions. For example, under reg 3 the maximum number of directors is 14 plus the chair, and the maximum number of executive directors is seven and there cannot be more executive directors than non-executive directors. Under reg 5, one of the executive directors must also be a person with experience of health-related functions of local authorities. Please see above for further analysis of the NHST(MP) Regs 1990.

NHS foundation trusts

7.135 NHS FTs were created by the HSC(CHS)A 2003, and the relevant provisions were then consolidated with other NHS statutory provisions when the NHS Act was passed in 2006. Substantial changes to the structures of the NHS were made by the Health and Social Care Act (HSCA) 2012, including changes to the law around FTs. These took effect both as free-standing provisions within the HSCA 2012 and as amendments to the NHS Act 2006.

7.136 However, while both government politicians and those opposed to FTs seek to stress the differences between FTs and NHS trusts, the reality is that FTs function in virtually the same way as NHS trusts and have very much the same tensions and challenges. There are differences at the edges but, particularly after the merger of the NHS Trust Development Agency and Monitor into NHS Improvement, these NHS provider bodies are accountable to the same regulator. Further the commercial freedoms which were enjoyed by FTs for the first ten years of their periods of authorisation have largely evaporated as a result of increasing intervention from NHSI, the worsening financial situation of the NHS (and hence the need for FTs to seek additional funding from the department) and a change in government policy away from a 'managed market' towards a planned NHS economy. All these factors mean that, in practice, there are relatively few surviving differences between NHS trusts and FTs. The commentary on FTs below will therefore concentrate on the areas where there are significant differences between the legal structures of FTs and those of trusts.

7.137 There are six key differences between NHS trusts and FTs, namely:

1) FTs have a governance structure which includes local people and staff as 'members' of the trust and 'governors', which makes FTs locally accountable in a manner which is lacking for NHS trusts;
2) FTs are required to be licensed by Monitor and accordingly are required to work within the framework of a complex licensing regime;
3) Monitor has specific statutory powers under the HSCA 2012 to intervene in the management of a failing FT; there are no such powers in relation to NHS trusts;
4) The contracts FTs sign with their commissioners are legally binding contracts as opposed to being NHS contracts; and
5) Unlike NHS trusts, FTs are not subject to the direction making powers of the secretary of state; and
6) The secretary of state has no power to require an FT to pay over any surplus funds held by the FT for the benefit of the rest of the NHS.

7.138 While any of these differences could be important in particular circumstances, with the exception of the different governance arrangements, now that the TDA and Monitor have merged to become NHSI, the occasions on which the differences matter in practice are likely to be relatively few.

The governance structures of foundation trusts

7.139 Section 30 of the NHS Act 2006 provides:

> (1) An NHS foundation trust is a public benefit corporation the function of which is to provide in accordance with this Chapter goods and services for the purposes of the health service in England.
> (2) A public benefit corporation is a body corporate which, in pursuance of an application under this Chapter, is constituted in accordance with Schedule 7.

7.140 An FT is thus a company, albeit not one registered under the Companies Acts, which is described in the Act as 'public benefit corporation'. As far as the authors are aware, FTs are the only companies that have been designated as being public benefit corporation. However, other bodies exist which have a similar role to, while not being formally called, public-benefit corporations including the BBC which is incorporated by Royal Charter.

7.141 The sole statutory function of an FT is to 'provide in accordance with this Chapter goods and services for the purposes of the health service in England'.[33] Thus while FTs may have powers to undertake other activities (such as providing privately funded healthcare services) these activities do not form part of the statutory purpose of an FT.

7.142 An application for registration as an FT must be made by an NHS trust to Monitor. Once granted, the trust ceases to be an NHS trust and becomes an FT. Section 35 of the NHS Act 2006 provides:

> (1) On an authorisation being given to a body corporate which is an NHS trust–
> (a) it ceases to be an NHS trust and becomes an NHS foundation trust,
> (b) the proposed constitution has effect, and
> (c) any order under section 25(1) is revoked.
> (2) . . . .
> (3) The authorisation is conclusive evidence that the body in question is an NHS foundation trust.
> (4) Subsections (1) to (3) do not affect the continuity of the body or of its property or liabilities (including its criminal liabilities).
> (5) The validity of any act of an NHS foundation trust is not affected by any vacancy among the directors or by any defect in the appointment of any director.
> (6) An NHS foundation trust must not be regarded as the servant or agent of the Crown or as enjoying any status, immunity or privilege of the Crown; and an NHS foundation trust's property must not be regarded as property of, or property held on behalf of, the Crown'

7.143 Subsections (1)–(4) of section 35 are due to be repealed if the relevant provisions of the HSCA 2012 are brought into force. However, as this repeal is contingent on all NHS trusts becoming FTs, there is no prospect of an imminent repeal. FTs, like NHS trusts, are not part of the Crown. It follows that, save as provided by statute, Ministers do not have decision making power over the actions of an FT.

33 There are no NHS foundation trusts in either Scotland or Wales.

The foundation trust constitution

7.144 Each FT is required to have a constitution which is its principal instrument of governance. This is provided for in paras 1 and 2 of Schedule 7 to the NHS Act 2006, which provides:

1 (1) A public benefit corporation must have a constitution.
(2) As well as any provision authorised or required to be made by this Schedule, the constitution may make further provision (other than provision as to the powers of the corporation) consistent with this Schedule.
2 (1) The constitution must name the corporation and, if the corporation is an NHS foundation trust, its name must include the words 'NHS foundation trust.
(2) If the corporation is an NHS foundation trust, the constitution must specify its principal purpose (as to which, see section 43(1)).

7.145 The draft constitution must be submitted to Monitor as part of the application process and, once the application is granted, the constitution takes effect. FTs publish their constitutions on their websites. Section 37 of the NHS Act 2006 contains rules to permit an FT to amend its constitution. It provides:

(1) An NHS foundation trust may make amendments of its constitution only if–
(a) more than half of the members of the council of governors of the trust voting approve the amendments, and
(b) more than half of the members of the board of directors of the trust voting approve the amendments.
(2) Amendments made under this section take effect as soon as the conditions in subsection (1)(a) and (b) are satisfied.
(3) But an amendment is of no effect in so far as the constitution would, as a result of the amendment, not accord with Schedule 7.
(4) The trust must inform the regulator of amendments made under this section; but the regulator's functions do not include a power or duty to determine whether or not the constitution, as a result of the amendments, accords with Schedule 7.

The members of a foundation trust

7.146 The original thinking that led to the creation of FTs centred on the idea that they would be organisations which were accountable downwards to the local people who used the services of the FT as opposed to being accountable upwards to Whitehall. While it is debatable how far this aspiration has been achieved in practice, the FT constitution is required to allow patients, local people and staff to become 'members' and to identify constituencies for the various types of public members. There also has to be a staff constituency. The relevant provisions are in paras 3–6 of Schedule 7 to the NHS Act 2006, and provide as follows:

Eligibility for membership
3 (1) The persons who may become or continue as members of a public benefit corporation are–
(a) individuals who live in any area specified in the constitution as the area for a public constituency,

(b) individuals employed by the corporation under a contract of employment and, if the constitution so provides, individuals who exercise functions for the purposes of the corporation otherwise than under a contract of employment with the corporation,

(c) if the constitution so provides, individuals who have attended any of the corporation's hospitals as either a patient or the carer of a patient within a period specified in the constitution.

(2) The constitution may specify one or more areas as areas for public constituencies, each of which must be an electoral area for the purposes of local government elections in England and Wales or an area consisting of two or more such electoral areas.

(3) A person may become or continue as a member of the corporation by virtue of sub-paragraph (1)(b) only if–

(a) he is employed by the corporation under a contract of employment which has no fixed term or has a fixed term of at least 12 months, or

(b) he has been continuously employed by the corporation for at least 12 months or, where he exercises functions for the purposes of the corporation as mentioned in that sub-paragraph, he has done so continuously for such a period.

(4) Chapter 1 of Part 14 of the Employment Rights Act 1996 applies for the purpose of determining whether an individual has been continuously employed by the corporation, or has continuously exercised functions for the purposes of the corporation, as it applies for the purposes of that Act.

(5) The constitution may divide those who come within sub-paragraph (1)(b) into two or more descriptions of individuals.

(6) An individual providing care in pursuance of a contract (including a contract of employment), or as a volunteer for a voluntary organisation, does not come within sub-paragraph (1)(c).

(7) The constitution may divide those who come within sub-paragraph (1)(c) into three or more descriptions of individuals, one of which must comprise the carers of patients.

(8) The constitution may make further provision as to the circumstances in which a person may not become or continue as a member.

Constituencies

4 (1) Members of a public benefit corporation are referred to as follows.

(2) Those who live in an area specified in the constitution as an area for any public constituency are referred to collectively as a public constituency.

(3) Those who come within paragraph 3(1)(b) are referred to collectively as the staff constituency and, if the power in paragraph 3(5) is exercised, each description of members is referred to as a class within that constituency.

(4) Those who come within paragraph 3(1)(c) are referred to collectively as the patient's constituency and, if the power in paragraph 3(7) is exercised, each description of members is referred to as a class within that constituency.

(5) A person who is a member of a constituency, or of a class within a constituency, may not while that membership continues be a member of any other constituency or class.

(6) A person who comes within paragraph 3(1)(b) may not become or continue as a member of any constituency other than the staff constituency.

5 The constitution must require a minimum number of members of each constituency or, where there are classes within the constituency, of each class.

Becoming a member

6 (1) An individual who is eligible to become a member of a public benefit corporation may do so on an application made to the corporation.

(2) The constitution may provide for any individual who is–

(a) eligible to become a member of the staff constituency, and

(b) invited by the corporation to become a member of that constituency (and, where there are classes within the constituency, a member of the appropriate class),

to become a member of the corporation as a member of that constituency (and class) without an application being made, unless he informs the corporation that he does not wish to do so.

(3) The constitution may provide for any individual who is–

(a) eligible to become a member of the patients' constituency (otherwise than as the carer of a patient), and

(b) invited by the corporation to become a member of a specified constituency (and where there are classes within the constituency, a member of the specified class),

to become a member of the corporation as a member of that constituency (and class) without an application being made, unless he informs the corporation that he does not wish to do so.

(4) The constituency and, where applicable, class to be specified–

(a) if he is eligible to be a member of any public constituency, is that constituency,

(b) otherwise, is the patients' constituency and, where applicable, the class of which he is eligible to become a member'

7.147 The Department of Health and Social Care has published a 'model NHS Foundation Trust constitution'[34] which sets out the way in which these statutory provisions could be incorporated into an FT constitution. Most constitutions of FTs closely follow the model constitution although there can be significant differences between FTs in the way in which public constituencies are defined.

Foundation trust council of governors

7.148 Although members of the FT may well become involved in the day-to-day running of the functions of the FT as volunteers, members of charitable boards or may work for the FT, their role as members is confined to voting for members of the council of governors of the FT, which is constituted in accordance with the terms of the constitution. The provisions relating to the election and duties of governors are in paras 7–14 of Schedule 7 to the NHS Act 2006, which provide:

Council of Governors

7 (1) A public benefit corporation has a council of governors.

(2) Only members of the corporation and persons appointed under the following provisions may become or continue as members of the council.

34 See www.gov.uk/government/uploads/system/uploads/attachment_data/file/298552/Model_Core_Constitution_-_April_2013_0.pdf.

(3) The members of the council other than the appointed members must be chosen by election.

(4) Members of a constituency or, where there are classes within it, members of each class may elect any of their number to be a member of the council.

8 (1) The following may not become or continue as members of the council of governors–

(a) a person who has been made bankrupt or whose estate has been sequestrated and (in either case) has not been discharged,

(aa) a person in relation to whom a moratorium period under a debt relief order applies (under Part 7A of the Insolvency Act 1986),

(b) a person who has made a composition or arrangement with, or granted a trust deed for, his creditors and has not been discharged in respect of it,

(c) a person who within the preceding five years has been convicted in the British Islands of any offence if a sentence of imprisonment (whether suspended or not) for a period of not less than three months (without the option of a fine) was imposed on him.

(2) The constitution may make further provision as to the circumstances in which a person may not become or continue as a member of [the council].

9 (1) More than half of the members of the council of governors must be elected by members of the corporation other than those who come within paragraph 3(1)(b).

(2) At least three members of the council must be elected by the staff constituency or, where there are classes within it, at least one member of the council must be elected by each class and at least three members must be elected altogether.

(3) . . .

(4) At least one member of the council must be appointed by one or more qualifying local authorities.

(5) A qualifying local authority is a local authority for an area which includes the whole or part of an area specified in the constitution as the area for a public constituency.

(6) If any of the corporation's hospitals includes a medical or dental school provided by a university, at least one member of the council must be appointed by that university.

(7) Any organisation specified in the constitution for the purposes of this sub-paragraph may appoint one or more members of the council (but no more than the number specified for those purposes in the constitution).

10 (1) An elected member of the council of governors may hold office for a period of three years.

(2) Such a member is eligible for re-election at the end of that period.

(3) But such a member ceases to hold office if he ceases to be a member of the corporation.

10A The general duties of the council of governors are–

(a) to hold the non-executive directors individually and collectively to account for the performance of the board of directors, and

(b) to represent the interests of the members of the corporation as a whole and the interests of the public.

10B A public benefit corporation must take steps to secure that the governors are equipped with the skills and knowledge they require in their capacity as such.

10C For the purpose of obtaining information about the corporation's performance of its functions or the directors' performance of their duties (and deciding whether to propose a vote on the corporation's or directors' performance), the council of governors may require one or more of the directors to attend a meeting.

11 The corporation may pay travelling and other expenses to members of the council of governors at rates decided by the corporation.

12 The constitution must provide for the chairman of the corporation or (in his absence) another person to preside at meetings of the council of governors.

13 (1) The constitution must provide for meetings of the council of governors to be open to members of the public.

(2) But the constitution may provide for members of the public to be excluded from a meeting for special reasons.

14 (1) The constitution must make provision as to–

(a) the conduct of elections for membership of [the council],

(b) the appointment of persons to membership,

(c) the practice and procedure of the council,

(d) the removal of a member from office.

(2) The constitution may make further provision about the council.

7.149 Monitor has published a guide to the legal duties of governors[35] and a guide to the duties of an FT governor.[36] The primary role of governors is to be the voice of patients and the local public, by appointing the chair and non-executive members of the board and then holding the board of directors of the FT to account for decisions they have made and the performance of the trust. They do this through holding regular meetings with directors at which the directors provide reports and submit to questions from the governors.

7.150 Section 39A of the NHS Act 2006 (as inserted by section 162 of the HSCA 2012) provides for NHSI to set up a panel to advise governors on specific issues that they seek to refer to NHSI. It provides:

39A Panel for advising governors

(1) The regulator may appoint a panel of persons to which a governor of an NHS foundation trust may refer a question as to whether the trust has failed or is failing–

(a) to act in accordance with its constitution, or

(b) to act in accordance with provision made by or under this Chapter.

(2) A governor may refer a question to the panel only if more than half of the members of the council of governors voting approve the referral.

(3) The panel–

(a) may regulate its own procedure, and

(b) may establish such procedures, and make such other arrangements, as it considers appropriate for the purpose of determining questions referred to it under this section.

(4) The panel may decide whether, or to what extent, to carry out an investigation on a question referred to it under this section.

(5) The panel may for that purpose, or for the purpose of carrying out such an investigation, request information or advice.

35 See www.gov.uk/government/uploads/system/uploads/attachment_data/file/284473/Governors_guide_August_2013_UPDATED_NOV_13.pdf.

36 See www.gov.uk/government/uploads/system/uploads/attachment_data/file/301286/BriefGuideForGovernors.pdf.

(6) Where the panel has carried out such an investigation, it must publish a report of its determination of the question referred to it.
(7) If a person refuses to comply with a request made under subsection (5), the report under subsection (6) may refer to the refusal.
(8) On any proceedings before a court or tribunal relating to a question referred to the panel under this section, the court may take the panel's report of its determination of the question into account.
(9) The regulator–
(a) must pay expenses properly incurred by the panel, and
(b) must make administrative support available to the panel.
(10) Regulations may make provision as to–
(a) eligibility for membership of the panel;
(b) the number of persons that may be appointed as members;
(c) the terms of appointment of members;
(d) circumstances in which a person ceases to be a member or may be suspended.

7.151 An independent panel for advising NHS FT governors has been formally established by NHSI and operates in accordance with its terms of reference, which more or less reflect section 39A.[37]

Foundation trust directors

7.152 Paragraphs 15–18E of Schedule 7 to the NHS Act 2006 provide the essential framework for the appointment and functioning of the board of directors of an FT. They provide:

Directors
15 (1) A public benefit corporation has a board of directors.
(2) The constitution must provide for all the powers of the corporation to be exercisable by the board of directors on its behalf.
(3) But the constitution may provide for any of those powers to be delegated to a committee of directors or to an executive director.
16 (1) The board consists of–
(a) executive directors, one of whom is the chief executive (and accounting officer) and another the finance director,
(b) non-executive directors, one of whom is the chairman.
(2) One of the executive directors must be a registered medical practitioner or a registered dentist (within the meaning of the Dentists Act 1984 (c 24)); and another must be a registered nurse or a registered midwife.
(3) A person may not be appointed as an executive director if he is within paragraph 8(1).
(4) A person may be appointed as a non-executive director only if–
(a) he is a member of a public constituency or the patients' constituency, or
(b) where any of the corporation's hospitals includes a medical or dental school provided by a university, he exercises functions for the purposes of that university,
and he is not within paragraph 8(1).

37 Available here: www.gov.uk/government/uploads/system/uploads/attachment_data/file/491759/The_panel_s_terms_of_reference.pdf. Further details about the panel are available here: www.gov.uk/government/groups/panel-for-advising-nhs-foundation-trust-governors#the-panels-independence.

17 (1) It is for the council of governors at a general meeting to appoint or remove the chairman and the other non-executive directors.

(2) Removal of a non-executive director under sub-paragraph (1) requires the approval of three-quarters of the members of the council.

(3) It is for the non-executive directors to appoint or remove the chief executive.

(4) It is for a committee consisting of the chairman, the chief executive and the other non-executive directors to appoint or remove the executive directors.

(5) The appointment of a chief executive requires the approval of [the council] of governors.

18 (1) It is for the council of governors at a general meeting to decide the remuneration and allowances, and the other terms and conditions of office, of the non-executive directors.

(2) The corporation must establish a committee of non-executive directors to decide the remuneration and allowances, and the other terms and conditions of office, of the executive directors; but the constitution may make provision for those matters to be decided pending the establishment of such a committee.

18A The general duty of the board of directors, and of each director individually, is to act with a view to promoting the success of the corporation so as to maximise the benefits for the members of the corporation as a whole and for the public.

18B (1) The duties that a director of a public benefit corporation has by virtue of being a director include in particular–

(a) a duty to avoid a situation in which the director has (or can have) a direct or indirect interest that conflicts (or possibly may conflict) with the interests of the corporation;

(b) a duty not to accept a benefit from a third party by reason of being a director or doing (or not doing) anything in that capacity.

(2) The duty referred to in sub-paragraph (1)(a) is not infringed if–

(a) the situation cannot reasonably be regarded as likely to give rise to a conflict of interest, or

(b) the matter has been authorised in accordance with the constitution.

(3) The duty referred to in sub-paragraph (1)(b) is not infringed if acceptance of the benefit cannot reasonably be regarded as likely to give rise to a conflict of interest.

(4) In sub-paragraph (1)(b), 'third party' means a person other than–

(a) the corporation, or

(b) a person acting on its behalf.

18C (1) If a director of a public benefit corporation has in any way a direct or indirect interest in a proposed transaction or arrangement with the corporation, the director must declare the nature and extent of that interest to the other directors.

(2) If a declaration under this paragraph proves to be, or becomes, inaccurate or incomplete, a further declaration must be made.

(3) Any declaration required by this paragraph must be made before the corporation enters into the transaction or arrangement.

(4) This paragraph does not require a declaration of an interest of which the director is not aware or where the director is not aware of the transaction or arrangement in question.

(5) A director need not declare an interest–
(a) if it cannot reasonably be regarded as likely to give rise to a conflict of interest;
(b) if, or to the extent that, the directors are already aware of it;
(c) if, or to the extent that, it concerns terms of the director's appointment that have been or are to be considered–
(i) by a meeting of the board of directors, or
(ii) by a committee of the directors appointed for the purpose under the constitution.

18D (1) Before holding a meeting, the board of directors must send a copy of the agenda of the meeting to the council of governors.
(2) As soon as practicable after holding a meeting, the board of directors must send a copy of the minutes of the meeting to the council of governors.]

18E (1) The constitution must provide for meetings of the board of directors to be open to members of the public.
(2) But the constitution may provide for members of the public to be excluded from a meeting for special reasons.

7.153 The general duty of directors of an FT is thus to 'act with a view to promoting the success of the corporation so as to maximise the benefits for the members of the corporation as a whole and for the public': see para 18A. This general duty gives a very great measure of discretion to directors to decide what decisions to make in order to deliver on this duty.

Governance and transparency

7.154 There are a series of provisions in Schedule 7 to the NHS Act 2006 which emphasise the ways in which the operation of an FT is required to be transparent, including the need for FTs to adopt policies for the management of conflicts of interest and to allow members of the public access to information concerning the office holders of the trust and the decision-making processes within the trust. Paragraphs 20–22 provide:

Register of members etc

20 (1) A public benefit corporation must have–
(a) a register of members showing, in respect of each member, the constituency to which he belongs and, where there are classes within it, the class to which he belongs,
(b) a register of members of the council of governors,
(c) a register of interests of the members of the council of governors,
(d) a register of directors,
(e) a register of interests of the directors.
(2) The constitution may make further provision about the registers including, in particular, admission to, and removal from, the registers.

21 The constitution must make provision for dealing with conflicts of interest of members of the council of governors and of the directors.

22 (1) A public benefit corporation must make the following documents available for inspection by members of the public free of charge at all reasonable times–
(a) a copy of the current constitution,
(b) . . .

(c) a copy of the latest annual accounts and of any report of the auditor on them,
(d) a copy of the latest annual report,
(e) . . .
(f) . . .
(g) a copy of any order made under section 65D, 65J, 65KC, 65L or 65LA,
(h) a copy of any report laid under section 65D,
(i) a copy of any information published under section 65D,
(j) a copy of any draft report published under section 65F,
(k) a copy of any statement provided under section 65F,
(l) a copy of any notice published under section 65F, 65G, 65H, 65J, 65KA, 65KB, 65KC or 65KD,
(m) a copy of any statement published or provided under section 65G,
(n) a copy of any final report published under section 65I,
(o) a copy of any statement published under section 65J or 65KC,
(p) a copy of any information published under section 65M.

(2) Any person who requests it must be provided with a copy of or extract from any of the above documents.

(3) The corporation is also to make the registers mentioned in paragraph 20 available for inspection by members of the public, except in circumstances prescribed; and, so far as the registers are required to be available–
(a) they must be available free of charge at all reasonable times,
(b) a person who requests it must be provided with a copy of or extract from them.

(4) If the person requesting a copy or extract under this paragraph is not a member of the corporation, the corporation may impose a reasonable charge for doing so.

7.155 The Public Benefit Corporation (Register of Members) Regulations 2004[38] provides that patients and others who ask should not have their details published in the register without their consent. Regulation 2 of those regulations provides:

A public benefit corporation must not make any part of its register available for inspection by members of the public that shows details of–
(a) where the constitution of the corporation provides for a patients' constituency, any member who belongs to that constituency [where that member has not consented to his details being made so available]; or
(b) any other member, if he so requests.

7.156 Paragraphs 24 and 25 of Schedule 7 to the NHS Act 2006 make provision for the FT to prepare annual accounts in a form complying with directions made by the secretary of state, and to publish them and law a copy before Parliament. Paragraph 26 provides that an FT is required to prepare annual plans which it is required to provide to the regulator, namely NHSI. These paragraphs provide:

Annual reports and forward plans

26 (1) A public benefit corporation must prepare annual reports and send them to the regulator.

38 SI No 539.

(2) The reports must give–
(a) information on any steps taken by the corporation to secure that (taken as a whole) the actual membership of any public constituency and (if there is one) of the patients' constituency is representative of those eligible for such membership,
(aa) information on any occasions in the period to which the report relates on which the council of governors exercised its power under paragraph 10C,
(ab) information on the corporation's policy on pay and on the work of the committee established under paragraph 18(2) and such other procedures as the corporation has on pay,
(ac) information on the remuneration of the directors and on the expenses of the governors and the directors,
(b) any other information the regulator requires.
(2A) Before imposing a requirement under sub-paragraph (2)(b) that the regulator considers is sufficiently significant to justify consultation, the regulator must consult such persons as it considers appropriate.
(3) It is for the regulator to decide–
(a) the form of the reports,
(b) when the reports must be sent to it,
(c) the periods to which the reports are to relate.

27 (1) A public benefit corporation must give information to the regulator as to its forward planning in respect of each financial year.
(2) The document containing the information must be prepared by the directors.
(3) In preparing the document the directors must have regard to the views of the council of governors.

Annual meetings

7.157 Paragraphs 27A–28 of Schedule 7 to the NHS Act 2006 provide for annual meetings of members of the FT and an annual meeting of the council of governors (which can be combined under para 28A) as follows:

Annual meeting of members
27A (1) A public benefit corporation must hold an annual meeting of its members.
(2) The meeting must be open to members of the public.
(3) At least one member of the board of directors of the corporation must attend the meeting and present the following documents to the members at the meeting–
(a) the annual accounts,
(b) any report of the auditor on them,
(c) the annual report.
(4) Where an amendment is made to the constitution in relation to the powers or duties of the council of governors of a public benefit corporation (or otherwise with respect to the role that the council has as part of the corporation)–
(a) at least one member of the council of governors must attend the next meeting to be held under this paragraph and present the amendment, and
(b) the corporation must give the members an opportunity to vote on whether they approve the amendment.

(5) If more than half of the members voting approve the amendment, the amendment continues to have effect; otherwise, it ceases to have effect and the corporation must take such steps as are necessary as a result.

Meeting of council of governors to consider annual accounts and reports

28 (1) The following documents must be presented to the council of governors of a public benefit corporation at a general meeting–
(a) the annual accounts,
(b) any report of the auditor on them,
(c) the annual report.

(2) Nothing in sub-paragraph (1) prevents the council of governors from holding a general meeting more than once a year.

7.158 Schedule 10 to the NHS Act 2006 has detailed provisions relating to the audit of the accounts of an FT. These provisions date from the HSC(CHS)A 2003 and only minor amendments were made to these rules by the HSCA 2012.

The registration duty and the powers of the regulator to intervene in the management of foundation trusts

7.159 Unlike NHS trusts, FTs are required to register with Monitor before they are entitled to deliver services to NHS patients. The terms of registration impose considerable duties on FTs, and the HSCA 2012 gives considerable powers to the regulator to intervene in the management of FTs when FTs are in breach of the conditions. These powers are discussed in chapter 8 on the powers and duties of Monitor.

Commissioning contracts concluded by foundation trusts

7.160 FTs will have commissioning contracts in the form of the NHS Standard Contract with a variety of CCGs and, if it delivers specialist services (as many FTs do) with NHS England. FTs are not included in the list of bodies set out in section 9 of the NHS Act 2006 which conclude NHS contracts. Accordingly, these commissioning contracts will be legally binding contracts.

7.161 Notwithstanding the fact that FTs and their commissioners are only able to conclude legally binding contracts, this does not mean that disputes between NHS commissioners and contractors will inevitably end up in court. The dispute resolution provisions in the NHS Standard Contract envisage that disputes will be resolved by an expert (who will conduct an expert determination) as opposed to an adjudicator appointed by the secretary of state. Full details of the dispute resolution provisions are in chapter 10 on acute contracting.

Foundation trusts and private patient income

7.162 There was a considerable parliamentary debate during the passing of the HSCA 2012 about the extent to which FTs should be entitled to fund themselves by offering services to fee paying patients. This debate was resolved by the passing of section 164 of the HSCA 2012, which created a new section 43 of the NHS Act 2006, which provides:

(1) The principal purpose of an NHS foundation trust is the provision of goods and services for the purposes of the health service in England.

(2) An NHS foundation trust may provide goods and services for any purposes related to–

(a) the provision of services provided to individuals for or in connection with the prevention, diagnosis or treatment of illness, and

(b) the promotion and protection of public health.

(2A) An NHS foundation trust does not fulfil its principal purpose unless, in each financial year, its total income from the provision of goods and services for the purposes of the health service in England is greater than its total income from the provision of goods and services for any other purposes.

(3) An NHS foundation trust may also carry on activities other than those mentioned in subsection (2) for the purpose of making additional income available in order better to carry on its principal purpose.

(3A) Each annual report prepared by an NHS foundation trust must give information on the impact that income received by the trust otherwise than from the provision of goods and services for the purposes of the health service in England has had on the provision by the trust of goods and services for those purposes.

(3B) Each document prepared by an NHS foundation trust under paragraph 27 of Schedule 7 (forward plan) must include information about–

(a) the activities other than the provision of goods and services for the purposes of the health service in England that the trust proposes to carry on, and

(b) the income it expects to receive from doing so.

(3C) Where a document which is being prepared under paragraph 27 of Schedule 7 contains a proposal that an NHS foundation trust carry on an activity of a kind mentioned in subsection (3B)(a), the council of governors of the trust must–

(a) determine whether it is satisfied that the carrying on of the activity will not to any significant extent interfere with the fulfilment by the trust of its principal purpose or the performance of its other functions, and

(b) notify the directors of the trust of its determination.

(3D) An NHS foundation trust which proposes to increase by 5% or more the proportion of its total income in any financial year attributable to activities other than the provision of goods and services for the purposes of the health service in England may implement the proposal only if more than half of the members of the council of governors of the trust voting approve its implementation'

7.163 Hence, the NHS income for an FT is required to be greater than the private patient income for the trust. Any projected level of private patient income of more than five per cent of the FT's turnover needs to be approved by the governors and the levels of private patient income are required to be set out in the FT annual accounts. In practice, very few FTs (other than those serving an international health market in central London) have private patient income which amounts to a substantial part of its income.

7.164 The HSCA 2012 also introduced provisions relating to the merger of FTs and their acquisition of trusts. These are rarely used powers and so no commentary is provided on these powers in this book.

CHAPTER 8

NHS regulators[1]

1 By Samantha Broadfoot QC, with special thanks to David Lock QC for his valuable insights and assistance, particularly in relation to paras 8.32–8.36 on the passage of the Health and Social Care Bill through Parliament.

Who regulates the NHS?

8.1 The question is a simple one, but, as with so many aspects of the NHS, the answer is far from straightforward. The 2015 report into the Morecambe Bay Trust Investigation,[2] which found a catalogue of missed opportunities in those responsible for regulating and monitoring the trust, stated that the system for monitoring NHS trusts was:

> . . . not only a complex and changing landscape to describe, the frequency of reorganization has introduced uncertainty while roles, relationships and demarcation are being resolved, upheaval as staff must become accustomed to working with new organisations and colleagues, and loss of corporate memory of how to work effectively with widely variable NHS organisations and where the high risk areas are. This repeated change to already complex systems has not helped them to function effectively.[3]

8.2 The array of publically available documentation and guidance on the internet is bewildering. For anyone unfamiliar with the complex and changing landscape of the NHS, it can be hard to work out which NHS regulatory bodies still exist (and what they are called) and what their statutory functions are.

8.3 As at March 2018, the primary regulators are:

a) NHS Improvement (NHSI) which operates as a single organisation but, as a matter of law, includes the following (legally separate NHS bodies):
   i) Monitor; and
   ii) NHS Trust Development Authority (TDA); and
b) the Care Quality Commission (CQC).

8.4 CQC regulates the delivery of health and social care within the NHS and outside it. It is thus not strictly an 'NHS regulator'. However, it has such an important role in regulating the activities of NHS providers that reference is made to CQC in a section at the end of this chapter.

8.5 There are other regulatory bodies which have a strong influence on staff activity within the NHS, such as the General Medical Council (GMC), which regulates doctors, and the Nursing and Midwifery Council (NMC), which regulates nurses and midwives. There are also regulators which set the framework for particular areas of medical activity, including the Human Fertilisation and Embryology Authority (HFEA) and the Human Tissue Authority (HTA). However, these regulators set the legal framework and regulate activity both within the NHS and for medical practice outside the NHS. Thus these bodies are not 'NHS regulators' as such, because

2 The Morecambe Bay Investigation was established by the Secretary of State for Health in September 2013, following serious incidents in the maternity department at Furness General Hospital (FGH), including a number of deaths of mothers and babies. The report concluded that the maternity unit at FGH was dysfunctional and that serious failures of clinical care led to many of these deaths. However, it also concluded that there were investigatory, organisational and regulatory failures which meant that the dysfunctional clinical system continued for far too long.

3 Report, p184, para 8.5, available at www.gov.uk/government/uploads/system/uploads/attachment_data/file/408480/47487_MBI_Accessible_v0.1.pdf.

their regulatory work is defined by the activity concerned and not the fact that this activity takes place within the NHS.

NHS Improvement

Overview

8.6 On 1 April 2016, Monitor and the NHS TDA were merged under a single leadership and operating model known as 'NHS Improvement'. This umbrella organisation brings together not only Monitor and the TDA, but also Patient Safety (including the National Reporting and Learning System), the Advancing Change Team and the Intensive Support Teams. Prior to their transfer to NHS TDA in 2016, Patient Safety and the other teams were part of NHS England and are involved in the patient safety obligations under National Health Service Act (NHS Act) 2006 s13R.

8.7 The rationale for the merger of these different NHS bodies is that NHS trusts (overseen by TDA) and foundation trusts (overseen by Monitor) face similar challenges and therefore they should be subject to the same kind of regulation and have access to similar kinds of support, even though they are organisationally different. A key part of this approach is the creation of the Single Oversight Framework[4] which sets out the oversight process which will be applied to all trusts. Other consolidated documentation and guidance will also be issued under the NHSI badge.

8.8 However, NHSI is not a legal body or an entity in its own right, even though it is starting to have the hallmarks of one such as NHSI Rules of Procedure. Monitor and NHS TDA continue to exist, and the legislation continues to refer to Monitor or NHS TDA rather than NHSI. Accordingly, this chapter examines the powers and duties of Monitor and NHS TDA separately, even though, on a day-to-day basis, these organisations now operate under the name of NHSI.

Monitor

Overview: history, functions and duties

8.9 Monitor originally came into being as the 'Independent Regulator of NHS Foundation Trusts' under the provisions of the Health and Social Care (Community Health and Standards) Act (HSC(CHS)A) 2003. Soon after its creation, it informally adopted the organisational name 'Monitor',[5] even though this was not the name of the organisation that parliament had given to it. This regulator was created as a body corporate, pursuant to section 2 of the HSC(CHS)A) 2003. It was set up to be independent of the secretary of state and, instead, directly accountable to parliament. The organisation's remit was to undertake the authorisation and regulation of NHS foundation trusts.

4 See https://improvement.nhs.uk/uploads/documents/Single_Oversight_Framework___update_Nov_2017_v2.pdf.

5 In the same way as the NHS Commissioning Board has adopted the name 'NHS England'.

8.10 The Health and Social Care Act (HSCA) 2012, and in particular Part 3 of that Act, brought in sweeping changes to Monitor's role, along with changes to the rest of the NHS. Section 61 of the HSCA 2012 made provision for the NHS to have an independent regulator. The government decided that, among the various NHS regulatory bodies then in existence, this role would be undertaken by Monitor. Thus the Independent Regulator of NHS Foundation Trusts continued to exist, but its name was now also formally changed to Monitor.

8.11 The HSCA 2012 extended Monitor's functions such that, from 1 April 2013, Monitor was established as the system regulator for all NHS-funded services in England.

8.12 There is also the potential, under section 65 of the HSCA 2012, for the secretary of state to extend Monitor's remit to cover adult social care services. However, to date this power has not been exercised. Unless there is a major change in government policy, there appears little prospect that this regulatory change will be implemented in the foreseeable future.

8.13 Monitor remains a body corporate and its governance arrangements are now contained in Schedule 8 to the HSCA 2012. The Schedule makes provision for membership and terms of appointment, gives Monitor a range of powers relating to the exercise of its functions and requires Monitor to prepare a set of accounts in each financial year which consolidates the annual accounts of all foundation trusts.[6] Monitor must also prepare its own annual accounts.[7] Paragraph 21 of Schedule 8 contains the important requirement that Monitor must publish an annual report on how it has exercised its functions. The report must, 'in particular', set out the measures that Monitor has taken to promote economy, efficiency and effectiveness in the use of resources for the exercise of its functions as well as include a statement as to what it did to comply with its duty to have regard to the secretary of state's guidance under sections 63(2) and 66(2)(h). The latest report, covering the period from 1 April 2016 to 31 March 2017, is published under the NHSI banner and, as with the earlier reports, is available online.[8]

8.14 The HSCA 2012 imposed a series of general duties on Monitor, which it was required to discharge when undertaking all of its functions, including the core duty – to protect and promote the interests of persons who use healthcare services.

8.15 Monitor's main functions are contained in Part 3 of the HSCA 2012, and are as follows:

a) *licensing functions* – all providers of NHS healthcare services are required to hold a licence with Monitor, unless they are exempt under regulations made by the Department of Health and Social Care;
b) *anti-competitive behaviour and competition functions* – Monitor is required to exercise its functions with a view to preventing anti-competitive behaviour; this applies to providers and commissioners of services, and NHS England;

6 Sch 8 para 17.
7 Sch 8 paras 18–20.
8 See www.gov.uk/government/uploads/system/uploads/attachment_data/file/630185/438953_Monitor_Annual_report_and_Accounts_2016–17_WEB.pdf

c) *pricing functions* – Monitor has various responsibilities around setting and regulating prices;
d) *managing the failure regime* where things go wrong with NHS providers.

8.16 These functions are considered in turn below. However, it is first necessary to consider the general duties which apply to the exercise of all of Monitor's functions.

Monitor's general duties

Core duty

8.17 Chapter 1 of Part 3 of the HSCA 2012 starts, after the name-change provision, with what is widely referred to as Monitor's 'core and overarching duty' – namely that Monitor's:

> . . . main duty in exercising its functions is to protect and promote the interests of people who use health care services by promoting provision of health care services which (a) is economic, efficient and effective, and (b) maintains or improves the quality of the services.[9]

In carrying out that duty Monitor must also 'have regard' to:

> . . . the likely future demand for health care services.[10]

8.18 The duty on Monitor to 'promote' services which have these defined characteristics is a relatively weak target duty which requires the decision-maker to focus on the stated objective, even though it may recognise that the objective may only be partially achieved. The nature of a 'promotion' duty was considered in *R v North and East Devon Health Authority ex p Coughlan*.[11] In that case, the Court of Appeal said a duty to 'promote' an objective was something a decision-maker had to have in mind (and thus should be referenced in documents to show it was in its mind) even if countervailing factors such as the availability of resources meant that the statutory objective may only be partially achieved (or possibly not achieved at all).

8.19 Even though the duty to promote is a relatively weak target duty, it is arguable that the words 'protect and promote' mean that Monitor may be acting unlawfully if it acts in a way which adversely affects the quality of existing NHS services. The scheme of the statutory duties in the HSCA 2012 requires Monitor to treat existing NHS services as a baseline. Monitor is then required to exercise its functions so as to ensure that the NHS maintains or improves the quality of the services it provides to patients.

8.20 Section 62(2) of the HSCA 2012 makes specific reference to the need to ensure that NHS services are not only fit for purpose now but will also be appropriate for the changing demands that will be made on the NHS in the future by requiring Monitor to 'have regard' to the likely future demand for healthcare services. Following the recent case of *R (The Pharmaceutical Services Negotiating Committee and another) v Secretary of*

9 HSCA 2012 s62(1).
10 HSCA 2012 s62(2).
11 [1999] EWCA Civ 1871, [2001] QB 213, (1999) 2 CCLR 285.

State for Health[12] a 'have regard' duty is to interpreted as being an onerous duty which is as pressing on a decision-maker as a 'due regard' duty.[13]

Other general duties

8.21 In addition to its main HSCA 2012 s62(1) duty, Monitor has a range of other general duties.

8.22 By section 62(3) of the HSCA 2012, Monitor must:

> ... exercise its functions with a view to preventing anti-competitive behaviour in the provision of health care services for the purposes of the NHS which is against the interests of people who use such services.

This duty would require Monitor to intervene if, for example, it became aware that providers had colluded to fix prices or to restrict the range of services available to commissioners. However, it should be noted that Monitor is not required to prevent *all* anti-competitive behaviour in the NHS. It is only required (and possible entitled) to exercise its functions with a view to preventing anti-competitive behaviour in the provision of healthcare services for the purposes of the NHS *which is against the interests of people who use such services.* It follows that the mischief that Monitor must guard against is not anti-competitive behaviour per se, but anti-competitive behaviour which it judges has the effect of being against the interests of patients. The amalgamation of specialist services in a single hospital in a locality may reduce the competition in the NHS market for such services, but may promote better patient outcomes. Thus such a set of service changes could be construed as being 'anti-competitive behaviour', but will not necessarily call for action by Monitor because Monitor could reach the view that these service changes would not be against the interests of NHS patients. However, an amalgamation of services that was designed solely to reduce costs or serve the interests of those who provide the services may well be judged by Monitor to be both anti-competitive behaviour *and* against the interests of patients, and thus justify an intervention.

8.23 Monitor is also required to exercise its functions with a view to enabling the integration of NHS healthcare services where it considers that this would improve outcomes or reduce inequalities. Section 62(4) and (5) of the HSCA 2012 provides:

> (4) Monitor must exercise its functions with a view to enabling health care services provided for the purposes of the NHS to be provided in an integrated way where it considers that this would–
> (a) improve the quality of those services (including the outcomes that are achieved from their provision) or the efficiency of their provision,
> (b) reduce inequalities between persons with respect to their ability to access those services, or
> (c) reduce inequalities between persons with respect to the outcomes achieved for them by the provision of those services.
> (5) Monitor must exercise its functions with a view to enabling the provision of health care services provided for the purposes of the NHS to be integrated with the provision of health-related services or social care services where it considers that this would–

12 [2017] EWHC 1147 (Admin).

13 See paras 3.22–3.24.

(a) improve the quality of those health care services (including the outcomes that are achieved from their provision) or the efficiency of their provision,
(b) reduce inequalities between persons with respect to their ability to access those health care services, or
(c) reduce inequalities between persons with respect to the outcomes achieved for them by the provision of those health care services.

8.24 An example of a 'health-related service' in this context could be a pharmaceutical service. In respect of these duties, Monitor must have regard to the way in which NHS England and clinical commissioning groups (CCGs) carry out their duties under sections 13N and 14Z1 of the NHS Act 2006 respectively.[14] The importance of NHS commissioners procuring services in a way that tackles the substantial health inequalities that exist in England is discussed elsewhere, and readers are referred to those passages for a description of the nature and effect of these duties.[15] However, it is of some significance that this is also required to be treated by Monitor as a key element in its decision-making.

8.25 Monitor is required to 'secure public participation in the exercise of its functions, albeit not in relation to decisions made in an individual case'.[16] An example where this duty would not apply is in a decision not to award a licence to a particular provider.

8.26 Monitor has a legal duty to obtain appropriate professional advice from persons who (taken together) have a broad range of relevant expertise.[17] It is also required to:

> Exercise its functions in a manner consistent with the performance by the Secretary of State of the duty under section 1(1) of the National Health Service Act 2006 (promotion of comprehensive health service).[18]

8.27 Section 66 of the HSCA 2012 provides a series of specific factors that Monitor needs to have regard to when discharging its functions. These are as follows:

a) the desirability of securing continuous improvement in the quality of NHS healthcare services and in the efficiency of their provision;[19]
b) the need for CCGs to ensure fair access to services based on clinical need and make best use of resources in doing so;[20]
c) the desirability of co-operation between providers in order to improve the quality of healthcare services;[21]
d) the need to promote research into matters relevant to the NHS;[22]
e) the need for high standards in the education and training of NHS healthcare professionals;[23]

14 See HSCA 2012 s62(6).
15 See chapter 3, paras 3.12–3.38 and chapter 4, paras 4.54–4.63 above
16 See HSCA 2012 s62(7).
17 See HSCA 2012 s62(8).
18 HSCA 2012 s62(9).
19 HSCA 2012 s66(2)(a).
20 HSCA 2012 s66(2)(b)–(d).
21 HSCA 2012 s66(2)(e).
22 HSCA 2012 s66(2)(f).
23 HSCA 2012 s66(2)(g).

f) any statutory guidance published by the secretary of state under section 13E of the NHS Act 2006 which the secretary of state considers to be particularly relevant to Monitor's exercise of its functions.[24]

8.28 The HSCA 2012 also contains a prohibition on Monitor exercising its functions 'for the purpose' of causing a variation in the proportion of healthcare services provided, by reference to whether the provider is in the public or private sector or some other aspect of their status.[25]

8.29 The HSCA 2012[26] makes it clear that Monitor's duties relate only to the regulation of the supply of services by NHS providers, but does not cover goods supplied to service providers, which presumably is a matter of commercial arrangements for each NHS provider.

Duty to review regulatory burdens

8.30 Monitor has a duty to keep its exercise of functions under review to ensure that it does not impose or maintain unnecessary regulatory burdens. The idea is that Monitor should only impose regulation that is necessary and proportionate and that this is reviewed over time.[27] This provision is based upon section 72 of the Regulatory Enforcement and Sanctions Act 2008, although neither provision appears to have formed the subject of any judicial consideration, perhaps because the high level of specialist judgment involved in imposing (or not removing) any particular regulatory burden has meant that such a case would be difficult to bring successfully.

Duty to carry out impact assessments

8.31 In some defined circumstances, Monitor has an obligation to carry out and publish an impact assessment in respect of a proposal (or publish reasons for not carrying out such an assessment).[28] Where an impact assessment is to be carried out, there must be a consultation period in respect of the proposal of at least 28 days from the date of publication of the impact assessment.

How should Monitor manage the conflicts between its various legal duties?

8.32 The general duties imposed on Monitor as the NHS's system regulator, and in particular the tensions between the requirement in section 62(3) of the HSCA 2012 to promote competition, and the requirement in section 62(4)–(5) of the HSCA 2012 to promote integration, reflect the tension between:

a) the desire of the government that the NHS should, as far as possible, operate as a 'managed market', with active competition between providers to secure contracts with commissioners; and
b) the recognition by the government that co-operation between different NHS bodies was vitally important if NHS patients were to experience

24 HSCA 2012 s66(2)(h).
25 HSCA 2012 s62(10).
26 HSCA 2012 s64(6).
27 HSCA 2012 s68.
28 HSCA 2012 s69.

a joined-up service between clinicians in primary, secondary and tertiary care and that co-operation between health and social care bodies (both commissioners and providers) was essential to making the services run effectively.

8.33 The underlying philosophy behind the Health and Social Care Bill that became the HSCA 2012 (as reflected in the white paper that preceded it) was that patient outcomes and value for money would be achieved if the NHS moved more towards operating as a managed market where there was greater competition for patients between NHS providers. However, a series of practical problems faced those who, during the passage of the bill that became the HSCA 2012, were promoting the idea that the NHS should operate as a legally managed market, notably that there were very significant barriers to entry for new economic entrants into the NHS market and that, unlike in other markets, any economic 'failure' of an existing NHS provider could not, for all practical purposes, lead to that provider going out of business. However badly a local hospital may have functioned, the experiences of cases such as Stafford showed that hospitals could not be allowed to fail and close down.[29] The traditional approach to NHS failure was to change the management (and sometimes leading clinicians) and to bring in a new management team that would attack the cultural and organisational practices which led to the failures. But a local NHS hospital cannot be allowed to close as a result of failures, however serious these may be. Equally, the barriers to entry for new providers of NHS services can be formidable. There are examples of new providers of specialist services who have been able to enter the NHS market and are competing with established NHS providers. However, there are no English private hospitals that have entered the market, seeking to compete with NHS hospitals in providing a full-range of emergency and elective services.

8.34 These tensions were frequently discussed as the Health and Social Care Bill progressed on its tortuous passage through parliament. The 'pro-market' lobby suffered a considerable defeat when ministers agreed to remove price competition from the operation of the NHS market (although there have been repeated attempts to re-interpret the provisions in the HSCA 2012 to attempt to argue that this concession was not made).[30] Another outcome was a series of duties on Monitor which required Monitor to stress the need for co-operation between providers of NHS services in a way that would be plainly anti-competitive and hence unlawful if, for example, Tesco and Sainsbury's engaged in the same conduct. These provisions also stressed that the 'managed NHS market' was required to operate in the interests of both present and future NHS patients and not

29 This refers to the Mid-Staffordshire Hospital scandal, in which up to 1,200 patients died unnecessarily between 2005 and 2009, leading to a public inquiry and a 1782-page report by Robert Francis QC, which catalogued failures at every level, from nursing through to management and watchdog bodies, all the way up to the Department of Health and Social Care.

30 Please see the relevant section of chapter 10 on acute care commissioning contracts to see a discussion on this point.

just in the interests of providers (which is, of course, the dominant motive of economic operators in other markets).

8.35 Hence, Monitor had a series of potentially conflicting duties placed on it by the HSCA 2012 as a result of different tensions in government policy between a 'competitive' NHS operating in a managed market and an NHS where the primary driver was co-operation between different providers. These tensions existed before the HSCA 2012, as shown by the Labour government's creation of a Co-Operation and Competition Panel.[31] An attempt to bridge the divide between the different approaches was taken in 2010 in the publication of a revised version of the document 'Principles and Rules for Co-operation and Competition' for the NHS.[32] This includes, for example, a recommendation on information sharing between providers where this was in the interests of patients. This is, of course, precisely the type of behaviour which cuts across against any notion of the NHS operating as a real market, with genuine competition between providers.

8.36 It is interesting to see that, in the years since the implementation of the HSCA 2012, the NHS England (and Department of Health and Social Care) commitment to competition within the NHS market as a way of improving NHS standards and efficiencies has largely been abandoned in favour of enforced co-operative behaviour between different providers of NHS services or even the entire amalgamation of primary and secondary care services in a single proposed provider.[33] This is most clearly seen with the promotion of the 'Accountable Care Organisation' model or, as they are now known 'Integrated Care Systems'.

8.37 Nonetheless, the legal framework within which Monitor is required to operate remains unchanged from the HSCA 2012. It follows that Monitor continues to be required to operate under a series of contradictory duties, the thrust of which is to require the NHS to operate in a competitive market whilst, at the same time, promoting the need for providers to plan and deliver services in a joined-up manner. Such co-operation is the antithesis of any form of genuinely competitive market.

8.38 It is perhaps in recognition of this potential conflict that section 67 of the HSCA 2012 was drafted, which provides:

> (1) In a case where Monitor considers that any of its general duties conflict with each other, it must secure that the conflict is resolved in the manner it considers best.
>
> (2) Monitor must act so as to secure that there is not, and could not reasonably be regarded as being, a conflict between–
>
> (a) its exercise of any of its functions under Chapter 5 of Part 2 of the National Health Service Act 2006 (regulation of NHS foundation trusts) or under sections 111 and 113 of this Act (imposition of licence conditions on NHS foundation trusts during transitional period) or under paragraph 17 of Schedule 8 to this Act (accounts of NHS foundation trusts), and
>
> (b) its exercise of any of its other functions.

31 Which still exists: see www.ccpanel.org.uk/about-the-ccp/index.html.

32 See www.gov.uk/government/uploads/system/uploads/attachment_data/file/216279/dh_118220.pdf.

33 This seems to be the motivation behind some of the move to promote accountable care contracts.

(3) Monitor must ignore the functions it has under sections 111 and 113 when exercising–
  (a) its functions under Chapter 2 (competition);
  (b) its functions under Chapter 4 (pricing).
(4) If Monitor secures the resolution of a conflict between its general duties in a case that comes within subsection (5), or that Monitor considers is otherwise of unusual importance, it must publish a statement setting out–
  (a) the nature of the conflict,
  (b) the manner in which it decided to resolve it, and
  (c) its reasons for deciding to resolve it in that manner.
(5) A case comes within this subsection if it involves–
  (a) a matter likely to have a significant impact on persons who provide health care services for the purposes of the NHS;
  (b) a matter likely to have a significant impact on people who use health care services provided for the purposes of the NHS;
  (c) a matter likely to have a significant impact on the general public in England (or in a particular part of England);
  (d) a major change in the activities Monitor carries on;
  (e) a major change in the standard conditions of licences under Chapter 3 (see section 94).
(6) Where Monitor is required to publish a statement under subsection (4), it must do so as soon as reasonably practicable after making its decision.
(7) The duty under subsection (4) does not apply in so far as Monitor is subject to an obligation not to publish a matter that needs to be included in the statement.
(8) Every annual report of Monitor must include–
  (a) a statement of the steps it has taken in the financial year to which the report relates to comply with the duty under subsection (2), and
  (b) a summary of the manner in which, in that financial year, Monitor has secured the resolution of conflicts between its general duties arising in cases of the kind referred to in subsection (5).
(9) Monitor's general duties for the purposes of this section are its duties under sections 62 and 66.

8.39 Thus, where Monitor considers that a conflict arises between its general duties under section 62 and 66 of the HSCA 2012, it is for Monitor to resolve any such conflict in the manner that Monitor considers best. It is suggested that the guiding principle in resolving any conflicts that may arise is Monitor's overarching duty in section 62(1). According to the 2016/17 report (published under the NHSI banner), no conflicts falling within section 67 were identified, and accordingly no statements were published.[34]

Monitor's licensing functions

Overview

8.40 Chapter 3 of Part 3 established a new licensing regime for providers of NHS services. In summary, unless exempt, all providers of NHS services should be licensed by Monitor and should deliver services in accordance with the licensing regime.

8.41 Two preliminary points should be noted at the outset:

34 See p78 of the report (for the link to the report see footnote 8).

a) The licence is a regulatory tool, not a kitemark of quality. Nor is it a badge of financial stability or a guarantee that the licensee will be awarded contracts by commissioners to provide NHS services. The licence was designed to entitle the holder to operate in the NHS market and compete with licensed holders for contracts from NHS commissioners.
b) The purpose of the licence criteria and application process is fundamentally different from that of the process for application for foundation trust status that Monitor is responsible for under Chapter 5 of, and Schedule 7 to, the NHS Act 2006, and is separate from the additional powers that Monitor has to intervene where a foundation trust is failing (which are considered below).

8.42 The licensing rules were implemented in April 2014. From that date, all providers of health care services for the purposes of the NHS required a Monitor licence[35] unless they were exempted pursuant to regulations made under section 83. Monitor sets the licencing criteria[36] but may not set or revise them without the secretary of state's prior approval of the proposed criteria (or revised criteria) and such approval is given by an order.[37]

8.43 The key distinction between this licensing regime and previous attempts to regulate NHS providers is that the licensing regime under the HSCA 2012 was designed to apply in the same way to all NHS providers: those consisting of public bodies and those NHS providers that were charities, other non-profit companies or private profit-making companies. Section 81 of the HSCA 2012 requires any person who provides NHS healthcare services to hold a licence from Monitor, unless exempt under regulations made under section 83 of the HSCA 2012.

8.44 The provider licence thus ought to have been one of the main tools Monitor was able to use when exercising its functions in line with its main general statutory duty to protect and promote the interests of people who use healthcare services.

8.45 However it is questionable whether the licensing system has any real practical effect – at least across the collective of providers of NHS services because (a) Monitor regulated FTs in any event and (b) the exemption Regulations are drafted very widely and exclude the vast majority of other NHS providers from the need to be licensed. The exemptions are contained in the National Health Service (Licence Exemptions, etc) Regulations (Licence Exemption Regs) 2013[38] as amended from time to time. The current exemptions under the Licence Exemption Regs 2013 are:

a) any NHS trust established under section 25 of the NHS Act 2006;[39]
b) providers of primary medical and dental services[40] – thus all general practitioner (GP) practices and community dental practices were exempt from the licensing system;

35 HSCA 2012 s81.
36 HSCA 2012 s86.
37 HSCA 2012 s86(3).
38 SI No 2677.
39 Licence Exemption Regs 2013 reg 4.
40 Licence Exemption Regs 2013 reg 5.

c) NHS providers who are providing NHS Continuing Healthcare and NHS funded nursing care[41] – hence virtually all care homes and nursing homes are exempt, even if they provide NHS commissioned services;
d) there are a variety of specialist medical services, such as the provision of psychotherapy, which do not require registration with CQC – these are exempt from the need for NHS registration;[42]
e) the provider's applicable turnover for the relevant business year is less than, or is reasonably expected to be less than £10 million.[43]

8.46 It should, however, be noted that pursuant to section 88 of the HSCA 2012, foundation trusts are treated as having made an application for a license and have met the criteria for holding a licence. Regulation 3 confirms that exemptions do not apply to foundation trusts.

Monitor's licensing criteria

8.47 There are only two licensing criteria, and these are contained in Schedule 1 to the National Health Service (Approval of Licensing Criteria) Order (Licensing Order) 2013,[44] namely:

1) registration with CQC; and
2) being fit to hold a licence – which in practical terms means not being a person banned from holding a licence as a result of a series of behaviours.

Criterion 1: Registration with CQC

8.48 The person must either be registered with CQC or must have made an application to be registered and CQC has informed Monitor that the person will be registered.[45] Criterion 1 applies to any person who, in providing a healthcare service for the purposes of the NHS, is, or on the grant of a licence would be, carrying on a regulated activity within the meaning of Chapter 2 of Part 1 (the Care Quality Commission) of the Health and Social Care Act 2008.

Criterion 2: Individual and/or corporate fitness

8.49 The person must be fit to hold such a licence.[46] A person is treated as a fit person unless he or she falls within the definition of an unfit person. If the applicant is an individual, he or she is unfit if he or she is:

a) a person who is under any one of a variety of orders relating to unpaid debts: including an undischarged bankrupted or a person whose estate has been sequestrated, a person to whom a debt relief order applies or a person who is under an undischarged arrangement with their creditors;[47]

41 Licence Exemption Regs 2013 reg 6.
42 Licence Exemption Regs 2013 reg 7.
43 Licence Exemption Regs 2013 reg 8.
44 SI No 2960.
45 Sch 1 para 1.
46 Sch 1 para 2.
47 Sch 1 para 2(4)(a)(i)–(iii).

b) a person who within the preceding five years has been convicted in the British Islands of any offence and a sentence of imprisonment (whether suspended or not) for a period of not less than three months;[48] or
c) a person subject to a disqualification order or a disqualification undertaking under the Company Directors Disqualification Act 1986.[49]

8.50 If the applicant (B) is not an individual, it is unfit if:
a) any of B's directors or governors would be unfit for the reasons relating to an individual set out above;[50]
b) where any director or governor of B is a body corporate, any of the directors or governors of that body or its parent body (if it has a parent body) are unfit for the reasons relating to an individual set out above;[51] or
c) it is a body corporate and that body or its parent body (if it has one) is subject arrangements made under the Insolvency Act 1986.[52]

8.51 In summary, where an applicant is an individual, that individual must not fall within the definition of an unfit person. Where the applicant is not an individual (such as a company, partnership or other organisation), its directors, governors or persons performing similar or equivalent functions must not fall within the definition of an unfit person.

8.52 The Monitor guidance on licensing can be accessed through the current licence application portal.[53]

The application

8.53 From 1 April 2014, providers who became required to hold an NHS provider licence and were already registered with CQC were to apply to Monitor for a licence, and normally this application must be made online. Unless changes are made to the Licence Exemptions Regs 2013, there are unlikely to be any new applications of this type.

8.54 For providers who are not already registered with CQC, they can choose to apply for both a CQC registration and NHS provider licence on the same form, called the Joint Licensing and Regulation (JLaR) form. The joint application consists of two parts: Part A (CQC registration) and Part B (NHS provider licence). This application can be accessed through CQC's website.[54] Providers will need to complete both Parts A and B of the JLaR form and submit it to CQC's National Customer Service Centre by email or post.

Licence conditions

8.55 Once a provider is licensed, it is required to comply with the licence conditions set by Monitor under section 94 (standard conditions) of the HSCA 2012. Licence conditions can take the form of standard conditions,

48 Sch 1 para 2(4)(a)(iv).
49 Sch 1 para 2(4)(a)(v).
50 Sch 1 para 2(3)(b)(i).
51 Sch 1 para 2(3)(b)(ii).
52 Sch 1 para 2(4)(b).
53 Guidance: https://licensing-gateway.monitor.gov.uk/sites/monitor/Documents/GuidanceDocumentation.pdf. Licensing Portal: https://licensing-gateway.monitor.gov.uk/sites/monitor/Pages/GuidanceConfirmation.aspx.
54 See www.cqc.org.uk/guidance-providers/registration/apply-new-provider.

which apply to all licence holders, or to particular types of licence holder; and special conditions,[55] which will apply to an individual provider. The standard set of conditions applicable to all holders of Monitor's licence is accessible on the government website.[56] The conditions are extensive and onerous, and include a duty to provide all services set out in NHS commissioning contracts held by the licence holder. By way of example, the following is a licence condition in section 4 of the NHS Provider Licence Standard Conditions, relating to the duties on all NHS bodies to promote integrated care:

> 1. The Licensee shall not do anything that reasonably would be regarded as against the interests of people who use health care services by being detrimental to enabling its provision of health care services for the purposes of the NHS to be integrated with the provision of such services by others with a view to achieving one or more of the objectives referred to in paragraph 4.
>
> 2. The Licensee shall not do anything that reasonably would be regarded as against the interests of people who use health care services by being detrimental to enabling its provision of health care services for the purposes of the NHS to be integrated with the provision of health-related services or social care services by others with a view to achieving one or more of the objectives referred to in paragraph 4.
>
> 3. The Licensee shall not do anything that reasonably would be regarded as against the interests of people who use health care services by being detrimental to enabling it to co-operate with other providers of health care services for the purposes of the NHS with a view to achieving one or more of the objectives referred to in paragraph 4.
>
> 4. The objectives referred to in paragraphs 1, 2 and 3 are:
>
> (a) improving the quality of health care services provided for the purposes of the NHS (including the outcomes that are achieved from their provision) or the efficiency of their provision,
>
> (b reducing inequalities between persons with respect to their ability to access those services, and
>
> (c) reducing inequalities between persons with respect to the outcomes achieved for them by the provision of those services.
>
> 5. The Licensee shall have regard to such guidance as may have been is sued by Monitor from time to time concerning actions or behaviours that might reasonably be regarded as against the interests of people who use health care services for the purposes of paragraphs 1, 2 or 3 of this Condition.

Enforcement of licence

8.56 Section 104 of the HSCA 2012 gives Monitor investigatory powers to require documents and information. Sections 105 to 107 and Schedule 11 give Monitor the powers to take action against actual or suspected licence breaches. These provisions give Monitor powers to take action to stop a breach continuing, rectify the breach and to impose a fine, and under section 89 of the HSCA 2012 Monitor may revoke a licence. It may also impose additional licence conditions.

55 HSCA 2012 s9.

56 See www.gov.uk/government/uploads/system/uploads/attachment_data/file/285009/Annex_NHS_provider_licence_conditions_-_20120207.pdf.

8.57 There is a right of appeal to the First-Tier Tribunal under section 92 of the HSCA 2012 against Monitor's refusal to issue or decision to revoke a licence. This is suspensive where the appeal is against the decision to revoke.

8.58 Monitor's (statutory) enforcement guidance sets out the principles it will follow in taking enforcement action.[57] However, this guidance does not apply to Monitor's enforcement powers under the National Health Service (Procurement, Patient Choice and Competition) (No 2) Regulations (NHS Procurement Regs) 2013,[58] which is addressed in chapter 21 of this book.

Additional powers in respect of foundation trusts

8.59 Pursuant to powers contained in sections 111–114 of the HSCA 2012 (which were supposed to be transitional, but have not yet been repealed), Monitor was provided with additional intervention powers over all foundation trusts. Under these provisions, Monitor may impose measures in order to prevent or remedy a breach of the foundation trust's licence. Measures include additional licence conditions and the ability to require the trust to remove one or more directors or governors of the trust.

8.60 These powers are without prejudice to any of Monitor's other powers, and are in addition to Monitor's continuing non-transitional powers to intervene where a licence holder is in breach of licence conditions.

Monitor's competition functions

8.61 As set out elsewhere in this book,[59] the HSCA 2012 brought significant changes to how NHS healthcare was commissioned and regulated in England. The new NHS Commissioning Board (now known as NHS England) and CCGs were to commission NHS healthcare in England and, between them, are now responsible for over £100 billion of annual public expenditure. The secretary of state was no longer to have extensive general powers to intervene in the NHS; his powers were replaced with specific and limited powers. It was therefore considered appropriate to impose a legal framework on the way these new bodies operated in the NHS market in order to provide for important safeguards to protect both patients' interests and the interests of the taxpayer. This was done in two main ways.

8.62 First, Monitor was given specific functions under the Part 1 of the Competition Act 1998 and under Part 4 of the Enterprise Act 2002 relating to anti-competitive practices and market investigations within the healthcare sector in England.[60] It shares these functions concurrently with the Competition and Markets Authority (CMA). The previously issued Monitor guidance has now been superseded by consolidated guidance issued by NHSI dated November 2017, which sets out how this will be

57 See www.gov.uk/government/publications/monitors-enforcement-guidance.

58 SI No 500.

59 See chapter 1.

60 See HCSA 2012 ss72–73, and also Sch 10.

approached and gives specific transaction guidance for trusts undertaking transactions, including mergers and acquisitions.[61]

8.63 Second, regulations were enacted pursuant to section 75 of the HSCA 2012 which imposed requirements upon NHS England[62] and CCGs relating to procurement, patient choice and competition. Monitor was given powers (partially) to enforce of these requirements pursuant to sections 76–77 and the regulations made thereunder.

8.64 The current regulations made under sections 75 and 76 are the National Health Service (Procurement, Patient Choice and Competition) (No 2) Regulations (NHS Procurement Regs) 2013. Details of the obligations these regulations put on NHS commissioners is explained in chapter 21 on procurement.

8.65 Part 3 of the NHS Procurement Regs 2013 provides Monitor with powers to investigate and take (limited) enforcement action in relation to breaches of the requirements imposed on relevant bodies by the NHS Procurement Regs 2013, and also in relation to breaches of regs 39, 42 and 43 of the National Health Service Commissioning Board and Clinical Commissioning Groups (Responsibilities and Standing Rules) Regulations 2012[63] relating to the choice of health service provider. Monitor's powers to investigate and take action in relation to breaches of the requirements include powers for Monitor to declare arrangements for the provision of healthcare services for the purposes of the NHS to be ineffective,[64] to give directions to a relevant body,[65] and to accept undertakings from a relevant body.[66] However, the NHS Procurement Regs 2013 do not give Monitor the power to direct where or when commissioners should introduce competition or patient choice of provider. In particular, the regulations provide that Monitor may not direct a commissioner to hold a competitive tender for a contract for the provision of healthcare services. Monitor's role is to investigate whether commissioners have respected due process, considered the full range of options and followed the requirements in the regulations when procuring healthcare services.

8.66 The NHS Procurement Regs 2013 apply alongside the Public Contracts Regulations 2006[67] and do not affect their application, although there are provisions preventing double recovery.[68] Section 78 of the HSCA 2012 places a duty on Monitor to publish guidance for commissioners on compliance with the regulations and how it intends to exercise its enforcement powers. Monitor must consult and must obtain the approval of the secretary of state before the guidance is published. The current guidance on the regulations is still the December 2013 guidance and is available online.[69]

61 See https://improvement.nhs.uk/uploads/documents/Transactions_guidance_2017_Final.pdf.

62 Referred to in the HSCA 2012 as the National Health Service Commissioning Board, the old name for NHS England (ie prior to 1 April 2013).

63 SI No 2996.

64 Reg 14.

65 Reg 15.

66 Reg 16.

67 SI No 5.

68 See reg 17.

69 See www.gov.uk/government/uploads/system/uploads/attachment_data/file/283505/SubstantiveGuidanceDec2013_0.pdf.

Pricing functions

8.67 Monitor has various responsibilities around setting and regulating prices. Once the HSCA 2012 ruled out price competition between providers for the delivery of NHS services, it became essential to identify a neutral body as between NHS commissioners and providers of NHS services to set the price that would be paid for those services that were fixed under the NHS National Tariff and to set the rules which commissioners and providers were required to follow to set local prices.

8.68 The rules for price fixing under the National Tariff are set out in Chapter 4 of Part 3 of the HSCA 2012. In summary, NHS England has a duty to specify those healthcare services for which it thinks a national price should be used, and Monitor (though the government website refers to NHS Improvement) has the duty to set that price. The National Tariff specifies rules governing not only how nationally set pricing will work, but also how local price-setting must operate.

Failure regime

8.69 The NHS failure regime was created to provide a solution to intractable problems, namely how interventions should be managed to assist NHS trusts (and NHS foundation trusts) that have significant financial or clinical challenges. One of the government's key aims in introducing the regime was to stop 'hidden bailouts' for these trusts.

8.70 The failure regime is designed to be used as a last resort and has only been used twice since its introduction by the Health Act 2009. It was used for South London Healthcare NHS Trust, in 2012; and the Mid Staffordshire NHS Foundation Trust, in 2013. Neither use of the powers was a total success. The main conclusion of the trust special administrator (TSA) in the South London Healthcare NHS Trust case was struck down by the High Court, a decision that was upheld by the Court of Appeal. The TSA report in the Stafford case resulted in services being moved to a combination of North Midlands and Wolverhampton, but the capital cost of the reorganisation ended up being far, far higher than predicted and there was considerable criticism of the costs of the TSA process. After the regime had been implemented at Mid Staffordshire NHS Foundation Trust, Monitor published a paper[70] reviewing the regime and stated that they would aim to take a local health economy-wide approach in the future. They also emphasised that they would avoid appointing a TSA unless absolutely necessary.

8.71 Trusts can either be deemed by Monitor to be failing financially, on governance or by significantly underperforming concerning the quality of care provided. Financial sustainability means that a trust is able to deliver the appropriate level of care to patients without it costing more than the money the trust receives. Failures in clinical quality means that trusts or services are failing to meet minimum clinical quality levels.

8.72 The process was legislated for in the Health Act 2009. It was then modified in the HSCA 2012 to reflect NHS foundation trusts' greater

70 As reported by the BMI at www.bma.org.uk/collective-voice/policy-and-research/nhs-structure-and-delivery/models-for-preventing-and-addressing-failure/the-failure-regime.

autonomy and to make it compatible with Monitor's regulatory role. The Care Act 2014 made further changes to allow the regime to legally make recommendations which may affect the services at other trusts (largely to overturn the decision of the Court of Appeal in *Trust Special Administrator Appointed to South London Healthcare NHS Trust and another v Lewisham LBC and another*[71]). However, the significant problems emerging from the two cases where this process was used means that it seems unlikely that the TSA route will ever be used by Monitor in the near future.

8.73 It should be noted that Chapters 5 and 6 of Part 3 of the HSCA 2012 introduced a 'health special administration' regime, based on insolvency legislation, for the purposes of securing the continued provision of NHS services by a company that becomes insolvent. The scheme applies only to 'relevant providers' as defined, and Monitor is tasked with various duties in relation to that regime. However, the provisions setting up the scheme have been shelved[72] and are not being brought into force, which means that if an independent provider of commissioner requested services becomes insolvent, Monitor will not be able to place them into a special administration regime in order to safeguard essential services and standard insolvency procedures will continue to apply.

Trust Development Authority

Generally

8.74 The TDA is a Special Health Authority, established by the National Health Service Trust Development Authority (Establishment and Constitution) Order 2012[73] (as amended), which is made pursuant to section 28 of the NHS Act 2006. The NHS TDA has two main functions:

a) regulatory functions in connection with the management of English NHS trusts;
b) safety functions following the transfer to it of the patient safety functions in section 13R of the NHS Act 2006.

Trust Development Authority regulatory functions

8.75 The TDA was established to exercise functions in connection with the management of the performance of English NHS trusts, supporting improvements in clinical quality, governance, and management of risk, with the objective of assisting them to become sustainable organisations, as the secretary of state may direct.[74] It has such functions, as well as others in connection with appointments relating to NHS trust boards and special trustees.

71 [2013] EWCA Civ 1409.

72 See www.nationalhealthexecutive.com/Health-Policy/health-special-administration-regime-plans-shelved.

73 SI No 901.

74 See NHS Act 2006 ss7 and 8; and 2012 Order art 3.

Trust Development Authority patient safety functions

8.76 In July 2015, following the announcement of the NHS TDA and Monitor organisational merger into the NHSI organisation, the secretary of state decided that the national safety function, as specified by section 13R of the NHS Act 2006 (at the time exercised by NHS England), would in the future be exercised by NHS TDA.[75] Section 13R provides:

> **13R Information on safety of services provided by the health service**
>
> (1) The Board must establish and operate systems for collecting and analysing information relating to the safety of the services provided by the health service.
>
> (2) The Board must make information collected by virtue of subsection (1), and any other information obtained by analysing it, available to such persons as the Board considers appropriate.
>
> (3) The Board may impose charges, calculated on such basis as it considers appropriate, in respect of information made available by it under subsection (2).
>
> (4) The Board must give advice and guidance, to such persons as it considers appropriate, for the purpose of maintaining and improving the safety of the services provided by the health service.
>
> (5) The Board must monitor the effectiveness of the advice and guidance given by it under subsection (4).
>
> (6) A clinical commissioning group must have regard to any advice or guidance given to it under subsection (4).
>
> (7) The Board may arrange for any other person (including another NHS body) to exercise any of the Board's functions under this section.
>
> (8) Arrangements made under subsection (7) do not affect the liability of the Board for the exercise of any of its functions.'

8.77 The transfer of responsibility to the TDA has been done through the National Health Service Trust Development Authority (Directions and Miscellaneous Amendments etc) Regulations 2016.[76] As the transfer of responsibility also involved the transfer of the relevant teams from NHS England, this instrument also made other amendments to the constitution of the NHS TDA regarding governance arrangements and to make provision for the transfer of staff, property and liabilities related to the safety function. All activity under this provision is now published under the NHSI banner.

Care Quality Commission

Overview: history and functions

8.78 CQC was established by section 1 of the Health and Social Care Act (HSCA) 2008 and came into being on 1 April 2009. Prior to the HSCA 2008:

a) the regulation of healthcare in England was carried out by the Commission for Healthcare Audit and Inspection (CHAI), known as the Healthcare Commission;

75 See www.gov.uk/government/speeches/making-healthcare-more-human-centred-and-not-system-centred.

76 SI No 214.

b) social care was regulated by the Commission for Social Care Inspection (CSCI); and
c) monitoring of key aspects of the operation of the Mental Health Act (MHA) 1983 was done by the Mental Health Act Commission (MHAC) which operated in England and Wales. The MHAC had other specific functions as well, notably: to appoint registered medical practitioners to give second opinions where this is required by the MHA 1983; to review decisions to withhold postal packages of patients detained in high security psychiatric hospitals; to visit and interview, in private, patients subject to the MHA 1983; and to investigate complaints.

8.79 CQC was thus established in a merger of those three watchdogs. It was reported at the time that the merger was the idea of the then prime minister, Rt Hon Gordon Brown MP, who wanted to cut the cost of regulation. CQC began operation with a smaller budget than the combined funding of its three predecessors and, according to both supporters and critics, too broad a remit.

8.80 Section 1 of the HSCA 2008 provides:

(1) There is to be a body corporate known as the Care Quality Commission (referred to in this Part as 'the Commission').
(2) The Commission for Healthcare Audit and Inspection, the Commission for Social Care Inspection and the Mental Health Act Commission are dissolved.
(3) Schedule 1 (which makes further provision about the Care Quality Commission) has effect.

8.81 CQC's functions are set out in section 2:

(1) The Commission has the functions conferred on it by or under any enactment.
(2) Those functions include–
  (a) registration functions under Chapter 2,
  (b) review and investigation functions under Chapter 3, and
  (c) functions under the Mental Health Act 1983.

8.82 CQC has had a range of functions imposed upon it, but this chapter focusses only upon the regulatory aspects of CQC's functions insofar as they apply to NHS trusts and foundation trusts. These are CQC's twin functions of registration and compliance (which includes investigation and enforcement).

8.83 CQC's objectives are contained in section 3:

(1) The main objective of the Commission in performing its functions is to protect and promote the health, safety and welfare of people who use health and social care services.
(2) The Commission is to perform its functions for the general purpose of encouraging–
  (a) the improvement of health and social care services,
  (b) the provision of health and social care services in a way that focuses on the needs and experiences of people who use those services, and
  (c) the efficient and effective use of resources in the provision of health and social care services.
(3) In this Chapter '*health and social care services*' means the services to which the Commission's functions relate.

8.84 This section is accordingly divided into two sections: registration and compliance activity.

Registration

8.85 The HSCA 2008, in Chapter 2 of Part 1, creates a system of registration for providers and, in some cases, managers of health and adult social care. The new registration system replaced (in England) the previous requirement for certain establishments and agencies providing independent healthcare or adult social care to be registered under the Care Standards Act 2000.

8.86 Regulations made under section 8 of the HSCA 2008 set out those health and social care activities (referred to as 'regulated activities'), which a person will not be able to carry on unless that person is registered to do so. The intention of the new scheme was that all providers, including, for the first time, NHS providers, would be brought within the ambit of registration and therefore regulation by an external body.

8.87 This was a significant task, as a Parliamentary Select Committee reported at the time:

> The timetable for registration of providers by the CQC was dictated by the Health and Social Care Act 2008 (Regulated Activities) Regulations 2010. The registration of different providers was staggered to enable the CQC to 'work with providers to build capability, so that the registration and ongoing compliance processes are implemented efficiently and effectively'. In the financial year 2009–10 the CQC registered all 378 NHS providers; by April 2011 the CQC was due to have registered 13,000 adult social care and independent health care providers, 8000 dentists and 350 private ambulance services; and by April 2012 the CQC was required to have registered some 8000 providers of primary care, including GP practices, out-of-hours primary care services and NHS walk-in centres.[77]

8.88 However, it is important to recall that registration was not the end in itself: it was preparing the ground for its main role of maintaining standards through its reviewing, inspection and enforcement role. In the event, this process of registration meant that the number of CQC inspections dramatically dropped. The cross-party Commons Select Committee on Health stated in September 2011 that this 'bias of the work in the CQC away from its core function of inspection and towards the essentially administrative task of registration represented a significant distortion of priorities'.[78]

8.89 The adverse impact on patient care was noted in real terms at the time – for example, the Committee concluded that action in the Winterbourne View case[79] was 'woefully inadequate'. Following this report, the Department of Health and Social Care launched its own investigation into the performance and capability of CQC, as did the National Audit Office, the latter also identifying serious concerns with CQC's ability to protect patients

77 See https://publications.parliament.uk/pa/cm201012/cmselect/cmhealth/1430/143004.htm at para 9.

78 See https://publications.parliament.uk/pa/cm201012/cmselect/cmhealth/1430/143004.htm at para 9.

79 Winterbourne View, a private hospital near Bristol for people with learning disabilities, where BBC Panorama exposed abuse and appalling standards of care.

and ensure that basic standards of care were met. Once the bias was exposed, various measures were taken to increase CQC's compliance activity.

8.90 Separately from issues of resources and staffing, the various scandals and the recommendations from the inquiries that followed, provoked a review of the regulations relating to registration. One of the key themes emerging from the second Mid-Staffordshire Hospital Inquiry,[80] also echoed in the Winterbourne Serious Case Review, was a lack of clarity in the registration requirements that inhibited CQC taking effective action against providers where harm to patients had occurred. It was recommended that fundamental standards of safety and quality below which care should never fall, be introduced.

8.91 This was done through the Health and Social Care Act 2008 (Regulated Activities) Regulations (Regulated Activities Regs) 2014,[81] which replaced the earlier regulations of the same name of 2010. The stated policy intention behind the fundamental standards was 'to clarify the requirements that providers must meet, and to make it more straightforward for CQC to bring prosecutions for the most serious breaches of the requirements'.[82] These standards are generally framed in terms of outcomes, for example that reg 14 requires providers to ensure that service users' nutrition and hydration needs are met. This has the advantage, in enforcement terms, that if there is evidence that the desired outcome has not been met, the regulation has been breached and the onus is on the provider to demonstrate that it had taken all reasonable steps to prevent that breach. These regulations have since been amended (in 2015) but the underlying structure and purpose remains the same.

8.92 The key requirements under the Regulated Activities Regs 2014 are:

a) a new 'fit and proper person' test for directors of a health service body that requires registration (ie NHS trust, NHS foundation trusts and some Special Health Authorities);[83]
b) fundamental standards[84] – these include requirements that care and treatment must be 'person centred' ie be appropriate, meet their needs and reflect their preferences;[85] that service users must be treated with dignity and respect;[86] that they receive suitable nutrition;[87] and that they are safeguarded from abuse;[88]
c) an entirely new requirement regarding the duty of candour,[89] imposed as a result of the various reviews and inquiries. This provision puts on a statutory footing the need for a culture of candour and transparency.

80 The second inquiry, also chaired by Robert Francis QC, was tasked with the wider remit of examining specifically the supervisory and regulatory failings which effectively allowed the serious failings at the hospital to go on for so long.
81 SI No 2936.
82 Explanatory Memorandum to the Regulated Activities Regs 2014.
83 Regulated Activities Regs 2014 reg 5.
84 Regulated Activities Regs 2014 regs 8–20.
85 Regulated Activities Regs 2014 reg 9.
86 Regulated Activities Regs 2014 reg 10.
87 Regulated Activities Regs 2014 reg 14.
88 Regulated Activities Regs 2014 reg 13.
89 See Care Act 2014 s81, which inserts a new subsection 5A into section 20 of the HSCA 2008 (regulation of regulated activities).

8.93 Failure to comply with some (but not all) of the regulations is a criminal offence.

8.94 Regulation 21 imposes a requirement on the registered person to have regard to the guidance issued by CQC under section 23 of the HSCA 2008 and any code of practice issue by the secretary of state under section 21.

8.95 The power to grant or refuse registration includes a power to grant it subject to conditions. There is a right of appeal under section 32 of the HSCA 2008 against a refusal, as well as against the decision to grant it subject to conditions.

Compliance activity

8.96 Compliance is CQC's core activity. Section 46 of the HSCA 2008 (as amended by the Care Act 2014) requires CQC to carry out periodic reviews of care and provides, so far as material for these purposes:

> **46 Reviews and performance assessments**
> (1) The Commission must, in respect of such regulated activities and such registered service providers as may be prescribed–
> (a) conduct reviews of the carrying on of the regulated activities by the service providers,
> (b) assess the performance of the service providers following each such review, and
> (c) publish a report of its assessment.
> (2) Regulations under subsection (1) may prescribe–
> (a) all regulated activities or regulated activities of a particular description;
> (b) all registered service providers or particular registered service providers;
> (c) the whole of a regulated activity or a particular aspect of it.
> (3) The assessment of the performance of a registered service provider is to be by reference to whatever indicators of quality the Commission devises.
> (4) The Commission must prepare a statement–
> (a) setting out the frequency with which reviews under this section are to be conducted and the period to which they are to relate, and
> (b) describing the method that it proposes to use in assessing and evaluating the performance of a registered service provider under this section.

8.97 In addition to this general duty, CQC may, and sometimes must, conduct a special review or investigation. This is contained in section 48 of the HSCA 2008, which provides, so far as material:

> **48 Special reviews and investigations**
> The Commission may conduct any special review or investigation, and must do so if the Secretary of State so requests; but the Commission may not conduct a review or investigation under subsection (2)(ba) or (bb) without the approval of the Secretary of State . . .

8.98 Subsections 48(2)(ba) and (bb), which would require the secretary of state's consent for a special review or investigation, refer to the exercise of the functions of NHS England or CCGs in arranging for the provision of NHS care, and the exercise of the functions of English local authorities in arranging for the provision of adult social services.

8.99 The regulations made under section 46 are the Care Quality Commission (Reviews and Performance Assessments) Regulations (CQC Assessments Regs) 2018,[90] which come into force on 1 April 2018. These replace earlier regulations of the same name which were made in 2014. The earlier regulations set out which providers and regulated activities were included in the section 46 duty. The CQC Assessments Regs 2018 effectively reverse the approach: all registered service providers and regulated activities fall within the section 46 duty unless they fall within a list of exempt services as set out in the CQC Assessments Regs 2018. CQC's duty to undertake periodic reviews therefore relates only to the provision of such regulated activities as is prescribed and not the commissioning of such services. Any performance review of health or social care commissioning would be undertaken under CQC's powers of special review under section 48 (as amended by section 91 of the Care Act 2014.)

8.100 The HSCA 2012 proposed to remove the duty for CQC to review English NHS providers, with the aim of providing that Monitor would be the sole NHS regulator. However, this change of policy has only been commenced insofar as it relates to primary care trusts (PCTs), which were themselves abolished by the HSCA 2012, and otherwise does not appear to have been progressed. In relation to other sectors, this repeal was not commenced (originally, it is understood that this was pending a review by the Nuffield Trust commissioned by the secretary of state as to whether aggregate ratings of providers' performance should be used in health and social care).

8.101 Insofar as frequency is concerned, CQC's position is that they aim to inspect each NHS trust at least once between June 2017 and summer 2019 and approximately annually after that. The maximum intervals for re-inspection depend upon the rating of the core services and range between one year for core services rated as inadequate, and five years for core services rated as outstanding.[91] CQC has published detailed guidance entitled *How CQC monitors, inspects and regulates NHS Trusts,* which is available on their website (the latest update at the time of writing being March 2018).[92]

8.102 As a result of the inspection, CQC awards a performance rating which must now be displayed at the premises and on any website maintained by or on behalf of any service provider, along with a link to the most recent CQC assessment and most recent rating.[93]

8.103 CQC has a range of powers in dealing with failures and has set out its enforcement policy in two guidance documents entitled *Enforcement policy*[94] and *Enforcement decision tree.*[95] Their main powers are as follows:

90 SI No 54.

91 See www.cqc.org.uk/guidance-providers/nhs-trusts/when-we-will-inspect-nhs-trusts.

92 See www.cqc.org.uk/sites/default/files/20180228-how-CQC-regulates-NHS-trusts-updated-March–2018-final.pdf.

93 Regulated Activities Regs 2014 reg 20A.

94 See www.cqc.org.uk/sites/default/files/20150209_enforcement_policy_v1–1.pdf.

95 See www.cqc.org.uk/sites/default/files/20170217_enforcement_decision_tree.pdf (January 2017).

a) *Requirement notice* – This is reserved for breaches at the lowest end of the seriousness scale, where the registered person is in breach of a regulation or has poor ability to maintain compliance but people using the service are not at immediate risk of harm. The notice requires the provider to take specific measures to remedy the breach. Failure to send CQC a report in the timescale set out in the requirement notice is an offence and may result in them using other enforcement powers.
b) *Warning notice* – CQC can issue a warning notice requiring action to be taken, under section 29 or section 29A of the HSCA 2008 if the quality of healthcare provided by an NHS trust 'requires significant improvement'. Note, however, that provisions are different and the applicable provision for NHS trusts and foundation trusts is section 29A. Warning notices are considered appropriate for risks assessed at a medium level of seriousness. Where the section 29A notice has not been complied with, section 29A(5) provides that CQC:
   (a) must decide what action to take in relation to the trust, and
   (b) in so deciding in the case of an NHS foundation trust, must consider in particular whether to require Monitor to make an order under section 65D(2) of the NHS Act 2006 (appointment of trust special administrator).

   CQC aim to follow up every warning notice through a check within three months of the date set out in the notice.[96] Warning notices may be published provided that the subject of them has been given an opportunity to make representations about the proposed publication.
c) *Civil enforcement powers*: These are the power to:
   i) *Impose, vary or remove conditions of registration* – Pursuant to section 12 of the HSCA 2008, CQC may 'at any time' vary or remove any condition or impose any additional condition.
   ii) *Suspend registration* – This power is available pursuant to section 18 of the HSCA 2008, however CQC's guidance indicates that they anticipate rarely using this power.
   iii) *Cancel registration* – Pursuant to section 17, CQC has power to cancel a person's registration (and must do so in certain circumstances).

   There are provisions which allow CQC to take any of these measures urgently (sections 30–31 of the HSCA 2008).
d) *Special measures:* This is an administrative (as opposed to statutory) scheme under which the NHS provider comes under close scrutiny. It is usually triggered by ratings of inadequate care, rather than by individual breaches of regulations although the latter is likely to form part of the former. Insofar as NHS trusts and foundation trusts are concerned, special measures require Monitor and NHS TDA as well as others to get involved with the aim of resolving the issues giving rise to the special measures.
e) *Criminal powers*: CQC has power
   i) *To issue simple cautions* – This is a formal record of an offence when a person has admitted to it, but is not prosecuted. There is no

96 *Enforcement policy* p19.

obligation on a provider to accept a caution, although refusal to do so may result in a prosecution being brought instead.

ii) *To issue penalty notices* – Pursuant to sections 86–87 of the HSCA 2008, and the Regulated Activities Regs 2014, CQC has discretion to issue a penalty notice as an alternative to prosecution. Failure to pay the sums under the penalty notice will normally lead to a prosecution.

iii) *To bring prosecutions* – The HSCA 2008 and the Regulated Activity Regs 2014 create various offences, which CQC has power to investigate and prosecute. CQC has published prosecution criteria[97] which essentially reserves, as one might expect, prosecution for the most serious of cases. There is, however, potential overlap between CQC's role and the powers of other bodies, such as the Health and Safety Executive, which also have a key role in prosecuting serious safety incidents. Accordingly, there are now memoranda of understanding setting out the arrangements for delineation of roles.[98]

97 See *Enforcement policy* p27.

98 See www.cqc.org.uk/about-us/our-partnerships/joint-working-agreements#hide1.

Part 3 The commissioning, provision and accessing of NHS services

CHAPTER 9

Commissioning NHS services

continued

Introduction

9.1 NHS organisations have been separated into commissioners, providers and regulators since 1993, although some organisations combine roles as commissioners and regulators or commissioners and providers. This chapter explores what is meant in law by 'NHS commissioning' and seeks to explain how commissioning decisions are taken.[1]

What is NHS commissioning?

9.2 There are many definitions of the word 'commissioning'. The NHS Improvement website previously described commissioning as the achievement of high-quality and value-for-money services for the NHS. It states:

> Commissioning is a cycle of activities that includes assessing the needs of a population; analysing 'gaps'; setting priorities and developing commissioning strategies; influencing the market to best secure services and monitoring and evaluating outcomes. In other words, it involves buying in services from a range of health service providers (including GPs, dentists, community pharmacists, NHS and private hospitals, and voluntary sector organisations) to meet the health needs of local people, and monitoring how well they are being delivered. Commissioning is an on-going process that applies to all services, whether they are provided by the local authority, NHS, other public agencies, or by the independent sector.

9.3 The main NHS commissioners are the National Health Service Commissioning Board (known as NHS England) and local clinical commissioning groups (CCGs). Please see chapter 13 on the responsible commissioner for an explanation as to which NHS services are commissioned by NHS England and CCGs for particular services.

9.4 The output of the commissioning process is usually a legal contract (or an NHS contract) under which the NHS commissioner enters into an enforceable arrangement with a provider of NHS services under which the provider agrees to provide defined categories of medical treatment to NHS patients as part of 'the health service'. The 'health service' is used as a term throughout the National Health Service Act 2006 (NHS Act 2006) to mean the collection of services which is known as the NHS. However, as the above definition makes clear, the placing of contracts with a provider is the final act of the commissioning process. The placing of the commissioning contract is just one step in a long sequence of events that ought to take place before the decision is made by a CCG or NHS England that the NHS ought to provide a specific service to NHS patients at a specific location. Placing the contract does not complete the commissioning process. Commissioning is a continuing process because, after the contract has been placed, the commissioner is responsible for monitoring the performance of the contract and considering whether the services

1 There is a good guide to the practical issues around commissioning and good practice at www.england.nhs.uk/wp-content/uploads/2014/03/serv-trans-guide.pdf.

should be renewed, extended, cut back or terminated in the next contracting year.

9.5 Hence, the commissioning process is complex. This chapter describes some of the legal challenges which arise in the commissioning process. It also contains an outline as to how NHS bodies are able to make lawful commissioning decisions. The model will not be followed by every NHS commissioner in every case, but the steps which are set out below are the essential building blocks of a lawful commissioning process. It does not explore the question as to whether the commissioning produces benefits to the NHS which exceed the costs of the commissioning process. There are deeply held views for and against, but an absence of clear evidence to prove the case either way. It also does not explore whether commissioning has any future if the NHS moves to an accountable care organisation (ACO) model, which effectively transfers commissioning from CCGs to provider organisations.

9.6 Commissioning presents particular challenges for all doctors and healthcare staff. The vast majority of medical training and professional medical practice is focused on the one-to-one relationship between a doctor and his or her patient. Commissioning is different because it is about population medicine, and is rarely about individual patients. Problems in commissioning regularly arise because the demand for clinically effective healthcare treatment for individual patients (suffering from both common and rare medical conditions) vastly exceeds the ability of the NHS to fund such treatment. NHS bodies have a finite budgets and this means that difficult choices have to be made about how services are organised and structured and, in the end, which drugs and other treatments can and cannot be provided to patients suffering from both common and rare conditions. Once it is recognised that choices have to be made as to which treatments the NHS can afford to provide to patients, it is a legal necessity that the process of making those policy choices should be transparent and rational. Hence, in practice the difficult commissioning decisions are where the NHS commissioner is saying 'No' to a treatment. Saying 'Yes the NHS will fund your treatment' is straightforward. Saying 'No' leaves a patient (and usually a proposed treating clinician) without the treatment that both clinician and the patient believe is necessary. Negative decisions lead to legal challenges, and often lead to an intense focus of the decision-making process which led up to the negative decision.

9.7 The proper approach to be taken by an NHS commissioner was set out in the evidence in *R (Condliff) v North Staffordshire Primary Care Trust*[2] and reproduced by Toulson LJ in his judgment as follows:

> 13. The PCT is under a legal duty to break even and our Chief Executive is the Accountable Officer responsible for ensuring that this requirement is met. This means that the PCT needs to consider carefully the costs of treatments and the benefits that a treatment delivers before we can agree to commission it. For the PCT, the decision to commission a particular type of treatment is not just a question of whether a medical treatment is clinically effective. If a treatment were not clinically effective, we would not commission it. However if a treatment is clinically effective, we would only

2 [2011] EWCA Civ 910, (2011) 14 CCLR 656.

commission the treatment if we could afford to do so. Our duty to break even means we need to judge whether clinically effective treatments are (a) a cost effective use of the limited resources available to the PCT and (b) affordable. As we have a fully committed and finite budget, the duty to break even means that if we commission additional services for any patient group where these are not funded at the moment, we need to pay for this by disinvestment in other services for other patient groups.

. . .

42. Each year the PCT undertakes a prioritisation process whereby the budget of the PCT for the present year is examined and plans are made for the treatments to be commissioned in the following financial year. As part of that process, the PCT considers the pressures that are likely to be placed on its services and budgets, the NICE (National Institute for Health and Clinical Excellence) Technology Appraisal Guidance that is likely to be published and thereby attract mandatory funding, and any other matters that are likely to affect the PCT budget. After ranking the competing demands on its financial resources in order of importance, the PCT reaches a conclusion about which treatments and interventions it will and will not fund in the coming financial year . . .

43. The PCT has adopted an Ethical Framework . . . These principles stand behind the PCT's decision making processes, especially those relating to our commissioning activities. The principles emphasise that decisions should be made on the evidence, should be non-discriminatory, should take into account that our budget can only be spent once and should result in the PCT maximising the welfare of our patient population within the resources available. Every decision we make to fund one treatment means that we are effectively taking a decision not to fund another treatment. As a result, the 3 components of the Ethical Framework – effectiveness, equity and patient choice – must be carefully balanced. Although patient choice is important, it may not outweigh the other relevant factors . . .

44. Our local prioritisation process involves evaluating healthcare interventions in order to decide what investments should be made with limited resources. It is a fundamental part of the commissioning business cycle.

9.8 Once a policy decision has been made as to which treatments will be funded by an NHS commissioner and which will not be funded, the court has no role to approve or disapprove of the choices made by the NHS commissioner. Lord Bingham said in *R v Cambridge Health Authority ex p B*:[3]

I have no doubt that in a perfect world any treatment which a patient, or a patient's family, sought would be provided if doctors were willing to give it, no matter how much it costs, particularly when a life was potentially at stake. It would however, in my view, be shutting one's eyes to the real world if the court were to proceed on the basis that we do live in such a world. It is common knowledge that health authorities of all kinds are constantly pressed to make ends meet . . . Difficult and agonising judgments have to be made as to how a limited budget is best allocated to the maximum advantage of the maximum number of patients. That is not a judgment which the court can make. In my judgment, it is not something that a health authority such as this authority can be fairly criticised for not advancing before the court.

3 [1995] 1 WLR 898.

9.9 It is not the role of the court to second-guess such decisions. Its role is generally limited to seeing that the decision-making is within the law. See *R (AC) v Berkshire West Primary Care Trust and another*[4] per Hooper LJ:[5]

> The court is not appropriately placed to make either clinical or budgetary judgments about publicly funded healthcare: its role is in general limited to keeping decision-making within the law. The claimant's point of view – that she is different from and more needy than a natal woman with a similar problem – matters; but it is a point of view which has to take its place within both legal and clinical criteria. The material legal criteria are that gender and clinical needs are both relevant characteristics. Their aetiology is relevant diagnostically, but what are more critically relevant are the ethical and clinical judgment of the PCT, provided these do not transgress the law.

9.10 Successful judicial challenges to commissioning decisions such as *R (S (a child)) v NHS England*[6] are almost always focused on the way in which decisions were made and involve a detailed analysis of the records made by the decision-maker. Hence the primary challenge for NHS commissioners is how to say 'No' in a legally defensible manner. It follows that following a proper process to reach commissioning decisions is an essential part of lawful commissioning. Following a proper process will not necessarily lead to NHS commissioners making the right decisions. However, failing to follow a proper process will leave any decisions open to legal challenge and thus, if they are challenged, will prevent the commissioners from giving effect to their decisions.

9.11 At the level of an individual patient, a positive outcome of commissioning process is that a decision to approve funding for a patient to be provided with NHS funded treatment. Patients are almost always unaware of the legal decision-making processes that exist behind decisions taken by doctors to provide them with treatment. Hence, for example, a patient attends the general practitioner (GP) to ask about pain in a hip. The GP considers that the patient may need a hip replacement operation and refers the patient to a consultant at the local hospital. The patient is seen by the consultant who then books the patient in for an operation and, hopefully within the 18-week target, the patient has a completed operation. However, unseen to the patient, each of these decisions is underpinned by a complex series of commissioning decisions and contracts, for example:

- The GP is entitled to make a referral to the hospital because a) the CCG (of which the GP's practice is a member) has an acute services contract with the hospital and b) the GP is a delegated decision-maker on behalf of the CCG under that contract.
- The consultant can see the patient as an out-patient and then perform the operation because a commissioning decision has been taken that hip replacement operations should be funded as part of NHS-funded care for patients referred by a GP under the contract.

4 [2011] EWCA Civ 247.
5 At para 56.
6 [2016] EWHC 1395 (Admin), (2016) 19 CCLR 336.

- Once the operation is completed, the episode of care will be coded and reported and, in due course, the hospital trust will be paid a national tariff fee for the activity.

9.12 Any decision to provide services to an NHS patient ought to be made by an NHS commissioner based on only one of three routes, namely:

1) by applying the terms of an approved CCG or NHS England commissioning policy (funding through a 'a commissioning policy decision');
2) by making a decision that a patient is within a recognised exception to a CCG or NHS England commissioning policy PCT (funding through an 'exception policy decision'); or
3) by making an individual funding decision outside of CCG or NHS England existing commissioning policies (an 'individual funding request (IFR) policy decision').

9.13 Detailed of each of these routes is set out below. However, in the above example, the patient was able to see the GP because NHS England placed a primary care commissioning contract with the GP practice. That funded the primary care service and hence the GP practice was able to run its business of providing NHS services to patients. The GP was able to refer the patient to the local hospital because the CCG had an acute services contract with the hospital trust, and that contract defined hip replacement operations as one of the services that the trust could provide to patients as part of NHS-funded services.

Commissioning and the duty to promote a comprehensive health service

9.14 Section 1 of the NHS Act 2006 imposes a duty on the Secretary of State for Health and Social Care to continue the promotion of 'a comprehensive health service'. Section 1H imposes this duty concurrently on NHS England. However, this does not impose any duty on the NHS to provide a comprehensive health service.[7] Section 1 of the NHS Act 2006 has comparatively little legal effect because it is difficult to imagine any set of circumstances in which a decision could be challenged on the grounds that the secretary of state had breached his or her section 1 duty. There has been no court case concerning reorganisation of NHS services or access to NHS-funded medical a treatment which (and there have been many), as far as the author is aware, has successfully criticised the secretary of state or any other NHS body for failing to discharge the section 1 duty. The Court of Appeal in *R (YA) v Secretary of State for Health*[8] noted that the secretary of state has a duty to continue the promotion in England of a comprehensive health service. The court then said:

> His duty under section 3 is subject to the qualification that his obligation is limited to providing the services identified to the extent that he considers that they are necessary to meet all reasonable requirements.

7 See chapter 1 for an explanation of this duty.
8 [2009] EWCA Civ 225, (2009) 12 CCLR 213.

> He does not automatically have to meet all the requirements and in certain circumstances he can exercise his judgment and legitimately decline to provide them. In exercising that judgment he is entitled to take into account the resources available to him and the demands on those resources.

9.15 It is therefore clear that the secretary of state has never had a statutory duty to deliver a comprehensive health service. NHS commissioners are required to remain focused on the fact that the secretary of state and NHS England have a duty to promote the delivering of a comprehensive health service. That target remains the ultimate aim of the NHS even if that is largely unachievable in practice.

Commissioning and the effect of the NHS Constitution

9.16 All NHS bodies, including CCGs, are required to 'have regard to the NHS Constitution': see section 2 of the Health Act (HA) 2009. The duty to 'have regard' to the NHS Constitution during a decision-making process means that the CCG is obliged to understand the terms of the NHS Constitution and act in accordance with the principles set out in that document unless it has a very good reason to depart from those principles.[9] The relevant part of the NHS Constitution on commissioning provides:

> The NHS commits to make decisions in a clear and transparent way, so that patients and the public can understand how services are planned and delivered.

9.17 Hence, throughout the commissioning process, there is a need for CCGs to act in a clear and transparent way, and to ensure that they can defend their reasoning at all times within the commissioning decision-making process. It also ties in to the central importance of public participation in the commissioning process which is considered at chapter 11 below.

The five-stage process to lawful commissioning decision-making by a CCG

9.18 While every stage of the commissioning process is not undertaken every year (because decisions referable to many treatment areas are rolled over from year to year), elements of the five-stage process should be present each year as part of any lawful commissioning process. The five main stages within the decision-making process for those commissioning NHS care, and thus carrying the responsibility for managing NHS budgets, are as follows:

1) a Joint Strategic Needs Assessment (JSNA);
2) a Joint Health and Wellbeing Strategy (JHWS);
3) an annual CCG commissioning plan;

9 For more details on the nature of the 'have regard' duty, please see paras 9.40–9.41.

4) commissioning policies for individual medical conditions which flow from the annual commissioning plan; and
5) agreeing policies concerning where exceptions will be made to policies; how 'in-year service developments' will be managed; and adopting a policy for IFRs.

9.19 Thus the 'arrangements' that the CCG is obliged to have in place in order to discharge its legal duties[10] ought to describe the processes that the CCG will follow to go through each of the above processes, and thus allow patients to understand the decision-making process which leads up to a final decision on whether the treatment they are requesting will or will not be routinely funded under a commissioning policy. It should also describe whether funding could be secured through exception policies, and how the CCG IFR process will operate.

9.20 Getting through the above procedures requires those involved in the difficult business of priority setting. In conducting this exercise, it is important for commissioners to bear in mind that it is potentially lawful for a CCG or NHS England to adopt a policy which provides that provides the NHS will *not* fund medically appropriate treatment even if this has the capacity to benefit a group of patients. Commissioning involves making tough (and sometimes near impossible) choices. NHS commissioners are entitled to decide that their substantial but nonetheless limited financial resources should be used to fund treatments for one group of patients in preference to another group. That will inevitably leave disappointed patients and clinicians where clinically effective medical interventions are decided not to have a sufficient priority to justify funding. These decisions will, almost inevitably, come under intense public scrutiny. It is thus essential that they are taken in a transparent and lawful manner. The primary duty on NHS commissioners is therefore for take these decisions in a rational way by following a lawful procedure. That procedure needs to ensure that the CCG or NHS England complies with all of its legal duties.

9.21 There are a large number of people who have either a legitimate or a commercial interest (and sometimes both) of having a say within the commissioning process. These include:

- patients (whose rights to be involved in decision-making are discussed elsewhere);
- the board members of a CCG;
- GPs who are not members of a CCG board;
- provider NHS trusts;
- other providers of healthcare services to the NHS;
- universities and other providers of training for clinical staff;
- persons who are engaged in clinical research which may be affected by CCG decisions;
- clinicians;
- locally elected politicians (both members of parliament (MPs) and local councillors); and

10 Under NHS Act 2006 s1(3).

- drug companies and other organisations that supply goods and services to the NHS.

9.22 A key part of a lawful decision-making process is recognising the right of everyone who has a proper interest in the outcome of the commissioning process to have their say during the process. The CCG will remain the final decision-maker but many of the above have the right to have an input into the process and to have their views properly considered by the CCG before final decisions are made. The commissioning process thus involves a series of complex challenges which CCGs need to surmount in order to be confident that CCG decisions are legally robust.

The legal duties on CCGs and NHS England in the commissioning process

9.23 Before considering the details of each of the steps that a CCG (and to a lesser extent NHS England) is required to follow in a lawful commissioning process, it is necessary to examine some of the overarching legal duties imposed on CCGs and NHS England throughout the commissioning process.

Overview

9.24 Regulations 34–36 of the National Health Service Commissioning Board and Clinical Commissioning Groups (Responsibilities and Standing Rules) Regulations (RSR Regs) 2012[11] impose a series of duties on NHS commissioning bodies governing the way in which commissioning decisions are required to be taken. The effects of these regulations was partially summarised by Mr Justice Jay in *R (Rose) v Thanet Clinical Commissioning Group*[12] as follows:

> 26. In my judgment, and insofar as is relevant to this case, there are three express regulatory obligations on the CCG and two implied ones. The express obligations are (i) to have in place arrangements and general policies for deciding whether to make available for persons particular health care interventions, (ii) to provide or make available its reasons for any general policy not to fund a particular intervention, and (iii) to include within its decision-making framework arrangements for dealing with specific requests by a person for funding in circumstances where there is no NICE-driven duty to make available the intervention at issue and the CCG's general policy is not to fund. Put in these terms it may be seen that express obligation (iii) is addressed to the determination of exceptional cases. It is to be noted that Regulation 34(1) refers to 'persons' and Regulation 34(2) to 'a person', underlining the distinction between general policies and special cases.
>
> 27. As for the CCG's implied obligations imposed by force of public law and/or the true construction of the regulatory scheme, the first is that the duty to have regard to NICE recommendations made under Regulation 5

11 SI No 2996.

12 [2014] EWHC 1182 (Admin) at paras 26–27.

must bear on the formulation of its general policies (see (i) above) rather than its exceptional policies (see (ii)). This flows from the structure of the regulatory scheme but I will be amplifying this point subsequently. The second implied obligation, and it flows from the first, is that the duty to give reasons for any general policy not to fund a particular intervention must encompass the giving of a reasoned explanation of why a NICE recommendation made under Regulation 5 is not being followed.

Arrangements

9.25 Regulation 34(1) of the RSR Regs 2012 imposes a legal obligation on every CCG and NHS England to have:

> . . . arrangements for making decisions and adopting policies on whether a particular health care intervention is to be made available for persons for whom the relevant body has responsibility.

This legal duty means that each CCG and NHS England have a legal duty to set up transparent processes which explain how that body will go about making decisions in its annual commissioning round, who will be consulted, who will take the decisions and how these will be translated into contracts with its providers.

9.26 The wording of the legal duty is to 'make arrangements'. This form of words is used in many other places in the NHS Act 2006 and in other legislation which imposes statutory duties on public bodies. The nature of the duty to make arrangements gives a considerable amount of discretion to CCGs and NHS England. Subject to other legal constraints (some of which are described below), CCGs and NHS England are able to decide for themselves what decision-making processes they should adopt. However, once the CCG or NHS England has put its 'arrangements' in place, the public body comes under a public law legal duty to follow its own procedures when making commissioning decisions.

9.27 Some guidance about the meaning of a duty to make 'arrangements' was given by Underhill J in the first instance decision of *R (Nash) v Barnet LBC (Capita plc and others, interested parties)*.[13] The case was only a permission decision and so is of limited weight, but it is a full judgment by a distinguished judge (now in the Court of Appeal) and was subsequently upheld by the Court of Appeal. The judge was concerned with a duty to make arrangements to secure best value under local government legislation. The judge said:[14]

> . . . the reference to 'making arrangements' would make it clear that the duty was concerned with intentions rather than outcome. It may also be that the draftsman wanted to emphasise the need to build the fulfilment of the best value duty into authorities' plans and procedures. Or perhaps it is just circumlocution. But, whatever the explanation, the important point for present purposes is what the arrangements are aimed at, namely securing improvements in the *way* in which authorities perform their functions.

9.28 Thus the legal duty is to ensure that the *way* in which a CCG of NHS England makes commissioning decisions and/or adopts commissioning

13 [2013] EWHC 1067 (Admin).

14 At para 70.

policies is clearly described. The published 'arrangements' need to describe the commissioning processes that the NHS commissioner will follow from its initial assessment of needs through to final contracting decisions. In *R v East Sussex CC ex p Tandy*,[15] Mummery LJ emphasised the width of the discretion on a public body which had a duty to make arrangements (in that case about the education of children with special educational needs). He said:

> In the interests of fairness, consistency and administrative efficiency a local education authority is entitled to formulate a policy setting norms, standards and criteria to be applied in the consideration of the circumstances of individual children. Such a policy is lawful if it promotes the specified statutory purpose and is sufficiently flexible not to fetter the decision-making process in individual cases. Further, once a policy has been formulated, it is permissible (and advisable) to review it from time to time in the light of experience and of changing circumstances.

9.29 The importance of NHS commissioners having clear policies which guide decision-making where decisions are made to fund some areas of treatment and not to fund others has been recognised by the courts long before the RSR Regs 2012 came into effect. In *R v North West Lancashire Health Authority ex p A and others*[16] where Auld LJ said:

> . . . it is an unhappy but unavoidable feature of state funded health care that Regional Health Authorities have to establish certain priorities in funding different treatments from their finite resources. It is natural that each Authority, in establishing its own priorities, will give greater priority to life-threatening and other grave illnesses than to others obviously less demanding of medical intervention. The precise allocation and weighting of priorities is clearly a matter of judgment for each Authority, keeping well in mind its statutory obligations to meet the reasonable requirements of all those within its area for which it is responsible. *It makes sense to have a policy for the purpose – indeed, it might well be irrational not to have one . . .* (emphasis added).

9.30 The overall purpose of the arrangements required by regulation 34 of the RSR Regs 2012 must be to describe the processes that the CCG will follow to make commissioning decisions so that those affected by those decisions[17] know what processes the NHS commissioner will take and when decisions will be made. Speaking in the House of Lords in the *Tandy* case Lord Browne-Wilkinson said:[18]

> The duty is to make arrangements for what constitutes suitable education for each child. That duty will not be fulfilled unless the arrangements do in fact provide suitable education for each child.

9.31 Thus the arrangements made by each CCG and NHS England will only comply with the terms of the statutory duty if they describe a proper system for decision-making and explain how policies will be adopted.

15 [1998] AC 714.

16 [1999] EWCA Civ 2022, (1999) 2 CCLR 419.

17 Ie those interested include patients, medical lobby groups, pharmaceutical companies and clinicians who wish to provide the treatment as part of NHS funded care.

18 At p747.

Reasons

9.32 Regulation 35(1) of the RSR Regs 2012 imposes a duty on each CCG and NHS England to give reasons for its decisions in favour or against funding any particular healthcare intervention. It provides:

> (1) A relevant body must–
>
> (a) publish on its website a written statement of its reasons for any general policy it has on whether a particular healthcare intervention is to be made available for persons for whom it has responsibility; or
>
> (b) where it has not published such a statement, provide a written statement of the reasons for any such policy when any person makes a written request for such a statement.
>
> (2) Where a relevant body–
>
> (a) makes a decision to refuse a request for the funding of a health care intervention for a person; and
>
> (b) its general policy is not to fund that intervention,
>
> the relevant body must provide that person with the reasons for that decision in writing.

9.33 These are potentially onerous responsibilities because they require the NHS commissioners to formulate *reasons* as to why they fund or decline to fund a particular healthcare intervention. There is a considerable amount of case-law on the duty to give reasons, which is beyond the scope of this guide. However, the general principle on reasons was explained by Lord Brown in *South Buckinghamshire DC v Porter (No 2)*[19] as follows:

> The reasons for a decision must be intelligible and they must be adequate. They must enable the reader to understand why the matter was decided as it was and what conclusions were reached on the 'principal important controversial issues', disclosing how any issue of law or fact was resolved. Reasons can be briefly stated, the degree of particularity required depending entirely on the nature of the issues falling for decision. The reasoning must not give rise to a substantial doubt as to whether the decision-maker erred in law, for example by misunderstanding some relevant policy or some other important matter or by failing to reach a rational decision on relevant grounds. But such adverse inference will not readily be drawn. The reasons need refer only to the main issues in the dispute, not to every material consideration.

9.34 If the CCG or NHS England fails to give proper reasons for a decision, then the decision itself may be unlawful because it will not be clear whether the CCG has properly understood the statutory function that it was undertaking: see *R v Westminster CC ex p Ermakov)*.[20] There are, however, occasions on which a public body is entitled to give supplementary detail to support initially inadequate reasons and may then, as a whole, be held to have acted lawfully.

Publication

9.35 Once a CCG or NHS England has resolved how it is going to make commissioning decisions and adopt commissioning policies, regulation 36

19 [2004] 1 WLR 1953.

20 [1995] EWCA Civ 42.

of the RSR Regs 2012 provides that the NHS body must publicise those arrangements. It provides:

> Each relevant body[21] must compile information in writing describing the arrangements it has made pursuant to the requirements in regulation 34 and must ensure that that information is–
> (a) published on the website of the relevant body; and
> (b) available to inspect at the head or main office of the relevant body.

9.36 Thus the 'arrangements' that each CCG and NHS England are required to have in place must be set out on its website. It is thus probably unlawful for a CCG or NHS England to make commissioning decisions in accordance with procedures which are not publicised.

9.37 There are vast differences between the extent to which both CCGs and NHS England comply or fail to comply with these statutory obligations. Some CCGs are excellent and provide a clear guide to members of the public about how decisions affecting them will be taken. Others fail to provide any proper guidance to show how they make decisions and fail to publicise policies. Those CCGs who fail to publish details of their decision-making processes are leaving themselves open to legal challenges.

The additional legal duties imposed on CCGs relevant to the commissioning process

9.38 The Health and Social Care Act (HSCA) 2012, which created CCGs, imposed a series of legal duties on the new NHS commissioning bodies. These are in general, target duties which are required to guide and focus the CCG's decision-making processes. The general legal duties imposed on CCGs are:[22]

a) a duty to act with a view to securing that health services are provided in a way which promotes the NHS Constitution: see section 14P of the NHS Act 2006;
b) a duty to exercise the CCG functions effectively, efficiently and economically: see section 14Q of the NHS Act 2006;
c) a duty to exercise CCG functions with a view to securing continuous improvement in the quality of services provided to individuals for or in connection with the prevention, diagnosis or treatment of illness: see section 14R(1) of the NHS Act 2006;
d) a duty to act with a view to securing continuous improvement in the outcomes that are achieved from the provision of the services: see section 14R(2) of the NHS Act 2006. 'Relevant outcomes' for these purposes means outcomes which show–
   i) the effectiveness of the services;
   ii) the safety of the services; and
   iii) the quality of the experience undergone by patients;

21 Relevant bodies under the RSR Regs 2012 are CCGs and NHS England: see reg 2.
22 See chapter 5 for more details of the legal duties on CCGs and chapter 6 for the duties on NHS England.

e) a duty to regard to any guidance published by NHS England on the discharge of their commissioning functions (see section 14Z8 of the NHS Act 2006);
f) a duty to assist NHS England in NHS England's duty to secure that there is continuous improvement in the quality of services provided to individuals for or in connection with the prevention, diagnosis or treatment of illness and continuous improvement in the outcomes that are achieved from the provision of the services: see section 14S of the NHS Act 2006;
g) a duty to have regard to the need to–
   i) reduce inequalities between patients with respect to their ability to access health services; and
   ii) reduce inequalities between patients with respect to the outcomes achieved for them by the provision of health services (see section 14T of the NHS Act 2006);
h) a duty to promote the involvement of patients, and their carers and representatives (if any), in decisions which relate to–
   i) the prevention or diagnosis of illness in the patients; or
   their care or treatment (see section 14U(1) of the NHS Act 2006);
i) a duty to have regard to guidance published by NHS England concerning the duty to involve patients in decision-making under section 14U(1) of the NHS Act (see section 14U(3) of the NHS Act 2006);
j) a duty to act with a view to enabling patients to make choices with respect to aspects of health services provided to them (see section 14V of the NHS Act 2006);[23]
k) a duty to promote innovation in the provision of health services (including innovation in the arrangements made for their provision) (see section 14X of the NHS Act 2006);
l) a duty to promote research on matters relevant to the health service and the use in the health service of evidence obtained from research (see section 14Y of the NHS Act 2006);
m) a duty to promote education and training for persons who are employed, or who are considering becoming employed, in an activity which involves or is connected with the provision of services as part of the health service in England (see a combination of section 1F(1) and section 14Y of the NHS Act 2006); and
n) a duty to promote integration between the services that the CCG commissions and other health and social care services (see section 14Z1 of the NHS Act 2006).

9.39 Each of these duties are legal obligations which are concerned with the way in which commissioning functions are undertaken and which impose duties on the CCG to have regard to particular factors when commissioning decisions are taken. They do not impose any requirement on CCG to make specific commissioning decisions (such as commissioning a specific service or keeping a specific hospital open). They are concerned with ensuring that CCG take into account defined factors when making these decisions. It is difficult to describe precisely what each of these duties mean in practice in any particular circumstances because the relevance of

23 For more details on patient choice rights, see chapter 12 on patient choice issues.

each factor will depend on the circumstances of each commissioning decision.

9.40 However, they are largely described as being duties to 'have regard' to specified factors. In *R (The Pharmaceutical Services Negotiating Committee and another) v Secretary of State for Health*[24] Collins J emphasised the scope and importance of a public body which was under a 'have regard' duty. He said:[25]

> I am equally wholly unpersuaded that there is in reality any material difference between the obligations to have regard and to have due regard. Merely to have regard in the sense that the existence of the statutory requirements is recognised is never likely to suffice, albeit much will turn on the nature of the matters to which regard must be had. In s1C it is a specific need to reduce inequalities so that the defendant is obliged to show that that need is recognised and that what is proposed does not in his view at the very least cause an increase in such inequalities. All that 'due' adds in my view is a specific recognition that the effect of the decision on the specified matters must be properly taken into account. It could indeed be argued that 'due' does not strengthen but rather weakens in that it recognises that there may be circumstances in which regard is not needed. But it seems to me in any event that the argument was a barren one having regard to the nature of the obligation in section 1C.

9.41 If there is no substantial difference between the duty to 'have regard' and the duty to 'have due regard', the following general guidance about the duty to have due regard is relevant to NHS decision-makers. The meaning of the 'due regard duty under the Equality Act 2010 was expressed as follows by Aitkens LJ in *R (Brown) v Secretary of State for Work and Pensions*[26] and, translated into the wording of the duties on a CCG, means that CCG decision-makers must take the following steps:

a) Decision-makers in a CCG must be made aware of each of the legal duties which are relevant when they are taking decisions. A CCG is likely to be in difficulties in asserting that it has followed its legal obligations in making commissioning decisions if those who have made the decisions were not aware of each one of the legal duties set out above.
b) The mind of the decision-maker must be focused on each of the above duties at some relevant point during the commissioning decision-making processes. Decision-makers must have a 'conscious approach and state of mind' which is focused upon the legal obligation when they are taking commissioning decisions.
c) Each legal duty must be exercised in substance, with rigour and with an open mind.
d) The duties are non-delegable duties. They bind whichever individual is delegated to take decisions on behalf of a CCG.
e) The duties are continuing duties throughout the commissioning process.
f) It is good practice for those exercising public functions in public authorities to keep an adequate record showing that they had actually considered their duties and pondered relevant questions. Proper

24 [2017] EWHC 1147 (Admin). Permission has been given for this case to go to the Court of Appeal.

25 At para 48.

26 [2008] EWHC 3158 (Admin).

record-keeping encourages transparency and will discipline those carrying out the relevant function. Further it will, in practice, be difficult if not impossible to show that the CCG has had regard to statutory factors if the records of the decision-making process make no reference to those factors.

9.42 There is a specific legal duty to seek public health advice. Interestingly, despite the myriad legal duties on a CCG, there is no duty to seek legal advice. The wording of the duty in section 14W of the NHS Act 2006 to seek public health advice is as follows:

> Each clinical commissioning group must obtain advice appropriate for enabling it effectively to discharge its functions from persons who (taken together) have a broad range of professional expertise in–
> (a) the prevention, diagnosis or treatment of illness, and
> (b) the protection or improvement of public health.

9.43 The reference to the requirement to seek advice from a 'broad range of professional expertise' inevitably means that the CCG is required to seek advice from more than one person before taking any key decision. The CCG almost certainly will not discharge this duty of it only relies on the expertise of its own GP professionals, because these individuals are potential decision-makers. NHS England has a power (but not a duty) to publish advice on how the CCG should seek advice in order to discharge this duty. No guidance has yet been published by NHS England about how they recommend CCGs exercise this statutory duty.

9.44 Unlike some of the target duties set out above, the duty to seek advice is clear. A CCG will act unlawfully if it fails to seek appropriate advice within the commissioning processes. There is no specific obligation in the NHS Act 2006 to require the CCG to publish the advice that it receives. However, the advice would not be covered by legal professional privilege because it is not legal advice. It is therefore difficult to see any exemption under the Freedom of Information Act 2000 which the CCG could rely on refuse to publish any advice that it has received.

The role of Health and Wellbeing Boards in NHS commissioning decisions

9.45 The first stage to any commissioning process is for a statutory provider of NHS or community care services to gain an understanding the needs of the population which the public body serves. These functions are required to be carried out by the Health and Wellbeing Board (HWB), acting on behalf of both the CCGs operating within a local authority area and the local social services authority. HWBs, as joint NHS and local authority committees, were created by section 194 of the HSCA 2012. Section 194(2) of the HSCA 2012 provides that the HWB must include the following persons:

> The Health and Wellbeing Board is to consist of–
> (a) subject to subsection (4), at least one councillor of the local authority, nominated in accordance with subsection (3),

(b) the director of adult social services for the local authority,
(c) the director of children's services for the local authority,
(d) the director of public health for the local authority,
(e) a representative of the Local Healthwatch organisation for the area of the local authority,
(f) a representative of each relevant clinical commissioning group, and
(g) such other persons, or representatives of such other persons, as the local authority thinks appropriate'

9.46 The primary functions of the HWBs are set out in section 195 of the HSCA 2012, which provides:

(1) A Health and Wellbeing Board must, for the purpose of advancing the health and wellbeing of the people in its area, encourage persons who arrange for the provision of any health or social care services in that area to work in an integrated manner.
(2) A Health and Wellbeing Board must, in particular, provide such advice, assistance or other support as it thinks appropriate for the purpose of encouraging the making of arrangements under section 75 of the National Health Service Act 2006 in connection with the provision of such services.
(3) A Health and Wellbeing Board may encourage persons who arrange for the provision of any health-related services in its area to work closely with the Health and Wellbeing Board.
(4) A Health and Wellbeing Board may encourage persons who arrange for the provision of any health or social care services in its area and persons who arrange for the provision of any health-related services in its area to work closely together.
(5) Any reference in this section to the area of a Health and Wellbeing Board is a reference to the area of the local authority that established it.
(6) In this section–
'the health service' has the same meaning as in the National Health Service Act 2006;
'health services' means services that are provided as part of the health service in England;
'health-related services' means services that may have an effect on the health of individuals but are not health services or social care services;
'social care services' means services that are provided in pursuance of the social services functions of local authorities (within the meaning of the Local Authority Social Services Act 1970).

9.47 Section 196(1) of the HSCA 2012 provides that the functions of preparing the JSNA and the JHWS under the Local Government and Public Involvement in Health Act (LGPIHA) 2007 are to be discharged by the HWB as follows:

The functions of a local authority and its partner clinical commissioning groups under sections 116 and 116A of the Local Government and Public Involvement in Health Act 2007 ('the 2007 Act') are to be exercised by the Health and Wellbeing Board established by the local authority.

9.48 HWBs have considerable powers to require CCGs and NHS England to provide them with information. Their powers to require the provision of information are set out in section 199 of the HSCA 2012, which provides:

(1) A Health and Wellbeing Board may, for the purpose of enabling or assisting it to perform its functions, request any of the following persons to supply it with such information as may be specified in the request—
(a) the local authority that established the Health and Wellbeing Board;
(b) any person who is represented on the Health and Wellbeing Board by virtue of section 194(2)(e) to (g) or (8);
(c) any person who is a member of a Health and Wellbeing Board by virtue of section 194(2)(g) or (8) but is not acting as a representative.
(2) A person who is requested to supply information under subsection (1) must comply with the request.
(3) Information supplied to a Health and Wellbeing Board under this section may be used by the Board only for the purpose of enabling or assisting it to perform its functions.
(4) Information requested under subsection (1) must be information that relates to—
(a) a function of the person to whom the request is made, or
(b) a person in respect of whom a function is exercisable by that person'

9.49 Further details of the functioning of HWBs are set out in the Local Authority (Public Health, Health and Wellbeing Boards and Health Scrutiny) Regulations 2013.[27]

Joint Strategic Needs Assessments

9.50 Each year the NHS has an established pattern of services but, with a changing society – and, in particular, with substantial immigration and with an ageing population – the footprint of existing services may not properly match the needs of the local population. There is a tendency in the NHS (as in all public services) to continue to fund any existing services that are serving a need for those services rather than examining whether the existing services are the best use of limited resources to meet population needs. However, continuing to fund existing services inevitably consumes resources and leaves little if any money for the expansion of other services that have seen increased demand, or the development of new services to meet gaps in provision.

9.51 The purposes of the JSNA is to create an objective assessment for the overall need for statutory health and social care services of the local population and thus ensure that planning is informed by a proper evidence base. This process should, to some extent, combat the inevitable tendency to continue to fund services as 'business as usual'. The statutory scheme imposes a series of steps that CCGs, working through the HWB, are required to take each year, in co-operation with their local authority colleagues, to assess needs and thus inform decisions whether the pattern of existing statutory services best meets the local needs and, if not, to make appropriate changes.

9.52 The commissioning process should start with the development of a JSNA which is carried out by the HWB on behalf of both the CCGs operating in a local authority area and the local authority. The duty to carry out a JSNA is set out in section 116(1) of the LGPIHA 2007 which provides:

27 SI No 218.

(1) An assessment of relevant needs must be prepared in relation to the area of each responsible local authority.

9.53 Section 116(4) then provides:

It is for–

(a) the responsible local authority, and
(b) each of its partner clinical commissioning groups,

to prepare any assessment of relevant needs under this section in relation to the area of the responsible local authority.

9.54 The term 'relevant needs' within the JSNA is widely defined by section 116(6) and (7) of the LGPIHA 2007 which provide:

(6) For the purposes of this section, there is a relevant need in relation to so much of the area of a responsible local authority as falls within the area of a partner clinical commissioning group if there appears to the responsible local authority and the partner clinical commissioning group to be a need or to be likely to be a need to which subsection (7) applies.

(7) This subsection applies to a need–

(a) which–
    (i) is capable of being met to a significant extent by the exercise by the responsible local authority of any of its functions; and
    (ii) could also be met, or could otherwise be affected, to a significant extent by the exercise by the partner clinical commissioning group or the National Health Service Commissioning Board of any of its functions; or

(b) which–
    (i) is capable of being met to a significant extent by the exercise by the partner clinical commissioning group or the National Health Service Commissioning Board of any of its functions; and
    (ii) could also be met, or could otherwise be affected, to a significant extent by the exercise by the responsible local authority of any of its functions.

9.55 Hence, each CCG is required, working through the HWB, on an annual basis to work with the local authority to carry out an assessment of all of the actual and potential needs in the local authority area for NHS or social care services. The identification of a 'need' as part of an assessment does not impose any direct legal obligation on either the NHS body or the local authority to provide a service to meet that need. The primary purpose of the assessment is to inform the priority setting decision-making process which is undertaken by both the NHS and by local authorities so as to ensure that the NHS and social services authorities are fully aware of the range of needs in their area and can thus make the best use of the resources available to them to fulfil as many of those needs as possible.

9.56 The local authority is under a specific duty to publish the joint strategic health needs assessment: see section 116(5) of the LGPIHA 2007.

9.57 The Department of Health and Social Care has published non-statutory 'best practice' guidance concerning these functions in March 2013.[28] This explains the purpose of these documents as follows:

28 See www.gov.uk/government/uploads/system/uploads/attachment_data/file/277012/Statutory-Guidance-on-Joint-Strategic-Needs-Assessments-and-Joint-Health-and-Wellbeing-Strategies-March–20131.pdf.

The purpose of JSNAs and JHWSs is to improve the health and wellbeing of the local community and reduce inequalities for all ages. They are not an end in themselves, but a continuous process of strategic assessment and planning – the core aim is to develop local evidence-based priorities for commissioning which will improve the public's health and reduce inequalities. Their outputs, in the form of evidence and the analysis of needs, and agreed priorities, will be used to help to determine what actions local authorities, the local NHS and other partners need to take to meet health and social care needs, and to address the wider determinants that impact on health and wellbeing.

9.58 The guidance explains the purpose of the JSNA as follows:

JSNAs are assessments of the current and future health and social care needs of the local community. – these are needs that could be met by the local authority, CCGs, or the NHS CB. JSNAs are produced by health and wellbeing boards, and are unique to each local area. The policy intention is for health and wellbeing boards to also consider wider factors that impact on their communities' health and wellbeing, and local assets that can help to improve outcomes and reduce inequalities. Local areas are free to undertake JSNAs in a way best suited to their local circumstances – there is no template or format that must be used and no mandatory data set to be included.

A range of quantitative and qualitative evidence should be used in JSNAs. There are a number of data sources and tools that health and wellbeing boards may find useful for obtaining quantitative data. Qualitative information can be gained via a number of avenues, including but not limited to views collected by the local Healthwatch organisation or by local voluntary sector organisations, feedback given to local providers by service users; and views fed in as part of community participation within the JSNA and JHWS process.

JSNAs can also be informed by more detailed local needs assessments such as at a district or ward level; looking at specific groups (such as those likely to have poor health outcomes); or on wider issues that affect health such as employment, crime, community safety, transport, planning or housing. Evidence of service outcomes collected where possible from local commissioners, providers or service users could also inform JSNAs. Boards will need to ensure that staff supporting JSNAs have easy access to the evidence they need to undertake any analysis they needed to support the board's decisions.

9.59 The JSNA thus ought to be a key document for the local all NHS and social services bodies.

Joint Health and Wellbeing Strategies

9.60 Once the joint strategic health needs assessment has been undertaken, the next step is for the local authority and the CCGs to work together through the HWB to produce a JHWS. The legal duty on the HWB to produce a JHWS is in section 116A of the LGPIHA 2007, which provides:

(1) This section applies where an assessment of relevant needs is prepared under section 116 by a responsible local authority and each of its partner clinical commissioning groups.

(2) The responsible local authority and each of its partner clinical commissioning groups must prepare a strategy for meeting the needs included in the assessment by the exercise of functions of the authority, the National Health Service Commissioning Board or the clinical commissioning groups ('a joint health and wellbeing strategy').

(3) In preparing a strategy under this section, the responsible local authority and each of its partner clinical commissioning groups must, in particular, consider the extent to which the needs could be met more effectively by the making of arrangements under section 75 of the National Health Service Act 2006 (rather than in any other way).

(4) In preparing a strategy under this section, the responsible local authority and each of its partner clinical commissioning groups must have regard to–

(a) the mandate published by the Secretary of State under section 13A of the National Health Service Act 2006, and

(b) any guidance issued by the Secretary of State.

(5) In preparing a strategy under this section, the responsible local authority and each of its partner clinical commissioning groups must–

(a) involve the Local Healthwatch organisation for the area of the responsible local authority, and

(b) involve the people who live or work in that area.

(6) The responsible local authority must publish each strategy prepared by it under this section.

(7) The responsible local authority and each of its partner clinical commissioning groups may include in the strategy a statement of their views on how arrangements for the provision of health-related services in the area of the local authority could be more closely integrated with arrangements for the provision of health services and social care services in that area.

(8) In this section and section 116B–

'partner clinical commissioning group', in relation to a responsible local authority, has the same meaning as in section 116, and

'health services', 'health-related services' and 'social care services' have the same meaning as in section 195 of the Health and Social Care Act 2012.

9.61 These provisions provide that CCGs are required to work with the relevant local authority (which in a two-tier local authority areas is the county council) to prepare a 'joint strategic health and wellbeing strategy', which describes how the NHS and local authority are planning to meet the needs of the local population for NHS and community care services. Each CCG is required to have regard to the mandate published by the Secretary of State for Health and Social Care under section 13A of the NHS Act 2006 and to any guidance published by the secretary of state.

9.62 The HWB has a duty under section 116A(5) of the LGPIHA 2007 to involve the Local Healthwatch organisation and to involve the 'the people who live or work in the area' in the preparation of that strategy. That is not a consultation duty but a duty to 'involve' local people in planning for NHS and community care services.

9.63 The guidance explains what the JHWS should contain as follows:

JHWSs are strategies for meeting the needs identified in JSNAs. As with JSNAs, they are produced by health and wellbeing boards, are unique to

> each local area, and there is no Statutory Guidance on Joint Strategic Needs Assessments and Joint Health and Wellbeing Strategies mandated standard format. In preparing JHWSs, health and wellbeing boards must have regard to the Secretary of State's mandate to the NHS CB which sets out the Government's priorities for the NHS.
>
> They should explain what priorities the health and wellbeing board has set in order to tackle the needs identified in their JSNAs. Again, it would not be appropriate to specify or dictate issues which should be prioritised. This is not about taking action on everything at once, but about setting a small number of key strategic priorities for action, that will make a real impact on people's lives. JHWSs should translate JSNA findings into clear outcomes the board wants to achieve, which will inform local commissioning – leading to locally led initiatives that meet those outcomes and address the needs.

9.64 The guidance explains that there is no requirement on NHS bodies and local authorities to rewrite these documents from scratch every year. It provides:

> JSNAs and JHWSs are continuous processes, and are an integral part of CCG and local authority commissioning cycles. Health and wellbeing boards will need to decide for themselves when to update or refresh JSNAs and JHWSs or undertake a fresh process to ensure that they are able to inform local commissioning plans over time. They do not need to be undertaken from scratch every year; however boards will need to assure themselves that their evidence-based priorities are up to date to inform the relevant local commissioning plans. To be transparent and enable wide participation, boards should be clear with their partners and the community what their timing cycles are and when outputs will be published.

9.65 There would be no benefit in undertaking the considerable amount of work needed to produce a proper JSNA and then a JHWS if the output of this work did not influence commissioning decisions by local authorities, CCGs and NHS England. Section 116B of the LGPIHA 2007 (as amended by the HSCA 2012) provides that, in exercising any functions, both a CCG and NHS England are required to 'have regard' to the JSNA and the JHWS. The section provides:

> (1) A responsible local authority and each of its partner clinical commissioning groups must, in exercising any functions, have regard to–
> (a) any assessment of relevant needs prepared by the responsible local authority and each of its partner clinical commissioning groups under section 116 which is relevant to the exercise of the functions, and
> (b) any joint health and wellbeing strategy prepared by them under section 116A which is so relevant.
>
> (2) The National Health Service Commissioning Board must, in exercising any functions in arranging for the provision of health services in relation to the area of a responsible local authority, have regard to–
> (a) any assessment of relevant needs prepared by the responsible local authority and each of its partner clinical commissioning groups under section 116 which is relevant to the exercise of the functions, and
> (b) any joint health and wellbeing strategy prepared by them under section 116A which is so relevant.

9.66 The duty to 'have regard' to a plan or set or assessment is a term of art in public law statutes.[29] In this context, it probably has the following general consequences:

a) Decision-makers in a CCG and in NHS England must be made aware of any relevant JSNA and JHWS when making commissioning decisions. A CCG cannot assert that it has followed its legal obligation to have regard to the joint strategic health needs assessment in making commissioning decisions if those who made the decisions were not aware of the relevant recommendations in the assessment document. In practice this means that relevant decision-makers must be focused on the recommendations of the joint strategic health needs assessment during the commissioning processes. Decision-makers must have a 'conscious approach and state of mind' which is focused upon this particular legal obligation when they are taking commissioning decisions.
b) The duty to have regard to the JSNA and JHWS means that the audit trail must show that the conclusions of these documents have been considered in substance, with rigour and with an open mind when the CCG are taking commissioning decisions.
c) The duty is non-delegable. It rests on the key decision-makers within the CCG or NHS England and cannot be discharged if the relevant 'regard' is given lower down in the organisations but not reported up to the key decision-makers.
d) The duty to have regard to the JSNA and the JHWS is a continuing duty which is engaged throughout the commissioning process.
e) It is good practice for both a CCG and NHS England to keep an adequate record showing that they had actually considered these documents and pondered the relevant questions raised by them as part of any decision-making process. Proper record-keeping encourages transparency and will discipline those carrying out the relevant function.

9.67 Whilst, the 'have regard' duty imposes a procedural obligation on NHS bodies, it does not mandate a particular outcome. Neither the CCG nor NHS England is bound to adopt each and every one of the priorities identified in either the JSNA or the JHWS. If either NHS body has good reasons to do so, it can depart from the collective views about the priorities for services set out in the JSNA and the JHWS. However, in order to ensure that it is acting lawfully, a CCG or NHS England would be required to demonstrate that it had carefully considered the recommendations of the JSNA and the JHWS and had identified precise reasons why it was taking a different course.

The CCG annual commissioning plan

9.68 The provisions of the HCSA 2012 imposed a statutory obligation on CCGs are required to consult key stakeholders about their annual commissioning plans and then publish a plan saying how they propose to exercise

29 See para 9.40 for details of the case-law on 'have regard' duties.

their functions in the coming financial year. This is an area of considerable legal risk for CCGs because NHS England Guidance appears to have largely forgotten about this legal duty. It recommends that CCG plans are absorbed within the wider plans of 'sustainability and transformation partnerships' (STPs).

9.69 While the STP process may be an entirely laudable, it is entirely non-statutory. Accordingly, notwithstanding the guidance from NHS England which has elevated the STP planning process above almost all other aspects of NHS planning, CCGs and NHS England need to take care to ensure that it does not take the place of the statutory planning processes which are set out in the HSCA 2012. The statutory processes may well have been found to be less than perfect, but the HSCA 2012 is an Act of Parliament and public bodies have a legal duty to comply with the provisions of the HSCA 2012 (at least until parliament is called on to repeal the relevant parts of the HSCA 2012).

9.70 The duty to publish an annual commissioning plan is set out in section 14Z11 of the NHS Act 2006, which provides:

> **14Z11 Commissioning plan**
>
> (1) Before the start of each relevant period, a clinical commissioning group must prepare a plan setting out how it proposes to exercise its functions in that period.
>
> (2) In subsection (1), 'relevant period', in relation to a clinical commissioning group, means–
>
> (a) the period which–
>
> (i) begins on such day during the first financial year of the group as the Board may direct, and
>
> (ii) ends at the end of that financial year, and
>
> (b) each subsequent financial year.
>
> (3) The plan must, in particular, explain how the group proposes to discharge its duties under–
>
> (a) sections 14R, 14T and 14Z2, and
>
> (b) sections 223H to 223J.
>
> (4) The clinical commissioning group must publish the plan.
>
> (5) The clinical commissioning group must give a copy of the plan to the Board before the date specified by the Board in a direction.
>
> (6) The clinical commissioning group must give a copy of the plan to each relevant Health and Wellbeing Board.
>
> (7) The Board may publish guidance for clinical commissioning groups on the discharge of their functions by virtue of this section and sections 14Z12 and 14Z13.
>
> (8) A clinical commissioning group must have regard to any guidance published by the Board under subsection (7).
>
> (9) In this Chapter, 'relevant Health and Wellbeing Board', in relation to a clinical commissioning group, means a Health and Wellbeing Board established by a local authority whose area coincides with, or includes the whole or any part of, the area of the group'

9.71 The purpose of the annual commissioning plan is to set out how the CCG 'proposes to exercise its functions' in the coming financial year. A CCG has powers under section 14Z12 of the NHS Act 2006 to revise its annual commissioning plan if it wishes to make any significant changes to the exercise of its functions within a financial year. This power is set out in section 14Z12, which provides:

(1) A clinical commissioning group may revise a plan published by it under section 14Z11.
(2) If the clinical commissioning group revises the plan in a way which it considers to be significant–
(a) the group must publish the revised plan, and
(b) subsections (5) and (6) of section 14Z11 apply in relation to the revised plan as they apply in relation to the original plan.
(3) If the clinical commissioning group revises the plan in any other way, the group must–
(a) publish a document setting out the changes it has made to the plan, and
(b) give a copy of the document to the Board and each relevant Health and Wellbeing Board'

9.72 The CCG is required to consult local people prior to publishing its annual commissioning plan. The full details of the statutory process which each CCG is required to follow a set out in section 14Z13 of the NHS Act 2006, which provides:

14Z13 Consultation about commissioning plans
(1) This section applies where a clinical commissioning group is–
(a) preparing a plan under section 14Z11, or
(b) revising a plan under section 14Z12 in a way which it considers to be significant.
(2) The clinical commissioning group must consult individuals for whom it has responsibility for the purposes of section 3.
(3) The clinical commissioning group must involve each relevant Health and Wellbeing Board in preparing or revising the plan.
(4) The clinical commissioning group must, in particular–
(a) give each relevant Health and Wellbeing Board a draft of the plan or (as the case may be) the plan as revised, and
(b) consult each such Board on whether the draft takes proper account of each joint health and wellbeing strategy published by it which relates to the period (or any part of the period) to which the plan relates.
(5) Where a Health and Wellbeing Board is consulted under subsection (4)(b), the Health and Wellbeing Board must give the clinical commissioning group its opinion on the matter mentioned in that subsection.
(6) Where a Health and Wellbeing Board is consulted under subsection (4)(b)–
(a) it may also give the Board its opinion on the matter mentioned in that subsection, and
(b) if it does so, it must give the clinical commissioning group a copy of its opinion.
(7) If a clinical commissioning group revises or further revises a draft after it has been given to each relevant Health and Wellbeing Board under subsection (4), subsections (4) to (6) apply in relation to the revised draft as they apply in relation to the original draft.
(8) A clinical commissioning group must include in a plan published under section 14Z11(4) or 14Z12(2)–
(a) a summary of the views expressed by individuals consulted under subsection (2),
(b) an explanation of how the group took account of those views, and
(c) a statement of the final opinion of each relevant Health and Wellbeing Board consulted in relation to the plan under subsection (4).

(9) In this section, 'joint health and wellbeing strategy' means a strategy under section 116A of the Local Government and Public Involvement in Health Act 2007 which is prepared and published by a Health and Wellbeing Board by virtue of section 196 of the Health and Social Care Act 2012.

9.73 Section 14Z14 of the NHS Act 2006 provides a power (but not a duty) for the HWB to provide NHS England with an opinion as to whether a CCG annual commissioning plan takes proper account of the JHWS published by the HWB. This is a power which enables the HWB to express its disagreement with the priorities identified by the CCG. A critical report may lay the ground for a legal challenge that, in making commissioning decisions, the CCG has failed to comply with its duty to have regard to the JHWS. A CCG may, of course, seek to defend that challenge by producing evidence that the CCG has properly had regard to the JHWS but, for defensible reasons, has come to a different view on the priorities for the local NHS.

9.74 The NHS England *Operational planning and contracting guidance 2017–2019*[30] makes no mention of the duties on CCGs to produce annual commissioning plans. In place of the statutory planning process, it requires joint plans between commissioners and providers to be submitted to NHS England for approval. This is a non-statutory process and NHS England have no clear statutory powers to require any CCG to engage in these procedures. This is the planning process which NHS England is enforcing currently seeing to impose on CCGs, under the umbrella of the STP process. However, NHS England has no power to permit CCGs to ignore their legal obligations to consult with the public about their annual commissioning plan. A CCG which fails to produce an annual commissioning plan will be acting unlawfully in the absence of a recommendation in the NHS *Operational planning and contracting guidance* document will be no defence. Further, any major commissioning decision which is taken without the CCG having annual commissioning plan which describes the decision and has been the subject of prior public consultation could be the subject of a judicial review challenge.

The development of CCG commissioning policies

9.75 Once the CCG annual commissioning plan has been agreed, the precise details of the services that are to be commissioned for each patient group or specialised service need to be formulated in commissioning policies, which must also be informed by the joint strategic health needs assessment. These policies set out agreed care pathways and define clinical criteria which set out which patients are entitled to NHS funded healthcare for each medical condition.

9.76 Once a policy has been agreed, patients are entitled to expect that the CCG will routinely agree to fund the medical treatment set out in the policy patients who fulfil for the stated clinical criteria. Patients whose

30 See www.england.nhs.uk/wp-content/uploads/2016/09/NHS-operational-planning-guidance–201617–201819.pdf.

clinical criteria are outside the scope of a policy will not be routinely funded for NHS care, even if the medical treatment has the potential to benefit an individual patient. However, there is always the possibility of the CCG making an individual decision to depart from its own policy.

9.77 CCGs and NHS England have a duty to publicise their commissioning policies on their website: see regulation 35(1) of the RSR Regs 2012 (see para 9.35 above). Thus, for example, patients are entitled to know what approach a CCG takes to funding in-vitro fertilisation (IVF) treatment and can thus know when they are and are not likely to be eligible for NHS-funded IVF treatment.

Exception policies and pick-up funding for clinical trials

Exception policies

9.78 Commissioning policies define what care will be funded by the NHS for defined cohorts of patients. However, there are always a minority of patients whose circumstances do not precisely fit the general pattern and thus are entitled to be treated separately from other patients. CCGs routinely develop 'exception policies' to apply to such patients. The essence of an exception policy is that a patient who comes within the policy will be provided with NHS funding to support a medical treatment even though the other patients with the same clinical presentation are denied funding for the same treatment.

9.79 The formulation of exception policies is problematic, but they are used to cover situations where the NHS has decided that particular circumstances justify making a different decision for one group of patients in comparison to other patients with a like condition. The CCG needs to formulate the justification for exception policies very carefully in order to avoid challenges by other patients who are denied the relevant treatment.

9.80 The following are examples of areas where exception policies have been developed:

- Funding can be agreed for patients who have taken part in an NHS-sponsored clinical trial of a new drug or medical treatment and have shown a capacity to benefit from the treatment. Thus such patients may continue to funded to receive the treatment after the trial has finished even if funding would not be made available to a new patient in the same clinical circumstances.
- To continue NHS-funded medical treatment which has been commenced by another NHS commissioner and now falls to the CCG as a result of the patient moving from one CCG area where a treatment is funded to an area where it is not routinely funded.

Pick-up funding for clinical trials

9.81 The limitations on funding for trial pick-up costs is a hugely contentious area. NHS commissioners can come under considerable pressure from patients, clinicians and drug companies to continue to fund the treatment after the trial has been completed. However, the policy position adopted by most NHS commissioners is that funding will only be provided to support successful treatment if an agreement to fund was obtained before the trial began. Funding for trial pick up costs should be rarely (if ever) agreed by NHS commissioners where funding has not been agreed in advance of the trial, because it ought to be unnecessary.

9.82 Every clinical trial is required by the Medicines for Human Use (Clinical Trials) Regulations 2004[31] to operate in accordance the Helsinki Declaration[32] published by the World Medical Association. The requirement to identify a source of funding to allow the treatment to continue for patients who have a capacity to benefit is part of the present version of the Helsinki Declaration. It provides:

> In clinical trials, the protocol must also describe appropriate arrangements for post-trial provisions.

9.83 There is an argument that the version of the Helsinki Declaration referred to in the regulations does not include this wording. However, the spirit of the regulations is that the Helsinki Declaration should be followed, and thus medical ethics committees ought only give approval for a clinical the trial if those running the proposed trial have identified the source of funding for post-trial treatment for successful patients at the outset.

The duties on CCGs and NHS England to commission treatments identified in National Institute for Health and Clinical Excellence's Technology Appraisal Recommendations and highly specialised technology recommendations

National Institute for Health and Clinical Excellence

9.84 Regulation 34 of the RSR Regs 2012 provides that the arrangements that the CCG has in place for making commissioning decisions must ensure that the CCG funds treatment for qualifying patients identified in any Technology Assessment Guidance published by the National Institute for Health and Clinical Excellence[33] (NICE). The Labour government of 1997 to 2001 recognised the tension between local decision-making and postcode prescribing. Its solution was to create the National Institute for Clinical Excellence, later renamed as the National Institute for Health and Care Excellence by section 232 of the HSCA 2012.

9.85 NICE's function is to evaluate specific medical interventions and make 'recommendations' to the NHS and local authorities about the intervention under consideration. NICE describes its own functions as follows:

31 SI No 1031.

32 See www.wma.net/policies-post/wma-declaration-of-helsinki-ethical-principles-for-medical-research-involving-human-subjects/.

33 See www.nice.org.uk/.

> NICE guidance supports healthcare professionals and others to make sure that the care they provide is of the best possible quality and offers the best value for money.
>
> We provide independent, authoritative and evidence-based guidance on the most effective ways to prevent, diagnose and treat disease and ill health, reducing inequalities and variation'

Hence NICE produce guidance which recognises that NHS services should be investing in the delivery of services that are both clinically effective and cost-effective.

9.86 NHS commissioners can thus divide the guidance that NICE produces broadly into two types:

1) Technology Appraisal Recommendations (TARs); and
2) all other NICE guidance.

Technology Appraisal Recommendations

Generally

9.87 The TAR process is used to assess the clinical and cost-effectiveness of health technologies, such as new pharmaceutical and biopharmaceutical products, but also include procedures, devices and diagnostic agents. NICE suggests that its intention is to attempt to ensure that 'all NHS patients have equitable access to the most clinically- and cost-effective treatments that are available'. However, that ambition would only be achieved if all medical treatments had been subject to binding NICE guidance. In fact only a tiny proportion of the medicine delivered by the NHS is set out in binding NICE guidance, and so this ambition is still a very long way from being achieved.

9.88 In 2003 the secretary of state converted the NICE TAR process which 'recommended' NHS commissioners fund a particular treatment for a particular patient group into a legal obligation by issuing directions to require primary care trusts (PCTs) to fund interventions in accordance with the relevant NICE TAR. The directions required the PCT to allocate funding for recommended treatment for patients within the cohort described in the TAR within 90 days of the publication of the final TAR (unless the secretary of state exempted the TAR from the scheme). There have been a few exemptions, but in the vast majority of cases a decision from NICE by-passed any prioritisation process because it effectively top sliced an NHS commissioner's budget by requiring funds to be made available for a particular treatment for a defined group of patients.

9.89 The HSCA 2012 abolished PCTs and replaced them with CCGs. One key difference between PCTs and CCGs was that the secretary of state was not given power by the HSCA 2012 to issue directions to CCGs. One effect of this policy was that from April 2013, the legal requirement on local NHS commissioners to fund medical treatments set out in NICE TARs could therefore not be enforced through directions.

9.90 The new mechanism to reduce postcode prescribing in the NHS is section 237 of the HSCA 2012. This allows the secretary of state to make regulations which replicate the former system which was enforced by directions. The relevant regulations are the National Institute for Health and Care Excellence (Constitution and Functions) and the Health and Social Care Information Centre (Functions) Regulations (NICE Regs) 2013.[34] Regulation 7 of the NICE Regs 2013 provides:

> NICE may make a technology appraisal recommendation–
> (a) in relation to a health technology identified in a direction given by the Secretary of State;
> (b) that recommends that relevant health bodies provide funding within a specified period to ensure that the health technology be made available for the purposes of treatment of patients'

9.91 Regulation 7(6) of the NICE Regs 2013 then provides that a CCG must comply with a TAR. CCGs must also provide funding to support patients who could benefit from TARs which were included in Directions to PCTs which were made prior to 1 April 2013 (see regulations 33 and 34 of the RSR Regs 2012). Every TAR contains clinical indicators which describe the patients that NICE considers should be permitted to benefit from a clinical intervention. The legal right to access NHS-funded treatment described in a TAR only applies to patients who satisfy the clinical indicators in the TAR. Thus the legally enforceable rights given by this statutory scheme do not apply to any patient who suffers from the condition described in a TAR and who may be able to benefit from the described clinical intervention. There is no absolute right to fund unless the patient's clinical indicators fall within those set out in the TAR.

Highly specialised technology recommendations

9.92 Regulation 8 of the NICE Regs 2013 produces a similar system for NICE to produce binding highly specialised technology recommendations which are required to be funded by NHS England.

Other NICE guidance

9.93 The remaining guidance produced by NICE is hugely useful for CCGs in assessing whether a particular medical intervention or care pathway provides clinically-effective and/or cost-effective medical treatment. However, other than TARs, there is no absolute legal requirement on CCGs to follow guidance issued by NICE. Some NICE guidance is routinely followed by virtually all CCGs but other guidance is departed from by many CCGs throughout the country. Hence, for example, NICE Guidance 156 recommends that CCGs should fund up to three cycles of IVF for infertile women up to the age of 42. There are relatively few CCGs which fund IVF to that extent.

9.94 Even though CCGs do not have an absolute legal obligation to implement CCG guidance, they have a legal obligation to look at the guidance, understand what it is recommending and to consider whether to

34 SI No 259.

implement it. This was explained by Dyson J in *R v North Derbyshire Health Authority ex p Fisher*,[35] who said:

> If the Circular provided no more than guidance, albeit in strong terms, then the only duty placed upon health authorities was to take it into account in the discharge of their functions. They would be susceptible to challenge only on *Wednesbury* principles if they failed to consider the Circular, or they misconstrued or misapplied it whether deliberately or negligently: see *Grandsden & Co Ltd and another v Secretary of State and Another* (1985) 54 P&CR 86, 93–94.

9.95 A CCG will act thus unlawfully if it does not consider relevant NICE guidance (or potentially other relevant guidance which it would be unlawful to fail to consider) when making a commissioning policy decision or if the CCG misunderstands the guidance or misapplies it. In contrast, the CCG will be acting lawfully if it considers relevant guidance as part of a decision-making process but makes the decision not to follow the guidance for a good reason. Allocating the medical treatment a lower level of priority than suggested by NICE is a potentially good reason. See, for example, *R (Condliff) v North Staffordshire Primary Care Trust*.[36] In order to ensure that the CCG can show that it has acted lawfully it is preferable if the document trail leading up to the commissioning decision shows on the face of the relevant documents that the relevant NICE Guideline has been properly considered.

Individual funding requests

9.96 It is inevitable that, from time to time, patients and the clinicians treating them will seek NHS funding for medical treatment where there is no established commissioning policy which provides that a particular treatment will be funded. The vast majority of NHS patients will be provided with wholly adequate medical treatment in accordance existing commissioning policies. However, where there is no commissioning policy which approves the funding for the treatment to be provided as part of NHS-funded care or the patient's clinical circumstances fall outside a commissioning policy, an NHS commissioner needs to make an individual decision as to whether to fund the requested treatment or to decline to do so. Regulation 34(2)(b) of the RSR Regs 2012 requires every CCG and NHS England to have:

> . . . arrangements for the determination of any request for the funding of a health care intervention for a person, where there is no relevant NICE recommendation and the relevant body's general policy is not to fund that intervention.

9.97 Thus both CCGs and NHS England must have an IFR policy which explains how decisions can be made by that body in cases where the general approach of the CCG or NHS England is not to fund a particular drug or other treatment generally or outside a defined patient population.

35 [1997] EWHC Admin 675.

36 [2011] EWHC 872 (Admin), (2011) 14 CCLR 656.

Patients generally seek NHS funding for medical treatment outside existing commissioning policies in the following circumstances:

a) the NHS commissioner has a policy which describes the treatment available for a particular medical condition, including the treatment in question, but the patient's clinical indicators fall outside the circumstances where the NHS is prepared to fund the treatment which the patient and his or her treating clinician is requesting; or
b) the NHS commissioner has a policy which describes the treatment available for a particular medical condition but the policy does not provide to NHS funding to be provided for the particular drug or other medical treatment which the patient and his or her treating clinician is requesting; or
c) the patient presents with a medical condition for which the NHS commissioner has no particular policy or which does not fall within a category of conditions for which the NHS commissioner has a policy and thus there is no policy to guide the decision-maker as to whether the patient should or should not be funded for have treatment in question.

9.98 IFR policies vary from one NHS commissioner to another, but they generally provide that, for the first two categories set out above, NHS funding should only be provided for drugs or other medical treatments which lie outside established policies where:

a) that patient can show that the application is supported by an NHS referring clinician. If the patient does not have a clinician who is prepared to provide the treatment for the patient then the CCG should not entertain the application because the NHS does not generally fund medical treatment which is not recommended by clinicians;
b) the patient, supported by his or her clinician, can show that the requested treatment is likely to be clinically effective;
c) the patient, supported by his or her clinician, can show that the requested treatment is likely to be cost effective;
d) the circumstances are such that there are not likely to be other patients in a clinically similar situation. If there are other patients then the CCG should respond to the request by devising a policy and/or considering the request as an 'in year service development' but should not process the request as an IFR case (unless the case has a degree of urgency); and
e) if all of the above tests are met, the patient is able to demonstrate that he or she has exceptional clinical circumstances.

9.99 The underlying assumption in the above cases is that the NHS commissioner has made a policy decision about what it is reasonable for the NHS to fund for a particular category of patients and thus is generally entitled to rely on its policy to make a negative decision. Hence, for example, patients who have a particular form of cancer will be entitled to treatment in accordance with protocols agreed between an oncologists and the CCG, and incorporated into an acute service contract. If a new, expensive but potentially life-extending cancer drug emerges, there will be an understandable desire by oncologists to have the benefit of this drug for their patients and, amongst relevant patients, an understandable desire to be treated with the drug. However, the issues for the NHS commissioner are different where the commissioner has no policy because there is no prior decision about what it is reasonable for the NHS to provide to this particular category of patients. Thus a requirement under an IFR policy for a patient to have to demonstrate exceptional clinical circumstances in the third category of cases would unlawfully set the bar too high. The question is such cases ought to be whether the patient has a 'reasonable requirement' for the requested treatment, and that would only engage the questions as to whether there was evidence that the treatment was both clinically effective and was cost effective (and possibly whether it was affordable in the case of a particularly expensive treatment).

9.100 The NHS Confederation has produced an excellent guide to the IFR process for the first two categories set out above. That guide[37] was specifically approved by the Court of Appeal in the *R (Condliff) v North Staffordshire Primary Care Trust.*[38] Commenting on the requirement to show exceptional clinical circumstances, the court approved a statement in the NHS Confederation guide saying:

> Exceptionality is essentially an equity issue that is best expressed by the question: 'On what grounds can the PCT justify funding this patient when others from the same patient group are not being funded?'

9.101 The reason that NHS bodies have traditionally operated an IFR process is that, within a patient group with the same disease, there may be patients with individual clinical situations which are so unusual that a decision to deny funding to that patient is inequitable. The patient may, for example, have a genetic condition which means that the patient cannot tolerate the treatment which is usually provided to patients with that medical condition. If another treatment is available, even if it is more expensive, then it would be justifiable to refuse access to the treatment for the majority but it may be equitable to permit the exceptional patient to have that more expensive treatment.

9.102 It is almost impossible to define what is meant by 'exceptional clinical circumstances'. Some policies ask the decision-maker to consider whether the patient is significantly clinically different to the group of patients in question at the same stage of the progression of the condition. The courts have said that it is permissible (and perhaps preferable) to leave the term undefined. In *R (AC) v Berkshire West Primary Care Trust and another*[39] Lord Justice Hooper said:

> The use of the phrase 'exceptional circumstances' tells the decision maker that the number of persons who will succeed under the proviso is expected to be a small minority. It does not otherwise provide a helpful legal test for the decision maker (see *Huang v Secretary of State for the Home Department* [2007] 2 AC 167 paragraph 20).

37 See www.nhsconfed.org/~/media/Confederation/Files/Publications/Documents/Priority%20setting%20managing%20individual%20funding%20requests.pdf.

38 [2011] EWCA Civ 910, (2011) 14 CCLR 656.

39 [2011] EWCA Civ 247.

9.103 However 'exceptional' does not mean 'unique' and the IFR policy will be operated in an unlawful way if, in practice, no one can ever secure funding for a treatment. In *R (S (a child)) v NHS England* Collins J said:[40]

> The [NHS England] policy[41] considers what is meant by exceptionality. I do not propose to burden this judgment with the four pages which deal with this. I shall summarise. It starts by stating that 'very few patients have clinical circumstances which are exceptional so as to justify funding for that patient which is not available for other patients'. Thus the approach to exceptionality must be to require considerably more than a failure of usual treatment. But it must be borne in mind that exceptional is not the same as unique and that there should not be an approach that denies that any but an extreme case is regarded as exceptional. In its ordinary meaning, exceptional can mean no more than a case which does not meet what is normal.

9.104 The IFR process is not intended to be an appeal on the merits of an individual case. Funding for a medical treatment that is requested by both a clinician and a patient can almost always be justified on an individual basis. The IFR process exists to preserve a measure of flexibility so as to balance the duties that the NHS has to each NHS patients with the need to ensure the equitable distribution of NHS resources in the competition between patients for scares resources. Whilst the individual clinical circumstances of each patient are, of course, unique, only very few patients are likely to be able to show that they genuinely have exceptional clinical circumstances. It follows that challenges to decisions of IFR Panels are almost always based on an attack on the decision-making process adopted by the IFR Panel rather than a challenge to the reasonableness of the decision.

9.105 The assessment as to whether a patient demonstrates exceptional clinical circumstances is a decision for the NHS commissioner, not the referring clinician. The NHS commissioner is required to consider any opinion expressed by the referring clinician but is not obliged to accept any opinion on clinical exceptionality. Despite the way in which Mr Justice Collins approached the issues in *R (S (a child)) v NHS England*, the real issue is often whether a decision by an NHS commissioner that a patient is not exceptional can be described as either irrational or a decision that has been reached without having paid proper regard to the evidence submitted by the treating team.

The largest area of risk for CCGs in the IFR process is probably showing that they have discharged all of the general duties imposed on them by the NHS Act 2006 (as described at para 9.38 above) when making an IFR decision. Most IFR policies make only the most general references to, for example, the need to promote patient choice or the need to tackle health inequalities, when making IFR decisions.

40 [2016] EWHC 1395 (Admin), (2016) 19 CCLR 336 at para 1.

41 NHS England is working under an 'interim' policy which is at www.england.nhs.uk/commissioning/wp-content/uploads/sites/12/2016/08/cp–03.pdf.

In-year service developments

9.106 During the lifetime of the annual commissioning plan there can be new unanticipated developments in the form of new drugs or medical treatments which emerge as options for CCG funding during the year. If there is insufficient evidence that a new treatment is clinically effective, then it is highly likely that the new treatment will not be supported with CCG funds (unless it is funded as an experimental treatment). However, the fact that there is evidence that a new treatment is likely to be clinically effective should not, of itself, be sufficient to justify funding because the annual CCG budget for commissioning healthcare will be fully committed. However, there will be the occasional new treatment which is so stunningly good (ie it is highly clinically-effective and cost-effective) that a responsible commissioner ought to fund it straightaway rather than waiting for the treatment to compete for funding in the next annual plan, and thus, deny patients funding until the following April (at the earliest).

9.107 Each CCG therefore needs to have a policy which sets out how it will respond to requests for funding for 'in-year service developments'. Policies usually provide that any such applications need to go through an in-year prioritisation process to determine:

a) the evidence base to support a case that the treatment is likely to be clinically-effective;
b) the evidence base to support a case that the treatment is likely to be cost-effective;
c) what level of relative priority should be applied to the new proposed treatment in comparison to the other treatments that are already funded; and
d) what services should cease to be funded (ie decommissioned) in order to redirect funding to any new investment area that has been viewed as a high priority.

9.108 The assessment of new treatments is therefore a process of re-evaluating the overall priorities for a new service. Even if a new service is considered an important priority, the service development still has to compete with other potential investments from other services in the annual commissioning process. Occasionally a treatment may be considered so important that it should be funded immediately (an in-year service development). Usually can only be done if reserves are available or funding can be released from elsewhere to fund the investment.

9.109 Difficult issues can arise where clinicians seek to introduce funding for a new treatment by a series of IFR applications and thus, in effect, create a precedent for funding for a new intervention. The clinician's perspective may be that the CCG does not have a policy to fund or not to fund the drug and accordingly the IFR process is only mechanism to secure funding for an individual patient. However, the perspective of the NHS commissioner is, of course, wholly different. The commissioner will say that the IFR process is not intended to permit a creeping extension of the range of services the NHS is prepared to fund outside of the annual prioritisation process. The in-year service development policy is there to square this circle by allowing genuinely innovative treatments to be considered outside the annual prioritisation process but also ensuring that the IFR process is not used to secure funding for medical treatments that failed to achieve funding through the annual prioritisation process.

Patient and public involvement in commissioning decision-making

9.110 A CCG is required to consult the public about its annual commissioning plan. That is a formal duty of consultation which is separate from the general duties on all NHS bodies to involve the patients and the public in their decision-making. See chapter 12 on the legal issues around public engagement in decision-making. However, both CCGs and NHS England are subject to wide-ranging duties of public involvement in making commissioning decisions.

9.111 A significant commissioning decision which was taken without any elements of public involvement will almost certainly leave the NHS commissioner to a legal challenge.

CHAPTER 10

NHS acute care contracting

Introduction

10.1 The separation of commissioning and providing within the NHS in England means that an 'arrangement' is required to be in place between a commissioner and a provider of NHS services so that the provider knows what services it is required to provide to NHS patients and also knows how it will be paid for providing those services. There is no 'contract' between the patient and the provider, and thus the role of monitoring whether services are being provided to appropriate standards falls to the commissioner. Any arrangement between a commissioner and a provider of NHS services needs to have performance standards which enable the commissioner to know how NHS patients are being treated and whether services are being provided in accordance with the standards defined in the contract.

10.2 Prior to the creation of NHS England, the Department of Health and Social Care (DHSC) published recommended forms of arrangement and developed payment mechanisms to support those arrangements. This was non-statutory until the implementation of the Health and Social Care Act (HSCA) 2012 when statutory rules were introduced to govern NHS contracting, with further restrictions imposed by the National Health Service Commissioning Board and Clinical Commissioning Groups (Responsibilities and Standing Rules) Regulations (RSR Regs) 2012.[1] These regulations require all NHS commissioners to use the NHS Standard Contract when contracting for NHS services (aside from primary care contracting).

10.3 Any arrangement between an NHS commissioner and an NHS provider operates under either an NHS contract or a legally binding contract, usually in the form of an NHS Standard Contract. This chapter looks at the rules and practice for NHS contracting (both under NHS contracts and legally binding contracts) in all circumstances other than for primary care contracting (ie contracts with GP and dental practices). This chapter does not consider the steps that NHS commissioners are required to follow before deciding which organisation is best placed to provide services to NHS patients – that is covered chapter 21.

10.4 The standard form of contract requires commissioners to pay providers on an activity basis, known as Payment by Results (PbR). But PbR has as many limitations as it has benefits and, in the years since the HSCA 2012 was passed, NHS commissioners have sought to work creatively with NHS providers to deliver alternative models of care. It remains to be seen whether, given the statutory straightjacket imposed by the HSCA 2012 enables alternative contractual models lawfully be put in place.[2]

NHS contracts

10.5 Arrangements between 'purchasers' of NHS services and providers were originally service level agreements, called 'NHS contracts'. The word

1 SI No 2996.

2 This is explored at para 10.110 below.

'contract' is something of a misnomer because, in law, these were not contracts. The National Health Service and Community Care Act (NHSCCA) 1990 first introduced NHS trusts and thus created NHS contracts as a way of health authorities contracting with the new provider organisations. Section 4 of the NHSCCA 1990[3] contained provisions which defined NHS contracts and provided they were not to give rise to legally enforceable obligations. There are a number of aspects of the statutory scheme under the NHSCCA 1990 describing NHS contracts which have survived into the present set of arrangements for NHS contracts. These provisions are now set out in section 9 of the National Health Service Act (NHS Act) 2006 which provides:

(1) In this Act, an NHS contract is an arrangement under which one health service body ('the commissioner') arranges for the provision to it by another health service body ('the provider') of goods or services which it reasonably requires for the purposes of its functions.
(2) Section 139(6) (NHS contracts and the provision of local pharmaceutical services under pilot schemes) makes further provision about acting as commissioner for the purposes of subsection (1).
(3) Paragraph 15 of Schedule 4 (NHS trusts and NHS contracts) makes further provision about an NHS trust acting as provider for the purposes of subsection (1).
(4) 'Health service body' means any of the following–
(za) the Board,
(zb) a clinical commissioning group,
(a) . . .
(b) . . .
(c) an NHS trust,
(d) a Special Health Authority,
(e) a Local Health Board,
(f) a Health Board constituted under section 2 of the National Health Service (Scotland) Act 1978,
(fa) a Special Health Board constituted under that section,
(g) a Health and Social Services Board constituted under the Health and Personal Social Services (Northern Ireland) Order 1972 (SI 1972/1265 (NI14)),
(h) the Common Services Agency for the Scottish Health Service,
(i) the Wales Centre for Health,
(j) . . .
(k) the Care Quality Commission,
(ka) NICE,
(kb) the Health and Social Care Information Centre,
(kc) Health Education England,
(l) the Scottish Dental Practice Board,
(m) the Secretary of State,
(n) the Welsh Ministers,
(na) the Scottish Ministers,
(nb) Healthcare Improvement Scotland,
(o) the Northern Ireland Central Services Agency for the Health and Social Services established under the Health and Personal Social Services (Northern Ireland) Order 1972,

3 As originally enacted.

(p) a special health and social services agency established under the Health and Personal Social Services (Special Agencies) (Northern Ireland) Order 1990,
(q) a Health and Social Services trust established under the Health and Personal Social Services (Northern Ireland) Order 1991,
(r) the Department of Health, Social Services and Public Safety.

(5) Whether or not an arrangement which constitutes an NHS contract would apart from this subsection be a contract in law, it must not be regarded for any purpose as giving rise to contractual rights or liabilities.

(6) But if any dispute arises with respect to such an arrangement, either party may refer the matter to the Secretary of State for determination under this section.

(7) If, in the course of negotiations intending to lead to an arrangement which will be an NHS contract, it appears to a health service body–
(a) that the terms proposed by another health service body are unfair by reason that the other is seeking to take advantage of its position as the only, or the only practicable, provider of the goods or services concerned or by reason of any other unequal bargaining position as between the prospective parties to the proposed arrangement, or
(b) that for any other reason arising out of the relative bargaining position of the prospective parties any of the terms of the proposed arrangement cannot be agreed,
that health service body may refer the terms of the proposed arrangement to the Secretary of State for determination under this section.

(8) Where a reference is made to the Secretary of State under subsection (6) or (7), he may determine the matter himself or appoint a person to consider and determine it in accordance with regulations.

(9) 'The appropriate person' means the Secretary of State or the person appointed under subsection (8).

(10) By the determination of a reference under subsection (7) the appropriate person may specify terms to be included in the proposed arrangement and may direct that it be proceeded with.

(11) A determination of a reference under subsection (6) may contain such directions (including directions as to payment) as the appropriate person considers appropriate to resolve the matter in dispute.

(12) The appropriate person may by the determination in relation to an NHS contract vary the terms of the arrangement or bring it to an end (but this does not affect the generality of the power of determination under subsection (6)).

(13) Where an arrangement is so varied or brought to an end–
(a) subject to paragraph (b), the variation or termination must be treated as being effected by agreement between the parties, and
(b) the directions included in the determination by virtue of subsection (11) may contain such provisions as the appropriate person considers appropriate in order to give effect to the variation or to bring the arrangement to an end.

10.6 The key differences between an NHS contract and other forms of NHS contracting are as follows:

a) The only organisations, companies or individuals who can be parties to an NHS contract are those listed in section 9 of the NHS Act 2006 or as a result of another statutory provision[4] which entitles the parties to an arrangement between an NHS commissioner and a provider to be treated as an NHS contract. Both parties to the contract thus must have statutory authority to enter into an NHS contract. If only one of the parties is permitted to do so, the arrangement cannot take effect in law as an NHS contract. The most significant (and deliberate) omission from the list of bodies that can enter into an NHS contract is an NHS foundation trust. NHS foundation trusts were first set up by the Health and Social Care (Community Health and Standards) Act 2003. No provision was made in this Act for the new form of NHS bodies to be permitted to contract on the basis of an NHS contract. That remains the position under the NHS Act 2006 and accordingly all contracts between an NHS commissioner and an NHS foundation trust are required to be in the form of legally binding contracts.[5]

b) Section 139 of the NHS Act 2006 provides that an individual or body corporate which wishes to enter into a pilot pharmaceutical service contract can apply to the Secretary of State for Health and Social Care to be treated as a 'health service body' and thus to contract on the basis of an NHS contract.

c) An NHS contract can be for any goods or services which a commissioner reasonably requires for the purposes of its functions. This form of contract is almost invariably used for services to be provided to NHS patients (often in primary care) but there is no limitation to patient services in the legislation and thus this form of arrangement could be used for the supply of a wide range of goods or services.

d) Section 9(5) of the NHS Act 2006 provides that an NHS contract gives rise no right to legal liabilities that can be enforced in the civil courts. The effect of section 9(5) was considered by the Court of Appeal in *Pitalia and another v The National Health Service Commissioning Board*[6] which emphasised that an NHS contract must not be regarded as giving rise to enforceable rights 'for any purpose'. It follows that it was, so the court held, wrong for the district judge to have held that an NHS contract (as the court found it to be) in that case could be interpreted as an arbitration clause. Such a clause could only be found in a legal contract and an NHS contract must not be regarded as a legal contract for any purpose.

e) Parties to an NHS contract have the right to refer a dispute to be determined by the secretary of state, since such a dispute cannot be litigated in the courts. However for acute care NHS contracts (ie those outside primary care, dental care and community pharmaceutical NHS contracts), this provision has become less important in recent years because the NHS Standard Contract has complex dispute resolution provisions which take the place of a reference to the secretary of state.

4 There are provisions in the GMS and PMS Regulations for general practitioners allowing NHS contracts; see chapter 11.

5 However, the dispute resolution provisions in the NHS Standard Contract mean that an NHS foundation trust contract cannot usually be enforced by way of standard court action.

6 [2014] EWCA Civ 474.

However for those contracting areas where disputes are referred to the secretary of state, the secretary of state has made a series of directions to require the Family Health Services Appeal Unit[7] (FHSAU), which is part of the National Health Service Litigation Authority, to make determinations on behalf of the secretary of state.

f) Section 9(7) of the NHS Act 2006 provides that, where health service bodies are 'in the course of negotiations intending to lead to an arrangement which will be an NHS contract' but cannot agree on the proposed terms, either health service body 'may refer the terms of the proposed arrangement to the Secretary of State for determination under this section'. Thus, in effect, the secretary of state is given a power to impose contractual terms on the parties to a proposed contract.

10.7 NHS contracts have a far greater impact in primary care commissioning than in acute care arrangements because acute care contracting is undertaken using the NHS Standard Contract. This provides for dispute resolution provisions which require expert determination as opposed to referring issues to the FHSAU.

The NHS Standard Contract

Background

10.8 Following the NHSCCA 1990, the DHSC developed a standard contract for acute commissioning between primary care trusts and NHS trusts. This form of contract evolved over the years and got gradually more complex. Although the form of contract was only contained in guidance, primary care trusts (PCTs) and NHS trusts almost invariably contracted on the basis of the standard contract (and could be directed by the secretary of state to do so if they attempted to use a different form of contract). When clinical commissioning group (CCGs) were created by the HSCA 2012, a decision was made that they would not be NHS bodies that could be subject to directions made by the secretary of state. As a result, many of the governance issues that were set out in guidance for PCTs (and were backed by the secretary of state's direction making power) were included in the RSR Regs 2012 as statutory duties imposed on CCGs and on the newly created NHS England.

10.9 One of the areas where NHS commissioners were affected by this change of legal structure was the requirement to use the NHS Standard Contract in acute care contracting. Under the RSR Regs 2012, the expression 'relevant body' is defined in reg 2 as 'a CCG or the Board'.

10.10 The term 'commissioning contract' is widely defined in reg 2 as follows:

> a contract, other than a primary care contract, entered into by a relevant body in the exercise of its commissioning functions

7 See www.nhsla.com/FHSAU/Pages/Home.aspx.

10.11 The width of this definition should be noted. A 'commissioning contract' is any arrangement put in place by a relevant body' in the exercise of its commissioning functions. The expression 'commissioning functions' is defined in reg 2 as follows:

> the functions of a relevant body in arranging for the provision of services as part of the health service, but it does not include, in relation to the Board, its functions in relation to services provided under a primary care contract

Thus any arrangement put in place by a CCG or NHS England which results in the provision of services which can be used by one or more NHS patients amounts to an exercise of commissioning functions, apart from services provided under a primary care contract.

10.12 Part 5 of the RSR Regs 2012 is headed 'Standing rules: commissioning contract terms'. Regulation 16 of the RSR Regs 2012 provides some technical requirements to ensure that providers under acute commissioning contracts are licensed by Monitor under the HSCA 2012 (or exempt from registration) and appropriately regulated by the Care Quality Commission (CQC). It provides:

> (1) A commissioning contract entered into by a relevant body must contain terms and conditions that ensure that the health service provider complies with all the duties imposed upon a registered person by regulation 20 of the Health and Social Care Act 2008 (Regulated Activities) Regulations 2014 (duty of candour) ('the 2014 Regulations'), as modified by paragraph (1B), irrespective of whether–
> (a) the health service provider is a registered person; or
> (b) the health service provider is carrying on a regulated activity.
>
> (1A) A commissioning contract entered into by a relevant body must contain terms and conditions that ensure that the health service provider–
> (a) co-operates with–
> (i) the LETB for each area in which it provides such services; and
> (ii) any LETB which represents that provider by virtue of arrangements made by HEE under paragraph 2(4)(c) of Schedule 6 to the Care Act 2014,
>
> in such manner and to such extent as the LETB in question may request, in planning the provision of, and in providing, education and training for health care workers; and
> (b) provides the LETB in question with such information as it may request.
>
> (1B) For the purposes of paragraph (1), regulation 20 of the 2014 Regulations is modified as follows–
> (a) for 'Registered persons' in paragraph (1), substitute 'Health service providers';
> (b) for 'registered person', in each place it appears, substitute 'health service provider';
> (c) in paragraph (1), omit 'in carrying on a regulated activity'; and
> (d) in paragraphs (8) and (9) for 'a regulated activity', substitute 'health care services'.
>
> (2) In this regulation–
>
> . . .
>
> 'LETB' means a local education and training board appointed by Health Education England under section 103 of the Care Act 2014;]
>
> . . .

> 'registered person' has the same meaning as in regulation 2(1) of the 2014 Regulations (interpretation);
> 'regulated activity' means an activity prescribed as a regulated activity for the purposes of section 8(1) of the Health and Social Care Act 2008 (regulated activity) by regulation 3 of the 2014 Regulations (prescribed activities)'

10.13 Regulation 17 of the RSR Regs 2012 then provides for the NHS Standard Contract to be drafted by NHS England as follows:

> (1) The Board must draft–
> (a) terms and conditions making provision for the matters specified in regulation 16; and
> (b) such other terms and conditions as the Board considers are, or might be, appropriate for inclusion in commissioning contracts entered into by a relevant body.
> (2) The Board may draft model commissioning contracts which reflect the terms and conditions it has drafted pursuant to paragraph (1).
> (3) A relevant body must incorporate the terms and conditions drafted by virtue of paragraph (1)(a) in commissioning contracts entered into by it.
> (4) The Board may require CCGs to incorporate the terms and conditions it has drafted pursuant to paragraph (1)(b) in commissioning contracts that a CCG enters into.
> (5) If a CCG is required by the Board to incorporate terms and conditions pursuant to paragraph (4), it must do so'

10.14 NHS England has complied with this obligation by publishing a variety of NHS Standard Contracts. The forms of these contracts tend to be revised on annual basis and published on the NHS England website. As from April 2017, there is a 'shorter form' contract, which runs to a mere 70 pages as opposed to the full form of the contract which is over 300 pages. The full-length NHS Standard Contract falls into three parts:[8]

1) the Particulars;
2) the Service Conditions; and
3) the General Conditions.

10.15 The shorter form contract is also in three parts, with the same division as the full-length NHS Standard Contract. It is beyond the scope of this book to describe every aspect of the NHS Standard Contract, but it contains numerous provisions governing the relationship between the NHS commissioner and the provider, and setting out the quality standards that the provider must adhere to.

10.16 NHS England has exercised the power in regulation 17(4) to require CCGs to use the NHS Standard Contract (or the shorter form contract), as confirmed in the *NHS England technical guidance*. The *NHS Standard Contract 2017/18* and 2018/19 *Technical guidance* document[9] sets out the legal obligations on NHS bodies to use the NHS Standard Contract as follows:

> **7 When should the NHS Standard Contract be used?**
> 7.1 The NHS Standard Contract exists in order that commissioners and providers operate to one clear and consistent set of rules which everyone

8 See www.england.nhs.uk/nhs-standard-contract/17–18/.

9 See www.england.nhs.uk/wp-content/uploads/2016/11/7-contract-tech-guid.pdf.

understands, giving a level playing field for all types of provider and allowing economies in the drafting and production of contracts, for example in respect of legal advice.

7.2 The NHS Standard Contract must be used by CCGs and by NHS England where they wish to contract for NHS-funded healthcare services (including acute, ambulance, patient transport, continuing healthcare services, community-based, high-secure, mental health and learning disability services). The Contract must be used regardless of the proposed duration or value of a contract (so it should be used for small-scale short-term pilots as well as for long-term or high-value services). Where a single contract includes both healthcare and non-healthcare services, the NHS Standard Contract must be used.

7.3 The only exceptions are:

- primary care services commissioned by NHS England, where the relevant primary care contract should be used; and
- any primary care improvement schemes agreed by CCGs with GP practices (with contractual arrangements, involving a variation or supplement to existing general practice contract, agreed between local NHS England teams and CCGs). Such Local Improvement Schemes (LIS) involve payments for improving the quality of services provided under an existing GP contract, not the commissioning of additional services.

7.4 CCGs must use the NHS Standard Contract for all community-based services provided by GPs, pharmacies and optometrists that were previously commissioned as Local Enhanced Services. This will apply where the CCG is commissioning services which expand the scope of services beyond what is covered in core primary care contracts or LIS agreements'

10.17 It follows that CCGs are under a public law duty to use the NHS Standard Contract whenever they were commissioning 'NHS funded healthcare services' unless the services were exempted because they come within the type of services set out in para 7.3 of the *Technical guidance* (as set out above).

10.18 The legal obligations on CCGs to use the NHS Standard Contract has the following implications:

a) There is no exemption from the legal duty to contract using the NHS Standard Contract where the proposed contract is of low value. The legal duty to use the NHS Standard Contract arises regardless of the value of the contract.
b) There is no exemption from the mandated duty to use the NHS Standard Contract where the commissioning decision has been made by an Individual Funding Request (IFR) panel.
c) There is no exemption from the duty to use the NHS Standard Contract where services are being commissioned by a CCG for a single patient as opposed to being commissioned for cohorts of patients.

10.19 This means that a CCG is under a legal duty to use an NHS Standard Contract when, for example, commissioning a care home place for a patient who is eligible for NHS Continuing Healthcare or a placement for a patient who requires mental health in-patient treatment. There has been a practice amongst CCGs of using an informal form of contract, called a 'spot purchase' arrangement, without using the full form NHS Standard Contract to set up these types of arrangements. There was even NHS England guidance which appears to endorse the use of such an arrangement.[10] However, the *Technical guidance* is clear that CCGs are under a legal duty to use the NHS Standard Contract for commissioning all services for NHS patients save for the exceptions set out above. This is confirmed at para 12.1 of the *Technical guidance* which provides:

> We expect the NHS Standard Contract to be used where an NHS commissioner is fully funding an individual's NHS Continuing Health Care (NHS CHC) placement in a care home or package of home care.

10.20 The *Technical guidance* gives the following advice about when NHS commissioners are entitled (and should) use the shorter form NHS Contract:

> **When to use the shorter-form Contract**
> 9.1 The shorter-form Contract must not be used for contracts under which acute, cancer, A&E, minor injuries, 111 or emergency ambulance services, or any other hospital inpatient services, including for mental health and learning disabilities, are being commissioned.
>
> 9.2 Restricting use of the shorter-form Contract in this way significantly reduces the number of detailed requirements which it has to include, and these providers (that is, providers of those services for which the shorter-form Contract must not be used) tend to be larger organisations.
>
> 9.3 Subject to the restriction around national prices above, commissioners may use the shorter-form Contract for all other services for which the NHS Standard Contract is mandated – for non-inpatient mental health and learning disability services, for any community services, including those provided by general practices, pharmacies, optometrists and voluntary sector bodies, for hospice care / end of life care services outside acute hospitals, for care provided in residential and nursing homes, for non-inpatient diagnostic, screening and pathology services and for patient transport services.
>
> 9.4 In response to feedback, however, we are amending the shorter-form Contract so that it can now be used for diagnostic, screening and pathology services, including where the National Tariff guidance sets a mandatory national price. We recognise that this will allow the shorter-form Contract to be used in a wider range of appropriate situations. Including the provisions relation to mandatory national prices adds to the length of the Contract, so we strongly recommend that commissioners use the e-Contract functionality, to ensure that this additional wording only appears in those contracts where it is required.
>
> 9.5 Within the parameters set out in this Guidance, it is for commissioners to determine when they wish to use the shorter-form version of the Contract, as opposed to the longer form.
>
> 9.6 We have not set a specific financial threshold for use of the shorter-form contract, but we strongly encourage commissioners to use it for appropriate services (as described in 9.3 above) with lower annual values, which will tend to include the great majority of contracts held by the smaller provider organisations which this new contract form is particularly intended to assist. The end result of this approach should be that the shorter-form Contract is used

10 The relevant guidance on patient choice rights was issued in 2014 and has now been rescinded.

for most contracts with smaller providers, including voluntary organisations, hospices (where grant agreements are not being used – see paragraph 11 below), care home operators and providers of enhanced services such as general practices, pharmacies and optometrists.

9.7 However, in deciding whether to use the shorter-form Contract to commission services for which it may be used, commissioners should consider carefully the differences in the management process and other provisions between the shorter-form and full-length Contracts. If the 'lighter touch' approach of the shorter-form is not thought appropriate to the services, the relationship or the circumstances, the full-length Contract may be used. Also, if the provider is providing other services under the full-length Contract, it may be more appropriate to keep all services on this form.

9.8 Note that when services are being tendered (whether competitively or under AQP) the same form of contract must be offered to all potential providers of those services. The form of contract offered (whether shorter-form or full-length) should be made clear in the Prior Information Notice, advertisements and other communications with potential providers'

Multiple commissioners under a single contract

10.21 The NHS Standard Contract can be used by multiple CCGs to commission services from a single provider of NHS services. This is particularly useful for services of a fairly specialised nature (but which do not fall to be commissioned by NHS England[11]). The *Technical guidance* explains the way in which the NHS Standard Contract can be used for multi-party contracting as follows:

13 Collaborative contracting
13.1 The NHS Standard Contract may be used for both bilateral and multilateral commissioning i.e. for commissioning by a single commissioner or by a group of commissioners collaborating to commission together, with one acting as the co-ordinating commissioner.

13.2 Clearly, it is for commissioners to determine the extent to which they choose to adopt the co-ordinating commissioner model – but it is an approach which NHS England strongly encourages. There can be great benefits for commissioners from working closely together to negotiate and manage contracts with providers. Using the co-ordinating commissioner model enables a consistent approach to contracting and is more efficient for both commissioners and providers, avoiding a proliferation of small, separate contracts.

13.3 In particular, we would encourage commissioners to work together to use, where they can, consistent contract metrics for the same provider – local quality and reporting requirements, local agreements, policies and procedures, Activity Planning Assumptions or Prior Approval Schemes. This will help to reduce the administrative burden which providers face.

13.4 Where commissioners choose to contract collaboratively, they should set out the roles and responsibilities that each commissioner will play in relation to the contract with the provider, and how they are to make decisions in relation to the contract and instruct the co-ordinating commissioner to act on their behalf, in a formal collaborative commissioning

11 See chapter 13 on the responsible commissioner to see the distinction between services commissioned by NHS England and those commissioned by CCGs.

agreement (CCA). The CCA is a separate document entered into by a group of commissioners and governs the way the commissioners work together in relation to a specific contract. A CCA should be in place before the contract is signed and takes effect. However, a contract which has been signed by all the parties (as outlined in paragraph 15 below) is still legally effective and binding on all the parties without a collaborative agreement in place. The CCA should not be included in the contract (though the allocation of roles and responsibilities between commissioners which are party to a contract can, where necessary, be set out in Schedule 5C (Commissioner Roles and Responsibilities) to that contract).

13.5 Model CCAs are available on the NHS Standard Contract 2017/18 web page.

13.6 Where NHS England is the sole party to a contract, but the lead for commissioning of particular services from the provider is being taken by different NHS England teams, use of a formal CCA is not appropriate – NHS England is one legal entity. However, it is important to ensure that the different teams understand what role each will play in managing the contract and communicate this clearly to the provider'

The period of an NHS contract

10.22 The period of an NHS contract is not set out in the standard form contract. It is thus up to NHS commissioners and providers to agree between themselves how long a contract should last. The guidance recommended that contracts starting in April 2017 should be for a two-year period, thus largely avoiding the annual contracting round for April 2018.[12] The *Technical guidance* give the following advice about the period of an NHS contract:

17.4 There is no nationally-mandated limit to contract duration, nor is there a central approval process for contract terms beyond a certain duration. It is for commissioners to determine locally, having regard to the guidelines below, the duration of the contract they wish to offer.

- Commissioners will need to consider carefully what benefits they can expect from offering providers the increased certainty of a longer-term contract, setting this against the need to ensure that they are able to use a competitive procurement approach when this will be in patients' best interests, in line with regulations and guidance. Commissioners should consider patient choice, competition, the likelihood of technological and other developments affecting service delivery models, all relevant commercial and market considerations, in determining the appropriate length of contract. Contract length should be considered in conjunction with consideration of including any right to extend the contract (see paragraph 18) and/or the consequences of early termination (see paragraph 47).
- Commissioners must ensure that they make clear the duration of the contract to be offered at the very outset of the procurement process.

12 NHS England then published updates for the NHS Standard Contract for April 2018, and asked CCGs to vary the contracts to include the new terms.

- Commissioners must ensure that the duration of any contract (and any proposed right to extend that period) is in compliance with their own standing financial instructions (SFIs) and other governance requirements, and that any approvals are obtained in line with those requirements. NHS England commissioners should note that, under NHS England SFIs, any proposal to let a contract with a potential duration of over five years (including any optional extensions) requires approval through the Efficiency Controls Committee prior to advertisement.

17.5 Alongside flexibility of contract duration, the Contract:

- includes an explicit acknowledgement of the parties' rights to terminate the Contract or any Service by mutual agreement (GC17.1); and
- continues to include provisions for early termination of the Contract or a Service on a no-fault basis, with flexibility as to notice periods (and note that different notice periods may be agreed for termination of the whole Contract or for a Service).

17.6 The Contract also continues to allow for National Variations to be mandated by NHS England, in particular to reflect annual updates to the NHS Standard Contract. Both commissioner and provider are able to propose other variations (for example to effect annual reviews'

10.23 The *Technical guidance* also provides the following guidance on the need for both commissioners and providers to act fairly in their dealings with other. It provides:

29 Contracting fairly

29.1 The contract is an agreement between the commissioner(s) and the provider. Once entered into, the contract is a key lever for commissioners in delivering high-quality, safe and cost-effective services. However, the contract in isolation will not achieve this. An effective working relationship between commissioner(s) and provider is a key element of successful contracting.

29.2 An effective relationship is unlikely to be a cosy one in which the partners are hesitant to address difficult issues for fear of upsetting each other – but nor will it be one where each party focusses, aggressively and continuously, on protecting what is perceives to be its own narrow, individual interests.

29.3 There is no perfect recipe, but an effective working relationship is more likely to be possible where commissioner and provider:

- have a shared vision for services, with the primary focus on what will produce the best outcomes for patients – but backed by a commitment to deal fairly with the consequences of this vision for individual organisations;
- are open and transparent in sharing information, ensuring early communication of new or changed intentions, emerging problems or potential disputes;
- take their contractual responsibilities seriously, but use contractual levers and processes in a reasonable and proportionate way; and
- tackle difficult discussions about financial pressures in a way which focusses on actions which will genuinely remove cost or increase efficiency in the local health system as a whole, rather than producing short-term, opportunistic gains for one party at the expense of the other'

10.24 This would be somewhat idealistic or even naive advice if the NHS operated in an entirely arms-length contractual manner, but that is not usually the overriding culture of the NHS. It remains to be seen how much this guidance is followed in practice.

Non-contract activity: how commissioning arrangements work without a contract in place

10.25 NHS commissioners will have contracts in place with their local providers of NHS services. However the patients for whom a CCG has commissioning responsibility will, in practice, be provided by NHS treatment by a vast variety of NHS providers, many of whom will not have a current contract in place with the responsible CCG. It would clearly be impracticable for CCGs to have contracts in place with every single NHS provider in the country just on the off chance that a patient from, say Newcastle, was treated by a hospital Trust in Devon. However where a patient who is resident in Newcastle falls ill whilst on holiday in Devon and is admitted to a Devon hospital, the Trust running the hospital needs to be able to charge the patient's home CCG in Newcastle for NHS treatment provided to the patient.[13]

10.26 The NHS England *Who pays? Determining responsibility for payments to providers* guidance[14] has the following guidance at paras 38–46:

> **Non-contract activity**
> 38. Non-contract activity is the term used to refer to NHS-funded services delivered to a patient by a provider which does not have a written contract with that patient's responsible commissioner, but which does have a written contract with another commissioner or commissioners.
>
> 39. Written contracts, using the NHS Standard Contract format, should be put in place by commissioners with a provider where there are established flows of patient activity with a material financial value. Non-contract activity billing arrangements are not intended as a routine alternative to formal contracting, but are likely to be required in some circumstances, usually for small, unpredictable volumes of patient activity delivered by a provider which is geographically distant from the commissioner.
>
> 40. The responsible commissioner for non-contract activity will be established in the usual manner, using paragraph 1, irrespective of the location or status of the provider.
>
> 41. The following arrangements apply, within England, in terms of commissioner approval processes for non-contract activity:
>
> a) No prior commissioner approval is required for emergency treatment on a non-contract basis.
>
> b) No prior commissioner approval is required for consultant-led elective care where the patient has exercised choice of provider under the legal rights set out in the NHS Constitution. A GP, dentist or optometrist referral is required in such cases, however.

13 Other than accident and emergency treatment which should be billed to the CCG local to the hospital trust. For more details on the division between different responsible commissioners, please see chapter 13 on the responsible commissioner.

14 See www.england.nhs.uk/wp-content/uploads/2014/05/who-pays.pdf.

c) For non-emergency treatment where the NHS Constitution does not set out a legal right for a patient to choose their provider, referral by the patient's GP, dentist or optometrist nonetheless constitutes authority for the provider to see and (depending on the content of the referral) treat the patient, and commissioners must pay for activity undertaken in such circumstances.

d) In other circumstances than those set out in paragraphs a) to c) above, there is no presumption that a provider may see and treat patients, on a non-contract basis, and expect to be paid by commissioners. Commissioners have the right to determine which services they wish to commission and from which providers. Where non-emergency non-contract referrals are made other than by the patient's GP, dentist or optometrist, including self-referrals, the provider must seek prior authorisation from the responsible commissioner before assessing and treating the patient. Where prior authorisation is not granted, commissioners are under no obligation to pay for activity which is carried out by providers on a non-contract basis.

42. The same arrangements apply for commissioner approval processes in respect of UK cross-border non-contract activity, except that for all elective referrals, prior approval from the commissioner must be sought and obtained by providers. Referral by a GP or consultant does not in itself constitute approval.

43. Emergency treatment should never be refused or delayed due to uncertainty or ambiguity as to which CCG is responsible for funding an individual's healthcare. Commissioners and providers should work together in good faith to ensure that, where prior authorisation is required, this is sought, and a response provided, as quickly as possible.

44. It is good practice for providers to put in place administrative systems to identify elective non-contract activity at the point of booking. Providers should inform responsible commissioners of any planned treatment(s) for a patient likely to result in claim for payment in excess of £10,000 and to keep them informed as necessary throughout the patient's stay, for example, if it becomes apparent that a patient's length of stay is likely to exceed 50 days. These arrangements can help to ensure that commissioners are informed about high-cost cases at the earliest opportunity and are appropriately involved in planning care for patients with complex needs. These are expected behaviours of organisations, not a lever for purposefully withholding non-contract activity funding.

45. Non-contract activity is undertaken by the provider on the terms of the NHS Standard Contract in place between that provider and its host commissioner(s). A contract on those terms will be implied as between the patient's responsible commissioner and the provider. Note in particular that:

- services will be delivered in accordance with the service specifications and other terms and conditions of the provider's contract with its host commissioner;
- prices for services will be in line with National Tariff guidance (Payment by Results guidance in 2013/14), as applicable, or the local prices set out in the provider's contract with its host commissioner(s);
- arrangements for submission of activity datasets, invoicing and payment reconciliation should follow National Tariff guidance (Payment by Results guidance in 2013/14) and the terms and conditions set out in the NHS Standard Contract. Commissioners will be

under no obligation to pay for activity where activity datasets and invoices are not submitted in line with these requirements;

- commissioners and providers should work together in good faith to minimise disagreements relating to payment for non-contract activity. However, any formal disputes over payment for non-contract activity should be resolved in accordance with the dispute resolution procedure set out in the NHS Standard Contract.

46. These arrangements may be applied to non-contract activity involving cross-border patient flows within the UK (eg cross border emergency treatment) under the arrangements set out in section C)'

10.27 This is all sensible, practical guidance, but it does not explain the legal basis upon which payments are required to be made by a commissioner to a provider where there is no contract in place between an NHS commissioner and a provider. It also appears to ground the right of the patient to make choices in the NHS Constitution whereas the source of the patient's legal rights is under the RSR Regs 2012 and the duties on commissioners, as explained in chapter 12 on patient choice.

10.28 The *Technical guidance* seeks to provide a legal basis for non-contract activity by applying either the terms of the contract or a model of an 'implied contract' to non-contract activity. It provides the following guidance:

25 Acceptance of referrals and non-contract activity

25.1 It is important for patients that providers of NHS-funded services accept referrals from all appropriate sources.

25.2 The Contract (full-length) includes a specific requirement on providers (SC6.6.2) to accept every referral, regardless of the identity of the Responsible Commissioner, where this is necessary to enable a patient to exercise his/her legal right of choice of provider. This applies whether or not the Responsible Commissioner for the patient affected is a party to a written contract with the provider. (Note, however, the new restrictions which will apply in respect of GP referrals not made via ERS from October 2018 – see paragraph 3.2 above.)

25.3 There is also an equivalent provision in relation to the acceptance of emergency referrals and presentations which are within the scope of the services it provides (SC6.6.3 of the full-length Contract). Again, this requirement applies whether or not the Responsible Commissioner for the affected patient is a party to a written contract with the provider. There will be instances where a provider cannot safely accept an emergency referral, and the Contract wording makes provision for this.

25.4 These provisions can be enforced by the Responsible Commissioner of any affected patient, either through the co-ordinating commissioner for the provider's main contract or via GC29.1 (Third Party Rights).

25.5 Conversely, we also set out clearly (SC6.8 in the full-length Contract, SC6.3 in the shorter form) that the existence of a contract with one commissioner does not automatically entitle a provider to accept referrals in respect of, provide services to, nor to be paid for providing services to, individuals whose Responsible Commissioner is not a party to the contract, except (where appropriate) where such an individual is exercising their legal right to choice as set out in the NHS Choice Framework or where necessary for the individual to receive emergency treatment.

25.6 Guidance on non-contract activity (NCA) (including what form of referral constitutes authority to treat) is set out in *Who Pays? Establishing the*

Responsible Commissioner[15]. Commissioners and providers should refer to this guidance for full detail, but it may be helpful to re-state certain key points here.

25.7 The guidance makes clear that 'Written contracts, using the NHS Standard Contract format, should be put in place by commissioners with a provider where there are established flows of patient activity with a material financial value. Non-contract activity billing arrangements are not intended as a routine alternative to formal contracting, but are likely to be required in some circumstances, usually for small, unpredictable volumes of patient activity delivered by a provider which is geographically distant from the commissioner.'

25.8 The concept of NCA is most relevant to acute hospital services, most of which are covered by national currencies and prices and where patients have choice of provider. As a guideline, we would strongly recommend that any CCG with activity of over £200,000 per annum with an acute provider should put in place a written contract, rather than relying on the NCA approach.

25.9 The guidance also explains that, where there is no written contract in place, there is nonetheless an implied contract (assumed to be on the terms of the NHS Standard Contract in place between the provider and its local commissioners). In particular, the guidance is clear that 'NCA' commissioners have the same rights to challenge payment as commissioners covered by written contracts, stating that 'Arrangements for submission of activity datasets, invoicing and payment reconciliation should follow National Tariff guidance (Payment by Results guidance in 2013/14) and the terms and conditions set out in the NHS Standard Contract. Commissioners will be under no obligation to pay for activity where activity datasets and invoices are not submitted in line with these requirements.'

25.10 We have heard of both commissioners and providers refusing to enter into written contract with their counterparts even where regular activity flows are substantially above the level referred to in paragraph 25.8 above, seemingly believing that it is in their interests to operate under NCA principles instead. We advise strongly against this sort of approach.

25.11 In practice, acute NCA will need to be reported via SUS, with invoices raised by providers in line with the timescale set out in SC36.35. It is essential that providers and commissioners comply with the requirements NHS England has published advice on access to personal confidential data for the purposes of invoice validation, *Who Pays? Information Governance Advice for Invoice Validation*, including the requirement for providers to submit detailed backing datasets to the same timescales as NCA invoices'

10.29 The contracting provisions work by placing an obligation on the NHS provider to accept a referral of a patient for treatment, even if the patient is not someone for whom the contracting CCG has commissioning responsibility. This is set out in Special Condition (SC) 6.6 which provides:

15 Please see chapter 13 on the responsible commissioner for a description of the system of allocating responsibility between commissioners. A degree of caution is needed because the 'Who Pays' guidance contains numerous statements that are at variance with the RSR Regulations.

Acceptance and Rejection of Referrals

6.6 Subject to SC6.2A and to SC7 (Withholding and/or Discontinuation of Service), the Provider must:

6.6.1 accept any Referral of a Service User made in accordance with the Referral processes and clinical thresholds set out or referred to in this Contract and/or as otherwise agreed between the Parties and/or as specified in any Prior Approval Scheme, and in any event where necessary for a Service User to exercise their legal right to choice as set out in the NHS Choice Framework; and

6.6.2 accept any clinically appropriate referral for any Service of an individual whose Responsible Commissioner (CCG or NHS England) is not a Party to this Contract where necessary for that individual to exercise their legal right to choice as set out in the NHS Choice Framework; and

6.6.3 where it can safely do so, accept a referral or presentation for emergency treatment, within the scope of the Services, of or by any individual whose Responsible Commissioner is not a Party to this Contract.

Any referral or presentation as referred to in SC6.6.2 or 6.6.3 will not be a Referral under this Contract and the relevant provisions of Who Pays? Guidance will apply in respect of it'

10.30 Thus, if a provider has an NHS Standard Contract with one CCG, the provider has a duty to accept referrals from other CCGs. The words 'referral' and 'referrer' are defined in the General Conditions (GCs) as follows:

Referral

the referral of any Service User to the Provider by a Referrer or (for a Service for which a Service User may present or self-refer for assessment and/or treatment in accordance with this Contract and/or Guidance) presentation or self-referral by a Service User

Referrer

(i) the authorised Healthcare Professional who is responsible for the referral of a Service User to the Provider; and

(ii) any organisation, legal person or other entity which is permitted or appropriately authorised in accordance with the Law to refer the Service User for assessment and/or treatment by the Provider'

10.31 General Condition (GC) 29 relates to third party rights. It provides:

GC29 Third Party Rights

29.1 A person who is not a Party to this Contract has no right under the Contracts (Rights of Third Parties) Act 1999 to enforce or enjoy the benefit of this Contract, except that, to the extent that it applies in its or their favour, this Contract may be enforced by:

29.1.1 a person who is the Provider's employee and is performing the Services for the Provider, if the matter to be enforced or the benefit to be enjoyed arises under GC5 (Staff), other than GC5.2, GC5.3.2 and GC5.15 to GC5.17 (Staff);

29.1.2 the Secretary of State;

29.1.3 a Regulatory or Supervisory Body

29.1.4 any CCG or Local Authority;

29.1.5 the NHS Business Services Authority;

29.1.6 a previous provider of services equivalent to the Services or any of them before the Service Commencement Date, or a new provider of services equivalent to the Services or any of them after the expiry or termination of this Contract or any Service, if the matter to be enforced or the benefit to be enjoyed arises under GC5.11 to GC5.14 (Staff);

29.1.7 the relevant NHS Employer, if the matter to be enforced or the benefit to be enjoyed arises under GC5.15 to GC5.17 (Staff).

29.2 Subject to GC13.2.2 (Variations), the rights of the Parties to terminate, rescind or agree any Variation, waiver or settlement under this Contract are not subject to the consent of any person who is not a party to this Contract.

10.32 Thus a CCG, or a person authorised to make referrals (such as a GP) can refer patients to any provider who has an NHS Standard Contract and, subject to the limited exceptions in SC6.6, the provider has a contractual duty to accept the referral and to provide appropriate NHS treatment to the patient who is referred. If the Provider refuses to accept the referral, the referring CCG has a contractual right under the Contracts (Rights of Third Parties) Act 1999 to enforce the obligation on the Provider to accept the referral and treat the patient by taking advantage of GC29.1.4.

10.33 That approach raises the question as to how the provider is entitled to bill the referring CCG for the activity that it has undertaken consequent upon that referral when the referring CCG has no contractual relationship with the provider. The answer provided by paragraph 25.9 of the *Technical guidance* is that there is an 'implied contract' on the terms of the NHS Standard Contract in place between the referring CCG and the provider under which the CCG agrees to remunerate the provider on the standard contractual terms. As a matter of law, this must be correct because the patient has been referred to the provider for NHS treatment against a clear expectation that the provider will have the duty to provide the treatment and that the provider will be entitled to charge standard fees as a result of providing that treatment. An alternative legal basis would be that the NHS guidance creates a public law duty or a legitimate expectation for the provider to be paid by the CCG. The provider's right to be paid could be enforced either by private law proceedings or possibly by way of judicial review proceedings if a CCG failed to pay.

Payment for delivering NHS services and the NHS National Tariff

Introduction

10.34 Over the years since the purchaser/provider model was first created, the DHSC developed a standard set of arrangements for paying NHS providers for providing services to NHS patients. The primary payment obligations in the NHS contract are set out in the Special Conditions, starting at SC36 which provides:

SC36 Payment Terms

Payment Principles

36.1 Subject to any express provision of this Contract to the contrary, each Commissioner must pay the Provider in accordance with the National

Tariff, to the extent applicable, for all Services that the Provider delivers to it in accordance with this Contract.

36.2 To avoid any doubt, the Provider will be entitled to be paid for Services delivered during the continuation of:

36.2.1 any Incident or Emergency, except as otherwise provided or agreed under SC30 (Emergency Preparedness, Resilience and Response); and

36.2.2 any Event of Force Majeure, except as otherwise provided or agreed under GC28 (Force Majeure)'

10.35 Thus the payment obligation extends to 'all Services that the Provider delivers to it in accordance with this Contract'. The price is defined by SC36.3 which provides:

Prices

36.3 The Prices payable by the Commissioners under this Contract will be:

36.3.1 for any Service for which the National Tariff mandates or specifies a price:

36.3.1.1 the National Price; or

36.3.1.2 the National Price as modified by a Local Variation; or

36.3.1.3 (subject to SC36.16 to 36.20 (Local Modifications)) the National Price as modified by a Local Modification approved or granted by NHS Improvement,

for the relevant Contract Year;

36.3.2 for any Service for which the National Tariff does not mandate or specify a price, the Local Price for the relevant Contract Year'

10.36 The term 'price' is defined by the General Conditions as:

Price

A National Price, or a National Price adjusted by a Local Variation or Local Modification, or a Local Price, as appropriate'

The lawfulness of NHS commissioners and providers agreeing a 'Local Variation' to the price for a service specified by the National Tariff is considered below.

10.37 The existence of a standard set of prices for the delivery of NHS services was also intended to dissuade NHS commissioners from choosing to place contracts with a provider which offered the lowest price for the delivery of a service. Where prices were set by the PbR system, providers were supposed to compete on service quality and patient experience but not on price. The NHS Digital website explained the purpose of the PbR system as follows:[16]

What is Payment by Results?
The aim of Payment by Results (PbR) is to provide a transparent, rules-based system for paying trusts. It rewards efficiency, supports patient choice and diversity and encourages activity for sustainable waiting time reductions. Payments are linked to activity and adjusted for Casemix. Importantly, this system ensures a fair and consistent basis for hospital funding rather than being reliant principally on historic budgets and the negotiating skills of individual managers.

16 This explanation was on the NHS Digital website until 2017. It has now been removed.

PbR encourages stronger incentives to ensure that extra money being invested into the NHS results in improved performance and accountability. This involves making changes to the way health care is financed and the way funding flows are managed across the NHS.

Healthcare Resource Groups version 4 (HRG4) supports PbR by providing a classification framework that represents current clinical practice. In addition, HRG4 supports service planning, costing and commissioning between PCTs and trusts by providing reliable and consistent presentation of activity data to:

- support the focus on patient-centred care, to enable patient choice
- support the analysis of healthcare needs and monitoring of service provision, to inform service planning.

Data collected through HRG4 allows commissioners to develop transparent service level agreements with trusts and other service providers'

10.38 The PbR system has only ever covered a proportion of NHS services outside of primary care (where a PbR system has never operated). Prior to the introduction of the new rules in the HSCA 2012, NHS commissioners and providers signed 'block contracts' to cover services that were not covered by prices defined within the PbR. These contracts defined the services that the provider would deliver and set quality and performance standards. However, the price to be paid was set for the contract as a whole rather than on a price per patient basis. There could be 'caps and collars' which provided an increased price if the provider treated more patients than a defined number or possibly a reduction in payment if fewer patients were referred.

10.39 The underlying purpose of the PbR system is that the 'money follows the patient'. Thus providers get paid for the treatment they provide to individual patients, with the income dependant on the volume of patients treated by a provider. This approach has both policy advantages and disadvantages. As this is a legal rather than NHS policy book, it is not appropriate to dwell on the policy issues. However, the advantages and disadvantages of a PbR system are explored in a King's Fund Report[17] *Payment by Results: How can payment systems help to deliver better care?* which was published in 2012.

10.40 The HSCA 2012 put the non-statutory payment rules on a statutory footing. The rules for the operation of NHS commissioning arrangements are now set out in Chapter 4 of Part 3 of the HSCA 2012. The Explanatory Notes to the Act explain the purpose of the Chapter as follows:

> Chapter 4 makes provision for Monitor, in conjunction with the NHS Commissioning Board, to regulate prices for NHS services through a national tariff. It also makes provision for references to the Competition Commission[18] to adjudicate over disputed changes to methodologies for determining prices under the national tariff.

10.41 Section 115 of the HSCA 2012 sets out the statutory obligation on NHS commissioners to pay providers of NHS services according to the National Tariff. It provides:

17 See www.kingsfund.org.uk/sites/default/files/field/field_publication_file/payment-by-results-the-kings-fund-nov–2012.pdf.

18 Now the Competition and Markets Authority.

Price payable by commissioners for NHS services

(1) If a health care service is specified in the national tariff (as to which, see section 116), the price payable for the provision of that service for the purposes of the NHS is (subject to sections 124 and 125) such price as is determined in accordance with the national tariff on the basis of the price (referred to in this Chapter as 'the national price') specified in the national tariff for that service.

(2) If a health care service is not specified in the national tariff, the price payable for the provision of that service for the purposes of the NHS is such price as is determined in accordance with the rules provided for in the national tariff for that purpose'

10.42 Section 116 of the HSCA 2012 sets out the provisions relating to the National Tariff. This section places an obligation on Monitor to publish the National Tariff as a single document that sets out the prices for NHS services which are to be paid by NHS commissioners to providers. The relevant provisions state:

(1) Monitor must publish a document, to be known as 'the national tariff', which specifies–
  (a) certain health care services which are or may be provided for the purposes of the NHS,
  (b) the method used for determining the national prices of those services,
  (c) the national price of each of those services, and
  (d) the method used for deciding whether to approve an agreement under section 124 and for determining an application under section 125 (local modifications of prices).

(2) The national tariff may provide for rules under which the commissioner of a health care service specified in the national tariff and the providers of that service may agree to vary–
  (a) the specification of the service under subsection (1)(a), or
  (b) the national price of the service.

(3) Where a variation is agreed in accordance with rules provided for under subsection (2), the commissioner of the service in question must maintain and publish a written statement of–
  (a) the variation, and
  (b) such other variations as have already been agreed in accordance with rules provided for under that subsection in the case of that service.

(4) The national tariff may also–
  (a) specify variations to the national price for a service by reference to circumstances in which the service is provided or other factors relevant to the provision of the service,
  (b) provide for rules for determining the price payable for the provision for the purposes of the NHS of health care services which are not specified under subsection (1)(a), and
  (c) provide for rules relating to the making of payments to the provider of a health care service for the provision of that service'

10.43 Further provisions for the operation of the National Tariff are set out at section 117 of the HSCA 2012, which provides:

(1) The ways in which a health care service may be specified in the national tariff under section 116(1)(a), or in rules provided for in the national tariff under section 116(4)(b), include in particular–

(a) specifying it by reference to its components,
(b) specifying it as a service (a 'bundle') that comprises two or more health care services which together constitute a form of treatment,
(c) specifying it as a service in a group of standardised services.

(2) In the case of a service specified in the national tariff under section 116(1)(a), the national tariff must–
(a) if the service is specified in accordance with subsection (1)(a), specify a national price for each component of the service;
(b) if it is specified in accordance with subsection (1)(b), specify a national price for the bundle;
(c) if it is specified in accordance with subsection (1)(c), specify a single price as the national price for each service in the group.

(3) In the case of a service specified in rules provided for in the national tariff under section 116(4)(b), the rules may–
(a) if the service is specified in accordance with subsection (1)(a), make provision for determining the price payable for each component of the service;
(b) if it is specified in accordance with subsection (1)(b), make provision for determining the price payable for the bundle;
(c) if it is specified in accordance with subsection (1)(c), make provision for determining the price payable for each service in the group.

(4) Where the commissioner of a health care service for the purposes of the NHS agrees to pay a price for the provision of the service other than the price that is payable by virtue of this Chapter, Monitor may direct the commissioner to take such steps within such period as Monitor may specify to secure that the position is, so far as practicable, restored to what it would have been if the commissioner had agreed to pay the price payable by virtue of this Chapter.

(5) Where the commissioner of a health care service fails to comply with rules provided for under section 116(2), (4) or (6), Monitor may direct the commissioner to take such steps within such period as Monitor may specify–
(a) to secure that the failure does not continue or recur;
(b) to secure that the position is, so far as practicable, restored to what it would have been if the failure was not occurring or had not occurred'

10.44 There is considerable disagreement between professional commentators about the meaning and effect of these provisions. NHS England, the DHSC and Monitor (now part of NHS Improvement) have interpreted these provisions to permit the NHS to operate an internal market with a measure of price competition. However, it is by no means clear whether their views are correct.[19] Further, it is far from clear that the rules are followed in practice by NHS commissioners and providers. There are also considerable inconsistencies between the way that NHS England, the DHSC and Monitor say payment provisions for the NHS now operate and assurances as to the effect of these rules given in parliament during the passage of the bill which became the HSCA 2012.

19 Two separate judicial reviews are due to be heard in April and May 2018 challenging the legality of arrangements that NHS England have proposed for Accountable Care Organisations. The outcomes of those cases may affect the text set out in this chapter and may be reported upon in the next edition of this book.

The meaning of a 'healthcare service' in the National Tariff

10.45 The starting point to understanding the potentially confusing set of provisions which govern how much an NHS commissioner should pay to an NHS provider for providing services to NHS patients starts by identifying the basic building block for the payment obligation, namely the provision of a 'health care service'. There is a definition of 'healthcare service' in section 64(3) of the HSCA 2012 which provides:

> 'Health care' means all forms of health care provided for individuals, whether relating to physical or mental health, with a reference in this Part to health care services being read accordingly; and for the purposes of this Part it does not matter if a health care service is also an adult social care service (as to which, see section 65).

It follows that a 'healthcare service' is any form of service which relates to the mental or physical health of an individual NHS patient. Whilst there is nothing in this section which requires a healthcare service to be linked to the activity provided to NHS patients, the National Tariff operates solely on the basis of payment for 'activity', namely the provision of services by a provider to an NHS patient.

10.46 Different rules operate depending on whether the healthcare service is 'specified in the National Tariff' or not. Section 115(1) of the HSCA 2012 sets pricing rules for services that are specified in the National Tariff. Section 115(2) covers those services which are not specified in the National Tariff. It sets different rules which apply to determining payment schemes for such services. Paragraphs 31 and 32 of the 2017/18 National Tariff explain how the rules apply to those services that are specified in the National Tariff. They provide:

> 31. Under the Health and Social Care Act 2012 ('the 2012 Act'), the national tariff must specify certain NHS healthcare services for which a national price is payable. The healthcare services to be specified must be agreed between NHS England and NHS Improvement. The 2012 Act also provides that the national tariff may include rules for determining which currency applies where there is more than one currency and price for the same service.
>
> 32. We are using healthcare resource group HRG4+ currency design as the basis for setting national prices for admitted patient care, outpatient procedures and accident and emergency (A&E) attendances. We are using 'phase 3' of the currency design, which was used for the collection of the 2014/15 reference costs.

10.47 Section 117(1) provides that the National Tariff can specify services in three ways, namely: a) by reference to its components, b) by specifying it as a service (a 'bundle') that comprises two or more health care services which together constitute a form of treatment or c) by specifying it as a service in a group of standardised services. The difference between these options is the extent to which a series of medical procedures are paid for under a single tariff payment. It would be possible for the NHS to remunerate providers for every blood test undertaken for a patient, every examination or every minute that a patient stays in hospital. Such a system would pay providers by the 'components' of healthcare. Alternatively, individual components could be 'bundled' together and attract a single payment.

10.48 A course of treatment can be 'grouped' from beginning to end under section 117(1)(c), so that a single payment is provided for each patient of a certain classification who requires a defined intervention such as a hip replacement, regardless of the number of tests done or length of stay in hospital. Such an approach has an element of 'swings and roundabouts' because, across a cohort of patients, some will be more straightforward and some will be more complex (and thus incur additional bed days or additional clinical interventions). The National Tariff uses this approach. This is explained at para 36 of the National Tariff as follows:

> 'Grouping' is the process of using clinical information such as diagnosis codes (in admitted patient care only), procedure codes (in admitted patient care and outpatient care), treatment codes (A&E only) and investigation codes (A&E only) to classify patients to casemix groups structured around healthcare resource groups. HRGs are groupings of clinically similar conditions or treatments that use similar levels of healthcare resources. The grouping is done using grouper software produced by NHS Digital. NHS Digital also publishes comprehensive documentation giving the logic and process behind the software's derivation of HRGs as well as other materials that explain and support the development of the currencies that underpin the national tariff.

10.49 The National Tariff uses the term 'Currency' to mean a unit of healthcare activity such as spell, episode, attendance which is grouped together under a single National Tariff price. Paragraphs 37–39 of the National Tariff states:

> 37. A 'currency' is a unit of healthcare for which a payment is made. Under the 2012 Act, a healthcare service for which a national price is payable must be specified in the national tariff. A currency can take one of several forms. We use spell-based HRGs as the currency for admitted patient care and some outpatient procedures. The currencies for A&E services are based on A&E attendances.
>
> 38. The HRG currency design used for the 2017/19 NTPS is known as HRG4+ and is arranged into chapters, each covering a body system. Some chapters are divided into subchapters. The specific design for the 2017/19 NTPS is that used to collect 2014/15 reference costs.
>
> 39. The currency used for outpatient attendances is based on attendance type and clinic type, defined by treatment function code (TFC). This is explained in more detail in Section 3.2.4.

10.50 Thus, an NHS provider that provides medical treatment to an NHS patient that qualifies as a 'currency' is entitled to claim a payment for the service which relates to that currency. The final sum payable may then be adjusted as described below. There are different definitions of currencies that apply to different types of care. Hence, for example, the currency for out-patient appointments operates as follows:

> **3.2.5. Outpatient care**
>
> 83. National prices for consultant-led outpatient attendances are based on clinic type categorised according to treatment function code (TFC) There are separate prices for first and follow-up attendances, for each TFC, as well as for single professional and multi-professional clinics.

84. To incentivise a change in the delivery of outpatient follow-up activity, to encourage a move to more efficient models and to free up consultant capacity, we over-reimburse first attendances and under-reimburse corresponding follow-up attendances. This transfer in cost is set at a TFC level and ranges from 10% to 30%. There is a full list in Annex A.

85. The outpatient attendance national price remains applicable only to pre-booked, consultant-led attendances and in accordance with the service conditions in the NHS Standard Contract'

10.51 The term 'HRG' in the National Tariff is a reference to 'Healthcare Resource Group'. The NHS Data Dictionary[20] explains this term as follows:

Healthcare Resource Groups offer Organisations the ability to understand their ACTIVITY[21] in terms of the types of PATIENTS they care for and the treatments they undertake. They enable the comparison of ACTIVITY within and between different Organisations and provide an opportunity to benchmark treatments and services to support trend analysis over time.

Healthcare Resource Groups are currently used as a means of determining fair and equitable reimbursement for care services delivered by Health Care Providers. Their use as consistent 'units of currency' supports standardised healthcare commissioning across the NHS. They improve the flow of finances within – and sometimes beyond – the NHS.

For further information on Healthcare Resource Groups, see the NHS Digital website at: Introduction to Healthcare Resource Groups.

10.52 The NHS Digital website contains a further explanation of HRGs as follows:[22]

What are Healthcare Resource Groups?
Healthcare Resource Groups (HRGs) are standard groupings of clinically similar treatments which use common levels of healthcare resource.

HRGs help organisations to understand their activity in terms of the types of patients they care for and the treatments they undertake. They enable the comparison of activity within and between different organisations and provide an opportunity to benchmark treatments and services to support trend analysis over time.

HRGs are currently used as a means of determining fair and equitable reimbursement for care services delivered by providers. Their use as consistent 'units of currency' supports standardised healthcare commissioning across the service.

They improve the flow of finances within – and sometimes beyond – the NHS. HRG version 4 has been in use for reference costs since April 2007 (for financial year 2006/7 onwards) and for Payment by Results (PbR) since April 2009 (for financial year 2009 onwards).

HRG4 was a major revision that introduced HRGs to new clinical areas, to support the Department of Health's policy of Payment by Results (PbR). It includes a portfolio of new and updated HRG groupings that accurately record patient treatment to reflect current practice and anticipated trends in healthcare.

20 See www.datadictionary.nhs.uk/data_dictionary/nhs_business_definitions/h/healthcare_resource_group_de.asp?shownav=1.

21 Words in capitals in the NHS Data Dictionary are defined terms.

22 See http://content.digital.nhs.uk/hrg.

Our aim is to ensure that HRG4 suits the needs of the NHS and meets the requirements of DH in implementing the policy of PbR'

10.53 The above definitions thus explain that, at least as far as services specified in the National Tariff are concerned, the term 'healthcare service' in section 115(1) is a reference to a pre-defined (and possibly 'grouped') episode of medical treatment for an individual NHS patient provided by an NHS provider. There is no scheme under the National Tariff which provides for a payment arrangement for the treatment of multiple patients other than as a multiplier of the national tariff price for an individual patient.

Is agreeing a changed price for a service specified in the National Tariff or 'price competition' lawful as part of any NHS procurement or contracting arrangement?

10.54 There is no definition of the term 'price' in the HSCA 2012. However, a 'price' appears to be a sum of money which, by virtue of the statutory scheme under the HSCA 2012, becomes payable by an NHS commissioner to a provider of NHS services for the provision of a healthcare service to an individual patient. Thus the term 'price' in Part 3 of the HSCA 2012 usually refers to the sum of money payable by an NHS commissioner to a provider for the provision of a health care service to an individual patient.

10.55 One of the unanswered questions relating to the proper interpretation of the HSCA 2012 is whether any departure from National Tariff prices (for those healthcare services which are specified in the National Tariff) and/or whether any substantial element of price competition is permissible when undertaking a procurement exercise for NHS services. These two issues are obviously linked.

10.56 In the years since the publication of the HSCA 2012, the NHS has embraced procurement processes with a focus on price competition. However, the material set out below suggests strongly that the scheme of the HSCA 2012 was intended to create statutory procedures for fixing pricing mechanisms which meant that 'prices' for the delivery of NHS services were determined on an objective basis, and that any competition between providers was limited to quality and delivery issues. If that construction of the HSCA 2012 is correct, this is an area, like so many, where there may be a significant distance between the day-to-day reality as to how the NHS operates and the statutory scheme set out in the HSCA 2012. A study of the parliamentary materials makes it very clear that one purpose of the bill which became the HSCA 2012 was to rule out price competition in relation to NHS contracts, and that Parliament was continually assured that the bill's provision operated to prevent price competition.

10.57 The Health and Social Care Bill, as originally published by the DHSC, proposed market mechanisms for the NHS, including the potential for price competition. That fitted with the policies of the incoming government which sought to drive the NHS towards adopting market mechanisms, including price competition for NHS services. Paragraph 5.43 of the NHS Operating Framework for 2011/12[23] which was published in December 2010, stated:

> The flexibilities set out in the 2010–11 NHS Operating Framework will remain largely in place for 2011–12. One new flexibility being introduced in 2011–12 is the opportunity for providers to offer services to commissioners at less than the published mandatory tariff price, where both commissioner and provider agree. Commissioners will want to be sure that there is no detrimental impact on quality, choice or competition as a result of any such agreement.

10.58 Clause 103(1) of the original bill[24] (which subsequently became section 115 of the HSCA 2012) proposed that the National Tariff price would be the 'maximum price' the NHS could pay for the delivery of an NHS service, leaving it open to NHS commissioners and providers to agree the final price, which could be lower than the maximum price. It provided:

> (1) If a health care service is specified in the national tariff (as to which, see section 104), the price payable for the provision of that service for the purposes of the NHS is–
> (a) the price specified in the national tariff for that service, or
> (b) where the national tariff specifies a maximum price for that service, such price not exceeding that maximum as the commissioner and the provider may agree'

10.59 Thus the proposal was that NHS commissioners could require all providers to compete to provide the best services at the lowest price. The intention to include regulated price competition as part of the NHS contracting environment was confirmed in an speech by the then Secretary of State for Health, Rt Hon Andrew Lansley, in January 2011[25] where he said:

> In the future, Monitor will have a vital new role in ensuring effective competition and a level playing field, acting in the interests of patients and the taxpayer. They will also oversee the process of price competition, which is to be allowed only where it is deemed appropriate and where it will not harm quality of service.

10.60 This aspect of the bill was the subject of considerable debate, especially at second reading in the House of Commons on 31 January 2011.[26] On 18 January 2011, the then Chief Executive of the NHS, Sir David Nicholson, told the Public Accounts Committee that he was very cautious about price competition. Speaking before the Public Accounts Committee[27] he said:

> The international evidence seems to show that, if you introduce price competition, you can get to a place where quality suffers. In a sense, people reduce quality in order to deliver. But it's not necessarily the case because the issues are first of all: have you got measures of quality? So, can you say what you expect from them? Have you got real good measures? Have you got real

23 See www.gov.uk/government/uploads/system/uploads/attachment_data/file/216187/dh_122736.pdf.

24 See https://publications.parliament.uk/pa/cm201011/cmbills/132/11132.pdf.

25 See http://webarchive.nationalarchives.gov.uk/20120503092949/http://www.dh.gov.uk/en/MediaCentre/Pressreleases/DH_123744.

26 See, for example, David Miliband MP at column 618: www.publications.parliament.uk/pa/cm201012/cmhansrd/cm110131/debtext/110131-0002.htm.

27 See https://publications.parliament.uk/pa/cm201011/cmselect/cmpubacc/741/11011802.htm.

> good measures of monitoring quality, and have you got patients who have the knowledge to be able to work out whether the service that they're getting themselves is the kind of quality that they'd expect? If you've got those three things in place, I think it's possible to start talking about price competition. But it seems to me, until you have that, it's a very dangerous thing to do.

10.61 The essential concern was that procurement exercises based on price competition would lead to a 'race to the bottom' on price because the public body paying the price for the services, namely the NHS commissioner, was not the person receiving the services (NHS patients). Hence there was a concern that financially stretched commissioners would accept an unrealistically low offer price from a provider who was desperate to secure the contract, and patients would suffer when the provider failed to deliver services to an acceptable quality. Expressions of concern about price competition were not confined to MPs, as the King's Fund Report[28] noted in its account of the history of the Act. It said:

> The academics attacked the operating framework, warning of a 'race to the bottom on price that would almost certainly threaten quality' – a concern that was echoed by the NHS Partners Network, the trade body for private and voluntary providers of NHS care, which declared itself 'very nervous about the idea'.
>
> Zack Cooper, the LSE health economist, said: 'I am about as pro-competition in health care as you are going to find. But price competition would be a hugely retrograde step. To introduce it is not to learn the lessons from the NHS's own experience and from abroad.'
>
> Julian Le Grand, another advocate of choice and competition in the NHS as Blair's health adviser, echoed the concerns. Shortly afterwards, in a letter to *The Times*, the leaders of six health service unions expressed their 'extreme concerns' over price competition. The Government had managed to unite reformers and opponents, and it floundered. It took weeks finally to rule out price competition over services covered by the NHS tariff.

10.62 The government came under increasing pressure and decided to make a virtue out of the fact that it would prevent price competition in NHS services. The change was explained by the then Secretary of State for Health, Rt Hon Andrew Lansley, who wrote to the *Financial Times* on 4 March 2011. The report in the *Financial Times* said:

> **Lansley U-turn over NHS price competition**
> Andrew Lansley is to amend his NHS bill to remove the right of the new health regulator to set 'maximum' prices for NHS care ....
>
> In a statement to the Financial Times on Wednesday, Mr Lansley said it was simply 'wrong' that he wanted 'to introduce price competition into the NHS'.
>
> 'Our modernisation plans have always been about competition on quality, not on price,' he said.[29] 'We want the tariff to be a nationally regulated price, not a starting point for price competition. These amendments will put our intentions beyond doubt.'
>
> Fixed prices were originally introduced by Labour with the aim of getting hospitals to compete on quality, not on price. They cover about 60 per cent

28 See page 81 at www.kingsfund.org.uk/sites/files/kf/field/field_publication_file/never-again-story-health-social-care-nicholas-timmins-jul12.pdf.

29 Whoever drafted this article for the minister does not appear to have been aware of the January 2011 statement in favour of price competition.

of hospital care, but are set to be extended to other parts of the NHS. Health economists and others warned that both UK and international evidence suggest that allowing price competition would lead to a 'race to the bottom' that would damage quality.

Health economists and others warned that both UK and international evidence suggest that allowing price competition would lead to a 'race to the bottom' that would damage quality'

10.63 However, Mr David Bennett, who was then Chair of Monitor, was quoted in the same article giving a slightly different view. He is quoted as saying:

> . . . . as measures of quality improve, there could be a role for price competition. Ruling it out entirely is 'neither necessary nor sensible' since it can help improve NHS productivity' In spite of the tariff remaining at a fixed price, Mr Lansley made clear that where services were not covered by the tariff, GP commissioners would still be able to put them out to tender. Speaking at a health summit run by the Nuffield Trust, he said it would still be possible for hospitals to offer spare capacity to commissioners at the financial year end at lower than the tariff price when commissioners could not afford the full price.

10.64 The freedom that Mr Bennett sought to retain for price competition was only in respect of those prices not fixed by the National Tariff. However, his view of the operation of the bill was not consistent with the message that ministers gave to parliament. The *Health Service Journal*[30] reported on 18 February 2011 as follows:

> **The government has performed a significant U-turn on allowing price competition between NHS trusts and independent providers**
> A letter to senior staff from NHS chief executive David Nicholson on February 17 said there was 'no question of introducing price competition' – contradicting the Health Bill which refers to the tariff being only 'a maximum price for that service'.
>
> The Department of Health is denying the comment represents a ministerial U-turn, saying in a statement today: 'There is no U-turn because we never intended to introduce price competition. There has been incorrect reporting around this and Sir David's letter simply sets that straight'

10.65 Amendments were thus drafted to the bill. The policy position of the government was set out by the Minister, Simon Burns, carefully explained the government's policy to the Bill Committee on 3 March 2011[31] in a letter sent to members of the committee:[32]

> We are writing to notify fellow Committee Members of amendments we have today tabled regarding Monitor's function to set prices, and how this relates to competition. As colleagues are aware, we have already spent a significant amount of Committee time discussing the Bill's provisions on competition. Unfortunately, not all of these discussions have been fully informed of the Government's intentions in this area. The amendments tabled today are designed to clarify our policy and close loopholes left by the previous Government. The amendments, if accepted, would:

30 See www.hsj.co.uk/topics/finance-and-efficiency/lansley-u-turn-on-price-competition/5025934.article.

31 See https://publications.parliament.uk/pa/cm201011/cmpublic/health/110303/pm/110303s01.htm.

32 This letter does not appear to be anywhere accessible.

a. clarify our position on the tariff by removing the ability of Monitor to set maximum prices; and
b. clarify that Monitor is not able to set differential prices on grounds of ownership.

Our policy on competition in the NHS is, and always has been, that it should be based on quality rather than price. We are fully aware of the academic evidence in this area; indeed, it was the Department that commissioned some of the key studies, for example the recent work led by Professor Carol Propper.

Under the existing legislative framework, Ministers have had complete freedom to introduce price competition should they so wish; the Bill as currently drafted continues to allow for the possibility of tariffs to be set as maximum prices, rather than set solely as fixed prices.

However, while the Government's intention not to introduce a general policy of price competition is clear, it is none the less a possibility that Monitor could in future seek to pursue a different approach, subject to agreement with the NHS Commissioning Board. This is not a scenario that we have considered to be at all likely; and in the Operating Framework, we made clear a range of safeguards and conditions that had to be met before prices could be treated as a maximum. However, to ensure clarity in this area, the amendments we have laid will remove the possibility of Monitor setting maximum prices.

The Bill also allows for some further national flexibility in price setting. Monitor can specify different prices depending on whether the service is designated (under Monitor's powers to preserve continuity of services), or due to different descriptions of the provider. The latter power was designed to allow prices to adequately reflect the higher unavoidable costs some providers face compared with others; for example, the differential costs based on location. It is important that we maintain such flexibility in the future.

It has never been the Government's intention to use this power to pay certain providers an increased tariff by virtue of their ownership status. We are not, for example, at all in favour of the approach adopted under the previous Government's Independent Sector Treatment Centre (ISTC) programme of paying providers a higher tariff.

However, this is another area where our proposals have been misinterpreted. To put the matter beyond doubt, the amendments laid remove Monitor's ability to vary prices by reference to whether a provider is in public or private ownership.

We look forward to debating these amendments with colleagues at the appropriate moment in Committee proceedings.'

10.66 The government then moved the amendments in committee on 22 March 2011. The Minister said:[33]

The amendments aim to clarify the provisions on pricing. The amendments in my name clarify that we do not want Monitor to have to specify every possible price payable for every service included in the national tariff. Instead, Monitor will set a national price, agreed with the NHS commissioning board, for the services covered by the national tariff and set an adjustment that will be applied in certain circumstances. Rules will be included to specify how the final price to be paid is calculated.

33 See https://publications.parliament.uk/pa/cm201011/cmpublic/health/110322/pm/110322s01.htm.

Under the amendment, Monitor will specify a base price for the service and a series of adjustments, based on, for example, location, the complexity of treating the patient or any other factors deemed to be appropriate. The provider would then be able to calculate the prices that it would receive for treating its patients by applying the rules and adjustments. For example, a specialist provider in central London would add the London uplift and specialist additional cost to the base price to easily calculate the price it will be paid for the service. The final price paid to providers will be transparent and simple to calculate. The need for Monitor to specify all prices in all circumstances for all providers is unnecessary.

Amendments 555, 559 and 562 ensure that the national tariff includes rules governing the application of variation to the national price. Such rules will be transparent, legally binding and enforceable by Monitor. Rules on variations in tariff will specify when the price set in the national tariff changes, which may include when adjustments are made to it to take account of volume–with a marginal rate being applied when fixed costs are covered–complexity of treatment and the location of provision.

The provisions are different from those outlined in clause 104(2), which provide a legally binding framework, within which the provider and commissioner may agree to vary the specified service and price. This measure will enforce rules that must be followed by commissioners and providers on services that are specified in the national tariff.

10.67 The Minister said at column 978 that the purpose of the amendments was:

To put it beyond any doubt, misrepresentation or misunderstanding, we intend to have competition based on quality, not price.

10.68 Thus the amendments 551–557, 559, and 561–574[34] were agreed to, removing the references to maximum prices in clause 103 and to introduce the form that now appears at section 115(1). However, the amendments also sought to introduce the following to clause 104 (which is now section 116) to provide as follows:

Monitor must publish a document, to be known as 'the national tariff' which:

(a) specifies certain health care services which are or may be provided for the purposes of the NHS,
(b) specifies the method used for determining the national prices of those services,
(c) specifies the national price of each of those services,
(d) provides rules for the variation of the national price of service according to such aspects of the provision of the service, and such other matters, as are specified in the national tariff,
(e) provides rules for determining the price payable for the provision for those purposes of health care services which are not specified under subsection (1)(a)'

10.69 However, by the date of the next published version of the bill on 18 July 2011,[35] this clause was re-named clause 119 and sub-clauses (d) and (e)

34 See https://publications.parliament.uk/pa/cm201011/cmbills/132/amend/pbc1321703a.421–427.html for the text of the amendments.

35 See https://publications.parliament.uk/pa/bills/cbill/2010–2012/0221/cbill_2010–20120221_en_14.htm#pt3-ch5-l1g119.

had been removed from the bill. On 12 July 2011 the Minister said in committee:[36]

> The hon. Member for Pontypridd asked whether the Bill prevents price competition. It most certainly does, ensuring that services covered by national tariffs have a fixed price attached to them that cannot be altered for the same service delivery. That is an important element, and I look forward to further discussion on the matter on Report.

10.70 The Minister then moved amendments to clause 115 (now section 116) to remove sub-clauses (d) and (e) which were agreed without further debate in the light of the assurances that the Minister gave that the bill prevented price competition.

10.71 When the bill came back to the House on Report stage[37] the secretary of state moved an amendment to add a sub-clause (d) to (what is now) section 116(1). This added the following as a mandatory requirement of the National Tariff:

> (d) the method used for deciding whether to approve an agreement under section 122 and for determining an application under section 123 (local modifications of national prices)

10.72 The consistent message from ministers was thus that price competition was ruled out for National Tariff prices and that prices for services outside the National Tariff had to be fixed in accordance with rules made under the National Tariff. Speaking in the House of Commons on 20 March 2012,[38] the Minister introduced a series of amendments and continued to advance this explanation of the effect of the bill. He said:

> The bill makes sure that in future there can be no scope for sweetheart deals to incentivise new entrants into the NHS, *it ensures that there cannot be price competition of the sort that was allowed under the 2006 Act*, and it ensures a protection for commissioners to decide when and if it is appropriate to use competition [emphasis added].

10.73 Ministers repeatedly assured parliament that prices would be set nationally so as to rule out local competition based on prices. This was repeated in the Impact Assessment[39] published by the government which said at para B82:

> As now, competition between providers of NHS services will be on the basis of quality, not price. There will be additional safeguards against price competition and cherry picking (where a provider accepts only the easier lower cost cases).

For example, Earl Howe said on 6 March 2012 at column 1714:[40]

> It is important to remember that Monitor will work with the Commissioning Board to design tariffs which best incentivise high-quality patient care,

36 See https://publications.parliament.uk/pa/cm201011/cmpublic/health/110712/pm/110712s01.htm at column 745.

37 See https://publications.parliament.uk/pa/cm201011/cmhansrd/cm110906/debtext/110906–0002.htm.

38 See https://publications.parliament.uk/pa/cm201212/cmhansrd/cm120320/debtext/120320–0003.htm.

39 See www.parliament.uk/documents/impact-assessments/IA11–038.pdf.

40 See https://hansard.parliament.uk/Lords/2012–03–06/debates/12030640001354/HealthAndSocialCareBill.

> including through integration. That brings me to the point made by the noble Baroness, Lady Meacher. The Bill addresses the situation where a private provider could cherrypick the most profitable services to deliver, leaving an NHS hospital with the most complex procedures. It requires Monitor and the NHS Commissioning Board to take account of variations in the range of services provided by different providers, and the complexity of the needs of patients treated, to ensure a fair level of pay for providers. As a result, providers undertaking only the more simple interventions would be paid a suitably lower price. We are not seeking to stop providers choosing which services to deliver; the issue is making sure that they are paid a fair price for each of them. If prices accurately reflected the cost of services, private providers simply would not have the incentive to cherry-pick and damage the viability of other providers.

It therefore seems very clear that parliament was repeatedly assured that price competition, at least for services covered by the National Tariff, was supposed to be prevented in NHS by the HSCA 2012.

10.74 However, if parliament intended to rule out the possibility of NHS commissioners and providers agreeing cut-price deals for less than National Tariff prices and wanted to rule out price competition, that raises the question as to what is the true meaning of section 116(2)(b)? Section 116(2) of the HSCA 2012 provides:

> The national tariff may provide for rules under which the commissioner of a health care service specified in the national tariff and the providers of that service may agree to vary–
> (a) the specification of the service under subsection (1)(a), or
> (b) the national price of the service.

10.75 An initial reading would appear to suggest that, provided NHS commissioners and providers followed the rules of the National Tariff when determining prices, they could run a procurement competition on price and then 'vary' the price to, say, 75 per cent or 50 per cent of the National Tariff price for a health care service. Thus a simple reading of the section appears to deliver precisely what ministers said was outlawed by the bill.

10.76 The answer appears to be that a 'variation' to a National Tariff price is something that is initially agreed between the NHS commissioner and the provider, but it only becomes an effective change to the terms of the contract between the parties if the variation becomes a Monitor approved 'modification' in accordance with sections 124 and 125. The draftsman has used the words 'variation' and 'modification' in Chapter 4 of Part 3 to the HSCA 2012 to refer to a change in a price from the price that would be fixed in accordance with the National Tariff. However, in this context, if both a 'variation' and 'modification' had contractual effect, the words mean the same thing. They both refer to a change to the amount of money that becomes owing for the provision to an NHS patient of a health care service specified in the National Tariff. Thus either:

a) the two words should be interpreted to have the same meaning, in which case any variation has to be approved by Monitor under section 124; or
b) a 'variation' is the first stage of agreeing a price which departs from the National Tariff price but that change does not have contractual effect unless approved by Monitor under section 124; or
c) price competition is permissible.

10.77 Options (a) and (b) are consistent with the wording of section 115(1) which provides a single method by which a provider of NHS services can be paid a different price to a price payable, namely by an application to Monitor approval under sections 124 or 125. In all other cases, the price payable has to be 'on the basis of . . . the national price'. The reference to 'on the basis of' allows changes to the national price caused by factors such as the Market Forces Factor which adjusts prices between regions of England to reflect differing underlying costs. NHS England and Monitor have construed the HSCA 2012 to provide two different methods of changing a national price, namely under either section 124/5 or by an agreement under section 116(2). However, if this construction was correct, it is arguable that section 115(1) ought to have referred to *both* methods of changing prices. Section 115(1) did not do that. It only gave one method of departing from a National Tariff, and provided that this was to be a payment 'on the basis of . . . the national price', not on the 'on the basis of . . . the national price as varied under section 116(2)(b)'.

10.78 The proposed construction of section 116(2) which suggests a second method of varying National Tariff prices also makes the Monitor process under section 124 largely redundant. Section 124(1) means that an application to Monitor to approve a change to a national price under section 124 can only be made (a) where there is agreement between the commissioner and the provider, and (b) where that agreement has been reached after following the rules of the National Tariff. However, if the term 'variation' in section 116(2)(b) prescribes a different process to a 'modification', then:

a) the section 124 process becomes entirely redundant since the commissioner and the provider can agree an increase or decrease in the price without going to Monitor; and
b) the protections build in by parliament which allow upward only price changes and, even then, only in defined circumstances become meaningless because a commissioner and a provider could agree a price reduction without reference to those protections.

10.79 Hence, interpreting the words 'variation' and 'modification' to mean different things brings back the possibility of NHS services which are specified in the national Tariff being subject to price competition when parliament was specifically assured that government amendments to the Bill which became the HSCA 2012 would prevent price competition.

10.80 It follows that if the bill had the effect that was explained to parliament, the proper interpretation of the words 'variation' and 'modification' in Chapter 4 of Part 3 of the HSCA 2012 is that they mean the same thing. Thus, any commissioner and provider that wish to change the price paid for a service which is specified in the National Tariff. If that is right, both Monitor and NHS England have misunderstood the price determination provisions in the HSCA 2012 by suggesting that NHS bodies are entitled to agree 'local prices' between themselves for health care services which are specified in the National Tariff which are less than the rates set out in the National Tariff.

10.81 Treating a variation and modification as the same process also means that NHS commissioners are fully entitled to run a competitive process to select a provider but cannot do so on the basis of price for services which are specified in the National Tariff. Thus, as Ministers repeatedly explained to Parliament, where services are specified in the National Tariff, competition can only be on the basis of quality and not on the basis of price.

How can prices for healthcare services be lawfully determined under the HSCA 2012?

10.82 There are potentially four different ways in which a price payable by an NHS commissioner to a provider of NHS services for the provision of a 'healthcare service' can be determined under the statutory scheme required by the HSCA 2012. These are:

a) If the healthcare service is specified in the National Tariff, the price payable can be the National Tariff set by Monitor for that service (referred to as 'Method A' below).
b) If the healthcare service is specified in the National Tariff (or has been reached National Tariff procedures for a non-tariff service) and Monitor has agreed a modification to that price under section 124 or 125, the price payable for that service will be the National Tariff as modified by Monitor (referred to as 'Method B' below).
c) If the healthcare service is not specified in the National Tariff, the price has to be determined between the commissioner and the provider following the rules set out in the National Tariff for determining prices for healthcare services that are not specified in the National Tariff (referred to as 'Method C' below).
d) If, contrary to the arguments advanced above, the healthcare service is specified in the National Tariff and the commissioner and the provider agree to 'vary' the National Tariff price, the price payable is the National Tariff price set by Monitor for that service as varied by agreement between the commissioner and the provider (referred to as 'Method D' below).

Method A: Paying the National Tariff price

10.83 If the healthcare service delivered by the provider is specified in the National Tariff and no other arrangements operate, the price payable by an NHS commissioner to the provider for any NHS patient who is provided with that service will be the National Tariff price. The national prices for a wide range of different services, 'grouped' into HRGs, are published annually by Monitor in the 'Workbook'.[41]

10.84 NHS bodies code their activity and submit returns via the Secondary Uses Service (SUS), operated by NHS Digital.[42] The NHS Digital website explains the purpose of SUS as follows:

> The Secondary Uses Service (SUS) is the single, comprehensive repository for healthcare data in England which enables a range of reporting and analyses to support the NHS in the delivery of healthcare services.

41 See www.gov.uk/government/publications/nhs-national-tariff-payment-system-201617.

42 See http://content.digital.nhs.uk/sus.

When a patient or service user is treated or cared for, information is collected which supports their treatment. This information is also useful to commissioners and providers of NHS-funded care for 'secondary' purposes – purposes other than direct or 'primary' clinical care – such as:

- Healthcare planning
- Commissioning of services
- National Tariff reimbursement
- Development of national policy

SUS is a secure data warehouse that stores this patient-level information in line with national standards and applies complex derivations which support national tariff policy and secondary analysis.

Access to SUS is managed using Role-Based Access Control (RBAC) which grants appropriate access levels to identifiable, anonymised or pseudonymised data based on the users job role.

10.85 Thus data on patients who are treated by NHS providers is channelled to SUS, which then passes it on to commissioners who use the data to pay providers at National Tariff prices.

10.86 The actual amount payable is not the national price itself, but the national price as varied by the rules of the National Tariff. There are four types of national variations to national prices within the National Tariff as published by Monitor:

1) variations to reflect regional cost differences;
2) variations to reflect patient complexity;
3) variations to help prevent avoidable hospital stays; and
4) variations to support transition to new payment approaches.

10.87 The most widely used variation is the 'Market Forces Factor' (MFF) which reflects the underlying cost differences between hospitals operating in different areas. The National Tariff explains the operation of the MFF as follows:

5.1. Variations to reflect regional cost differences: the market forces factor
266. National prices are calculated on the basis of average costs and do not take into account some features of cost that are likely to vary across the country. The purpose of the market forces factor (MFF) is to compensate providers for the cost differences of providing healthcare in different parts of the country. Many of these cost differences are driven by geographical variation in land, labour and building costs, which cannot be avoided by NHS providers, and therefore a variation to a single national price is needed.

267. The MFF takes the form of an index. This allows a provider's location-specific costs to be compared with every other organisation. The index is constructed to always have a minimum value of 1.00. The MFF payment index operates as a multiplier to each unit of activity. The example below explains how this works in practice.

A patient attends an NHS trust for a first outpatient attendance, which has a national price of £168.
The NHS trust has an MFF payment index value of 1.0461.
The income that the trust receives from the commissioner for this outpatient attendance is £176 (£168 x 1.0461).

10.88 Paragraphs 273–279 of the National Tariff explain the adjustments that are made to the National Tariff for a comparatively small number of providers where the case-mix is significantly more complex than the average case-mix. These are mostly teaching hospitals with predominantly tertiary referrals where the 'average' payment does not recognise the complexities of the types of patients who are referred to these hospitals.

10.89 The third marginal variation is the 'Marginal Emergency Rate Rule'. The first part this tariff change, in effect, penalises A&E departments that treat too many patients. The full text of the rule is as follows:

> **5.3. Variations to help prevent avoidable hospital stays**
>
> *5.3.1. Marginal rate emergency rule*
>
> 280. The marginal rate emergency rule was introduced in 2010/11 in response to a growth in emergency admissions in England that could not be explained by population growth and A&E attendance growth alone. It was made up primarily of emergency spells lasting less than 48 hours.
>
> 281. The purpose of the marginal rate emergency rule is twofold. It is intended to incentivise:
>
> a. lower rates of emergency admissions
> b. acute providers to work with other parties in the local health economy to reduce the demand for emergency care.
>
> 282. The marginal rate emergency rule sets a baseline monetary value (specified in GBP) for emergency admissions at a provider. A provider is then paid 70% of the national price for any increases in the value of emergency admissions above this baseline. Further guidance for commissioners on investing retained funds can be found on our website.[43]

10.90 The second part of this rule applies a marginal rate to penalise re-admissions of patients within 30 days (see para 302 and following).

10.91 The final change is in section 5.4 concerning variations to support transition to new payment approaches. Paragraph 313 of the National Tariff provides:

> **5.4. Variations to support transition to new payment approaches**
> 313. New or changing payment approaches can alter provider income or commissioner expenditure. For some organisations, the financial impact can be significant and could be difficult to manage in one step'

10.92 However the only area of clinical practice where the rules can be varied under this part concerns 'Best Practice Tariffs' for hip and knee replacements (see para 313 and following). Thus, at least under the 2017/18 version of the National Tariff, this does not permit wider variations to the prices paid for services specified in the National Tariff to support new payment approaches.

10.93 It is beyond the scope of this book to attempt to describe every aspect of the rules of the National Tariff. In any event, these rules change on an annual basis. However, the essential purpose of the National Tariff is to provide a rules based system which ought to ensure that NHS providers in different organisations are paid the same price for delivering the same type of care for cohorts of NHS patients. That does not mean that an NHS provider is compensated precisely for the cost of treatment to each individual patient because, across a cohort, there will be clinical variations. However the system is designed to operate in a 'swings and roundabouts' manner, under which the provider is provided with a fixed payment for

43 See www.nhsimprovement.nhs.uk.

carrying out a procedure which, given the variation in complexities across different patients, will provide a reasonable level of remuneration to compensate the provider for the costs of delivering the service.

Method B: Modifying the price under sections 124 and 125 of the HSCA 2012

10.94 Section 124 enables NHS commissioners and providers of NHS services to agree that a provider should be paid a higher price for a service than the price set out in the National Tariff. Section 124 provides:

(1) The commissioner and the provider of a health care service may agree that the price payable to the provider for the provision of the service for the purposes of the NHS in such circumstances or areas as may be determined in accordance with the agreement is the price determined in accordance with the national tariff for that service as modified in accordance with the agreement.
(2) An agreement under this section must specify the date on which the modification is to take effect; and a date specified for that purpose may be earlier than the date of the agreement (but not earlier than the date on which the national tariff took effect).
(3) An agreement under this section has effect only if it is approved by Monitor.
(4) An agreement submitted for approval under subsection (3) must be supported by such evidence as Monitor may require.
(5) Monitor may approve an agreement under this section only if, having applied the method specified under section 116(1)(d), it is satisfied that, without a modification to the price determined in accordance with the national tariff for that service, it would be uneconomic for the provider to provide the service for the purposes of the NHS.
(6) Where an agreement is approved under subsection (3), Monitor must send a notice to the Secretary of State and such clinical commissioning groups, providers and other persons as it considers appropriate.
(7) Monitor must also publish the notice.
(8) The notice must specify–
 (a) the modification, and
 (b) the date on which it takes effect.
(9) If the Secretary of State considers that the modification gives or may give rise (or, where it has yet to take effect, would or might give rise) to liability for breach of an EU obligation, the Secretary of State may give a direction to that effect; and the modification is (or is to be) of no effect in so far as it is subject to the direction'

10.95 Section 116(1)(d) provides that the National Tariff should set out rules for such applications. The key limitation is in section 124(5) which provides that Monitor is only entitled to approve a modification if it is satisfied that, without a modification to the price, 'it would be uneconomic for the provider to provide the service for the purposes of the NHS'. This means that, in practice, this provision only allows upward price increases. The wording of the test suggests that Monitor ought to ask itself whether it would be uneconomic for this particular provider to provide the service for the NHS at the National Tariff price. This could be because, for example, the provider will only see a limited number of patients with a particular condition, and therefore will not have the advantage of economies of scale available to larger providers. However, it could also be uneconomic for the provider to provide services at the National Tariff rate because its cost base is particularly high. That could be due to any number of different factors, but the test appears to focus on the objective costs to the provider as opposed to benchmarking that provider's costs against the average (which of course is the purpose of the National Tariff). However, Monitor has a discretion to decide whether to approve a proposed higher price, even if the test in section 124(5) is met. The exercise of discretion allows Monitor to refuse to agree a higher price, even if the test is met, if the higher price is not considered by Monitor to be objectively justifiable.

10.96 Section 125 covers a situation where an NHS commissioner is seeking to require a provider to provide a service but the provider considers that it would not be economic to provide that service at National Tariff rate, but where there is no agreement between the NHS commissioner and the provider about the price. It allows a provider of NHS services to apply to Monitor to set a price for a health care service specified in the National Tariff which is higher than the price that would be payable applying the rules of the National Tariff. Section 125 of the HSCA 2012 provides:

> (1) Monitor may, on an application by a provider of a health care service who has failed to reach an agreement under section 124 with the commissioner, decide that the price payable to the provider for the provision of the service for the purposes of the NHS in such circumstances or areas as Monitor may determine is to be the price determined in accordance with the national tariff for that service as modified in such way as Monitor may determine.
>
> (2) An application under this section must be supported by such evidence as Monitor may require.
>
> (3) Monitor may grant an application under this section only if, having applied the method under section 116(1)(d), it is satisfied that, without a modification to the price determined in accordance with the national tariff for that service, it would be uneconomic for the provider to provide the service for the purposes of the NHS.
>
> (4) Subsections (5) to (8) apply where Monitor grants an application under this section.
>
> (5) The decision by Monitor on the application takes effect on such date as Monitor may determine; and a date determined for that purpose may be earlier than the date of the decision (but not earlier than the date on which the national tariff took effect).
>
> (6) Monitor must send a notice of the decision to the Secretary of State and such clinical commissioning groups, providers and other persons as it considers appropriate.
>
> (7) Monitor must also publish the notice.
>
> (8) The notice must specify–
> (a) the modification, and
> (b) the date on which it takes effect.
>
> (9) If the Secretary of State considers that the modification gives or may give rise (or, where it has yet to take effect, would or might give rise) to liability for breach of an EU obligation, the Secretary of State may give a direction to that effect; and the modification is (or is to be) of no effect in so far as it is subject to the direction'

10.97 The power for Monitor to impose a higher price on a commissioner where the commissioner and the provider cannot agree a price between then can only be exercised by Monitor if it is satisfied that 'it would be uneconomic for the provider to provide the service for the purposes of the NHS' at the National Tariff price. It is thus the same test as where the parties are agreed that a higher price should be paid. However if Monitor exercises its powers to set a higher price, the provider is entitled to be paid the higher price. However, just as under section 124, Monitor has a discretion to exercise to decide whether to approve a price rise, even if the statutory test met.

10.98 If Monitor does approve the higher price, there does not appear to be any provision to entitle an NHS commissioner to refuse to enter into a contract with the provider at this price.

Method C: Determining prices for health care services that are not specified in the National Tariff

10.99 There are a substantial number of health care services which are either not specified in the National Tariff or where the health care service is specified in the National Tariff but no 'price' has been specified for the provision that service.[44] Section 115(2) of the HSCA 2012 provides:

> If a health care service is not specified in the national tariff, the price payable for the provision of that service for the purposes of the NHS is such price as is determined in accordance with the rules provided for in the national tariff for that purpose.

10.100 It follows that the absence of a national tariff price does not permit NHS commissioners and providers a free hand to set prices at a purely market rate where there is no National Tariff price. The NHS commissioner and the provider are required to follow the rules of the National Tariff to work together (and with both clinicians and the public) to determine a fair price for the services that are to be provided.

10.101 The relevant rules are explained at para 449 and following of the National Tariff which provides:

> 449. For many NHS services there are no national prices. Some of these services have nationally specified currencies, but others do not. In both cases, commissioners and providers must work together to agree prices for these services. The 2012 Act confers on Monitor the power to set rules for local price-setting of such services, as agreed with NHS England, including rules specifying national currencies for such services. We have set both general rules and rules specific to particular services. There are two types of general rule:
>
> a. Rules that apply in all cases when a local price is set for services without a national price. See Section 6.4.1.
>
> b. Rules that apply only to local price-setting for services with a national currency (but no national price). See Section 6.4.2.
>
> 450. As well as the general rules, there are rules specific to particular services. See Sections 6.4.3 to 6.4.7.

44 The services where there is a 'national currency' which specifies the services but no national price are described at para 453 of the National Tariff.

10.102 Paragraph 452 then provides:

> 452. Rules 1 and 2 apply when providers and commissioners agree local prices for services without national prices. The rules apply irrespective of whether or not there is a national currency specified for the service.
>
> Local pricing rules: general rules for all services without a national price
>
> Rule 1: Providers and commissioners must apply the principles in Section 6.1 when agreeing prices for services without a national price.
>
> Rule 2: Commissioners and providers should have regard to the efficiency and cost uplift factors for 2017/18 and 2018/19 (as set out in sections 4.7 and 4.8 of this document) when setting local prices for services without a national price for 2017/18 and 2018/19, respectively.

10.103 The requirement to 'apply the principles' in section 6.1 means, in effect, that NHS commissioners and providers are required to follow the procedures set out at that part of the National Tariff when fixing prices. However the requirement to 'apply the principles' suggests that there may be an element of discretion to permit NHS commissioners and providers to decide precisely how they are going to follow the procedures set out in the National Tariff and could depart from the precise form of the procedures specified in the National Tariff without acting unlawfully. If NHS commissioners and providers depart from the procedures specified in the National Tariff, there is a danger that their prices will be subject to a later legal challenge (either by one of the contracting parties or by a third party).

10.104 The procedures specified in section 6.1 of the National Tariff are as follows:

> **6.1. Principles applying to all local variations, local modifications and local prices**
>
> 326. Commissioners and providers must apply the following three principles when agreeing a local payment approach:
>
> a. the approach must be in the best interests of patients
> b. the approach must promote transparency to improve accountability and encourage the sharing of best practice, and
> c. the provider and commissioner(s) must engage constructively with each other when trying to agree local payment approaches.
>
> 327. These principles are explained in more detail in sections 6.1.1 to 6.1.3 and are additional to other legal obligations on commissioners and providers. These include other rules set out in the national tariff, and the requirements of competition law, procurement law, regulations under Section 75 of the 2012 Act, and NHS Improvement's provider licence.
>
> *6.1.1. Best interest of patients*
>
> 328. Local variations, modifications and prices must be in the best interest of patients today and in the future. In agreeing a locally determined price, commissioners and providers must therefore consider the following factors:
>
> a. Quality: how will the agreement maintain or improve the outcomes, patient experience and safety of healthcare today and in the future?
> b. Cost effectiveness: how will the agreement make healthcare more cost effective, without reducing quality, to enable the most effective use of scarce resources for patients today and in the future?
> c. Innovation: how will the agreement support, where appropriate, the development of new and improved service delivery models which are in the best interest of patients today and in the future?

d. Allocation of risk: how will the agreement allocate the risks associated with unit costs, patient volumes and quality in a way that protects the best interests of patients today and in the future?

6.1.2. Transparency

329. Local variations, modifications and prices must be transparent. Increased transparency will make commissioners and providers more accountable to each other, patients, the general public and other interested stakeholders. Transparent agreements also mean that best practice examples and innovation in service delivery models or payment approaches can be shared more widely. In agreeing a locally determined price, commissioners and providers must therefore consider the following factors:

a. Accountability: how will relevant information be shared in a way that allows commissioners and providers to be held to account by one another, patients, the general public and other stakeholders?
b. Sharing best practice: how will innovations in service delivery or payment approaches be shared in a way that spreads best practice?

6.1.3. Constructive engagement

330. Providers and commissioners must engage constructively with each other to decide on the mix of services, delivery model and payment approach that deliver the best value for patients in their local area. This process should involve clinicians, patient groups and other relevant stakeholders where possible. It should also facilitate the development of positive working relationships between commissioners and new or existing providers over time, as constructive engagement is intended to support better and more informed decision-making in both the short and long term.

331. In agreeing a locally determined price, commissioners and providers must therefore consider the following factors:

- Framework for negotiations: have the parties agreed a framework for negotiating local variations, modifications and prices that is consistent with the existing guidelines in the NHS Standard Contract and procurement law (if applicable)?
- Information-sharing: are there agreed policies for sharing relevant and accurate information in a timely and transparent way to facilitate effective and efficient decision making?
- Involvement of relevant clinicians and other stakeholders: are relevant clinicians and other stakeholders, such as patients or service users, involved in the decision-making process?
- Short and long term objectives: are clearly defined short and long term strategic objectives for service improvement and delivery agreed before starting price negotiations?

6.1.4. Guidance on applying the principles applying to all local variations, local modifications and local prices

Record-keeping

332. Providers and commissioners should maintain a record of how local payment approaches comply with the principles. The content and level of detail of this record will vary depending on the circumstances. For example, more information is likely to be required for high value contracts than for lower value contracts. Further (non-exhaustive) examples are provided in the box below.

Examples of what information a record might contain

Providers and commissioners should consider whether to include the following in their record:

- reasons for choosing to use a local payment approach
- details of any engagement with patients, community groups, carers and other third parties and how their views have been taken into account before agreeing the approach
- reasons for specifying the services in a particular way
- rationale for combining payment for several different services as a bundle and the composition of that bundle, if applicable
- analysis of how the services will be delivered in a way that is co-ordinated from the perspective of patients alongside other health-care, health-related and social care services
- details of the due diligence applied to the information used to inform the local payment approach
- rationale for key terms of the agreement, for example, prices, quality requirements that the provider must satisfy, how performance will be assessed during the contract, the consequences of breaches, and the duration of the contract.

How we will assess whether local payment approaches are in the best interests of patients

333. When assessing compliance with the requirement to apply the principle that local payment approaches must be in the best interests of patients, we will examine whether providers and commissioners have considered all relevant factors. The extent to which, and way in which, the four factors listed in Section 6.1.1 need to be considered will differ according to the characteristics of the services and the circumstances of the agreement.

334. To have considered a relevant factor properly, we would expect providers and commissioners to have:

a. obtained sufficient information
b. used appropriately qualified/experienced individuals to assess the information
c. followed an appropriate process to arrive at a conclusion.

335. It is up to providers and commissioners to determine how to consider the factors set out above based on the matter in hand.

Evaluation and sharing of best practice

336. We encourage commissioners and providers to use the rules for locally determined prices as a basis for considering how they can improve the payment system, especially where care is being delivered in a new way. We are interested in learning from commissioners and providers that are implementing new payment approaches to enhance system-wide incentives: for example, to focus on prevention, integration of care, improved outcomes and improved patient experiences. Such payment approaches might include pathway, capitation or outcomes-based payments.

337. To determine whether local payment approaches have achieved their desired objectives and inform future decision-making, we recommend that commissioners and providers plan to evaluate the success of new payment approaches. We encourage commissioners and providers to share the results of any evaluation processes.

Guidance on a framework for constructive engagement

338. We believe that the principles will be consistent with existing practice for many providers and commissioners. However, we recognise that this will not always be the case, particularly where providers and commissioners do not have existing contractual relationships.

339. Below we set out a framework that could be used as a guide to facilitate constructive engagement where commissioners and providers do not already have a framework. It has been designed with local payment approaches agreed through negotiation rather than competitive procurement in mind. It includes four stages, which are explained in more detail below. In summary, to implement the framework in full, providers and commissioners would have to:

a. **establish a working group** for contract negotiations in relation to locally determined prices
b. **define roles and responsibilities** for members of the working group, including relevant clinicians and other stakeholders, where appropriate
c. **agree objectives, timescales and rules** for the working group, including rules on information sharing, deadlines and the responsibilities of each party when providing or handling information for contract negotiations
d. **document progress and outputs** for the working group and contract negotiation, including any planned evaluation, if appropriate'

10.105 Thus NHS commissioners and providers who follow the above rules are entitled to reach mutually agreeable 'prices' under a contract which requires the provider to provide health care services that are not specified in the National Tariff to NHS patients. Once a 'price' for a healthcare service has been agreed following the above procedures, section 115(2) means that the NHS commissioner is under a statutory duty to pay the provider the agreed price every time the provider provides a healthcare service of the type defined in the contract to an NHS patient for whom the NHS commissioner has commissioning responsibility. If the provider provides a healthcare service to another NHS commissioner (with whom the provider does not have a contract), the guidance set out above explains that this is 'non-contract activity' and the provider is entitled to bill the relevant NHS commissioner for providing that service at the agreed price.

10.106 However, what happens (as is regrettably the norm) if an NHS commissioner and a provider agree prices for the provision of services to NHS patients without following the procedures set out in the National Tariff? The High Court has not considered the contractual effect of NHS bodies agreeing terms which breach the statutory requirements of the HSCA 2012.[45] However, the House of Lords considered a similar issue in *Johnson v Moreton.*[46] The question in *Johnson* was whether a contract could be enforced if the parties had purported to contract out of a statutory rights. Mr and Mrs Johnson let a farm on an agricultural lease to Mr Moreton. The Agricultural Holdings Act 1948 gave security of tenure to tenant farmers. However, the agricultural lease purported to contract out of that

45 The only occasion on which these provisions were considered (to the knowledge of the author) was an expert dispute resolution process relating to Corby Urgent Care Centre. The outcome was reported in the professional press but has not been formally published. However the expert found that the requirements in the National Tariff were mandatory and thus the failure by the Corby CCG to follow those requirements meant that a purported to agreement to pay the operators of Corby Urgent Care Centre a price that was below the National Tariff was unenforceable. The outcome was that the operators of Corby Urgent Care Centre were entitled to substantial back-payments based on the National Tariff rate.

46 [1980] AC 37.

statutory right. The court was required to decide whether a contract which had been agreed in a manner which departed from statutory protections was nonetheless enforceable as a private law contract between the parties. Lord Salmon observed that:

> Accordingly if clause 27 is enforceable the security of tenure which Parliament clearly intended to confer, and did confer upon tenant farmers for the public good would have become a dead letter.

10.107 The conclusion reached by the House of Lords was that parties to a private law contract could contract out of statutory processes and protections if these were introduced solely for the private benefit of the contracting parties. However, if parliament intended these terms to operate in all relevant contracts and/or the statutory provisions existed for public good (as opposed to being solely for the private benefit of the contracting parties), a term seeking to contract out of the mandated statutory protections would be unenforceable. The same principle applies to the duty to pay workers the National Minimum Wage (under the National Minimum Wage Act 1998).

10.108 The rules by which prices for the provision of NHS services which are not specified in the National Tariff are to be determined have a clear 'public interest' purpose. The aim of the processes is to ensure that a price is fixed which is in the best interests of NHS patients. Thus, it seems highly likely that a contractual agreement on price between an NHS commissioner and a provider of NHS services (which are not specified in the National Tariff) where the price has been fixed through a process which fails to comply with the rules of the National Tariff may be an unenforceable agreement.

10.109 Unfortunately, NHS commissioners have generally failed to follow the procedures under the National Tariff set out above when seeking to agree prices for services which are not specified in the National Tariff. In principle, there seems no reason why a provider should not register a dispute about the 'price' paid under the contract and seek to have this re-evaluated in accordance with the procedures which ought to have been followed at a point that the contract was originally signed.

Method D: Varying the price under section 116(2)(b)

10.110 The difficulties in working out the effect of HSCA 2012 s116(2) is described above. However, if this section provides an alternative route by which commissioners and providers are able to vary the price of a healthcare service that is specified in the National Tariff, as a minimum, NHS commissioners and providers are required to follow the rules of National Tariff in any process to seek to agree a varied price. A variation to the price may (or may not) be accompanied by a variation to the specification of the healthcare service which is the subject of the price variation. The National Tariff rules that a commissioner and provider have to follow to agree such a variation are the same rules as those for setting local prices (see para 10.104 above). In practice, the National Tariff rules are not followed because NHS commissioners tend to run procurement competitions which largely seek to secure the best price for a service and then seek to 'vary' the national price to the competitively achieved price by way of an agreement with the successful tenderer. Such a process may well give rise to a series of difficult legal issues (see para 10.106 above).

Are 'block contracts' legally permissible under the HSCA 2012 statutory scheme?

10.111 An NHS 'block contract' is an arrangement under which an NHS commissioner pays a defined sum of money to an NHS provider in order to deliver defined NHS services to the patients for whom the NHS commissioner has commissioning responsibility. These are frequently used in mental health and community services contracts. A feature of these 'block' contracts is that the payment is not linked to the number of patients treated by the provider or the complexity of the treatments provided. These types of arrangements existed before the HSCA 2012 was implemented and have largely remained unchanged.

10.112 One of the consequences of this type of contracting arrangement is that the provider cannot expand its services to meet additional demand because the amount of money that is provided is fixed, irrespective of the number of patients. Hence, by way of example, there is an acute shortage of child and adolescent specialist inpatient mental health beds provided by NHS mental health trusts. Many of these trusts have block contracts with their commissioners and accordingly cannot increase the amount they charge their commissioners if additional services are provided. In contrast, an acute hospital providing hip replacement services to the same commissioners will increase its charges if more patients are referred to the acute trust for this type of operation.

10.113 There are serious questions to as to whether this type of contracting arrangement complies with section 115(2) of the HSCA 2012. A 'healthcare service' is probably the provision of a service or group of services to a particular, individual patient. Section 115(2) requires a price to be determined for that 'healthcare service'. The money is supposed to follow individual patients, so any arrangement which pays the same amount, regardless of the number of patients treated and/or the complexity of the treatment is failing to identify a price for each of the healthcare services provided by that provider to NHS patients. Further, the procedures which are required to be followed under the National Tariff before prices for healthcare services can be agreed are difficult to reconcile with the outcome being a 'block contract'.

10.114 In practice, block contract arrangements are used by NHS commissioners and providers even though the statutory mandated rules have not been followed. However, as austerity continues to affect the NHS, groups representing patient interests may well challenge the lawfulness of any arrangements which fail to comply with the statutory provisions. Accordingly, maintaining block contracts or agreeing contracts prices for non-tariff services otherwise than in accordance with the rules of the National Tariff, gives rise to considerable legal risks for NHS bodies.

How can the rules for determining prices be operated within a competitive procurement exercise?

10.115 This is considered under chapter 21 on procurement. However, the strong message from the parliamentary materials is that NHS procurement ought to be conducted on quality alone and not on a combination of price and quality.

The dispute resolution provisions within the NHS Standard Contract

10.116 If there is a dispute between the commissioner and the provider who hold an NHS standard contract, the dispute resolution provisions in GC14 provide for a three-stage process, namely:

1) escalated negotiation;
2) mediation; and
3) expert determination.

10.117 The terms of GC14 provide as follows:

GC14 Dispute Resolution

14.1 The provisions of GC14.2 to 14.21 will not apply when any Party in Dispute seeks an injunction relating to a matter arising out of GC20 (Confidential Information of the Parties).

Escalated Negotiation

14.2 If any Dispute arises, the Parties in Dispute must first attempt to settle it by any of them making a written offer to negotiate to the others. During the Negotiation Period each of the Parties in Dispute must negotiate and be represented:

14.2.1 for the first 10 Operational Days, by a senior person who where practicable has not had any direct day-to-day involvement in the matter and has authority to settle the Dispute; and

14.2.2 for the last 5 Operational Days, by their chief executive, director, or member of its Governing Body who has authority to settle the Dispute.

14.3 Where practicable, no Party in Dispute should be represented by the same individual under GC14.2.1 and 14.2.2.

Mediation

14.4 If the Parties in Dispute are unable to settle the Dispute by negotiation, they must, within 5 Operational Days after the end of the Negotiation Period, submit the Dispute:

14.4.1 to mediation arranged jointly by NHS Improvement and NHS England, where the Commissioners are CCGs and/or NHS England and the Provider is an NHS Trust; or

14.4.2 to mediation by CEDR or other independent body or organisation agreed between the Parties and set out in the Particulars, in all other cases.

14.5 Mediations under GC14.4.1 will follow the mediation process agreed between NHS Improvement and NHS England from time to time:

14.6 Mediations under GC14.4.2 will follow the mediation process of CEDR or other independent body or organisation named in the Particulars.

Expert Determination

14.7 If the Parties in Dispute are unable to settle the Dispute through mediation, the Dispute must be referred to expert determination, by one Party in Dispute giving written notice to that effect to the other Parties in Dispute following closure of the failed mediation. The Expert Determination Notice must include a brief statement of the issue or issues which it is desired to refer, the expertise required in the expert, and the solution sought.

14.8 If the Parties in Dispute have agreed upon the identity of an expert and the expert has confirmed in writing their readiness and willingness to embark upon the expert determination, then that person will be appointed as the Expert.

14.9 Where the Parties in Dispute have not agreed upon an expert, or where that person has not confirmed their willingness to act, then any Party in Dispute may apply to CEDR for the appointment of an expert. The request must be in writing, accompanied by a copy of the Expert Determination Notice and the appropriate fee and must be copied simultaneously to the other Parties in Dispute. The other Parties in Dispute may make representations to CEDR regarding the expertise required in the expert. The person nominated by CEDR will be appointed as the Expert.

14.10 The Party in Dispute serving the Expert Determination Notice must send to the Expert and to the other Parties in Dispute within 5 Operational Days of the appointment of the Expert a statement of its case, including a copy of the Expert Determination Notice, the Contract, details of the circumstances giving rise to the Dispute, the reasons why it is entitled to the solution sought, and the evidence upon which it relies. The statement of case must be confined to the issues raised in the Expert Determination Notice.

14.11 The Parties in Dispute not serving the Expert Determination Notice must reply to the Expert and to the other Parties in Dispute within 5 Operational Days of receiving the statement of case, giving details of what is agreed and what is disputed in the statement of case and the reasons why.

14.12 The Expert must produce a written decision with reasons within 30 Operational Days of receipt of the statement of case referred to in GC14.11, or any longer period as is agreed by the Parties in Dispute after the Dispute has been referred.

14.13 The Expert will have complete discretion as to how to conduct the expert determination, and will establish the procedure and timetable.

14.14 The Parties in Dispute must comply with any request or direction of the Expert in relation to the expert determination.

14.15 The Expert must decide the matters set out in the Expert Determination Notice, together with any other matters which the Parties in Dispute and the Expert agree are within the scope of the expert determination.

14.16 The Parties in Dispute must bear their own costs and expenses incurred in the expert determination and are jointly liable for the costs of the Expert.

14.17 The decision of the Expert is final and binding, except in the case of fraud, collusion, bias, manifest error or material breach of instructions on the part of the Expert, in which case a Party will be permitted to apply to Court for an Order that:

14.17.1 the Expert reconsider his decision (either all of it or part of it); or
14.17.2 the Expert's decision be set aside (either all of it or part of it).

14.18 If a Party in Dispute does not abide by the Expert's decision the other Parties in Dispute may apply to Court to enforce it.

14.19 All information, whether oral, in writing or otherwise, arising out of or in connection with the expert determination will be inadmissible as evidence in any current or subsequent litigation or other proceedings whatsoever, with the exception of any information which would in any event have been admissible or disclosable in any such proceedings

14.20 The Expert is not liable for anything done or omitted in the discharge or purported discharge of their functions, except in the case of fraud or bad faith, collusion, bias, or material breach of instructions on the part of the Expert.

14.21 The Expert is appointed to determine the Dispute or Disputes between the Parties in Dispute and the Expert's decision may not be relied upon by third parties, to whom the Expert will have no duty of care.

10.118 The reference to 'CEDR' is a reference to the Centre for Effective Dispute Resolution,[47] 70 Fleet Street, London EC4Y 1EU. CEDR can be approached by either party and, for a fee, will appoint an expert to conduct the expert determination process. Once the expert is appointed, the expert will have a wide discretion to set the process and to issue directions to both parties as to the material that the expert needs in order to determine the dispute.

10.119 Once the expert has made his or her decision, the expert determination is generally binding. The recent case of *Walton Homes Ltd v Staffordshire County Council*[48] emphasised the very limited scope that the court has to interfere with a decision by an expert. The fact that the expert may have made an error of law or fact in his determination is usually insufficient to get the determination set aside: see *Veba Oil Supply & Trading GmbH v Petrotrade Inc.*[49] An expert determination will only usually be set aside if a party can prove one of the following:

a) *Material departure from instructions*, in a case such as *Shafi v Rutherford.*[50]
b) *Failure to state reasons*: If the expert does not adequately state the reasons for his decision, a court can direct an expert to do so (*Halifax Life Ltd v The Equitable Life Assurance Society*[51]).
c) *Fraud or collusion*: If the expert has reached his determination due to fraud or collusion with one of the parties, then the determination can be set aside by the court (*Campbell v Edwards*[52]).
d) *The certificate not being certain:* If an expert is determining a situation which requires the expert to produce a certificate (as is sometimes the case in accounting scenarios) then the certificate cannot be uncertain or qualified (*Shorrock Ltd v Meggitt plc*[53]).
e) *Partiality:* If an expert has shown actual bias or there is a real danger of injustice resulting from the alleged bias, then the court has the power to set aside the expert determination (*Hickman v Roberts*[54]).

10.120 Thus, in practice, a NHS commissioner and provider are likely to be bound by the consequences of the expert determination. This high level of finality can be contrasted with decisions of the FHSAU where either party can issue judicial review proceedings to challenge the lawfulness of the decision: see *R (Hussain and others) v Secretary of State for the Health Department and another.*[55]

47 See www.cedr.com/.
48 [2013] EWHC 2554 (Ch).
49 [2001] EWCA Civ 1832.
50 [2014] EWCA Civ 1186.
51 [2007] EWHC 503 (Comm).
52 [1976] 1 WLR 403.
53 [1991] BCC 471.
54 [1913] AC 229.
55 [2011] EWCA Civ 800.

CHAPTER 11

Primary medical care contracting

continued

Introduction

11.1 Unlike doctors working in hospitals, NHS general practitioners (GPs) have never been required to be employees of the NHS. General practices operated as private sector businesses prior to World War II, with many patients covered by insurance schemes. As a result, the British Medical Association (BMA) rejected the government's original proposal that GPs working in the NHS[1] should become local authority employees and argued that they should remain as self-employed individual professionals, contracting into the new NHS as required. This reality was accepted by the Minister for Health, Rt Hon Aneurin Bevan, MP, and thus when the NHS was set up in 1948 (as a result of the National Health Service Act (NHS Act) 1946), general practices continued without general practice doctors being required to become NHS employees. GPs have largely remained as self-employed professionals, operating 'for profit' businesses since the NHS was created.

11.2 Although there have been various experiments with directly employed GPs working for NHS bodies, in general these have not been successful or popular with doctors[2]. Hence the vast majority of GP practices are staffed by doctors who are not employees of the NHS, but who work under a variety of contractual relationships to deliver services to NHS patients. For the greater part of the history of the NHS, the vast majority of GP practices operated as single-handed practices or medical partnerships where the partners were the GPs who delivered the majority of the services to patients. Thus, the GP both delivered professional medical services to NHS patients, and was a 'business owner' because he or she owned a share of the business in which those medical services were delivered.

11.3 In recent years, the complex demands of general practice, the investment needed to deliver an effective GP service and the transfer of medical work from hospitals into the community has created more of a distinction between the GPs who provide professional services to NHS patients and the individuals who own the medical businesses within which those services are delivered. 'Super practices', federated practices and medical companies all compete for NHS general practice contracts. It should, of course, be largely irrelevant to the patient whether the GP who sits on the other side of the consulting room table is a partner, salaried partner, salaried employee of a practice or a locum – the services provided by the GP should be driven by the professional obligations owed by the GP, as a professional doctor, to the patient. There would be something seriously awry if the services that patients receive were affected by the status of their NHS GP. However, the legal duties owed by an individual

1 This chapter is concerned with GPs who work within the NHS. There are also GPs who work in private medical practices where the fees are covered by payments made by patients, employers or insurance companies. Those types of medical practices are outside the scope of this chapter.

2 However, there are an increasing number of PMS practices where the doctors are employees of NHS foundation trusts, and where the push for integration in the NHS is causing the foundation trust to employ both primary and secondary care staff. This appears to be a model which is working well in places where there is good leadership in the foundation trust. It remains to be seen whether it can be scaled up to other areas and/or is a long-term sustainable model for general practice.

GP to everyone other than the patient are vastly different depending on the status of the GP.

GP contracting – a brief history

11.4 Section 29 of the National Health Service Act (NHS Act) 1977 provided that health authorities were required to 'arrange as respects their area with medical practitioners to provide personal medical services for all persons in the area who wish to take advantage of the arrangements'. Thus, under the NHS 1977 Act (and the NHS Act 1946 which preceded it), GP practices were licensed by the NHS to deliver services to NHS patients, and were paid for providing primary care services to those NHS patients under a statutory scheme. The terms of service for GPs were set out in regulations, and the payment scheme was governed by directions made by the secretary of state. This scheme was known as 'General Medical Services'(GMS) and, at the time, was the only mechanism under which GPs could provide primary care services for NHS patients.

11.5 With effect from April 1993, the Conservative government created the division between 'purchasers' and 'providers' in the NHS. The legislation which brought this about was the National Health Service and Community Care Act (NHSCCA) 1990. It created two models of commissioning – one based on health authorities, and the other based on general practice. General practices were encouraged to become commissioners through a route that became known as 'fundholding'. This broadly meant that the GP practice held a real or notional budget that was used to commission secondary care for the patients of the practice.

11.6 Under GP fundholding, GPs held real budgets with which they purchased primarily non-urgent elective and community care for their patients; they had the right to keep any savings and had the freedom to deliver new services. The aim was to give GPs a financial incentive to manage costs and to apply some competitive pressure to hospital providers.[3] Some GP practices came together in consortia, creating larger organisations to pool financial risk and share resources. From 1994 the total purchasing pilot scheme (TPP) allowed general practices – either individually or in groups – to commission all services for their patients, though most were highly selective in what they chose to purchase. TPPs acted as sub-committees of health authorities and used an indicative, rather than a real, budget. However, payments to GPs for their own work continued to be made under the general statutory scheme. Section 29(4) of the NHS Act 1977 provided, somewhat cryptically, that payment to a GP:

3 The practical effect of fundholding was explained by a GP to one of the authors. He said that, prior to fundholding, he used to send a bottle of whisky each Christmas to the local surgeons to persuade them to see and treat his patients when he referred them to a hospital for elective surgical treatment. After fundholding, the surgeons sent the whisky to the GP practice to seek to persuade the GP to refer patients to the surgeons; because the income of the surgeons depended on the GP practice referring patients to them. The flow of Christmas whisky indicated (for good or bad) the way that the balance of power between GPs and the hospitals was changed by fundholding.

> ... shall not, except in special circumstances, consist wholly or mainly of a fixed salary which has no reference to the number of patients for whom he has undertaken to provide such services.

11.7 The details of the payment to GPs under GMS contracts is set out in the annual 'statement of financial entitlements' (SFE). This was (and remains) a direction made by the secretary of state every year which sets out the sums that GP practices[4] are entitled to be paid for every aspect of their work. The secretary of state issues amended directions to update the details of payments to GPs. Payment under many 'Personal Medical Services' (PMS) agreements or 'Alternative Provider Medical Services' (APMS) agreements is linked to the sums paid under the SFE.

11.8 The incoming Labour government abolished GP fundholding in 1997, but retained the purchaser/provider split. However, just before the 1997 general election, parliament passed the National Health Service (Primary Care) Act (NHS(PC)A) 1997. The NHS(PC)A 1997 introduced a new form of 'arrangement' for primary care contracting called a 'Personal Medical Services' (PMS) agreement. This was the first opportunity for GP practices to work under a contract, and thus move away from working under a statutory scheme. The original PMS agreements were pilot agreements (under Part 1 of the NHS(PC)A 1997) which were only designed to last for a limited period. There was no 'standard' form of wording for a PMS agreement, because the idea was to allow local health authorities to be flexible in agreeing new ways of working with innovative GPs. A doctor who provided GP services to NHS patients under a PMS agreement was not permitted to deliver General Medical Services, but could revert back to a GMS arrangement at any point.

11.9 Part 2 of the NHS(PC)A 1997 proposed amendments to the NHS Act 1977 which allowed Health Authorities to enter into permanent PMS agreements. However, these powers were not implemented until March 2004 because the Department of Health wanted to evaluate the success or otherwise of the temporary pilot PMS agreements which had been brought into existence under Part 1 of the NHS(PC)A 1997.

11.10 By 2004, the government had decided that all GP practices should have contracts with their local NHS commissioners (who were primary care trusts (PCTs) at that stage). This signalled an end to GPs being paid under a statutory scheme. This policy changed the primary legal relationship between the NHS commissioner and the GP, which ceased to be based on statutory duties and became a contractual relationship.

11.11 The transition from pilot agreements to permanent PMS agreements was not a straightforward process. The government decided that all pilot agreements should become transitional agreements under articles 1 and 58 of the General Medical Services and Personal Medical Services Transitional and Consequential Provisions Order (PMS Transitional Order) 2004.[5] NHS commissioners and PMS practices were then required to negotiate contracts with each other with a view to agreeing variations to the transitional agreement that would ensure that the terms of the transitional agreement complied with the National Health Service

4 It now applies solely to GMS practices.

5 SI No 865.

(Personal Medical Services Agreements) Regulations (PMS Regs) 2004.[6] However, the final agreement between the parties was not required in all respects to follow the form agreement set out in the PMS Regs 2004. All that was required was that NHS commissioners and PMS practices were not permitted to agree terms which were 'contrary to' the PMS Regs 2004.[7]

Overview of the current legal framework governing primary medical care contracts

11.12 The statutory duty to commission primary care services rests with NHS England. Section 83(1) of the National Health Service Act (NHS Act) 2006 provides:

> The Board must, to the extent that it considers necessary to meet all reasonable requirements, exercise its powers so as to secure the provision of primary medical services throughout England.

11.13 The nature of this duty means that there is no absolute requirement on NHS England to ensure that every individual is able to register with a GP practice which is local to their home. The duty requires NHS England to set up a network of GP services to meet the 'reasonable requirements' of patients. What is 'reasonable' will depend on a number of things, in particular what the needs are of the local population for which NHS England is commissioning primary care services, but it is axiomatic that one relevant factor will be the level of resources available. However, NHS England is also under duties to tackle health inequalities in exercising its commissioning functions, and this duty may affect the way it is required to commission primary care services.[8]

11.14 Once NHS England has discharged its duty by ensuring that such a network of primary care services is available, it is a matter of choice for individual patients as to whether to register themselves with a GP practice to receive such services or not to do so. There is no obligation on anyone living in England to register with an NHS GP practice. As is explored below, however, there are limited circumstances in which a patient can receive primary care services if they do not register with a GP.

11.15 NHS England complies with the duty under section 83(1) of the NHS Act 2006 by 'making arrangements' for the provision of primary medical services with GP practices or those running such practices. Section 83(2) of the NHS Act 2006 provides:

> The Board may (in addition to any other power conferred on it) make such arrangements for the provision of primary medical services as it considers appropriate; and it may, in particular, make contractual arrangements with any person.

11.16 There is no definition of 'primary medical services' in the NHS Act 2006, but section 83(5) provides:

6 SI No 627.

7 The complexities of these arrangements were explored by the Court of Appeal in *Pitalia and another v The National Health Service Commissioning Board* [2014] EWCA Civ 474.

8 See para 4.54 above.

> Regulations may provide that services of a prescribed description must, or must not, be regarded as primary medical services for the purposes of this Act.

11.17 Thus the definition as to what constitutes 'primary medical services' is a matter to be set out in regulations and, accordingly, the definition could be changed by the making of new regulations. The details of the primary medical services that a GP practice is required to provide under the GMS and PMS regulations is described in detail in chapter 18 on GP practice management.

11.18 The way that NHS England discharges this duty in each area is to set up a series of contracts (either legally binding contracts or NHS contracts) with GP practices who agree to provide primary medical services to patients in that area.[9] It is becoming increasingly common for GP practices to join 'federations' or 'super partnerships', which broadly can be described as more than one practice working collaboratively to varying degrees legally and organisationally. That federation or super partnership may hold a contract with NHS England rather than the individual practices holding the contract.

11.19 In recent years, NHS England has moved to a model of primary care co-commissioning, whereby it either partially or wholly delegates its responsibility for primary care commissioning to local CCGs. NHS England, however, retains ultimate responsibility for primary care commissioning under the section 83 duty to provide primary care services to meet reasonable requirements, and is named as the commissioning party in any primary care contract. The CCG is also often a party to the contract, either as agent for NHS England or as co-commissioner.

11.20 Under sections 83(2), 84 and 92 of the NHS Act 2006 (respectively), NHS England has created three types of contract, by which it discharges its duty to make arrangements to meet reasonable requirements throughout England:

1) a General Medical Services (GMS) Contract;
2) a Personal Medical Services (PMS) Agreement;
3) an Alternative Provider Medical Services (APMS) Contract.

11.21 The conditions and terms that are required to be in the various forms of contract are set out in regulations, in the case of GMS and PMS contracts; and in directions, in the case of APMS contracts:

a) GMS contracts are governed by the National Health Service (General Medical Services Contracts) Regulations (GMS Regs) 2015;[10]
b) PMS agreements are governed by the National Health Service (Personal Medical Services Agreements) Regulations (PMS Regs) 2015;[11] and
c) APMS contracts are governed by the Alternative Provider Medical Services Directions (APMS Directions) 2016 (as amended by the Alternative Provider Medical Services (Amendment) Directions 2017).

The differences between the three types of contract are set out in the next section.

9 Please see below for the distinction between legally binding contracts and NHS contracts

10 SI No 1862.

11 SI No 1879.

11.22 Once the NHS commissioner and the practice have agreed the contract (which ought to comply with the statutory duties on NHS England as set out in the relevant regulations or directions), the terms of the agreement take effect as a normal commercial contract between the parties (see *Tomkins v Knowsley Primary Care Trust*[12]). The GP practice will owe various duties under private law of negligence to patients, which will be informed by the services specified in the contract. But the duty to provide the services under the terms set out in the contract will be a separate contractual duty owed to the commissioner.

11.23 In addition to fulfilling their contractual obligations, as noted in the GMS and PMS Regs 2004, and remarked upon by Arnold J in *Generics (UK) Limited (Trading as Mylan) v Warner-Lambert Company LLC*,[13] GPs are also required to have regard to guidance issued by NHS England, although they are not obliged to follow it if they have good reasons to depart from it.

11.24 In November 2017, NHS England published a comprehensive guidance document entitled, *Primary medical care policy and guidance manual (PGM)*.[14] This document contains guidance and standard templates for many of the issues discussed in this chapter and in chapter 18 on GP practice management.

Details of the different types of GP contracts

11.25 As stated above, the different types of 'primary medical services' that GPs are required to provide under their practice contracts – be they GMS, PMS or APMS contracts – is set out in the GMS and PMS Regs 2015 and APMS Directions 2016, is discussed in chapter 18 on GP practice management. That is therefore not repeated here.

GMS contracts

Generally

11.26 Section 84 of the NHS Act 2006 provides that NHS England is entitled to deliver on its statutory duty under section 83 of arranging for the provision of primary medical services by entering into GMS contracts. The GMS contract is the only type of contract which is specifically referred to in the NHS Act 2006, and the legal structures around GMS contracts are set out in the GMS Regs 2015.

11.27 The GMS Regs 2015, along with the PMS Regs 2015, came into force on 7 December 2015. They consolidate a number of amendments made to the previous 2004 regulations. For more details on the rights and obligations of GPs under GMS contracts, please see chapter 18 on GP practice management.

12 [2010] EWHC 1194 (QB) per Hickinbottom J at para 5. This was affirmed by the Court of Appeal in *Krebs v NHS Commissioning Board* [2014] EWCA Civ 1540.

13 [2016] RPC 3 at para 555.

14 See www.england.nhs.uk/publication/primary-medical-care-policy-and-guidance-manual-pgm/.

11.28 A GMS contract is a nationally negotiated contract which takes effect between NHS England and a GP practice. Its central features are:

a) that it potentially exists in perpetuity for the practice
b) if it is a contract with a partnership, it exists with the partners as they exist from time to time;[15] and
c) the contractual fees payable are set by the SFE Directions made by the secretary of state.

11.29 The GMS contract is the default option for many GP practices since a PMS contractor has a statutory right to revert to a GMS contract. Although APMS contracts became a popular method of contracting for reasons explored below, the majority of practice contracts are still GMS contracts and many PMS contracts are now being changed to operate far more like GMS contracts.

11.30 Indeed, the recent advice of the BMA General Practitioners Committee (GPC) is for practices to consider converting their PMS contracts to GMS contracts:

> The GPC strongly encourages consideration of a return to the nationally negotiated GMS contract. The GMS contract offers greater stability and security than PMS agreements. It is not subject to local negotiation, which is likely to place obligations on practices over and above those required by the regulations; or to unilateral termination with six months notice without reason.
>
> Under national arrangements, Minimum Practice Income Guarantee (MPIG) payments once available to some GMS practices are being removed over a seven year period and reinvested in core global sum payments. This will increase the value of global sum funding and is likely, over time, to make a return to GMS a more attractive and viable option for some, if not most, PMS practices. This consideration may not apply to some practices with unusual populations, for whom PMS contracts may remain the best option.[16]

Who is able to hold a GMS contract?

Qualifying persons

11.31 Section 86(1) of the NHS Act 2006 provides restrictions on the identity of the persons with whom NHS England may enter into a GMS contract. It provides that a GMS contract can only be held by:

a) a medical practitioner;
b) a medical partnership, provided defined requirements are met in respect of the partnership; or
c) a medical company, provided defined requirements are met in respect of the company.

15 There is substantial and unresolved question as to whether this type of perpetual contract with a floating body of persons who can change their identity and thus 'inherit' the rights under a contract let by a contracting authority is compatible with the UK's legal obligations under the EU procurement directives since it means, in effect, that a new group of GPs who join a partnership can secure a contract without any form of competitive process.

16 Available at: www.bma.org.uk/advice/employment/contracts/gp-partner-contracts/gms-contract-and-pms-agreement-how-they-compare (last updated 15 March 2018).

11.32 A 'medical practitioner' for these purposes means a fully registered person within the General Medical Council.[17] Regulation 5 of the GMS Regs 2015 provides that 'where the Board enters, or is proposing to enter into a contract with a medical practitioner, that practitioner must be a general medical practitioner'. A 'general medical practitioner' means a person whose name is included on the General Practitioner Register held by the GMC under section 2 of the Medical Act 1983. Hence a GMS contract with a single doctor can, in practice, only be entered into with a practising GP.

11.33 Section 86(2) of the NHS Act 2006 provides that a medical partnership which holds a GMS contract must contain at least one member who is a medical practitioner. Regulation 5 of the GMS Regs 2015 limits this to a GP because it provides that at least one partner (who must not be a limited partner) must be a general medical practitioner. The reference to a 'limited partner' is a reference to the Limited Partnerships Act 1907. A 'limited partner' is a person who, at the time of entering into the partnership, has contributed a sum or sums as capital or property valued at a stated amount, and who the partnership agreement states shall not be liable for the debts or obligations of the partnership beyond the amount so contributed. There must also be general partners in such a partnership who are liable for the entire debts of the partnership and the limited partnership must be registered. Accordingly, this provision requires a medical partnership to have at least one GP who is a full partner (and hence liable for the entire debts of the partnership) before a GMS contract could be awarded to the partnership.

11.34 Under reg 5 of the GMS Regs 2015, the other partners in a medical partnership that are a party to a GMS contract must fall into one of further two categories, namely:

a) one or more other doctors; or
b) a limited class of persons who are not doctors, as described below.

11.35 Any other doctor partner in a medical partnership that wishes to enter into a GMS contract is entitled to be a limited partner (provided the partnership is set up in accordance with the Limited Partnership Act 1907). However, each such doctor partner must either be a general medical practitioner or, if not a GP, must (in England) be an employee of an NHS trust (see reg 5(1)(b)(ii)(bb) of the GMS Regs 2015).

11.36 Any partner in a medical partnership holding a GMS contract who is not a doctor must satisfy one of the conditions in section 86(2)(b) of the NHS Act 2006. These conditions are that the person is:

a) an NHS employee,[18] which term includes a person who is providing services under a GMS contract or a General Dental Services (GDS) contract; or

17 See NHS Act 2006 s275; and the Interpretation Act 1978.

18 Section 93(3) provides that an 'NHS employee' means an individual who, in connection with the provision of services in the health service, the Scottish health service or the Northern Ireland health service, is 'employed by–(a) an NHS trust, an NHS foundation trust or (in Northern Ireland) a Health and Social Services Trust, (b) a . . . Local Health Board, (c) a person who is providing services under a general medical services contract or a general dental services contract or a Welsh general medical services contract or a Welsh general dental services contract, (d) an individual who is providing services as specified in subsection (1)(d)(iii)'.

b) a person who is employed by a person delivering services under section 92 arrangements (ie a practice that is delivering primary medical services under a PMS agreement or another form of agreement sanctioned by section 92 of the NHS Act 2006) or employed in a Welsh, Scottish or Northern Ireland equivalent service; or
c) a person who is employed by a person delivering services under section 107 arrangements (ie a practice that is delivering primary medical services under a Personal Dental Services (PDS) agreement or another form of agreement sanctioned by section 107 of the NHS Act 2006) or employed in a Welsh, Scottish or Northern Ireland equivalent service; or
d) a healthcare professional who is engaged in the provision of services under the NHS Act 2006 or the National Health Service (Wales) Act 2006; or
e) an individual who is 'providing services' under a GMS contract, a GDS contract, section 92 arrangements or in a Welsh, Scottish or Northern Ireland equivalent service.

11.37 If the non-doctor partner is employed by a GMS or PMS contract, there is no requirement that the partner has medical qualifications. Hence, for example, a practice manager or a nurse or pharmacist working at the practice is entitled to become a partner in a medical partnership even though that person is not a qualified doctor.

11.38 Section 86(1)(c) of the NHS Act 2006 permits NHS England to enter into contracts with a limited company, provided the members and directors of the company satisfy certain criteria under section 86(3). At least one share in the company must be legally and beneficially owned by a medical practitioner who, under reg 5 of the GMS Regs 2015 must be a registered general medical practitioner. Section 86(3)(b) of the NHS Act 2006 provides that all other shares in the medical company must be legally and beneficially owned by persons who come within section 86(2)(b) of the NHS Act 2006, namely those persons (as set out above) who would be entitled to be partners in a medical partnership.

Conditions which disqualify a person from holding a GMS Contract

11.39 Regulation 6 of the GMS Regs 2015 provides a list of criteria which prevent a person (whether a doctor or not) from being a party to a GMS contract. The language of the regulation refers to the position prior to the entry into the contract. However, variation provisions (such as the inclusion of a new partner to a partnership contract) also include reference to the same provisions. The restrictions apply to:

a) a sole contractor;
b) any member of a medical partnership;
c) a medical company, anyone legally and beneficially owning shares in a medical company and any director or company secretary of a medical company.

11.40 The exclusion criteria are of two types. First, there are a series of absolute exclusions where NHS England has no power to enter into a GMS contract with a person to whom the exclusion applies. Second, there are a more limited set of qualified exclusions where NHS England has the power to give consent if it reaches the view that the person is suitable to be a contractor.

Absolute exclusions

11.41 The absolute exclusions from the power to sign a GMS contract in reg 6(2) of the GMS Regs 2015 are as follows:

(a) the contractor is the subject of a national disqualification;
(b) subject to paragraph (3), the contractor is disqualified or suspended (other than by interim suspension order or direction pending an investigation) from practising by any licensing body anywhere in the world;
(c) the contractor has, within the period of five years before the signing of the contract or commencement of the contract (whichever is the earlier), been dismissed (otherwise than by reason of redundancy) from any employment by a health service body, unless–
  (i) if the contractor was employed as a member of a health care profession at the time of the dismissal, the contractor has not subsequently been employed by that health service body or by another health service body, and
  (ii) the dismissal was the subject of a finding of unfair dismissal by any competent tribunal or a court;
(d) the contractor has, within the period of five years before the signing of the contract or commencement of the contract (whichever is the earlier), been removed from, or refused admission to, a primary care list by reason of inefficiency, fraud or unsuitability (within the meaning of section 151(2), (3) and (4) of the Act (disqualification of practitioners)), or a performers list held by the Board by virtue of regulations made under section 91(3) (persons performing primary medical services) of the Act, unless the contractor's name has subsequently been included in such a list;
(e) the contractor has been convicted in the United Kingdom of murder;
(f) the contractor has been convicted in the United Kingdom of a criminal offence other than murder committed on or after 14th December 2001 and has been sentenced to a term of imprisonment of longer than six months;
(g) subject to paragraph (3), the contractor has been convicted outside of the United Kingdom of an offence which would, if committed in England and Wales, constitute murder and–
  (i) the offence was committed on or after 14th December 2001, and
  (ii) the contractor was sentenced to a term of imprisonment of longer than six months;
(h) the contractor has been convicted of an offence, referred to in Schedule 1 to the Children and Young Persons Act 1933 (offences against children and young persons, with respect to which special provisions of this Act apply), or in Schedule 1 to the Criminal Procedure (Scotland) Act 1995 (offences against children under the age of 17 years to which special provisions apply), committed on or after 1st March 2004;
(i) the contractor has at any time been included in–
  (i) any barred list within the meaning of section 2 of the Safeguarding Vulnerable Groups Act 2006 (barred lists), or

(ii) any barred list within the meaning of article 6 of the Safeguarding Vulnerable Groups (Northern Ireland) Order 2007 (barred lists),

unless the contractor was removed from the list either on the grounds that it was not appropriate for the contractor to have been included in it or as the result of a successful appeal;

(j) the contractor has, within the period of five years before the signing of the contract or commencement of the contract (whichever is the earlier), been removed from the office of charity trustee or trustee for a charity by an order made by the Charity Commission, the Charity Commission for Northern Ireland or the High Court, and that order was made on the grounds of misconduct or mismanagement in the administration of a charity for which the contractor was responsible or to which the contractor was privy, or which was contributed to, or facilitated by, the contractor's conduct;

(k) the contractor has, within the period of five years before the signing of the contract or commencement of the contract (whichever is the earlier), been removed from being concerned with the management or control of any body in a case where the removal was by virtue of section 34(5)(e) of the Charities and Trustee Investment (Scotland) Act 2005 (powers of Court of Session);

(l) the contractor–

(i) has been [made] bankrupt and has not been discharged from the bankruptcy or the bankruptcy order has not been annulled, or

(ii) has had sequestration of the contractor's estate awarded and has not been discharged from the sequestration;

(m) the contractor is the subject of a bankruptcy restrictions order or an interim bankruptcy restrictions order under Schedule 4A to the Insolvency Act 1986 (bankruptcy restrictions order and undertaking), Schedule 2A to the Insolvency (Northern Ireland) Order 1989 (bankruptcy restrictions order and undertaking), or sections 56A to 56K of the Bankruptcy (Scotland) Act 1985 (bankruptcy restrictions order, interim bankruptcy restrictions order and bankruptcy restrictions undertaking), unless the contractor has been discharged from that order or that order has been annulled;

(n) the contractor–

(i) is subject to moratorium period under a debt relief order under Part VIIA of the Insolvency Act 1986 (debt relief orders), or

(ii) is the subject of a debt relief restrictions order or an interim debt relief restrictions order under Schedule 4ZB to that Act (debt relief restrictions orders and undertakings);

(o) the contractor has made a composition agreement or arrangement with, or granted a trust deed for, the contractor's creditors and the contractor has not been discharged in respect of it;

(p) the contractor is subject to–

(i) a disqualification order under section 1 of the Company Directors Disqualification Act 1986 (disqualification orders: general) or a disqualification undertaking under section 1A of that Act (disqualification undertakings: general),

(ii) a disqualification order or disqualification undertaking under article 3 (disqualification orders: general) or article 4 (disqualification undertakings: general) of the Company Directors Disqualification (Northern Ireland) Order 2002, or

(iii) a disqualification order under section 429(2) of the Insolvency Act 1986 (disabilities on revocation of an administration order against an individual);

(q) the contractor has had an administrator, administrative receiver or receiver appointed in respect of the contractor;
(r) the contractor has had an administration order made in respect of the contractor under Schedule B1 to the Insolvency Act 1986 (administration); or
(s) the contractor is a partnership and–
(i) a dissolution of the partnership is ordered by any competent court, tribunal or arbitrator, or
(ii) an event happens that makes it unlawful for the business of the partnership to continue, or for members of the partnership to carry on in partnership.

Qualified exclusions

11.42 Where a person fulfils the conditions of a qualified exclusion, the person is not automatically barred from holding a GMS contract. However, in each case NHS England is required to reach a decision as to whether the person is suitable to hold a GMS contract or not. If NHS England reach the decision that the person is not suitable to hold a GMS contract, then the person falls within the category of persons who cannot be granted a GMS contract.

11.43 The first qualified exclusion arises where an individual or medical company is disqualified or suspended (other than by an interim suspension order or direction pending an investigation) from practising by a licensing body (so would prima facie fall within reg 6(2)(b), but that licensing body that disqualified or suspended the person was one outside the United Kingdom.

11.44 In such a case, reg 6(3)(b) provides for the following 'unsuitability test' to be applied:

(b) the Board is satisfied that the disqualification, suspension or, as the case may be, the conviction does not make that person unsuitable to be–
(i) a contractor,
(ii) a partner, in the case of a contract with two or more persons practising in partnership, or
(iii) in the case of a company limited by shares–
(aa) a person who both legally and beneficially owns a share in the company, or
(bb) a director or secretary of the company.

11.45 The other qualified exclusion arises where a person has been convicted of a criminal offence, but this was either outside the United Kingdom or the sentence was less than six months. It applies to a person who has been convicted elsewhere of an offence:

a) which would, if committed in England and Wales, constitute murder; or
b) which was committed on or after 14 December 2001, and which would if committed in England and Wales, constitute a criminal offence other than murder, and been sentenced to a term of imprisonment of over six months.

In such a case, NHS England has to apply the same suitability test under reg 6(3)(b).

11.46 *The exclusion of some medical companies from holding a GMS contract.* Under reg 6(1)(c) of the GMS Regs 2015, the same exclusions apply to a medical company as they apply to individual. The restrictions apply to:

a) the company,
b) any person both legally and beneficially owning a share in the company, or
c) any director or secretary of the company.

11.47 One of the peculiarities of the wording in reg 6 is that a medical company cannot be automatically excluded if a person who would otherwise be excluded is the beneficial owner of shares in a company but is not registered as the legal owner. The 'beneficial' owner of shares is the person who has the real ownership of shares. However, shares can be held in the name of another person who is the 'legal' owner but is required to act in accordance with the instructions of the beneficial owner.

11.48 It is not clear why the exclusion test under the GMS Regs 2015 is that such a person should be *both* the legal and beneficial owner of shares as opposed to being either the legal or beneficial owner of shares. This wording appears to enable a person who would otherwise be excluded from arranging for shares in a medical company to be registered in the name of a nominee and thus will avoid the exclusions.

PMS agreements

Generally

11.49 A PMS agreement is a local contract where some of the terms can be agreed between NHS England and the practice, including funding arrangements. However, many of the terms of the PMS contract are governed by the PMS Regs 2015, which require the contract to contain terms which replicate a GMS contract. Key features of PMS contracts are that:

a) they are almost always time-limited contracts;
b) any GP practice which operates under a PMS agreement has the right to terminate the PMS agreement and insist on having a GMS contract in its place;[19] and
c) the commissioner (or the contracting practice) may unilaterally terminate the contract with six months' notice. This is in contrast to the GMS contract, where the right to unilaterally terminate the contract without cause is reserved to the contractor alone. For this reason, a GMS contract may afford more stability to practices.

11.50 Section 92 of the NHS Act 2006 permits NHS England to enter into 'arrangements' for the delivery of primary care services which are not GMS contracts (and are not contracts entered into using the reserve power in section 83(2)). However, section 92(2) provides that any such agreement must be made in accordance with Regulations passed under section 94. Although a PMS agreement can be a legally binding contract, they are usually referred to as 'agreements' rather than contracts because the

19 PMS Regs 2015 reg 32.

default position is that a PMS agreement is an NHS contract rather than a legally binding contract.

11.51 Section 94 contains detailed provisions about how the secretary of state is entitled to make regulations for defining arrangements for the provision of primary care services (other than GMS contracts). This was the power that was used by the secretary of state to make the PMS Regs 2015, which define how PMS agreements are to be set up and the contents of every PMS agreement.

11.52 However, the NHS commissioner and the GP practice still have a measure of freedom to negotiate specific terms in a PMS agreement because they are not tied to a nationally agreed form of model agreement. The terms of PMS agreements are not negotiated on a national basis between the Department of Health and Social Care and the General Practitioners Committee of the British Medical Association,[20] as is the case with the GMS contract. However, Part 5 of the PMS Regs 2015 sets out various terms which are required in PMS agreements. In addition, reg 27 provides that agreements must also contain provisions which are equivalent in their effect to the provisions set out in Parts 6–14 of and Schs 1 and 2 to the PMS Regs 2015. These provisions are numerous, and are very substantially the same terms as are required to be included in a GMS contract.

Who can hold a PMS agreement?

Qualifying persons

11.53 The list of persons who can be party to a PMS contract are much wider than those persons who can hold a GMS contract. The full list is set out in section 93(1) of the NHS Act 2006, as follows:

> The Board may make an agreement under section 92 only with one or more of the following–
> (a) an NHS trust or an NHS foundation trust,
> (b) a medical practitioner who meets the prescribed conditions,
> (c) a health care professional who meets the prescribed conditions,
> (d) an individual who is providing services–
> (i) under a general medical services contract or a general dental services contract or a Welsh general medical services contract or a Welsh general dental services contract,
> (ii) in accordance with section 92 arrangements, section 107 arrangements, section 50 arrangements, section 64 arrangements, section 17C arrangements or Article 15B arrangements, or
> (iii) under section 17J or 25 of the 1978 Act or Article 57 or 61 of the Health and Personal Social Services (Northern Ireland) Order 1972 (SI 1972/1265 (NI14)),
> or has so provided them within such period as may be prescribed,
> (e) an NHS employee, a section 92 employee, a section 107 employee, a section 50 employee, a section 64 employee, a section 17C employee or an Article 15B employee,
> (f) a qualifying body.

20 Which may in part explain the BMA preference for GMS contracts.

11.54 Thus NHS trusts and an NHS foundation trusts are entitled to be PMS contractors (but these bodies cannot hold a GMS contract). A 'medical practitioner' and a 'healthcare professional' can also hold a PMS contract, even if the medical practitioner is not a GP. A 'healthcare professional' means a person who is a member of a profession regulated by a body mentioned (at the time the agreement in question is made) in section 25(3) of the National Health Service Reform and Health Care Professions Act 2002. The list of relevant bodies is:

a) the General Medical Council;
b) the General Dental Council;
c) the General Optical Council;
d) the General Osteopathic Council;
e) the General Chiropractic Council;
f) the General Pharmaceutical Council;
g) the Pharmaceutical Society of Northern Ireland;
h) the Nursing and Midwifery Council;
i) the Health and Care Professions Council (which regulates arts therapists, biomedical scientists, chiropodists / podiatrists, clinical scientists, dietitians, hearing aid dispensers, occupational therapists, operating department practitioners, orthoptists, paramedics, physiotherapists, practitioner psychologists, prosthetists / orthotists, radiographers, social workers in England and speech and language therapists); and
j) any other regulatory body (within the meaning of Schedule 3 to the Health Act 1999) established by an Order in Council under section 60 of that Act.

11.55 This means that NHS England can award a PMS contract to a nurse, a physiotherapist or a dentist.[21] The person who held the contract would have to employ or engage GPs to deliver any part of the services under the contract which required a GP, but the contract could be held by a professional with any of the above professions. A practice manager who was employed by a GP practice could also hold a PMS contract.

11.56 There is no list of other conditions in the PMS Regs 2015 that need to be fulfilled before such a person can hold a PMS contract. However, there are requirements for medical practitioners and healthcare professionals practising under the agreement in terms of their qualifications, see regs 33 and 34 of the PMS Regs 2015, and regs 40 and 41 in the GMS Regs 2015, although this is a separate matter to the nature of the person who can contract. There is a list of conditions which disqualify a person from holding a PMS contract. These are considered below.

Conditions which disqualify a person from holding a PMS contract

11.57 Regulation 5 of the PMS Regs 2015 sets out a long list of conditions which would disqualify a person from being awarded a PMS contract. The list of disqualifying conditions is almost identical to the list in the GMS Regs 2015 above, except some of the dates relating to when crimes were committed are slightly different, and there is no subparagraph(s), which concerns partnership.

21 The authors are aware of a number of PMS contracts where one or more nurses are the main contractor.

11.58 Like the GMS Regs 2015, there are qualified exceptions and there are special provisions about healthcare professionals who are suspended by licensing bodies other than those operating in the UK under reg 5(3). The conditions for disqualification of persons who can hold PMS contracts thus substantially mirror the list of those who cannot hold GMS contracts.

APMS agreements

Generally

11.59 NHS England has been given a wide power under section 83(2) of the NHS Act 2006 to enter into different types of arrangements to provide primary medical services with anyone it considers fit and on such terms as it considers fit as follows:

> The Board may (in addition to any other power conferred on it) make such arrangements for the provision of primary medical services as it considers appropriate; and it may, in particular, make contractual arrangements with any person.

11.60 This allows NHS England to contract with 'any person' to provide primary care services under local commissioning arrangements. APMS contracts are individually negotiated, although some of the terms found in PMS contracts (themselves based on the GMS contract) are mandatory under directions published by the secretary of state. They are time-limited.

11.61 The power under section 83(2) would theoretically enable NHS England to enter into a contract with anyone to provide primary medical services. There is no specific requirement under section 83(2) that the person who contracts to provide services has to be a registered general practitioner or even a doctor, although the services for patients would need to be provided by registered doctors in order not breach the terms of the Medical Act 1983 and to comply with the National Health Service (Performers Lists) (England) Regulations 2013[22] (and substantially the same performers' qualifications contractual terms are required in APMS contracts are required under direction 7 of the APMS Directions 2016). Unlike GMS contracts and PMS agreements, the terms of a section 83 contract, including the payment terms, are not set out in regulations, but are left to be agreed between NHS England and the contractor.

11.62 This power was previously available to primary care trusts. However, the secretary of state introduced a series of directions which permitted the power to be used to set up alternative forms of contract with GP practices which were called APMS contracts. These directions introduced additional flexibilities which could be agreed locally to the arrangements set out in PMS agreements. The power for the secretary of state to issue directions to NHS England is now in section 98A(1) of the NHS Act 2006, which provides:

> The Secretary of State may direct the Board to exercise any of the Secretary of State's functions relating to the provision of primary medical services.

22 SI No 335.

11.63 The secretary of state has used this power to make the APMS Directions 2016[23] (as amended[24]). Part 3 of those directions refers to a large number of terms that are required to be inserted into an APMS agreement.

11.64 Like PMS agreements, APMS contracts are time-limited, although the APMS Directions 2016 do not specify a maximum contract length. While, typically, APMS agreements have been awarded for shorter periods such as three or five years, increasingly APMS contracts are being awarded on a longer-term basis, particularly as the focus of NHS England moves from increasing competition to achieving 'integration'.

11.65 APMS contracts can also be used to 'wrap around' service provision by GP practices under GMS contracts, given that they allow for contracting on a more flexible basis.

Who can hold an APMS contract?

11.66 As stated above, APMS contracts can theoretically be awarded to 'any person'. This includes, as well as the persons who can enter into GMS and PMS contracts, companies, voluntary organisations and NHS trusts. Under the APMS Directions 2016, however, the same restrictions as in the PMS Regs 2015 apply to the proposed contractor. For NHS trusts, entering into APMS contracts creates multiple conflicts of interests issues: first, under the APMS Directions a contractor providing 'essential services' (see chapter 18 on GP practice management) is required to be a member of the clinical commissioning group (CCG), which commissions local hospital services from providers that might include the trust in question. Second, NHS trusts as GP contractors would, in theory, be in a position to refer patients for services at their own hospital. Direction 11 of the APMS Directions 2016 requires an APMS contractor to ensure that in making such a decision, however, it does so 'without regard to its own financial interests'. Trust APMS contractors would be advised to carefully consider where potential conflicts of interest might arise.

11.67 NHS England has now published a Standard APMS Contract.[25] Thus, new APMS contracts will be expected to conform to the standard terms (which incorporate the terms set out in the directions). However, the publication of a new contract will not affect the legal relationships existing under contracts which were signed before the new standard contract was published.

The legal relationship between the parties to a GP contract and the NHS

11.68 The vast majority of GPs are not employees of an NHS organisation despite the fact that GPs are entitled to become members of the NHS

23 See www.gov.uk/government/uploads/system/uploads/attachment_data/file/588880/APMS_Directions_2016.pdf.

24 Amendments tend to be made annually. The 2017 amendments are at www.gov.uk/government/uploads/system/uploads/attachment_data/file/657146/The_Alternative_Provider_Medical_Services__Amendment__Directions_2017.FINAL__2_.pdf.

25 See www.england.nhs.uk/wp-content/uploads/2018/01/17-18-apms-contract.pdf.

pension scheme (a feature normally limited to employees of an organisation). This is clearly stated in clause 2.1.1 of the standard form 2017/18 GMS contract, which provides:

> The Contract is a contract for the provision of services. The Contractor is an independent provider of services and is not an employee, partner or agent of the Board. The Contractor must not represent or conduct its activities so as to give the impression that it is the employee, partner or agent of the Board.

The same position arises under PMS agreements and APMS agreements.

11.69 The legal relationship between a GP practice and the NHS commissioner is accordingly defined by the terms of the practice contract which exists between the parties. For most purposes, the fact that the terms of the contract are governed by regulations does not prevent the contract operating and being interpreted by the courts as a normal commercial contract. The contractual relationship between the GP practice and NHS England means that NHS England (and/or CCGs if responsible for commissioning primary care services under delegated commissioning arrangements) do not owe GPs working in NHS practices a duty of care at common law and do not have direct responsibility for the conditions in which GPs work.

Legal relationships between a GP and a primary care practice

11.70 GPs who work in general practice can hold one of the following relationships with the GP practice within which NHS services are delivered:

a) in the cases of a sole practitioner, the GP owns the practice and is a self-employed professional;
b) in the case of a GP equity partner in a partnership, the GP is a part owner of the practice and is in a contractual relationship with his or her fellow partners, the terms of which are defined by the partnership agreement;
c) the GP may be a director and/or shareholder of the medical company which has entered into the practice contract with the NHS; in this case the GP may be self-employed (in the case of a director) or may also be an employee of the medical company;
d) the GP may be a 'salaried partner' of a GP practice, which means that the GP is an employee of the partnership (as opposed to being a part owner of the practice) but is presented to the outside world as a partner and has some rights to become involved in partnership matters as defined in the contract of employment;
e) the GP may be an employee of the GP practice or the company which holds the contract; or
f) a GP may be a self-employed contractor who contracts with the GP practice to provide professional medical services to patients on either a regular or occasional basis (either arranged directly with the partnership or through an agency). These doctors are often referred to as 'locum GPs'.

11.71 However, all of the legal relationships set out in the paragraph above are relationships between the GP and the practice. None of these relationships (of themselves) create any direct legal relationship between the GP and the NHS commissioner.

The distinctions between NHS contracts and legally binding contracts

Overview

11.72 Arrangements between NHS bodies were traditionally regarded as 'service level agreements' within the NHS, namely agreements between different parts of the same organisation which did not give rise to contractual obligations that either party could enforce in the courts. If one party failed to comply with the terms of an agreement or required additional money in order to meet the costs of a commitment, this was seen as a management problem to be resolved within the NHS. If a compromise solution could not be negotiated between NHS bodies, the secretary of state undertook an adjudication and reached a decision which was de facto binding on both NHS bodies that were parties to the service level agreement. This process reduced the legal fees that NHS bodies were required to meet, but it meant that commitments taken on by NHS bodies never had the same force as those which were subject to legal enforcement.

11.73 This position was formalised by section 4 of the NHSCCA 1990, which defined the concept of an 'NHS contract' as follows:

> . . . an arrangement under which one health service body ('the acquirer') arranges for the provision to it by another health service body ('the provider') of goods or services which it reasonably requires for the purposes of its functions.

11.74 The principal feature of an NHS contract is that it does not give rise to legally enforceable rights by any person in the civil courts. This was confirmed by the courts in *Pitalia v NHS Commissioning Board*[26] and more recently in *NHS England v Bargain Dentist.com*.[27] This is set out in section 9(5) and (6) of the NHS Act 2006, which provide:

> (5) Whether or not an arrangement which constitutes an NHS contract would apart from this subsection be a contract in law, it must not be regarded for any purpose as giving rise to contractual rights or liabilities.
>
> (6) But if any dispute arises with respect to such an arrangement, either party may refer the matter to the Secretary of State for determination under this section.

11.75 Although the purpose of NHS contracts is that disputes between the parties are dealt with by way of alternative dispute resolution, this does not mean there is no role whatsoever for the courts, as was confirmed in *Jones*

26 [2014] EWCA Civ 474, (2014) 138 BMLR 89.

27 [2014] EWHC 1994 (QB), [2014] Med LR 301. NHS England sought permission to appeal this judgment and then abandoned the appeal.

v NHS Commissioning Board.[28] In *Jones* the claimant doctors succeeded in obtaining an injunction to prevent NHS England from termination their contract by service of a 'clause 591 notice', and thereby taking steps to introduce a new practice, until all the disputes surrounding the termination had been resolved under the NHS Family Health Services Appeal Unit (FHSAU) disputes procedure (see below). NHS England had refused to give a commitment to hold back from taking any steps to remove the doctors from their practice before the adjudication process had been determined, and thus Soole J noted that 'public law may have a complementary role to support the statutory process of dispute resolution'.[29] Central to this conclusion was the fact that 'the statutory provisions (Part 12 of the 2015 GMS Regs) make no provision for FHSAU to make interim orders. Nor, of course, can FHSAU grant an injunction'.[30] An injunction was therefore an appropriate remedy.[31]

11.76 Similarly, since there is no power for the FHSAU to review or conduct appeals of its decisions, once a decision has been made and the procedure exhausted, the appropriate way of challenging a decision of the FHSAU is to apply to challenge it by way of judicial review in the High Court (see below).

GMS contracts and NHS contracts

11.77 The NHSCCA 1990 contained a list of NHS bodies which were designated to be 'health service bodies' for the purpose of section 4 of that Act. GP practices were not initially included on the list and therefore could contract as a health service body. However, at that stage, the arrangements between GP practices and the secretary of state were set out in the statutory General Medical Services scheme. In 1990, contracting was not the usual method for the NHS to procure primary care services from GPs. In any event, the relationship between NHS commissioners and GP practices was always somewhat different because GP practices were not 'NHS bodies' and thus it was not seen by NHS management as just being a case of moving money (or obligations) from one NHS body to another. However, the relationship between GP practices and NHS managers has also usually not been an arms-length contractual relationship with both sides sticking to their legal rights, but more in the nature of a 'partnership'.

11.78 The first 'GP contracts' were the pilot scheme agreements introduced by the National Health Service (Primary Care) Act (NHS(PC)A) 1997. This Act provided that both pilot scheme agreements and (later) permanent PMS agreements could treat GP practices as health service bodies for the purpose of section 4 of the NHSCCA 1990 and thus could be set up as NHS contracts (see, for example, section 22 of the NHS(PC)A 1997, which brought section 28E of the NHS Act 1977 into effect which provided that

28 [2017] EWHC 3457 (QB).

29 Para 59.

30 Para 59.

31 The decision of the FHSAU was made in January 2018 – it concluded that after the termination of the GPs' contract on 14 October 2016, an implied GMS contract has been in place – and is available at: www.nhsla.com/fhsau/Documents/18808%20et%20al%20-%20Dispute%20Resolution.pdf.

the PMS Regs 2015 could provide that the contractor was to be a health service body).

11.79 The present position is that GP practices are entitled to enter into NHS contracts through a variety of provisions. For GMS contracts, section 90(3) of the NHS Act 2006 provides:

> Regulations may make provision for a person or persons entering into a general medical services contract to be regarded as a health service body for any purposes of section 9, in circumstances where he or they so elect.

11.80 This power (previously in the NHS Act 1977) has been used to make reg 10 of the GMS Regs 2015, which provides:

> (1) A person who proposes to enter into a contract with the Board (a 'proposed contractor') may elect, by giving notice in writing to the Board prior to entering into the contract, to be regarded as a health service body for the purposes of section 9 of the Act (NHS contracts).
> (2) An election made by a proposed contractor under paragraph (1) has effect from the date on which the contract is entered into.
> (3) If, by virtue of paragraph (1), a proposed contractor elects to be regarded as a health service body, the nature of, or any rights or liabilities under, any other contract previously entered into by that proposed contractor with a health service body before the date of that election remains unaffected.

11.81 Regulation 10(3) of the GMS Regs 2015 means that the fact that a party has elected to become an NHS body for a proposed GMS contact does not affect the nature of, or any rights or liabilities arising under, any other contract that the contractor may have been a party to before the date on which the election to be an NHS body is made.

11.82 Once a GMS contractor who is an individual or a medical partnership has elected to become an NHS body, reg 10(5) of the GMS Regs 2015 provides that this status will continue notwithstanding any change in the individuals who become parties to the GMS contract. Thus, if a sole practitioner were to take on a partner under his or her GMS contract and then resign from the partnership, the new contractor will continue to be treated as an NHS body.

11.83 Regulation 11(1) of the GMS Regs 2015 permits any contractor who wishes to change the contractor's status to become an NHS body or to cease to be an NHS body shall be able to do so by serving notice on the Board. Thus a legally binding contract can be changed to being an NHS contract at the election of a contractor and vice versa. Regulation 11(1) provides:

> (1) A contractor may at any time request in writing a variation of the contract to include in, or remove from, the contract provision to the effect that the contract is an NHS contract and, if it does so–
> (a) the Board must agree to the variation; and
> (b) the procedure specified in regulation 29 and Part 8 of Schedule 3 for the variation of contracts applies.

11.84 It follows that if a request is made by a GP practice to change the status of a GMS practice contract, the Board comes under a statutory duty to agree to the change in the status of the contract. In the unlikely event that the Board refuses to fulfil that duty then the dispute can be enforced by an application to the FHSAU of the NHS Resolution (formerly the NHS

Litigation Authority). The reference to reg 29 and Part 8 of Schedule 3 is a reference to the requirement that a GMS contract must include a term that no amendment or variation shall have effect unless it is in writing and signed by or on behalf of the Board and the contractor.[32] In the case of a change of status, the notice from the contractor would constitute evidence of the change. However, the change of status will not be legally effective until there has been a signed notice back from the Board confirming the change in status.

11.85 The date that the change in status takes effect is the date when the contract is varied (see reg 10(2)). Thus, the change in status occurs at the date when the Board provides a signed approval to the change in status, and not the date when the contractor serves his or her notice.

11.86 Regulation 12(1) provides that a contractor shall cease to be a health service body for the purposes of section 9 of the NHS Act 2006 if the contract terminates. Accordingly, if NHS England has a claim against a contractor for something that has happened after the termination of a GMS contract, that claim has to be litigated in the courts unless it comes within the exceptions in reg 12, which are fairly self-explanatory and are as follows:

> (2) Where, by virtue of paragraph (1), a contractor ceases to be regarded as a health service body in relation to a contract ('the relevant contract'), the contractor is to continue to be regarded as a health service body for the purposes of any other NHS contract to which it became a party between the date on which it entered into the relevant contract and the date on which it ceased to be regarded as a health service body for the purposes of that contract (but it ceases to be a health service body for the purposes of such other NHS contract on the termination of that contract).
>
> (3) Where–
> (a) a contractor ceases to be regarded as a health service body in relation to a contract by reason of a variation of the contract by virtue of regulation 11(1); and
> (b) the contractor or the Board–
> (i) has referred any matter to the NHS dispute resolution procedure before it ceases to be a health service body, or
> (ii) refers any matter to the NHS dispute resolution procedure, in accordance with regulation 82, after it ceases to be a health service body, the contractor is to continue to be regarded as a health service body (and accordingly the contract is to continue to be regarded as an NHS contract) for the purposes of the consideration and determination of the dispute.
>
> (4) Where a contractor ceases to be regarded as a health service body by virtue of regulation 11(1) but continues to be regarded as a health service body for the purposes of the NHS dispute resolution procedure where that procedure was commenced–
> (a) before the termination of the contract; or
> (b) after the termination of the contract (whether in connection with or arising out of the termination of the contract or otherwise),
> the contractor ceases to be regarded as a health service body for those purposes on the conclusion of that procedure.'

32 See GMS Regs 2015 Sch 3 Part 8 para 57(1).

PMS agreements and NHS contracts

11.87 Section 92(3)(g) of the NHS Act 2006 provides that regulations can be made that permit contractors who enter 'section 92 arrangements to be treated, in such circumstances and to such extent as may be prescribed, as health service bodies for the purposes of section 9'. Thus the secretary of state was given power to make regulations to permit PMS agreements (which are a form of section 92 arrangements) to operate as NHS contracts.

11.88 Regulation 9(1) of the PMS Regs 2015 provides:

> (1) A contractor is to be regarded as a health service body for the purposes of section 9 of the Act (NHS contracts) from the date on which it enters into an agreement unless, in the case of–
> (a) an agreement with a contractor who is an individual or which is a qualifying body, that individual or qualifying body; or
> (b) any other agreement, any of the proposed parties to the agreement (other than the Board),
> objects by giving notice in writing to the Board at any time prior to the agreement being made.

11.89 PMS agreements are different from GMS contracts because a PMS agreement is presumed to be an NHS contract unless the contractor makes an election not to be a health service body and thus elects to have a legally binding contract. The position is the reverse for a GMS contract. Regulation 12 of the PMS Regs 2015 provides that the PMS agreement must state that the contractor has the status of being a health service body.

11.90 Regulation 9(2) of the PMS Regs 2015 provides:

> If, by virtue of paragraph (1), a contractor is to be regarded as a health service body, any change in the parties comprising the contractor does not affect the status of the contractor as a health service body.

This provision ensures that a PMS agreement with a partnership shall not change from an NHS contract to a legally binding contract because of a change in the identity of the partners.

11.91 Regulation 10(1) of the PMS Regs 2015 permits a PMS agreement to switch from being an NHS contract to be a legally binding contract or vice versa. It provides:

> A contractor may at any time request in writing a variation of the agreement to include in, or remove from, the agreement provision to the effect that the agreement is an NHS contract and, if it does so–
> (a) the Board must agree to the variation; and
> (b) the procedure specified in regulation 24 and Part 8 of Schedule 2 for the variation of agreements applies.

11.92 Thus, the contractor can change the status of the contract by making a request to NHS England to change the status of the agreement. The PMS Regs 2015 require the request to be in writing. The reference to reg 24 and Part 8 of Schedule 2 for the variation of agreements is a reference to the requirement to include a term in the PMS agreement that 'a variation of, or amendment to, an agreement is not effective unless it is in writing and signed by or on behalf of the Board and the contractor'.[33] It follows that if a contractor makes a request to change the

33 See PMS Regs 2015 Sch 2 Part 8 para 52(1).

status of a PMS agreement, NHS England is required to serve a signed notice on the contractor agreeing to the change of the status of the contract. However, the change will not take effect until the contractor also signs a document (which could in some circumstances be the original request) confirming the change in the contract status. The date of the change is confirmed in reg 10(2) and (3) of the PMS Regs 2015, which provide:

> (2) If, by virtue of a request under paragraph (1), the agreement is varied so as to remove provision from it to the effect that is an NHS contract, the contractor is, subject to regulation 11, to cease to be regarded as a health service body for the purposes of section 9 of the Act from the date on which that variation takes effect.
>
> (3) If, by virtue of a request under paragraph (1), the agreement is varied so as to include provision in it to the effect that it is an NHS contract, the contractor is to be regarded as a health service body for the purposes of section 9 of the Act from the date on which that variation takes effect.

11.93 The provisions in the PMS Regs 2015 about post-termination matters, pre-existing matters at the date of transfer of status and existing disputes are set out in reg 11. These provisions mirror those for GMS contracts which are set out above.

APMS agreements and NHS contracts

11.94 APMS agreements are contracts which are entered into by NHS England using the wide default powers in section 83 of the NHS Act 2006. There is no specific provision in the NHS Act 2006 which permits a person entering into an APMS agreement to become a 'health service body' and therefore no direct route by which an APMS agreement can be treated as an NHS contract. However:

a) An APMS agreement could be treated as an NHS contract if the person providing the GP practice is a body of a type set out in section 9(4) of the NHS Act 2006.
b) An APMS agreement could be treated as an NHS contract if the person providing the GP practice is already party to another NHS contract. Thus if a medical company runs multiple GP practices under a variety of contracts, at least one of which is an NHS contract, a new APMS agreement can be treated as being an NHS contract because it is being entered into with a person who has the status of being a 'health service body'.
c) Even if the contract takes effect as a legally binding contract, the standard terms of the contract will still require (or permit) the contractor to use the NHS disputes resolution process, and thus refer disputes to the FHSAU. If the APMS agreement requires disputes between the contractor and the NHS commissioner to be referred to the FHSAU, the term ought to be regarded as an arbitration agreement for the purposes of the Arbitration Act 1996.[34] It follows that any contractor who commences court proceedings to resolve a dispute may face

34 Although the Court of Appeal decided not to found a decision on that basis in a dental case: see *R (Hussain and others) v Secretary of State for the Health Department and another* [2011] EWCA Civ 800. The observations must be obiter as the PCT's appeal was allowed on other grounds.

an application by the NHS commissioner for those proceedings to be stayed pending a referral to the FHSAU. If the relevant term of the APMS agreement provides that contractor has an option to use the NHS disputes resolution process (as opposed to being obliged to do so), then it will be a matter for the GP practice to decide whether to resolve the dispute in the courts or using the FHSAU.

The NHS disputes resolution procedure

11.95 Disputes between parties to an NHS contract, including on termination matters, breaches of contract and sanctions (about which see below) are required to be adjudicated upon by the secretary of state.[35] The secretary of state has delegated the discharge of this function to NHS Resolution, which delivers this service through the FHSAU.

11.96 The FHSAU have published guidance concerning the procedures they will use to resolve disputes, and also publish all determinations on its website.[36]

The differences between an NHS contract and a legally binding contract when litigating

11.97 The main differences between litigating in the courts and litigating in the FHSAU of NHS Resolution are as follows:

a) The main advantage of an NHS contract is that the contactor cannot be sued in the civil courts by NHS England, with all of the cost implications associated with such a court case. On the other hand, the corresponding disadvantage of an NHS contract is that contactor cannot sue for their rights in the civil courts.
b) The FHSAU is a specialist tribunal which deals with NHS disputes all the time. It has great expertise and is likely to get to a result which accords with the regulations in a far shorter time than a civil court case would take. It is also likely to apply far more expertise in getting to the result than a civil judge who may never have come across these types of contract before.
c) The FHSAU will generally decide matters on paper without a hearing (its decisions are available on its website[37]). This reduces costs, but can be unsatisfactory if there are substantial disputes of fact that need to be resolved between the contractor and the NHS body before a decision can be reached. There are facilities for the FHSAU to hold hearings and make decisions on disputed points of fact, but this power is rarely used.
d) The FHSAU procedures often operate with parties not being legally represented but, if a party does engage lawyers, the determination does

35 NHS Act 2006 s9(6).
36 See www.nhsla.com/FHSAU/Pages/Home.aspx.
37 See www.nhsla.com/FHSAU/Pages/Home.aspx.

not generally result in any order for costs payable by either side. Thus a winning party who engages lawyers cannot get an order for the other side to pay their legal costs.

e) There is no statutory provision to permit an appeal against a legally incorrect decision of the FHSAU to the First-tier Tribunal. However, either side is entitled to apply for judicial review of the decision of the FHSAU. For an example of this in a case that went to the Court of Appeal, see *R (Hussain and others) v Secretary of State for the Health Department and another*.[38] The court adjudicated on the dispute within the judicial review procedure, despite the fact that this was essentially a private contractual matter which did not give rise to public law issues. There have been a series of recent cases which suggest that a more restrictive approach may now be taken to the extent to which a private contractual dispute can be the subject of judicial review proceedings: see *Krebs v NHS Commissioning Board*[39] and the cases cited therein including *Hampshire County Council v Support Wave Community Services Ltd*[40] (which was not referred to by the Court in *Hussain*).

Resolving disputes before a primary care contract is signed

11.98 It is rare for parties who are negotiating for a commercial agreement to acquire legal rights or obligations before a contract is concluded. The usual position is that the parties negotiate and, if they reach an agreement on all terms of a proposed contract, the terms are set out in the final contract which both parties sign. However, if the negotiations do not lead to the parties reaching agreement on all terms of a proposed contract, both parties can walk away from the negotiating table. Neither party is usually under an obligation to continue negotiating or is obliged to accept terms imposed by a third party. The position is different in negotiations for a GP practice contract between NHS commissioners and proposed providers.

11.99 If an NHS commissioner and a proposed provider are in the course of negotiations intending to lead to a contract but cannot agree a term, either party can refer the dispute to the FHSAU which can make a determination on the dispute. However, once the FHSAU have adjudicated, the outcome is only binding on the NHS commissioner – the GP practice can still refuse to sign the contract with that term included.

11.100 For GMS contracts, the pre-contract dispute resolution process is set out in reg 9 of the GMS Regs 2015, which provides:

> (1) If, in the course of negotiations intending to lead to a contract, the parties to the proposed contract ('the prospective parties') are unable to agree on a particular term of the contract, either party may refer the dispute to the Secretary of State to consider and determine.
>
> (2) Where the prospective parties are health service bodies, any dispute which arises in the course of the negotiation of the proposed contract

38 [2011] EWCA Civ 800.
39 [2014] EWCA Civ 1540.
40 [2006] EWCA Civ 1035.

may be referred to the Secretary of State for determination under section 9 of the Act (NHS contracts).

(3) Any dispute referred to the Secretary of State in accordance with paragraph (1), or to which section 9 of the Act applies by virtue of paragraph (2), must be considered and determined in accordance with the provisions of regulations 83(3) to (15) and 84(1) and, where applicable, paragraph (4) of this regulation.

(4) Where the Secretary of State determines a dispute referred under paragraph (1), the determination–

(a) may specify terms to be included in the proposed contract;

(b) may require the Board to proceed with the proposed contract, but may not require the intended contractor to proceed with the proposed contract; and

(c) is binding upon the prospective parties.

11.101 The resolution of disputes before the GMS contract commences accordingly operates in the following way:

a) The parties (ie NHS England and the proposed contractor) must be 'in the course of negotiations intending to lead to a contract' before the regulation applies. This appears to assume that, at the very least, both parties wish the contract to happen even if the terms cannot be agreed. If a contractor has made a request for a contract which NHS England has not agreed to provide, it seems probable that no right arises to refer the case to the FHSAU for determination.

b) If the parties cannot agree a term of the proposed contract, either NHS England or the proposed contractor can refer the dispute to the FHSAU to determine.

c) Once the FHSAU has reached its decision, that decision is binding on NHS England but is not binding on the contactor (possibly unless the contractor is already an NHS body and has referred the dispute to the secretary of state under section 9 of the NHS Act 2006, in which case the decision is binding as a result of section 9(10) of the NHS Act 2006, which provides: 'by the determination of a reference under subsection (7) the appropriate person may specify terms to be included in the proposed arrangement and may direct that it be proceeded with'. In practice, the contractor has the choice at that stage of accepting the contract on the terms set by the FHSAU, or walking away from the agreement (unless NHS England come up with an offer of other acceptable terms).

11.102 The same scheme for the resolution of disputes before a contract is signed is set out at reg 8 of the PMS Regs 2015. There is no right if the parties are negotiating for an APMS agreement, because there are no regulations which govern the terms of such contracts.

11.103 There is an unresolved legal problem with this procedure because it appears to assume that NHS England is in the process of negotiating with a single prospective supplier of GP services. That approach sits somewhat uncomfortably with the duty on NHS England to tender all GP contracts under the Public Contract Regulations 2015[41] and the National Health Service (Procurement, Patient Choice and Competition) (No 2) Regulations

41 SI No 102.

(NHS Procurement Regs) 2013[42] which came into force on 1 April 2013. It is difficult to see many circumstances in which NHS England would be entitled to enter into negotiations with a prospective contractor (after a selection of that contactor through a procurement process) without the negotiation process prejudicing the rights of the other potential contractors who took part in the competitive process but were unsuccessful. However, this is something that may need to be worked out in litigation concerning the meaning of the Public Contract Regulations 2015 and NHS Procurement Regs 2013. Nonetheless, at present there appears to be a fairly stark contradiction between the two sets of regulations.

Variation and updating of GMS and PMS contracts

11.104 When an NHS general practice enters into a GMS contract or a PMS agreement, the contractors ought to sign a large paper document which records the terms of the agreement between the parties before the services are commenced. In practice, the signing of the formal contract can often take place months or years after the services start being provided. There are also occasions known to the authors where, many years on, neither the commissioner nor the practice can locate a signed NHS primary care commissioning contract. Such a situation means that the legal rights of both the commissioner and the practice can be wholly unclear.

11.105 Under para 57(2)(a) of Part 8 of Schedule 3 to the GMS Regs 2015, NHS England may vary a contract where 'it is reasonably satisfied that the variation is necessary to comply with the Act, any regulations made under or by virtue of the Act or any direction given by the Secretary of State under or by virtue of the Act'. This power is used by NHS England to bring the contractual terms of both GMS and PMS contracts up to date following changes to the relevant regulations, and to reflect any relevant directions made by the secretary of state. All other changes require the written consent of both parties.

11.106 Where an NHS commissioner wishes to vary the terms of the contract with the GP practice, pursuant to para 57(2)(b) and (3) of Part 8 of Schedule 3 to the GMS Regs 2015, it must give notice in writing to the contractor of the wording of the proposed variation and the date on which that variation is to take effect. That date must fall at least 14 days after the date on which notice of the proposed variation is given.

11.107 A like provision is included in para 52 of Part 8 of Schedule 2 to the PMS Regs 2015, which requires all PMS agreements to have a term with the same wording.

11.108 There are no regulations affecting APMS agreements or former pilot scheme contracts. It follows that those contracts can only be varied to bring them in line with any directions issued by the secretary of state if the terms of such a contract include a provision which is modelled on a GMS or PMS agreement.

11.109 From time to time NHS England publishes updated versions of a 'standard' GMS contract. This document is used as a template by primary

42 SI No 500.

care organisations which are entering into new contracts with GMS providers. However, the standard document also reflects the current position under the GMS Regs 2015, and any relevant directions made by the secretary of state, and thus (provided the requisite notices have been served on each GMS practice) probably reflects the present terms of the GMS contract between NHS England and the GP practice. The changes to PMS Regs 2015 tend to mirror those under the GMS scheme (but do not always do so).

11.110 NHS England also publishes 'standard' versions of APMS and PMS contracts, which are also in effect templates.

11.111 The most reliable method to determine the present terms of a contract between a GP practice and NHS England is to start with the paper document issued to the practice at the date that the contract was originally agreed (if that can be located) and then work through every contract notice that has been served on the practice by any former primary care trust and then NHS England in order to determine the present state of any particular clause. It may, however, be impossible to conduct such a contractual audit trail because neither the commissioner nor the practice are able to locate all the relevant contractual documents.

11.112 Each year there are negotiations between the BMA General Practice Committee and the DHSC, represented by 'NHS Employers' to make changes to the terms of the GP contracts. A joint guidance note is published by the BMA, NHS Employers (the organisation representing NHS provides) and NHS England, outlining new contractual requirements of the GMS contract. A summary of the outcome of the most recent negotiations was published in March 2018.[43] However, these contractual changes will only take effect if steps are taken to incorporate them into the individual contracts held by each GP practice using the procedures set out above.

'Entire agreement' clauses and exclusion of prior representations clauses

11.113 An 'entire agreement' clause is a clause in a commercial contract which provides that all of the terms agreed between the parties are contained within the document. Where such a clause is present, it makes it difficult (if not nearly impossible in most cases) for either party to allege that the true agreement between the parties contained implied terms which added to or contradicted the express terms. An effective entire agreement clause prevents either party to the contract from relying on something that was said or done prior to the contract being signed giving rise to enforceable rights.

11.114 These clauses are not included in the mandatory list of clauses that GMS and PMS agreements are required to contain under the relevant regulations. However, all of the standard GMS contracts have contained

43 See www.nhsemployers.org/-/media/Employers/Documents/Primary-care-contracts/GMS/Summary-of-the-2018-19-GMS-contract-agreement.pdf?la=en&hash=3CAFA50ECF88B1E21BD69186270334DCF12399D8.

such clauses since the contracts were first drafted in 2004, and many PMS and APMS agreements contain such clauses.

11.115 The 2017/18 GMS standard form contract contains entire agreement and exclusion of representations clauses as follows:

> **27.2. Entire Agreement**
> 27.2.1. Subject to Part 11 (opts outs of additional and out of hours services), clauses 15.9.8 and 15.10.8 and any variations made in accordance with Part 26, this Contract constitutes the entire agreement between the parties with respect to its subject matter.
>
> 27.2.2. The Contract supersedes any prior agreements, negotiations, promises, conditions or representations, whether written or oral, and the parties confirm that they did not enter into the Contract on the basis of any representations that are not expressly incorporated into the Contract. However, nothing in this Contract purports to exclude liability on the part of either party for fraudulent misrepresentation.

11.116 The effect on an entire agreement clause was considered by Lightman J in *Inntrepreneur Pub Company Ltd v East Crown Ltd*,[44] which followed *Deepak Fertilisers & Petrochemicals Ltd v Davy McKee (London) Ltd and another*.[45] The judge said:[46]

> The purpose of an entire agreement clause is to preclude a party to a written agreement from threshing through the undergrowth and finding in the course of negotiations some (chance) remark or statement (often long forgotten or difficult to recall or explain) on which to found a claim such as the present to the existence of a collateral warranty. The entire agreement clause obviates the occasion for any such search and the peril to the contracting parties posed by the need which may arise in its absence to conduct such a search. For such a clause constitutes a binding agreement between the parties that the full contractual terms are to be found in the document containing the clause and not elsewhere, and that accordingly any promises or assurances made in the course of the negotiations (which in the absence of such a clause might have effect as a collateral warranty) shall have no contractual force, save insofar as they are reflected and given effect in that document. The operation of the clause is not to render evidence of the collateral warranty inadmissible in evidence as is suggested in *Chitty on Contracts* 28th ed. Vol 1 para 12–102: it is to denude what would otherwise constitute a collateral warranty of legal effect.

11.117 In *Ravennavi SpA v New Century Shipbuilding*,[47] Moore-Bick LJ said as follows about entire agreement clauses:[48]

> The effect of an entire agreement clause of the kind to be found in Article XIX.4 of the two formal shipbuilding contracts executed in this case must depend primarily on its terms, since it is the language chosen by the parties to express their agreement (wherever it appears) which, construed in its proper context, provides the primary source of their intentions. It is for that reason that I am unable to accept the suggestion in the Buyer's skeleton argument that clauses of this kind can be construed by reference to their supposed purpose or that their significance is diminished if

44 [2000] 2 Lloyd's Rep 611.
45 [1999] 1 All ER (Comm) 69.
46 At para 7.
47 [2007] EWCA Civ 58, [2007] 2 Lloyd's Rep 24.
48 At para 25.

> they are found among what are sometimes called the 'boilerplate' provisions of a formal contract of this kind. There may be circumstances, of course, in which the court can be satisfied that a clause of that kind, although apparently couched in language wide enough to encompass the particular matter on which one or other party seeks to rely, was not intended by the parties to operate in the way in which its terms would suggest, but any such conclusion must be borne out by the particular circumstances of the case.

11.118 Thus, the effect of entire agreement clauses generally is to give rise to a contractual estoppel which prevents a party from asserting that something outside the four corners of the contract was either i) a term or ii) a collateral contract.

11.119 The standard form GMS contract not only includes an entire agreement clause but also a clause which provides that the terms of the agreement superseded any 'prior agreements, negotiations, promises, conditions or representations'. Hence, other than in a case of fraud, neither party ought to be able to rely on anything that was said prior to the contract being signed to change the terms of legal obligations between the parties.

11.120 There are, however, some limitations to the extent to which an entire agreement clause can be relied upon if the evidence shows that the GMS contract did not contain all of the terms which had been agreed by the parties and was not intended to contain all such terms. See, for example, *Tomkins v Knowsley Primary Care Trust*.[49] In such a case, depending on the precise evidence in the case, the courts may give effect to parallel agreements which exist alongside the formal GMS contract.

Third party rights under GP practice contracts

11.121 Prior to 1999, save in highly unusual circumstances, legally enforceable contracts only gave legally enforceable rights to the parties to the contract. Rights under contracts are 'private law rights' which are enforceable in the normal civil courts. Private law rights need to be distinguished from 'public law rights', the latter of which can only be enforced against a public body by way of judicial review.

11.122 The legal theory was that a contract between A and B gave rights to A and B alone and that, unless the contract specifically provided that enforceable rights were to be acquired by a person other than A and B, no one else got any rights. This was changed by the Contracts (Rights of Third Parties) Act 1999. However, section 1(2) of the 1999 Act permitted the parties to a contract to exclude the rights of third parties by an express term of the contract.

11.123 Regulation 95 of the GMS Regs 2015 provides that a term is required to be included in a GMS contract to provide that the contract does not

49 [2010] EWHC 1194 (QB). While this case was not the subject of an appeal, it is a first instance judgment that is not binding on any other judge. There must, at least, be questions whether this case should be followed on the construction of the entire agreement clause in the light of the hard contractual approach taken by the Court of Appeal in *National Health Service Commissioning Board v Silovsky and another* [2017] EWCA Civ 1389.

create any enforceable right by any person who is not a party to the contract. This is now contained in clause 2.1.3 of the standard form 2017/18 GMS contract. This clause will mean that third parties, and in particular patients of the practice, cannot acquire additional private law enforceable rights by seeking to rely on the terms of a GMS contract.

11.124 The same position arises under PMS agreements as a result of reg 87 of the PMS Regs 2015.

11.125 Under direction 7 of the APMS Directions 2016, any APMS contract must contain a term that has the same effect as reg 87 of the PMS Regs 2015 and thus in effect exclude third party rights.

Payments under primary medical care contracts

11.126 The payment which is due to the service provider under a commercial contract is one of the key features of any contract. However, in GP practice contracts, payment terms are not straightforward. The payment obligation depends on the type of GP practice contract, and on whether the services which the contractor agrees to provide are essential, additional or enhanced services. Further, the payment terms (as well as other terms) are reviewed on an annual basis and, for those practices holding GMS contracts, can be changed by the unilateral action of a person who is not a party to the contract, namely the secretary of state. Changes cannot be made to PMS agreements without the consent of the contract holder.

Payment due to GP Practices under GMS contracts

11.127 The sums due to a GP practice that holds a GMS contract are only partially set out in the GMS contract, but are mainly set out in directions made by the secretary of state. The directions are known as the General Medical Services Statement of Financial Entitlement Directions (SFE Directions). This document defines the amounts that are payable for essential, additional and enhanced services to GP practices that hold a GMS contract.

11.128 The legal basis for payments being set by directions is in section 87 of the NHS Act 2006, which provides as follows concerning payments to GP practices that hold a GMS contract:

> (1) The Secretary of State may give directions as to payments to be made under general medical services contracts.
> (2) A general medical services contract must require payments to be made under the contract in accordance with directions under this section.
> (3) Directions under subsection (1) may in particular–
> (a) provide for payments to be made by reference to compliance with standards or the achievement of levels of performance,
> (b) provide for payments to be made by reference to–
> (i) any scheme or scale specified in the direction, or
> (ii) a determination made by any person in accordance with factors specified in the direction,
> (c) provide for the making of payments in respect of individual practitioners,

(d) provide that the whole or any part of a payment is subject to conditions (and may provide that payments are payable by the Board only if it is satisfied as to certain conditions),

(e) make provision having effect from a date before the date of the direction, provided that, having regard to the direction as a whole, the provision is not detrimental to the persons to whose remuneration it relates.

(4) Before giving a direction under subsection (1), the Secretary of State–

(a) must consult any body appearing to him to be representative of persons to whose remuneration the direction would relate, and

(b) may consult such other persons as he considers appropriate.

(5) 'Payments' includes fees, allowances, reimbursements, loans and repayments.

11.129 Consideration of changes to the GP contract and the payment rates follows an annual cycle. The secretary of state has delegated the job of negotiating the changes to GP contracts to staff at NHS Employers, who hold the consultations referred to in section 87(4). The 'representative' tends to be the General Practice Committee of the BMA. These discussions are often described as 'negotiations' to seek to reach a common conclusion about changes to the GP contract and payment rates but, in law, this is a consultation. This means that the secretary of state has to take due account of the views expressed by the GPC on behalf of working doctors, but the secretary of state remains as the ultimate decision-maker. Hence, the GPC can register its support or objection to a proposed change of terms but, once those consultations are completed, the secretary of state makes the final decision. The secretary of state then issues directions which set out the changes to the existing SFE that affect GMS practices will be paid in the coming year.

11.130 In 2013 the secretary of state revised the SFE Directions and published an entirely new document rather than making directions which contained reference to previous versions. The 2013 document runs to 141 pages. There are a number of amendment directions that have made amendments to the SFE, known in these directions as the 'principal directions'.

11.131 The directions take effect as a term of the GMS contract by clause 18.1.2 (of the standard 2017/18 GMS contract published by NHS England), which provides:

> The Board shall make payments to the Contractor in such amount and in such manner as specified in any directions given by the Secretary of State for the time being in force under section 87 or 98A of the 2006 Act. Where, pursuant to directions made under section 87 or 98A of the 2006 Act, the Board is required to make a payment to the Contractor under the Contract but subject to conditions, those conditions must be a term of the Contract.

11.132 Thus the directions made by the secretary of state form a term of the GMS contract. The contract also includes 'set off' provisions under which NHS England are entitled to set off any sums which are due to NHS England from the contractor against any sums payable under the directions. All payments must be made promptly by NHS England under clause 18.1.1, which provides:

> The Board and the Contractor shall make any payments under the Contract promptly and in accordance with both the terms of the Contract (including,

for the avoidance of doubt, any payment due pursuant to clause 18.1.2), and any other conditions relating to payment contained in directions given by the Secretary of State under section 87 of the 2006 Act, subject to any right the Board may have to set off against an amount payable to the Contractor under the Contract any amount that:

(a) is owed by the Contractor to the Board under the Contract; or
(b) the Board may withhold from the Contractor in accordance with the terms of the Contract or any other applicable provisions contained in directions given by the Secretary of State under section 87 of the 2006 Act.

In practice, payments are made monthly by the NHS Business Services Authority (BSA) on behalf of NHS England to GMS practices.[50]

11.133 The scheme for all the payments due to GP practices under the SFE is complex. The SFE sets down a number of formulae and calculations for determining exactly how much money is owed to each practice. It is beyond the scope of this book to analyse all the various payment routes, and GP practices should seek advice on payment matters relating to their particular practice, but broadly the SFE contains provisions to make the following payments:

a) global sum payments, which are a monthly contribution towards the contractor's costs in delivering essential and additional services, including its staff costs;
b) Minimum Practice Income Guarantee;
c) payments under the Quality and Outcomes Framework (QOF), a voluntary payment scheme which rewards practices for the provision of 'quality care' and helps to fund further improvements in the delivery of clinical care. Changes to the QOF are negotiated annually by NHS Employers (on behalf of NHS England) and the BMA GPC. NHS Employers publishes guidance each year on the changes. The QOF, although voluntary, is a key area where GPs can increase their income. QOF is a points-based system by reference to a number of 'indicators', to assess the GP practice's performance;
d) payment for Directed Enhanced Services, such as the Extended Hours Access Scheme, Alcohol Related Risk Reduction Scheme, Learning Disabilities Health Check Scheme, Patient Participation Scheme, Childhood Immunisations;
e) Payments for Specific Purposes, such as seniority payments, particular vaccines, payment for locums, the flexible careers scheme, and dispensing, among others.

Practice premises costs

11.134 Many GP practices own their own premises, and there can be significant costs associated with running and maintaining such premises. On 1 April 2004, the National Health Service (General Medical Services – Premises Costs) (England) Directions 2004 replaced the sections of the statement of fees and allowances (SFA) relating to practice premises costs.

50 The NHS BSA has contracted out this duty to Capita. There are numerous problems reported with the functioning of this contract.

11.135 On 1 April 2013, the National Health Service (General Services – Premises Costs) Directions 2013 came into force. They provide for payments to contractors in respect of:

a) premises developments or improvements;
b) professional fees and related costs incurred in occupying significantly refurbished premises;
c) relocation of, or re-mortgaging by, the contractor;
d) recurring premises costs.

11.136 The BMA provides a useful summary of what premises payments involve:

> GPs borrow the capital to build the premises and there are schemes that compensate the practice for this, for example borrowing costs (formerly known as cost rent) or notional rent reimbursement.
>
> Payments to contractors are calculated on the amount of rent the practice would pay if renting the premises and this is agreed with the District Valuer (DV).
>
> Other contractors rent their premises, in which case they receive rent reimbursement for actual leasehold rent. The level of reimbursement is calculated by the DV in relation to local current market rents (CMR).
>
> NHS England area teams are responsible for rent reimbursement payments to GP contractors.[51]

11.137 The Premises Costs Directions 2013, however, do not apply where, under reg 20(5) of the GMS Regs 2015, at the point of entering into the practice contract NHS England has drawn up a plan jointly with the contractor to specify the steps to be taken by the contractor to bring the premises up to the required standard and which provides for NHS England to give financial assistance in carrying out such steps.

11.138 Direction 6 provides that the Premises Costs Directions 2013 do not prevent NHS England from providing such financial assistance as it thinks fit in order to pay, or contribute towards, the premises costs of a contractor in circumstances not contemplated by the Premises Costs Directions.

Payment due to GP practices under PMS contracts

11.139 Regulations 16 and 17 of the PMS Regs 2015 make provision for payment to PMS contractors. They provide as follows:

> **16 Finance**
>
> (1) The agreement must contain a term which has the effect of requiring payments to be made under the agreement promptly and in accordance with–
>
> (a) the terms of the agreement;
> (b) any other terms based on which the payment is made; and
> (c) any other conditions relating to the payment contained in regulations made by the Secretary of State under section 94(4) (regulations about section 92 arrangements) or directions given by the Secretary of State under section 98A (exercise of functions) of the Act.

51 See www.bma.org.uk/advice/employment/gp-practices/service-provision/prescribing/advice-for-dispensing-gps/the-gp-practice/nhs-contracts-for-primary-medical-services.

(2) The obligation referred to in paragraph (1) is subject to any right that the Board may have to set off against any amount payable to the contractor under the agreement any amount that–

(a) is owed by the contractor to the Board under the agreement; or

(b) the Board may withhold from the contractor in accordance with the terms of the agreement or any other applicable provisions contained in regulations made by the Secretary of State under section 94(4) of the Act (regulations about section 92 arrangements) or directions given by the Secretary of State under section 98A of the Act (exercise of functions).

17 Conditions about payments

Where, as a consequence of regulations made under section 94(4) of the Act (regulations about section 92 arrangements) or in accordance with directions given by the Secretary of State under section 98A of the Act (exercise of functions), the Board is required to make a payment to a contractor under an agreement which is subject to conditions, the agreement must contain a term which requires those conditions to be a term of the agreement.

11.140 The secretary of state has not made any directions which fix the sums that PMS contractors are required to be paid for the provision of essential services or many other aspects of the contract, because these remain a matter for local negotiation.

11.141 The absence of directions to cover essential services and terms such as premises costs means that PMS contracts need to be read carefully to determine the payments due without necessarily any reference to the equivalent GMS terms. A large number of PMS agreements define that the sums paid to the practice will be fixed by reference to the SFE. If this is the case then, as the terms of the SFE are varied each year, so the terms of the PMS contract are varied. However, in the absence of an express term incorporating the SFE as a term of the PMS agreement, in principle, terms agreed for GMS contracts will only apply to PMS agreements if there is a written agreement between the parties that varies the contractual terms to incorporate the new term: see *National Health Service Commissioning Board v Silovsky and another*.[52]

11.142 In terms of payment to PMS practices, the 2017/18 'standard' PMS agreement published by NHS England provides the following in relation to calculation of service price/charges:

> For local agreement: Reference should be made where appropriate to SFE entitlement, PCR, QOF, seniority payments, superannuation, national insurance contributions, growth, administration, premises costs, any applicable KPIs and LMC levy deductions. Calculation of annual funding changes and uplifts should make reference to NHS England guidance on the arrangements it will apply to ensure fair and equitable treatment of all GP practices.

Situations where there is specific provision for payment to PMS practices

11.143 The secretary of state issued directions in 2013 (Personal Medical Services Agreements (Payments for Specific Purposes) Directions 2013) to PMS practices which cover payments due to doctors working on the Flexible

52 [2017] EWCA Civ 1389.

Careers Scheme, the Returners Scheme and the Doctors' Retainer Scheme, all of which were designed to keep as many GPs as possible working within the NHS.

11.144 In addition, the Primary Medical Services (Directed Enhanced Services) Directions 2017 (which apply to both GMS and PMS contracts) have been made, and provide for payments to be made to PMS contractors for the following Enhanced Services:

a) Extended Hours Access Scheme;
b) Learning Disabilities Health Check Scheme;
c) Childhood Immunisation Scheme;
d) Influenza and Pneumococcal Immunisation Scheme;
e) Violent Patients Scheme;
f) Minor Surgery Scheme.

11.145 The Directed Enhanced Services Directions 2017 do not fix the sums that a PMS practice is required to be paid if the practice agrees to participate in any of the above schemes. The directions either leave payment to be negotiated, or provide, additionally, that in the case of PMS contractors the appropriate level of payment is to be made 'having regard' to the amounts payable under the SFE. The amounts in the SFE must be a starting point for any negotiations between the PMS practice and NHS England for the provision of an Enhanced Service but the parties may agree a higher or lower sum to be paid for the provision of the service.

11.146 If the practice and NHS England were unable to agree the amount to be paid to a PMS practice for an additional service, then theoretically NHS England would be able to define the sum that was to be paid and, if the PMS practice wished to continue to provide the service, it would have to accept the sum that was stipulated by NHS England to challenge the sum by way of an application to the FHSAU. However, in that case, NHS England would need to have considered the sum payable under the SFE for the provision of the services and to have justifiable reason for departing from that sum in the PMS agreement with the practice.

Payment due to GP practices under APMS contracts

11.147 APMS contracts are awarded by NHS England exercising its general powers under section 83(2) of the NHS Act 2006. There is no provision for the secretary of state to make directions to govern payments under such contracts. It follows that the payment terms must be governed by the terms of any such contract (as varied by agreement between NHS England and the contractor from time to time).

Remedies for a failure to pay monies due under a GP practice contract

11.148 Under the GMS and PMS Regs 2015, NHS England is required to make payments to the GP practice 'promptly'. If payments are not made by NHS England to a GP practice, then the GP practice can either register a dispute with the FHSAU or, if it is a legally binding contract, sue NHS England for the monies owing in the county court.

11.149 In addition, both the GMS and PMS Regs 2015 give the GP practice grounds to terminate the contract following a procedure involving serving a 'late payment notice', which involves NHS dispute resolution with the FHSAU. Paragraph 63 of Part 8 of Schedule 3 to the GMS Regs 2015, and para 56 of Part 8 of Schedule 2 to the PMS Regs 2015, provide as follows:

> (1) The contractor may give notice in writing (a 'late payment notice') to the Board if the Board has failed to make any payments due to the contractor in accordance with a term of the agreement regarding prompt payments which has the effect specified in regulation 16(1), and the contractor must specify in the late payment notice the payments that the Board has failed to make in accordance with that term.
> (2) Subject to sub-paragraph (4), the contractor may, at least 28 days after the date on which a late payment notice under sub-paragraph (1) was given, terminate the agreement by giving a further written notice to the Board in the event of the Board's continuing failure to make the payments that are due to the contractor as specified in the late payment notice.
> (3) Sub-paragraph (4) applies if, following receipt of a late payment notice, the Board–
> (a) refers the matter to the NHS dispute resolution procedure before the end of a period of 28 days beginning with the date on which the Board received the late payment notice; and
> (b) gives notice in writing to the contractor that it has done so before the end of that period.
> (4) Where this sub-paragraph applies, the contractor may not terminate the agreement in accordance with sub-paragraph (2) until–
> (a) there has been a final determination of the dispute under the NHS dispute resolution procedure and that determination permits the contractor to terminate the agreement; or
> (b) the Board ceases to pursue the NHS dispute resolution procedure,
> whichever is the earlier.
> (5) This paragraph does not affect any other rights to terminate the agreement that the contractor may have.

Breaches of contract, sanctions and terminations

11.150 As set out above, the rights and obligations of both GP practices and NHS England are set out in the GMS, PMS or APMS contract, which then takes effect as if it is a normal contract between the parties. The contract will also specify how each party is entitled to respond if the other party breaches the contract.

11.151 There are a large number of obligations that GP practices take on within a practice contract. NHS England is thus entitled to require GP practices to perform all of the obligations. Thus, for example, the practice is obliged to be open for core hours as defined in the GMS Regs 2015. Christmas Day is excluded from core hours, but the practice must be open on Christmas Eve. A practice that fails to provide services to NHS patients on Christmas Eve would be acting in breach of contract and NHS England would therefore be entitled to take enforcement action against the practice for that breach.

11.152 However, NHS England is rarely able to terminate a GP practice for a single breach of contract of that type. The contract sets out a scheme under which NHS England is entitled to respond to breaches of contract in a measured and proportionate way. This scheme requires the contractor to respond appropriately to an alleged breach. The scheme seeks to avoid unnecessary confrontation and to manage the relationship between the contractor and NHS England in a sensible way. However, a contractor that does not co-operate with NHS England by responding appropriately to action by NHS England under the contract can find that his, her or its contract is lawfully terminated.

11.153 In November 2017 NHS England published a comprehensive guidance document on primary care commissioning, *Primary medical care – policy and guidance manual* (PGM), which is aimed at CCGs and NHS England. Part C of the PGM is entitled 'When things go wrong' and contains information on contract breaches, sanctions and terminations. The PGM sets out the options open to a commissioner that considers a breach of the contract has occurred:

> 1.2.1 Where the Commissioner considers that a breach has occurred, there are a number of options on how to proceed. The Commissioner can:
>
> - take no action;
> - agree an action with the contractor;
> - issue a Remedial Notice;
> - issue a Breach Notice;
> - apply a Contract Sanction; or
> - terminate the contract.
>
> 1.2.2 Doing nothing and agreeing an action with the contractor are options that are always available to the Commissioner. The remaining options may only be applied in specific situations as envisaged by the contract.
>
> 1.2.3 The following paragraphs set out the circumstances in which a Remedial Notice or a Breach Notice may be issued, a Contract Sanction may be applied or the contract may be terminated with an explanation of the relevant process that the Commissioner must follow.
>
> 1.2.4 The Commissioner must ensure that, when issuing a Remedial or Breach Notice, applying a Contract Sanction or terminating a contract, it follows the proper internal processes around approval of the action, compliance with any standing orders and due consideration of all relevant factors in the decision making process.

11.154 NHS England also issued guidance to its own staff in June 2013 about how to respond to breaches of contract by GP practices called *Contract breaches, sanctions and termination for primary medical services: Standard operating policies and procedures for primary care.* Notwithstanding the existence of the PGM, the 2013 guidance does not appear to have been withdrawn. The 2013 guidance set out the policies that NHS England expects its staff to follow when responding to actual or perceived breaches of contract by GP practices. The 2013 guidance starts with the following:

> Whilst most health care professionals practise to a very high standard, some individuals may occasionally work in ways that pose a serious risk to patient

safety. In many instances this can be unintentional and the clinician's performance may be affected by a combination of personal and situational factors, such as illness or professional isolation and in these cases NHS England shall refer to the policy for Identification management and support of independent contractors whose performance gives cause for concern.

11.155 At paras 14–16 the 2013 guidance then explains the basic approach that NHS England staff are expected to take to contract breaches as follows:

> 14. In most cases, the issue of a breach notice, application of a sanction or a move to terminate a contract should be considered as the final stages in a process where NHS England and contractor have endeavoured to resolve matters satisfactorily, without the need to take formal contractual steps.
>
> 15. However, there will be occasions when a contract or is either unable or unwilling to change their behaviour or remedy a situation which may then result in a direct breach of their contracted terms and/or pose a significant risk to patient safety, requiring immediate action by NHS England to quickly resolve the matter.
>
> 16. This policy is designed to give an overview of the procedure to be followed by NHS England when taking formal steps in resolving contractual and performance related issues of independent contractors providing primary medical care services.

11.156 In practice, NHS England and the CCGs who work on their behalf under co-commissioning are in a difficult position as a result of the shortage of GPs who are willing to take on NHS general practice contracts. Accordingly, NHS England is usually required to persuade a GP practice to comply with the terms of its contracts because enforcement action which results in the contract being terminated may well result in a temporary permanent vacuum with no GP service being available to patients. However, NHS England will act to terminate a contract if there are serious threats to patient safety or substantial financial irregularities.

Remedial and breach notices

11.157 Under GMS and PMS contracts, NHS England is entitled to respond to a breach by the GP practice of any of the terms of the contract by serving either a 'remedial notice' or a 'breach notice'. These are two different types of notices, which have subtly different consequences for the GP practice. The APMS Directions 2016 do not require APMS contracts to contain provisions relating to remedial or breach notice, however the 'standard' APMS agreement 2017/18 published by NHS England does contain such provisions (at para 62).

11.158 Paragraph 70 of Part 8 of Schedule 3 to the GMS Regs 2015, which is replicated in para 61 of Part 8 of Schedule 2 to the PMS Regs 2015, creates the following scheme for remedial and breach notices:

> (1) Where a contractor's breach of the contract is not one to which any of paragraphs 65 to 69[53] apply and that breach is capable of remedy,

53 These concern rights of termination on the following grounds: provision of untrue information; fitness to practise matters; a serious risk to patient safety or risk of financial loss to NHS England; unlawful sub-contracting; and in the case of a GMS contract, issues relating to the contractor's eligibility to hold the contract.

the Board must, before taking any action it is otherwise entitled to take by virtue of the contract, give notice in writing to the contractor requiring it to remedy the breach (a 'remedial notice').

(2) A remedial notice must specify–
   (a) details of the breach;
   (b) the steps that the contractor must take to the satisfaction of the Board in order to remedy the breach; and
   (c) the period during which those steps must be taken (the 'notice period').

(3) The notice period must not be less than a period of 28 days beginning with the date on which the notice is given unless the Board is satisfied that a shorter period is necessary to protect–
   (a) the safety of the contractor's patients; or
   (b) itself from material financial loss.

(4) Where the Board is satisfied that the contractor has not taken the required steps to remedy the breach by the end of the notice period, the Board may give a further notice in writing to the contractor terminating the contract with effect from such date as the Board specifies in the notice.

(5) Where the contractor's breach of the contract is not one to which any of paragraphs 65 to 69 apply and the breach is not capable of remedy, the Board may give notice in writing to the contractor requiring the contractor not to repeat the breach (a 'breach notice').

(6) If, following a breach notice or a remedial notice, the contractor–
   (a) repeats the breach that was the subject of the breach notice or the remedial notice; or
   (b) otherwise breaches the contract resulting in either a remedial notice or a further breach notice,

   the Board may give notice in writing to the contractor terminating the contract with effect from such date as the Board specifies in the notice.

(7) The Board may not exercise its right to terminate the contract under sub-paragraph (6) unless the Board is satisfied that the cumulative effect of the breaches is such that to allow the contract to continue would prejudice the efficiency of the services to be provided under the contract.

(8) If the contractor is in breach of any obligation under the contract and a breach notice or a remedial notice in respect of the default giving rise to the breach has been given to the contractor, the Board may withhold or deduct monies which would otherwise be payable under the contract in respect of the obligation which is the subject matter of the default.

11.159 The PGM makes clear that:

> **GMS/PMS** – Where a breach is capable of remedy, a Remedial Notice must be issued before the Commissioner takes any other action under the contract (such as termination). Where a breach is not capable of remedy, a Breach Notice must be issued before the Commissioner takes any other action under the contract (such as termination).

Remedial notices

11.160 The service of a remedial notice thus gives rights to both NHS England and the contractor. It can be served for any breach (however trivial) of the obligations of the GP practice as set out in the GMS contract. Once it is served, the GP practice has the notice period (which must be not less than 28 days) to remedy the breach.

11.161 The PGM says:[54]

> A breach capable of remedy is where the breach continues but the contractor could take action to stop the breach. Examples of breaches that may be capable of remedy include:
> - failure to compile a practice leaflet; or
> - failure to provide information to the Commissioner.

11.162 The PGM then sets out the steps a commissioner may take if it determines that a breach is capable of remedy:

> 1.3.9 Where the Commissioner has determined that a breach is capable of remedy, the Commissioner may, depending on the nature and circumstances of a breach take the following steps. These steps do not prejudice or delay a Commissioners right to issue a Remedial Notice at any point before or during any of these steps being taken where the Commissioner reasonably considers it is appropriate to do so:
>
> 1.3.9.1 The Commissioner should contact the contractor to discuss the breach and the action that they may be entitled to take, i.e. the issue of a Remedial Notice.
>
> 1.3.9.2 This discussion should provide the contractor with an opportunity to provide an explanation as to the circumstances that led to the breach. An accurate minute of any discussions should be retained.
>
> 1.3.9.3 The Commissioner should review the evidence related to the breach including any information received during the discussion or in representations .
>
> 1.3.9.4 If the Commissioner is satisfied that the matter is a breach which is capable of remedy, then the Commissioner may issue a Remedial Notice to the contractor, requiring the contractor to remedy the breach.
>
> 1.3.9.5 It is important that when the steps above are undertaken, this is completed as quickly as is reasonably possible as long delays between the breach occurring, or the Commissioner becoming aware of the breach, and the Remedial Notice being issued, could lead to an argument that the Commissioner has accepted the breach and waived its right to take action. The Commissioner will need to decide what action it considers would be reasonable to take before issuing a Remedial Notice taking into account the circumstances of an individual breach'

11.163 The PGM contains template remedial notices in its appendices and suggests what a remedial notice should contain:[55]

> 1.3.10 A Remedial Notice must specify:
>
> 1.1.5 details of the breach, which led to the Remedial Notice being issued and any evidence gathered in respect of the breach;
>
> 1.1.6 the steps the contractor must take in order to remedy the breach to the Commissioner's satisfaction;
>
> 1.1.7 the period in which the steps must be taken;
>
> 1.1.8 any arrangements for reviewing the matter to ensure that the requirements of the Remedial Notice have been met; and

54 At Part C 1.3.7.

55 The strange numbering is taken from the original document published by NHS England.

1.1.9 the actions that the Commissioner shall take if the contractor fails to satisfactorily remedy the breach.

11.164 If the GP practice does not act to remedy the breach to NHS England's satisfaction (or later repeats the same breach or breaches the contract in a different way), NHS England acquires the right to terminate the contract by serving a further notice after the notice period has ended. The wording provides that NHS England obtains the right to terminate if NHS England is not 'satisfied' that the breach has been remedied. This provision has not been, as far as these authors are aware, ever been tested in the High Court. However, it is possible to envisage a situation where the contractor contends that he or she has taken sufficient steps to remedy the breach, but NHS England say that they are not satisfied with those actions. In such a case (unless possibly the dispute about whether the breach is remedied is referred to the FHSAU for determination) NHS England would still appear to have the contractual right to terminate the contract, provided that it had reasonable grounds for its position.

11.165 There is also no time period set within the terms of the contract within which NHS England have to respond to a failure to remedy a breach. The contractual terms appear to permit NHS England (at least in theory) to continue to have the right to serve a termination notice throughout the remaining period of the contract. However, if there is a significant delay of many months or years, there may be arguments that NHS England has affirmed the contract and thus cannot serve a termination notice.

Breach notices

11.166 There are other breaches of contract which cannot be remedied. For example, the GP practice is required to be open from Monday to Friday for all days except Good Friday, Christmas Day and bank holidays (see the definition of 'core hours' in the GMS contract). If a GP practice failed to open on, say, Christmas Eve, this would be a breach of contract. However, it cannot be 'remedied' because, by the time a notice is served, it is all in the past. However, NHS England is entitled to respond to such a breach by serving a breach notice. The primary effect of the breach notice is that it acts as a 'yellow card' to warn the GP practice that NHS England considers that they have breached the contract and to warn the GP practice not to repeat the breach.

11.167 The first effect of a breach notice under para 70 of Part 8 of Schedule 3 to the GMS Regs 2015 is that if the GP practice breaches the same term of the contract for a second time following the service of a breach notice, NHS England can respond to the second breach by serving a notice to terminate the GP practice contract. Second, there is a wider effect; if, following the service of a breach notice, the GP practice act in breach of *any* of the terms of a GP contract, NHS England are entitled to serve a further breach notice or, as the case may be, a remedial notice and then get the right to serve a termination notice. However, this seemingly wide power is cut down by para 70(7), which provides that NHS England:

> . . . may not exercise its right to terminate the contract under sub-paragraph (6) unless the Board is satisfied that the cumulative effect of the breaches is such that to allow the contract to continue would prejudice the efficiency of the services to be provided under the contract.

11.168 This is the 'cumulative effect' clause under which NHS England consider must be satisfied before they have the right to terminate the contract. It is thus not quite a 'two strikes and you are out' provision. However, the power to serve a termination notice applies if NHS England are 'satisfied' that the breaches have a cumulative effect, and thus gives a considerable amount of discretion to NHS England staff to determine whether the breaches have this effect or not.

11.169 Neither the PGM nor the 2013 guidance provide any clear guidance on the meaning of the 'cumulative effect' test. However, the expression 'prejudicial to the efficiency of the services' has a specific meaning under reg 14 of the National Health Service (Performers List) (England) Regulations 2013, which refers to the test that NHS England must apply when considering the removal of a GP from the Performers List. Regulation 15 sets out a list of factors that NHS England (or the First-tier Tribunal on appeal) must take into account when considering whether to remove a practitioner from the Performers List under the 2013 Performers List Regulations. The factors are as follows:

> (5) Where the Board is considering whether to remove a Practitioner from a performers list under regulation 14(3)(b) (an efficiency case), it must consider–
> (a) any information relating to that Practitioner which it has received under regulation 9;
> (b) any information held by the NHSLA about past or current investigations or proceedings involving or relating to that Practitioner, which information the NHSLA must supply if the Board so requests; and
> (c) the matters referred to in paragraph (6).
>
> (6) Those matters are–
> (a) the nature of any incident which was prejudicial to the efficiency of the services which the Practitioner performed;
> (b) the length of time since the last incident occurred and since any investigation into it was concluded;
> (c) any action taken by any regulatory or other body (including the police or courts) as a result of any such incident;
> (d) the relevance of the incident to the Practitioner's performance of the services which those included in the relevant performers list perform, and the likely risk to patients or to public finances;
> (e) whether the Practitioner has ever failed to comply with a request to undertake an assessment by the NCAA on or before 31st March 2005, by the NPSA between 1st April 2005 and 31st March 2012 inclusive, by the NICE between 1st April 2012 and 31st March 2013 inclusive, or thereafter by the NHSLA;
> (f) whether the Practitioner has previously failed to supply information, make a declaration or comply with an undertaking required on inclusion in a performers list;
> (g) whether, in respect of any list, the Practitioner–
> (i) was refused inclusion in it,
> (ii) was included in it subject to conditions,
> (iii) was removed from it, or
> (iv) is currently suspended from it,
> and, if so, the facts relating to the incident which led to such action and the reasons given for such action by the holder of the list; and
> (h) whether, in respect of any list, the Practitioner was at the time of the originating event or in the six months preceding that event, a director of a body corporate, which–

(i) was refused inclusion in it,
(ii) was included in it subject to conditions,
(iii) was removed from it, or
(iv) is currently suspended from it,

and, if so, the facts relating to that event and the reasons given for such action by the holder of the list.

11.170 The use of the same language in both the GMS contract and the Performers List Regulations 2013 means that it seems that NHS England ought to consider each of these factors before making a decision whether the 'cumulative effect' test has been met.

Termination of the practice contract

11.171 In addition to the termination route explored above, after the serving of a remedial or breach notice, there are several other means by which a practice contract may be terminated. There are slight differences between the GMS and PMS scheme. APMS agreements must contain some terms which have the same effect as some of the termination provisions in the PMS Regs 2015 (see direction 7 of the APMS Directions 2016), but not all, and the parties are afforded some latitude to specify the grounds under which an APMS contract may or must be terminated and any contract sanctions may be imposed.

11.172 The termination routes below, therefore, are predominantly relevant to GMS and PMS contracts.

Termination by agreement

11.173 Both the GMS and PMS Regs 2015 provide that the practice and NHS England can mutually agree to terminate the contract and the date at which the contract will end. Paragraph 60 of Part 8 of Schedule 3 to the GMS Regs 2015 and para 53 of Part 8 of Schedule 2 to the PMS Regs 2015 provide as follows:

> The Board and the contractor may agree in writing to terminate the contract, and if the parties so agree, they must agree the date upon which that termination is to take effect and any further terms upon which the contract is to be terminated.

Termination on the death of an individual medical practitioner

11.174 Both the GMS and PMS Regs 2015 provide for termination of the contract when a sole medical practitioner dies. The default position is that the contract will end after seven days from the date of the death, however both sets of regulations provide for an extension of this time. Paragraph 61 of Part 8 of Schedule 3 to the GMS Regs 2015 provides as follows:

> (1) Where the contractor is an individual medical practitioner and the contractor dies, the contract terminates at the end of the period of seven days beginning with the date of the contractor's death unless, before the end of that period sub-paragraph (2) applies.
> (2) This sub-paragraph applies where–
> (a) the Board agrees in writing with the contractor's personal representatives that the contract is to continue for a further

period, not exceeding 28 days, from the end of the period of seven days; and

(b) the contractor's personal representatives confirm in writing to the Board that they wish to employ or engage one or more general medical practitioners to assist in the continuation of the provision of clinical services under the contract and, after discussion with the Board–

(i) the Board agrees to provide reasonable support which would enable clinical services under the contract to continue,

(ii) the Board and the contractor's personal representatives agree the terms on which the provision of clinical services can continue,

(iii) the Board and the contractor's personal representatives agree the period during which clinical services must be provided being a period of not more than 28 days beginning on the day after the end of the period of seven days referred to in sub-paragraph (1).

(3) This paragraph does not affect any other rights to terminate the contract which the contractor may have.

11.175 There are a number of potential difficulties with the operation of this scheme. It appears that it was originally drafted to allow the widow or widower of the GP to find another GP to take over the practice with the intention that the incoming GP would take over the practice and would purchase any part of the practice that could be sold from the widow or widower. GPs are prohibited from selling the goodwill of a GP practice, but there is nothing to prevent the widow or widower of a GP from selling the buildings from which the practice was delivered (if owned by the deceased GP) and the fixtures, fittings and equipment of the practice.

11.176 However, this scheme meant that, subject to NHS England giving its agreement, the selection of the incoming GP was mainly made by the widow or widower of the deceased GP. Such an arrangement may have benefitted the financial position of the widow or widower of the GP but was not a defensible process for the selection of the holder of a contract to deliver public services. NHS England is now obliged to follow a transparent and open process under the National Health Service (Procurement, Patient Choice and Competition) (No 2) Regulations 2013 and/or the Public Contracts Regulations 2015 before appointing a new contractor to take over any GP practice.[56]

11.177 Paragraph 54 of Part 8 of Schedule 2 to the PMS Regs 2015 is slightly different and provides as follows:

(1) Where the agreement is with an individual medical practitioner and that medical practitioner dies, the agreement terminates at the end of the period of seven days beginning with the date of the contractor's death unless sub-paragraph (2) applies.

(2) This sub-paragraph applies where, before the end of the period of seven days referred to in sub-paragraph (1), the Board agrees in writing with the contractor's personal representatives that the agreement should continue for a further period, not exceeding 28 days, from the end of the period of seven days.

56 Please see chapter 27 on procurement for further information about what a proper procurement process should look like.

(3) This paragraph does not affect any other rights to terminate the agreement which the Board may have under paragraphs 57 to 60.

Termination by notice

11.178 Both the GMS and PMS Regs 2015 provide for termination by notice, although there is a crucial and fundamental distinction between the two provisions, which lies at the heart of why GPs may choose to contract under a GMS rather than PMS contract.

11.179 Paragraph 62 of Part 8 of Schedule 3 to the GMS Regs 2015 gives the *contractor*, and not NHS England, the right to terminate the contract in six months, or three months if the contractor is a sole practitioner, by giving notice. It provides as follows:

(1) A contractor may terminate the contract at any time by giving notice in writing to the Board.
(2) Where a contractor gives notice to the Board under sub-paragraph (1), the contract terminates six months after the date on which the notice was given ('the termination date') unless the termination date does not fall on the last calendar day of a month, in which case the contract terminates instead on the last calendar day of the month in which the termination date falls.
(3) If the contractor is an individual medical practitioner, sub-paragraph (2) applies to the contractor as if the references to 'six months' were instead references to 'three months'.
(4) This paragraph does not affect any other rights to terminate the contract that the contractor may have'

11.180 The PMS Regs 2015 also provide for termination by notice, except the right is reserved to *both* parties. Paragraph 55 of Part 8 of Schedule 2 to the GMS Regs 2015 provides as follows:

(1) The contractor or the Board may at any time terminate the agreement by giving notice in writing to the other party or parties to the agreement.
(2) Subject to sub-paragraphs (3) and (4), notice given under sub-paragraph (1) must specify the date on which the termination is to take effect and the agreement terminates on the date so specified.
(3) Where the period of notice in relation to the termination (which must be a period of at least six months) has previously been agreed between the parties and provided for in the agreement, the date of termination specified in the notice must be calculated in accordance with the agreed period of notice.
(4) Where a period of notice in relation to the termination has not previously been agreed between the parties and provided for in the agreement, the period of notice required must be six months and the date of termination specified in the notice must be calculated accordingly and the agreement terminates on the date so calculated.
(5) This paragraph does not affect any other rights to terminate the agreement which the contractor and the Board may have.

11.181 The period of notice must be at least six months but is otherwise as the parties have agreed. However, as stated above, PMS contractors have a right under reg 32 of the PMS Regs 2015 to a GMS contract. Regulation 32(1) provides:

(1) Where a contractor is providing essential services under the agreement and would like to enter into a general medical services contract by virtue of this regulation, the contractor must give notice

in writing to the Board to that effect at least three months before the date on which the contractor would like to enter into the general medical services contract.

11.182 It follows that the 'six month notice' provision under the above regulations does not make the business run by PMS practices as precarious as they might have thought because, as long as they act swiftly, they can use reg 32 to convert from PMS to GMS status.

Termination by NHS England for the provision of untrue information

11.183 Those who hold GP practice contracts are required to provide a large amount of information to satisfy NHS England that they satisfy the conditions in regs 5 and 6 of the GMS Regs 2015 and reg 5 of the PMS Regs 2015 (analysed above) and have contractual changes to inform NHS England if, for example, there are changes to the partners in a GP contract.

11.184 Paragraph 66 of Part 8 of Schedule 3 to the GMS Regs 2015, which is substantively replicated in para 57 of Part 8 of Schedule 2 to the PMS Regs 2015, give NHS England a *right* but not a duty to terminate the contract for the provision of untrue information:

(1) The Board may give notice in writing to the contractor terminating the contract with immediate effect or from such date as may be specified by the Board in the notice where sub-paragraph (2) applies.

(2) This sub-paragraph applies if, after the contract was entered into, it comes to the Board's attention that written information–

(a) provided to the Board by the contractor before the contract was entered into; or

(b) included in a notice given to the Board by the contractor under paragraph 50(1)(a) or (b) or 51(1), relating to the conditions set out in regulations 5 and 6 (and compliance with those conditions)

was, when given, untrue or inaccurate in a material respect.

Termination by NHS England because a GP is struck off or suspended by the GMC

11.185 Paragraph 65 of Part 8 of Schedule 3 to the GMS Regs 2015 provides:

(1) Subject to paragraph (2), the Board must give notice in writing to the contractor terminating the contract with immediate effect where, in any case, a contractor who is an individual medical practitioner has ceased to be a general medical practitioner.

(2) Where the contractor referred to in sub-paragraph (1) has ceased to satisfy the condition specified in regulation 5(1)(a) by reason of a suspension of the type described in sub-paragraph (7), the Board is not required to give notice to the contractor under sub-paragraph (1) unless–

(a) the contractor is unable to satisfy the Board that it has in place adequate arrangements for the provision of clinical services under the contract for so long as the suspension continues; or

(b) the Board is satisfied that the circumstances of the suspension are such that if the contract is not terminated with immediate effect–

(i) the safety of the contractor's patients would be at serious risk, or

(ii) the Board would be at risk of material financial loss.

(3) Sub-paragraph (4) applies where–
(a) except in a case to which paragraph 59(4) applies, the contractor consists of two or more persons practising in partnership and the condition specified in regulation 5(1)(b) is no longer satisfied; or
(b) the contractor is a company limited by shares, and the condition specified in regulation 5(1)(c) is no longer satisfied.
(4) Where this sub-paragraph applies, the Board must–
(a) give notice in writing to the contractor terminating the contract with immediate effect; or
(b) give notice in writing to the contractor confirming that the Board is prepared to allow the contract to continue, for a period specified by the Board, in accordance with sub-paragraph (5) ('the interim period').
(5) The period specified by the Board under sub-paragraph (4)(b) must not exceed–
(a) six months; or
(b) where the failure of the contractor to continue to satisfy the condition in regulation 5(1)(b) or 5(1)(c), is by reason of a suspension described in sub-paragraph (7), the period for which that suspension continues.
(6) The Board must, during the interim period and with the consent of the contractor, employ or supply the contractor with one or more general medical practitioners for the interim period to assist the contractor in the provision of clinical services under the contract.
(7) The suspensions described in this sub-paragraph are suspension–
(a) by a Fitness to Practise Panel under–
(i) section 35D of the Medical Act 1983 (functions of a fitness to practise panel) in a health case, other than an indefinite suspension under section 35D(6) of that Act, or
(ii) section 38(1) of the Medical Act 1983 (power to order immediate suspension etc. after a finding of impairment of fitness to practise); or
(b) by a Fitness to Practise Panel or an Interim Orders Panel under section 41A of the Medical Act 1983 (interim orders).
(8) Before deciding which of the options in sub-paragraph (4) to pursue, the Board must, if it is reasonably practicable to do so, consult the Local Medical Committee (if any) for the area in which the contractor provides services under the contract.
(9) If the contractor does not, in accordance with sub-paragraph (6), consent to the Board employing or supplying a general medical practitioner during the interim period, the Board must give notice in writing to the contractor terminating the contract with immediate effect.
(10) If, at the end of the interim period, sub-paragraph (3)(a) or (b) continues to apply to the contractor, the Board must give notice in writing to the contractor terminating the contract with immediate effect.

11.186 Paragraph 65 thus provides for immediate termination where a single-handed GP has 'ceased to be a general medical practitioner', which includes having been struck off by the GMC, and the potential for termination where a single-handed GP has been suspended. The GMS Regs 2015 give NHS the *option* to terminate in the latter case if:

a) the contractor is unable to satisfy the Board that it has in place adequate arrangements for the provision of clinical services under the Contract for so long as the suspension continues; or

b) the Board is satisfied that the circumstances of the suspension are such that if the contract is not terminated with immediate effect:
    i) the safety of the contractor's patients is at serious risk; or
    ii) the Board is at risk of material financial loss.

11.187 If the contract is terminated when a GP is suspended, NHS England can continue it during the interim period of the suspension. The GMS contract is silent about what is supposed to happen if the GP's suspension is lifted by the GMC but it appears to be implicit that the contract has to be reinstated. There are no equivalent provisions for PMS contractors, but there equally no automatic termination of a PMS contract when a PMS doctor is suspended or removed from practice. It follows that a similar decision-making process needs to be followed if NHS England wishes to terminate a PMS contract in such circumstances.

11.188 Under para 65, a GP practice contract with multiple partners does not necessarily come to an end if one of the partners is struck off. However, NHS England may have a duty to terminate the contract if the other GP partners who are not stuck off are only limited partners (ie they have a limited liability under the Limited Partnerships Act 1907) because, in such a case, the partnership cannot continue to hold a GMS contract under reg 5(1)(b) of the GMS Regs 2015. The same situation arises where a GP shareholder in a medical company is struck off, if that means the company no longer satisfies the requirements in reg 5(1)(c) that:

(i) at least one share in the company must be both legally and beneficially owned by a general medical practitioner, and
(ii) any other share or shares in the company that are both legally and beneficially owned by a medical practitioner must be so owned by–
    (aa) a general medical practitioner, or
    (bb) a medical practitioner who is employed by a Local Health Board, (in England and Wales and Scotland) an NHS Trust, an NHS foundation trust, (in Scotland) a Health Board, or (in Northern Ireland) a Health and Social Services Trust.

11.189 In these latter two scenarios, NHS England has a choice whether to terminate with immediate effect or allow the contract to continue for an interim period, which cannot exceed six months, or the period of the suspension. When choosing between these two options, para 65(8) of Part 8 of creates a qualified duty for NHS England, 'if it is reasonably practicable to do so, consult the Local Medical Committee (if any) for the area in which the contractor provides services under the contract'.

11.190 These provisions do not apply to PMS practices because NHS England is not under a mandatory obligation to terminate the contract if a GP is struck off by the GMC.

Termination of the contract by NHS England for being in breach of the conditions disqualifying GPs from holding practice contracts

11.191 Under para 67 of Part 8 of Schedule 3 to the GMS Regs 2015, NHS England has the right to terminate (either with immediate effect or from such date as specified in the notice) a GMS contract if the conditions in reg 6 of the GMS Regs 2015 (discussed above at para 11.31 above) are not satisfied.

11.192 There is a similar provision under para 58 of Part 8 of Schedule 2 to the PMS Regs 2015 in relation to the disqualifying conditions for PMS contractors under reg 5 of the PMS Regs 2015 (discussed above at para 11.53 above).

Termination of the contract by NHS England where patients' safety is at risk or where there is risk of financial loss to the Board

11.193 Paragraph 68 of Part 8 of Schedule 3 to the GMS Regs 2015 and para 59 of Part 8 to Schedule 2 to the PMS Regs 2015 provide as follows:

> The Board may give notice in writing to the contractor terminating the contract with immediate effect or with effect from such date as may be specified in the notice if–
> (a) the contractor has breached a term of the contract and, as a result of that breach, the safety of the contractor's patients would be at serious risk if the contract is not terminated; or
> (b) the Board considers that contractor's financial situation is such that the Board would be at risk of material financial loss.

11.194 In practice, only a very serious risk to patient safety could justify NHS England from relying on this forthwith notice provision. The scope for NHS England terminating the contract for 'material financial loss' is also only likely to arise in the most serious of situations. Any GP practice which finds itself in receipt of a termination notice under these provisions should seek urgent specialist legal advice.

Termination by NHS England for unlawful sub-contracting

11.195 Under para 69 of Part 8 of Schedule 3 to the GMS Regs 2015 and para 60 of Part 8 of Schedule 2 to the PMS Regs 2015, NHS England is under a duty to terminate the contract with immediate effect if the contractor has been sub-contracting clinical services in breach of the agreement or give an instruction to terminate the sub-contracting arrangements that give rise to the breach forthwith (where any failure to do so will result in the contract being terminated forthwith). The relevant regulations, which require terms in GMS and PMS contracts preventing sub-contracting unless certain conditions are met, are reg 44 of the GMS Regs 2015 and reg 43 of the PMS Regs 2015.

Termination due to a change in the identity of the partners to a GMS contract

11.196 A GMS partnership contract is held between NHS England and the partners in a partnership as it is form time to time constituted. This means that the GPs can take someone into partnership and, on doing so, that person becomes a party to the practice contract. Regulation 15 of the GMS Regs 2015 provides:

> Where a contract is with two or more individuals practising in partnership–
> (a) the contract is to be treated as made with the partnership as it is from time to time constituted, and the contract must make specific provision to this effect; and
> (b) the terms of the contract must require the contractor to ensure that any person who becomes a partner in the partnership after the contract has come into force is automatically bound by the contract whether by virtue of a partnership deed or otherwise.

11.197 If a partner leaves the partnership, then that person ceases to be a contracting party to the GMS contract. This right to have a contract with a fluctuating number of individuals (all of whom must satisfy the conditions in regs 5 and 6 of the GMS Regs 2015) may lead to a situation where NHS England is not satisfied that the remaining partners have the skills or experience to hold a GMS contract or there are other factors operating which make it inappropriate for the remaining partners to hold the contract.

11.198 In these circumstances, para 71(2)–(3) of Part 8 of Schedule 3 to the GMS Regs 2015 provides as follows:

> (2) Where the contractor consists of two or more persons practising in partnership and one or more of those persons has or have left the partnership during the existence of the contract, the Board may give notice in writing to the contractor terminating the contract on such date as may be specified in the notice if, in the Board's reasonable opinion, the change in the membership of the partnership is likely to have a serious adverse impact on the ability of the contractor or the Board to perform its obligations under the contract.
>
> (3) A notice given to the contractor under sub-paragraph (2) must specify–
> (a) the date on which the contract is to terminate; and
> (b) the Board's reasons for considering that the change in the membership of the partnership is likely to have a serious adverse impact on the ability of the contractor or the Board to perform its obligations under the contract'

11.199 The test is whether NHS England considers that the change in the identity of the partners is likely to have a *serious adverse impact* on the ability of the contractor or the Board to perform its obligations under the contract. NHS England would need to have conducted a proper investigation and have reasoned grounds before it could say that it was likely (ie more probable than not) that the remaining partners could not manage the practice so that the practice continued to deliver on its obligations. In practice, this situation is likely to occur most often then the partner who leaves the practice has departed 'under a cloud' and there are serious questions as to whether the remaining partners are able to turn the practice around so that it is able to deliver services to patients.

11.200 This problem does not arise with PMS practices because there is no provision in the PMS Regs 2015 which permits the GPs to change the identity of the contracting parties. Accordingly, if a PMS contract is concluded with a partnership it can only be varied when a partner leaves or joins by signing a new PMS contract or by agreeing a variation with NHS England.

Termination for carrying on business 'detrimental' to the contract

11.201 Under para 71(1) of Part 8 of Schedule 3 to the GMS Regs 2015, NHS England has the following right to terminate the contract:

> (1) If the Board becomes aware that a contractor which is a company limited by shares is carrying on any business which the Board considers to be detrimental to the contractor's performance of its obligations under the contract–

(a) the Board may give notice in writing to the contractor requiring it to cease carrying on that business before the end of a period of at least 28 days beginning with the date on which the notice is given ('the notice period'); and
(b) if the contractor has not satisfied the Board that it has ceased carrying on that business by the end of the notice period, the Board may give a further notice in writing to the contractor terminating the contract with immediate effect or from such date as may be specified in the notice.

11.202 A similar provision applies in relation to qualifying bodies under the PMS Regs 2015 in para 62 of Part 8 of Schedule 2:

> If the Board becomes aware that a contractor which is a qualifying body is carrying on any business which the Board considers to be detrimental to the contractor's performance of its obligations under the agreement–
> (a) the Board may give notice in writing to the contractor requiring it to cease carrying on that business before the end of a period of not less than 28 days beginning with the date on which the notice is given ('the notice period'); and
> (b) if the contractor has not satisfied the Board that it has ceased carrying on that business by the end of the notice period, the Board may give a further notice in writing to the contractor terminating the agreement with immediate effect or from such date as is specified in the notice.

11.203 This appears to be a wide and general provision which could cover a range of different behaviours by a GP. There is, as far as the authors are aware, no guidance indicating what is meant by carrying on any business which the Board considers to be detrimental to the contractor's performance of its obligations under the agreement.

Contract sanctions

11.204 One of the key features of GP practice contracts is the power of NHS England to impose 'contract sanctions' on a GP practice that acts in breach of contract as an alternative to termination of the contract. The imposition of contract sanctions is thus a 'half way house' between informal management of a contract breach and termination of the contract.

11.205 The power to impose contract sanctions is found in para 72 of Part 8 of Schedule 3 to the GMS Regs 2015, which provides as follows:

> (1) In this paragraph and in paragraph 73, 'contract sanction' means–
> (a) termination of specified reciprocal obligations under the contract;
> (b) suspension of specified reciprocal obligations under the contract for a period of up to six months; or
> (c) withholding or deducting monies otherwise payable under the contract.
>
> (2) Where the Board is entitled to terminate the contract under paragraphs 66, 67, 68, 69, 70(4) or (6) or 71, it may instead impose any of the contract sanctions if the Board is reasonably satisfied that the contract sanction to be imposed is appropriate and proportionate to the circumstances giving rise to the Boardís entitlement to terminate the contract.

(3) The Board may not, under sub-paragraph (2), impose any contract sanction that has the effect of terminating or suspending any obligation to provide, or any obligation that relates to, essential services.

(4) If the Board decides to impose a contract sanction, the Board must–
  (a) give notice in writing to the contractor of the contract sanction that it proposes to impose and the date upon which that sanction is to be imposed; and
  (b) include in the notice an explanation of the effect of the imposition of the sanction.

(5) Subject to paragraph 73 the Board may not impose the contract sanction until the end of a period of at least 28 days beginning with the date on which the Board gives notice to the contractor under sub-paragraph (4) unless the Board is satisfied that it is necessary to do so in order to protect–
  (a) the safety of the contractor's patients; or
  (b) itself from material financial loss.

(6) Where the Board imposes a contract sanction, the Board may charge the contractor the reasonable costs of any additional administration that the Board has incurred in order to impose, or as a result of imposing, the contract sanction.

11.206 There is a similar power on the part of NHS England for PMS agreements, where the sanctions are referred to as 'agreement sanctions', under para 63 of Part 8 of Schedule 2 to the PMS Regs 2015. This provides:

(1) In this paragraph and in paragraph 64, 'agreement sanction' means–
  (a) termination of specified reciprocal obligations under the agreement;
  (b) suspension of specified reciprocal obligations under the agreement for a period of up to six months; or
  (c) withholding or deducting monies otherwise payable under the agreement.

(2) Where the Board is entitled to terminate the agreement in accordance with paragraph 57, 58, 59, 61(4) or (6) or 62, it may instead impose any of the agreement sanctions if the Board is reasonably satisfied that the agreement sanction to be imposed is appropriate and proportionate to the circumstances giving rise to the Board's entitlement to terminate the agreement.

(3) If the Board decides to impose an agreement sanction, the Board must–
  (a) give notice in writing to the contractor of the agreement sanction that it proposes to impose and the date upon which that sanction is to be imposed; and
  (b) include in the notice an explanation of the effect of the imposition of the sanction.

(4) Subject to paragraph 64, the Board may not impose the agreement sanction until the end of a period of at least 28 days beginning with the date on which the Board gives notice to the contractor under to sub-paragraph (3) unless the Board is satisfied that it is necessary to do so in order to protect–
  (a) the safety of the contractor's patients; or
  (b) itself from material financial loss.

(5) Where the Board imposes an agreement sanction, the Board may charge the contractor the reasonable costs of any additional administration that the Board has incurred in order to impose, or as a result of imposing, the agreement sanction.

11.207 It follows that NHS England only obtains the right to impose contract sanctions where it has a contractual right to terminate the GP practice contract. As the PGM makes clear, the following are circumstances where sanctions can be imposed:

- provision of untrue information;
- fitness to practice matters;
- where there is a serious risk to patient safety or NHS England is at risk of material financial loss;
- where the Commissioner is satisfied that the contractor has not taken the steps required by a Remedial Notice to remedy a breach within the required period;
- where, after a Remedial Notice or Breach Notice has been issued, the contractor:
  - repeats a breach that was the subject of a Remedial Notice or a Breach Notice; or
  - otherwise breaches the contract resulting in a further Remedial Notice or Breach Notice;
- where the contractor carries on business detrimental to the contract; and/or
- for GMS contracts only, where changes in membership of the partnership is likely to have a serious adverse impact on the ability of the contractor or the Commissioner to perform obligations under the contract.

11.208 The PGM also gives the following guidance when considering whether to impose a contract sanction, and the level of sanction if it is a financial one:

> 1.4.7 The choice of which Contract Sanction to use would ordinarily depend on the nature of the breach, or cumulative effect, and what is felt to be the most appropriate and proportionate action in those circumstances. For example, if the breaches have occurred in relation to a specific service element under the contract, it might be most appropriate to move to terminate that specific service, such as an additional service.
>
> 1.4.8 Where the Commissioner is considering imposing a Contract Sanction and the contractor has a GMS contract, it is a statutory requirement that the Commissioner consults the relevant LMC before it imposes the Contract Sanction, where it is reasonably practicable to do so. There is no such statutory requirement in respect of PMS or APMS contracts and the Commissioner should ensure it considers any relevant wording in the contract.
>
> 1.4.9 Where the Commissioner decides that the most appropriate sanction would be to withhold or deduct monies, this must be calculated in order to establish a consistent, fair and measured approach. Annex 7 provides further information on calculating a financial Contract Sanction.

11.209 Paragraph 73 of Part 8 of Schedule 3 to the GMS Regs 2015 prevents a sanction being imposed in circumstances where there is a parallel dispute about that sanction:

> (1) If there is a dispute between the Board and the contractor in relation to a contract sanction that the Board is proposing to impose, the Board may not, subject to sub-paragraph (5), impose the contract

sanction except in the circumstances specified in sub-paragraphs (2) and (3).

(2) The circumstances specified in this sub-paragraph are if the contractor–

(a) refers the dispute relating to the contract sanction to the NHS dispute resolution procedure before the end of a period of 28 days beginning with the date on which the contractor was given notice in accordance with paragraph 72(4) (or such longer period as may be agreed in writing with the Board); and

(b) gives notice to the Board in writing that it has done so.

(3) Where the circumstances specified in sub-paragraph (2) apply, the Board may not impose the contract sanction unless–

(a) there has been a final determination of the dispute in accordance with regulation 83 (or by a court) and that determination permits the Board to impose the contract sanction; or

(b) the contractor ceases to pursue the NHS dispute resolution procedure,

whichever is the sooner.

(4) If the contractor does not invoke the NHS dispute resolution procedure before the end of the period specified in sub-paragraph (2)(a), the Board may impose the contract sanction with immediate effect.

(5) If the Board is satisfied that it is necessary to impose the contract sanction before the NHS dispute resolution procedure is concluded in order to protect–

(a) the safety of the contractor's patients; or

(b) itself from material financial loss,

the Board may impose the contract sanction with immediate effect, pending the outcome of that procedure (or any court proceedings).

11.210 Paragraph 64 of Part 8 of Schedule 2 to the PMS Regs 2015 contains a substantively similar provision.

CHAPTER 12

Patient choice

continued

Background to patient choice issues

12.1 The principle that NHS patients should be entitled to choose where they are treated has become a key part of government policy in recent years. The underlying concept is that patients should be able to choose the clinician who they want to provide them with healthcare and that the money should follow the patient. Turning this political aspiration into reality is far from straightforward, but this chapter attempts to explain how the systems are supposed to operate to deliver patient choice. Whether the choices made by patients are respected in practice is, of course, an entirely different matter.

12.2 The importance of patient choice was reflected in the key *Five year forward view* document published by NHS England which said:

> We will make good on the NHS' longstanding promise to give patients choice over where and how they receive care.

12.3 The importance of patient choice was also set out in the Mandate[1] issued by the Secretary of State for Health and Social Care for 2016/17 which said:[2]

> We want people to be empowered to shape and manage their own health and care and make meaningful choices, particularly for maternity services, people with long term conditions and end-of-life care.

12.4 The 2020 goals in the Mandate included a requirement to 'significantly improve patient choice'. NHS England has responded to this part of the Mandate by saying on its website:[3]

> NHS England is therefore committed to a major programme of work to realise the NHS' longstanding promise to give patients choice over where and how they receive care, as highlighted in the *NHS Five Year Forward View*.

12.5 NHS England has set up a 'Patient Choice Unit' and refers to the government guidance called the *NHS Choice framework*. The ambit of this guidance is considered below.

The rights under the NHS Constitution

12.6 The NHS Constitution was created in 2009 to be a single summary of the 'rights' that NHS patients have and the rights and expectations of NHS staff. Section 2(1) of the Health Act (HA) 2009 provides that NHS bodies[4] 'must, in performing [their] . . . health service functions, have regard to the NHS Constitution'. The duty to 'have regard' to the NHS Constitution

1 See www.gov.uk/government/uploads/system/uploads/attachment_data/file/494485/NHSE_mandate_16–17_22_Jan.pdf.

2 At pp12–13.

3 See www.england.nhs.uk/about/gov/patientchoice/.

4 There is a list of NHS bodies which have a legal duty to have regard to the NHS Constitution. It includes NHS England, CCGs, NHS trusts, NHS foundation trusts and local authorities exercising NHS functions. It does not include the Secretary of State for Health and Social Care, but a like duty is imposed on the secretary of state by section 1B of the NHS Act 2006.

is a legal duty to consider the patient 'rights' created by the NHS Constitution when exercising functions. However, it is a procedural duty and does not necessarily make it unlawful for an NHS body to act in a way that contravenes the NHS Constitution. However, in order to take a lawful decision to depart form the NHS Constitution, an NHS body would have to have very carefully considered the relevant provisions of the NHS Constitution and to have departed from it for very good reasons.[5]

12.7 There are provisions of the NHS Constitution relating to patient choice in both primary care and secondary care. These provisions are referred to below.

Patient choice of GP

12.8 The NHS Constitution provides as follows concerning choice and general practitioner (GP) services:

> You have the right to choose your GP practice, and to be accepted by that practice unless there are reasonable grounds to refuse, in which case you will be informed of those reasons.
>
> You have the right to express a preference for using a particular doctor within your GP practice, and for the practice to try to comply.

This wording is a summary of the rights given to patients by the rules under which NHS GP practices operate and does not materially add to those rights.

12.9 Patients living in the catchment area of an NHS GP practice have the right to apply to be registered at that practice. Please see para 18.114 for details of the application process and the limited grounds on which a GP practice with an open list can refuse to register a patient.

12.10 Once a patient is registered at a GP practice, the rules about patient preferences for seeing a particular doctor within are set out in reg 22 of the National Health Service (General Medical Services Contracts) Regulations (GMS Regs) 2015.[6] These provide by para 22 of Schedule 3 that every GMS contract must contain a term to the following effect:

> **22** (1) Where the contractor has accepted an application made under paragraph 18 or 20, the contractor must–
> (a) give notice in writing to the person (or, in the case of a child or an adult who lacks capacity, to the person who made the application on the applicant's behalf) of that person's right to express a preference to receive services from a particular performer or class of performer either generally or in relation to any particular condition; and
> (b) record in writing any such preference expressed by or on behalf of that person.
>
> (2) The contractor must endeavour to comply with any reasonable preference expressed under sub-paragraph (1) but need not do so if the preferred performer–
> (a) has reasonable grounds for refusing to provide services to the person who expressed the preference; or
> (b) does not routinely perform the service in question within the contractor's practice.

5 See chapter 2 for more guidance on the effect of the NHS Constitution.

6 SI No 1862.

An identical provision is in reg 21 of the National Health Service (Personal Medical Services Agreements) Regulations 2015.[7]

12.11 In accordance with these regulations, once a patient is accepted onto the list of an NHS GP practice, the contractor must inform the patient of the right to:

> ... express a preference to receive services from a particular performer or class of performer either generally or in relation to any particular condition

and that, if a patient expresses a preference, the practice:

> ... must endeavour to comply with any reasonable preference.

12.12 Thus if a patient expresses a preference to see a particular doctor, the practice must operate a system which endeavours to comply with this preference. Patients can also request to be treated by a 'class of performer'. This may raise some difficult issues about discrimination. This provision is commonly used to permit a female patient to express a preference to see a woman doctor, particularly if she needs to be treated for gynaecological or family planning matters. Equally, a male patient may express a preference for being treated by a male doctor if he has erectile dysfunction problems. Patients for whom English is a second language may properly ask to be seen by a 'class' of doctors who can speak their language. However, it is almost certainly not permissible to use this part of the contract for a patient to express a preference only to be seen by a 'white doctor'.

12.13 There are different ways that the practice can comply with this requirement in practice, including ensuring that the practice computer system informs the receptionist where a patient has expressed a preference and prompts the receptionist to offer an appointment with the patient's preferred GP.

Patient choice in secondary care

12.14 Patient choice in secondary care is more complex than in primary care. The rules are both substantive and procedural but there is considerable ambiguity about what the rules mean and there have been attempts (now abandoned) to cut down the ambit of the rules by 'Guidance' produced by NHS England. Accordingly, the extent to which patients can exercise any meaningful choice in secondary care is somewhat unclear.

The gatekeeping role of the GP or other primary care professional

12.15 Patients make their own choices about when they visit primary care. In contrast, NHS patients can only make their own choices about the provider that delivers NHS-funded secondary care where they seek care on an emergency basis or where a patient is referred for a specific secondary care procedure by their GP, community dentist or an optometrist. The vast majority of referrals are made by GPs and so this chapter will describe

7 SI No 1879.

patient choice rights by reference to a GP. However, the same principles apply to referrals by community dentists and optometrists.

12.16 Patient choice is generally concerned with elective procedures as opposed to emergency procedures, and the role of the GP as 'gatekeeper' in the system is essential. Giving effect to patient choice for secondary care is not, in reality, giving effect to a choice for the patient alone. It is giving effect to joint decision-making between a GP and the patient. The GP makes the decision to offer a referral and, if the patient agrees to the proposed referral, the patient has the right to be referred to any clinically appropriate provider who contracts with the NHS.

The sources of the legal right to exercise choice in secondary care

12.17 Patient choice is delivered by two complimentary processes, namely:

1) specific occasions on which a patient can establish a legal right to choose his or her secondary care provider in defined circumstances; and
2) general procedural duties which are imposed on NHS England and clinical commissioning groups (CCGs) (which are only relevant where 1 above does not apply).

The duty on CCGs and NHS England to make patient choice arrangements

12.18 Part 8 of the National Health Service Commissioning Board and Clinical Commissioning Groups (Responsibilities and Standing Rules) Regulations (RSR Regs) 2012[8] sets up the system of legal rights of patients to make their own choices about which provider should provide treatment to them. Subject to the terms of the regulations, patients have a legal right to choose the secondary care provider to whom they are referred for a first appointment by their NHS GP (and certain other NHS primary care professionals) where the GP decides that the patient requires an 'elective referral'.

12.19 Regulation 38 defines the meaning of an 'elective referral' as follows:

> 'elective referral' means referral by a general medical practitioner, general dental practitioner or optometrist to a health service provider for treatment that is not identified as being immediately required at the time of referral.

12.20 Hence, a patient cannot 'self-refer' for secondary NHS care and claim to exercise patient choice rights in respect of that referral. The person making the referral must be a GP, community dentist or optometrist. The rules about choice for elective referrals do not apply to emergency procedures and so a referral by a GP for treatment that is 'immediately required' does not give rise to patient choice rights.

12.21 The elective referral must be made to a 'health service provider'. This term is widely defined in reg 2 of the RSR Regs 2012 to mean:

8 SI No 2996. These regulations have been amended on a number of occasions since they were made in 2012. References in this chapter are to the form of the 2012 regulations in force in September 2016.

> 'health service provider' means a person, other than a relevant body, who has entered into a commissioning contract.

12.22 Accordingly, a health service provider can be any public body, commercial organisation or third sector body, provided it holds a 'commissioning contract' with any CCG or NHS England (referred to in the regulations as the 'relevant body'). There was some controversy about what is meant by a 'commissioning contract'. This term is defined in reg 2 as follows:

> 'commissioning contract' means a contract, other than a primary care contract, entered into by a relevant body in the exercise of its commissioning functions.

Hence, the regulations appear to define the term 'commissioning contract' as including *any* contract entered into by a CCG or NHS England in exercise of their commissioning functions other than a primary care contract. NHS England guidance originally suggested that a 'commissioning contract' could only refer to an NHS Standard Contract. That does not seem to be consistent with the above definition and that part of the Guidance has now been changed.

12.23 Regulation 39 of the RSR Regs 2012 provides:

> (1) A relevant body must make arrangements to ensure that a person–
> (a) who requires an elective referral; and
> (b) for whom that body has responsibility,
> is given the choices specified in paragraph (2).
> (2) Subject to regulations 40 and 41, the choices specified for the purposes of this paragraph are the choice–
> (a) in respect of a first outpatient appointment with a consultant or a member of a consultant's team, of–
> (i) any clinically appropriate health service provider with whom any relevant body has a commissioning contract for the service required as a result of the referral, and
> (ii) any clinically appropriate team led by a named consultant who is employed or engaged by that health service provider; and
> (b) in relation to an elective referral for mental health services in respect of which the patient's first outpatient appointment is not with a consultant or a member of a consultant's team, of—
> (i) any clinically appropriate health service provider with whom any relevant body has a commissioning contract for the service required as a result of the referral, and
> (ii) any clinically appropriate team led by a named health care professional who is employed or engaged by that health service provider.
> (3) . . .
> (4) . . .
> (5) The arrangements referred to in paragraph (1) must include such arrangements as are necessary to ensure that a person may make the choices specified in those paragraphs where that person–
> (a) has not been offered that choice by the person making the initial referral; and
> (b) notifies the relevant body who has responsibility for that person that that choice was not offered.
> (6) For the purposes of this Part, a health service provider, or a team led by a consultant or a health care professional, is clinically appropriate if, in

the opinion of the person making the referral, they offer services that are clinically appropriate for that person in respect of the condition for which that person is referred.

12.24 Regulation 39(1) imposes a legal duty on each CCG and NHS England to 'make arrangements' to give effect to the right of patients to exercise their patient choice rights. The imposition of a legal duty 'to make arrangements' is used throughout the National Health Service Act (NHS Act) 2006. It thus imposes a legal obligation on the CCG to operate systems which ensure that patients can access those services that are within the scope of the arrangements. In *R v East Sussex CC exp Tandy*[9] the House of Lords was concerned with a duty to make arrangements to provide suitable education services to children in its area. While emphasising that the council had a discretion to decide the form of these arrangements, Lord Browne-Wilkinson said:[10]

> The duty is to make arrangements for what constitutes suitable education for each child. That duty will not be fulfilled unless the arrangements do in fact provide suitable education for each child.

12.25 It follows that, when making decisions as to whether to fund medical treatment for an NHS patient, reg 39(1) requires both CCGs and NHS England to put in place a decision-making processes, which asks four questions, namely:

1) Is this patient a person for whom the CCG/NHS England has commissioning responsibility?
2) Is this patient a person that a GP has decided should have – ie 'requires' – an elective referral?
3) Do the patient's circumstances come within reg 39(2)?
4) Is the patient entitled to exercise patient choice rights for this particular episode of treatment?

12.26 The decision-making process in the policy which constitutes the 'arrangements' must provide that, if the answer to all four questions is 'yes', the CCG or NHS England *must* make a decision to fund the initial consultation with the preferred secondary care clinician which is the subject of the referral. That appointment must be funded because the patient's 'legal right' to have NHS-funded treatment have been established and so the CCG or NHS England no longer has a discretion to decide whether to fund the treatment or not as part of NHS funded care. It follows that any set of legal 'arrangements' must set up a decision making process that guide a decision-maker to ask whether the answer to all four questions set out above are answered in the affirmative.

12.27 Regulation 39(6) provides that the assessment as to whether the referral is clinically appropriate is exclusively a matter for the person making the referral, not for the CCG or NHS England. Hence, the decision-making processes cannot allow the commissioner to reach their own view as to whether the referral is appropriate treatment to be funded as part of NHS care.

9 [1998] AC 714.
10 At p747.

The limitation of secondary care patient choice rights to a first out-patient appointment

12.28 The right of patients to choose their secondary care provider under the regulations is limited to a 'first appointment'. On the face of it this seems a strange limitation because it suggests that a patient only has a very limited right to choose who the patient should be treated by and thereafter must accept the choice made by the NHS commissioner. As far as the author is aware, neither the government nor NHS England has advanced a policy reason why the right to patient choice under Part 8 of the RSR Regs 2012 is limited to a first out-patient appointment.

12.29 In the absence of any other explanation, it seems that the limitation of the right to a first out-patient appointment reflects a compromise between the interests of NHS commissioners and those of individual NHS patients. NHS commissioners have no absolute duty to commission every clinically appropriate service for an NHS patient. CCGs are entitled to adopt policies to define the services that they wish to commission for the patients for whom they are responsible in order to manage their budgets: see, for example, *R v Cambridge Health Authority ex p B*[11] and *R (AC) v Berkshire West Primary Care Trust and another*.[12] In contrast, NHS England and CCGs are not entitled to have blanket policies to refuse to fund particular treatments and have a legal duty to consider requests to commission care for a patient outside their usual policies and to make decisions whether to commission the requested treatment: see *R v North West Lancashire Health Authority ex p A*[13] and regs 34 and 35 of the RSR Regs 2012.

12.30 It follows that the purpose of limiting the legal right of a patient to choose their provider for a first out-patient appointment appears to be designed to enable the provider of the patient's choice to have a first meeting with the patient, funded by the NHS, to discuss treatment options. Following this first appointment, the patient can request funding from the NHS commissioner to support a full course of treatment with the patient's favoured provider (either as part of an existing CCG or NHS England policy or as an individual funding request outside the policy).

12.31 The purpose of limiting the legal right to a first out-patient appointment thus appears to allow the patient to be seen by the secondary care provider of the patient's choice and for the CCG (or NHS England) to be informed by the secondary care provider what treatment that provider recommends for the patient. The CCG (or NHS England) is then in a better position to make a decision whether to commission further treatment for the patient from the provider. It is also relevant to note:

a) when making decisions about funding further treatment, both NHS England and CCGs must comply with their general procedural duties (see below) to exercise their functions with a view to enabling patients to make choices with respect to aspects of health services provided to them; and

11 [1995] 1 WLR 898.

12 [2011] EWCA Civ 247.

13 [2000] 1 WLR 977, (1999) 2 CCLR 419.

b) each CCG must have regard to the guidance issued by NHS England concerning whether to commission any further treatment in accordance with the patient's choice: see section 14Z8 of the NHS Act 2006.

12.32 Accordingly, properly understood, the legal framework appears to represent a balance between the interests of the individual patient and the interests of the NHS commissioner, who acts on behalf of the general body of patients for whom the NHS commissioner is required to commission services.

Does NHS England have patient choice arrangements in place?

12.33 NHS England has no policy on its website which informs patients how decision-makers within NHS England are required to give effect to patient choice rights when services are commissioned by NHS England. It is therefore unclear what arrangements, if any, have been put in place by NHS England to ensure that patients can exercise their choice rights when referred for care commissioned by NHS England. It thus appears that NHS England may be acting in breach of its legal duty to have in place patient choice arrangements that make clear to patients who are entitled to services funded by NHS England how to exercise their choice rights.

12.34 The department of NHS England which regulates CCGs appears to be focused solely on making sure CCGs respect the patient choice rights of patients. The NHS England website[14] says:

> Clinical commissioning groups (CCGs) have a duty to enable patients to make choices, and to promote their involvement in decisions related to their care or treatment. NHS England will work alongside CCGs to help them meet their legal responsibilities and build on their offer of choice to patients, to ensure that choices are meaningful and deliver positive improvements to patient outcomes including patient experience of the services they access and use.
>
> The initial priorities of this programme of work are:
>
> - Strengthening choice in elective services
> - Enhancing the choice available in maternity services, including through a programme of Pioneers to develop and test ways of improving choice in maternity services for national replication
> - Improving choice in end of life care (EOLC) (including ensuring more people are able to achieve their preferred place of care and death)
> - Securing choice in the new care models that some Vanguard areas of the country are developing.

12.35 However, it is less clear how (if at all) NHS England is complying with its own patient choice obligations. If NHS England does not have any 'patient choice' arrangements in place, then it may be acting in breach of its duty under reg 39. As a consequence, any decisions which fail to respect patient choice rights could be challenged by way of judicial review.

14 See www.england.nhs.uk/about/gov/patient-choice/.

Patient choice arrangements by CCGs

12.36 There are some CCGs with well-developed 'patient choice polices'. A good example is Blackpool CCG.[15] However, there are many other CCGs that have no specific policy that explains patient choice to patients and, crucially, to decision-makers within the CCG. As with NHS England, CCGs will be acting unlawfully if they do not have a policy that guides decision-makers to identify and respect appropriate choices made by patients.

12.37 The legal rights given by Part 8 of the RSR Regs 2012 need to be seen within the overall legal structures operating in the NHS. These structures provide that that decisions about which NHS-funded medical treatment should be provided to an NHS patient are primarily a matter to be decided between the patient and his or her treating NHS GP or other primary care clinician. This balance between the decision-making power of GPs and the powers of the CCG is seen in three areas in particular, namely:

1) drugs or medical appliances prescribed for patients by a GP;
2) National Institute for Health and Care Excellence (NICE) recommended treatments for NHS patients (usually prescribed within secondary care); and
3) patient choice rights for secondary care recommended by a GP or other primary care clinician.

Drugs or medical appliances prescribed for patients by a GP

12.38 The question as to whether a pharmaceutical drug should be provided to a patient of a GP practice is, in the first instance, a matter exclusively for the GP. A CCG cannot impose any fixed cost limit on the pharmaceutical drugs a GP can prescribe for an NHS patient. Any drug prescribed by a GP must be funded by a CCG as part of NHS funded care. See reg 56 of the GMSC Regs 2015. The only exceptions are the 'black list' of drugs published by the secretary of state that an NHS GP cannot prescribe and a 'grey' list of products, such as Viagra, which can only be prescribed in limited circumstances. However, outside these limited examples, the only restraint on GPs and other primary care clinicians on prescribing is in reg 64 of the GMS Regs 2015, which provides:

> (1) The contractor must not prescribe drugs, medicines or appliances the cost or quantity of which, in relation to a patient, is, by reason of the character of the drug, medicine or appliance in question, in excess of that which was reasonably necessary for the proper treatment of the patient.
>
> (2) In considering whether a contractor has breached its obligations under paragraph (1), the Board must seek the views of the Local Medical Committee (if any) for the area in which the contractor provides services under the contract.

12.39 Save where GPs are prescribing branded drugs when generics are available, the requirement not to prescribe drugs where the cost or quantity is 'in excess of that which was reasonably necessary for the proper treatment of that patient' is almost impossible to enforce because the GP must

15 See http://blackpoolccg.nhs.uk/patient-choice/.

follow GMC guidance in prescribing the most appropriate drug for the patient regardless of the cost. A drug should only be prescribed for a patient where the patient agrees to take the drug (or it is a waste of NHS resources), but a joint decision between the GP and the patient on the choice of drug binds the CCG. Once the prescription is written, the patient goes to an NHS pharmacy which dispenses the drug to the patient. The pharmacist then makes a financial claim from the NHS Business Services Agency for payment for dispensing the drug (where the payment depends on the type of the drug). The cost of the drug eventually makes its way back to the local clinical commissioning group. CCGs can encourage GPs to limit costs when prescribing drugs but have no powers to prevent GPs exercising their clinical judgement to prescribe the drug GP considers most appropriate for the NHS patient.

NICE recommended treatments for NHS patients (usually prescribed within secondary care)

12.40 There is, in principle, no limit on the types of drugs or other treatments that a secondary care provider, such as a hospital trust, can provide to an NHS patient. However, the contract between a CCG (or NHS England) and a secondary care provider can place limits on the costs that a secondary care provider can recover from the CCG. Secondary care providers will usually prevent clinicians providing expensive drugs or other medical interventions for an NHS patient unless the secondary care provider can recover the costs of those drugs or interventions from the CCG.

12.41 CCGs are obliged to fund drugs or other treatments provided to patients where the drug or medical appliance is recommended in a Technology Appraisal Guidance (TAG) by NICE. A combination of section 237(8) of the Health and Social Care Act 2012 and reg 34 of the RSR Regs 2012 means that CCGs must have arrangements in place which require the CCG to fund drugs or treatments for patients with medical conditions which come within a cohort defined by a NICE TAG. Regulation 34 provides:

> (1) A relevant body must have in place arrangements for making decisions and adopting policies on whether a particular health care intervention is to be made available for persons for whom the relevant body has responsibility.
>
> (2) Arrangements under paragraph (1) must–
>
> (a) ensure that the relevant body complies with relevant NICE recommendations; and
>
> (b) include arrangements for the determination of any request for the funding of a health care intervention for a person, where there is no relevant NICE recommendation and the relevant body's general policy is not to fund that intervention[16]'

12.42 This right is repeated in the NHS Constitution[17] which says:

16 This is the regulation which requires a CCG and NHS England to have an individual funding arrangement policy and to operate IFR panels. Where an IFR request is turned down the CCG or NHS England must give reasons: see reg 35.

17 See www.gov.uk/government/publications/the-nhs-constitution-for-england/the-nhs-constitution-for-england.

> You have the right to drugs and treatments that have been recommended by NICE for use in the NHS, if your doctor says they are clinically appropriate for you.

12.43 Thus, a CCG is obliged to reimburse a secondary care provider for providing drugs or treatments to patients with medical conditions which come within a cohort defined by a NICE TAG.

The requirements that must be fulfilled before a patient can establish 'patient choice' rights under Part 8 of the RSR Regs 2012

12.44 The wording of Part 8 of the RSR Regs 2012 provides that NHS patients have a legal right to have a referral funded by their CCG or NHS England for the first consultation with the clinician to whom they are referred by their GP if the following conditions are satisfied:

1) *Condition 1:* The patient is a patient for whom the CCG has responsibility (reg 39(1)(b)).
2) *Condition 2:* The patient requires an elective referral (reg 39(1)(a)). The wording of the regulation is that the patient requires *an* elective referral, not that the patient requires an elective referral for a form of treatment that the CCG considers she ought to receive. Regulation 39(6) provides that the exercise of clinical judgement to determine what treatment the patient requires is for the GP and not the CCG.
3) *Condition 3:* A referral has been made by the patient's GP[18] to a 'clinically appropriate provider' (reg 39(2)(a) and (b)). However, reg 39(6) provides that whether a provider is clinically appropriate is solely a decision for the person making the referral.
4) *Condition 4:* The provider to whom the patient is referred has a commissioning contract with a 'relevant body' for the service required by the referral (see reg 39(2)(a) and (b)). The expression 'relevant body' is also defined in reg 2 as 'a CCG or the Board'. Thus, this condition is satisfied if *any* CCG or NHS England has a commissioning contract for the service required by the referral with the proposed provider. It is not necessary for the patient's own CCG to have an existing contract with the proposed provider for the proposed service.
5) *Condition 5:* The service is not of a type listed in reg 40 where the choice right does not apply. The services that are exempted from patient choice rights are:
   a) cancer services (where a two-week wait right arises – as to which see below);
   b) maternity services; and
   c) services for which the patient has a need for urgent care.
6) *Condition 6:* The patient is not a person who comes within reg 41 (which defines those patients who cannot exercise choice). The following patients do not have patient choice rights under reg 41:
   a) patients detained under the Mental Health Act 1983;

18 Or another person who can make a referral under reg 38.

b) patients who are detained in or on temporary release from prison, in an immigration removal centre, secure training centre or detained other accommodation described in reg 10(2) of the RSR Regs 2012; or
c) patients who are serving as a member of the armed forces.

12.45 Mental health services were excluded from patient choice rights when the RSR Regs 2012 were originally made. However, mental health services were removed from the list of excluded services with effect from 1 April 2014 by the National Health Service Commissioning Board and Clinical Commissioning Groups (Responsibilities and Standing Rules) (Amendment) Regulations 2013.[19] It follows that, from 1 April 2014, mental health patient gained the same legal rights to choose a secondary care provider from that date as other NHS patients.

The guidance on patient choice published by the Department of Health and Social Care

12.46 The Department of Health and Social Care has published guidance concerning the 2015/16 *Choice framework*.[20] This suggests that the only occasions where a patient does not get the legal right to access treatment following a GP referral to a secondary care provider are those set out in the regulations. An example of the exercise of patient rights is given in the recent guidance from the secretary of state as follows:

> Fatima is suffering from a mental health condition and visits her GP to be referred for treatment. She would like to exercise her entitlement to choose a named health care professional, whose team will then be responsible for her care. She has heard of a particular consultant that she would like to go to for her treatment and discusses this with her GP. He uses the NHS e-Referral Service to search for this named consultant and show Fatima the list of organisations and locations where the consultant works. Her GP creates a shortlist from these options and gives her log-in details for the NHS e-Referral service so she can do some research at home before deciding which one she would like to choose for her first outpatient appointment.
>
> Fatima uses NHS Choices to research each organisation before choosing one that is close to where she lives and has a number of convenient available appointments. A close friend of hers has also received treatment at this organisation and tells her that the quality of care is good. Fatima logs into the NHS e-Referral Service, selects her chosen organisation and books an appointment. She will be treated by her chosen health care specialist or a member of their team.

12.47 There is no suggestion in the secretary of state's guidance (or in the example above) that the legal right to choose is constrained by whether the patient's chosen provider holds a 'Standard NHS Contract' or whether the treatment for which the patient is referred is treatment that is routinely commissioned by the patient's CCG.

19 SI No 2891.
20 See www.gov.uk/government/publications/the-nhs-choice-framework/the-nhs-choice-framework-what-choices-are-available-to-me-in-the-nhs.

NHS England's guidance concerning patient choice rights

12.48 Prior to guidance published in 2018, NHS England took a substantially different approach to the conditions which must be satisfied before patient choice rights arise. Despite the many statements made by NHS England in support of the concept of patient choice and the existence of a team within NHS England which promotes patient choice, guidance issued by NHS England in December 2014 sought to place additional restrictions on the ability of all NHS patients to exercise patient choice rights. This guidance was issued after mental health patients came within the patient choice rights framework and appears to be an attempt to restrain the rights of all patients to exercise patient choice rights.

12.49 NHS England published interim guidance on patient choice in mental health services in May 2014[21] and then published final guidance in December 2014. The December 2014 NHS England guidance suggested that, in addition to the qualifying criteria set out in the RSR Regs 2012, there were two further restrictions on patient choice rights, namely:

a) the referral must be for treatment which is of a type which the patient's own CCG routinely commissions; and
b) the 'commissioning contract' held by the provider must be in the form of an NHS Standard Contract and not any other form of contract.

12.50 The legality of the additional conditions in this Guidance was challenged in *R (AA) v Haringey CCG*.[22] Haringey CCG had relied on the restrictions set out above to deny a patient funding for the treatment she was seeking. The CCG relied on the NHS England Guidance and, as a result, NHS England was invited by the Court to take part in the litigation in order to explain and defend the legality of its own Guidance. NHS England refused and the CCG capitulated in December 2015, a few days before trial. However, the December 2014 Guidance remained in place until February 2018, when fresh Guidance was released by NHS England which, in effect, removed any reference to additional conditions.[23]

Were the additional NHS England restrictions on patient choice part of the law?

12.51 Although the additional conditions have now been removed from the current version of the guidance, NHS practice often takes time to catch up with current guidance. It is thus still worth identifying the reasoning that led to the challenge in *BB v Haringey CCG* as to why the additional proposed restrictions were unlawful. This should ensure that no patient is denied access to patient choice rights based on the previous guidance.

12.52 A conventional approach to statutory construction would suggest that a patient who could show that he or she satisfied each of the six conditions laid down by the RSR Regs 2012 would have a legal right to require the CCG to fund a referral made by his or her GP.

21 See www.england.nhs.uk/wp-content/uploads/2014/05/guid-choice-prov-health.pdf.
22 CO/4263/2015.
23 See www.england.nhs.uk/mental-health/about/choice/.

12.53 There would have been serious issues about the legality of any CCG refusing to recognise a patient choice had been established where the patient satisfied the six conditions set out in the RSR Regs 2012 but was denied the right to exercise patient choice based on the previously published NHS England additional restrictions.

The suggestion in previous NHS England Guidance that the referral must be for treatment which is of a type which the patient's own CCG routinely commissions

12.54 The 2014 NHS England interim guidance provided:[24]

> Since 1 April 2013, people with mental health conditions who have been referred for a first outpatient appointment have had a right to choose who treats them within the organisation providing their care and treatment. This means having a right to choose which team, led by a named healthcare professional, delivers their care and treatment. Until April 2014, this right was limited to a mental health provider with which the patient's clinical commissioning group (CCG) or NHS England had contracted.
>
> The right to choice is no longer limited to mental health providers that have a contract with the CCG responsible for that patient, but is extended to other providers with a contract with any CCG, in the same way there is a right to choice of provider in physical health. This is an important step both towards establishing 'parity of esteem', or equal status, between mental and physical health services in the NHS and towards improving access, personalising and improving both the quality of care that people receive and, ultimately, their health outcomes.

12.55 That part of the interim guidance was correct. However, the interim guidance went on to say:

> These changes mean that a patient who requires an elective referral for mental health services has a right from 1 April 2014 to choose any clinically appropriate health service provider (whether an NHS mental health trust, a Foundation Trust or a mental health provider in the independent or third sector) for the their first outpatient appointment *as long as the provider has a contract with any CCG or with NHS England for the service required, and that the service or treatment is routinely commissioned by the patient's CCG or NHS England, or is approved by the relevant Independent Funding Review Panel.* This brings mental health services a step closer towards 'parity of esteem', or equal status, with physical health services in the NHS [emphasis added].

12.56 That guidance thus suggested patient choice rights were restricted to services that are already 'routinely commissioned' by a CCG or where a specific commissioning decision was made by a CCG to support the commissioning of the service. This proposed restriction was repeated in the next part of the interim guidance which said:

> Consistent with the operation of choice in physical health care, patients cannot generally choose services or treatments which are not routinely commissioned by their local CCG or NHS England. Patients wishing to access services not commissioned by their CCG or (where relevant) NHS England, may seek to demonstrate exceptionality and so access funding for the treatment through the commissioner's Independent Funding Review

24 At pp4–5.

Panel. Patients should discuss their options with their GP who is required to support such an application.

12.57 In December 2014, NHS England published further guidance on *Choice in mental health care*.[25] In the introduction, the NHS England Medical Director, Prof Sir Bruce Keogh, states:

> The changes in law that have given patients with mental health conditions the same legal rights as they have in physical health services are a significant step towards parity. They are part of the more significant shift to increase the direct control patients have over their care and every one of us working in mental health has a part to play to help implement these rights and make them work well for patients.

12.58 The December 2014 guidance provided:[26]

> This guidance seeks to interpret these regulations and set out the principles for how these legal rights to choice should operate. It is important to note that the right choice does not mean that a patient only has their first outpatient appointment with their chosen provider: consistent with physical health care, once a patient has chosen a provider, that provider will normally treat the patient for their entire episode of care unless the patient's diagnosis changes significantly.

12.59 However, the guidance departed from the terms of the regulations in suggesting that a patient's legal right to choose a provider was limited as follows:

> As is the case in physical health, the legal rights to choose in mental health do not give a legal right to choose their treatment. It is for commissioners to decide which services to secure in order to meet the needs of their local population. Where commissioners routinely commissioned particular mental health services, eligible patients may choose any provider team, in line with the description above, to access those services. Where patients, with the support of their GP, wish to access services that are not routinely commissioned by their responsible commission, they may apply through the Commissioner's Individual Funding Request ('IFR') process or if in receipt of a personal health budget through the care planning process.

12.60 This wording followed the interim guidance, but it appeared to confuse two different matters, namely: a) whether patients can choose which NHS medical services they wish to access without the support of their GP; and b) whether the clinical decision-maker should be the patient's referring clinician or the CCG. Neither the 2009 Choice Directions which preceded Part 8 of the RSR Regs 2012, nor Part 8 of the RSR Regs 2012 gives the patient a 'choice of treatment' which is not supported by the patient's clinician. However, neither the 2009 Choice Directions nor Part 8 of the RSR Regs 2012 contain any wording which suggest that the CCG has the right to restrict the choices agreed between the patient and the patient's referring GP.

12.61 If it were to have been the secretary of state's intention that patient choice rights should be restricted to services that are routinely commissioned by the patient's CCG or approved by way of that CCG's individual funding request (IFR) panel, this important restriction would have been referred to in either the regulations or in the DOH guidance, but it was not.

25 At p6. See www.england.nhs.uk/wp-content/uploads/2014/12/choice-mhc–14.pdf.

26 At p4.

12.62 The duty on a CCG under reg 39(1) is to make arrangements to fund a first appointment for patients who 'require' an elective referral. The use of the word 'require' appears to echo the duty on the CCG under section 3(1) of the NHS Act 2006, namely that:

> A clinical commissioning group must arrange for the provision of the following to such extent as it considers necessary to meet the reasonable requirements of the persons for whom it has responsibility . . .

12.63 However, the RSR Regs 2012 were made by the secretary of state in exercise of his powers under section 6E of the NHS Act 2006, which provides that the secretary of state may make regulations which direct CCGs how they are required to exercise their commissioning responsibilities. There are wide powers in section 6E(2) to make regulations directing CCGs as follows:

> The regulations may, in relation to the commissioning functions of the Board or clinical commissioning groups, make provision–
> (a) requiring the Board or clinical commissioning groups to arrange for specified treatments or other specified services to be provided or to be provided in a specified manner or within a specified period;
> (b) as to the arrangements that the Board or clinical commissioning groups must make for the purpose of making decisions as to–
> (i) the treatments or other services that are to be provided;
> (ii) the manner in which or period within which specified treatments or other specified services are to be provided;
> (iii) the persons to whom specified treatments or other specified services are to be provided;
> (c) as to the arrangements that the Board or clinical commissioning groups must make for enabling persons to whom specified treatments or other specified services are to be provided to make choices with respect to specified aspects of them'

12.64 These powers add to the commissioning responsibilities under section 3(1) and thus the limitation suggested by the previous NHS England guidance was not consistent with these extensive powers. Further, reg 39(1) of the 2012 Regulations makes it clear that the decision-maker as to whether a patient 'requires' a secondary care referral is the patient's GP as opposed to the CCG.

12.65 The ambit of the right was also important. It is a right for a first consultation and the strict legal right does not extend beyond the first consultation. Hence, a right to a first consultation with a secondary care clinician in an area of treatment that the CCG would not routinely fund does not necessarily lead to the CCG having any further extended liability for treatment. It follows that this part of the NHS England guidance was legally incorrect mainly because a limitation to a referral for treatment that the CCG routinely commissions is not a limitation which is set out in the RSR Regs 2012. NHS England has thus correctly abandoned this attempt to restrict patient choice rights.

The observations in the previous NHS England guidance about the need for the provider to have an NHS Standard Contract

12.66 The December 2014 NHS England guidance suggested that a provider would only qualify for patient choice rights if the provider held an NHS Standard Contract for the service in question, and that any other type of contracting arrangement would not suffice to give rise to patient choice rights. This additional requirement was not in the guidance and appeared to be even more problematic than the suggestion that the service is limited to a service that the CCG routinely commissions. It has been abandoned in the February 2018 Guidance.

12.67 This suggested limitation was not included in the May 2014 interim guidance but was set out for the first time in the December 2014 NHS guidance. This said at p6:[27]

> Routinely commissioned services are the types of treatments that commissioners secure for their populations on an ongoing basis, through the award of NHS Standard Contracts. These treatments exclude spot contracts between a commissioner and a provider on a one-off basis for the treatment of a specific patient.

12.68 Thus, the guidance suggested that if a CCG enters into a 'spot contract' with a provider to treat a specific patient, that contract cannot be relied on by other patients in order to establish a right to be referred to that provider. There were two major problems with this suggested limitation. First, in entering into these contracts, CCGs are discharging commissioning functions in relation to particular patients under section 3(1) of the NHS Act 2006. Accordingly, these contracts constitute 'commissioning contracts' within the definition of that term in reg 2 of the RSR Regs 2012. There is a full definition of the term 'commissioning contract' in reg 2 of the RSR Regs 2012 as follows:

> 'commissioning contract' means a contract, other than a primary care contract, entered into by a relevant body in the exercise of its commissioning functions.

12.69 The attempt in the December 2014 NHS England guidance to restrict the meaning of the term 'commissioning contract' to a contract which was concluded using the NHS Standard Contract was thus not contained within the wording of the RSR Regs 2012.

12.70 The second difficulty in suggesting that a 'commissioning contract' should mean 'a commissioning contract in the form of an NHS Standard Contract and not in any other form' is that a CCG that entered into a commissioning contract in any form other than the NHS Standard Contract would be acting in breach of NHS England's own rules. Hence, a CCG would not be acting lawfully in entering into a 'spot contract' with a provider for the delivery of NHS services to a patient in any form other than the NHS Standard Contract.

12.71 The requirement on CCGs to use the NHS Standard Contract when commissioning all NHS services is set out in Part 5 of the RSR

27 See www.england.nhs.uk/wp-content/uploads/2014/12/choice-mhc–14.pdf.

Regs 2012, which is headed 'Standing rules: commissioning contract terms'.

12.72 Regulation 16 provides:

(1) The Board must draft–
  (a) terms and conditions making provision for the matters specified in regulation 16; and
  (b) such other terms and conditions as the Board considers are, or might be, appropriate for inclusion in commissioning contracts entered into by a relevant body.
(2) The Board may draft model commissioning contracts which reflect the terms and conditions it has drafted pursuant to paragraph (1).
(3) A relevant body must incorporate the terms and conditions drafted by virtue of paragraph (1)(a) in commissioning contracts entered into by it.
(4) The Board may require CCGs to incorporate the terms and conditions it has drafted pursuant to paragraph (1)(b) in commissioning contracts that a CCG enters into.
(5) If a CCG is required by the Board to incorporate terms and conditions pursuant to paragraph (4), it must do so.

12.73 NHS England has complied with this obligation by publishing the NHS Standard Contract,[28] which is revised on annual basis. NHS England has also exercised the power under reg 17(4) to require CCGs to use the NHS Standard Contract. The NHS England website says:

> The NHS Standard Contract is mandated by NHS England for use by commissioners for all contracts for healthcare services other than primary care.

12.74 NHS England also produces *Technical guidance* each year concerning the legal obligations on NHS bodies to use the NHS Standard Contract. Although these documents describes themselves as being 'guidance', the documents set out the rules set by NHS England exercising its powers under reg 17 of the RSR Regs 2012. Accordingly, CCGs have a legal duty to follow the rules set out in the *Technical guidance* document as opposed to merely having a duty to have regard to them. Paragraphs 5.2 and 5.3 of the 2015/16 *Technical guidance*[29] provides:

> 5.2 *The NHS Standard Contract must be used by CCGs and by NHS England where they wish to contract for NHS-funded healthcare services* (including acute, ambulance, patient transport, continuing healthcare services, community-based, high-secure, mental health and learning disability services). The Contract must be used regardless of the proposed duration or value of a contract (so it should be used for a small-scale short-term pilots as well as for long-term or high-value services). Where a single contract includes both healthcare and non-healthcare services, the NHS Standard Contract must be used.
>
> 5.3 *The only exceptions are:*
>
> - primary care services commissioned by NHS England, where the relevant primary care contract should be used; and
> - any primary care improvement schemes agreed by CCGs with GP practices (with contractual arrangements, involving a variation or supplement

28 See www.england.nhs.uk/nhs-standard-contract/.

29 See www.england.nhs.uk/wp-content/uploads/2015/03/7-nhs-contrct-tech-guid-fin.pdf.

> to existing general practice contract, agreed between local NHS England teams and CCGs). Such Local Improvement Schemes involve payments for improving the quality of services provided under an existing GP contract, not the commissioning of additional services. [Emphasis added.]

12.75 The compulsory nature of the obligations set out in these paragraphs is shown by the use of the word 'must' in the first line of para 5.2. It follows that, at least until April 2016, CCGs were under a legal obligation to use the NHS Standard Contract whenever they were commissioning 'NHS funded healthcare services' unless the services were exempted because they came within the type of services set out in para 5.2. CCGs may now use an approved form of 'NHS contract light' but cannot enter into commissioning contracts in any other form.

12.76 Three points emerged from the 2015/16 rules concerning the extent of the legal obligations on CCGs to use the NHS Standard Contract which are relevant to the issue of patient choice, namely:

a) There is no exemption from the legal duty where the proposed contract is of low value. The legal duty to use the NHS Standard Contract arises regardless of the value of the contract.
b) There is no exemption from the mandated duty to use the NHS Standard Contract where the commissioning decision has been made by an IFR panel. The *Technical guidance* shows that the fact that the commissioning decision has been made through an IFR process as opposed to be made by any other process does not exempt a CCG from using an NHS Standard Contract when putting the IFR commissioning decision into effect.
c) There is no exemption from the duty to use the NHS Standard Contract where services are being commissioned by a CCG for a single patient as opposed to being commissioned for cohorts of patients. This is clear from the rules in para 5.2 which provides that the only exceptions to the mandated rule under para 5.1 others exemption set out in para 5.2. Further the use of the NHS Standard Contract is emphasised at para 12.1 of the *Technical guidance*.

12.77 It follows that every CCG was under a public law legal obligation to use an NHS Standard Contract when placing a contract with a chosen provider following an IFR decision for an individual patient. It is therefore difficult to see that this part of the NHS England Guidance can ever have been correct because it failed to give effect to NHS England's own rules on the type of contracts that must be used by CCGs. Thus the February 2018 guidance properly abandoned any attempt to rely on this requirement.

The general duties on CCGs and NHS England to commission services in accordance with preferences expressed by patients

12.78 Section 13I of the NHS Act 2006 provides:

> The Board must, in the exercise of its functions, act with a view to enabling patients to make choices with respect to aspects of health services provided to them.

12.79 A like provision is imposed on CCGs by section 14V of the NHS Act 2006 which provides:

> Each clinical commissioning group must, in the exercise of its functions, act with a view to enabling patients to make choices with respect to aspects of health services provided to them.

12.80 This general duty is clearly not relevant where a patient seeks to establish a right to exercise patient choice under Part 8 of the RSR Regs 2012. However, this duty is relevant to categories of patients who are outside the patient choice rights under Part 8 of the RSR Regs 2012 and to any request for funding for treatment that goes beyond an initial consultation.

12.81 Sections 13I and 14V of the NHS Act 2006 impose procedural duties which require NHS England and each CCG to act *at all times* 'with a view' to enabling patients to make their own choices about inter alia their selected healthcare provider. It is thus a general duty which applies to all commissioning decision-making processes by NHS England and every CCG. It therefore applies to CCGs when formulating general policies as well as when they are considering IFRs.

12.82 A CCG has a legal duty to have regard to NHS England guidance when making commissioning decisions in accordance with this duty. This duty is set out in section 14Z8 of the NHS Act 2006, which provides:

> (1) The Board must publish guidance for clinical commissioning groups on the discharge of their commissioning functions.
> (2) Each clinical commissioning group must have regard to guidance under this section.
> (3) The Board must consult the Healthwatch England committee of the Care Quality Commission–
> (a) before it first publishes guidance under this section, and
> (b) before it publishes any revised guidance containing changes that are, in the opinion of the Board, significant.

12.83 The December 2014 NHS England guidance to CCGs provides:[30]

> It is important to note that the right to choice does not mean that the patient only has their first outpatient appointment with their chosen provider: consistent with physical health care, once the patient has chosen a provider, that provider will normally treat the patient for their entire episode of care unless the patient's diagnosis changes significantly.

12.84 This is statutory guidance that each CCG must follow unless it has a good reason to depart from the guidance. The courts scrutinise those 'good reasons' carefully and they need to be very good reasons: see *R v North Derbyshire Health Authority ex p Fisher*[31] and *R (Rose) v Thanet Clinical Commissioning Group*.[32] NHS England has no specific statutory duty to follow its own guidance, but may well be acting irrationally if it has identical legal duties and yet fails to follow guidance it issues to CCGs about how the duties under the section are to be discharged.

12.85 However, sections 13I and 14V of the NHS Act 2006 only impose procedural duties. It follows that there can be countervailing factors on which a CCG or NHS England could rely upon to reach a final decision

30 At p4.
31 [1997] EWHC Admin 675, (1997–98) 1 CCLR 150.
32 [2014] EWHC 1182 (Admin).

which does not enable a patient to make choices with respect to aspects of health services provided to him or her. That raises the interesting question as to how a CCG or NHS England should approach a request for a provider to fund treatment which the CCG or NHS England has made a specific decision not to commission. The factors would have to be balanced in the decision-making, but it is probably lawful to override the patient's preference and to apply the general policy. It is probably not, however, permissible to adopt a general policy not to fund any medical treatments where no specific decision has been taken to fund the form of treatment.

12.86 These legal structures probably mean that NHS England and CCGs can only discharge the duty by adopting a starting-point that it should enable a patient to make choices with respect to aspects of health services provided to them, and then depart from that position if driven to do so by other factors. Some helpful guidance on the meaning of the section 14V duty can be drawn from the observations of Aitkens LJ in *R (Brown) v Secretary of State for Work and Pensions*,[33] which was concerned with the similarly worded 'due regard' duty under section 149 of the Equality Act 2010. It follows that, in order to act lawfully:

a) Decision-makers in a CCG and NHS England must record their awareness of the duty when making decisions. A CCG or NHS England decision-maker will be in difficulties in asserting that he or she complied with this legal obligations in making a commissioning decision if the person who made the decision was not aware of the legal duty and/or made no reference to the legal duty in the decision making process.
b) The mind of the decision-maker must be focused on the duty during each stage of the commissioning decision making processes. Decision-makers must have a 'conscious approach and state of mind' which is focused upon the legal obligation when they are taking commissioning decisions.
c) The legal duty must be exercised in substance, with rigour and with an open mind.
d) The duty is a non-delegable duty.
e) The duty is a continuing duty throughout the commissioning process.
f) It is good practice for those exercising public functions in public authorities to keep an adequate record showing that they had actually considered this duty and pondered relevant questions.

Conclusion

12.87 Patient choice rights are powerful rights for patients to exercise a measure of control over the services they wish to receive. However, these rights are complex, are not generally well understood and are rarely exercised in practice. However, these legal rights are likely to become more important as NHS resources become tighter and patients are therefore increasingly denied treatment that they seek, in order to balance the books.

33 [2008] EWHC 3158 (Admin).

CHAPTER 13

The responsible commissioner

continued

Wales and Northern Ireland • Category 12: Other qualifying mental health patients • Category 13: Patients usually resident in Scotland, Northern Ireland or Wales • Category 14: Mental Health Act 1983 s117 aftercare patients

13.150 Resolving disputes about which CCG is the responsible commissioner

Introduction

13.1 Ever since the 'purchaser/provider' split was first introduced into the NHS in 1993, and later merged into the commissioner/provider split,[1] the question as to which NHS body was responsible for commissioning (and in particular paying for) care for which patients, and whether care costs should be divided between different NHS commissioners, has been a source of conflict both between NHS patients and NHS commissioning bodies and between different NHS commissioning bodies.

13.2 The aim of this chapter is to provide a guide to the legal structures which define which NHS body is responsible for commissioning which services for which patients. Working out which NHS body is responsible for commissioning services is complicated by three elements.

13.3 First, the present rules are set out in Part 2 and sections 3 and 3A of the National Health Service Act (NHS Act) 2006 and in the National Health Service Commissioning Board and Clinical Commissioning Groups (Responsibilities and Standing Rules) Regulations (RSR Regs) 2012.[2] These are drafted in a way that is nearly impenetrable for trained lawyers, and are thus near to impossible for non-lawyers to follow.

13.4 Second, NHS England produced guidance called *Who Pays? Determining responsibility for payments to providers* in August 2013, which was in reasonably plain English, but which was incorrect in a number of respects.[3] This was updated in April 2006 to reflect amendments made to the identification of the relevant commissioner for section 117 services under the Mental Health Act (MHA) 1983 as a result of changes made by the Care Act 2014. However, the remaining errors in the August 2013 guidance were not corrected.

13.5 Third, there is no statutory dispute resolution system operating to allow independent evaluation of disputes between different NHS bodies about which NHS body is responsible for commissioning services for high-cost patients. The Secretary of State for Health and Social Care has an adjudication function where local authorities disagree over which of them should fund a community care place, but neither the secretary of state nor NHS England have a statutory adjudication function in responsible commissioner disputes.[4]

13.6 As a result of these three elements, disputes about which NHS body is responsible for expensive care packages often drag on for many years without being resolved. It is hoped that this chapter will assist all sides to understand what the regulations provide and thus aid the swift, non-legal resolution of any disputes. However, given the complexity of the legislation, NHS bodies are increasingly agreeing that a single lawyer

1 See chapter 10 for details of the policy changes leading to the creation of the purchaser/provider split and how this became the commissiner/provider division.

2 SI No 2996.

3 See www.england.nhs.uk/wp-content/uploads/2014/05/who-pays.pdf. This replaced 2006 guidance which was also called *Who pays?* The earlier guidance is at http://webarchive.nationalarchives.gov.uk/20130107105354/http:/dh.gov.uk/prod_consum_dh/groups/dh_digitalassets/@dh/@en/documents/digitalasset/dh_126387.pdf.

4 NHS England offers a non-statutory dispute resolution process but that does not assist with questions of vires.

(including the author of this chapter) should be jointly instructed to assist the resolution of such disputes. This can be a quick and relatively inexpensive way to achieve clarity in a complex matter.

Identifying the responsible commissioner in primary care

13.7 Issues around 'who is the responsible commissioner' do not generally arise in primary care. General practitioner (GP) commissioning contracts have their own rules about which patients are required to be provided with services by a GP practice.[5] NHS community dental practices and NHS community pharmacies are both commissioned by NHS England (see below). NHS dentists do not have 'patient lists' operating under GDS or PDS contracts and so can provide NHS services to any patient and make the appropriate claim for providing the service, provided that the dentist has unused Units of Dental Activity in a financial year which can be used to make the claim. Similar rules apply where NHS community optician or optometrist services are available.

13.8 Para 99 of the statutory guidance *Who pays?* accurately explains that clinical commissioning groups (CCGs) are responsible for commissioning the following services that are related to primary care:

- out-of-hours (OOH) primary medical services (where practices have opted out of providing OOH services under the GP contract);
- community-based services that go beyond the scope of the GP contract (akin to previous Local Enhanced Services);
- meeting the costs of prescriptions written by member practices (but not the associated dispensing costs);
- secondary ophthalmic services and any associated community-based eye care services.

Identifying the responsible commissioner for secondary care services

13.9 Wherever NHS care (outside of primary medical or dental care) is provided to a patient by a provider who seeks payment from an NHS commissioner for the provision of that care, it is necessary for the provider to identify the NHS commissioner with statutory responsibility for paying for the relevant NHS care for that NHS patient. Once the responsible commissioner has been identified, the next step for the provider is to establish whether the contractual arrangements between the relevant NHS commissioner and an NHS provider entitle the provider to charge for the treatment provided to the patient. That question is addressed in chapter 10.

13.10 Since the implementation of the Health and Social Care Act (HSCA) 2012, identifying the responsible NHS commissioner involves addressing two questions:

5 Readers are referred to chapter 11 which provides details of these services.

1) is a CCG is the responsible commissioner or is NHS England the responsible commissioner for the services provided to the patient? and
2) if this is care where a CCG is the responsible commissioner, which CCG is the responsible commissioner?

The commissioning responsibilities of NHS England

Overview

13.11 Section 3(1) of the NHS Act 2006 provides a range of services that each CCG is required to commission for patients for whom the CCG has commissioning responsibility. However, section 3(1E) provides:

> The duty in subsection (1) does not apply in relation to a service or facility if the Board has a duty to arrange for its provision.

13.12 A reference to 'the Board' in the NHS Act 2006 is a reference to the National Health Service Commissioning Board, which operates under the name of 'NHS England'. Thus if NHS England has commissioning responsibility for a 'service or facility', a CCG does not have a duty to commission such a service under section 3(1). CCGs have powers (but not duties) to commission a wide range of NHS and social care services under section 3A(1), but section 3A(2) provides:

> A clinical commissioning group may not arrange for the provision of a service or facility under subsection (1) if the Board has a duty to arrange for its provision by virtue of section 3B or 4.

It follows that a CCG has no power (ie no 'vires') to expend money on commissioning services where NHS England has commissioning responsibility for that service.[6] Hence, commissioning responsibility for NHS services under Part 1 of the NHS Act 2006 (namely services beyond those provided as part of primary care services) either falls to NHS England or to a CCG but cannot lawfully be funded by both bodies.

13.13 It is possible for NHS England to delegate commissioning responsibility for a service for which it has statutory responsibility to a CCG. However, where NHS England has delegated commissioning responsibility for a service to a CCG, the cost of the service *must* be paid by NHS England and not the CCG (because the CCG has no vires to pay for the service itself).

13.14 The power to make regulations which define the services for which NHS England has commissioning responsibility is set out in section 3B of the NHS Act 2006 which provides:

> (1) Regulations may require the Board to arrange, to such extent as it considers necessary to meet all reasonable requirements, for the provision as part of the health service of–
> (a) dental services of a prescribed description;

6 This was recently confirmed in *R (Wolverhampton City Council) v South Worcestershire CCG and another* (Garnham J). The judgment was not yet available at the time of publication.

(b) services or facilities for members of the armed forces or their families;
(c) services or facilities for persons who are detained in a prison or in other accommodation of a prescribed description;
(d) such other services or facilities as may be prescribed.

(2) A service or facility may be prescribed under subsection (1)(d) only if the Secretary of State considers that it would be appropriate for the Board (rather than clinical commissioning groups) to arrange for its provision as part of the health service.

(3) In deciding whether it would be so appropriate, the Secretary of State must have regard to–
(a) the number of individuals who require the provision of the service or facility;
(b) the cost of providing the service or facility;
(c) the number of persons able to provide the service or facility;
(d) the financial implications for clinical commissioning groups if they were required to arrange for the provision of the service or facility.

(4) Before deciding whether to make regulations under this section, the Secretary of State must–
(a) obtain advice appropriate for that purpose, and
(b) consult the Board.

(5) The reference in subsection (1)(b) to members of the armed forces is a reference to persons who are members of–
(a) the regular forces within the meaning of the Armed Forces Act 2006, or
(b) the reserve forces within the meaning of that Act.

13.15 It follows that the NHS Act 2006 gives the power for the secretary of state to make regulations which define the types of services or facilities which should be commissioned by NHS England as opposed to CCGs. The relevant regulations are in Part 3 of the RSR Regs 2012. These regulations provide that NHS England has commissioning responsibility for a range of general and specialist services.

NHS England commissioned dental services

13.16 Regulation 6 of the RSR Regs 2012 provides:

> The Board must arrange, to such extent as it considers necessary to meet all reasonable requirements, for the provision as part of the health service of–
> (a) community dental services; and
> (b) the dental services specified in Schedule 2.

13.17 Community dental services are defined in reg 3 as:

> 'community dental services' means dental services provided as part of the health service other than–
> (a) emergency services,
> (b) dental services provided pursuant to arrangements made by the Board under Part 5 of the 2006 Act, or
> (c) the dental services specified in Schedule 2.

13.18 The reference to dental services provided under Part 5 of the NHS Act 2006 is a reference the duty under section 99 of the NHS Act 2006 which provides:

> The Board must, to the extent that it considers necessary to meet all reasonable requirements, exercise its powers so as to secure the provision of primary dental services throughout England.

13.19 Hence, 'primary' dental services are commissioned by NHS England under Part 5 of the NHS Act 2006 and secondary dental services, including 'community dental services' are commissioned by NHS England under reg 3 of the RSR Regs 2012. Schedule 2 provides the following list of dental services to supplement community dental services:

> 1. Oral surgery.
> 2. Restorative dentistry.
> 3. Paedodontic/paediatric dentistry.
> 4. Orthodontics.
> 5. Oral and maxillofacial surgery.
> 6. Endodontics.
> 7. Periodontics.
> 8. Prosthodontics.
> 9. Oral medicine.
> 10. Oral microbiology.
> 11. Oral and maxillofacial pathology.
> 12. Dental and maxillofacial radiology.
> 13. Special care dentistry.

13.20 It follows that the only dental services that fall to be commissioned by CCGs are emergency dental services since these are excluded from the definition of 'community dental services'. Emergency services are defined in reg 2 as:

> 'emergency services' means ambulance services and accident and emergency services provided as part of the health service, whether provided at a hospital accident or emergency department, a minor injuries unit, a walk-in centre or elsewhere.

Services for members of the Armed Forces

13.21 Regulation 7 of the RSR Regs 2012 provides that NHS England has the responsibility for commissioning most NHS services for members of the armed services and their families. It provides:

> (1) This regulation applies to–
>   (a) a person who is a serving member of the armed forces; and
>   (b) that person's family.
> (2) The Board must arrange, to such extent as it considers necessary to meet all reasonable requirements, for the provision as part of the health service to persons to whom this regulation applies of–
>   (a) community services;
>   (b) secondary care services; and
>   (c) the services specified in Schedule 4.
> (3) The arrangements to be made by the Board under paragraph (2)(b) in respect of a person referred to in paragraph (1)(a) must include the provision of any infertility treatment to that person and to that person's partner.
> (4) The infertility treatment referred to in paragraph (3) must–
>   (a) where a person referred to in paragraph (1)(a) has been injured in service and is in receipt of compensation for infertility under the Armed Forces Compensation Scheme, include funding the cost of

sperm storage facilities from the date on which the injury was sustained (where clinically necessary and where provision for such storage has previously been made); and

(b) where, and to the extent that, the Board is satisfied that this is clinically appropriate in the circumstances of any case, include the provision of up to three cycles of in vitro fertilisation treatments or other means of assisted conception.

(5) In paragraph (1)(b), 'family', in relation to a person to whom this regulation applies, means that person's immediate family registered for primary care services with Defence Medical Services.

(6) The Board must regard a person ('A') as the partner of a person referred to in paragraph (1)(a) ('B') if–

(a) A is the spouse or civil partner of B; or

(b) A and B are cohabiting as partners in a substantial and exclusive relationship in circumstances where either–

(i) A is financially dependent on B, or

(ii) A and B are financially interdependent.

(7) In deciding whether A is in a substantial relationship with B, the Board must–

(a) have regard to any evidence which A considers demonstrates that the relationship is substantial; and

(b) in particular, have regard to the examples of evidence specified in paragraph (8) which could, either alone or together, indicate that the relationship is substantial.

(8) The evidence referred to in paragraph (7)(b) is–

(a) evidence of regular financial support of A by B;

(b) evidence of a will or life insurance policy, valid at the time at which the infertility treatment is sought in which–

(i) B nominates A as principal beneficiary or co-beneficiary, or

(ii) A nominates B as the principal beneficiary;

(c) evidence indicating that A and B have purchased or are purchasing accommodation together as joint owners or evidence of joint ownership of other valuable property, such as a car or land;

(d) evidence of a joint savings plan or joint investments of a substantial nature;

(e) evidence that A and B operate a joint account for which they are co-signatories;

(f) evidence of joint financial arrangements such as joint repayment of a loan or payment of each other's debts;

(g) evidence that either A or B has given the other the power of attorney;

(h) evidence that the names of both A and B appear on a lease or, if they live in rental accommodation, rental agreement; and

(i) evidence of the length of the relationship.

(9) For the purposes of paragraph (6)(b), a relationship is not an exclusive relationship if one or both of the parties is a party to another relationship which is, or could be considered to be, a substantial and exclusive relationship having regard to the provisions of this regulation.

13.22 This is a somewhat confusingly worded provision, but in summary:

a) NHS England has lead NHS commissioning responsibility for members of the armed services and those members of the immediate family of a member of the armed services who registered for primary care services with Defence Medical Services.

b) As a result of the definition of 'community services' in reg 5 of the RSR Regs 2012, NHS England is responsible for commissioning all NHS services for members of the armed forces and their families other than emergency services and primary care services (which are already a commissioning responsibility of NHS England under Part 4 of the NHS Act 2006).
c) There are special rules for fertility services where a member of the armed services is injured in service and is in receipt of compensation for infertility under the Armed Forces Compensation Scheme. The regulations provide:
   i) an extended definition of 'partner' for fertility services;
   ii) special rules about infertility services are extended to armed forces veterans by reg 8 and by reg 9 for deceased members of the armed forces who have had sperm preserved before death and proper consent has been given.

Services for prisoners and other detained persons

13.23 Regulation 10 of the RSR Regs 2012 provides that NHS England has commissioning responsibility for individuals who are detained by the state. It provides:

> **10** (1) Where a person is detained in a prison or in other accommodation described in paragraph (2), the Board must arrange, to such extent as it considers necessary to meet all reasonable requirements, for the provision to that person as part of the health service of–
> (a) community services;
> (b) secondary care services; and
> (c) the services specified in Schedule 4.
> (2) The other accommodation referred to in paragraph (1) is–
> (a) a court;
> (b) a secure children's home (except those specified in Part 1 of Schedule 3);
> (c) a secure training centre specified in the first column of Table 1 in Schedule 3 from the date specified in the corresponding entry in the second column of that Table;
> (d) an immigration removal centre specified in the first column of Table 2 in Schedule 3 from the date specified in the corresponding entry in the second column of that Table; and
> (e) a young offender institution (except Ashfield Young Offender Institution).
> (3) In this regulation, 'court' means any court in which criminal proceedings against a person are heard.

13.24 'Secondary care services' are defined in reg 5 as:

> services provided as part of the health service in a hospital setting, or by those working in or based in a hospital setting, other than emergency services, primary care services or the services specified in Schedule 4.

13.25 Schedule 4 services are services for patients with rare and very conditions and are considered below. 'Community services' are defined in reg 5 to mean:

> services provided as part of the health service other than–
> (a) emergency services,
> (b) primary care services,

(c) secondary care services, or
(d) the services specified in Schedule 4.

13.26 NHS England already has general commissioning responsibility for primary care services (see section 83 of the NHS Act 2006). It follows that NHS England is responsible for commissioning all NHS services for detainees other than emergency services, which have to be commissioned by the CCG which covers the area where the services are provided. It follows that if a detainee is transferred from detention to a hospital for secondary care, the local CCG has to meet the cost of any emergency care provided to the detainee but NHS England is responsible for funding all other NHS secondary care provided to a detainee.

13.27 NHS England's responsibility covers detainees held in the following institutions;

- a prison (including those run by private prison operators);
- a court;
- a secure children's home;
- a secure training centre specified in the first column of Table 1 in Schedule 3 to the RSR Regs 2012 from the date specified in the corresponding entry in the second column of that Table;
- an immigration removal centre specified in the first column of Table 2 in Schedule 3 from the date specified in the corresponding entry in the second column of that Table; and
- a young offender institution.

13.28 The above list does not cover services to individuals who are detained in police stations. Responsibility for providing physical and mental health medical care to detainees in police stations rests with the police who engage their own doctors. That is beyond the scope of this chapter, but details can be obtained from the guidance published by the College of Policing.[7] However, the policy objective is to ensure that this potentially vulnerable group of individuals are provided with healthcare which is equivalent to that provided in the NHS.

13.29 Prison health services have been run by the NHS since they were transferred from Home Office control in 2004. However, the unique situation within detention establishments and the difficulties in recruiting and retaining appropriate staff has meant that NHS has struggled to deliver services in prisons which match the ambition to ensure that prisoners have the same access to services as the rest of the community. The NHS England strategy document *Strategic direction for health services in the justice system: 2016–2020*[8] 'contains a number of clearly stated objectives to improve the health of those being held in secure accommodation. In its foreword it notes:

> Children, young people and adults in contact with the criminal justice system, or in detained settings are more likely to smoke, misuse drugs or alcohol, have mental and physical health problems, report having a disability, self-harm or attempt suicide. Their lives are often further complicated by complex social and personal issues such as unemployment, low educa-

7 See www.app.college.police.uk/app-content/detention-and-custody–2/detainee-care/.
8 See www.england.nhs.uk/wp-content/uploads/2016/10/hlth-justice-directions-v11.pdf.

> tional attainment or even homelessness. They are marginalised by society. As a consequence of all these influences their lives are often cut short in a brutal manifestation of social and health inequality.

13.30 The document then commits NHS England to a strategic direction of improving health services in prisons and contains the relatively weak commitment:[9]

> . . . they are generally expected to access the same healthcare services as the rest of the population.

13.31 The document contains commitments to improving health outcomes for prisoners and those at risk in the early stages of the criminal justice system, but it says virtually nothing about the allocation of additional resources to offender health in the short term. It is worth noting the eventual laudable aim is to use NHS resources to provide these vulnerable individuals with more targeted, personalised support and thus divert those with mental health or substance abuse problems away from the criminal justice system. It could be thought that the document looks far into the future when it says:[10]

> By extending availability of these approaches, we will do more to address the specific needs of this particular population group, break the cycle of offending and improve the quality of care and experience of individuals. This will also deliver better value for money and furthermore may cut costs for both health and justice systems.

13.32 While, as a statement of ambition, that appears laudable, it is difficult to see how this aim can ever be achieved without significant additional resources being diverted from other areas of NHS spending into commissioning health and justice services. However, this document is a statement of NHS England's strategy and thus NHS England may be acting unlawfully if it continues to adopt this strategy but fails to take decisions, including resource allocation decisions, which are consistent with the published strategy. Thus, the document may be useful for lawyers representing prisoners who find themselves receiving substandard services primarily because they are in custody.

Specialised services

13.33 In 2015/16, £15.6 billion was allocated by NHS England to the commissioning of 'specialised services' for NHS patients who suffer from rare and very rare conditions.[11] This is a very significant element of the NHS expenditure in England. The bill for commissioning specialised services is, for example, almost double the entire cost of commissioning general practice services across the NHS (which is £8.2 billion[12]).

13.34 The duty on NHS England to commission specialised services is set out in reg 11 of the RSR Regs 2012, which provides:

9 At p9.
10 At p29.
11 See www.england.nhs.uk/commissioning/spec-services/.
12 See http://content.digital.nhs.uk/catalogue/PUB21318/nhspaymentsgp–15–16-rep.pdf.

The Board must arrange, to such extent as it considers necessary to meet all reasonable requirements, for the provision as part of the health service of the services specified in Schedule 4.

13.35 Schedule 4 lists the services that have been classified as 'specialised services', starting with 'Adult ataxia telangiectasia services' and ending with 'Xeroderma pigmentosum service'. There are a huge variety of services listed in Schedule 4. Some are plainly not 'rare' diseases, such as 'Adult specialist cardiac services', but others are very rare indeed, such as the 'Ataxia telangiectasia service for children'.[13]

13.36 Specialised services are an area of huge political controversy and regular legal challenge: see, for example, *R (S (a child)) v NHS England*.[14] Regulation 35 of the RSR Regs 2012 provides that reasons must be given for a commissioning decision and these decisions (probably) engage the European Convention on Human Rights (ECHR) Article 8 rights (right to privacy) of the patient, and thus require anxious scrutiny of the decision.[15] However, there are dilemmas throughout the processes for commissioning specialised services. Pharmaceutical companies can argue, with some justification, that developing drugs or other treatments for patients with rare conditions is just as expensive as developing other treatments but that a high price of a successfully developed treatment is justified by the limited number of patients to whom the drug can be provided. Clinicians treating these patients often have huge levels of specialist knowledge arising from their involvement in research and development for new treatments and naturally wish to use any treatment that may be successful for their patients, many of whom will have rare and life-threatening conditions. There are a series of highly effective pressure groups whose purposes are to support patients with rare conditions and to promote the interests of such patients, including lobbying for new treatments to be made available to patients with their particular condition. Some of these pressure groups support 'All Party Parliamentary Groups' (APPGs) of members of parliament (MPs) who take an interest in patients with a particular condition. This can lead to the pressure groups having a huge influence on the contents of reports produced by the APPG, and thus increase the standing and media coverage of treatment options for small groups of patients.

13.37 The Department of Health and Social Care is also the government department which promotes the UK pharmaceutical industry, and rolling out new treatments into the NHS is seen as vital to the success of this industry. Finally, and not to be underestimated, NHS England comes under media pressure whenever a new drug or treatment is not available as part of NHS-funded treatment for an identified individual.

13 Which has a prevalence of about one patient in every 400,000: see www.atsociety.org.uk/data/files/William/A-T_Clinical_Guidance_Document_Final.pdf.

14 [2016] EWHC 1395 (Admin), (2016) 19 CCLR 336.

15 There is a debate about this following differing views expressed by the Court of Appeal in *R (Condliff) v North Staffordshire PCT* [2011] EWCA Civ 910, (2011) 14 CCLR 656 and *R (Tracey) v Cambridge University Hospitals NHS Foundation Trust and others* [2014] EWCA Civ 822.

13.38 NHS England is thus under huge political pressure to fund specialised services at a cost per patient which far exceeds the costs that would be permitted to support virtually any other patient where the CCG is the responsible commissioner. NHS England has attempted to manage this pressure by introducing a system of prioritisation and budget control but it remains to be seen whether senior management at NHS England have the courage to take difficult decisions.[16] The substantial additional resources which are made available to support patients with a condition which comes within specialised services in comparison to resources for supporting services which fall outside specialist services appears unjustifiable. It is difficult to see why a patient who has a 'common' life threatening condition should be denied a life-saving or life-extending drug which costs £40,000 per year when a patient with a less common condition will be funded for a life-saving or life-extending drug that costs £400,000 per year. In an appropriate case, there may be an argument that failing to fund the drug for the patient with the common condition is a breach of ECHR Articles 2, 3 or 8 combined with Article 14.

13.39 There is an unresolved issue about whether community services which are required to treat a patient who has a condition listed in Schedule 4 should be funded by a CCG or NHS England. The wording of the RSR Regs 2012 suggests that such services should be funded by NHS England because reg 11 and Schedule 4 make no distinction between the type of location at which services for the specified patient groups should be provided. Hence where, for example, a patient suffers from severe obsessive compulsive disorder (see para 103 of Schedule 4), both acute and community NHS services which are provided to meet that patients' needs appear to be required to be funded by NHS England and not the local CCG. Practice appears to vary across the country, with some community-based specialised services being funded by NHS England and others funded by CCGs. The test should be whether the community services are being commissioned because a patient has a particular medical condition. If that medical condition is one which is listed in Schedule 4, statutory responsibility for funding all services to treat that condition (including community services) appears to rest with NHS England. Thus, if that is correct, local CCGs have no vires to fund such services.

Mental health patients

Generally

13.40 The *Who pays?* guidance suggests that the responsible commissioner for detained mental health patients will generally be the CCG where the patient was registered with a GP practice before the patient was detained. It states:[17]

16 Please see chapter 9 for more details about the difficulties of commissioning decision-making.

17 At para 33.

If a person is detained for treatment under the Mental Health Act (MHA) 1983, the responsible commissioner will be as set out in paragraph 1.[18] Every effort should be made to determine GP practice registration or establish an address where they are usually resident, but if this fails and the patient refuses to assist, then as a last resort the responsible commissioner should be determined by the location of the unit providing treatment.

13.41 This does not appear to be correct for secure mental health services because paragraph 7 of Schedule 4 provides that NHS England has commissioning responsibility for adult secure mental health services.

13.42 Secure mental health services are divided into High, Medium and Low Secure services. The consequence of including secure mental health services in Schedule 4 is that NHS England has sole commissioning responsibility for providing NHS services to all patients who are detained under the MHA 1983 and CCGs have no power to expend monies funding detained mental health patients. However, although all patients who are detained in a hospital under the MHA 1983 are, by definition, deprived of their liberty, not all detained MHA patients are classified by the NHS as being in 'secure' services. There are mental health wards where patients are detained (and which are locked wards) but are not classified by the NHS as being 'secure' accommodation. There does not appear to be a centrally approved definition as to the clinical characteristics that need to be fulfilled in order for mental health accommodation to be classified as 'secure'. It follows that, in practice, the meaning given to above paragraph appears somewhat circular. NHS England is responsible for commissioning High, Medium and Low Secure mental health services, and CCGs are responsible for commissioning other mental health services for detained patients. However a unit is defined as being a High, Medium and Low Secure service based on whether the services at the unit are commissioned by NHS England or not. If it is not commissioned by NHS England then, by definition, it appears not to be a 'secure' mental health service and thus detained patients at that unit must be funded by the relevant CCG.

Informal mental health patients

13.43 CCGs will remain responsible for funding services for informal mental health patients. The relevant CCG will be identified by the location of the patient's GP in the usual way. For informal mental health patients who are not on the list of any GP practice, the responsible commissioner will be worked out by reference to the patient's place of residence. A detained mental health patient does not become 'resident' at the hospital at which he or she is forcibly detained: see *R v Mental Health Review Tribunal ex p Hall*.[19] Hence, the detained mental health patient will not change their place of residence as a result of being detained in hospital. In contrast, an

18 The reference to para 1 of the guidance is a reference to the general rule that commissioning responsibility lies with the CCG where the patient is registered with a GP practice or, where the patient is not registered with any GP practice, the place where the patient is usually resident.

19 [1999] 3 All ER 132, (1999) 2 CCLR 383.

informal patient (with capacity) may change their place of residence to the hospital if the patient chooses to remain in the hospital for an extended period and, in particular, if the patient does not have anywhere to 'return' to live in their former area.

13.44 However, if a patient is registered with a GP practice local to the psychiatric hospital after they have been admitted as an informal patient (or has their GP registration transferred to that practice after admission without action by their home CCG) the CCG local to the new GP practice is likely to become the responsible commissioner.

Other services commissioned by NHS England

13.45 Regulation 12 of the RSR Regs 2012 provides that NHS England has commissioning responsibility for the Independent Sector Treatment Centre programme, which was originally commissioned directly by the DHSC. Regulation 13 provides that NHS England has responsibility for fixated threat assessment services. Regulation 13(1) provides:

> The Board must arrange, to such extent as it considers necessary to meet all reasonable requirements, for the provision as part of the health service of specialised clinical risk assessment and management services for people with mental health problems who may present a risk to prominent people or locations.

13.46 In practice, this means that NHS England funds the Fixated Threat Assessment Centre (FTAC) which is a joint Home Office, DHSC and Metropolitan Police Service unit. The purpose of the FTAC[20] is:

> . . . to assess and manage the risks from lone individuals who harass, stalk or threaten public figures. Many such people are suffering from serious mental illnesses and have fallen through the care net.
>
> FTAC helps such people get the care they need and, by doing so, decreases any risk they might pose, not just to prominent people, but to the individuals' families and to those around them.

13.47 The FTAC observes that:

> The main risks to elected politicians in western countries come not from terrorist or criminal groups, but from fixated loners.

That statement rings true in the light of tragic cases such as the murder in 2016 of Labour MP Jo Cox. It must be justifiable to use additional resources to protect those who are elected or appointed to public office and thus come under a greater level of threat because of the public office that they hold. It may be less justifiable to expend resources to protect actors, media figures, sports stars or those who become public figures for other reasons, but the definition of 'prominent people' covered by FTAC appears to exclude this because it defines its subjects as follows:

> 'Prominent people' are those who are in the public eye due to their public service role. These include the main members of the British Royal Family, senior politicians and members of parliament'

20 See http://fixatedthreat.com/ftac-welcome.php.

Commissioning for patients who have multiple conditions

13.48 Patients may present with a variety of conditions, some of which fall into NHS England's commissioning responsibilities and others of which fall to a CCG. As far as the author is aware, there is no clear guidance on how commissioners are supposed to work together where a patient presents with multiple conditions, some of which require services to be commissioned by NHS England and others of which require services which fall to be commissioned by a CCG. In practice, NHS England interpret their commissioning responsibilities as largely being limited to contracts that they place with specialist secondary care providers to deliver the acute phase of services to patients suffering from conditions which come within those described in Schedule 4 to the RSR Regs 2012.

13.49 However, NHS England's duties appear to be wider because a patient who is living outside hospital and has a rare condition may be entitled to NHS Continuing Healthcare. That raises the question as to whether the costs of delivering a package of services for an NHS Continuing Healthcare patient who lives in the community but suffers from a condition which falls within Schedule 4 to the RSR Regs 2012 should fall on NHS England or a local CCG. There is no clear answer to this conundrum, but the duty to assess and make decisions about NHS Continuing Healthcare falls both on NHS England and on CCGs (depending on the status of the patient: see reg 21(2) of the RSR Regs 2012). However, at present, NHS England does not appear to have any mechanisms to make decisions to fund NHS Continuing Healthcare for patients who suffer from conditions for which it has commissioning responsibility.

Allocating commissioning responsibility between CCGs

Introduction

13.50 Disputes between commissioners as to which CCG is responsible for which commissioning services for a patient are just as much a feature of the NHS as disputes between local authorities as which local authority has statutory responsibility to provide community care services to a service user.

13.51 The rules are concerned with the allocation of responsibility between different public bodies. Accordingly, they should be interpreted so that there is only one CCG which acts as the 'responsible commissioner' for a patient for a particular episode of care: see by analogy *R (Cornwall Council) v Secretary of State for Health and Somerset CC*.[21] However, the fact that a CCG is the responsible commissioner for a patient for one episode of care does not necessarily mean that the same CCG is the responsible commissioner for that patient for other episodes of care. Hence, for example, section 1C of the NHS Act 2006 provides:

21 [2015] UKSC 46, (2015) 18 CCLR 497.

> The power conferred by subsection (1B)(b) must be exercised so as to provide that, in relation to the provision of services or facilities for emergency care, a clinical commissioning group has responsibility for every person present in its area.

13.52 Hence, the responsible commissioner for all emergency patients must be the CCG in whose area the emergency facility is located. This means that a CCG becomes the responsible commissioner for every patient who attends a local hospital A&E department. However, responsibility for funding ongoing care for a patient who is admitted to a hospital ward will revert to the patient's home CCG.

13.53 Section 3 of the NHS Act 2006 and Part 2 and Schedule 1 to the RSR Regs 2012 contain a series of reasonably clear rules which define the 'responsible commissioner' in different circumstances. The secretary of state has also made the National Health Service (Clinical Commissioning Groups – Disapplication of Responsibility) Regulations (CCGDR Regs) 2013.[22] Thus, in determining which CCG is responsible for a patient for a particular episode of care:

a) reference needs to be made the primary rules in the NHS Act 2006 to determine which CCG starts as the responsible commissioner;
b) reference then needs to be made to the RSR Regs 2012 to determine whether the primary rules need to be varied by the rules set out in those regulations;
c) finally, a CCG needs to bear the rules in the CCGDR Regs 2013 to determine if they disapply either the primary rules in the NHS Act 2006 or the rules in the RSR Regs 2012.

13.54 There is also the useful guidance published by NHS England accurately called *Who Pays? Determining responsibility for payments to providers*. However, the guidance needs to be treated with some care because, while it is generally useful and CCGs have a statutory duty to have regard to the guidance under section 14Z8 of the NHS Act 2006, it contains a series of errors. As a matter of law, the statutory scheme takes precedence over the guidance and thus, if in doubt, a CCG is obliged to follow the statutory scheme and not the guidance: see for example *R (Simpson) v Police Medical Appeal Board and others*[23] as an example of a case where the guidance was quashed for being inconsistent with a statutory scheme.

13.55 In order to make sense of the complex rules, groups of patients can be divided into a series of categories:

1) Category 1: Patients who require emergency treatment
2) Category 2: Patients for whom a CCG member GP practice provides medical services
3) Category 3: Patients who are not on any GP practice list but who are usually resident in the CCG area

And additional categories of patients described in Schedule 1 to the RSR Regs 2012:

22 SI No 350.
23 [2012] EWHC 808 (Admin).

4) Category 4: Adult continuing care patients placed in a facility in the area of another CCG
5) Category 5: Placed children falling within paragraph 4 of Schedule 1 to the RSR Regs 2012
6) Category 6: Placed children who become adults
7) Category 7: Adult patients who have been placed out of area by a primary care trust
8) Category 8: Children who have been placed out of area by a primary care trust
9) Category 9: Children placed at special schools by local authorities before 1 April 2013
10) Category 10: Patients who are resident outside the United Kingdom
11) Category 11: Mental health patients resident in Scotland, Wales and Northern Ireland
12) Category 12: Other qualifying mental health patients
13) Category 13: Patients usually resident in Scotland, Northern Ireland or Wales
14) Category 14: MHA 1983 s117 aftercare patients

Categories 1–3

Category 1: Patients who require emergency treatment

13.56 Section 1C of the NHS Act 2006 provides that the responsible commissioner is the CCG in whose area the patient is present. That is reproduced in para 2(a) of Schedule 1 to the RSR Regs 2012, which provides that a CCG has commissioning responsibility for:

> . . . every person present in the CCG's area, in relation to the provision of ambulance services or accident and emergency services, whether provided at a hospital accident and emergency department, a minor injuries unit, a walk-in centre or elsewhere (but excluding any services provided after the person has been accepted as an in-patient, or at an out-patient appointment).

13.57 This is also confirmed in the *Who pays?* guidance which provides:[24]

> A CCG is responsible for commissioning emergency care for anyone present in its geographic area, regardless of where the person in question is usually resident or which GP practice (if any) they are registered with.

13.58 If a patient is transferred from one A&E to another A&E for more specialist emergency care, the first CCG continues to have a duty to fund the accident and emergency services: see reg 3(a) of the CCGDR Regs 2013.

13.59 Paragraph 5 of the *Who pays?* guidance provides:

> The rules on payment for emergency care are that:
> - For A&E attendances and emergency admissions, the CCG that would ordinarily be the responsible commissioner for a patient (under the rules in paragraph 1 and subject to the other relevant exceptions in Section C) or NHS England (for example, for members of the armed forces) is responsible for paying the provider for the costs of that patient's care;

24 At p3.

- The costs of all other emergency care will be met by the CCG that commissions the care, except where cost-sharing arrangements have been voluntarily agreed by CCGs or NHS England;
- As set out in the 2013/14 Payment by Results (PbR) Guidance, residents of Scotland, Wales and Northern Ireland attending English A&E departments, the cost is covered by the host CCG, not the patient's responsible health board.

13.60 This part of the guidance is not consistent with the statutory scheme. Where a patient is provided with A&E services (as defined in para 2(a) of Schedule 1 to the RSR Regs 2012), the CCG with commissioning responsibility for those services is the CCG covering the area in which the hospital is located. The part of the guidance set out above about cost sharing conflicts with section 3(1C) in as much as it recommends that the normal GP practice or usual residence rules shall apply where a patient accesses emergency services. The only CCG that should meet the cost of the provision of those services is the CCG where those services are located.

Category 2: Patients for whom a CCG member GP practice provides medical services

13.61 Section 3(1A) of the NHS Act 2006 provides:

> (1A) For the purposes of this section, a clinical commissioning group has responsibility for–
> (a) persons who are provided with primary medical services by a member of the group, and
> (b) persons who usually reside in the group's area and are not provided with primary medical services by a member of any clinical commissioning group'

13.62 The 'members of the group' are the GP practices in the CCG's area which hold primary medical care commissioning contracts: see section 14A(1) of the NHS Act 2006, which provides that NHS England must exercise its functions so that 'each provider of primary medical services is a member of a clinical commissioning group'. The persons who are 'provided with primary medical services by a member of the group' are the persons to whom a GP practice has a contractual duty to provide primary care services. These are:

a) those who are permanently on the list of patients of a GP practice;
b) those who are accepted onto a GP practice list as 'temporary patients';[25] and
c) persons to whom the contractor is required to provide immediately necessary treatment as part of its obligation to provide 'essential services'.[26]

Permanent patients on a GP practice list

13.63 Each NHS GP practice has a list of patients who are registered with the practice. The GP practice has a duty to provide primary medical services to those patients. The CCG to which the GP practice belongs has the duty

25 See chapter 18 for details about the process of management of lists of patients by GP practices.

26 The definition of essential services is explained at para 18.21.

to commission secondary care services for all of the patients on the GP practice list.

Temporary residents

13.64 The position of 'temporary patients' is described as follows in the guidance:[27]

> This applies to patients permanently registered as well as those registered as a temporary patient – if a person is registered with a GP who is a member of CCG A and then becomes registered as a temporary patient with a GP who is a member of CCG B under the regulations the patient ceases to be the responsibility of CCG A under s3 for the period of that temporary registration.

13.65 A patient who is temporarily registered on the list of a GP practice may also be permanently on the list of another GP practice. Where a patient has been temporarily admitted to the list of a GP practice, the CCG covering the area where the patient is permanently registered ceases to be the responsible commissioner for NHS services for that patient for as long as the patient is registered as a temporary resident in the area of another CCG: see reg 2(2)(d) of the CCGDR Regs 2013.

GP emergency services

13.66 An NHS GP has a duty to attend to anyone who is physically present in his or her practice area and who seeks emergency medical care. This duty is set out in reg 17(7) of the National Health Service (General Medical Services Contracts) Regulations (GMS Regs) 2015[28] as follows:

> A contractor must provide primary medical services required in core hours for the immediately necessary treatment of any person to whom the contractor has been requested to provide treatment owing to an accident or emergency at any place in the contractor's practice area.

13.67 Thus if, for example, a GP is asked to attend someone who has collapsed in the street outside the surgery, and provides immediate medical assistance to the person before an ambulance attends, and the patient is then taken to hospital for further treatment, the GP's local CCG may have a duty to fund the treatment.

Category 3: Patients who are not on any GP practice list but who are usually resident in the CCG area

13.68 Section 3(1A) of the NHS Act 2006 provides that if a person is 'usually resident' in the CCG's area and is not on the list of any GP practice (in the area or otherwise), the test for commissioning responsibility is based on 'usual residence'. Annex B to the *Who pays?* guidance explains what is meant by the usual residence test. It provides:

> **Annex B: Defining 'usually resident'**
> 1. It is important to note that:

27 At n8 on p7.
28 SI No 1862.

- the 'usually resident' test must only be used to establish the responsible commissioner when this cannot be established based on the patient's GP practice registration;
- 'usually resident' is different from 'ordinarily resident'. If a person is not ordinarily resident in the UK and not covered by an exemption in regulations then they are liable for NHS hospital treatment costs themselves (see Annex A). The 'usually resident' test may still be needed to establish the responsible commissioner for non-hospital services;
- by contrast, local authority responsibility in relation to the public health services they commission is based on a duty to take steps to improve the health of the people in their area. The duty is not limited to residents, or people permanently in the area. It can include people who are only temporarily in the area, eg a visiting student or worker, or a tourist, or a commuter. It is therefore for the local authority to determine who is the relevant population (residents or wider) in relation to the services they commission, deciding whether any step to improve their health is appropriate, given their resources, other priorities etc.;
- local authority responsibility for the provision of accommodation and community care services is largely based on the concept of 'ordinary residence'.

2. The main criterion for assessing 'usual residence' is the patient's perception of where they are resident in the UK (either currently, or failing that, most recently). The same principles apply in determining usual residence for determining which CCG has responsibility for arranging care for a patient.

3. Where the patient gives an address, they should be treated as usually resident at that address.

4. Certain groups of patients may be reluctant to provide an address. It is sufficient for the purpose of establishing usual residence that a patient is resident in a location (or postal district) within the CCG geographical area, without needing a precise address. Where there is any uncertainty, the provider should ask the patient where they usually live. Individuals remain free to give their perception of where they consider themselves resident. Holiday or second homes should not be considered as 'usual' residences.

5. If patients consider themselves to be resident at an address, which is, for example, a hostel, then this should be accepted. If they are unable to give an address at which they consider themselves resident, but can give their most recent address, they should be treated as usually resident at that address.

6. Another person (for example, a parent or carer) may give an address on a patient's behalf.

7. Where a patient cannot, or chooses not to, give either a current or recent address, and an address cannot be established by other means, they should be treated as usually resident in the place where they are present'

13.69 There has been considerable litigation about where individuals are 'resident'. Statutory regimes use the terms 'ordinary residence', 'habitual residence' and 'normal residence' to assign responsibility for the allocation of statutory services, to indicate submission to the jurisdiction of a court or to incur a liability to various forms of tax. Community care responsibilities are allocated on the basis of an 'ordinary residence' test: see section 39 of the Care Act 2014. The DHSC has provided guidance[29] on the meaning of

29 See chapter 19 of the guidance at www.gov.uk/government/publications/care-act-statutory-guidance/care-and-support-statutory-guidance.

the 'ordinary residence' test following the Supreme Court case of *R (Cornwall Council) v Secretary of State for Health*.[30] Save for one issue, there appears to be no policy justification for the NHS allocating responsibility between CCGs on the basis of a 'usual residence' test while local authorities allocate responsibility between themselves on an 'ordinary residence' test. It is also both not helpful and not necessarily legally correct for Annex B of the *Who pays?* guidance to suggest that the meaning of '"usually resident" is different from "ordinarily resident"'. The High Court has held that these terms usually mean the same thing: see *R (M) v Hammersmith and Fulham LBC and another*,[31] where Mr Justice Mitting said at para 25:

> There seems to me to be no perceptible difference between the three phrases, 'resident', 'ordinarily resident' and 'normally resident'. All three connote settled presence in a particular place other than under compulsion.

13.70 'Usual residence' fell into the same category as 'resident', 'ordinarily resident' and 'normally resident' according to the Court of Appeal in *Varsani v Relfo Ltd (in liquidation)*.[32] This case considered the meaning of a 'usual residence' test in wholly different circumstances, namely whether a Nigerian businessman was usually resident in London for the purposes of the Civil Procedure Rules (CPR) 1998 when he had multiple homes in different countries because a 'usual residence' test applies under the CPR. The case may thus only be of limited assistance in determining the meaning of usual residence under the NHS Act 2006. However, Etherton LJ approved the following explanation of the meaning of 'usual residence' used by the deputy judge:[33]

> 'Usual' is an ordinary English word. It is not a term of art. It means, in its ordinary signification, that which is in ordinary use . . . It may not add very much to the simple word 'residence', although it does serve to emphasise the element of regularity and continuity of occupation of the property concerned . . .

13.71 Hence the correct approach is probably to treat the concept of 'usual residence' under section 3(1A)(b) as analogous to 'ordinary residence' in almost all circumstances and for NHS bodies to rely on the statutory guidance issued by the DHSC under the Care Act 2014 where there is a dispute as to where someone is usually resident.

13.72 One key difference between an 'ordinary residence' test and a 'usual residence' test may be that 'ordinary residence' requires a person to be lawfully living at the place at which he or she resides, whereas a 'usual residence' test does not: see *R v Barnet LBC ex p Shah*.[34] Despite the observations set out at Annex B of the *Who Pays?* Guidance, that requirement is almost certainly not part of the test for the allocation of commissioning responsibilities because people who are unlawfully resident in the UK are still entitled to access NHS services.

13.73 The NHS Act 2006 makes specific provision to enable charges to be levied for NHS services provided to anyone who is not ordinarily resident

30 [2015] UKSC 46.
31 [2010] EWHC 562 (Admin).
32 [2010] EWCA Civ 560.
33 At para 19.
34 [1983] 2 AC 309.

in the UK: see section 175 of the NHS Act 2006. Hence, for example, overseas visitors and failed asylum-seekers, who are not lawfully in the UK, are required to pay charges for some NHS services. In *R (YA) v Secretary of State for Health*[35] the Court of Appeal focused on the secretary of state's duty to promote a comprehensive health service for the people of England. Ward LJ said:[36]

> Note that it is the people *of* England, not the people *in* England, which suggests that the beneficiaries of this free health service are to be those with some link to England so as to be part and parcel of the fabric of the place. It connotes a legitimate connection with the country. The exclusion from this free service of non-residents and the right conferred by section 175 to charge such persons as are not ordinarily resident reinforces this notion of segregation between them and us. This strongly suggests that, as a rule, the benefits were not intended by Parliament to be bestowed on those who ought not to be here.

13.74 That case confirmed that (at that time) NHS trusts had a discretion to withhold treatment from an overseas visitor who could be required to pay for the treatment.

13.75 There is a list of secondary care treatments for overseas visitors (whether lawfully in the UK or not) for which no charges can be levied. Hence, by way of example, no charges can be made for human immunodeficiency virus (HIV) treatment provided to an overseas visitor: see Schedule 1 to the National Health Service (Charges to Overseas Visitors) Regulations 2015.[37] In such a case, the NHS trust or private hospital providing the treatment will need to know which CCG should meet the costs of the treatment. If that patient is not on the list of GP practice, the responsible CCG will be the CCG in the area where the patient usually resides even if that residence is unlawful because, for example, the individual has no legal right to be in the UK.

Additional categories of patients described in Schedule 1 to the RSR Regs 2012

Introduction

13.76 Schedule 1 to the RSR Regs 2012 provides a series of confusingly worded categories of additional patients for whom a CCG has commissioning responsibility. These are tightly drawn categories of patients which are also described in the *Who pays?* guidance. Unfortunately this is an area where the guidance describes common NHS practice but, in place, that practice departs from the wording of the Schedule. The wording of the regulations takes precedence over the guidance and so it is necessary to look carefully at the descriptions of additional patients for whom a CCG is allocated commissioning responsibility.

13.77 The regulations are worded in a way that is far from straightforward. However, in order to work through the statutory definitions there are three questions that need to be addressed:

35 [2009] EWCA Civ 225, (2009) 12 CCLR 213.

36 At para 55.

37 SI No 238.

a) Is the patient within the categories defined in Schedule 1 as someone for whom a CCG may have commissioning responsibility?
b) If so, is the CCG's commissioning responsibility excluded by virtue of the rules in reg 4(4)?
c) If the answer to question a) is 'Yes' and the answer to question b) is 'No', is the CCG's responsibility limited to 'accommodation and services' by virtue of reg 4(2).

13.78 Regulation 4(1) of the RSR Regs 2012 provides:

> Subject to paragraphs (2) to (4), for the purposes of sections 3 and 3A of the 2006 Act (which relate respectively to a CCG's duty to commission services and its power to do so), a CCG has responsibility for the persons listed in paragraph 2 of Schedule 1 (in addition to those mentioned in section 3(1A) of that Act).

13.79 This regulation means that, in addition to the patients referred to in section 3(1A) of the NHS Act 2006, a CCG may have commissioning responsibility for some or all of the NHS services CCGs commission for that patient (depending on the answer to the next questions). The details of the categories listed in para 2 of Schedule 1 are considered below.

13.80 Regulation 4(4) defines the categories of patients who do not become the responsibility of a local CCG even though they come within the terms of para 2 of Schedule 1 to the RSR Regs 2012. They provide:

> (4) The responsibility for persons listed in paragraph 2(b) to (j) of Schedule 1 does not apply where the person is detained in–
> (a) an immigration removal centre;
> (b) a secure training centre; or
> (c) a young offender institution.

13.81 This regulation provides that a CCG does not acquire commissioning responsibility, in any circumstances, for patients in an immigration removal centre, a secure training centre or a young offender institution even if that otherwise person comes within the scope of Schedule 1. That is confirmed in reg 2(2)(f) of the CCGDR Regs 2013 which provides that a CCG shall not have commissioning responsibility for anyone detained in the three institutions listed above. It is noteworthy that this list does not include patients in a regular prison. NHS England has statutory responsibility for such patients.

13.82 Regulation 4(2) provides that where a CCG gains commissioning responsibility for an additional person as a result of a person being within para 2(a), (b), (d), (e) or (f) of Schedule 1, the CCG only gains responsibility for commissioning 'accommodation or services specified in the sub-paragraph of paragraph 2 which relates to that person'. Regulation 4(2)(c) is necessary to ensure that section 3(1C) takes effect, namely that commissioning responsibility for commissioning emergency services is not transferred from one CCG to another.

13.83 Paragraph 2 of Schedule 1 to the RSR Regs 2012 contains the following list of additional categories:

> The list of persons referred to in regulation 4(1) is as follows–
> (a) every person present in the CCG's area, in relation to the provision of ambulance services or accident and emergency services, whether provided at a hospital accident and emergency department, a minor

injuries unit, a walk-in centre or elsewhere (but excluding any services provided after the person has been accepted as an in-patient, or at an out-patient appointment);

(b) every person aged 18 or over who falls within paragraph 3, in relation to the provision of the accommodation or services referred to in paragraph 3(b);

(c) every child who falls within paragraph 4;

(d) every person who falls within paragraph 5 in relation to the provision of the accommodation or services referred to in paragraph 5(b);

(e) every person who falls within paragraph 6 in relation to the provision of the accommodation or services referred to in paragraph 6(b);

(f) every child who falls within paragraph 7 in relation to the provision of the accommodation or services referred to in paragraph 7(b);

(g) every child who falls within paragraph 8;

(h) every person present in the CCG's area who is resident outside the United Kingdom and not provided with primary medical services by a member of any CCG;

(i) every person resident in Scotland, Wales or Northern Ireland and present in the CCG's area who is a qualifying patient within the meaning of section 130C of the 1983 Act (section 130A:supplemental), and not provided with primary medical services by a member of any CCG;

(j) every person who is a qualifying patient within the meaning of section 130C of the 1983 Act and liable to be detained under that Act in a hospital or registered establishment (within the meaning of that Act) in the CCG's area'

13.84 This list refers to a series of different categories of patients, and the rules operate in subtlety different ways in relation to each category. Hence, it is necessary to look at each category to work out which CCG has any commissioning responsibility for providing which services to a patient and then to ask which services are the responsibility of which CCG. Inclusion in a category under para 2 will not necessarily result in a transfer from one CCG to another of all commissioning responsibility for the patient. The rules retain part of the NHS commissioning responsibility for patients for services described in the wording of the Schedule but provide that part rests with another CCG.

Category 4: Adult continuing care patients placed in a facility in the area of another CCG

Overview

13.85 Where a patient needs specialist care, provided in dedicated accommodation, a CCG with commissioning responsibility can properly exercise its commissioning responsibilities by 'placing' a patient in a care home or other institution located in the area of another CCG. The patient then registers with a GP practice in the area of the specialist facility and, at that point, a question can arise whether commissioning responsibility transfers to the CCG in the place of the specialist facility or remains with the CCG that placed the patient. For these purposes, there are two CCGs, namely the 'placing CCG' (ie the CCG whose officers made the placement) and the 'local CCG' (ie the CCG which is local to where the services are provided).

13.86 Rules have been in existence since at least 2006 to prevent NHS commissioners from having a financial incentive to place their patients out of area and thereby transfer commissioning responsibilities onto neighbouring CCGs. This has been pejoratively labelled as 'dumping': see *R (Greenwich LBC) v Secretary of State for Health and another*.[38] The rules are now in Schedule 1 to the RSR Regs 2012 and the broad effect is to ensure that a CCG that places an NHS Continuing Healthcare patient in a care home or other facility the area of another CCG retains commissioning responsibility for funding the costs of NHS Continuing Healthcare for that patient. However, a) these rules have a series of peculiarities and go wider than just of NHS Continuing Healthcare patients and b) they only apply to the costs of NHS Continuing Healthcare, with other services being funded by the local CCG to the care placement.

13.87 Paragraph 2(b) of Schedule 1 to the RSR Regs 2012 provides that the category of persons where the placing CCG retains commissioning responsibility is:

> . . . every person aged 18 or over who falls within paragraph 3, in relation to the provision of the accommodation or services referred to in paragraph 3(b).

13.88 Paragraph 3 of Schedule 1 to the RSR Regs 2012 provides:

> A person falls within this paragraph if–
> (a) the CCG has made an arrangement in the exercise of its commissioning functions (by itself or jointly with a local authority) by virtue of which the person is to be provided with services to meet his or her continuing care needs,
> (b) those services consist of or include the provision of the following accommodation and services to meet the person's continuing care needs–
> (i) accommodation in a care home or independent hospital situated in the area of another CCG or of a Local Health Board, and
> (ii) at least one planned service (other than a service consisting only of NHS-funded nursing care) which is connected to the provision of such accommodation (whether or not the accommodation is arranged by the CCG referred to in sub-paragraph (a)),
> (c) the person is resident in that accommodation and continues to need that planned service (or those planned services), and
> (d) the person would not be a person for whom the CCG is responsible under section 3(1A)(a) of the 2006 Act.

Conditions

13.89 In order for the placing CCG to retain commissioning responsibility under para 3 of Schedule 1 to the RSR Regs 2012, six conditions must be satisfied:

1) the patient must cease to be registered with a GP practice in the area of the placing CCG ('the GP registration requirement');
2) the patient must be provided with accommodation in a care home or independent hospital by a placing CCG situated in the area of the local CCG ('the accommodation requirement');

38 [2006] EWHC 2576 (Admin), (2007) 10 CCLR 60.

3) the patient must be placed to meet a need for continuing care ('the continuing care requirement');
4) the CCG must commission at least one other planned service for the patient (other than a service consisting only of NHS-funded nursing care) ('the other service requirement');
5) the patient must become resident at the accommodation so provided ('the residence requirement'); and
6) the patient must continue to need that planned service (or those planned services) (the continuity requirement').

1) The GP registration requirement

13.90 A patient who spends time living in a care home or independent hospital will remain the responsibility of the placing CCG for as long as the patient remains registered with a GP practice in the area of the placing CCG. However, care home residents are usually registered on a permanent basis with a GP practice which is local to the care home. Where this happens, the registration with the former GP practice comes to an end, and thus the placing CCG's responsibility for the patient would also come to an end unless continued by the placing rules contained within Schedule 1 to the RSR Regs 2012.

2) The accommodation requirement

13.91 The placing rules only apply if the patient is placed by a CCG in a care home or an independent hospital to meet the patient's continuing care needs. Hence, if a patient is placed in supported living accommodation in the area of another CCG or in an NHS hospital, the placing rules do not prevent commissioning responsibility transferring when the patient changes his or her GP.

13.92 A 'hospital' is widely defined in section 275 of the NHS Act 2006 as follows:

> 'hospital' means–
> (a) any institution for the reception and treatment of persons suffering from illness,
> (b) any maternity home, and
> (c) any institution for the reception and treatment of persons during convalescence or persons requiring medical rehabilitation, and includes clinics, dispensaries and out-patient departments maintained in connection with any such home or institution, and 'hospital accommodation' must be construed accordingly.

13.93 Section 3(4) of Care Standards Act 2000 provides that 'An establishment in England is not a care home if it is a hospital (within the meaning of the National Health Service Act 2006'. The extended definition of 'hospital' under section 275 of the NHS Act 2006 thus precludes a nursing home from being defined as a 'care home' if it comes within the definition of a hospital. The meaning of the word 'hospital' was considered by the Court of Appeal in *Minister of Health v General Committee of the Royal Midland Counties Home for Incurables at Leamington Spa*.[39] The issue in that case was whether a 'home for incurables' should be transferred from the charity

39 [1954] Ch 530.

which operated it to the newly created national health service.[40] That depended on whether the home was classified as a 'hospital'. The court decided that it was a hospital even though there were no doctors on site all of the time and 'the atmosphere of the place was much more homelike than that of any hospital'. Evershed MR said:

> . . . the word 'hospital' is intended to have, and has, a wider significance for the purposes of the Act than that of what may be called an ordinary general hospital.

13.94 The continuing effect of this case was affirmed in both *Botchett v The Chief Adjudication Officer*[41] and in *R (Whapples) v Birmingham CrossCity Clinical Commissioning Group*.[42]

13.95 The decision to move a patient to a hospital must be a decision of the CCG (at least in part). If the accommodation is arranged solely by a local authority as part of a package of community care services under the Care Act 2014, the NHS placing rules do not apply. If a patient is entitled to NHS Continuing Healthcare, but the accommodation arrangements are made wholly by the patient themselves or by the family, as opposed to being arranged by the CCG, the placing rules do not apply: see *R (Greenwich LBC) v Secretary of State for Health and another*.[43]

3) The continuing care requirement

13.96 The placing rules require that the CCG places the patient in accommodation because the patient has a need for 'continuing care'. Paragraph 1 of Schedule 1 to the RSR Regs 2012 defines 'continuing care' to mean:

> 'continuing care' means care provided over an extended period of time to a person to meet physical or mental health needs which have arisen as the result of illness.

13.97 Patients who are eligible for NHS Continuing Healthcare will be patients who have a need for 'continuing care'. However the term 'continuing care' is wider than patients who are eligible for NHS Continuing Healthcare. It could, for example, cover a patient who is informally admitted to a mental hospital for an extended stay. It may also cover patients who receive NHS-funded Nursing Care payments. Paragraphs 59–64 of the guidance *Who pays?* appears to equate the term 'continuing care' with 'NHS Continuing Healthcare', despite the statutory definition of continuing care which is wider than patients who are eligible for NHS Continuing Healthcare.

4) The other service requirement

13.98 The placing rules only apply if a patient is in receipt of continuing care arranged by CCG and receives at least one planned service other than nursing care. The term 'planned service' is defined in para 1 of Schedule 1 to mean:

> any service whose provision is planned and arranged by a CCG as part of the health service in response to the results of an assessment of a person's

40 Without any compensation being paid for the state acquisition of the property.

41 (1999) 2 CCLR 121, (1996) 32 BMLR 153.

42 [2015] EWCA Civ 435, (2015) 18 CCLR 300.

43 [2006] EWHC 2576 (Admin), (2007) 10 CCLR 60.

physical or mental health needs and which is intended to bring about or promote a specific outcome in relation to those needs.

13.99 Paragraph 3(b)(ii) of Schedule 1 requires the patient to be placed in accommodation by the CCG and to receive at least one planned service (other than a service consisting only of NHS-funded nursing care) which is connected to the provision of such accommodation.

5) The residence requirement

13.100 Responsibility for commissioning services for a patient who lives in a care home or independent hospital will only be retained by the placing CCG if the patient becomes 'resident' in the care home or independent hospital. However, a patient is highly unlikely to move their GP registration to a practice which is local to the care home or independent hospital unless the patient is anticipating remaining there for an extended period. A place of 'residence' indicates an intention to live at a location for an extended period as opposed to a short period with a defined end-point.

6) The continuity requirement

13.101 The patient must continue to have a need for a planned service (or those planned services) for the period when the patient is resident at the care home or independent hospital. Hence, a service which is provided for a short period but then is no longer required will not qualify under the placing rules. However, a CCG is highly unlikely to commission a placement at a care home or independent hospital over an extended period if no additional medical services are needed.

Responsibility for secondary care services provided in accommodation which is not a care home or independent hospital

13.102 If a patient with continuing care needs is placed by a CCG in accommodation which is not a care home or independent hospital, the placing rules will not apply and commissioning responsibility will transfer to the CCG which is local to the accommodation. Hence commissioning responsibility will transfer to the CCG local to the accommodation where a patient who is placed by a CCG in supported living accommodation, a shared lives scheme or in an NHS facility as soon as the patient registers with a GP local to his or her accommodation.

13.103 If a CCG has continuing commissioning responsibility for a patient under this paragraph, the responsibility only extends to funding the placement but not secondary care or other services that the patient needs outside of the placement.

Category 5: Placed children falling within paragraph 4 of Schedule 1 to the RSR Regs 2012

13.104 The next group of patients for whom a CCG retains commissioning responsibility despite the patient being registered in a GP practice in the area of a different CCG is defined in para 4 of Schedule 1 to the RSR Regs 2012. This paragraph relates to children who become resident in accommodation outside of the area of a CCG as a result of being placed by either a CCG or a local authority, and then join the list of a GP practice in the area in which they are placed. Paragraph 2(c) states that a placing CCG will retain commissioning responsibility for 'every child who falls within paragraph 4'.

13.105 Paragraph 4 provides:

> 4 (1) A child falls within this paragraph if both of sub-paragraphs (2) and (3) apply to the child.
>
> (2) This sub-paragraph applies to a child if any of the following is the case–
>
> (a) the child is looked after by a local authority within the meaning of section 22 of the Children Act 1989 (general duty of local authority in relation to children looked after by them), other than by way of being accommodated in a secure children's home in respect of which the National Health Service Commissioning Board must arrange for the provision of services to children detained there;
>
> (b) the child is a relevant child within the meaning of section 23A of that Act (the responsible authority and relevant children);
>
> (c) the child is a person to whom section 24(1A) or (1B) of that Act (persons qualifying for advice and assistance) applies;
>
> (d) the child is provided with accommodation at a school to which he or she is admitted in accordance with a statement of special educational needs made under section 324 of the Education Act 1996 (statement of special educational needs); or
>
> (e) the child requires accommodation in a care home, a children's home or an independent hospital to meet the child's continuing care needs.
>
> (3) This sub-paragraph applies to a child if–
>
> (a) the child is provided with–
>
> (i) services which consist of or include the provision of accommodation situated in the area of another CCG or of a Local Health Board, under arrangements made by the CCG in the exercise of its commissioning functions (by itself or jointly with a local authority), or
>
> (ii) such services under arrangements made by the local authority and immediately before those arrangements were made the CCG was responsible for the child under section 3(1A) of the 2006 Act; and
>
> (b) the child is both–
>
> (i) resident in that accommodation, and
>
> (ii) would not be a person for whom the CCG is responsible under section 3(1A)(a) of the 2006 Act.

13.106 Accordingly, this part of the placing rules only applies to children, namely patients under the age of 18: see para 1. The placing rules will apply to the child if one of the conditions in para 4(2) is satisfied and the conditions in both paras 4(3)(a) and (b) are both satisfied. A child will come within para 4(2) if any one of the following conditions applies to the child:

a) The child is a 'looked after child' within the meaning of section 22 of the Children Act 1989. A looked after child is a child which is within the care of the local authority or is provided with accommodation by the authority in the exercise of any of its functions. However children who are accommodated in a secure children's home are excluded because commissioning responsibility for such children lies with NHS England.

b) The child is a 'relevant child' under the Children Act 1989. This is a child who is aged 16 or 17 who has been provided with accommodation by a local authority for at least 13 weeks after the age of 14: see para 19B of Schedule 2 to the Children Act 1989 and reg 40 of the Care Planning, Placement and Case Review (England) Regulations 2010 SI No 959. A child is also a 'relevant child' if, on attaining the age of 16, the child was detained, or in hospital, and, immediately before being detained or admitted to hospital, had been looked after by a local authority for a period or periods amounting in total to at least 13 weeks that began after the child attained the age of 14: see reg 3 of the Care Leavers (England) Regulations 2010 SI No 2571.

c) The child comes within section 24(1A) of the Children Act 1989, namely if the child has reached the age of 16 but not the age of 21, and where a special guardianship order is in force (or, if he or she has reached the age of 18, was in force when he reached that age) and who was, immediately before the making of that order, looked after by a local authority.

d) The child comes within section 24(1B) of the Children Act 1989, namely the child has been accommodated or fostered by a local authority at any time after the age of 16.

e) The child is provided with accommodation at a school to which he or she is admitted in accordance with a statement of special educational needs made under section 324 of the Education Act 1996 (statement of special educational needs).

f) The child requires accommodation in a care home, a children's home or an independent hospital to meet the child's continuing care needs. Please see above for a discussion on the meaning of 'continuing care'.

13.107 Both of the conditions in para 4(3)(a) and (b) have to be satisfied in order to prevent commissioning responsibility for a child transferring to the local CCG when the child's GP registration transfers. The condition in para 4(3)(a) will be satisfied if the child is provided with either:

a) services which consist of or include the provision of accommodation situated in the area of another CCG or of a Local Health Board, under arrangements made by the CCG in the exercise of its commissioning functions (by itself or jointly with a local authority), or

b) such services under arrangements made by the local authority and immediately before those arrangements were made the CCG was responsible for the child under section 3(1A) of the NHS Act 2006.

13.108 Hence, in contrast to adults, where a local authority acts alone in placing a child away from his or her home area, *both* the home CCG and the home local authority continue to have statutory responsibility for providing NHS and community care services to the child. In contrast, the placing rules do not apply where a local authority acts alone in placing an adult in a care home in the area of another CCG and the adult is registered with a GP practice close to the care home. In such a case, responsibility for funding NHS services transfers to the CCG for the new GP practice.

13.109 The conditions in para 4(3)(b) are that the child is 'resident in that accommodation' which means that the child's period of stay in the accommodation is long enough to mean that the child acquires a residence at that place. Second, and somewhat strangely, the paragraph provides that the child is not someone for whom the CCG would have commissioning responsibility under section 3(1A)(a) of the NHS Act 2006, namely someone who is on the list for a GP practice in the area of the CCG. It is unclear why this provision is needed because these provisions only apply where a CCG is not allocated commissioning responsibility by virtue of GP registration.

13.110 Where a CCG continue to have commissioning responsibility for a child under this paragraph, the CCG's commissioning responsibilities extend to all services that the child needs (other than those which fall within the responsibility of NHS England) and not just meeting the costs of the placement. Accordingly, if a placed child is admitted to hospital from the placement, in contrast to the position of adults, the placing CCG retains full responsibility for meeting the cost of the child's NHS treatment.

Category 6: Placed children who become adults

13.111 Paragraph 5 of Schedule 1 to the RSR Regs 2012 provides for cases where a CCG has placed a child in accommodation for his or her continuing care needs (which has become that person's residence) once the child reaches the age of 18. The paragraph provides that the CCG will continue to have commissioning responsibility for the adult, notwithstanding that the adult is on the list of a GP practice local to their accommodation. However, there can be circumstances where the CCG retains commissioning responsibility for the child but does not continue to have commissioning responsibility when the child reaches the age of 18 because, for example, no nursing services are provided as part of the placement.

13.112 Paragraph 5 of Schedule 1 to the RSR Regs 2012 provides:

> A person falls within this paragraph if–
>
> (a) the CCG has made an arrangement in the exercise of its commissioning functions (by itself or jointly with a local authority) by virtue of which immediately before attaining 18 the person was provided with services to meet his or her continuing care needs;
>
> (b) those services consist of or include the provision of the following accommodation and services to meet the person's continuing care needs–
>
> (i) accommodation in a care home, a children's home or an independent hospital situated in the area of another CCG or of a Local Health Board, and
>
> (ii) nursing and another service which is a planned service, as part of the health service to meet his or her continuing care needs;
>
> (c) the person is resident in that accommodation and continues to need that planned service (or those planned services), and
>
> (d) the person would not be a person for whom the CCG is responsible under section 3(1A)(a) of the 2006 Act.

13.113 This formulation follows the same structure as that described above. It refers to a child being provided with services to meet their 'continuing care' needs, which is probably wider than children's NHS Continuing Healthcare. The arrangements to provide the placement can either be made by the CCG alone or by the CCG in combination with the relevant local authority (which is highly likely to be the case for any child with significant disabilities). However, this part of the placing rules does not apply if the placement was made by the local authority alone (ie without any significant part being played by the CCG in the placement decision).

13.114 The placement is only a qualifying placement under this paragraph if it provides both nursing services and another 'planned service'. Please see above for a discussion on the meaning of the term 'planned service'. If the accommodation provides one or more planned services but does not provide nursing services, the patient falls outside this paragraph. This is likely to be the case for children with learning difficulties who are provided with specialist support accommodation but which does not necessarily include nursing services.

13.115 If a CCG has continuing commissioning responsibility for a patient under this paragraph, the responsibility only extends to funding the placement but not secondary care or other services that the patient needs outside of the placement.

Category 7: Adult patients who have been placed out of area by a primary care trust

13.116 Primary care trusts (PCTs) were the local NHS commissioners prior to the creation of CCGs and NHS England in April 2013. In contrast to the position under the NHS Act 2006 (as amended by the HSCA 2012), PCTs acted as the delegate of the secretary of state in making commissioning decisions. The placing rules were set out in reg 3 of the National Health Service (Functions of Strategic Health Authorities and Primary Care Trusts and Administration Arrangements) (England) Regulations (PCT Regs) 2002.[44] These rules were slightly different to the rules now operating under the RSR Regs 2012. The rules operated until 31 March 2013 when CCGs came into existence and PCTs were abolished.

13.117 Paragraph 2(e) of Schedule 1 to the RSR Regs 2012 provides that a CCG shall have continuing commissioning responsibility for adult patients placed out of area where the placing rules under the PCT Regs 2002 meant that the placing PCT retained commissioning responsibility. Paragraph 2(e) of Schedule 1 to the RSR Regs 2012 provides:

> . . . every person who falls within paragraph 6 in relation to the provision of the accommodation or services referred to in paragraph 6(b).

13.118 Paragraph 6 of Schedule 1 to the RSR Regs 2012 provides:

> A person falls within this paragraph if–
> (a) a Primary Care Trust has made an arrangement before the relevant date in the exercise of its functions by virtue of regulation 3 of the National Health Service (Functions of Strategic Health Authorities and Primary Care Trusts and Administration Arrangements)(England) Regulations 2002 by virtue of which the person was provided with services to meet his or her continuing care needs;
> (b) the rights and liabilities under that arrangement are transferred to the CCG by virtue of a scheme made under section 300 of the 2012 Act (transfer schemes);
> (c) the person continues to need the provision of the following accommodation and services to meet the person's continuing care needs–

44 SI No 2375. These were amended from their original form many times.

(i) accommodation in a care home or independent hospital situated in the area of another CCG, and
(ii) at least one planned service (other than a service consisting only of NHS-funded nursing care) which is connected to the provision of such accommodation (whether or not the accommodation is arranged by the CCG); and

(d) the person would not be a person for whom the CCG is responsible under section 3(1A)(a) of the 2006 Act.

13.119 This paragraph thus provides that the CCG has continuing commissioning responsibility for a person where the predecessor PCT made a lawful placement for a person for whom it had commissioning responsibility under the PCT Regs 2002 to meet his or her continuing care needs[45] and retained commissioning responsibility for that patient because of the placing rules in force under the PCT Regs 2002. Regulation 3 provided that a PCT had commissioning responsibility for patients on the lists of GP practices in its area and those who were resident in its area but not on the list of any GP practice. It also contained a series of placing rules.

13.120 When CCGs were created there were a series of 'Transfer Orders' which transferred assets, liabilities and statutory responsibilities from a PCT to a CCG or, if the CCG area was not coterminous with the area of the PCT, between the CCGs that were created to operate in the area of the former PCT. The new CCGs were created as membership organisations of GP practices operating in a defined area. Accordingly for the majority of patients, statutory responsibility for patients of a GP practice was transferred by reference to the GP practice where the patient was registered. Paragraph 6(b) of Schedule 1 to the RSR Regs 2012 provides that a CCG has continuing commissioning responsibility for a placement made by a predecessor PCT if the relevant Transfer Order transferred rights and liabilities for that patient to the PCT.

13.121 Paragraph 6(c) contains the same formulation as set out in other paragraphs, namely that the patient is placed in a care home or independent hospital[46] and that he or she is receiving at least one planned service other than nursing care. Finally, the paragraph contains the superfluous condition that the person is not someone who the CCG would otherwise have statutory responsibility for because the person is on the list of a GP practice in the CCG's area.

13.122 If a CCG has continuing commissioning responsibility for a patient under this paragraph, the responsibility only extends to funding the placement but not secondary care or other services that the patient needs outside of the placement.

Category 8: Children who have been placed out of area by a primary care trust

13.123 Paragraph 7 of Schedule 1 to the RSR Regs 2012 contains identical provisions to paragraph 6 (which relates to adults only) relating to children who

45 Please see paras 16.1–16.5 above for a discussion on what is meant by 'continuing care' needs.

46 See paras 13.91–13.93 above for a discussion on what is meant by an independent hospital or care home.

were placed by a primary care trust in accommodation to meet their continuing care needs. If a child was placed by a primary care trust out of area in circumstances where the primary care trust retained commissioning responsibility for the NHS services provided to the child, the liability for funding the placement is transferred to the CCG.

13.124 If a CCG has continuing commissioning responsibility for a child under this paragraph, the responsibility only extends to funding the placement but not secondary care or other services that the child needs outside of the placement.

Category 9: Children placed at special schools by local authorities before 1 April 2013

13.125 The RSR Regs 2012 provide that children placed by a local authority at a school outside their local area with a statement of special educational needs (SEN) before 1 April 2013 should continue to be the responsibility of their home CCG. This is achieved by a combination of para 2(g) and para 8 of Schedule 1 to the RSR Regs 2012.

13.126 Paragraph 2(g) provides that the category of persons for which a CCG has continuing responsibility is as follows:

> Every child who falls within paragraph 8 . . .

13.127 Paragraph 8 defines the relevant cohort of children as follows:

> (1) A child falls within this paragraph if–
> (a) a local authority has made an arrangement before the relevant date by virtue of which the child is provided with accommodation at a school in the area of another CCG or a Local Health Board, to which the child is admitted in accordance with a statement of special educational needs made under section 324 of the Education Act 1996;
> (b) immediately before the child was accommodated at that school the child was either–
> (i) provided with primary medical services by a person who is now a member of the CCG; or
> (ii) usually resident in the area of the CCG and not provided with primary medical services by a person who is now a member of the CCG; and
> (c) the child would not be a person for whom the CCG is responsible under section 3(1A)(a) of the 2006 Act.

13.128 The 'relevant date' is 1 April 2013: see reg 2. Accordingly, this cohort of children is confined to children who have a statement of SEN and have been provided with accommodation at a school in the area of another CCG as a result of the decision of a local authority prior to 1 April 2013. For any child coming within this category, commissioning responsibility is retained by the CCG where the child had a GP registration immediately before moving to the school or, if the child was not on the list of any GP practice, the CCG which covered the area where the child was usually resident before moving to the school.

Category 10: Patients who are resident outside the United Kingdom

13.129 Paragraph 2(h) of Schedule 1 to the RSR Regs 2012 extends the responsibility of each CCG to commission NHS services for persons who are resident outside the UK and are not on the list of any GP practice but are physically present in the CCG's area. Some of these individuals will be entitled to access NHS services on the same basis as those permanently resident in the UK. Others will be required to pay charges for some NHS services. Details of this are set out in chapter 15 on charging for NHS services. This paragraph provides that, as between different CCGs, the CCG that has commissioning responsibility for an overseas resident is the CCG where that individual is physically present. The paragraph provides as follows:

> . . . every person present in the CCG's area who is resident outside the United Kingdom and not provided with primary medical services by a member of any CCG

13.130 There are different ways in which this paragraph could be interpreted. Commissioning responsibility could change as the individual moves from one CCG area to another CCG area. Hence, if a patient was seen by ambulance staff in the area CCG A and then transferred to hospital in the area of CCG B, it is unclear from the wording whether commissioning responsibility for the hospital services should be met by CCG A or CCG B. It seems likely that commissioning responsibility changes as the location of the patient changes. Thus, in the above example, CCG B would be liable for all costs of the providing services to the patient and not just the cost of providing emergency services.

13.131 Paragraph 20 of the *Who pays?* guidance suggests that commissioning responsibility for an overseas resident lies with the CCG where the person is resident in the UK. This appears to be incorrect because responsibility is allocated under this part of the regulations to the CCG where the person is physically present, not the CCG where the person is resident. Paragraph 21 of the guidance states:

> It is particularly important to identify a responsible commissioner for a person who becomes mentally ill whilst living abroad, and who intends to return home for treatment, so that they remain entitled to care without charge. Wherever possible, the principles outlined in paragraph 1 should be applied to identify the responsible commissioner. If this fails, a unit which will offer an appropriate service should be identified (if possible in an area to which the person in question is willing to return voluntarily) and the CCG covering the location of that unit should become the responsible commissioner.

13.132 This paragraph appears to confuse a number of different concepts. First, UK nationals who are resident abroad have no greater rights to access free NHS care than any other individual of any nationality who lives abroad. Entitlement to free NHS care is based on residence in the UK, and not on nationality. Second, there is no general right to access free mental health services for overseas residents. However, all NHS services provided outside of a hospital are not presently subject to charges: see reg 9(b) of the National Health Service (Charges to Overseas Visitors) Regulations 2015. Accordingly, community-based mental health services are not subject to charges for any overseas patient. If an overseas patient is provided with hospital-based mental health services, charges are required to be made unless the patient is able to claim an exemption (for example, because they are resident in the

European Union (EU) or in a country with a reciprocal agreement). No charges can be levied for NHS services to a detained mental health patient, a patient received into guardianship or a patient subject to a community treatment order under the MHA 1983: see reg 18 of the National Health Service (Charges to Overseas Visitors) Regulations 2015.

13.133 Where an overseas patient is suffering from a mental health condition which means that the patient is a 'qualifying patient' under section 130C of the MHA 1983, the CCG with commissioning responsibility for that patient will be the CCG where the relevant mental hospital is located (see category 12 below). In all other circumstances, the CCG with commissioning responsibility will be the CCG where the patient is physically present (unless the patient has registered with an English NHS GP practice). However, the suggestion in the guidance that a residence test can be used to identify the responsible commissioning CCG is inaccurate. Commissioning responsibility for overseas residents who need mental health treatment can only be fixed by either being on the practice list of a GP practice or by physical presence, not by residence.

Category 11: Mental health patients resident in Scotland, Wales and Northern Ireland

13.134 Paragraph 2(i) of Schedule 1 to the RSR Regs 2012 extends the commissioning responsibilities of CCGs to the following additional group of patients:

> . . . every person resident in Scotland, Wales or Northern Ireland and present in the CCG's area who is a qualifying patient within the meaning of section 130C of the 1983 Act (section 130A:supplemental), and not provided with primary medical services by a member of any CCG.

13.135 There are four conditions which need to be satisfied to bring a patient within this group:

1) the patient needs to be resident in either Scotland, Wales or Northern Ireland;
2) the patient needs to be physically present in the CCG's area;
3) the patient needs to be a 'qualifying patient' within the meaning of section 130C of the MHA 1983; and
4) the patient needs to be someone who is not on the list of any English NHS GP practice.

13.136 The term 'qualifying patient' as defined by section 130C of the MHA 1983 means a patient who has a mental disorder which means that he or she is liable to be detained under the MHA 1983 otherwise than by virtue of excepted sections of the MHA 1983 or is subject to a guardianship under the MHA 1983 or is a community mental health patient. The excepted sections are:

a) section 4 of the MHA 1983 (admission for assessment in cases of emergency);
b) section 5(2) and (4) of the MHA 1983 (application for admissions for patients who are already in hospital);
c) section 135 of the MHA 1983 (persons who are detained by the police or an approved mental health professional following the issue of a magistrate's warrant); and

d) section 136 of the MHA 1983 (mentally disordered persons who are detained after being found in public places by the police).

13.137 Section 130C(3), (3A) and (4) of the MHA 1983 also relevant and provides:

> (3) A patient is also a qualifying patient if the patient is to be regarded as being in England for the purposes of this subsection and–
> (a) not being a qualifying patient falling within subsection (2) above, he discusses with a registered medical practitioner or approved clinician the possibility of being given a form of treatment to which section 57 above applies; or
> (b) not having attained the age of 18 years and not being a qualifying patient falling within subsection (2) above, he discusses with a registered medical practitioner or approved clinician the possibility of being given a form of treatment to which section 58A above applies.
> (3A) For the purposes of subsection (3), a patient is to be regarded as being in England if that has been determined in accordance with arrangements made for the purposes of that subsection and section 130I(4), and published, by the Secretary of State and the Welsh Ministers.
> (4) Where a patient who is a qualifying patient falling within subsection (3) above is informed that the treatment concerned is proposed in his case, he remains a qualifying patient falling within that subsection until–
> (a) the proposal is withdrawn; or
> (b) the treatment is completed or discontinued.

13.138 Accordingly para 2(i) of Schedule 1 to the RSR Regs 2012 generally extends commissioning responsibility to mental health patients who are community patients, subject to guardianship under the MHA 1983 or are liable to be detained in an English hospital under either section 2 or section 3 of the MHA 1983 who are physically present in the area of a CCG, have no English GP and are usually resident in Scotland, Wales or Northern Ireland.

13.139 Where a CCG acquires continuing commissioning responsibility for a mental health patient under this paragraph, the CCG's commissioning responsibilities extend to all services that the patient needs (other than those which fall within the responsibility of NHS England) and not just meeting the costs of the mental health placement.

Category 12: Other qualifying mental health patients

13.140 Paragraph 2(j) of Schedule 1 to the RSR Regs 2012 provides that a CCG has the commissioning responsibility for the following mental health patients:

> . . . every person who is a qualifying patient within the meaning of section 130C of the 1983 Act and liable to be detained under that Act in a hospital or registered establishment (within the meaning of that Act) in the CCG's area.

13.141 This paragraph generally extends NHS commissioning responsibility to 'qualifying patients' within the meaning of section 130C of the MHA 1983 who are also liable to be detained in a hospital in the CCG's area under either section 2 or section 3 of the MHA 1983. If a patient is actually detained in a mental health hospital, commissioning responsibility for the provision of mental health services may lie either with a CCG or with

NHS England depending on whether the unit is 'secure'. However, the category of patients who are 'liable to be detained' is wider than those who are actually detained.

13.142 Where a CCG acquires continue commissioning responsibility for a mental health patient under this paragraph, the CCG's commissioning responsibilities extend to all services that the patient needs (other than those which fall within the responsibility of NHS England) and not just meeting the costs of the mental health placement.

Category 13: Patients usually resident in Scotland, Northern Ireland or Wales

13.143 Patients who are usually resident in Scotland, Northern Ireland or Wales can nonetheless register with an English GP. However reg 2(2)(a)–(c) provide that a CCG shall not have commissioning responsibility for other healthcare services for anyone who is usually resident in Scotland, Northern Ireland or Wales. Thus, where such persons need services other than primary care services, the responsible commissioner is:

a) the Local Health Board in Wales covering the area where the individual is usually resident in Wales;
b) the Scotland Health Board where the individual is usually resident in Scotland; and
c) the Health and Social Care Board for Northern Ireland where the individual is usually resident in Northern Ireland.

Category 14: Mental Health Act 1983 s117 aftercare patients

13.144 Section 117 of the MHA 1983 imposes a duty jointly on a CCG and a local authority to provide 'after-care' services for a mental health patient who has been detained in hospital under defined parts of the MHA 1983. The section provides as follows:

> (1) This section applies to persons who are detained under section 3 above, or admitted to a hospital in pursuance of a hospital order made under section 37 above, or transferred to a hospital in pursuance of a hospital direction made under section 45A above or a transfer direction made under section 47 or 48 above, and then cease to be detained and (whether or not immediately after so ceasing) leave hospital.
>
> (2) It shall be the duty of the clinical commissioning group or . . . And of the local social services authority to provide or arrange for the provision of, in co-operation with relevant voluntary agencies, after-care services for any person to whom this section applies until such time as the clinical commissioning group or . . . and the local social services authority are satisfied that the person concerned is no longer in need of such services[; but they shall not be so satisfied in the case of a community patient while he remains such a patient.
>
> (2A) . . .
>
> (2B) Section 32 above shall apply for the purposes of this section as it applies for the purposes of Part II of this Act.
>
> (2C) References in this Act to after-care services provided for a patient under this section include references to services provided for the patient–
>
> (a) in respect of which direct payments are made under–

(i) sections 31 to 33 of the Care Act 2014 (as applied by Schedule 4 to that Act),
(ii) sections 50, 51 and 53 of the Social Services and Well-being (Wales) Act 2014 (as applied by Schedule A1 to that Act), or
(iii) regulations under section 12A(4) of the National Health Service Act 2006, and

(b) which would be provided under this section apart from those sections (as so applied) or the regulations.

(2D) Subsection (2), in its application to the clinical commissioning group, has effect as if the words 'provide or' were omitted.

(2E) The Secretary of State may by regulations provide that the duty imposed on the clinical commissioning group by subsection (2) is, in the circumstances or to the extent prescribed by the regulations, to be imposed instead on another clinical commissioning group or the National Health Service Commissioning Board.

(2F) Where regulations under subsection (2E) provide that the duty imposed by subsection (2) is to be imposed on the National Health Service Commissioning Board, subsection (2D) has effect as if the reference to the clinical commissioning group were a reference to the National Health Service Commissioning Board.

(2G) Section 272(7) and (8) of the National Health Service Act 2006 applies to the power to make regulations under subsection (2E) as it applies to a power to make regulations under that Act.

(3) In this section 'the clinical commissioning group . . . means the clinical commissioning group . . . and 'the local social services authority' means the local social services authority–

(a) if, immediately before being detained, the person concerned was ordinarily resident in England, for the area in England in which he was ordinarily resident;
(b) if, immediately before being detained, the person concerned was ordinarily resident in Wales, for the area in Wales in which he was ordinarily resident; or
(c) in any other case, for the area in which the person concerned is resident or to which he is sent on discharge by the hospital in which he was detained.

(4) Where there is a dispute about where a person was ordinarily resident for the purposes of subsection (3) above–

(a) if the dispute is between local social services authorities in England, section 40 of the Care Act 2014 applies to the dispute as it applies to a dispute about where a person was ordinarily resident for the purposes of Part 1 of that Act;
(b) if the dispute is between local social services authorities in Wales, section 195 of the Social Services and Well-being (Wales) Act 2014 applies to the dispute as it applies to a dispute about where a person was ordinarily resident for the purposes of that Act;
(c) if the dispute is between a local social services authority in England and a local social services authority in Wales, it is to be determined by the Secretary of State or the Welsh Ministers.

(5) The Secretary of State and the Welsh Ministers shall make and publish arrangements for determining which of them is to determine a dispute under subsection (4)(c); and the arrangements may, in particular, provide for the dispute to be determined by whichever of them they agree is to do so.

(6) In this section, 'after-care services', in relation to a person, means services which have both of the following purposes–

(a) meeting a need arising from or related to the person's mental disorder; and
(b) reducing the risk of a deterioration of the person's mental condition (and, accordingly, reducing the risk of the person requiring admission to a hospital again for treatment for mental disorder)'

13.145 This section imposes a legal obligation on a CCG and a local authority jointly to provide 'aftercare' services to a person who was previously a detained mental health patient. This duty is owed directly to an individual patient and takes precedence over the target duty imposed patient generally by section 3(1) of the NHS Act 2006. There are a wide range of services that potentially fall within the duty to provide after-care services, including accommodation (where that is part of the patient's need), community psychiatric services and social care and support services. There is no guidance as to how the relevant CCG and local authority ought to divide the costs of complying with this duty between the two public bodies. Most CCGs and local authorities agree to divide the costs of providing the services equally between the two public bodies but other arrangements are possible.

13.146 Where the patient was ordinarily resident in any part of England prior to being detained, the CCG with responsibility for providing section 117 of the MHA 1983 services is defined in section 117(3)(a) as the CCG covering the location where the patient was ordinarily resident. Accordingly, the responsible CCG is determined by the application of an ordinary residence test and not by the location of the GP practice where the patient is registered.

13.147 Paragraph 34 of the *Who pays?* guidance provides:

> It is the duty of the CCG and local social services authority to commission after-care for those persons discharged from hospital following detention under section 117 of the Mental Health Act. The responsible CCG should be established by the usual means (see paragraph 1). If a patient who is resident in one area (CCG A) is discharged to another area (CCG B), it is then the responsibility of the CCG in the area where the patient moves (CCG B) to pay for their aftercare under section 117 of the Act as agreed with the appropriate local social services authority.

13.148 This guidance was written prior to the amendments to section 117 of the MHA 1983 brought in by the Care Act 2014. However, those amendments did not substantially change the law. Unfortunately, the guidance was incorrect. Responsibility for providing services under section 117 is not determined by the 'usual means' (namely GP registration or in default a residence test) but solely by an ordinary residence test. It is also incorrect to suggest that a patient who is discharged from detention in hospital to a new area should have after-care services funded by the CCG in that new area. The duty to fund after-care services remains with the CCG in the area in which the patient was ordinarily resident prior to being detained in hospital.

13.149 There is newer guidance dated April 2016 but it still suggests that detained mental health patients should be funded by CCGs rather than NHS England. That approach appears to conflict with other NHS England guidance, which confirms that secure mental health patients are funded by NHS England.[47]

Resolving disputes about which CCG is the responsible commissioner

13.150 Disputes between local authorities as to which has responsibility to provide community care services to a service user are subject to a statutory adjudication process by the secretary of state under the Care Act 2014 (and previously under the National Assistance Act 1948). There is no similar provision under the NHS Act for dispute resolution by either the secretary of state or by NHS England. Nonetheless para 9 of the *Who pays?* guidance provides:

> NHS England expects that all disputes will be resolved locally, ideally at CCG level, with reference to the guidance in this document and coming to pragmatic solutions where responsibility is not immediately obvious or where it may be shared. In cases that cannot be resolved at CCG level, Area Teams of NHS England should be consulted and should arbitrate where necessary.

13.151 Section 14Z8 of the NHS Act 2006 (as imposed by the HSCA 2012) enables NHS England to publish commissioning guidance, and CCGs are required to have regard to the guidance. Accordingly, CCGs that are in dispute about the allocation of commissioning responsibilities are required to consider referring the matter to NHS England to arbitrate. While that appears a sensible and cost-effective option, the numerous mistakes in the *Who pays?* guidance could make it very difficult for a CCG to have confidence that the NHS England decision maker would reach a decision that was in accordance with the NHS Act 2006 and the RSR Regs 2012. It thus may be preferable for two CCGs to commission an independent legal opinion to assist resolving the dispute.

47 See www.england.nhs.uk/wp-content/uploads/2013/06/c03-med-low-sec-mh.pdf.

CHAPTER 14

Direct payments and personal health budgets

continued

Introduction

14.1 The introduction of direct payments, often referred to as personal health budgets (PHBs), could be seen as a quiet revolution in the way that the NHS delivers on its statutory duties to fund NHS services to patients.

14.2 The traditional model is for the patient to be provided with services commissioned by an NHS commissioner and provided by an NHS provider which is under contract to the commissioner. There is no contractual or financial relationship between the patient and the NHS provider, and the services that the patient has access to are those set out in the commissioning contract.

14.3 Direct payments could not be more different. The whole purpose of a direct payment is to make *the patient* the commissioner for his or her own care. Hence health care (and potentially social care) is delivered to the patient pursuant to a direct payment arrangement under contracts between the patient and the care provider, not set up by an NHS commissioner. Operating a direct payment thus involves a substantial transfer of control, risk and responsibility from the NHS commissioner to the patient. Direct payments raise a series of potentially difficult legal issues, including establishing systems to ensure there is proper financial and clinical governance in the operation of the packages.

Background

14.4 Direct payments were trialled by the NHS and a 215-page report was published concerning the outcome of a research project.[1] The main findings were:

> The main benefit-related implications of personal health budgets were as follows (unless otherwise noted, significance is assessed at the 95% confidence level):
>
> - The use of personal health budgets was associated with a significant improvement in the care-related quality of life (ASCOT) and psychological well-being (GHQ–12) of patients (at 90% confidence).
> - Personal health budgets did not appear to have an impact on health status per se over the 12 month follow-up period. No significant effects were found with regard to two clinical measures (HbA1C and lung-function tests, used where relevant) and there was no significant difference in mortality rates between the groups. Consistent with these results, the study did not find that personal health budgets had a significant effect on EQ–5D compared to the control group.

14.5 Hence, patients felt significantly better if they had a measure of control over their own healthcare services, but it did not necessarily improve objective health outcomes. The research findings about cost were as follows:

1 See www.personalhealthbudgets.dh.gov.uk/_library/Resources/Personalhealthbudgets/2012/PHBE_personal_health_budgets_final_report_Nov_2012.pdf.

The main findings of the cost analysis were:

- The cost of inpatient care (an 'indirect' cost) was significantly lower for the personal health budget group compared to the control group after accounting for baseline differences.
- The ('direct') costs of well-being and other health services were both significantly higher for the personal health budget group compared to controls.
- Other categories of direct and indirect cost showed no difference between the groups.
- The difference in direct and indirect total costs between personal health budget and control groups after accounting for baseline differences were not statistically significant.

14.6 Perhaps the message from this finding was that it cost more NHS money directly to provide care to someone under a direct payment, but the patient ended up in hospital for in-patient treatment less and so overall direct payments represented value for money.

14.7 Direct payments are now governed by the National Health Service (Direct Payments) Regulations (DP Regs) 2013[2] and, for patients in receipt of NHS Continuing Healthcare or Continuing Care for Children, by Part 6A of the National Health Service Commissioning Board and Clinical Commissioning Groups (Responsibilities and Standing Rules) Regulations (RSR Regs) 2012[3] (as amended by the National Health Service Commissioning Board and Clinical Commissioning Groups (Responsibilities and Standing Rules) (Amendment) Regulations 2013[4]). The DP Regs 2013 have been amended since they were first made. The version referred to here is the version in effect on 1 April 2018. The DP Regs 2013 are supplemented by statutory guidance published by NHS England: *Guidance on direct payments for healthcare: understanding the regulations*.[5] There is separate guidance on the 'right to have' a direct payment for patients who are eligible for NHS Continuing Healthcare[6] as a result of changes to the legal regime around direct payments arising from the National Health Service Commissioning Board and Clinical Commissioning Groups (Responsibilities and Standing Rules) (Amendment) (No 3) Regulations 2014.[7]

14.8 The first attempt to persuade an NHS body to use direct payments occurred in *R (Harrison) v Secretary of State for Health and others*.[8] Mr Harrison[9] had a social care direct payment, but he was then assessed to be eligible for NHS Continuing Healthcare. As a result, responsibility for funding services for him switched from the local authority to the NHS.

2 SI No 1617.
3 SI No 2996.
4 SI No 2891.
5 See www.personalhealthbudgets.england.nhs.uk/_library/Resources/Personalhealthbudgets/2014/Guidance_on_Direct_Payments_for_Healthcare_Understanding_the_Regulations_March_2014.pdf.
6 See www.personalhealthbudgets.england.nhs.uk/_library/Resources/Personalhealthbudgets/2014/Personal_health_budgets_right_to_have_guidance.pdf.
7 SI No 1611.
8 [2009] EWHC 574 (Admin).
9 There was a second claimant who was in a similar position.

He had had the benefit of social care direct payments, an arrangement which he had asked to be continued once his care became funded by the NHS. However, the NHS said that it had no power to provide direct payments and could only fund services provided to Mr Harrison. The judge noted that the Department of Health and Social Care acknowledged the benefits of direct payments. He said:[10]

> There is clear evidence that direct payments for medical care increase both the claimants' degree of choice and flexibility in relation to medical care as well as enhancing their autonomy so that a greater degree of independent living can be enjoyed by each of them. Indeed this is not in dispute as in the witness statement adduced by the defendant from Mr Andrew Sanderson a civil servant in the Department of Health, he accepted that:
>
> > 'research suggests that direct payments have substantially increased the satisfaction of the recipient as well as delivering better outcomes and greater independence than traditional social care models'.

14.9 However, the judge accepted the secretary of state's submissions that the duty to provide 'services' under section 3(1) of the National Health Service Act (NHS Act) 2006 could not be discharged by the provision of money to a patient, even if that money was provided with the intention of allowing the patient to purchase his own services.

14.10 This legislative lacuna was corrected by section 11 of the Health Act (HA) 2009 which introduced a new section 12A into the NHS Act 2006. The present version of section 12A is as follows:

> (1) The Secretary of State, the Board, a clinical commissioning group or a local authority may, for the purpose of securing the provision to a patient of anything to which this subsection applies, make payments, with the patient's consent, to the patient or to a person nominated by the patient.
>
> (2) Subsection (1) applies to–
>
> (a) anything that the Secretary of State or a local authority has a duty or power to provide or arrange under section 2A or 2B or Schedule 1;
>
> (aa) anything that the Board or a clinical commissioning group may or must arrange for the provision of under this Act or any other enactment.
>
> (b) . . .
>
> (c) . . .
>
> (3) Subsection (1) is subject to any provision made by regulations under section 12B.
>
> (4) If regulations so provide, a clinical commissioning group may, for the purpose of securing the provision for a patient of services that the group must provide under section 117 of the Mental Health Act 1983 (after-care), make payments, with the patient's consent, to the patient or to a person nominated by the patient; and the references in this subsection to a clinical commissioning group are, so far as necessary for the purposes of regulations under subsection (2E) of that section, to be read as references to the Board.
>
> (5) A payment under subsection (1) . . . is referred to in this Part as a 'direct payment'.
>
> (6) . . .
>
> (7) In this section and sections 12B to 12D, 'local authority' has the same meaning as in section 2B.

10 At para 21.

14.11 Section 12B provided regulation-making powers which were used to make the DP Regs 2013. Section 12C provided for direct payments to be subject to pilot arrangements. Those pilot arrangements have now come to an end and direct payments are generally available to NHS patients in appropriate circumstances.

14.12 The next significant change arose in October 2014 when changes were made to the RSR Regs 2012 to give patients who were eligible for NHS Continuing Healthcare and Children and Young Person's Continuing Care a qualified 'right' to insist that they have direct payments. The nature of this right and the qualifications are examined below.

14.13 Today direct payments are an established method of funding community health services for large numbers of patients. They are widely used but, as far as the author is aware, there are no published statistics about how many direct payment arrangements are operating in the English NHS. It is possible for patients to have both profound physical and mental health needs. In that case, a patient would fall to be assessed for his or her physical needs under the Continuing Healthcare system and would be entitled to support under section 117 of the Mental Health Act 1983. Aside from such unusual circumstances, patients being discharged from compulsory in-patient mental health should not be assessed for Continuing Healthcare.

14.14 This chapter will look at the rules on direct payments that apply to all cases. The special rules concerning patients in receipt of NHS Continuing Healthcare or Continuing Care for Children will be considered at chapter 16 below.

Who is ineligible to apply for a personal health budget?

14.15 Most NHS patients have the right to apply for a direct payment (although no patient can be forced to have one). However, there is a list of patients who are excluded from the right in the Schedule to the DP Regs 2013. None of the following persons have a right to have a direct payment:

(a) *Anyone subject to a drug rehabilitation requirement*, as defined by section 209 of the Criminal Justice Act 2003 (drug rehabilitation requirement), imposed by a community order within the meaning of section 177 of that Act (community orders), or by a suspended sentence of imprisonment within the meaning of section 189 of that Act (suspended sentences of imprisonment).

(b) *Anyone subject to an alcohol treatment requirement* as defined by section 212 of the Criminal Justice Act 2003 (alcohol treatment requirement), imposed by a community order, within the meaning of section 177 of that Act, or by a suspended sentence of imprisonment, within the meaning of section 189 of that Act.

(c) *Anyone released on licence* under Part 2 of the Criminal Justice Act 1991 (early release of prisoners), Chapter 6 of Part 12 of the Criminal Justice Act 2003 (release, licences and recall) or Chapter 2 of Part 2 of the Crime (Sentences) Act 1997 (life sentences) subject to a non-standard licence condition requiring the offender to undertake offending behaviour work to address drug- or alcohol-related behaviour.

(d) *Anyone required to submit to treatment for their drug or alcohol dependency by virtue of a community rehabilitation order* within the meaning of section 41 of the Powers of Criminal Courts (Sentencing) Act 2000 (community rehabilitation orders) or a community punishment and rehabilitation order within the meaning of section 51 of that Act (community punishment and rehabilitation orders).

(e) *Anyone subject to a drug treatment and testing order* imposed under section 52 of the Powers of Criminal Courts (Sentencing) Act 2000 (drug treatment and testing orders).

(f) *Anyone subject to a youth rehabilitation order* imposed in accordance with para 22 (drug treatment requirement) of Schedule 1 to the Criminal Justice and Immigration Act (CJIA) 2008 which requires the person to submit to treatment pursuant to a drug treatment requirement.

(g) *Anyone subject to a youth rehabilitation order* imposed in accordance with para 23 of Schedule 1 to the CJIA 2008 (drug testing requirement) which includes a drug testing requirement.

(h) *Anyone subject to a youth rehabilitation order* imposed in accordance with para 24 of Schedule 1 to the CJIA 2008 (intoxicating substance treatment requirement) which requires the person to submit to treatment pursuant to an intoxicating substance treatment requirement.

(i) Anyone who is either–
   (i) *subject to a drug treatment and testing order* within the meaning of section 234B of the Criminal Procedure (Scotland) Act 1995 (drug treatment and testing order); or
   (ii) *subject to a community payback order* under section 227A of that Act imposing requirements relating to drug or alcohol treatment.

(j) *Anyone released on licence* under section 22 (release on licence of persons serving determinate sentences) or section 26 of the Prisons (Scotland) Act 1989 (release on licence of persons sentenced to imprisonment for life, etc) or under section 1 (release of short-term, long term and life prisoners) or section 1AA of the Prisoners and Criminal Proceedings (Scotland) Act 1993 (release of certain sexual offenders) and subject to a condition that they submit to treatment for their drug or alcohol dependency.

14.16 These are fairly narrow categories and mostly involve persons who are within the criminal justice system. Any other patient has the right to seek direct payments.

14.17 Where a patient sets up a direct payment arrangement and subsequently comes within one of the above categories, the health body is obliged to bring the direct payment to an end and resume commissioning services for the patient because the health body has no vires to continue with a direct payment for anyone in the categories set out in the Schedule to the DP Regs 2013.

What services cannot be funded by direct payments?

14.18 The DP Regs 2013 do not define a list of NHS services that can be funded by direct payments. Instead, it defines a list of services that are outside the scope of direct payments. Regulation 8(5) provides that a direct payment arrangement *cannot* be entered into to fund the provision of any of the following services to a patient:

a) primary care services, namely those arranged or provided under sections 83 (primary medical services), 84 (general medical services contracts) or 92 (arrangements by the Board for the provision of primary medical services) of the NHS Act 2006;
b) any services where a charge is made to the patient for the service (by virtue of sections 172 (charges for drugs, medicines or appliances, or pharmaceutical services), 176 (dental charging) or 179 (charges for optical appliances) of the NHS Act 2006);
c) planned surgical procedures;
d) providing vaccination, immunisation or screening, including population-wide immunisation programmes;
e) services provided under the National Child Measurement Programme;
f) services provided as part of an NHS Health Check;
g) services which consist of the supply or procurement of alcohol or tobacco;
h) services which consist of the provision of gambling services or facilities; or
i) services to repay a debt otherwise than in respect of a service specified in the care plan.

14.19 In addition, the guidance provides:[11]

> A direct payment cannot be used for urgent or emergency treatment services, such as unplanned in-patient admissions to hospital or accident and emergency. This is because by their very nature they are unplanned and so will not have been included in a care plan. Whilst CCGs should not include services which require unplanned emergency access they may want to develop advance directives or crisis planning to ensure that people's wishes are taken into account when a crisis happens or that they have increased support or services to prevent the need for emergency care or hospital admission.

14.20 The guidance also notes in a cautionary way:[12]

> In addition they cannot be used to purchase anything illegal or unlawful.

So, at least for the time being, medicinal cannabis probably cannot be funded out of a direct payment.

14.21 It follows that a direct payment arrangement can be set up to fund any other health, social care or other service that a patient needs on a regular basis other than those described above and which is a service of a nature that the health body would commission for the patient. This is confirmed in the guidance which says as follows:[13]

> In principle, other than the services listed in paragraphs 22 to 27, a direct payment can be spent on a broad range of things that will enable the person to meet their health and wellbeing needs.

11 At para 24.
12 At para 27.
13 At para 28.

Which health bodies can set up a direct payment arrangement?

14.22 Direct payments can be set up by:[14]

a) a clinical commissioning group (CCG);
b) NHS England;
c) some local authorities; and
d) the Secretary of State for Health and Social Care.

14.23 The only local authorities that can set up NHS direct payments are:

a) a county council in England;
b) a district council in England, other than a council for a district in a county for which there is a county council;
c) a London borough council;
d) the Council of the Isles of Scilly; and
e) the Common Council of the City of London.

14.24 CCGs and NHS England can set up a direct payment arrangement under the DP Regs 2013 in order to provide services that they are authorised to provide under any Act of parliament. In contrast, local authorities can only set up a direct payment arrangement under the DP Regs 2013 where they have duties to a patient under the NHS Act 2006. Local authorities have powers to set up direct payments in discharge of their community care duties under the Care Act 2014 under the Care and Support (Direct Payments) Regulations 2014.[15] Community care direct payment arrangements under those regulations have a number of features which are different to NHS direct payment arrangements.[16]

14.25 In practice, local authorities are most likely to become parties to NHS direct payment arrangements involving complex services to disabled children (as to which see below). It is hard to see how local authorities are likely to make use of direct payments to discharge their public health duties under the NHS Act 2006.

The key players in any direct payment arrangement

14.26 The DP Regs 2013 define a series of roles that can be or are required to be carried out in the setting up and operation of a direct payment arrangement. The primary roles are:

a) the patient;
b) the representative;
c) the nominated person;
d) the care co-ordinator; and
e) support organisations.

14 See the definition of 'health body' in reg 2 of the DP Regs 2013.
15 SI No 2871.
16 The operation of community care direct payment arrangements is beyond the scope of this chapter.

The patient

14.27 The patient is the person to whom the health body owes the primary legal duty to provide services, and is the beneficiary of the direct payment arrangement. The health body owes public law duties to provide health and/or social care services to the patient and seeks to discharge that duty by making payments under a direct payment arrangement instead of commissioning services from one or more providers to provide services to the patient.

14.28 The patient can be a child or an adult, and may or may not have capacity to make his or her own medical treatment decisions or have capacity to manage the direct payment (in which case, it must be managed via a representative).

The representative

14.29 The representative is the person who takes legal responsibility for the direct payment arrangements when the patient is unable to do so because the patient is either a child or is an adult who lacks capacity.

14.30 Regulation 2 of the DP Regs 2013 defines the list of persons who can be appointed to be a representative as follows:

a) any deputy who has been appointed by the Court of Protection under section 16(2)(b) of the Mental Capacity Act (MCA) 2005 (powers to appoint deputies) to make decisions on that person's behalf in relation to matters in respect of which direct payments may be made;
b) any donee of a lasting power of attorney within the meaning of section 9 of the MCA 2005 (lasting powers of attorney) to make decisions on that person's behalf in relation to matters in respect of which direct payments may be made;
c) any attorney in whom the power is vested in the case of a person who has created an enduring power of attorney within the meaning of Schedule 4 to the MCA 2005 (provisions applying to existing enduring powers of attorney), which is registered in accordance with paras 4 and 13 of that Schedule or in respect of which an application has been made for such registration;
d) any person with parental responsibility for a child who is the beneficiary of a direct payment arrangement;
e) any person with parental responsibility for a child who lacks capacity between the ages of 16 and 18; or
f) any other person appointed by the health body to be a representative for a person who lacks capacity under reg 5(4), which permits the appointment of someone to be a representative for a patient who lacks capacity where no one is proposed on behalf of the patient.

14.31 The references to 'capacity' in the above paragraphs are a reference to the capacity of the patient to consent to the making of a direct payment to them, applying the capacity tests under the MCA 2005: see reg 5(1). Capacity is, of course, a decision-specific test and a patient with limited cognitive functions may have capacity to take some types of decision for himself or herself but not have capacity to take other decisions. Patients can also have fluctuating capacity. The legal structures arsing in connection with direct payment arrangements for patients who lacks capacity are considered in more detail below.

14.32 The categories of persons who can be a representative are limited to those set out in para 14.30 above. The DP Regs 2013 do not permit a patient who has capacity to nominate someone to be their representative, even if this would assist the smooth operation of the direct payment arrangements. Hence, a patient with capacity who wants the benefit of a direct payment arrangement must be prepared to become a party to the direct payment arrangement and take on the legal responsibilities associated with the arrangement. The capacitous patient can be assisted by a 'nominated person' (as explained below), but must take on the legal burden of being a party to the direct payment arrangement. The guidance explains the role of the representative as follows:[17]

> 83. A representative is responsible for managing direct payments on behalf of the person receiving care. They, or their nominee, must:
> - act on behalf of the person, e.g. to help develop care plans and to hold the direct payment;
> - act in the best interests of the person when securing the provision of services;
> - be the principal person for all contracts and agreements, e.g. as an employer;
> - use the direct payment in line with the agreed care plan;
> - comply with any other requirement that would normally be undertaken by the person as set out in this guidance (eg review, providing information).
>
> 84. If a representative believes that the person for whom they are acting has regained capacity they should notify the CCG as soon as possible (see paras 47–49 on fluctuating capacity)

The nominated person

14.33 Regulation 6 of the DP Regs 2013 refers to the role of the 'nominated person'. This is a person who is nominated by the patient or the patient's representative to 'receive a direct payment': see reg 6(1). The guidance explains the difference between nominees for NHS direct payments and nominees for social care direct payments as follows:[18]

> It is important that CCGs and their commissioning and provider partners understand that the role of nominee for direct payments for healthcare is different from the role of nominee for direct payments for social care. For social care direct payments, a nominee does not have to take on all the responsibilities of someone receiving direct payments, but can simply carry out certain functions such as receiving or managing direct payments on behalf of the person receiving them. In direct payments for healthcare, however, the nominee is responsible for fulfilling all the responsibilities of someone receiving direct payments, as described below in Box 2. People aged 16 or over with capacity and representatives receiving direct payments for healthcare, and those who act as their nominees need to be made fully aware of this particularly if they have previous experience of appointing or acting as a nominee under the social care arrangements.

17 At para 83.

18 At para 66.

14.34 The wording in 'Box 2' explaining the legal duties of the nominee is as follows:

> **What is a nominee?**
> A nominee is responsible for managing the direct payment on behalf of the person receiving care. They are responsible for fulfilling all the responsibilities of someone receiving direct payments. These include:
> a. acting as the principal person for all contracts and agreements with care providers, employees, etc;
> b. using the direct payment in line with the agreed care plan; and
> c. complying with any other requirement that would normally be undertaken by the person receiving care as set out in this guidance (e.g. review, providing financial information)'

14.35 Regulation 6(3) sets out the legal duties of the nominee as follows:

> A nominee to whom a direct payment is made in respect of a patient must–
> (a) be responsible as a principal for all contractual arrangements entered into for the benefit of the patient and secured by means of the direct payment;
> (b) use the direct payment in accordance with the care plan; and
> (c) comply with the relevant provisions of these Regulations'

14.36 In practice, this means that a nominee takes on considerable legal obligations. The nominee must be a joint employer with the patient or representative under any contract of employment with a care worker. The nominee must also become a contracting party with an agency which is providing care workers for the patient. Thus, if the care worker is dismissed, both the nominee and the patient would be respondents to an application to an employment tribunal. The nominee has a legal duty to ensure that the NHS money provided under the direct payment is used for the purposes set out in the care plan and for no other purposes. The nominee also has a duty to ensure that there is compliance with all of the duties under the regulations.

14.37 No one can be forced to act as a nominee. The nominee must give their consent to take on this role, and can resign his or her responsibilities at any time. A nominee can be a company as well as an individual. There is nothing expressly set out in the DP Regs 2013 or the guidance which refers to the question as to whether a nominee can be paid for undertaking these duties. However, in practice nominees are regularly paid by CCGs for supporting direct payment arrangements. Paragraph 72 of the guidance recognises that organisations can be established to act as nominees to support direct payment arrangements. These organisations perform a valuable role in assisting the patient or their representative to employ care staff, manage timesheets, wages, rotas and pension arrangements. Such organisations could only operate if they were paid for undertaking this role and the costs of the nominee must therefore be built into the costs of the care plan.

14.38 Paragraph 70 of the guidance explains the need for the nominee (or individuals representing a corporate nominee) to provide Criminal Record Bureau (CRB) clearance as follows:

> If the proposed nominee is not a close family member of the person living in the same household as the person, or a friend involved in the person's care, then the CCG must require the nominee to apply for an enhanced Disclosure and Barring Service (DBS) certificate (formerly a CRB check) with a check of

the adults' barred list and consider the information before giving their consent. If a proposed nominee in respect of a patient aged 18 or over is barred the CCG must not give their consent. This is because the *Safeguarding Vulnerable Groups Act 2006* prohibits a barred person from engaging in the activities of managing the person's cash or paying the person's bills.

The care co-ordinator

14.39 Regulation 8(3) of the DP Regs 2013 provides that the health body must appoint a specific individual to be the care co-ordinator in relation to every direct payment. The regulation provides that the duties of the care co-ordinator are as follows:

> A health body must nominate a care co-ordinator who is to be responsible for the following functions in respect of the patient–
> (a) managing the assessment of the health needs of the patient for the care plan;
> (b) ensuring that the patient or their representative has agreed to the matters listed in paragraph (7);
> (c) monitoring or arranging for the monitoring of–
> (i) the making of direct payments, and
> (ii) the health conditions of the patient in respect of which the direct payments are made;
> (d) arranging for review of the direct payments; and
> (e) liaising between the patient or the representative or nominee and the health body in relation to the direct payments.

14.40 The reference to a 'the matters in paragraph (7)' in reg 8(3) above is a reference to reg 8(7) which provides that, before a direct payment is set up, the patient or their representative must agree:

a) that the patient's specified health needs can be met by the services specified in the care plan;
b) that the amount of the direct payments is sufficient to provide for the full cost of each of the services specified in the care plan; and
c) that the patient's requirements may be reviewed in accordance with regulation 14(2) which provides for monitoring and review of direct payments.

14.41 The care co-ordinator is not required to have any specific qualifications but is typically a nurse or other healthcare professional employed by a CCG. The role of the care co-ordinator is explained in the guidance as follows:[19]

> 115. The care coordinator should normally be someone who has regular contact with both the individual receiving care, and their representative or nominee if they have one. They do not need to have 'care coordinator' in their job title – the important thing is that they fulfil the responsibilities above and that the direct payment recipient is aware of who they are and their role. While they are able to arrange with others to undertake actions, such as monitoring or review, the care coordinator should be the primary point of contact between the individual and the CCG. This is a similar role to the care coordinator in many mental health services and community matrons in NHS Continuing Healthcare.

19 At paras 115 and 116.

116) It is the responsibility of CCGs to decide who is best placed in their organisations to take up the role of care coordinator. Different services such as mental health services already have best practice guidance around the role of the care coordinator. CCGs may also find it helpful to build on the experience of local authorities.

Support organisations

14.42 There is no reference in the DP Regs 2013 to 'support organisations'. However, support organisations are involved in many direct payment arrangements. The roles undertaken by such organisations is noted in the guidance as follows:[20]

> **The status of support organisations with regard to the role of nominee**
> An organisation which does not have the status of a nominee but provides financial management and support services to the person who receives and manages direct payments for an individual, their representative or nominee, is not considered to be acting as a nominee as defined by the regulations. In this situation the individual, their representative or nominee remain fully responsible for the direct payment, including acting as the employers of any personal assistant/s and the making of decisions about their direct payment. The organisation may offer advice and support around a number of elements including being an employer, in addition to coordinating the financial element of the direct payment but they do not take on full responsibility for the person's care and budget.

14.43 This guidance suggests that a care plan can build in the costs of an organisation whose role is to support the patient or representative in managing the arrangements. A support organisation differs from a nominee because it is not a party to a direct payment agreement, does not receive the direct payment money and does not become the employer of any staff engaged to support the patient or contractually responsible under, for example, a domiciliary care contract. However, even though it is not formally a nominee under the regulations, a support organisation could provide the same type of practical support as a nominee, namely assisting in employing staff, managing rotas, making payments and handling the paperwork. The key difference is that a nominee has a direct relationship with the commissioning health body whereas a support organisation provides these services under contract to the patient or representative.

The decision-making process leading to offer of a direct payment arrangement

Overview

14.44 The scheme of the DP Regs 2013 envisages the following stages to the setting up of a direct payment arrangement with a patient or the patient's representative:

20 At para 75.

1) the patient or the patient's representative approaches the health body to request a direct payment;
2) the health body makes a 'capability' decision;
3) the health body nominates a care co-ordinator and then prepares the care plan;
4) the cost of delivering the care plan is calculated and a budget is proposed;
5) the care plan and the amount of the direct payment are agreed with the patient or the patient's representative; and
6) once the care plan and the budget are agreed, the health body and the patient (or the patient's representative) makes a final decision whether to proceed with the direct payment arrangement and, at that point, the health body stops commissioning relevant services for the patient and services are commissioned under the direct payment arrangement.

14.45 Although the regulations separate out the capability decision from decisions about the care plan and financial decisions, in practice none of these stages are wholly independent since they all depend on each other. However, as the regulations identify different decisions at different stages, it is necessary to consider the stages separately in order to describe the legal structures around direct payment decision-making.

Capability decisions under reg 7 of the DP Regs 2013

Overview of the decision-making process

14.46 Regulation 7 of the DP Regs 2013 contains a detailed, mandatory decision-making process that the health body is required to follow when making an 'in principle' decision whether to set up a direct payment arrangement. It provides:

> (1) A health body must make any decision to make a direct payment to, or in respect of, a patient in accordance with this regulation.
> (2) Before deciding whether to make a direct payment to a patient, a health body–
> (a) may consult the following persons–
> (i) anyone identified by the patient as a person to be consulted for the purpose,
> (ii) if the patient is a person aged 16 or over but under the age of 18, a person with parental responsibility for the patient,
> (iii) the person primarily involved in the care of a patient,
> (iv) any other person who provides care for the patient,
> (v) any independent mental capacity advocate or independent mental health advocate appointed for the patient,
> (vi) any health care professional or other professional person who provides health services to the patient,
> (vii) any local authority social care team that is responsible for ensuring that the patient's social care needs are met, or
> (viii) any other person who appears to a health body to be able to provide information of relevance;
> (b) may require the patient to provide information relating to–
> (i) the patient's state of health,
> (ii) any health condition of the patient in respect of which a direct payment is contemplated, and

(iii) any bank, building society, post office or other account into which a direct payment may be made; and

(c) must be satisfied that the patient is capable of managing a direct payment by themselves or with the assistance that may be available to them.

(3) Before deciding whether to make a direct payment in respect of a patient to the representative of the patient, a health body may consult–

(a) the patient;

(b) any deputy appointed in respect of the patient by the Court of Protection under section 16(2)(b) of the 2005 Act (powers to appoint deputies) who lacks authority to make decisions on behalf of the patient in relation to matters in respect of which direct payments may be made;

(c) any donee of a lasting power of attorney within the meaning of section 9 of the 2005 Act (lasting powers of attorney) in respect of the patient but who lacks authority to make decisions on behalf of the patient in relation to matters in respect of which direct payments may be made;

(d) the persons mentioned in paragraph (2)(a)(iii) to (viii); and

(e) anyone named by the patient, when the patient had capacity, as a person to be consulted for this purpose.

(4) Before deciding whether to make a direct payment in respect of a patient to the representative of the patient, a health body–

(a) may require the representative to provide information relating to any bank, building society, post office or other account into which the direct payment may be made; and

(b) must be satisfied that the representative is capable of managing a direct payment by themselves or with the assistance that may be available to them.

(5) When deciding whether to make a direct payment in respect of a patient to a representative, a health body may, in particular, consider–

(a) whether the patient has in the past, when the patient had capacity, expressed in writing, or by other means which are understandable, a wish for direct payments to be made to them or for their benefit;

(b) so far as reasonably ascertainable, the beliefs and values that would be likely to influence the patient's decision as to whether or not to consent to receive a direct payment if the patient had capacity; and

(c) any other factors that the patient would be likely to consider on the issue of whether to consent to receive a direct payment if the patient were able to do so, including the patient's wishes and feelings.

(6) Before deciding whether to make a direct payment in respect of a patient to a nominee, a health body may–

(a) consult the persons mentioned in paragraphs (2)(a) and (3)(a) to (c) and, where relevant, (e);

(b) require a patient with the necessary capacity or competence to provide information relating to the patient's state of health or any health condition in respect of which the direct payment is contemplated; and

(c) require the nominee to provide information relating to any bank, building society, post office or other account into which the direct payment may be made.

(7) Before deciding whether to make a direct payment in respect of a patient to a nominee, a health body must–

(a) be satisfied that the nominee is capable of managing a direct payment by themselves or with the assistance that may be available to them;

(b) where the nominee is an individual, require the nominee to apply for an enhanced criminal record certificate issued under section 113B of the Police Act 1997 including suitability information relating to vulnerable adults under section 113BB of that Act, unless the nominee is an individual living in the same household as the patient, a family member mentioned in paragraph (8) or a friend involved in the provision of the patient's care; and

(c) where the nominee is a body corporate or an unincorporated body of persons, require that the individual whom the nominee has decided will, on behalf of the nominee, have overall responsibility for the day-to-day management of the patient's direct payments, applies for an enhanced criminal record certificate issued under section 113B of the Police Act 1997 including suitability information relating to vulnerable adults under section 113BB of that Act.

(8) The family members referred to in paragraph (7)(b) are–

(a) the spouse or civil partner of the patient;

(b) a person who lives with the patient as if their spouse or civil partner;

(c) a person who is the patient's–

(i) parent or parent-in-law,

(ii) son or daughter,

(iii) son-in-law or daughter-in law,

(iv) stepson or stepdaughter,

(v) brother or sister,

(vi) aunt or uncle, or

(vii) grandparent;

(d) the spouse or civil partner of any person specified in sub-paragraph (c); and

(e) a person who lives with any person specified in sub-paragraph (c) as if that person's spouse or civil partner.

(9) In deciding whether a patient, representative or nominee is capable of managing a direct payment, a health body may, in particular, consider whether–

(a) the patient, representative or nominee would be a suitable person to arrange with any person or body to provide, or assist in providing, any services secured by means of direct payments for the patient;

(b) the patient, representative or nominee has not been able to manage a direct payment or a direct payment to secure relevant services for social care under the Community Care, Services for Carers and Children's Services (Direct Payments) (England) Regulations 2009; or

(c) the patient, representative or nominee is capable of taking all reasonable steps to prevent fraudulent use of the direct payment.

(10) If a health body considers making a direct payment to a patient in accordance with this regulation and decides not to make such a payment, they must inform the patient and any representative or nominee in writing of the decision, and state the reasons for the decision.

(11) Where a health body decides under paragraph (10) not to make a direct payment, a patient, representative or nominee may require the health body to re-consider the decision, and may provide evidence or relevant information for the health body to consider as part of that deliberation.

(12) A health body must inform the patient and any representative or nominee in writing of the decision on a re-consideration, and state the reasons for the decision.

(13) A health body may not be required to undertake more than one re-consideration following a decision under paragraph (10) in any six month period.

14.47 The wording of reg 7 is not especially clear, but it appears to set up a series of different decision-making processes, depending on whether the patient has capacity or is a child, and whether a nominee is to be appointed or not. The structure is:

a) where the patient is over the age of 16 and has capacity, the decision-making process in reg 7(2) and (9) applies;
b) where the patient is under the age of 16 or lacks capacity and a direct payment is being made to a representative, the decision-making process in reg 7(3), (4), (5) and (9) applies;
c) where it is proposed that a nominee is to be appointed (irrespective as to whether the patient is an adult or child and whether the patient has capacity or not), the decision-making process in reg 7(6), (7) and (9) applies.

14.48 The regulation thus sets up a series of steps and tests that a health body is required to follow when going through this decision-making process as to whether to set up a direct payment arrangement for a particular patient. The decision-making processes are, however, subtly different depending on whether the patient has capacity or not, and whether a nominee is to be appointed or not. The health body would be well advised to keep proper records of the decision-making process in order to be able to demonstrate that it has followed the process properly and thus has made a lawful decision (particularly if the eventual decision is to refuse to set up a direct payment arrangement).

Capability decisions where the patient has capacity

Overview

14.49 The NHS body with power to set up a direct payment is the NHS commissioner, not the existing provider of NHS services to the patient. The commissioner will know the nature of the services commissioned for the patient, but may well be unaware of all of the details of the patient's medical condition. Accordingly, where a patient makes a request for a direct payment, the first step is for the health body to collect information about the patient's medical condition so that it can understand the nature of the services that would be included in any direct payment arrangement. Regulation 7(2)(b) provides that the health body may require the patient to provide information to the health body relating to:

a) the patient's state of health;
b) any health condition of the patient in respect of which a direct payment is contemplated.

14.50 There are further provisions about the provision of personal data relating to the patient in reg 12 which provides:

> Any information that must be provided under these Regulations to a health body must be–

(a) legible;
(b) accompanied by the relevant authorisation enabling the taking of copies or making of extracts, where appropriate;
(c) if so requested by a health body, accompanied by–
   (i) an explanation by the information provider of anything which has been provided, or
   (ii) a statement to the best of the knowledge and belief of the information provider as to where information or evidence that the person has failed to provide is held'

14.51 Regulation 12 only applies where the patient has capacity to make decisions to release data to the health body. The regulations provide that a patient with capacity who seeks a direct payment arrangement is required to provide any relevant information sought by the health body, even though this is sensitive personal data relating to the patient under the Data Protection Act (DPA) 1998. In practice, much of the information that the patient or the patient's representative will be called on to provide will be held by whoever presently provides services to the patient. This could be a general practitioner (GP), an NHS community trust, an NHS acute trust, a care home or a domiciliary care provider. Thus, if a capacitous patient wishes to set up a direct payment arrangement, the patient is required to authorise those holding information about him or her to provide all relevant information about the patient's medical condition to the health body that is thinking about setting up the direct payment.

14.52 Any information which is passed to the health body as a result of a request made under reg 7(3)(b) will be highly likely to be both 'personal data' and 'sensitive personal data' within the meaning of the DPA 1998. Any data controller is entitled to rely on the explicit consent given by the patient to process the data by providing it to the health body. The health body is, in turn, entitled to use that data for the purpose of assisting it to make its own decisions about the direct payment. However, health bodies are not, without more, entitled to share the data with any third party. The health body also needs to be careful to ensure that this data is not used for any other purpose because, in doing so, the health body may be contravening its obligations under the DPA 1998.

14.53 It would be possible for the health body to seek 'explicit consent' from the patient to the health body sharing data about the patient's condition with a limited range of other persons outside the health body as part of this decision-making process but the health body probably cannot insist that such consent is provided. The conditions which must be satisfied before sensitive personal data can be shared are set out at Schedules 1–3 to the DPA 1998. Unless the health body both has explicit consent (or satisfies one of the other criteria in Schedule 3 to the DPA 1998) and acts both fairly and lawfully, it will be unlawful for the health body to divulge any details of the patient's medical condition to any third party.

Information about a proposed bank account to be used for direct payments

14.54 Regulation 7(2)(b)(iii) of the DP Regs 2013 enables the health body to require the patient to provide information about any 'any bank, building society, post office or other account into which a direct payment may be made'. Any such bank account must comply with the provisions set out in reg 10 which provides:

(1) Where a health body has decided to make direct payments to or in respect of a patient, a health body must only make the payments into an account approved by the health body for the benefit of the patient if they are satisfied that the requirements in paragraphs (2), (3) and (5) are met.
(2) The account mentioned at paragraph (1) must be capable of–
 (a) providing for monies paid into the account to be held only for the purposes of securing services by means of–
  (i) direct payments under these Regulations,
  (ii) direct payments to secure relevant services for social care,
  (iii) payments made by the Independent Living Fund (2006), or
  (iv) other payments to secure relevant services for a disabled person; and
 (b) being audited (by reference to statements setting out the source of monies deposited and the destination of monies withdrawn) by–
  (i) a health body, or
  (ii) anyone authorised in writing by a health body.
(3) The account mentioned in paragraph (1) must be–
 (a) accessible only by named persons approved by a health body; and
 (b) used only to hold monies paid into the account by way of the payments mentioned in paragraph (2)(a).
(4) A health body may require a patient, representative or nominee to provide the health body with access to information about an account into which a direct payment is, or may be made.
(5) A health body must ensure that an account mentioned in paragraph (1) is subject to arrangements or procedures that the health body considers adequate to–
 (a) enable the monitoring and review mentioned in regulation 14(1)(a) and (6)(c) to be carried out; and
 (b) ensure that direct payments paid into it will be used only for services agreed in a patient's care plan.
(6) Paragraphs (1) to (5) do not apply where a patient is in receipt of a one-off direct payment.

14.55 The regulations thus require a patient, the patient's representative or any proposed nominee to set up a dedicated bank account to handle direct payments (and for the other purposes set out in reg 10(2)(a)). The bank account cannot be used for any other purpose, and must be capable of being audited by the health body to ensure that the payments are used for their intended purposes. This bank account will exclusively handle public money and must be used solely to fund care services for the patient. Money paid under a direct payment becomes the property of the patient or representative once it is paid over by the health body, but the patient or representative comes under a series of statutory obligations in relation to the money. However, the DP Regs 2013 do not provide that the patient or their representative holds the money on trust for the purposes of the care plan. Thus any money paid over becomes the property of the patient or representative, albeit with the right of the health body to seek repayment in the circumstances set out below.

Consultation by the health body

14.56 The next step in setting up a direct payment for a patient with capacity is consultation with a series of individuals who may have legitimate perspectives on the wisdom of setting up a direct payment arrangement for a particular patient.

14.57 The health body has a power (but not a duty) to consult those people listed in reg 7(2)(a). The categories of people who can be consulted is not closed because reg 7(2)(a)(viii) provides that the health body can consult 'any other person who appears to a health body to be able to provide information of relevance'. The purpose of the consultation is to assist the health body to make a decision 'whether to make a direct payment' and in particular to make the decision set out in reg 7(2)(c), namely whether 'the patient is capable of managing a direct payment by themselves or with the assistance that may be available to them'.

14.58 This consultation needs to be handled with care because, unless the health body has been provided with explicit consent by (or possibly on behalf of) the patient to disclose medical information about the patient to family members and others, the health body will have to be cautious about what information is disclosed about the patient to consultees during the consultation. The health body needs to disclose to consultees that the patient is seeking a direct payment and ask them whether, in their opinion, the patient (and any proposed representative) will be able to manage a direct payment and to invite the consultee to provide the health body with any information held by that person that may be relevant to the decisions that the health body has to take about setting up or operation of a direct payment arrangement.

14.59 However, as part of the process of seeking views, the health body must be careful to preserve the confidentiality in personal data relating to the patient. Those providing care to the patient may well know something about the patient's medical condition, but care must be taken not to disclose additional information relating to the patient's health as part of the consultation. There is no general right for family members to know the details of a medical condition suffered by another family member and, absent explicit consent, the health body may be acting in breach of its duty under the DPA 1998 if it makes disclosures as part of the consultation exercise.

14.60 The health body is not under an absolute duty to consult anyone listed in reg 7(2)(a). However, the existence of the power suggests that the health body ought carefully to consider carefully whether there is likely to be any benefit in seeking views from any person and, if so, ought to seek and record their views.

Consideration of the proposed care plan with the patient

14.61 The DP Regs 2013 separate out the decision-making process as to whether a direct payment arrangement should be set up (reg 7) with a care plan to be put in place once the direct payment is put in place (reg 8). In practice, it is difficult to see how the health body could properly follow the decision-making process under reg 7 unless it had started to develop a care plan and was thus able to discuss the risks of the direct payment arrangement with the patient. Until work on the care plan is commenced, the health body will not necessarily know whether the patient has the capacity to manage a direct payment arrangement. Both the health body and the patient need carefully to consider what would be involved in passing over responsibility for commissioning services to the patient.

14.62 The statutory requirements relating to the care plan are set out below but, unless it becomes clear to the health body at an early stage that a direct payment arrangement is unsuitable, the care plan (including the discussion of the risks) will need to be developed and agreed with the patient before the reg 7 decision can be made. The health body will also need to agree the amount of direct payment with the patient (as to which see below) before any reg 7 decision can be made to go ahead with the direct payment arrangement.

The capability question for a direct payment to a patient with capacity

14.63 Once the health body has:

a) collected relevant information about the capacitous patient;
b) undertaken its consultations;
c) developed a suitable care plan;
d) discussed the risks and satisfied itself that the patient understands them and can take on those risks; and
e) agreed the amount of the direct payment,

the health body has to:

f) address the question in reg 7(2)(c), namely whether it is satisfied that the patient is 'capable of managing a direct payment'.

The health body can reach this view by looking at the patient's capacity together with the assistance that may be available to the patient.

14.64 At this stage of the decision-making process, the health body also has the power (but not the duty) to address the additional factors in reg 7(9) as part of its overall assessment of the capability question. For a patient with capacity, these factors cover the following broad issues:

i) Whether the patient (with or without assistance from a nominee or support organisation depending on the proposal) has the capability to manage the contracts needed to deliver care to the patient. In particular, the health body will need to consider whether the patient, with or without a nominee, has the ability to become an employer of his or her own care workers, to manage the rotas, make the required payments (including Pay As You Earn (PAYE) tax and National Insurance (NI) and pension sums), and generally act as an appropriate employer;
ii) Whether the patient has been unable to manage a social care direct payment in the past; and, if so, what is likely to be different this time?
iii) Whether the patient is capable of taking all reasonable steps to prevent fraudulent use of the direct payment. Direct payment monies are taxpayers' money which is passed to the patient under arrangements which impose a statutory requirement on the patient to use the money for a particular purpose. The relatively high level of autonomy which is provided for patients means that there can be a substantial risk of fraud, and thus proper processes need to be put in place to prevent fraud. The health body needs to ensure that it is satisfied that the patient is capable of taking all reasonable steps to prevent the money being used for fraudulent purposes before reaching the decision that

the patient (with or without a nominee) is capable of managing a direct payment.

14.65 The health body therefore has to consider all of these factors as part of addressing the statutory test set up by reg 7(2)(c). It is essential for the decision maker to make a written record of the decision and the reasons for making this decision, whether the decision is to approve a direct payment or not.

14.66 If the health body decides that a patient with capacity is *not* capable of managing a direct payment by himself or herself, even with the assistance of such persons as the patient proposes (or someone else as a nominee that the health body proposes), that is the end of the decision-making process because no direct payment arrangement can lawfully be set up. The health body has no power to proceed to make a direct payment arrangement unless it is satisfied on the capability question. In making this decision, the health body has to take into account the information provided by the patient and on his or her behalf and the views expressed as part of its consultations. However, the health body has a wide margin for making a discretionary decision to decide whether it is or is not satisfied that the patient is capable of managing a direct payment by themselves or with the assistance of a nominee. A failure to give proper reasons would make the decision-making process unlawful: *R v Westminster City Council ex p Ermakov*[21] and *R v Parole Board ex p Oyston and others.*[22]

The capability decision-making process for a child under the age of 16 or for a patient who lacks capacity

Overview

14.67 The decision-making process in reg 7(2) only relates to a decision to make a direct payment to a patient who is over the age of 16 and has capacity. If the patient is a child under the age of 16 or does not have capacity, the direct payment is made to either the representative or a nominee (if there is to be one) and not to the patient. The decision-making process the health body has to follow in this case leads up to the test in reg 7(4)(b) which is whether the health body is:

> . . . satisfied that the representative is capable of managing a direct payment by themselves or with the assistance that may be available to them.

14.68 The stages to the process are similar to the stages for the patient with capacity, namely:

a) information gathering;
b) consultation;
c) development of the care plan and the risk;
d) financial proposals; and
e) capability decision, including by reference to the reg 7(9) factors.

21 [1966] 2 All ER 302.
22 [2000] EWCA Crim 3552.

Information gathering

14.69 Regulation 7 does not give the health body a specific power to require any third party to provide information to the health body about the patient's health conditions where the patient is under the age of 16 or lacks capacity. It follows that the proposed representative or nominee, or anyone else holding information about the patient, is under no legal duty to provide information to the health body in response to such a request.

14.70 However, if the patient lacks capacity, any decision-maker acting on behalf of the patient would be under a legal duty (pursuant to the MCA 2005) to make disclosure decisions which are in the best interests of the patient. If a parent, care worker, doctor, nurse or any other person who held information about a patient was asked by a health body to provide information about a child patient or an adult who lacks capacity in order to assist a health body make a decision as to whether to set up a direct payment arrangement, that person would have to decide whether it was in the best interests of the patient to do so. If, for example, a CCG asked for relevant information about a young person with learning disabilities, it is hard to envisage any circumstances in which such a person would consider that it was not in the best interests of the patient not to provide the required information to the CCG. Provided appropriate confidentiality assurances were provided by the CCG, it would almost always be in the best interests of the patient to co-operate with the CCG in providing the information. If there was a dispute, that dispute could be referred to the High Court (for a child under the age of 16) or to the Court of Protection for adjudication.

Consultation where a representative is proposed

Overview

14.71 If it is proposed that a representative should be appointed, reg 7(3) provides a list of persons whom the health body has a power to consult. Although the health body is not under an absolute duty to consult any of these individuals about the suitability and capability of the representative, the health body ought to do so if it considers that any of them may have information which will assist it in deciding if the suitability and capability of the representative. The list of people includes the patient. The procedural requirements of Article 8 ECHR apply notwithstanding the patient has lost capacity and would almost certainly be breached if the health body did not consult a patient who was capable of expressing a view on a change to their healthcare arrangements. The health body is not bound to act in accordance with any view expressed by a patient who lacks capacity, but is required to consider the patient's views as part of the decision-making process.

14.72 Regulation 7(4)(a) provides that the health body may require the representative to provide information relating to the bank account into which the direct payment will be made. The bank account must satisfy the reg 10 requirements (see para 14.54 above).

14.73 There are another set of considerations which a health body is encouraged to consider before deciding that a representative is capable of managing a direct payment arrangement in reg 7(5). These revolve around the past and present wishes and feelings of the patient, along with the beliefs and values of the patient. Where the health body is making the decision whether to set up a direct payment arrangement for a patient who lacks capacity or a child, the health body has to act in the best interests of the patient. Section 4 of the MCA 2005 sets up a specific decision-making process that has to be followed by any best interests decision-maker, including the health body when it is making this decision for anyone over the age of 16. A similar process must be followed by a health body which is acting in the best interests of a child under the age of 16. The factors set out in reg 7(5) are all factors that, where appropriate on the facts of an individual case, the health body needs to take into account in order to follow the section 4 of the MCA 2005 process.

The capability question where a direct payment is proposed to be made to a representative

14.74 Once the health body has:

a) collected relevant information about the representative;
b) undertaken its consultations about the representative;
c) developed a suitable care plan in conjunction with the representative;
d) discussed the risks and satisfied itself that the representative understands them and can take on those risks; and
e) agreed the amount of the direct payment with the representative,

the health body has to address the question in reg 7(4)(b), namely whether it is satisfied that the representative is 'capable of managing a direct payment'. The health body can reach this view by looking at the representative's capacity, together with the assistance that may be available to the representative.

14.75 At this stage of the decision-making process the health body also has the power (but not the duty) to address the additional factors in reg 7(9) as part of its overall assessment of the capability question. For a child patient or a patient who lacks capacity, these factors cover the following broad issues:

f) Whether the representative (with or without assistance from a nominee or support organisation depending on the proposal) has the capability to manage the contracts needed to deliver care to the patient. In particular does the representative have the ability to become an employer of any care workers needed for the patient, to manage the rotas, make the required payments (including PAYE and pension sums), and generally act as an appropriate employer.
g) Whether the representative has been unable to manage a social care direct payment in the past; and, if so, what is likely to be different this time?
h) Whether the representative is capable of taking all reasonable steps to prevent fraudulent use of the direct payment.

14.76 The health body has to consider all of these factors as part of addressing the statutory test set up by reg 7(4)(b) concerning the capacity of the representative. It is thus essential for the decision-maker to make a written record of the decision and the reasons for making this decision.

14.77 If the health body decides that a representative is not capable of managing a direct payment by himself of herself or with the assistance of such persons as the representative proposes, that is the end of the decision-making process because no direct payment arrangement can lawfully be set up. The health body must provide the patient and the representative with reasons for any decision to refuse to provide a direct payment.

The capability test where a nominee is proposed

14.78 A nominee can be proposed both in cases where the adult patient has capacity and, for a child or patient who lacks capacity, where a representative is appointed. Regulation 7 of the DP Regs 2013 provides for steps to be taken leading up to an additional capacity test for the nominee. The test is in reg 7(7)(a) namely that the health body is:

> . . . satisfied that the nominee is capable of managing a direct payment by themselves or with the assistance that may be available to them.

14.79 The structure of the obligations is similar to the previous cases. It involves:

a) consultation with all the persons who can be consulted where a patient has capacity (ie those listed in reg 7(2)(a));
b) consultation with extra persons who have to be consulted where a representative is being considered (ie those listed in reg 7(3)(a)–(c));
c) provision of information about the proposed bank account to check that it satisfies reg 12.

14.80 Regulation 7(6)(b) provides that a health body can:

> . . . require a patient with the necessary capacity or competence to provide information relating to the patient's state of health or any health condition in respect of which the direct payment is contemplated.

14.81 This is a slightly strangely worded provision, since it contemplates a category of patients who do not have capacity to provide information about their own health conditions to a health body but who have the 'competence' to do so. This may refer to individuals with borderline or fluctuating capacity, but is difficult to understand what the draftsman of the regulations had in mind. A health body already has the right to seek this information from a patient with capacity under reg 7(2)(b), and so this additional power appears to adds nothing. However, if the patient does not have capacity, the patient is not a lawful decision maker to decide whether to pass over this information. It is therefore unclear what this regulation adds to the existing powers for the health body.

14.82 Regulation 7(7) provides that a where a nominee is an individual, he or she must have to apply for an enhanced criminal record certificate issued, including suitability information relating to vulnerable adults. There is an exception to this requirement where a nominee is an individual living in the same household as the patient, a family member of the patient or a 'friend' involved in the provision of the patient's care. The term 'friend' is not defined but is presumably intended to differentiate an informal carer who had a relationship with the patient before the direct payment was set up from someone a who is brought in to act as a nominee in order to help manage the direct payment arrangement (and is probably paid for doing so). If the nominee is a company then reg 7(7)(b) requires the individual with 'overall responsibility for the day-to-day management of the patient's direct payments' to be approved.

14.83 If the health body decides not to approve the nominee and hence not to go ahead with a direct payment arrangement, the patient, any proposed representative and any proposed nominee must be informed and reasons for the decision must be given: see reg 7(10).

The care plan and the care plan co-ordinator

14.84 Regulation 7(3) of the DP Regs 2013 provides that the health body has to appoint a person to be a care co-ordinator whose functions are described above (see para 14.39 above). Regulation 8(4) provides that the care plan must specify the following:

(a) the health needs to be met by services secured by means of direct payments, and the health outcomes intended to be achieved through the provision of the services;
(b) the services to be secured by means of direct payments that the health body considers necessary to meet the health needs of the patient;
(c) the amount to be paid by way direct payments, and the intervals at which monies are to be paid;
(d) the name of the person who is the care co-ordinator in respect of the patient;
(e) who is to be responsible for monitoring each health condition of the patient in respect of which direct payments may be made;
(f) the anticipated date of the first review mentioned in regulation 14(2)(a) (monitoring and review of direct payments) and how it is intended to be carried out; and
(g) the period of notice that is to apply if, following a review under regulation 14(2)(a), a health body decides to reduce the amount of the direct payments or to stop making the direct payments.

14.85 The guidance explains the role of the care plan as follows:

> **5.1 Care Planning**
> 89. The care plan is at the heart of a personal health budget. Drawing up of a care plan should involve a series of discussions between the person receiving the care, their nominee or representative, their care coordinator . . . and the appropriate health and social care professionals involved in the individual's care. The personal health budget toolkit includes information and examples that provide CCGs with additional information on care planning.
>
> 90. Wherever possible, CCGs should work with local authorities and other healthcare providers to ensure that the person has a single plan covering their health and wellbeing needs across both the NHS and social care. This could include all the services and support provided, whether traditionally commissioned or through notional or third party budgets, as well as direct payments. For children with special educational needs and disabilities, who have a single education, health and care plan, this could also include their educational needs.
>
> 91. The regulations and thus the use of the term 'care plan' in this guidance only applies to that part of a person's care plan related to services purchased by direct payments for healthcare, although the principles are applicable to all ways of managing a personal health budget.
>
> 92. The care plan is an agreement between the CCG and the person receiving direct payments, and includes responsibilities on both sides. It is therefore vital that people are supported throughout the care planning

process. This will help ensure that they are able to make informed decisions in their best interests, and that they do not find the process overly burdensome or overwhelming. This support could take many forms – it may be from their healthcare professional, but some people may prefer an independent person to guide them through the process and liaise with the relevant parties. As with each aspect of personal health budgets, the best approach is to enable choice and not assume that the same option suits everyone. The personal health budget toolkit contains information and examples which will help CCGs and others consider the best ways for supporting their local population.

93. As a result of the care planning discussion, the care plan should clearly set out the health needs that the direct payment is to address. These may be reasonably broad, but it should be clear to both the CCG and the people involved what the direct payments are meant to achieve.

94. Having set out the health needs, the care plan should also set out the outcomes that are intended to be achieved. These may relate to both health and 'wellbeing' outcomes. CCGs have broad powers to address people's health and wellbeing needs, and a good care plan should address people's needs holistically.

95. Having set out the health needs and the intended outcomes, the care plan must specify the services to be secured by the direct payment in order to achieve these. This should be done in such a way to enable the CCG to be satisfied that the health needs and identified outcomes are likely to be met.

96. The CCG must make arrangements for the person, their representative or nominee to obtain information, advice or support in connection with the direct payments. These arrangements should be specified in the care plan and could be a service for which direct payments may be made'

14.86 The NHS England published materials include a useful handbook[23] on care planning for people with long-term conditions.

14.87 There is no requirement that a care plan has to propose funding for every service that a disabled person might have a need or which the patient may find helpful. The primary duty on NHS bodies is to provide services to meet the 'reasonable requirements' of a patient: see section 3(1) of the NHS Act 2006. The courts have repeatedly said that NHS commissioners are entitled to take the available budget into account in deciding what services it is reasonable for the NHS to provide. More details on this subject are set out in chapter 9 on commissioning and priority setting. However, health bodies should be careful to ensure that the care planning process provides patients with an equivalent level of service under a direct payment as can be secured by services that are directly commissioned. Any marked differential in levels of service could give rise to indirect discrimination claims.

14.88 Regulation 8 provides that the services described in the care plan should be those which the health body 'considers necessary to meet the health needs of the patient'. The reference in reg 8 to 'health needs' must mean the same as 'reasonable requirements' in section 3(1) of the NHS Act 2006.

23 See www.england.nhs.uk/wp-content/uploads/2016/04/core-info-care-support-planning–1.pdf.

Setting the budget for direct payments

14.89 Having described the services to be provided in the care plan, the health body then has to set the budget. Regulation 13 of the DP Regs 2013 provides:

> **13** (1) A health body must ensure that the amount of the direct payments paid to or in respect of a patient is sufficient to provide for the full cost of each of the services specified in the care plan.
>
> (2) Where a health body is notified, or becomes aware, that the state of health of the patient has changed significantly, but in the view of the health body a review mentioned in regulation 14 is not necessary, the health body must be satisfied that the amount of the direct payments continues to be sufficient in accordance with paragraph (1).
>
> (3) A health body may at any time increase or reduce the amount of the direct payments if satisfied that the new amount is sufficient in accordance with paragraph (1).
>
> (4) A health body may reduce the amount paid by way of direct payments by an amount not exceeding the amount due in respect of a period for which payment falls to be made where–
>
> (a) direct payments have been accumulated and remain unused; and
>
> (b) the health body considers that it is reasonable to offset the monies accumulated against the outstanding amount to be paid for that period.
>
> (5) Where a health body decides to reduce the amount of the direct payments, the health body must provide reasonable notice in writing to the patient, representative or nominee stating the reasons for the decision'

14.90 The DP Regs 2013 thus impose a requirement that the direct payment must be sufficient to meet the cost of all of the services set out in the care plan. This means that the CCG must satisfy itself that the patient, or those making decisions on behalf of the patient, is provided with sufficient money so that he or she will actually be able to purchase services to meet the needs set out in the care plan. Thus, by way of example, if the care plan includes the cost of a carer or a nurse for 20 hours per week, the health body needs to be satisfied that the direct payment will meet the full cost of employing one or more staff to provide those services. The direct payment will thus need to cover:

a) wages;
b) NI payments;
c) pension payments;
d) recruitment costs;
e) training costs;
f) insurance costs;
g) any consumables that the member of staff will use;
h) the administration of costs associated with employing staff; and
i) any other employment costs that will arise in a particular case.

14.91 The breadth of the costs that must be included in the budgeting is set out in the guidance, which provides:

> 117. Direct payments must be set at a level sufficient to cover the full cost of each of the services agreed in the care plan.
>
> 118. When calculating the budget, CCGs should ensure that they recognise the additional 'hidden' costs. For example, if someone is employing an

assistant, they must ensure that there is sufficient funding available to cover the additional necessary costs of employment such as tax, National Insurance, training and development, pension contributions, any necessary insurance such as public liability, emergency cover and so on.

119. Direct payments must cover the full cost of the care agreed in the care plan. However, they do not circumvent existing Government policy around additional private care. In no circumstances should the budget be set at a level where someone is expected to pay for care privately in order to meet their agreed health needs. If someone wishes to purchase additional care privately, they may do so, so long as it is additional to their assessed needs, and it is a separate episode of care, with clearly separate lines of clinical accountability and governance.

120. If the amount of a direct payment is not set at a suitable level, it must be reviewed and adjusted.

121. CCGs may wish to consider including a contingency fund in the direct payment, either for the individual or as part of a collective risk pool, to ensure that the budget is available to fully fund the care plan.

122. The personal health budget toolkit contains two budget setting documents which set out the learning from the pilot programme – one focuses on budget setting in NHS Continuing Healthcare and the other explores different methods used by pilot sites to set budgets beyond NHS Continuing Healthcare.

14.92 There is limited publicly accessible guidance on how health bodies should set budgets. In November 2012 the DOH published *Personal Health Budgets Guide – How to set budgets – early learning.*[24] However, the guidance is of marginal benefit as it only describes a series of methods that different primary care trusts (PCTs) developed within the pilot, without providing enough details to be of any real benefit to either patients or commissioners.

14.93 Some CCGs and local authorities have developed 'Resource Allocation Systems' (RAS) for setting the amounts of a direct payment. An RAS can be a useful tool for a CCG to work out the cost of the direct payment, provided the figures used to populate the RAS are realistic. Hence, for example, if a patient has a need for 20 hours of carer support at home, the care plan may suggest that the patient employs one or more carers to fulfil this role. The RAS can be helpful in setting the likely cost of employing a suitably trained carer and calculating the additional costs needed on top of wages. However, these costs need to be realistic costs that reflect the true costs employing the relevant service. The RAS cannot be moderated to reflect the amount of money that the health body is prepared to make available to support a service or the amount it considers it can afford.

The operation of a direct payment arrangement

14.94 Once a direct payment arrangement has been set up, payments will be made to the nominated bank account. Those payments must be used by

24 See www.personalhealthbudgets.england.nhs.uk/_library/Resources/Personalhealthbudgets/Toolkit/HowPHBwork/SettingBudget/Phb_guide_HowToSetBudgets.pdf.

the patient to purchase goods and services, as set out in the care plan. This is set out in reg 11(1) of the DP Regs 2013, which provides:

> A patient, representative or nominee must–
> (a) use the direct payments to procure services specified in the care plan;
> (b) only use the direct payments in accordance with the patient's care plan, in particular, to secure the provision of the whole of the services specified in the care plan.

14.95 There are two duties imposed by this regulation – the first is a positive duty and the second is a prohibition. The positive duty is under a combination of reg 11(1)(a) and the second half of the wording of reg 11(1)(b). This wording requires the patient or representative to use the money provided by the NHS to 'procure services specified in the care plan' and to 'secure the provision of the whole of the services so specified'. Even though the patient is a consultee concerning the care plan, responsibility for writing the care plan lies on the health body, not the patient. However once the care plan is written, the regulations require the patient (or representative) to agree that he or she will procure services precisely in accordance with the care plan. Thus, if the care plan states that the patient will have 20 hours' care worker support a week, the patient or representative takes on a legal duty to procure 20 hours' care support for the patient every week. The normal rule in healthcare is that the NHS has the duty to offer services to an NHS patient, but the patient has the right to accept or refuse the services. However, it is different for a patient who signs up to a direct payment arrangement because the regulations impose a positive duty on the patient (or the representative) to accept the whole range of services set out in the care plan.

14.96 The second part of reg 11(1) duty is a negative duty. The patient agrees that he or she will only use the direct payment money for procuring services in accordance with the care plan. This constitutes a legal bar on using the money provided by direct payment to fund any form of care for the patient or any benefit for the patient which is not set out in the care plan. This regulation removes any freedom for patients or their representative to use direct payment money in the way the patient or the representative considers most beneficial for the individual patient, save to the extent that these decisions are supported by the health body as part of the care plan. The wording of this regulation thus cuts across the freedom that a direct payment is supposed to give to the patient.

14.97 In practice, patients have a greater degree of freedom than the DP Regs 2013 suggest, because CCGs appear not to enforce their rights to re-charge patients if direct payment monies are used to procure services which are of benefit to the patient but are not precisely in accordance with the care plan. However, the strict legal position under the DP Regs 2013 is that a tight legal duty is imposed on the patient or representative to use the money provided to procure all of services set out in the plan and not to use a single penny to procure any other type of service.

14.98 The remainder of reg 11 of the DP Regs 2013 covers a variety of requirements to ensure that direct payment money is used appropriately. These are:

a) Regulation 11(2)(a)(i) requires any provider who is carrying out a 'regulated activity' under the reg 3 and Schedule 1 to the Health and Social Care Act 2008 (Regulated Activities) Regulations 2014 SI No 2936 is required to be registered with the Care Quality Commission (CQC). This provision does not apply to individual care staff who are employed by the patient but will apply where staff are employed by a domiciliary care agency. It is the agency which carries out the regulated activity and thus needs to be registered.
b) Regulation 11(2)(a)(ii) provides that the patient must ascertain that any individual providing services to the patient is registered with the relevant professional body. Hence, for example, the patient must check to ensure that any nurses employed or engaged in providing services must be registered with the Nursing and Midwifery Council (NMC) and physiotherapists are registered with the Health and Care Professions Council (HCPC).
c) Regulation 11(2)(a)(iii) is about professional indemnity insurance. It requires the patient to find out whether a provider is under a legal duty to maintain appropriate professional indemnity insurance.

14.99 Regulation 11(3) allows the patient or a representative to ask the health body to carry out the checks required under reg 11(2). Hence, in the usual case, the patient can ask the CCG to find out the regulatory status of an provider and whether any provider has appropriate insurance.

Monitoring and reporting on changes in the health of the patient

14.100 The care plan is only appropriate for a patient if it is up to date. A patient who has an improving, fluctuating or deteriorating condition may well find that the support set out in a care plan becomes out of date because it either provides too much or, more likely, too little support as the patient's medical condition changes. The health body has a duty under reg 14 of the DP Regs 2013 to monitor the making of direct payments and the 'health conditions of the patient in respect of which direct payments are made'. In addition to the duty of regular monitoring, the health body has a duty to conduct a review at appropriate intervals which must be at least:

a) within the first three months after the direct payment arrangement is set up; and
b) annually thereafter (see reg 14(2)).

14.101 A patient can request a review and, if a request is made, the health body has a duty to consider whether to carry out a review: see reg 14(7). The health body is not required to carry out a review on every occasion on which a request is made. However, if the patient or a representative provides information which suggests that the direct payment is insufficient to purchase sufficient services to meet the patient's reasonable needs, the health body probably has a duty to carry out a review in order to determine whether the care plan and budget properly meets the patient's reasonable needs.

14.102 The relevant information about the patient will be held by the patient and those caring for him or her and not by the CCG or NHS England. Although this is patient sensitive personal data and is legally confidential information, the patient has a duty to provide any information that the health body requests about:

a) the state of health or any condition of the patient in respect of which the direct payment is made; or
b) the health outcomes expected from the provision of any service: see reg 11(4).

14.103 There is a specific duty to consider carrying out a review if the health body becomes aware that the state of health of the patient has changed significantly: see reg 14(3). A health body is not required to carry out a review on every occasion where there is a significant change, but has a duty to consider whether to do so. In contrast, there is a duty to carry out a review if the health body 'becomes aware' that the direct payments have not been sufficient to secure the services specified in the care plan: see reg 14(4). This duty may arise where the patient's health means that he or she has a greater need for services. However, it can also arise if the health body is aware that local factors mean that the patient cannot, in practice, purchase the services he or she needs for the sum of money provided by direct payments. Hence, if the care plan and budget is based on a cost of employing a care worker for £X per hour, but the local market conditions mean that care workers cannot be employed on a secure basis at a cost of less than £Y per hour, the health body has the duty to carry out a review and will be obliged to increase the budget to meet the real cost of employing a care worker.

14.104 Regulation 14(5) sets out the matters that the health body is required to consider as part of a review. As part of every review the health body must:

a) review the care plan to establish whether it continues to provide appropriately for the health needs of the patient;
b) consider whether the direct payments have been used effectively;
c) consider whether the amount of the direct payments paid to or in respect of the patient is sufficient to provide for the full cost of each of the services specified in the care plan; and
d) consider whether the patient, representative or nominee has complied with the obligations imposed on them by or under reg 11.

14.105 Regulation 14(6) sets out a series of steps that health body may take as part of a review (but which are not required to be part of every review). These steps are:

> (a) re-assess the health needs of the patient for services to be secured by way of direct payments;
> (b) consult any of the persons mentioned in regulation 7(2)(a) or (3)(a) to (c) or, where relevant, (e) (consultation by a health body in relation to a decision to make a direct payment to or in respect of a patient);
> (c) review receipts, bank statements or other information relating to the use of the direct payments;
> (d) consider whether the direct payments have been effectively managed, including whether any provider of services secured by means of the direct payments–

(i) if carrying on a regulated activity, is registered as a service provider in respect of that activity with the Care Quality Commission,
(ii) has complied with any obligation that the provider has to be registered as a member of a profession regulated by a body mentioned in section 25(3) of the 2002 Act, or
(iii) operates under insurance or indemnity cover which is proportionate to the risks involved in providing the service and otherwise appropriate in relation to the services provided to the patient'

14.106 The actions that a health body can take following a review are set out in reg 14(8) as follows:

(8) Following a review, a health body may, having regard to the purposes of the care plan and the consultations and enquiries under regulation 7–
(a) amend the care plan;
(b) substitute the patient for the nominee or representative of the patient, or substitute a representative or nominee for the patient, as the person to whom the direct payments are made;
(c) increase, maintain or reduce the amount of the direct payments;
(d) impose on the patient, representative or nominee either or both of the following conditions in connection with the making of direct payments–
(i) the recipient, whether the patient, their representative or their nominee, must not secure a service from a particular person, or
(ii) the patient, their representative or their nominee must provide information that the health body considers necessary other than as described at regulation 7(2)(b), (4)(a) or (6)(c) (information that can be required in relation to a decision to make a direct payment) or regulation 11(4), (7) or (8)(b) (conditions relating to information that are to be complied with by the patient, representative or nominee); or
(e) take other action that the health body considers appropriate.

14.107 The health body has wide powers to act following a review. These powers include making changes to the care plan, making changes to the amount of direct payments and changing the decision-maker. The health body could decide that a particular care worker or agency should not be employed and paid for under direct payments including, for example, a family member who appears to be failing to provide appropriate care to the patient. The final general power allows the health body to take such other action in relation to the direct payment arrangement as the health body considers appropriate.

14.108 There are, however, probably three restrictions on the types of action that a health body can take under this regulation. First, there are specific conditions under reg 17 that must be satisfied before the health body can take the decision to stop the direct payments. Hence, any decision to stop the direct payments altogether ought to be by exercising the powers under reg 17 and not by the exercise of the general power under reg 14(8)(e). Second, the range of actions that the health body can lawfully take under reg 14(8)(e) is limited to actions of the same kind as the actions listed in reg 14(8)(a)–(d) as a result of the 'ejusdem generis' rule. Third, the health body can only use this power to take actions which promote the overall purpose of the health service and the management of direct payments in particular, and must respect the human rights of the patient. Hence if, for example, the health body considers that the patient's health would be likely to improve significantly if the patient consented to have a particular surgical operation or agreed to take a particular pharmaceutical drug, the powers under reg 14(8) could not be used to require the patient to undergo that procedure even if the result would be an improvement in the patient's health and hence a reduction in the level of the direct payment.

14.109 If the health body decides to stop the direct payments after a review (by exercising the reg 17 powers) or to reduce the direct payments, the health body is required to give the patient or a representative written reasons for its decision: see reg 14(9). The patient can respond to the decision to stop or reduce direct payments by requiring the health body to carry out a further review: see reg 14(10). Although there is no express requirement in the DP Regs 2013 to have any such review carried out by a different person to the original decision-maker, there is a strong argument that the duty to carry out a 'review' could only be validly discharged in practice by having a different decision-maker looking at the case. Thus, when asked to review a decision, health bodies will protect their own positions by setting up systems to ensure that any review under the DP Regs 2013 is carried out by someone other than the original decision-maker.

14.110 The health body must give reasons for the outcome of a further review (see reg 14(11)), but if that review decides to uphold the decision, there is no right for the patient to request a third review (see reg 14(12)).

Decisions to reduce or stop direct payments

14.111 A direct payment arrangement may seem a good idea to a patient or those who care for a patient but these arrangements do not always work out well in practice. The patient or the representative takes on considerable administrative responsibilities and some patients find that the burdens of taking on the arrangements do not justify the benefits that the arrangements provide. Equally, a health body has to ensure that the public money which is provided under a direct payment arrangement is being used properly and that there is a sufficient level of accountability in the arrangements. The health body also needs to be confident that appropriate clinical governance is being maintained, particularly where the decisions are being made for the patient by a representative. Hence a decision to terminate a direct payment arrangement can come from either the patient (or representative) or the health body.

14.112 The health body has the power to reduce the direct payment if the circumstances come within under reg 13(4) of the DP Regs 2013. This provides:

> A health body may reduce the amount paid by way of direct payments by an amount not exceeding the amount due in respect of a period for which payment falls to be made where–
> (a) direct payments have been accumulated and remain unused; and
> (b) the health body considers that it is reasonable to offset the monies accumulated against the outstanding amount to be paid for that period.

Where a health body decides to reduce the direct payment for a period it must give a written notice to the patient or representative setting out its reasons for taking this decision.

14.113 The health body has powers to stop a direct payment arrangement under reg 17. Regulation 17(1) provides that the health body must stop the direct payment arrangement if:

a) the patient (other than a child under the age of 16) has capacity and withdraws his or her consent to the direct payment arrangement;
b) the representative withdraws consent and there is no other representative who can consent to replace the existing representative;
c) the child reaches the age of 16 and does not consent to the direct payment arrangement continuing (see regs 4(4)(b) and regs 17(1)(c)); or
d) the patient lacked capacity when the direct payment arrangement was set up but has now regained capacity and not consent to the direct payment arrangement continuing (see regs 5(8)(b) and regs 17(1)(c)).

14.114 Regulation 17 does not specifically provide that a health body is required to stop a direct payment arrangement if the patient comes within the categories of persons who cannot have a direct payment, as listed in the Schedule to the Regulations. However, reg 3(3)(c) provides that direct payments may not be made to a person who is within the category of persons set out in the Schedule (see para 14.75 above for details of the excluded persons). Thus, once a person comes within the category of persons in the Schedule the health body has no vires to continue the direct payment arrangement and must cancel it. The health body is also required to cease to operate a direct payment arrangement with a representative who comes within the terms of the Schedule because there is no vires to continue to operate direct payments with that person as a representative: see regs 4(1)(b) and 5(1)(b).

14.115 Regulation 17(2) gives a health body a general power to stop the direct payment arrangement and sets out a number of circumstances in which a health body may wish to consider whether to do so. It provides:

> A health body may stop making direct payments if satisfied that it is appropriate to do so and in particular if–
> (a) a person in respect of whom a direct payment is made is not a patient;
> (b) the health body does not consider that the representative or nominee is a suitable person to receive direct payments in respect of the patient;
> (c) the nominee does not agree to receive the direct payments in respect of the patient;
> (d) the person who has nominated the nominee pursuant to regulation 6(1) (nominated person) has withdrawn the nomination;
> (e) the direct payments have been used otherwise than for a service specified in the care plan;
> (f) the health body considers that theft, fraud or another offence may have occurred in connection with the direct payments;
> (g) the health body considers that the health needs of the patient cannot be, or are not being, met by services secured by means of direct payments; or
> (h) the patient has died.

14.116 The health body has a duty to give reasons to the patient or the patient's representative when a direct payment arrangement is stopped: see reg 17(3). Notice must be given to the personal representative if the patient dies, although it is not clear to whom notice must be given if the patient dies intestate and no personal representative is appointed. The patient or representative has the same rights to seek a reconsideration as when payments are reduced (see para 14.112 above).

14.117 When a decision is taken to stop payments, the health body is required to give 'reasonable notice' before the decision takes effect: see reg 17(8). The period of notice will depend on the circumstances and the reasons for the decision to stop the direct payments. However, the guidance notes as follows:

> In some cases, it may be necessary to stop the direct payment immediately, for example if fraud or theft has occurred. In these cases, 'reasonable notice' may include immediate termination of the direct payment. In these circumstances, the CCG should endeavor (*sic*) to protect public money as far as possible, whilst being mindful that they are still under a duty to provide healthcare if the individual requires it. No person should ever be denied the care they need. Where possible, CCGs should also endeavour to continue to provide a personalised service and maintain a continuity of care. For example, an independent user trust could be established to manage the budget or the CCG could directly commission the services agreed in the care plan.

14.118 Regulation 17(9) and (10) execute a formal assignment of contractual and employment liabilities from the patient to the health body at the point that a direct payment arrangement is brought to an end. These regulations provide:

> (9) Any right or liability of the patient, personal representatives, representative or nominee in respect of or to a third party, acquired or incurred in respect of a service secured by means of a direct payment, shall transfer to a health body when the health body stops making direct payments pursuant to paragraph (1) or (2).
>
> (10) The transfer of any liability under paragraph (9) is binding on the third party, even though, apart from this paragraph, it would have required the consent or concurrence of that party.

14.119 Thus any person who is employed by the patient under a direct payment becomes an employee of the health body at the point that a direct payment arrangement ceases. Equally, any contracts to which the patient was a party transfer to the health body. Unwinding a direct payment arrangement could thus give rise to some difficult decisions for health bodies because, for example, a health body would need to consider whether there was any suitable alternative employment available for an employee before making a care worker redundant. That could lead to a duty on the health body to offer an employee work to support another patient before an employee could be fairly dismissed. Equally, the health body is required to take over the contractual liability liable under contracts with domiciliary care agencies or other providers even though the health body never signed up to those contracts in the first place.

14.120 It is slightly strange that the health body only has a power but not a duty to stop the direct payment arrangement if the patient dies. The death of the patient will, of course, mean that the patient no longer has any health needs and thus has no need for services. However, unwinding the employment and support arrangements which had been set up for the patient may incur some costs and take some time. The health body probably has a power but not a duty to bring the direct payment arrangement to an immediate end so as to allow it to continue the arrangement with a representative for a short period so as to allow contracts to be terminated and employees to be made redundant while the direct payment arrangement remains operative. That would prevent any contractual or employment liabilities being transferred to the health body. However, save to the extent needed to wind up the arrangements, the health body has no vires to continue the arrangement after the death of the patient and so should terminate the arrangements as quickly as possible.

14.121 One of the main circumstances in which a direct payment is stopped in practice is when a patient with a chronic condition moves from his or her home into full-time care in a hospital, care home or other institution. In such a case, the justification for the direct payment no longer exists and the direct payment arrangement will usually come to an end (as opposed to being used to pay the care home fees).

When can a health body seek repayment of direct payments?

14.122 The DP Regs 2013 give wide powers to the health body to seek repayment of monies which have been paid to a patient or the patient's representative. There is a general power in reg 15(1) to seek repayment in the following terms:

> A health body may require that part or all of a direct payment must be repaid to the health body, if satisfied that it is appropriate to require repayment having regard in particular to whether–
> (a) the care plan has changed substantially;
> (b) the patient's circumstances have changed substantially;
> (c) a substantial proportion of the direct payments received by a patient, representative or nominee have not been used to secure services specified in the care plan and have accumulated;
> (d) the direct payments have been used otherwise than for a service specified in the care plan;
> (e) theft, fraud or another offence may have occurred in connection with the direct payments; or
> (f) the patient has died.

14.123 These wide powers appear to give the health body the right to make the decision that money should be repaid even the direct payment money has been used to employ care workers to provide services to the patient in accordance with the care plan. The only absolute condition that needs to be satisfied before a repayment claim can be made is that the health body is satisfied that it is 'appropriate' that all or part of a direct payment should be repaid. However, the guidance suggests this power should be used more sparingly. The guidance states:

> 138. CCGs should be aware that genuine errors can occur. The power to reclaim direct payments should not be used to penalise people for making mistakes or when the individual has been the victim of fraud.

> 139. If a substantial amount of money accumulates in the individual's account due to an underspend for any reason, the CCG should consider whether it is appropriate to reclaim that money. In some circumstances, it may be more appropriate to simply reduce subsequent direct payments, factoring in the existing surplus. CCGs should also assess the reasons for the build up of the surplus as part of the review process – either the individual is not receiving the care they need or too much money was allocated.
>
> 140. When reclaiming money from someone with a representative or nominee, the CCG should approach the person holding the money, rather than the individual receiving care. The CCG should also ensure that, as far as possible, the person receiving care is also aware of their intention, and the reasons for this.
>
> 141. When reclaiming money from the estate of someone who has died, the CCG must approach the personal representatives of the individual to seek repayment. They should do so sensitively, and may wish to leave a period of grace to allow the executors of the will to ensure the estate is in order. The CCG should bear in mind that if the person, their representative or nominee was an employer, their employees will have employment rights, which may include a paid period of notice or redundancy payment.

14.124 This seems sensible guidance, with the possible exception of the guidance in para 141 which does not appear to have taken account of the effect of the transfer of rights and liabilities under reg 17(9). Employees of the patient become employees of the health body on the stopping of the direct payment arrangement and thus, following the stopping of a direct payment arrangement, any redundancy notices should be given by the health body and not by the patient's estate (unless the health body continues the direct payment to the extent necessary to allow the estate to wind up these arrangements).

14.125 A health body must comply with the procedural requirements set out at reg 15(2) of the DP Regs 2013 when making a decision to seek repayment. This regulation provides:

> Where a health body decides under paragraph (1) that a sum must be repaid, the health body must give reasonable notice in writing to the patient and any representative or nominee, stating–
> (a) the reasons for the decision;
> (b) the amount to be repaid;
> (c) the time within which the sum must be repaid; and
> (d) the person who must repay.

14.126 The person who is required to make the repayment is entitled to ask for a review under reg 15 in the same way as a review can be sought if the amount of the direct payment is reduced or the direct payment is stopped. A health body should arrange for the decision-maker who conducts the review to be a different person to the original decision-maker or there is probably no proper compliance with the duty to carry out a review.

14.127 The regulations give an express power to the health body to waive any requirement that a sum be repaid: see reg 15(7). This power can only be exercised after a decision has been made to seek repayment (whether communicated to the patient or not). Hence, if a patient or representative asks the health body to exercise this power, the health body has a duty to do so and must consider whether to waive a repayment or not to do so. If the health body informs the patient or a representative that it has made a decision to waive a repayment, it would face considerable legal difficulties in attempting to reverse that decision, because the statement that the repayment claim was being waived may well have given rise to a legitimate expectation that no repayment would be sought, and that legitimate expectation could be enforced by the patient or representative.

14.128 Where monies are owing by the patient or representative, and the health body considers that there may have been theft, fraud or any other criminal offence, it is entitled to take summary proceedings to enforce this right to collect monies it has decided to reclaim. This right is set out at reg 16 of the DP Regs 2013, which provides:

> (1) Where a sum must be repaid to a health body pursuant to regulation 15 and the reasons for the decision to require repayment is that theft, fraud or another offence may have occurred in connection with a direct payment, that sum may be recovered summarily as a civil debt.
> (2) Paragraph (1) does not affect any other method of recovery.

14.129 It follows that there are two different means open to a health body which seeks to recover monies paid under a direct payment arrangement. First, if the reason for the repayment demand is that there may have been 'theft, fraud or another offence', the health body has the right to recover the sum summarily. It is not necessary for the health body to provide that there has, been in fact, any theft, fraud or another offence. It is only necessary for the health body to show:

a) there may have been theft, fraud or another offence; and
b) this was the reason why the health body made the decision to issue a recovery notice.

14.130 The procedure for summary recovery is set out at section 58(1) of the Magistrates' Courts Act 1980 which provides:

> A magistrates' court shall have power to make an order on complaint for the payment of any money recoverable summarily as a civil debt.

14.131 Once the magistrates' court has made an order that the health body recovers a specified sum, the sum is payable pursuant to the terms of the order made by the magistrates' court. Once the order is made, there are a variety of enforcement methods available to the health body.

14.132 In any case, where the reason for the repayment demand is not that there may have been theft, fraud or another offence, or where the health body elects not to use the summary procedure route, the health body has the right to issue debt proceedings in the county court. Although this is untested territory, it is probable that a person against whom proceedings are issued has the right to challenge the lawfulness of the decision (on public law grounds) to require the repayment. Hence there could be a 'judicial review' trial of the reasonableness or other alleged unlawfulness of the decision to impose the payment in the county court: see *Wandsworth LBC v Winder (No 1)*.[25]

25 [1984] UKHL 2.

Direct payments rules for patients in receipt of NHS Continuing Healthcare or Continuing Care for Children

14.133 The categories of patients who are eligible for NHS Continuing Healthcare or Continuing Care for Children are discussed elsewhere. However, there are special rules relating to direct payments and the management of budgets for any patients who are eligible for NHS Continuing Healthcare or Continuing Care for Children. There are subtle legal differences between the direct payment rights for patients who are eligible for NHS Continuing Healthcare or Continuing Care for Children and the legal rights of all other patients. It is too early to tell whether these will make any difference in practice but it seems unlikely that they will have any real impact.

14.134 The rules for eligible for patients who are eligible for NHS Continuing Healthcare or Continuing Care for Children are set out in reg 32B of the RSR Regs 2012. This regulation, which took effect from 1 April 2014, provides:

(1) A relevant body must ensure that it is able to arrange for the provision of a relevant health service to an eligible person by means of a personal health budget which is managed in accordance with paragraph (2).

(2) A personal health budget must be managed in at least one of the following ways–
  (a) the making of a direct payment;
  (b) the application of the personal health budget by the relevant body in accordance with the outcome of discussions with the eligible person or that person's representative as to how best to secure the provision of the relevant health service to the person; or
  (c) the transfer of the personal health budget by a relevant body to a person who applies the money in accordance with the outcome of discussions with the eligible person or that person's representative as to how best, with the agreement of the relevant body, to secure the provision of the relevant health service to the eligible person.

(3) A relevant body must–
  (a) publicise and promote the availability of personal health budgets to eligible persons and their representatives; and
  (b) provide information, advice and other support to eligible persons and their representatives to assist them in deciding whether to request a personal health budget in respect of a relevant health service.

(4) A relevant body must–
  (a) give due consideration to a request made by or on behalf of an eligible person for a personal health budget;
  (b) decide whether it is appropriate in the circumstances of the eligible person's case to arrange for the provision of the relevant health service to that person by means of a personal health budget; and
  (c) if it decides that it would be appropriate, decide which of the ways mentioned in paragraph (2) would be the most appropriate way in which to manage the personal health budget.

(5) A relevant body must make arrangements for eligible persons for whom a personal health budget has been arranged, and their representatives, to obtain information, advice and other support in connection with the management of the personal health budget.

(6) The duty in paragraph (5) does not apply in relation to any part of a personal health budget to which regulation 9 of the National Health Service (Direct Payments) Regulations 2013 (information, advice and other support) applies.

(7) If a relevant body decides to refuse a request for a personal health budget made by or on behalf of an eligible person, it must provide that person and their representatives with the reasons for that decision in writing.

(8) On receipt of written reasons in accordance with paragraph (7), an eligible person or a person acting on the eligible person's behalf may require a relevant body to undertake a review of the decision and may provide evidence or information for the relevant body to consider as part of that review.

(9) A relevant body must inform the eligible person or their representatives in writing of the decision following a review, and state the reasons for the decision.

(10) A relevant body may not be required to undertake more than one review following a decision under paragraph (7) in any six month period.

14.135 In September 2014, NHS England issued guidance about reg 32B of the RSR Regs 2012 called *Guidance on the 'right to have' a personal health budget in Adult NHS Continuing Care Healthcare and Children and Young People's Continuing Care.*[26] While the guidance speaks of a 'right' to a personal health budget, a close examination of the regulations shows that an eligible patient does not have any legal rights to a health budget. Regulation 32A(1) provides that the health body (ie a CCG or NHS England) has to ensure that it is *able* to arrange for the provision of a relevant health service to an eligible person by means of a personal health budget which is managed in accordance with para (2). Hence, the regulation imposes a duty on the CCG and NHS England to have decision-making systems in place to ensure that it is *able* to offer a health budget by any of the means set out at reg 32A(2). It does not provide that a patient who is eligible for NHS Continuing Healthcare or Continuing Care for Children has a legal right to have a direct payment. However, the guidance makes it clear that CCGs ought to provide a personal health budget (via one of the options) to eligible patients. It states:

> If an individual comes within the scope of the 'right to have' a personal health budget, as outlined in section 4 above, then the expectation is that one will be provided.
>
> There may be some exceptional circumstances when a CCG considers a personal health budget to be an impracticable or inappropriate way of securing NHS care for an individual. This could be due to the specialised clinical care required or because a personal health budget would not represent value for money as any additional benefits to the individual would not outweigh the extra cost to the NHS. However, evidence from the pilot and learning from CCGs that are already rolling out personal health budgets in these areas suggests that there will be few cases where a personal health budget cannot be provided.

26 See www.personalhealthbudgets.england.nhs.uk/_library/Resources/Personalhealthbudgets/2014/Personal_health_budgets_right_to_have_guidance.pdf.

14.136 However, many patients in residential care are eligible for NHS Continuing Healthcare. The guidance makes it clear that a personal health budget would not be appropriate for such patients. It provides:

> **Can personal health budgets be provided to people in nursing/residential care home settings?**
> The Government's intention is for all people receiving NHS CHC or CC to have the 'right to have' a personal health budget where they would benefit.
>
> The National Health Service (Direct Payments) Regulations 2013 and 'right to have' announcement do not explicitly limit this to people living in their own homes. Individuals assessed as eligible for NHS CHC or CC funding may live in nursing or residential care and they too may benefit from receiving care via a personal health budget.
>
> Where a request for a direct payment for healthcare is made for a person living in a residential setting the CCG must be certain that providing care in this way adds value to the person's overall care. Generally, direct payments should not be used to pay for care and support services being commissioned by the NHS that a person will continue to access in the same way whether they have a personal health budget or not. In such instances, where no additional choice or flexibility has been achieved by giving someone a personal health budget, then allocating a direct payment only adds an additional financial step and layer of bureaucracy into the commissioning of the care.
>
> CCGs need to be clear that the use of a direct payment in such settings is cost effective and is a sensible way to provide care to meet or improve the individual's agreed outcomes.
>
> The use of direct payments for adults within residential settings was not tested as part of the personal health budget pilot and the benefits of providing care in this way are not known. There is a pilot programme underway in residential settings considering the use of direct payments for personal budgets in social care and the Department of Health will use the learning and evidence from this programme to inform guidance. This will then be used to support the introduction of direct payments for people receiving social care and living in residential care from April 2016.
>
> Learning from the residential care pilot will help inform national policy developments in the NHS around the use of direct payments in residential settings. In the meantime, although there is no prohibition on using direct payments for those in residential care, CCGs should be cautious about offering a personal health budget in this form.
>
> Other types of personal health budget, for example notional budgets, can be used where direct payments are not a practical route and many people may find great benefit in planning their care using the personalised care planning process associated with developing a personal health budget'

14.137 No steps have yet been taken to introduce direct payments for people receiving social care and living in residential care. It is unclear if this is still government policy or whether further regulations will be made in the future to carry forward this policy.

14.138 Where a health body does agree to provide a personal health budget, there are three ways in which a personal health budget can be delivered. The three options are identified at reg 32A(2), namely:

a) A direct payment arrangement in accordance with the DP Regs 2013. If this is set up for an NHS Continuing Care Healthcare patient or for a representative where a child is in receipt of Children and Young People's Continuing Care, it will operate in the same way as any other direct payment arrangement.

b) A 'notional' personal health budget set by the health body in accordance with the outcome of discussions with the eligible person or that person's representative as to how best to secure the provision of the relevant health service to the person. This is described in the guidance as:[27]

> A notional budget – where the commissioner (for example the CCG) holds the budget but utilises it to secure services bases on the outcome of discussions with the service user.

c) The third option is to make a direct payment to a person who applies the money in accordance with the outcome of discussions with the eligible person or that person's representative as to how best, with the agreement of the relevant body, to secure the provision of the relevant health service to the eligible person. This is described as follows in the guidance:[28]

> A third party budget – where an organisation independent of the individual and the NHS manages the budget on the individual's behalf and arranges support by purchasing services in line with the agreed care plan.

14.139 The RSR Regs 2012 do not define the types of services that are required to be included in a 'personal health budget'. However, the guidance suggests that these should be the same services that could be part of a direct payment arrangement (and should not include services that are excluded from a direct payment arrangement. The guidance states:[29]

> Personal health budgets are not appropriate for all types of healthcare. There are particular exclusions for their use where the personal health budget is received as a direct payment and a full list can be found in the National Health Service (Direct Payments) Regulations 2013. Although the regulations refer specifically to direct payments, for consistency and good practice the exclusions should be applied to all types of personal health budgets.

14.140 The guidance suggests that the third option should be limited to circumstances where an independent third party organisation acts as a commissioner of healthcare for the patient, in accordance with the outcome of discussions with the patient or the patient's representative as to how best, with the agreement of the health body, to secure the provision of the relevant health service to the eligible person. The need for the health body to 'agree' the provision means that the health body has the final say as to how NHS money should be used. It is thus difficult to see that this option adds anything substantial to the direct payment arrangements. The governance arrangements under this option are also not spelled out in the RSR Regs 2012.

14.141 The changes to the RSR Regs 2012 appear to have been driven by a desire by the government to increase the take up in direct payment arrangements for patients who are eligible for NHS Continuing Healthcare or Continuing Care for Children. However badging this as a case where a

27 At para 3.2.
28 At para 32.
29 At para 5 (p12).

patient has a 'right' to a personal health budget is misleading the RSR Regs 2012 do not create a right for a patient to have a personal health budget. However the RSR Regs 2012 may have caused a change in practice by emphasising the normality of direct payment arrangements for patients with long-term conditions.

Legal issues that can arise with direct payments

14.142 There are several legal issues that can arise as part of care planning under direct payment arrangements. The following particular legal issues can arise:

a) the employment of family members;
b) top-ups, wealthy patients and patients with substantial damages payments; and
c) whether to support a direct payment to for a home care package or commission a care home placement.

These are discussed in turn below.

The employment and payment of family members as part of the care plan

14.143 Section 3(1) of the Children Act 1989 defines the term 'parental responsibility' as meaning 'all the rights, duties, powers, responsibilities and authority which by law a parent of a child has in relation to the child and his property'. However, a general parental duty to 'look after' a child cannot amount to a legal duty to provide 24-hour, seven-day-a-week specialist medical care to a disabled child.

14.144 Many parents of disabled children become 'expert carers'. Their exposure to the child's medical condition over an extended period, their own interaction with doctors, nurses and care staff and seeing the first-hand effects of different treatment regimes means parents (or those standing in the place of parents such as foster carers) can become as knowledgeable about their child's condition as any formally qualified medical professional. This can both be a source of high-quality care but also, on rare occasions, a serious risk to the health of the child, particularly if parents provide treatment for their child which deviates significantly from established clinical practice.

14.145 If parents are delivering far more care than they could be called upon to provide as part of their parental responsibilities, there is no reason in principle why the NHS should not permit a direct payment to be used to pay a parent for delivering these services. Parents of disabled children often give up jobs or forgo career advancement in order to free up time to provide round the clock care to a disabled child. If the parent did not provide these services, a non-family carer would have to be employed to provide care to a child in place of a family member. However, where the family member knows the child far better, it is often possible for the family member to deliver excellent care in place of external carers. Further, keeping the family finances afloat is plainly in the child's best interests and can be in the

NHS's interests, particularly if payment to the parents keeps the household viable and thus avoids the need for an expensive care home package.

14.146 The position with adults patients is more straightforward. Family members may have a moral duty to support adults in their family, but there is no legal duty to do so. Prior to the National Assistance Act 1948, the Poor Law schemes placed a legal duty on families to provide care and support to a wide range of relatives. The only people who ended up in the workhouse were those who had no relatives who could be prevailed upon to support them. However, that all changed in 1948 when the legal duty to support family members was abolished. Despite the absence of a legal duty, many disabled adults receive care and support from their family members, including parents of disabled adults and those caring for a disabled parent. The observations above about parents looking after disabled children apply equally to the care of adults by family members. At its best, it can be superb levels of care and, at its worst, it can be inadequate care where the control of the property prevents the NHS being able to deliver on its duties to the patient. The 'best case' scenario is far, far more common than the worst case scenario.

14.147 However, the paid employment of family members to provide care to an NHS patient gives rise to some difficult issues and tricky conflicts of interest which need to be managed carefully. A paid member of the family becomes someone who is paid by public funds to deliver a care service, and is thus accountable for the services that the carer provides. He or she can be required to follow care protocols and make proper notes, when that may not be the case where care is unpaid. On 14 October 2013 the DP Regs 2013 were amended by the National Health Service (Direct Payments) (Amendment) Regulations 2013[30] to provide specific provisions concerning the employment of family members. The provisions were further changed by the National Health Service (Direct Payments) (Amendment) Regulations 2017.[31] The relevant provisions now read:

> (5A) A health body may specify in a care plan that a service may be secured in respect of a patient from a connected person only if a health body is satisfied that to secure a service from that person is necessary–
> (a) to meet satisfactorily the patient's need for that service; or
> (b) to promote the welfare of a patient who is a child.
> (5B) In paragraph (5A), 'connected person' in relation to a patient means any of the following who lives in the same household as the patient whether or not the person is a nominee–
> (a) a family member mentioned in regulation 7(8); or
> (b) a friend of the patient.

14.148 Thus a person 'in the same household as the patient' who is a friend or family member can only be employed to provide services to the patient if the test in (5A)(a) or (b) is met and provided the person is specified in the care plan. In this context, the word 'necessary' probably does not mean 'essential so no other option is possible' but 'appropriate and proportionate' in all the circumstances of the case. The guidance says as follows about the employment of family members (although this says little more than reproduce the wording of the regulations):

30 SI No 2354.
31 SI No 219.

153) A direct payment can only be used to pay an individual living in the same household, a close family member (see Box 3 for a definition of a 'close family member'[32]) or a friend if the CCG is satisfied that to secure a service from that person is necessary in order to satisfactorily meet the person receiving care's need for that service; or to promote the welfare of a child for whom direct payments are being made. CCGs will need to make these judgements on a case by case basis.

154) These restrictions are not intended to prevent people from using their direct payments to employ a live-in personal assistant, provided that person is not someone who would usually be excluded by the regulations. The restriction applies where the relationship between the two people is primarily personal rather than contractual, for example if the people concerned would be living together in any case.

14.149 The test introduced by the amended regulations is, in practice, pretty meaningless. A care co-ordinator could almost always conclude that it is necessary for an appropriate family member or friend to be employed to provide support to a patient. Equally, if the care co-ordinator concluded that it was inappropriate for a family member or friend to be employed to provide support to a patient, care for the patient from that person should not be included in the care plan. If a proposal is made to pay a family member or friend to provide care the health body may wish to pay particular attention to this proposal as part of its consultations.

14.150 There are a series of governance issues which arise where family members are providing paid care to a patient as part of NHS funded care, including:

a) *Should there be separation of the 'representative' and the paid carer:* There is nothing in the DP Regs 2013 which prevents the representative also being paid to provide care to the patient. The representative could not be 'employed' because he or she would be both the employer and the employee. He or she would thus have to be a self-employed carer and would be responsible for his or her own income tax and NI payments. The direct payment should also allow funds to enable the representative to make pension arrangements in the same way as if the representative were an employee. In order to ensure conflicts of interest are properly managed, the care plan should set out clearly that the representative will be employed and should detail the level of payment to be made to the representative.
b) *The need for proper contracts of employment:* Family members (other than any representative) should be provided with proper contracts of employment by the patient or the representative. The contract should set out the responsibilities on both sides.
c) *Adherence to professionally agreed care plans:* Family members who are paid to provide care to a vulnerable patient should be asked to confirm that they will provide care in accordance with the care plan and will follow any protocols set up by professional medical staff for the patient. Where a home care package is working well, professionals and family members will pool their knowledge and skills to devise care plans. However, once protocols are agreed, the health body needs to know that family members will provide appropriate care, and that normally

32 The box refers to the list of close family members in reg 7(8).

means agreeing to provide care in accordance with protocols devised under the care plan.

d) *Suitable amounts of time off and holidays:* The health body should be cautious to ensure that a family member does not agree to take on an excessive workload and that proper arrangements are put in place to allow time off for the family member, with funded respite care if needed. It has to be in the interests of all parties that any direct payment is a long-term, sustainable arrangement, and this will require a key family member having time away from delivering care.
e) *Record-keeping:* Professional care staff keep records of the care provided to a patient. If family members are paid by the NHS to provide care, the health body needs to reach agreement with the family member about how records will be made about the number of hours that a family member provides care and the material events that occur during any period when care is provided.
f) *Insurance:* Care staff should be insured for the mutual benefit of themselves and the patient. Family members who provide care should be in the same position, with appropriate insurance funded by the direct payment.
g) *Reviews and the suitability of a home care placement:* The existence of an income for family members from a direct payment will inevitably mean that the family finances will become dependent on the continuance of this source of revenue. If a patient has a progressive condition, there may come a time when a care home placement is more clinically appropriate but some family members may be understandably reluctant to agree to this because, in part, it will lead to cessation of the direct payment income. Health bodies should be mindful of this potential conflict of interest when conducting reviews.

14.151 None of these issues should prevent a care plan providing for paid care to be provided by family members in a suitable case. However, the health body needs to be acutely aware of the potential conflicts of interest that arise where a family member's personal financial interests are involved.

Top-ups, wealthy patients and patients with substantial damages payments

14.152 Top-ups are arrangements under which service users pay part of the fees for a care home which provides an enhanced service above the base level that the state is prepared to fund, and are common in social care. However, they are generally prohibited when a patient is getting NHS-funded care. The NHS Choices website explains:[33]

> **Is it possible to pay top-up fees for NHS continuing healthcare?**
> No, it is not possible to top up NHS continuing healthcare packages, like you can with local authority care packages.
>
> The only way that NHS continuing healthcare packages can be topped up privately is if you pay for additional private services on top of the services

33 See www.nhs.uk/Conditions/social-care-and-support-guide/Pages/nhs-continuing-care.aspx.

you get from the NHS. These private services should be provided by different staff and preferably in a different setting'

14.153 Thus, wealthy patients are generally left with a choice between a care home placement at a level that the NHS is prepared to fund or accepting the whole cost of funding a higher quality placement for themselves. This can be a source of tension between patients, families and NHS commissioners, particularly where a patient has received a damages payout which is supposed to include the cost of funded care.

14.154 The law around personal injury (and in particular clinical negligence) payments provides that a claimant has the right to claim privately funded health services as part of a damages claim: see section 2(4) of the Law Reform (Personal Injuries) Act 1948. Provided a claimant genuinely has an intention to seek privately funded medical treatment at the time the damages award is made, the court cannot look into the reasonableness or otherwise of the decision to seek private medical care as opposed to accessing NHS services: see *Eagle v Chambers (No 2)*.[34]

14.155 However, once a settlement of a personal injury claim has been agreed, particularly if the settlement is by way of a lump sum payment, the claimant is fully entitled to 'change his or her mind' and claim NHS services. At that point, the patient is entitled to be treated in the same way as any other patient. Hence, a patient who has been the subject of a clinical negligence award based on negligent NHS treatment and which claimed compensation based on privately funded care is nonetheless entitled to seek NHS-funded care (which will be free at the point of use). An NHS commissioner cannot conclude that a patient does not have a 'reasonable requirement' for healthcare services because of a damages award in favour of the patient: see *R (Booker) v NHS Oldham and another*.[35] However, a patient who is wealthy is only entitled to the same level of NHS services as a patient who is destitute. The 'needs' of the patient are not adjusted to reflect the lifestyle of the patient prior to the provision of NHS services. This can often lead to difficulties and to requests by a patient to 'upgrade' services funded by the NHS.

14.156 Outside of direct payments, there are continuing difficulties around the extent to which direct payments may be used to sidestep restrictions which the NHS commissioner seeks to put on the level or cost of care for a patient or to support a home care package when care could be commissioned in a care home at a cheaper rate. It is often considerably more expensive for individuals with long-term conditions to be provided with a comprehensive package of specialist care in their own homes as opposed to being provided with care in a care home environment where economies of scale can, to some extent, reduce the cost for each individual patient. CCGs and NHS England have a duty under section 3(1) of the NHS Act 2006 to provide services to meet the reasonable requirements of relevant patients for a range of health and social care services. Arranging to have these services delivered to the patient way of a direct payment is one method by which the CCG or NHS England can discharge the duty under section 3(1) (and indeed is a method by which the CCG or NHS England

34 [2004] 1 WLR 3081 at paras 69–72.

35 [2010] EWHC 2593 (Admin), (2011) 14 CCLR 315.

could discharge any other duty to the patient as long as the services are not exempt under the regulations). However, the fact that payments to support a care plan are being sought by way of direct payments does not impose any legal duty on the CCG or NHS England to expend more money on supporting an individual patient than is required to discharge the primary duty. CCGs are often confronted with the problem that continuing a bespoke arrangement under which a package of services is provided at a person's own home is more expensive than funding a care home placement. This can arise whether the care is funded by a direct payment or in the traditional way.

14.157 This issue was considered by the High Court in *R (Gunter) v South Western Staffordshire Primary Care Trust.*[36] This case arose prior to direct payments but the family attempted to persuade the NHS commissioner to set up a 'User Independent Trust' (UIT), which was an attempt by Rachel Gunter's family to get around the then bar on direct payments by setting up a contract between the UIT. The UIT would then use the money provided by the PCT to employ the staff needed to provide care to Rachel Gunter at home, supplemented by care provided by family members. The PCT was concerned whether there was power to set up a contract and agreed that it may be a sensible way to avoid the care agency's profit, which was estimated at add 35 per cent to the overall cost. The UIT was thus seen by the family as making a home care package more affordable. Mr Justice Collins confirmed that the PCT had power to explore this option and would need to justify any decision that moved her from her home when this was not her preferred option. The judge said:[37]

> It is apparent that to remove Rachel from her home will interfere with her right to respect for her family life. Mr Wise has also relied on the positive need to give an enhanced degree of protection to the seriously disabled. This is in my view an unnecessary refinement. The interference with family life is obvious and so must be justified as proportionate. Cost is a factor which can properly be taken into account. But the evidence of the improvement in Rachel's condition, the obvious quality of life within her family environment and her expressed views that she does not want to move are all important factors which suggest that to remove her from her home will require clear justification.

14.158 However, bearing in mind cost was a factor, the judge also added the following cautionary words:[38]

> The claimant and her parents cannot assume that home care will necessarily result. I certainly hope that it can since it is obviously benefiting Rachel. But cost is an important consideration and it may turn out that the IUT route is not satisfactory or does not provide the sort of saving which can to a sufficient extent bridge the gap between care at home and residential care. The risks to Rachel must also be carefully assessed.

Thus, the case supported the general framework but let the parties sort out the details.

36 [2005] EWHC 1894 (Admin), (2006) 9 CCLR 121.

37 At para 20.

38 At para 28.

14.159 The next relevant case was *R (S) v Dudley PCT*.[39] This was an application for permission to apply for judicial review by the patient who challenged the failure of the PCT to pay the entire cost of care for Mr S who was discharged to Prestwood House near Stourbridge after a stay in hospital. The case has limited weight because permission was refused, albeit after a full judgment by Mr Justice Mitting. However, it shows the level of discretion available to a NHS commissioner and is thus of some use.

14.160 Mr S was eligible for NHS continuing healthcare and thus this was NHS funded care rather than social care. The judge explained that:

> There are two buildings within the grounds of Prestwood House; the house itself and the Coach House. Different rates of charge are made by the operators of the house for residents in two buildings. The claimant was discharged to the Coach House at, it seems, his own and his family's request.

14.161 The PCT was prepared to fund Mr S in the main house at their standard rate, but his family insisted that he should be accommodated in the Coach House. Thus the PCT entered into a contract with the care home for the standard rate and the family 'topped up' the care by a separate contract. Mr S then challenged this arrangement on various grounds saying it was an unlawful top up. The judge noted that the PCT's position was as follows:[40]

> The defendant had a standard rate which it was willing to pay for continuing health care of £471 per week. She noted that NHS continuing health care was required to be provided free of charge and that it was not the policy of the defendant or the practice of the wider NHS to agree to pay part of the cost of the continuing health care, leaving the balance to be paid privately by the patient or his family. However, it has always been the case within the National Health Service that those who wish to enjoy what are known in National Health Service jargon as 'hotel-type services', may do so at their own cost. Thus, ever since the foundation of the National Health Service there have been available within National Health Service hospitals enhanced facilities, such as individual rooms, available to patient who are willing to pay for such facilities, but the principle has always been, and remains, subject to exceptions recently canvassed in relation to drugs administered to those with life-threatening illnesses, that health care services are provided free.

14.162 The PCT justified its position by reference to various provisions allowing NHS patients to pay for enhanced services within hospitals. That argument was accepted by Mr Justice Mitting who rejected the patient's challenge. Thus, on the particular facts of this case, the NHS had acted lawfully in part-funding the cost of the care home. However, the arrangement would have been unlawful if the care home had not offered to fund a placement at the standard rate.

14.163 That raises the question as to whether a 'direct payment' arrangement could be used to circumvent the general prohibition on co-funding NHS services. This is not a subject which is covered in the guidance but, as a matter of principle, there could be no legitimate objection to a patient or

39 [2009] EWHC 1780 (Admin).

40 At para 21.

representative committing to using their own funds to meet a certain part of the care needs from their own resources. If that commitment were to be given, the health body would not be obliged to provide services to meet that 'need' because it would be met from the patient's own resources. There is a possible analogy here with an NHS Continuing Healthcare patient who has their own home (funded from their own resources) and thus does not have a 'need' for accommodation funded by the NHS. Thus if, by way of example, the patient has a need for a single overnight carer, but commits to funding that need from a damages claim, the health body can legitimately exclude that 'need' when calculating the level of a direct payment. That may make the continuance of a home care package affordable for a health body whereas, without that element of care being funded by the health body, a care home place may be significantly cheaper and so a home care package may not be offered.

14.164 The same logic could be used to fund a care home placement if the care home was prepared to divide the cost into services that the patient agreed to fund and those that the health body agreed to fund. Regulation 13(1) of the DP Regs 2013 provides that the health body must be satisfied that the direct payment meets the 'full cost of the services specified in the care plan'. However, if a care home's basic charges were £X per week but the patient required additional services costing £Y per week, there is probably no reason why the patient should not commit to meeting the cost of the additional services and thus leaving the NHS only funding the core service provision. This is an area where the lawfulness of top-up payments will depend on the way that packages of care are structured. In a time of tight constraints, it seems unlikely that the NHS will be able to hold to the principle that there should be no co-funding of care home packages.

Whether to support a direct payment to for a home care package or commission a care home placement

14.165 Commissioning care for patients with complex needs in their own homes is often the ideal. However, creating all the facilities to enable a patient to have a bespoke 'hospital at home' can be prohibitively expensive. NHS commissioners thus frequently have to face the difficult question as to whether to discharge their duties to the patient by offering to commission a care home placement or whether to continue to meet the escalating costs of a home care package. Patients who seek a direct payment do not avoid the resource constraints involved in any NHS commissioning decision. Accordingly, the question as to whether a home care package provides value for money for the NHS arises in the context of a direct payment arrangement in the same way as it does with directly commissioned packages of care.

14.166 Health bodies have a duty to 'respect' the home of a patient as a result of their duties under Article 8 of the European Convention on Human Rights (ECHR). However, it is questionable whether that duty extends to a requirement to spend more resources on the patient in order to keep them in their own home where there is intense competition for resources between patients: see the discussions of the interplay of ECHR rights and resources in *R (Condliff) v North Staffordshire Primary Care Trust.*[41]

14.167 Some CCGs have adopted policies which operate a 'buffer' under which a home care package will continue to be funded as long as the cost is not more than a fixed percentage (say, ten per cent) more than the cost of an appropriate care home package. The lawfulness of such a policy has never been challenged, but it is hard to see any basis on which such an approach could be alleged to be unlawful.

41 [2011] EWHC 872 (Admin), (2011) 14 CCLR 656.

CHAPTER 15

Who can access NHS care: charges for overseas visitors

continued

Introduction: NHS charges for overseas visitors

Background

15.1 There are few subjects that get tabloid newspapers and right-wing members of parliament (MPs) more worked up that the perception that vast numbers of 'foreigners' are descending on the UK for the sole purpose of using free NHS services and, as a result, all the shortcomings of the NHS can be put down to foreigners clogging up general practitioners' (GPs') waiting rooms, wards and clinics. However, attention paid by politicians to the use of NHS services by overseas visitors appears to be out of all proportion to the real cost to NHS bodies of providing services to overseas visitors. Moreover, the NHS has always relied on vast numbers of healthcare staff trained abroad. So a person on the ward who was born and raised abroad is far more likely to be a doctor or a nurse than an overseas visitor patient.

15.2 Nonetheless, the NHS operates in a political environment and decisions about the way it operates are made by politicians, and politics is driven by sentiment as much as it is by evidence. Thus the rules relating to overseas visitors using the NHS have been continually tightened by governments responding to public opinion, loosened in response to legal challenges and then tightened once more in response to tabloid pressure. The result is a complex set of rules where there are numerous categories of individuals who may or may not be able to access NHS care and may or may not be required to pay for the care provided to them (either up-front or after the care is delivered).

15.3 Aside from anti-foreigner prejudice, there is considerable policy justification for seeking to charge overseas visitors for having the benefit of NHS services. The NHS is a taxpayer-funded public service which works on a system of reciprocity. All taxpayers in the UK pay into the government's coffers by both direct and indirect taxation, and in return the same people receive NHS services. Thus those who are not UK taxpayers should not have the benefit of free NHS services. The principles were set out by the former Minister of State, John Hutton, explained the government's thinking behind a previous set of charging regulations[1] as follows:

> The National Health Service is first and foremost for the benefit of people who live in the United Kingdom. . . .
>
> With the changes to the charging Regulations, and their proper enforcement, we can ensure that, as far as possible, NHS resources are being used to meet the health care needs of people who live in the UK, not those who don't.

15.4 That approach was endorsed by the Court of Appeal in *R (YA) v Secretary of State for Health*[2] which was called upon to determine whether NHS services should be made available, free of charge, to a failed asylum-seeker.[3] Ward LJ said:

1 Quoted at para 16 of the judgment of the Court of Appeal in *R (YA) v Secretary of State for Health* [2009] EWCA Civ 225, (2009) 12 CCLR 213.

2 [2009] EWCA Civ 225, (2009) 12 CCLR 213.

3 There are now statutory provisions dealing with failed asylum-seekers which are considered below at para 15.148 ff.

> Here the statute in need of construction is the 2006 NHS Act. As set out at [8] above, the Secretary of State's duty prescribed by section 1 is to continue the promotion in England of a comprehensive health service designed to secure improvement in the health 'of the people of England'. Note that it is the people *of* England, not the people *in* England, which suggests that the beneficiaries of this free health service are to be those with some link to England so as to be part and parcel of the fabric of the place. It connotes a legitimate connection with the country. The exclusion from this free service of non-residents and the right conferred by section 175 to charge such persons as are not ordinarily resident reinforces this notion of segregation between them and us. This strongly suggests that, as a rule, the benefits were not intended by Parliament to be bestowed on those who ought not to be here.

15.5 The present rules are set out in the National Health Service (Charges to Overseas Visitors) Regulations (COV Regs) 2015,[4] as amended by the National Health Service (Charges to Overseas Visitors) (Amendment) Regulations 2015[5] and the National Health Service (Charges to Overseas Visitors) (Amendment) Regulations (COVA Regs) 2017.[6] The changes made to the COV Regs 2015 came out of a consultation which was run by the government between December 2015 and February 2016. This was a one-way series of changes, as the consultation document[7] explained:[8]

> Our aim now is to further extend charging of overseas visitors and migrants who use the NHS. This consultation seeks your views on how best to do this, including exploring changes in primary care, secondary care, community healthcare and changing current residency requirements.

15.6 Hence, the consultation was not focused upon reducing the charges paid by overseas visitors but only looked at ways of increasing them. The government produced a response to that consultation in February 2017: *Making a fair contribution: Government response to the consultation on the extension of charging overseas visitors and migrants using the NHS in England.*[9] The decision of the government was as follows:[10]

> Other than for A&E and ambulance services, for which more reflection is necessary, it is therefore our intention for all NHS funded care to be chargeable to those not living here or making a financial contribution to the country, except where there are good reasons for some services to be freely available to all overseas visitors, for example because of the need to protect public health. However, in recognition of the need to ensure these major changes can be implemented effectively, we will take a phased approach to extending charging into new areas of NHS care.

4 SI No 238.
5 SI No 2025.
6 SI No 756.
7 See www.gov.uk/government/uploads/system/uploads/attachment_data/file/483870/NHS_charging_acc.pdf.
8 At para 1.5.
9 See www.gov.uk/government/uploads/system/uploads/attachment_data/file/590027/Cons_Response_cost_recovery.pdf.
10 At para 4.5.

15.7 That response led to the COVA Regs 2017. The majority of the changes made by the COVA Regs 2017 came into force on 21 August 2017, but there are also changes which came into force on 23 October 2017.

15.8 The Department of Health and Social Care (DHSC) has also published guidance[11] about the operation of the COV Regs 2015, namely the *Guidance on implementing the overseas visitors charging regulations*. This replaced interim guidance which was published in August 2017.

Primary care services

15.9 The rules at present do not provide for charges to be made for primary care services. The guidance published in August 2017 said:[12]

> We will work with stakeholders including the Royal College of GPs, BMA's General Practitioners' Committee and General Dental Council to consider how best to extend the charging of overseas visitors and migrants into primary care.

However, this paragraph was omitted from the guidance published in October 2017. Hence, the policy question as to whether to extend charges to overseas visitors who use primary care services may not be settled. However, the government has included primary care in the current regulations and, contrary to the position in August 2017, it does not appear that the government has any current plans to extend charges for these services.

The February 2017 government response concerning charges for NHS community services

15.10 The February 2017 response also indicated the government was considering extending charges to other areas. It said:[13]

> We will consider further the options listed below, where additional analysis is required to better understand the potential usage of certain services by overseas visitors and migrants and establish a robust cost/benefit case before deciding whether to pursue charging in these areas:
>
> - If NHS continuing care and NHS-funded nursing care should become chargeable to overseas visitors
> - If introducing charges to overseas visitors for NHS sight tests is implementable and cost-effective
> - If individuals who provide third party support to an overseas visitor as part of their visa application should be liable for the overseas visitor's unpaid NHS bills, and work with the Home Office to do so
> - If areas of care which are part-funded by charitable donations (e.g. hospice care) should become chargeable to overseas visitors.

15.11 Some of these services are now chargeable as a result of the COVA Regs 2017. It therefore looks as if the government intends to continue to expand

11 See assets.publishing.service.gov.uk/government/uploads/system/uploads/attachment_data/file/697626/guidance_on_implementing_the_overseas_visitor_charging_regulations_april_2018.pdf. Although this guidance gives its publication date as October 2017, it was not actually released until April 2018.

12 At para 4.25.

13 At para 4.28.

the number of NHS services for which charges will be made to overseas visitors over the coming years. It remains to be seen, of course, whether a government without a parliamentary majority will be able to achieve this.

The general right to free NHS services

15.12 The vast majority of NHS services are available to everyone who lives in the UK and are free of charge at the point of use. Charges are made in England[14] to some patients for some NHS services, such as prescriptions, eye tests and dental services. This chapter looks at NHS charges for individuals who have come to England from overseas. The general rule is set out in section 1 of the National Health Service Act (NHS Act) 2006, which provides:

> (4) The services provided as part of the health service in England must be free of charge except in so far as the making and recovery of charges is expressly provided for by or under any enactment, whenever passed.

15.13 Accordingly, the default position is that all NHS services must be provided to all NHS patients unless the NHS body has a specific right to impose a charge. However, section 175 of the NHS Act 2006 provides:

> (1) Regulations may provide for the making and recovery, in such manner as may be prescribed, of such charges as the Secretary of State may determine in respect of the services mentioned in subsection (2).
> (2) The services are such services as may be prescribed which are–
> (a) provided under this Act, and
> (b) provided in respect of such persons not ordinarily resident in Great Britain as may be prescribed.
> (3) Regulations under this section may provide that the charges may be made only in such cases as may be determined in accordance with the regulations.
> (4) The Secretary of State may calculate charges under this section on any basis that he considers to be the appropriate commercial basis

15.14 Section 175 of the NHS Act 2006 thus permits the secretary of state to make regulations to provide that charges shall be made for the provision of categories of NHS services for anyone who is not 'ordinarily resident in Great Britain'.

15.15 There is a useful chart in the guidance which summarises the way the regulations operate, as follows:[15]

14 Separate rules operate for Wales, Scotland and Northern Ireland.
15 At p101 of the Guidance.

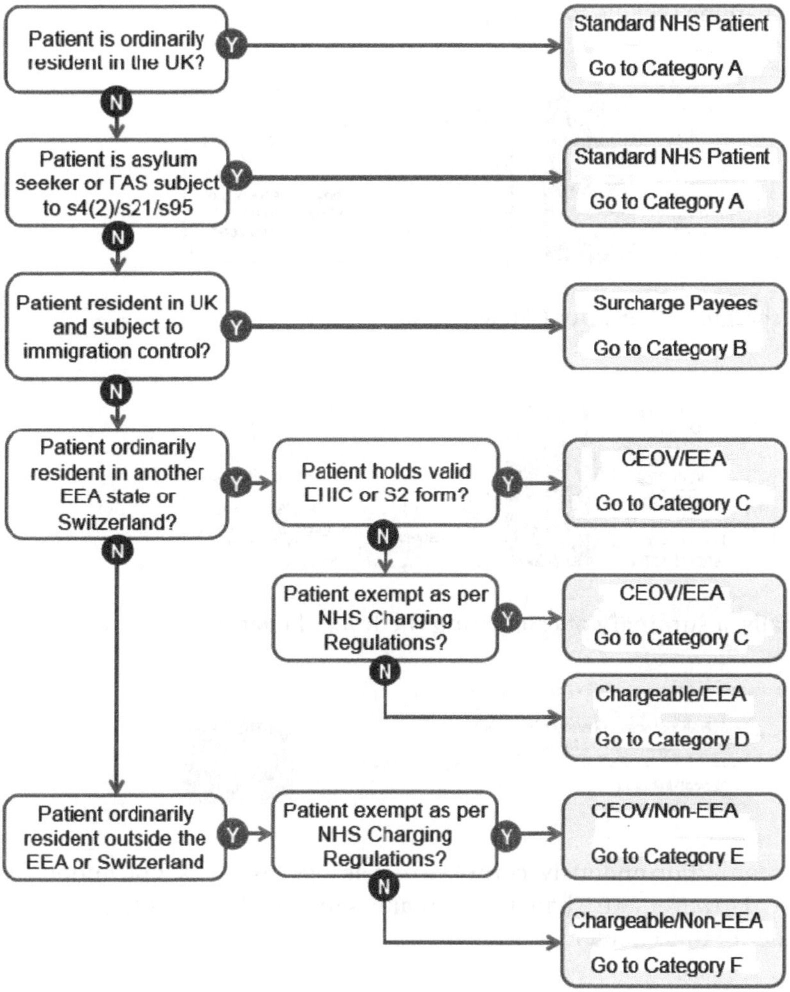

15.16 This then leads to a series of further charts which explains the approach that is to be taken to charging. These explain each 'category'. The scheme for Category A is:

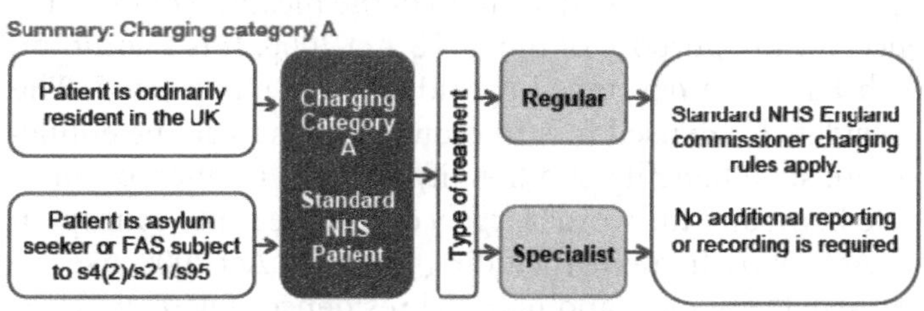

The charging scheme for Category B is:

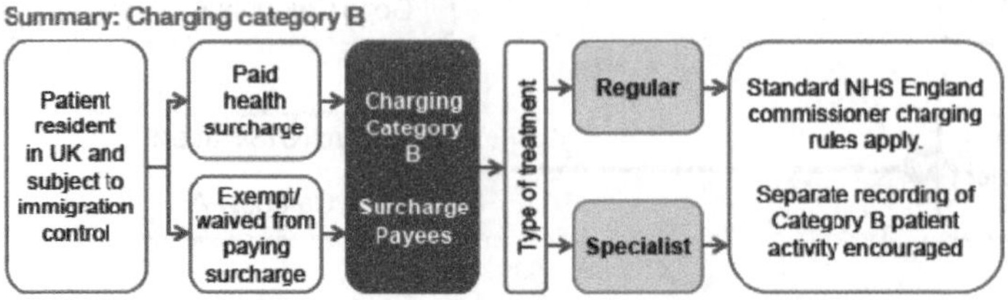

The charging scheme for Category C is:

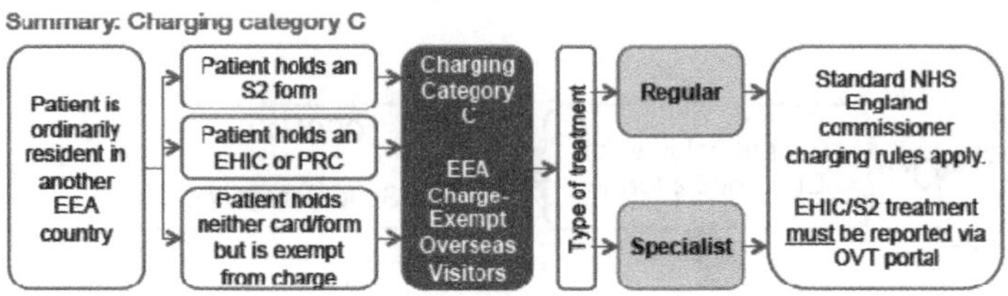

15.17 And finally, a summary of calculating the level of charging:

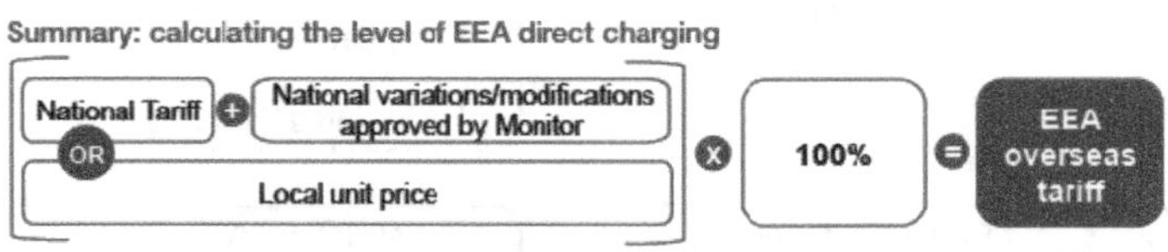

15.18 If this seems horrendously complex – it is because it is horrendously complex. However, we shall try to make sense of the concepts in the remainder of this chapter.

The 'ordinary residence' test under section 175 of the NHS Act 2006

Background

15.19 There is no comprehensive statutory definition of the meaning of the term 'ordinary residence' for the purpose of the NHS Act 2006. It is a common law concept which has been developed by judges over many years. The words 'ordinary residence' are used in numerous statutes to define entitlement to one or more state benefits or a liability to make taxation or other payments to a state body, and the words largely define the same concept in every Act.[16] Other Acts of parliament, including the NHS Act 2006, use the terms 'residence', usual residence and habitual residence. There are clear differences in meaning between 'habitual residence' and the term 'ordinary residence'. However, the words 'residence', 'normally resident' and 'ordinary residence' generally mean the same thing. This was confirmed

16 Save that for some Acts, such as the Care Act 2014, a person can only have one place of OR whereas for other Acts a person can have multiple places of OR.

by Mitting J in *R (M) v Hammersmith and Fulham LBC and another*[17] who said:

> There seems to me to be no perceptible difference between the three phrases, 'resident', 'ordinarily resident' and 'normally resident'. All three connote settled presence in a particular place other than under compulsion.

15.20 The leading case on the meaning of 'ordinary residence' is *R v Barnet LBC ex p Shah,*[18] which concerned the eligibility of foreign-based students for UK student grants. Eligibility was based on an 'ordinary residence' test and the students argued (successfully) that once they were settled in the UK, they were ordinarily resident here and so entitled to a grant. Lord Scarman relied upon the definition of 'ordinary residence' in *Levene v Commissioners of Inland Revenue,*[19] a tax case, in which reference was made to the Oxford English Dictionary definition of 'reside' as meaning:

> . . . to dwell permanently or for a considerable time, to have one's settled or usual abode, to live in or at a particular place.

15.21 The court in *Levene* also said that 'ordinary residence', was said to connote:[20]

> . . . residence in a place with some degree of continuity and apart from accidental or temporary absences.

15.22 Lord Scarman thus concluded that, unless 'the statutory framework or the legal context' pointed to a different meaning, the expression 'ordinarily resident' should be taken as referring to:[21]

> . . . a man's abode in a particular place or country which he has adopted voluntarily and for settled purposes as part of the regular order of his life for the time being, whether of short or of long duration.

15.23 Lord Scarman decided that a place of ordinary residence had to be 'voluntarily adopted' and hence a residence which was an 'enforced presence by reason of kidnapping or imprisonment' did not count. However, he said that the issue did not depend on the identification of a person's 'real home', nor on his or her long-term future intentions or expectations but where he or she lived at this point in a reasonably settled manner. Choice is not part of the ordinary test unless a person is living under compulsion. A person can be either resident or ordinarily resident in a place where he or she does not particularly wish to be, provided it is a place of settled residence. In *Mohammed v London Borough of Hammersmith and Fulham,*[22] Lord Slynn considered the meaning of the expression 'normally resident' for the purposes of the Housing Act 1996. The judge said:[23]

> So long as that place where he eats and sleeps is voluntarily accepted by him, the reason why he is there rather than somewhere else does not prevent that place from being his normal residence. He may not like it, he

17 [2010] EWHC 562 (Admin). The judgment was upheld in the Court of Appeal on slightly different grounds.

18 [1983] 2 AC 309.

19 [1928] AC 217.

20 Per Lord Viscount Cave LC, p225.

21 At 343G–H.

22 [2002] 1 AC 547.

23 At 553C–D.

may prefer some other place, but that place is for the relevant time the place where he normally resides . . . Where he is given interim accommodation by a local housing authority even more clearly is that the place where for the time being he is normally resident.

15.24 A person who is detained in a mental health institution or in a prison will not acquire an ordinary residence at that institution, and so will be deemed to continue to be ordinarily resident in the place that he or she was prior to being detained, even if there is nowhere for him or her in fact to go to live at that place: *R v Mental Health Review Tribunal ex p Hall*.[24] However, in all other cases, a person cannot continue to be ordinarily resident in a place unless there is property that he or she could occupy at that place: see *R (Sunderland City Council) v South Tyneside Council*.[25]

15.25 It is not usually relevant how long a person has been living at their place of residence before they become ordinarily resident. If someone moves house from location A to location B, thus giving up their place of residence at location A, they will instantly acquire location B as their place of ordinary residence: see *Macrae v Macrae*[26] where it was said:

From the moment he travelled to Inverness . . . it seems to me that all the evidence tends to show that he was ordinarily resident in Scotland.

The need for the residence to be lawful

15.26 A key feature of 'ordinary residence' in a place is that the residence is required to be lawful. However, this element of the ordinary residence test has been extended by section 39 of the Immigration Act (IA) 2014, which provides that the person's residence in the UK must be lawful and cannot be for a limited period. It provides:

A reference in the NHS charging provisions to persons not ordinarily resident in Great Britain or persons not ordinarily resident in Northern Ireland includes (without prejudice to the generality of that reference) a reference to–

(a) persons who require leave to enter or remain in the United Kingdom but do not have it, and
(b) persons who have leave to enter or remain in the United Kingdom for a limited period.

15.27 This provision only impacts on non-EEA nationals. The practical effect of this section is explained in the guidance, as follows:[27]

It is important to note that since 6 April 2015, non-EEA[28] nationals who are subject to immigration control must have indefinite leave to remain (ILR) in the UK in order to be ordinarily resident in the UK. They must also still meet the other requirements of the test set out at paragraph 3.12; having ILR on its own is not sufficient since that person may no longer be, for

24 [2000] 1 WLR 1323, (1999) 2 CCLR 383.
25 [2012] EWCA Civ 1232.
26 [1949] 2 All ER 34.
27 At paras 3.10 and 3.12.
28 A list of EEA countries is at paras 15.96–15.98.

> example, residing in the UK on a properly settled basis, and may only be visiting.
>
> ...
>
> Non-EEA nationals usually need permission to be in the UK, except in some circumstances when they are not subject to immigration control, eg due to their relationship to an EEA national who is resident here, or when a diplomat.

15.28 Hence, non-EEA nationals who only have limited right to remain in the UK must be treated as individuals who are not ordinarily resident within section 175 of the NHS Act 2006.

The position of British nationals who live abroad

15.29 British nationals who are ordinarily resident abroad and do not have a sufficiently settled residence in the UK to be ordinarily resident at an address in the UK will not be ordinarily resident in the UK for the purposes of section 175 of the NHS Act 2006. This is explained in the guidance as follows:[29]

> British citizens have automatic right of abode in the UK, so are always here lawfully. EEA nationals are almost always here lawfully. It is important to note that a person does not need to meet the 'right to reside test' for certain benefits, for example, in order to be considered ordinarily resident in the UK.

15.30 It follows that a British national (other than a UK pensioner who lives in the European Union (EU) or European Economic Area (EEA)[30]) who lives abroad and is taken ill while visiting the UK on a temporary basis will not be entitled to free NHS care. Such a person will be treated as being an overseas resident in the same way as someone who does not have British nationality.

15.31 This could be explicable on the reciprocity principle. A British national who lives abroad is unlikely to be a UK taxpayer and hence will not be contributing to the cost of the NHS, and thus should not be entitled to have the same benefits as someone who lives here and pays taxes. However, the regulations do not consistently apply principle of reciprocity because foreign-based workers who are here on a temporary basis and pay tax here are potentially charged for treatment.

Having more than one place of ordinary residence

15.32 A person can have more than one place of ordinary residence, including residences in different countries at the same time. Hence, by way of example, a university student who divides his or her time between halls of residence at University in Hull and a parental home in Cornwall will be ordinarily resident at both locations (see *Fox v Stirk*[31]) and hence will be ordinarily resident in the UK for the purposes of section 175 of the NHS

29 At para 3.12.

30 See para 15.96 below.

31 [1970] 2 QB 463 at 475E.

Act 2006. In the same way, a student who studies in France but maintains a place of residence at his parents' house in Bristol, will probably continue to be ordinarily resident in Bristol and thus be entitled to free NHS care.

Other guidance

15.33 In 2013, the DHSC published extensive guidance about the meaning of the expression 'ordinary residence' for the purposes of the Care Act 2014.[32] That guidance was updated in 2016 to take account of the decision of the Supreme Court in *R (Cornwall Council) v Secretary of State for Health and Somerset CC*.[33] New guidance was issued primarily to assist with the identification of the place of ordinary residence of a person who lacked capacity.[34] DHSC has also published guidance on the tests for ordinary residence for the purposes of the COV Regs.[35]

15.34 All of this guidance could be useful to determine whether, on the facts on individual case, a person is or is not ordinarily resident in Great Britain. No charges can be made pursuant to the COV Regs 2015 in respect of anyone who is ordinarily resident in Great Britain.

The NHS services that are exempt from charges for overseas visitors

15.35 Part 3 of the COV Regs 2015 sets out a list of NHS services for which no charges can be levied, even if they are provided to overseas visitors who would otherwise be liable to pay charges under the regulations. Some NHS services do not attract charges for overseas visitors because they are not 'relevant services' services for the purposes of the COV Regs 2015. Other services are relevant services but are specifically exempt from charges.

NHS services that are not 'relevant services'

Definition

15.36 'Relevant' NHS services are defined in reg 2 of the COV Regs 2015, as follows:

> 'relevant services' means accommodation, services or facilities which are provided, or whose provision is arranged, under the 2006 Act other than–
> (a) primary medical services provided under Part 4 (medical services);
> (b) primary dental services provided under Part 5 (dental services);
> (c) primary ophthalmic services provided under Part 6 (ophthalmic services); or
> (d) equivalent services which are provided, or whose provision is arranged, under the 2006 Act.

32 See www.gov.uk/government/uploads/system/uploads/attachment_data/file/252864/OR_Guidance_2013-10-01_Revised__with_new_contact_details_New_DH_template.pdf.

33 [2015] UKSC 46, (2015) 18 CCLR 497.

34 See www.gov.uk/government/uploads/system/uploads/attachment_data/file/575956/OR_update_acc.pdf.

35 See assets.publishing.service.gov.uk/government/uploads/system/uploads/attachment_data/file/697626/guidance_on_implementing_the_overseas_visitor_charging_regulations_april_2018.pdf.

15.37 Accordingly, no charges under the COV Regs 2015 can be levied for primary care services, primary dental services or primary ophthalmic services (or any equivalent services). That does not mean that overseas visitors will necessarily be able to access these services free of charge because, for example, other regulations provide that charges can be made to some patients for primary dental services. However, apart from these defined NHS services (and the slightly ambiguously worded 'equivalent services which are provided, or whose provision is arranged, under the 2006 Act'), all other NHS-funded services are 'relevant services' for the purposes of the COV Regs 2015.

The removal of the 'out of hospital services' limitation

15.38 Until 23 August 2017, reg 9(b) of the COV Regs 2015 used to provide that any NHS services that were provided outside of a hospital would be exempt from charges, despite being 'relevant services' for the purposes of the regulations. The regulation previously provided:

> No charge may be made or recovered in respect of any of the following relevant services provided to an overseas visitor– . . . (b) services provided otherwise than at, or by staff employed to work at, or under the direction of, a hospital.

15.39 When that provision was in place, all NHS community services were exempt from charges for overseas visitors. Hence, for example, an overseas visitor who qualified for NHS Continuing Healthcare and was accommodated in a care home (which was not a hospital within the meaning of section 275 of the NHS Acts 2006) received services free of charge. That part of reg 9 was repealed by the COVA Regs 2017 with effect from 23 August 2017. It follows that, as from 23 August 2017, all NHS community services (other than those deemed not to be 'relevant services' within the definition under reg 2) are services which come within the scope of the COV Regs 2015. This is confirmed in the Q&A section of the guidance which provides:[36]

> Q: I provide NHS community services, including to some overseas visitors. Should I be charging them?
>
> A: This will depend on if the community services are 'relevant services' or not. Some services provided in the community are not relevant services, such as those provided by school nurses and health visitors. In that case they remain outside the scope of the Charging Regulations and not chargeable.
>
> However, provided that the services provided fall within the definition of 'relevant services' and no exemption applies, charges may be payable in relation to those services, regardless of whether they are provided within a hospital setting or in the community (for example, district nursing services).
>
> Therefore, as long as the services provided are not:
>
> - primary medical services
> - primary dental services
> - primary ophthalmic services or
> - equivalent services which are provided, or whose provision is arranged, under the 2006 Act
>
> then you should charge overseas visitors for them, unless an exemption category applies to the overseas visitor or the service you are providing.

36 At p32.

15.40 It follows that any overseas visitor who has been in receipt of a package of NHS Continuing Healthcare support, including those in a care home, may have to pay for the services after 23 August 2017, whereas those services will have been free of charge before that date. There has been no publicity about this change, and no guidance has been issued about it because the published guidance only covers hospital-based services. It also appears to contradict the government's intentions as set out in the February 2017 response (see para 15.10 above).

NHS relevant services which are exempt from charges

15.41 The new form of reg 9 of the COV Regs 2015 lists those services which, from 23 October 2017, are exempt from charges for overseas visitors despite being relevant services. Regulation 9 of the COV Regs 2015 provides:[37]

> No charge may be made or recovered in respect of any of the following relevant services provided to an overseas visitor–
>
> (a) accident and emergency services, but not including any services provided–
>   (i) after the overseas visitor has been accepted as an in-patient at a hospital; or
>   (ii) at an outpatient appointment;
>
> (aa) services provided as part of the telephone advice line commissioned by a clinical commissioning group or the National Health Service Commissioning Board;
>
> ...
>
> (c) family planning services;
>
> (d) services provided for the diagnosis and treatment of a condition listed in Schedule 1;
>
> (e) services provided for the diagnosis and treatment of sexually transmitted infections;
>
> (f) services provided for the treatment of a condition caused by–
>   (i) torture;
>   (ii) female genital mutilation;
>   (iii) domestic violence; or
>   (iv) sexual violence,
>
>   provided that the overseas visitor has not travelled to the United Kingdom for the purpose of seeking that treatment;
>
> (g) palliative care services provided by–
>   (i) a company referred to in section 26 of the Companies (Audit, Investigations and Community Enterprise) Act 2004 (community interest companies); or
>   (ii) a palliative care charity within the meaning given in section 33D of the Value Added Tax Act 1994 (charities to which section 33C applies).

Accident and emergency services

15.42 The regulations contain no definition of accident and emergency (A&E) services. However, the guidance states that among exempt services are:[38]

37 As from 23 October 2017.
38 At para 4.3.

accident and emergency (A&E) services (whether provided at an A&E department or similar eg urgent care centre, walk-in centre or minor injuries unit) but not including services provided after the overseas visitor is accepted as an inpatient or at a follow-up outpatient appointment. So, where emergency treatment is given after admission to the NHS hospital, eg intensive care or coronary care, it is chargeable to a non-exempt overseas visitor. Note that some walk-in centres provide primary care services rather than A&E-type services and overseas visitors cannot be charged for such services either because primary care services are not within the scope of the regulations.

15.43 The guidance also states as follows regarding ambulance services:[39]

> Q: Can I charge for ambulance services?
>
> A: No. Ambulance services are considered to be part of A&E care and should be provided free of charge where they are part of the patient's clinical need. However, whilst European visitors and students with valid EHICs cannot be charged directly for ambulance services, all A&E treatment costs (including ambulance services) should be recorded and reported via the Department of Work and Pensions OVT EHIC Portal (see para 9.14) portal.

15.44 The guidance also extends 'A&E services' to patients who are treated on a Medical Assessment Unit or Clinical Decisions Unit which is attached to the A&E department, despite the fact that the services are generally treated as being outside of A&E services the purpose of the national tariff.[40] The guidance provides:

> Q: Can I charge someone for A&E services while on an observation ward?
>
> A: No, patients kept in observation wards or similar that are attached to A&E departments are usually still under the care of the A&E consultant and should not be charged unless and until they are formally admitted to NHS hospital as an inpatient.

Telephone advice services

15.45 Services such as 111 or Out-of-Hours (OOH) telephone advice services are exempt from charges. Further, if a call is made to the GP OOH services resulting in a visit by GP, that is probably not a 'relevant service' because it would be an 'equivalent service' to primary care medical services. Thus, no charge should be levied for such a visit if the patient is an overseas visitor.

Family planning services

15.46 Family planning services are exempt from charges. They are defined in the guidance as follows:

> . . . services that supply contraceptive products and devices to prevent pregnancy (termination of an established pregnancy is not a method of contraception or family planning).

Accordingly, any services associated with a proposed abortion or any other services connected to the termination of pregnancy are outside the definition of family planning services.

39 At p32.

40 This commonly adopted approach may well be inconsistent with the wording of the national tariff, although it is a somewhat 'grey' area.

Schedule 1 condition services

15.47 Schedule 1 to the COV Regs 2015 sets out a list of medical conditions where there is a public health interest in ensuring that patients receive prompt medical treatment in order to protect others from the spread of the condition. The list of diseases in Schedule 1 is as follows:

- Acute encephalitis
- Acute poliomyelitis
- Anthrax
- Botulism
- Brucellosis
- Cholera
- Diphtheria
- Enteric fever (typhoid and paratyphoid fever)
- Food poisoning
- Haemolytic uraemic syndrome (HUS)
- Human immunodeficiency virus (HIV)
- Infectious bloody diarrhoea
- Invasive group A streptococcal disease and scarlet fever
- Invasive meningococcal disease (meningococcal meningitis, meningococcal septicaemia and other forms of invasive disease)
- Legionnaires' disease
- Leprosy
- Leptospirosis
- Malaria
- Measles
- Middle East Respiratory Syndrome (MERS)[41]
- Mumps
- Pandemic influenza (defined as the 'Pandemic Phase') or influenza that might become pandemic (defined as the 'Alert Phase') as defined by WHO in the World Health Organisation's ('WHO') Pandemic Influenza Risk Management Interim Guidance
- Plague
- Rabies
- Rubella
- Severe Acute Respiratory Syndrome (SARS)
- Smallpox
- Tetanus
- Tuberculosis
- Typhus
- Viral haemorrhagic fever
- Viral hepatitis
- Whooping cough
- Yellow fever

15.48 Accordingly, no charges should be made for any treatment provided to an overseas visitor for, or arising out of, any of the Schedule 1 medical conditions. Patients may, of course, present for treatment with multiple conditions. This is addressed in the guidance as follows:

> Q: Clinicians are treating a patient for TB. Do I charge for other conditions the patient has?

41 This condition was added to the list by SI 2015 No 2025. Other conditions may be added at a later date, and a full list should be maintained on the NHS England website.

> A: Yes, unless treatment of the other condition is also an exempt service, or the patient is exempt from charges under another exemption, then you must charge for the treatment of the other condition, even if the other condition impacts on the treatment of the TB.
>
> Q: An overseas visitor says they have forgotten to bring their antiretroviral (ARV) therapy for their HIV. Do we provide it free of charge?
>
> A: HIV is a disease for which treatment is free on public health grounds. Guidance to the NHS advises that in such circumstances the supply of free ARVs should be limited to an amount that will last until the overseas visitor returns home or has arranged for ARVs to be sent to them. Further guidance on this can be found at *HIV treatment for overseas visitors: Guidance for the NHS*.

15.49 The guidance makes it clear that free NHS care includes testing and treatment for somebody who is suspected of having a Schedule 1 condition even if it is subsequently shown that the person does not have that condition. The guidance provides:

> the diagnosis and treatment, including routine screening and routine vaccinations, of the conditions specified in Schedule 1 to the Charging Regulations which is necessary to protect the wider public health. This exemption from charge will apply to the diagnosis of the condition, even if the outcome is a negative result. It will also apply to any treatment provided for a suspected specified condition, up to the point that it is negatively diagnosed. It does not apply to any secondary illness that may be present even if treatment is necessary in order to successfully treat the condition.

15.50 The DHSC has published specific guidance to assist NHS staff who are called upon to treat overseas visitors with HIV.[42] The August 2017 guidance made it clear that HIV treatment is provided to overseas visitors for the benefit of other people within the UK, as opposed to being provided on a philanthropic basis. It stated:[43]

> From 1 October 2012, an amendment to the Charging Regulations means that HIV treatment is no longer chargeable to any overseas visitors and is provided in the same way as treatment for other sexually transmitted infections for which NHS treatment is free to all. This amendment responds to the significant evidence on the benefits to public health of providing HIV treatment to all in clinical need. Left untreated, HIV presents a significant risk of transmission to people in the UK. The availability of treatment should increase the acceptance of confidential HIV testing in people from abroad living in the UK and hence contribute to reducing undiagnosed HIV'

That policy was carried forward into the COV Regs 2015. However, the guidance also makes it clear that treatment, including prescribing of antiretroviral therapy, is available only the duration of a person's stay in the UK.

Services provided for the diagnosis and treatment of sexually transmitted infections

15.51 Regulation 9(e) of the COV Regs 2015 provides that no charges will be made for the diagnosis and treatment of sexually transmitted infections (STIs). While no charges should be made to the patient for the provision

42 See www.gov.uk/government/uploads/system/uploads/attachment_data/file/212952/DH-Guidance-HIV-and-NHS-Charging-fORMATED.pdf.

43 At para 2.3. This is omitted from the current guidance.

of STI services, the guidance suggests that charges could still be recovered from EEA governments in respect of EEA nationals who present seeking such treatment. It provides:[44]

> Q: Do I need to assess patients attending sexually transmitted diseases clinics for charges?
>
> A: The diagnosis and treatment of sexually transmitted infections is free to all, so charging issues will arise less often in those settings. Regulations prevent the disclosure of any identifying disease other than to a medical practitioner (or to a person employed under the direction of a medical practitioner). This applies to information in connection with, and for the purpose of, the treatment of the patient and/or the prevention of the spread of the disease.
>
> However, this does not mean that sexually transmitted diseases clinics do not have to apply the Charging Regulations or should not allow Overseas Visitor Managers (OVMs) access to do their job. Overseas visitors being provided with treatment for sexually transmitted diseases will still be liable for charges for other types of treatment unless another exemption applies, so it can still be helpful for awareness of charging issues to be raised in these settings.
>
> Reimbursement claims can be made to other EEA countries for providing treatment for sexually transmitted infections whenever the patient has a valid EHIC/PRC/S2, so sexually transmitted diseases clinics can be encouraged to take down these details and provide OVMs with them. There would be no question of treatment being charged, or delayed, if no EHIC/PRC/S2 was presented'

NHS services provided to treat victims of torture

15.52 Services provided to overseas visitors who have been victims of torture to treat conditions arising out of or related to torture are services for which no charges can be made. 'Torture' is defined at reg 8(1) of the COV Regs 2015 as follows:

> 'torture' has the meaning given in Article 1(1) of the United Nations Convention Against Torture and other Cruel, Inhuman or Degrading Treatment or Punishment (agreed in New York on 4th February 1985.

15.53 The United Nations Convention against Torture and other Cruel, Inhuman or Degrading Treatment or Punishment (UNCAT) was ratified by the UK on 7 January 1989. Article 1(1) provides:

> For the purposes of this Convention, the term 'torture' means any act by which severe pain or suffering, whether physical or mental, is intentionally inflicted on a person for such purposes as obtaining from him or a third person information or a confession, punishing him for an act he or a third person has committed or is suspected of having committed, or intimidating or coercing him or a third person, or for any reason based on discrimination of any kind, when such pain or suffering is inflicted by or at the instigation of or with the consent or acquiescence of a public official or other person acting in an official capacity. It does not include pain or suffering arising only from, inherent in or incidental to lawful sanctions.

15.54 Article 3(1) of the UNCAT provides that a state which ratifies the convention shall not:

44 See p34.

> ... expel, return ('refouler') or extradite a person to another State where there are substantial grounds for believing that he would be in danger of being subjected to torture.

15.55 Hence, a person who has suffered torture and remains at danger of being subjected to torture cannot be extradited. Further, Article 14 provides:

> Each State Party shall ensure in its legal system that the victim of an act of torture obtains redress and has an enforceable right to fair and adequate compensation, including the means for as full rehabilitation as possible.

15.56 The UK state thus has a duty under the UNCAT to provide 'as full rehabilitation as possible' to torture victims. Any requirement that torture victims should pay charges for NHS services would be a breach of Article 14. Thus, any provision that NHS services should only be provided to overseas visitors who paid charges would be a breach of the government's duties under Article 14 of the UNCAT.

15.57 Regulation 8(2)(a) provides that 'treatment' for torture victims includes:

> ... any subsequent or on-going treatment provided to an overseas visitor for any condition, including a chronic condition, that is directly attributable to the torture, female genital mutilation, domestic violence or sexual violence.

In practice, overseas visitors who have been tortured cannot be charged for treatment for the initial physical injuries caused by the torture and for any mental health treatment for the enduring psychological consequences suffered by torture victims.

15.58 The exemption does not apply to a torture victim who has travelled to the UK for the purpose of seeking treatment. It is unclear whether this provision applies if the victim has come to the UK for multiple purposes – eg escaping torture and seeking medical help for the consequences of torture. However, given the terms of Article 14 of the UNCAT, it seems probable that this provision would only be relevant if the overseas visitor came to the UK for the sole reason of seeking medical treatment for the effects of torture. If the victim was also claiming asylum or came here to get away from the place where he or she was tortured, then the proviso probably does not apply. It thus seems that this limitation is only likely to apply where a torture victim is settled in another safe country and has travelled to the UK for the sole purpose of gaining NHS treatment for the medical effects of torture.

NHS services provided to treat victims of female genital mutilation

15.59 Regulation 9(f)(ii) of the COV Regs 2015 provides that no charges shall be made to patients who are seeking treatment for a condition caused by female genital mutilation (FGM). FGM is defined in reg 8(1) as follows:

> 'female genital mutilation' means the excision, infibulation or other mutilation (collectively referred to as mutilation) of the whole or any part of a female's labia majora, labia minora or clitoris where–
>
> (a) that mutilation constituted an offence under the Female Genital Mutilation Act 2003 ('the 2003 Act');
>
> (b) if the mutilation was performed prior to the coming into force of the 2003 Act, that mutilation would have constituted an offence under the 2003 Act if the Act had been in force at the time the mutilation was performed;

(c) if the mutilation was performed outside the United Kingdom but did not constitute an offence under the 2003 Act, that mutilation would have constituted an offence under the 2003 Act had it been performed in the United Kingdom; or
(d) if the mutilation was performed outside the United Kingdom prior to the coming into force of the 2003 Act, that mutilation would have constituted an offence under the 2003 Act if–
(i) the mutilation had been performed in the United Kingdom; and
(ii) the 2003 Act had been in force at the time the mutilation was performed

'girl' includes woman

15.60 The Female Genital Mutilation Act 2003 creates a series of offences around FGM. The extended definitions set out in reg 8 extend the protection against charges for any woman who is a victim of FGM even if the relevant act was not an offence under the Female Genital Mutilation Act 2003 because of the time the act occurred or place where it occurred. The extended causation definition in reg 8(2) applies to the meaning of 'treatment' in this part of the regulations (see para 15.57 above). However, the definition of NHS treatment for which no charges can be made is extended by reg 9(b), which provides:

(b) in the case of female genital mutilation, any antenatal, perinatal and postpartum treatment provided to an overseas visitor the need for which is directly attributable to the mutilation

15.61 Regulation 6A relates to services provided to victims of FGM between 6 April 2015 (when the COV Regs 2015 came into force) and 31 January 2016 when the COVA Regs 2015 came into force. Regulation 6A of the COVA Regs 2015 provides:

(1) This paragraph applies to an overseas visitor who received relevant services from a *relevant NHS body* [relevant body[45]] during the period beginning on 6th April 2015 and ending on 31st January 2016, where–
(a) those services were provided for the treatment of a condition, which was caused by female genital mutilation in the circumstances described in paragraph (d) of the definition of 'female genital mutilation' in regulation 8(1) (interpretation of this part); or
(b) at the time the relevant services were provided–
(i) the overseas visitor was a person in respect of whom an application to be granted temporary protection, asylum or humanitarian protection under the immigration rules had been rejected; and
(ii) the overseas visitor was supported under Part 1 (care and support) of the Care Act 2014 by the provision of accommodation.
(2) relevant body which, in respect of an overseas visitor to whom paragraph (1) applies, has–
(a) yet to make a charge under regulation 3 (obligation to make and recover charges), must not make the charges; or
(b) made charges under regulation 3 but has yet to recover the charges, must not recover the charges'

45 The change from 'relevant NHS body' to 'relevant body' applies from 23 October 2017 when private providers of NHS services became liable to impose charges.

15.62 This provision was necessary because the original definition of FGM under the COV Regs 2015 did not include the wording now in reg 8(1)(d) of the definition. When those words were added, the above provision required NHS bodies to cease enforcing payment of any charges that had been made. However, it did not impose any obligation on an NHS body to refund any charges which had been paid.

15.63 The proviso that charges only apply if the patient has not travelled to the UK specifically for the purpose of securing treatment for medical problems caused by FGM also applies. This probably means that charges can only be imposed if the person travelled to the UK for the sole or predominant purpose of seeking treatment, as opposed to travelling to the UK for other reasons (even if the person hoped to be able to secure NHS treatment once the person arrived in the UK).

NHS services provided to treat victims of domestic violence

15.64 Regulation 9(f)(iii) of the COV Regs 2015 provides that no charges may be made or recovered from any person who is a victim of domestic violence. There is no definition of 'domestic violence' in the regulations, but there is the following agreed cross-government definition of domestic violence and abuse:[46]

> **Domestic Violence and Abuse:**
> Any incident or pattern of incidents of controlling, coercive, threatening behaviour, violence or abuse between those aged 16 or over who are, or have been, intimate partners or family members regardless of gender or sexuality.
>
> The abuse can encompass, but is not limited to:
>
> - psychological
> - physical
> - sexual
> - financial
> - emotional
>
> *Controlling behaviour*
>
> Controlling behaviour is a range of acts designed to make a person subordinate and/or dependent by isolating them from sources of support, exploiting their resources and capacities for personal gain, depriving them of the means needed for independence, resistance and escape and regulating their everyday behaviour.
>
> *Coercive behaviour*
>
> Coercive behaviour is an act or a pattern of acts of assault, threats, humiliation and intimidation or other abuse that is used to harm, punish, or frighten their victim'

15.65 The government website unhelpfully states that the above is not to be treated as a 'legal definition'. While the precise meaning of that limitation is unclear, if there were to be a dispute about the meaning of the term 'domestic violence', it seems highly likely that the court would adopt the government's own meaning of the term, particularly given the absence of a definition of the term 'domestic violence' in the COV Regs 2015.

46 See www.gov.uk/guidance/domestic-violence-and-abuse.

15.66 There is no requirement in the regulations that the domestic violence must have taken place in the UK. It follows that a person who comes to the UK with a need for NHS services arising from domestic violence which was committed overseas is entitled to free NHS services for medical conditions related to or arising out of the domestic violence. The extended causation definition in reg 8(2) applies to the meaning of 'treatment' in this part of the regulations (see para 15.57 above).

15.67 The proviso that charges only apply if the patient has not travelled to the UK specifically for the purpose of securing treatment for medical problems caused by domestic violence also applies. This probably means that charges can only be imposed if the person travelled to the UK for the sole or predominant purpose of seeking treatment, as opposed to travelling to the UK for other reasons (even if the person hoped to be able to secure NHS treatment once the person arrived in the UK).

NHS services provided to treat victims of sexual violence

15.68 Regulation 9(f)(iv) provides that no charges may be made or recovered from any person who is a victim of sexual violence. The World Health Organization (WHO) has defined the term 'sexual violence' as follows:[47]

> Sexual violence is defined as:
>
> any sexual act, attempt to obtain a sexual act, unwanted sexual comments or advances, or acts to traffic, or otherwise directed, against a person's sexuality using coercion, by any person regardless of their relationship to the victim, in any setting, including but not limited to home and work.
>
> Coercion can cover a whole spectrum of degrees of force. Apart from physical force, it may involve psychological intimidation, blackmail or other threats – for instance, the threat of physical harm, of being dismissed from a job or of not obtaining a job that is sought. It may also occur when the person aggressed is unable to give consent – for instance, while drunk, drugged, asleep or mentally incapable of understanding the situation.
>
> Sexual violence includes rape, defined as physically forced or otherwise coerced penetration – even if slight – of the vulva or anus, using a penis, other body parts or an object. The attempt to do so is known as attempted rape. Rape of a person by two or more perpetrators is known as gang rape.
>
> Sexual violence can include other forms of assault involving a sexual organ, including coerced contact between the mouth and penis, vulva or anus.

15.69 Both men and women can be victims of sexual violence. While the majority of sexual violence is directed against women, and services are mainly focused on women survivors of sexual violence, the problem of sexual violence against men is recognised by the WHO, which says:[48]

> Sexual violence against men and boys is a significant problem. With the exception of childhood sexual abuse, though, it is one that has largely been neglected in research. Rape and other forms of sexual coercion directed against men and boys take place in a variety of settings, including in the

47 See www.who.int/violence_injury_prevention/violence/global_campaign/en/chap6.pdf.

48 See p154 at www.who.int/violence_injury_prevention/violence/global_campaign/en/chap6.pdf.

home, the workplace, schools, on the streets, in the military and during war, as well as in prisons and police custody.

In prisons, forced sex can occur among inmates to establish hierarchies of respect and discipline. Sexual violence by prison officials, police and soldiers is also widely reported in many countries. Such violence may take the form of prisoners being forced to have sex with others as a form of 'entertainment', or to provide sex for the officers or officials in command. Elsewhere, men who have sex with other men may be 'punished', by rape, for their behaviour which is perceived to transgress social norms.

15.70 The extended causation definition in reg 8(2) applies to the meaning of 'treatment' in this part of the regulations (see para 15.57 above).

15.71 The proviso that charges only apply if the patient has not travelled to the UK specifically for the purpose of securing treatment also applies. This probably means that the person travelled to the UK for the sole or predominant purpose of seeking treatment for medical problems caused by sexual violence, as opposed to travelling to the UK for other reasons (even if the person hoped to be able to secure NHS treatment once the person arrived in the UK).

The categories of overseas visitors who are exempt from NHS charges

15.72 Part 4 of the COV Regs 2015 defines the categories of individuals who are exempt from the payment of NHS charges despite being classified as 'overseas visitors', in the sense that they are individuals who are not ordinarily resident in the UK. There are a large number of different categories of overseas visitors who do not have to pay charges for accessing NHS services. The main categories are as follows:

a) individuals who have paid or are exempt from paying the immigration health charge (also known as the immigration health surcharge);
b) EU citizens and others with EU/EEA rights;
c) asylum-seekers and failed asylum-seekers and their families;
d) victims of modern slavery:
e) persons granted the right to NHS treatment without charge for exceptional humanitarian reasons;
f) persons detained in an NHS hospital or subject to court-ordered treatment;
g) prisoners and other detainees;
h) persons from countries with whom the UK has a reciprocal arrangement;
i) members of the regular and reserve forces, Crown servants and others;
j) NATO forces personnel;
k) war pensioners and armed forces compensation scheme payment recipients;
l) Turkish nationals where the need for accessing NHS services arose during a visit and who cannot afford payment;
m) family members of overseas visitors.

Each of these categories is discussed in turn below.

15.73 Regulation 18 of the COV Regs 2015 covers the position of staff on UK registered ships who were previously entitled to NHS services without charge but are now included within the charging regime, albeit that the charges have to be paid by the shipowner and not the patient.

Overseas visitors within the scope of the immigration health charge (also known as the immigration health surcharge)

Overview

15.74 Section 38 of the IA 2014 brought in provisions to enable the secretary of state to set an 'immigration health charge' (also known as the immigration health surcharge or IHS) to be paid by visitors who come to the UK on visitors visas. The purpose of the policy change was to collect a fixed annual fee from a category of overseas visitors as part of the visa application process and then to allow such persons to use the NHS on the same basis as UK permanent residents. Section 38 of the IA 2014 provides:

38 Immigration health charge

(1) The Secretary of State may by order provide for a charge to be imposed on–
- (a) persons who apply for immigration permission, or
- (b) any description of such persons.

(2) 'Immigration permission' means–
- (a) leave to enter or remain in the United Kingdom for a limited period,
- (b) entry clearance which, by virtue of provision made under section 3A(3) of the Immigration Act 1971, has effect as leave to enter the United Kingdom for a limited period, or
- (c) any other entry clearance which may be taken as evidence of a person's eligibility for entry into the United Kingdom for a limited period.

(3) An order under this section may in particular–
- (a) impose a separate charge on a person in respect of each application made by that person;
- (b) specify the amount of any charge (and different amounts may be specified for different purposes);
- (c) make provision about when or how a charge may or must be paid to the Secretary of State;
- (d) make provision about the consequences of a person failing to pay a charge (including provision for the person's application to be refused);
- (e) provide for exemptions from a charge;
- (f) provide for the reduction, waiver or refund of part or all of a charge (whether by conferring a discretion or otherwise).

(4) In specifying the amount of a charge under subsection (3)(b) the Secretary of State must (among other matters) have regard to the range of health services that are likely to be available free of charge to persons who have been given immigration permission.

(5) Sums paid by virtue of an order under this section must–
- (a) be paid into the Consolidated Fund, or
- (b) be applied in such other way as the order may specify.

(6) In this section–

'entry clearance' has the meaning given by section 33(1) of the Immigration Act 1971;

'health services' means services provided as part of the health service in England, Wales, Scotland and Northern Ireland;

and the references to applying for leave to enter or remain for a limited period include references to applying for a variation of leave to enter or remain which would result in leave to enter or remain for a limited period.

15.75 This section gave the secretary of state power to make an order which specified how the IHS was to operate. The secretary of state used that power to make the Immigration (Health Charge) Order (HC Order) 2015,[49] which came into effect on 6 April 2015. This order was amended by the Immigration (Health Charge) (Amendment) Order 2016[50] and then further amended by the Immigration (Health Charge) (Amendment) Order 2017.[51]

Who has to pay the IHS

15.76 Article 3 of the HC Order 2015 defines who is required to pay the IHC, namely:

(1) A person who applies for–
(a) entry clearance of a type mentioned in section 38(2)(b) or (c) of the 2014 Act, or
(b) leave to remain in the United Kingdom for a limited period,
must pay a charge to the Secretary of State, subject to article 7.
(2) A person is required by paragraph (1) to pay a separate charge in respect of each application made by the person.

15.77 Schedule 2 to the HC Order 2015 sets out the persons who are exempt from paying the charge despite falling within article 3. The general position is summarised on the government website which explains that, for visa applications made outside the UK, applicants need to pay the IHC if:

a) the applicant is a national of a country outside the EEA;[52] and
b) the applicant is applying for a visa to work, study or to join family in the UK for more than six months (but is not applying to remain in the UK permanently).

15.78 There are different rules in article 3 of the HC Order 2015 for applicants who make immigration applications from within the UK. Such applicants need to pay the IHS if:

a) the applicant is a national of a country outside the EEA; and
b) the applicant is making an immigration application for any length of time, including applications for six months or less (but not applying to remain in the UK permanently).

15.79 Even if an applicant comes within article 3, the applicant is exempt from paying the IHS as a result of Schedule 2 to the HC Order 2015 if:

a) the applicant is applying for indefinite leave to enter or remain. However, an applicant will need to pay the healthcare surcharge if he or

49 SI No 792.
50 SI No 400.
51 SI No 420.
52 The EEA consists of the EU countries plus Iceland, Liechtenstein and Norway. The EU countries (until the UK leaves the EU) are Austria, Belgium, Bulgaria, Croatia, Republic of Cyprus, Czech Republic, Denmark, Estonia, Finland, France, Germany, Greece, Hungary, Ireland, Italy, Latvia, Lithuania, Luxembourg, Malta, Netherlands, Poland, Portugal, Romania, Slovakia, Slovenia, Spain, Sweden and the UK.

she applies for indefinite leave to remain but are only given limited leave. The applicant will need to pay before he or she is given the leave;

b) the applicant is a diplomat or a member of a visiting armed forces and not subject to immigration control;
c) the applicant is a dependant of a member of the UK's armed forces;
d) the applicant is a dependant of a member of another country's armed forces who is exempt from immigration control;
e) the applicant is a family member of a European national with EU treaty rights;
f) the applicant is applying for a visa for the Isle of Man or Channel Islands;
g) the applicant is a British Overseas Territory citizen resident in the Falkland Islands;
h) the applicant is an asylum-seeker or applying for humanitarian protection (or the asylum-seeker's dependant);
i) the applicant is a domestic worker who has been identified as a victim of slavery or human trafficking;
j) the applicant is applying for discretionary leave to remain in the UK as someone who has been identified as a victim of slavery or human trafficking (or the applicant's dependant);
k) the Home Office's domestic violence concession[53] applies to the applicant (or the applicant's dependant); or
l) being made to leave the UK would be against the applicant's rights under Article 3 of the European Convention of Human Rights (ECHR) (or the applicant's dependant).

15.80 A person who applies for a visitor's visa or a visa for six months or less from outside the UK does not need to pay the IHS or get an IHS reference number. However, such a person will have to pay charges for any NHS services that he or she uses.

15.81 Applicants who come within the terms of the HC Order 2015 still need to pay the IHS even if they have private medical insurance.

How much is the IHS?

15.82 The amounts of the IHS are set out in Schedule 1 to the HC Order 2015 as follows:

Type of application	Annual amount
Application for entry clearance or leave to remain as a student, in accordance with the immigration rules.	£150
Application for entry clearance or leave to remain as the dependant of a student, in accordance with the immigration rules.	£150

53 See www.gov.uk/government/publications/application-for-benefits-for-visa-holder-domestic-violence.

Application for entry clearance as a Tier 5 (Youth Mobility Scheme) Temporary Migrant in accordance with the immigration rules.	£150
All other applications for entry clearance or leave to remain.	£200

What is the consequence of paying the IHS

15.83 With the exception of chargeable assisted conception services, the effect of the IHS on the payment of NHS charges is covered in reg 10 of the COV Regs 2015, which broadly exempts anyone from NHS charges who has paid the IHS and has NHS services (which would otherwise be chargeable) provided to that person at a relevant time. This is set out in reg 10(2), which provides:

> (2) Subject to paragraph (2A), no charge may be made or recovered under these Regulations in respect of any relevant services provided during the relevant period to an overseas visitor in respect of whom–
> (a) an immigration health charge has been paid;
> (b) an exemption from paying such an immigration health charge applies, unless paragraph (3) applies;
> (c) a reduction or waiver from paying such an immigration health charge applies; or
> (d) a refund for part, but not all, of an immigration health charge has been made,
> in accordance with an order made under section 38 of the 2014 Act.
> (2A) Paragraph (2) does not apply in respect of chargeable assisted conception services.

15.84 The expression 'relevant period' is defined in reg 10(1) as follows:

> In this regulation 'relevant period' means–
> (a) where–
> (i) an immigration health charge is payable;
> (ii) an exemption from paying an immigration health charge applies as a consequence of any exemption provided for in an order made under section 38 (immigration health charge) of the 2014 Act;
> (iii) the Secretary of State has exercised discretion to reduce or waive all or part of an immigration health charge in accordance with such an order; or
> (iv) the Secretary of State has exercised discretion to refund part, but not all of an immigration health charge paid under such an order,
> the period of leave to enter or remain in the United Kingdom which is granted to the overseas visitor, or has effect on their arrival in the United Kingdom, in respect of the application for entry clearance or leave to remain to which the immigration health charge, exemption, reduction or waiver relates; and
> (b) in a case where the overseas visitor's leave to enter or remain in the United Kingdom is extended by virtue of–
> (i) section 3C (continuation of leave pending variation decision); or
> (ii) section 3D (continuation of leave following revocation),
> of the 1971 Act, the period in respect of which leave is extended under those sections'

15.85 Regulation 10(3) provides an exception to the exemption from NHS charges for someone who is exempt from paying the IHS. Thus a person who comes within regulation 10(3) is exempt from paying the IHS, but nonetheless has to pay NHS charges. Regulation 10(3) provides:[54]

> (3) This paragraph applies where a person is exempt from payment of an immigration health charge under an order made under section 38 of the 2014 Act by virtue of having made an application–
> (a) for entry clearance where, if granted in accordance with the immigration rules, the entry clearance would have effect on arrival in the United Kingdom as leave to enter for 6 months or less, or where the leave to enter which may be granted pursuant to that entry clearance would be for 6 months or less if granted in accordance with the immigration rules; or
> (b) for entry clearance–
> (i) before 6th April 2016, under Part 2 of the immigration rules (visitors to the UK); or
> (ii) on or after 6th April 2016, under Appendix V to the immigration rules (immigration rules for visitors).

15.86 The guidance explains the broad effect of paying the IHS as follows:[55]

> Payment of the health surcharge entitles the payer to NHS-funded healthcare on a similar basis as someone who is ordinarily resident. They are entitled to NHS services free at the point of use, including NHS hospital care, with, from 21 August 2017, the exception of assisted conception services (e.g. IVF) (see paragraph 5.16). They must also pay for services for which a UK ordinary resident must also pay, such as dentistry and prescriptions in England, unless they also meet the particular exemption criteria of those services.

15.87 The guidance also explains:[56]

> An individual who pays for the health surcharge is only entitled to free treatment once their application for a visa has been granted, and not from the date when the health surcharge is paid. The exemption from NHS charges applies to the period of leave to enter or remain in the UK granted to the person. Once that leave expires or is curtailed, the person becomes liable for charges from then on, including where the person is part-way through a course of treatment.

15.88 There are special rules for overseas visitors who have made applications for entry clearance or leave to remain prior to the commencement of the immigration health charge. This is set out in regulation 11(3), which provides:[57]

> (3) Subject to paragraph (3A), no charge may be made or recovered under these Regulations in respect of any relevant services provided to an overseas visitor during the relevant period who–
> (a) made an application for entry clearance or leave to remain in the United Kingdom before the relevant date and was granted leave to enter or remain in the United Kingdom or entry clearance which has effect on the overseas visitor's arrival in the United Kingdom as leave to enter or remain in the United Kingdom in respect of that application;
> (b) has entered, or remained in, the United Kingdom by virtue of that leave to enter or remain; and

54 As from 21 August 2017 as a result of SI 2017 No 756.
55 At para 5.2.
56 At para 5.8.
57 As from 21 August 2017.

(c) had that application for entry clearance or leave to remain been made on or after the relevant date, would be–
(i) liable to pay an immigration health charge; or
(ii) exempt from paying an immigration health charge as a consequence of an exemption provision under an order made under section 38 of the 2014 Act, unless paragraph (4) applies.
(3A) Paragraph (3) does not apply in respect of chargeable assisted conception services'

15.89 The relevant date for the purposes of reg 11 of the 2015 Regulation is 6 April 2015. The term 'relevant period' for the purposes of Article 11 is defined at reg 11(1) as follows:

In this regulation 'relevant period' means–
(a) the period of leave to enter or remain in the United Kingdom granted to the overseas visitor in respect of the application for entry clearance or leave to remain to which paragraph (3)(a) refers; and
(b) in a case where the overseas visitor's leave to enter or remain in the United Kingdom is extended by virtue of–
(i) section 3C (continuation of leave pending variation decision); or
(ii) section 3D (continuation of leave following revocation),
of the 1971 Act, the period in respect of which leave is extended under those sections

15.90 There is a similar exemption to reg 10(3)[58] in reg 11(4) which provides that a person who satisfies the following conditions will be liable for NHS charges:

(4) This paragraph applies where an overseas visitor–
(a) would be exempt from an immigration health charge under an order made under section 38 of the 2014 Act by virtue of having made an application of a kind described in regulation 10(3)(a) or (b) (immigration health charge); or
(b) has been granted leave to enter or remain in the United Kingdom outside the immigration rules for 6 months or less.

15.91 From 21 August 2017 there are rules to prevent most overseas visitors who have paid the IHS being entitled to free in-vitro fertilisation (IVF) services. However, there are exceptions to this. This is explained in the guidance as follows:

Assisted Conception Services
5.15. Since 21 August 2017, those exempt from charge under Regulation 10 (health surcharge arrangements) or 11 (transitional arrangements) are not exempt from charge in relation to assisted conception services.

5.16. Assisted conception services are defined in the Charging Regulations as any medical, surgical or obstetric services provided for the purpose of assisting a person to carry a child. Broadly speaking, this means any medicines, surgery or procedures that are required to diagnose and treat infertility so a person can have a child. It includes procedures such as intrauterine insemination (IUI), in vitro fertilisation (IVF) and egg and sperm donation.

5.17 However, it is important to understand a number of points in relation to this exclusion. Firstly, assisted conception services do not include services that are commissioned by NHS England as follows:

- services for serving members of the armed forces and their families;

58 See para 15.85 above.

- infertility treatment for seriously injured serving members and veterans; and,
- infertility treatment: further provisions.

5.18 Therefore, dependants of a member of HM forces, or of a member of a force who is exempt from immigration control, will still be able to receive assisted conception services free of charge due to the above exclusion within the definition.

5.19 Secondly, there are some groups who, whilst they may choose to make an application for leave to remain in the UK (under a category that means they are exempt from paying the health surcharge, thereby entitling them to free NHS services except for assisted conception services), there are some overlapping exemptions within the Charging Regulations to consider. These groups are:

- people, and their dependants, who make an application for asylum, temporary protection or humanitarian protection;
- children who are looked after by a Local Authority;
- victims of modern slavery (which includes victims of trafficking or slavery, servitude and forced or compulsory labour) with a positive conclusive grounds decision; and,
- people who make applications for leave to remain under the Home Office Destitution Domestic Violence Concession (would only be entitled to free assisted conception services on the same basis as a resident, if the need to the services was as a result of domestic violence and the person had not travelled to the UK to receive treatment)

5.20 This means that when assessing if charges will apply for assisted conception services, relevant bodies must consider whether Regulations 15(b), 16 or 9(f), or any other exemption, also apply to the patient. If they do, this will mean that no charge can be made to that person for assisted conception services, despite the exclusion of those services from the ones that those covered by health surcharge arrangements alone can receive without further charge.

5.21 Thirdly, those applying for leave to remain as either:

- a person granted entry clearance or leave to remain pursuant to an EU obligation; or
- a British Overseas Territories citizen who is resident in the Falklands Islands,

remain entitled to assisted conception services without further charge if they are covered for those services under the exemption for people with rights under EU law or under the terms of a reciprocal agreement.

5.22 Finally, a person who is exempt under Regulation 10 or 11 and who has begun a course of assisted conception treatment before 21 August 2017 will be entitled to the remainder of that course of treatment free of charge. New courses of assisted conception treatment begun on or after 21 August 2017 will not be free of charge and the overseas visitor will be required to pay for that service. It is a clinical decision as to what constitutes a particular course of treatment. Where two people are seeking assisted conception services with NHS funding, and one of the two people is covered by health surcharge arrangements and the other is ordinarily resident in the UK and therefore not subject to charge, the services required by the health surcharge payer will be chargeable. Any services required by the ordinarily resident person will continue to be freely available, subject to the established local or national commissioning arrangements'

15.92 Hence, unless within the exceptions listed above, an overseas visitor who has paid the IHS will have to pay for NHS assisted conception services.

15.93 There is no general exemption from paying charges for NHS services for family members of the person who pays the IHS (or would have been liable to pay the IHS if the person had arrived in the UK after the IHS came into effect). Each person who wants to come to the UK is required to apply for his or her own visa and will have to pay the IHS as part of that visa application process. However, there is an exemption for children born to someone who pays the IHS for the first three months of life. This is set out in reg 25(3), which provides:

> No charge may be made or recovered in respect of any relevant services provided to an overseas visitor who is a child who–
> (a) is born in the United Kingdom to a parent who is exempt from charges by virtue of–
> (i) regulation 10 (immigration health charge); or
> (ii) regulation 11 (overseas visitors who have made applications for entry clearance or leave to remain prior to the commencement of the immigration health charge);
> (b) is aged 3 months or less; and
> (c) has not left the United Kingdom since birth.

15.94 Once the child reaches the age of three months, an application should be made for the child to have leave to remain in the UK. The IHS will have to be paid for the child as part of that application in order for the child to be able to continue to receive NHS services without incurring charges under the COV Regs 2015.

Overseas visitors with EU and EEA rights

Overview

15.95 Regulation 12 of the COV Regs 2015 provides that EU citizens and others with EU rights are exempt from charges. It provides:

> No charge may be made or recovered in respect of any relevant services provided to an overseas visitor who has an entitlement to the provision of the services in question without charge under or by virtue of any of the following–
> (a) regulations made under Article 48 of the Treaty on the Functioning of the European Union;
> (b) an agreement entered into between the European Union and any other country; or
> (c) any other enforceable EU right.

15.96 The EU consists of the 28 member states of the EU (at least until the UK leaves the EU) which are as follows: Austria, Belgium, Bulgaria, Croatia, Cyprus (Southern), Czech Republic, Denmark, Estonia, Finland, France, Germany, Greece, Hungary, Ireland, Italy, Latvia, Lithuania, Luxembourg, Malta, Netherlands, Poland, Portugal, Romania, Slovakia, Slovenia, Spain, Sweden and the UK. In addition, EU regulations apply to the EEA countries of Iceland, Liechtenstein and Norway, and so persons who have rights to reside in those countries come within reg 12.

15.97 The position of residents of Switzerland is explained in the guidance as follows:[59]

> Switzerland has a separate agreement with the EU which, in effect, applies the EU Regulations to Switzerland.

15.98 The guidance also explains:[60]

> It should be noted that:
>
> a) for the purposes of the relevant EU Regulations:
>   - France includes the overseas departments of Guadeloupe, Martinique, Guyane (French Guiana) and Réunion;
>   - Spain includes the Balearic Islands, the Canary Islands, Ceuta and Melilla;
>   - Portugal includes the Azores and Madeira.
>
> b) the territory of Denmark excludes the Faroe Islands and Greenland. However, a separate reciprocal healthcare agreement between the EU and Greenland allows Greenland nationals visiting EEA countries to receive immediately necessary treatment under state healthcare;
>
> c) Andorra, Monaco, San Marino and Vatican City are not part of the EEA;
>
> d) EU law is suspended in the north Cyprus. It only applies in the rest of Cyprus. Therefore, visitors from north Cyprus are not covered by the EU Regulations. Visitors who are ordinarily resident in north Cyprus and chargeable directly at the point of use for NHS services should be counted as ordinarily resident in the EEA and should therefore be charged on that basis (i.e. at 100% of tariff);
>
> e) the UK sovereign bases in Cyprus do not count as part of the UK in this context, nor as part of the EU;
>
> f) for the purposes of healthcare, relations between the UK and Gibraltar are governed by a bilateral healthcare agreement (Chapter 10). The EU Regulations do not apply;
>
> g) though not covered under the EU Regulations, Bosnia and Herzegovina, Kosovo, Macedonia, Montenegro and Serbia have reciprocal agreements with the UK (see Regulation 14 and Chapter 10).

What NHS services are holders of EU rights entitled to access without charge?

15.99 The rights of EU residents to obtain healthcare services in another member state is an area of some complexity. There are a variety of rules which have been set up to support the single market in goods and services across the EU.

15.100 The essential premise is that workers and nationals from EU states have free movement rights to enable them to travel for both business and other purposes across the EU and should not be discriminated against by individual members states. Limiting access to state-provided health services would be a severe limitation on that right of free movement. However, the rules governing the operation of each member state's national health service are outside the EU's competence.[61] It follows that

59 At para 9.6.

60 At para 9.67.

61 See Article 168(7) of the Treaty for the Functioning of the European Union. There is competency on public health measures but that is outside the scope of this chapter.

freedom of movement would be abused if it permitted citizens in a low tax, low public service state to cross the border every time they needed healthcare services to take advantage of the more extensive range of services provided in a higher taxed state with better public services. Hence a system of recharges operates so that the government which funds healthcare services in members state A for residents of member state B is entitled to recoup the cost of providing those services from the government of member state B. However, the right to access to healthcare under the systems of other member states is not designed to allow individuals to expand the services that they can access. Hence, for example, if IVF treatment or a specific cancer drug is not available in member state A as part of state-funded healthcare, a resident of that state should not be able to access that treatment by travelling to member state B where it is provided as part of the state healthcare system for member state B.

15.101 Even though the organisation of healthcare services by national governments is a matter for the individual governments, there is a 'market' in the delivery of healthcare services and hence EU citizens have the right to travel across borders to access specialist health services in other countries. It follows that it would be a breach of the principles of the single European market for the national rules under which each member state purchases healthcare for their own citizens to unduly favour healthcare services operating in their own countries. Hence, the rules provide that a person who has a contractual right under a state insurance system to have a particular medical procedure carried out cannot only access that service in his or her home country. There is thus, within certain constraints, a right for persons who are covered by healthcare rights under their home state to exercise those rights in any member state. This right is expressed in Article 56 of the Treaty of the Functioning of the European Union[62] which provides:

> Within the framework of the provisions set out below, restrictions on freedom to provide services within the Union shall be prohibited in respect of nationals of Member States who are established in a Member State other than that of the person for whom the services are intended.
>
> The European Parliament and the Council, acting in accordance with the ordinary legislative procedure, may extend the provisions of the Chapter to nationals of a third country who provide services and who are established within the Union.

15.102 This Article provides for rights which are directly enforceable by UK residents who seek services abroad, as well as EU-based residents who seek services in the UK. However, those are not absolute rights since they can be limited to the extent needed to protect the legitimate interests of a state healthcare system.

15.103 EU residents also acquired specific rights under Regulation (EEC) 1408/71 on the application of social security schemes to employed persons and their families moving within the Community. The rights under Regulation 1408/71 were separate from the rights under the Article 56 of

62 See http://eur-lex.europa.eu/legal-content/EN/TXT/?uri=celex%3A12012E%2FTXT.

the Treaty.[63] Those rights are now replaced by Regulation (EC) No 883/2004 of the European Parliament and of the Council of 29 April 2004 on the coordination of social security systems (Text with relevance for the EEA and for Switzerland) ('the 2004 EU Regulation'). The 2004 EU Regulation came into force on 1 May 2010. The EU also made Regulation (EC) No 987/2009 of the European Parliament and of the Council of 16 September 2009 laying down the procedure for implementing Regulation (EC) No 883/2004 on the coordination of social security systems[64] ('the 2009 EU Regulation') which implement the 2004 EU Regulation.

15.104 In 2011 the EU passed a Directive (2011/24/EU)[65] on the application of patients' rights in cross-border healthcare ('the 2011 EU Directive'). There had been extensive litigation in the EU Court of Justice about cross-border healthcare rights. Recital 8 provides:

> Some issues relating to cross-border healthcare, in particular reimbursement of healthcare provided in a Member State other than that in which the recipient of the care is resident, have already been addressed by the Court of Justice. This Directive is intended to achieve a more general, and also effective, application of principles developed by the Court of Justice on a case-by-case basis.

15.105 It is beyond the scope of this chapter to describe the full operation of the rules of cross-border healthcare since this chapter is focused on NHS charges. However, where NHS services are provided to a person with EU rights, in order to determine which legal regime operates, the first question to ask is whether:

a) the need for medical treatment arose during the visit to the UK without the patient having travelled to the UK for the purpose of seeking medical treatment; or
b) the patient travelled to the UK for the purpose of seeking medical treatment.

Medical treatment where the need arises while the EU rights holder is in the UK

15.106 The 2004 EU Regulation draws a distinction between the NHS services that a person exercising EU rights is entitled to where that person resides in another EU country and the NHS services a person is entitled to who visits (or stays in) another EU country.

15.107 Article 17 of the 2004 EU Regulation covers the position of EU rights holders who reside in a different member state. It provides:

> An insured person or members of his family who reside in a Member State other than the competent Member State shall receive in the Member State of residence benefits in kind provided, on behalf of the competent institution, by the institution of the place of residence, in accordance with

63 The fact that the rights under the Treaty were separate to the rights under EU Regulations was established by Munby J in *R (Watts) v Bedford Primary Care Trust and others* [2003] EWHC 2228 (Admin).

64 See http://eur-lex.europa.eu/LexUriServ/LexUriServ.do?uri=OJ:L:2009:284:0001:0042:en:PDF.

65 See http://eur-lex.europa.eu/LexUriServ/LexUriServ.do?uri=OJ:L:2011:088:0045:0065:en:PDF.

> the provisions of the legislation it applies, as though they were insured under the said legislation

Hence, a French person who resides in the UK is entitled to the same benefits from the NHS as other people living in the UK. A person with EU rights who resides in the UK is highly likely to become 'ordinarily resident' in the UK. That residence will be lawful because the EU rights holder will be able to exercise freedom of movement rights in order to be able lawfully to reside in the UK. It follows that the COV Regs 2015 will not generally apply to an EU rights holder who resides here, even if the EU rights holder also maintains a residence in their home EU country. It follows that such a person can access NHS services without having to show a European Health Insurance Card (EHIC) or PRC card before accessing NHS services.

15.108 There is a separate set of rules in the 2004 EU Regulation for individuals who are resident in one member state and 'stay' in another member state (without becoming 'ordinarily resident' in the UK). The word 'stay' is used in the 2004 EU Regulation to contrast with 'reside'. It thus suggests that the person with EU rights has a need for healthcare services in a different country to the country where he or she resides. Article 19 of the 2004 EU Regulation provides:

> 1. Unless otherwise provided for by paragraph 2, an insured person and the members of his family staying in a Member State other than the competent Member State shall be entitled to the benefits in kind which become necessary on medical grounds during their stay, taking into account the nature of the benefits and the expected length of the stay. These benefits shall be provided on behalf of the competent institution by the institution of the place of stay, in accordance with the provisions of the legislation it applies, as though the persons concerned were insured under the said legislation.
>
> 2. The Administrative Commission shall establish a list of benefits in kind which, in order to be provided during a stay in another Member State, require for practical reasons a prior agreement between the person concerned and the institution providing the care.

15.109 The right to healthcare for people who visit another EU state under Article 19 of the 2004 EU Regulation is subject to the limitation that these services must be 'necessary on medical grounds during their stay, taking into account the nature of the benefits and the expected length of the stay'. The Article 19 right is further qualified where the person has travelled for the purpose of seeking treatment (see para 5.115 below).

15.110 Article 25(3) of 2009 EU Regulation, which implements the 2004 EU Regulation, provides the following definition of the benefits to which an EU rights patient is entitled to under the 2004 EU Regulation as follows:

> The benefits in kind referred to in Article 19(1) of the basic Regulation[66] shall refer to the benefits in kind which are provided in the Member State of stay, in accordance with its legislation, and which become necessary on medical grounds with a view to preventing an insured person from being

66 This is reference to the 2004 EU Regulations.

forced to return, before the end of the planned duration of stay, to the competent Member State to obtain the necessary treatment.

15.111 The guidance has interpreted this set of rights as follows:[67]

> 9.16 A person with a valid EHIC/PRC is entitled to free treatment for 'all treatment that is medically necessary before their planned date of return,' except where charges also apply to residents in England, such as prescription and dental fees. In other words, this means treatment that it is medically necessary to provide a visitor during their temporary stay in the UK, with a view to preventing them from being forced to return home for treatment before the end of their planned duration of stay. The patient does not need to have a specific leaving date or duration of stay, as long as the stay is temporary. This means the following is covered:
>
> - diagnosis of symptoms or signs occurring for the first time after the visitor's arrival in the UK;
> - any other treatment which, in the opinion of a registered medical or dental practitioner, is required promptly for a condition which:
>   - arose after the visitor's arrival; or
>   - became acutely exacerbated after their arrival; or
>   - would be likely to become acutely exacerbated without treatment; plus
> - the treatment of chronic or pre-existing conditions, including routine monitoring.
>
> 9.17 It should be noted that the above definition of 'medically necessary treatment' is different from the entitlement to free treatment that applies to visitors from reciprocal agreement countries which are not covered by EU regulations (see regulation 14 and Chapter 10).

15.112 The guidance also refers to maternity and dialysis services, and explains how these can be accessed. This wording gives guidance about how the NHS should strike the balance between treatment which is necessary for an EU rights overseas visitor during a temporary stay in the UK, which is covered by the Article 19/EHIC system, and the need for more extensive medical treatment for such a patient which lies outside of the Article 19/ EHIC system.

15.113 Both EU residents and visitors have to prove their entitlement to NHS services under the Article 19/EHIC set of rights before they can access services free of charge. Article 25 of the 2009 EU Regulation provides:

> 1. For the purposes of the application of Article 19 of the basic Regulation, the insured person shall present to the health care provider in the Member State of stay a document issued by the competent institution indicating his entitlement to benefits in kind. If the insured person does not have such a document, the institution of the place of stay, upon request or if otherwise necessary, shall contact the competent institution in order to obtain one.
>
> 2. That document shall indicate that the insured person is entitled to benefits in kind under the conditions laid down in Article 19 of the basic Regulation on the same terms as those applicable to persons insured under the legislation of the Member State of stay.

15.114 The guidance explains how this works in practice as follows:

> **European Health Insurance Card (EHIC)**
>
> 9.9. A valid EHIC or Provisional Replacement Certificate (PRC) for the EHIC can demonstrate that a visitor (including a student) is exempt from

67 At paras 9.16 and 9.17.

charge under the EU Regulations, and therefore entitled to free NHS treatment that is medically necessary during their visit until their planned date of return. This is because the other country is responsible for the healthcare costs of the visitor. The UK can reclaim back the cost of providing treatment to the patient, if the details of the EHIC or PRC are recorded on the OVM portal.

9.10. However, an arrangement between the UK and the Republic of Ireland means that visitors from the Republic of Ireland do not have to present an EHIC to obtain free NHS treatment under the EU Regulations. They only need to present evidence that they are resident in the Republic of Ireland, although a valid EHIC can be used as evidence of this. Visitors from the Republic of Ireland do need to be referred with an S2 for pre-planned treatment.

9.11. Visitors who are resident in Switzerland or the EEA (except Ireland) who do not 9 provide an EHIC/PRC must be charged for their NHS hospital treatment at 100% of the NHS tariff or equivalent, unless they are ordinarily resident in the UK or a different exemption applies to them under the Charging Regulations.

9.12. A person who has been charged because they did not provide an EHIC/PRC may be entitled to a reimbursement from their home state on their return. Alternatively, if they provide a valid EHIC/PRC covering the period of treatment within a reasonable timescale after treatment, they should be reimbursed by the relevant body.

9.13. Visitors from the EEA/Switzerland may be exempt under a different exemption category within the Charging Regulations and it is very important that this is considered before the patient is charged. EEA and Swiss nationals as well as some non-EEA nationals not subject to immigration control, who are ordinarily resident in the UK are entitled to free treatment on that basis.

9.14. However, if the visitor is able to show a valid EHIC or PRC from another EEA member state or Switzerland, the UK can claim back the cost of their treatment from that country. It is possible to be ordinarily resident in the UK and still be insured by another country. This is often the case with EEA students coming to study in the UK Consequently, if a patient from another EEA country or Switzerland presents for treatment and the treating NHS provider suspects they are ordinarily resident in the UK, the provider should still ask the patient if they have an EHIC/ PRC and report their details via the OVT web portal.

9.15. In order for the UK to make a claim to the relevant EEA state or Switzerland for treating its residents, it is imperative that the data from the EHIC/PRC is recorded and reported to the Overseas Healthcare Team at the Department for Work and Pensions (DWP) via the OVT web portal (see paragraphs 9.49–9.54 below).

15.115 Article 20 of the 2004 EU Regulation places limits on these rights for persons who travel for the purpose of accessing healthcare services. It provides:

1. Unless otherwise provided for by this Regulation, an insured person travelling to another Member State with the purpose of receiving benefits in kind during the stay shall seek authorisation from the competent institution.

2. An insured person who is authorised by the competent institution to go to another Member State with the purpose of receiving the treatment

appropriate to his condition shall receive the benefits in kind provided, on behalf of the competent institution, by the institution of the place of stay, in accordance with the provisions of the legislation it applies, as though he were insured under the said legislation. The authorisation shall be accorded where the treatment in question is among the benefits provided for by the legislation in the Member State where the person concerned resides and where he cannot be given such treatment within a time-limit which is medically justifiable, taking into account his current state of health and the probable course of his illness.

3. Paragraphs 1 and 2 shall apply mutatis mutandis to the members of the family of an insured person.

15.116 The requirement to provide authorisation from the home state 'competent institution' before EU cross border healthcare rights can be exercised only applies where a person travels 'with the purpose of receiving benefits in kind during the stay'. That can be a fact sensitive assessment because, by way of example, a person who has a long-term condition which needs regular medication may travel to another EU country for a family or social event or even for a holiday, but may need healthcare during the visit. Even if it was foreseeable that the person would have a need for healthcare services during the trip, he or she will be entitled to exercise rights under the regulation as long as the primary purpose of the trip was not to secure healthcare services in another country.

15.117 Article 35 of the 2004 EU Regulation provides that the benefits in kind provided by the institution of a member state on behalf of the institution of another member state under this chapter gives rise to full reimbursement by the home member state. Hence, where the NHS provides services to a person who exercises EU rights, the NHS cannot charge the person exercising rights but the UK government can recover the costs of providing the treatment from the home EU state. Details of the procedures that NHS bodies should follow to process payment claims are set out in the guidance.

15.118 Family members of overseas visitors who have EU/EEA rights (known as the 'principal overseas visitor') will usually have their own rights to medical treatment as an EU/EEA citizen. However, there can be occasions where a principal overseas visitor can assert EU/EEA rights but members of his or her family do not have their own EU/EEA rights. In such circumstances, reg 25(4) extends the right to be exempt from charges in a like way to a member of the family[68] of the principal overseas visitor provided:

a) the overseas visitor who is seeking the exemption from NHS charges is lawfully present in the UK;
b) the overseas visitor who is seeking the exemption from NHS charges is visiting the United Kingdom with the principal overseas visitor; and
c) the principal overseas visitor would be exempt from the relevant NHS charges for the NHS treatment in question.

15.119 Even though no charges are made against the individuals with EU rights who access NHS services, the UK government can recover the costs of

68 Please see para 15.193 for the meaning of 'member of a family' of an overseas visitor.

providing NHS services to these individuals through the reciprocal agreements set up by the EU. The UK government also has to pay for healthcare services provided to UK residents who are treated by the health services operating other EU member states. Almost all other EU states operate under a mandatory insurance system, and the rights to free NHS treatment in the UK only apply to those who are eligible for state-funded healthcare services in their home state. The guidance explains this as follows:[69]

> Only residents 'insured' under any public healthcare system of an EEA country or Switzerland are covered by the EU Regulations when they are visiting the UK. In detail, this covers:
> - EEA nationals, stateless persons or refugees, plus their family members and survivors (irrespective of nationality) of these groups of people, insured in each case under any public healthcare system in an EEA country (N.B. they may be 'insured' by the UK even if they are living abroad. See paragraph 9.55 onwards);
> - Swiss or EU nationals, stateless persons or refugees, plus their family members and survivors (irrespective of nationality) of these groups of people, insured in each case in Switzerland;
> - non-EEA nationals legally resident and insured in any EU country (except Denmark).

15.120 Thus bodies providing NHS services are required to assess the level of charges payable in respect of persons exercising EU and EEA rights so that the Department for Work and Pensions (DWP) can make the appropriate claim from their host healthcare service.

EU rights holders who come to the UK for planned treatment

15.121 The rights discussed above under Article 19 of the 2004 EU Regulation do not apply where an EU rights holder comes to the UK for the specific purpose of seeking medical treatment. Entirely different considerations arise where a patient seeks to exercise EU rights to come to the UK for the specific purpose of having medical treatment. The real issue here is not securing NHS treatment from an NHS provider. NHS bodies are not allowed to discriminate on the grounds of the racial origin of place of residence of a patient (as that would be unlawful discrimination contrary to the Equality Act 2010). As Munby J noted in *R (Watts) v Bedford Primary Care Trust and others*:[70]

> . . . the entire debate in relation to Article 49 is not about the right to travel abroad for treatment – for which, of course, one needs no more than a passport – but about the right to be reimbursed for the cost of treatment obtained abroad. And, moreover, it shows that in this context it matters not whether the cost of such treatment is to be reimbursed to the patient or paid direct to the foreign service provider. Nor does it matter if the reimbursement comes from a sickness fund *or from the national budget.*

15.122 There are broadly five routes by which holders of EU rights can come to the UK and seek treatment at an NHS hospital or other NHS provider. These are:

69 At para 9.8.

70 [2003] EWHC 2228 (Admin), (2003) 6 CCLR 566 at para 105.

1) as a patient who pays NHS charges or arranges for NHS charges to be paid on the patient's behalf by an employer, an insurance company or any other third party. In such a case, the patient is accessing NHS services but is doing so on a fee-paying basis;
2) an EU-based healthcare provider or EU member state healthcare organisation directly contracts with an NHS body to provide healthcare services to persons covered by their state healthcare system.[71] In such an arrangement, the NHS provider bills the EU-based healthcare provider or EU member state healthcare organisation in accordance with the terms of contract. This would be an entirely private law arrangement and the rights of each party would be governed by the terms of the contract. No 'NHS charges' would be payable because the remuneration for the NHS provider would be fixed by the contract (unless the contract also provided that the patient was to make a defined financial contribution);
3) by exercising the patient's rights under the 2011 EU Directive;
4) by the 'S2' route; or
5) by the 'S1' route.

15.123 Different considerations apply regarding NHS charges depending on the route chosen by the patient. However, the first two do not need to be considered further here as they do not give rise to charges under the COV Regs 2015. The latter three routes will be discussed in turn.

The 2011 EU Directive

15.124 The secretary of state has implemented the 2011 EU Directive in England by the National Health Service (Cross-Border Healthcare) Regulations 2013.[72] However, these regulations are almost entirely focused on the position of UK residents who are entitled to NHS services but wish to access services in another EU country. The regulations do not generally assist in describing the way in which the NHS should react to patients from abroad who are EU rights holders who want to exercise their right to have treatment provided within the NHS.

15.125 Rights under the directive can be exercised by those having rights in EU and EEA states, but not those having rights in Switzerland. It applies to both planned and unplanned medical treatment. Further, the person exercising the rights is not limited to seeking treatment in NHS facilities but can seek to access healthcare from any Care Quality Commission (CQC) registered provider of healthcare services in the UK.

15.126 The general effect of the 2011 EU Directive is to allow a patient to seek healthcare in another EU country at his or her own cost and then to make a retrospective claim against his or her home state healthcare system to be reimbursed for the costs the patient has incurred. The patient meets the costs of travel and any other costs which arise as a result of the choice to seek treatment in another EU member state.

15.127 NHS bodies are obliged to charge the patient the full cost of any medical treatment provided where a patient is seeking to exercise his

71 Both NHS trusts and NHS foundation trusts are entitled to undertake private healthcare.

72 SI No 2269.

or her rights under the 2011 EU Directive. NHS bodies also have duties to ensure that they provide full information to any prospective patient. Article 4.2(b) of the 2011 EU Directive provides:

> The Member State of treatment shall ensure that: . . .
>
> (b) healthcare providers provide relevant information to help individual patients to make an informed choice, including on treatment options, on the availability, quality and safety of the healthcare they provide in the Member State of treatment and that they also provide clear invoices and clear information on prices, as well as on their authorisation or registration status, their insurance cover or other means of personal or collective protection with regard to professional liability. To the extent that healthcare providers already provide patients resident in the Member State of treatment with relevant information on these subjects, this Directive does not oblige healthcare providers to provide more extensive information to patients from other Member States.

15.128 NHS providers must not discriminate against EU-based patients who wish to exercise their rights under the 2011 EU Directive. This is explained in Article 4.3 of the 2011 EU Directive, which provides:

> **3. The principle of non-discrimination with regard to nationality shall be applied to patients from other Member States.**
> This shall be without prejudice to the possibility for the Member State of treatment, where it is justified by overriding reasons of general interest, such as planning requirements relating to the aim of ensuring sufficient and permanent access to a balanced range of high-quality treatment in the Member State concerned or to the wish to control costs and avoid, as far as possible, any waste of financial, technical and human resources, to adopt measures regarding access to treatment aimed at fulfilling its fundamental responsibility to ensure sufficient and permanent access to healthcare within its territory. Such measures shall be limited to what is necessary and proportionate and may not constitute a means of arbitrary discrimination and shall be made publicly available in advance.

15.129 The guidance suggests that this gives rise to grounds on which an NHS provider could refuse to treat an EU-based patient exercising rights under the directive on the grounds that the provider needed its facilities to treat locally based patients. It states:

> 9.41. The Directive does not require providers to accept visiting patients for planned healthcare if this would be to the detriment of ensuring sufficient access for their own patients with similar health needs. It also does not require providers to prioritise visitors to the detriment of other patients, for instance by increasing waiting times. However, acute trusts or other providers would need to be able to explain and evidence the lack of capacity, demonstrate that refusal is necessary and show they were not discriminating against nationals of other states on grounds of nationality if rejecting a request for treatment.
>
> 9.42. In principle, the strongest ground for refusing a visiting patient is a lack of service capacity. However, the provider would need to consider whether the patient could be offered the option of joining the waiting list, to be treated alongside domestic patients on the basis of clinical priority. The patient may also consider the option of approaching a different provider.

15.130 Those paragraphs appear to suggest that NHS providers have a greater level of discretion to turn away patients than the limited level of discretion suggested by the wording of the 2011 EU Directive, particularly as any NHS body which wishes to turn away patients exercising rights under the 2011 EU Directive has to have publicised its position in advance in order to be acting lawfully. The wording of Article 4.3 appears to suggest that the ability of NHS providers to refuse to permit EU-based patients to join the queue for treatment may be more restricted than the approach set out in the guidance.

15.131 Part of that non-discrimination involves charging the same fees as UK patients (albeit these are usually paid by an NHS commissioner and not by the patient themselves). This is set out in Article 4.4 of the 2011 EU Directive, which provides:

> Member States shall ensure that the healthcare providers on their territory apply the same scale of fees for healthcare for patients from other Member States, as for domestic patients in a comparable medical situation, or that they charge a price calculated according to objective, non-discriminatory criteria if there is no comparable price for domestic patients.

15.132 The guidance summarises the obligations on NHS bodies as follows:

> 9.35 OVMs [Overseas Visitors Managers] should be aware that healthcare providers in England who are providing treatment to visiting patients under the provisions of the Directive need to observe some key requirements. They must:
> - provide patients with relevant information on treatment options, quality and safety;
> - provide clear invoices and price information;
> - apply fees in a non-discriminatory manner;
> - ensure transparent complaints procedures and procedures to obtain redress are in place;
> - apply adequate systems of professional liability insurance or similar;
> - respect privacy in the processing of personal information; and,
> - supply patients with a copy of the record of their medical treatment.

The S2 Route (formerly the E112 route)

15.133 Article 20 of the 2004 EU Regulation provides a route by which EU-based patients can apply to their home state healthcare provider to approve the patient securing NHS treatment in advance of a visit to the UK. It provides:

> **Travel with the purpose of receiving benefits in kind – Authorisation to receive appropriate treatment outside the Member State of residence**
> 1. Unless otherwise provided for by this Regulation, an insured person travelling to another Member State with the purpose of receiving benefits in kind during the stay shall seek authorisation from the competent institution.
> 2. An insured person who is authorised by the competent institution to go to another Member State with the purpose of receiving the treatment appropriate to his condition shall receive the benefits in kind provided, on behalf of the competent institution, by the institution of the place of stay, in accordance with the provisions of the legislation it applies, as though he were insured under the said legislation. The authorisation shall be accorded where the treatment in question is among the benefits provided for by the legislation in the Member State where the person concerned resides and where he cannot be given such treatment within

a time-limit which is medically justifiable, taking into account his current state of health and the probable course of his illness.

3. Paragraphs 1 and 2 shall apply mutatis mutandis to the members of the family of an insured person'

15.134 There has been extensive litigation about when a home member state is required to give authorisation for a patient to seek healthcare in another member state. This issue was examined by the High Court in *Watts*,[73] and the issues have been examined in a series of cases in the European Court of Justice. The regulation cannot be used by patients to access NHS treatment which would not be funded under their home state healthcare system and only acquire a right to have treatment funded by their home state in the healthcare system of another member state where there is a measure of failure in the home provision, usually because there are capacity problems and so treatment will be unduly delayed. The test is whether 'he cannot be given such treatment within a time-limit which is medically justifiable, taking into account his current state of health and the probable course of his illness'. However, where a patient with EU rights is able to exercise rights under Article 20 of the 2004 EU Regulation, the 'competent institution' in his or her home state will issue the patient with a form S2.

15.135 Where an EU-based patient has a valid S2 form from his or her home competent institution, the patient has a right to seek treatment from an NHS provider. The guidance states that such patients should join the waiting list and be treated in the same way as other NHS patients. The NHS provider then passes the information on to the DWP which makes a claim from the home competent institution. The guidance states as follows:

> 9.46. To avoid the complications that may occur if a patient authorised to seek NHS treatment in the UK is inadvertently treated privately, NHS hospitals and consultants are advised to establish when accepting such referrals whether the treatment should be at the cost of the patient's relevant foreign authority or at the patient's own cost, and if they wish to be a chargeable NHS or private patient.
>
> 9.47. Where an NHS hospital has agreed to accept a patient under these arrangements, but on arrival the patient cannot produce the appropriate form, only treatment under the 'all medically necessary treatment' definition should be provided without charge (assuming they can show their EHIC or PRC). The patient can pay in advance for the planned treatment and should be charged the tariff cost or equivalent (if no national tariff exists) for the treatment. The patient may be able to claim reimbursement for this cost from their state of residence. If the relevant form is subsequently received, the charge should be refunded. If the form has not been received by the time the patient is discharged from NHS hospital they should be told to take the matter up with their social security institution.
>
> 9.48. The number of referred patients from Malta who are treated free under these arrangements is governed by a strict quota and is monitored by the Department of Health. Arrangements exist by which NHS hospitals are notified in advance of patients authorised to come under these arrangements. The Maltese High Commission in London allocates quota numbers

73 See *R (Watts) v Bedford Primary Care Trust and others* [2003] EWHC 2228 (Admin), (2003) 6 CCLR 566.

to patients referred to the UK. When the quota is exhausted, further patients may be referred to the UK by the health authorities of Malta, but these patients should be charged for their treatment. Reclaiming the costs of treating EEA/Swiss residents under the EHIC and S2 routes

9.49. In order for the UK to make a claim to the relevant EEA country or Switzerland for the cost of treating their residents, it is imperative that the data from a valid EHIC/PRC/S2 /or Maltese quota number is recorded and reported to the Overseas Healthcare Team at DWP. Without this data, the UK cannot make a claim for reimbursement and is in effect subsidising the healthcare costs of other countries.

9.50. All treatment carried out whenever a valid EHIC/PRC/S2 is presented, including 'exempt' services such as treatment in A&E, and including when the person with an EHIC might be exempt in another way or if they are ordinarily resident, should be reported using the OVT portal, which NHS trusts and foundation trusts can access at: www.ovt.dh.nhs.uk/

9.51. The full cost of treatment should be recovered. To calculate the cost, relevant NHS bodies should use the latest national tariff guidance at: https://www.england.nhs.uk/nhsstandard-contract18 supplementing this with local tariffs calculated in accordance with the rules set out in the national tariff document where the treatment does not have a national tariff price.

9.52. Relevant NHS bodies should note that recording and reporting this data so that the UK can claim reimbursement from the appropriate country does not mean that relevant NHS bodies do not have to invoice the appropriate commissioner. If this commissioner is not invoiced, then the relevant NHS body will not be paid for treating the patient.

9.53. Full instructions on how to submit this data can be found in the Department of Health Finance Manual, which can be accessed via the internet at: http://www.info.doh.gov.uk/doh/finman.nsf

9.54. For advice on how to operate the web portal/submit data contact DWP Overseas Healthcare Team. Email: OHT.Overseasvisitorsteam@DWP.gsi.gov.uk.

Patients with S1 status

15.136 There are three categories of overseas visitors who have S1 status. This status enables the patient to access free NHS treatment despite being ordinarily resident overseas. These are people who have a sufficient connection with the UK so that they are exempt from NHS charges even though they are overseas visitors for the purposes of the COV Regs 2015 (in that they are not ordinarily resident in the UK at the time when they seek treatment). These groups are:

a) frontier workers;
b) posted workers and their families; and
c) UK pensioners living abroad.

Frontier workers

15.137 Frontier workers are defined in Article 1(f) of the 2004 EU Regulation as follows:

'frontier worker' means any person pursuing an activity as an employed or self-employed person in a Member State and who resides in another Member State to which he returns as a rule daily or at least once a week.

Hence someone who works in London but returns to their family home in Northern France every weekend is a 'frontier worker'. Such a worker may well be able to prove that living in the UK, working in the UK and paying taxes in the UK means that the worker is 'ordinarily resident' in the UK, possibly as well as retaining a place of ordinary residence in France.

15.138 However, the term 'frontier worker' extends beyond those who have a sufficiently settled pattern of life that they can establish an ordinary residence in a member state where they work because, for example, it covers workers who return to a family home in an adjoining member state every evening. This may well be the position for a significant number of workers who live in the Republic of Ireland and work in Northern Ireland. Problems can arise for frontier workers and their families who become eligible for state health benefits arising out their work even though this not the state in which the worker and his or her family primarily resides. Article 18 of the 2004 EU Regulation provides:

> **Stay in the competent Member State when residence is in another Member State – Special rules for the members of the families of frontier workers**
> 1. Unless otherwise provided for by paragraph 2, the insured person and the members of his family referred to in Article 17 shall also be entitled to benefits in kind while staying in the competent Member State. The benefits in kind shall be provided by the competent institution and at its own expense, in accordance with the provisions of the legislation it applies, as though the persons concerned resided in that Member State.
>
> 2. The members of the family of a frontier worker shall be entitled to benefits in kind during their stay in the competent Member State, unless this Member State is listed in Annex III. In this event, the members of the family of a frontier worker shall be entitled to benefits in kind in the competent Member State under the conditions laid down in Article 19(1).

15.139 Annex III lists the countries where there are restrictions on the rights of the families of frontier workers, namely Denmark, Spain, Ireland, Netherlands, Finland, Sweden and the UK. The effect of this restriction is explained in the guidance as follows:

> 9.55. Under the EU Regulations, some people who are resident in other EEA member countries or Switzerland (for example frontier and posted workers, and pensioners) may have their healthcare costs paid for by the UK by virtue of the UK being the 'competent country' for them and therefore responsible for their healthcare costs. These persons should have a valid UK-issued S1 registered in their EEA country of residence or Switzerland (except some posted workers, who will have a UK A1 and UK EHIC). OVMs need to be aware that there will be times when visitors from the EEA or Switzerland fall within this category.
>
> 9.56. Except for family members of frontier workers (see paragraph below), people in this category are entitled to not be charged for planned and unplanned NHS treatment, except where charges would also apply to UK residents, for example prescription and dental charges. They will need to show evidence of their entitlement and may have to make arrangements before accessing care.
>
> **Family members of frontier workers**
> 9.57. As set out above, there is one group of persons within this category who are not entitled to all NHS treatment on the same basis as people ordinarily resident in the UK. These are family members of 'frontier

workers'. 'Frontier workers' are people who are resident in one EEA country but work in the UK, with a valid UK S1 registered in their country of residence. While 'frontier workers' are entitled to full NHS treatment, as explained in the paragraph above, their family members, also resident in the other EEA country with a UK S1, are only entitled, free of charge, to treatment which becomes medically necessary during a temporary visit to England. However, they will still need to pay any charges which also apply to residents in England, such as prescription and dental charges. They do not need to show an EHIC for this, but may be asked to show a copy of their S1, failing this, OVMs should contact DWP OHT (see para 9.54 for details) to verify the status of their S1.

15.140 Frontier workers who work in the UK but are resident in another EU country should therefore be granted an S1 certificate to enable them to access NHS services free of charges under the COV Regs 2015. They are persons who are exercising EU rights and are thus entitled to claim an exemption from charges under reg 12 of the COV Regs 2015.

Posted workers and their families

15.141 Article 12 of the 2004 EU Regulation has special provisions for workers who are posted to work in another EU country for a period of less than two years, or self-employed people who are in a like position. It provides:

> 1. A person who pursues an activity as an employed person in a Member State on behalf of an employer which normally carries out its activities there and who is posted by that employer to another Member State to perform work on that employer's behalf shall continue to be subject to the legislation of the first Member State, provided that the anticipated duration of such work does not exceed twenty-four months and that he is not sent to replace another person.
>
> 2. A person who normally pursues an activity as a self-employed person in a Member State who goes to pursue a similar activity in another Member State shall continue to be subject to the legislation of the first Member State, provided that the anticipated duration of such activity does not exceed twenty-four months.

15.142 Thus a person who is 'posted' continues to enjoy healthcare rights in his or her home country for up to two years. Such a person is thus entitled to the benefits under the EHIC system for treatment to meet his or her immediate health needs without paying charges under Article 19 of the 2004 EU Regulation as a person who is 'staying' but not residing in the UK. The guidance explains:

> 9.21. 'Posted workers' are those sent to the UK on a time-limited posting by their employer from another EEA country or Switzerland, or the other way around, rather than those who have chosen to move to another country to take up employment or to seek work. Posted workers here for less than two years should show an EHIC and an A1 document. The details of the EHIC should be recorded on the portal. Posted workers who are in the UK for more than two years should be covered by an S1 document, but may also be classed as ordinarily resident in the UK.

UK state pensioners living in an EU or EEA country

15.143 The guidance explains the position of UK state pensioners who live abroad as follows:

9.58. In April 2015, there was a change in law which meant that all UK state pensioners who are living in the EEA or Switzerland and have registered an S1 form from the UK with the local authorities in their EEA country of residence are entitled to not be charged for NHS secondary healthcare, just like someone who is ordinarily resident in England. This rule also applies to any of their family members who also possess a UK-issued S1. However, they will need to pay any charges which also apply to UK residents, such as prescription and dental charges. Individuals who have registered a UK S1 in another EEA country should be asked to provide some evidence confirming this. If they present a UK-issued EHIC, their EHIC information should not be entered into the portal for reimbursement. Regulation 13 of the Charging Regulations concerns this category of patient.

15.144 Thus a person in receipt of a UK state pension who resides in Spain is entitled to return to the UK to seek medical treatment at an NHS hospital without being classified as an overseas visitor, and thus having his or her right to treatment limited under Article 19 of the 2004 EU Regulation to that needed for their immediate care. This objective is achieved through reg 13 of the COV Regs 2015, which provides:

Overseas visitors who are treated as if entitled under the Social Security Coordination Regulation
No charge may be made or recovered in respect of any relevant services provided to an overseas visitor who would have an entitlement to the provision of the services in question under Article 27(2) of Regulation (EC) No 883/2004 if the United Kingdom had opted in as described in that Article and was listed in Annex IV to that Regulation.

15.145 Article 27 of the 2004 EU Regulations provides:

1. Article 19 shall apply mutatis mutandis to a person receiving a pension or pensions under the legislation of one or more Member States and entitled to benefits in kind under the legislation of one of the Member States which provide his pension(s) or to the members of his family who are staying in a Member State other than the one in which they reside.

2. Article 18(1) shall apply mutatis mutandis to the persons described in paragraph 1 when they stay in the Member State in which is situated the competent institution responsible for the cost of the benefits in kind provided to the pensioner in his Member State of residence and the said Member State has opted for this and is listed in Annex IV.

15.146 Article 18 provides for full entitlement to healthcare services for frontier workers as set out above (see para 15.137). The UK is not listed in Annex IV as a country which has opted in to Article 27(2). Hence, UK state pensioners do not have the same rights as frontier workers under Article 18 as a matter of EU law. However, the effect of reg 13 of the COV Regs 2015 is that it gives UK state pensioners who reside in an EU or EEA country the same rights under UK domestic law as if the UK had opted in to Article 27(2) of the 2004 EU Regulation. The net effect is as described in the guidance, namely that UK state pensioners who are resident in EU or EEA countries are entitled to access all NHS services in the UK free of charge. The guidance correctly states that this means that UK state pensioners cannot be charged for NHS secondary healthcare. However, the rights under Article 18 of the 2004 EU Regulation extend to all aspects of healthcare and thus a UK state pensioner living in another EU or EEA country would be entitled to access all NHS services on the same basis as a UK resident, not just secondary healthcare services. UK state pensioners can establish their rights by seeking a form S1 from NHS England and then registering it with their home local authority.

15.147 Family members[74] of EU/EEA resident UK state pensioners may have their own rights to access NHS services without incurring charges under the COV Regs 2015. However, family members may also be ordinarily resident overseas and thus may not, in their own right, come within any of the categories which exempt them from charges for NHS treatment in the UK under the COV Regs 2015. In such a case, reg 25(4) of the COV Regs 2015 extends the right to exemption from charges for NHS treatment to family members of an EU/EEA resident UK state pensioner (known as the 'principal overseas visitor') where:

a) the overseas visitor (ie the family member) who is seeking the exemption from NHS charges is lawfully present in the UK;
b) the overseas visitor who is seeking the exemption from NHS charges is visiting the UK with the principal overseas visitor; and
c) the principal overseas visitor would be exempt from the relevant NHS charges for the NHS treatment in question.

The right of asylum-seekers and failed asylum-seekers and their families to be exempt from NHS charges

Overview

15.148 Regulation 15 of the COV Regs 2015 makes provision to exempt a series of individuals from NHS charges. It covers refugees and asylum-seekers, as well as looked-after children. Regulation 15 of the COV Regs 2015 provides:[75]

> No charge may be made or recovered in respect of any relevant services provided to an overseas visitor who–
> (a) has been granted temporary protection, asylum or humanitarian protection under the immigration rules;
> (aa) has leave to enter or remain in the United Kingdom as the dependant of a person granted temporary protection, asylum or humanitarian protection under the immigration rules;
> (b) has made an application, which has not yet been determined, to be granted temporary protection, asylum or humanitarian protection under those rules the immigration rules;
> (ba) is treated as a dependant of a person described in paragraph (b) for the purposes of an application described in that paragraph;
> (c) is currently supported under section 95 (persons for whom support may be provided) of the Immigration and Asylum Act 1999 ('the 1999 Act');
> (d) has made an application to be granted temporary protection, asylum or humanitarian protection under the immigration rules which was rejected and who is supported under–
> (i) section 4(2) (facilities for the accommodation of a person) of the 1999 Act; . . .

74 Please see para 15.193 for the meaning of 'member of a family' of an overseas visitor.
75 As from 21 August 2017.

(ii) . . .
(iii) Part 1 (care and support) of the Care Act 2014 or section 35 or 36 of the Social Services and Well-being (Wales) Act 2014, by the provision of accommodation; or

(da) is treated as the dependant of a person described in paragraph (d) for the purposes of the provision of support under that paragraph; or

(e) is a child who is looked after by a local authority within the meaning of section 22(1) (general duty of local authority in relation to children looked after by them) of the Children Act 1989 [or, as the case may be, section 74(1) of the Social Services and Well-being (Wales) Act 2014 (child or young person looked after by a local authority)'

15.149 The UK is a signatory to the United Nations Refugee Convention 1951 ('the 1951 Refugee Convention'). A refugee, according to the convention, is someone who is unable or unwilling to return to his or her country of origin owing to a well-founded fear of being persecuted for reasons of race, religion, nationality, membership of a particular social group or political opinion. Section 94 of the Immigration and Asylum Act (IAA) 1999 defines an 'asylum-seeker' and 'claim for asylum' as follows:

> *'asylum-seeker'* means a person who is not under 18 and has made a claim for asylum which has been recorded by the Secretary of State but which has not been determined
>
> *'claim for asylum'* means a claim that it would be contrary to the United Kingdom's obligations under the Refugee Convention, or under Article 3 of the Human Rights Convention, for the claimant to be removed from, or required to leave, the United Kingdom

The reference to the 'Human Rights Convention' in section 94 is a reference to the ECHR. Article 3 is the right not to be subjected to torture or to inhuman or degrading treatment or punishment.

15.150 Section 94(3) of the IAA 1999 defined the date when a claim is 'determined' as follows:

> (3) For the purposes of this Part, a claim for asylum is determined at the end of such period beginning–
> (a) on the day on which the Secretary of State notifies the claimant of his decision on the claim, or
> (b) if the claimant has appealed against the Secretary of State decision, on the day on which the appeal is disposed of,
> as may be prescribed.
> (4) An appeal is disposed of when it is no longer pending for the purposes of the Immigration Acts or the Special Immigration Appeals Commission Act 1997.

15.151 There are three groups of people affected by this provision, namely:

1) refugees, ie persons who have claimed asylum where a decision has been made in their favour;
2) asylum-seekers, ie persons who have claimed asylum, where a decision has not yet been made or the individual is appealing against an adverse decision; and
3) failed asylum-seekers, ie persons who have had their claim for asylum (and any subsequent appeal) rejected but remain resident in the UK.

Refugees

15.152 Anyone who is granted asylum, temporary protection or humanitarian protection under the Immigration Rules is recognised as a refugee for the purposes of the 1951 Refugee Convention and is exempt from charges for NHS services. Such a person will be lawfully permitted to live in the UK. However, if a refugee is given leave to remain in the UK for five years, the person will still not be treated as being 'ordinarily resident' because of the provisions of section 39 of the IA 2014[76] which prevent a person having ordinary residence if he or she is granted leave to remain in the UK for a limited period. It follows that such a person continues to be an 'overseas visitor' under the COV Regs 2015, but is exempt from charges for all NHS services.

15.153 Family members of a person who has been granted asylum, temporary protection or humanitarian protection under the Immigration Rules have refugee status. It follows that anyone who has been given like status as a dependant of a refugee is exempt from paying charges for NHS services under the COV Regs 2015.

Asylum-seekers (ie persons applying for refugee status)

15.154 An asylum-seeker – namely anyone whose application for asylum, temporary protection or humanitarian protection under the Immigration Rules has not yet been determined – is exempt from paying charges for NHS services. Asylum-seekers are entitled to register with a GP practice and to receive the full range of NHS services which are appropriate to their needs in the same way as any other UK resident has access to NHS services.

15.155 A person whose claim for refugee status has been rejected by a Home Office decision-maker can challenge that decision by way of an appeal to the First-tier Tribunal (and then, with permission, on appeal to the Upper Tribunal if an error of law has been made). The exemption from NHS charges for asylum-seekers continues until any appeal against an adverse decision has been determined. In practice this usually means:

a) an application to the First-tier Tribunal has been rejected with any application for permission to appeal being refused, and the period for a proposed appeal to the Upper Tribunal has expired without an application for permission to appeal being made;
b) an application for permission to appeal to the Upper Tribunal has been refused by the Upper Tribunal (since there is no route for a further appeal against a decision to refuse permission to appeal other than a judicial review);
c) an appeal to the Upper Tribunal has been refused along with any application to for permission to appeal to the Court of Appeal, and the period for making an application to the Court of Appeal has expired[77] without any appeal being made;

76 This is 14 days from the date of the decision.
77 This is 21 days from the date of the decision.

d) an application for permission to appeal to the Court of Appeal is refused by the Court of Appeal; or
e) an appeal the Court of Appeal is refused and there is no pending appeal to the Supreme Court.

Failed asylum-seekers

15.156 A failed asylum-seeker is a person whose application for refugee status has been rejected and who has been unsuccessful in any appeal against that decision. However, many such persons are, in practice, unable to be deported by the government to their country of origin for a variety of reasons, and so remain in the UK for extended periods without having a legal right to remain living in the UK. The position of such persons is explained in the guidance as follows:

> 7.37. A person who has had their asylum/humanitarian protection application and all appeals rejected becomes a 'failed asylum seeker'. They will become liable for charges for their NHS community or secondary care at that point, unless one of the following situations applies to them.
>
> 7.38. Persons who are being supported by the Home Office under section 95 of the Immigration and Asylum Act 1999 are exempt from charges. Section 95 support is provided to asylum seekers where they would otherwise be destitute and this normally continues for those failed asylum seekers who have children under the age of 18.
>
> 7.39. Some failed asylum seekers are supported under other provisions of the 1999 Act because, whilst making reasonable efforts to leave the UK, there are genuine recognised barriers to their return home. Any failed asylum seeker receiving support from the Home Office under s4(2) of the 1999 Act, and anyone treated as their dependent in the provision of the support, is exempt from charges.
>
> 7.40. Failed asylum seekers being supported by a local authority under section 21 of the National Assistance Act 1948 or Part 1 (care and support) of the Care Act 2014 by the provision of accommodation are also exempt from charges. Such failed asylum seekers receive this support due to a need for care and attention (usually because of a disability), and are in an analogous situation to those receiving section 4(2) support, who are usually able bodied.
>
> 7.41. Failed asylum seekers in England now receive support from the Local Authority under Part 1 of the Care Act 2014 and not section 21 of the National Assistance Act 1948 Act.
>
> 7.42. An OVM might come across a failed asylum seeker who was provided with relevant services between 6 April 2015 and 31 January 2016 and who was, at that time, supported under Part 1 of the Care Act 2014 by the provision of accommodation. In this circumstance, any outstanding charges already made to such a person should be cancelled and any charges for such services not yet made, should not be made. In the event that the Department of Health becomes aware that charges have been made and recovered prior to 1 February 2016, the Department will look at the particular facts of the case and consider whether a refund of those charges can and should be made. Consideration will be undertaken on a case by case basis. Failed asylum seekers who were supported by section 21 before it was repealed will continue to be exempt from charge even though they are now supported by the provision of accommodation under the Care Act 2014.

7.43. Relevant bodies in England should note that section 21 of the National Assistance Act 1948 continues to apply in Wales and therefore eligible failed asylum seekers in Wales may receive support under the 1948 Act and then receive relevant NHS services in England.

7.44. The following should be provided as evidence of being supported by the Home Office or a local authority:

- confirmation from the Home Office that the person is being supported under section 95 of the 1999 Act, or is a failed asylum seeker supported under s4(2) of the 1999 Act; or
- Confirmation by a local authority that the person is being supported under section 21 of the NAA Act or Part 1 of the Care Act.

15.157 It follows that the question as to whether a failed asylum-seeker is exempt from paying NHS charges depends on their status under the asylum support system and/or as to whether they are recognised as someone who should be provided with support by a local authority. Thus NHS organisations may need to make inquiries of other organisations in order to be able to establish whether a person is or is not exempt from paying charges for NHS treatment.

15.158 A failed asylum-seeker can make a 'fresh claim' for asylum after an initial application has been rejected. The guidance explains that a person who makes a fresh claim will be entitled to be treated as an asylum-seeker once their fresh claim has been registered with the Home Office. It provides:[78]

> A failed asylum seeker who makes a fresh application for asylum, temporary protection or humanitarian protection will become an asylum seeker again and will therefore be exempt from charges again under Regulation 15(b), until that new application, including any appeals, is determined. A person does not become an asylum seeker again at the point they make a fresh claim for asylum or the claim is received by the Home Office, but only when that claim has been 'recorded' by the Home Office. Charges will still apply during any period between the first application, including appeals, being 'rejected' and the second, fresh, application being 'recorded' by the Home Office.

Looked-after children

15.159 There are a significant number of unaccompanied children who come to the UK from overseas. Many of these children will be taken into the care of a local authority. Regulation 15(e) of the COV Regs 2015 provides that children who are looked after by a local authority within the meaning of section 22(1) of the Children Act 1989 are exempt from charges for NHS services. The guidance explains that this will include the following children who are accommodated by a local authority in the following circumstances:

a) children in the care of the local authority by virtue of a care order (by a court);
b) children who are unaccompanied by a parent or guardian in the UK or abandoned or for whom there is no one with parental responsibility; and

78 At para 7.45.

c) children who are voluntarily accommodated by a local authority (without the need for intervention by a court).

15.160 The guidance sets out the approach that should be taken where there is a doubt about the status of a child:

> 7.47. There may be occasions when a relevant body treats an overseas visitor child who is unaccompanied or abandoned, or for whom there is no one with parental responsibility, and whom the relevant body believes should be in the care of or looked after by the local authority. Where that child is subsequently taken into the care of the local authority, there will be no charge for the treatment prior to the child being taken into the care of, or becoming looked after by, the local authority.
>
> 7.48. OVMs and frontline staff should be aware that some of these children will make applications to the Home Office for leave to remain in the UK. They are exempt from paying the health surcharge, and are entitled to all their NHS healthcare free of charge on the same basis as an ordinary resident. They will have a 'Green: Paid or exempt from the health surcharge' banner on their record when viewed through the Summary Care Record application.
>
> 7.49. Confirmation from the local authority should be obtained to confirm that the child is looked after by that local authority'

Victims of modern slavery

15.161 Regulation 16 of the COV Regs 2015 contains specific provisions relating to overseas visitors who are victims of modern slavery. Such persons are exempt from charges for all NHS treatment under the COV Regs 2015, not just for medical treatment to respond to the immediate effects of having been a victim of modern slavery. It provides:

> (1) No charge may be made or recovered in respect of any relevant services provided to an overseas visitor, where a competent authority–
> (a) has identified the overseas visitor as a victim of modern slavery; or
> (b) considers that there are reasonable grounds to believe that the overseas visitor is a victim of modern slavery, and–
> (i) a competent authority is required to make a conclusive determination; and
> (ii) there has not been a conclusive determination by a competent authority that the overseas visitor is not a victim of modern slavery.
>
> (2) In this regulation–
> 'competent authority' means a designated competent authority of the United Kingdom for the purposes of the Trafficking Convention;
> 'Trafficking Convention' means the Council of Europe Convention on Action against Trafficking in Human Beings (agreed at Warsaw on 16th May 2005);
> 'victim of modern slavery' means a victim of–
> (a) trafficking in human beings, which has the same meaning as in the Trafficking Convention, as set out in article 4 of that Convention; or
> (b) slavery, servitude, or forced or compulsory labour, which have the same meaning as they have for the purposes of article 4 of the Convention for the Protection of Human Rights and Fundamental Freedoms (agreed at Rome on 4th November 1950).

15.162 The 2005 Council of Europe Convention on Action against Trafficking in Human Beings[79] ('the 2005 Trafficking Convention') defines 'trafficking in human beings' in Article 4 as follows:

> For the purposes of this Convention:
>
> a. 'Trafficking in human beings' shall mean the recruitment, transportation, transfer, harbouring or receipt of persons, by means of the threat or use of force or other forms of coercion, of abduction, of fraud, of deception, of the abuse of power or of a position of vulnerability or of the giving or receiving of payments or benefits to achieve the consent of a person having control over another person, for the purpose of exploitation. Exploitation shall include, at a minimum, the exploitation of the prostitution of others or other forms of sexual exploitation, forced labour or services, slavery or practices similar to slavery, servitude or the removal of organs;
>
> b. The consent of a victim of 'trafficking in human beings' to the intended exploitation set forth in subparagraph (a) of this article shall be irrelevant where any of the means set forth in subparagraph (a) have been used;
>
> c. The recruitment, transportation, transfer, harbouring or receipt of a child for the purpose of exploitation shall be considered 'trafficking in human beings' even if this does not involve any of the means set forth in subparagraph (a) of this article;
>
> d. 'Child' shall mean any person under eighteen years of age;
>
> e. 'Victim' shall mean any natural person who is subject to trafficking in human beings as defined in this article'

15.163 The UK government signed the Trafficking Convention on 23 March 2007.[80] The convention was ratified by the UK on 17 December 2008, and came into force on 1 April 2009. This led to the creation of the UK's National Referral Mechanism (NRM) in 2009. The NRM is a victim identification and support process. It is designed to make it easier for all the different agencies that could be involved in a trafficking case (for example, the police, Home Office – including Border Force, UK Visas and Immigration and Immigration Enforcement – the National Crime Agency, local authorities, and non-governmental organisations) to co-operate, share information about potential victims and facilitate their access to advice, accommodation and support.

15.164 The Trafficking Convention requires that potential victims of trafficking are provided with a period of a minimum of 30 days recovery and reflection, during which they will receive support, including accommodation, subsistence and access to relevant medical and legal services, and potential eligibility for discretionary leave if they are recognised as a victim. The UK provides this support to potential victims referred to the NRM for a longer period of 45 days.

15.165 The decision as to whether a person is a victim of modern slavery or whether there are reasonable grounds to believe that a person is a victim of modern slavery is not a decision that an NHS body needs to make. It is a decision for the UK's 'competent authority'. The UK's two competent

79 See https://rm.coe.int/168008371d.

80 See the Home Office Guidance at www.antislaverycommissioner.co.uk/media/1059/victims_of_modern_slavery_-_competent_authority_guidance_v3_0.pdf.

authorities are: the Modern Slavery Human Trafficking Unit (MSHTU),[81] which deals with referrals from the police, local authorities, and non-governmental organisations (NGOs) and the Home Office Visas and Immigration (UKVI), which deals with referrals identified as part of the immigration process. The MSHTU replaced the UK Human Trafficking Centre which was previously the competent authority for the UK under the Trafficking Convention.

15.166 The government estimates that there are between 10,000 and 13,000 potential victims of modern slavery in the UK, originating from around the world and the UK itself.[82] Once identified, many of these victims will have both immediate and longer term healthcare needs. Hence, NHS services are likely to be required in many cases where victims of modern slavery have been discovered, often by the police or other statutory agencies, and are referred for NHS treatment before any decision is made whether that person should be classified as a victim of modern slavery. The guidance makes it clear that potential victims of modern slavery should be provided with NHS services without charges being levied prior to a decision being made as to whether a person is classified as a victim of modern slavery. It provides:

> 7.50. A 'victim of modern slavery' means a victim of:
> - trafficking in human beings;
> - slavery;
> - servitude; or
> - forced or compulsory labour.
>
> 7.51. A person who is thought to be a victim of modern slavery can be referred to the 'competent authorities' (CA) of the UK to be identified as such. The CA are currently the UK Human Trafficking Centre (UKHTC)[83] and, where cases are linked to asylum and immigration issues, the Home Office[84]. The CA will then consider if there are reasonable grounds to consider the person to be such a victim and if so, will issue a 'reasonable grounds' decision. Individuals given a reasonable grounds decision are suspected victims of modern slavery and are exempt from charge until a final determination is given by one of the CAs (unless a final determination is not required, which would be highly unusual). They will continue to be exempt from charge if the CA confirms them as being a victim of modern slavery with a 'conclusive grounds' decision.
>
> 7.52. Those whom the CA confirm not to be victims of modern slavery are no longer exempt from charge, other than for courses of treatment already under way, which remain free of charge until complete or until the person leaves the country.
>
> 7.53. It may be that NHS treatment is provided prior to a person being referred to the CA for identification. Charges incurred prior to a referral to the CA for assessment as a victim of modern slavery must be refunded or, if not yet paid, cancelled, when the CA provide a reasonable grounds decision. If the CA does not provide a reasonable grounds decision, these

81 This Unit is led by the National Crime Agency: see www.nationalcrimeagency.gov.uk/about-us/what-we-do/specialist-capabilities/uk-human-trafficking-centre.

82 See summary at https://publications.parliament.uk/pa/cm201617/cmselect/cmworpen/803/803.pdf.

83 This is an error in the guidance as it should refer to the MSHTU.

84 This should refer to the UKVI.

charges are not cancelled or refunded. If the CA goes on to establish that the person is not, in fact, a victim of modern slavery, no treatment provided during the time that the person was suspected as being a victim of modern slavery, or provided prior to being referred to the CA for such an assessment, will become chargeable.

7.54. The spouse/civil partner and dependent children of those exempt under this regulation are also exempt from charges in their own right, as long as they are here lawfully. They do not have to have been here with the victim of modern slavery during the entire period of their stay.

7.55. Victims of modern slavery are often in powerless situations and frontline staff may come across them before they have had a chance to escape their oppressors and seek help. They may be unwilling to disclose their situation, although frontline staff are often trusted individuals who might be best placed to identify signs of trafficking and/or slavery. A leaflet and e-learning resources are available for health professionals, to raise awareness about the issue of modern slavery and enable health professionals to identify and respond to victims more effectively. A copy of the leaflet is available at: https://www.gov.uk/government/publications/identifying-and-supporting-victims-of-human-trafficking-guidance-for-health-staff

The e-learning resources can be accessed at: http://www.e-lfh.org.uk/programmes/modern-slavery/

7.56. Consequently, it may be that NHS staff are concerned that a person they are treating or assessing for charges is a victim of modern slavery. OVMs should speak to their safeguarding lead for advice. If the patient appears to be in danger, the relevant NHS body should contact the police.

7.57. There are also charitable 'First Responder' organisations that are trained to identify and provide support to victims, and suspected victims, that can be contacted for advice. OVMs are encouraged to engage with these organisations to ensure that victims of modern slavery who are not exempt from charges (because they are unwilling to be referred to the CA) still receive the support they need. The current list of First Responder organisations can be found here: http://www.nationalcrimeagency.gov.uk/about-us/what-we-do/specialist-capabilities/uk-human-trafficking-centre/national-referral-mechanism

Some victims of modern slavery go on to make applications to the Home Office for leave to remain as victims of modern slavery. They are likely to be exempt from paying the health surcharge. In the circumstance, while their visa is valid, they are entitled to all their NHS healthcare free of charge on the same basis as an ordinary resident. They will have a 'Green: Paid or exempt from the health surcharge' banner on their record when viewed through the Summary Care Record application. Victims of modern slavery may make applications for a period of discretionary leave, and may not be required to pay the health surcharge.

7.58. The following should be provided as evidence:

- a letter from the CA confirming their status as a victim (a 'conclusive grounds' decision), or suspected victim (a 'reasonable grounds' decision) for whom the recovery and reflection period has not elapsed;
- those who make an immigration application for leave to remain as a victim of modern slavery will have a 'Green: Paid or exempt from the health surcharge' banner on their NHS record, when it is viewed through the Summary Care Record application, indicating their access to NHS services on the same basis as a person who is ordinarily

resident. Note that not all victims will make such an application to the Home Office, so they will not all have a green banner indicating their status.

7.59. Prior to 1 February 2016 only victims, or suspected victims, of human trafficking were exempt from charge for NHS hospital treatment. The competent authority of the UK will now also consider suspected victims of modern slavery, as well as victims of human trafficking, within this formal process'

15.167 Regulation 25 of the COV Regs 2015 provides that the exemption from charges under the COV Regs 2015 extends to members of the family[85] of an overseas visitor who is a victim of modern slavery, provided that family member is lawfully present in the UK.

Persons granted the right to NHS treatment without charge for exceptional humanitarian reasons

15.168 Regulation 17 of the COV Regs 2015 provides that the secretary of state is entitled to designate a person has having exceptional humanitarian reasons for being provided with NHS treatment without charge. Regulation 17 provides:

(1) Where an overseas visitor who has been granted leave to enter the United Kingdom outside the immigration rules–
  (a) applies (or someone applies on the overseas visitor's behalf) for exemption from charges in respect of relevant services for a course of treatment; and
  (b) the Secretary of State determines that exceptional humanitarian reasons justify it,

no charge may be made or recovered in respect of relevant services provided to that overseas visitor for that course of treatment.

(2) A determination under paragraph (1)(b) may only be made by the Secretary of State if the Secretary of State is satisfied, in the case of that overseas visitor, that–
  (a) the treatment specified is not available in that person's home country;
  (b) the necessary arrangements have been made for temporary accommodation for that person, any authorised companion and authorised child for the duration of the course of treatment; and
  (c) the necessary arrangements have been made for the return of that person, any authorised companion and any authorised child to their home country when the course of treatment is completed'

15.169 This is a relatively unusual basis for exempting a person from charges, and the decision needs to be made on an individual basis by the secretary of state (although in practice it will be taken on the secretary of state's behalf by an official). The guidance explains the approach NHS bodies should take in such cases as follows:

7.60. This regulation allows the Secretary of State for Health to designate an individual as exempt from charges on exceptional humanitarian grounds, as long as certain specified criteria are met. This designation can only be made by the Secretary of State. It is envisaged that the powers will

85 See para 15.193 for the meaning of 'members of the family' of an overseas visitor.

only be used very rarely, where there is a clear humanitarian imperative to do so (e.g. the UK is responsible for causing the injury needing treatment or there are humanitarian reasons for treating the person in the UK). As far as relevant bodies are concerned, their role in the context of the Charging Regulations is to establish whether such a determination has been made, not to make the determination themselves.

7.61. The following should be noted with regard to evidence:

- The relevant NHS body will be advised that the appropriate determination has been made and supporting documentation will be provided (although in an emergency this may arrive after the patient).

7.62. Where such a determination is made, the person will be allowed to be accompanied by an authorised companion (which need not be their spouse/civil partner) and any authorised children, who will be exempt from charges for treatment the need for which arises while they are here, but not for other treatment'

Persons detained in an NHS hospital or subject to court ordered treatment

15.170 Regulation 18 of the COV Regs 2015 exempts anyone detained in a UK hospital or who is deprived of their liberty from being charged for the NHS services that that person receives under compulsion. The regulation provides:

> No charge may be made or recovered in respect of relevant services provided to an overseas visitor–
>
> (a) who is liable to be detained in a hospital, received into guardianship or subject to a community treatment order under the Mental Health Act 1983;
>
> (b) who is detained in a hospital in circumstances which amount to deprivation of the overseas visitor's liberty and that deprivation of liberty is authorised under any of the following provisions of the Mental Capacity Act 2005–
>
> (i) section 4A (restriction on deprivation of liberty);
>
> (ii) section 4B (deprivation of liberty necessary for life-sustaining treatment etc);
>
> (iii) section 16 (powers to make decisions and appoint deputies: general); or
>
> (iv) Schedule A1 (hospital and care home residents: deprivation of liberty);
>
> (c) whose detention in hospital is authorised by any other enactment authorising detention in a hospital; or
>
> (d) who is required to submit to a specified form of treatment that is imposed by, or included in, an order of a court and paragraph (a), (b) or (c) does not apply'

15.171 This provision covers all NHS medical treatment that is provided to a person in circumstances where treatment is provided without the person being required to give their consent. That includes individuals who are detained in a hospital under the Mental Health Act 1983, are subject to a guardianship order or are subject to a Community Treatment Order. It also covers individuals who are cared for in circumstances where they are deprived of their liberty under a urgent or standard authorisation under Schedule A1 to the Mental Capacity Act 2005, or where an order has been made authorising the deprivation of their liberty by the Court of Protection.

Prisoners and other detainees

15.172 Regulation 19 of the COV Regs 2015 provides that no charges for NHS services shall be made for anyone who is detained in prison or under the immigration system. It provides:

> (1) No charge may be made or recovered in respect of any relevant services provided to an overseas visitor–
>   (a) who is detained in prison or in a place in which a person may be detained that is provided by the Secretary of State under section 43(1) (remand centres and young offender institutions) of the Prison Act 1952; or
>   (b) who is detained under any of the following provisions–
>   (i) Schedule 2 (administrative provisions as to control on entry etc) or Schedule 3 (supplementary provisions as to deportation) to the 1971 Act;
>   (ii) section 62 (detention by Secretary of State) of the Nationality, Immigration and Asylum Act 2002;
>   (iii) section 40(7)(c) (searches: contracting out) of the Immigration, Asylum and Nationality Act 2006; or
>   (iv) section 2 (detention) or 36 (detention) of the UK Borders Act 2007.
>
> (2) In this regulation, 'prison' has the meaning given in section 53(1) of the Prison Act 1952.

15.173 The government has made a series of commitments that anyone who is subject to compulsory detention in prison, in custody as a young person or in an immigration removal centre ought to have access to the same level of NHS services (without any charges being levied) as a person who is not in detention. Those commitments have proved to be extremely hard to deliver in practice but the COV Regs 2015 make it clear that no charges can be made for any NHS services that are provided to detained persons.

Full or partial exemption from NHS charges for persons from countries with whom the UK has a reciprocal arrangement

15.174 The UK has a series of reciprocal arrangements with other countries under which residents of that country are entitled to NHS care without charge (either wholly or in part) and, in return, UK residents are entitled to access government paid healthcare when visiting that country. This is set out in reg 14 of the COV Regs 2015 which provides:

> No charge may be made or recovered in respect of any relevant services provided to an overseas visitor where those services are provided in circumstances covered by a reciprocal agreement with a country or territory specified in Schedule 2.

15.175 The countries listed in Schedule 2 with effect from 21 August 2017 are:

- Anguilla
- Australia

- Bosnia
- British Virgin Islands
- Falkland Islands
- Gibraltar
- Isle of Man
- Israel
- Jersey
- Kosovo
- Macedonia
- Montenegro
- Montserrat
- New Zealand
- Serbia
- St Helena
- Turks and Caicos Islands

15.176 This list has been amended on many occasions, usually by removing countries that were previously subject to reciprocal arrangement. Hence, by way of example, Barbados, Russia and a series of former soviet republics have been removed on dates between February 2016 and August 2017. However, patients from these countries who were receiving a course of treatment at the point Schedule 2 was amended may be able to take advantage of the 'easement clause' in reg 3(5) of the COV Regs 2015 to complete their course of treatment without charges.[86]

15.177 Residents of a country which has a reciprocal arrangement are only entitled to access NHS services without paying charges to the extent that the individual agreement between the UK and that country provides for free NHS treatment. There are four categories of entitlement under these arrangements, namely:

1) Level 1: A right to immediate NHS medical treatment only.
2) Level 2: A right to NHS treatment on the same basis as UK residents if the medical treatment is required promptly for a condition which arose after arrival into the UK or became (or but for treatment would have become) acutely exacerbated after such arrival. Services such as the routine monitoring of chronic/pre-existing conditions are not included and free treatment should be limited to that which is urgent in that it cannot wait until the patient can reasonably return home.
3) Level 3: A right to NHS treatment on the same basis as UK residents on the same basis as for a person insured in the other country, including services such as routine monitoring of pre-existing conditions, but not including circumstances where a person has travelled to the other country for the purpose of obtaining healthcare.
4) Level 4: A right to all NHS treatment on the same basis as UK residents including elective treatment.

15.178 The guidance contains a table which explains which residents of which countries with reciprocal arrangements are entitled to NHS service without charges. It provides:

86 See para 15.195 for details of the operation of the easement clause.

Country	Level of cover	Further information
Anguilla	1*	Applies to all residents of that country. Can also refer four patients to the UK for free NHS hospital treatment.
Australia	1*	Applies to all residents of that country.
Bosnia and Herzegovina	3	Applies to all insured persons of that country.
British Virgin Islands	1*	Applies to all residents of that country. Can also refer four patients to the UK for free NHS hospital treatment.
Falkland Islands	4	Applies to all residents of that country. Can refer an unlimited number of patients to the UK for free elective treatment.
Gibraltar	3	Applies only to citizens resident in that country when that citizen is not expected to stay in the UK for more than 30 days. Can also refer an unlimited number of patients to the UK for free elective treatment (see 10.4).
Isle of Man	2	Applies to all residents of the Isle of Man for a period of stay in the UK that has not exceeded, nor is expected to exceed, three months.
Jersey	2	Applies to all residents of Jersey for a period of stay in the UK that has not exceeded, nor is expected to exceed, three months.
Kosovo	3	Applies to all insured persons of that country
Macedonia	3	Applies to all insured persons of that country.
Montenegro	3	Applies to all insured persons of that country.
Montserrat	1*	Applies to all residents of that country. Can also refer four patients per year for free NHS hospital treatment.
New Zealand	2	Applies only to citizens resident in that country.

Serbia	3	Applies to all insured persons of that country.
St Helena	1*	Applies to all residents of that country. Does not include Ascension Island or Tristan da Cunha. Can also refer four patients per year for free NHS hospital treatment.
Turks and Caicos Islands	1*	Applies to all residents of that country. Can also refer four patients per year for free NHS hospital treatment.

The * in the above table provides that for these countries, the agreement will also apply to those persons requiring treatment if they are a member of the crew, or a passenger, on any ship, vessel or aircraft travelling to, leaving from or diverted to the UK and the need for urgent treatment has arisen during the voyage or flight.

15.179 There are particular issues about referral of patients from these countries to the NHS for elective medical treatment. The Guidance explains the approach that NHS bodies should take as follows:

> 10.3. Depending on the terms of the particular country's reciprocal healthcare agreement, the exemption also applies to those who have been referred to the UK specifically for NHS treatment. Normally the referrals can be made only when the countries do not have adequate facilities to provide the treatment needed.
>
> 10.4. Referrals from Gibraltar are commissioned by Gibraltar itself. Trusts should not bill back the Clinical Commissioning Group for treatment provided to someone referred from Gibraltar under the terms of the reciprocal healthcare agreement.
>
> 10.5. The British Overseas Territories of Anguilla, the British Virgin Islands, Montserrat, St Helena and the Turks and Caicos Islands can refer up to four patients each per year. In respect of the Falkland Islands, there is no limit on the number of referrals that can be made. Referral arrangements are made by the relevant British Overseas Territory through the DWP Overseas Healthcare Team (see Chapter 9 for their contact details). Persons hoping to be referred should contact the relevant British Overseas Territory in the first instance.
>
> 10.6. For all people who are referred for NHS treatment as per paragraphs 10.3 to 10.4 above, advance arrangements for their acceptance should be made and the patients must be given the same priority as patients living in the UK.
>
> 10.7. A number of reciprocal healthcare agreements ended on 31 December 2015 and the agreement with Barbados ended on 30 September 2016. If the overseas visitor began an ongoing course of treatment which was exempt under the reciprocal agreement on or before 31 December 2015 or 30 September 2016 respectively, there should be no charge for the remainder of that course of treatment provided after the date of termination, under the easement clause.

10.8. However, it should be noted that a change to the easement clause now means that, from 21 August 2017, should any reciprocal healthcare agreements be terminated in the future or cease to apply in respect of an overseas visitor for some other reason, charges will apply to overseas visitors that cease to be covered by the agreement for the remaining part of a course of treatment that is already underway, as well as any new courses of treatment. The overseas visitor will remain exempt from charge if another exemption applies.

15.180 Where there are issues about the entitlement of a person to NHS care without charge from a country with a reciprocal arrangement, it may be necessary to examine the precise terms of the reciprocal arrangement agreement. Copies of the relevant documents ought to obtainable from the Visitor and Migrant NHS Cost Recovery Programme at Richmond House, 79 Whitehall, London SW1A 2NS or via email at NHScostRecovery@dh.gsi.gov.uk.

Members of the regular and reserve forces, Crown servants and others

15.181 Regulation 20 of the COV Regs 2015 contains provisions to exempt members of the regular and reserve UK forces, Crown servants and others from NHS charges. It provides:

(1) No charge may be made or recovered in respect of any relevant services provided to an overseas visitor who is–
  (a) a member of the regular or reserve forces within the meaning of the Armed Forces Act 2006;
  (b) a qualifying employee who is visiting the United Kingdom in the course of the qualifying employment; or
  (c) where paragraph (b) does not apply, a qualifying employee who–
    (i) was ordinarily resident in the United Kingdom immediately prior to becoming a qualifying employee; or
    (ii) where the qualifying employee has been employed in more than one position of qualifying employment, the qualifying employee was ordinarily resident in the United Kingdom immediately prior to taking up one of the positions of qualifying employment.

(2) An overseas visitor will be a 'qualifying employee' if the overseas visitor was recruited in the United Kingdom and is–
  (a) a Crown servant (other than a person falling within paragraph (1)(a)) employed by, or in the service of, the Government of the United Kingdom;
  (b) an employee of the British Council or the Commonwealth War Graves Commission; or
  (c) working in employment, whether or not the overseas visitor derives a salary or wage from that employment, that is financed in part by the Government of the United Kingdom in accordance with arrangements with the Government of some other country or territory or a public body in such other country or territory.

(3) In this regulation 'qualifying employment' means any period of employment during which the overseas visitor was a qualifying employee

15.182 This regulation refers to specific categories of persons who have a strong connection to the British government and who get access to NHS services (without charge) arising out of that connection. The operation of this exemption is explained in the guidance as follows:

Armed forces members, Crown servants and UK Government funded employment (Regulation 20)

Armed forces members

6.4. Members of the regular and reserve forces (collectively referred to as UK forces) are exempt from charge for all treatment. The armed forces member does not have to have been a former UK resident, but the exemption will also cover those who are serving overseas and who might not be considered ordinarily resident in the UK.

6.5. The spouse/civil partner and children under 18 of the armed forces member are also exempt from charge, even if the armed forces member is not in the UK with them at the time of treatment. The spouse/civil partner or child must be in the UK lawfully. Note that those dependants of armed forces members who apply to reside in the UK for six months or more will be entitled to free NHS healthcare by virtue of the health surcharge arrangements (they are exempt from having to pay the health surcharge – see Chapter 5 for more details).

Examples of evidence include proof that they are a serving member of the UK forces, e.g. valid UK forces ID card or confirmation from the Ministry of Defence.

Crown servants, British Council staff, Commonwealth War Graves Commission staff, and those in employment (paid or unpaid) financed in part by the UK Government (in arrangements with the government or public body of another country or territory).

6.6. A person from any of the above groups (called a 'qualifying employee' in the regulation) is exempt from charge for all treatment, provided that they are either:

- visiting the UK in the course of the qualifying employment; or
- if visiting for leisure/other purposes, they were ordinarily resident in the UK immediately prior to being posted overseas as a qualifying employee. A qualifying employee who was not ordinarily resident in the UK immediately prior to their current post will still be exempt if they had previously held another post as a qualifying employee, and were ordinarily resident in the UK immediately prior to taking up that earlier post.

6.7. The spouse/civil partner or children under 18 of the qualifying employee are also exempt from charge, even if the qualifying employee is not in the UK with them at the time of treatment. The spouse/civil partner or child must be in the UK lawfully. However, if the qualifying employee was not previously ordinarily resident as described in the paragraph above, and is only exempt because they are visiting the UK as a requirement of their employment, their spouse/civil partner or child will only be exempt when visiting the UK with that qualifying employee.

Examples of evidence include proof of such employment, and of being ordinarily resident in the UK prior to taking up such a post. For more information about evidence of ordinary residence, see Chapter 3.

15.183 Regulation 25 of the COV Regs 2015 provides that the exemption from charges under the COV Regs 2015 extends to members of the family[87] of

87 See para 15.193 for the meaning of 'members of the family' of an overseas visitor.

an overseas visitor who is entitled to exemption from charges for NHS treatment under reg 20, provided that family member is lawfully present in the UK.

NATO forces personnel

15.184 Regulation 21 of the COV Regs 2015 provides that, in specified circumstances, NATO forces are entitled to receive free NHS care. Regulation 21 provides:

> (1) No charge may be made or recovered in respect of any relevant services provided to an overseas visitor who is a person to whom Article IX(5) of the Agreement regarding the Status of Forces of Parties to the North Atlantic Treaty (agreed in London on 19th June 1951) applies.
> (2) This regulation applies where the services in question cannot readily be provided by the medical services of the armed forces of–
> (a) the overseas visitor's own country; or
> (b) the United Kingdom.

15.185 The guidance explains this provision as follows:

> **North Atlantic Treaty Organisation (NATO) (Regulation 21)**
> 10.10. The eligibility of NATO personnel and attached civilians stationed in the UK is governed by the Agreement Regarding the Status of Forces of Parties to the North Atlantic Treaty. This regulation provides for free treatment to be given to a person, or the spouse/civil partner and/ or dependent children of a person, who is serving with the armed forces of a country which is part of NATO. The only NATO country to have bases in the UK and maintain substantial numbers of service personnel here is the USA, but members of the armed forces of the other countries may spend time on duty in the UK.
>
> 10.11. NATO personnel and their exempt family members are expected to use their own or UK armed forces hospitals, but if the services they require cannot readily be provided by the medical services of their own or the UK armed forces (eg because NHS services are significantly more accessible to the patient) then NHS hospital services may be provided free of charge.
>
> Example of evidence:
>
> – Will be in receipt of appropriate documentation confirming NATO status'

15.186 Regulation 25 of the COV Regs 2015 provides that the exemption from charges under the COV Regs 2015 extends to members of the family[88] of an overseas visitor who is entitled to exemption from charges for NHS treatment under reg 21 by being a member of NATO forces, provided that family member is lawfully present in the UK.

War pensioners and armed forces compensation scheme payment recipients

15.187 Regulation 21 of the COV Regs 2015 provides that overseas visitors who are war pensioners or armed forces compensation scheme payment recipients are exempt from NHS charges. Regulation 21 provides:

88 See para 15.193 for the meaning of 'members of the family' of an overseas visitor.

No charge may be made or recovered in respect of any relevant services provided to an overseas visitor who is in receipt of–

(a) any pension or other benefit under a Personal Injuries Scheme or Service Pensions Instrument, which Scheme and Instrument are defined in regulation 2(1) (interpretation) of the Social Security (Overlapping Benefits) Regulations 1979; or

(b) a payment made under article 15(1)(c) (description of benefits–injury) or article 29(1) (description of benefits–death) of the Armed Forces and Reserve Forces (Compensation Scheme) Order 2011.

15.188 The guidance explains the basis of this part of the regulations as follows:

War pensioners and armed forces compensation scheme payment recipients (Regulation 22)

6.8. People who receive UK war pensions or war widows' pensions are exempt from charges for all NHS hospital treatment, as are recipients of armed forces compensation scheme payments. This exemption extends to their spouse/civil partner and/or dependent children if they are lawfully present and visiting the UK with the exempt overseas visitor.

6.9. Examples of evidence include proof of appropriate pension/compensation scheme payment – pension book/slip, letter from the Ministry of Defence or the Department for Work and Pensions. The relevant NHS body should contact the Departments for confirmation if necessary'

15.189 Family members[89] of war pensioners or armed forces compensation scheme payment recipients may have their own rights to access NHS services without incurring charges under the COV Regs 2015. However, family members of war pensioners or armed forces compensation scheme payment recipients may also be 'ordinarily resident' overseas and thus may not, in their own right, come within any of the categories which exempt them from charges for NHS treatment in the UK under the COV Regs 2015. In such a case, reg 25(4) of the COV Regs 2015 extends the right to exemption from charges for NHS treatment to family members of a war pensioner or armed forces compensation scheme payment recipient (known as the 'principal overseas visitor') where:

a) the overseas visitor (ie the family member) who is seeking the exemption from NHS charges is lawfully present in the UK;
b) the overseas visitor who is seeking the exemption from NHS charges is visiting the UK with the principal overseas visitor; and
c) the principal overseas visitor is exempt from the relevant NHS charges under the COV Regs 2015.

Treatment for Turkish nationals where the need for which arose during a visit and who cannot afford payment

15.190 Regulation 24 of the COV Regs 2015 provides that charges should not be made for NHS treatment provided for a medical condition, the need for which arose during a visit, to nationals of states that are contracting parties to two treaties where that person is lawfully in the UK and is without sufficient resources to pay the charge. The treaties are the European Convention on Social and Medical Assistance (agreed in Paris on 11 December 1953)

89 Please see para 15.193 for the meaning of 'member of a family' of an overseas visitor.

or the European Social Charter (agreed in Turin on 18 October 1961). However, these rights are (in virtually all cases) only relevant to Turkish nationals because all other nationals of contracting parties are covered by the rights of EU and EEA citizens.

15.191 Regulation 24 provides:

> No charge may be made or recovered in respect of any relevant services, consisting of treatment the need for which arose during the visit, provided to an overseas visitor who is any of the following–
> (a) a national of a state which is a contracting party to the European Convention on Social and Medical Assistance (agreed in Paris on 11th December 1953) or the European Social Charter (agreed in Turin on 18th October 1961) and is–
> (i) lawfully present in the United Kingdom; and
> (ii) without sufficient resources to pay the charge;
> (b) an authorised child or an authorised companion.

15.192 The guidance explains this as follows:

> 10.9. Nationals of countries that are contracting parties to the European Convention on Social and Medical Assistance or the European Social Charter are exempt from charges for treatment the need for which arises during the visit here when they are lawfully present in the UK and without sufficient resources to pay. Other reciprocal arrangements have generally superseded these arrangements, although not in the case of Turkey. The regulation will apply when lawfully present nationals from Turkey are genuinely without the resources to pay a charge for their treatment. However, since visitors from Turkey are required to have sufficient funds available to finance their stay, as well as their onward or return journey, they are unlikely to be genuinely without resources to pay, at least by instalments, or other assets, so this exemption is unlikely to apply.
>
> Examples of evidence:
>
> – Proof of nationality and lawful presence in the UK, e.g. passport.
>
> – Evidence of inability to pay, e.g. they are destitute.

Family members of overseas visitors

15.193 Regulation 25 of the COV Regs 2015 provides for like rights to be provided in some cases for family members of overseas visitors. Regulation 25 provides:

> (1) For the purposes of this regulation, unless otherwise provided, 'member of the family' means–
> (a) the spouse or civil partner of an overseas visitor; or
> (b) a child in respect of whom an overseas visitor has parental responsibility.
> (2) No charge may be made or recovered in respect of any relevant services provided to an overseas visitor who is a member of the family of another overseas visitor ('the principal overseas visitor') and is lawfully present if the principal overseas visitor is exempt from charges under any of the following regulations–
> (a) regulation 16 (victims of modern slavery);
> (b) regulation 20 (members of the regular and reserve forces, Crown servants and others);
> (c) regulation 21 (NATO forces).

(3) No charge may be made or recovered in respect of any relevant services provided to an overseas visitor who is a child who–
   (a) is born in the United Kingdom to a parent who is exempt from charges by virtue of–
      (i) regulation 10 (immigration health charge); or
      (ii) regulation 11 (overseas visitors who have made applications for entry clearance or leave to remain prior to the commencement of the immigration health charge);
   (b) is aged 3 months or less; and
   (c) has not left the United Kingdom since birth.

(4) Subject to paragraphs (5) to (7) of this regulation, no charge may be made or recovered in respect of any relevant services provided to an overseas visitor who is a member of the family of a principal overseas visitor if–
   (a) the overseas visitor is lawfully present in the United Kingdom;
   (b) the overseas visitor is visiting the United Kingdom with the principal overseas visitor; and
   (c) the principal overseas visitor is exempt from charges under–
      (i) regulation 12 (EU rights);
      (ii) regulation 13 (overseas visitors who are treated as if entitled under the social security coordination regulation); or
      (iii) regulation 22 (war pensioners and armed forces compensation scheme payment recipients).

(5) Where the overseas visitor is a member of the family of a principal overseas visitor who is exempt from charges under–
   (a) regulation 12 (EU rights); or
   (b) regulation 13 (overseas visitors who are treated as if entitled under the social security coordination regulation),

   the exemption in paragraph (4) only applies if both the conditions in paragraphs (6) and (7) are satisfied.

(6) The first condition is that–
   (a) the overseas visitor–
      (i) where paragraph (5)(a) applies, does not have an enforceable EU right of the kind described in regulation 12; or
      (ii) where paragraph (5)(b) applies, would not have an enforceable EU right of the kind described in regulation 13 if the United Kingdom had opted in as described in Article 27(2) of Regulation 883/2004 and was listed in Annex IV to that Regulation; and
   (b) the reason that the overseas visitor does not, or would not, have an enforceable EU right of the kind described in those regulations is because the overseas visitor is not recognised as a member of the family (within the meaning in Article 1(i) of Regulation (EC) 883/2004 or any other relevant regulations or agreements which provide for an enforceable EU right of the kind described in regulation 12 for family members) of the principal overseas visitor.

(7) The second condition is that the relevant services provided to the overseas visitor are services that the overseas visitor would be entitled to receive without charge by virtue of an enforceable EU right under regulation 12 or 13 if the overseas visitor had such a right.

(8) None of the provisions of this regulation affect any entitlement which any member of the family of an overseas visitor may have to an exemption from charges for relevant services by virtue of an enforceable EU right or any other exemption which they may be entitled to in their own right'

15.194 These are complex provisions which are considered above in relation to each category of exempt person. However in each case the term 'member of the family' is limited to the spouse or civil partner of an overseas visitor and a child (that is someone under the age of 18) in respect of whom an overseas visitor has parental responsibility.

The easement clause: the liability of persons who become liable to charges for NHS services during a course of medical treatment

15.195 Regulation 3(5) of the COV Regs 2015 covers the liability of a person to charges for NHS treatment where that person starts a course of treatment when he or she is exempt from charges but becomes liable to pay NHS charges during a course of treatment. It provides[90] that such a person shall not pay charges for the remainder of the course of treatment. Regulation 3(5) provides:[91]

> (5) Subject to paragraph (6), where–
> (a) a relevant body has determined that an overseas visitor is exempt from being charged for relevant services under these Regulations, except where the overseas visitor is exempt from being charged by virtue of–
> (i) regulation 10 (immigration health charge);
> (ii) regulation 11 (overseas visitors who have made applications for entry clearance or leave to remain prior to the commencement of the immigration health charge);
> (iii) regulation 25(3) (family members of overseas visitors–children born to a parent exempt under regulation 10 or 11); or
> (iv) regulation 14 (reciprocal health care agreements);
> (b) the overseas visitor has received relevant services from a relevant body as part of a course of treatment; and
> (c) prior to the course of treatment being completed, a relevant body has determined that the overseas visitor is no longer exempt from being charged for relevant services under these Regulations,
> a relevant body may not make and recover charges under paragraph (1) in respect of relevant services provided as part of that course of treatment during a period where the overseas visitor has remained in the United Kingdom without absence.
> (6) Paragraph (5) does not apply where a relevant body has determined that a person is exempt from being charged for relevant services as a result of that body receiving fraudulent or misleading information'

15.196 This exemption is referred to in the guidance as the 'easement clause'. The effect is explained as follows:

> 7.65. Under the easement clause, any particular course of treatment under way when either:
> - an asylum seeker's application, including all appeals, is rejected; or
> - a person stops receiving section 95 support from the Home Office; or

90 Subject to reg 3(6).
91 As from 23 October 2017.

- a failed asylum seeker stops receiving support from the Home Office under section 4(2) of the 1999 Act, or section 21 or Part 1 support from a local authority; or
- a person ceases to be a child looked after by a local authority; or
- a prisoner is released from prison or immigration detention; or
- a person is no longer detained in a hospital or liable to court ordered treatment; or
- a person suspected of being a victim of modern slavery by a competent authority (having issued a 'reasonable grounds' decision), who is then found by the competent authority not to be a victim of modern slavery,

will continue free of charge until that course of treatment concludes or the person leaves the country.[92]

7.66. However, they must be charged for any new courses of treatment, although relevant NHS bodies are reminded that, regardless of the lack of advance payment, they must not withhold treatment that is medically considered immediately necessary or urgent in that it cannot wait until the patient can reasonably be expected to return home. They are also reminded that they have the option to write off debts and not pursue them when the person is genuinely without funds. See Chapter 8 for more details'

Employees on UK registered ships and aircrew employees

15.197 Until 23 August 2017, reg 23 of the COV Regs 2015 provided that overseas visitors who were employees or engaged to work on a ship that is registered in the UK were exempt from charges for NHS treatment. Regulation 23 has been repealed. The guidance explains that from 21 August 2017, the employer of an overseas visitor working, in any capacity, on a ship registered in the UK is liable for the cost of that ship worker's treatment. The employer is the owner of the ship on which they are employed or engaged. This brings the liability for charges into line with those who are employed on ships registered outside the UK. The ship worker himself or herself is not liable for the cost of their treatment, because the liability rests on the shipowner: see reg 4(2) of the COV Regs 2015.

15.198 Regulation 4(3) provides that where an overseas visitor is an air crew member and is present in the UK in the course of that employment, the person liable to pay charges under the COV Regs 2015 is the employer of the aircrew member.

The legal duty to make charges for NHS treatment

15.199 Regulation 3 of the COV Regs 2015 imposes[93] a statutory duty on all providers of NHS services to make and recover charges for relevant NHS services that are provided to overseas visitors who are not exempt from the charges. From 23 October 2017, reg 3 of the COV Regs 2015 provides:

92 The guidance document does not make it clear that the sentence starting 'will continue' refers to all of the categories. However that is plainly the effect of reg 3(5).

93 As from 23 October 2017. Before that date the statutory duty only rested on NHS bodies who provided NHS services to overseas visitors.

(1) Where the condition specified in paragraph (2) is met, a relevant body must make and recover charges for any relevant services it provides to an overseas visitor from the person liable under regulation 4 (liability for payment of charges).

(1A) Where the condition specified in paragraph (2) is met, before providing a relevant service in respect of an overseas visitor, a relevant body must secure payment for the estimated amount of charges to be made under paragraph (1) for that relevant service unless doing so would prevent or delay the provision of–

(a) an immediately necessary service; or

(b) an urgent service.

(1B) The person from whom payment is to be secured under paragraph (1A) in respect of a relevant service is the person who it appears to the relevant body, at the time that the request for that payment is made, will be the person to whom a charge will be made under paragraph (1) in respect of that relevant service at the time that it is provided.

(2) The condition is that the relevant body, having made such enquiries as it is satisfied are reasonable in all the circumstances, including in relation to the state of health of that overseas visitor, determines that the case is not one in which these Regulations provide for no charge to be made.

(3) Where more than one relevant body is to provide relevant services to an overseas visitor, each relevant body must secure the advance payment sum in respect of each relevant service that it is to provide.

(3A) Where more than one relevant body provides relevant services to an overseas visitor, each relevant body must make and recover the actual charge in respect of each relevant service that it provides.

(4) A relevant body that makes and recovers a charge in accordance with paragraph (1) or secures payment in accordance with paragraph (1A) must give or send to the person making the payment a receipt for the amount paid.

(4A) In making and recovering an actual charge from a person in respect of a relevant service, a relevant body must–

(a) deduct any advance payment sum secured by the relevant body from that person in respect of that relevant service; and

(b) refund any amount by which an advance payment sum secured by the relevant body from that person in respect of that relevant service exceeds the amount of the actual charge that person is liable to pay.

(5) Subject to paragraph (6), where–

(a) relevant body has determined that an overseas visitor is exempt from being charged for relevant services under these Regulations, except where the overseas visitor is exempt from being charged by virtue of–

(i) regulation 10 (immigration health charge);

(ii) regulation 11 (overseas visitors who have made applications for entry clearance or leave to remain prior to the commencement of the immigration health charge); *or*

(iii) regulation 25(3) (family members of overseas visitors–children born to a parent exempt under regulation 10 or 11); or

(iv) regulation 14 (reciprocal health care agreements);

(b) the overseas visitor has received relevant services from relevant body as part of a course of treatment; and

(c) prior to the course of treatment being completed, relevant body has determined that the overseas visitor is no longer exempt from being charged for relevant services under these Regulations, relevant body may not make and recover charges under paragraph (1) in respect of relevant services provided as part of that course of treatment during a period where the overseas visitor has remained in the United Kingdom without absence.

(6) Paragraph (5) does not apply where relevant body has determined that a person is exempt from being charged for relevant services as a result of that body receiving fraudulent or misleading information.

(7) In this regulation–

'actual charge' means a charge to be made under paragraph (1);

'advance payment sum' means a sum to be secured under paragraph (1A);

'immediately necessary service' means–

(a) antenatal services provided in respect of a person who is pregnant;

(b) intrapartum and postnatal services provided in respect of–

(i) a person who is pregnant;

(ii) a person who has recently given birth; or

(iii) a baby; and

(c) any other relevant service that the treating clinician determines the recipient needs promptly–

(i) to save the recipient's life;

(ii) to prevent a condition becoming immediately life-threatening; or

(iii) to prevent permanent serious damage to the recipient from occurring;

'urgent service' means a service that the treating clinician determines is not an immediately necessary service but which should not wait until the recipient can be reasonably expected to leave the United Kingdom'

15.200 Prior to the amendments made by the COVA Regs 2017, the statutory duty to charge overseas visitors for the provision of NHS services was only placed on NHS bodies. As from 23 October 2017, the duty to make and collect charges applies to any 'relevant body'. This term is defined in reg 2 of the COV Regs 2015 to mean:

'relevant body' means–

(a) an NHS foundation trust;

(b) an NHS trust;

(c) a local authority within the meaning of section 2B of the 2006 Act (functions of local authorities and Secretary of State as to improvement of public health) exercising public health functions (within the meaning of that Act); or

(d) any other person providing relevant services,

except in respect of regulation 6A, for which purposes a person mentioned in paragraph (d) is not a 'relevant body';

15.201 The term 'relevant services' is also defined in reg 2 to mean:

'relevant services' means accommodation, services or facilities which are provided, or whose provision is arranged, under the 2006 Act other than–

(a) primary medical services provided under Part 4 (medical services);

(b) primary dental services provided under Part 5 (dental services);

(c) primary ophthalmic services provided under Part 6 (ophthalmic services); or

(d) equivalent services which are provided, or whose provision is arranged, under the 2006 Act'

15.202 It follows that any provider of NHS services other than those defined in sub-paragraphs (a)–(d) above will be under a duty to make and collect charges in the same way as that duty lies on NHS bodies. The duty to make and collect charges only covers services under the NHS Act 2006. It does not extend to services that are provided by way of aftercare services under section 117 of the Mental Health Act 1983. It means that, by way of example, as from 23 October 2017 a nursing home which is providing accommodation, medical and social care to an overseas visitor who is eligible for NHS Continuing Healthcare will be obliged to make and collect charges for the provision of those services.

The level of NHS charges under the COV Regs 2015

15.203 The amount of charges to be levied on an overseas visitor for the provision of NHS services under the COV Regs 2015 is defined by reg 7, which from 23 October 2017 provides as follows:

(1) The relevant body must calculate charges made under these Regulations, including where charges are estimated for the purposes of determining an advance payment sum, in accordance with this regulation.
(2) Where the overseas visitor is ordinarily resident in another EEA state or Switzerland the charge payable in respect of a relevant service provided to the overseas visitor shall be calculated in the same way as provided for by regulation 13(1) (NHS charges) of the National Health Service (Cross-Border Healthcare) Regulations 2013.
(3) In any other case, the charge payable in respect of each relevant service provided to an overseas visitor shall be equal to the tariff for that relevant service multiplied by 150 per cent.
(4) In this regulation 'the tariff' has the meaning set out in paragraphs (5) to (8), subject to paragraphs (9) to (12).
(5) Unless paragraph (6) applies, where a relevant service is specified in the national tariff under section 116(1)(a) (national tariff) of the 2012 Act, the tariff for the provision of that service to an overseas visitor is such price as is determined in accordance with the national tariff on the basis of the national price specified in the national tariff for that service in relation to that relevant body including any applicable modification referred to in paragraph (10).
(6) Where–
  (a) a relevant body provides a relevant service to an overseas visitor that is included in a bundle of services to which a pathway payment applies in accordance with the national tariff;
  (b) that relevant service constitutes part, but not all, of the bundle of services; and
  (c) the relevant body is unable to determine the price of that relevant service as an individual service within the bundle of services to which the pathway payment relates,

  the tariff is such reasonable price for the provision of the relevant service that the relevant body determines having had regard to the matters set out in paragraph (7).
(7) The matters to which the relevant body must have regard for the purposes of determining the tariff for a relevant service under paragraph (6) are–

(a) the amount of the pathway payment which would be payable to the relevant body in accordance with the national tariff, by the commissioner with responsibility for commissioning services in respect of the overseas visitor to whom the relevant service was provided, if that overseas visitor were ordinarily resident in the United Kingdom;
(b) the relevant service that the overseas visitor received as a proportion of the bundle of services to which the pathway payment applies; and
(c) the complexity of the relevant service provided to the overseas visitor.

(8) Where a relevant service is not specified in the national tariff under section 116(1)(a) of the 2012 Act, the tariff is such price for the provision of that service as is determined in accordance with the rules provided for in the national tariff for that purpose including any applicable modification referred to in paragraph (10).

(9) The following variations to the national price of a relevant service made under the 2012 Act shall not apply to the determination of the national price for that relevant service for the purpose of paragraph (5)–
(a) a variation agreed to by the commissioner of the service and the relevant body that is providing that service in accordance with rules made under section 116(2);
(b) a variation specified in the national tariff under section 116(4)(a), except for a variation–
(i) to reflect regional cost difference; or
(ii) to reflect patient complexity.

(10) An applicable modification is any modification to the price, as determined in accordance with the national tariff, of the relevant service where that modification is–
(a) made in accordance with an agreement made under section 124(1) of the 2012 Act; or
(b) determined by Monitor under section 125(1) of the 2012 Act.

(11) For the purposes of determining the tariff for a relevant service provided to an overseas visitor–
(a) under paragraph (5) or (8) (whichever is applicable), a modification of the kind specified in paragraph (10) will apply to the relevant service only when the modification applies to the price payable to the relevant body by the commissioner with responsibility for commissioning services in respect of that overseas visitor; and
(b) under paragraph (8), an agreement between a commissioner and the relevant body made in accordance with the rules will be relevant for the determination of the tariff only when the commissioner which is party to the agreement is the commissioner with responsibility for commissioning services in respect of that overseas visitor.

(12) Where rules made under section 116(6) provide for which specification of a relevant service is to apply in a particular case or cases of any particular description, the relevant body must comply with those rules when calculating charges under this regulation for that relevant service.

(13) For the purposes of this regulation–
'the 2012 Act' means the Health and Social Care Act 2012;
'national price' has the meaning given in section 115(1) (price payable by commissioners for NHS services) of the 2012 Act;
'national tariff' is the document known as the national tariff published by Monitor under section 116(1) of the 2012 Act;

'the rules' mean the rules provided for in the national tariff under section 116 and 117 (the national tariff: further provision) of the 2012 Act.

15.204 Regulation 7(1) provides that the charging scheme set out in reg 7 is mandatory. Accordingly both NHS bodies and private providers do not have the freedom to use any other scheme to calculate the level of charges to be made to an overseas visitor.

15.205 Regulation 7(2) provides that where the overseas visitor is ordinarily resident in another EEA state or Switzerland, the charge payable in respect of a relevant service provided to the overseas visitor shall be calculated in the same way as provided for by reg 13(1) (NHS charges) of the National Health Service (Cross-Border Healthcare) Regulations 2013.[94] Regulation 13 of those regulations provides that, where a service is provided to an overseas patient:

> . . . the amount of the charge to the visiting patient for that service must not exceed the amount that the person or body responsible for providing the service, as mentioned in paragraph (2)(b), would assess as the cost of that service if it had been provided to a resident patient.

15.206 Hence, this regulation imposes a ceiling of the cost that an NHS body would recover from the NHS commissioner for providing the relevant service. If the service is covered by the NHS national tariff, that ceiling is set at the national tariff rate. If the service is not covered by the NHS national tariff, that ceiling is set at the rate that the NHS provider would charge an NHS body for the service in question. The guidance recommends that the NHS body charges the patient at the full rate. This is 'Category D' at para 13.28 of the guidance. The guidance suggests that the 'responsible commissioner' should pay 50 per cent of the costs of the treatment to the provider. If the provider is successful in securing repayment of the full charge, the 50 per cent paid by the commissioner should be returned. However, depending on the status of the patient, it may well be ultra vires a CCG to act in accordance with this scheme. A CCG will have power to make these payments if the overseas visitor is on the list of a GP practice in the CCG area. The CCG will also be able to make a 50 per cent payment if the overseas visitor is 'usually resident' in the CCG area (see the test in section 3(1A)(b) of the NHS Act 2006) and is not on the list of any NHS GP practice. However, if an overseas visitor is neither on the list of a local GP practice or usually resident in a CCG area, the CCG will have no vires to make any payment to the provider for providing non-A&E NHS medical treatment to the individual. Payments can be made for providing such a person with emergency treatment, but that treatment is exempt from charges.[95]

15.207 Regulation 7(3) provides that, where the patient is not an EU/EEA resident, the charge payable in respect of each relevant service provided to an overseas visitor shall be equal to the NHS tariff price for any services provided to the patient multiplied by 150 per cent. If the price payable for the service has been increased as a result of a Monitor approved modifica-

94 SI No 2269.

95 See para 15.42 above.

tion under section 124 of the Health and Social Care Act (HSCA) 2012, the price charged to the overseas visitor shall include that increase. However, if the CCG and the provider have negotiated a price below the national tariff under section 116 of the HSCA 2012,[96] the price charged to the overseas visitor shall be the national tariff price without the agreed reduction.

15.208 Where the particular service provided to the overseas visitor is part of a pathway payment for a bundle of services with no price for the service the overseas visitor received, reg 7(6) provides that the tariff is such reasonable price for the provision of the relevant service that the relevant body determines having had regard to national tariff price (if it had applied), the relevant service that the overseas visitor received as a proportion of the bundle of services to which the pathway payment applies and the complexity of the relevant service provided to the overseas visitor.

Who is liable to charge and pay charges under the COV Regs 2015?

15.209 Regulation 4 of the COV Regs 2015 sets out who is liable to pay charges under the COV Regs 2015. It provides:

(1) The person liable to pay charges under these Regulations is, unless paragraph (2), (3) or (4) applies, the overseas visitor in respect of whom the relevant services are provided.

(2) Where–

(a) an overseas visitor is employed or engaged or works in any capacity on board a ship and whose normal place of work is on board a ship; and

(b) that overseas visitor is present in the United Kingdom in the course of that employment, engagement or work,

the person liable to pay charges under these Regulations is the shipowner of the ship on which the overseas visitor is employed, engaged or works.

(3) Where an overseas visitor is an air crew member and is present in the United Kingdom in the course of that employment, the person liable to pay charges under these Regulations is the employer of that overseas visitor.

(4) Where an overseas visitor is a child, the person liable to pay charges under these Regulations is the person with parental responsibility for that child.

(4A) Where, due to a change in circumstances occurring during the period in which a relevant service is provided, more than one person is liable under paragraphs (1) to (4) to pay charges under these Regulations in respect of that relevant service, each such person is liable to pay charges only in respect of relevant services provided during the period during which those paragraphs apply to that person.

(5) In this regulation–

'air crew member' means any person employed or engaged in an aircraft in flight on the business of the aircraft;

96 There is an unresolved legal question as to whether such price reductions are lawful. This issue will be addressed elsewhere.

'shipowner' has the meaning given in regulation 2(1) (interpretation) of the Merchant Shipping (Maritime Labour Convention) (Minimum Requirements for Seafarers etc) Regulations 2014.

15.210 Hence the primary rule is that the person who is liable to pay the charges is the overseas visitor. However, there are separate rules in respect of staff working on ships or aeroplanes who need NHS treatment. In those case cases the person who is liable to pay the charges is the shipowner or employer of the air crew member.

15.211 The duty to impose charges for NHS services for overseas visitors only applies to NHS treatment provided by NHS bodies. However, this changed on 23 October 2017 when the duty applies to any provider (whether an NHS body or not) that provides relevant NHS services to patients.

15.212 There are provisions in reg 5 to provide for repayment of charges to anyone who has been wrongly charged or has been overcharged. There are also provisions in regs 6 and 7 for charges to be refunded to persons who subsequently prove their right to receive NHS services without charge because the person is recognised as a refugee, a victim of modern slavery or a victim of FGM.

When can or should treatment be provided without advance payment?

15.213 In *R (Reffell) v Hammersmith Hospitals NHS Trust*[97] the Court of Appeal decided that it was lawful for an NHS provider to treat without seeking payments in advance, but it has a discretion as to whether it should do so. Thus a provider could insist that an overseas visitor should pay for the treatment up-front or provide security for the costs of the treatment by a third party guarantee before commencing any treatment. That general rule has been amended by the COV Regs 2015, which provides that treatment will be required to be provided to an overseas visitor in specific cases before any payment is made. However, it changed as from 23 October 2017 when, in all other cases, NHS providers will come under a statutory duty to recover the costs of treatment in advance for all but urgent or immediately necessary medical treatment.

15.214 The guidance provides:

This chapter gives important advice on the safeguards that relevant bodies must employ to protect the lives of overseas visitors who are not exempt from charges under the Charging Regulations, and guidelines on how relevant bodies should handle such people without the resources to pay, including when to withhold treatment.

What are the relevant bodies' responsibilities?

8.1. Chapter 2 sets out the legal obligations under the Charging Regulations of all relevant bodies.

8.2. Relevant bodies must also ensure that treatment which clinicians consider to be immediately necessary or urgent is provided to any patient, even if they have not paid in advance. Failure to provide immediately necessary treatment

97 Unreported but noted on LexisNexis under number 2000 WL 1274140 from 26 July 2000.

may be unlawful under the Human Rights Act 1998. Urgent treatment should also always be provided to any person, even if deposits have not been secured. Non-urgent treatment should not be provided unless the estimated full charge is received in advance of treatment. See paragraphs 8.10; 8.14 and 8.29 for more important information on non-urgent treatment.

What is immediately necessary, urgent and non-urgent treatment?

8.3. Only clinicians can make an assessment as to whether a patient's need for treatment is immediately necessary, urgent or non-urgent. In order to do this they may first need to make initial assessments based on the patient's symptoms and other factors, and conduct further investigations to make a diagnosis. These assessments and investigations will be included in any charges.

Immediately necessary treatment?

8.4. Immediately necessary treatment is that which a patient needs promptly:

- to save their life; or
- to prevent a condition from becoming immediately life-threatening; or
- to prevent permanent serious damage from occurring.

8.5. Relevant bodies must always provide treatment which is classed as immediately necessary by the treating clinician irrespective of whether or not the patient has been informed of, or agreed to pay, charges, and it must not be delayed or withheld to establish the patient's chargeable status or seek payment. It must be provided even when the patient has indicated that they cannot afford to pay.

Maternity treatment

8.6. Due to the severe health risks associated with conditions such as eclampsia and pre-eclampsia, and in order to protect the lives of both mother and unborn baby, all maternity services must be treated as being immediately necessary. Maternity services include all antenatal, intra-partum and postnatal services provided to a pregnant person, a person who has recently given birth or a baby. No one must ever be denied, or have delayed, maternity services due to charging issues. Although a person must be informed if charges apply to their treatment, in doing so they should not be discouraged from receiving the remainder of their maternity treatment. OVMs and clinicians should be especially careful to inform pregnant patients that further maternity healthcare will not be withheld, regardless of their ability to pay.

Urgent treatment

8.7. Urgent treatment is that which clinicians do not consider immediately necessary, but which nevertheless cannot wait until the person can be reasonably expected to leave the UK. Clinicians may base their decision on a range of factors, including the pain or disability a particular condition is causing, the risk that delay might mean a more involved or expensive medical intervention being required, or the likelihood of a substantial and potentially life-threatening deterioration occurring in the patient's condition if treatment is delayed until they return to their own country.

8.8. For urgent treatment, relevant bodies are strongly advised to make every effort, taking account of the individual's circumstances, to secure payment in the time before treatment is scheduled. However, if that proves unsuccessful, the treatment should not be delayed or withheld for the purposes of securing payment.

8.9. Treatment is not made free of charge by virtue of being provided on an immediately necessary or urgent basis. Charges found to apply cannot be waived and if payment is not obtained before treatment then every effort must be made to recover it after treatment has been provided.

Non-urgent treatment

8.10. Non-urgent treatment is routine elective treatment that can wait until the patient leaves the UK. Relevant bodies must not provide non-urgent treatment until the estimated full cost of treatment has been received (see paragraph 8.19).

Clinicians and OVM collaboration

8.11. The decision on whether a patient's need for treatment is immediately necessary, urgent or non-urgent is only for clinicians to make, and they should be asked to complete an Advice from Doctors or Dentists Form (https://www.gov.uk/government/collections/nhs-visitor-and-migrant-cost-recovery-programme), which should then be documented in the patient's notes and a copy sent to the relevant service/delivery manager.

8.12. However, in determining whether or not a required course of treatment should proceed even if payment is not obtained in advance, or if it can safely wait until the patient can return home (ie whether it is urgent or non-urgent), clinicians will need to know the patient's estimated return date.

8.13. It is the responsibility of OVMs to gather the information on when the patient can return home in such cases, based on the patient's ability to do so. It is also the OVM's responsibility to establish whether or not the patient is entitled to free NHS treatment in the first place'

15.215 Until 22 October 2017, NHS bodies had a discretion to decide whether to treat treatment patients who are overseas visitors who need non-urgent treatment and to seek to recover the costs later or whether to insist on pre-payment. However, that discretion was removed on 23 October 2017 when reg 4(1A) came into effect. It provides:

(1A) Where the condition specified in paragraph (2) is met, before providing a relevant service in respect of an overseas visitor, a relevant body must secure payment for the estimated amount of charges to be made under paragraph (1) for that relevant service unless doing so would prevent or delay the provision of–
(a) an immediately necessary service; or
(b) an urgent service.

(1B) The person from whom payment is to be secured under paragraph (1A) in respect of a relevant service is the person who it appears to the relevant body, at the time that the request for that payment is made, will be the person to whom a charge will be made under paragraph (1) in respect of that relevant service at the time that it is provided.

15.216 The effect of this provision is explained in the guidance as follows:[98]

It is very important to note that the law will change on 23 October 2017 so that it will be a legal requirement to recover in advance the estimated full cost of a course of treatment unless doing so would prevent or delay the provision of immediately necessary or urgent treatment. In practice this will mean that where a clinician has determined a patient's need for care to be non-urgent, payment from the person liable will be required upfront and in full, where no exemption category applies, before the treatment can

98 At para 8.14.

be provided. Where services are immediately necessary or urgent, full upfront payment should be secured wherever possible, unless doing so would prevent or delay the treatment. Providers of NHS-funded community and secondary care will therefore need to prepare for how they will ensure that they meet this legal requirement.

15.217 It follows that the discretion to treat first and recover fees later for non-urgent treatment was removed when this regulation came into effect. It means, in effect, that NHS providers are obliged to refuse to provide medical treatment to patients whose need for treatment is not urgent. This may, of course, mean that the underlying condition for which medical treatment is being sought progresses and the need for treatment will become urgent. This is already a serious problem for some NHS providers that, for example, provide renal dialysis. It appears that fees for routine renal dialysis will have to be paid in advance by overseas visitor patients (unless they are exempt under one of the categories set out above). However, where patients are unable to pay for routine renal dialysis, the charging rules may mean that some of these patients suffer serious renal problems and thus need emergency treatment. That emergency treatment will have to be provided. Charges will be made but, in practice, the patient has no money and so will be unable to pay the fees. However, once a renal crisis is abated, an NHS provider will not be able to provide routine dialysis unless clinicians can say that there is an 'urgent' need for this treatment. It remains to be seen how this will work itself out in practice.

CHAPTER 16

NHS Continuing Healthcare and NHS-funded nursing care

continued

Introduction: what is NHS Continuing Healthcare?

16.1 This chapter is a general guide to the law and practice around NHS Continuing Healthcare (referred to as 'CHC'). CHC is the name given to a package of care that is arranged and funded solely by the NHS for individuals who are (generally) not in hospital and who have complex ongoing healthcare needs to such an extent that the patient can be described as having a 'primary health need'.[1] The Department of Health and Social Care (DHSC) has published a summary about CHC in the form of a leaflet – *NHS Continuing Healthcare and NHS-funded nursing care: public information leaflet* (2013)[2] – which is a good start to explaining the complexities of a service that is widely misunderstood.

16.2 The core legal documents governing CHC are Part 6 of the National Health Service Commissioning Board and Clinical Commissioning Groups (Responsibilities and Standing Rules) Regulations (RSR Regs)[3] 2012 and the 'National Framework on NHS Continuing Healthcare and NHS-funded Nursing Care' ('the National Framework')[4] which was published in November 2012 and came into effect on 1 April 2013. In March 2018, shortly before this book went to press, the DHSC published a revised version of the National Framework which will come into effect in October 2018.[5] The law set out in this chapter is based on the 2012 version of the National Framework. However, readers who are considering matters related to CHC after 1 October 2018 should review matters in the light of the new framework. A full description of the effect of the new National Framework will be provided in the second edition of this book.

16.3 The present version of the National Framework defines CHC as follows:

> 'NHS continuing healthcare' means a package of ongoing care that is arranged and funded solely by the NHS where the individual has been found to have a 'primary health need' as set out in this guidance. Such care is provided to an individual aged 18 or over, to meet needs that have arisen as a result of disability, accident or illness. The actual services provided as part of the package should be seen in the wider context of best practice and service development for each client group. Eligibility for NHS continuing healthcare places no limits on the settings in which the package of support can be offered or on the type of service delivery.

16.4 CHC is thus a package of health and social care services (and possibly accommodation if that is part of the patient's needs) to meet a patient's reasonable requirements for such services, all of which is funded by the NHS. This is shown in the *National framework*, which provides:[6]

1 See www.nhs.uk/chq/Pages/2392.aspx.

2 See www.gov.uk/government/uploads/system/uploads/attachment_data/file/193700/NHS_CHC_Public_Information_Leaflet_Final.pdf.

3 SI No 2996.

4 See https://www.gov.uk/government/uploads/system/uploads/attachment_data/file/213137/National-Framework-for-NHS-CHC-NHS-FNC-Nov-2012.pdf.

5 See https://assets.publishing.service.gov.uk/government/uploads/system/uploads/attachment_data/file/690426/National_Framework_for_CHC_and_FNC_-_October_2018_Revised.pdf.

6 At para 25.

Where an individual has a primary health need and is therefore eligible for NHS continuing healthcare, the NHS is responsible for providing all of that individual's assessed needs – including accommodation, if that is part of the overall need.

16.5 A decision that the patient is eligible for NHS CHC means, in practice, that the whole of the care package for that patient will be funded by the NHS, as opposed to the costs being shared between the NHS and social services authorities (ie the local authority). This has the practical benefit for patients (and their families) that none of the services for a CHC patient are designated as being 'means tested' services under the social care system but are provided by the NHS, ie generally free of charge. Frequently CHC patients are provided with care in care homes as opposed to being provided with care directly by staff employed by NHS bodies, because clinical commissioning groups (CCGs) contract with private care homes to provide the required services (as they are permitted to do under section 10 of the National Health Service Act (NHS Act) 2006). The care home fees thus become costs that are required to be met by the local Clinical Commissioning Group ('CCG').

A brief history of government policy concerning NHS CHC

Background

16.6 The concept of NHS CHC emerged out of concerns in the 1980s and early 1990s that patients with complex conditions were being treated outside NHS hospital, where the same patients would previously have received this care within an NHS hospital. Patients who receive their health and social care in an NHS hospital are provided with their medicines, food, accommodation and social care free of charge. Although this is often taken for granted, the provision of food, accommodation and social care is the provision of 'non-medical' support to hospital patients, funded by the NHS. Thus, the provision of food, accommodation and social care funded by the NHS comes as part of an overall 'NHS hospital' package of care. However, the NHS does not generally provide 'non-medical' support for patients outside an NHS hospital environment. Where such services are needed by patients, they are either paid for by patients themselves or are community care services which are the responsibility of a local authority under the Care Act 2014. Community care services are subject to means testing and thus for those with means charges fall to be paid.

16.7 When the NHS was created in 1948, a large number of individuals were provided with long-term care in NHS hospitals. There were 'back-wards' in NHS hospitals which provided long-term care to the elderly. Although it is dangerous to generalise, these 'patients' were often the frail elderly and often had minimal acute medical input. The NHS also supported patients with learning difficulties who mainly needed social care in larger mental health hospitals. Patients with long-term conditions were also managed within a hospital environment. In the early 1950s, the NHS maintained 32,000 TB beds and had a considerable estate of 'mental health' institutions providing care for those with learning difficulties, many of whom would not now be considered to have a mental health disorder. Most patients with learning difficulties had social care needs, but far fewer had physical or mental health needs. There is an excellent history of the changes to the NHS and how these long-term beds were phased out in the King's Fund interim report *A new settlement for health and social care*.[7] This explains how, over an extended period, starting in the 1960s, these long-term beds were phased out, with many former long-stay patients being provided with social care services in place of an NHS bed (often called 'care in the community').

16.8 There are two crucial differences between NHS services and community care services. First, as far as the service user/patient is concerned, NHS services are largely funded out of government money (ie provided by taxpayers) and thus provided free of charge to the individual patient. In contrast, community care services have always been subject to a means-tested contribution, being paid by the service user.[8] Second, NHS services are funded by NHS bodies exercising target legal duties. In contrast, community care services are provided by local social services authorities (unitary councils or county councils) under duties imposed by the Care Act 2014. These are not target duties, but are duties owed by local authorities directly to individual service users.

16.9 Hence, one effect of changing medical patterns of care which moved medical treatment for patients with complex conditions out of the hospital environment was to transfer responsibility for the duty to provide accommodation and social care away from the NHS and, at least in a majority of cases, to a local authority. This change also changed the services from being 'free at the point of use' to being a service where the user had to pay, subject to a means test. However, that statutory change also resulted in the costs of provision of these services being transferred from the NHS (ie nationally managed state funds) to either patients or local authorities.

National Health Service and Community Care Act 1990 and guidance

16.10 The first relevant guidance that attempted to describe the dividing line between statutory health and social care responsibilities was Health Service Guidance (92)50 which was issued when the National Health Service and Community Care Act (NHSCCA) 1990 came into force in April 2003. The NHSCCA 1990 imposed a statutory duty on social services authorities to conduct assessments of the needs of service users who required community care services. The coming into force of the NHSCCA 1990 was accompanied by a guideline document, HSG(92)50, issued by the NHS Management Executive to district health authorities called

7 See www.kingsfund.org.uk/press/press-releases/independent-commission-calls-new-settlement-health-and-social-care.

8 This distinction goes back to the National Assistance Act 1948 and the National Health Act 1946, both of which emerged out of the 1941 Beveridge Report.

Local authority contracts for residential and nursing home care: NHS related aspects. It provided:

> This guidance sets out district health authority and local authority responsibilities, from April 1993, for funding community health services for residents of residential care and nursing homes who have been placed in those homes by local authorities.

16.11 The guidance proposed a distinction between 'specialist' nursing services, which would continue to be provided by the NHS, and 'general nursing care', which the guidance proposed should be for the local authority to fund. The guidance said:

> Full implementation of the White Paper 'Caring for People' will mean that local authorities will have responsibilities for purchasing nursing home care for the great majority of people who need it and who require to be publicly supported. When, after April 1993, a local authority places a person in a nursing home after joint health authority/local authority assessment, the local authority is responsible for purchasing services to meet the general nursing care needs of that person, including the cost of incontinence services (e g laundry) and those incontinence and nursing supplies which are not available on NHS prescription. Health authorities will be responsible for purchasing, within the resources available and in line with their priorities, physiotherapy, chiropody and speech and language therapy, with the appropriate equipment, and the provision of specialist nursing advice, e.g. continence advice and stoma care, for those people placed in nursing homes by local authorities with the consent of a district health authority. Health authorities can opt to purchase these services through directly managed units, NHS trusts, or other providers including the nursing home concerned. Health authorities continue to have the power to enter into a contractual arrangement with a nursing home where a patient's need is primarily for health care. Such placements must be fully funded by the health authority.

16.12 The guidance thus suggested that the NHS would continue to have a power (but possibly not a duty) to purchase a nursing place for an NHS patient where the 'patient's need is primarily for health care'. However, the guidance gave no indication as to how the NHS was supposed to determine whether a patient's needs were primarily for healthcare as opposed to having a primary need for social care. It was also unclear from this guidance whether the NHS would have a duty or only a power to provide a nursing home place (and hence a package including accommodation and social care services) for a patient whose needs were primarily for healthcare.

16.13 The practical consequence of this policy was that, once patients with complex conditions moved out of the NHS hospital environment, accommodation, social care and support was generally funded by patients themselves or by local authorities. Health authorities limited themselves to providing 'specialist' health services, but looked to the local authority to provide accommodation and social care services pursuant to their community care obligations.

16.14 Further guidance was issued in 1995 called *Continuing care: NHS and local councils' responsibilities*. The 1995 guidance included some general principles which attempted to define where the line lay between the duties of local authorities and those of NHS bodies. It said the NHS was responsible for arranging and funding in-patient continuing care in a hospital or nursing home, on a short- or long-term basis, for people:

a) where the complexity or intensity of their medical, nursing care or other care or the need for frequent not easily predictable interventions requires the regular (in the majority of cases this might be weekly or more frequent) supervision of a consultant, specialist nurse or other NHS member of the multidisciplinary team;
b) who require routinely the use of specialist health care equipment or treatments which require the supervision of specialist NHS staff; or
c) who have a rapidly degenerating or unstable condition which means that they will require specialist medical or nursing supervision.

16.15 The DHSC issued supplementary guidance in February 1996, which referred to the danger of these eligibility criteria being interpreted in an over-restrictive way. It specifically mentioned the risk of over-relying on the needs of a patient for specialist medical opinion when determining eligibility for continuing NHS-funded care. It said that there would be a limited number of cases where the complexity or intensity of nursing or other clinical needs might mean that a patient was eligible for continuing care even though that patient no longer required medical supervision.

The *Coughlan* case

16.16 The next step on the history of the development of CHC was the seminal case of *R v North and East Devon Health Authority ex p Coughlan.*[9] The Court of Appeal was required to consider whether the health authority had acted lawfully in seeking to close Mardon House and to transfer care responsibilities for the residents to the local authority. At first instance, Hidden J explained that the residents needed nursing services and that, in his view, these could only be provided by an NHS body. He said the provision of both general and specialist nursing services were 'health care' and can never be 'social care'. His view was that the health authority was wrong because:

> . . . both general and specialist nursing care remain the *sole responsibility* of the health authorities.

16.17 The health authority appealed, and the Court of Appeal had to decide where the line was to be drawn between health and social care services. The Court of Appeal did not see the divide in such clear terms as the judge at first instance. The conclusions of the Court of Appeal are worth setting out in full as follows:

> (a) The Secretary of State can exclude some nursing services from the services provided by the NHS. Such services can then be provided as a social or care service rather than as a health service.
>
> (b) The nursing services which can be so provided as part of the care services are limited to those which can legitimately be regarded as being provided in connection with accommodation which is being provided to the classes of persons referred to in section 21 of the 1948 Act who are in

9 [2001] QB 213, (1999) 2 CCLR 285.

need of care and attention; in other words as part of a social services care package.

(c) The fact that the nursing services are to be provided as part of social services care and will have to be paid for by the person concerned, unless that person's resources mean that he or she will be exempt from having to pay for those services, does not prohibit the Secretary of State from deciding not to provide those services. The nursing services are part of the social services and are subject to the same regime for payment as other social services. Mr Gordon submitted that this is unfair. He pointed out that if a person receives comparable nursing care in a hospital or in a community setting, such as his or her home, it is free. The Royal Commission on Long Term Care, in its report, 'With Respect to Old Age' (Cm 4192-I) (March 233 1999), chapter 6, pp 62 et seq, not surprisingly agrees with this assessment and makes recommendations to improve the situation. However, as long as the nursing care services are capable of being properly classified as part of the social services responsibilities, then, under the present legislation, that unfairness is part of the statutory scheme.

(d) The fact that some nursing services can be properly regarded as part of social services care, to be provided by the local authority, does not mean that all nursing services provided to those in the care of the local authority can be treated in this way. The scale and type of nursing required in an individual case may mean that it would not be appropriate to regard all or part of the nursing as being part of 'the package of care' which can be provided by a local authority. There can be no precise legal line drawn between those nursing services which are and those which are not capable of being treated as included in such a package of care services.

(e) The distinction between those services which can and cannot be so provided is one of degree which in a borderline case will depend on a careful appraisal of the facts of the individual case. However, as a very general indication as to where the line is to be drawn, it can be said that if the nursing services are (i) merely incidental or ancillary to the provision of the accommodation which a local authority is under a duty to provide to the category of persons to whom section 21 of the 1948 Act refers and (ii) of a nature which it can be expected that an authority whose primary responsibility is to provide social services can be expected to provide, then they can be provided under section 21. It will be appreciated that the first part of the test is focusing on the overall quantity of the services and the second part on the quality of the services provided.

(f) The fact that care services are provided on a means tested contribution basis does not prevent the Secretary of State declining to provide the nursing part of those services on the NHS. However, he can only decline if he has formed a judgment which is tenable and consistent with his long-term general duty to continue to promote a comprehensive free health service that it is not necessary to provide the services. He cannot decline simply because social services will fill the gap.

16.18 This Court of Appeal judgment appears to be the origin of the 'incidental or ancillary' test concerning residential accommodation which defines the type of care placements that can properly be classified as being social care. This test continues to be part of the process of assessing eligibility to CHC today: see regulation 21(7) of the RSR Regs 2012. This part of the *Coughlan* case was primarily about whether a local authority was lawfully obliged to provide nursing services. It was not (at least at this stage of the argument) a case about whether the NHS was under a duty to fund accommodation and social care services. It thus left open the possibility of a gap between health and social care provision.

Section 49 of the Health and Social Care Act 2001

16.19 The next significant step was section 49 of the Health and Social Care Act (HSCA) 2001 which effectively prevented local authorities from employing registered nurses as part of the package of care provided at local authority care homes or funding care to be provided by nurses at homes run in the private sector. This legislation was, in part, a government response to the Royal Commission on Long Term Care chaired by Sir Stewart Sutherland ('the Sutherland Report'). The Sutherland Report had recommended that state-funded personal care for elderly people in need should be made available to everyone. It recommended that personal care for elderly people should be paid for from general taxation and that, for others, it should be subject to co-payment arrangements according to means. The then government were not prepared to accept the recommendations (or pay the cost of this bold recommendation) but as a compromise it enacted section 49 of the HSCA 2001. This provided:

> (1) Nothing in the enactments relating to the provision of community care services shall authorise or require a local authority, in or in connection with the provision of any such services, to–
> (a) provide for any person, or
> (b) arrange for any person to be provided with,
> nursing care by a registered nurse.
> (2) In this section 'nursing care by a registered nurse' means any services provided by a registered nurse and involving–
> (a) the provision of care, or
> (b) the planning, supervision or delegation of the provision of care,
> other than any services which, having regard to their nature and the circumstances in which they are provided, do not need to be provided by a registered nurse.

16.20 The broad effect of section 49 of the HSCA 2001 was thus to prevent local authorities from having either the legal power or legal duty to employ or pay for nursing services as part of their community care obligations. The idea was to ensure that, where the services of a nurse were required by a patient outside of a hospital environment, those services should be funded by the NHS and not by a local authority.

Continuing Care guidance

16.21 Following the *Coughlan* judgment, the DHSC released some fairly unhelpful guidance, *Continuing Care: NHS and local council's responsibilities* (HSC 2001/015).[10] This guidance introduced a distinction between 'continuing care' and 'Continuing NHS healthcare' for the first time. It defined continuing care as follows:

10 See http://webarchive.nationalarchives.gov.uk/20120503185631/http://www.dh.gov.uk/prod_consum_dh/groups/dh_digitalassets/@dh/@en/documents/digitalasset/dh_4012280.pdf.

> 'Continuing care' (or 'long term care') is a general term that describes the care which people need over an extended period of time, as the result of disability, accident or illness to address both physical and mental health needs. It may require services from the NHS and/or social care. It can be provided in a range of settings, from an NHS hospital, to a nursing home or residential home, and people's own homes.

In contrast, it defined 'Continuing NHS Healthcare' as follows:

> 'Continuing NHS healthcare' describes a package of care arranged and funded solely by the NHS. It does not include the provision by local councils of any social services.

16.22 The guidance then recommended that local health authorities set their own eligibility criteria to determine which patients were and were not entitled to Continuing NHS healthcare (ie a package of health and community care services care funded exclusively by the NHS). Annex C gave some guidance about what should be contained within local NHS policies. It said:

> 1. The eligibility criteria or application of rigorous time limits for the availability of services by a health authority should not require a local council to provide services beyond those they can provide under section 21 of the National Assistance Act (see point 20 of the guidance for the definition of nursing care used in the *Coughlan* judgment).
>
> 2. The nature or complexity or intensity or unpredictability of the individual's health care needs (and any combination of these needs) requires regular supervision by a member of the NHS multidisciplinary team, such as the consultant, palliative care, therapy or other NHS member of the team.
>
> 3. The individual's needs require the routine use of specialist health care equipment under supervision of NHS staff.
>
> 4. The individual has a rapidly deteriorating or unstable medical, physical or mental health condition and requires regular supervision by a member of the NHS multidisciplinary team, such as the consultant, palliative care, therapy or other NHS member of the team.
>
> 5. The individual is in the final stages of a terminal illness and is likely to die in the near future.
>
> 6. A need for care or supervision from a registered nurse and/or a GP is not, by itself, sufficient reason to receive continuing NHS health care.
>
> 7. The location of care should not be the sole or main determinant of eligibility. Continuing NHS health care may be provided in an NHS hospital, a nursing home, hospice or the individual's own home.
>
> Guidance on free nursing care will include more details on determining registered nurse input to services in a nursing home, where the care package does not meet continuing NHS health care eligibility criteria.

16.23 This guidance demonstrated the tensions in government which have always been present in CHC policy. There are two primary sets of tensions.

16.24 First, there are tensions between health and social care organisations. A patient with serious disabilities represents a long-term resource commitment for the state. Thus working out which side of the NHS/social care line such a patient falls is important because both NHS and local budgets have been under immense pressure and will remain under pressure for the foreseeable future.

16.25 Second, there are tensions between patients (and their families) and the NHS. Patients naturally want to fall under NHS CHC because this will result in the patient getting social care and accommodation which is free at the point of use. The practical consequence of 'going into [social] care' is that many family homes have to be sold to pay care fees. Thus the entirely understandable aspiration of both the patient and their relatives that the home should be an asset to be passed on to the next generation is thwarted. While this is an entirely legitimate perspective, some of the mechanisms used by families to avoid the state getting their hands on the home may have less legitimacy. From the NHS perspective, the expression 'where there's a will, there's a relative' has come to the mind of many NHS officials struggling to define the boundary and trying to explain to an insistent relative why their elderly mother or father is not entitled to CHC.

16.26 Those two sets of tensions – the NHS/local authority tension and the NHS/patient and family tension – run through CHC policy like the word Brighton runs through a stick of seaside rock. They are always present, albeit often just below the surface.

Response to the *Continuing Care* guidance

16.27 In 2003, the Parliamentary and Health Service Ombudsman (PHSO) issued a special report, *NHS funding for long term care*,[11] which criticised both central government and individual NHS bodies in relation to their approach to eligibility for CHC, and upheld a large number of specific complaints from members of the public where a patient had been denied free NHS and social care. The PHSO reported on the DHSC's 2001 *Continuing Care* guidance in the following unflattering terms:

> A pattern is emerging from the complaints I have seen of NHS bodies struggling, and sometimes failing, to conform to the law and central guidance on this issue, resulting in actual or potential injustice arising to frail elderly people and their relatives (paragraph 1).
>
> I do not underestimate the difficulty of setting fair, comprehensive and easily comprehensible criteria. The criteria have to be applied to people of all ages, with a wide range of physical, psychological and other difficulties. There are no obvious, simple, objective criteria that can be used. But that is all the more reason for the Department to take a strong lead in the matter: developing a very clear, well-defined national framework. One might have hoped that the comments made in the *Coughlan* case would have prompted the Department to tackle this issue. However, efforts since then seem to have focused mainly on policy about free nursing care. Authorities were left to take their own legal advice about their obligations to provide continuing NHS health care in the light of the *Coughlan* judgment. I have seen some of the advice provided, which was, perhaps inevitably, quite defensive in nature. The long awaited further guidance in June 2001 [HSC 2001/015] gives no clearer definition than previously of when continuing NHS health care should be provided: if anything it is weaker, since it simply lists factors authorities should 'bear in mind' and details to which they should 'pay attention' without saying how they should be taken into account. I have criticised some Authorities for having criteria which were out of line with previous guidance: except in extreme cases I fear I would find it even harder

11 February 2003, HC 399.

now to judge whether criteria were out of line with current guidance. Such an opaque system cannot be fair. (paragraph 31).

16.28 Two significant and legitimate criticisms can be made of the PHSO report. First, it criticised variations between the polices adopted by different health authorities. That is a misguided criticism because the NHS has always been set up a national service with local decision-makers. Whenever there are local decision-makers, there will be differences between the decisions that are made. Hence, differences between services being made available in different areas are an inevitable consequence of the decision-making system, not necessarily evidence that the system is failing. Second, it is arguable that the report only considered the perspective of prospective CHC patients and their families. It gave insufficient weight to the needs of other patients who were also seeking funding for NHS treatment out of the same limited budget. However, the NHS was probably too timid to point out these errors and largely adopted a 'mea culpa' approach.

16.29 The 2001 guidance was also subsequently the subject of some pointed criticism by Mr Justice Charles in *R (Grogan) v Bexley NHS Care Trust and others*.[12] However, the judge in that case importantly noted:[13]

> . . . the divide between the duties relating to the provision of health services and social services is not between two duties that are enforceable by individuals. This is because the duties of the local authority are so enforceable but the relevant duties of the [secretary of state] in respect of the NHS are 'target duties'.

16.30 The judge also said:[14]

> I accept as submitted on behalf of the [secretary of state] that the extent of her duties to provide health services is governed by the health legislation and not by the limits of the duties of local authorities. Thus I accept that there is potential for a gap between what the [secretary of state] (through the relevant health bodies) provides, or is under a duty to provide, as part of the NHS, and 'health services' that could lawfully be supplied by local authorities.

16.31 The judge complained that the 2001 DHSC guidance was 'far from being as clear as it might have been' and concluded that it was partially to blame for the failure of local NHS bodies to adopt a consistent approach to eligibility for CHC. However, one significant feature of the *Grogan* case was that the local authority were not parties to the action and hence not represented at court. Thus, the court only had the perspectives of the patient, the secretary of state and the NHS, but was not assisted by the perspective of the local authority.

Primary care trusts and strategic health authorities

16.32 The adoption of different eligibility criteria by different health authorities and the then newly emerging local commissioners, known as 'primary care trusts' (PCTs), led to a plethora of complaints about a 'postcode

12 [2006] EWHC 44 (Admin), (2006) 9 CCLR 188.
13 At para 37.
14 At para 39.

lottery' around the entitlement of individual patients to CHC. Complaints about a postcode lottery are a standard of any debate on NHS services. Critics of decisions often affirm the benefits of 'local decision-making', assuming a local decision will be in their favour, but equally complain about decisions varying between localities when they go against them. A 'postcode lottery' is, of course, the inevitable result of local decision-making. However, the perceived unfairness of different CHC eligibility policies in different areas led the DHSC to require CHC eligibility criteria to be set by 'strategic health authorities' (SHAs) from 1 April 2004.

16.33 PCTs remained as the statutory decision-makers to decide which patients were eligible for CHC but, in making this decision after 1 April 2004, PCTs were required to use the SHA eligibility criteria to determine eligibility for NHS CHC. This change was aimed at delivering a greater level of consistent approach over the area of the SHA. At this stage, there were ten (later nine) SHAs covering the whole of England. However, there were still elements of postcode lottery in this system because the interpretation of the SHA criteria differed between different PCTs within the SHA area and, even if a patient was eligible, the package of care that an eligible patient received was determined by the policies of individual PCTs.

16.34 The 2001 guidance introduced a further stage for patients, namely the SHA Review Panel. These panels were commonly referred to as 'appeal panels' but they were not final decision-makers. The panels reviewed cases and made 'recommendations' back to the PCTs, but could not take their own decisions. However, few if any of the recommendations were not accepted by PCTs.

National framework

16.35 The adoption of SHA eligibility criteria and SHA appeal panels did not lead to a completely uniform approach across the country, and hence complaints continued. The government responded by introducing national CHC criteria covering the whole of England. These were set out in the first *National framework for NHS Continuing Healthcare*, which was published in October 2007. The *National framework* was updated in 2009 and a further edition was published in 2012. A new version of the National Framework has now been published. That will take effect from October 2018. A detailed description of the new National Framework will be provided in the next edition of this book.

Present position

16.36 The present position is that a person's eligibility for CHC is determined by applying rules in Part 6 of the RSR Regs 2012,[15] which, in turn, follows the decision-making process set out in the 2012 version of the *National framework*. The details of the eligibility decision-making process are explained below. However, the package of services that an eligible patient receives is still governed by the policies of the local NHS commissioners, which is now (almost always) the relevant CCG.

15 SI No 2996.

16.37 The present version of the *National framework* has a 'Part 2'[16] which consists of a series of questions and answers called 'Practice Guidance'. This part is a record of the accumulated guidance provided by Departmental officials to NHS bodies over the years. It is perhaps inevitable that there is not complete uniformity between the main section of the Guidance and the 'Practice Guidance'. This leads to the unfortunate position that, in the case of disputes, both patients and NHS bodies can find parts of the Guidance to support their positions. Where such disputes arise, the court will have to interpret the Guidance in order to seek to draw out a consistent meaning. The proper interpretation of guidance is for the courts, not for a CCG or even NHS England.[17]

The legal basis for the provision of NHS CHC

16.38 The 1995 *Continuing care: NHS and local councils' responsibilities* guidance grappled with the problem as to when the NHS should provide a comprehensive package of health and social care services for a seriously ill patient, which was free at the point of use but was delivered outside of a hospital environment. That conundrum has remained the central issue for subsequent policy-makers in this area.

16.39 Section 3 of the NHS Act 2006 requires CCGs, who are the statutory successors of PCTs, to make arrangements to provide the following services:

> (1) A clinical commissioning group must arrange for the provision of the following to such extent as it considers necessary to meet the reasonable requirements of the persons for whom it has responsibility:
> (a) hospital accommodation;
> (b) other accommodation for the purpose of any service provided under this Act;
> (c) medical, dental, nursing and ambulance services;
> (d) such other facilities for the care of expectant and nursing mothers and young children as the group considers are appropriate as part of the health service;
> (e) such facilities for the prevention of illness, the care of persons suffering from illness and the after-care of persons who have suffered from illness as the group considers are appropriate as part of the health service;
> (f) such other services as are required for the diagnosis and treatment of illness'

16.40 CHC involves the provision of a 'package' of care and support services to meet the needs of someone who has a primary healthcare need. This can include medical care (ie the services of medical professionals plus drugs and other medical inventions). However, it can also include accommodation and social care in addition to medical care. The legal basis for the provision of such services is a combination of section 3(1)(c) (for medical and nursing services), section 3(1)(b) (for accommodation) and section 3(1)(e) (for social care and other services). In *R (Whapples) v Birmingham CrossCity*

16 Starting at page 50.

17 See *Tesco Stores Ltd v Dundee City Council (Scotland)* [2012] UKSC 13.

Clinical Commissioning and another,[18] the Court of Appeal accepted that the power to create the *National framework* was contained in section 2 of the NHS Act 2006.

16.41 The obligation to provide accommodation to CHC patients, when this is part of their overall needs, probably arises under section 3(1)(b), although a clear view on this is somewhat difficult as a result of the judgments in *Whapples*, which specifically left the matter open. It appears reasonably clear that the duty to provide accommodation to a CHC patient outside a hospital arises when the patient has a 'reasonable requirement' for accommodation for the purpose of any service provided under the NHS Act 2006. That raises the slightly difficult question as the meaning of the term 'hospital' in the NHS Act 2006.

16.42 The word 'hospital' is widely defined in section 275 of the NHS Act 2006 to include 'any institution for the reception and treatment of persons suffering from illness'. A care home can amount to a 'hospital' where the resident requires and is provided with nursing services: see *Minister of Health v General Committee of the Royal Midland Counties Home for Incurables at Leamington Spa*;[19] *Chief Adjudication Officer v White*;[20] and *Botchett v Chief Adjudication Officer*.[21] See also *R (DLA 2/06)* which explains the legislative history in some detail.

16.43 However, the obligation to provide accommodation will rarely, if ever, result in the NHS having a duty to provide 'ordinary accommodation' to a patient outside of a care home environment. In *Whapples* the Court of Appeal said:

> Read as a whole, the National Framework does not, in circumstances where a patient is receiving NHS continuing healthcare in his own home, generally contemplate that the NHS will be responsible for defraying the costs of that accommodation.

16.44 However, that case made it clear that, where a person needs accommodation which is different from the accommodation in which they are presently living in order to deliver health and social care services, a local authority may well have a duty to provide suitable accommodation to such a person under its community care powers. These powers were under section 21 of the National Assistance Act 1948 in *Whapples* and are now under the Care Act 2014 after 1 April 2015.

16.45 The extent of the NHS's obligation to provide 'other services' under section 3(1)(e) is subject to the additional qualification that they are only such services as the CCG considers to be 'appropriate as part of the health service'. That clearly gives the CCG a wider discretion to determine the circumstances in which CHC services should and should not be provided to NHS patients. However, in exercising that discretion, the CCG must follow the guidelines set out in the *National framework* unless it has a good reason to depart from the guidance.

18 [2015] EWCA Civ 435, (2015) 18 CCLR 300.
19 [1954] Ch 530.
20 Reported as R(IS) 18/94.
21 Reported as R(IS) 10/96.

Who qualifies for NHS CHC?

Overview

16.46 From 1 October 2007, a *National framework* is required to be used by local NHS decision-makers to determine eligibility. The *National framework* has been updated from time to time and the present version dates from November 2012.[22] The rules on CHC eligibility are now contained in the RSR Regs 2012. Part 6 of the RSR Regs[23] sets out the tests to be applied by each CCG to determine whether a patient is eligible for CHC.

16.47 The CCG or NHS England decision-making process to determine whether a patient is eligible for CHC ought to be completed and a decision made and communicated to the patient within a maximum of 28 days. The *National framework* sets out the timescales as follows:[24]

> The time that elapses between the Checklist (or, where no Checklist is used, other notification of potential eligibility) being received by the CCG and the funding decision being made should, in most cases, not exceed 28 days. In acute services, it may be appropriate for the process to take significantly less than 28 days if an individual is otherwise ready for discharge. The CCG can help manage this process by ensuring that potential NHS continuing healthcare eligibility is actively considered as a central part of the discharge planning process, and also by considering whether it would be appropriate to provide interim or other NHS-funded services, as set out in paragraph 65 above.

16.48 Regulation 20 transposes the definitions of 'NHS Continuing Healthcare' into statute for the first time. The definition is the same as in the *National framework*, namely:

> 'NHS Continuing Healthcare' means a package of care arranged and funded solely by the health service in England for a person aged 18 or over to meet physical or mental health needs which have arisen as a result of disability, accident or illness.

16.49 The word 'care' is not defined in the regulations or in the NHS Act 2006, and so the meaning of the services that can be provided as part of a package of 'care' must be taken from the guidance.

Assessments to inform eligibility decisions

16.50 Regulation 21(1) of the RSR Regs 2012 provides:

> A relevant body must take reasonable steps to ensure that an assessment of eligibility for NHS Continuing Healthcare is carried out in respect of a person for which that body has responsibility in all cases where it appears to that body that–

22 See www.gov.uk/government/uploads/system/uploads/attachment_data/file/213137/National-Framework-for-NHS-CHC-NHS-FNC-Nov-2012.pdf. The 2018 version of the National framework will come into force on 1 October 2018. This text does not cover the 2018 document.

23 The National Health Service Commissioning Board and Clinical Commissioning Groups (Responsibilities and Standing Rules) Regulations 2012 SI No 2996 as amended by a series of subsequent amendment regulations.

24 At para 95.

(a) there may be a need for such care; or
(b) an individual who is receiving NHS Continuing Healthcare may no longer be eligible for such care.

16.51 The RSR Regs 2012 thus impose a statutory duty on the CCG to take reasonable steps to carry out an assessment if the CCG comes under a legal duty to carry out the assessment if the CCG is aware of the existence of the individual and has information that 'may' suggest a patient could become eligible for CHC or there has been a variation in the care services for a CHC eligible patient.

16.52 CCGs are not under an absolute duty to carry out a CHC assessment, but only to take 'reasonable steps' to do so. In practice, the patient with capacity is required to give their consent to the CCG using the patient's records to carry out the assessment. If a patient who has capacity to give or refuse consent to medical treatment refuses to give their consent, it will be practically impossible for the CCG to carry out any assessment.

16.53 The *National framework guidance* at PG6 (page 58) does not deal satisfactorily with this point, suggesting that NHS bodies and local authorities should proactively seek to escalate cases where individuals with capacity refuse assessments. That comes close to an attempt to force NHS treatment on reluctant patients. The better view is that patients with capacity have an absolute right to refuse treatment for good reasons, bad reasons or no reasons: see *Re T (adult: refusal of treatment)*.[25] Hence if a patient with capacity refuses to be assessed for CHC, that is a decision that the NHS commissioning body is required to accept. Thus the 'reasonable steps' that a CCG is required to take in such cases may well be no steps at all.

16.54 Regulation 20(2) of the RSR Regs 2012 provides:

(2) For the purposes of this Part a relevant body has responsibility for a person if the body is responsible–
  (a) in the case of a CCG, by virtue of–
    (i) section 3(1A) of the 2006 Act, except where the person is a person for whom another CCG is responsible by virtue of paragraph 2(b), (d), (e) or (f) of Schedule 1 to these Regulations, or
    (ii) paragraph 2, other than paragraph 2(a), of Schedule 1 to these Regulations; or
  (b) in the case of the Board, by virtue of regulation 7 (secondary care services and community services: serving members of the armed forces and their families) or regulation 10 (services for prisoners and other detainees)'

16.55 Accordingly, NHS England only has duties to assess and make decisions about the eligibility of patients for CHC for serving members of the armed forces and their families and for prisoners and other detainees. The responsibility for conducting assessments and making eligibility decisions lies with CCGs in all other cases, even if the main services that the patient needs are specialised services and thus fall to be commissioned by NHS England.

25 [1993] Fam 95.

16.56 This means the vast majority of CHC eligibility decisions are made by CCGs and not by NHS England. The decision-maker for CHC eligibility is thus referred to in this chapter as 'the CCG'. However the same decision-making processes are required to be followed by NHS England in the limited number of cases where NHS England is the 'relevant body' under the RSR Regs 2012.[26]

16.57 The information which can lead a CCG or NHS England to have the assessment duty can come from any source, including a local authority, provided there is enough information to lead the CCG to believe that the patient may have need for CHC. The duty to carry out a CHC assessment can thus arise whether there is a request by the patient or not. The wording of the duty is substantially the same as the duty on a local authority to carry out an assessment of an individual's entitlement to community care services under section 9 of the Care Act 2014 (formerly section 47 of the NHSCCA 1990). The case-law suggests that there is a low threshold before the duty to carry out an assessment arises (see *R v Bristol CC ex p Penfold*[27]). All that is needed to trigger a duty to carry out an assessment is for the CCG to have sufficient information that a patient 'may' be eligible for CHC.

16.58 There is an unresolved question as to whether an NHS patient who is in hospital and will remain in hospital for the foreseeable future is a person who comes within regulation 21(2)(a) of the RSR Regs 2012 (ie is a person where there may be a need for CHC). CHC is defined as a '*package of care arranged and funded solely by the health service*'. It is not wholly clear from this wording whether someone who is in long-term care in a hospital could be a person who is in receipt of a 'package' of NHS-funded care.

16.59 Paragraph 13 of the *National framework* provides:

> Eligibility for NHS continuing healthcare places no limits on the settings in which the package of support can be offered or on the type of service delivery.

16.60 This wording suggests that a CHC eligible patient could have their needs met within an NHS hospital and thus suggests that a long-term NHS patient may well be entitled to an assessment and eligibility decision. The better view is probably that the word 'package' of care is looking to arrangements for care outside of a hospital setting, and that a patient who will be remaining in hospital for the foreseeable future is not entitled to demand a CHC assessment. However, if there is any real possibility that such a patient should continue to receive care in a hospital or community setting, the patient will be someone who 'may' have an entitlement to CHC and thus should be subject to the assessment process.

26 NHS England has no published procedures for making its own decisions concerning CHC eligibility, but is required to follow the decision-making processes under the National Framework.

27 (1997–98) 1 CCLR 315.

Hospital discharge cases

16.61 Patients are often assessed for their eligibility for CHC at the point that they are ready to be discharged from hospital. Paragraphs 62 to 67 of the *National framework* set out the approach to be taken in such cases as follows:

> 62. In a hospital setting, before an NHS trust, NHS foundation trust or other provider organisation gives notice of an individual's case to an LA, in accordance with section 2(2) of the Community Care (Delayed Discharges etc) Act 2003, it must take reasonable steps to ensure that an assessment for NHS continuing healthcare is carried out in all cases where it appears to the body that the patient may have a need for such care. This should be in consultation, as appropriate, with the relevant LA.
>
> 63. CCGs should ensure that local protocols are developed between themselves, other NHS bodies, LAs and other relevant partners. These should set out each organisation's role and how responsibilities are to be exercised in relation to delayed discharge and NHS continuing healthcare, including responsibilities with regard to the decision-making on eligibility. There should be processes in place to identify those individuals for whom it is appropriate to use the Checklist and, where the Checklist indicates that they may have needs that would make them eligible for NHS continuing healthcare, for full assessment of eligibility to then take place.
>
> 64. Assessment of eligibility for NHS continuing healthcare can take place in either hospital or non-hospital settings. It should always be borne in mind that assessment of eligibility that takes place in an acute hospital may not always reflect an individual's capacity to maximise their potential. This could be because, with appropriate support, that individual has the potential to recover further in the near future. It could also be because it is difficult to make an accurate assessment of an individual's needs while they are in an acute services environment. Anyone who carries out an assessment of eligibility for NHS continuing healthcare should always consider whether there is further potential for rehabilitation and for independence to be regained, and how the outcome of any treatment or medication may affect ongoing needs.
>
> 65. In order to address this issue and ensure that unnecessary stays on acute wards are avoided, there should be consideration of whether the provision of further NHS-funded services is appropriate. This might include therapy and/or rehabilitation, if that could make a difference to the potential of the individual in the following few months. It might also include intermediate care or an interim package of support in an individual's own home or in a care home. In such situations, assessment of eligibility for NHS continuing healthcare should usually be deferred until an accurate assessment of future needs can be made. The interim services (or appropriate alternative interim services if needs change) should continue in place until the determination of eligibility for NHS continuing healthcare has taken place. There must be no gap in the provision of appropriate support to meet the individual's needs.
>
> 66. Where NHS-funded care, other than on an acute ward, is the next appropriate step after hospital treatment, this does not trigger the responsibilities under the Community Care (Delayed Discharges etc) Act 2003.
>
> 67. Whenever an individual outside a hospital setting is having their health or social needs assessed or reviewed by a CCG or an LA, consideration

should always be given to whether their needs suggest that it might be appropriate to use the Checklist (see below) to identify whether or not there is potential eligibility for NHS continuing healthcare.

16.62 The above Guidance does not appear controversial. However, there is a chart at page 23 of the *National framework* which raises some difficult legal issues. It seeks to explain how a CCG should respond where a patient is identified as '*possibly eligible for NHS CHC*'. It suggests that, unless a patient is on the 'fast-track' because the patient has a rapidly deteriorating condition, the first question CCG staff should ask themselves is:

> Could NHS Services enable further improvements in health/functioning that might alter outcome of eligibility decision.

16.63 The flowchart suggests that, if the answer to that question is 'yes', the NHS rehabilitation/reablement or other services should be provided. That part of the Guidance is uncontroversial. However, it suggests that, in such a case, the CCG should not, at that stage, undertake the assessment and eligibility decision-making process. This approach is supported in the Guidance by paragraph 65 which provides:

> In order to address this issue and ensure that unnecessary stays on acute wards are avoided, there should be consideration of whether the provision of further NHS-funded services is appropriate. This might include therapy and/or rehabilitation, if that could make a difference to the potential of the individual in the following few months. It might also include intermediate care or an interim package of support in an individual's own home or in a care home. In such situations, assessment of eligibility for NHS continuing healthcare should usually be deferred until an accurate assessment of future needs can be made. The interim services (or appropriate alternative interim services if needs change) should continue in place until the determination of eligibility for NHS continuing healthcare has taken place. There must be no gap in the provision of appropriate support to meet the individual's needs.

16.64 While this is Guidance produced by the secretary of state to which CCGs have a legal duty to consider, where there is contradiction between the Guidance and a statutory duty imposed by regulations, the statutory duty must take precedence. The circumstances envisaged above relate to a person who, by definition, 'may' have a need for CHC and thus the CCG has a statutory duty to carry out an assessment and decision-making process. The possibility that an individual patient, who may well have a 'primary health need' at that point, may (or may not) cease to be have such a need after being in receipt of rehabilitation services for some months cannot relieve the CCG of undertaking the assessment duty under regulation 21 of the RSR Regs 2012. If the patient is due to leave hospital and, at that point, may have a primary health need, the CCG is under a legal duty to carry out an assessment to determine whether the patient is eligible for CHC.[28]

16.65 The error in this Guidance can be illustrated by considering the circumstances of a patient who is discharged from hospital to a care home in order to receive a course of therapy and rehabilitation in accordance

28 See PG18 of the *National framework guidance* p66.

with the terms of this paragraph. The package of medical therapy and rehabilitation services will, of course, be funded by the CCG.

16.66 A question may arise as to whether the care home accommodation and social care fees should be funded by the NHS or by social care (which, for a patient with means, will effectively mean that the patient is funding the care home fees himself or herself). Care home fees are generally only paid for patients who have been determined to be eligible for CHC. In all other cases, the care home services are treated as being social care services which may (depending on the needs of the service user) be social care services that a local authority may be required to fund under the Care Act 2014.

16.67 However, Care Act services are means tested and thus the service in these circumstances use may well end up funding their own services even though a CHC assessment would show that, at that time, the patient is eligible for NHS funded social care and accommodation. Thus CCGs should be extremely wary about seeking to delay CHC assessments in an attempt to transfer the costs of accommodation and social care to local authorities while patients are undertaking medical therapy and rehabilitation services. Patients and their relatives may well wish to challenge any failure by a CCG to undertake a full CHC assessment and decision-making process in such circumstances.

16.68 The potential problems with this Guidance are, to some extent, ameliorated by PG14: How does NHS continuing healthcare link with intermediate care?[29] which suggests that intermediate care or the type described should be funded by the NHS. It provides:

> 14.1 Intermediate care is aimed at people who would otherwise face unnecessarily prolonged hospital stays or inappropriate admission to acute or longer-term in-patient care or long-term residential care. It should form part of a pathway of support. For example, intermediate care may be appropriately used where a person has received other residential rehabilitation support following a hospital admission and, although having improved, continues to need support for a period prior to returning to their own home. It should also be used where a person is at risk of entering a care home and requires their needs to be assessed in a non-acute setting with rehabilitation support provided where needed. This is irrespective of current or potential future funding streams, but is clearly important in the context of consideration for NHS continuing healthcare.
>
> 14.2 CCGs should have regard to the most recent guidance in relation to Intermediate Care.
>
> 14.3 Individuals should not be transferred directly to long-term residential care from an acute hospital ward unless there are exceptional circumstances. Such circumstances might include:
> a) those who have already completed a period of specialist rehabilitation, such as in a stroke unit
> b) those who have had previous failed attempts at being supported at home (with or without intermediate care support)
> c) those for whom the professional judgement is that a period in residential intermediate care followed by another move is likely to be unduly distressing.

29 See *National framework* pp64–65.

> 14.4 The guidance referred to above sets out what intermediate care should look like as well as how to commission it, with an emphasis on partnership working. CCGs should seek to ensure that this pathway is followed prior to any long-term placement apart from exceptional circumstances'

Carrying out assessments for patients who are due to leave hospital

16.69 The duty in the RSR Regs 2012 to carry out a CHC assessment can arise where a patient is being discharged from hospital if, at the point of discharge, the CCG believes that the patient may qualify for CHC. There is also a duty on the CCG and a hospital trust to consider whether a patient qualifies for CHC when discharging a patient from hospital if there is a delayed discharge.

16.70 Further guidance on assessing CHC eligibility at the hospital discharge point is provided at PG13 which provides:

> 13.1 Arrangements for applying the Framework should form an integral part of local hospital discharge policies, and should be implemented in such a way that delays are minimised. Timely assessments will prevent whole system delays within the acute hospital sector. LAs, CCGs and other NHS bodies providing hospital services should ensure that there is clarity in local discharge protocols and pathways about how NHS continuing healthcare fits into these processes, and what their respective responsibilities are.
>
> 13.2 CCGs should ensure that discharge policies with providers who are not NHS trusts are clear. Where appropriate, the CCG may wish to make provisions in its contract with the provider.
>
> 13.3 The 'delayed discharges' procedures (such as the issuing of section 2 and section 5 notices under the Community Care (Delayed Discharges etc) Act 2003 as amended) are not triggered until the NHS trust or NHS foundation trust are satisfied that the relevant individual is not entitled to NHS continuing healthcare.
>
> 13.4 Where it appears to an NHS trust or NHS foundation trust that a person planned to be discharged from hospital may have a need for NHS continuing healthcare, a decision on eligibility should be made prior to notices being issued under delayed discharges legislation unless alternative NHS-funded services are provided.
>
> 13.5 It is preferable for eligibility for NHS continuing healthcare to be considered after discharge from hospital when the person's long-term needs are clearer, and for NHS-funded services to be provided in the interim. This might include therapy and/or rehabilitation, if that could make a difference to the potential further recovery of the individual in the following few months. It might also include intermediate care or an interim package of support in an individual's own home or in a care home. Where a person is discharged from hospital with such interim services in place delayed discharges legislation does not apply.
>
> 13.6 Social care practitioners should work jointly with NHS staff throughout the NHS continuing healthcare eligibility process, and should be involved as part of the MDT wherever practicable. Therefore, where the LA receives a referral for involvement in the MDT process for NHS continuing healthcare they should respond positively and promptly. The LA should

usually be represented on the MDT completing the NHS continuing healthcare eligibility process. This means that, in most cases, the key assessment information needed for LA support is already available if the delayed discharge process is triggered subsequently. Therefore, where a person is found to be ineligible for NHS continuing healthcare and delayed discharge notices are then issued, the LA should be in a position to respond and action their responsibilities within a short timeframe.

13.7 CCGs and LAs could consider developing an agreed format for the NHS continuing healthcare multidisciplinary assessment that is also suitable for use as a community care assessment if the person is found ineligible for NHS continuing healthcare and delayed discharge processes are triggered.

13.8 In summary, CCGs should have appropriate processes and pathways in place to ensure that, where an individual may have a need for support after hospital discharge, one of the following scenarios will apply:

a) prior to completing a Checklist in hospital a decision is made to provide interim NHS-funded services to support the individual after discharge (in which case the delayed discharge provisions would not be triggered). In such a case, before the interim NHS-funded services come to an end, consideration of NHS continuing healthcare eligibility should take place through use of the Checklist and, where appropriate, the full MDT process using the DST;
b) a Checklist is completed which indicates the person may have a need for NHS continuing healthcare and interim NHS-funded services are put in place to support the individual after discharge until a full MDT NHS continuing healthcare assessment is completed (in which case the delayed discharge provisions would not be triggered); or
c) a Checklist is completed which indicates the person may have a need for NHS continuing healthcare and a full MDT NHS continuing healthcare assessment takes place before discharge. If this results in eligibility for NHS continuing healthcare then the delayed discharge procedures do not apply as the NHS continues to have responsibility for the individual's care; or
d) a Checklist is completed which indicates the person may have a need for NHS continuing healthcare and a full MDT NHS continuing healthcare assessment takes place before discharge. If this does not result in eligibility for NHS continuing healthcare then the appropriate delayed discharge notices should be issued; or
e) a Checklist is completed before discharge which does not indicate the person may have a need for NHS continuing healthcare in which case the appropriate delayed discharges notices should be issued.

If a local area does not use the Checklist either generally or in individual cases then a full MDT NHS continuing healthcare assessment should take place before delayed discharge notices are issued'

16.71 The procedures under the Community Care (Delayed Discharges etc) Act 2003 ('the 2003 Act') are mandatory and the Act remains in force. Many NHS bodies and local authorities have elected not to use the provisions of the 2003 Act despite its mandatory nature but, as a matter of law, NHS bodies are required to do so.

The CHC checklist as an initial screening tool

16.72 If the CCG has a legal duty to conduct a CHC assessment, the first step is decide whether to use the CHC checklist as an initial screening tool to screen out patients who are clearly not eligible for CHC (although there is no absolute legal duty to do so). Regulation 21(4) of the RSR Regs 2012 provides:

> If a relevant body wishes to use an initial screening process to decide whether to undertake an assessment of a person's eligibility for NHS Continuing Healthcare it must–
> (a) complete and use the NHS Continuing Healthcare Checklist issued by the Secretary of State and dated 28th November 2012 to inform that decision;
> (b) inform that person (or someone lawfully acting on that person's behalf) in writing of the decision as to whether to carry out an assessment of that person's eligibility for NHS Continuing Healthcare; and
> (c) make a record of that decision.

16.73 The *National framework* suggests that the checklist procedure should be used as a first step in most cases. The procedure can be conducted by a nurse, doctor, social worker or other qualified healthcare professional. The *National framework* states that:

> . . . the tool could form part of the discharge pathway from hospital, a GP or a nurse could use it in an individual's home, and Social Services workers could use it when carrying out a Community Care assessment. This list is not exhaustive, and in some cases it may be appropriate for more than one person to be involved.[30]

16.74 The purpose of the checklist is to help practitioners identify people who need a full assessment for NHS CHC and those who do not have sufficient needs to justify a full assessment. The form that should be completed goes through the care domains set out in the full assessment process and is attached to the checklist document. Completion of the checklist fulfils the duty in regulation 21(4) of the RSR Regs 2012 to make a record of the decision. If a decision is made that a person is not CHC eligible after following the checklist procedure, that is usually a sound basis for a CCG concluding that the person is not eligible for CHC

16.75 The CHC checklist requires the multi-disciplinary team to assess whether the individual meets or exceeds the described need across 11 Care Domains (Column A) or is Borderline (Column B). A full consideration of eligibility is required if there are:

- two or more ticks in column A.
- five or more ticks in column B; or one tick in A and four in B;
- one tick in column A in one of the boxes marked with an asterisk (ie, the domains which carry a priority level in the Decision Support Tool), with any number of ticks in the other two columns.

16.76 There may be special circumstances where a full consideration for NHS CHC is necessary even though the individual does not appear to meet the

30 PG17.

indicated threshold. If the patient does not pass the above tests, then the CCG can be confident that the patient does not qualify for fully funded CHC. However, getting through the initial screening tool does *not* mean that a patient will qualify for fully funded CHC. There are many patients who get through the initial screening but will not be entitled to fully funded CHC.

16.77 The form to be completed as part of the initial screening tool contains a section where the healthcare worker who completes the forms records their reasons for or against a full assessment. Completing the form with reasons is a legal requirement under the regulations.

16.78 The Guidance PG22[31] explains what should happen once the Checklist has been completed. It provides:

> 22.1 If full consideration for NHS continuing healthcare is required the Checklist should be sent to the CCG where the individual's GP is registered unless alternative arrangements have been made by the CCG. If the individual does not have a GP, the responsible CCG should be identified using the approaches set out in the 'Who Pays' guidance. Checklists should be sent in the fastest, but most appropriate, secure way, which could include e-mail (if secure) or fax. The use of either internal or external postal systems can delay the receipt of the Checklist and should only be used if no other referral mechanism is available. Each CCG should have appropriate secure arrangements for the receipt of Checklists and these should be publicised to all relevant partners. The CCG will then arrange for a case coordinator to be appointed who will ensure that an MDT (including those currently treating or supporting the individual) carries out an assessment and uses this to complete a DST.
>
> 22.2 CCGs have the responsibility for ensuring that arrangements are in place so that individuals who are screened out at the Checklist stage are informed of the outcome, are given a copy of the Checklist, are given details of how to seek a review of the outcome by the CCG and are offered the opportunity for their case to be referred to the LA for consideration for social care support. This could be delegated by agreement to other organisations that have staff completing Checklists but CCGs have the ultimate responsibility.
>
> 22.3 Where a Checklist indicates that a referral for consideration for NHS continuing healthcare is not necessary, it is good practice for the Checklist to still be sent to the relevant CCG for information, as the individual may wish to request the CCG to reconsider the decision and the CCG will need a copy of the Checklist in order to do this'

The full assessment process

16.79 Regulation 21(5) of the RSR Regs 2012 describes the process a CCG must follow when undertaking the full CHC assessment process. It provides:

> When carrying out an assessment of eligibility for NHS Continuing Healthcare, a relevant body must ensure that–
>
> (a) a multi-disciplinary team–
>
> (i) undertakes an assessment of needs, or has undertaken an assessment of needs, that is an accurate reflection of that

31 See *National framework* pp68–69.

person's needs at the date of the assessment of eligibility for NHS Continuing Healthcare, and

(ii) uses that assessment of needs to complete the Decision Support Tool for NHS Continuing Healthcare issued by the Secretary of State and dated 28th November 2012; and

(b) the relevant body makes a decision as to whether that person has a primary health need in accordance with paragraph (7), using the completed Decision Support Tool to inform that decision.

16.80 The Guidance recommends each CCG to appoint an NHS continuing healthcare co-ordinator whose role is to manage the process from the point that a full assessment has been commenced through to the delivery of the final package. The details of this role are set out as follows at PG26:[32]

> 26.1 Once an individual has been referred for full assessment for NHS continuing healthcare, the CCG has the responsibility for coordinating the whole process until the eligibility decision is made. The CCG should identify an individual or individuals to carry out the coordination role. Whilst this is likely to be a CCG staff member, it could (by agreement) be a staff member from another organisation such as the LA, an NHS Trust or independent sector organisation. This could be part of a wider inter-agency agreement, or could be negotiated in specific cases due to the skills or responsibilities that the practitioner(s) have in relation to a client group or individual.
>
> 26.2 The coordination role includes:
>
> a) receiving and acting upon a referral for assessment of eligibility for NHS continuing healthcare, ensuring appropriate consent has been given
>
> b) identifying and securing the involvement of the MDT which will assess the individual's needs and will then use this information to complete the DST. The MDT should comprise health and social care staff presently or recently involved in assessing, reviewing, treating or supporting the individual
>
> c) supporting MDT members to understand the role they will need to undertake in participating in a multidisciplinary assessment and completing the DST
>
> d) helping MDT members to identify whether they will need to undertake an updated or specialist assessment to inform completion of the multidisciplinary assessment
>
> e) supporting the person (and those who may be representing them) to play a full role in the eligibility consideration process, including ensuring that they understand the process, they have access to advocacy or other support where required, and organising the overall process in a manner that maximises their ability to participate
>
> f) ensuring that there is a clear timetable for the decision-making process, having regard to the expectation that decisions should usually be made within 28 days of the Checklist being received
>
> g) ensuring that the assessment and DST processes are completed in accordance with the requirements in the Framework and relevant Responsibilities Directions
>
> h) acting as an impartial resource to the MDT and the individual on any policy or procedure questions that arise

32 See *National framework* pp70 onwards.

i) ensuring that the MDT's recommendation on eligibility is sent for approval through the relevant local decision-making processes in a timely manner
j) where local arrangements place the responsibility for informing the individual of the eligibility decision within the role of the coordinator, ensuring that this happens in a timely manner and in accordance with the requirements of the Framework.

26.3 Care should be taken by CCGs to ensure an appropriate separation between the coordinator role and those responsible for making a final decision on eligibility for NHS continuing healthcare.

Keeping the individual informed
26.4 Individuals should be kept fully informed throughout the process. The coordinator should ensure that this takes place, including:

- explaining timescales and key milestones
- making the person aware of other individuals likely to be involved
- informing them of any potential delays
- providing the individual with a key contact person and ensuring a clear channel of communication between them and the MDT
- helping the individual to understand the eligibility process as it progresses. In addition to the national public information leaflet it may be helpful to provide a locally produced information leaflet explaining local processes and giving key contact numbers
- keeping family members appropriately informed, including where the individual indicates that s/he wishes this to take place and where family members will be involved in providing support to the individual and so need to be involved in agreeing their role.

16.81 Where a full CHC assessment is needed, the RSR Regs 2012 require an assessment by a multi-disciplinary team ('MDT'). There are a number of points to note. First, an MDT is defined in reg 21(13) of the RSR Regs 2012 to mean a team consisting of either:

(a) two professionals who are from different healthcare professions, or
(b) one professional who is from a healthcare profession and one person who is responsible for assessing persons for community care services under section 9 of the Care Act 2014 (assessment of an adult's needs for care and support).

16.82 It is best practice to include a professional with a social care background as part of the MDT where it is clinically appropriate to do so, but it is lawful to have an MDT with two different healthcare professionals.[33]

16.83 The role of the MDT is to carry out the assessment. However, the MDT is not the final decision-making body as to whether a patient qualifies for CHC. The team's role is to complete the assessment process and to provide the information to the CCG, and thus support the CCG decision-maker to decide whether the patient is eligible for CHC.

16.84 Membership of the MDT should be recorded with a full record made of the conclusions of the MDT and the reasons for any recommendations that are put forward by the MDT.

33 See *National framework* PG30 at p74.

16.85 The MDT is required to meet and make decisions using the Decision Support Tool. ('DST').[34] The Guidance strongly advises against a 'virtual' meeting or the members of the MDT filling in the forms separately without meeting. It provides:[35]

> **PG31: What happens if the co-ordinator is unable to engage relevant professionals to attend an MDT meeting?**
>
> 31.1 CCGs should not make decisions on eligibility in the absence of an MDT recommendation, unless exceptional circumstances require an urgent decision to be made.
>
> 31.2 Apart from ensuring that all the relevant information is collated, it is crucial to have a genuine and meaningful multidisciplinary discussion about the correct recommendation to be made. This should normally involve a face-to-face MDT meeting (including the individual and/or their representative). If a situation arises where a relevant professional is unable or unwilling to attend an MDT meeting every possible effort should be made to ensure their input to the process in another way, such as participating in the MDT meeting as a teleconference call. Where this is not possible then submission of a written assessment or other documentation of views could be used but this should be the least favoured option. Where professionals use this route, the CCG should explain to them that, whilst their views will be taken into account, the eligibility recommendation will by necessity be made by MDT members physically present or participating by teleconference.
>
> Care should be taken to ensure that alternative approaches for MDT participation still enable the individual being assessed to fully participate in the process.
>
> 31.3 If, even after having followed the above processes, there are still difficulties with the participation of, or obtaining assessment information from, a specific professional, CCGs should consider (in liaison with the individual) whether they have sufficient wider assessment information to reach a full picture of the individual's needs, having regard to the minimum MDT membership set out above. CCGs should record the attempts to secure participation.
>
> 31.4 In order to ensure effective MDT decision-making, CCGs should:
>
> a) have arrangements in place for coordinators to obtain senior support to secure participation of other practitioners where necessary
>
> b) consider agreeing protocols on MDT participation with organisations that frequently have staff who participate in MDTs.

16.86 In practice this means that the multi-disciplinary team needs to meet in person and ensure that the paperwork is completed for each of the Care Domains after a detailed discussion which seeks to reconcile any conflicting views. That involves an assessment of the level of need for each of the domains before a decision can be reached on CHC eligibility. The *National framework*[36] contains the following guidance about the MDT assessment:

34 The present version of the DST is dated June 2016 and is available at https://www.gov.uk/government/publications/national-framework-for-nhs-continuing-healthcare-and-nhs-funded-nursing-care.

35 See *National framework* p75.

36 See *National framework* pp70–72.

PG28: What are the elements of a good multidisciplinary assessment?

28.1 Assessment in this context is essentially the process of gathering relevant, accurate and up-to-date information about an individual's health and social care needs, and applying professional judgement to decide what this information signifies in relation to those needs. Both information and judgement are required. An assessment that simply gathers information will not provide the rationale for any consequent decision; an assessment that simply provides a judgement without the necessary information will not provide the evidence for any consequent decision. Assessment documentation should be obtained from any professional involved in the individual's care and should be clear, well recorded, factually accurate, up to date, signed and dated. As a minimum a good quality multidisciplinary assessment of an individual's health and social care needs will be:

- preceded by informed consent or an appropriate 'best interests' decision as discussed in paragraph 50 of the National Framework
- proportionate to the situation, ie in sufficient depth to enable well-informed judgements to be made but not collecting extraneous information which is unnecessary to these judgements. If appropriate this may simply entail updating existing assessments
- person-centred, making sure that the individual and their representative(s) are fully involved, that their views and aspirations are reflected and that their abilities as well as their difficulties are considered
- informed by information from those directly caring for the individual (whether paid or unpaid)
- holistic, looking at the range of their needs from different professional and personal viewpoints, and considering how different needs interact
- taking into account differing professional views and reaching a commonly agreed conclusion
- considerate of the impact of the individual's needs on others
- focused on improved outcomes for the individual
- evidence-based – providing objective evidence for any subjective judgements made
- clear about needs requiring support in order to inform the commissioning of an appropriate care package
- clear about the degree and nature of any risks to the individual (or others), the individual's view on these, and how best to manage the risks.

28.2 Local assessment arrangements and processes differ around the country, though a number of models have formed the basis for assessment and care and support planning processes including the Single Assessment Process for older people, the Care Programme Approach and the Common Assessment Framework. Person-centred plans (which were originally developed for use by people with learning disabilities, but which can be used by anyone – and are increasingly being used more widely) are not assessments. Rather, they represent the individual's own view of their desired outcomes and support needs. As such, they can offer key evidence to be considered when completing both the assessment and the DST. Health action plans and health checks can also provide useful evidence.

28.3 Effective assessment processes and documentation are key to making swift decisions on eligibility for NHS continuing healthcare and for commissioning the right care package at the right time and in the right place, so that the individual can move to their preferred place of choice as quickly and safely as possible.

28.4 CCGs and LAs should consider agreeing joint models of assessment documentation and having regular training or awareness events to support them.

16.87 The question as to which sources of information should be accessed by the MDT when undertaking the DST process will, of course, depend on the circumstances of an individual case. However, PG29 of the *National framework* suggests the following sources:

> **PG29 Potential Sources of Information/Evidence (not an exhaustive list):**
> - Health needs assessment
> - Community care assessment
> - Nursing assessment
> - Individual's own views of their needs and desired outcomes
> - Person-centred plan
> - Carer's views
> - Physiotherapy assessment
> - Behavioural assessment
> - Speech and Language Therapy (SALT) assessment
> - Occupational Therapy assessment
> - Care home/home support records
> - Current care plan
> - 24-hour/48-hour diary indicating needs and interventions (may need to be 'good day' and 'bad day' if fluctuating needs)
> - GP information
> - Specialist medical/nursing assessments (eg tissue viability nurse, respiratory nurse, dementia nurse, etc)
> - Falls risk assessment
> - Standard scales (such as the Waterlow score)
> - Psychiatric/community psychiatric nurse assessments.

16.88 An assessment which was completed without making reference to one or more significant sources of clinical information may well be unlawful unless the departure from the above guidance can be justified on the facts of an individual case.

16.89 One of the key elements in the CHC process is to attempt to secure consistency of decision-making across a CCG and between CCGs. The variations between areas led to complaints of a 'post-code lottery' around CHC. Discrepancies between decisions made by different NHS bodies was one of the primary criticisms of the 2003 PHSO Report and a concern for uniformity across the English NHS was, in part, a driver behind the creation of the *National framework*. However, the assessment process involves an element of professional judgment and thus an element of variation is inevitable. The Guidance contains the following passages which are aimed at keeping variations to a minimum:

> **PG33: What process should be used by MDTs to ensure consistency when completing the DST?**
>
> 33.1 Whilst local conditions and therefore local processes will vary, the following elements are recommended as being core to achieving consistency:
>
> a) The coordinator should gather as much information as possible from professionals involved prior to the MDT meeting taking place, including agreeing where any new/updated specialist assessments are required prior to the meeting.
> b) The coordinator (or someone nominated by them) should explain the role of the MDT to the individual in advance of the meeting, together with details of the ways that the individual can participate.

Where an individual requests copies of the documentation to be used this should be supplied.

c) Information from the process above and any additional evidence should be discussed within the MDT meeting to ensure common agreement on individual needs. Where copies of assessments are circulated to MDT members at the meeting, copies should also be made available to the individual if they are present.
d) Relevant evidence (and sources) should be recorded in the text boxes preceding each of the domain levels within the DST and this information should be used to identify the level of need within that domain, having regard to the user notes of the DST.
e) Depending upon local arrangements the MDT members may decide to reach the final recommendation on eligibility after the individual and their representative have left the meeting. However, the above gives clear expectations on their involvement in the wider process. If the MDT is to reach its final recommendation privately it is best practice to give the individual/representative an opportunity before they leave the meeting to state their views.
f) Having completed the care domains, the MDT should consider what this information signifies in terms of the nature, complexity, intensity and unpredictability of the individual's needs. It should then agree and record its recommendation, based on these concepts, providing a rationale which explains why the individual does or does not have a primary health need. It is important that MDT members approach the completion of the DST objectively without any preconceptions that specific conditions or diagnoses do or do not indicate eligibility or fit a particular domain level without reference to the actual needs of the individual (see below for more detail on recommendations).
g) The recommendation should then be presented to the CCG, who should accept this, except in exceptional circumstances. These circumstances could for example include insufficient evidence to make a recommendation or incomplete domains.
h) If the CCG, exceptionally, does not accept the MDT recommendation (see PG41 for circumstances when this can happen) it should refer the DST back to the MDT identifying the issues to be addressed. Once this has been completed the DST should be re-presented to the CCG who should accept the recommendation (except in exceptional circumstances).
i) The decision should be communicated in writing as soon as possible in an accessible format and language to the individual or their representative so that it is meaningful to them. They should also be sent a copy of the DST and information on how to ask for a review of the decision if the individual is dissatisfied with the outcome.

This whole process should usually be completed within 28 (calendar) days. This timescale is measured from the date the CCG receives the completed Checklist indicating the need for full consideration of eligibility (or receives a referral for full consideration in some other acceptable format) to the date that the eligibility decision is made. However, wherever practicable, the process should be completed in a shorter time than this.

16.90 One of the key issues in practice is assessing the level of a 'need' with the DST demonstrated by a patient if medical and social care interventions mean that the need is being effectively managed. The DST provides at paragraph 28:

> Needs should not be marginalised because they are successfully managed. Well-managed needs are still needs. Only where the successful management of a healthcare need has permanently reduced or removed an ongoing need will this have a bearing on NHS continuing healthcare eligibility. However, there are different ways of reflecting this principle when completing the DST. For example, where psychological or similar interventions are successfully addressing behavioural issues, consideration should be given as to the present-day need if that support were withdrawn or no longer available and this should be reflected in the Behaviour domain.

16.91 Thus a well-managed need remains as a 'need' for the purposes of the assessment process. Further guidance on this tricky area is provided in PG11[37] which provides:

> **PG11 How should the well-managed need principle be applied?**
>
> 11.1 This Framework provides that the decision-making rationale should not marginalise a need just because it is successfully managed: well-managed needs are still needs. The DST user notes provide additional guidance on the application of this principle at paragraphs 27–29. An example of this might occur in the context of the behaviour domain where an individual's support plan includes support/interventions to manage challenging behaviour, which is successful in that there are no recorded incidents which indicate a risk to themselves, others or property. In this situation, the individual may have needs that are well-managed and if so, these should be recorded and taken into account in the eligibility decision. In applying the principle of well-managed need, consideration should be given to the fact that specialist care-providers may not routinely produce detailed recording of the extent to which a need is managed. It may be necessary to ask the provider to complete a detailed 24/48 hour diary to demonstrate the nature and frequency of the needs and interventions, and their effectiveness.
>
> 11.2 Care should be taken when applying this principle. Sometimes needs may appear to be exacerbated because the individual is currently in an inappropriate environment rather than because they require a particular type or level of support – if they move to a different environment and their needs reduce this does not necessarily mean that the need is now 'well managed', the need may actually be reduced or no longer exist. For example, in an acute hospital setting, an individual might feel disoriented or have difficulty sleeping and consequently exhibit more challenging behaviour, but as soon as they are in a care home environment, or their own home, their behaviour may improve 2 without requiring any particular support around these issues.
>
> 11.3 The fact that an individual has a well-managed need does not, of itself, mean that they are either eligible or not eligible for NHS continuing healthcare. However, well-managed needs should be considered as part of the eligibility decision-making process. For more information see DST user notes paragraph 27.

16.92 This suggests that the patient's reduced level of need in a particular domain arising from good management care should largely be ignored unless the intervention has '*has permanently reduced or removed an ongoing need*'.

37 *National framework* p61.

Scoring the levels of need within the DST

16.93 The level of need for any care domain can be assessed at:

- Low;
- Moderate;
- High;
- Severe;
- Priority (but only for four of the behaviour, breathing, drug-therapies or altered states of consciousness domains).

16.94 It will inevitably be the case that not all assessors agree on the appropriate domain for an individual. The DST does not provide for decisions to be taken on a majority basis but instead provides that where there is an agreement which cannot be reconciled, the higher score by an assessor must be treated as the score of the panel. Paragraph 22 of the DST states:

> If, after considering all the relevant evidence, it proves difficult to decide or agree on the level, the MDT should choose the higher of the levels under consideration and record the evidence in relation to both the decision and any significant differences of opinion. Please do not record an individual as having needs between levels. It is important that differences of opinion on the appropriate level are based on the evidence available and not on presuppositions about a person's need or generalised assumptions about the effects of a particular condition.

16.95 This part of the process is also described at PG35[38] which states as follows:

> PG35: What happens if MDT members cannot agree on the levels within the domains of the DST?
>
> 35.1 The DST (paragraph 22) advises practitioners to move to the higher level of a domain where agreement cannot be reached but there should be clear reasoned evidence to support this. If practitioners find themselves in this situation they should review the evidence provided around that specific area of need and carefully examine the wording of the relevant DST levels to cross-match the information and see if this provides further clarity to move forwards or seek further evidence, although this should not prolong the 8 process unduly. If this does not resolve the situation, the disagreement about the level should be recorded on the DST along with the reasons for choosing each level and by which practitioner. This information should also be summarised within the recommendation so that the CCG can note this when verifying recommendations.
>
> 35.2 The practice of moving to the higher level where there is disagreement should not be used by practitioners to artificially steer individuals towards a decision that they have a primary health need where this is not justified. It is important that this is monitored during the CCG audits of recommendations and processes so that individual practitioners found to be using the 'higher level' practice incorrectly can be identified. Discussion may need to take place with these practitioners and possibly further training offered.
>
> 35.3 If practitioners are unable to reach agreement, the higher level should be accepted and a note outlining the position included within the recommendation on eligibility. As part of CCGs' governance responsibilities, they should monitor occurrences of this issue. Where regular patterns are

38 See *National framework* pp77–78.

identified involving individual teams or practitioners this should be discussed with them and where necessary their organisations to address any practice issues.

16.96 Thus, in effect, the final score involves levelling up to the score of the member of the MDT who gives the domain the highest score. In contrast, the patient or members of the patient's family are entitled to be present at the meeting but their views on the severity of a domain are not decisive. PG36 explains:

PG36: What happens if the individual concerned or their representative disagrees with any domain level when the DST is completed?

36.1 Whilst the individual and/or their representative should be fully involved in the process and be given every opportunity to contribute to the MDT discussion, the formal membership of the MDT consists of the practitioners involved. The approach described in PG35 above applies to disagreements between practitioners and not when an individual or their representative disagrees with individual domain levels chosen in the completion of the DST. However, concerns expressed by individuals and representatives should be fully considered by reviewing the evidence provided. If areas of disagreement remain these should be recorded in the relevant parts of the DST.

16.97 The DST suggests that a patient is likely to be eligible for CHC if he or she has:

- a level of *priority* needs in any one of the four domains that carry this level;
- a total of two or more incidences of identified *severe* needs across all care domains.

16.98 The Guidance requires the MDT to complete the DST. However, it also suggests that the panel provide a detailed report to assist the CCG panel which is charged with the final decision-making process. This is set out at PG37[39] which provides:

PG37: What does the DST recommendation need to cover?

37.1 The recommendation should:

a) provide a summary of the individual's needs in the light of the identified domain levels and the information underlying these. This should include the individual's own view of their needs.
b) provide statements about the nature, intensity, complexity and unpredictability of the individual's needs, bearing in mind the explanation of these concepts provided in paragraphs 77–89 of the National Framework.
c) give an explanation of how the needs in any one domain may interrelate with another to create additional complexity, intensity or unpredictability.
d) in the light of the above, give a recommendation as to whether or not the individual has a primary health need (with reference to paragraphs 77–89 of the National Framework). It should be remembered that, whilst the recommendation should make reference to all four concepts of nature, intensity, complexity and unpredictability, any one of these could on their own or in combination with others be sufficient to indicate a primary health need.

39 See *National framework* pages 78–79.

37.2 Although the core responsibility of MDTs is to make a recommendation on eligibility for NHS continuing healthcare, the recommendation could also indicate any particular factors to be considered when commissioning/securing the placement or care/support package required to meet the individual's needs (whether or not the individual has a primary health need).

37.3 Where the outcomes of the individual care domains do not obviously indicate a primary health need (eg a priority level in one domain or severe levels in two domains being found), but the MDT is using professional judgement to recommend that the individual does nonetheless have a primary health need, it is important to ensure that the rationale for this is clear in the recommendation.

37.4 Where an individual has a deteriorating condition, practitioners need to take this into account in reaching their conclusion on primary health need, considering the approaches set out in paragraph 38 of this Framework and being mindful of how that condition and the associated needs are going to progress before the next planned review. Where an individual has a deteriorating condition but eligibility for NHS continuing healthcare is not presently recommended, consideration should be given to setting an early review date. This should be clearly highlighted in the recommendation to the CCG who should ensure that the review is arranged at the appropriate time.

37.5 The recommendation for eligibility for NHS continuing healthcare should not be based upon an individual's specific condition or disease (eg stroke, cancer, Alzheimer's disease, dementia, etc) but on the needs that are identified. Needs that give rise to eligibility can be from any condition or disease. Just because individuals with a particular condition or disease have previously been found to be eligible for NHS continuing healthcare does not mean that every individual with a similar condition or disease will be eligible. Each individual should be assessed in their own right and evidence provided around the range of their needs; the identification of a primary health need should not be prejudged without going through the proper process in each individual case.

37.6 All of the above information should be provided even if the recommendation is that the individual does not have a primary health need. The CCG is responsible for care planning and commissioning all services that are required to meet the needs of all individuals who qualify for NHS continuing healthcare, and for the healthcare part of a joint care package. However, it is beneficial if the MDT makes recommendations on the care package to be provided, based on the assessment and any care plan already developed, whether the CCG, LA or both will have responsibilities.

37.7 The written recommendation needs to provide as much detail as possible, but should be clear and concise, to enable the CCG and the individual to understand the rationale behind the recommendation.

37.8 As the individual or their nominated representative should receive a copy of the DST it is important that it is legible, and free from jargon and abbreviations.

37.9 A copy of the completed assessment, DST and other documents should be forwarded to the CCG.

16.99 The test for the decision-maker under the RSR Regs 2012 is solely whether the patient has a 'primary healthcare need'. The multi-disciplinary team is usually expected to recommend that the patient has a 'primary health need' if the patient has a priority need in one domain or two or more instances of severe needs. However, the DST only provides indicators to assist in the 'Primary Healthcare Need' decision, but does not mandate an outcome.

16.100 The decision-maker is fully entitled to conclude that, given the individual clinical circumstances, the patient does not have a primary health need despite having a priority level of needs in one of the four domains that carry this level or two or more identified severe needs. The ultimate decision is a matter for the clinical judgment of the decision-maker (usually a CHC panel acting as a decision-maker on behalf of the CCG). The panel should be informed by the outcome of the DST as reported by the multi-disciplinary team, but must reach its own decision on the tests set out in the RSR Regs 2012. The guidance states that the assessment should not be carried out in a mechanistic way and, depending on the clinical facts, the team is entitled to recommend that the patient has a primary health need if there is:

- one domain recorded as severe, together with needs in a number of other domains, or
- a number of domains with high and/or moderate needs,

16.101 In these cases, the team needs to look at overall level and severity of medical needs, the interactions between needs in different care domains, and the evidence from risk assessments. All these should be taken into account in deciding whether to make a recommendation of eligibility for NHS CHC. The guidance, however, notes that it is *not* possible to equate a number of incidences of one level with a number of incidences of another level. The team should not, for example, conclude that 'two moderates equals one high'.

16.102 Ultimately, the recommendation must be one of professional judgment by the multi-disciplinary team. It is therefore inevitable that there will be some variations between the assessments conducted by different professionals. A single set of national criteria and a single DST assist in improving consistency between decisions within a CCG and between different CCGs, but some degree of inconsistency is inevitable given the professional judgments that need to made within the multi-disciplinary team. Provided the assessments are carried out conscientiously, it is more important to carry out accurate assessments on the clinical information available than to be over concerned about consistency between this case and another which, however similar, cannot ever be identical.

Consultation with social services

16.103 Regulation 22(1) of the RSR Regs 2012 provides that CCGs must, as far as reasonably practicable, consult with social services before making a final decision about whether a patient qualifies for CHC. There is a duty on social services departments to provide advice and assistance to CCGs when they are consulted. If the local authority has any paperwork concerning the patient including any assessment that a local authority has conducted to determine if the patient is in need of community care services, there is a duty on the local authority to disclose this to assist the

CCG. The consultation stage should happen after the completion of the assessment using the DST but before the eligibility decision is made.

16.104 PG76[40] explains the role of local authorities as follows:

> **PG76: What is the role of the LA in NHS continuing healthcare?**
>
> 76.1 The Standing Rules require CCGs to consult, so far as is reasonably practicable, with the relevant social services authority before making a decision on a person's eligibility for NHS continuing healthcare. (The Ordinary Residence Guidance 2011 should be used to identify the relevant social services authority.)
>
> 76.2 Social services authorities shall provide advice and assistance to a CCG over individual cases as far as reasonably practicable. This duty applies regardless of whether a community care assessment is needed and is separate from the LA's duty to carry out assessments under section 47 of the NHS and Community Care Act 1990.
>
> 76.3 However, once such a case has been brought to the attention of the social services authority, in addition to giving advice and assistance it should, having regard to the facts of the case, also consider whether a community care assessment is required. Where community care assessments have been carried out, the LA should use information from these assessments to assist the CCG in carrying out its responsibilities.
>
> 76.4 The roles that a LA should undertake as part of this duty include:
>
> - making staff available wherever practicable to be part of multidisciplinary teams (MDTs) which will undertake joint assessments and jointly complete the DST (including where the individual is a self-funder)
> - contributing to eligibility panels (where these exist) and participating in the decision-making process on eligibility
> - making staff available to undertake joint reviews
> - having systems for responding promptly to requests for information when the CCG has received a referral for NHS continuing healthcare
> - working jointly with the CCG in the planning and commissioning of care/ support for individuals deemed eligible for NHS continuing healthcare wherever appropriate, sharing expertise and local knowledge (whilst recognising that CCGs retain formal commissioning and care planning responsibility for those eligible for NHS continuing healthcare).
>
> 76.5 LAs shall make nominations to the Board of potential members of Independent Review Panels (IRPs) whenever requested by the Board and, where appointed, to make their nominees available to participate in IRPs as far as reasonably practicable.

16.105 The CCG should provide as much information to the local authority about the case as the local authority reasonably requires. Provided assurances are given by both sides about maintaining professional confidentiality (which should not be a problem with professional social workers), the Data Protection Act 1998 should not prevent the flow of relevant clinical information between the local authority. The CCG can rely on the statutory duty to consult under reg 22 of the RSR Regs 2012 to justify the disclosure of sensitive personal data about the patient to the local authority. It thus appears that, unless there are very special circumstances, the local

40 See *National framework* p100.

authority is entitled to see all the case papers concerning the patient to assist them to respond to the application for CHC.

16.106 However, the local authority does not have an automatic right to see the information for other purposes, such as following up any concerns they may have about other service users. CCG staff should seek advice if they are concerned that there is a request from the local authority or anyone else (including the police) to use the information collected in the CHC process for any purpose other than assessing if a patient is entitled to CHC.

16.107 The role of local authority at this stage is to have the chance to comment on the assessment and its recommendations, and to feed their views into the decision-making process. But the local authority does not hold a veto. The CCG is the sole decision-maker on CHC eligibility as the Court of Appeal confirmed in *R (St Helens Borough Council) v Manchester PCT and another*.[41]

16.108 The CCG must take any views expressed by local authority colleagues into account when taking the CHC eligibility decision. Tensions between the CCG and the local authority can mean that the CCG ends up disagreeing with the local authority's views on the right outcome of an individual case. The local authority may consider that a patient is eligible for CHC and thus seek to press the CCG to fund a patient's ongoing care (supported by the patient and/or the family). However, it is not unknown for the CCG to disagree with views strongly expressed by local authority colleagues. Any such disagreement should not prevent the CCG making a decision because the duty on the CCG under the regulations is to *consult* the local authority. This process does not require consensus decision-making. The local authority holds no veto and the decision-making process should not be set up so as to give the local authority a veto. Disputes between CCGs and local authorities are considered below.

16.109 If the local authority fails to respond to a request to provide input into the CHC process relating to a particular patient, the CCG are entitled to press ahead to the decision-making phase without the local authority input.

Who within the CCG makes the eligibility decision?

16.110 The eligibility decision can be made by a person or committee authorised under the CCG's standing orders to take the decision on behalf of the CCG. This will usually be a nominated officer or a panel which is constituted to review the assessments and reach a decision. There is considerable flexibility in the DHSC Model Standing Orders for CCGs to permit CCGs to delegate decision-making by a CCG to a committee which includes individuals who are not employed by the CCG. Thus, the CCG panel could include colleagues from social services or patient user groups, provided that the body is constituted as a committee of the CCG.

16.111 The membership, terms of reference and decision-making powers of the panel should be approved by the CCG governing body. Many CCGs

41 [2008] EWCA Civ 931, (2008) 11 CCLR 774.

have colleagues from social services on the panel which makes the final decisions on eligibility, but it is not appropriate to set up the decision-making process of the committee in such a way that those from outside the CCG have a right of veto or constitute a majority for a vote on the issue of eligibility. The CCG should not leave itself in a position where CCG staff are unable to take a decision that a patient is or is not eligible for CHC.

What weight should be given to the MDT's assessment as set out in the DST?

16.112 Regulation 21(5)(b) of the RSR Regs 2012 provides that the purpose of the DST is to 'inform' the decision of the CCG as to whether the patient has a 'primary health need'. The wording of the regulation thus suggests that the panel is required to take the DST into account in reaching a decision but is not bound to adopt the same conclusions as the MDT which complied the DST. However, the *National framework* suggests that the DST should do more than 'inform' the decision of the panel, in that it suggests that the panel should only depart from the recommendation of the MDT as set out in the DST in exceptional cases. This approach is explained at paragraphs 91 to 93 of the *National framework* which provide:

> 91. The CCG may choose to use a panel to ensure consistency and quality of decision-making. However, a panel should not fulfil a gate-keeping function, and nor should it be used as a financial monitor. Only in exceptional circumstances, and for clearly articulated reasons, should the multidisciplinary team's recommendation not be followed. A decision not to accept the recommendation should never be made by one person acting unilaterally'
>
> 92. The CCG may ask a multidisciplinary team to carry out further work on a Decision Support Tool if it is not completed fully or if there is a significant lack of consistency between the evidence recorded in the Decision Support Tool and the recommendation made. However, the CCG should not refer a case back, or decide not to accept a recommendation, simply because the multidisciplinary team has made a recommendation that differs from the one that those who are involved in making the final decision would have made, based on the same evidence.
>
> 93. CCGs should not make decisions in the absence of recommendations on eligibility from the multidisciplinary team, except where exceptional circumstances require an urgent decision to be made. The final eligibility decision should be independent of budgetary constraints, and finance officers should not be part of a decision-making panel.

16.113 The suggestion that the panel should only depart from the conclusions of the MDT in exceptional circumstances is reinforced in PG40[42] which provides:

> **PG40: What should the role of the CCG decision-making process be?**
>
> 40.1 The role of the CCG decision-making processes, whether by use of a panel or other processes should include:

42 See *National framework* pp82–83.

- verifying and confirming recommendations on eligibility made by the MDT, having regard to the issues in PG41 below;
- agreeing required actions where issues or concerns arise.

40.2 CCG decision-making processes should not have the function of:

- financial gatekeeping
- completing/altering DSTs
- overturning recommendations (although they can refer cases back to an MDT for further work in certain circumstances – see below).

16.114 PG41[43] also provides more details about the 'exceptional circumstances' in which a panel is said to be entitled to depart from a recommendation from the MDT. It provides:

> PG41: What are the 'exceptional circumstances' under which a CCG or panel might not accept an MDT recommendation regarding eligibility for NHS continuing healthcare?
>
> 41.1 Eligibility recommendations must be led by the practitioners who have met and assessed the individual. Exceptional circumstances where these recommendations may not be accepted by a CCG include:
>
> - where the DST is not completed fully (including where there is no recommendation)
> - where there are significant gaps in evidence to support the recommendation
> - where there is a obvious mismatch between evidence provided and the recommendation made
> - where the recommendation would result in either authority acting unlawfully.
>
> 41.2 In such cases the matter should be sent back to the MDT with a full explanation of the relevant matters to be addressed. Where there is an urgent need for care/support to be provided, the CCG (and LA where relevant) should make appropriate interim arrangements without delay. Ultimately responsibility for the eligibility decision rests with the CCG.

16.115 However, this part of the Guidance is open to the objection that, if the statutory scheme in the RSR Regs 2012 had wanted decision-making panels to be bound by the conclusions of the MDT as expressed in the DST in all but exceptional circumstances, it could have said so but it did not. In contrast regulation 23(8) of the RSR Regs 2012 provides that a CCG is required to implement the decision of the NHS England review panel 'unless it determines . . . that there are exceptional reasons not to do so'. It is therefore probably an unacceptable gloss on the statutory decision-making scheme for the decision-making panel to be required to find 'exceptional circumstances' before it is entitled to reach a different decision from the MDT as expressed in the DST. The better view is that the panel has a duty to make its own decision as to whether the patient has a primary health need, duly informed by the views of the MDT as expressed in the DST, and that in doing so it should place considerable weight on the views of the DST. However, notwithstanding the duty to give considerable weight to the contents of the DST, the panel has to reach its own conclusions and is not limited to following the DST unless it finds there are exceptional circumstances.

43 See *National framework* p82.

How should the CCG decision-making panel make its decision?

16.116 Regulation 21(5)(b) provides that the first question the decision-making panel has to decide is whether the patient has a primary health need. Regulation 21(6) then provides:

> If a relevant body decides that a person has a primary health need in accordance with paragraph (5)(b), it must also decide that that person is eligible for NHS Continuing Healthcare.

16.117 The CCG's judgment as to whether a person has a primary health need will be reached in part by looking at the medical support the patient requires on a day-to-day basis to meet his or her needs using the assessment produced by the DST. The *National framework* states that a primary healthcare need is assessed according to the following aspects of a patient's needs:[44]

- *Nature:* the type of needs, and the overall effect of those needs on the individual, including the type ('quality') of interventions required to manage them.
- *Intensity:* both the extent ('quantity') and severity (degree) of the needs, including the need for sustained care ('continuity').
- *Complexity:* how the needs arise and interact to increase the skill needed to monitor and manage the care;
- *Unpredictability:* the degree to which needs fluctuate, creating difficulty in managing needs; and the level of risk to the person's health if adequate and timely care is not provided.

16.118 The *National framework* goes on to state that:[45]

> Each of these characteristics may, in combination or alone, demonstrate a primary health need, because of the quality and/or quantity of care required to meet the individual's needs.

16.119 Paragraphs 3.5 and 3.6 of the Guidance[46] additionally state:

> 3.5 Whilst there is not a legal definition, in simple terms an individual has a primary health need if, having taken account of all their needs (following completion of the DST), it can be said that the main aspects or majority part of the care they require is focused on addressing and/or preventing health needs.
>
> 3.6 Primary health need is not about the reason why someone requires care or support, nor is it based on their diagnosis; it is about their overall actual day-to-day care needs taken in their totality. Indeed, it could be argued that most adults who require a package of health and social care support do so for a health-related reason (eg because they have had an accident or have an illness or disability). It is the level and type of needs themselves that have to be considered when determining eligibility. for NHS continuing healthcare.

16.120 At paragraph 3.8 the Practice Guidance then gives the following advice about how to approach the four characteristics of nature, intensity, complexity and unpredictability of a patient's needs:

44 At para 35.
45 At para 36.
46 See *National framework* p51.

3.8 Four characteristics of need, namely 'nature', 'intensity', 'complexity' and 'unpredictability' 'may help determine whether the 'quality' or 'quantity' of care required is beyond the limit of an LA's responsibilities, as outlined in the Coughlan case (a summary of the case can be found at Annex B). It is important to remember that each of these characteristics may, alone or in combination, demonstrate a primary health need, because of the quality and/or quantity of care that is required to meet the individual's needs.

3.9 It may be helpful for MDTs to think about these characteristics in terms of the sorts of questions that each generates. By the MDT answering these questions they can develop a good understanding of the characteristic in question. The following questions are not an exhaustive list and are not intended to be applied prescriptively.

'Nature' is about the characteristics of both the individual's needs and the interventions required to meet those needs.

Questions that may help to consider this include:

- How does the individual or the practitioner describe the needs (rather than the medical condition leading to them)? What adjectives do they use?
- What is the impact of the need on overall health and well-being?
- What types of interventions are required to meet the need?
- Is there particular knowledge/skill/training required to anticipate and address the need? Could anyone do it without specific training?
- Is the individual's condition deteriorating/improving?
- What would happen if these needs were not met in a timely way?

'Intensity' is about the quantity, severity and continuity of needs.

Questions that may help to consider this include:

- How severe is this need?
- How often is each intervention required?
- For how long is each intervention required?
- How many carers/care workers are required at any one time to meet the needs?
- Does the care relate to needs over several domains?

'Complexity' is about the level of skill/knowledge required to address an individual need or the range of needs and the interface between two or more needs.

Questions that may help to consider this include:

- How difficult is it to manage the need(s)?
- How problematic is it to alleviate the needs and symptoms?
- Are the needs interrelated?
- Do they impact on each other to make the needs even more difficult to address?
- How much knowledge is required to address the need(s)?
- How much skill is required to address the need(s)?
- How does the individual's response to their condition make it more difficult to provide appropriate support?

'Unpredictability' is about the degree to which needs fluctuate and thereby create challenges in managing them.

Questions that may help to consider this include:

- Is the individual or those who support him/her able to anticipate when the need(s) might arise?
- Does the level of need often change? Does the level of support often have to change at short notice?

- Is the condition unstable?
- What happens if the need isn't addressed when it arises? How significant are the consequences?
- To what extent is professional knowledge/skill required to respond spontaneously and appropriately?
- What level of monitoring/review is required?

16.121 Panels should bear in mind that all sick and vulnerable adults require a level of social support and, if they cannot be cared for in their own homes or with relatives, have a need for suitable accommodation. Patients with complex medical conditions will inevitably need a measure of daily healthcare support as well. The panel must focus on what the patient needs at this time. For many patients, there is a possibility that their condition will change in the near future. The patient may improve or his or her medical condition may deteriorate. If this happens then eligibility for CHC should be reconsidered when the changed facts are known. However, the panel needs to make a decision on the patient's clinical condition as it is at the date of the decision. A patient should not become eligible for CHC because he or she has a medical condition which, if not managed properly, may be life threatening or require intensive medical intervention unless there is an intense intervention at present to avoid a deterioration. The panel should focus on the nature, intensity, complexity and unpredictability of the patient's condition at that point to determine eligibility for CHC.

16.122 There are particularly difficult issues where a patient has a deteriorating. The medical condition (but where the fast-track pathway tool conditions are not met). Paragraph 38 of the *National framework* provides as follows:[47]

> It is also important that deterioration is taken into account when considering eligibility, including circumstances where deterioration might reasonably be regarded as likely in the near future. This can be reflected in several ways:
>
> - Where it is considered that deterioration can reasonably be anticipated to occur before the next planned review, this should be documented and taken into account. This could result in immediate eligibility for NHS continuing healthcare (i.e. before the deterioration has actually occurred). The anticipated deterioration could be indicative of complex or unpredictable needs.
> - Where eligibility is not established at the present time, the likely deterioration could be reflected in a recommendation for an early review, in order to establish whether the individual then satisfies the eligibility criteria.
> - If an individual has a rapidly deteriorating condition that may be entering a terminal phase, they may need NHS continuing healthcare funding to enable their needs to be met urgently (eg to allow them to go home to die or appropriate end of life support to be put in place). This would be a primary health need because of the rate of deterioration. In all cases where an individual has such needs, consideration should be given to use of the Fast Track Pathway Tool, as set out in paragraphs 97–107.
> - Even when an individual does not satisfy the criteria for use of the Fast Track Pathway Tool, one or more of the characteristics listed in paragraph 35 may well apply to those people approaching the end of their lives, and eligibility should always be considered.

47 At para 38.

16.123 A balance of medical and non-medical needs need is probably not sufficient to lead to a conclusion that the patient has a primary health need. The issue for the CCG is whether the above factors suggest that the patient's main or predominant need is for healthcare support, with a subsidiary need for accommodation and social care, or whether the patient has a main or predominant need for accommodation and social care, albeit that the patient also has a variety of healthcare needs. There will be cases where a patient with a complex medical condition is properly managed by staff who know the patient very well. This may lead to a situation where a previously unpredictable medical condition is now much less uncertain. It may mean that the intensity and severity of the patient's needs is less than it was a few months previously. Panels need to give proper recognition to carers who are able to bring about such benefits and should not underestimate the complexity of the patient's condition because it is managed predominantly by non-specialist staff. However, it should give due weight to such improvements and may well conclude that, as a result, the patient no longer qualifies for CHC. The issue should always come back to the single issue as to whether the patient has a primary health need.

16.124 The setting in which the patient is provided with care is not usually relevant to a decision about CHC entitlement. CHC can be provided to patients in their own home or in a care home.

The alternative ground: needs beyond what a local authority can be expected to provide

16.125 Regulation 21(7) of the RSR Regs picks up the tests outlined in *Coughlan*[48] and requires the CCG to apply them as an alternative route for the panel to reach the conclusion that the patient has a primary medical need. It provides:

> In deciding whether a person has a primary health need in accordance with paragraph (5)(b), a relevant body must consider whether the nursing or other health services required by that person are–
> (a) where that person is, or is to be, accommodated in relevant premises, more than incidental or ancillary to the provision of accommodation which a social services authority is, or would be but for a person's means, under a duty to provide; or
> (b) of a nature beyond which a social services authority whose primary responsibility is to provide social services could be expected to provide,
>
> and, if it decides that the nursing or other health services required do, when considered in their totality, fall within sub-paragraph (a) or (b), it must decide that that person has a primary health need.

16.126 It follows that, in reaching the decision as to whether a patient has a primary health need, the CCG is required to take two further steps. The CCG panel is required to look at the 'nursing or other health services required by that person' and then ask itself two questions. First, if the person is in a care home or is required to be placed in a care home. If so, the CCG needs to ask itself whether the individual's needs are:

48 See paras 16.16 onwards above.

> ... more than incidental or ancillary to the provision of accommodation which a social services authority is, or would be but for a person's means, under a duty to provide.

16.127 If the patient does have a need for 'nursing or other health services' which is more than is appropriate to be provided within social care accommodation (ie accommodation funded by the local authority under the Care Act 2014), the CCG is required to reach the conclusion that the patient has a primary health need and hence is eligible for CHC.

16.128 The second part of reg 21(7) applies where the patient is *not* in a care home, which will usually mean that the person is living in his or her own home or with relatives. This part of the test looks at the nature of the package of domiciliary services that are required by a patient who is living outside of a care. In such a case the CCG is required to consider the 'nursing or other health services required by that person' and ask whether these needs are of a nature beyond which a social services authority could be expected to provide. If the services are beyond those which a social services authority could be expected to provide, the CCG panel must find that the patient is eligible for CHC.

16.129 It is good practice to have these questions set out on the form that those undertaking the assessment have to complete to ensure that the CCG addresses its mind to them as part of the assessment process. The thinking in this part of the regulation (which is identical to the directions which preceded the regulations), emerges from the observations of the Court of Appeal in *R v North and East Devon Health Authority ex p Coughlan.*[49] The wording means that if the CCG decides that, looking at the patient's needs as a whole, it is inappropriate to look to social services to provide day-to-day care for the person, the CCG is required to conclude that the patient qualifies for CHC.

16.130 These provisions exist to ensure that patients are not left in circumstances where their needs are not serious enough to qualify for CHC but their nursing or other health service needs are too medically complex to be provided by a local authority. However, CCG panels need to bear a number of points in mind when addressing this issue:

- There are a wide range of health functions which local authorities are required to provide under a variety of statutes. The range and quality of health and health related services that local authorities can provide appears to be far greater than some local authorities assume.
- The test asks the CCG to focus on what the CCG considers it is reasonable to ask the local social services to provide. That may well be a higher or lower level of services than the local authority social services are in fact prepared to provide. The range of service users supported by the social services department of a local authority may be more generous in their provision of services than the CCG considers is reasonable. In that case, a patient may qualify for CHC even if the local social services could have provided support for the patient. Equally, however local authority social services cannot cut back on social care provision and thereby seek to shift patients from social to health care

49 [2001] QB 213, (1999) 2 CCLR 285.

by simply failing to provide classes of services. If the CCG considers that a patient's needs could properly be met by the local authority (even if the local authority social services may refuse to provide such services), it may be entirely appropriate for the CCG to decline to provide CHC support for the patient.

- The NHS does not walk away from a patient if the patient is not eligible for CHC. CCGs provide a wide range of medical support services to a patient in a nursing home or in the community who do not qualify for CHC, including NHS-funded nursing care.

16.131 Once the decision has been made, it needs to be communicated to everyone who has a legitimate interest in knowing the decision. PG42[50] provides:

> **PG42: How should decisions be communicated to the individual/ representative?**
>
> 42.1 Once the recommendation is confirmed by the CCG, the individual should be informed in writing in an appropriate language or format as soon as possible (although this could be preceded by verbal confirmation where appropriate), including the reasons for the decision and details of who to contact if they wish to seek further clarification or request a review of the decision. In most circumstances a fully completed DST with a covering letter confirming the decision and giving the above details will be sufficient for this purpose. Confirmation of the care package to be provided could be included within the letter or, if not known at that stage, should be supplied as soon as available.

The Fast Track Pathway decision-making processes

16.132 The CHC processes recognise that there will be patients whose needs are so urgent that a decision needs to be taken more urgently than permitted by the usual processes. The Fast Track Pathway Tool is available for such cases. The statutory framework for this is set out in regulation 21(8) to (10) of the RSR Regs 2012 which provide:

> (8) Paragraphs (2) to (6) do not apply where an appropriate clinician decides that–
> an individual has a primary health need arising from a rapidly deteriorating condition; and
> the condition may be entering a terminal phase,
> and that clinician has completed a Fast Track Pathway Tool stating reasons for the decision.
>
> (9) A relevant body must, upon receipt of a Fast Track Pathway tool completed in accordance with paragraph (8), decide that a person is eligible for NHS Continuing Healthcare.
>
> (10) Where an assessment of eligibility for NHS-funded nursing Continuing Healthcare has been carried out, or a relevant body has received a Fast Track Pathway Tool completed in accordance with paragraph (8), the relevant body must–
> (a) notify the person assessed (or someone lawfully acting on that person's behalf), in writing, of the decision made about their eligibility for NHS Continuing Healthcare, the reasons for that

50 See *National framework* p83.

decision and, where applicable, the matters referred to in paragraph (11); and

(b) make a record of that decision.

16.133 It follows that the key differences between the Fast Track and the normal track are:

a) The Fast Track is only appropriate where a patient has a 'rapidly deteriorating condition' which may be entering a 'terminal phase';
b) The decision-maker as to whether these conditions are met is an 'appropriate clinician' and not the CCG; and
c) Once the decision is made by an appropriate clinician that the statutory test is met, the CCG has a statutory duty to make the decision that the patient is eligible for CHC. The appropriate clinician is thus a delegated decision-maker on behalf of the CCG: see by analogy *R (Crudace) v Northumbria Police Authority*.[51]

16.134 The term 'appropriate clinician' is defined in regulation 21(13) as follows:

> 'appropriate clinician' means a person who is–
> (a) responsible for the diagnosis, treatment or care of the person under the 2006 Act in respect of whom a Fast Track Pathway Tool is being completed, and
> (b) a registered nurse or a registered medical practitioner.

16.135 The 'Fast Track Pathway Tool' is published by the Department of Health and Social Care.[52] The purpose of is explained at paragraph 13:

> The purpose of the Fast Track Pathway Tool is to ensure that individuals with a rapidly deteriorating condition, which may be entering a terminal phase, are supported in their preferred place of care as quickly as possible. It means that a CCG takes responsibility for commissioning and funding appropriate care. Once this has happened, a CCG, and its partners can proceed, where appropriate, with reaching a decision on longer-term NHS continuing healthcare eligibility. No one who has been identified through the fast-track process as being eligible for NHS continuing healthcare should have this funding or support removed without their eligibility being reviewed in accordance with the review processes set out in the National Framework. The review should include completion of the Decision Support Tool (DST) by a multidisciplinary team, including a recommendation on eligibility. This overall process, including how personal information will be shared between different organisations and healthcare professionals involved in delivering care, should be carefully and sensitively explained to the individual and, where appropriate, their family. Careful decision-making is essential to avoid the undue distress that might result from a person moving in and out of NHS continuing healthcare eligibility within a very short period of time. Where an individual receiving services through use of the Fast Track Pathway Tool is expected to die in the very near future, CCGs should continue to take responsibility for the care package until the end of life.

16.136 This approach is replicated at paragraphs 97 to 107 of the *National framework* which provide:

51 [2012] EWHC 112 (Admin) at paras 63–70.

52 See https://www.gov.uk/government/publications/national-framework-for-nhs-continuing-healthcare-and-nhs-funded-nursing-care.

Fast Track Tool

97. Individuals with a rapidly deteriorating condition that may be entering a terminal phase, may require 'fast tracking' for immediate provision of NHS continuing healthcare. The Fast Track Tool should be completed by an appropriate clinician, who should give the reasons why the person meets the criterion required for the fast-tracking decision. 'Appropriate clinicians' are those persons who are, pursuant to the 2006 Act, responsible for an individual's diagnosis, treatment or care and who are medical practitioners (such as consultants, registrars or GPs) or registered nurses. The clinician should have an appropriate level of knowledge or experience of the type of health needs, so that they are able to comment reasonably on whether the individual has a rapidly deteriorating condition that may be entering a terminal phase.

98. Appropriate clinicians can include clinicians employed in voluntary and independent sector organisations that have a specialist role in end of life needs (for example, hospices), provided they are offering services pursuant to the 2006 Act. Others involved in supporting those with end of life needs, including those in wider voluntary and independent sector organisations, may identify the fact that the individual has needs for which use of the Fast Track Tool would be appropriate. They should contact the appropriate clinician who is responsible for the diagnosis, care or treatment of the individual and ask for consideration to be given to completion of the Fast Track Tool.

99. The completed Fast Track Tool should be supported by a prognosis, if available. However, strict time limits that base eligibility on some specified expected length of life remaining should not be imposed: it is the responsibility of the appropriate clinician to make a decision based on the needs

100. Where a recommendation is made for an urgent package of care via the fast-track process, this should be accepted and actioned immediately by the CCG. It is not appropriate for individuals to experience delay in the delivery of their care package while concerns over the use of the Fast Track Tool are resolved. CCGs should carefully monitor use of the tool and raise any specific concerns with clinicians, teams and organisations. Such concerns should be treated as a separate matter from the task of arranging for service provision in the individual case.

101. No one who has been identified through the fast-track process as eligible for NHS continuing healthcare should have this funding removed without the eligibility being reviewed in accordance with the review processes set out in paragraphs 139–144. The review should include completion of a Decision Support Tool by a multidisciplinary team, including them making a recommendation on eligibility.

102. The purpose of the Fast Track Tool is to ensure that individuals with a rapidly deteriorating condition that may be entering a terminal phase are supported in their preferred place of care as quickly as possible. This overall process including how personal information will be shared between different organisations and healthcare professionals involved in delivering care, should be carefully and sensitively explained to the individual and (where appropriate) their representative. Careful and sensitive decision-making is essential in order to avoid the undue distress that might result from a person moving in and out of NHS continuing healthcare eligibility within a very short period of time.

103. Where an individual who is receiving services from use of the Fast Track Tool is expected to die in the very near future, the CCG should continue to take responsibility for the care package until the end of life.

104. It is important to bear in mind that this is not the only way that someone can qualify for NHS continuing healthcare towards the end of their life. The Decision Support Tool asks practitioners to document deterioration (including observed and likely deterioration) in a person's condition, so that they can take this into account in determining eligibility using the Decision Support Tool. However, this should not be used as a means of circumventing use of the Fast Track Tool when individuals satisfy the criteria for its use.

105. Where deterioration can be reasonably anticipated to take place in the near future, this should also be taken into account, in order to avoid the need for unnecessary or repeat assessments.

106. In end of life cases, CCGs and LAs should take particular account of paragraphs 169–171 regarding person-centred commissioning and procurement arrangements.

107. NHS continuing healthcare assessments, care planning and commissioning for those with end of life needs should be carried out in an integrated manner, as part of the individual's overall end of life care pathway, and should reflect the approaches set out in the national End of Life Care Strategy19, with full account being taken of patient preferences, including those set out in advance care plans.

16.137 Further guidance on the use of the Fast Track Tool is provided in the Practice Guidance sections at pages 83–84 of the *National framework*.

16.138 Care planning for those in a terminal phase may need to be completed quickly once an eligibility decision is made. PG52 recommends care planning should be completed within 48 hours if the Fast Track Tool is used. It provides:

PG52: How quickly could a hospital discharge take place following the completion of the Fast Track Tool?

52.1 Standing Rules state that the CCG must, upon receipt of a completed Fast Track Pathway Tool, decide that the individual is eligible for NHS continuing healthcare. Action should be taken urgently to agree and implement the care package. CCGs should have processes in place to enable such care packages to be implemented quickly. Given the nature of the needs, this time period should preferably not exceed 48 hours from receipt of the completed Fast Track Pathway Tool. CCGs who receive significant numbers of Fast Track Pathway Tools could consider having staff dedicated to implementing fast-track care packages as this will avoid a conflict of time priorities with dealing with non-fast-track applications. Having dedicated staff could also facilitate close working with end of life care teams. CCGs should also consider wider arrangements that need to be in place to facilitate implementation of packages within 48 hours, such as protocols for the urgent provision of equipment. The CCG coordinator and the referrer should communicate effectively with each other to ensure well-coordinated discharge/support provision arrangements.

16.139 This Guidance thus suggests that CCGs are required to move very quickly to make suitable arrangements for a person in a terminal phase of life.

NHS-funded nursing care

16.140 NHS-funded nursing care is covered by Part 6 of the RSR Regs 2012. Regulation 20 defines 'nursing care' as follows:

> 'nursing care' means nursing care by a registered nurse and 'nursing care by a registered nurse' has the same meaning as in section 49(2) of the Health and Social Care Act 2001.

16.141 The definition of 'nursing care' in section 49(2) of the 2001 Act is:

> In this section 'nursing care by a registered nurse' means any services provided by a registered nurse and involving–
> (a) the provision of care, or
> (b) the planning, supervision or delegation of the provision of care,
>
> other than any services which, having regard to their nature and the circumstances in which they are provided, do not need to be provided by a registered nurse'

16.142 Regulation 28 of the RSR Regs 2012 defines the decision-making process for determining if a patient is eligible for NHS-funded nursing care as follows:

> 28(1) Subject to paragraphs (2) and (3), where it appears to a relevant body in respect of a person for whom it has responsibility that that person–
> (a) is resident in relevant premises or may need to become resident in such premises; and
> (b) may be in need of nursing care,
>
> that body must carry out an assessment of the need for nursing care.
>
> (2) Before carrying out an assessment under paragraph (1), the relevant body must consider whether its duty under regulation 21(2) is engaged, and if so, it must comply with the requirements of regulation 21 prior to carrying out any assessment under this regulation.
>
> (3) Paragraph (1) does not apply if a relevant body has made arrangements for providing the person with NHS Continuing Healthcare.
>
> (4) Where–
> (a) the relevant body has carried out an assessment pursuant to regulation 21(2); but
> (b) paragraph (3) does not apply because a decision has been made that the person is not eligible for NHS Continuing Healthcare,
>
> that body must nevertheless use that assessment, wherever reasonably practicable, in making its assessment under paragraph (1).
>
> (5) Where–
> (a) the relevant body determines that a person has a need for nursing care pursuant to this regulation; and
> (b) the person has agreed with that body that that person does want to be provided with such nursing care,
>
> paragraph (6) applies.
>
> (6) The relevant body must pay to a registered person for the relevant premises the flat rate in respect of that person's nursing care unless or until that person–
> (a) has their need for nursing care assessed and it is determined that that person no longer has any need for nursing care;
> (b) is no longer resident in the relevant premises;
> (c) becomes eligible for NHS Continuing Healthcare pursuant to this Part; or
> (d) dies.

16.143 This regulation makes it clear that NHS-funded nursing care is an NHS contribution towards the cost of care home fees for patient that are not eligible for fully funded CHC. Guidance on determining the need for NHS-funded nursing care is provided at Annex D to the Guidance.[53] This provides:

Annex D: Determining the Need for NHS-funded Nursing Care

1. In all cases, individuals should be considered for eligibility for NHS continuing healthcare before a decision is reached about the need for NHS-funded nursing care (NHS-funded nursing care provided by registered nurses) in residential accommodation. In most cases, therefore, the individual will already have been considered for NHS continuing healthcare and will have had an associated assessment, which should provide sufficient information to gauge the need for nursing care in residential accommodation. In certain circumstances, an individual who has been found not to be eligible for NHS continuing healthcare at the Checklist stage may still need an assessment of needs for NHS-funded nursing care. In such cases, an appropriate assessment should be completed. It may, therefore, be appropriate to use the Single Assessment Process (or similar), to ensure that all needs are identified and that the decisions reached are proportionate, reasoned and recorded.

2. Where the local authority (LA) also carries out an assessment of the individual's needs, it may be appropriate for the CCG to carry out an assessment for NHS-funded nursing care jointly with this process. Where an individual is funding his or her own care needs (apart from NHS-funded nursing care), CCGs should take particular care to ensure that there is clarity on the part of themselves, the relevant LA and the individual as to who is taking responsibility for the assessment, case management and review of the individual's needs on an ongoing basis.

3. The outcome of the above process should provide the CCG with sufficient information to establish an agreement with a care home for NHS-funded nursing services, and will trigger the CCG's responsibility to fund the care from a registered nurse through a single rate of payment.

4. Individuals who were in receipt of the high band of NHS-funded nursing care under the three-band system that was in force until 30 September 2007 are entitled to continue on the high band until:

a) on review, it is determined that they no longer have any need for nursing care;
b) on review, it is determined that their needs have changed, so that under the previous three-band system, they would have moved onto the medium or low bands. In this situation, the individual should be moved onto the single rate;
c) they are no longer resident in a care home that provides nursing care;
d) they become eligible for NHS continuing healthcare; or
e) they die.

16.144 Patients cannot qualify both for CHC and NHS-funded nursing care: see reg 28(3). Patients who have a need for nursing services but live at home do not qualify for the payment. This provision assumes that a patient living in their own home who needs nursing services will have those provided by district nurses or by a domiciliary care agency which is contracted by the relevant CCG to provide this service.

53 See *National framework* p127.

16.145 Regulation 28 imposes a duty on the CCG (or possibly NHS England) to carry out an assessment of the patient's need for nursing care. However, reg 28(4) provides that where a patient is found not to be eligible for CHC, the CHC assessment or the CHC checklist should be used to determine the patient's eligibility for NHS-funded nursing care.

16.146 The level of payment in November 2016 was £156.25 per week (supposedly on an 'interim basis'). Before 1 October 2007, there were three different levels or bands of payment for NHS-funded nursing care – low, medium and high. If a patient moved into a care home before 1 October 2007, and was awarded the low or medium bands, the patient should have been transferred to the standard rate from that date. If the patient moved into a care home before 1 October 2007 and was awarded the high band, NHS-funded nursing care continues to be paid at the higher rate. For 2015/16, the standard rate was fixed at £156.25. This represented a 40 per cent increase on the previous rate. However the rate payable from 1 April 2017 was reduced to £155.05[54] and the higher rate was fixed at £213.32. The standard rate is due to rise to £158.16 on 1 April 2018 and the higher rate will increase to £217.59.

16.147 Patients are entitled[55] to continue on the standard rate unless:

a) the patient no longer has nursing needs;
b) the patient no longer lives in a care home that provides nursing;
c) the patient's nursing needs have reduced and, applying the previous tests, he or she is would no longer be eligible for the high band; in that case the patient will drop from the higher rate to the standard rate of £112.00 a week; or
d) the patient becomes entitled to CHC.

The relationship between NHS and local authority funded services

16.148 Care for a service user which is delivered by a registered nurse cannot be delivered by the local authority. Local authorities also do not employ doctors, apart from for the discharge of their public health functions and care to an individual patient by a doctor will fall on the NHS, not on social care. However, all other highly specialised community care services that a CCG can expect to be provided to individuals who are accommodated outside an NHS hospital.

16.149 If a package of care services is needed to support someone who is disabled or ill, or to prevent them getting ill, and the care is of such a nature that it does *not* require a substantial and regular care input by a registered nurse or doctor, the primary duty to provide care for those with eligible needs will usually rest on the local authority. There is, for example, a wide range of duties to the sick and disabled on local authorities under the Care Act 2014.

54 See https://www.gov.uk/government/news/nhs-funded-nursing-care-rate-for-2017-to-2018.

55 The entitlement is set out on the NHS Choice website at www.nhs.uk/chq/Pages/what-is-nhs-funded-nursing-care.aspx.

16.150 However, where a patient is eligible for CHC, a local authority will generally decide that the patient has no 'need' for community care services because a package of accommodation, social and health care service should be funded by the NHS to meet all of the service user's eligible needs.

Reviews and appeals to NHS England by patients or relatives on eligibility grounds

Reviews and appeals

16.151 Regulation 21(11) of the RSR Regs 2012 provides for the patient to be informed of the CHC decision as follows:

> (11) Where a relevant body has decided that a person is not eligible for NHS Continuing Healthcare, it must inform the person (or someone acting on that person's behalf) of the circumstances and manner in which that person may apply for a review of the decision if they are dissatisfied with–
> (a) the procedure followed by the relevant body in reaching that decision; or
> (b) the primary health need decision made in accordance with paragraph (5)(b).

16.152 Unlike other provisions within the RSR Regs 2012, reg 21(11) does not specifically require the CCG to give reasons for its decision. However, the *National framework* states:[56]

> . . . the CCG should give clear reasons for its decision.

The duty to have regard to the *National framework* thus probably means that the CCG has a legal duty to give coherent reasons for its eligibility decision.

16.153 Regulation 21(11) provides that the patient must be told that he or she can seek a review of the decision. The *National framework* provides:[57]

> Each CCG should agree a local review process. These review processes should include timescales and should be made publicly available, and a copy should be sent to anybody who requests a review of a decision.

16.154 The CCG should devise and operate a procedure to enable staff who were not involved in the original decision to review decisions on CHC eligibility. This should be undertaken as quickly and thoroughly as is possible in the circumstances. This will rarely require the CCG to repeat in full the multi-disciplinary assessment. Nonetheless if there are areas of substantial concern identified in the review, this review may lead to the CCG re-running the assessment process. Once the review is completed, the CCG should provide a response to the patient or their relatives explaining the decision that has been reached and the reasons for the decision.

16.155 If the patient or his or her relatives remain dissatisfied with the review they can appeal to a panel set up by NHS England. The options for the patient or their family are explained in PG73 which provides:

> **PG73: What if the individual wishes to challenge the final eligibility decision made by the CCG?**

56 At para 146.

57 At para 151.

> 73.1 If the individual or their representative wishes to dispute the decision made and/or the process used to reach it, they can request an independent review through the Board as set out in this Framework. However, CCGs should always work with the individual and their representatives to seek to resolve the matter informally without the need for an IRP. Even when an IRP has been requested, CCGs should continue to seek to informally resolve the matter, up to the date of the IRP hearing itself. When the Board receives an IRP request they should contact the relevant CCG to establish what efforts have been made to achieve local resolution and the outcome. The Board can consider asking CCGs to attempt further local resolution prior to the IRP hearing. CCGs and the Board may receive requests that are outside the remit of the IRP process (ie that are not about the application of the eligibility criteria or the process followed to reach the decision). The eligibility criteria are set nationally by Standing Rules and so are not a matter for local review or complaints processes. If CCGs and the Board receive review requests about other non-IRP matters (for example, the nature of the care package to be provided) they should advise the individual to pursue the matter through the NHS complaints process. CCGs should consider publishing local processes and timescales for responding to complaints and concerns relating to NHS continuing healthcare on issues that fall outside of the IRP process.

16.156 The NHS England panel is under a duty to 'review' the decision: see reg 23 of the RSR Regs 2012. Regulation 23(8) and (9) provide that the CCG must follow the recommendation of the NHS England review panel unless it has exceptional reasons not to do so. Those 'exceptional reasons' could be that the review panel has failed to apply the *National framework* properly, has failed properly to understand the assessments that the CCG made of the patient's needs or has come to an irrational conclusion.

16.157 CCG staff should co-operate fully with the operation of such panels which will make final decisions on entitlement to CHC.

16.158 If the NHS England appeal panel decides that the patient is eligible for CHC and that decision is accepted by the CCG, the CCG has a liability to meet the costs from the date of the decision. If the decision-making process has taken more than 28 days, the CCG should reimburse the patient or family members for relevant care and accommodation costs involved from 28 days after the date when an application was made to the CCG for CHC support. If the CCG turns down the patient for CHC and this decision is reversed by the NHS England panel, an ex-gratia payment should be made to cover the costs incurred by whoever has funded the care whilst the decision-making process was continuing: see para 18 of Annex F to the *National framework*.

16.159 A CCG is highly unlikely to have any legal responsibility to meet care costs incurred before the date when an application was first made to the CCG for CHC support (although a claim can be made under the maladministration provisions which have been used for the extra-statutory CHC retrospective review processes).

Support for the patient while the review or appeal procedure is continuing

16.160 If the CCG makes the decision that a patient is not entitled to CHC, the CCG should nonetheless provide a package of appropriate health care for the patient but is entitled to refuse to enter into new agreements to fund accommodation or social care costs, even if the patient is challenging the CHC eligibility decision.

16.161 There can be considerable difficulties if the patient is ready to be discharged from hospital and there is a dispute with either the relatives or social services about a package of services at home or about meeting care home fees while the review procedures are being carried out.

16.162 There are a number of options that CCGs can consider in such circumstances:

a) It may be possible to agree with the local authority that the patient should go to a care home or have a package of domiciliary care at home to be funded by either the local authority or the CCG, and the paying party will be reimbursed by the CCG or local authority for the care home costs if the NHS England appeal is upheld.
b) The same arrangement could be reached with the patient or with family members. Under such an arrangement, the CCG could enter into a similar arrangement with the patient or relatives to meet the costs in the short term, and for the CCG to be reimbursed if appeal is unsuccessful.

16.163 If agreement cannot be reached for any of the above options and this is preventing a patient being discharged from in-patient care, reference should be made to the relevant National Institute for Health and Care Excellence (NICE) guidance on transition between inpatient hospital settings and community or care home settings for adults with social care needs[58] to manage the process to ensure that a patient is moved out of hospital as soon as possible. However, the existence of a dispute with either the local authority or with the patient (or the patient's relatives) is not a good reason for holding back from serving notices.

16.164 If the patient or the patient's relatives makes it clear to social services that they do not wish to seek support from social services then the local authority generally have no duty to arrange accommodation for the patient. In those circumstances the usual route is for the either the CCG or the acute trust to seek legal advice about evicting the patient from the in-patient bed. A patient who remains in an NHS hospital bed after the time when the NHS trust has decided that the patient has clinical needs to justify the bed is a trespasser. If necessary, an eviction order can be obtained from the county court: see *Barnet PCT v X*.[59]

Disputes between CCGs and local authorities over CHC eligibility

16.165 Unlike patients or their relatives, local authorities are unable to appeal to NHS England panels. Disputes between local authorities and CCGs need to be resolved using dispute resolution procedures agreed between the two public bodies. Regulation 22(2) of the RSR Regs 2012 provides:

58 See www.nice.org.uk/guidance/ng27/chapter/Recommendations.

59 [2006] EWHC 787 (QB).

(2) Where there is a dispute between a relevant body and the relevant social services authority about–
   (a) a decision as to eligibility for NHS Continuing Healthcare; or
   (b) where a person is not eligible for NHS Continuing Healthcare, the contribution of a relevant body or social services authority to a joint package of care for that person,

the relevant body must, having regard to the National Framework, agree a dispute resolution procedure with the relevant social services authority, and resolve the disagreement in accordance with that procedure.

16.166 Thus there is a statutory duty on the CCG to have regard to the National Framework and they must 'agree a dispute resolution procedure with the relevant social services authority'. Once the dispute resolution procedure has been agreed, the CCG is under a statutory duty to use the procedure to resolve the disagreement.

16.167 The *National framework* provides:[60]

> CCGs and LAs in each local area should agree a local disputes resolution process to resolve cases where there is a dispute between them about eligibility for NHS continuing healthcare, about the apportionment of funding in joint funded care/support packages, or about the operation of refunds guidance (see Annex F). Disputes should not delay the provision of the care package, and the protocol should make clear how funding will be provided pending resolution of the dispute. Where disputes relate to LAs and CCGs in different geographical areas, the disputes resolution process of the responsible CCG should normally be used in order to ensure resolution in a robust and National Framework for NHS Continuing Healthcare and NHS-funded Nursing Care timely manner. This should include agreement on how funding will be provided during the dispute, and arrangements for reimbursement to the agencies involved once the dispute is resolved.

16.168 Annex F to the *National framework* sets out the general statutory duties imposed on both NHS bodies and local authorities and urges them to comply with those duties until a CHC eligibility decision is made. It provides:[61]

> No individual should be left without appropriate support because statutory bodies are unable to agree on respective responsibilities.

16.169 Paragraph 19 of Annex F to the *National framework* provides some more detail about dispute resolution procedures as follows:

> It is important that the Board/ CCGs and LAs have clear jointly agreed local processes for resolving any disputes that arise between them on the issues covered in this guidance. The Standing Rules Regulations and Directions to LAs require the Board or CCGs and LAs to have an agreed local process for resolving disputes between them on issues relating to eligibility for NHS continuing healthcare and for the NHS elements of joint packages. The Board, CCGs and LAs could extend the remit of their local disputes process to include disputes over refunds. Whatever disputes process is selected, it is important that it should not simply be a forum for further discussion but includes an identified mechanism for final resolution, such as referring the case to another CCG and LA and agreeing to accept their recommendation.

60 At para 159.

61 At para 7.

16.170 Further guidance is provided at PG71 and PG72 which provide:

> **PG71 What factors need to be considered in local disputes processes?**
>
> 71.1 It is important that local disputes processes include levels of escalation of the references to 'dispute disputes, for example, by the matter initially being considered further by team managers from the CCG and LA and then increasing to senior management involvement as necessary. Disputes processes should also include a level by which the matter has to be finally resolved, even if it has not been resolved at lower levels. This could, for example, be by the matter being referred jointly to another to another CCG and LA, and agreeing to accept their recommendation. CCGs and LAs should carefully monitor the use of their disputes process. Disputes should be reviewed after resolution procedures' arefor learning points and these should be fed back to those involved in the decision-making process in the case and also built into the training of MDT members as appropriate.
>
> **PG72 What if the dispute crosses CCG/LA borders?**
>
> 72.1 Where a dispute occurs between a CCG and LA in different areas (and therefore without a shared disputes resolution agreement) it is recommended that the local process applying to the CCG involved in the case is used. Where a dispute involves two CCGs, it is recommended to use the disputes process for the CCG area where the individual is residing at the outset of the relevant decision-making process. Thus if CCG A had made a placement in CCG B's area, it is CCG A's dispute process that should be used, even if the person is now physically residing in CCG B's area. Both CCGs should be able to play a full and equal role in the dispute resolution. Consideration could be given to identifying an independent person (who is not connected with either CCG) to oversee the resolution of the dispute. CCGs and LAs should consider agreeing and publishing local processes and timescales for responding to complaints and concerns relating to NHS continuing healthcare on issues that fall outside of the IRP process'

16.171 However well-meaning this may be, a statutory duty to 'agree a procedure' or to operate an existing procedure which has been agreed with a different local authority is largely incapable of being enforced. Further, the reference to 'dispute resolution procedures' being used to take decisions is somewhat problematic because the CCG is required by statute to remain as the ultimate decision-maker throughout the process. Further there is no specific duty on the local authority to follow the procedures. The locally agreed procedures should provide, in effect, a further opportunity for the local authority to require the CCG to examine its own decision. They should cover:

a) who in the local authority and CCG should review the dispute in the first instance;
b) an agreed timetable for that review;
c) a set of principles to guide the review which should include a recognition that it is not the role of the CCG to take decisions which are the statutory responsibility of the local authority and that it is not the role of the local authority to take decisions which are the statutory responsibility of the CCG, but that either body can ask the other to review their decisions;
d) an agreed process for the involvement of senior officers in the process;

e) an agreement that, in the event that the review procedures changes or modifies a decision, one public body will provide full reimbursement to the other in an agreed form over the relevant period without the need to review the details of the expenditure or determine whether such expenditure would have been met by that body, together with interest;
f) an agreement to refer disputes to mediation (possibly with an independent legal view being provided if that is needed) if the dispute cannot be resolved by this process.

16.172 The CCG has a duty agree procedures for seeking to resolve the dispute once it has arisen. This could involve agreeing a dispute resolution process with the local social services authority in advance of a dispute or could involve a 'one-off' procedure once a dispute has arisen. There are many CCGs and local authorities where protocols are not in place between CCGs and local authorities. There are many model policies in existence, but the Sheffield CCG dispute resolution policy is an example of one which is straightforward and sensible.[62]

16.173 The guidance does not specifically explain what happens if the CCG and the local authority have not been able to agree local dispute resolution protocols as has happened in a number of areas. In those circumstances, there is probably a duty on the CCG to offer a form of mediation. However, as the Court of Appeal made clear in *R (St Helens Borough Council) v Manchester Primary Care Trust and another*,[63] the NHS commissioning body is the ultimate decision-maker and its decision will only be set aside if the court considers that it is a *Wednesbury* unreasonable decision.

What package of NHS funded services should be provided to an NHS CHC eligible patient?

16.174 The CCG has two different types of decision to make:
1) Does the patient qualify for CHC?
2) If the patient does qualify, what package of support should be provided by the CCG and others including the local authority to support the patient.

16.175 Once the CCG has made the decision that the patient is eligible for CHC, the CCG comes under a legal duty to offer an appropriate package of services to meet the patient's needs for medical services, social care services and accommodation (where that is part of the need). This duty is explained in paragraphs 108 to 111 of the *National framework* which provide:

> 108. Where an individual is eligible for NHS continuing healthcare, the CCG is responsible for care planning, commissioning services and for case management. It is the responsibility of the CCG to plan strategically, specify outcomes and procure services, to manage demand and provider performance for all services that are required to meet the needs of all individuals who qualify for NHS continuing healthcare, and for the healthcare part of a joint care package. The services commissioned must

62 See www.sheffieldccg.nhs.uk.
63 [2008] EWCA Civ 931, (2008) 11 CCLR 774.

include ongoing case management for all those entitled to NHS continuing healthcare, as well as for the NHS elements of joint packages, including review and/or reassessment of the individual's needs.

109. As with all service contracts, commissioners are responsible for monitoring quality, access and patient experience within the context of provider performance. This is particularly important in this instance, as ultimate responsibility for arranging and monitoring the services required to meet the needs of those who qualify for NHS continuing healthcare rests with the CCG. CCGs should ensure that there is clarity on the respective responsibilities of commissioners and providers with regard to NHS continuing healthcare.

110. CCGs should take a strategic as well as an individual approach to fulfilling their NHS continuing healthcare commissioning responsibilities. CCGs may wish to commission NHS-funded care from a wide range of providers, in order to secure high-quality services that offer value for money. As part of their joint commissioning responsibility, CCGs and LAs should work in partnership, and share information (where reasonable) to enable them to commission the most appropriate packages of care for their populations.

111. Many individuals in receipt of NHS continuing healthcare and joint care packages will have long-term conditions. CCGs and LAs should take into account the policy set out in *Supporting People with Long Term Conditions: Commissioning Personalised Care Planning*. The approaches set out may also be helpful in care planning for those in receipt of NHS continuing healthcare who do not have a long-term condition. The individual and personalised approaches described in Valuing People Now for people with learning disabilities are similarly relevant. Care planning for needs to be met under NHS continuing healthcare should not be carried out in isolation from care planning to meet other needs, and, wherever possible, a single, integrated and personalised care plan should be developed.

16.176 There is further guidance on care planning at paragraphs 166–167 which provides:

166. Whether or not a person is eligible for NHS continuing healthcare, if they have ongoing care needs, the care planning process helps in the decision on how best to meet those needs.

167. Where a person qualifies for NHS continuing healthcare, the package to be provided is that which the CCG assesses is appropriate to meet all of the individual's assessed health and associated social care needs. Although the CCG is not bound by the views of the LA on what services the individual requires, the LA's assessment under section 47 of the National Health Service and Community Care Act 1990, or its contribution to a joint assessment, will be important in identifying the individual's needs and, in some cases, the options available for meeting them.

16.177 This guidance is expanded at PG4.[64] PG78 also provides:

PG78 How should care planning be approached for a person entitled to NHS continuing healthcare?

78.1 It is important that the services commissioned and provided for a person in receipt of NHS continuing healthcare are based on supporting the outcomes identified in a care plan jointly developed and agreed with the

64 *National framework* pp53–55.

individual and regularly updated and reviewed. There should therefore be strong linkages between the care planning and commissioning processes in CCGs.

78.2 Supporting People with Long-Term Conditions; Commissioning Personalised Care Planning. A Guide for Commissioners sets out how to adopt a personalised approach for individuals with a long-term condition and how to reflect this in the commissioning of services. Clearly most people who are eligible for NHS continuing healthcare have a long-term condition or other long-term health need. Even for those who qualify for other reasons, the approaches in the guidance are still applicable. It sets out that the care planning process:

- puts the individual, their needs and choices that will support them to achieve optimal health and well-being at the centre of the process
- focuses on goal setting and outcomes that people want to achieve, including carers
- is planned, anticipatory and proactive with contingency planning to manage crisis episodes better
- promotes choice and control by putting the person at the centre of the process and facilitating better management of risk
- ensures that people, especially those with more complex needs, the socially excluded and particularly vulnerable or those approaching the end of life, receive coordinated care packages, reducing fragmentation between services
- provides information that is relevant and timely to support people with decision-making and choices
- provides support for self care so that people can self care/self manage their condition(s) and prevent deterioration
- facilitates joined-up working between different professions and agencies, especially between health and social care, and
- results in an overarching, single care plan that is owned by the person but can be accessed by those providing direct care/services or other relevant people as agreed by the individual, e.g. their carer(s). The important aspect of this is that the care planning discussion has taken place with an emphasis on goal setting, equal partnership, negotiation and shared decision-making.

78.3 There are other models of personalised care planning using similar approaches which could also be used when appropriate.

16.178 These are patients with complex and unpredictable needs, many of whom will require a bespoke package of services. Thus the CCG needs to undertake active case management to ensure that the services that are provided are suitable to meet the patient's reasonable requirements. This case management duty is explained at PG80[65] and the commissioning responsibilities at PG81. These provide:

PG80 Case management

80.1 Once an individual has been found eligible for NHS continuing healthcare, the CCG is responsible for their case management, including monitoring the care they receive and arranging regular reviews. This could be through joint arrangements with LAs, subject to local agreement. CCGs should ensure arrangements are in place for an ongoing case management role for all those entitled to NHS continuing healthcare, as well as for the NHS elements of joint packages.

65 *National framework* p104.

80.2 Case management should be person-centred. The individual should be encouraged to have an active role in their care, be provided with information or signposting to enable informed choices, and supported to make their own decisions.

80.3 In the context of NHS continuing healthcare case management necessarily entails management of the whole package, not just the healthcare aspects. The key elements of the role include:

a) ensuring that a suitable care plan has been drawn up for and with the individual in line with the approaches set out in PG78 above – this might best be done initially by the MDT involved in their care, in consultation with the person concerned or their representative
b) ensuring that the care/support package meets the individual's assessed needs and agreed outcomes and is appropriate to achieve the identified intended outcomes in the care plan
c) where the care plan includes access to non-NHS services, for example leisure services, ensuring that the arrangements for these are in place and are working effectively
d) monitoring the quality of the care and support arrangements and responding to any difficulties/concerns about these in a timely manner
e) acting as a link person to coordinate services for the individual
f) ensuring that any changes in the person's needs are addressed
g) reviewing the situation on a regular planned basis, and if necessary undertaking additional unplanned reviews where circumstances require. Reviews need to consider not just whether the individual is still eligible for NHS continuing healthcare but also the effectiveness and appropriateness of the care/support arrangements.

PG81: How should commissioning be approached for a person entitled to NHS continuing healthcare?

81.1 This Framework sets out a number of responsibilities of CCGs in relation to NHS continuing healthcare commissioning:

a) NHS continuing healthcare commissioning involves actions at both strategic and individual levels.
b) NHS continuing healthcare commissioning actions by CCGs should include strategic planning, specifying outcomes, procuring services, and managing demand and provider performance (including monitoring quality, access and the experience of those in receipt of NHS continuing healthcare). In managing the quality and performance of providers and the experiences of those using their services, CCGs should take into account the role and areas of focus of the Care Quality Commission and, where relevant, LA commissioners of the relevant provider's services in order to avoid duplication and to support the mutual development of an overall picture of each provider's performance.
c) There should be clarity on the roles of commissioners and providers. The services commissioned should include an ongoing case management role as well as the assessment and review of individual needs.
d) CCGs should consider commissioning from a wide range of providers in order to secure high quality, value for money services. In exercising this responsibility, CCGs should have regard to the case management role set out in 11.4 above of ensuring that the care/support package meets the individual's assessed needs and agreed outcomes and is appropriate to achieve the identified intended outcomes in the care plan. To help inform this approach,

CCGs should have an understanding of the market costs for care and support within the relevant local area.

e) CCGs should commission in partnership with LAs wherever appropriate.

f) CCGs should ensure clarity regarding the services being commissioned from providers, bearing in mind that those in receipt of NHS continuing healthcare continue to be entitled to access the full range of primary, community, secondary and other health services. The services that a provider of NHS continuing healthcare-funded services is expected to supply should be clearly set out in the contract between the provider and the CCG. CCGs should commission services using models that maximise personalisation and individual control and that reflect the individual's preferences as far as possible. It is particularly important that this approach should be taken when an individual who was previously in receipt of an LA direct payment begins to receive NHS continuing healthcare; otherwise they may experience a loss of the control they had previously exercised over their care. CCGs should also be aware of the personal health budgets programme as set out in *Personal Health Budgets: First Steps* and particularly that it is only direct payments that will be restricted to approved pilots. The other models of personal health budgets are available under existing powers for any CCG to use.

g) CCGs and LAs should operate person-centred commissioning and procurement arrangements, so that unnecessary changes of provider or of care package do not take place purely because the responsible commissioner has changed.

h) CCGs should take into account other policies and guidance relevant to the individual's needs.

16.179 However, CCGs also need to bear in mind that these services need to be subject to strict cost-effectiveness tests, in the same way as the provision of all other NHS services are subject to such tests. Once a CCG has reached a decision that a patient is eligible for CHC, it is necessary for the CCG to decide what services should be provided to support the patient. Eligibility for CHC is not a 'blank cheque' which means that every one of the patient's social and healthcare needs are required to be met by the NHS.

Funding for aids and adaptations

16.180 PG79 provides the following guidance about funding aids and adaptations for a person who is eligible for CHC:

> **PG79: Who is responsible for equipment and adaptations if someone is eligible for NHS continuing healthcare and is in their own home?**
>
> 79.1 The focus of NHS continuing healthcare should be on enabling the delivery of the desired outcomes of the individual and promoting their physical and psychological well-being. Care planning should therefore consider the need for equipment to assist with activities of daily living and the provision of healthcare, personal care, social care support and wider housing adaptation needs.
>
> 79.2 As set out in the Framework (paragraph 172), those in receipt of NHS continuing healthcare should have access to local joint equipment services on the same basis as any other patient of their CCG. Local agreements on the funding of joint equipment services should take into account the fact

that the NHS has specific responsibilities for meeting the support needs of those entitled to NHS continuing healthcare. Some individuals will require bespoke equipment (and/or specialist or other non-bespoke equipment that is not available through joint equipment services) to meet specific assessed needs identified in their NHS continuing healthcare care plan. CCGs should make appropriate arrangements to meet these needs.

79.3 For larger adaptations, Disabled Facilities Grants (DFGs) may be available from local housing authorities towards the cost of housing adaptations that are necessary to enable a person to remain living in their home (or to make a new home appropriately accessible). DFGs are means that the patient has an entitlement to a package of services from the CCG. That the package is likely to include a range of social care services, as well as health services as explained above-tested. However, housing authorities, CCGs and LA social services authorities all have discretionary powers to provide additional support where appropriate. Further details can be found in the guidance Delivering Housing Adaptations for Disabled People; A Good Practice Guide. This guidance encourages the above bodies, together with home improvement agencies and registered social landlords, to work together locally on integrated adaptations services. Whether or not such integrated services are in place, CCGs should consider having clear arrangements with partners setting out how the adaptation needs of those entitled to NHS continuing healthcare should be met, including referral processes and funding responsibilities.

16.181 Although some patients who are eligible for CHC are provided with accommodation, others are supported with a package of services in their own homes. This can lead to difficult divisions of responsibilities between CCGs and local authorities:

79.4 CCGs should be aware of their responsibilities and powers to meet housing-related needs for those entitled to NHS continuing healthcare:

a) CCGs have a general responsibility under section 3(1)(e) of the NHS Act 2006 to provide such after-care services and facilities as it considers appropriate as part of the health service for those who have suffered from illness.
b) The Board has responsibility for arranging, under section 3B(1) of the NHS Act 2006 and under Standing Rules Regulations, secondary care and community services for serving members of the armed forces and their families, and prisoners, as part of the health service to such an extent as it considers necessary to meet all reasonable requirements.
c) CCGs may make payments in connection with the provision of housing to housing authorities, social landlords, voluntary organisations and certain other bodies under sections 256 and 257 of the above Act.
d) CCGs also have a more general power to make payments to LAs towards expenditure incurred by the LA in connection with the performance of any LA function that has an effect on the health of any individual, has an effect on any NHS function, is affected by any NHS function or are connected with any NHS function.
e) Housing can form part of wider partnership arrangements under section 75 of the above Act.

79.5 LAs should be aware that they may continue to have responsibilities under section 47 of the NHS and Community Care Act 1990 and under section 2 of the Chronically Sick and Disabled Persons Act 1970 to those in receipt of NHS continuing healthcare. However, in deciding whether it is necessary to provide services under these provisions the LA should take into account services that are/will be provided by the NHS, either as NHS continuing healthcare or as other NHS services. They may also continue to have some responsibilities for those in their own homes entitled to NHS continuing healthcare where the services needed are not ones that the Secretary of State requires the NHS to provide. This can include support for housing-related needs where appropriate. When carrying out an assessment for a property adaptation or the provision of equipment for someone receiving NHS continuing healthcare funding, LAs should respond positively to requests for a community occupational therapy assessment to assist and advise the individual and the CCG on deciding on appropriate equipment/adaptation and whether or not the adaptation is necessary to meet the assessed NHS continuing healthcare needs.

79.6 Whilst LAs and CCGs have some overlapping powers and responsibilities in relation to supporting individuals eligible for NHS continuing healthcare in their own home, a reasonable division of responsibility should be negotiated locally. In doing this, CCGs should be mindful that their responsibility under NHS continuing healthcare involves meeting both health and social care needs based on those identified through the MDT assessment. Therefore, whilst LAs and CCGs have overlapping powers, in determining responsibilities in an individual case, CCGs should first consider whether the responsibility to meet a specific need lies with them as part of their NHS continuing healthcare responsibilities. LAs should be mindful of the types of support that they may provide in such situations as outlined in PG85 below.

Choice of accommodation

16.182 It is good practice for CCG policies to cover the issue of choice of accommodation. Some CCGs follow the scheme set out in Annex A to the statutory guidance under the Care Act 2014.[66] However, the patient's choice must be subject to certain conditions. Some guidance on this is provided at PG83:

PG83: What limits (if any) can be put on individual choice where, if followed, this would result in a CCG paying for a very expensive care arrangement? Under what circumstances can a CCG decline to provide care in the preferred setting of the individual?

83.1 This Framework says (paragraph 167) that 'the package to be provided is that which the CCG assesses is appropriate for the individual's needs'.

83.2 In many circumstances there will be a range of options for packages of support and their settings that will be appropriate for the individual's needs. The starting point for agreeing the package and the setting where NHS continuing healthcare services are to be provided should be the individual's preferences. Individuals will not always be aware of the models of support that it is possible to deliver (for example, they may assume that it is only possible to receive support in a care home). Those involved in working with individuals to plan their future support should advise them of the options

66 See www.gov.uk/government/uploads/system/uploads/attachment_data/file/366104/43380_23902777_Care_Act_Book.pdf.

> and the benefits and risks associated with each one. CCGs should be aware of the models of support offered by partners and in the case of CCGs, by other CCGs, and of evidence about their benefits and risks so that the options offered are maximised and that generalised assumptions are avoided.
>
> 83.3 In some situations a model of support preferred by the individual will be more expensive than other options. CCGs can take comparative costs and value for money into account when determining the model of support to be provided but should consider the following factors when doing so:
>
> a) The cost comparison has to be on the basis of the genuine costs of alternative models. A comparison with the cost of supporting a person in a care home should be based on the actual costs that would be incurred in supporting a person with the specific needs in the case and not on an assumed standard care home cost.
>
> b) Where a person prefers to be supported in their own home, the actual costs of doing this should be identified on the basis of the individual's assessed needs and agreed desired outcomes. For example, individuals can sometimes be described as needing 24-hour care when what is meant is that they need ready access to support and/or supervision. CCGs should consider whether models such as assistive technology could meet some of these needs. Where individuals are assessed as requiring nursing care, CCGs should identify whether their needs require the actual presence of a nurse at all times or whether the needs are for qualified nursing staff or specific tasks or to provide overall supervision. The willingness of family members to supplement support should also be taken into account, although no pressure should be put on them to offer such support. CCGs should not make assumptions about any individual, group or community being available to care for family members.
>
> c) Cost has to be balanced against other factors in the individual case, such as an individual's desire to continue to live in a family environment. . . .

16.183 There is reference in the Guidance to the *Gunter* case at PG84 which states:

> 84.1 In the case of *Gunter v South Western Staffordshire Primary Care Trust* [2005] EWHC 1894 (Admin), a severely disabled woman wished to continue living with her parents whereas the PCT's preference was for her to move into a care home. Whilst not reaching a final decision on the course of action to be taken, the court found that Article 8 of the European Convention of Human Rights had considerable weight in the decision to be made, that to remove her from her family home was an obvious interference with family life and so must be justified as proportionate. Cost could be taken into account but the improvement in the young woman's condition, the quality of life in her family environment and her express view that she did not want to move were all important factors which suggested that removing her from her home would require clear justification'

16.184 However that decision did not reach a definitive conclusion and probably needs to be seen in the light of the later Court of Appeal case of *R (Condliff) v North Staffordshire Primary Care Trust*[67] which decided that Article 8

67 [2011] EWCA Civ 910, (2011) 14 CCLR 656.

rights were not engaged in NHS commissioning decisions where those decisions were based on the allocation of resources.

16.185 A number of CCGs have policies which set up a series of conditions for considering choice of accommodation for CHC patients which CCGs may wish to adopt along the following lines:

a) Having regard to the Care Quality Commission (CQC) registration and inspection reports, does the preferred accommodation appear to the CCG to be suitable in relation to the patient's needs as assessed by the CCG?
b) Would the cost of making arrangements for the patient at the preferred accommodation require the CCG to pay more than they would usually expect to pay having regard to the patient's assessed needs?
c) Is the preferred accommodation available?
d) Are the persons in charge of the preferred accommodation willing and able to provide it to the patient subject to the CCG usual terms and conditions, having regard to the nature of the accommodation, for providing accommodation for such a person for NHS CHC?

16.186 If the above approach is followed, CCG policies provide that the CCG usually will find the patient in his or her preferred care home. This could be in another part of the UK if, for example, the patient has reached a stage in life where his or her priority is to live near a relative.

16.187 The patient's Article 8 rights under the European Convention on Human Rights (ECHR) are probably, to a limited degree, engaged in any placement decision-making process, and so the CCG would only be entitled to insist on being placed in another care home if the preferred care home failed the above tests. There is a particular problem where a patient is living in a care home where the fees are higher than the CCG considers that it ought to pay to provide services to the patient. The CCG may offer of a package of services for the patient at a different and less expensive home and thus discharge its statutory duty. Patients are not obliged to accept NHS services and the CCG discharges its duties to a patient if it makes an offer of a package of services, including accommodation, to a patient.

16.188 There does not appear to be any legal presumption that a care package for a CHC eligible patient should enable a patient to remain in their present home and there is no absolute right. Contrary to the position taken by the Equality and Human Rights Commission, it is hard to see that the patient's rights under Article 8 ECHR imposes an obligation on a CCG to spend significantly more of its resources to support a patient in his or her own home than offering to fund a package of care for the patient in a suitable care setting. While the preferences of the patient are an important factor which the CCG needs to take into account in making the overall decision, cost is also a key factor: see *R (Gunter) v South Western Staffordshire PCT*.[68]

16.189 This is a complex and contentious area, and it would be helpful if CCG policies, endorsed by the CCG governing body, made this policy position clear from the outset. CCGs need to ensure that there is a measure of

68 [2005] EWHC 1894 (Admin), (2006) 9 CCLR 121.

equity in the levels investment provided by the CCG in supporting different groups of patients. This can therefore mean that:

a) The CCG offers to discharge its duty by providing a package of services for a patient in a care or nursing home which is not the patient's preferred home. The CCG offers to discharge its duty to a patient who, to date, has had a package of services in his or her own home by moving the patient to a care home (since the costs of providing such care may be significantly less than providing care for an isolated individual patient).
b) Or, the CCG offers to provide a package of domiciliary care services in the patient's own home which is the same broad cost of a package of services in a care home and either:
   i) the patient funds the provision of other services from his or her own resources, which can typically be a personal injury pay-out;
   ii) relatives or family members agree to provide additional support to fill any gaps left by NHS provision which is not being provided; or
   iii) the patient is content to accept a service which is less than required to meet his or her assessed needs but prefers to accept such a package than move to a care home.

16.190 If agreement cannot be reached with the patient on a package of domiciliary care services in the patient's own home and the CCG continues to offer a care home placement that the patient refuses, the CCG will discharge its legal duties to the patient by offering the care home placement (albeit that this placement is refused). In such circumstances the CCG may be able lawfully withdraw an existing package of domiciliary care services in the patient's own home.

No top up fees or fee sharing for NHS services

16.191 There is a key difference between NHS and social services care in that there is no provision within the NHS for cost sharing, or for families to provide top-up fees to augment the cost of a care home package in the individual's chosen care home if that is higher than the cost of a package at a care home that the CCG is prepared to fund. The reason for this difference is that NHS services are required to be provided free of charge and thus the traditional view is that fee sharing is not permissible for core NHS services.[69] The NHS Choices website[70] explains:

> **Is it possible to pay top-up fees for NHS continuing healthcare?**
> No, it is not possible to top up NHS continuing healthcare packages, like you can with local authority care packages.
>
> The only way that NHS continuing healthcare packages can be topped up privately is if you pay for additional private services on top of the services you get from the NHS. These private services should be provided by different staff and preferably in a different setting'

16.192 Guidance on this is provided at PG96 and PG99 which provide:

69 See section 1(3) of the NHS Act 2006.

70 See www.nhs.uk/conditions/social-care-and-support-guide/pages/nhs-continuing-care.aspx.

PG96: Can an individual pay for additional services themselves in addition to their NHS continuing healthcare package?

96.1 DH published guidance (referred to below as the 'Additional Private Care guidance') in March 2009 on NHS patients who wish to pay for additional private care, in addition to their NHS care package. Although it is primarily aimed at situations where NHS patients want to buy additional secondary and specialist care services that the NHS doesn't fund, it contains a set of principles applicable to all NHS services:

a) As affirmed by the NHS Constitution:

- the NHS provides a comprehensive service, available to all
- access to NHS services is based on clinical need, not an individual's ability to pay, and
- public funds for healthcare will be devoted solely to the benefit of the people that the NHS serves.

b) The fact that some NHS patients also receive private care separately should never be used as a means of downgrading or reducing the level of service that the NHS offers. NHS organisations should not withdraw any NHS care simply because a patient chooses to buy additional private care.

c) As overriding rules, it is essential that:

- the NHS should never subsidise private care with public money, which would breach core NHS principles, and
- patients should never be charged for their NHS care, or be allowed to pay towards an NHS service (except where specific legislation is in place to allow this) as this would contravene the founding principles and legislation of the NHS.

96.2 To avoid these risks, there should be as clear a separation as possible between private and NHS care.

96.3 CCGs should seek to ensure that providers are aware of the above principles. Where a provider receives a request for additional privately-funded services from an individual who is funded by NHS continuing healthcare they should refer the matter to the CCG for consideration.

96.4 The following specific issues should be considered when dealing with additional private care issues in relation to NHS continuing healthcare:

- The NHS care package provided should be based on the individual's health and social care needs as identified in their care plan, developed from the multidisciplinary assessment in the NHS continuing healthcare eligibility process (including any changes to the care plan following review of the individual's needs).
- The care plan should set out the services to be funded and/or provided by the NHS. It may also identify services to be provided by other organisations such as LAs but the NHS element of the care should always be clearly identified. Any care which would normally have provided in the course of good NHS practice should continue to be offered free of charge on the NHS.
- Where an individual advises that they wish to purchase additional private care or services, CCGs should discuss the matter with the individual to seek to identify the reasons for this. If the individual advises that they have concerns that the existing care package is not sufficient or not appropriate to meet their needs, CCGs should offer to review the care package in order to identify whether a different package would more appropriately meet the individual's assessed needs.
- CCGs should also be aware that individuals in receipt of NHS continuing healthcare continue to be eligible for all other services

available to patients of their CCG. In developing or reviewing care packages, CCGs should consider whether other services commissioned or provided by the CCG would help meet the individual's needs.

- The decision to purchase additional private care services should always be a voluntary one for the individual. Providers should not require the individual to purchase additional private care services as a condition of providing, or continuing to provide, NHS-funded services to them.
- In the Additional Private Care guidance, 'separation' is defined as usually requiring the privately-funded care to take place in a different location and at a different time to the NHS-funded care. However, many individuals eligible for NHS continuing healthcare have limitations on their ability to leave their home due to their health needs. Moreover, the majority of the care they receive is often by its nature focused on supporting them within their own home and any additional private care may well also be focused on home-based support. Therefore, although the principle of separation still applies to NHS continuing healthcare, a different approach may be necessary. For example, where a person receives 24-hour NHS-funded support by way of a care home package it may not be possible for privately-funded care to be provided at a time that is separate to NHS-funded care. However, in such circumstances, the private care should be delivered by different staff to those involved in delivering the NHS-funded care at the time it takes place and they should not be delivering treatment, care or support identified within the care plan as being part of the NHS-funded service.
- Although NHS-funded services must never be reduced or downgraded to take account of privately-funded care, the CCG and the organisations delivering NHS-funded care should, wherever clinically appropriate, liaise with those delivering privately-funded care in order to ensure safe and effective coordination between the services provided. Transfers of responsibility between privately-funded and NHS care should be carried out in a way which avoids putting individuals receiving services at any unnecessary risk. The CCG, the NHS-funded provider and the privately-funded provider should work collaboratively to put in place protocols to ensure effective risk management, timely sharing of information, continuity of care and coordination between NHS-funded and privately-funded care at all times. If different staff are involved in each element of care, these protocols should include arrangements for the safe and effective handover of the patient between those in charge of the NHS care, and those in charge of the privately-funded care.
- As when patients are transferred from one NHS organisation to another, it should always be clear which clinician/care provider staff and which organisation is responsible for the assessment of the patient, the delivery of any care and the delivery of any follow-up care.

PG99: Can an individual 'top-up' their care package to pay for higher-cost services or accommodation?

99.1 The funding provided by CCGs in NHS continuing healthcare packages should be sufficient to meet the needs identified in the care plan, based on the CCG's knowledge of the costs of services for the relevant needs in the locality where they are to be provided. It is also important that the models of support and the provider used are appropriate to the individual's needs and have the confidence of the person receiving the services.

99.2 Unless it is possible to separately identify and deliver the NHS-funded elements of the service, it will not usually be permissible for individuals to pay for higher-cost services and/or accommodation (as distinct from purchasing additional services). However, there may be circumstances where the CCG should consider the case for paying a higher-than-usual cost. For example, where an individual indicates a desire to pay for higher-cost accommodation or services, the relevant CCG should liaise with them to identify the reasons for the preference. Where the need is for identified clinical reasons (for example, an individual with challenging behaviour wishes to have a larger room because it is identified that the behaviour is linked to feeling confined, or an individual considers that they would benefit from a care provider with specialist skills rather than a generic care provider), consideration should be given as to whether it would be appropriate for the CCG to meet this.

99.3 In some circumstances individuals become eligible for NHS continuing healthcare when they are already resident in care home accommodation for which the fees are higher than the relevant CCG would usually meet for someone with their needs. This may be where the individual was previously funding their own care or where they were previously funded by an LA and a third party had 'topped up' the fees payable. 'Topping-up' is legally permissible under legislation governing LA social care but is not permissible under NHS legislation. For this reason, there are some circumstances where a CCG may propose a move to different accommodation or a change in care provision.

99.4 In such situations, CCGs should consider whether there are reasons why they should meet the full cost of the care package, notwithstanding that it is at a higher rate, such as that the frailty, mental health needs or other relevant needs of the individual mean that a move to other accommodation could involve significant risk to their health and well-being.

99.5 There may also be circumstances where an individual in an existing out of area placement becomes entitled to NHS continuing healthcare and where, although the care package is of a higher cost than the responsible CCG would usually meet for the person's needs, the cost is reasonable taking into account the market rates in the locality of the placement. CCGs should establish this by liaison with the CCG where the placement is located. In such circumstances CCGs should consider whether there are particular circumstances that make it reasonable to fund the higher rate. This could be because the location of the placement is close to family members who play an active role in the life of the individual or because the individual has resided in the placement for many years so that they have strong social links with the area and it would be significantly detrimental to the individual to move them.

99.6 CCGs should deal with the above situations with sensitivity and in close liaison with the individuals affected and, where appropriate, their families, the existing service provider and the local authority if they have up to this point been funding the care package. Where a CCG determines that circumstances do not justify them funding an existing higher cost placement or services that they have inherited responsibility for, any decisions on moves to other accommodation or changes in care provider should be taken in full consultation with the individual concerned and put in writing with reasons given. Advocacy support should be provided where this is appropriate.

99.7 Where an individual become entitled to NHS continuing healthcare and has an existing high-cost care package, CCGs should consider funding the full cost of the existing higher-cost package until a decision is made on whether to meet the higher cost package on an ongoing basis or to arrange an alternative placement.

99.8 Where separation of NHS and privately funded care arrangements is possible, the financial arrangements for the privately funded care is entirely a matter between the individual and the relevant provider and it should not form part of any service agreement between the CCG and the provider.

99.9 Where an individual wishes to dispute a decision not to pay for higher-cost accommodation, they should do this via the NHS complaints process. The letter from the CCG advising them of the decision should also include details of the complaints process and who to contact if the individual wishes to make a complaint.

99.10 The new accommodation and/or services should reflect the individual's assessed needs as identified in their care plan, including taking into account personal needs such as proximity to family members. Individuals should be provided with a reasonable choice of 119 providers. A transition care plan should be developed by the existing and new providers that identifies key needs and preferences, including how any specific needs and risks in the transition process should be addressed. The CCG should keep in regular liaison with the new provider and with the individual during the initial weeks of the new services to ensure that the transition has proceeded successfully and to ensure that any issues that have arisen are being appropriately addressed.

99.11 Further details are given in Personal Health Budgets: First Steps'

16.193 This Guidance is potentially confusing and may not be wholly consistent. It is an area where CCGs should bear in mind that patients have a right to use their own money as they wish and that interferences with that right under Article 1 of Protocol 1 of the ECHR have to justified. So this is, perhaps, 'guidance' which should be treated lightly.

16.194 It is clearly permissible for the patient or relatives to agree a package of additional services with the care home owners (such as a visits from a chiropodist, hairdresser or even to pay for a larger room). See for example *R (S) v Dudley PCT*.[71] However, in order to comply with NHS Guidance, the CCG ought to be able to enter into a contract with the home owners which is capable of standing on its own without the support of others.

16.195 The absence of a fee sharing arrangement can lead to significant difficulties where a patient has chosen a social care setting in circumstances where patient or relatives are making a contribution towards the cost. This can either supplement the sums paid by the local authority or may represent the whole of the cost. A change from local authority/patient funding to NHS funding can then arise where and the patient's medical condition deteriorates, the patient becomes eligible for CHC. In such a case, the CCG may offer to discharge its obligations by funding care for the patient at a less expensive care home.

16.196 There are two potential routes a patient could take to avoid having to make the choice between continuing to pay the fees in their existing care home or moving to a less expensive care home. These are:

71 [2009] EWHC 1780 (Admin). This case is reported on Lawtel and LexisNexis but not in any open source website.

(a) Asking for a personal health budget to meet the costs of the care that the individual needs. The budget would be set at the costs of the less expensive care home, but the patient could then use their own money to use the funds to purchase care at the more expensive care home; or
(b) The more expensive care home could divide its offer of services into two separate contracts; one for the accommodation costs and the other for care services. CHC only meets accommodation costs if the patient has a 'need' for the NHS to pay for accommodation. A CHC patient in their own home does not have the rent or mortgage paid by the NHS. Accordingly, a care home which created a separate 'accommodation contract' could allow the patient to argue that he or she had no accommodation needs, and that it was therefore cost-effective for the CCG to purchase care services from his existing care home.

16.197 There is no established case-law to demonstrate that either of these approaches will be successful and any patient seeking to use these arrangements would be well advised to seek individual legal advice.

Contracting with care homes and other providers of care under NHS CHC

16.198 If the CCG agrees to provide care to a patient at a care home, a written contract in the form of an NHS Standard Contract should be entered into between the care home and the CCG. CCGs are under a statutory duty to use the NHS Standard Contract: see Part 5 of the RSR Regs and the NHS England technical guidance.[72]

16.199 The contract should set out the level of service that the care home agrees to provide, define clinical governance regimes, review mechanisms and state the price to be paid. It should limit the extent to which the care home can increase the fees and require the care home to report to the CCG if the patient's medical condition changes.

16.200 From April 2016, CCGs have been permitted to use the shorter form contract.[73] However, this contract is still 70 pages long and so is only 'shorter' than the full contract, which runs to over 200 pages.

Direct payments for NHS CHC patients

16.201 Patients who have long term conditions which require support from either the NHS or social services are entitled to have sums paid to them and then, in effect, to purchase and arrange their own care under a system of direct payments. PG90[74] provides the following guidance about the use of direct payments:

72 See www.england.nhs.uk/nhs-standard-contract/16-17/.
73 See www.england.nhs.uk/wp-content/uploads/2016/04/nhse-contrcts-shrt-frm-guid.pdf.
74 See *National framework* p110.

PG90: Can a personal health budget be used for people eligible for NHS continuing healthcare?

90.1 Yes, CCGs are encouraged to use personal health budgets where appropriate. A personal health budget helps people to get the services they need to achieve their health outcomes, by letting them take as much control over how money is spent on their care/support as is appropriate for them. It does not necessarily mean giving them the money itself. Personal health budgets could work in a number of ways, including:

- a notional budget held by the CCG commissioner
- a budget managed on the individual's behalf by a third party, and
- a cash payment to the individual (a 'healthcare direct payment').

90.2 Direct payments for healthcare can only currently be offered by the Board, or by CCGs that are pilot sites approved by the Secretary of State. However, CCGs already have powers to offer other forms of personal health budgets, either as a notional budget or a real budget held by a third party.

Further details are given in Personal Health Budgets: First Steps.

16.202 The system for NHS direct payments is governed by the National Health Service (Direct Payments) Regulations 2013[75] (as amended by the National Health Service (Direct Payments) (Amendment) Regulations 2013[76]). Readers are referred to separate chapter about direct payments and the inter-relationship between CHC and direct payments is considered in that chapter.

16.203 Direct payments can often deliver value for money to the local authority, properly reward members of the family who provide voluntary care and give control to patients and their families. It can result in carers being directly employed by the service user. Patients who are entitled to CHC are entitled to seek a direct payment from April 2014.[77] The amount of the direct payment must be:

> . . . sufficient to provide for the full cost of each of the services specified in the care plan.

16.204 It is hard to see how a direct payment can be appropriate where a CHC patient is accommodated in a care home save where this is part of an arrangement to enable a patient to remain in a care home of their own choice. However, direct payments can be used by CHC-eligible patients who live in their own homes or in supported living.

Providing a care package in a patient's home

Requirements, issues and considerations

16.205 If the patient is to be provided with a care package in his or her own home, the details of the care to be provided should be set out clearly in a care plan which describes the level of service to be provided to the patient and how

75 SI No 1617.

76 SI No 2354.

77 This is explained in the statutory guidance which is at www.gov.uk/government/uploads/system/uploads/attachment_data/file/366104/43380_23902777_Care_Act_Book.pdf.

it is to be delivered. CCGs are entitled to contract out such care packages to domiciliary care providers. If this happens, the CCG should ensure there is an NHS Standard Contract (possibly in the shorter form) between the domiciliary care provider and the CCG which covers the same areas as a contract with a care home (see above).

16.206 Guidance on this is provided in PG85 which provides:

PG85: What are the responsibilities of CCGs and LAs when a person is supported in their own home?

85.1 Where someone is assessed as eligible for NHS continuing healthcare but chooses to live in their own home in order to enjoy a greater level of independence, the expectation in the Framework is that the CCG would remain financially responsible for all health and personal care services and associated social care services to support assessed health and social care needs and identified outcomes for that person, e.g. equipment provision (see PG79), routine and incontinence laundry, daily domestic tasks such as food preparation, shopping, washing up, bed-making, support to access community facilities, etc. (including additional support needs for the individual whilst the carer has a break). However, people who choose to live in their own home may have additional community care needs which it may be appropriate for the LA to address subject to their local eligibility threshold and charging policy, eg assistance with property adaptation (see PG79), support with essential parenting activities, support to access other community facilities, carer support services that may include additional general domestic support, or indeed any appropriate service that is specifically required to enable the carer to maintain his/her caring responsibilities (bearing in mind PG89 below).

85.2 There is a range of circumstances in which CCGs have overlapping powers with other statutory organisations. Where this is the case, CCGs and other statutory bodies should work in partnership locally to determine how each partner's responsibilities will be exercised. CCGs should not simply assume that another organisation will meet the need. Active liaison should take place. The needs appropriate for the CCG to meet will depend upon the circumstances of the individual case, having regard to the overall purpose of the health service – to improve physical or mental health, and to prevent, diagnose or treat illness.

85.3 Where other agencies/organisations have potentially overlapping powers/ responsibilities there should be a discussion between the parties involved. If someone is receiving NHS continuing healthcare in their own home their benefits are unaffected (although they will not be able to receive support from the Independent Living Fund). There is a range of everyday household costs that are expected to be covered by personal income or through welfare benefits (ie food, rent/mortgage interest, fuel, clothing and other normal household items). In addition, disability-related benefits (eg Disability Living Allowance and Attendance Allowance) are intended to cover some disability-related costs. As individual circumstances will differ considerably, it is not possible to give hard and fast rules on how best to divide responsibilities where overlapping powers exist. However, the following questions may help inform the decision-making process:

a) Is this service part of the support plan necessary to meet the individual's assessed health, personal care and associated social care needs?

b) What support is necessary for the CCG to fund/provide in order for the individual to access essential services?
c) What responsibilities do other organisations/agencies have to enable the person to access essential services?
d) What would happen if a CCG or a partner organisation did not fund/ provide the service in question – what would the outcome be?

16.207 Where the CCG delivers care using its own staff, it needs a clear policy about the approach to be taken by its staff in designing packages to support patients in their own homes. While there can be enormous merit for both the patient and the CCG in maintaining the patient at home (and the CCG does not need to pay for accommodation costs) as patients with chronic conditions require an increasing level of services, there can come a time when the overall cost of the package is substantially higher than providing services to patients in a nursing home. There can also be significant problems with sustaining staff in a home if there are continuous disagreements between carers and the patient and/or the patient's family.

16.208 The CCG needs to be mindful that, any provider that is using staff to deliver services in the patient's own home will result in the patient's home being the employee's place of work. A provider should be mindful of the need to balance its duties to the patient with the duty to provide the member of staff with a reasonably safe place of work.

16.209 Problems can arise if the provider uses staff to deliver care in a patient's own home. The patient's home is the staff's place of work and the provider therefore has a duty to deliver a reasonably safe place of work for its staff. The duties to staff are not defined by the best interest of the patient, but exist independently of such obligations. There are a series of issues that managers should consider:

a) *The interests and rights of other occupants of the home:* A CHC package can only be delivered to a patient in his or her own home if the legal owners of the home agree to staff coming into the home to deliver care. Where the patient is not the legal owner of the property, clear agreement is needed from the property owner to enable care to be delivered. The CCG should ensure that it is not left in the position where care staff do not have unimpeded access to the property.
b) *Health and safety issues:* The CCG must consider whether the patient's home is a reasonably safe environment for staff to work in. While some allowance can be made for the fact that the home environment does not need to be maintained to the same standard as a hospital, a risk assessment should be carried out and action taken to avoid any very obvious risks. The patient's home needs to be a reasonably safe place of work for that particular member of staff. So if, for example, a member of staff is allergic to dog hair and the patient has a dog, it would be unreasonable to expect that member of staff to work in the patient's home, even if would be fine for others.
c) *Harassment issues:* Predictable and/or repeated harassment from the patient, members of the patient's family or visitors could leave the domiciliary care provider in breach of its duty to its own staff. While some allowance must be made to permit the patient to live life in their own way, verbal or physical abuse, racially or sexually improper

comments or any other action which is designed or likely to impede staff in their ability to deliver care must be addressed. In extreme cases, this can arise where members of the patient's family (who may be expert in managing the patient's medical condition) are so insistent on their own ways of doing things and/or can be so directing that they impede the ability of staff to do their job. These problems require balancing duties to staff with duties to patients. If CCG staff are aware of these types of problems, they should report them and seek advice and support without delay.

16.210 While CCG decision-makers obviously wish to do the best for individual patients, they should also bear in mind that the CCG has a statutory duty under the NHS Act 2006 to break even financially. This means that the services that the CCG is able to provide under section 3 are inevitably subject to a degree or rationing or prioritisation (as is the case with all NHS-provided health services and indeed virtually all health services across the world). Thus if the CCG has reached the point where it would be able to provide an appropriate package of care for a patient in a care home at a significantly lower cost, CCG staff should look very carefully to decide whether it is justifiable under their own policies to pay a higher sum to the maintain the patient in his or her own home. This is an area where specialist legal advice is often sought.

The extent of services (other than accommodation) that are required to be provided as part of the CHC package

16.211 Patients often require a wide range of nursing and other services as part of a package of CHC. While this needs to be considered on a case-by-case basis, CCGs should be mindful that they have a duty to act fairly between different classes of patients and there are many patients whose healthcare needs cannot be fulfilled by the NHS, either in part or in whole. An assessment may, for example, indicate that a patient has a need for ten hours' nursing support a week. That assessment does not lead to a statutory duty to provide ten hours' support a week. The CCG has a statutory duty to break even financially each year and is entitled to apply its policies fairly and to provide a package of support which is consistent with the level of support provided to other patients.[78] That may, in the above example, mean that the CCG is only able to offer five hours' nursing support a week. Provided the CCG has followed its own procedures it is highly unlikely that such a decision could be challenged in the courts. As Mr Justice Ouseley said in *R (T and others) v Haringey LBC*:[79]

> If [the CCG] is providing the resources, it is entitled to decide how they should be used.

16.212 CCGs should have policies to assist officers making decisions about what level of support should be provided to patients who qualify for CHC. In reaching these decisions it is entirely proper, and probably inevitable, that

78 See the observations of Mr Justice Ouseley in *R (T and others) v Haringey LBC* [2005] EWHC 2235 (Admin), (2006) 9 CCLR 58.

79 [2005] EWHC 2235 (Admin), (2006) 9 CCLR 58.

the CCG will take into account the cost of services. The courts have consistently upheld the right of NHS bodies to ration services for patients so that the CCG can make a rational and fair allocation of services to the wide range of people that it needs to serve out of its limited budget.

Support for patients who do not qualify for NHS CHC or NHS-funded care

16.213 If a patient does not qualify for CHC, the NHS is under no legal obligation to meet all or any part of the accommodation or social care costs of a patient who is not in hospital. However, the CCG may still be responsible for providing a broad range of healthcare services to the patient, including offering to provide primary care services from a general practitioner (GP) practice. Thus, the CCG is obliged to consider how much of the healthcare needs it is able to meet, including meeting nursing needs and to balance those needs against the other demands on its budget.

16.214 The guidance states that, for patients who do not qualify for CHC includes the following:

> The range of services which the NHS is expected to arrange and fund includes but is not limited to:
> - Primary health care
> - Assessment involving doctors and registered nurses
> - Rehabilitation and recovery (where this forms part of an overall package of NHS care as distinct from intermediate care)
> - Respite health care
> - Community health services
> - Specialist health care support
> - Palliative care.

16.215 If a patient does not qualify for CHC, the local authority may have a responsibility for providing such social care, including personal care, to the patient (depending on the patient's circumstances and the local authority's policies). The local authority cannot be expected to provide specialist NHS care (either in quantity or quality). However, if the CCG has properly followed the responsibilities directions, the issue as to whether the patient needs specialist care which is beyond that able to be provided by a local authority will already have been considered as part of the CHC process. Hence, as long as the process is followed correctly, by the time the CCG has got to the point of deciding that a patient does not qualify for CHC, the overall level of social care needed by the patient should not be beyond that which a local authority is entitled to provide. The range of social care and personal support services to be provided by the local authority will be determined by the local authority applying their own policies. This may well not meet all the social and personal care needs of the patient but that decision does not impose any duty on the CCG to plug the gaps.

16.216 There may, of course, be elements in the overall care package which comes out of the care planning process which need to be provided by a doctor or nurse or other NHS specialist. Those elements, if they are to be provided (and the CCG does not of course need to meet every healthcare need), will have to be provided by CCG staff or otherwise funded by the CCG. The core accommodation and social care costs, however, should not be met by the CCG.

Cost-sharing arrangements with local authorities outside CHC

16.217 There is a widespread practice or dividing up the costs of meeting services for patients outside hospital who have significant health needs but do not qualify for CHC between the NHS and local authorities, often on a 50:50 basis. These arrangements result in NHS funds being used to meet part of the costs of accommodation and social care services for non-CHC patients. There is no legal basis for making such payments.

16.218 The *National framework* guidance states:[80]

> It is the responsibility of the CCG to plan strategically, specify outcomes and procure services, to manage demand and provider performance for . . . the healthcare part of a joint care package

16.219 Thus where a patient is not eligible for CHC, the responsibility on the CCG is to fund the 'healthcare part' of a joint care package. However, the costs of accommodation and social care services for patients who are not eligible for CHC should generally not be paid by an NHS commissioning body. That guidance accurately identifies that, where a patient is not eligible for CHC, CCGs should only fund the 'healthcare part of a joint care package'. That means the cost of services of those healthcare professionals who are needed to provide support to a community-based patient. This duty is made clearer further on in the guidance:[81]

> There will be some individuals who, although they are not entitled to NHS continuing healthcare (because 'taken as a whole' their needs are not beyond the powers of a local authority to meet), but nonetheless have some specific needs identified through the Decision Support Tool that are not of a nature that an LA can solely meet or are beyond the powers of an LA to solely meet. CCGs should work in partnership with their LA colleagues to agree their respective responsibilities in a joint package of care, including which party will take the lead commissioning role.

16.220 The Practice Guidance also addresses some of the problems associated with such arrangements:[82]

> **PG58: What are joint packages of care?**
> 58.1 Where an individual's care/support package is supported by both the NHS and the LA this is known as a 'joint package of care'. The Framework advises that if an individual does not qualify for fully funded NHS continuing healthcare the NHS may still have a responsibility to contribute to meeting that individual's healthcare needs. The respective powers and responsibilities of each organisation should be identified by considering

80 At para 108.
81 At para 114.
82 See *National framework* pp89–90.

the needs of the individual. Where there are overlapping powers and responsibilities, a flexible, partnership-based approach should be adopted based on the most appropriate organisation to meet the specific need.

58.2 Although the LA can provide some healthcare services (within legal limitations of LA social care powers) the assessment and DST may have identified some healthcare needs that are not of a nature that the LA could solely meet, or that are beyond the powers of the LA to solely meet, and therefore these may be the responsibility of the NHS to provide. Practitioners should draw on their knowledge and skills regarding the assessed needs and their organisation's powers to meet them, and work together to agree respective responsibilities for care provision in a joint package of care.

58.3 In a joint package of care the CCG and the LA can each contribute to the package by:

(a) delivering direct services to the individual
(b) commissioning care/services to support the care package, or
(c) transferring funding between their respective organisations (where the needs are ones that the NHS and the LA both have the power to meet).

58.4 Although the funding for a joint package comes from more than one source it is quite possible that one provider, or the same worker(s), could provide all the support. Joint care packages can be provided in any setting. Examples can include:

- someone in their own home with a package of support who does not have a primary health need but has a package of support comprising both health and social care elements
- someone in a care home with nursing who has nursing or other health needs that, whilst not constituting a primary health need, are clearly above the level of needs intended to be covered by NHS-funded nursing care
- someone in a care home (without nursing) who, although not eligible for NHS continuing healthcare, has some specific health needs beyond the power of the LA to meet, requiring skilled intervention or support where these needs cannot practically be met by community nursing services.

58.5 Joint/coordinated CCG and LA reviews should be considered for any joint package in order to maximise effective care and support for the individual.

16.221 The importance of the NHS only funding 'healthcare costs' of a joint package is also emphasised in PG61:

PG61 In a joint package does the DST define which elements are the responsibility of the NHS and which are the responsibility of social services?
61.1 No. The completed DST will help to indicate the nature and levels of need of an individual, but it does not attribute responsibility for individual elements of a care package. Where a person is not entitled to full NHS continuing healthcare the cost of a jointly funded support package are a matter of negotiation between the CCG and the local authority based on the assessed needs of the person and the limits of what a local authority can fund.

61.2 One approach to identifying respective funding responsibilities is to analyse a 24 hour/48 diary of the tasks and interventions required to meet the individual's needs in order to identify which elements are beyond local

> authority powers, which are areas where both health and social care have power to provide, and which areas which are clearly social care responsibility.
>
> 61.3 CCGs and local authorities should agree protocols for dealing with jointly funded packages/placements. Local dispute resolution processes should cover both disputes over joint funding as well as NHS continuing healthcare eligibility.

16.222 However, the duty to fund services to meet 'specific needs' will not generally (if ever) extend to a duty to contribute to the costs of accommodation or social care services for such a patient. Outside CHC arrangements it would generally be beyond the powers of the CCG[83] to expend monies to support social and personal care services because they are likely to be outside the range of services that the CCG has a statutory power to deliver under section 3 of the NHS Act 2006.

16.223 The scope and limits on the duties of the NHS to provide accommodation as part of its overall responsibilities are not always fully understood. The correct position was set out by HHJ Hickinbottom (now Hickinbottom LJ) in *Secretary of State for Work and Pensions v Vale and others*[84] where the Judge said:

> Perhaps because it appears not to be mentioned in circulars issued by the Department of Health, it seems often to be overlooked that, where a person requires accommodation because of his or her need for nursing services (rather than because of a need for 'care and attention' to which any nursing services required are merely incidental or ancillary), it is the duty of the National Health Service to make such accommodation available under section 3 of the 1977 Act, either directly or by making arrangements under section 23 to place a person in a nursing home. That is because the implication of *Coughlan, White* and *Botchett* is that the accommodation that is required in those circumstances falls within the scope of section 3(1)(a) or (b) of the 1977 Act. A local authority has no power to provide such accommodation due to the effect of section 21(8) of the 1948 Act. Of course, a person who is entitled to services may choose not to take advantage of the National Health Service and instead to pay for his accommodation and nursing from his own resources or with help from a relative or friend. However, that must be a matter of choice, exercised by someone competent to make the relevant decision.

This is probably still good law despite the Court of Appeal's decision in *Whapples* but legal advice should be sought if needed.

16.224 Thus if the CCG enters into a 50:50 cost sharing arrangement for a patient who does not qualify for CHC, the CCG may well be contributing to the cost of the patient's accommodation in circumstances where the CCG has not power to meet any part of the patient's accommodation costs. The better approach is for the CCG to work out the (approximate) cost of the healthcare inputs into the package which the CCG is prepared to fund, and then to make a contribution to the overall package which is consistent with the level of its commitment. If there are disputes about the right division of costs between the local authority and the CCG this can be resolved using the dispute resolution process set out above.

83 The CCG's powers are limited by statute and it would be ultra vires for the CCG to act beyond these powers.

84 CDLA/3161/2003 dated 27 July 2005.

Subsequent review of CHC decisions for eligible patients

16.225 When a decision is made that a patient is eligible for CHC, the panel should fix a date for reviewing that decision. The initial review should be after three months, and then the review should happen at least annually. However, if a patient's medical condition is expected to change (for the better or worse) within the year a review after less than a year may well be appropriate.

Special categories of patients

16.226 There are some categories of patients whose special needs stand apart from the CHC process, or who require special consideration. These include:

a) children;
b) palliative or near death care for patients who are in a terminal phase of life;
c) patients with learning difficulties;
d) former long-stay patients;
e) patients where there are section 28A agreements;[85] and
f) patients leaving in-patient mental health care under section 117 of the Mental Health Act (MHA) 1983.

Children

16.227 The *National framework* for CHC only applies to adults. The *National framework for Children and Young People's Continuing Care*[86] provides a framework for making decisions relating to children. The scheme is somewhat different to CHC for adults for a variety of reasons, including: the need for educational input for the child, the impact of special educational needs and the fact that the child will almost certainly be a 'child in need' under section 17 of the Children Act 1989 and thus the duties on the local authority will be different to the local authority's duties to an adult who needs services under the Care Act 2014. Hence, no assumption can be made that the legal framework set out above applies in the case of children.

Palliative or near death care for patients who are in a terminal phase of life

16.228 CHC has always been awarded on a more generous basis to patients who are in the final few months or weeks of their lives. While the principles set out above continue to apply to those in a terminal phase, CCGs are expected to work swiftly to resolve applications where there is clear

85 Agreements made under section 28A of the NHS Act 1977 now section 256 of the NHS Act 2006.

86 See www.gov.uk/government/publications/children-and-young-peoples-continuing-care-national-framework.

evidence that patients are in a terminal phase of life and to flexible about the nature of the package to be offered to such patients. Such patients should be assessed using the Fast Track Tool as described above. However those patients who do not fulfil all of the strict criteria to come within the Fast Track Tool have generally found a substantially more generous approach is afforded to the allocation of support in their cases.

Patients with learning disabilities

16.229 There are no special rules for patients with learning disabilities in relation to CHC, although the inclusion of 'challenging behaviour' as one of the domains in the Decision Support Tool which can lead to a 'priority need' can often lead to such patients being treated in a separate way to other groups of patients.

16.230 The recognition that the vast majority of learning difficulty patients have a primary need for social care support rather than having a primary healthcare need has led to the transfer of responsibility for this group of patients from the NHS to community care over the last 30 years. However, there remain large numbers of learning disabled patients who continue to be funded by the NHS solely because they are assessed as having a high level of challenging behaviour. The Decision Support Tool indicates that patients with the highest level of challenging behaviour can qualify for CHC on this ground alone, provided the level of severity is at the very highest end of the spectrum. However even with such patients, the test under the RSR Regs 2012 is whether the highest level of challenging behaviour gives rise to a primary *health* need. If the challenging behaviour gives rise to hugely complex social care management without the direct input on a regular basis of healthcare professionals, the primary *health* need test is unlikely to be satisfied even if the Decision Support Tool points towards CHC eligibility.

16.231 The issues are accurately summarised at PG38[87] which provides:

> **PG38: How does the Decision Support Tool (DST) and primary health need eligibility test apply to people with learning disabilities?**
> 38.1 The DST should be used for all adults who require assessment for NHS continuing healthcare, irrespective of their client group/diagnosis. The tool focuses on the individual's needs, not on their diagnosis. Directions require that the DST is used to inform the decision as to whether someone has a primary health need, and if they do they must be deemed eligible for NHS continuing healthcare.
>
> 38.2 In all cases eligibility for NHS continuing healthcare should be informed by good quality multi-disciplinary assessment. Where the individual has a learning disability it will be important to involve professionals with expertise in learning disability in the assessment process as well as those with expertise in NHS continuing healthcare. It will also be important to ensure that the assessment process is person-centred and that family members/carers are fully and appropriately involved.
>
> 38.3 Standing Rules set out the meaning of 'Primary Health Need' in relation to the limits of local authority responsibility and paragraph 33 of this Framework explains the primary health need test in some detail. It is

87 See *National framework* p80.

important to understand that this test is about the balance of needs once all needs have been mapped onto the DST.

38.4 This Framework makes it clear (see paragraph 58) that 'the reasons given for a decision on eligibility should not be based on . . . the use or not of NHS employed staff to provide care; the need for/presence of "specialist staff" in care delivery or any other input related (rather than needs-related) rationale'.

38.5 The question is not whether learning disability is a health need, but rather whether the individual concerned, whatever client group he or she may come from, has a 'primary health need'.

38.6 The indicative NHS continuing healthcare eligibility threshold levels of need as set out in the user notes apply equally to all individuals irrespective of their condition or diagnosis.

38.7 Previous or current pooled budget, joint funding, Section 75 agreements or legacy funding arrangements and the funding transfer to local authorities in April 2009 do not alter the underlying principles of NHS continuing healthcare entitlement.

38.8 The Department of Health made it clear that the funding transfer to local authorities in 2009 was for social care and did not include those eligible for NHS continuing healthcare. However, this Framework points out that some historic local agreements relating to particular groups of clients with learning disabilities (for example following hospital/campus closures) can mean that these individuals are not required to be considered separately for NHS continuing healthcare.

38.9 It is crucial that the detail of these local agreements are examined in order to clarify whether or not the Framework applies. It is important to ensure that all adults are treated equitably under the Framework.

38.10 Some people have concerns about the potential loss of personalisation/control for people with learning disabilities (and other client groups) if their care is commissioned/provided/funded by the NHS. However, CCGs have considerable existing legal powers to maximise choice and control, including the provision of 'personal health budgets'. The Government has announced that from April 2014, anyone in receipt of NHS continuing healthcare will have the right to ask for a personal health budget, including a 'direct payment'.

38.11 Whatever the outcome of the eligibility decision regarding NHS continuing healthcare, commissioning should be person-centred and needs-led. NHS commissioners for people with learning disabilities should be familiar with and apply the principles of 'Valuing People' and 'Valuing People Now'. For further information on commissioning and care planning please see paragraphs 108–111 of this Framework. This is an area where local authorities and CCGs need to work closely in partnership to ensure the best outcome for the individuals concerned, whether or not the care package is to be fully funded by the NHS.

38.12 Where an individual is eligible for NHS continuing healthcare, CCGs have responsibility to ensure that effective case management is commissioned. Consideration should be given as to who is best placed to provide this function, and clear responsibilities agreed. Amongst other options it may be appropriate to secure this from the local authority who may have previous knowledge of the individual concerned or have staff with particular skills and experience to undertake this function on behalf of the CCG. Please see PG80 below regarding responsibilities for case management.

16.232 While cases are, of course, fact-specific, a number of CCGs have undertaken review processes of patients who have been awarded CHC on the basis of challenging behaviour alone in order to determine whether this genuinely leads to a primary health need.

Former long-stay patients

16.233 There are a limited group of former residents of long-stay mental hospitals where the NHS has been provided with dowry funding to support the patient for the rest of their lives. If a patient falls into this category then, if they do not qualify for CHC under the *National framework* and are being supported by local authority provided social care, the money provided under the dowry should be passported through to the local authority under 'section 28A' agreements – now agreements under section 256 of the NHS Act 2006. However, these are payments by CCGs to support the discharge by local authority social services departments of social services functions – ie the provision of community care services by social services authorities and not services for which the CCG has statutory responsibility.

16.234 Otherwise, there are no special rules for former long-stay patients. Over the years this group of patients have been supported by the NHS, by the benefits system and are now, where appropriate, supported by local authorities. Large sums of government funding have been passed from one department to another as responsibility has moved. The fact that a patient, who does not have a dowry payment, was once supported in an NHS facility does not create a responsibility on the NHS to meet the costs of that patient for the rest of his or her life. However, there may well be circumstances where the NHS chooses to provide some support for such patients even though under no legal obligation to do so. The details of such support are outside the scope of this chapter.

Patients where there are agreements

16.235 There are some patients or groups of patients where the NHS has entered into long-term agreements with local authorities for support the social care costs for those patients. These agreements can take one of two forms, namely:

a) Section 75 agreements in which local authorities agreed to provide specified health care services on behalf the CCG; or
b) Section 256 agreements under which the CCG provides resources to a local authority to enhance the delivery of local authority social care services so as to reduce the demand for healthcare services.

16.236 There may well be CHC patients who can benefit from local authority services provided under either type of agreement. However, the existence of such a service arrangement should not affect a patient's eligibility for CHC. It may however affect the identity of service provider who delivers services under a package for a CHC eligible patient.

16.237 Guidance on this is provided by PG95 which states:

> **PG95: Can a local authority act as a third party to administer direct payments to someone who has been deemed eligible for NHS Continuing Healthcare?**
> 95.1 Where a CCG has been authorised to have powers to make NHS Direct Payments, they can reach a formal agreement (under Section 75 of the NHS Act 2006) to transfer these powers (and funding) to the relevant local authority. This would enable the local authority to make direct payments to individuals receiving NHS continuing healthcare.
>
> 95.2 Where an individual is not entitled to NHS continuing healthcare but is receiving a joint package of care between the LA and CCG, they can reach agreement for the local authority to make a direct payment for the elements of the care package that are within local authority powers. The remaining elements of the care package (beyond local authority powers) should be arranged by the CCG in a manner that, as far as possible, is compatible with the direct payment arrangements.
>
> 95.3 Where the CCG has not been given powers to offer direct payments, there is currently no provision to allow a local authority to make direct payments for NHS continuing healthcare on their behalf. However, the CCG should always consider the other models of personal health budget that are available for all CCGs to use, including a) notional personal health budget held by the CCG and used in partnership with the individual; and b) a real personal health budget held by a 3rd party such as a brokerage organisation, who should agree with the individual how it is to be spent.
>
> 95.4 CCGs should commission services using models that maximise personalisation and individual control and that reflect the individual's preferences, as far as possible. It is particularly important that this approach should be taken when an individual who was previously in receipt of an LA direct payment begins to receive NHS continuing healthcare; otherwise they may experience a loss of the control they had previously exercised over their care.

Thus, in the right case, these arrangements may well assist an individual patient.

Patients leaving mental health care – section 117 of the Mental Health Act 1983

16.238 Patients who are leaving detention under the MHA 1983 have a legal right under section 117 of the MHA 1983 to after care services. This is entirely separate from CHC funding. Section 117 sets up a legal duty which is jointly owed to relevant patients jointly by a CCG and the relevant local authority. Such patients are entitled to a package of support arising from their mental health needs without the need to be assessed under the CHC regime. This is explained in PG64 and PG65[88] which provide:

> **PG64: What is the relationship between NHS continuing healthcare and section 117 after-care under the Mental Health Act?**
> 64.1 Services for needs that fall to be met as after-care services under section 117 of the Mental Health Act 1983 should be provided under that legislation rather than as NHS continuing healthcare. Only needs that are not section 117 after-care needs should be considered for NHS continuing healthcare

88 See *National framework* p93.

eligibility in the usual way. For example, the individual might have or develop physical health needs which are distinct from the section 117 needs, and which separately constitute a primary health need. There should be no charge to the individual for section 117 services, regardless of whether they are being funded by a CCG or an LA.

64.2 LAs and CCGs should have agreements in place detailing how they will carry out their section 117 responsibilities, and these agreements should clarify which services fall under section 117 and which authority should fund them. LAs and CCGs may use a variety of different models and tools as a basis for working out how section 117 funding costs should be apportioned. However, where this results in a CCG fully funding a section 117 package this does not constitute NHS continuing healthcare.

64.3 It is preferable for the CCG to have separate budgets for funding section 117 and NHS continuing healthcare. Where they are funded from the same budget they still continue to be distinct and separate entitlements

PG65: Is there any additional guidance on the relationship between NHS continuing healthcare and the Mental Health Act 1983?

65.1 Arrangements under the Mental Health Act are separate and different from NHS Continuing Healthcare and the two should not be confused. The above guidance particularly deals with Section 117, however the same principle (regarding the need to determine whether the services are provided under the Mental Health Act or under NHS continuing healthcare) applies where an individual is subject to Section 17 leave or to a Section 17A Supervised Community Treatment Order.

16.239 In the unusual case of a patient who has physical and mental health needs, the patient would fall to be assessed for their physical needs under the CHC system and would be entitled to support for their mental health needs under section 117. Aside from such unusual circumstances, patients being discharged from compulsory in-patient mental health should not be assessed for CHC. The division of responsibility between health and social services should be set out in a local agreement and this is a rare occasion on which CCGs can agree to meet 50 per cent of the costs of a care package.

CHAPTER 17

Reconfiguration of NHS services

continued

Introduction

17.1 There are few more vexed and contentious subjects in the NHS than the management of major service change to NHS services and buildings. In his introduction to his judgment in *R (Lewisham LBC and another) v Secretary of State for Health and others*,[1] Silber J said:

> There are few issues which prompt such vociferous protest as attempts to reduce the services at a hospital which is highly regarded and which is much used by those who live in its neighbourhood.

17.2 However, running the NHS without change is virtually impossible, and delaying essential change is hugely inefficient and may lead to poorer services for patients. Medicine is changing all the time, often at a faster rate than the public understand, and so the management of change is and has always been part of NHS management. Maintaining an efficient and effective service often means changing the way that the service is delivered or the place at which it is delivered. However, there can be a marked difference of perspective between the public, hospital staff and NHS managers about the reasons for change and its likely effects.

17.3 One approach is that the 'bricks and mortar' of a hospital are merely the setting within which NHS services are delivered by caring, dedicated professionals. On this analysis, the services are more important than the buildings in which the services are delivered, and if the way that the buildings are used needs to change to make the services more efficient or effective, then the demand to deliver efficient and effective services takes precedence over maintaining the existing footprint of services in existing buildings. That may be a sensible and logical approach which commends itself to an NHS manager or a health economist, but NHS services are 'human' services at all levels and reactions to service change proposals are governed by the heart as well as the head.[2]

17.4 Staff who work at the hospital may see service change in a totally different way to NHS managers (who may not work at that site) or external consultants. There is a strong belief among many NHS staff that reconfiguration exercises are largely driven by a desire to save money, but that they are dressed as being for patient benefit when, in fact, they are all about cutting budgets, reducing staff and thus making existing staff 'deliver the impossible'. Many staff will have been through numerous previous change programmes and have seen the extent to which they have (or often have not) delivered on the promised improvements for patients or working efficiencies, and thus a degree of cynicism can be justified by past experience.

1 [2013] EWHC 2381 (Admin).

2 The author does not suggest that these passages are anything but his anecdotal musings on the causes and effects of disputes concerning NHS service change, but they are informed by multiple experiences. He served as the MP for Wyre Forest, until displaced by a candidate who opposed service change at Kidderminster Hospital (despite having no alternative plan for the services and the changes subsequently saving many lives). He has also advised numerous NHS bodies about service change issues and also acted for patients opposing service change as, for example, in the Lewisham Hospital case. He has lectured about these issues on many occasions, including to the NHS Confederation annual conference.

Usually, there is a good deal of truth in these broader concerns. Perhaps the worst perennial 'sin' around reconfigurations is for NHS management to fail to be honest with both staff and the public by not admitting that one of the primary drivers for change, if not the sole driver, is cost saving.

17.5 Any proposed change to the existing services that NHS staff deliver can, if not communicated properly, be seen as an attack on the professionalism of those same staff. Staff will have developed their own ways of working, may be operating within a comfort zone and service change will impose unwelcome change, threatening their security and possibly their jobs. Staff, especially senior clinical staff, working for the NHS can have incredible power and, on occasions, groups of clinicians have proved themselves hugely resistant to change. Any opposition will, of course, always be expressed as being mediated through the interests of the patients, but this may be coincidental with the staff's own financial and professional interests. On other occasions senior clinical staff are leaders and promoters of change, even if it is to their personal or professional disadvantage, and are in the vanguard of persuading other staff and the public that change will deliver improved services.

17.6 Local authorities may see things differently again. Local authority officers and members may well be primarily concerned about how changes in the delivery of NHS services will affect their delivery of social services, particularly around delayed discharges of care. Local authority members will be concerned that the NHS is communicating its plans effectively and sympathetically with the public, or members who do not oppose change in a sufficiently robust way may become victims at the ballot box.

17.7 The perspective of the public can be very different again. Where service change is properly managed, communicated well and the public feel they have had a genuine say in final decisions, major service change may not attract support but public opposition can be muted. However in the author's experience over several decades, this is sadly a rarity. There are a huge variety of reasons for this but the following are (anecdotally) relevant:

a) The public are suspicious of change in NHS services and will tend to link any changes to a 'cuts agenda'. Closing an NHS community hospital because, for example, beds for patients can be purchased at nursing homes for half the cost, with the savings being delivered as increased community services can attract huge opposition despite its obvious common sense.[3] This can be seen as 'cutting' community services, not investing in them.
b) NHS managers often underestimate the extent to which the public have a profound emotional attachment to particular NHS buildings. This attachment can be out of all proportion to the medical importance of the buildings and may be based on a false understanding of the type of services that are delivered there. However, such myths are persistent and can endure in the popular imagination. Hence, 'saving' a hospital A&E or maternity unit can become a 'cause celebre' based on a belief

3 This is an example from a recent reconfiguration exercise in the Midlands.

that this is needed to save lives, even if more patients with life threatening conditions are not in fact treated at the local hospital, but are routinely referred to another centre with greater facilities.

c) Having a fully functioning hospital with a full range of services can be seen as being symbolic of the standing of a community. Thus, removing services from a hospital can be seen as diminishing the importance of the local area. This emotional attachment to buildings often starts at birth and ends with the death of loved ones.

d) In the balance between safety and convenience, the public have the ability to measure convenience but are reluctant to engage with safety arguments. Local services are convenient for local people and the opposition arising from the inconvenience of moving services to a distant hospital, with associated parking problems, is often underestimated by those planning services. In contrast, the prevailing culture is a disbelief of experts who rely on population cohort statistics to conclude that, for example, patients needing emergency treatment will have better outcomes if they are treated in larger centres by specialist staff. The history of change in the NHS is full of well researched plans to centralise services which, where implemented, have saved lives, that attracted disbelief when they were proposed and continue to attract opposition from the public.

e) Finally, there is the fact that NHS change will inevitably become a hot local political issue. MPs and local councillors who have to respond to NHS service change can be in a difficult (if not impossible) position. However much they may be intellectually convinced of the case for change, it can be electoral suicide for an elected politician to take the moral high ground of supporting change. There are always those who will campaign against NHS changes, characterise them as 'cuts' even if they will cost hundreds of millions of pounds to implement and seek to get elected on the back of manufactured public opposition to NHS service change. Ultimate responsibility for NHS services lies with the secretary of state, and so service change is inevitably political.

17.8 It is thus entirely understandable that the NHS has been wary about implementing widespread service change, whatever the compelling medical and financial case that change will deliver benefits for patients, staff and the wider community. However, the factors driving change have not stayed constant. At the time of writing there are an increasing number of schemes coming forward, driven by a variety of factors:

1) First, the NHS does not have the resources to continue to work inefficiently. Hence austerity drives the change process.
2) Second, and perhaps more importantly, many change programmes are driven by the inability of smaller hospitals to recruit and retain sufficient clinical staff to meet Care Quality Commission (CQC) standards.
3) Third, the *Five year forward view* programme published by NHS England (whatever its flaws and unfulfilled ambitions) is driving a service change programme which gives local health economies permission to propose reconfiguration schemes even if these are politically unpopular.

17.9 Thus, it seems inevitable that NHS managers and clinical leaders will have to grapple with unpopular service change issues in the months and years ahead. This chapter seeks to guide them through the steps they need to take to deliver a lawful reconfiguration scheme, as well as assisting those who want to object to change proposals to understand what the NHS should be doing in advance of any final decision.

Terminology used in this chapter

17.10 A decision to make significant changes to NHS services can be made by a commissioner or a provider. This chapter concentrates on proposals for change which are led by commissioners. Changes to NHS services made by providers, without the involvement of commissioners, tend to be unplanned changes to services made in response to urgent situations such as emerging clinical problems or staff shortages. However, in general, planned reconfigurations are led by commissioners and not providers. Changes can be led by a single Clinical Commissioning Group (CCG), a joint committee of a number of CCGs, NHS England (in its role as a commissioner) or a combination of NHS England and CCGs. The same principles apply regardless as to whether the body bringing forward the changes is a CCG or NHS England, and whether it is a single CCG or a group of CCGs. For convenience, the body bringing forward proposals to make the proposed services changes in this chapter will be referred to as 'the CCG', but the same approach should be taken by a group of CCGs or NHS England.

The NHS England guidance concerning reconfigurations

17.11 In 2013, NHS England published detailed guidance about the processes to be followed in order to implement major service change called *Planning, assuring and delivering service change for patients: A good practice guide for commissioners on the NHS England assurance process for major service changes and reconfigurations* (the NHS service change guidance)[4]. This guidance was revised in 2015 and then revised again in March 2018.[5] References in this chapter are to the 2018 revised document. It sets out the internal NHS processes that commissioners and providers are recommended (but in reality required) to follow in order to give effect to major NHS service changes. The NHS service change guidance needs to be read with some care as it focuses on the management processes that should be followed without having full regard to the legal duties that are imposed on NHS bodies whilst they are following the processes.

4 Available on the NHS England website: www.england.nhs.uk.

5 The 2015 document states 'This guidance will be revised annually to take into account changes in the commissioning landscape and feedback from stakeholders'. No revisions were published in 2016 or 2017 but the new version was published in March 2018: see www.england.nhs.uk/wp-content/uploads/2018/03/planning-assuring-delivering-service-change-v6-1.pdf. Readers should check the NHS England website before relying on the text above as the document may be further updated.

17.12 Although the NHS service change guidance does not expressly provide that it is statutory guidance, the tone of the guidance is worded in a way that CCGs are expected to follow it closely. It thus seems likely that the guidance has the status of being formal guidance issued by NHS England under section 14Z8 of the National Health Service Act (NHS Act) 2006. It follows that CCGs have a legal duty to have regard to the guidance when undertaking reconfiguration exercises. Thus, a CCG may well be challenged by way of judicial review if it fails properly to have regard[6] to the guidance. NHS England will also have a legal duty to have regard to its own guidance document.

The relationship between procurement duties and NHS reconfiguration exercises

17.13 Implementing any NHS service reconfiguration decision will almost certainly involve making substantial changes to the contracts between the CCG and the NHS body (or private provider) that is delivering changed NHS services. CCGs should therefore satisfy themselves that they are complying with their procurement obligations before any contracts are signed. The reconfiguration decision is usually about the type of services that the CCG wishes to commission. There will be occasions where there is only one possible provider of those services such as, for example, where changes are made to consultant led maternity services at a local hospital. Procurement issues are unlikely to arise in such cases because there are no other economic operators who could have delivered those services. However, in other cases the reconfiguration decision is about 'what' services should be delivered. A procurement decision may then need to be made about 'who' should be contracted to deliver those services.

17.14 The details of the procurement obligations on a CCG are set out in chapter 21 on procurement, but CCGs need to be mindful of the way in which procurement obligations can arise throughout a reconfiguration exercise.

Which NHS body makes final decisions about NHS service change?

17.15 The question as to which NHS body is the final decision-maker about NHS service change can be far from straightforward. NHS commissioners (CCGs and NHS England) make decisions about the services they wish to commission from NHS providers and the places at which they wish to commission particular services. However, CCGs do not deliver services to NHS patients and do not run hospitals. Hence, once a CCG (or group of CCGs) has made a decision to go forward with a particular form of service change, the CCGs have to change the contracts with providers of NHS

6 See also in chapter 9 on commissioning, paras 9.39–9.41 on the meaning of a 'have regard duty'.

services to implement the changes determined by the CCG. However, CCGs cannot insist that NHS trusts, NHS foundation trusts or other providers of NHS services sign contracts which change the way in which the provider[7] operates. Contracts can only be agreed if both parties consent to the terms, and so changes to the terms of an ongoing service can only be delivered with changes to the terms of the contract, and that requires the consent of the trust. A CCG that was seeking to decommission a service entirely would need to terminate an existing contract with a trust. In all other cases, the changes can only be brought into effect once the contracts have been changed so that the CCG is commissioning services in accordance with the new arrangements for the delivery of services.

17.16 Changes to services are not solely matters for a commissioner. A trust that was substantially changing the way in which it functioned would have to seek consent from Monitor (now part of NHS Improvement) to change the terms of its NHS licence in order to vary the services that it provided to NHS patients. If consent is not given, the trust will remain under a statutory duty (pursuant to the terms of its licence) to deliver the services even though it is not commissioned by any CCG to do so and, perhaps more importantly, has no basis to charge any CCG for the provision of these services. Thus, in practice, decisions about changes to NHS services can only be made by commissioners and providers working in partnership throughout the processes leading up to final decisions.

17.17 The March 2018 guidance included a new para 3.2 entitled 'Who is the decision maker around service change.' This paragraph recognised that decisions about service change were not matters for a single NHS Body. The relevant paragraphs read as follows:

> The public involvement and consultation duties of commissioners are set out in NHS Act 2006 s13Q (as amended by the Health and Social Care Act 2012) for NHS England and NHS Act 2006 s14Z2 for CCGs.
>
> NHS trusts and foundation trusts are also under a duty to make arrangements for the involvement of the users of health services when engaged with the planning or provision of health services (NHS Act 2006 s242).
>
> Amendments to the NHS Act 2006 introduced by the Health and Social Care Act 2012, have changed the NHS architecture and placed a number of further duties on NHS commissioners, which need to be considered and complied with in making any decision on changes to service delivery. In particular there are procurement obligations on commissioners which need to be considered when making decisions.
>
> Where substantial changes are proposed to NHS services, there is a separate duty to consult the local authority under the Local Authority (Public Health, Health & Wellbeing Boards and Health Scrutiny) Regulations 2013 (the 2013 Regulations) made under NHS Act 2006 s244. This is additional to the duties on commissioners and providers for involvement and consultation and can trigger a referral to the Secretary of State and the Independent Reconfiguration Panel.

7 The word 'trust' is used in this chapter to refer to NHS trusts, NHS foundation trusts and can include other providers of NHS services. Substantially the same issues arise whether the provider is a trust, an NHS foundation trust or a commercial provider of NHS services. Almost all of the case-law concerns changes which have been proposed for services by NHS bodies and thus the word trust is used here in a 'generic' sense meaning 'any provider of NHS services'.

Where a proposal for substantial service change is made by the provider rather than the commissioner, the 2013 Regulations require the commissioner to undertake the consultation with the local authority on behalf of the provider. Where there is a duty for the commissioner to consult the local authority under the Regulations s244, it will almost invariably be the case that public consultation is also required.

In practice, public consultation requirements for commissioners and providers may be satisfied with one public consultation, but it is for each organisation with a public involvement duty to satisfy themselves that the consultation properly addresses their responsibilities. Therefore both commissioners and providers need to ensure that they have satisfied their statutory duties to involve and consult. Where there are public involvement and consultation duties on both commissioners and providers it should be possible to coordinate and consolidate any involvement and consultation requirements so that they are run in parallel to consultation with any relevant local authorities.

In practice, substantial service change consultation will normally be commissioner led and in those circumstances a provider can make arrangements to satisfy its duty to involve service users through a commissioner led consultation. Nevertheless, providers would need to engage with commissioners and address consultation responses in order to comply with their duties.

Good governance and clear and effective public decision-making are critical to effective major/significant change programmes. Programmes must be clear who the decision-makers are and how they will go about making consultation launch, and post-consultation, service change decisions. These arrangements should be referenced in consultation documents and ensure the public are clear how and by whom decisions will be made.

17.18 Thus, in practice, although final decisions about NHS service change will usually be made by CCGs or joint committees of multiple CCGs, successful NHS change processes can only be delivered by commissioners and providers working in partnership from an early stage. Final decisions will only come at the end of a long and complex process, which is described in the guidance and is explained below, all of which has to be delivered co-operatively between commissioners and providers.

The roles of other public bodies (and others) within the reconfiguration process

17.19 There are a large number of bodies that are involved in any successful reconfiguration process. The involvement of other bodies is, in part, a result of the complex processes set out in the NHS service change guidance and partly the result of the legislative schemes within which CCGs and NHS England are required to operate.

17.20 It may be helpful to summarise the roles played by different bodies before describing the processes in detail. The key players are as follows:

a) *Health and wellbeing boards (HWBs):* The role played by HWBs is described elsewhere.[8] HWBs consist of CCG and local authority

8 See chapter 9 on commissioning NHS services.

representatives. The HWB devises the Joint Strategic Needs Assessment (JSNA) and then produces the Joint Health and Wellbeing Strategy (JHWS). Section 116B of the Local Government and Public Involvement in Health Act 2007 (as amended by the Health and Social Care Act (HSCA) 2012) provides that, in exercising any functions including proposing service changes, both a CCG and NHS England are required to 'have regard' to the JSNA and the JHWS. This is a potentially onerous duty and, in effect requires CCGs to produce service change plans which are consistent with the plans set out in the JHWS or could only depart from the terms of the JHWS if the CCGs had clear, rational reasons for doing so. This requirement is reflected in para 5.2 of the NHS service change guidance, which says that CCGs should:

> . . . work with Health and Wellbeing (H&WB) Boards to ensure service reconfiguration proposals reflect JSNA and JHWS . . .

b) *NHS England and NHS Improvement:* Neither NHS England nor Monitor (now part of NHS Improvement) have any direct statutory role in approving CCG service reconfiguration plans. However, the NHS service change guidance provides that NHS England has a substantial 'assurance' role and recommends that CCGs 'have early and ongoing discussions with their local NHS England team'. There is also a practical reason why CCGs have to work co-operatively with NHS England in any change management process, namely that NHS England and NHS Improvement are key decision-makers concerning the availability of NHS capital funding. Almost all reconfiguration schemes require amounts of capital to implement them. Accordingly, securing the agreement of NHS England and NHS Improvement to the plans is a key part of the planning process leading up to any final decision. NHS England makes capital investment decisions through its Investment Committee. NHS England has set up an Oversight Group for Service Change and Reconfiguration (OGSCR) which the guidance explains:

> Oversight Group for Service Change and Reconfiguration (OGSCR) – Supports the Investment Committee to oversee the implementation and continued working of the assurance process. Membership includes (but is not limited to) Regional Directors, Medical Director (Acute), Director of Strategic Finance, and Director of Operations and Information.

Thus, in practice, few reconfiguration proposals can progress unless supported by the OGSCR (who make recommendations to the Investment Committee). The Guidance thus confirms that, in practice, NHS England and NHS Improvement should be closely involved in any major reconfiguration exercise.

c) *The affected clinicians:* The NHS service change guidance repeatedly emphasises the need for NHS trust managers and those acting for commissioners to involve the clinicians whose practices will be affected by any proposed changes, so that there is a clear input from the clinical frontline. This does not only include doctors, but all clinical staff whose roles will be affected by NHS changes, and so should include nursing, physiotherapists, radiographers and the many other clinical roles needed to make the modern NHS function.

d) *The clinical senate:* The creation of clinical senates was an administrative as opposed to statutory process. CCGs are not legally required to seek the views of the clinical senate about reconfiguration proposals but often assume they are required to do so. The NHS service change guidance recommends CCGs to seek independent assurance of any reconfiguration proposals. As part of this process it provides:

  Where the clinical case for change is more complex, commissioners may require an independent clinical review. This would usually be through the clinical senate, although in some cases (for example, very specialist services) it may be appropriate to obtain a review from another independent source such as a royal society or clinical networks.

e) *Local authority officers:* Any changes to NHS acute services will have effects on the delivery of social care services and may affect public health services. The NHS service change guidance thus stresses the importance of the involvement of key local authority officers as follows:[9]

  Directors of public health, directors of adult social services and directors of children's social services have an important role in bringing their professional perspectives where reconfigurations span health, social care and public health.

f) *Local authority members:* The local services authority will have a Health Overview and Scrutiny Committee (HOSC). Proposals for substantial changes to NHS services are required to be referred to the HOSC as part of the consultation process, as described below. A HOSC that does not support the proposals is entitled to refer the proposals to the secretary of state for a final decision.

g) *The secretary of state:* Although the secretary of state is politically responsible for the NHS to parliament, the secretary of state can only directly act as a decision-maker on local reconfiguration proposals where a referral has been made to the secretary of state by a HOSC. In all other cases the secretary of state is required to accept that NHS services operate under a system of local decision-making and, however much he or she may disagree with a local decision, a CCG or group of CCGs have the right to make whatever decisions they consider most appropriate for the NHS in their area. While that is the legal theory as set out in the legislation, the secretary of state and junior ministers have substantial practical 'influence' over the final shape of all politically contentious reconfiguration decisions, usually mediated through NHS England.

h) *The Independent Reconfiguration Panel (IRP):* Where a referral is made by a HOSC to the secretary of state, the secretary of state will usually seek a view on the wisdom of the plans from the IRP. The secretary of state is not bound to follow the advice of the IRP but almost invariably does so.

The five tests

17.21 The NHS service change guidance sets out four tests which NHS England recommends should be met by any reconfiguration proposal. The latest

9 At para 5.3.

version of the guidance also formally introduces a fifth test. The relevant part of the guidance provides:

> **4.1 The five tests of service change**
> There must be clear and early confidence that a proposal satisfies the governments four tests, NHS England's test for proposed bed closures (where appropriate), best practice checks3 and is affordable in capital and revenue terms.
>
> The government's four tests of service change are:
> - Strong public and patient engagement.
> - Consistency with current and prospective need for patient choice.
> - Clear, clinical evidence base.
> - Support for proposals from clinical commissioners.
>
> NHS England introduced a new test applicable from 1 April 2017. This requires that in any proposal including plans to significantly reduce hospital bed numbers NHS England will expect commissioners to be able to evidence that they can meet one of the following three conditions:
> i. Demonstrate that sufficient alternative provision, such as increased GP or community services, is being put in place alongside or ahead of bed closures, and that the new workforce will be there to deliver it; and/or
> ii. Show that specific new treatments or therapies, such as new anti-coagulation drugs used to treat strokes, will reduce specific categories of admissions; or
> iii. Where a hospital has been using beds less efficiently than the national average, that it has a credible plan to improve performance without affecting patient care (for example in line with the Getting it Right First Time programme).
>
> The application of these conditions will be agreed as part of an assurance process that will be proportionate to the proposals in question – see section 6 for details.

The four tests

17.22 There is a considerable history behind the 'four tests', which was partially explored in *R (Lewisham LBC and another) v Secretary of State for Health and others.*[10] It may be worthwhile to recount the background in order to set the present policy in its proper context. The policy position of the Labour government in office prior to 2010 was set out in guidance issued in May 2008 called *Changing for the better*. The 2008 guidance sets out various principles, principles 3 and 4 of which were:

> 3. **All change will be locally-led.** Meeting the challenge of being a universal service means the NHS must meet the different needs of everyone. Universal is not the same as uniform. Different places have different and changing needs – and local needs are best met by local solutions.
>
> 4. **You will be involved.** The local NHS will involve patients, carers, the public and partners. Those affected by proposed changes will have the chance to have their say and offer their contribution. NHS organisations will work openly and collaboratively'

10 [2013] EWHC 2381 (Admin).

17.23 Thus it was the policy of the previous government that reconfiguration decisions should be made locally by NHS managers as opposed to being made by the secretary of state. The guidance provided at that:

> The Interim Report of the NHS Next Stage Review recognised the benefit of clinical involvement when considering major service change proposals. It also set out a recommendation that any proposals to change services should, prior to consultation, be subject to independent clinical and management assessments
>
> . . .
>
> The Gateway Review Process is a series of short, focused, independent peer reviews carried out at key stages of a programme or project. The reviews are designed to highlight key risks and issues, which if not addressed would threaten the successful delivery of the business outcomes.

17.24 In 2010, the newly elected coalition government signalled a substantial change in policy. This was shown in a letter from Sir David Nicholson, the Chief Executive of the NHS in England, to all NHS chief executives dated 20 May 2010, which said:

> I am writing to let you know how we intend to take forward the Secretary of State's policy commitments on service reconfiguration. This will have an immediate impact on those of you currently undertaking consultation on service reconfiguration, and contains important information about how the system will change for any future reconfiguration plans.
>
> The Secretary of State has identified four key areas in which reconfiguration processes need to improve as plans for significant service change are developed and consulted upon.
>
> 1. support from GP commissioners will be essential;
> 2. arrangements for public and patient engagement, including local authorities, should be further strengthened;
> 3. there should be greater clarity about the clinical evidence base underpinning proposals.
> 4. that proposals should take into account the need to develop and support patient choice.
>
> Future reconfiguration proposals will be expected to meet clear standards in each of these areas, which I intend to set out in further detail during June.
>
> . . .
>
> PCTs and other NHS bodies with current reconfiguration proposals will be asked to revisit their processes to date to ensure they meet these new requirements. This applies to all future reconfigurations and those that are ongoing. I expect that in many cases this will require further work to be done locally and, in consultation with the IRP, assure the Department that these standards are now being applied.
>
> Clearly the detail of these new standards will be important, but I thought I should write to you with these clear signals so that you can begin to think about how you should respond.
>
> Given the complexity and scale of the change issues in London, I have asked NHS London to make separate recommendations about how service change in the capital should be taken forward to meet these requirements.

17.25 The secretary of state followed up this letter by an article in the *Daily Telegraph*[11] on the following day, 21 May 2010, which explained the purpose

11 See www.telegraph.co.uk/health/7747870/The-NHS-must-put-patients-first.html.

of the new policy. The article was in the name of the secretary of state and plainly was intended to be a clear public statement of the position adopted by the new government. The beginning of the article set out the promises made by the secretary of state as follows:

> **The NHS must put patients first.**
> *Bureaucracy and a top-down approach have undermined the health service, writes Andrew Lansley. Patients and clinicians must be put in control.*
>
> The first duty of any health service is to serve its patients – to ensure that people do not have to fit their lives around an inflexible system, but that the system bends to fit them. It sounds like a simple aim, yet too often in recent years, the reality has been quite different.
>
> Perhaps the most frustrating example of this is the closure of local A&E and maternity units around the country – against the wishes not just of clinical staff, but also of the communities that they are there to serve. It reminds me of Bertolt Brecht's dark joke that a government which has lost the faith of its people and is contemplating reform might find it easier simply to 'dissolve the people and elect another.
>
> ...
>
> As of today, I am calling a halt to the current process. I have asked Sir David Nicholson, the chief executive of the NHS, to inform the service of this immediately and to signal a complete change to the way we deal with these issues. This moratorium will provide a chance to reset every proposal, to reconsider every decision and to ensure that in each case they are consistent with the following key criteria.
>
> First, there must be clarity about the clinical evidence base underpinning the proposals. Second, they must have the support of the GP commissioners involved. Third, they must genuinely promote choice for their patients. Fourth, the process must have genuinely engaged the public, patients and local authorities.
>
> This will not merely be another tick-box exercise – it will be a tough test, which every proposal must pass if it is to proceed.
>
> More importantly, this will not be about me, as the Secretary of State, going back over these decisions. This time the power won't be at the centre, it will be at the grassroots – in the hands of the patients, the communities and the clinicians who are directly involved. The critical point is that the key criteria are met.
>
> So I am issuing a challenge to GPs to work with community leaders and their local authorities, to take the reins and steer their local services to meet the quality standards and achieve the outcomes that people expect.
>
> It is time we recognised that the real headquarters of the NHS is not on Whitehall, it's wherever there are patients, it's the doctors and nurses whom we register with at our local practice. These are the people whom we rely on and trust. They should be the ones making the decisions about the management of our services as well. That is how we will create a service that is centred on the needs and the wishes of patients.
>
> And it is only by pushing power to the front line that we will get away from the stultifying focus on inputs and processes that has dominated the healthcare debate.
>
> I've talked to staff in hundreds of hospitals, surgeries and clinics across the country and there's one thing predominant in their minds – how to improve the service and care they provide to their patients.

> By instituting this moratorium and putting patients and clinicians in control we are taking a first, and immediate, step towards improving outcomes and creating a less centralised, less bureaucratic, stronger NHS.

17.26 A revised 2010 Operating Framework for the NHS was then published on 21 June 2010. Paragraph 15 was headed 'New rules on reconfiguration'. It said:

> These [referring to specific reconfiguration proposals referred to earlier in the paragraph] and any other current and future reconfiguration proposals must meet four new tests before they can proceed. These tests are designed to build confidence within the service, with patience and communities.

17.27 The document repeated the four tests set out in the newspaper article and in the letter of 20 May 2010, namely:

1) support from GP commissioners;
2) strengthened public and patient engagement;
3) clarity on the clinical evidence base; and
4) consistency with current and prospective patient choice.

17.28 Further guidance on the meaning of the four tests emerged from the then Chief Executive of the NHS, Sir David Nicholson, in a letter dated 29 July 2010. This letter said:

> The Secretary of State has identified four key tests service change, which are designed to build confidence within the service, with patients and communities. The tests were set out in the revised Operating Framework for 2010–11 and require existing and future reconfiguration proposals to demonstrate:
>
> - support from GP commissioners;
> - strengthened public and patient engagement;
> - clarity on the clinical evidence base; and
> - consistency with current and prospective patient choice'
>
> . . .
>
> 'The Secretary of State has also made it very clear that GP commissioners will lead local change in the future. With that in mind, I am asking local GP commissioners, in conjunction with PCTs, to lead this process locally and assure themselves, and their SHAs, that proposals pass each of the tests.

17.29 The revised 2010 Operating Framework also provided:

> **New and future reconfiguration schemes.**
> The four tests also apply to all future proposals for substantial service change. As GP commissioning structures develop, GP commissioners will want to take a greater role in proposing and leading future service reconfigurations. The tests should be embedded as an integral part of pre-reconfiguration discussions between GP commissioners, PCTs, providers, SHAs, LINks, OSCs and other relevant local stakeholders. This is illustrated in the flowchart overleaf.
>
> This means that, in future, schemes would not proceed to formal OGC and NCAT review, and then formal consultation, without a robust assessment being made first of compliance with the four tests'

17.30 The effect of this guidance was considered by Silber J in the *Lewisham* case. The judge decided that the ministerial statements constituted guidance to which those arranging NHS reconfigurations were required to 'have regard'. That conclusion was plainly correct given the judgment of Dyson J about the effect of NHS ministerial guidance in *R v North Derbyshire*

Health Authority ex p Fisher,[12] which has been approved by the Court of Appeal on repeated occasions.

17.31 Second, Silber J decided, following *Tesco Stores Limited v Dundee City Council*[13] that the meaning of the four tests was a matter for the courts and not a matter where the NHS (or those advising the secretary of state) were entitled to reinterpret the policy to fit the circumstances of the individual case. In that case, Lord Reed explained that a meaning of a policy 'should be interpreted objectively in accordance with the language used, read always in its proper context'. Thus if, as the judge decided in the *Lewisham* case, the secretary of state had misunderstood the meaning and effect of his own policy when making a decision, the secretary of state was acting unlawfully.

17.32 It is important to note that this does not mean that an NHS reconfiguration will be unlawful if CCG decision-makers fail to satisfy themselves that all of the four tests, or five if applicable, are met. CCG decision-makers need properly to understand the tests and to demonstrate they have considered them. It is potentially lawful for a CCG to consider the tests, and proceed with a reconfiguration even if the CCG concludes that one or more of the tests are not satisfied, provided the CCG has good reasons for departing from the recommended policy that all reconfigurations should comply with the four or five tests. However, decision-makers will act unlawfully if they wrongly claim the tests are all satisfied when, objectively considered, one or more of the tests is not in fact met.

17.33 It may be helpful to consider the practical effect of the 'tests' in reverse order. The final test is 'support from GP commissioners'. Some guidance is provided on this test in the guidance. It states:[14]

> **Support for proposals from clinical commissioners test**
> - CCGs should assure themselves that those proposals have the support of their member practices.
> - For directly commissioned services, regional teams should ensure proposals have support of their medical directors and understand the views of CCGs on the proposed change to ensure alignment between commissioners.
> - Commissioners need to be sensitive to any actual or perceived conflicts of interest. For more information please refer too: [sic] https://www.england.nhs.uk/ourwork/coi/.
> - Disputes should be acted upon in accordance with the CCG's dispute resolution process as set out in its Constitution.

17.34 As per the *Lewisham* case, this will usually be interpreted to mean that the CCG which is actually commissioning the relevant services supports the proposals. It is not sufficient for a wider group of CCGs to be supportive if the key local CCG is against the reconfiguration exercise. In the normal case, the relevant CCG governing body will be the decision-maker and so 'support' can be assumed from the decision to proceed with the reconfiguration. However, this test will be relevant where the commissioning decision is made by a party other than the local CCG (such as where it is made by a committee of CCGs). The reference above to proposals having the support of

12 [1997] EWHC Admin 675, (1997–98) 1 CCLR 150.
13 [2012] UKSC 13, [2012] PTSR 983.
14 At p30.

'member practices' probably does not mean that every single member practice needs to be supportive, but the test will probably not be met unless a majority of the practices indicate their support. Thus a set of proposals which was supported by the CCG elected governing body but which was opposed by a majority of the GP practices within the CCG (ie a situation where a CCG elected governing body had not managed to secure the positive support of members) may well fail this test.

17.35 The requirement that the reconfiguration should be supported by a clear clinical evidence base is explained in the guidance by the need for decision-makers to show that they have sought independent clinical assessments concerning the proposed changes. This independent assessment can come from Monitor, NHS England, the clinical senate or possibly one or more of the Royal Colleges. This does not mean, of course, that the independent assessment is required to support every detail of the proposed changes or that the CCG is required to comply with every single recommendation contained within an independent report. There will be occasions when the independent assessment offers broad support but comes with caveats or makes additional assurance recommendations, which may or may not be either sensible or affordable. A view should be reached by the CCG about the overall level of support demonstrated by the assessments in determining whether they can say that there is a clear clinical evidence base to support the proposals. As long as the CCG properly understands the test, the question as to whether it is met is a discretionary decision for the CCG (and thus can only be challenged on rationality grounds).

17.36 The requirement that the changes should meet the test of 'consistency with current and prospective need for patient choice' is perhaps the most opaquely worded of the tests. In the *Lewisham* case, there was evidence that removing consultant led maternity services from Lewisham Hospital was not what women in Lewisham wanted. It was thus argued that this test was not met because the proposed changes were not consistent with 'patient choice', since women in Lewisham wanted to choose to give birth at their local hospital. Although this was, perhaps, the original meaning of the test (for the reasons explained above), interpreting the test in this way would give a local population an effective veto over NHS changes. While that is probably the natural meaning of the words of the test (adopting Lord Reed's analysis in the *Tesco Stores* case), it would mean that local campaigns against NHS changes would be placed in a very strong position to block changes (or more changes would have to happen with this test not being met but departed from for good reason).

17.37 The judgment given by Silber J on this argument is not wholly convincing,[15] albeit it is perhaps understandable in policy terms. Silber J accepted a slightly convoluted submission from the secretary of state's counsel that the:

> . . . requirement to be '*consistent with*' in this requirement cannot and does not mean '*the same as*'. The Secretary of State was quite entitled to accept

15 The author declares an interest since he was leading counsel for the successful campaign claimants in this case, albeit the claimants were not successful on this point.

the view that concentrating clinical sites to drive up clinical quality so that although it inevitably reduces patient's choice, it still increases choice between high quality services.

In connection with this requirement, there was the Equality and Health Impact Assessment commissioned by the TSA to understand the impact of the proposals on patient choice. It noted that the reduction of maternity facilities meant that patients would benefit from centres with a large number of consultant surgeons and multidisciplinary team and a wide choice of surgeons. In addition the midwife-led maternity unit would increase choice.

17.38 Thus, assuming that Silber J's interpretation is accepted by other judges,[16] it appears that the test will be met as long as the reconfiguration proposals continue to offer choices to patients, even if these are not the choices that patients wish to make based on the present footprint of services.

17.39 However, this part of the decision was obiter and, in any event, the doctrine of precedent does not apply as the Court of Appeal did not rule on this point. It would thus be open to another judge to depart from this interpretation to give the words of the test their natural meaning. It might be thought that Silber J's interpretation of the wording of the test makes it fairly meaningless since the ability of NHS patients to access or be referred to other NHS hospitals means that 'patient choice' will be maintained (to a greater or lesser extent) in almost every case. The only case where the test is not met will be where a reduction in the locations at which specialist services are provided means that there is no effective 'choice' remaining for an NHS patient with that particular condition.

17.40 The first test is 'strong public and patient engagement'. The public engagement requirements in any major reconfiguration are considered below.

The fifth test – added assurance when in-patient beds are closed

17.41 On 3 March 2017, Mr Simon Stevens, the NHS England Chief Executive announced a test or criterion which should be met by NHS commissioners where bed closures were proposed, in addition to the existing four general tests. This additional bed-closure-specific test was to take effect on 1 April 2017 and is now included in the March 2018 guidance. The fifth test concerns an NHS body which is proposing to make changes to NHS services that will result in a significant reduction in in-patient beds. Such a body must now:

a) demonstrate that sufficient alternative provision, such as increased GP or community services, is being put in place alongside or ahead of bed closures, and that the new workforce will be there to deliver it; and/or
b) show that specific new treatments or therapies, such as new anti-coagulation drugs used to treat strokes, will reduce specific categories of admissions; and/or

16 This point was argued in the Court of Appeal in the case but the court decided the issue purely on the vires question and thus there was no judgment on the effect of the four tests.

c) where a hospital has been using beds less efficiently than the national average, that it has a credible plan to improve performance without affecting patient care (for example, in line with the Getting it Right First Time programme).

17.42 The status of this new 'test' was considered by Mostyn J in *Cherwell District Council and others v Oxfordshire CCG*.[17] The judge decided that the new test had the same status as the other tests and that the public ought to have been consulted about their views as to whether the new test was satisfied. However, judicial review is a flexible remedy and the judge decided that the legal flaw by the CCG in not seeking public views on the new test was not sufficiently serious to justify a finding that the consultation was unfair. The judge thus refused to quash the consultation despite the fact that this test was not properly the subject of public comment. This was, perhaps, a benevolent interpretation which allowed the CCG to rely on a consultation document which became inadequate during the consultation process (since the new test was announced during the consultation process). NHS bodies will not be able to rely on such an approach again. Accordingly, any reconfiguration proposals that involve a reduction of in-patient beds should seek public views on the fifth test and decision makers should be carefully advised on the outcome of the consultation responses on this area, along with the responses on the other four tests.

The danger of pre-determination

17.43 Throughout the decision making process, CCGS need to be careful about the language they use to avoid any later claim that the CCG had a closed mind to any option other than its preferred option. At this point the CCG can only have developed proposals and should not put out any document that indicates a substantial degree of commitment by the CCG to follow any course set out in the documents. The requirements of a lawful consultation are considered in some detail below, but one of the key considerations is that consultation must take place when proposals are at a 'formative stage'. That means that the documents generated by the CCG must all speak of these proposals in a conditional sense and not give the impression that the CCG (or its lead officials) have made up their minds that this is the way in which service changes will be managed. If the documents suggest that there has been any 'pre-determination', any subsequent consultation may well be struck down as unlawful. It is not open to a public body to make a decision to proceed with a set of service changes and then seek to 'consult' the public about the proposals (because the consultation will not be held at a time when the proposals are at a formative stage): see *Sardar v Watford Borough Council*.[18]

17.44 The question as to what amounts to unlawful 'pre-determination' was examined by the High Court in *R (Royal Brompton and Harefield NHS*

17 [2017] EWHC 3349 (Admin).
18 [2006] EWHC 1590 (Admin).

Foundation Trust) v Joint Committee of Primary Care Trusts and another.[19] The issue was whether the joint committee of primary care trusts (PCTs) had decided that there would only be two NHS centres in London providing paediatric heart surgery prior to consulting on whether there would be two or three such centres. The judge, Mr Justice Owen, carefully looked at all the relevant material and asked himself whether it demonstrated that the joint committee had a 'closed mind' to the possibility of retaining three centres.[20] The judge said it was:

> . . . open to a consultee to take issue with the proposal for two London centres, and . . . to take issue with the exclusion of the RBH Trust. A fair reading of both documents does not lead to the conclusion that either issue had been pre-determined.

17.45 There are three important points to note from this judgment and the subsequent decision of the Court of Appeal in the same case (reported as *R (Royal Brompton and Harefield NHS Foundation Trust) v Joint Committee of Primary Care Trusts and another*[21]). First, the key evidence relevant to any claim of predetermination is contained within the relevant documents. This has far greater standing than witness statements produced after the event which seek to explain the mind of decision-makers. The court will look at all of the contemporaneous documents to ask whether they show that the decision-makers had already de facto decided to proceed with the proposals and were only going through the motions of a consultation. There is no objection to the documents promoting a 'preferred option' and there is no duty to evaluate all potential options. The question is whether the documents show that the public body had moved beyond having a preferred option to having taken a de facto decision that these changes would be implemented, so that no other outcome was reasonably open to decision-makers.

17.46 Second, proving pre-determination by a decision-maker is not straightforward. The fact that there are some statements in documents which appear to show that a clear path has been set in favour of an option falls a long way short of showing that the relevant decision-makers had a closed mind. The key issue is the mind of the public body. Thus showing that a junior official who prepared a report had not understood that a decision had not yet been made will not necessarily amount to a decision that the public body had a closed mind.

17.47 Third, the Court of Appeal made the additional point that, as long as it was open to a consultee to raise the issue that concerned them (ie it was not removed as a possible consultation response), the consultation process can be 'self-correcting' to avoid any concern about pre-determination.[22] The court said:[23]

> One of the functions of a consultation process is to winnow out errors in the decision-maker's provisional thinking. The JCPCT [Joint Committee Primary Care Trust] owes a public law duty to reconsider matters in the light of responses.

19 [2011] EWHC 2986 (Admin).

20 At para 98.

21 [2012] EWCA Civ 472.

22 At para 93.

23 At para 87.

17.48 Thus a challenge to a consultation process on the ground that the decision-maker had a closed mind may well be met by an objection that the challenge is premature because the consultee can point this out in a consultation response and the decision maker can correct the mistake. Thus a judicial review challenge to the consultation process may be premature because the objector has an alternative way of putting things right. Nonetheless, CCGs would be well advised to ensure that committee members understand the dangers of expressing views orally at an early stage which are indicative of final decisions having been made and should go through documents carefully to ensure that they do not suggest that key decisions have already been taken.

The various stages to a reconfiguration process

17.49 The NHS service change guidance does not divide the reconfiguration process into clear steps. However, it describes a series of steps which should be taken in virtually all reconfiguration decision making processes and thus it is possible to outline the way in which NHS bodies are encouraged to organise their work.

Stage 1: Developing proposals

Overview

17.50 The first stage is for commissioners to develop outline proposals for service change. The NHS service change guidance states:[24]

> Commissioners should build their proposal by identifying the range of service change options that could improve outcomes within available resources.

17.51 The crucial role played by the Joint Strategic Needs Assessment (JSNA) and Joint Health and Wellbeing Strategy (JHWS) in the statutory scheme governing the development of NHS services is reflected in the guidance. The guidance arguably goes beyond the statutory duty on CCGs to 'have regard' to the JSNA and JHWS and states that 'there is an expectation' of 'clear alignment' with these jointly agreed documents. The full wording of the relevant part of the guidance is as follows:

> In light of the legal duty consider JSNA and JHWS, there is an expectation that proposals will have a clear alignment to the JSNA and JHWS. There are a number of advantages to this:
> - H&WB boards can bring a multi-service and professional perspective, meaning proposals can be considered holistically across the local health and care system.
> - H&WB boards must involve local diverse communities when preparing JSNAs and JHWSs.
> - Where communities have already been involved in the shape of health services in their area it provides a strong platform for more in-depth conversations on potential changes.

24 At para 7.2.

- Where there is local consensus about health and care needs and priorities it creates space for conversations on what this could mean for the configuration of front line services.

17.52 It thus seems that, in order to act lawfully, a CCG would need to have well-reasoned and clearly developed justifications for developing a set of proposed changes which departed from the plans and priorities which had been jointly agreed between CCG and local authority representatives in the JSNA and JHWS.

17.53 It is also essential that the proposals are consistent with the CCG's own annual commissioning plan (as required under section 14Z11 of the NHS Act 2006). That plan requires advance public consultation and so developing proposals that contradict the annual plan (if it exists) may lead a CCG into areas of significant legal risk. Proceeding with a substantial reconfiguration without having complied with the statutory duty to have an Annual Commissioning Plan in place would place a CCG at considerable risk of legal challenge.

17.54 The NHS service change guidance makes the following recommendations at Annex 5 about how a CCG should work to develop initial proposals:

> A proposal should cover:
> - analysis of the full range of potential service changes that can achieve the desired improvement in quality and outcomes;
> - the development of a range of options based on the above analysis;
> - an assessment against legal duties and obligations including the Public Sector Equality Duty (PSED) and the duty to have regard to the need to reduce inequalities;
> - dialogue that seeks to align proposals with the plans and priorities of STPs and partners;
> - consideration of whether proposals represent a substantial service change (to be agreed locally);
> - assessment against the government's [sic] four tests and NHS England's tests and best practice checks;
> - any potential financial implications (capital spend, transactional or transitional funds, savings, core costs etc.) which may impact on the range of options taken forward;
> - any outline plans which can demonstrate how each of the options would be implemented and show that there are plans to ensure that safe services are maintained in the interim;
> - consideration of whether proposals can be implemented in a phased approach in order to secure the required funding;
> - a privacy impact assessment identifying requirements for lawful information sharing and, from May 2018, consideration should be given to GDPR obligations;
> - analysis of demographic and other factors likely to influence future demand for the service;
> - service models and learning from elsewhere including national/international experience;
> - deliverability in estates terms (if the change proposals imply change to physical infrastructure); and
> - show consideration of and progress towards meeting the clinical standards of seven-day services.
>
> The level of planning, clinical and management input should be proportionate to the and complexity of the change being proposed scale.

17.55 It follows that the development of initial proposals is a far from straightforward task. Later in the guidance,[25] CCGs are recommended to develop a 'pre-consultation business case' (PCBC) which sets out the proposals and is used for the various assurance steps that are recommended. The guidance explains at Annex 6 what should be in a PCBC as follows:

> **Pre-consultation business case**
> The PCBC will vary, however they should:
> - be clear about the impact in terms of outcomes;
> - outline how stakeholders, patients and the public have been involved, proposed further approaches and how their views have informed options;
> - outline the case for change;
> - identify governance and decision making arrangements;
> - be explicit about the number of people affected and the benefits to them;
> - identify indicative implementation timelines;
> - include an analysis of travelling times and distances;
> - outline how the proposed service changes will promote equality, tackle health inequalities and demonstrate how the commissioners have met PSED;
> - explain how the proposed changes impact on local government services and the response of local government;
> - demonstrate how the proposals meet the government's four tests and NHS England's test for proposed bed closures (where appropriate);
> - demonstrate links to relevant JSNAs and JHWSs, STPs and CCG and NHS England commissioning plans;
> - summarise information governance issues identified by the privacy impact assessment;
> - identify any clinical co-dependency issues, including any potential impact on the current or future commissioning or provision of specialised or other services; and
> - show that options are affordable, clinically viable and deliverable:
>   - Demonstrate evaluation of options against a clear set of criteria.
>   - Demonstrate affordability and value for money (including projections on income and expenditure and capital costs/receipts for affected bodies) and satisfaction of any applicable return on investment (ROI) criteria.
>   - Demonstrate proposals are affordable in revenue and capital terms, proposals are deliverable on site, and transitional and recurrent revenue impact have been robustly defended.

17.56 In most cases, the PCBC eventually evolves into the full business case to support the final shape of the proposed changes.

Public involvement at the initial stages

17.57 The NHS service change guidance recommends that the PCBC explains the steps that the CCG proposes to take to discharge the duty to involve patients and the public in its decision-making processes. It states:

> The pre-consultation business case should include clear involvement plans.
>
> Involvement activity should:

25 At p28.

- Be proactive to local populations.
- Be accessible and convenient.
- Take into account different information and communication needs.
- Consider how clinicians should be involved.

Commissioners should assure they have taken appropriate involvement for each stage of the process.

Further guidance on public participation is available in NHS England's website.

17.58 This guidance appears to assume that CCGs should devise a special set of public involvement procedures for a major reconfiguration exercise. However, that may be a mistaken approach. Section 14Z2 of the NHS Act 2006 requires CCGs to have a set of arrangements which define how they commit themselves to involving all of their patients and the public in their decision making. These 'arrangements' ought to be a 'patients and public involvement' (PPI) policy which describes how the CCG commits itself to involving patients in all of its commissioning decisions. Thus, in devising the precise way in which the public are able to influence decisions in any proposed major reconfiguration exercise, CCGs should start by working out how to implement their existing PPI policy for the reconfiguration exercise. There may, of course, need to be supplemental steps taken to involve patients and the public in a significant reconfiguration exercise, but these should be additional to the working out of the processes set out in the PPI policy and not a substitute for following the PPI policy.

17.59 However, planning for public involvement later in any process cannot be used to justify excluding public involvement at the initial stages. Possibly contrary to established NHS management practice, the guidance confirms that the public have the right to be involved in discussion around the development of proposals. The fact that there is likely to be formal public consultation later in the process is not a proper reason for developing proposals away from the public eye at the early stage. CCGs have a duty under section 14Z2 of the NHS Act 2006 to have arrangements which give the public the right to be involved:

(a) in the planning of the commissioning arrangements by the group,
(b) in the development and consideration of proposals by the group for changes in the commissioning arrangements where the implementation of the proposals would have an impact on the manner in which the services are delivered to the individuals or the range of health services available to them, and
(c) in decisions of the group affecting the operation of the commissioning arrangements where the implementation of the decisions would (if made) have such an impact.

17.60 The details of the steps that a CCG is required to take to satisfy this obligation are explained elsewhere[26] but, for present purposes, it is sufficient to note that the public must be involved from the start of anything that could be described as a reconfiguration proposal that will have an effect on how or where patients access NHS services. This is recognised in the NHS service change guidance which states:[27]

26 See chapter 5 on CCGs.
27 At p25.

> Commissioners have a statutory duty to involve service users in the development of proposals. It is good practice for commissioners to involve stakeholders in the early stages of building a case for change.

17.61 A standard practice has built up in many NHS reconfiguration exercises of retaining strict confidentiality about the early stages of the development of proposals on the grounds that NHS staff need space to develop contentious proposals internally without exposing them to public scrutiny at any early stage because either this would only confuse the public or would generate scare stories about changes which may, in the end, never be seriously considered. Whatever the attractions for NHS staff and the external consultants who support them of such an approach, this is not a legally permissible way to proceed as it is inconsistent with the obligations under section 14Z2 of the NHS Act 2006. NHS staff are paid public servants and are using public money when discussing the future shape of public services. Parliament has decided that the public have a right to know what proposals are being discussed and developed and to have their say at all stages.

17.62 Having said that, 'public involvement' around the development of proposals does not mean continuous 'public consultation'. The statutory duty is likely to be satisfied if information relating to the development of proposals is available to patients and the public and they have the chance to feed their views back to those who are concerned with the development of any proposals. Any feedback which comes from the public must be considered as part of the development of any proposals.

17.63 Part of the guidance suggests that a degree of caution should be exercised before sharing any proposals with the public. It states:[28]

> If the commissioner is content the options are viable, it should then progress with undertaking an assessment of these proposals against the government's four tests, NHS England's test for proposed bed closures (where appropriate) and best practice checks . . .
>
> For each option to be shared with the public, consideration of the financial proposal in terms of both capital and revenue and its sustainability should be made in conjunction with NHS England and NHS Improvement prior to launching consultation. It is essential that only those options that are sustainable in service, economic and financial terms are offered publicly. No service change option should be exposed for public engagement/consultation unless prior to launch there is a high degree of confidence that it would be capable of being delivered as proposed, that it does not imply an unsustainable level of capital expenditure and/or projected spend profiles that cannot be reconciled to available resources and will not be affordable in revenue terms. All options must be affordable within commissioner revenue allocations and provider revenue financial targets.

17.64 There appears a measure of contradiction between this part of the guidance and another part which says:[29]

> It is critical that patients and the public are involved throughout the development, planning and decision making of proposals for service change. Early involvement with the diverse communities, local Healthwatch organisations, and the local voluntary sector is essential, as well as engaging NHS Improvement where appropriate. Early involvement will give early

28 At p26.

29 At p17.

warning of issues likely to raise concerns in local communities and gives commissioners' time to work on the best solutions to meet those needs.

17.65 In resolving this contradiction, primacy should be given to the statutory duty on the CCG to involve the public in the 'development and consideration of proposals' for possible service changes (the wording of the statutory duty under section 14Z2(b)) and the guidance which suggests that proposals should only be 'offered publicly' which have already been shown to be sustainable in service, economic and financial terms. The statutory duties must take precedence over the guidance and thus CCGs should share emerging proposals with the public as and when they are developed. However, it may be sensible to make it clear at this stage that the proposals are only in the very early stages of consideration and thus cannot be taken to amount to fully worked up proposals.

Stage 2: The initial assurance process concerning the emerging proposals

17.66 NHS England's service change guidance suggests that it should conduct an initial 'Strategic sense check' to viability of the proposals. The guidance explains:[30]

> **6.3 National oversight of the assurance framework**
>
> The oversight of the national work programme for service change takes place by the sub-committee of the Investment Committee: the Oversight Group for Service Change and Reconfiguration.
>
> NHS England will operate a two stage assurance process:
>
> - a strategic sense check; and
> - an assurance checkpoint.
>
> An overview of the service change assurance process can be seen at Annex 2.
>
> Decisions about the extent of assurance required by NHS England will be informed by the scale of the service change proposals under consideration.
>
> **Stage 1 – Strategic sense check**
>
> This will determine the level for the next stages of assurance and decision making. Clinical senates may at this stage be asked to review a service change proposal against the appropriate key tests (clinical evidence base). Engagement with NHS Improvement should have commenced, and if capital is likely to be required, discussions with the relevant NHS England and NHS Improvement finance teams should have begun.

17.67 The guidance suggests that a CCG should engage with the clinical senate at this stage for complex reconfiguration schemes. If a scheme is rejected by NHS England at the initial 'strategic sense check' stage, the CCG will have significant problems in making progress with the proposals.

Stage 3: The NHS England assurance process

17.68 The guidance suggests that the next stage is to seek assurance from NHS England in accordance with a fairly prescriptive process. The NHS service change guidance suggests that the next stage is to seek external assurance on the proposals. The guidance states:

30 At p20.

> **. . . Assurance checkpoint**
>
> Takes place in advance of any wider public involvement or public consultation process or a decision to proceed with a particular option. For substantial service change, it is best practice to seek the clinical senate's advice on proposals again at this stage.
>
> Support for proposals from providers and other commissioners impacted to a significant degree by the proposals' will be tested as part of the assurance process and where relevant, letters of support may be required as part of the assurance evidence. Your local NHS England regional team will be able to advise where and when these are required.
>
> Examples of the types of questions and other evidence required at the assurance checkpoint are available in Annex 4.
>
> Decisions about the extent of assurance required by NHS England will be informed by the scale of the service change proposals under consideration. An assurance panel will be put together consisting of suitable members and any conflict of interest will be declared. The advice of specialised commissioning colleagues should be sought to ensure that any involvement of specialist services commissioned by NHS England are considered and either included as part of consultation process or that any impact on remaining services is adequately considered through assurance.
>
> Before public consultation is launched, proposals should be tested to ensure there is a high degree of confidence that all options would be capable of being delivered as proposed and do not imply an unsustainable level of capital expenditure or revenue funding. NHS England will review this as part of the assurance process. Service change schemes which require capital financing will require the support of NHS England and NHS Improvement (in writing) before public consultation on options requiring capital commences.
>
> Full detail on the assurance process can be found in 'Service change – a support and guidance toolkit' available from NHS England regional teams.

17.69 Thus, in effect, NHS England become the decision maker as to whether a reconfiguration scheme should go ahead. There is no statutory basis for NHS England assuming this role and it is not consistent with the 'hands off' approach envisaged for NHS England under the HSCA 2012. It is more akin to the role previously played by Strategic Health Authorities. However CCGs are, in effect, required to follow this process and thus have to seek approval from NHS England for any major reconfiguration scheme. Annex 2 to the guidance provides a flow chart of the process followed internally by NHS England and Annex 4 provides details of the questions that any proposal will need to address to get through the NHS England assurance process. The papers seeking assurance and any responses provided by any public body considering the proposals should, in principle, be publicly available documents.

Stage 4: Initial discussions with the Health Overview and Scrutiny Committee of the local authority

17.70 Regulation 23 of the Local Authority (Public Health, Health and Wellbeing Boards and Health Scrutiny) Regulations 2013[31] creates a power on a local

31 SI No 218.

authority to scrutinise the functioning of local NHS services. Where local government operates 'two tiers' of local authorities, the HOSC is a committee of the local authority that discharges social functions, which will usually be the county council as opposed to a district council.

17.71 Regulation 23(1) provides:

> A local authority may review and scrutinise any matter relating to the planning, provision and operation of the health service in its area.

17.72 Thus the HOSC has a power (but not a duty) to scrutinise any aspect of local NHS services that it is minded to look into. Following preparation of the PCBC and the obtaining of positive views from NHS England, NHS Improvement and the clinical senate (or other body undertaking the external clinical assurance process), the next stage is for the CCG to approach the HOSC of the relevant local authority or local authorities (if more than one are affected by the proposals) for their views on the proposals. The guidance provides:

> **7.5 Discussion of formal proposal with local authorities**
> Commissioners should discuss their proposals with local stakeholders prior to any public consultation, in particular with STP leads and local authorities. The discussion ensures alignment of the case for change, avoids proposals being developed in isolation, and ensures the wider health system is considered. Discussions should continue throughout the life of the proposal.
>
> The purpose of this stage is to:
> - Ensure commissioners' legislative requirements on consulting local authorities responsible for discharging health scrutiny functions are met.
> - Follow good practice that Health & Wellbeing Boards have an opportunity to feed into the development of proposals.

17.73 There is a slightly difficult question for a CCG as to whether the HOSC should be formally consulted before or after public consultation. The guidance recommends that the HOSC is consulted before the CCG goes out to public consultation but, in practice, that does not seem appropriate because the final proposals for service change may well change after public consultation. It thus seems far better for a CCG to make initial contact with the HOSC before public consultation but only to undertake final (legal) consultation with the HOSC once public consultation has been completed and the CCG have clearly worked up proposals to put to its governing body (or other decision making body). The role of the HOSC as a legal consultee is thus considered below.

17.74 However, in advance of formal consultation, CCGs should work closely with relevant HOSCs to explain the emerging thinking and hopefully build a consensus in support of change.

Stage 5: Public consultation

Overview

17.75 There has, on occasion, been a degree of cynicism expressed by some NHS managers as to the utility of consulting the public before changes are made to NHS services. A traditional NHS management view could be characterized as 'decide first, consult afterwards'.[32] This misunderstands both the legal duties and the practical utility of consultation. NHS services are not 'free'. They are paid for by the public out of their taxes and the public make a continuing commitment to support the NHS by electing politicians who pledge to support the NHS. However, the 'quid pro quo' is that the public have a key say in how the health service they fund should be organised. The public also offer a 'consumer perspective' on NHS services, and frequently this differs substantially from the perspective of those whose role is to supply health services. Genuine and sustained public engagement in NHS services is vital to prevent the arrangement of services being organized around 'supplier interests'.

17.76 There is a short and helpful guide from the Cabinet Office concerning consultation which is worth repeating in full. It provides:

> **Consultation Principles 2016**
>
> **1. Consultations should be clear and concise**
> Use plain English and avoid acronyms. Be clear what questions you are asking and limit the number of questions to those that are necessary. Make them easy to understand and easy to answer. Avoid lengthy documents when possible and consider merging those on related topics.
>
> **2. Consultations should have a purpose**
> Do not consult for the sake of it. Ask departmental lawyers whether you have a legal duty to consult. Take consultation responses into account when taking policy forward. Consult about policies or implementation plans when the development of the policies or plans is at a formative stage. Do not ask questions about issues on which you already have a final view.
>
> **3. Consultations should be informative**
> Give enough information to ensure that those consulted understand the issues and can give informed responses. Include validated assessments of the costs and benefits of the options being considered when possible; this might be required where proposals have an impact on business or the voluntary sector.
>
> **4. Consultations are only part of a process of engagement**
> Consider whether informal iterative consultation is appropriate, using new digital tools and open, collaborative approaches. Consultation is not just about formal documents and responses. It is an on-going process.
>
> **5. Consultations should last for a proportionate amount of time.**
> Judge the length of the consultation on the basis of legal advice and taking into account the nature and impact of the proposal. Consulting for too long will unnecessarily delay policy development. Consulting too quickly will not give enough time for consideration and will reduce the quality of responses.
>
> **6. Consultations should be targeted**
> Consider the full range of people, business and voluntary bodies affected by the policy, and whether representative groups exist. Consider targeting specific groups if appropriate. Ensure they are aware of the consultation and can access it. Consider how to tailor consultation to the needs and preferences of particular groups, such as older people, younger people or people with disabilities that may not respond to traditional consultation methods.

32 An extreme version of this approach was illustrated by a senior NHS manager who, when advised to conduct a consultation exercise before closing an in-patient facility, asked the author: 'Why should the public tell me how to do my job?' It is difficult to know where to start in unpicking the mindset which leads to this perspective.

7. Consultations should take account of the groups being consulted
Consult stakeholders in a way that suits them. Charities may need more time to respond than businesses, for example. When the consultation spans all or part of a holiday period, consider how this may affect consultation and take appropriate mitigating action.

8. Consultations should be agreed before publication
Seek collective agreement before publishing a written consultation, particularly when consulting on new policy proposals. Consultations should be published on gov.uk.

9. Consultation should facilitate scrutiny
Publish any response on the same page on gov.uk as the original consultation, and ensure it is clear when the government has responded to the consultation. Explain the responses that have been received from consultees and how these have informed the policy. State how many responses have been received.

10. Government responses to consultations should be published in a timely fashion
Publish responses within 12 weeks of the consultation or provide an explanation why this is not possible. Where consultation concerns a statutory instrument publish responses before or at the same time as the instrument is laid, except in exceptional circumstances. Allow appropriate time between closing the consultation and implementing policy or legislation.

11. Consultation exercises should not generally be launched during local or national election periods.
If exceptional circumstances make a consultation absolutely essential (for example, for safeguarding public health), departments should seek advice from the Propriety and Ethics team in the Cabinet Office.

17.77 While this document comes with the rider 'This document does not have legal force and is subject to statutory and other legal requirements', it is suggested that this rider is unnecessary. The guidance is a model of good governance and, with suitable adaptions to reflect that the consultation is by an NHS body and not central government, it entirely reflects the approach that should be taken by public bodies to a consultation exercise.

17.78 There is no explicit statutory duty on a CCG to conduct a formal consultation exercise before making a decision on a reconfiguration proposal. The duty on a CCG under section 14Z2 of the NHS Act 2006 is to have PPI arrangements which 'involve' the public in its decision making. Consultation is one of the stated methods by which the public can be 'involved' in decision making by NHS commissioners, but there are other methods apart from a formal consultation exercise, including a regular dialogue with the public under which emerging proposals and the arguments for and against them are published, with a continuing invitation for the public to respond to the material which is put into the public domain. However, the courts have long held that the 'involvement' duty should be fulfilled by a pro-active consultation exercise where there are substantial or locally contentious proposals so all of the public have a say, rather than just the provision of information online for the benefit of IT savvy or particularly interested members of the public who tend to get involved in informal communication exercises. A proactive consultation exercise may also be needed to discharge the CCG's duty to tackle health inequalities.

17.79 The meaning of the duty to 'involve' the public in decision making was explored by Collins J in *Smith v North Eastern Derbyshire Primary Care Trust and another.*[33] This concerned the re-provision of a primary care practice where the local PCT wanted to contract with a commercial provider of GP services to deliver the GP practice services, as opposed to contracting with a more traditional GP-led service. The PCT argued unsuccessfully that the involvement duty did not arise because the services to the public would be unchanged.[34] That argument was rejected by the judge (on the then wording of the duty). Collins J appears to have been unclear what was meant by the statutory duty to 'involve' patients in decision making. He said:[35]

> Thus 'involved in' really means no more than informed and able to express a view (which adds little to 'consulted on'). What is important is that the public must know what is proposed or what changes are to take place or how the services which affect them are to be operated and must have the opportunity, at least through a representative body, to comment on such matters. Their views must be obtained.

17.80 The reference to 'through a representative body' reflected the wording of the then PPI duty (in section 11 of the Health and Social Care Act 2001). The option to discharge the duty through an allegedly 'representative body' is not in the wording of the section 14Z2 duty and thus is not a permissible option for a CCG. The duty under section 14Z2 is designed to ensure that *all* patients affected by a decision or who may be affected by a decision have the opportunity to express their views and influence decision-making. This means that it is almost certainly not open to a CCG to argue that it has fulfilled its patient involvement duty by inviting only members of a Patient Participation Group, or a representative from the local Healthwatch, for example, to (possibly confidential) meetings to discuss the proposed service change. The guidance does not appear to recognise the significant differences between the previous section 11 duty and the section 14Z2 duty and advises that the PPI duty can be discharged through representatives. However a close reading of this wording of the PPI duty shows this to be mistaken.

17.81 There was a discussion in the first instance judgment in *Smith* about whether the duty to 'involve' meant a duty to consult, or could be discharged by a more informal approach to involving patients. The trial judge said:

> It will only be necessary to undertake a more formal and wider consultation exercise if the proposals are for major changes.

17.82 That limited view of the circumstances where a duty to consult arose did not commend itself to the Court of Appeal. Lord Justice May said:[36]

> The simple fact is that the defendants had a duty to consult and they did not properly perform it.

33 [2006] EWHC 1338 (Admin).

34 The present PPI duty under section 14Z2 may not be engaged by such an exercise now because the duty only arises 'where the implementation of the proposals would have an impact on the manner in which the services are delivered to the individuals or the range of health services available to them'. However, if the services are to be delivered at a different location or with different access arrangements, the PPI duty will be engaged.

35 At para 4.

36 [2006] EWCA Civ 1291, (2006) 9 CCLR 663 at para 9.

Thus the Court of Appeal appear to have treated 'involvement' and 'consultation' as being substantially the same concept. That does not appear to be correct and the remarks may well not be binding (as they are arguably obiter dicta) but nonetheless they carry some weight. That approach is consistent with the decision of Hodge J in *R (Morris) v Trafford Healthcare NHS Trust*[37] who was faced by an NHS body that tried to argue that the public involvement duty did not arise where the case for change was based on urgent patient safety issues. That argument was robustly rejected by the judge, who said:

> The section 11 duty to consult is of high importance. The public expect to be involved in decisions by healthcare bodies, particularly when the issues involved are contentious as they clearly were with AGH. I do not accept that the need to close the wards at Altrincham General Hospital was so urgent that it was right that no public consultation should take place. There ought to have been consultation under section 11 about the closure of the wards in so important a local provision as Altrincham General Hospital. In those circumstances I regard the decision to close the wards as unlawful and will quash it.

This case also equated the duty to 'involve' patients with a duty to consult patients. However, it is noteworthy that, while the judge quashed the decision in that case, he did not order the services to be reinstated.

17.83 The guidance makes it clear that NHS bodies which are involved in substantial reconfigurations of NHS services ought to undertake formal public consultation because it provides that public consultation should be a key part of any reconfiguration process. The question as to how a CCG can 'involve' patients in lesser sets of changes, short of consultation, thus does not arise within the context of this chapter. It should, however, be treated as an area where NHS commissioners should seek detailed legal advice in the light of the conflicting case-law. The guidance makes it clear that it is 'good practice' for NHS bodies undertaking substantial configurations to consult the public in a formal way, stating:

> **7.8 Public consultation**
> Subject to feedback from local authorities, the proposing body may decide to progress to public consultation on the range of options that will be tested with staff, patients and the public, subject to assurance by NHS England.
>
> NHS England has a role in the assurance of all commissioner-led schemes. This will ensure consistency across the NHS commissioning system and ensure that good practice and lessons learnt are shared.
>
> It is advisable to engage an independent body to run the consultation analysis ahead of finalising any consultation documents, and to include a suitable budget for this piece of work in plans including the pre-consultation business case. There are also many private companies and organisations who can offer advice to running effective consultations.
>
> For NHS England's advice on undertaking consultations see https://www.england.nhs.uk/commissioning/primary-care-comm/involving-the-public/
>
> Schemes have struggled to build public support where they have not adequately addressed public concerns that:

37 [2006] EWHC 2334 (Admin), (2006) 9 CCLR 648.

- The proposals are perceived to be purely financially driven.
- Patients and their carers will need to make journeys that may reduce access.
- Emergency services will be too far away, putting people at risk.

By the time a scheme moves to public consultation, effective involvement will have identified any potential issues or barriers from within the local population and health economy which could compromise plans. Final proposals should take into consideration these concerns and seek to address them where appropriate.

17.84 It is beyond the scope of this book to provide an exhaustive explanation on the law on consultation or to explain how every reconfiguration consultation can be conducted in a lawful manner (or how a defective consultation process can be challenged). Nonetheless, as the Court of Appeal made clear in *R v North & East Devon Health Authority ex p Coughlan*:[38]

> . . . whether or not consultation of interested parties and the public is a legal requirement, if it is embarked upon it must be carried out properly.

17.85 The key issue in determining whether a consultation has been carried out properly, is whether it is 'fair' process. Fairness was described in *R (Moseley) v Haringey LBC*[39] as being a 'protean concept, not susceptible of much generalised enlargement'. That has, however, not prevented judges ruling on numerous occasions as to whether an NHS consultation has been run fairly or not. In *Moseley* the Supreme Court decided that the 'Sedley rules' were 'a prescription for fairness' for the consultation process. These 'rules' can be summarised as follows:

> First that consultation must be at a time when proposals are still at a formative stage. Second, that the proposer must give sufficient reasons for any proposal to permit of intelligent consideration and response. Third . . . that adequate time must be given for consideration and response and, finally, fourth that the product of consultation must be conscientiously taken into account in finalising any statutory proposals.

17.86 Webster J observed in *R v Secretary of State for Social Services ex p Association of Metropolitan Authorities*[40] that:

> In any context the essence of consultation is the communication of a genuine invitation to give advice and a genuine receipt of that advice.

Thus, as a minimum, NHS bodies should ensure that they both act in accordance with these principles when conducting a public consultation and have an audit trail of documents to be able to demonstrate clearly that they have conducted the consultation in accordance with these principles. It must be a genuine attempt by NHS decision-makers to seek advice from the public and, once they get that advice, carefully to consider the responses and decide on a reasoned basis whether to accept or reject the advice that the public have given.

38 [1999] EWCA Civ 1871, (1999) 2 CCLR 285.
39 [2014] UKSC 56.
40 [1986] 1 WLR 1 at 4.

17.87 How much information to put in a consultation document is always a difficult judgment. In *R v Devon County Council, ex p Baker*[41] Simon Brown LJ said:[42]

> . . . the demands of fairness are likely to be somewhat higher when an authority contemplates depriving someone of an existing benefit or advantage than when the claimant is a bare applicant for a future benefit.

Hence a greater level of detail is likely to be required to justify a proposal to remove existing NHS services than where services are being expanded.

17.88 The main purpose of the consultation document is enabling members of the public to know which services the CCG is proposing should be the subject of change and why the CCG is making these proposals. Over many years there has been a tendency for NHS bodies to shy away from admitting that reconfiguration decisions are primarily driven by the need to make the best use of the limited financial resources available to the NHS. In contrast, the courts have long accepted that NHS funds are limited and that NHS decision-makers have to make choices between what services to support and which they should not support. The 'locus classicus' of this is Lord Bingham's oft-quoted words in *R v Cambridge Health Authority ex p B*[43] where the judge said:

> It is common knowledge that health authorities of all kinds are constantly pressed to make ends meet . . . Difficult and agonising judgments have to be made as to how a limited budget is best allocated to the maximum advantage of the maximum number of patients.

17.89 The author has seen numerous consultation documents which suggest that the proposed service changes are being driven solely by a commitment to improving outcomes for patients, when the internal NHS documents show that saving money is the driving force behind the plans. NHS bodies who misrepresent the justifications for plans for service change run very serious legal risks because it could be argued that the second Sedley principle has been breached. This requires a public body to put forward 'sufficient reasons for any proposal' to allow an intelligent response by the public. However, a key part of that duty involves being honest with the public about the reasons for the proposed changes. The paradox here is that CCGs who pretend that they are only making changes to improve patient outcomes and not (also) to save money (or make the best use of limited NHS resources) are unlikely to persuade the public that this is true (and it is usually not wholly true). The public tend to assume that all service change is 'cuts' by any other name. They will thus assume that money is at the heart of NHS service change plans, and are very unlikely to accept any other explanation. There are, of course, reconfigurations where the delivery of the service will cost more than the current costs of delivering the service, but are justified by the need to recruit and retain appropriate staff and/or to improve clinical outcomes. Where this is the case, a CCG can overcome public scepticism by setting out the financial implications of the change plans in the document and

41 [1995] 1 All ER 73.

42 At p91. An observation that was quoted by Lord Reed with approval in *Moseley*.

43 [1995] 1 WLR 898 at 906.

hence explaining very carefully and clearly that the objective is not to save the NHS money. However, even then, the public may take some convincing.

17.90 One of the most difficult questions for any NHS consultation is what options to put forward for public consultation. The cases suggest three key principles should be adopted by those making these decisions.

a) First, NHS bodies should seek the views of the public about any clinically and financially sustainable options. Refusing to set out the arguments for or against a particular option in a consultation exercise merely because the CCG prefers a different option could well give rise to a complaint that the consultation was unfair because, instead of genuinely seeking the views of the public on options, it was used by the CCG as an attempt to persuade the public of the acceptability of a single option.
b) Second, the consultation document should expressly make it clear that the CCG remains open to consultees devising their own options and putting them forward as part of the consultation, and that if they do so additional options will form part of the post-consultation analysis.
c) Third, there is no duty to seek public views on options that the CCG honestly and reasonably believes cannot be delivered either because they are too expensive or because they cannot be staffed or for other justifiable reasons.

17.91 It is legally acceptable for a consultation document to advance a 'preferred option' for change and, if the CCG has formed a clear view on which option is preferable, there is an argument that the public are entitled to know which option has emerged as the CCG's preferred option in the work undertaken prior to formal public consultation. In *R v Hillingdon Health Authority ex p Goodwin*[44] Woolf J said:

> Whenever there has to be consultation, there has to be an indication of what there is to be consultation about; and, although an authority must enter into the consultation without a closed mind, it seems to me that there is nothing objectionable in the authority having decided on a course it would seek to adopt, if after consultation it decided that that is the proper course to adopt.

17.92 A CCG is likely to have taken considerable steps to analyse the options before public consultation and sought external assurance about its plans. It thus ought to have a clear body of evidence upon which to rely in making the case in favour of its preferred option. This needs to be explained in the consultation document, along with the reasons that other options did not attract provisional support, whether or not the public is invited to express their views about alternative options. However, a CCG is not obliged to put all of the technical information available to it in the public domain as part of the consultation document (although it may need to make this information available in response to requests under the Freedom of Information Act 2000). It also may not have complete answers to all of the questions likely to be raised by the public or relevant to a service change programme, and will act lawfully by properly putting such information that it does have in the public domain.

44 [1984] ICR 800 at p809.

17.93 This issue was explored in *R (Copson) v Dorset Healthcare University NHS Foundation Trust*,[45] where a challenge to a proposed closure of an in-patient mental health unit (with a transfer to home based services) was partly based on a failure of the trust to explain how patients who still needed in-patient treatment would travel to get it. The trust accepted that this would be an issue for a minority of patients and, in effect, said it was working on solutions. That was not held to be unlawful. HHJ Keyser QC said:[46]

> It was for the defendant to judge what information to disclose for the purposes of the consultation and that judgement had to be exercised with regard to the factors that were liable to affect the ultimate decision on the proposals and to the purpose of the consultation. In that regard, the decision was a practical one; the edge of the consultation might as well be dulled by a surfeit as by a lack of information. I hold that the manner in which the defendant approached the consultation was well within the scope of its discretion, and I reject the contention that the consultation was so unfair that it was unlawful.

Thus the CCG will have a considerable area of discretion to decide what level of information to put into the consultation document (and associated documents) and will only act unlawfully if a paucity of information makes the consultation exercise unfair.

17.94 There will be occasions where so much consultative work has been undertaken with stakeholders (including the public) prior to public consultation that there is, in the view of the NHS commissioner, only one realistic option. That raises the question as to whether it is lawful for an NHS body to seek views on only one option, whilst still indicating that it remains open to consultees putting forward other options in response to the consultation process. That was the situation in *R v (Kidderminster and District Community Health Council) v Worcestershire Health Authority*.[47] The argument that there was anything unlawful in consulting on one option was firmly rejected by the Court of Appeal. Simon Brown LJ said:

> If, as is clearly established (and is, in any event, only plain common sense) an authority can go out to consultation upon its preferred option, per O'Connor LJ, or with regard to 'a course it would seek to adopt if after consultation it had decided that that is the proper course to adopt' per Woolf J, then it seems to me plain that it can choose not to consult upon the less preferred options. It does not, in other words, have to consult on all possible options merely because at some point they were developed, crystallised, canvassed and considered.

17.95 However, following *Moseley*, there can be risks in not consulting on other options because it gives the impression that the CCG is only considering a single option and so has, in effect, already made up its mind. As a minimum, the CCG needs to make it very clear that it is open to other proposals or to the possibility of rethinking the whole reconfiguration exercise.

The consultation process

17.96 The NHS England statutory guidance *Patient and public participation in commissioning health and care: Statutory guidance for clinical commissioning*

45 [2013] EWHC 732 (Admin).

46 At para 51(9).

47 [1999] EWCA Civ 1525.

groups and NHS England[48] outlines a wide variety of ways in which patients can become involved in consultation exercises. A CCG will want to publish a 'consultation document' which explains the proposals, the options under consideration and the reasons why the CCG proposes to make changes to local NHS services. That document will seek views from the public and may well ask specific questions to help guide the decision-making process. CCGs should resist the temptation to frame closed questions in a way that points to their preferred outcome. Open questions which give the public the chance to express their views are far better guides to the public mood.

17.97 Respondents should be offered a wide variety of ways to make their views known, including electronic and 'paper and ink' responses. Many CCGs hold meetings as which those who are promoting the proposals have the chance to explain the details and to answer questions. These should be properly minuted and reported faithfully, whatever the level of opposition expressed to the CCG plans. Such meetings need careful handing where there are sensitive or controversial proposals, but they can be an important opportunity for NHS decision-makers to understand the public views.

17.98 The duty to tackle health inequalities is particularly relevant here because it requires a CCG to consider how to ensure that voices of those who are rarely heard are listened to within the consultation exercise. If, for example, the proposals affect mental health patients, children or the elderly, the design of the consultation process will have to ensure that these voices are heard. There are also groups of patients such as travellers or those living in nursing homes who, for different reasons, may not make their voices heard unless arrangements are made to seek out their views. The duty to tackle health inequalities may not be discharged if insufficient attention is paid to the needs of under-represented groups.

The length of the consultation process

17.99 Former Cabinet Office guidance recommended a period of 13 weeks for consultation. There is now no set length for a consultation exercise. Longer than 13 weeks will rarely be necessary, but it is good practice to avoid large parts of a consultation period covering public holiday periods (namely Christmas, Easter and August) or to extend the consultation to take account of those who are away. For example, this is particularly relevant if the proposals are for changes to services which are used by transient or seasonal populations such as students.

17.100 In practice, four weeks is probably the shortest period for any serious consultation exercise and there will rarely be a need to conduct a consultation that is longer than 13 weeks. The choice between those periods is a matter for the discretionary judgment of the body holding the consultation.

Changes to the plan – when is there a need to conduct further consultation?

17.101 As proposals develop, so it is perhaps inevitable that changes will be made to the final details of changes to NHS services. Thus a CCG can find itself

48 See www.england.nhs.uk/wp-content/uploads/2017/05/patient-and-public-participation-guidance.pdf.

consulting on one set of proposals but find that, by the time of the final decision, the final shape of the proposals is somewhat different to the proposals set out in the consultation document. Part of the reason for change can, of course, be a desire to accommodate the views of the public as expressed during the consultation process. However, there may be a myriad of other reasons which mean that the CCG comes to the view that the original proposed model is no longer the most appropriate way to deliver local NHS services. This can lead to complaints that the final model for services has never been the subject of public consultation.

17.102 The question as to when an NHS body has a duty to conduct a further public consultation exercise was considered in *R (Smith) v East Kent Hospital NHS Trust and another*.[49] In that case, Silber J considered a number of previous cases which had wrestled with the extent of the duty of a public body to conduct a further round of consultation. He finally settled on a 'fundamental difference' test, saying:[50]

> In determining whether there should be further re-consultation, a proper balance has to be struck between the strong obligation to consult on the part of the health authority and the need for decisions to be taken that affect the running of the Health Service. This means that there should only be re-consultation if there is a fundamental difference between the proposals consulted on and those which the consulting party subsequently wishes to adopt.

17.103 In that case, the NHS body consulted on four options and then implemented a fifth option which had elements from various of the options. That was not fundamentally different and hence the duty to re-consult did not emerge. However, different considerations may arise if the factor which causes the changes is not a response to consultation but an entirely new or independent factor. This was the subject of the following observations from Lord Justice Sullivan in *R (Stirling) v Haringey LBC*:[51]

> 23. . . . we heard submissions on the relevance of the *Smith* case, and I think it appropriate to express my view on the applicability 'fundamental change' test in the context of the present case. While I do not doubt the correctness of Silber J's decision in *Smith*, I do not consider that it is of assistance in this case. As Underhill J pointed out, Silber J was dealing with a case where four options were consulted upon, and having considered the consultees' responses, the decision maker decided to proceed with a fifth option which incorporated elements from the other options. Underhill J rightly identified the distinction between those cases where, following consultation the decision maker decides to adopt a new proposal, and cases, such as the present case, where a new factor emerges during the course of a consultation
>
> 24. In the latter type of case, I am not persuaded that the 'fundamental change' test is appropriate. Mr. Wise accepted that there would often be a 'moving target', and a decision maker was not obliged to draw each and every change of circumstance during what might be a lengthy consultation process to the attention of consultees. It is easy to postulate the test – that the new factor must be of such significance that, in all the circumstances, fairness demands that it must (not may) be drawn to the attention of consultees; it is much more difficult to decide what fairness demands in any particular set of circumstances. A holistic approach should be adopted, all relevant factors should be

49 [2002] EWHC 2640 (Admin), (2003) 6 CCLR 251.

50 At para 45.

51 [2013] EWCA Civ 116.

considered, and these may include, in addition to the nature and significance of the new material, such matters as the extent to which the new material is in the public domain, thereby affording consultees the opportunity to comment upon its relevance to the proposal the subject of the consultation, and the practical implications, including cost and delay, of further consultation'

17.104 Thus the real issue is not whether there is a fundamental difference between the original proposals and those implemented in the light of the new factors, but whether fairness requires a period of further consultation. This approach seems consistent with the approach taken by the Supreme Court in the same case, which was known as *Moseley* albeit that the Supreme Court reached a different final decision on the lawfulness of the consultation under challenge in that case.

17.105 In practice, if new factors which could affect the commissioning decision to any substantial extent arise during a consultation, CCGs would be well advised to publicise them and expressly seek public views on the new factors, and if necessary extend the period of formal consultation to allow for additional responses. This should ensure that the 'fairness' of the consultation is maintained. It will rarely be necessary to commence an entirely fresh consultation process.

Stage 6: Assessing the results of public consultation

17.106 A public body undertaking consultation must ensure that the product of consultation must be conscientiously taken into account in finalising any proposals. There is no right or wrong way to assess the outcome of a consultation because the assessment process depends on the facts of an individual process. However, the following pointers may assist CCG staff who are preparing a response for decision-makers:

a) If the consultation paper asked the public a series of questions, decision-makers should be provided with an analysis of the responses provided by the public.
b) Qualitative comments in response to the consultation should be provided as well as quantitative. These should be selected (there is no need to report all comments), but a balanced selection of the representative and the perceptive should be provided.
c) If there is a very strong public expression of support or opposition to proposals, this should be carefully explained along with the reasons for the expression of views.
d) If alternative models for the provision of services are advanced by the public (or pressure groups on behalf of the public), these should be reported together with any analysis that has been conducted of the viability and preferability of this alternative model.
e) Particular attention should be paid to the views and perspectives of those patients or patient groups who are directly affected by the service changes, 'hard to reach' or suffer from significant health inequalities.

17.107 However, one of the significant problems that NHS bodies often find is that the public express very strong views in favour of the existing pattern of services, but do so without engaging with the reasons that a CCG is advancing a case for change. Hence, for example, there may be strong support for retaining a 'full' A&E service at a small hospital when this cannot be staffed in a sustainable manner and is delivering outcomes which are below those possible at a larger unit. The report of the consultation responses must faithfully report this expression of opinion and it is a factor which the CCG has to take into account when making the final decision. However, decision-makers are also required by law to discharge their functions in an effective and efficient way. Hence they may well lawfully conclude that delivering services in accordance with the strongly expressed opinions of the public is not possible. Nonetheless, decision-makers need to ask themselves how far they can accommodate the strong views of the public, consistent with their overriding legal duties. There will, however, be occasions where a CCG is faced with a 'binary' decision. If, for example, full A&E services are currently provided at two hospitals and the CCG's assessment is that continuing to deliver services at both hospitals is not clinically sustainable, decision-makers can be put in a position where there is no viable middle ground. One set of supporters will have their views supported, and the other set will be bitterly disappointed.

17.108 However, as the court emphasised in *Copson*, a consultation process does not turn those consulted into decision-makers. Their views have to influence the final decision-makers, but this process is not a plebiscite. Hence there is nothing inherently unlawful in a CCG preferring a minority view or indeed adopting a decision which has little, if any, support, provided the decision-makers have genuinely and carefully considered the views expressed by the public as part of the consultation process.

Stage 7: Preparing the decision-making business case

17.109 Once the results of consultation have been carefully considered, CCG staff should move to the preparation of final proposals for the CCG Board, as set out in a DMBC. The NHS service change guidance explains the process as follows:

> **8 Decision**
> Following consultation it is important to ensure that the Decision Making Business Case (DMBC) validates consultation outcomes and that progress to implementation is fully informed by solid detailed analysis of consultation outcomes. NHS Improvement and the Department of Health and Social Care should remain sighted on any capital that has been planned for and NHS England should be informed of the proposed next steps once all feedback from the consultation has been gathered and analysed.
>
> The commissioners' decision is to be based on the best balance of clinical evidence and evidence gained through public engagement and consultation. A clear audit trail to evidence how the decision was reached and the considerations taken, is to be captured.
>
> Once a decision has been made as to the preferred option following consultation, organisations can develop SOCs based on this preferred option. Before individual organisations incur major cost on any scheme they should ensure that they have agreed with NHS England and NHS Improvement, including written confirmation in principle as to the availability, level and source(s) of funding for the scheme. Until approval for the SOC is in place organisations should not incur material costs progressing to the next formal stages of the scheme (OBCs and FBCs), the implementation phase.

17.110 The DMBC is essential to support any application for capital funding and thus, in practice, is a key document for both internal and external consumption.

Stage 8: Formal consultation with the local authority Health Overview and Scrutiny Committee

Procedures

17.111 The role of the local authority HOSC has been introduced above. Regulation 23 of the 2013 Regulations explains the procedures which have to be followed if a CCG is proposing any 'substantial development' to local NHS services. It provides:

> 23 (1) Subject to paragraphs (2) and (12) and regulation 24, where a responsible person ('R') has under consideration any proposal for a substantial development of the health service in the area of a local authority ('the authority'), or for a substantial variation in the provision of such service, R must–
> (a) consult the authority;
> (b) when consulting, provide the authority with–
> (i) the proposed date by which R intends to make a decision as to whether to proceed with the proposal; and
> (ii) the date by which R requires the authority to provide any comments under paragraph (4);
> (c) inform the authority of any change to the dates provided under paragraph (b); and
> (d) publish those dates, including any change to those dates.
> (2) Paragraph (1) does not apply to any proposals on which R is satisfied that a decision has to be taken without allowing time for consultation because of a risk to safety or welfare of patients or staff.
> (3) In a case such as is referred to in paragraph (2), R must notify the authority immediately of the decision taken and the reason why no consultation has taken place.
> (4) Subject to regulation 30(5) (joint committees) and any directions under regulation 32 (directions as to arrangements for discharge of health scrutiny functions), the authority may make comments on the proposal consulted on by the date or changed date provided by R under paragraph (1)(b)(ii) or (c).
> (5) Where the authority's comments under paragraph (4) include a recommendation to R and R disagrees with that recommendation–
> (a) R must notify the authority of the disagreement;
> (b) R and the authority must take such steps as are reasonably practicable to try to reach agreement in relation to the subject of the recommendation; and
> (c) in a case where the duties of R under this regulation are being discharged by the responsible commissioner pursuant to paragraph (12), the authority and the responsible commissioner must involve R in the steps specified in sub-paragraph (b).
> (6) This paragraph applies where–
> (a) the authority has not exercised the power in paragraph (4); or
> (b) the authority's comments under paragraph (4) do not include a recommendation.
> (7) Where paragraph (6) applies, the authority must inform R of–
> (a) its decision as to whether to exercise its power under paragraph (9) and, if applicable, the date by which it proposes to exercise that power; or

(b) the date by which it proposes to make a decision as to whether to exercise that power.

(8) Where the authority has informed R of a date under paragraph (7)(b), the authority must, by that date, make the decision referred to in that paragraph and inform R of that decision.

(9) Subject to paragraph (10), the authority may report to the Secretary of State in writing where–

(a) the authority is not satisfied that consultation on any proposal referred to in paragraph (1) has been adequate in relation to content or time allowed;

(b) in a case where paragraph (2) applies, the authority is not satisfied that the reasons given by R are adequate; or

(c) the authority considers that the proposal would not be in the interests of the health service in its area.

(10) The authority may not make a report under paragraph (9)–

(a) in a case falling within paragraph (5), unless the authority is satisfied that–

(i) the steps specified in paragraph (5)(a) to (c) have been taken, but agreement has not been reached in relation to the subject of the recommendation within a reasonable period of time;

(ii) R has failed to comply with its duty under paragraph (5)(b) within a reasonable period of time; or

(b) in a case to which paragraph (6) applies, unless the authority has complied with the duty in paragraph (7) and, where applicable, paragraph (8).

(11) A report made under paragraph (9) must include–

(a) an explanation of the proposal to which the report relates;

(b) in the case of a report under paragraph (9)(a) or (b), the reasons why the authority is not satisfied of the matters set out in paragraph (9)(a) or (b);

(c) in the case of a report under paragraph (9)(c), a summary of the evidence considered, including any evidence of the effect or potential effect of the proposal on the sustainability or otherwise of the health service in the area of the authority;

(d) an explanation of any steps the authority has taken to try to reach agreement with R in relation to the proposal or the matters set out in paragraph (9)(a) or (b);

(e) in a case falling within paragraph (10), evidence to demonstrate that the authority has complied with the applicable condition in that paragraph;

(f) an explanation of the reasons for the making of the report; and

(g) any evidence in support of those reasons.

(12) In a case where R is a service provider and the proposal relates to services which a clinical commissioning group or the Board is responsible for arranging the provision of–

(a) the functions of R under this regulation must be discharged by the responsible commissioner on behalf of R; and

(b) references to R in this regulation (other than in paragraph (5)(c)) are to be treated as references to the responsible commissioner.

(13) Where the functions of R under this regulation fall to be discharged by more than one body under paragraph (12)(a), the duties of those bodies under that paragraph may be discharged by those bodies jointly or by one or more of those bodies on behalf of those bodies.

(14) In this regulation–

'service provider' means an NHS trust, an NHS foundation trust or a relevant health service provider;

'the responsible commissioner' means the clinical commissioning group or groups or the Board, as the case may be, responsible for arranging the provision of the services to which the proposal relates.

What is a 'substantial development of the health service in the area of a local authority'?

17.112 The duty on a CCG to consult the HOSC arises where the CCG is considering any 'substantial development of the health service in the area of a local authority'. There is no definition of 'substantial development' in the regulations. However, the guidance published by the secretary of state in 2003[52] gave the following explanation as to what is meant by these words:

> **10.6 Understanding 'substantial variation and substantial development'**
> 10.6.1 The Regulations for overview and scrutiny do not define 'substantial'. Local NHS bodies should aim to reach a local understanding or definition with their overview and scrutiny committee(s). This should be informed by discussions with other key stakeholders including patients' forums.
>
> 10.6.2 In considering whether the proposal is substantial, NHS bodies, committees and stakeholders should consider generally the impact of the change upon patients, carers and the public who use or have the potential to use a service.
>
> 10.6.3 More specifically they should take into account:
>
> a) **changes in accessibility of services**, for example both reductions and increases on a particular site or changes in opening times for a particular clinic. Communities attach considerable importance to the local provision of services, and local accessibility can be a key factor in improving population health, especially for disadvantaged and minority groups. At the same time, development in medical practice and in the effective organisation of health care services may call for reorganisation including relocation of services. Thus there should be discussion of any proposal which involves the withdrawal of in-patient, day patient or diagnostic facilities for one or more speciality from the same location;
> b) **impact of proposal on the wider community** and other services, including economic impact, transport, regeneration;
> c) **patients affected**, changes may affect the whole population (such as changes to accident and emergency), or a small group (patients accessing a specialised service). If change affects a small group it may still be regarded as substantial, particularly if patients need to continue accessing that service for many years (for example, renal services). There should be an informed discussion about whether this is the case and which level of impact is considered substantial;
> d) **methods of service delivery**, altering the way a service is delivered may be a substantial change – for example moving a particular service into community settings rather than being entirely hospital-based. The views of patients and patients' forums will be essential in such cases'

52 See *Overview and scrutiny of health – guidance* (July 2003).

17.113 Further guidance was published in 2014, namely *Guidance to support local authorities and their partners to deliver effective health scrutiny* ('the 2014 guidance'), although it does not offer any views on what is meant by the term 'substantial development'. It thus seems that the best guide to the meaning of this term remains in the 2003 guidance.

When does the CCG not have to refer a reconfiguration to the HOSC?

17.114 The 2014 guidance explains the provisions in the regulations that govern when consultation is not required. It states:

> The Regulations set out certain proposals on which consultation with health scrutiny is *not* required. These are:
> - Where the relevant NHS body or health service commissioner believes that a decision has to be taken without allowing time for consultation because of a risk to safety or welfare of patients or staff (this might for example cover the situation where a ward needs to close immediately because of a viral outbreak) – in such cases the NHS body or health service provider must notify the local authority that consultation will not take place and the reason for this.
> - Where there is a proposal to establish or dissolve or vary the constitution of a CCG or establish or dissolve an NHS trust, unless the proposal involves a substantial development or variation.
> - Where proposals are part of a trusts special administrator's report or draft report (i.e. when a trust has financial difficulties and is being run by an administration put in place by the Secretary of State) – these are required to be the subject of a separate 30-day community-wide consultation.

17.115 However, as explained below, the HOSC has the power to refer a proposal to the secretary of state if it was not consulted but considers that it ought to have been consulted.

When can a referral be made by the HOSC to the secretary of state?

17.116 Where the HOSC is satisfied that there has been adequate information as part of the consultation and adequate time for the consultation, the primary test for the HOSC is whether:

> . . . the authority considers that the proposal would not be in the interests of the health service in its area . . .[53]

17.117 Where the HOSC and the CCG disagree on the proposed changes, the regulation sets up a process under which the HOSC and the CCGs are required to attempt to resolve their differences. Regulation 23(5) provides that the HOSC and the CCG:

> . . . must take such steps as are reasonably practicable to try to reach agreement in relation to the subject of the recommendation.

17.118 There will, however, be occasions on which the CCG and the HOSC cannot agree on the final shape of a proposed NHS reconfiguration. If this point is reached, or if the HOSC is dissatisfied with the quality of the consultation exercise undertaken by the CCG or objects to the fact that there has been no consultation of the HOSC, the HOSC has the power to

53 See reg 23(9)(c).

refer the matter to the secretary of state. The 2014 guidance explains when an HOSC can and cannot refer a case to the secretary of state. It states:

> 4.7.4 The circumstances for referral of a proposed substantial development or variation remain the same as in previous legislation. That is, where a health scrutiny body has been consulted by a relevant NHS body or health service provider on a proposed substantial development or variation, it may report to the Secretary of State in writing if:
>
> - It is not satisfied that sufficient time has been allowed for consultation.
> - It considers that the proposal would not be in the interests of the health service in its area.
> - It has *not* been consulted, and it is not satisfied that the reasons given for not carrying out consultation are adequate.
>
> 4.7.5 However, there are certain limits on the circumstances in which a health scrutiny bodies may refer a proposal to the Secretary of State.
>
> In particular, where a health scrutiny body has made a recommendation and the relevant NHS body or health service provider has disagreed with the recommendation, the health scrutiny body may not refer a proposal unless:
>
> - it is satisfied that reasonably practicable steps have been taken to try to reach agreement (with steps taken to involve the provider where NHS England or a CCG is acting on the provider's behalf) but agreement has not been reached within a reasonable time; or
> - it is satisfied that the relevant NHS body or health service provider has failed to take reasonably practicable steps to try to reach agreement within a reasonable period.
>
> In a case where a health scrutiny body has not commented on the proposal or has commented without making a recommendation, the health scrutiny body may not refer a proposal unless:
>
> - It has informed the relevant NHS body or health service provider of-
>   - its decision as to whether to exercise its power of referral and, if applicable, the date by which it proposed to exercise that power, or
>   - the date by which it proposes to make a decision as to whether to exercise its power of referral.
> - In a situation where it informed the relevant NHS body or health service provider of the date by which it proposed to decide whether to exercise the power of referral, it has made that decision by that date and informed the body or provider of the decision'

17.119 However, the 2014 guidance explains more of the government's thinking about the way in which referral powers should be used. It observes:[54]

> The backdrop to consultation on substantial reconfiguration proposals is itself changing. The ideal situation is that proposals for change emerge from involving service users and the wider public in dialogue about needs and priorities and how services can be improved. Much of this dialogue may take place through representation of service users and the public on health and wellbeing boards and through the boards' own public engagement strategies. With increasing integration of health and care services, many proposals for change may be joint NHS-local authority proposals which may have been discussed at an early stage through the health and wellbeing board. Health scrutiny bodies should be party to such discussions – local circumstances will determine the best way for this to happen. If informally involved and consulted at an early enough stage, health scrutiny bodies in collaboration with local Healthwatch, may be able to advise on how patients and the public

54 Para 4.1.2.

can be effectively engaged and listened to. If this has happened, health scrutiny bodies are less likely to raise objections when consulted.

17.120 The guidance thus emphasises that formal consultation under the 2013 regulations should be the last stage in an on-going dialogue between the NHS commissioners and the local authority about the future shape of NHS services in the area of the local authority (as well as ongoing dialogue with patients and the public).

17.121 The HOSC is not obliged to refer the matter to the secretary of state, even if the test is met. It could properly decide not to make a referral. However, the political reality is usually that, where there is a fundamental disagreement between the HOSC and the CCG (over, for example, the relocation of an A&E unit or a reduction from a consultant-led maternity service to a nurse-led service), the depth of local feeling means the HOSC has little choice but to refer a matter to the secretary of state.

The report which must accompany a referral to the secretary of state

17.122 Where the HOSC decides that it wishes to refer a proposed reconfiguration to the secretary of state, the HOSC has to prepare a detailed report to explain the basis of the referral. Regulation 23(11) requires the HOSC to provide the secretary of state with a report covering the following areas:

- An explanation of the proposal to make substantial changes to the local NHS services.
- If the referral is made because the HOSC is dissatisfied with the quality of the consultation exercise undertaken by the CCG or objects to the fact that there has been no consultation, the report needs to set out why the authority is not satisfied with the actions of the CCG.
- If the referral is made because the HOSC considers that the proposal would not be in the interests of the health service in its area, the report needs to include a summary of the evidence considered, including any evidence of the effect or potential effect of the proposal on the sustainability or otherwise of the health service in the area of the authority.
- The HOSC must provide an explanation of any steps the authority has taken to try to reach agreement with the CCG and that it is not barred from being able to report because of the conditions in reg 23(10) (namely that it did try to reach agreement but failed to do so within a reasonable time or the CCG failed to attempt to reach agreement and that it did follow the processes to try to reach agreement before the referral was made).
- The report must set out an explanation of the reasons for the making of the report and any evidence in support of those reasons.

The powers of the secretary of state when an HOSC referral is made

17.123 Regulation 25 of the 2013 Regulations provides the powers for the secretary of state to act as decision maker when an HOSC referral is made. It provides:

> 25 (1) Where a local authority has reported to the Secretary of State under regulation 23(9) in relation to a proposal, the Secretary of State may–
>
> (a) in the case of a referral under regulation 23(9)(a) or (b), make a decision in relation to the subject matter of the referral;

(b) in the case of a referral under regulation 23(9)(c), make a final decision on the proposal; and
(c) in the case of a referral under regulation 23(9), give directions to the Board, including directions as to the exercise of its power under paragraph (2), in relation to the proposal.

(2) Where a local authority has reported to the Secretary of State under regulation 23(9) in relation to a proposal, and the Secretary of State has made a decision pursuant to paragraph (1)(a) or (b), the Board may, subject to any directions under paragraph (1)(c), give directions to a clinical commissioning group in relation to the proposal.

(3) The powers conferred by paragraphs (1)(c) and (2) include powers to require the person to whom the direction is given–
(a) to consult (or consult further) with the authority in relation to the proposal;
(b) to determine the matter in a particular way;
(c) to take, or not to take, any other steps in relation to the matter.

17.124 The secretary of state thus has wide decision-making powers concerning the proposals referred to him or her by the HOSC. It has been the established practice of successive secretaries of state to refer contentious reconfigurations to the Independent Reconfiguration Panel (IRP) for an independent assessment of the proposals and for advice as to what decision to make on the referral. This has the distinct advantage for the secretary of state of 'de-politicising' a decision, particularly where the issues have become of local political interest (as will often be the case). The IRP publishes reports of its findings in the form of reports.[55] These explain the way that the IRP has assessed the robustness of the cases.

The interim position where a referral is made

17.125 There is nothing in the 2013 Regulations which governs the management of the interim position. There have been occasions where an NHS commissioner has, in effect, taken a final decision and implemented the changes before the secretary of state has reached a final decision, accepting that this process may have to be reversed if the secretary of state reaches a decision that is adverse to the NHS commissioner. However, the usual position is that the CCG seeks to maintain the status quo pending the decision of the secretary of state. This often occurs because NHS England is unlikely to agree to release capital to finance change programmes until there is clarity about the way forward.

17.126 Nonetheless, there does not seem to be any basis to suggest that a CCG is deprived of its decision-making powers in the interim period merely because a referral has been made to the secretary of state. However if the secretary of state were to uphold the complaint, the CCG would be obliged to act in accordance with the secretary of state's decision.

Stage 9: Final decision-making

17.127 Having gone through all of the above processes, the last stage of decision-making is for the CCG governing body, or often a committee of multiple CCGs, to meet to consider all of the relevant material and to make the

55 See www.gov.uk/government/publications?departments%5B%5D=independent-reconfiguration-panel&page=1.

final decision concerning any proposed reconfiguration. The papers for this final meeting should carefully consider all of the factors set out in the NHS service change guidance, as described above. Board members should be provided with:

- a clear explanation of the decision that the CCG is invited to make, including its financial implications, the benefits for patients and staff implications;
- the CCG's assessment of the 'five tests';
- a detailed explanation of the outcome of public consultation;
- details of any capital requirements of the scheme and the proposed source of the capital;
- views expressed in support or against the proposal by the HOSC, local councillors or members of parliament;
- views expressed in support or against the proposal by NHS England and Monitor (NHS Improvement);
- how the CCG has satisfied itself that it has discharged each of its procedural duties regarding the said proposal,[56] and in particular how the proposals will discharge the CCG duty to tackle health inequalities.

17.128 The meeting should be held in public, and a detailed note should be taken of the discussions, recording any views in favour or against the proposals. It is important that there is a clear vote of members of the decision making body in favour or against the proposals. The minutes need to record clearly what decision has been reached.

17.129 Particular attention should be paid to the management of any conflicts of interest which might arise for members of the body which has been charged with making the final decision.[57]

Stage 10: Implementation of the decision

17.130 While making a decision to change NHS services may appear complex, these difficulties can seem small in comparison to the challenges of implementing a decision to change the way that NHS services are delivered. This should be an NHS management process rather than a legal process, but it is often a protracted and complex process which is far more expensive than originally anticipated. Legal issues can arise where the proposed decision turns out to be difficult (if not impossible to implement) and thus the final model can involve substantial changes from that originally anticipated. In such a case, the CCG needs to monitor the position carefully to ensure that its services on the ground reflect decisions made by the governing body, and that there is no breach of the continuing duty to involve the public in commissioning decisions.

17.131 Prior to implementing a decision by making changes to contracts, the CCG also needs to satisfy itself that it has satisfied any procurement obligations that arise as a result of the proposed changed to the contractual arrangements.

56 These are described in detail in chapter 5 on the duties of a CCG. Like duties are imposed on NHS England.

57 For details of the law on managing conflicts of interest, please see paras 5.95–5.104.

CHAPTER 18

GP practice management[1]

continued

1 By Hannah Gibbs and Ben Fullbrook.

Introduction

18.1 General practice has always been at the front line in terms of providing essential medical care to the population. It is a vital component of the NHS as the gateway by which the majority of NHS secondary care services are accessed by NHS patients. In order to access such services, patients must register with an NHS general practitioner (GP) practice as a permanent or temporary patient in order to receive services from an NHS GP and to be referred by that GP to secondary care providers.

18.2 In what is a seemingly constantly changing policy context, GPs remain of central importance to the Department of Health and Social Care (DHSC) and NHS England's[2] vision for an increasingly integrated health and social care system. As part of its *General practice forward view* published in April 2016, NHS England announced its intention, in conjunction with clinical commissioning groups (CCGs), to commission extended access to primary care appointments and encourage new models of providing primary care. This includes integrating primary care with community, urgent and acute services. By way of example, from December 2017 patients all across London have been able to access GP services across extended hours on weeknights and Saturdays for the first time ever.

18.3 However, it is widely reported that general practice is 'in crisis', with GPs complaining of growing pressures as a result of an increased demand and consequent work-load, under-staffing and the burden of keeping up-to-date with constantly evolving models of care.[3] Part of the reason is that the management of patients with long term conditions has moved from hospital-based services to GP services inexorably over the last 25 years as the number of patients with one or more long-term conditions increases. This relieves pressure on NHS acute care but makes the role of GPs more complex, particularly as the promised secondary care support is uneven across the country.

18.4 Against this background this chapter seeks to explain exactly *which* services GP practices are required to provide under their contracts (and what other services they can contract to provide); *when* they must provide those services; to *whom*; *how* they must manage the services provided to their patients; and when they can *charge* for services provided to patients.

18.5 It should be noted that, to the best of the authors' knowledge, this chapter represents the law at the time of publication. However, as stated above, the policy context within the NHS and the models of primary care proposed by NHS England and the DHSC are in constant flux. The legality of many of these models and their associated contracts is uncertain (particularly given the proposal to change the contracting structures entirely by creating the 'accountable care organisation' (ACO) model and draft ACO contract, concerning which there may be clarification from the

2 The legal title of NHS England is the National Health Service Commissioning Board. It refers to itself as 'NHS England', although this has no bearing on its legal functions. Please see chapter 5 on the powers and duties of NHS England for further information.

3 See, for example, Beccy Baird, The King's Fund, *Is general practice in crisis?* (1 June 2017): www.kingsfund.org.uk/publications/articles/big-election-questions-gp-crisis.

courts in future[4]). Changes to primary and secondary legislation may be forthcoming to address this. Readers should therefore ensure that they read this chapter along with any updates that may be issued.

Overview of the legal framework governing general practice management

18.6 The primary duty to commission primary care services rests with NHS England. Section 83(1) of the National Health Service Act (NHS Act) 2006 provides:

> The Board [ie NHS England] must, to the extent that it considers necessary to meet all reasonable requirements, exercise its powers so as to secure the provision of primary medical services throughout England.

18.7 The nature of this duty means that there is no absolute requirement on NHS England to ensure that every individual is able to register with a GP practice which is local to their home. The duty requires NHS England to set up a network of GP services to meet the 'reasonable requirements' of patients. What is 'reasonable' will depend on a number of things, in particular what the needs are of the local population for which NHS England is commissioning services, but it is axiomatic that one relevant factor will be the level of resources available. However, NHS England is also under duties to tackle health inequalities in exercising its commissioning functions, and this duty may affect the way it is required to commission primary care services.[5]

18.8 Once NHS England has discharged its duty by ensuring such a network of primary care services is available, it is a matter of choice for individual patients as to whether to register themselves with a GP practice to receive such services or not to do so. There is no obligation on anyone living in England to register with an NHS GP practice. As is explored below, however, there are limited circumstances in which a patient can receive primary care services if they do not register with a GP.

18.9 NHS England complies with the duty under section 83(1) of the NHS Act 2006 by 'making arrangements' for the provision of primary medical services with GP practices or those running such practices. Section 83(2) of the NHS Act 2006 provides:

> The Board may (in addition to any other power conferred on it) make such arrangements for the provision of primary medical services as it considers appropriate; and it may, in particular, make contractual arrangements with any person.

18.10 The way that NHS England discharges this duty in each area is to set up a series of contracts (either legally binding contracts or NHS contracts) with GP practices who agree to provide primary medical services to patients in that area.[6] It is becoming increasingly common for GP practices to join

4 At the time of writing there are two challenges proceeding against the DHSC/NHS England models concerning ACOs.

5 See paras 3.18–3.28 above.

6 Please see chapter 11 on primary care contracting for further information.

'federations' or 'super partnerships', which broadly can be described as more than one practice working collaboratively to varying degrees legally and organisationally. That federation or partnership may hold a contract with NHS England rather than the individual practices.

18.11 In recent years, NHS England has moved to a model of primary care co-commissioning, whereby it either partially or wholly delegates its responsibility for primary care commissioning to local CCGs. NHS England, however, retains ultimate responsibility for primary care commissioning under the section 83 primary duty to meet reasonable requirements and is named as the commissioning party in any primary care contract.

18.12 As explained in chapter 11 on primary care contracting,[7] under sections 83(2), 84 and 92 of the NHS Act 2006, NHS England has created three types of contract, by which it discharges its duty to make arrangements to meet reasonable requirements throughout England:

a) *A General Medical Services (GMS) contract.* This is a nationally negotiated contract which takes effect between NHS England and a GP practice. Its central features are: i) that it potentially exists in perpetuity for the practice; ii) if it is a contract with a partnership, it exists with the partners as they exist from time to time; and iii) the contractual fees payable are set by directions made by the Secretary of State for Health and Social Care. The GMS contract is the default option for many GP practices since a PMS (Personal Medical Services) contractor has a statutory right to revert to a GM contract. Although Alternative Provider Medical Services (APMS) contracts (see below) became a popular method of contracting, for reasons that are explored in chapter 17 on primary care contracting, the majority of practice contracts are still GMS contracts and many Personal Medical Services (PMS) contracts (see below) are now being changed to operate far more like GMS contracts.

b) *A Personal Medical Services (PMS) agreement.*[8] This is a local contract and some of the terms can be agreed between NHS England and the practice, including funding arrangements. However, many of the terms of the PMS contract are governed by the regulations which require the contract to contain terms which replicate a GMS contract. PMS contracts are almost always time-limited contracts (but the practice can 'convert' to a GMS contract which has no time limit).

c) *An Alternative Provider Medical Services (APMS) contract.* This allows NHS England to contract with 'any person' to provide primary care services under local commissioning arrangements. APMS contracts are individually negotiated although some of the terms found in PMS contracts (themselves based on the GMS contract) are mandatory under Directions published by the Secretary of State for Health and Social Care. They are time-limited.

18.13 The conditions and terms that are required to be in the various forms of contract are set out in regulations, in the case of GMS and PMS contracts, and directions, in the case of APMS contracts:

7 And thus the relevant statutory provisions are not intended to be addressed in detail here.

8 Technically, PMS contracts are refered to as PMS 'agreements' for reasons explained at para 11.50, although the terms are used here interchangeably.

a) GMS contracts are governed by the National Health Service (General Medical Services Contracts) Regulations (GMS Regs) 2015;[9]
b) PMS contracts are governed by the National Health Service (Personal Medical Services Agreements) Regulations (PMS Regs) 2015;[10] and
c) APMS contracts are governed by the Alternative Provider Medical Services Directions 2016 (as amended by the Alternative Provider Medical Services (Amendment) Directions 2017).

18.14 Once the NHS commissioner and the practice have agreed the contract (which ought to comply with the statutory duties on NHS England as set out in the relevant regulations or directions), the terms of the agreement take effect as a normal commercial contract between the parties (see *Tomkins v Knowsley Primary Care Trust*[11]). The GP practice will owe various duties under the private law of negligence to patients, which will no doubt be informed by the services specified in the contract, but the duty to provide the services under the terms set out in the contract will be a separate contractual duty owed to the commissioner.

18.15 In addition to fulfilling their contractual obligations, as noted in the GMS and PMS Regs 2015, and remarked upon by Arnold J in *Generics (UK) Limited (t/a Mylan) v Warner-Lambert Company LLC*,[12] GPs are also required to have regard to guidance issued by NHS England, although they are not obliged to follow it if they have good reasons to depart from it.

18.16 In November 2017, NHS England published a comprehensive guidance document entitled *Primary medical care policy and guidance manual* (PGM). This document contains guidance on many of the issues discussed in this chapter and in chapter 11 on primary care contracting.

18.17 This chapter will explore which services GPs are contractually obliged to provide, when and under what terms; what types of other services they might provide; how a practice must manage its list of registered patients and deal with unregistered patients; and when it can charge for services. In doing so, it will predominantly focus on the GMS Regs 2015, since not only do they direct the content of GMS contracts, but they also inform to a large extent the content of PMS contracts, and are the basis for some mandatory terms in APMS contracts.

The services provided by GP practices

What are primary medical services?

18.18 Sections 83(5) and (6) of the NHS Act 2006 provide:

> (5) Regulations may provide that services of a prescribed description must, or must not, be regarded as primary medical services for the purposes of this Act.

9 SI No 1862.
10 SI No 1879.
11 [2010] EWHC 1194 (QB) per Hickinbottom J at para 5.
12 [2016] RPC 3 at para 555.

(6) Regulations under this section may in particular describe services by reference to the manner or circumstances in which they are provided.

18.19 The GMS Regs 2015 contain a somewhat circular definition of 'primary medical services', describing them in reg 3 'as medical services provided under or by virtue of a contract or agreement to which the provisions of Part 4 of the 2006 Act applies'. However, as set out above, section 83 of the NHS Act 2006 states that regulations may provide that certain services are 'primary medical services', which those delivering primary care within the NHS are obliged to or may provide.

18.20 Part 5 of the GMS Regs 2015 contains a number of terms which must be included within practice contracts with NHS England held by GP practices. Some of these terms relate to services that must or may be provided under a contract. From these, it can be deduced that 'primary medical services' include the following categories of service, which are explored below:

a) essential services (including emergency services);
b) additional services;
c) enhanced services;
d) out of hours services; and
e) other services provided for in the regulations.

Essential services

18.21 The current definition of 'essential services' for primary care is set out at reg 17 of the GMS Regs 2015 as follows:

(1) Subject to paragraph (2), for the purposes of section 85(1) of the Act (requirement to provide certain medical services), the services which must be provided under a contract ('essential services') are the services described in paragraphs (4), (6), (7) and (9).
(2) Essential services are not required to be provided by the contractor during any period in respect of which the Care Quality Commission has suspended the contractor as a service provider under section 18 of the Health and Social Care Act 2008 (suspension of registration).
(3) Subject to regulation 20(2)(b) and (c), a contractor must provide the services described in paragraphs (4) and (6) throughout the core hours.
(4) The services described in this paragraph are services required for the management of a contractor's registered patients and temporary residents who are, or believe themselves to be–
  (a) ill, with conditions from which recovery is generally expected;
  (b) terminally ill; or
  (c) suffering from chronic disease,
  (d) which are delivered in the manner determined by the contractor's practice in discussion with the patient.
(5) For the purposes of paragraph (4)–
  'disease' means a disease included in the list of three-character categories contained in the tenth revision of the International Statistical Classification of Diseases and Related Health Problems 1 . . .

This definition is incorporated into the PMS Regs 2015 in its entirety by reg 3.

18.22 The above provisions, and the scope of 'primary medical services', need to be interpreted in the light of the NHS Act 2006 as a whole, which divides healthcare services into different categories. Acute medical services come within Part 1 of the NHS Act 2006 and primary care services fall within Part 4 of the NHS Act 2006. Other parts of the Act provide for dental and pharmaceutical services to be delivered as part of NHS funded care.[13]

18.23 Although there is an inevitable measure of overlap between acute services and primary care services, where services are classified as 'acute services' under Part 1, they are generally not primary care services under Part 4. Acute services are widely defined in section 3(1) of the NHS Act 2006 as follows:

(a) hospital accommodation,
(b) other accommodation for the purpose of any service provided under this Act,
(c) medical, dental, ophthalmic, nursing and ambulance services,
(d) such other services or facilities for the care of pregnant women, women who are breastfeeding and young children [as the group considers] are appropriate as part of the health service,
(e) such other services or facilities for the prevention of illness, the care of persons suffering from illness and the after-care of persons who have suffered from illness [as the group considers] are appropriate as part of the health service,
(f) such other services or facilities as are required for the diagnosis and treatment of illness'

18.24 Where a CCG, which has responsibility for commissioning acute services, commissions relevant services under section 3(1) of the NHS Act 2006, a GP can discharge his or her obligations as a provider of primary care by referring an NHS patient onto another NHS provider where his or her patient requires one of those acute services. The 'essential services' that are required to be provided by GPs are therefore a much narrower group of services.

18.25 The core requirement on a GP who provides essential services to NHS patients is 'the management of' such patients. Regulation 17(5) of the GMS Regs provides that 'management' of a patient includes:

(a) offering consultation and, where appropriate, physical examination for the purposes of identifying the need, if any, for treatment or further investigation; and
(b) making available such treatment or further investigation as is necessary and appropriate, including the referral of the patient for other services under the Act and liaison with other health care professionals involved in the patient's treatment and care.

18.26 This is expanded by reg 17(6), which provides that management of the GP's patients includes the provision of appropriate ongoing treatment and care to all registered patients and temporary residents taking account of their specific needs, including:

a) the provision of advice in connection with the patient's health, including relevant health promotion advice; and

13 See chapters 10, 11 and 19.

b) the referral of the patient for other services under the NHS Act 2006 (which normally means referral for acute and community services under section 3 of the NHS Act 2006).

To whom must GPs provide 'essential services'?

18.27 The persons to whom the GP is obliged to offer this 'management' service are:

a) the patients on the list for the GP practice held by NHS England; and
b) temporary patients.

These are precisely defined terms under the GMS Regs 2015, and are explored below in the section on patient list management.

18.28 The GP practice is not obliged to offer 'management services' to every patient on their list for every minute of the core hours (because that would be an impossible task to fulfil and would mean offering services where they were not needed). The contractual duty is to provide services to patients who are, or *believe* themselves to be:

a) ill, with conditions from which recovery is generally expected;
b) terminally ill; or
c) suffering from chronic disease.

18.29 The expression 'illness' is defined in section 275 of the NHS Act 2006 as follows:

> 'illness' includes any disorder or disability of the mind and any injury or disability requiring medical or dental treatment or nursing.

18.30 There are thus two important implications of the scope of this duty. The first is that the duty to provide management services to a patient is engaged by the patient's own *subjective* belief that they are ill. Thus, a GP practice is obliged to see and offer management services to a patient who believes himself or herself to be ill even if that person is not, in fact, suffering from any diagnosable illness. Of course, a patient who was suffering from hypochondria and continually believed themselves to be ill might indeed require treatment of some sort. Which leads into the second implication of the duty, which is that 'illness' is defined extremely broadly. The wide definition means that, for example, a drug addiction is likely to be an 'illness' because drug addiction changes the brain in fundamental ways, disturbing a person's normal hierarchy of needs and desires and substituting new priorities connected with procuring and using the drug. The resulting compulsive behaviours that override the ability to control impulses despite the consequences are similar to hallmarks of other mental illnesses. The behaviour can be classified as an illness in ICD-10 the *International statistical classification of diseases and related health problems,* and thus GP practices have the same management duty to such patients as they have to patients with any other illness.

18.31 A GP is obliged to provide a management service to a patient 'in the manner determined by the contractor's practice in discussion with the patient' (reg 17(4) of the GMS Regs 2015). Thus, the patient is entitled to be consulted about the way in which general medical services are provided to the patient, but the final decision about the manner in which services should be provided (including the location at which the services should be provided) rests with the GP.

When are GPs obliged to provide essential services?

18.32 The GMS contract (and virtually all PMS contracts) provides that the contractual duty on the GP practice to provide the essential services is only operative during 'core hours'. These hours are defined in regs 3 of the GMS and PMS Regs 2015 as follows:

> 'core hours' means the period beginning at 8.00am and ending at 6.30pm on any day from Monday to Friday except Good Friday, Christmas Day or bank holidays.

18.33 However, the GMS contract does not require the GP practice to make a GP available in person to provide routine services to patients throughout the core hours. Under reg 20 of the GMS Regs the duty to provide services within core hours has two parts, namely:

a) to provide the essential services and additional services funded under the global sum[14] within core hours, 'as are appropriate to meet the reasonable needs' of its patients; and
b) to have in place arrangements for its patients to access such services throughout the core hours in case of emergency.

18.34 Thus, if GP practice premises are closed at any point during the core hours, the GP practice either must provide a means for patients to be able to access one of the practice GPs throughout that period or must make arrangements with an out of hours provider to provide emergency GP services to patients during that period. There are no set surgery hours within the GMS contract but the opening hours need to be sufficient to 'meet the reasonable needs of its patients'.

18.35 There has been considerable discussion in the professional press about practices that do not provide sufficient surgery slots to meet the needs of patients and thus patients find themselves having to wait for an appointment. In the past, the Labour government had a policy that patients should have a maximum period of waiting of 48 hours before seeing a GP. However, that target was abandoned by the coalition government in 2010. The present position is that there is no specific time target, but the NHS website states:

> Your surgery should be able to offer you an appointment to see a GP or other healthcare professional quickly if you need it. However, you should also be able to book appointments in advance if this is more convenient.[15]

18.36 GP practices that fail to provide a sufficient number of surgery appointments to meet the reasonable needs of their patient populations

14 The 'global sum' is defined in reg 3 of the GMS Regulations as 'having the meaning given in the GMS Statement of Financial Entitlements', which are directions as to payments to be made under GMS contracts. The 'global sum' is a contribution towards the contractor's costs in delivering essential and additional services, including its staff costs. It represents the core funding for GP practices and is calculated by reference to a formula. See chapter 11 on primary care contracting.

15 See www.nhs.uk/chq/Pages/2555.aspx?CategoryID=68&SubCategoryID=158.

are probably acting in breach of the contractual requirement to provide services to 'meet the reasonable needs of its patients' and could find that NHS England/the CCG serve a Remedial Notice to require them to extend the number of surgery appointments. However, NHS England (or its delegate the CCG) is the only party that can enforce compliance with the contract. Patients can, however, seek to put pressure on NHS England to enforce the terms of the contract and could consider a judicial review action against NHS England if it failed to do so.

The duty on GP practices to provide emergency services

18.37 GPs are not paramedics and will not usually be called to a medical emergency within their practice area. However, under reg 17 of the GMS Regs 2015, as part of the 'essential services' provided by the GP practice, it must also provide a range of emergency services in defined circumstances: as a result of an accident or emergency in its practice area or when emergency care for certain patients who are not on its registered list is required. Given that the definition of 'essential services' is incorporated into the PMS Regs 2015 in its entirety, PMS contractors will also be obliged to provide emergency services in the core hours as defined in the contract.

Accident and emergency care

18.38 Regulation 17(7) and (8) of the GMS Regs 2015 provides:

> (7) A contractor must provide primary medical services required in core hours for the immediately necessary treatment of any person to whom the contractor has been requested to provide treatment owing to an accident or emergency at any place in its practice area.
>
> (8) In paragraph (7), 'emergency' includes any medical emergency whether or not related to services provided under the contract.

18.39 This is an obligation to react to requests for assistance made at any time throughout the core hours. The contractual duty to provide services only comes into effect if the GP practice has been 'requested' to provide emergency primary care services in the event of an accident or emergency taking place anywhere in the practice area. The identity of the person making the request is not specified in the regulations and the request therefore could be made by the police, fire brigade, paramedics or a member of the public (whether a patient is on the practice list or not). The regulation does not specify what sort of service the GP is required to provide beyond saying that the GP must provide primary medical services. Thus, the GP has to provide the same type of 'management' services for the patient in an emergency situation as he or she would provide in the surgery. This includes:

a) physical examination for the purpose of identifying the need, if any, for treatment or further investigation; and
b) the making available of such treatment or further investigation as is necessary and appropriate, including the referral of the patient for other services under the NHS Act 2006 and liaison with other healthcare professionals involved in the patient's treatment and care.

18.40 It seems clear that, in order to comply with the contractual obligation, the practice would have to send out a qualified GP who could administer such services as could be reasonably expected from a GP as opposed to a specialist in emergency medicine. The contractual obligation is likely to be fulfilled if the GP arrives at the scene of the accident or emergency reasonably promptly and provides a primary medical service whilst, at the same time, calling for help from specialist emergency practitioners.

Emergency care for certain patients who are not on the registered list

18.41 The second type of emergency service that a GP practice is required to provide is 'immediately necessary treatment' to someone who is not on the list of patients for the practice and is not a temporary patient but who comes within certain specified categories. Regulation 17(9)–(11) provides the contractual duty is as follows:

> (9) A contractor must provide primary medical services required in core hours for the immediately necessary treatment of any person to whom paragraph (10) applies who requests such treatment for the period specified in paragraph (11).
>
> (10) This paragraph applies to a person if–
>
> (a) that person's application for inclusion in the contractor's list of patients has been refused in accordance with paragraph 21 of Schedule 3, and that person is not registered with another provider of essential services (or their equivalent);
>
> (b) that person's application for acceptance as a temporary resident has been refused under paragraph 21 of Schedule 3; or
>
> (c) that person is present in the contractor's practice area for a period of less than 24 hours.
>
> (11) The period specified in this paragraph is, in the case of a person to whom–
>
> (a) paragraph (10)(a) applies, 14 days beginning with the date on which that person's application was refused or until that person has been subsequently registered elsewhere for the provision of essential services (or their equivalent), whichever occurs first;
>
> (b) paragraph (10)(b) applies, 14 days beginning with the date on which that person's application was rejected or until that person has been subsequently accepted elsewhere as a temporary resident, whichever occurs first; or
>
> (c) paragraph (10)(c) applies, 24 hours or such shorter period as the person is present in the contractor's practice area.'

18.42 The contractual duty on a GP practice to provide emergency services is thus limited in three ways:

a) It is not a duty to provide a full primary care service to these patients, but only to provide immediately necessary treatment to such patients. There is clearly a measure of judgment that the GP practice will have to make as to what services are within this requirement and which services can be left for another GP to provide in due course.
b) The duty is limited to those categories of patients set out in reg 17(10), namely individuals who have applied to join the practice list and been refused, who have been rejected as temporary residents or are in the practice area for less than 24 hours.
c) The duty is time-limited in that for patients who have been rejected from the practice list either as permanent or temporary patients, the duty only lasts for a maximum of 14 days, but can come to an end if the

patient secures another GP in that period and, in the case of a person only in the practice area for 24 hours, is limited to a maximum of 24 hours.

18.43 A person who has been accepted onto the practice list and is then removed from the list because, for example, the patient has been violent to staff members, does not come within reg 17(10) of the GMS Regs 2015 unless that person applies to re-join the practice list and is refused. Equally, a person who has applied to join the practice list but has not yet been accepted or refused does not come within this provision. The GP practice is therefore under no contractual duty to provide services to such a patient.

18.44 The regulations do not explain what happens if, at the end of the 14-day period, the rejected patient presents at the surgery seeking a further course of 'immediately necessary treatment'. It seems likely that the duty under reg 17(10) of the GMS Regs 2015 is a 'one off' duty to an individual and that, once the period specified in reg 17(11) has ended the GP practice has no further duty to provide medical services to that individual. If it were otherwise, a patient who had been refused entry onto the practice list as a result of violence to staff could, for example, keep seeking services under this provision and thus remain a threat to staff.

Additional services

18.45 Essential services are the range of services that GP practices are obliged to provide as a minimum to their practice patients and temporary residents. However, pursuant to reg 19 of the GMS Regs 2015, GP practices can contract to provide extra services to patients and thus avoid the need for the GP practice to refer patients who need such services elsewhere. Services which are extra to the essential services (as described above) are classified as 'additional services' and 'enhanced services'. GP practices are not obliged to contract to provide additional services but they are paid additional sums (usually as part of the global sum) where they agree to do so.

18.46 'Additional services' are defined in reg 3 of the GMS Regs 2015 as follows:

> 'additional services' means one or more of–
> (a) cervical screening services;
> (b) contraceptive services;
> (c) vaccines and immunisations;
> (d) childhood vaccines and immunisations;
> (e) child health surveillance services;
> (f) maternity medical services; and
> (g) minor surgery.

18.47 Under reg 19, where a GP practice opts to provide such a service, it must include, within its contract:

a) a term which has the same effect as that specified in Schedule 1 para 1 (ie that the contractor must provide, in relation to each additional service, such facilities as are necessary to enable the contractor to properly perform that service); and

b) a term which has the same effect as that specified in in Schedule 1 insofar as they are relevant to the specific service which the practice is opting to provide

18.48 Schedule 1 to the GMS Regs 2015 contains specific requirements when GP practices provide the defined 'additional services'. Hence, for example, GP practices that agree to provide contraceptive services are required to provide services in the following way (Schedule 1 para 3):

(1) A contractor whose contract includes the provision of contraceptive services must make the services described in sub-paragraph (2) available to all of its patients who request those services.
(2) The services described in this sub-paragraph are–
(a) the giving of advice about the full range of contraceptive methods;
(b) where appropriate, the medical examination of patients seeking such advice;
(c) the treatment of such patients for contraceptive purposes and the prescribing of contraceptive substances and appliances (excluding the fitting and implanting of intrauterine devices and implants);
(d) the giving of advice about emergency contraception and, where appropriate, the supplying or prescribing of emergency hormonal contraception or, where the contractor has a conscientious objection to emergency contraception, prompt referral to another provider of primary medical services who does not have such an objection;
(e) the giving of advice and referral in cases of unplanned pregnancy including advice about the availability of free pregnancy testing in the contractor's practice area and, where appropriate, where the contractor has a conscientious objection to the termination of pregnancy, prompt referral to another contractor who does not have such an objection;
(f) the giving of initial advice about sexual health promotion and sexually transmitted infections; and
(g) the referral as necessary to specialist sexual health services, including tests for sexually transmitted infections.'

18.49 The contract can specify that the GP practice should provide additional services to the practice patients and persons accepted by the GP practice as temporary residents. However, the GMS contract can also be extended so that such services are provided to a wider range of patients. Hence, for example, a GP practice could develop a specialism in minor surgery or be contracted to provide contraceptive services to a wider range of patients than just those on its practice list.

When are GPs obliged to provide additional services?

18.50 The same requirements as to providing essential services in the core hours apply to additional services that are funded under the global sum. Readers are asked to refer to the section above on essential services.

Enhanced services

18.51 Enhanced services are defined in reg 3 of the GMS Regs 2015 as follows:

'enhanced services' are–
(a) services other than essential services, additional services or out of hours services; or

(b) essential services, additional services or out of hours services or an element of such a service that a contractor agrees under a contract to provide in accordance with specifications set out in a plan, which requires of the contractor an enhanced level of service provision compared to that which it needs generally to provide in relation to that service or element of service.

18.52 Enhanced services are therefore something that goes above and beyond the essential services, additional services, or out of hours services required by the regulations, be that the *type* of service altogether that is provided or the hours or intensity of service provision. There is no limit on the type of enhanced services that a commissioner and a GP practice can agree will be provided to NHS patients, provided that the service can properly be considered to be part of the health service. The terms fall to be agreed between the commissioner and the provider.

18.53 The archetypal 'enhanced services' are extended hours. There is a present focus among commissioners on extending the hours during which GP practices provide routine primary care appointments, as a means to tackle the pressures on urgent and emergency services. This is not without controversy, however, in the professional GP press.

18.54 Certain enhanced services schemes are provided for nationally as 'Directed Enhanced Services'. The nature of those services is set out in directions, the most recent of which are the Primary Medical Services (Directed Enhanced Services) Directions 2017. They provide that NHS England must operate the following enhanced services schemes to meet its reasonable requirements duty under section 83 of the NHS Act 2006, which it must offer to GP practices to be part of their GMS or PMS contract:

a) an Extended Hours Access Scheme, the underlying purpose of which is to enable patients to consult a healthcare professional, face-to-face, by telephone or by other means at times other than during the core hours specified in the contractor's primary medical services contract, as agreed with the Board – these are not 'out of hours' services, which are explained below, but are routine bookable appointments;
b) a Learning Disabilities Health Check Scheme;
c) a Childhood Immunisation Scheme;
d) an Influenza and Pneumococcal Immunisation Scheme;
e) a Violent Patients Scheme; and
f) a Minor Surgery Scheme.

18.55 These schemes apply on a yearly basis, after which the terms might change. For example, in this year's Extended Hours Access Scheme, the directions have introduced a requirement that a practice that closes for a half-day on a weekly basis cannot join the scheme, unless by written prior agreement with NHS England. It is understood by these authors that this requirement is a reaction to the perception that (often single handed) practices that close for long periods during the day produce worse clinical outcomes for their patients.

18.56 Another example of enhanced services provision is the recent introduction in London of the London Extended GP Access Service, which allows all Londoners registered with a GP practice to book routine GP, and in some case nurse, appointments in the evenings, weekends and on bank holidays. This scheme was proposed in the *General practice forward view*. These services were commissioned by NHS England and CCGs working together under the *Transforming primary care in London: a strategic commissioning framework*. As with the Directed Extended Hours Access Scheme, practices do not necessarily provide these services individually, but CCGs have typically contracted strategically with a number of practices so that they provide these services collectively. Therefore, a patient might have to go to a different practice to see a GP or see a GP other than the patient's usual GP. These kind of enhanced services can 'wrap around' a practice's GMS or PMS contract, and are often procured by way of an APMS contract.

Out of hours services

18.57 Regulation 3 of the GMS Regs 2015 defines out of hours (OOH) services as 'the services required to be provided in all or part of the out of hours period which (a) would be essential services if provided by a contractor to its registered patients in core hours; or (b) are included in the contract as additional services funded under the global sum'. The OOH period is the remainder of the time outside the core hours as defined by the GMS Regs 2015, so from 6.30pm on Monday to Thursday to 8am the following day, the weekend starting at 6.30pm on Friday and ending at 8am on Monday, and Good Friday, Christmas Day and bank holidays.

18.58 Therefore, and as explained above, the OOH period does not include any period where a GP practice closes during contracted hours, during which time the practice has a responsibility (including a financial responsibility) to provide cover.

18.59 If a GP has signed up to an extended access scheme, either the Directed Enhanced Services scheme, or a local scheme, it is likely that these appointments will be routine bookable appointments. OOH services therefore would co-exist with this enhanced provision, since there will still be patients who require urgent primary care in a community setting and have not booked an appointment in advance. However, in practice, patients will access these services via an Extended Hours scheme rather than through an OOH provider (which is likely to be different to the GP practice).

18.60 Until 2004, GP practices were required to provide essential service to patients at all times of the day and night. Many practices used deputising services to provide services to patients outside of core hours. Thus, in practice, prior to 2004 many patients would not see their family doctor if they sought GP OOH services. However, from 2004 GP practices were entitled to opt out of responsibility for providing OOH services. The vast majority of GP practices did so and accordingly the responsibility for OOH GP provision fell to primary care trusts (the predecessors of CCGs) to arrange.

18.61 The present duty to commission OOH primary care services for GP practices which have opted out of OOH responsibilities lies with the CCG and not NHS England. It follows that CCGs need to be careful to observe the rules on conflicts of interest in any contract process where one of the bidders includes GPs who work within a local GP practice (and are therefore connected to members of the CCG).[16]

18.62 The way OOH services are structured varies. CCGs typically arrange for the provision of OOH services by entering into contracts with specific OOH providers, including co-operatives of local GPs. There have been a series of scandals concerning OOH providers, such as Serco in Cornwall, which was issued with a warning notice by the Care Quality Commission (CQC) for failing to meet essential health and safety standards and subsequently gave notice to terminate the contract. It is becoming increasingly common for OOH providers to be GP-led social enterprises or community interest companies, such as Devon Doctors.

18.63 Despite the widely reported problems with OOH providers, analysis by Urgent Health UK of data from approximately half of all GP urgent care providers found that they have an important role to play in reducing pressure on the acute system, ensuring that patients are cared for in the community when appropriate.[17] Nonetheless, worrying stories about understaffing of OOH provision continue to emerge. A freedom of information request by Pulse magazine, a major professional publication for GPs and healthcare professionals, found ten areas of the country where patients were left with no GP available during out of hours shifts in 2016.[18] Any failure by the OOH provider to fulfil its contractual obligations with the CCG could lead to enforcement action by the CCG. However that will not, of itself, inevitably leave the CCG in breach of the terms of its statutory obligation to make the appropriate OOH arrangements. This is because the arrangements are in place, albeit not being performed. There may, however, on any particular set of facts, come a time when the failure to provide a robust service will leave the CCG in breach of this duty.

Obligations on GPs who have not opted out of OOH services

18.64 Regulation 18(2) of the GMS Regs 2015 provides that, where a GP practice has contracted to provide OOH services, it:

- (a) is only required to provide out of hours services to a patient if, in the contractor's reasonable opinion having regard to the patient's medical condition, it would not be reasonable in all the circumstances for the patient to wait to obtain those services; and
- (b) must, in the provision of out of hours services–
  - (i) meet the quality requirements set out in the document entitled 'National Quality Requirements in the Delivery of Out of Hours Services' published on 20th July 2006, and
  - (ii) comply with any requests for information which it receives from, or on behalf of, the Board about the provision by the contractor of out of hours services to its registered patients in such manner, and before the end of such period, as is specified in the request.

16 Please see chapter 5 on the powers and duties of CCGs, which explores how CCGs should manage conflicts of interest.

17 See www.pulsetoday.co.uk/news/commissioning/commissioning-topics/urgent-care/out-of-hours-gps-are-keeping-hundreds-of-thousands-of-patients-out-of-ae/20033831.article.

18 See www.pulsetoday.co.uk/your-practice/practice-topics/out-of-hours/revealed-why-out-of-hours-is-on-a-knife-edge/20033775.article.

18.65 A judgment call is therefore required by the contractor as to whether a patient presenting out of hours could wait until the morning to receive services. It is also a matter for the judgment of the GP whether advice given over the telephone is sufficient, whether the GP should visit the patient or whether the patient should be advised to attend a local A&E.

Obligations on GPs who have opted out of OOH

18.66 However, even where a GP practice has opted out of providing OOH services, it will have some responsibility relating to the OOH care that its patients receive, including quality monitoring and reporting requirements. This is set out in reg 18(3) of the GMS Regs 2015:

> (3) Where a contractor is not required to provide out of hours services under a contract or, by virtue of Part 6, has opted out of the provision of such services under the contract, the contractor must–
> (a) monitor the quality of the out of hours services which are offered or provided to the contractor's registered patients having regard to the National Quality Standards referred to in paragraph (2)(b), and record, and act appropriately in relation to, any concerns arising;
> (b) record any patient feedback received, including any complaints;
> (c) report to the Board, either at the request of the Board or otherwise, any concerns arising about the quality of the out of hours services which are offered or provided to patients having regard to–
> (i) any patient feedback received, including any complaints, and
> (ii) the quality requirements set out in the National Quality Standards referred to in sub-paragraph (2)(b).

18.67 It should be noted that, since 2013, the NHS has also been operating the NHS 111 telephone service. The NHS website describes the function of NHS 111 with respect to OOH care as follows:

> The NHS pledges to provide services at a time that's convenient for you. Outside normal surgery hours you can still phone your GP practice, but you'll usually be directed to an out-of-hours service. The out-of-hours period is from 6.30pm to 8.00am on weekdays and all day at weekends and on bank holidays.
>
> Consider calling NHS 111 if you urgently need medical help or advice, but it's not a life-threatening situation. You can also call NHS 111 if you're not sure which NHS service you need.[19]

18.68 Thus, patients who need primary care support out of hours have the alternative of calling NHS 111 in order to be directed towards the appropriate service.

18.69 Following the Urgent and Emergency Care Review led by Sir Bruce Keogh, which was announced in 2013, NHS England has set out in the *General practice forward view* its intention to move towards integrated 24/7 urgent care services, which includes the NHS 111 service as well as OOH and other urgent care services. NHS England has also published guidance for commissioners with responsibility for OOH and urgent care commissioning: *Commissioning standards integrated urgent care.*[20]

19 See www.nhs.uk/NHSEngland/AboutNHSservices/Emergencyandurgentcareservices/Pages/NHS-111.aspx.

20 See www.england.nhs.uk/wp-content/uploads/2015/10/integrtd-urgnt-care-comms-standrds-oct15.pdf.

Where must GPs provide services to patients?

18.70 The default position is that a contractor must provide 'premises', that is to say a GP practice building, from where services may be provided. Regulation 20(1)(b) of the GMS Regs 2015 (and reg 13(1)(b) of the PMS Regs 2015) provides that the contract must specify the name of the premises. However, reg 20(4) of the GMS Regs 2015 (and reg 13(3) of the PMS Regs 2015) provides that those premises do not include the homes of any patients or any other premises where services are provided on an emergency basis.

18.71 Patients who seek assistance from their GP are, by definition, ill (or at least consider themselves to be ill). Some of these patients will be too ill to be able to attend the surgery premises, or, if they have an infectious condition, it may not be medically appropriate for them to attend the GP surgery because they may spread their condition to other patients. Thus treating patients at their own home has always been part of the work of a GP.

18.72 Schedule 3 para 5 to the GMS Regs 2015 (and Schedule 2 para 6 to the PMS Regs 2015) has the following provision which sets out when a GP is obliged to treat a patient outside the surgery premises:

> (1) Where the medical condition of a patient is such that, in the reasonable opinion of the contractor–
> (a) attendance on the patient is required; and
> (b) it would be inappropriate for the patient to attend the contractor's practice premises,
> the contractor must provide services to the patient at whichever of the places described in sub-paragraph (2) is, in the contractor's judgement, the most appropriate.
> (2) The places described in this sub-paragraph are–
> (a) the place recorded in the patient's medical records as being the patient's last home address;
> (b) such other place as the contractor has informed the patient and the Board is the place where the contractor has agreed to visit and treat the patient; or
> (c) another place in the contractor's practice area.
> (3) Nothing in this paragraph prevents the contractor from–
> (a) arranging for the referral of the patient without first seeing the patient in any case where the patient's medical condition makes that course of action appropriate; or
> (b) visiting the patient in circumstances where this paragraph does not place the contractor under an obligation to do so.

18.73 Thus a patient is entitled to medical treatment from home from a GP if, in the reasonable opinion of the GP, two conditions are satisfied, namely:

a) attendance on the patient is required; and
b) it would be inappropriate for him to attend at the practice premises.

18.74 At the stage that the GP is making this assessment, it is likely that the GP will not have seen the patient and therefore can only make this decision based upon the information that the patient has given to the GP practice (or has been provided on the patient's behalf) and on the medical history of the patient as set out in their notes. It seems clear, however, that the decision whether to make a home visit is a matter for the GP's judgment and is not something that could properly be left to reception staff or even the practice nurse, because the contract requires 'the contractor' to make the assessment and accordingly this must be an assessment made by a qualified person. Assessments as to whether a person needed a home visit could be made by practice nurses provided there was a system to enable the nurse to seek guidance from a GP in cases of doubt.

18.75 The first test is whether the patient requires 'attendance', which must mean that the patient has a need for the the type of patient management services defined in the regulations as being essential services.

18.76 The second test is whether it is inappropriate for the patient to attend at the practice premises. There is no limit to the reasons why a GP might consider that it could be inappropriate for the patient to attend at the practice premises. It may be that the patient is too ill to attend, has an infectious illness which makes it inappropriate to attend or has a medical condition such as agoraphobia which makes it difficult for the patient to attend the surgery. This provision could also be used to manage a violent patient who the GP practice does not wish to remove from its list but nonetheless wishes to treat in a location where there is a measure of protection for the GP (such as a room at a local police station if the police were to agree to that arrangement).

18.77 Once the GP has reached the opinion that the patient needs treatment outside the surgery, the place at which the GP must offer treatment is set out in the regulations. It must be offered at the 'most appropriate' of the following places:

a) at the patient's home;
b) at another place agreed between the GP practice and the patient; or
c) at some other place within the practice area.

18.78 The final provision appears to be a catch-all provision, but that place must still pass the test of being the most appropriate place to provide services to the patient.

18.79 A GP practice which asserted that it did not offer home visits under any circumstances or applied a requirement for a patient who sought a home visit which was different to those set out above would be acting in breach of contract and could, in an extreme case, have contract sanctions imposed or, in extremis, have the contract cancelled by NHS England (either through the Area Team or by the CCG under delegated powers).

Other services that a GP practice is obliged to provide

18.80 Part 1 of Schedule 3 to the GMS Regs 2015 provides a list of other services that all GMS practice contracts must specify are provided to the patients of the practice. There is a similar list in Part 1 of Schedule 2 to the PMS Regs 2015. The following points summarise these requirements.

- *Premises:* The contract provides that the contractor shall ensure that the premises used for the provision of services under the contract are:
  a) suitable for the delivery of those services; and
  b) sufficient to meet the reasonable needs of the contractor's patients.

- *Telephone lines:* NHS GP practices are prohibited from using premium rate telephone numbers which start with the digits 087, 090 or 091 or consist of a personal number, unless the service is provided free to the caller. There are also provisions to prevent NHS GP practices using other types of premium rate telephone services.
- *Attendance by patients at the practice premises:* GP practices must take steps to ensure that any patient who has not previously made an appointment and attends at the practice premises during the normal hours for essential services is provided with such services by an appropriate healthcare professional during that surgery period. There is an exemption to this obligation if it is more appropriate for the patient to be referred elsewhere or if the patient is offered an appointment at another time, which is appropriate and reasonable, at the practice and the patient's health would not be jeopardised as a result.
- *Newly registered patients:* Patients who are new to the practice list (but are not temporary residents) must also be offered a 'consultation' with the GP practice within six months, at which the GP must make such inquiries and undertake such examinations as appear to be appropriate in all the circumstances. This appointment is to enable the GP to conduct a baseline assessment of the patient's health and thus offer such advice and/or other services as are appropriate to that individual. It is a pro-active requirement, and thus is an exception to the general approach of GP practices which is to be responsive to requests for services initiated by patients. The wording of this requirement (in para 6 of Schedule 3 to the GMS Regs 2015) is as follows:

  (1) Where a patient has been–
    (a) accepted on a contractor's list of patients; or
    (b) assigned to that list by the Board,
    the contractor must invite the patient to participate in a consultation either at the contractor's practice premises or, if the patient's medical condition so warrants, at one of the places described in paragraph 5(2).

  (2) An invitation under sub-paragraph (1) must be issued by the contractor before the end of the period of six months beginning with the date of the acceptance of the patient on, or assignment of the patient to, the contractor's list of patients.

  (3) Where a patient (or, where appropriate, in the case of a patient who is a child, the patient's parent) agrees to participate in a consultation mentioned in sub-paragraph (1), the contractor must, during the course of that consultation, make such inquiries and undertake such examinations as appear to the contractor to be appropriate in all the circumstances.

  (4) This paragraph and does not affect the contractor's other obligations under the contract in respect of the patient.

  Either as part of this consultation, or separately, the practice is also required to offer an alcohol dependency assessment to newly registered patients over the age of 16. The practice must also in certain circumstances provide follow up services for alcohol dependency.
- *Accountable GP:* Contractors must ensure that each of their patients, if they so wish, is assigned a GP that is accountable for ensuring that necessary services to meet the needs of the patients are co-ordinated and delivered. The requirements in relation to the accountable GP for

those aged 75 and over are found in para 11 of Part 1 of Schedule 3 to the GMS Regs 2015 and are more stringent, including an obligation on the GP to work co-operatively with other health and social care professionals to ensure the delivery of a multi-disciplinary care package. Another significant difference is that all patients over the age of 75 must have an accountable GP.

- *Patients who are not seen for three years:* Where a registered patient between the ages of 16 and 75 who has not attended the surgery for three years requests a consultation, the GP practice must take advantage of the opportunity of this individual attending the surgery to 'make such inquiries and undertake such examinations as appear to it to be appropriate in all the circumstances'. However, there is no duty on the GP practice to seek out patients who have not attended for three years to offer them a check-up. The duty only arises if the patient requests a consultation.
- *Patients over the age of 75:* The time period of non-attendance which needs to elapse before the GP practice has a duty to 'make such inquiries and undertake such examinations as appear to it to be appropriate in all the circumstances' is reduced to 12 months. However, once again, there is no duty on the GP practice to seek out patients over the age of 75 who have not attended the practice for 12 months to offer them a check-up. The duty only arises if such a patient requests a consultation with the GP practice.
- *Patients living with frailty:* GP practices must take steps to identify any registered patient aged 65 years and over who is living with moderate to severe frailty. Such patients are to be identified by the use of the electronic Frailty Index (eFI) or another appropriate assessment tool.[21] Once identified, the practice must:
  a) undertake a clinical review in respect of the patient, which includes:
     i) an annual review of the patient's medication; and
     ii) where appropriate, a discussion with the patient about whether the patient has fallen in the last 12 months;
  b) provide the patient with any other clinically appropriate interventions; and
  c) where the patient does not have an enriched Summary Care Record, advise the patient about the benefits of having an enriched Summary Care Record and activate that record at the patient's request.

  Where an intervention is provided, any appropriate information relating to it must be recorded in the patient's Summary Care Record.
- *Clinical reports on patients on the list of another practice:* Where the GP practice provides any clinical services, other than under a private arrangement, to a patient who is not on its list of patients, it shall, as soon as reasonably practicable, provide a clinical report relating to the consultation, and any treatment provided, to NHS England. Thus every time medical care is provided to a temporary resident or

21 More detail on the eFI can be found in the NHS Updated guidance on supporting routine frailty identification and frailty care through the GP Contract 2017/2018, www.england.nhs.uk/wp-content/uploads/2017/04/supporting-guidance-on-frailty-update-sept-2017.pdf.

emergency care is provided to a patient who is not registered with the practice, a report should be sent to NHS England explaining what care has been provided and the clinical findings. NHS England then has the task of sending the report to the patient's own practice so that it can form part of the clinical notes for that practice.

- *Storage of vaccines:* GP practices must ensure that all vaccines are stored in accordance with the manufacturer's instructions and that all refrigerators in which vaccines are stored have a maximum/minimum thermometer and that readings are taken on all working days.
- *Infection control:* Each GP practice must ensure that it has appropriate arrangements for infection control and decontamination. The content of infection control policies are a matter for each GP surgery. However, the National Institute for Health and Care Excellence (NICE) has published guidance about infection control in primary care.[22] While there is a measure of discretion, GP practices would have to have good reasons for adopting policies which departed from the infection control guidance published by NICE. In addition, infection control is one of the CQC fundamental standards under the Health and Social Care Act 2008 (Regulated Activities) Regulations 2014.[23]

  The Medical Protection Society (MPS) has identified the following as the most common breaches of infection control in GP practices, after having analysed data from more than 120 Clinical Risk Self Assessments of practices conducted in 2012:[24]

  a) the cleaning of premises was inadequate because no schedule of cleaning was available;
  b) reception staff were handling specimens at the reception desk;
  c) hand washing was not addressed within the practice;
  d) risks associated with clinical waste and the management of sharps. For example, not using pedal-operated clinical waste bins, clinical waste bins not being provided in the consulting room and inappropriate storage of clinical waste awaiting collection;
  e) GP practices were not providing spillage kits, either purchased or made up in-house, for dealing with spillages such as body fluids, blood and mercury (if applicable);
  f) failing to provide staff training on infection control;
  g) waiting room toys that were not cleaned routinely. The guidance observed that soft toys are hard to disinfect and tend to rapidly become re-contaminated after cleaning and that conversely, hard toys can be cleaned and disinfected easily.

  Their headline finding was that 85 per cent of those practices had some problems with infection control, which suggests that this an area of risk for many GP practices.
- *Duty of co-operation:* Paragraph 15 of Schedule 3 to the GMS Regs 2015 provides that GP practices which do not provide additional services, enhanced services or OOH services, either at all or for some

22 See www.nice.org.uk/guidance/cg139.

23 SI No 2936.

24 See www.medicalprotection.org/uk/practice-matters-issue-4/risk-alert-infection-control.

parts of the day or in relation to some services, must co-operate with those providers which do deliver those services for NHS patients. The GP practice must:

(a) co-operate, insofar as is reasonable, with any person responsible for the provision of that service or those services;
(b) comply in core hours with any reasonable request for information from such a person or from the Board relating to the provision of that service or those services; and
(c) in the case of out of hours services–
    (i) take reasonable steps to ensure that any patient who contacts the contractor's practice premises during the out of hours period is provided with information about how to obtain services during that period,
    (ii) ensure that the clinical details of all out of hours consultations received from the out of hours provider are reviewed by a clinician within the contractor's practice on the same working day as those details are received by the practice or, exceptionally, on the next working day,
    (iii) ensure that any information requests received from the out of hours provider in respect of any out of hours consultations are responded to by a clinician within the contractor's practice on the same day as those requests are received by the contractor's practice, or on the next working day,
    (iv) take all reasonable steps to comply with any systems which the out of hours provider has in place to ensure the rapid, secure and effective transmission of patient data in respect of out of hours consultations, and
    (v) agree with the out of hours provider a system for the rapid, secure and effective transmission of information about registered patients who, due to chronic disease or terminal illness, are predicted as more likely to present themselves for treatment during the out of hours period.

- *Handover requirements:* Where a contractor ceases to be required to provide a particular additional service, a particular enhanced service or out of hours services, either at all or in respect of some periods or some services, the GP practice is obliged to comply with any reasonable request for information relating to the provision of that service or those services made by NHS England or by any person with whom NHS England intends to enter into a contract for the provision of such services.

Management of the practice list of patients

18.81 As set out above, the primary statutory duty on NHS England is to make arrangements to meet the 'reasonable requirements' of patients for primary care services throughout England. That does not mean that NHS England has a duty to ensure that every single person is registered with a GP practice, but does mean that everyone must have reasonable access to a GP practice which is reasonably local to their home. Thus NHS England is responsible for the overall 'footprint' of GP practices but it is up to individual patients and GP practices to decide which patient is registered with which practice.

18.82 The GMS and PMS Regs 2015 make provision for GP practices to manage the admission of patients onto their list, either as a registered patient or temporary patient. The management of practice lists and patients wishing to be treated by practices is generally consigned to the domain of the GP practice's contractual obligations, except, for example, in circumstances where there are no GP practices accepting patients across a whole area, such that NHS England is in breach of its statutory duty to make arrangements for reasonable requirements.

18.83 GP practice lists may be 'open' for applications, or 'closed', meaning that the GP practice is not accepting applications for patients to join their list other than from immediate family members. As a general rule, GP practices are allowed to refuse applications from patients who are not resident in a particular area.

18.84 This section explores the legal rules which apply to GP practices admitting patients to their lists, removing patients from their lists and the powers of NHS England to force an NHS GP practice to take a patient onto their practice list.

Who are the patients to whom a GP practice is obliged to provide primary care services?

18.85 The word 'patient' is defined in reg 2 of the GMS Regs 2015 (and replicated materially in reg 3 of the PMS Regs 2015) as:

(a) a registered patient;
(b) a temporary resident;
(c) persons to whom the contractor is required to provide immediately necessary treatment under regulation 17(7) or (9) respectively;
(d) any other person to whom the contractor has agreed to provide services under the contract; and
(e) any person in respect of whom the contractor is responsible for the provision of out of hours services.

The nature of the services set out in (c), (d), (e) are explored in the section above.

18.86 Regulation 20(1)(c) of the GMS Regs 2015 and reg 13(1)(c) of the PMS Regs 2015 require every GMS and PMS contract to specify 'the persons to whom such services are to be provided'. These must be the patients as defined in reg 2 of the GMS Regs 2015. The obligations owed to the different types of patients are explored below.

The registered patients of the practice

18.87 Regulation 2 of the GMS Regs 2015 and reg 3 of the PMS Regs 2015 define a 'registered patient' of a GP practice as follows:

(a) a person who is recorded by the Board[25] as being on the contractor's list of patients; or
(b) a person whom the contractor has accepted for inclusion in its list of patients, whether or not notification of that acceptance has been received by the Board, and who has not been notified by the Board as having ceased to be on that list

25 'The Board' is a reference to NHS England.

18.88 There are two categories of patients or patients who are clearly included as registered patients with a GP practice, namely:

a) patients who are on the GP practice list held by NHS England (because the practice has notified NHS England that the person is on the practice list and NHS England have put that name on the list); and
b) patients who have been accepted by the practice into the practice list but where the practice has yet to pass their name on to NHS England.

18.89 A patient will remain on the practice list until his or her name is removed by NHS England. This will usually be because the patient has moved to another practice and thus is registered on the list of that other practice. A patient can only be on the list of one practice at a time (which can cause difficulties for students who have to decide whether to register with a GP practice at their home or at their place of study). If a patient gives notice to the GP practice they are leaving the practice but then changes his or her mind before NHS England gives effect to the removal, the patient will remain on the practice list.

18.90 At the time of publication, NHS England has sub-contracted the management of practice to a private company under a service contract. There are reports that service performance by this company is well below a level that GPs find acceptable. This may well be an area for future litigation as GP practices become exasperated with the failure of NHS England's agents to deliver on the contractual obligations around the management of patient lists.

18.91 The regulatory scheme is such that persons who have been removed from the list of a practice, for whatever reason, can only regain their status as a practice patient by a separate decision being made by NHS England to include a person's name on the practice list. One objective of this arrangement appears to be to ensure that disruptive or violent patients who are excluded from a practice list and are properly notified cannot claim that the practice has accepted them back as a result of an informal agreement. Once a notified former patient is excluded, the patient can only regain their status as a practice patient by getting onto the list for the practice held by NHS England. In practice, this will mean that the practice has to forward the relevant name to NHS England and ask that the patient be restored to the list of registered patients.

Temporary residents

18.92 A person can only be permanently on the list of one NHS GP practice at a time. However, a person may be in need of primary care services when temporarily away from the area in which he or she is registered as a GP. Both the GMS and PMS contracts enable patients to access services in such circumstances by registering with a GP as a 'temporary resident'.

18.93 Paragraph 20 of Schedule 3 to the GMS Regs 2015 and para 19 of Schedule 2 to the PMS Regs 2015 set out the scheme for dealing with temporary residents and the clauses that must be included within the contracts:

> (1) The contractor may, if the contractor's list of patients is open, accept a person as a temporary resident provided the contractor is satisfied that the person is–

(a) temporarily resident away from their normal place of residence and is not being provided with essential services (or their equivalent) under any other arrangement in the locality where that person is temporarily residing; or
(b) moving from place to place and not for the time being resident in any place.

(2) For the purposes of sub-paragraph (1), a person is to be regarded as temporarily resident in a place if, when that person arrives in that place, they intend to stay there for more than 24 hours but not for more than three months.

18.94 It is irrelevant whether the proposed temporary resident is registered with another GP practice (either as part of the NHS or in another part of the world) or is someone who is not registered with any GP practice. A person can thus apply to be accepted by a practice as a temporary resident if they have a GP in another part of the country and if they have no other GP. In practice, temporary residents are often patients who fall ill whilst on holiday, away from home for work or are staying with relatives. They can also be patients who have never registered with a GP and present on a very occasional basis, but do not wish to become permanent patients of a GP practice for any reason.

18.95 The proposed temporary resident is not required to be living on a temporary basis in the GP practice area. However, if the person is temporarily living outside the GP 'practice area', the contractor has the *right* to refuse to register the person as a temporary resident. See below for a further discussion on the definition of a GP practice area.

18.96 If the person intends to be resident in his or her present 'temporary' home for more than three months, then the person cannot be registered as a temporary resident. The only option here would be for the GP practice to register the patient as a permanent patient (and thus for them to give up their existing GP practice registration).

18.97 Once a person is registered as a temporary resident, the GP practice has the same range of duties to that patient as the GP practice has to all its other patients, and the CCG has the same range of duties to the patient regarding secondary care. These duties last for three months or such shorter period as is agreed between the temporary resident and the practice. This could be, for example, a two-week period during which a person is on holiday.

18.98 A GP practice is not obliged to continue to provide services to a temporary resident for as long as the patient wants. It is entitled to terminate its responsibility for a person accepted as a temporary resident before the end of three months provided a shorter period was agreed between the contractor and the patient and that period has expired. Hence, a GP practice is entitled to say to a temporary patient that he or she can be accepted as a temporary patient for, say, one month only (as long as that is consistent with the GP's duty of care to the patient). At the end of that period the contractor is entitled to give seven days' notice of that fact to the person, either orally or in writing, and the contractor's responsibility for that person will cease.

18.99 It is irrelevant whether the temporary resident is or is not usually, ordinarily or habitually resident in the UK at the time that he or she seeks primary care services from a GP, or is a UK citizen. A temporary resident will often be someone who is usually resident abroad. Although NHS services are provided primarily for the 'physical and mental health of the people of England' (see section 1(1) of the NHS Act 2006) there is nothing in the statutory scheme which requires a person to be a UK national or usually, ordinarily or habitually resident in the UK before that person can take advantage of NHS services. Hence, it is highly likely to be unlawful to refuse to register someone as a temporary resident solely on the grounds that the person is not usually, ordinarily or habitually resident in the UK.

How can patients join the list of a GP practice?

18.100 Before moving on to a discussion of the process by which patients may apply to become a permanent or temporary patient at a practice, it is necessary to discuss three concepts inherent to that issue.

What is the 'list' of patients?

18.101 First, what is it that one is talking about when discussing the 'list' of a GP practice? Primarily the duty to keep a list of registered patients for each GP practice falls on NHS England. Under para 17 of Part 2 of Schedule 3 to the GMS Regs 2015 and para 13 of Part 2 of Schedule 2 to the PMS Regs 2015, the practice contract must contain a term that requires NHS England to keep an up-to-date list of the patients who have been accepted by the contractor for inclusion in its list of patients and who have not subsequently been removed from that list or who have been assigned by NHS England to that contractor's list of patients.

18.102 This being said, in reality practices will keep their own lists of patients, which is an administrative necessity and thus GP practices manage the patients on that list accordingly. Applications to join a practice's list will be made to the practice, not NHS England. Under para 18 of Schedule 3 to the GMS Regs 2015, a contractor must give notice to NHS England as soon as it has accepted a patient onto its list. Thereafter, NHS England is required to include the patient in the list from the date on which the notice was received and give notice to that applicant (or their representative, see below).

Open or closed list

18.103 Second is whether a GP practice's list is 'open' or 'closed'. Under the GMS and PMS Regs 2015, unless they are an immediate family member of an existing patient, a person can only apply to become a patient of a practice if its list is open. If a practice list is open, the GP practice has no absolute duty to accept the patient onto its list. However, there is a defined list of grounds which must not be relied upon by a GP practice to refuse admission to its list and thus, in practice, a GP practice with an open list has little alternative but to accept virtually all applications from potential patients who live in the practice catchment area.

18.104 Whether, at the date on which the practice contract comes into force, the practice's list of patients is open or closed is something that the contract is required to specify under reg 20 of the GMS Regs 2015 and reg 13 of the PMS Regs 2015.

18.105 The circumstances in which a GP practice list may be 'closed' are discussed further below.

The 'practice area'

Overview

18.106 Third, reg 20 of the GMS Regs 2015 and reg 13 of the PMS Regs 2015 require a GP contract to specify the 'practice area' for the GP practice.

18.107 The purpose of the practice area is to create a geographical area outside of which the GP practice is entitled, as of right, to refuse to register patients on the grounds that the patient lives outside the area that the practice is intended to serve. However, a contractor is not obliged to refuse to register someone who lives outside the practice area. The practice can register a patient at a GMS practice regardless of whether that person lives within the practice area or not but, where the area is defined, the contractor is under no duty to do so. The practice retains the same obligations on providing home visits and so taking on patients that live far from the practice can impose additional obligations on the practice.

18.108 The GMS and PMS Regs 2015 (under para 21 of Schedule 3 and para 20 of Schedule 2, respectively) provide that an application by the patient can be refused because living outside the area gives the contractor 'reasonable grounds' to refuse to register the patient. However, the fact that the patient does not live in the contractor's practice area is not a 'reasonable ground' for refusing an application to become a temporary resident.

18.109 The regulations use the test as to whether a person 'lives' in the contractor's practice area. There is no definition of the meaning of 'lives' in the GMS or PMS Regs 2015, but it seems likely that this refers to a person's place of ordinary residence. It is well-established that a person can be ordinarily resident in more than one place at a time. However, the GMS and PMS schemes only permit an NHS patient to be registered with one GP practice at a time. Accordingly, individuals who live in more than one place need to decide where to register for primary care services. For example, students regularly register with a GP practice near their university and thus can only be treated during the vacation by registering as a temporary resident on the practice list at the place they reside outside term-time (which may be their parental home). If they re-register at their home practice, they will end up being removed from the practice list of their university residence.

18.110 GP practices will routinely identify their 'catchment area' by way of a map on their website, or a list of street names, so prospective patients can determine if they live within the practice area.

The 'outer-boundary area'

18.111 As well as the practice area, the GMS and PMS Regs 2015 have a separate concept of the 'outer-boundary area'.

18.112 There are instances of people who continue to be registered with a practice, despite living outside its practice area. As explained above, a GP practice is entitled (but not obliged) to register a person who lives outside the practice area. However, changes to the GMS contract in 2012 made provision for patients who were originally living inside the GP practice area but then moved to live in an area which was reasonably proximate to the practice but is nonetheless outside the GP practice area.

18.113 Under reg 20(3) of the GMS Regs 2015 and reg 13(2) of the PMS Regs 2015, a practice is not obliged to identify an outer practice area, but *may* identify one. If a patient who was living in the practice area moves into the outer-boundary area and would like to remain on the contractor's list of patients, they may remain on that list, if the contractor agrees. The regulations then provide that, once a patient remains on the list because of this provision, the outer boundary area is to be treated as if it were the practice area for the purposes of the application of any other terms and conditions of the practice contract in relation to that patient; in other words, they are not to be treated any differently or offered a lesser service as a result.

Applications to join a practice list

18.114 Applications to join a practice list are governed by para 18 of Part 2 of Schedule 3 to the GMS Regs 2015 and replicated in para 17 of Part 2 of Schedule 2 to the PMS Regs 2015.

18.115 Anyone can apply to join the practice list either as a permanent or temporary resident by 'delivering to the practice premises a medical card or an application signed (in either case) by the applicant or a person authorised by the applicant to sign on his behalf'. The application is made by the patient themselves if the person is an adult and is capable of making the application.

18.116 For children and adults who lack capacity, these regulations provide that:

> (4) An application may be made–
> (a) where the patient is a child, on behalf of the patient by–
> (i) either parent, or in the absence of both parents, the guardian or other adult who has care of the child,
> (ii) a person duly authorised by a local authority to whose care the child has been committed under the Children Act 1989, or
> (iii) a person duly authorised by a voluntary organisation by which the child is being accommodated under the provisions of the Children Act 1989; or
> (b) where the patient is an adult who lacks capacity to make such an application, or to authorise such an application to be made on their behalf, by–
> (i) a relative of that person,
> (ii) the primary carer of that person,
> (iii) a donee of a lasting power of attorney granted by that person, or
> (iv) a deputy appointed for that person by the court under the provisions of the Mental Capacity Act 2005.

18.117 A 'medical card' under reg 3 of the GMS Regs 2015 means 'a card issued by the Board or a Local Health Board, Health Authority, Health Board or Health and Social Services Board to a person for the purpose of enabling that person to obtain, or to establish entitlement to receive, primary medical services'. However, the regulations allow practices to use 'an application' as an alternative to a medical card. Therefore, any document which can reasonably be taken by the contractor as being an application by a person to be registered at the practice and is signed by or on behalf of the patient is sufficient to constitute an application by the prospective patient.

18.118 Once the contractor receives the application, the GP practice must decide whether to accept the patient onto the practice list as either a permanent patient or a temporary resident, or refuse to register the patient.

18.119 If the practice list is closed the only person who can be accepted onto the list is an 'immediate family member' of a registered patient, which is defined in reg 3 as:

(a) a spouse or civil partner;
(b) a person whose relationship with the registered patient has the characteristics of the relationship between spouses;
(c) a parent or step-parent;
(d) a son or daughter;
(e) a child of whom the registered patient is–
  (i) the guardian, or
  (ii) the carer duly authorised by the local authority to whose care the child has been committed under the Children Act 1989; or
(f) a grandparent . . .

18.120 This provision prevents a GP practice from having a closed list, but being selective about who is admitted to the practice in the period when the list is closed (so as to avoid a situation where, for example, only patients who are straightforward to manage are accepted onto the practice list). Only immediate family members can be added to a closed list regardless of where that person lives. However, there is no obligation on a GMS contracting practice to take an immediate family member who lives outside the practice area onto the list. In the case of immediate family members who live in the practice area, the practice needs to have reasonable grounds for refusing to take the person onto the list. Although this is not expressly stated in the regulations, the fact that the practice list is closed is capable of amounting to such a reason (depending on the circumstances).

18.121 If the practice list is open then, by virtue of para 21 of Schedule 3 to the GMS Regs 2015 and para 20 of Schedule 2 to the PMS Regs 2015:

(1) The contractor may only refuse an application made under paragraph 18 or 20 if the contractor has reasonable grounds for doing so which do not relate to the applicant's age, appearance, disability or medical condition, gender or gender reassignment, marriage or civil partnership, pregnancy or maternity, race, religion or belief, sexual orientation or social class.
(2) The reasonable grounds referred to in sub-paragraph (1) may, in the case of an application made under paragraph 18, include the ground that the applicant–
  (a) does not live in the contractor's practice area; or
  (b) lives in the outer boundary area (the area referred to in regulation 20(3)).

18.122 It follows that an NHS practice cannot refuse to admit a patient to its list either on a permanent basis or as a temporary resident because the patient suffers from a medical condition which will be time-consuming for the doctors working at the practice or will result in the practice having to prescribe expensive drugs or other treatment for the patient. Equally the patient cannot be refused admission to the practice list on grounds which might give rise to a free-standing discrimination claim under the Equality Act 2010, such as on the basis of race or sexual orientation. It should be noted, however, that although the grounds in reg 21(1) of the GMS Regs 2015 broadly correspond with the protected characteristics under the Equality Act, they are not identical.

18.123 This provision raises some interesting and potentially difficult questions as to whether GP practices can refuse to register patients with alcohol or drug problems. A GP practice would not be entitled to refuse to register a person because the person suffered from such an addiction, but may be entitled to refuse to register such a patient if the patient's conduct (related to his or her addiction) makes it difficult or impossible for the GP to be able to provide primary care services to the patient. This can be a difficult area in practice, and GP practices may well find it sensible to seek legal advice in borderline cases.

18.124 If a contractor refuses an application of a person to join the list, be that as a registered patient or temporary resident, then by reg 21(3) the contractor has 14 days to provide reasons in writing:

> . . . the contractor must give notice in writing of that refusal and the reasons for it to the applicant (or, in the case of a child or an adult who lacks capacity, to the person who made the application on their behalf) before the end of the period of 14 days beginning with the date of its decision to refuse.

What options do patients have if their application to join a practice list has been refused?

Appeals to NHS England

Overview

18.125 A patient who has been refused admission to a practice list by a GMS or PMS contractor (either on a permanent or temporary basis) is entitled to apply to NHS England to be admitted to the practice list, even if that list is closed, after the contractor has made the decision to refuse to permit the patient to be admitted to the list. The fact that the decision was made by the GP practice for a good reason (as the GP practice sees matters) does not prevent the patient from having this right.

18.126 Paragraphs 38–43 of Schedule 3 to the GMS Regs 2015 and paras 37–42 of Schedule 2 to the PMS Regs 2015 provide how the decision is to be made by NHS England when a patient appeals against the refusal by the practice to admit a patient to its list (either permanently or on a temporary basis).

18.127 The first step in this process is that the patient is required to approach the practice to apply to be admitted to the list, and the practice is required to make the initial decision. NHS England has no power to impose a patient on a practice unless the patient has first applied and been refused admission to the practice (either on a permanent basis or as a temporary patient).

18.128 If the practice list is closed, there are only very limited circumstances in which NHS England is entitled to require a practice to take on a new patient. The scheme for requiring admission of a patient to a closed list is looked at in detail in the section of this chapter relating to closed practice lists.

18.129 If the practice list is open, NHS England has a discretion to decide whether to require a practice to accept a patient onto its list or to accept a patient as a temporary resident. The decision is generally made on paper by NHS England officials. Where the list is open, in making that decision, the terms of the contract (as mandated by GMS Regs 2015 Sch 3 para 40) require NHS England to take account of the following factors:

a) *The preferences and circumstances of the person.* The 'preferences' of the patient to be admitted to the practice list are a material factor, but they are not conclusive. NHS England is also required to take account of the 'circumstances of the person', which in practice must mean such of the circumstances as are known to NHS England and the practice. There can be no duty on the patient to disclose all of their personal circumstances but clearly NHS England can only take account of circumstances that are known.
b) *The distance between the person's place of residence and the contractor's practice premises.* The usual significance of this will be that the nearer the patient lives to the practice premises (or one of the practice premises), the stronger the case that can be made for the patient being admitted to that particular practice.
c) *Any request made by any contractor to remove the person from its list of patients within the preceding period of six months starting on the date on which the application for assignment is received by the Board.* It is a relevant factor as to whether the practice has asked NHS England to remove the person from the list within the previous six months and the circumstances which led to that request being made (whether it was granted or not). The person may be applying to be re-admitted to the list after NHS England agreed to remove the patient from the list. Alternatively, it is possible that the request was refused but that the patient had been removed from the practice list for a different reason and is now seeking to rejoin the list.
d) The wording under para 40(d) requires NHS England to take into account whether, during the preceding period of six months starting on the date on which the application for assignment is received by the Board, the patient has been removed from the list of patients of any NHS GP practice either at the request of the contractor or because the patient had been violent.
e) Para 40(e) requires NHS England to take into account whether, in a case where the patient has been removed from the list of patients of any NHS GP practice because the patient has been violent, the contractor has appropriate facilities to deal with such patients.
f) NHS England is required to take such other matters into account as it considers relevant.

18.130 There is no provision in the rules for an oral hearing, but NHS England is a public body making a decision which potentially affects the European Convention on Human Rights (ECHR) Article 8 rights of the patient. It would be required to follow a fair process in reaching the decision. The procedural requirements of this decision have not been tested in the courts, but are likely to necessitate:

a) giving the person the opportunity in writing (or to speak with an NHS England official if writing is not appropriate for any reason) to explain why he or she wishes to be included on the practice list;
b) giving the practice the opportunity to explain why the person has been refused admission to the list;
c) giving both the practice and the patient the chance to see and comment on the observations made by the other before a decision is made;
d) taking reasonable steps to consider any other relevant information provided by the patient or any third party; and
e) although this is not expressly stated in the regulations, it seems highly likely that a fair decision could only be given by NHS England if reasons are given for the decision. Those reasons should explain how the decision-maker has taken account of the various factors set out above and the weight given to each factor. Some weight should be given by the decision-maker to every factor because each factor is one which is required to be included by the GMS Regs 2015. However, provided some weight is attached to each factor, the decision-maker is entitled to exercise a wide margin of discretion in reaching the view as to which factor or factors are more important than other factors in the particular circumstances of each case.

18.131 There is no right of appeal provided within the GMS or PMS Regs 2015 for either the patient or the practice against the decision of NHS England to order or to not order a patient to be admitted to a GP practice list. If NHS England refused the patient's appeal, that decision may be the subject of a challenge by way of judicial review if the patient considered that the decision was made unlawfully. However, this would not be an appeal on the merits, because the regulations make NHS England the discretionary decision-making body. It could only be a challenge asserting that the decision was made in an unlawful way by, for example, failing to take account of one of the mandatory factors, or was an irrational decision.

What can a practice do if it disagrees with NHS England's decision?

18.132 If NHS England decides in favour of the patient and the GP practice still disagrees with the decision, it has two options. First, it may accept the decision but then exercise its power to remove the patient from the list. Removal of patients from the practice list is considered below. This is a high-risk strategy which may well be successfully challenged by the patient (assuming that there are no new grounds to justify removal).

18.133 Second, if the practice believed that the decision had been taken on an improper basis (as opposed to a decision on the merits with which they disagreed) it may be possible for the practice to refer the matter to the NHS Resolution under the contractual dispute resolution process. The details of the dispute resolution process are considered in chapter 11. However, the NHS Resolution ought to recognise that decision-making about this matter is given to NHS England, and accordingly it will only look to see whether the decision has been properly taken by NHS England.

The NHS Resolution ought not to attempt to reconsider the decision on its merits, but only ask itself whether NHS England has reached a proper decision. However, the patient would remain on the practice list and thus must be provided with general practice services until (at least) the NHS Resolution has reached a decision.

Other remedies or routes of challenge for patients

18.134 In theory, it is possible for a patient who feels their application has been refused on grounds which constitute discrimination under the Equality Act 2010 to commence a discrimination claim under that Act in the county court. There is some overlap between the contractual obligations of the GP practice not to refuse a patient on specified grounds and the protected characteristics under the Equality Act. However, the contractual grounds are wider because these include appearance or social class and any medical condition, whether it led to the patient being disabled or not.

18.135 It would be difficult for a patient to judicially review the decision of the GP practice to refuse his or her application if it had not appealed to NHS England because the patient would have an alternative remedy and thus it could be argued that permission should be refused because judicial review should only operate as a remedy of last resort.

18.136 The patient may feel aggrieved if he or she believes that the practice has turned down an application on grounds that are impermissible under the GP contract (such as a refusal based on the patient's medical condition). However, it is hard to see how a patient can enforce the terms of the contract because the practice's contractual obligations are owed to the commissioner, ie NHS England (and potentially also the CCG) but not to the patient. Further, the standard form of contract excludes any right for a third party (such as a patient) to enforce the terms of the contract (thereby excluding any rights the patient may have claimed under the Contracts (Rights of Third Parties) Act 1999. However, in making the decision as to whether a patient can join an NHS GP practice, it is probable that the GP practice is acting as a public body and hence, if all other obstacles could be overcome, a claim to quash the refusal to admit the patient may be possible as a judicial review action.

18.137 However, a patient who was refused admission to a practice list in a manner which amounted to a breach of the GMC Code of Conduct (which is likely to be rare) could report the GPs to the General Medical Council (GMC). The issue of reports to the GMC is considered in more detail below in relation to the removal of patients from a GP list, but it could apply equally to a refusal to take a patient onto a list in the first place.

18.138 If NHS England considered that the practice had refused one or more patients access to the patient list in circumstances which amounted to a breach of contract (because the practice did not have good reasons for the refusal), NHS England would be obliged to enforce the contract by allowing an appeal. If the practice still refused to accept the patient, it would be entitled to serve a Remedial Notice on the practice.[26]

26 See chapter 11.

Removal of patients from a practice list

18.139 The removal of patients from the lists of GP practices is a hugely contentious area. It is the subject of a specific paragraph in the GMC Code of Conduct and several bodies including the British Medical Association (BMA) and the GMC have published guidance on this issue.[27] There can be particularly difficult issues arising from both violent patients and patients who make excessive demands upon limited practice resources by, for example, seeking a GP appointment several times a week without proper justification.

GMC professional standards

18.140 The GMC's *Good medical practice* code of conduct provides:

> 62. You should end a professional relationship with a patient only when the breakdown of trust between you and the patient means you cannot provide good clinical care to the patient.[28]

18.141 Thus a doctor will potentially act in breach of the GMC Code of Practice by ending a relationship with a patient unless two things are present, namely:

a) there must be a breakdown of trust between the doctor and the patient; and
b) the doctor must be unable to provide good clinical care to the patient as a result of that breakdown.

18.142 Asking NHS England to remove a patient from a practice list because of one or more complaints is a breach of the professional standards unless the number and/or nature of the complaints means that there has been a breakdown of trust between the patient and the doctor. Examples given for situations where there may have been a breakdown of trust include where a patient has been violent, threatening or abusive to their GP or a member of practice staff; stolen from their GP or the premises; persistently acted inconsiderately or unreasonably; or made a sexual advance.

18.143 It is also clear, even in the face of such scenarios, that a doctor must work at a relationship with a patient and cannot seek to exclude the patient at the first sign of difficulties. A warning must usually be given, and then the doctor must attempt to make the relationship work before concluding that it is the interests of both parties for medical care for the patient to be provided by someone else. A GP is also advised to discuss the decision with (a more senior) colleague. However, there will be occasions where the patient has acted in a way that leads a doctor genuinely to conclude that trust and confidence has broken down to such a degree that the doctor cannot continue to provide medical services to the patient. In such circumstances, it is in the interests of the doctors, the patient and the rest of the patients served by the practice for the patient to be moved to another practice or provided with primary care services in another way.

27 See the BMA guidance: www.bma.org.uk/advice/employment/gp-practices/service-provision/removal-of-patients-from-gp-lists.

28 The associated guidance is found here: www.gmc-uk.org/Ending_your_professional_relationship_with_a_patient.pdf_58834078.pdf.

Grounds for removal of the practice list under the regulations

18.144 The GMS and PMS Regulations, however, do provide for a number of special situations in which a patient can be removed from a practice list without there being a breakdown of trust between the doctor and the patient, including when patients are violent.

18.145 These grounds are fairly numerous and are set out in Part 2 of Schedule 3 to the GMS Regs 2015 and Part 2 of Schedule 2 to the PMS Regs 2015. The exact conditions and requirements of each ground are not explored in detail here, and readers should go to the regulations for more information, but they include removal of a patient from the list:

a) on discretionary grounds by the practice (discussed in further detail below);
b) when the patient's period as a temporary resident expires;
c) following the death of a registered patient;
d) at the patient's request;
e) when a patient registers with another practice;
f) when a patient moves out of the practice area (although a practice is entitled to keep a patient on its list even if a patient moves out of the practice area);
g) when a patient's address is unknown to NHS England and a notice period of six months has expired;
h) when a patient is sentenced to more than two years in prison (the rationale being that specialist services for prisoners are commissioned by NHS England and thus this aims to avoid double funding);
i) when a patient joins HM Forces (again the rationale for this is that specialist services for members of HM Forces can access services specially commissioned for them by NHS England);
j) when a patient is abroad for more than three months;
k) when a patient who has registered as a temporary resident elsewhere remains in that location for a long term basis and thus now 'lives' in the practice area where they registered as a temporary resident;
l) if the patient was receiving services by virtue of being a pupil at a (usually residential) school and is no longer on the roll of that school;
m) if the patient is violent.

Removal of violent patients from GP lists

18.146 The last of these categories, violent patients, merits further consideration.

18.147 There is a specific scheme under para 25 of Schedule 3 to the GMS Regs 2015 and replicated in para 24 of Schedule 2 to the PMS Regs 2015 for removal from the list of patients who are violent 'with immediate effect'. It provides:

> (1) Where a contractor wants a person to be removed from its list of patients with immediate effect on the grounds that–
> (a) the person has committed an act of violence against any of the persons specified in sub-paragraph (2) or has behaved in such a way that any of those persons has feared for their safety; and
> (b) the contractor has reported the incident to the police,

the contractor must give notice to the Board in accordance with sub-paragraph (3).

(2) The persons specified in this sub-paragraph are–

(a) the contractor, where the contractor is an individual medical practitioner;

(b) in the case of a contract with two or more persons practising in partnership, a partner in the partnership;

(c) in the case of a contract with a company limited by shares, a person who is both a legal and beneficial owner of shares in that company;

(d) a member of the contractor's staff;

(e) a person engaged by the contractor to perform or assist in the performance of services under the contract; or

(f) any other person present–

(i) on the contractor's practice premises, or

(ii) in the place where services were provided to the person under the contract.

(3) Notice under sub-paragraph (1) may be given by any means but, if not in writing, must subsequently be confirmed in writing before the end of a period of seven days beginning with the date on which notice was given.

(4) The Board must acknowledge in writing receipt of a request for removal from the contractor under sub-paragraph (1).

(5) A removal requested in accordance with sub-paragraph (1) takes effect at the time at which the contractor–

(a) makes a telephone call to the Board; or

(b) sends or delivers the notice to the Board.

(6) Where, under this paragraph, the contractor has given notice to the Board that it wants to have a person removed from its list of patients, the contractor must inform that person of that fact unless–

(a) it is not reasonably practicable for the contractor to do so; or

(b) the contractor has reasonable grounds for believing that to do so would–

(i) be harmful to that person's physical or mental health, or

(ii) put the safety of any person specified in sub-paragraph (2) at risk.

(7) Where a person is removed from the contractor's list of patients under this paragraph, the Board must give that person notice in writing of that removal.

(8) The contractor must record the removal of any person from its list of patients under this paragraph and the circumstances leading to that removal in the medical records of the person removed.'

18.148 The notification can be given to NHS England orally or in writing but, if given orally, must be confirmed in writing within seven days. Emails are sufficient to constitute written confirmation.

18.149 There is no precise definition in the contract of the phrase 'committed an act of violence'. However, the World Health Organisation published a report on *Violence and health* in 2002. This defines violence as follows:

> The intentional use of physical force or power, threatened or actual, against oneself, another person, or against a group or community, that either results in or has a high likelihood of resulting in injury, death, psychological harm, maldevelopment or deprivation.

18.150 This seems an appropriate test against which to judge the act complained about. It can include a threat of violence if the threatened act, if carried out, would result in injury. The alternative formulation of conduct which can lead to a patient being removed instantly from a practice list is that the patient must have 'behaved in such a way that any such person has feared for his safety'. This test has a potentially wider scope because it focuses on the reaction of the person to the actions of the patient and not just on the actions of the patient himself or herself.

18.151 It is important to note that in order to come within the terms of the immediate removal provisions in the contract, the incident must be reported to the police. The trigger, however, is a report to the police and not any defined action by the police themselves. Thus a police response which suggests that no criminal offence has been committed does not prevent the GP practice from relying on the incident.

18.152 The regulations provide that a removal shall take effect at the time the contractor makes the telephone call to NHS England, or sends or delivers the notification to NHS England. It follows that the duty on the contractor to provide continuing medical care to the patient ceases immediately when the contractor has made a report to NHS England of violence and made a 'request' for the patient to be removed from the practice list. If the patient was in need of emergency care, then the contractor would have a duty to continue to provide emergency care to the patient in the same way as emergency care is required for any other individual, whether a registered patient or not. However, there is no contractual duty on the GP practice to take steps to ensure that the violent patient is able to access alternative primary medical services before the patient is removed from the list.

18.153 However, under the Primary Medical Services (Directed Enhanced Services) Directions 2017, NHS England is obligated to establish, operate and, as appropriate, revise a Violent Patient Scheme. The Violent Patient Scheme was introduced as a Directed Enhanced Service in 2004, with the aim of providing a secure environment in which patients who have been violent can still receive primary care services. Typically, NHS England commissions these services via APMS contracts with single providers for a geographical area. These services can include security escorts who accompany violent patients to appointments to protect the safety of GPs and other staff.

Discretionary removal of patients from a GP list

Overview

18.154 There are, of course, numerous reasons why a GP practice may wish to remove a patient from a practice list. The BMA guidance and the GMC Code of Practice make it clear that this should be an exceptional and rare event.

18.155 Both GMS and PMS contracts are required to contain terms which prevent a GP practice applying to NHS England to remove a patient for any of the following reasons:

- age;
- appearance;
- disability or medical condition;
- gender or gender reassignment;
- marriage or civil partnership;

- pregnancy or maternity;
- race;
- religion or belief;
- sexual orientation;
- social class.

18.156 The approach of the GMS and PMS Regs 2015 (paras 24 of Schedule 3 and para 23 of Schedule 2, respectively) is generally to permit a contractor to require NHS England to remove a patient from the practice list when:

a) the contactor has a good reason for wanting to remove the patient (the reason cannot be a prohibited reason);
b) (save in a specified set of cases) the patient has been warned about the conduct which led to the decision and has failed to heed the warning; and
c) the patient is generally entitled to know the reason that the GP wants to remove the patient from the practice list.

18.157 However, a practice will continue to have clinical responsibility for a patient until the removal of the patient comes into effect in accordance with the contractual scheme described below. The practice has a full duty to provide services to the patient until the removal takes effect.

The warning for the patient

18.158 The first stage in the process of removing a patient from a GP practice list is that a warning has to be given to the patient about the patient's conduct which is causing the practice concern and which may lead to the practice seeking to have the patient removed. The regulations provide that:[29]

> (3) Except in the circumstances specified in sub-paragraph (4), a contractor may only request the removal of a person from its list of patients under sub-paragraph (1) if, before the end of the period of 12 months beginning with the date of the contractor's request to the Board, the contractor has–
> (a) warned that person of the risk of being removed from that list; and
> (b) explained to that person the reasons for this.

18.159 There are a limited number of exceptions to the need to warn the patient before a request is made to NHS England to remove the patient from the practice list:

> (4) The circumstances specified in this sub-paragraph are that–
> (a) the reason for the removal relates to a change of address;
> (b) the contractor has reasonable grounds for believing that the giving of such a warning would–
> (i) be harmful to the person's physical or mental health, or
> (ii) put at risk the safety of one or more of the persons specified in sub-paragraph (5); or
> (c) the contractor considers that it is not otherwise reasonable or practical for a warning to be given.

18.160 The persons specified in subparagraph (5) are as follows:

29 GMS Regs 2015 Sch 3 para 24 and PMS Regs 2015 Sch 2 para 23.

(a) the contractor, where the contractor is an individual medical practitioner;
(b) in the case of a contract with two or more persons practising in a partnership, a partner in the partnership;
(c) in the case of a contract with a company limited by shares, a person who is both a legal and beneficial owner of shares in that company;
(d) a member of the contractor's staff;
(e) a person engaged by the contractor to perform or assist in the performance of services under the contract; or
(f) any other person present–
 (i) on the practice premises, or
 (ii) in the place where services are being provided to the patient under the contract.

18.161 The contractor is then required to keep a written record of: a) the date of any warning given in accordance with subparagraph (3) and the reasons for giving such a warning as explained to the person concerned; or b) the reason why no such warning was given.

Notifying NHS England and the patient

18.162 Once a warning has been given and the GP practice reaches the view that it has not been heeded, or if the contractor considers that it is entitled to dispense with a warning in accordance with the above provisions, the regulations provide that the contractor should write to NHS England saying that it 'wants' to remove the patient. At the same time the GP practice is required to notify the patient of the *specific reasons* for requesting removal. Those reasons cannot be any of the prohibited reasons.

18.163 Subject to these specific limitations, there are a wide range of potential reasons why a practice could seek to have a patient removed from its list. The most obvious reasons are that the patient has moved out of the practice area or that the doctors do not feel able to continue to provide services to the patient. Some guidance on reasons is provided in reg 24(2) of the GMS Regs 2015 (replicated in the PMS Regs 2015), which provides that:

> . . . where, in the reasonable opinion of the Contractor, the circumstances of the removal are such that it is not appropriate for a more specific reason to be given; and there has been an irrevocable breakdown in the relationship between the patient and the Contractor, the reason given under subparagraph (1) may consist of a statement that there has been such a breakdown.

18.164 This language echoes the grounds on which a doctor can terminate a relationship with a patient in the GMC Code. The NHS practice contract does not give the patient a right to object to the proposed removal or to challenge the factual basis of the decision to remove him or her from the practice list. The provisions in the contract treat this matter as one solely to be decided between the practice and NHS England. There is no legal right for a patient to object to being removed from a practice list.

Removal takes effect

18.165 Where notification is given to NHS England that a practice wishes to remove a patient from its list, there is no provision for a separate decision to be made by NHS England as to whether the practice has properly made out a case to have the patient removed. The next step is that the removal takes effect automatically on the date when the patient is registered with another practice or eight days after the notice is sent to NHS England, whichever is the sooner unless the patient is being treated at intervals of less than seven days. If the patient is in receipt of medical treatment at less than seven-day intervals, the removal does not take effect until the eighth day after NHS England receives notification from the contractor that the person no longer needs such treatment, or on the date on which the person is registered with another provider of essential services, whichever is the sooner.

18.166 This scheme seeks to preserve the balance between the interests of the contractor who wishes to have the patient removed from the practice list, and the interests of the patient who may have a need for ongoing medical treatment. It, however, has the potential to cause a difficulty in the case of a patient who has a chronic condition which will require treatment at less than seven-day intervals indefinitely. The patient is under no obligation to seek out a new GP practice and cannot be registered with a new practice unless he or she makes an application to join the list of that practice. If the patient prefers to stay with his or her existing practice, then the patient cannot be compelled to join another practice. The contractor continues to have a full duty to provide medical treatment to the patient until the removal notice takes effect, and cannot reduce the level of input for the patient because a removal has been requested. In these circumstances, a mediation may be the appropriate way forward if mutually agreed.

18.167 The GP is a contractor who seeks to discharge NHS England's statutory duty to make arrangements for patients to have access to primary care services. Accordingly, any public law action by a patient who is left without access to GP services would have to be against NHS England and not the GP practice. However, that could only be based on an overall alleged failure by NHS England to provide primary care services in a particular area, and so could be cured by NHS England offering to arrange for the patient to be registered at another practice or offering the GP services under arrangements for patients who are excluded from GP practices generally in an area. It is therefore difficult, if not impossible, to see how a patient could construct a cause of public law action arising out of the decision of a GP practice to remove a patient from its list of registered patients (unless that left the patient with no possible alternative provision). The patient's only remedies appear to be to sue in defamation or to complain to the GMC.

18.168 If the patient is removed from the practice list pursuant to this scheme, NHS England has a duty to write to both the patient and the contractor to inform them that the patient has been removed and the date of removal. However, NHS England does not need to explain the reasons for the patient's removal, since this will usually have already been explained by the contractor to the patient.

18.169 NHS England and the contracting GP are required to keep proper records relating to the removal of patients from a list of registered patients including, in the case of the GP practice, proper records of any warnings that have been given in advance of any removal.

Closure and reopening of GP practice lists

18.170 GP practice list sizes vary enormously, but it is not in the interests of patients or doctors for a GP practice to have too many patients and not enough doctors. A GP practice has a contractual and professional duty to deliver services of an acceptable quality for patients, and this will not be possible if the GP practice does not have enough capacity. As referenced above, there is often talk of a 'crisis' in general practice, with GPs struggling to cope with overwhelming demand for their services. This is particularly problematic where GPs retire and cannot be replaced, leaving the remaining partners with responsibility for a list that is too large for them to manage properly.

18.171 One way of managing demand is for a GP practice to close its list to new patients. However, a closure is assumed in the regulations to be a strictly temporary measure while the GP practice takes the necessary steps to increase its capacity to deliver services to patient. The regulations do not make provision for the present (possibly chronic) shortage of GPs which inevitably means that some practices are simply unable to recruit and thus are left with lists that are too large on a semi-permanent basis.

18.172 Lists are held by NHS England and not the individual practice, and therefore the decision on any closure application is strictly a decision for NHS England and not the GP practice. Although it is becoming increasingly common for GP practices to make requests to NHS England/CCGs to close their lists, it is understood by the authors that a sizeable proportion of these requests are refused. It seems likely that this reluctance to allow GP practices to close their lists is a result of NHS England not wanting to prevent new patients having a practice with which they can register. However, that decision could be the subject of an action by a GP practice (probably to the NHS Resolution) that felt that it had done everything reasonable to be able to staff up the practice and had failed to recruit sufficient GPs.

How can practices apply to close their list?

18.173 The scheme for closure of GP practice lists is found in Part 3 of Schedule 3 to the GMS Regs 2015 and Part 3 of Schedule 2 to the PMS Regs 2015.

Application

18.174 The first step when a contractor wants to close its list of patients is to send a written application to that effect to NHS England. The application must contain the following information:

(a) the options which the contractor has considered, rejected or implemented in an attempt to alleviate the difficulties which the contractor has encountered in respect of its open list and, if any of the options were implemented, the level of success in reducing or extinguishing such difficulties;

(b) details of any discussions between the contractor and its patients and a summary of those discussions including whether or not, in the opinion of those patients, the list of patients should be closed;

(c) details of any discussions between the contractor and the other contractors in the contractor's practice area and a summary of the opinion of the other contractors as to whether or not the list of patients should be closed;
(d) the period of time, being a period of not less than three months and not more than 12 months, during which the contractor wants its list of patients to be closed;
(e) any reasonable support from the Board which the contractor considers would enable its list of patients to remain open or would enable the period of the proposed closure to be minimised;
(f) any plans which the contractor may have to alleviate the difficulties mentioned in the application during the period of the proposed closure in order for that list to re-open at the end of that period without the existence of those difficulties; and
(g) any other information which the contractor considers ought to be drawn to the attention of the Board.

18.175 NHS England must acknowledge receipt of the application within seven days from when it receives the application. It must consider that application and make requests for any other information it requires to determine it.

Discussions

18.176 NHS England must then enter into discussions with the practice, about what support it can provide or any changes that can be made, with both parties doing everything possible to keep the list open. The Local Medical Committee (LMC) may be invited at any stage during these discussions to attend any meetings that have been arranged. Also, NHS England may consult anyone who might be affected by the closure of the list, and if so, must provide the practice with a summary of any views expressed. NHS England must give the practice the opportunity to comment on all the information relating to the application before they make their decision.

18.177 The practice may withdraw its application at any time before NHS England makes its decision. This must be made within 21 days from the date it received the application (or within a longer period if both parties agree).

Decision

18.178 The decision by NHS England will be either to:

a) approve the application and set the dates of closure and reopening of the list; or
b) reject the application.

18.179 A practice will not be able to make another application to close its list within 12 months of the date of this decision unless the application has been rejected (in which case different time limits apply) or there has been a change in circumstances affecting the ability of the practice to deliver services under its contract.

Approval

18.180 A decision by NHS England to give approval to an application to close a list of patients must be sent in writing to the practice as soon as possible.

This should also be copied at the same time to others who were involved in this process, such as the LMC and/or anyone affected by the list closure who was consulted.

18.181 The closure notice must include:

a) the period of time the list will be closed, which must be either the period stated in the practice's application, or a period agreed subsequently. In either case, this must be three months or more, but cannot be longer than 12 months;
b) the date the list will close; and
c) the date the list will reopen (which may change should the practice and NHS England agree that the closure period will be extended or the list will reopen sooner).

Rejection

18.182 A decision by NHS England to reject an application to close a list of patients must be sent in writing to the practice as soon as possible. This should also be copied at the same time to others who were involved in this process, such as the LMC and/or anyone who was consulted.

18.183 A practice will not be able to make another application to close its list within three months of the date of NHS England's decision to reject an application, or the date of any final determination in a dispute on this matter, whichever is the later. This time limit will not apply where there has been a change in circumstances affecting the ability of the practice to deliver services under its contract.

18.184 Although the regulations do not provide that NHS England has a duty to give reasons, there is probably a common law duty on NHS England to do so.

18.185 A practice that disagrees with the rejection of its application to close its list could refer the matter to the NHS Resolution under the contractual NHS dispute resolution provisions.

Extension of the closure period

18.186 A practice may apply to have the closure period extended. The application must be made in writing at least eight weeks in advance of the date the list will reopen. The application to extend must include:

a) any options the practice has considered, rejected or implemented to try to relieve the difficulties it has encountered during the closure period and, if any of these options were implemented, the level of success in reducing or eliminating these difficulties;
b) the period of time during which the practice wishes its list to remain closed, which must not be more than 12 months;
c) any reasonable support from NHS England which the practice considers would enable its list to reopen or would enable the period of proposed extension of closure to be minimised;
d) details of any plans the practice may have to reduce or eliminate the difficulties mentioned in their application to extend the closure which would allow their list to reopen when this period elapses; and
e) any other information which the practice considers necessary to bring to the attention of NHS England.

18.187 NHS England must acknowledge receipt of the application within seven days of receiving it. It must consider the application and may request any information from the practice to enable it to do so. NHS England may enter into discussions with the practice, about what support it can provide or any changes that can be made, with both parties doing everything possible to enable the list to reopen.

18.188 Within 14 days of the receipt of the application to extend the closure period, NHS England must make a decision either to approve or reject it.

18.189 Where NHS England approves an application to extend the closure period, it must notify the practice in writing as soon as possible. A copy of the decision letter should be sent to others who were involved in discussions on the original list closure application. This can include the LMC and/or anyone affected by the list closure who was consulted. The extended closure notice must include:

a) the period of time the list will be closed, which must be either the period stated in the practice's application to extend the closure period, or a period agreed in writing between NHS England and the practice subsequently. In either case, this must be three months or more, but not longer than 12 months;
b) the date from when the closure period will be extended; and
c) the date the list will reopen.

18.190 GP practices that disagree with decisions made by NHS England on patient list matters can invoke the NHS disputes resolution process by registering a dispute with NHS Resolution.

18.191 NHS England has published guidance on list closure entitled, *Managing closed lists*.[30] This guidance summarises the statutory provisions but provides little additional information about how the processes should be handled.

Assignment of patients to closed lists

18.192 Under the regulations, there is a special procedure that NHS England must adopt (under Part 4 of Schedule 3 to the GMS Regs 2015 and replicated under Part 4 of Schedule 2 to the PMS Regs 2015) if it wishes to assign patients to the list of a GP practice that is closed. NHS England can only do this after having constituted a special assessment panel to determine whether new patients may be assigned to the GP practice in question, and if that that determination has not been overturned by the secretary of state, to whom a right of review lies. Finally, before doing so, NHS England must have entered into discussions with the GP practice if required under the regulations.

30 See www.england.nhs.uk/wp-content/uploads/2013/07/mng-close-list.pdf.

Services for which GPs can charge fees

Introduction

18.193 NHS services are generally free at the point of use for patients. However, the NHS has always imposed charges for some services which are not included within NHS commissioned care or where regulations require charges to be imposed.[31] There are also other functions undertaken by NHS doctors which are outside their NHS duties and hence attract a fee. It follows that the full legal position is somewhat more nuanced. The requirement that services should generally be provided free of charge is set out in section 1(4) of the NHS Act 2006, which provides:

> The services provided as part of the health service in England must be free of charge except in so far as the making and recovery of charges is expressly provided for by or under any enactment, whenever passed.

18.194 There are a number of areas where regulations provide that charges may be imposed for NHS services including:

- prescriptions;
- dental services;
- optical services;
- contraceptive services;
- hospital services for persons who are not usually ordinarily resident in the UK.

18.195 Primary care services provided under a GMS or PMS contract to patients on the practice list or temporary residents are required to be provided free of charge. As outlined above, the GMS and PMS contracts also provide that GP practices have a contractual obligation to provide a range of other services to patients. However, GP practices are (almost all) private sector businesses that have contracted with NHS England to provide defined primary care services to a defined group of patients and to provide a defined level of emergency medical services in limited circumstances. If a registered patient or temporary resident seeks primary care services from an NHS GP practice outside the terms of the contract held by that practice, the NHS GP practice has no obligation to provide services to that person. A GP may choose to do so; however, he or she may not charge for treatment provided outside the GP practice contract unless the service falls within a limited categories of specific services.

The general prohibition on an NHS GP practice charging fees to patients

18.196 The general prohibition on an NHS GP practice charging fees for services provided to patients is set out in reg 24 of the GMS Regs 2015, which provides:

31 Charges are and remain a hugely contentious area. The original Minister of Health, Rt Hon Nye Bevan, resigned from the government over the imposition of charges for drugs prescribed by GPs.

> (2) The contractor must not, either itself or through any other person, demand or accept from any of its patients a fee or other remuneration, for its own benefit or for the benefit of another person for–
> (a) the provision of any treatment whether under the contract or otherwise; or
> (b) any prescription or repeatable prescription for any drug, medicine or appliance,
> except in the circumstances set out in Regulation 25.

There is a like provision in reg 18 of the PMSC Regs 2015.

18.197 The prohibition covers any charge which is made for the provision of treatment or any prescription to a patient, not just treatment that the GP is required to provide under the practice contract. A GP practice cannot therefore charge a third party, such as an employer or the parent of a child, for medical treatment provided to a patient.

18.198 A 'patient' in these circumstances is defined as set out above.

18.199 The general prohibition on imposing charges for treatment means that a GP with a GMS or PMS contract cannot charge a 'patient' for the delivery of any form of medical treatment even if that treatment is not provided as part of NHS funded healthcare. Thus a GP who provides, for example, osteopathy, acupuncture or homeopathy outside of NHS-funded care is prohibited from charging 'patients' (as that term is defined above) for the provision of such a service. There is nothing to prevent a GP practice from offering such services on a commercial basis to persons who are not patients of the practice and do not otherwise come within the definition of being a 'patient' under the GMS or PMS Regulations. However, in summary, reg 24 provides that a GP practice which holds an NHS contract cannot charge for offering any form of medical treatment (even outside NHS services) to patients of an NHS practice.

Medical certificates

18.200 The GMS and PMS Regs 2015 contain a list of statutory certificates that GP practices are required to provide without charge. Regulation 22 of the GMS Regs 2015 provides:

> (1) Subject to paragraphs (2) and (3), a contract must contain a term which has the effect of requiring the contractor to issue any medical certificate of a description prescribed in column 1 of Schedule 2 under, or for the purposes of, the enactments specified in relation to that certificate in column 2 of that Schedule if that certificate is reasonably required under or for the purposes of the enactments specified in relation to that certificate.
> (2) A certificate referred to in paragraph (1) must be issued free of charge to a patient or to a patient's personal representatives.
> (3) A certificate must not be issued where, for the condition to which the certificate relates, the patient is–
> (a) being attended by a medical practitioner who is not–
> (i) engaged or employed by the contractor,
> (ii) in the case of a contract with two or more persons practising in a partnership, one of those persons, or
> (iii) in the case of a contract with a company limited by shares, one of the persons legally or beneficially owning shares in that company; or

(b) not being treated by or under the supervision of a health care professional.

18.201 The exception in para (3)(a) does not apply where the certificate is issued in accordance with reg 2(1) of the Social Security (Medical Evidence) Regulations 1976[32] (evidence of incapacity for work, limited capability for work and confinement) or reg 2(1) of the Statutory Sick Pay (Medical Evidence) Regulations 1985[33] (medical information).

18.202 This provision is somewhat clumsily worded, but it means that a GP must issue one or more statutory certificates without charge where the following apply:

a) the GP is asked to produce the certificate by a patient (as that term is defined, as to which see above) or his personal representative;
b) the certificate is of a description prescribed in column 1 of Schedule 2 to the GMS Regs 2015 (these are listed below);
c) the certificate must be reasonably required under or for the purposes of the enactments specified in relation to the certificate in column 2 of Schedule 2 to the GMS Regs 2015;
d) the exemptions in reg 22(3)(a) and (b) do not apply (as to which see below); and
e) the exemption in reg 22(4) to the exception in (3)(a) applies.

18.203 Column 1 of Schedule 2 to the GMS Regs 2015 lists the types of certificates which have to be provided free of charge and column 2 lists the Acts of Parliament under which the certificates have to be provided.

Column 1: Purpose of certificate	Column 2: Enactments
To support a claim or to obtain payment either personally or by proxy; to prove incapacity to work or for self-support for the purposes of an award by the Secretary of State; or to enable proxy to draw pensions etc	Naval and Marine Pay and Pensions Act 1865 Air Force (Constitution) Act 1917 Pensions (Navy, Army, Air Force and Mercantile Marine) Act 1939 Personal Injuries (Emergency Provisions) Act 1939 Pensions (Mercantile Marine) Act 1942 Polish Resettlement Act 1947 Social Security Administration Act 1992 Social Security Contributions and Benefits Act 1992 Social Security Act 1998
To establish pregnancy for the purpose of obtaining welfare foods	Section 13 of the Social Security Act 1988 (Benefits under schemes for improving nutrition: pregnant women, mothers and children)

32 SI No 615.
33 SI No 1604.

To secure registration of still-birth	Section 11 of the Births and Deaths Registration Act 1953 (special provision as to registration of still-birth)
To enable payment to be made to an institution or other person in case of mental disorder of persons entitled to payment from public funds	Section 142 of the Mental Health Act 1983 (pay, pensions etc of mentally disordered persons)
To establish unfitness for jury service	Juries Act 1974
To support late application for reinstatement in civil employment or notification of non-availability to take up employment owing to sickness	Reserve Forces (Safeguard of Employment) Act 1985
To enable a person to be registered as an absent voter on grounds of physical incapacity	Representation of the People Act 1985
To support applications for certificates conferring exemption from charges in respect of drugs, medicines and appliances	National Health Service Act 2006
To support a claim by or on behalf of a severely mentally impaired person for exemption from liability to pay the Council Tax or eligibility for a discount in respect of the amount of Council Tax payable	Local Government Finance Act 1992

18.204 The wording of the exemption in reg 22(1) means that none of the above certificates have to be provided free of charge where the medical condition to which the certificate relates is being treated by a doctor or other healthcare professional who is not either a partner of the practice (including a corporate partner) or employed by the GP practice. In such a case, the regulations effectively signpost the patient to obtaining the certificate from the doctor or other healthcare professional who is treating the patient. This could be a private doctor, or is more likely to be a consultant in secondary care. This exception does not apply where the certificate is sought in accordance with reg 2(1) of the Social Security (Medical Evidence) Regulations 1976 (evidence of incapacity for work, limited capability for work and confinement) or reg 2(1) of the Statutory Sick Pay (Medical Evidence) Regulations 1985 (medical information). In such cases, the GP practice must issue the certificate free of charge, even though the patient is being treated by another doctor or other healthcare professional.

18.205 The exemption in reg 22(3)(b) provides that where the medical condition to which the certificate relates is not being treated by a healthcare professional at all, the GP practice is not required to provide a certificate free of charge.

18.206 The BMA reports that it has clarified with the Department for Work and Pensions (DWP) that it is not obligatory for GPs to fill in statements of incapacity when requested for the purposes of social security benefits by DWP. These forms attract a separate fee payable by the DWP.

18.207 Once a certificate has been issued to the DWP, the person to whom the certificate is sent is entitled to come back with follow up questions. The terms of the GMS and PMS contracts provide that the GP practice must be satisfied that the patient has consented before any questions are answered but, if consent is given, no charge can be made by the GP practice for answering questions which follow on from a report that must be provided free of charge. This is set out in reg 76 of the GMS Regs 2015, which provides that GMS contract must contain a term that:

> (1) The contractor must, if satisfied that the patient consents–
> (a) supply in writing to a person specified in paragraph (3) (a 'relevant person'), before the end of such reasonable period as that person may specify, such clinical information as a person specified in paragraph (3)(a) to (d) considers relevant about a patient to whom the contractor, or a person acting on behalf of the contractor, has issued or has refused to issue a medical certificate; and
> (b) answer any inquiries by a relevant person about–
> (i) a prescription form or medical certificate issued or created by, or on behalf of, the contractor, or
> (ii) any statement which the contractor, or a person acting on behalf of the contractor, has made in a report.

18.208 For the purpose of being satisfied that a patient consents, a contractor may rely on an assurance in writing from a relevant person that the consent of the patient has been obtained, unless the contractor has reason to believe that the patient does not consent.

18.209 For the purposes of reg 76(3), 'a relevant person' is:

(a) a medical officer;
(b) a nursing officer;
(c) an occupational therapist;
(d) a physiotherapist; or
(e) an officer of the DWP who is acting on behalf of, and at the direction of, any person specified in subparas (a)–(d).

18.210 Paragraph (f)(ii) of reg 25 of the GMS Regs 2015 provides that where a GP practice is asked by a commercial, educational or not-for-profit organisation to attend and/or examine (but not otherwise treat) a patient for the purpose of creating any other form of medical report or certificate, the GP practice is entitled to charge a reasonable fee. This seems to cover virtually all types of reports that are requested concerning patients other than the certificates issued under the various statutes listed above.

Charges where the GP practice has reasonable doubts as to whether a patient is on the practice list

18.211 Regulation 24 of the GMS Regs 2015 and reg 18 of the PMS Regs 2015 contain a provision to cover situations where a person presents seeking treatment, but where the GP has genuine doubts about whether the GP practice has a duty to provide services to that person. In such a case, the GP practice may impose a charge. Regulation 24(3)–(4) of the GMS Regs 2015 states as follows:

(3) Subject to paragraph (4), where–
(a) a person–
(i) applies to a contractor for the provision of essential services,
(ii) claims to be on that contractor's list of patients, and
(iii) fails to produce a medical card relating to that person on request; and
(b) the contractor has reasonable doubts about that person's claim,
the contractor must give any necessary treatment to that person and may demand and accept from that person a reasonable fee in accordance with regulation 25(e).
(4) Where–
(a) a person from whom the contractor has received a fee under regulation 25(e) applies to the Board for a refund within 14 days from the date of payment of the fee (or within such longer period not exceeding one month as the Board may allow if it is satisfied that the failure to apply within 14 days was reasonable); and
(b) the Board is satisfied that that person was on the contractor's list of patients when the treatment was given,
the Board may recover the amount of the fee from the contractor, by deduction from the contractor's remuneration or otherwise, and must pay the amount recovered to the person who paid the fee.'

18.212 This regulation imposes a duty on the GP to provide 'essential services' to the person, notwithstanding the fact that the GP practice has 'reasonable doubts' that the practice contract requires the GP practice to treat the person. However, in such a case the GP practice can impose a reasonable charge and recover this sum from the patient.

18.213 The reasonable fee will, of course, depend on the circumstances and the precise nature of the treatment provided. The regulations provide that the individual can then claim the fee back from NHS England if that person can prove they were on the list of patients for the practice at the relevant time. NHS England will then claim the fee back from the GP practice if the patient was a 'patient' of the practice.

18.214 The above provision only applies if a GP practice has 'reasonable doubts' whether a person is on the practice list or not. If the GP practice knows (without any reasonable doubt) that the patient is not on the practice list, then there is no duty to provide essential services to that person. Hence if, for example, a patient that has been removed from the practice list because they have moved away, registered with anther GP practice or have been violent, attends the surgery seeking treatment, the GP practice owes no duty to provide essential services to that person (unless there is a medical emergency) and can require the patient to leave the premises. The person will be a trespasser and thus, if the person does not leave, the person may commit a civil wrong. If there is a suggestion of a breach of the peace the police can be called.

Charges permitted by reg 25 of the GMS Regs 2015 and reg 19 of the PMS Regs 2015

18.215 The specific circumstances in which GP practices can impose charges on 'patients' is set out in reg 25 of the GMS Regs 2015. There is a like provision in reg 19 of the PMS Regs 2015. The particular circumstances relating to each of these exemptions is set out below. APMS contractors are likely to have the same restrictions on charging and the same exemptions introduced through a contractual term (see para 10 of Part 4 of the APMS Directions).

18.216 Regulation 25 of the GMS Regs 2015 provides as follows:

> The contractor may demand or accept (directly or indirectly) a fee or other remuneration–
> (a) from a statutory body for services rendered for the purposes of that body's statutory functions;
> (b) from a body, employer or school for–
> (i) a routine medical examination of persons for whose welfare the body, employer or school is responsible, or
> (ii) an examination of such persons for the purpose of advising the body, employer or school of any administration action that they might take;
> (c) for treatment which is not primary medical services or is otherwise required under the contract and which is given–
> (i) at accommodation made available in accordance with the provisions of paragraph 11 of Schedule 6 to the Act (accommodation and services for private patients), or
> (ii) in a registered nursing home which is not providing services under the Act,
> if, in either case, the person administering the treatment is serving on the staff of a hospital providing services under the Act as a specialist providing treatment of the kind the patient requires, and if, within seven days of giving the treatment, the contractor or the person giving the treatment supplies the Board, on a form provided by the Board for that purpose, with such information as the Board may require;
> (d) under section 158 of the Road Traffic Act 1988 (payment for emergency treatment of traffic casualties);
> (e) when the contractor treats a patient under regulation 24(3), in which case the contractor is entitled to demand and accept a reasonable fee (recoverable in certain circumstances under regulation 24(4)) for any treatment given, if the contractor gives the patient a receipt;
> (f) for attending and examining (but not otherwise treating) a patient–
> (i) at a police station, at the patient's request, in connection with possible criminal proceedings against the patient,
> (ii) for the purpose of creating a medical report or certificate, at the request of a commercial, educational or not for profit organisation,
> (iii) for the purpose of creating a medical report required in connection with an actual or potential claim for compensation by the patient;

(g) for treatment consisting of an immunisation for which no remuneration is payable by the Board and which is requested in connection with travel abroad;
(h) for prescribing or providing drugs, medicines or appliances (including a collection of such drugs, medicines or appliances in the form of a travel kit) which a patient requires to have in their possession solely in anticipation of the onset of an ailment or occurrence of an injury while that patient is outside of the United Kingdom but for which that patient is not requiring treatment when the drug, medicine or appliance is prescribed;
(i) for a medical examination–
    (i) to enable a decision to be made whether or not it is inadvisable on medical grounds for a person to wear a seat belt, or
    (ii) for the purpose of creating a report–
        (aa) relating to a road traffic accident or criminal assault, or
        (bb) that offers an opinion as to whether the patient is fit to travel;
(j) for testing the sight of a person to whom none of paragraphs (a) to (e) of section 115(2) of the Act (primary ophthalmic services) applies (including by reason of regulations made under section 115(7) of the Act);
(k) where the contractor is authorised or required in accordance with arrangements made with the Board under section 126 of the Act (arrangements for pharmaceutical services) and in accordance with regulations made under section 129 of the Act (regulations as to pharmaceutical services) to provide drugs, medicines or appliances to a patient and provides for that patient, otherwise than by way of dispensing services, any Scheduled drug; and
(l) for prescribing or providing drugs or medicines for malaria chemoprophylaxis.

Charges for meeting the requirements of other statutory bodies

18.217 Under reg 25 of the GMSC Regs 2015, a GP practice may demand or accept (directly or indirectly) a fee or remuneration from a statutory body for services rendered for the purposes of that body's statutory functions.

18.218 GP practices are under contract to NHS England (and sometimes CCGs too). They are obliged to undertake the functions set out in the contract but are not obliged to spend time responding to requests from other statutory bodies including local authorities unless the request is based on another form of statutory authority including, for example, requests under the Freedom of Information Act 2000. In practice, it can often be difficult for GP practices to set out clear limits on what they are prepared to do because statutory bodies assume that GP practices have a duty to co-operate with them in the discharge of their public functions.

18.219 The right to charge for doing work in response to requests by other public bodies includes where a GP is asked to attend a Child Protection Conference at the request of the local authority for a child who is a practice patient or who the GP has seen. According to the BMA, some CCGs have suggested that, although GP contracts contain no provision requiring them to participate in the safeguarding process, GPs would nonetheless have to justify non-compliance, with regard to their statutory safeguarding duties, and that non-compliance could justify a referral to the GMC, with the implication that disciplinary action could be taken against defaulting GPs. While the extent of GPs' safeguarding duties is outside the scope of this chapter, it is clear that GPs are entitled to charge a fee for this work. The BMA recommends that such fees should be indicated by the GP in advance of preparing reports or attending case conferences.[34]

18.220 If a GP is called to a Child Protection Conference by another statutory body (usually the local authority or the police) and no fee is agreed, the right course is probably for the GP to make it clear in advance that he or she is attending in response to the request and the GP practice expects to be remunerated for the GP's time. The GP should attend the Child Protection Conference (in discharge of his or her duties as a doctor) and then the GP Practice should send an invoice to the public body that called the GP seeking a reasonable fee. Although the authors are unaware of any case in which this issue has been tested in court, it seems likely that the GP practice would be entitled to a reasonable fee in quasi-contract and thus ought to succeed in such a claim.

18.221 The BMA has also provided guidance on so-called 'collaborative arrangements'.[35] This term refers to work done by GPs on behalf of local authorities in the fields of education, social services and public health. With the exception of family planning, fees for collaborative arrangements are not agreed nationally. Instead they must be agreed at a local level in accordance with local needs. GP practices are advised to agree these fees in advance because this avoids difficult arguments over quasi-contract claims. The BMA reminds GPs that:

> . . . basic health information provided by GPs for community care purposes does not attract a fee. [However] community care work that goes beyond the provision of basic health data . . . does attract a fee.[36]

18.222 If a GP practice is asked to undertake work for any other statutory agency, the GP practice is entitled to levy a reasonable fee. However, no fee can be claimed if a GP is required to do something under a different statutory scheme (which may or may not give rise to a right to payment depending on that statutory scheme). Hence if a GP is summoned to court as a witness of fact by the Crown Prosecution Service, no fee is payable because the legal duty to attend arises from the summons. It is, of course, different if the GP is attending court as an expert where fees can be claimed.

Fees for conducting routine medical examinations

18.223 It is not part of the duties of a GP to undertake medical examinations of persons who are not and do not believe themselves to be ill. Hence, the second exemption to the rule against charges in reg 25 provides that if an employer, a school or any other body (including the patient themselves) asks a GP to do a medical examination of a well patient 'for the purpose of advising the body, employer or school of any administrative

34 See www.bma.org.uk/advice/employment/fees/safeguarding-children-and-adults.

35 See www.bma.org.uk/advice/employment/fees/collaborative-arrangements.

36 See www.bma.org.uk/advice/employment/fees/collaborative-arrangements.

action they might take', a fee can be charged. The request for such a service is outside the terms of the duty to provide 'essential services' under a GMS or PMS contract and yet it is not in the interests of the patient for the GP to refuse to provide such a report. Hence the regulations allow the GP practice to charge a fee for this work. A fee cannot be claimed for the health checks that are required for new patients or those over the age of 75.

18.224 If a patient of the practice asks for a medical examination to provide reassurance to an employer that they can undertake a physical job or a student wants a report to confirm he or she is fit to go on an expedition, the GP practice is entitled to charge a reasonable fee for this service.

Services provided by a specialist GP for private patients in hospitals or a care home

18.225 The third circumstance in which a GP practice can charge a fee in reg 25 needs a little explanation.

18.226 There is no difficulty in a GP practice charging a fee for providing services to a nursing home or receiving remuneration for working in an NHS hospital if the patients who are being treated are not 'patients' of the GP practice within the above definition. However, there are only very limited circumstances in which a GP practice can charge for medical services provided in a hospital or care home to practice patients or others who come within the above definition. In order for the GP practice lawfully to be able to lawfully impose a charge under the above exemption:

a) The *location requirement* must be met. The services must be provided in either a registered care home or to a private patient in an NHS hospital. This exemption does not extend to providing services in a private hospital.
b) The *services requirement* must be met. The services provided to the patient must not be 'primary care services' under this exemption. The meaning of 'primary care services' is explored above. The fact that a general management service for a resident patient in a care home or a private patient in an NHS hospital is provided in the home rather than requiring the patient to come to the surgery does not take the service outside the scope of being a primary care service. Thus charges can only be made if the service provided by the GP practice is something which cannot properly be described as a primary care service. It effectively means that the GP is contracted by the care home (or private wing in an NHS hospital) to provide a service that is different to the services that GPs usually provide in the surgery.
c) The *person requirement* must be met. The person from the GP practice who is providing the services must be employed by a hospital providing services under the NHS Act 2006 as a specialist providing treatment of the kind the patient requires.
d) The *procedural requirement* must be met. Within seven days of giving the treatment, the contractor or the person providing the treatment must supply NHS England with such information about the treatment as NHS England may require on a form provided by it for this purpose.

18.227 This is the provision which is used by some GP practices to charge for providing medical cover to nursing homes. If the patients at a nursing home are not registered patients of a GP practice (because they are registered with another practice) and do not come within the definition of 'patients' as set out above, then there is no prohibition on a GP practice providing medical cover for the care home and charging for that service. However, if the residents are registered patients of the GP practice, the right to charge is strictly limited by the above four provisions. This exemption probably only applies in practice to a partner or salaried doctor in a GP practice who is employed by a local NHS Trust to deliver a specialist skill and, as part of that work, finds himself or herself treating a patient from his or her own practice. It is thus a very limited exemption.

Payment for emergency treatment of traffic casualties

18.228 Section 158 of the Road Traffic Act 1988 provides for very modest payments to any doctor who treats a victim of a road traffic accident.

18.229 This exemption to the general rules against charging practice patients only applies if a GP attends on a road accident on a road or in some other public place (ie not in the doctor's surgery) and the victim happens to be a 'patient' within the meaning of the above definition. In such a case, a GP who administers any treatment to such a patient is allowed to claim a fee of £21.30 from the accident victim and 41p per mile for any travelling over two miles. The fee must be claimed from the patient, and it can then be reclaimed from whoever caused the accident in the first place (unless that was the person being so treated, of course).

18.230 If the person who is treated by the GP is not a 'patient' of the practice, then the GP can still claim the fee under section 158. However this arrangement is entirely outside the contract and so there are no relevant restrictions on the GP.

Fees for attending a police station

18.231 Many GPs are under contract to the police service to attend police stations in order to provide healthcare services to those who are arrested or otherwise detained by the police. There will, of course, be occasions where the person who the GP is called upon by the police to treat is a patient of the practice where the GP is a partner or works as a salaried doctor. Exemption 25(f)(i) of the GMS Regs 2015 provides that a GP can still claim his fee (usually from the police) in such circumstances.

18.232 This exemption would also entitle a GP to claim a fee if he or she was asked to attend a police station by anyone else to see a patient of the practice (or any other person coming within the definition of 'patient') including, for example, a solicitor for the patient.

Fees for preparing a medical report or certificate

18.233 Regulation 25(f)(ii) of the GMS Regs 2015 provides that where a GP practice is asked to attend and/or examine (but not otherwise treat) a patient for the purpose of creating a medical report or certificate at the request of a commercial, educational or not for profit organisation, the GP practice is entitled to charge a reasonable fee.

Fees for preparing medico-legal reports

18.234 Regulation 25(f)(iii) of the GMSC Regs 2015 provides that where a GP practice is asked to attend and/or examine (but not otherwise treat) a patient for the purpose of creating a medical report required in connection with an actual or potential claim for compensation by the patient, the GP practice is entitled to charge a reasonable fee.

18.235 The fee can be payable by the patient or by the solicitor's firm who have made the request, depending on the circumstances.

Requests by patients who are about to travel abroad

18.236 Where a patient has asked for treatment consisting of an immunisation for which no remuneration is payable by NHS England (because it is not usually provided as part of NHS funded treatment) and which is requested in connection with travel abroad, a fee can be charged.

18.237 Travellers also frequently request a prescription of drugs to prevent them from contracting a condition. The GP practice can also charge for prescribing or providing drugs, medicines or appliances (including a collection of such drugs, medicines or appliances in the form of a travel kit) which a patient requires to have in his possession solely in anticipation of the onset of an ailment or occurrence of an injury while he is outside the UK but for which he is not requiring treatment when the medicine is prescribed.

18.238 A fee can also be charged for prescribing or providing drugs or medicines for malaria chemoprophylaxis.

Fees for preparing reports for seat belt purposes, following a traffic accident, a criminal assault or for fitness to travel

18.239 A fee can be charged where a GP practice is asked to undertake a medical examination to enable a decision to be made whether or not it is inadvisable on medical grounds for a person to wear a seat belt.

18.240 A fee can also be charged where a GP practice is asked to undertake a medical examination for the purpose of creating a report relating to a road traffic accident or criminal assault or that offers an opinion as to whether a patient is fit to travel.

Eye examinations by GPs

18.241 Part 6 of the NHS Act 2006 places a requirement on NHS England to arrange ophthalmic services for specific classes of people, notably those who are under 16, over 60, who are on state benefits or have defined medical conditions. These services are generally delivered by opticians and not by GPs. However, unlike other areas of NHS services, the ophthalmic service is not universal and there are individuals who are not included in NHS provision. If such persons come to a GP practice, then a fee can be charged for undertaking an eye examination.

Dispensing doctors and scheduled drugs

18.242 The last exemption in reg 25 of the GMS Regs 2015 only applies to dispensing GP practices. It permits dispensing practices to charge a fee to patients if a 'scheduled drug' is prescribed to that patient. A 'scheduled drug' means a drug which has been prohibited by the secretary of state from being prescribed to NHS patients generally or has been prohibited for prescription as part of NHS funded treatment apart from a limited class of patients.[37] This is known as the 'black list' or the 'black/grey list'.

37 Reg 3 of the GMS Regs 2015 define a 'scheduled drug' as follows:
'Scheduled drug' means–

(a) a drug, medicine or other substance specified in any directions given by the Secretary of State under section 88 of the Act (GMS contracts: prescription of drugs etc.) as being a drug, medicine or other substance which may not be ordered for patients in the provision of medical services under the contract; or
(b) except where the conditions in regulation 61(3) are satisfied, a drug, medicine or other substance which is specified in any directions given by the Secretary of State under section 88 of the Act as being a drug, medicine or other substance which can only be ordered for specified patients and specified purposes.

CHAPTER 19

Community dental services[1]

1 By Andrew Byass.

Introduction: background to contracting for community dental services[2]

19.1 As with general medical practitioners (GPs), dentists providing community dental services have never been required to be employees of the NHS. The majority of dentists in the past have been operating, and still do operate, as independent practitioners.

19.2 Those dentists operating as independent practitioners previously provided NHS dental services pursuant to a statutory regime provided under section 35 of the National Health Service Act (NHS Act) 1977. That regime was in turn overtaken by the new general dental services (GDS) contracts introduced in 2006, by way of amendments made to the NHS Act 1977 by the Health and Social Care (Community Health and Standards) Act 2003 and the National Health Service (General Dental Services Contracts) Regulations (GDS Regs) 2005,[3] which came into force on 1 January 2006.[4] The relevant provisions were consolidated in the National Health Service Act (NHS Act) 2006 when that Act came into force on 1 March 2007.

19.3 Prior to the 2006 reforms, several pilot schemes were undertaken (as they were with GPs) by which dentists entered what were known as 'personal dental services' agreements with a health authority or primary care trust (PCT). This was by way of provisions introduced under the National Health Service (Primary Care) Act (NHS(PC)A) 1997. Personal dental service agreements trialled several different forms of remuneration systems, and so did not operate under any standard form of wording.

19.4 The NHS(PC)A 1997 also provided for permanent personal dental services agreements to be entered with a health authority. This was introduced by way of amendments made to the NHS Act 1977. Reflective again of the approach taken with GPs, these powers were not implemented until March 2004. The delay allowed the Department of Health and Social Care (DHSC) an opportunity to evaluate the success or otherwise of the pilot agreements.

19.5 The changes made to dental services contracts in 2006 reflected the desire to bring NHS community dentistry broadly in line with other NHS services, principally by giving PCTs (now NHS England) responsibility for the commissioning of dental practitioners to provide an agreed level of activity and thus allowing NHS commissioners to be able to control the expenditure on NHS community dentistry. There was little effective financial control until the reforms, because NHS dentists were allowed to charge for every patient they saw. The charging system was changed under the new contracts, with dentists being only being able to charge the NHS for a fixed number of agreed units of dental activity (UDA) within a financial year. The stated aspirations at the time were to provide better coverage of NHS dental services across the country, and to better incentivise the

2 This chapter explains the law as it relates to England.

3 SI No 3361.

4 For an explanation of certain of the transitional provisions operating in respect of the Health and Social Care (Community Health and Standards) Act 2003, see *R (Hussain) v Secretary of State for the Health Department and Warwickshire PCT* [2011] EWCA Civ 800.

provision of preventative care and advice. However, it was primarily driven by a desire to gain financial control over the cost to the NHS of community dentistry.

19.6 Since it operates as a consolidating Act, the law as consolidated in the NHS Act 2006 has continuing effect, including in relation to both GDS contracts and personal dental services (PDS) agreements.[5] Express provision was made for any subordinate legislation to continue to have effect as if it was made, or done under, or for the purposes of, the corresponding provision in the NHS Act 2006, and for references to previous provisions to be construed as if they are references to the corresponding provision in the NHS Act 2006.[6]

19.7 This explains why the relevant regulations (see below) relating to GDS contracts and PDS agreements continue to refer to provisions within the NHS Act 1977. Those provisions have now been consolidated within the NHS Act 2006 and the regulations operate as if made under the NHS Act 2006 and as if the references to the NHS Act 1977 are references to the NHS Act 2006.

19.8 The commissioning of primary dental services by NHS England must now be undertaken in compliance with its general duties, which are discussed in chapter 3. Thus, maintaining and increasing access to NHS dentistry should now be a key objective for NHS England's commissioners, as will effective contract management. The focus of commissioners should be on ensuring the universal availability, quality and value of commissioned community dental services.[7]

How the NHS Act 2006 provides for different types of dental contracts

19.9 The NHS Act 2006 provides that NHS England must, to the extent that it considers necessary to meet all reasonable requirements, exercise its powers so as to secure the provision of primary dental services throughout England.[8] The NHS Act 2006 does not define the term 'primary dental services', but instead provides that the definition may be provided in regulations. Again, this overarching structure has aligned dentists with the structure applicable to GPs.

19.10 The form of legal duty upon NHS England is not directed to individual patients. It is instead a target duty to make arrangements to 'secure the provision of' primary dental services. This duty is discharged by setting up an appropriate number of contracts with a network of community dental providers, thus creating a primary dental service across the country, which is supposed to be sufficient to meet all reasonable requirements.

5 Paragraph 1 of Schedule 2 to the National Health Service (Consequential Provisions) Act 2006.

6 Paragraphs 2–4 of Schedule 2 to the National Health Service (Consequential Provisions) Act 2006.

7 See the *Dental handbook: A guide for commissioners, practices and dentists in England*, produced by the NHS Business Services Authority.

8 Section 99(1).

19.11 The means by which the NHS Act 2006 then provides powers to secure the provision of primary dental services is by way of dental contracts. The two types of contracts provided for by the NHS Act 2006 are:

a) GDS contracts, under section 100; and
b) PDS agreements, under section 107 (described in the NHS Act 2006 as 'section 107 arrangements').

19.12 There may also be former pilot scheme agreements made under the NHS(PC) Act 1997 which have continued under transitional provisions. These, however, are not provided for by the NHS Act 2006, but instead under previous legislation. Since 2015, trials have also taken place in respect of 'prototype agreements'. These agreements (initially 100 in number) are GDS or PDS agreements which have been temporarily varied as part of the Prototype Agreements Scheme.[9]

19.13 Regulations made under the NHS Act 2006 provide for much of the detail of the terms that will be included within GDS contracts and PDS agreements. These are, respectively, the GDS Regs 2005 and the National Health Service (Personal Dental Services Agreements) Regulations (PDSA Regs) 2005.[10] The regulations also provide for some of the details relating to prototype agreements. The remaining provisions relating to prototype agreements are found in the National Health Service (Dental Services) (Prototype Agreements) Directions 2015. All of these regulations are amended from time to time. References in this chapter are to the versions of the regulations in force on 1 January 2018, but readers are cautioned to check the up to date versions of any relevant regulations.

19.14 GDS contracts are referred to as 'contracts' within the NHS Act 2006. However, a GDS contract can take effect as a legally binding contract or as an NHS contract.[11] PDS arrangements are referred to as 'agreements' as opposed to 'contracts'. There does not appear to be any significance in the different wording. A PDS agreement can take effect either as a legally binding contract or as an NHS contract. However, the default position set out in the PDSA Regs 2005 is that the contractor to a PDS agreement is a health service body for the purposes of section 9 of the NHS Act 2006[12] and thus the agreement take effect as an NHS contract.[13] However, the contractor has the ability to service notice on NHS England to change the status of the agreement to being a legally binding contract.

9 The 'Prototype Agreements Scheme' is referred to in the GDS Regs 2005 as being the scheme 'introduced by the secretary of state on 1st November 2015, that the Secretary of State has developed to assist in continuing to promote and secure improvement in the provision of dental services in accordance with the [NHS Act 2006]': see footnote 41 within the definition for prototype agreement in reg 2.

10 SI No 3373.

11 See para 10.5 for the distinction between an NHS contract and a legally binding contract.

12 Previously section 4 of the National Health Service and Community Care Act 1990.

13 For a discussion of the legal effect of a NHS contract, see paras 19.86–19.92 below.

General dental services contracts

GDS contracts under the NHS Act 2006

19.15 Section 100 of the NHS Act 2006 provides that NHS England may enter into GDS contracts under which primary dental services are provided in accordance with Part 5 of the Act. Unsurprisingly, much of the detail in respect of the content of a GDS contract is left to regulations that may be made under section 101(2).[14] This includes the definition of 'primary dental services'.

19.16 The NHS Act 2006 does, however, provide the general outline of what a GDS contract may constitute, and makes provision for the persons entitled to enter a GDS contract (section 102), the powers to make directions as to payments to be made under a GDS contract (section 103), and for the matters that may be included within regulations.

19.17 The persons who may enter into a GDS contract are as follows:

a) a dental practitioner;[15]
b) a dental corporation;
c) two or more persons practicing in partnership, providing that at least one of the partners is a dental practitioner and either: i) that partner is able to secure that the partnership's affairs are conducted in accordance with that partner's wishes; or ii) a combination of partners is able to secure that the partnership's affairs are conducted in accordance with their wishes, and at least one of them is a dental practitioner or an employee of the type defined in section 102(3C);
d) a limited liability partnership, providing that at least one of the members is a dental practitioner and either: i) that member is able to secure that the LLP's affairs are conducted in accordance with that member's wishes; or ii) a combination of members is able to secure that the LLP's affairs are conducted in accordance with their wishes, and at least one of them is a dental practitioner or an employee of the type defined in section 102(3C).

19.18 Regulation 12 of the GDS Regs 2005 provides:

> (1) Where the contract is with two or more individuals practising in partnership, the contract shall be treated as made with the partnership as it is from time to time constituted, and the contract shall make specific provision to this effect.
> (2) Where the contract is with two or more individuals practising in partnership, the contractor must be required by the terms of the contract to ensure that any person who becomes a member of the partnership after the contract has come into force is bound automatically by the contract whether by virtue of a partnership deed or otherwise.

19.19 This provision means that the contract continues with whoever the partners in the relevant practice choose to take into partnership. Thus, a dental

14 The GDS Regs 2005 are now deemed to have been made under section 101(2): see paras 2–4 of Schedule 2 to the National Health Service (Consequential Provisions) Act 2006.

15 Section 274 defines a 'dental practitioner' as meaning a person registered in the dentists register under the Dentists Act 1984.

partnership that holds a GDS contract is able to change its partners (and thus change the identity of the persons delivering these public services and being paid for doing so) without going through any form of procurement process. NHS England must be informed of the identity of any new partner (see para 42 of Schedule 3 to the GDS Regs 2005) but has no general right to object to anyone being a contractor provided that person is eligible to hold a GDS contract.

19.20 Paragraph 63 of Schedule 3 to the GDS Regs 2005 allows the partners to dissolve the partnership and for all of the partners to agree that one of the former partners to elect to continue to hold the GDS contract and para 65 provides for the possibility of the contract continuing after the death of a sole practitioner. The right to have a contract with the partners in a partnership as it exists from time to time only applies to GDS contracts, but not to PDS contracts.

19.21 The GDS Regs 2005 in turn make specific provision for those who are not entitled to enter into a GDS contract. The persons disentitled from entering a GDS contract include those who are subject to a national disqualification, those who within the past five-years have been dismissed from employment with a health service body, and those who have committed serious criminal offences.[16]

19.22 So far as payments are concerned, section 103 provides that a GDS contract must require payments to be made in accordance with directions made by the secretary of state. Before issuing any such directions, the secretary of state must consult with any body appearing to the secretary of state to be representative of those who would receive payment in accordance with the direction. In practice, the secretary of state consults with the British Dental Association (BDA) which represents NHS community dentists.

The GDS Regs 2005

19.23 The legal status of a GDS contract as governed by private contractual law principles (as is generally the case) is discussed below. There is, however, the possibility for a contractor to elect to be regarded as a health service body for the purposes of section 9 of the NHS Act 2006, in which event the GDS contract would become an 'NHS contract'. Such an election takes the GDS agreement outside of being able to be enforced through the courts based on private contractual law principles. This election can be unilaterally withdrawn by the contractor at any time.[17]

19.24 Detailed requirements are provided in Schedule 3 to the GDS Regs 2005 as to the terms that must be included within a GDS contract. These terms can be amended at any time and thus it is necessary to refer to an up-to-date version of the regulations when addressing any matters relating to the terms of a new contract, or modifications to an existing contract.

19.25 NHS England has produced a standard form GDS contract which complies with the GDS Regs 2005 and also contains a series of other

16 There are others also not entitled to enter a GDS contract. See reg 4.

17 Reg 9(4).

standard clauses, including a specific obligation on NHS England to act reasonably. However, once a GDS contract is signed (and providing the contractor has not elected to enter a NHS contract), the meaning of the contract falls to be construed by the court in the same way as any other commercial contract: see *Tomkins v Knowsley Primary Care Trust.*[18]

Mandatory services (reg 14)

19.26 Regulation 14 provides for the mandatory services that must be provided under a GDS contract. It is these service that define the core obligations of a dentist who takes on a contract to provide primary dental services. It defines the services he or she is expected to provide in order to enable NHS England to comply with its duty in section 99 of the NHS Act 2006 to secure the provision of all reasonable requirements for dental services throughout England.

19.27 The services are: a) urgent treatment (during normal surgery hours) and b) routine treatment at a surgery to include the treatment set out in reg 14(4). These matters are as follows:

- (a) examination;
- (b) diagnosis;
- (c) advice and planning of treatment;
- (d) preventative care and treatment;
- (e) periodontal treatment;
- (f) conservative treatment;
- (g) surgical treatment;
- (h) supply and repair of dental appliances;
- (i) the taking of radiographs;
- (j) the supply of listed drugs and listed appliances; and
- (k) the issue of prescriptions.

19.28 The contractual terms provided for in Schedule 3 to the GDS Regs 2005, among many other matters, address how the above mandatory services are to be provided to NHS patients. This includes by a requirement for the contractor to comply with any relevant guidance issued by the National Institute for Health and Care Excellence (NICE) when providing services.

19.29 In particular, para 14 of Schedule 3 stipulates that contractors must provide services in accordance with the guidance entitled *Dental recall – Recall interval between routine dental examinations.* This guidance is reflective of the desire to move away from fixed dental review periods (previously as frequently as six-monthly), so as to make better use of NHS resources. The guidance makes clear that patients should be informed that recall periods may vary over time to take into account any changes in their level of risk of or from oral disease (with recall periods ranging from three to 24 months).

Additional services (reg 15)

19.30 Non-routine treatment, defined in the GDS Regs 2005 as 'additional services', may also be provided for under a GDS contract. Insofar as such services are provided for, then the GDS contract is required to have terms

18 [2010] EWHC 1194 (QB) at [8].

that have the same effect as those specified in Schedule 1 to the GDS Regs 2005.

Units of dental or orthodontic activity (regs 17 and 18)

19.31 Regulations 17 and 18 of the GDS Regs 2005 make provision for a GDS contract to specify the number of UDA or (where a contract includes the provision of orthodontic services) units of orthodontic activity (UOA) that is the maximum level that the contractor must provide and hence is entitled to charge for in each financial year.[19] It is the completion of these units of activity that provides the basis under a GDS contract both for payment to be recovered from a patient (if applicable) and to claim any payment from NHS England having taken account of the patient charge revenue received from the patient.

19.32 There is no fixed amount payable for a UDA. The amount is subject to local negotiation and can vary significantly from one NHS dental practice to another.

Personal dental services agreements

19.33 The provisions contained within the NHS Act 2006 and in the PDSA Regs 2005 which relate to PDS agreements in many respects mirror the provisions that apply to GDS contracts. There are, however, important differences. These include that:

a) the default position is that the contractor is a health services body, such that the PDS agreement must be treated as a NHS contract (reg 9(1));
b) a PDS agreement is for a fixed duration, unlike GDS agreements which subsist until terminated (reg 12(1)(b)); and
c) no mandatory services are required to be included within a PDS agreement, there instead being greater flexibility in the nature of services to be provided.

PDS agreements under the NHS Act 2006

19.34 The NHS Act 2006 provides in section 107 that NHS England may make agreements, other than GDS contracts, under which primary dental services are to be provided. Under the NHS Act 2006 these are described as 'section 107 arrangements' and as 'agreements' under the PDSA Regs 2005.

19.35 Section 107 provides the principal vires for PDS agreements. It provides at section 107(2) that all such PDS agreements must be in accordance with regulations made under section 109 (ie the PDSA Regs 2005), that PDS agreements may not combine arrangements for the provision of primary dental services with primary medical services (section 107(3)) or local pharmaceutical services (section 107(4)), but that they may combine with the provision of other services (section 107(5)).

19 See paras 19.49–19.70 below.

19.36 The persons who may enter into a PDS agreement are set out in section 108. The list of persons is complicated and requires careful reading if an issue ever arises as to whether a person is entitled to be a party to a PDS agreement. In general terms, permissible parties include an NHS trust or NHS foundation trust, a dental practitioner, a healthcare professional, certain individuals providing general medical services, certain NHS and other employees, dental corporations and certain companies and partnerships so long as rules about control of those companies and partnerships are met.

19.37 The PDSA Regs 2005 in turn make specific provision for those who are not entitled to enter into a PDS agreement. The persons barred from entering a PDS agreement include those who are subject to a national disqualification, those who within the past five years have been dismissed from employment with a health service body, and those who have committed serious criminal offences.[20]

The right to a GDS contract

19.38 A PDS contractor which is providing 'mandatory services'[21] and which wishes a GDS contract to be entered may terminate a PDS agreement and elect to enter a GDS contract.[22] Providing that the usual qualifying criteria are met, NHS England is required to enter a GDS contract in place of the PDS agreement.

The PDSA Regs 2005

19.39 Unlike with GDS Regs 2005, the default position with PDS agreements is that a contractor is to be regarded as a health services body for the purposes of section 9 of the NHS Act 2006.[23] A contractor may at any time unilaterally elect to be a health services body, or to cease to be regarded as such, and NHS England must agree to the variation.[24] If a contractor is to be regarded as a health services body, reg 10 provides that the PDS agreement must state that it is a NHS contract.

General terms

19.40 A PDS agreement must specify the services that are to be provided by the contractor (the extent of these are left to individual agreement, unlike with a GDS contract), the duration of the agreement, to who services are to be provided, and the premises at which those services will be provided (reg 12).

19.41 Detailed requirements are also provided in Schedule 3 to the PDSA Regs 2005 as to the terms that must be included within a PDS agreement. As with GDS contracts, these terms are able to be amended at any time and thus it is necessary to refer to an up-to-date version of the regulations

20 There are others also not entitled to enter a PDS agreement. See reg 4.
21 See para 19.26 above.
22 See reg 21 of the PDSA Regs 2005.
23 Reg 9(1).
24 Reg 9(4).

when addressing any matters relating to the terms of a new contract, or modifications to an existing contract. NHS England has produced a standard form PDS agreement which complies with the GDS Regs 2005 and also contains a series of other standard clauses.

19.42 PDS agreements must otherwise specify the number of UDA or (where a contract includes the provision of orthodontic services) UOA that a contractor must provide in each financial year. As with GDS contracts, it is the completion of these units of activity that provides the basis under a PDS agreement both for payment to be recovered from a patient (if applicable) and to claim any payment from NHS England having taken account of the patient charge revenue received from the patient.

Additional services (reg 11)

19.43 Non-routine treatment, defined in the GDSC Regs 2005 as 'additional services', may also be provided for in a PDS agreement. These services are defined in reg 2 as meaning one or more of:

a) advanced mandatory services, being any mandatory service generally provided under a GDS contract but provided on a referral basis due to the high level of facilities, experience or expertise required in respect of a particular patient;
b) dental public health services, meaning services provided by a contractor under section 111 of the NHS Act 2006 (previously section 16CB(4)(c) of the NHS Act 1977);
c) domiciliary services, meaning services provided other than at a surgery, a mobile surgery or a prison;
d) orthodontic services, meaning, generally, treat of, or treatment to prevent, malocclusion of the teeth and jaws, and irregularities of the teeth; and
e) sedation services.

19.44 Insofar as such services are provided for, the PDS agreement is required to have terms that have the same effect as those specified in Schedule 1 to the PDSA Regs 2005.

Prototype agreements

19.45 Prototype agreements are being used to trial alternative contractual arrangements for NHS community dentistry, with the stated aim of assisting the NHS to change the focus of dental service provision from delivery of treatment to address disease, to a system whereby prevention is the focus, with the patient participating in their own care to minimise the occurrence of disease.

19.46 Both the GDS Regs 2005[25] and the PDSA Regs 2005[26] provide for the terms of a GDS or PDS agreement, as the case may be, to be varied upon a contractor and NHS England electing to enter into a prototype agreement.

25 Reg 24C.
26 Reg 20C.

The key differences in the terms provided for under prototype agreements are set out in the National Health Service (Dental Services) (Prototype Agreements) Directions 2015, and the related *Prototype agreement scheme statement of financial entitlements*.[27]

19.47 The prototype agreements have trialled different forms of payments, which are based on a blend of payments for capitation and for activity. Capitation is based on the number of actual patients a practice is expected to have on its 'list' by the year-end, and provides for payments to be made based on this number of patients in place of payments for certain types of activity. The differences in the agreements relate to the blend of capitation payments versus activity payments (Blend A provided for approximately 60 per cent capitation payments and Blend B provided for approximately 83 per cent). This is a return to the system of 'practice lists' which took effect prior to 2006. The 2006 reforms abolished the concept of a practice list but many NHS dentists continued to operate de facto patient lists. The prototype arrangements are a return to this type of arrangement.

19.48 Should these prototype agreements be rolled out more generally, then it will be necessary to give close regard to the means by which capitation is calculated for any dental practice, in addition to having regard to units of activity.

Units of dental activity

19.49 Both the GDS Regs 2005[28] and the PDSA Regs 2005[29] require relevant dental contracts to specify the number of UDA that a contractor must provide in each financial year. Where a contract includes the provision of orthodontic services, the contract will also specify the number of UOA that a contractor must provide in each financial year.

19.50 The requirement upon a contractor to complete a specified number of UDA or UOA in a financial year is the principal means by which NHS England can seek to incentivise (or require) dentists to provide a measurable amount of primary dental services in any given year and thus maintain financial control of the cost of NHS community dentistry. In this regard, para 1 of Schedule 3 to the GDS Regs 2005 simply provides that a contractor 'may' provide NHS primary care dental services to any person if a request is made by a person who requires the services, or a request is made on behalf of a person who requires the services.

19.51 However, subparagraph 1(4) provides that the contractor is not entitled to refuse to provide services to a person who makes a request unless the contractor has reasonable grounds for doing so. There is a list of impermissible grounds in subparagraph 1(4) relating, broadly speaking, to equality matters. An NHS dentist is also not entitled to refuse to provide NHS services in order to persuade a person to accept privately paying services. Thus, as mentioned above, the 2006 reforms abolished each NHS dental practice having a list of patients who had preferential status within the practice.

27 See assets.publishing.service.gov.uk/government/uploads/system/uploads/attachment_data/file/463529/Prototypes_SFE_acc.pdf.

28 Regs 17 and 18.

29 Regs 13 and 14.

19.52 However, it is reasonable to refuse to provide services to NHS dental patients because the contractor has exceeded his annual allocation of UDA or (where a contract includes the provision of orthodontic services) UOA, and therefore cannot charge the NHS for providing treatment to a patient in the financial year.

19.53 It follows that if a patient seeking dental treatment presents himself or herself to a dentist who holds a GDS contract and the contractor has unused UDAs (or UOAs) that could be allocated to that treatment, there is a contractual obligation on the contractor to provide NHS dental treatment to that patient unless the contractor has reasonable grounds for refusing to provide the requested treatment. If the patient is not exempt from paying NHS dental charges, the contractor is entitled to seek payment of the relevant charge from the patient and is entitled to refuse to go ahead with the treatment if the charge is not paid: see para 4 of Schedule 3 to the GDS Regs 2005. A dentist can only recover the balance of the fee from the NHS Business Services Agency (NHS BSA) which administers dental payments on behalf of NHS England). Thus, the dentist is left with the loss if the patient refuses to pay the dental charge.

19.54 However, in the usual case, the contractor performs its contractual obligations to NHS England by providing appropriate dental treatment to the patient and the patient pays the charge, and the balance of the UDA sum is recovered from the NHS BSA.

Treatment bands and charge exempt courses of treatment

19.55 Schedule 2 in both the GDS Regs 2005 and the PDSA Regs 2005 specifies how a UDA or a UOA are to be calculated. UDAs are split between a) banded courses of treatment and b) charge-exempt courses of treatment. Both forms of treatment attract UDAs (of varying amounts), but as the name suggests, the charge exempt courses of treatment are free to the patient.

19.56 Chargeable treatment is divided into three bands. The course of treatment falling within each respective band is defined within Schedules 1 to 4 to the National Health Service (Dental Charges) Regulations (Dental Charges Regs) 2005.[30] A course of activity falling within band 1 attracts one UDA (1.2 units in the case of urgent treatment), while band 2 attracts three units and band 3 attracts 12 units. The more routine courses of treatment fall within band 1, with the complexity of treatment increasing commensurately within bands 2 and 3 respectively.

Payments to GDS contractors based on UDAs and UOAs

19.57 By section 103(2) of the NHS Act 2006, a GDS contract must require payments to be made under the contract to a contracting party in accordance with directions made under section 103(1). The sorts of matters that may be included within such a direction are set out in section 103(3), which provides as follows:

> (3) A direction under subsection (1) may in particular–
>
> (a) provide for payments to be made by reference to compliance with standards or the achievement of levels of performance,

30 SI No 3477.

(b) provide for payments to be made by reference to–
   (i) any scheme or scale specified in the direction, or
   (ii) a determination made by any person in accordance with factors specified in the direction,
(c) provide for the making of payments in respect of individual practitioners,
(d) provide that the whole or any part of a payment is subject to conditions (and may provide that payments are payable by the Board only if it is satisfied as to certain conditions),
(e) make provision having effect from a date before the date of the direction, provided that, having regard to the direction as a whole, the provision is not detrimental to the persons to whose remuneration it relates.

19.58 The relevant directions made on behalf of the secretary of state are the *General Dental Services statement of financial entitlements* (SFE). The SFE is produced annually although the form of the directions can be structured by way of an amendment of the previous consolidated directions. The most recent consolidated version of the SFE was published in 2013. Accordingly, current amendments are cumulative amendments to the form of the SFE published in 2013.

19.59 The SFE provides that the NHS BSA, which administers the dental payment scheme on behalf of the secretary of state, must pay a monthly sum to all GDS contractors. The monthly sum is based on one-twelfth of the annual contract value, but is reduced by the amount of declared patient charge revenue notified by the dentist each month. This is, in effect, a payment on account to dentists.

19.60 Unlike other areas of NHS treatment, dental services are not universally free at the point of use. The secretary of state has made the Dental Charges Regs 2005 which define the categories of NHS dental patients who are obliged to make financial contributions towards the cost of their dental care (which in practice is everyone who is not exempt through age, financial status or medical condition) and which set the amount required to be paid by the NHS patient for different types of treatment.

19.61 Regulation 8(2) of the Dental Charges Regs 2005 provides:

(2) A provider of relevant primary dental services, in providing relevant primary dental services for which a charge may be made under regulations 4(1) to (3), (5) or 12A(2)–
(a) may, on arranging to provide a course of treatment or urgent course of treatment, make the appropriate charge;
(b) shall require the patient to acknowledge, on the appropriate part of the form supplied for that purpose by the Board, and before that form is sent to the Secretary of State, his obligation to pay a charge which is made;
(c) may, on completing the course of treatment or urgent course of treatment, recover the charge from the patient (if it has not previously been paid);
(d) shall, on receiving a sum for payment (in full or in part) of the charge payable under these Regulations, give a receipt for it on–
   (i) a paper form provided for that purpose by the Board; or
   (ii) an electronic form which identifies the provider of the relevant primary dental services, the patient, the amount of the charge paid and the date on which it is paid.

19.62 Accordingly, a GDS contractor is entitled but not obliged to recover a charge determined in accordance with the regulations which is payable by an NHS patient who is not exempt from paying the charge. However, reg 12 of the Dental Charges Regs 2005 provides:

> Where a provider of relevant primary dental services has provided relevant primary dental services for which a charge is payable under these Regulations, the remuneration which would otherwise be payable by the Board to that Provider shall be reduced by the amount of charge, irrespective of whether or not that charge has been recovered by the provider.

19.63 The usual arrangement is that a potential patient presents himself or herself at the dental surgery and requests NHS treatment. If the contractor has no reasonable grounds for refusing to treat the patient, it is under a contractual obligation to provide NHS primary care dental treatment to the patient. Either before or (more usually) after providing the relevant treatment, an appropriate amount is demanded (and hopefully collected) from the patient. This sum ought to cover any charges payable by that patient under the Dental Charges Regs 2005. The charge is paid to the contractor and is retained by the contractor.

19.64 This sum then reduces the amount of payment received by the contractor under the SFE. NHS England has suggested in correspondence with various dental contractors that patient charge revenue (known as 'PCR') is the property of the secretary of state. There is no basis in the regulations for making this suggestion. The patient is under a statutory duty to pay the charges, but they are payable to the contractor, not to the secretary of state. Further, once the sum is paid, it becomes the property of the contractor and not the secretary of state. It follows that there does not appear to be any basis for suggesting that PCR is held by a contractor on behalf of the secretary of state. The correct legal position is that the contractor is free to treat the money as its own as soon as the sums are paid over by an NHS patient.

Payments to PDS contractors based on UDAs and UOAs

19.65 The system for payments to dental contractors under PDS agreements is largely the same as under GDS contracts. There is however no obligation for the secretary of state to consult upon the terms of any directions that are made in respect of payments under PDS agreements. The directions that have been made for PDS agreements are the Personal Dental Services Statement of Financial Entitlements 2013.[31]

19.66 The Dental Charges Regs 2005 also apply to PDS agreements. The relevant regulations (discussed above) apply in respect of 'relevant primary dental services', which are defined in the regulations to include dental treatment (including urgent treatment and orthodontic treatment) provided and dental appliances and orthodontic appliances supplied under a PDS agreement.

31 Available at the NHS Business Services Authority website at www.nhsbsa.nhs.uk/fp17-processing-and-payments/sfe-payments.

Mid-year review of dental activity

19.67 The GDS Regs 2005 and the PDSA Regs 2005 provide identical provisions relating to the mid-year review of dental activity.

19.68 Paragraph 58 of Schedule 3 to both regulations provides that NHS England must conduct mid-year reviews to determine the amount of UDAs and UOAs, as the case may be, that a contractor has provided. Such a review provides a mechanism to ensure that overpayments to a contractor are monitored, and also presumably to monitor the level of dental services being provided within any particular area.

19.69 NHS England is empowered (and encouraged[32]) to take steps to seek to remedy underperformance at a mid-year review, which is referable to a contractor which has provided less than 30 percent of the total number of UDAs or UOAs that the contractor is required to provide in the first six months of a financial year. Those steps consist of the following:

a) notifying the contractor of concerns about underperformance (para 58(5)(a) of Schedule 3);
b) requiring the contractor to participate in a mid-year review to inform decision-making as to the appropriate remedial steps (para 58(5)(b) of Schedule 3);
c) having assessed any information provided by the contractor, NHS England may then: i) require the contractor to comply with a written plan drawn up by NHS England to ensure that the level of activity meets the contractor's target of UDAs and/or UOAs; or ii) withhold monies under the GDS contract; or iii) agree a contract variation with the contractor.

19.70 Insofar as monies are withheld by NHS England, the objective will be to support service delivery in-year elsewhere, so as to maintain the level of primary dental care assessed as being required to meet the reasonable requirements of an area.

Variation and termination of GDS contracts and PDS agreements

Contract length

19.71 By regulation 13 of the GDS Regs 2005, GDS contracts must provide that they are to subsist until terminated. By this means, GDS contracts, like General Medical Services (GMS) contracts, are perpetual contracts which can only be terminated by the contractor resigning the contract, mutual consent or as a result of NHS England terminating the contract for breaches of contract by the contractor. The perpetual nature of the contracts gives contractors security, because they are able to invest in dental practices knowing that, subject to not breaching the contract, the contract will continue indefinitely. The only exception is when NHS England has terminated the contract of another provider of primary dental

32 See the *Dental handbook: A guide for commissioners, practices and dentists in England*, produced by the NHS Business Services Authority.

services and wishes to make temporary arrangements with another contractor. No maximum duration is provided for such a contract, though it will be in the interest of any temporary contractor to move to a permanent contract with no fixed duration should they wish to do so.

19.72 In contrast, PDS agreements are required to specify the duration of the agreement,[33] so will in the normal course be for a fixed period, and subject to renegotiation at the end of that period.

19.73 There is an interesting legal argument as to whether such perpetual contracts are lawful under EU law on the grounds that they may not be compatible with EU procurement principles. The primary objection is the identity of a contractor providing public services is, for all practical purposes, determined by the contractor and not by the contracting authority. The issues arise in practice where, for example, a two-partner partnership that holds a GDS contract consists of individual dentists who wish to retire. The existing partners advertise for new partners to 'buy into' the partnership and two younger dentists do so, paying a considerable sum for the 'goodwill' in the partnership. Unlike the case with NHS medical partnerships, there is no statutory restriction on the sale of goodwill in NHS dental partnerships. Once the younger dentists have become partners in the partnership, the outgoing partners retire, and the new partners carry on with the perpetual contract. Thus, in effect, the younger partners have purchased the right to deliver public services and be paid by the NHS for doing so. However, the selection of the new partners is a matter for the outgoing partners (and thus the contract is in effect 'auctioned') as opposed to being selected by the NHS commissioner as a contracting authority. This is a procedure for the selection of a person to hold a public contract which seems difficult to reconcile with the EU procurement directives.

Variation

19.74 Although there is generally no power to limit the period of a GDS contract, NHS England does have power to unilaterally vary a GDS contract. Similar power exists in respect of a PDS agreement. The parties may of course also agree between them to vary the contract or agreement. However, an unresolved issue is the extent to which these wide powers of variation need to be substantially constrained by the limitations on reg 72 of the Public Contracts Regulations 2015.[34]

19.75 The circumstances in which such a variation may be made are set out in largely identical terms in para 60 of Schedule 3 to both the GDS Regs 2005 and PDSA Regs 2005. The GDS Regs 2005 provide as follows:

> (1) Subject to paragraph 31(3), no amendment or variation shall have effect unless it is in writing and signed by or on behalf of the Board and the contractor.
>
> (2) In addition to the specific provision made in paragraphs 62(6), 63(6) and 75, the Board may vary the contract without the contractor's consent where it–

33 See reg 12(1)(b) of the PDSA Regs 2005.

34 SI No 102.

(a) is reasonably satisfied that it is necessary to vary the contract so as to comply with the Act, any regulations made pursuant to the Act, or any direction given by the Secretary of State pursuant to the Act; and
(b) notifies the contractor in writing of the wording of the proposed variation and the date upon which that variation is to take effect,

and, where it is reasonably practicable to do so, the date that the proposed variation is to take effect shall be not less than 14 days after the date on which the notice under paragraph (b) is served on the contractor.

19.76 The PDSA Regs 2005 provide as follows:

(1) Subject to paragraph 32(3), no amendment or variation shall have effect unless it is in writing and signed by or on behalf of the Board and the contractor.
(2) In addition to the specific provision made in paragraph 73, the Board may vary the agreement without the contractor's consent where it–
(a) is reasonably satisfied that it is necessary to vary the agreement so as to comply with the Act, any regulations made pursuant to that Act, or any direction given by the Secretary of State pursuant to that Act; and
(b) notifies the contractor in writing of the wording of the proposed variation and the date upon which that variation is to take effect,

and, where it is reasonably practicable to do so, the date that the proposed variation is to take effect shall be not less than 14 days after the date on which the notice under paragraph (b) is served on the contractor.

19.77 Thus, the parties can agree between them to vary the contact, in which event that variation must be in writing and signed by both parties. NHS England's powers to unilaterally vary a GDS contract or PDS agreement otherwise depend on it being reasonably satisfied that such a variation is necessary so as to comply with the NHS Act 2006 or relevant regulations, and where appropriate notice is given.

Termination

19.78 A contractor may terminate a GDS contract or PDS agreement at any time, by giving written notice to NHS England.[35] On the other hand, termination by NHS England may only be for one of the reasons set out in Schedule 3. This includes by reason of a contractor ceasing to be an eligible party to a GDS contract, risk to patient safety, or risk of material financial loss to NHS England by reason of the contractor's financial situation.

19.79 Upon receipt of a notice of termination, a GDS contractor may elect to invoke the NHS dispute resolution procedure (see below). The incentive for doing so, as compared to relying on a private law claim, is that the GDS contract in issue will usually not be terminated so long as there remains a pending dispute within the dispute resolution procedure, and a) providing that termination is not on grounds relating to patient safety or risk of material financial loss to NHS England[36] and b) the contract is not suspended (as to which, see below).

35 Paragraph 66 of Schedule 3 to the GDS Regs 2005, and para 64 of Schedule 3 to the PDSA Regs 2005.

36 Paragraph 77 of Schedule 3 to the GDS Regs 2005.

19.80 A PDS contractor also has the right to refer a dispute about a notice of termination to the NHS dispute resolution procedure. As with a GDS contract, upon referral to the NHS dispute resolution procedure, a notice of termination will not take effect until that procedure is completed, save if termination was on the grounds of patient safety or risk of material financial loss to NHS England.[37]

19.81 By para 75 of Schedule 3 to the GDS Regs 2005, and para 73 of Schedule 3 to the PDSA Regs 2005, contracts and agreements must also make provision for NHS England to be able to impose a 'contract sanction'. These are defined as meaning:

(a) termination of specified reciprocal obligations under the contract;
(b) suspension of specified reciprocal obligations under the contract for a period of up to six months; or
(c) withholding or deducting monies otherwise payable under the contract.

19.82 A contact suspension may be imposed when NHS England is otherwise entitled to terminate a GDS contract or PDS agreement on specified grounds, providing that NHS England is reasonably satisfied that the sanction is appropriate and proportionate to the circumstances. A contract sanction cannot have the effect of terminating or suspending any obligation to provide a mandatory service[38] under a GDS contract. Under both the PDSA and the GDS Regs 2005, a contractor may refer any dispute about a contract sanction to the NHS dispute resolution procedure.

The legal relationship between the parties to a dental contract and NHS England

19.83 As with GPs, the vast majority of dentists are not employees of an NHS organisation. This is reflected in the GDS standard contract produced by the DHSC, which at clause 6 provides as follows:

> The Contract is a contract for the provision of services. The Contractor is an independent provider of services and is not an employee, partner or agent of the Board. The Contractor must not represent or conduct its activities so as to give the impression that it is the employee, partner or agent of the Board.

19.84 The standard PDS agreement contains a materially identical clause. In many instances, a dentist may instead be an employee of the dental practice for which she or he works, but that (legal) relationship is necessarily then not one that is with NHS England.

19.85 The legal relationship between a dentist or a dental practice and NHS England will thus be defined by the terms of the contract or agreement under which GDS or PDS are provided. That contract will for most purposes be construed by the courts in accordance with general principles of contractual interpretation.

37 Paragraph 75 of Schedule 3 to the PDSA Regs 2005.
38 See para 19.26 above.

The distinctions between NHS contracts and private law contracts

19.86 As set out above, a contractor to either a GDS contract or a PDS agreement may choose to be recognised as a health services body so that the dental services contract then entered into is a NHS contract. Indeed, the default position in respect of PDS agreements is that these will be a NHS contract, subject to the right of a contractor to elect to not be a health service body prior to the agreement being made,[39] or to request a variation to a PDS Agreement which NHS England is required to agree.[40]

Section 9 of the NHS Act 2006 makes provision for NHS contracts as follows:

> (1) In this Act, an NHS contract is an arrangement under which one health service body ('the commissioner') arranges for the provision to it by another health service body ('the provider') of goods or services which it reasonably requires for the purposes of its functions.
>
> . . .
>
> (5) Whether or not an arrangement which constitutes an NHS contract would apart from this subsection be a contract in law, it must not be regarded for any purpose as giving rise to contractual rights or liabilities.
>
> (6) But if any dispute arises with respect to such an arrangement, either party may refer the matter to the Secretary of State for determination under this section.
>
> (7) If, in the course of negotiations intending to lead to an arrangement which will be an NHS contract, it appears to a health service body–
>
> (a) that the terms proposed by another health service body are unfair by reason that the other is seeking to take advantage of its position as the only, or the only practicable, provider of the goods or services concerned or by reason of any other unequal bargaining position as between the prospective parties to the proposed arrangement, or
>
> (b) that for any other reason arising out of the relative bargaining position of the prospective parties any of the terms of the proposed arrangement cannot be agreed,
>
> that health service body may refer the terms of the proposed arrangement to the Secretary of State for determination under this section.
>
> (8) Where a reference is made to the Secretary of State under subsection (6) or (7), he may determine the matter himself or appoint a person to consider and determine it in accordance with regulations.
>
> (9) 'The appropriate person' means the Secretary of State or the person appointed under subsection (8).
>
> (10) By the determination of a reference under subsection (7) the appropriate person may specify terms to be included in the proposed arrangement and may direct that it be proceeded with.
>
> (11) A determination of a reference under subsection (6) may contain such directions (including directions as to payment) as the appropriate person considers appropriate to resolve the matter in dispute.

39 Reg 9(1) of the PDSA Regs 2005.

40 Reg 9(3) and (4) of the PDSA Regs 2005.

(12) The appropriate person may by the determination in relation to an NHS contract vary the terms of the arrangement or bring it to an end (but this does not affect the generality of the power of determination under subsection (6)).

(13) Where an arrangement is so varied or brought to an end–

(a) subject to paragraph (b), the variation or termination must be treated as being effected by agreement between the parties, and

(b) the directions included in the determination by virtue of subsection (11) may contain such provisions as the appropriate person considers appropriate in order to give effect to the variation or to bring the arrangement to an end.

19.87 The principal consequence of entering a NHS contract is that such a contract does not give rise to legally enforceable rights by any person in the civil courts. This is by operation of section 9(5). Provision is also made in section 9 for the resolution of disputes either relating to the terms of a proposed agreement, or relating to an existing agreement. Both the GDS Regs 2005 and the PDSA Regs 2005 also make provision for the resolution of disputes (see below). Thus, a NHS dental contactor who is party to an NHS contract cannot either sue or be sued in the courts: see *Pitalia and another v The National Health Service Commissioning Board*.[41]

19.88 Once a GDS contractor who is an individual or in a partnership has elected to become an NHS body, reg 9(3) of the GDS Regs 2005 provides that this status will continue notwithstanding any change in the individuals who become parties to the GMS contract. Thus, if a sole practitioner were to take on a partner under his or her GMS contract and then resign from the partnership, the new contractor will continue to be treated as an NHS body.

19.89 Under reg 9(2) of the PDSA Regs 2005, any change in the identity of the parties comprising the contractor (such as a change of partners) does not affect the health service body status of the contractor. In other words, unlike the position with GDS contracts, the continuation of status as a health service body is not dependent upon the original contractor being an individual or a partnership.

19.90 Regulation 9(4) of both the GDS Regs 2005 and PDSA Regs 2005 permits any contractor who wishes to change the contractor's status to become an NHS body or to cease to be an NHS body shall be able to do so by serving notice on NHS England. Upon receipt of such a notice, NHS England is required to agree the variation, which will take effect once the variation procedures in para 60 of Schedule 3 are complied with. Thus, a legally binding contract can be changed to being an NHS contract at the election of a contractor and vice versa, and upon completion of the requisite formalities.

19.91 Regulation 9(7) in both the GDS Regs 2005 and PDSA Regs 2005 provides that a contractor shall cease to be a health service body for the purposes of section 4 of the National Health Service and Community Care Act (NHSCCA) 1990 (now section 9 of the NHS Act 2006) once a variation takes effect following an election under reg 9(4) being made, or if the

41 [2014] EWCA Civ 474.

contract or agreement terminates. Accordingly, if NHS England has a claim against a contractor for something that has happened after the termination of a dental services (PDS or GDS) contract, or indeed after a switch from being a health service body, that claim has to litigated in the courts unless it comes within the exceptions in reg 9(7).

19.92 These exceptions are again in identical terms in each of the regulations, and are as follows:

> (7) Where a contractor ceases to be a health service body pursuant to–
> (a) paragraph (5) [variation] or (6) [termination], it shall continue to be regarded as a health service body for the purposes of being a party to any other NHS contract entered into after it became a health service body but before the date on which the contractor ceased to be a health service body (for which purposes it ceases to be such a body on the termination of that NHS contract);
> (b) paragraph (5), where it or the Board–
> (i) has referred any matter to the NHS dispute resolution procedure before it ceases to be a health service body, or
> (ii) refers any matter to the NHS dispute resolution procedure, in accordance with paragraph 54(1)(a) of Schedule 3, after it ceases to be a health service body,
> the contractor is to continue to be treated as a health service body (and accordingly the agreement is to continue to be regarded as an NHS contract) for the purposes of the consideration and determination of the dispute; or
> (c) paragraph (6), it shall continue to be regarded as a health service body for the purposes of the NHS dispute resolution procedure where that procedure has been commenced–
> (i) before the termination of the agreement; or
> (ii) after the termination of the agreement, whether in connection with, or arising out of, the termination of the agreement or otherwise,
> for which purposes it ceases to be such a body on the conclusion of that procedure.

Dispute resolution

Pre-contract dispute resolution

19.93 Both the GDS Regs 2005 and PDSA Regs 2005 provide a mechanism by which a dispute about the terms of a proposed GDS contract or PDS agreement can be referred to the secretary of state to resolve. In practice, that dispute will be resolved by the Family Health Services Appeal Unit (FHSAU).

19.94 The opportunity to refer pre-contract disputes to the FHSAU is peculiar to this type of category of NHS contracts. A failure to agree contractual terms in an arm's-length commercial negotiation usually results in the prospective parties not entering a contract. The pre-contract resolution procedure can thus operate as a means to put pressure on a proposed commissioner, probably NHS England, to offer reasonable terms to a proposed contractor. A ruling of the FHSAU on such a reference will be binding on NHS England but is not binding on the contractor. By this means, the contractor can gain some measure of confidence that any terms to be included within a relevant contract or agreement are objectively justified, while at the same time still being able to walk away from a contract if the adjudicated terms remain unsatisfactory.

19.95 The resolution procedure operates in the following way:

a) The parties must be 'in the course of negotiations intending to lead to' a contract or an agreement: reg 8(1). At the least, then, negotiations must have commenced with the intention of agreeing a GDS contract or PDS agreement. If a person has a request for a contract or agreement rebuffed, the pre-contract dispute resolution will not apply.
b) The dispute must be about a particular term of the agreement or contract: reg 8(1). Guidance issued by primary care contracting suggests that NHS England should discourage referral of disputes about mandatory terms (ie those that properly reflect the terms set out in the regulations) since such disputes will be rejected. More common will be disputes about negotiable terms such as contract value and UDAs.
c) Before referring a dispute, both parties must 'make every reasonable effort to communicate and co-operate with each other with a view to resolving' the dispute: reg 8(3) of the GDS Regs 2005; reg 8(2) of the PDSA Regs 2005.
d) The dispute so referred (either under the regulations or under section 9 of the NHS Act 2006) is then required to be determined in accordance with the dispute resolution procedures provided in Schedule 3 to each set of regulations (see below).
e) The FHSAU will issue a determination which may specify terms to be included in the proposed contract or agreement and which may require NHS England (insofar as the dispute is referred under the GDS Regs 2005 or PDSA Regs 2005) to proceed with the proposed contract or agreement.

19.96 The FHSAU's determination binds NHS England, but the contactor has the right to reject the terms proposed by the FHSAU and walk away from the proposed contract (unless the contractor is already an NHS body, in which case the decision is binding as a result of section 9(10) of the NHS Act 2006). In practice, the contractor has the choice at that stage of either accepting the contract on the terms set by the FHSAU or walking away from the agreement (unless NHS England come up with an offer of other acceptable terms).

The NHS disputes resolution procedure

19.97 Section 9(6) of the NHS Act 2006 requires that any dispute about an NHS contract must be referred to the Secretary of State for Health and Social Care for resolution. As with pre-contract disputes, it is the FHSAU which has the delegated authority to resolve such disputes.

19.98 In addition, in the case of either a GDS contract or a PDS agreement that is not a NHS contract, a dispute may also be referred to the secretary of state to resolve. Such a referral can only be made by the contractor, or with the contractor's agreement in writing if the referral is made by NHS England. If a dispute in respect of a non-NHS contract is referred, both the GDS Regs 2005 and PDSA Regs 2005 provide that the parties agreed to be bound by the determination then made.[42]

19.99 Both the GDS Regs 2005 and the PDSA Regs 2005 provide details regarding the means as to how disputes will be resolved, in para 55 of Schedule 3. The procedure to be followed is as follows (assuming it is the FHSAU that is ruling on a dispute):

a) Notice must be provided to the secretary of state in writing of the names and addresses of the parties to the dispute, together with a copy of the contract or agreement and a brief statement describing the nature of the dispute.
b) Any such notice must be provided within three years beginning with the date on which the matter giving rise to the dispute happened or should reasonably have come to the attention of the party wishing to refer the dispute. No provision is made in the regulations to extend time.
c) The FHSAU provides the respondent to any dispute with a copy of the notice of the dispute and provides a time frame within which any written observations may be made in response.
d) The FHSAU will then decide whether it will determine the dispute on paper or whether oral representations will be requested. In most instances, an oral hearing does not take place, meaning that the representations made in writing need to be thorough.
e) The FHSAU will issue a determination in writing. Reasons for the determination will be provided.

19.100 If a party is dissatisfied with a determination of the FHSAU, that decision can be challenged by way of judicial review proceedings in the High Court: see *R (Hussain others) v Secretary of State for the Health Department and another*[43] where the Court of Appeal rejected an argument from the NHS commissioner that this was a form of private arbitration and lacked the necessary public law elements to be challengeable by way of judicial review. However, the Court of Appeal went on to find in favour of the PCT in that case.

19.101 Where a GDS contract or a PDS agreement is not a NHS contract and there is no agreement to refer a dispute to the Secretary of State, such a dispute will be resolved through the courts who can be expected to apply normal private law contractual principles: see *Krebs v NHS Commissioning Board*.[44]

42 Paragraph 54(2) of Schedule 3 to both the GDS Regs 2005 and PDSA Regs 2005.
43 [2011] EWCA Civ 800.
44 [2014] EWCA Civ 1540.

CHAPTER 20

NHS complaints and the Health Service Commissioner

Introduction

20.1 Even when those providing and commissioning NHS services strive to deliver the highest possible standards of clinical care and service, it is inevitable that complaints will from time to time be made by patients or those, such as relatives, who are concerned with the welfare of patients. These may range from the vexatious to the highly meritorious, for example a complaint about potentially negligent clinical practice that caused an otherwise avoidable death. Clinicians and managers in NHS organisations may feel that administrative and clinical resources are over-employed in the area of complaints handling. However, the right to complain and the complaints process is a fundamental part of NHS service provision. It is also a right protected by the NHS Constitution and is a matter for regulation by the Care Quality Commission (CQC).[1] It is something that all healthcare providers and commissioners should take very seriously. Complaints also provide an invaluable source of information for senior managers to understand patient perspectives and thus assist with service improvement programmes. Bill Gates, the founder of Microsoft observed, 'your most unhappy customers are your greatest source of learning'.

20.2 Data on written complaints in the NHS, which is published on a yearly basis by NHS Digital, shows that the number of complaints made by or on behalf of patients is rising.[2] In 2016–2017, 208,415 reported written complaints were made about NHS services. This is the equivalent to 4,008 written complaints a week or 571 complaints a day. This increase in the number of complaints is not *necessarily* a bad thing, however. In recent years, particularly following the 2013 report *A review of the NHS hospitals complaints system: Putting patients back in the picture* by Rt Hon Ann Clwyd MP and Professor Tricia Hart, there has been a drive to highlight awareness among patients of their right to complain, either directly or by a representative, about issues with the care and service provided to them. There is also a greater emphasis, at least in theory, on the complaints process being part of an aspiration for a more honest and open NHS culture devoted to continuous learning and improvement of patient safety. It goes hand in hand, for example, with the development of an improved patient safety reporting system and the introduction of the 'duty of candour' under reg 20 of the Health and Social Care Act 2008 (Regulated Activities) Regulations 2014,[3] which form the basis of CQC regulation. The duty of candour requires registered providers to act in an open and transparent way and provide an apology in relation to any 'notifiable safety incident'.

20.3 The NHS complaints system allows for complaints to be made on an informal or formal basis. It is also a way for patients who feel there has been a failure with his or her care to seek appropriate redress, be that a

1 Please see chapter 2 for further discussion of how NHS bodies must have regard to the NHS Constitution; and chapter 8 on the CQC.

2 See NHS Digital's report, *Data on written complaints in the NHS 2016–2017*, 14 September 2017.

3 SI No 2936.

clarification or a fuller explanation of 'what went wrong', an apology, a promise to implement service improvements, or financial compensation.

20.4 If a complainant has exhausted all complaints processes at the NHS stage and is not satisfied by the substantive outcome, or with the way in which their complaint was handled by the relevant health service organisation, the patient has the right to ask the Health Service Commissioner for England, known colloquially as the Parliamentary and Health Service Ombudsman (hereafter referred to as 'the PHSO'), to investigate. The PHSO has a discretion to decide whether to investigate an individual complaint or not to do so. The PHSO conducts a number of investigations but it has limited resources and frequently declines to investigate complaints referred by individual patients. There are certain circumstances, discussed below, where the PHSO is statutorily barred from investigating a complaint. If the PHSO agrees to investigate and upholds or partially upholds a complaint, he can make recommendations as to remedy to the body complained about. He can also lay reports before parliament in particularly egregious cases.

20.5 At this stage, it should be emphasised that making a complaint is an alternative, and different, method of seeking redress, to, for example, making a legal claim based on negligence for medical malpractice, judicially reviewing a decision of an NHS body, or making a claim under the Equality Act 2010 for discrimination. It is possible, however, in some limited circumstances for a complaints procedure to run alongside these other methods of redress. There are also different mechanisms by which patients can raise concerns about poor clinical care or unacceptable conduct by NHS staff including referring individual doctors to the General Medical Council (GMC) or making a complaint to the CQC. They do not come within the scope of this chapter, but readers should be aware of their existence.

The NHS complaints procedure

20.6 Under reg 3(2) of the Complaints Regs 2009 the NHS complaints procedure is governed by the Local Authority Social Services and National Health Service Complaints (England) Regulations (Complaints Regs) 2009,[4] made under sections 113, 114, 115 and 195 of the Health and Social Care (Community Health and Standards) Act 2003. They govern when, how, by whom and to whom complaints can be made, as well as setting out requirements for the complaints procedure itself and how it ought to be managed.

Informal complaints

20.7 The Complaints Regs 2009 create a formal statutory complaints process, which must be adhered to by NHS bodies complained about (and must be followed by complainants who wish to follow through the process). There is, however, the option for patients and NHS bodies to attempt to try and resolve any issues that have arisen informally prior to the patient making

4 SI No 309.

a formal complaint. If a patient makes a complaint orally, and this is resolved to the complainant's satisfaction 'not later than the next working day after the day on which the complaint was made' then by virtue of reg 8(1)(c) of the Complaints Regs 2009, the body complained about is not required to handle the complaint in accordance with the process. This gives patients and bodies the chance to resolve issues informally, although it is incumbent on them to bring the complaint to a swift resolution.

20.8 A patient who wishes to make an informal complaint within a hospital setting may want to seek advice from the Patient Advice and Liaison Service (PALS) based within the hospital. As described on the NHS Choices website, this service 'offers confidential advice, support and information on health-related matters. They provide a point of contact for patients, their families and their carers'. They can therefore help patients with health-related questions or help them to resolve any concerns. If informal resolution is not possible, they can also advise about the formal complaints procedure.

Formal complaints under the Complaints Regs 2009

Responsible bodies

20.9 The Complaints Regs 2009 came into force on 1 April 2009 and made transitional arrangements for complaints made before that date. Fundamentally, they require what is known as the 'responsible body' to 'make arrangements' for the handling and consideration of complaints in accordance with the Complaints Regs 2009. Responsible bodies, and thus those bodies who must have regulations-compliant arrangements in place, are:

a) local authorities (county councils, metropolitan district councils, a non-metropolitan district council for an area where this is no county council, a London borough council, the Common Council of the City of London and the Council of the Isles of Scilly);
b) NHS bodies (special health authorities, clinical commissioning groups (CCGs), NHS England, NHS trusts and foundation trusts);
c) primary care providers (general practices under General Medical Services (GMS), Personal Medical Services (PMS) and Alternative Provider Medical Services (APMS) contracts, General Dental Services (GDS) contractors or a provider or dental services in accordance with section 107 of the National Health Service Act (NHS Act) 2006, general ophthalmic services contractors, and providers of pharmaceutical services under the NHS Act 2006); and
d) independent providers (any person or body who provides healthcare in England under arrangements made with an NHS body and who is not an NHS body or primary care provider – this would therefore include private companies running care homes, for example).

The complaints arrangements

20.10 The complaints arrangements must be 'such as to ensure that':

(a) complaints are dealt with efficiently;

(b) complaints are properly investigated;
(c) complainants are treated with respect and courtesy;
(d) complainants receive, so far as is reasonably practical–
 (i) assistance to enable them to understand the procedure in relation to complaints; or
 (ii) advice on where they may obtain such assistance;
(e) complainants receive a timely and appropriate response;
(f) complainants are told the outcome of the investigation of their complaint; and
(g) action is taken if necessary in the light of the outcome of a complaint.

20.11 Regulation 16 of the Complaints Regs 2009 requires the responsible body to make information available to the public as to:

a) its arrangements for dealing with complaints; and
b) how further information about those arrangements may be obtained.

20.12 It is difficult to see how an NHS body can comply with the duty to have 'arrangements' to manage complaints unless the NHS adopts a policy which sets out how it is going to respond to complaints. That policy constitutes the NHS body's arrangements and thus complies with the duty under the Complaints Regs 2009 to have arrangements in place. NHS bodies should make this policy available to the public on its website, and, for example, in paper copy and in other formats and languages on request. The arrangements must also be such as to ensure that complainants receive assistance to understand the process or advice on where they can receive such assistance. Responsible bodies may have PALS which achieve this function. The NHS Complaints Advocacy Service, which was funded by the Department of Health (now Department of Health and Social Care (DHSC)), has now ceased to exist. It is supposed to have been replaced by a number of independent complaints advocacy services commissioned by local authorities. Section 223A of the Local Government and Public Involvement in Health Act 2007 requires each local authority to 'make such arrangements as it considers appropriate for the provision of independent advocacy in relation to its area' in the provision of assistance for individuals making or intending to make an NHS complaint or a complaint to the PHSO. Responsible bodies should be aware of local advocacy services (such as VoiceAbility, SEAP, Impetus and POhWER[5]) and inform potential complainants of these, as well as of other resources available from organisations like Healthwatch and the PHSO.

20.13 Under reg 4 of the Complaints Regs 2009, a responsible body must designate persons to fulfil two roles:

1) The first is the 'responsible person', who is responsible for ensuring compliance with the arrangements and in particular ensuring that action is taken if necessary in light of the outcome of a complaint. This person must be the chief executive officer of a local authority or NHS body, or if it is another type of responsible body, such as a primary care provider or independent provider, it must be the person who is the

5 There are many others and patients looking for a service should seek advice from the relevant responsible body and/or their local authority and/or Healthwatch but these are some known to this author.

sole proprietor, a partner where the body is partnership (such as a general practitioner (GP) partnership), or in any other case a director or person with managerial responsibility of the body.

2) The second is a 'complaints manager', who is responsible for managing the procedures for handling and considering complaints. The complaints manager does not need to be an employee of the responsible body, can be the same person as the responsible person, and may also act for another responsible body as a complaints manager. This allows for the possibility of outsourcing or bodies joining together to provide this function.

20.14 Both responsible persons and complaints manager can delegate their functions to another person.

20.15 Other management responsibilities in relation to the complaints process include monitoring and the preparation of annual complaints reports. Regulation 17 in relation to monitoring provides that:

> For the purpose of monitoring the arrangements under these Regulations each responsible body must maintain a record of the following matters–
> (a) each complaint received;
> (b) the subject matter and outcome of each complaint; and
> (c) where the responsible body informed the complainant of–
> (i) the response period specified in regulation 13(7)(b); or
> (ii) any amendment to that period,
>
> whether a report of the outcome of the investigation was sent to the complainant within that period or any amended period.

20.16 Under reg 18, a responsible body must prepare and make available on request an annual report for each year, ending on 31 March, which must:

> (a) specify the number of complaints which the responsible body received;
> (b) specify the number of complaints which the responsible body decided were well-founded;
> (c) specify the number of complaints which the responsible body has been informed have been referred to–
> (i) the Health Service Commissioner to consider under the 1993 Act; or
> (ii) the Local Commissioner to consider under the Local Government Act 1974; and
> (d) summarise–
> (i) the subject matter of complaints that the responsible body received;
> (ii) any matters of general importance arising out of those complaints, or the way in which the complaints were handled;
> (iii) any matters where action has been or is to be taken to improve services as a consequence of those complaints.

20.17 A responsible body that is not a CCG or NHS England must send a copy of its annual report to whichever of those commissioners commissioned its services.

20.18 In terms of communications with any complainant, they may be made by email where a complainant has consented in writing or electronically and has not withdrawn that consent (reg 15(1)). Regulation 15(2) also allows for electronic signatures.

Who may make a complaint?

20.19 Regulation 5 of the Complaints Regs 2009 sets out who may make complaints. A complaint may be made by:

(a) a person who receives or has received services from a responsible body; or
(b) a person who is affected, or likely to be affected, by the action, omission or decision of the responsible body which is the subject of the complaint.

20.20 A representative may make a complaint on another person's behalf if the person has died, is a child or is unable to make the complaint himself or herself because of physical capacity or because they lack capacity to make a complaint within the meaning of the Mental Capacity Act 2005, or because that representative has been requested to make the complaint on someone else's behalf.

20.21 When a representative has made a complaint on behalf of a child, the responsible body cannot consider the complaint unless there are 'reasonable grounds' for the complaint being made by a representative instead of the child. If the responsible body is not so satisfied, it must notify the representative in writing, and state the reason for its decision. Similarly, where a representative makes a complaint on behalf of a person without capacity, if the responsible body is not satisfied that the representative is conducting the complaint in the best interests of the incapacitated person, it should cease to consider the complaint and must notify the representative in writing. This best interests assessment requirement is also applied to complaints made on behalf of children.

20.22 There is no limit on the factors that a responsible body can consider as 'reasonable grounds'. There will therefore be considerable latitude for a responsible body to make a decision on this matter provided its decision is rational. It is unclear what the 'reasonable grounds' requirement adds beyond the best interests assessment, since it is likely if a representative is making a complaint in a child's best interests that it is reasonable he or she is acting as the child's representative. This may be relevant, however, for 'Gillick competent' children, who have been deemed to have capacity to consent to and make decisions regarding their own medical treatment notwithstanding that they are under the age of 16, or a child who is 16–17 years and has consented to treatment by virtue of section 8 of the Family Law Reform Act 1969. One possible area of complaint would be around the provision of treatment to a child who was refusing consent to treatment. While clinicians cannot overrule a refusal by a competent child to give consent to serious medical treatment (and parents cannot give consent on behalf of competent child), it is possible for an NHS body to apply to the High Court to do so. Hence, it would be possible for parents of a competent child who is refusing treatment to complain that the NHS body has failed to ask a judge to overrule their child's refusal to provide consent to medical treatment.

What types of complaints must be handled under the Complaints Regs 2009?

20.23 Under reg 6 of the Complaints Regs 2009 responsible bodies have a duty to handle the following broad range of complaints made in accordance with the regulations:

(1) This regulation applies to a complaint made on or after 1st April 2009 in accordance with these Regulations to–
   (a) a local authority about the exercise by the local authority of the following functions–
      (i) its social services functions; or
      (ii) any function discharged or to be discharged by it under arrangements made between it and an NHS body under section 75 of the 2006 Act in relation to the functions of an NHS body;
   (b) an NHS body about–
      (i) the exercise of its functions; or
      (ii) the exercise of any function discharged or to be discharged by it under arrangements made between it and a local authority under section 75 of the 2006 Act in relation to the exercise of the health-related functions of a local authority;[6]
   (ba) a clinical commissioning group or the National Health Service Commissioning Board about the exercise by it of any functions in pursuance of arrangements made under section 7A of the National Health Service Act 2006;[7]
   (c) a primary care provider about the provision of services by it under arrangements with an NHS body; or
   (d) an independent provider about the provision of services by it under arrangements with an NHS body.

20.24 Regulation 6(5) and (6) create a deeming provision where by, if it appears to a responsible body that complaint, if it had been made to another responsible body, would have fallen to be handled by that second responsible body, and it sends that complaint on to the second responsible body, is deemed to have been made to the second responsible body. This would cover, for example, a complaint about care in an NHS foundation trust that was made to a patient's GP's practice, to be passed onto the foundation trust and treated as if the complaint had been made to the foundation trust in the first place.

20.25 It does not cover, however, situations where a complaint is materially a complaint about both bodies. There is a duty to cooperate in that situation under reg 9 of the Complaints Regs 2009, which provides as follows:

(1) This regulation applies where–
   (a) a responsible body ('the first body') is considering a complaint made in accordance with these Regulations; and
   (b) it appears to the first body that the complaint contains material which, if it had been sent to another responsible body ('the second body'), would be a complaint which would fall to be handled in accordance with these Regulations by the second body.
(2) The first body and the second body must co-operate for the purpose of–
   (a) co-ordinating the handling of the complaint; and
   (b) ensuring that the complainant receives a co-ordinated response to the complaint.
(3) The duty to co-operate under paragraph (2) includes, in particular, a duty for each body–
   (a) to seek to agree which of the two bodies should take the lead in–
      (i) co-ordinating the handling of the complaint; and
      (ii) communicating with the complainant;

6 Please see the section on care trusts in chapter 7 on NHS trusts.
7 Public health functions of the secretary of state.

(b) to provide to the other body information relevant to the consideration of the complaint which is reasonably requested by the other body; and
(c) to attend, or ensure it is represented at, any meeting reasonably required in connection with the consideration of the complaint.

20.26 Complaints which are *not* required to be dealt with under the Complaints Regs 2009 are set out in reg 8(1). They are the following:

(a) a complaint by a responsible body;
(b) a complaint by an employee of a local authority or NHS body about any matter relating to that employment;
(c) a complaint which–
  (i) is made orally; and
  (ii) is resolved to the complainant's satisfaction not later than the next working day after the day on which the complaint was made;
(d) a complaint the subject matter of which is the same as that of a complaint that has previously been made and resolved in accordance with sub-paragraph (c);
(e) a complaint the subject matter of which has previously been investigated under–
  (i) these Regulations;
  (ii) the 2004 Regulations, in relation to a complaint made under those Regulations before 1st April 2009;
  (iii) the 2006 Regulations, in relation to a complaint made under those Regulations before 1st April 2009; or
  (iv) a relevant complaints procedure in relation to a complaint made under such a procedure before 1st April 2009;
(f) a complaint the subject matter of which is being or has been investigated by–
  (i) a Local Commissioner under the Local Government Act 1974; or
  (ii) a Health Service Commissioner under the 1993 Act;
(g) a complaint arising out of the alleged failure by a responsible body to comply with a request for information under the Freedom of Information Act 2000; and
(h) a complaint which relates to any scheme established under section 10 (superannuation of persons engaged in health services, etc) or section 24 (compensation for loss of office, etc) of the Superannuation Act 1972, or to the administration of those schemes.

Complaints about an NHS provider that are made to an NHS commissioner

20.27 One of the perceived weaknesses in the complaints system is that an NHS body is able to both investigate and adjudicate on complaints made about it. Hence there is a concern that NHS body could be seen to be biased towards believing its own staff if there is a conflict of evidence or could be more forgiving of systemic failings. The concern is that the NHS body is, in effect, 'marking its own homework'. One potential answer to this concern, which is provided in the Complaints Regs 2009, is for a complaint about an NHS provider to be made to the relevant commissioner. For example, a patient complains to the local CCG about unacceptable care provided by the local NHS hospital.

20.28 Regulation 7 of the Complaints Regs 2009 explains how a commissioner is required to handle a complaint made to it about services provided by an NHS provider. A patient may choose to complain to the commissioner for various reasons, including what the patient perceives to be his or her ability to take a more distanced and objective position on the matter, or because of a breakdown in relations with and lack of trust in the provider. This might be particularly so, for example, if a patient wanted to make a complaint to NHS England about the care provided by a small GP partnership with only two GPs or where the complaint is about defects in the overall systems operated by a provider as opposed to the conduct of individual clinicians.

20.29 When a CCG or NHS England receives such a complaint, they must:

1) first ask the complainant whether he or she consents to details of the complaint being sent to the provider; and
2) if the complainant so consents, the CCG or NHS England must as soon as reasonably practicable send details of the complaint to the provider.

The regulations do not explain what steps the CCG or NHS England are required to take if the patient does not provide consent to the details of the complaint to the provider. The CCG or NHS England is still required to conduct an investigation into the complaint and to reach a conclusion, but would have to do so without informing the provider that it had received a complaint from the patient. It is possible that the complaint could give rise to generic issues which could be investigated without reference to the individual circumstances of the patient. However, if the complaint is solely about the individual experience of the patient, it is hard to see how the commissioner can conduct any effective investigation without the patient allowing the details of the complaint to be put to the provider.

20.30 A CCG or NHS England may feel that it would be better for the complaint to be investigated and adjudicated upon by the NHS provider itself rather than by the commissioner. Regulation 7 sets up a two-stage process. The first stage is for the CCG or NHS England to decide if it is 'appropriate' for it to deal with the complaint itself. If so, the CCG or NHS England must notify the complainant and provider and continue to handle the complaint itself. If, however the commissioner considers it would be 'more appropriate' for the complaint to be dealt with by the provider, *and* (crucially) the complainant 'consents', then under reg 7(5):

> (a) the group or Board must so notify the complainant and the provider;
> (b) when the provider receives the notification given to it under sub-paragraph (a)–
> (i) the provider must handle the complaint in accordance with these Regulations; and
> (ii) the complainant is deemed to have made the complaint to the provider under these Regulations.

20.31 There are some important things to note with regards to this ability of the commissioner to pass over the complaint to the provider. The first is that the test is whether it is *more* appropriate for the complaint to be dealt with by the provider rather than the commissioner, not merely whether it would be appropriate for the provider to deal with the complaint. The commissioner's assessment of this matter must be rational, taking into account all the relevant factors put forward by the complainant, including the fact that the complainant chose to complain to the commissioner rather than the provider. If the rationale is that there has been a breakdown in trust and communication, and the patient has complained to the commissioner for that very reason, it is, in the author's view, highly unlikely to be *more* appropriate that the complaint be dealt with by the provider.

20.32 Second, and crucially, the complainant must *consent to his or her complaint being passed from the commissioner to the provider*, regardless of the commissioner's view of the appropriateness. If consent is not given, the commissioner must continue to handle the complaint itself. It is not lawful for the commissioner to create a hybrid process whereby it lets the provider investigate and adjudicate on the complaint and then reviews their decision after an investigation. A patient's choice is protected by the need for consent.

20.33 Third, if the complaint is passed on to the provider, it is deemed to have been made to them and the provider must handle the complaint in accordance with the Complaints Regs 2009.

When must a complaint be made?

20.34 Under reg 12 of the Complaints Regs 2009 there is a 12-month time limit for making a complaint, although a responsible body may waive this time limit:

> (1) Except as mentioned in paragraph (2), a complaint must be made not later than 12 months after–
> (a) the date on which the matter which is the subject of the complaint occurred; or
> (b) if later, the date on which the matter which is the subject of the complaint came to the notice of the complainant.
> (2) The time limit in paragraph (1) shall not apply if the responsible body is satisfied that–
> (a) the complainant had good reasons for not making the complaint within that time limit; and
> (b) notwithstanding the delay, it is still possible to investigate the complaint effectively and fairly.

20.35 The question of whether the time limit should be waived is a matter for the responsible body's discretion and is inherently fact-specific. Situations where the discretion could be exercised include, for example, where a person has been grieving the death of a person whose care the person is complaining about; where there have been difficulties in obtaining advice or advocacy services from the independent advocacy provider; or where the complainant has been pursuing other avenues, such as a legal claim or attempts at informal resolution.

Investigation and response to a complaint

20.36 Regulation 13 of the Complaints Regs 2009 concerns the procedure that must be adopted before investigation. It provides:

> (1) A complaint may be made orally, in writing or electronically.
> (2) Where a complaint is made orally, the responsible body to which the complaint is made must–

(a) make a written record of the complaint; and
(b) provide a copy of the written record to the complainant.

(3) Except where regulation 6(5) or 7(1) applies in relation to a complaint, the responsible body must acknowledge the complaint not later than 3 working days after the day on which it receives the complaint.

(4) Where paragraph (5) of regulation 6 applies, and a responsible body ('the recipient body') receives a complaint sent to it by another responsible body in accordance with that paragraph, the complaint must be acknowledged by the recipient body not later than 3 working days after the day on which it receives the complaint.

(5) Where regulation 7(1) applies to a complaint–
(a) clinical commissioning group or National Health Service Commissioning Board which receives the complaint must acknowledge the complaint not later than 3 working days after the day on which it receives it; and
(b) where a responsible body receives notification given to it under regulation 7(5)(a), it must acknowledge the complaint not later than 3 working days after the day on which it receives the notification.

(6) The acknowledgement may be made orally or in writing.

(7) At the time it acknowledges the complaint, the responsible body must offer to discuss with the complainant, at a time to be agreed with the complainant–
(a) the manner in which the complaint is to be handled; and
(b) the period ('the response period') within which–
(i) the investigation of the complaint is likely to be completed; and
(ii) the response required by regulation 14(2) is likely to be sent to the complainant.

(8) If the complainant does not accept the offer of a discussion under paragraph (7), the responsible body must–
(a) determine the response period specified in paragraph (7)(b); and
(b) notify the complainant in writing of that period.

20.37 Regulation 14 governs the investigation. Regulation 14(1) provides as follows:

(1) A responsible body to which a complaint is made must–
(a) investigate the complaint in a manner appropriate to resolve it speedily and efficiently; and
(b) during the investigation, keep the complainant informed, as far as reasonably practicable, as to the progress of the investigation.

It is axiomatic, but the duty is therefore to 'investigate' the complaint, which may involve requesting and assessing clinical records, requesting further information from any clinicians implicated in the complaint or the complainant himself or herself, or seeking clinical advice. The investigation should be directed at the subject of the complaint itself. The investigation should be resolved speedily and efficiently, and the complainant should be kept informed of its progress. Where there is a statutory duty on a public body to investigate a complaint, the public body has a duty to reach conclusions on the key elements of the complaint. That duty is not discharged if the public body simply notes a conflict of evidence without reaching a conclusion as to where the truth lies or adopts the approach that it can only accept evidence of facts which are recorded in medical records: see *R (Williams) v Merseyside Police Authority*.[8]

8 [2011] EWHC 1119 (Admin).

20.38 Once the investigation is complete, the responsible body should come to a conclusion as to whether the complaint is upheld (which may be partially) or not, and what the outcome of the complaint is in terms of any remedy. Under reg 14(2) the responsible body must produce the conclusions of their investigation in a report:

> (2) As soon as reasonably practicable after completing the investigation, the responsible body must send the complainant in writing a response, signed by the responsible person, which includes–
> (a) a report which includes the following matters–
> (i) an explanation of how the complaint has been considered; and
> (ii) the conclusions reached in relation to the complaint, including any matters for which the complaint specifies, or the responsible body considers, that remedial action is needed; and
> (b) confirmation as to whether the responsible body is satisfied that any action needed in consequence of the complaint has been taken or is proposed to be taken;
> (c) where the complaint relates wholly or in part to the functions of a local authority, details of the complainant's right to take their complaint to a Local Commissioner under the Local Government Act 1974; and
> (d) except where the complaint relates only to the functions of a local authority, details of the complainant's right to take their complaint to the Health Service Commissioner under the 1993 Act.

20.39 NHS England's Complaint Policy published on 12 June 2017 provides that its response, if it is the investigating body, will include:

- An explanation of how the complaint has been considered.
- An apology if appropriate
- An explanation based on facts.
- Whether the complaint in full or in part is upheld.
- The conclusions reached in relation to the complaint including any remedial action that the organisation considers to be appropriate.
- Confirmation that the organisation is satisfied any action has been or will be actioned.
- Where possible, we will respond to people about any lessons learnt.
- Information and contact details of the Parliamentary and Health Service Ombudsman as the next stage of the NHS complaints process.

20.40 It also makes clear that:

> A key consideration is to make arrangements flexible; treating each case according to its individual nature with a focus on satisfactory outcomes, organisational learning and those lessons should lead to service improvement.

20.41 As stated above, remedial action might include: an apology; further clarification or an explanation; promises to implement service improvements; or financial redress. Good complaints handling will mean the responsible body's process is informed by the expectations of the complainant and what he or she seeks to achieve from the process. As part of the process, or after the responsible body has concluded its investigation, it may want to consider holding local resolution meetings with the complainant, for example if the complainant has indicated that he or she may take the complaint further to the PHSO. If appropriate, a responsible body could consider offering reconciliation or mediation. If so, and in any event, it should make clear to the complainant what options there are for obtaining the assistance of an NHS complaints advocacy service.

20.42 Unless the complainant and responsible body agreed a different response period, by reg 14 the response must be provided within six months from the day the complaint was received:

> (3) In paragraph (4), 'relevant period' means the period of 6 months commencing on the day on which the complaint was received, or such longer period as may be agreed before the expiry of that period by the complainant and the responsible body.
> (4) If the responsible body does not send the complainant a response in accordance with paragraph (2) within the relevant period, the responsible body must–
> (a) notify the complainant in writing accordingly and explain the reason why; and
> (b) send the complainant in writing a response in accordance with paragraph (2) as soon as reasonably practicable after the relevant period.

Contractual obligations with regards to complaints

20.43 As well as their statutory duties under the Complaints Regs 2009, all NHS providers who work under contracts with NHS commissioners ought to have contractual obligations concerning complaints handling and their cooperation with any complaints handling by the commissioner.

20.44 There are provisions in the NHS Standard Contract which require NHS providers to operate complaints systems which comply with the Complaints Regs 2009. GP practices holding GMS contracts are under a like duty. Regulations 79–80 of the National Health Service (General Medical Services Contracts) Regulations 2015[9] provide that the commissioning contract must require the practice to have a Complaints Regulations compliant procedure in place, and also that the practice must co-operate with any investigation which it is implicated in. A failure to do so might mean the contractor is in breach of its contractual obligations:

> **79 Complaints procedure**
> (1) The contractor must establish and operate a complaints procedure to deal with complaints made in relation to any matter that is reasonably connected with the provision of services under the contract.
> (2) The complaints procedure must comply with the requirements of the Local Authority Social Services and National Health Service Complaints (England) Regulations 2009.
>
> **80 Co-operation with investigations**
> (1) The contractor must co-operate with–
> (a) the investigation of any complaint made in relation to a matter that is reasonably connected with the provision of services under the contract by–
> (i) the Board, or
> (ii) the Health Service Commissioner; and
> (b) the investigation of any complaint made by an NHS body or local authority which relates to a patient or former patient of the contractor.

9 SI No 1862.

(2) In paragraph (1)–
'NHS body' means–
(a) in relation to England, the Board or a CCG; and
(b) in relation to England and Wales, Scotland and Northern Ireland, an NHS trust, an NHS foundation trust, a Local Health Board, a Health Board, a Health and Social Services Board or a Health and Social Services Trust;
'local authority' means–
(a) a local authority within the meaning of section 1 of the Local Authority Social Services Act 1970 (local authorities);
(b) the Council of the Isles of Scilly;
(c) a council constituted under section 2 of the Local Government etc. (Scotland) Act 1994 (constitution of councils); [or]
(d) the council of a county or county borough in Wales; and

'Health Service Commissioner' means the person appointed as Health Service Commissioner for England in accordance with section 1 of, and Schedule 1 to, the Health Service Commissioners Act 1993 (The Commissioner).

(3) For the purposes of paragraph (1), co-operation includes–
(a) answering any questions which are reasonably put to the contractor by the Board;
(b) providing any information relating to the complaint which is reasonably required by the Board; and
(c) attending any meeting held to consider the complaint (if held at a reasonably accessible place and at a reasonable hour and if due notice has been given) if the contractor's presence at the meeting is reasonably required by the Board.

The Health Service Commissioner for England

20.45 The Health Service Commissioner for England is a statutory appointment under section 1 of the Health Service Commissioners Act (HSCA) 1993. The Parliamentary and Health Service Ombudsman (PHSO), as it is colloquially known, combines the two statutory roles of a) Parliamentary Commissioner for Administration (the Parliamentary Ombudsman, whose powers are set out in the Parliamentary Commissioner Act 1967) and b) Health Service Commissioner for England (Health Service Ombudsman). The legislation governing the powers of the Parliamentary Ombudsman and the Health Service Ombudsman is materially the same in most respects. As a general rule, case-law applicable to one ombudsman is applicable to any discussion of the powers of the other. The current ombudsman is Rob Behrens CBE, who was appointed on 6 April 2017 to succeed the previous ombudsman, Dame Julie Mellor.

20.46 As set out on the PHSO website:

> We were set up by Parliament to provide an independent complaint handling service for complaints that have not been resolved by the NHS in England and UK government departments.
>
> We share findings from our casework to help Parliament scrutinise public service providers. We also share our findings more widely to help drive improvements in public services and complaint handling.

20.47 The PHSO[10] is accountable to the Parliamentary Public Administration and Constitutional Affairs Committee. The PHSO's role is primarily to investigate individual complaints against health service providers where the complainant has sustained injustice or hardship in consequence of a service failure or maladministration (a term which is broadly defined). The PHSO also has the power under section 14 of the HSCA 1993 to lay reports before each House of Parliament, either in relation to a specific case where the injustice sustained has still not been remedied or pursuant to any of his functions. A recent example of the latter is a report published by the PHSO on 6 December 2017, *Ignoring the alarms: How NHS eating disorder services are failing patients,* a study of failures in several NHS organisations to properly care for patients with eating disorders. This report was triggered by a specific complaint about the tragic death of Averil Hart, who had anorexia nervosa and died on 15 December 2012, aged only 19.[11] The PHSO therefore has an important public function.

20.48 As a general rule, complainants will be able to take a complaint about NHS care or services they have received to the PHSO after they have exhausted the NHS complaints process explained above. The process is statutorily designed to be an informal one, and inquisitorial rather than adversarial. As explained by Sir Ernest Ryder, Senior President of Tribunals, in the recent Court of Appeal case, *Miller v Health Service Commissioner for England*:[12]

> I would also emphasise that it is important that this court does not import into the informal, non-judicial process of administrative and complaints adjudicators like the ombudsman the procedures of courts and tribunals. The adjudication process is an informal resolution of a complaint or problem where other remedies are not reasonably available or appropriate. The procedure is a matter entirely within the gift of the ombudsman provided that her decision-making process is lawful, rational and reasonable.

20.49 Despite the informality of the procedure, however, courts appear increasingly likely to scrutinise the fairness of the PHSO's processes, particularly in relation to the treatment of those complained about, influenced by the fact that the outcome of a complaint could lead to 'serious criticism of the [body or person complained about's] professional practice [which] might ruin their reputation, professional standing and ability to earn a livelihood'.[13]

The PHSO's powers and duties

The PHSO's discretionary powers and their amenability to judicial review

20.50 By way of a preliminary point, the HSCA 1993 confers on the PHSO a number of broad discretions, including whether to investigate a complaint

10 I refer hereafter to the 'PHSO', although this should be taken as a reference to the PHSO insofar as it relates to the specific functions of the Health Service Commissioner under the Health Service Commissioners Act 1993.

11 Available at: www.ombudsman.org.uk/sites/default/files/page/ACCESSIBILE%20PDF%20-%20Anorexia%20Report.pdf.

12 [2018] EWCA Civ 144 at [55].

13 See *Miller* at [46].

in the first place, whether to discontinue an investigation, whether to investigate notwithstanding that the complainant may have another remedy, what standard he shall adopt to assess whether there has been a service failure or maladministration, what procedure for conducting an investigation is appropriate in the circumstances, and so on. In these circumstances, the Ombudsman's exercise of discretion will only be reviewable by the courts on public law grounds, including whether the exercise of discretion was a reasonable one. The requirements of procedural fairness are also particularly relevant to the Ombudsman's procedure, given that it is designed by statute to be informal and flexible. What fairness demands in a particular situation will depend upon the context and the nature of the complaint (see *R v Secretary of State for the Home Department ex p Doody*[14]). It has thus traditionally been difficult for claimants to successfully challenge a range of decisions taken by the PHSO.

20.51 Case-law has consistently established the threshold for challenging a matter of the PHSO's discretion is 'a very high one indeed'. In *R (Morris) v The Health Service Commissioner*,[15] Jay J, quoting Collins J, who was himself quoting Simon Brown LJ in the seminal case of *Dyer*, said:

> ... the courts have consistently recognised that the defendant's investigatory powers under section 3 of the Health Service Commissioners Act 1967 are very widely drawn. In *R (Mencap) v Parliamentary and Health Service Ombudsman* [2011] EWHC 3351 (Admin), Mitting J referred to 'an unfettered discretion'. I interpret that as meaning a very broad discretion, reviewable only on a conventional Wednesbury basis, including demonstrating that the decision maker has plainly asked itself the wrong question or has plainly misinterpreted the complaint. In *R (Jeremiah) v Parliamentary and Health Service Ombudsman* [2013] EWHC 1085 (Admin), Collins J said this:
>
>> '30. The law, as set out by both the Act and its interpretation in previous decisions, is that the hurdle which has to be surmounted by any claimant seeking to persuade a court that an exercise of discretion by the Ombudsman is unlawful is a very high one indeed. The relevant leading decision is *R v Parliamentary Commissioner for Administration ex p Dyer* [1994] 1 WLR 621 where Simon Brown LJ, as he then was, giving the judgment of the Divisional Court made it clear that the width of the discretion was, as he put it, made 'strikingly clear' by the legislature. That is a reference to the provision which is now in section 3(5) that the Commissioner should act in accordance with his own discretion. He said that it would always be difficult to mount an effective challenge on what may be called the conventional ground of Wednesbury unreasonableness. While manifest absurdity perhaps did not have to be shown, it would be almost as difficult to demonstrate that the Commissioner had exercised one or other of his discretions unreasonably in the public law sense ...'

20.52 One caveat should be given here with respect to the application of the case-law above to the PHSO's discretion to set aside the statutory one-year time bar (discussed below) and investigate a complaint if he considers it reasonable to do so under section 9(4) of the HSCA 1993. It was held in a

14 [1994] 1 AC 531.
15 [2014] EWHC 4364 (Admin).

recent case, *R (Newman) v PHSO*[16] by Jefford J that the decision to investigate if reasonable was not a broad discretion but a specific decision, and thus the usual rationality standard would apply:

> ... the authorities that consider the nature and breadth of the discretion under s.3(1) and (2) (or their equivalent) are not directly relevant. The decision that is challenged in this case is a decision under s.9(4). That does not involve the exercise of the broad discretion under s. 3(2) but involves the specific decision as to whether it is reasonable to investigate a complaint made out of time and the issue I have to consider is whether the decision that it was reasonable to do so was irrational (in particular in the sense of lacking logic) or failed to take into account relevant considerations.

There is an argument (which may well have merit) that this judgment was wrongly decided. Section 9(4) gives the PHSO an ability to investigate if he considers that it is reasonable to do so. This appears to give the PHSO a wider discretion than the judge suggests. There is the question of compatibility of this decision with the power in section 3(2) to act in accordance with his own discretion in determining whether to initiate an investigation, which comes within section 3 establishing the 'general remit' of the commissioner. A first instance judgment is not binding as a matter of precedent and so it will remain to be seen whether this case is followed by the court in future.

What does the PHSO investigate?

20.53 In terms of the PHSO's investigatory remit, section 3 of the HSCA 1993 gives him a discretion to investigate a complaint made by a member of the public who claims to have sustained injustice in consequence of service failure by, or maladministration in connection with an, action taken by or on behalf of a 'health service body'. That power is extended to independent providers on materially the same terms, and to investigating actions in connection with services provided by 'family health service providers' broadly speaking (primary care providers). It is important to note that the PHSO will only uphold a complaint if a complainant has actually *sustained* injustice as a consequence of a service failure or maladministration. If there has been poor service, but the organisation or person complained about has already made amends and put things right to a level the PHSO deems acceptable, he may acknowledge failures but will not uphold a complaint if there is nothing left to remedy.

20.54 The PHSO's overview guidance explains to complainants:

> If we uphold your complaint it means that we found the organisation got things wrong that have had a negative effect on you that hasn't been put right. We can recommend what the organisation should do about this. We investigate around 4,000 complaints a year and we uphold, in full or in part, around 40% of these.[17]

20.55 Although the PHSO's primary function is to investigate maladministration, by virtue of amendments made to the HSCA 1993 in 1996, he is

16 [2017] EWHC 3336 (TCC), a case in which this author appeared for the PHSO with James Maurici QC, also of Landmark Chambers.

17 Available at: www.ombudsman.org.uk/sites/default/files/PHSO_Overview_leaflet_0.pdf.

empowered to investigate the merits of an action taken by a medical practitioner in the exercise of his or her clinical judgment (see section 3(7)). This means the PHSO can consider complains about unsatisfactory care or treatment.

20.56 Section 3 provides as follows:

(1) On a complaint duly made to the Commissioner by or on behalf of a person that he has sustained injustice or hardship in consequence of–
(a) a failure in a service provided by a health service body,
(b) a failure of such a body to provide a service which it was a function of the body to provide, or
(c) maladministration connected with any other action taken by or on behalf of such a body,
the Commissioner may, subject to the provisions of this Act, investigate the alleged failure or other action.

(1ZA) Any failure or maladministration mentioned in subsection (1) may arise from action of–
(a) the health service body,
(b) a person employed by that body,
(c) a person acting on behalf of that body, or
(d) a person to whom that body has delegated any functions.

(1A) Where a family health service provider has undertaken to provide any family health services and a complaint is duly made to the Commissioner by or on behalf of a person that he has sustained injustice or hardship in consequence of–
(a) action taken by the family health service provider in connection with the services,
(b) action taken in connection with the services by a person employed by the family health service provider in respect of the services,
(c) action taken in connection with the services by a person acting on behalf of the family health service provider in respect of the services, or
(d) action taken in connection with the services by a person to whom the family health service provider has delegated any functions in respect of the services,
the Commissioner may, subject to the provisions of this Act, investigate the alleged action.

(1C) Where an independent provider has made an arrangement with a health service body or a family health service provider to provide a service (of whatever kind), or has undertaken to provide direct payment services, and a complaint is duly made to [the Commissioner by or on behalf of a person that he has sustained injustice or hardship in consequence of–
(a) a failure in the service provided by the independent provider,
(b) a failure of the independent provider to provide the service, or
(c) maladministration connected with any other action taken in relation to the service,
the Commissioner may, subject to the provisions of this Act, investigate the alleged failure or other action.

(1D) Any failure or maladministration mentioned in subsection (1C) may arise from action of–
(a) the independent provider,
(b) a person employed by the provider,
(c) a person acting on behalf of the provider, or
(d) a person to whom the provider has delegated any functions.

(1E) Where a complaint is duly made to [the Commissioner by or on behalf of a person that the person has sustained injustice or hardship in consequence of maladministration by any person or body in the exercise of any function under section 113 of the Health and Social Care (Community Health and Standards) Act 2003 (complaints about health care), the Commissioner may, subject to the provisions of this Act, investigate the alleged maladministration.

20.57 'Maladministration' as a concept is a broad one. It encompasses things like poor administration, including poor complaints handling, rudeness, misleading advice, refusal to provide information to which an individual is entitled, or clerical error. Summarising the powers in the Parliamentary Commissioner Act 1967, Andrews J in *R (Rapp) v PHSO*[18] said about the meaning of 'maladministration':

> 'Maladministration' is not defined in the 1967 Act. It will cover 'bias, neglect, delay, incompetence, ineptitude, perversity, turpitude, arbitrariness and so on'. The list is open-ended, but the type of behaviour that qualifies concerns the manner in which a decision is reached or a discretion is exercised, rather than the merits of that decision or of the discretion itself: *R v Local Commissioner ex p Liverpool CC* [2001] 1 All ER 262 per Henry LJ at [3], adopting a passage in the judgment of Lord Denning MR in *R v Local Commissioner for Administration for the North and East Area of England ex p Bradford Metropolitan CC* [1979] QB 287 at 311–312.

Which bodies or persons can the PHSO investigate?

20.58 The health service bodies subject to the PHSO's investigatory powers are set out in section 2 of the HSCA 1993 and are as follows:

a) special health authorities (if they have been designated as ones to which the HSCA 1993 is applicable);
b) NHS trusts managing a hospital, or other establishment or facility, in England;
c) NHS foundation trusts;
d) NHS England; and
e) CCGs.

20.59 A 'family health service provider' subject to the PHSO's investigatory powers is, broadly speaking, a reference to a primary care provider, and is defined in section 2A:

(a) persons (whether individuals or bodies) providing services under a contract entered into by them with the National Health Service Commissioning Board under section 84, 100 or 117 of the National Health Service Act 2006;
(b) persons (whether individuals or bodies) undertaking to provide in England pharmaceutical services under that Act;
(c) individuals performing in England primary medical services or primary dental services in accordance with arrangements made under section 92 or 107 of that Act (except as employees of, or otherwise on behalf of, a health service body or an independent provider); or
(d) individuals providing in England local pharmaceutical services in accordance with arrangements made under a pilot scheme established

18 [2015] EWHC 1344 (Admin).

under section 134 of the National Health Service Act 2006 (except as employees of, or otherwise on behalf of, a health service body or an independent provider).

20.60 An 'independent provider' subject to the PHSO's investigatory powers is defined in section 2B as follows (importantly, it extends to providers providing direct payments services, where patients arrange for and pay for their own care services out of a payment or budget allotted to them[19]):

(1) Persons are subject to investigation by the Commissioner if–
(a) they are or were at the time of the action complained of persons (whether individuals or bodies) providing services in England under arrangements with health service bodies or family health service providers, and
(b) they are not or were not at the time of the action complained of themselves health service bodies or family health service providers.

(1A) Persons are subject to investigation by the Commissioner if–
(a) they are, or were at the time of the action complained of, providing direct payment services, and
(b) they are not, or were not at the time of the action complained of, health service bodies.

The PHSO's decision to investigate

20.61 Before the PHSO investigates a complaint, he will first come to an in-principle decision to 'propose' to investigate a complaint. This decision involves a consideration of matters set out in the statute, which might preclude an investigation, such as whether a complaint has been properly made, whether there is an alternative remedy, and whether the complaint is in time, but also discretionary factors such as whether there are indications of unremedied injustice sustained such that the PHSO should investigate. The PHSO's guidance on *Deciding whether to investigate* explains that he will consider the following matters:

- Who brought the complaint – whether you have suffered personally or been affected in some other way because of what happened, or whether you are making the complaint for someone else.
- Timings – when you first became aware of the problem.
- Whether legal action is open to you.
- Whether there is another organisation that is better placed to deal with your complaint.
- What led you to complain: what did the organisation do wrong, what happened because of this, and what has been done to respond to your concerns.[20]

20.62 The discretion as to whether to treat a complaint to the PHSO as 'duly made' and whether to initiate, continue or discontinue an investigation under the 1993 Act are matters for the PHSO, subject only to review by the courts on public law grounds. The relevant section, 3(2) and (3), provide:

19 See chapter 14 on direct payments.

20 See www.ombudsman.org.uk/sites/default/files/PHSO_Step_Two_Info_leaflet_1.pdf.

(2) In determining whether to initiate, continue or discontinue an investigation under this Act, the Commissioner shall act in accordance with his own discretion.

(3) Any question whether a complaint is duly made to the Commissioner shall be determined by him.

20.63 In terms of whether a complaint is duly made, section 8(1) of the HSCA 1993 provides that 'a complaint may be made by an individual or a body of persons, whether incorporated or not, other than a public authority'. Section 9 of the HSCA 1993 sets out the requirements that must be followed:

(2) A complaint must be made in writing.

(3) The complaint shall not be entertained unless it is made–
  (a) by the person aggrieved, or
  (b) where the person by whom a complaint might have been made has died or is for any reason unable to act for himself, by–
    (i) his personal representative,
    (ii) a member of his family, or
    (iii) some body or individual suitable to represent him.

(4) The Commissioner shall not entertain the complaint if it is made more than a year after the day on which the person aggrieved first had notice of the matters alleged in the complaint, unless he considers it reasonable to do so.

(4A) In the case of a complaint against a person who is no longer of a description set out in section 2A(1), but was of such a description at the time of the action complained of, the Commissioner shall not entertain the complaint if it is made more than three years after the last day on which the person was a family health service provider.

(4B) In the case of a complaint against a person falling within section 2B(1) in relation to whom there are no longer any such arrangements as are mentioned there, the Commissioner shall not entertain the complaint if it is made more than three years after the last day on which the person was an independent provider.

20.64 Section 10 of the HSCA 1993 gives a health service body the power to refer to the PHSO a complaint made to it that a person has, in consequence of a failure or maladministration for which that body is responsible, sustained injustice or hardship as mention in section 3(1).

20.65 Section 9(4) creates a statutory bar to the PHSO investigating a complaint if it is made more than a year after the day on which the person aggrieved (ie who alleges to have sustained injustice) first had notice of the matters alleged. However, he may investigate nonetheless if he considers it reasonable to do so (although see above for the decision in *Newman* about the applicability of the general case law on the breadth of the PHSO's discretions). It is worth pointing out here that both the NHS complaints procedure and PHSO legislation create a prima facie one-year time limitation period. They technically run concurrently, and complainants at the NHS stage may want to consider this if they think they will refer their complaint onto the PHSO. However, exhaustion of the local resolution process will be a highly relevant factor to the PHSO's decision as to whether it is reasonable to investigate after a year has passed. This decision is inherently fact-specific. The personal circumstances of the complainant, the reasons for any delay, and potentially the impact on the person or body being complained about, will be relevant. For family health service providers and independent providers there is a long-stop period of three years after the person has ceased to act in that capacity, after which the PHSO has no discretion to extend time and investigate.

20.66 It is the practice of the PHSO, once he has received a complaint, to liaise with the complainant to ascertain the exact scope of his or her complaint and the scope of the investigation the complainant wishes for him to conduct if the complaint is accepted for investigation. This is proper; however, it was held by the Court of Appeal in *R (Cavanagh) v Health Service Commissioner*[21] that the PHSO's functions were limited to an investigation of the complaint and he had no power of investigation at large. In addition, the statutory discretions that he possessed neither enabled him to expand the ambit of a complaint beyond what it contained, nor his investigation of it beyond what the complaint warranted.

20.67 Another matter that the PHSO must consider under section 4 of the HSCA 1993 before he can decide to investigate the complaint is whether a complainant has an alternative remedy. As described in *Miller*, section 4 'provides a qualified prohibition which guards against conflict and inconsistency where judicial or quasi-judicial remedies are otherwise reasonably available giving them a priority over the ombudsman'. It provides:

(1) The Commissioner shall not conduct an investigation in respect of action in relation to which the person aggrieved has or had–
  (a) a right of appeal, reference or review to or before a tribunal constituted by or under any enactment or by virtue of Her Majesty's prerogative, or
  (b) a remedy by way of proceedings in any court of law,
  unless the Commissioner is satisfied that in the particular circumstances it is not reasonable to expect that person to resort or have resorted to it.

(2) The Commissioner shall not conduct an investigation in respect of action which has been, or is, the subject of an inquiry under section 84 of the National Health Service Act 1977 or section 76 of the National Health Service (Scotland) Act 1978 (general powers to hold inquiries).

(3) A Commissioner shall not conduct an investigation in respect of action [by a health service body other than the Mental Welfare Commission for Scotland if it is action in relation to which the protective functions of the Mental Welfare Commission for Scotland have been, are being or may be exercised under the Mental Health (Scotland) Act 1984.

(4) Subsection (5) applies where–
  (a) action by reference to which a complaint is made under section 3(1), (1A) or (1C) is action by reference to which a complaint can be made under section 113(1) or (2) of the Health and Social Care (Community Health and Standards) Act 2003 or under a procedure operated by a health service body, a family health service provider or an independent provider, and
  (b) subsection (1), (2) or (3) does not apply as regards the action.

(5) In such a case the Commissioner shall not conduct an investigation in respect of the action unless he is satisfied that–
  (a) the other procedure has been invoked and exhausted, or
  (b) in the particular circumstances it is not reasonable to expect that procedure to be invoked or (as the case may be) exhausted.

21 [2005] EWCA Civ 1578.

(6) Section 1(2) of the Hospital Complaints Procedure Act 1985 (which provides that no right of appeal etc. conferred under section 1 of that Act is to preclude an investigation under this Act) shall have effect subject to subsection (5) above.

20.68 The effect of this section is that if, when a complaint is made to the PHSO, there are already existing or contemplated proceedings – for example, by way of judicial review, a claim for negligence, or proceedings before the GMC – the PHSO cannot investigate until those proceedings have been concluded. Where they are concluded or no longer contemplated, the PHSO has to be satisfied that it was not reasonable for the complainant to have resorted to those alternative remedies. In addition, for health complaints, section 4(4) and (5) provide that the PHSO shall not conduct an investigation where a complaint could be made under the NHS complaints procedure set out above, unless that procedure has been invoked and exhausted or it is not reasonable to expect that procedure to be invoked or exhausted. Complainants should be aware that if they bypass the NHS complaints procedure under the Complaints Regs 2009 and go straight to the PHSO, or refuse a reasonable offer of mediation or local conciliation from the NHS body or provider, then the PHSO may well refer them back to complete the local resolution process.

20.69 As explained in *Miller*:[22]

> Ultimately, two questions need to be answered under section 4 of the 1993 Act: (1) is there a legal remedy? (2) is the ombudsman satisfied that in the particular circumstances it is not reasonable to expect that person to resort to it?

And:[23]

> The question of reasonableness is one for the ombudsman, and this court can only interfere if the ombudsman's approach discloses an error of law or the conclusion is irrational. The following principles appear to be clear:
> (1) The presence of an alternative legal remedy does not preclude the ombudsman from investigating. Any other conclusion would defeat the purpose of the provision in section 4 questioning whether it is reasonable to expect the other person to resort to it.
> (2) The decision is a matter of weighing several factors. If the complainant is primarily seeking financial redress, that points to the legal remedy being appropriate. If the person is primarily seeking an apology or wider systemic change, that points to the legal remedy being inappropriate. Neither factor is, however, conclusive. It is a sliding scale, and all the circumstances of the person, including their financial circumstances should be considered.

20.70 It is important that the decision-maker clearly records all the possible alternative routes of address, then records and weighs up the relevant factors, coming to a specific conclusion on the presence of an alternative legal remedy and whether the complaint should be investigated nonetheless.

22 At [87].
23 At [88].

The PHSO's investigation procedure

20.71 Section 11 governs the procedure the PHSO must adopt in respect of investigations. The first point is that under section 11(1)–(1C), when the Ombudsman 'proposes' to conduct an investigation of a complaint, before he actually proceeds with the investigation, he must give the body complained about the chance to comment on any of the allegations in the complaint. As a matter of fairness, the allegations must be disclosed with sufficient particularity to allow the person complained about to have a meaningful opportunity to comment (see *Miller*). At this stage, the PHSO has not exercised his discretion to decide to investigate formally so the comments of a body complained about could change an in-principle decision that a complaint is suitable for investigation. For example, a body or person complained about may highlight that there are parallel proceedings in front of a court or the GMC or that a complaint was not made under the Complaints Regs 2009.

20.72 Section 11(2) provides that an investigation shall be conducted in private.

20.73 Otherwise section 11(3) gives the PHSO a broad discretion to conduct the investigation in a way that he considers 'appropriate', however it must be a fair process, which will depend on the individual circumstances of the complaint. Section 11(3) provides:

> (3) In other respects, the procedure for conducting an investigation shall be such as the Commissioner considers appropriate in the circumstances of the case, and in particular–
> (a) he may obtain information from such persons and in such manner, and make such inquiries, as he thinks fit, and
> (b) he may determine whether any person may be represented, by counsel or solicitor or otherwise, in the investigation.

20.74 In terms of the standard of review adopted by the PHSO in determining whether there has been a service failure or maladministration, Burnett J in *R (Attwood) v Health Service Commissioner*,[24] confirmed in *Miller*, held as follows:[25]

> The purpose of the Health Service Commissioner ... is to adjudicate over complaints and provide redress by making findings and recommendations. It is, in my judgment, clear that Parliament was not seeking to create a parallel jurisdiction to courts and tribunals, which jurisdiction should apply the same principles by reading over established legal concepts into the language of various Acts governing the jurisdiction of the ombudsmen.

The judge explained the key issue and concluded saying:[26]

> As a matter of principle, it is for the ombudsman to decide and explain what standard she applies before making a finding of a failure in a service. That standard as defined will not be interfered with by a reviewing court unless it reflects an unreasonable approach.

20.75 The PHSO's adopted standard must therefore be a rational one and that standard ought to be clearly communicated to the public and those

24 [2008] EWHC 2315 (Admin).

25 At [27].

26 At [27].

involved in the complaint. The PHSO's current literature explains in relation to its adopted approach:

> To help us understand what should have happened, we look at how the organisation was expected to act at the time of the events. We look at any standards, legislation or established good practice that was in place at the time, and we use advice we have gathered from experts. We also refer to our Principles of Good Administration and Principles of Good Complaint Handling. These set out what we expect from organisations when they carry out their work and how they should reply when things go wrong. You can find them on our website.[27]

20.76 The PHSO has long had a practice of producing a draft report of the investigator's findings, along with a draft decision as to whether the complaint will be upheld, partially upheld or not upheld; and if upheld, what remedies he or she suggests are appropriate.

20.77 It is possible at this stage for a complainant or person or body complained about to provide further comment and/or evidence. The PHSO may also commission further specialist advice at this stage from his clinical advisors. The investigator should be careful to ensure he or she acts fairly. Any comments on the draft report or further information obtained should be carefully considered and taken into account in any final decision. To avoid pre-determination, the investigator should keep an open mind to the new information changing the conclusions and outcome of the complaint, even if he or she has reached a provisional view.

20.78 Under section 12 of the HSCA 1993, the PHSO has the same powers in relation to evidence as the High Court and may require disclosure by those bodies and persons he is investigating.

The PHSO's final report

20.79 Under section 14(1) of the HSCA 1993, the PHSO is obliged to send a report of the results of his investigation to the following people:

(a) to the person who made the complaint,
(b) to any member of the House of Commons who to the Commissioner's knowledge assisted in the making of the complaint (or if he is no longer a member to such other member as the Commissioner thinks appropriate),
(c) to the health service body who at the time the report is made provides the service, or has the function, in relation to which the complaint was made, and
(d) to any person who is alleged in the complaint to have taken or authorised the action complained of.

20.80 In the case of an investigation into the actions of a primary care provider or an independent provider, there is also a requirement to send the report to the relevant commissioning body or the health service body or primary care provider with whom any independent provider made the arrangement to provide the services concerned. If the complaint was about complaints handling within the NHS, then the report must be sent to the

27 At the time of writing, however, the PHSO website states that it is currently updating this guidance. Readers should check whether there have been any changes since publication of this book.

complaints handler and any other provider about whom the complaint was originally made. An example would be if a complaint was made to NHS England, about a GP, then the complaint about NHS England's complaint handling was made to the PHSO. The PHSO would have to send the report to the GP too under section 14(2E).

20.81 Section 14 does not state what the report must contain, or define what 'the results' of an investigation should be. The PHSO therefore has a broad discretion as to what that report will contain and what remedies he will suggest are appropriate to remedy the injustice he has found the complainant has sustained. The PHSO's guidance explains that the final report will mean that the complainant will:

- know our final decision on your complaint,
- have a clear understanding of how we made our decision, what information we used, and how we took into account any feedback we received on our draft report,
- know what action we may have asked the organisation to take and by when,
- know how you can give us feedback.

It says:

> If we have made recommendations for the organisation to carry out, our report will clearly explain what action we expect and by when. We will check to make sure the organisation does what we have asked, and we will keep you updated about this.[28]

20.82 In terms of remedy, the PHSO's guidance makes clear that the remedy could include an organisation or person complained about:

- acknowledging its mistakes,
- apologising to you,
- making a payment to you – for example, to pay you back if you have been left out of pocket because of its errors, or to acknowledge distress it has caused you,
- taking action to prevent the same mistakes happening to someone else, and to make services better for everyone.

20.83 If the PHSO decides not to investigate, under section 14(2) he must send a statement or reasons to the person who made the complainant and to any MP who he knows assisted in making the complaint.

20.84 Section 14(2I) provides a catch-all provision about report recipients, and states:

> Where the Commissioner is required by this section to send a report or statement of reasons to certain persons, the Commissioner may send the report or statement to such other persons as the Commissioner thinks appropriate.

20.85 Under section 14(2HA), if the PHSO:

> ... has not concluded an investigation before the end of the 12 month period beginning with the date the complaint was received, the Commissioner must send a statement explaining the reason for the delay to the person who made the complaint.

28 Available at: www.ombudsman.org.uk/sites/default/files/PHSO_Step_Three_Info_leaflet_1.pdf.

20.86 Moreover, the PHSO has the power to lay reports before the Houses of Parliament in certain circumstances. The first is under section 14(3) if it appears to him that the injustice or hardship sustained by the complainant has not been and will not be remedied.

20.87 The second is under section 14(4)(a), whereby the PHSO is required to lay an annual report before parliament providing a general report on the performance of his functions under the HSCA 1993. This must include information about: a) how long investigations that were concluded in the year to which the report relates took to be concluded; b) how many of those investigations took more than 12 months to be concluded; and c) the action being taken with a view to all investigations being concluded within 12 months.

20.88 Finally, the PHSO has the power to lay reports before parliament 'with respect to those functions as he thinks fit'. The PHSO relies on this power to publish reports such as the one referenced above about care of patients with eating disorders, where he has amassed a certain amount of evidence and wisdom about potential service failures on a broader scale as a result of his investigation of individual complaints.

Remedies against a decision of the PHSO

20.89 If a complainant is not happy with the decision of the PHSO, it is possible to apply to the High court for permission for judicial review to challenge the lawfulness of a PHSO decision. As explained above, the substantial areas of discretion available to the PHSO mean that it is not straightforward for claimants to prove that various of the PHSO's discretions have been exercised unlawfully.

The parallel jurisdiction of the PHSO and the court

20.90 A tricky question often arises relating to the parallel jurisdiction of ombudsmen and the courts where a decision made by an NHS service-provider is one that is both amenable to the review jurisdiction of the courts and is one about which a complaint could be made to the PHSO. Issues arise particularly in the context of the three-month judicial review time limit under Part 54 of the Civil Procedure Rules (CPR) 1998 and what a claimant should do in the circumstances where he or she might want to pursue both forms of redress. This issue was recently considered by Hickinbottom J (as he was) in *R (Zahid) v University of Manchester*,[29] albeit in the context of complaints to the Office of the Independent Adjudicator. He made the following observations about the correct approach:

> 67. The early finality of executive and administrative decisions is an important principle, and consequently, as a general principle, prompt resolution of public law claims by the courts is considered to be in the public interest – hence the relatively tight and strict time limit for the issuing of judicial review proceedings. However, the courts have also recognised that that principle may sometimes have to bow in the face of other interests, both

29 [2017] EWHC 188 (Admin) although readers should be aware that an appeal decision from the Court of Appeal is outstanding.

public and private. Where there is an available ADR procedure – especially when it is provided by Parliament – the interests of the public body and citizen in having a more attractive procedure and, very importantly, the public interest in resolving claims outside the court system where possible, will be of such weight that the balance of interests will be in favour of giving a proper opportunity for the dispute to be resolved, in whole or in part, by the alternative procedure; even if that may delay the final resolution of the dispute, if recourse to the courts is in the event necessary.

68. Consequently, where there is such a complaints procedure as provided by the 2004 Act through the OIA, the court should be slow to become engaged with issues arising out of the same subject matter, unless and until that procedure has been given reasonable time and opportunity to run to a conclusion; and, where either a claimant or a defendant (or both) wish to progress court proceedings before then, they must provide the court with good reasons for doing so. In my view, both parties and the court should approach the issues raised in the applications such as those before me – and all issues that arise as a result of the relationship between a reference to the OIA and judicial review proceedings – with this uppermost in mind.

20.91 Against this background, he suggested that 'the court is in any event unlikely to refuse a student [a complainant] an extension of time'[30] for judicial review if they have missed the three-month time limit mandated by CPR Part 54 because they were pursuing an alternative complaints procedure, such as to an ombudsman.

20.92 However, the safest approach is likely to be that a judicial review claim is issued protectively within the three-month time limit, in conjunction with an application to the court for a stay of proceedings at the earliest reasonably practicable stage. The consent of the body under challenge to a stay should also be sought. If a stay is granted, the PHSO can consider the matter before the claimant resorts to judicial review proceedings. This can raise complex issues given section 4 of the HSCA 1993, however, so potential claimants/ complainants are very much advised to seek legal advice in these circumstances.

30 At para 83.

CHAPTER 21

The impact of procurement law in the NHS[1]

continued

1 By James Neill. The author is particularly grateful to David Lock QC and Simon Taylor of Keating Chambers for their invaluable assistance in reviewing this chapter and providing extremely useful suggestions. Any errors remain the responsibility of the author.

Introduction: the nature and scope of procurement law and its application to the NHS

21.1 In broad terms, procurement law is the law governing the way in which public bodies award contracts to a third party for the supply of goods and services. The general UK public procurement regime is, at least whilst the UK is a member of the European Union (EU), derived from EU law,[2] as set out in three EU directives on public procurement issued in 2014 as part of a package of reforms, namely the Public Procurement Directive,[3] the Concessions Directive,[4] and the Utilities Directive.[5] Procurement law is a complex area that has given rise to a number of high profile legal challenges, some of which have resulted in significant embarrassment for central and local government as a result of the abandonment of procurement competitions and sizeable damages awards. It is therefore important for anyone concerned with NHS contracting to be aware of the nature of the obligations that procurement law imposes and the risks of breaching those laws.

21.2 The EU directives referred to above are implemented in England and Wales by various sets of regulations, in particular the Public Contracts Regulations (PC Regs) 2015.[6] The PC Regs 2015 impose various general obligations on contracting authorities when carrying out tender processes for public services or works contracts, the most significant ones being the obligations of: a) equal treatment, b) non-discrimination, c) proportionality and d) transparency. Legal duties under the PC Regs 2015 are enforceable by economic operators, including aggrieved bidders who have been unsuccessful in bidding for an NHS contract. In limited circumstances, third parties who are not economic operators may also bring challenges to procurement competitions carried out by public contracting authorities by judicial review. Domestic remedies under the PC Regs 2015 include orders setting aside the decision to award the contract, declarations of ineffectiveness (where contracts have already been entered into) and damages.[7]

21.3 NHS England, clinical commissioning groups (CCGs), NHS (as opposed to private) providers and the Department of Health and Social Care (DHSC) are all 'contracting authorities' for the purposes of the PC Regs 2015. They are therefore subject in principle to the same general obligations contained in those regulations as other UK contracting authorities when seeking to award public contracts.

2 Although the shape of the future procurement regime post Brexit is unclear, it is reasonably certain that some form of regulation will still apply after the UK leaves the EU: the UK government is seeking powers via the Trade Bill 2017 to implement the WTO Government Procurement Agreement which sets out minimum standards for procurement competitions.

3 Directive 2014/24/EU of the European Parliament and of the Council of 26 February 2014 on public procurement and repealing Directive 2004/18/EC.

4 Directive 2014/23/EU of the European Parliament and of the Council of 26 February 2014 on the award of concession contracts.

5 Directive 2014/25/EU of the European Parliament and of the Council of 26 February on procurement by entities operating in the water, energy, transport and postal services sector and repealing Directive 2004/17/EC.

6 SI No 102.

7 Remedies are discussed in detail at para 21.112 below.

21.4 However, in the case of contracts for healthcare services (health services contracts), for those contracts under €750,000, the PC Regs 2015 do not apply at all. For those over that threshold, unless they fall within certain specific exemptions and derogations, a specific Light Touch Regime (LTR) applies.[8] Under the LTR, the most significant differences to the standard procurement regime are first, that the key duty of advertisement via a contract notice does not apply; and second, the use of the standard procurement competition procedures (ie the open, restricted, and negotiated procedures) become discretionary rather than obligatory. The main features of the LTR as set out in regs 74–77 and the accompanying guidance issued by the UK government are considered in detail below.

21.5 In addition to the PC Regs 2015, CCGs and NHS England are also subject to duties under the National Health Service (Procurement, Patient Choice and Competition) (No 2) Regulations (PPCC2 Regs) 2013[9] and the National Health Service Act (NHS Act) 2006, which sometimes overlap with and potentially conflict with duties under the PC Regs 2015.

21.6 The scope of the two sets of regulations is discussed in detail below, but the position in summary is as follows:

a) the PC Regs 2015 apply to all contracts (whether for health services or otherwise) above the defined financial thresholds entered into by *all* NHS bodies;
b) the PPCC2 Regs 2013 apply to all health services contracts (of whatever value) entered into by CCGs and NHS England on the one hand and health service providers on the other;
c) the PC Regs 2015 *and* the PPCC2 Regs 2013 apply where the subject of the contract is the provision of health services, with a value of over EUR750,000, and where the contracting authority is either a CCG or NHS England.

21.7 The existence of two tiers of regulation (which are not always consistent between themselves) poses additional legal hurdles and constraints (not least arising from the application of the National Tariff for some services) for NHS contracting authorities seeking to award contracts. Chapter 10 on NHS acute care contracting (which should be read in conjunction with this chapter) addresses in particular the extent to which price competition can form part of a procurement competition for services specified in the National Tariff.

21.8 This chapter describes both tiers of regulation and sets out the various obligations they contain. It is in four main sections:

1) *An overview of the key rules and standard procurement procedures set out in the PC Regs 2015.* The majority of health services contracts are likely to be of a sufficiently high value to fall within the LTR and therefore these standard procedures will not apply to those particular types of contract. However, a number of specific rules and principles that apply to standard procurements under the PC Regs 2015 remain relevant in certain

8 For procurement commenced before 18 April 2016, the Public Contract Regulations 2006 SI No 5 (as amended) apply. This regulated the procurement of health care services as 'Part B' services.

9 SI No 500.

respects to healthcare contracts above the LTR threshold, in particular the application of a set of specified derogations and exemptions that remove the requirement to advertise altogether. In any event, they also provide important background to understanding the principles applying to procurements governed by the PPCC2 Regs 2013, and so are addressed in this section.

2) *The Light Touch Regime.* A description of the obligations that arise in respect of health services contracts that fall within the LTR and the principles for awarding such contracts.
3) *The PPCC2 Regs 2013.* A consideration of the PPCC2 Regs 2013 and the relatively few cases where the courts have considered their interpretation.
4) *Breach of the regulations.* A description of the various remedies available for breach of either or both sets of regulations, including an overview of procedural issues involved in challenging or defending NHS procurement decisions.

The Public Contract Regulations 2015 – an outline

The concept of contracting authorities

21.9 The PC Regs 2015 apply to all 'contracting authorities'. Contracting authorities are defined in Article 2 of the Public Procurement Directive as follows:

> . . . the State, regional or local authorities, bodies governed by public law or associations formed by one or more such authorities or one or more such bodies governed by public law.

21.10 Article 2(4) of the directive defines 'bodies governed by public law' as bodies that have all of the following characteristics:

(a) they are established for the specific purpose of meeting needs in the general interest, not having an industrial or commercial character;
(b) they have legal personality; and
(c) they are financed, for the most part, by the State, regional or local authorities, or by other bodies governed by public law; or are subject to management supervision by those authorities or bodies; or have an administrative, managerial or supervisory board, more than half of whose members are appointed by the State, regional or local authorities, or by other bodies governed by public law.

21.11 The definition in reg 2 adopts this definition verbatim, with the additional clarification that it includes central government authorities. Central government authorities are specified in Schedule 1, which includes the DHSC, all NHS trusts, and the NHS Business Services Authority.

21.12 In light of that definition, it is clear that the following are contracting authorities within the health sector for the purposes of the PC Regs 2015:

a) DHSC;
b) NHS commissioners: CCGs, NHS commissioning board and local authorities;
c) NHS trusts;
d) NHS foundation trusts (insofar as they meet the definition of bodies governed by public law in reg 2).

21.13 NHS GP and dental practices would not be caught by the regulations as they are not financed by the state, but rather are private for-profit businesses; nor would private providers of NHS services.

Public contracts

21.14 The rules apply to all 'public contracts', of which there are three defined types: a) contracts for the execution of work, b) contracts for the supply of products or c) contracts for the provision of services.[10] A contract is only covered by the Public Procurement Directive if it is a contract for pecuniary interest (ie the service provider gets paid under the contract). Issues can arise in situations where goods or services are provided free to NHS bodies by the private sector, in the expectation of an increase in publicity (for example, the free supply of particular clinical equipment). The test is not whether there is 'consideration' in the common law sense, but rather where there is direct economic benefit to the provider: see the opinion of Advocate General Leger in *La Scala*, as applied by Forbes J in *R (Chandler) v Secretary of State for Children, Schools and Families.*[11]

Contract thresholds

21.15 Article 4 of the Public Procurement Directive sets out a set of thresholds for determining contracts are subject to the directive, together with a number of expressly excluded categories of contracts.

21.16 The current thresholds which apply as from 1 January 2018 (which are revised every two years by the European Commission) are as follows:

Type of contract	**Threshold from 1 January 2018**
Supply and services contracts (central government)	€144,000
Supply and services contracts (non-central government)	€221,000
Works and subsidised works contracts	€5,548,000
Social and other services contracts falling within the LTR	€750,000

21.17 Unless a specific exemption or derogation applies removing these contracts from outside the scope of the PC Regs 2015 altogether,[12] the specific LTR referred to above in applies to health services contracts above €750,000.

21.18 Contracts below the €750,000 threshold do not fall within the scope of the PC Regs 2015 and so do not need to be advertised in the European Journal via an Official Journal of the European Union (OJEU) notice, nor is it likely that the general EU principles of equal treatment and non-discrimination apply to them (on the assumption that they would not attract cross-border interest). However, it is important to note that very

10 PC Regs 2015 reg 2.

11 [2009] EWHC 219 (Admin). See also the discussion in *Arrowsmith, The Law of Public and Utilities Procurement* (3rd edn, 2014, Sweet & Maxwell) at 6.12–6.14.

12 See, for example, the reg 32 derogations discussed below at para 21.51.

similar (if not identical) principles apply by virtue of the PPCC2 Regs 2013, and thus a CCG that breaches those principles runs the risk of being liable in damages to a bidder who was excluded in breach of the rules. This is discussed further at paras 21.112 onwards below.

Excluded contracts, 'in-house' exceptions and 'public-to-public co-operation'

21.19 There are a number of contracts that are excluded altogether from the scope of the Public Procurement Directive. These are set out at Articles 7–12 of the directive. The following are the main exclusions relevant to health service contracts:

a) service contracts awarded on the basis of an exclusive right (Article 11);
b) public contracts between entities within the public sector (Article 12);
c) contracts subsidised by contracting authorities (Article 13);
d) particular types of research and development (R&D) services contracts (Article 14).

The section below focusses on the exceptions contained in Articles 12 and 14.

21.20 Article 12 of the Public Procurement Directive codifies the previous Court of Justice of the European Union (CJEU) case-law that developed under the so-called the *Teckal* doctrine. In *Teckal*,[13] the European Court of Justice (ECJ) established that under certain conditions the procurement rules do not apply to arrangements between a contracting authority and another public body, where that public body is closely controlled by the awarding entity (and therefore effectively 'in-house'). They are incorporated by reg 12(1)–(3) of the PC Regs 2015.

21.21 For the exemption to apply, pursuant to Article 12(1) the following conditions have to be fulfilled (known as the control, activity and private participation conditions):

> (a) the contracting authority exercises over the legal person concerned a control which is similar to that which it exercises over its own departments;
> (b) more than 80% of the activities of the controlled legal person are carried out in the performance of tasks entrusted to it by the controlling contracting authority or by other legal persons controlled by that contracting authority; and
> (c) there is no direct private capital participation in the controlled legal person with the exception of non-controlling and non-blocking forms of private capital participation required by national legislative provisions, in conformity with the Treaties, which do not exert a decisive influence on the controlled legal person.

21.22 Article 12(2) states that:

> . . . a contracting authority shall be deemed to exercise over a legal person a control similar to that which it exercises over its own departments within the meaning of point (a) of the first subparagraph where it exercises a decisive influence over both strategic objectives and significant decisions of the controlled legal person. Such control may also be exercised by another

13 Case C-107/98, *Teckal Srl v Commune di Viano* [1999] ECR I-8121.

legal person, which is itself controlled in the same way by the contracting authority.

21.23 Article 12(3) creates an exemption for contracts awarded to *jointly* controlled public bodies, with similar exemptions to those specified in Article 12(2). These are incorporated into the PC Regs 2015 at reg 12(4)–(6).

21.24 In the context of healthcare services, CCGs have powers under section 223 of the NHS Act 2006 to set up companies to provide healthcare services (although such powers are circumscribed by section 223A).[14] In such circumstances, such a company could in principle satisfy the 'in-house' requirements of reg 12. Whether or not such an 'in-house' exemption is however removed by the operation of the PPCC2 Regs 2013 is discussed at para 21.91 below.

21.25 Article 12(4) states that a contract concluded exclusively between two or more contracting authorities is excluded from the directive where all of the following conditions are fulfilled:

(a) the contract establishes or implements a cooperation between the participating contracting authorities with the aim of ensuring that public services they have to perform are provided with a view to achieving objectives they have in common;
(b) the implementation of that cooperation is governed solely by considerations relating to the public interest; and
(c) the participating contracting authorities perform on the open market less than 20% of the activities concerned by the cooperation.

21.26 This reflects the principle established by the ECJ in Case C-480/06 *Commission v Germany* (the *Hamburg* doctrine), to the effect that certain co-operative arrangements between two or more public bodies (so called 'horizontal co-operation' or 'public-to-public co-operation') falls outside the directive and Treaty on the Functioning of the European Union (TFEU) principles. This is incorporated into domestic law by reg 12(7) of the PC Regs 2015.

21.27 CCGs and NHS England commission healthcare services but do not *provide* them, so it is difficult to see a situation arising whereby there could be co-operation between two or more commissioners for the provision of healthcare services, thus meeting the first of the requisite conditions for the public-to-public co-operation exemption.

21.28 However, two companies established under section 223 of the NHS Act 2006 could co-operate in this way and this could fall within the exception.[15] But it is doubtful that the condition set out at Article 12(4)(a) would be met if a contract between a commissioner and an NHS Trust were entered into, given the commissioner/provider split that was at the centre of the major NHS reforms introduced by the Health and Social Care Act (HSCA) 2012 and embodied in the PPCC2 Regs 2013. However, it seems it would be possible for two NHS trusts to pool resources with a view to providing a service to themselves and potentially to other Trusts and take advantage of this exception.

21.29 Article 14 is a general exclusion clause which excludes contracts for all research and development services, unless the two specified conditions

14 See chapter 5 on the powers and duties of CCGs.

15 A view shared by the Procurement Law Association Working Paper at para 4.23.

are satisfied. It is an important exclusion which enables research services carried out by NHS bodies to be procured without the need to conduct procurement competitions that comply with the Directive or PC Regs 2015. It states the following:

> This Directive shall only apply to public service contracts for research and development services which are covered by CPV codes 73000000-2 to 73120000-9, 73300000-5, 73420000-2 and 73430000-5 provided that both of the following conditions are fulfilled:
> (a) the benefits accrue exclusively to the contracting authority for its use in the conduct of its own affairs, and
> (b) the service provided is wholly remunerated by the contracting authority.

21.30 The effect of the conditions is to exclude from the scope of the directive the funding by a contracting authority of research whose aim is to develop products for the benefit of the market as a whole. As an exclusion clause, it is likely to be construed narrowly by the CJEU particularly in light of the recitals to the directive which seek to prevent contracting authorities taking advantage of this exclusion clause. Recital 35 of the 2014 Directive states that 'fictitious sharing of the results of the R & D' will not be sufficient to trigger the exclusion and re-iterates that the exclusion will not apply if the contracting authority 'retains an exclusive right to use the outcome of the R & D in the conduct of its own affairs'. On the face of it, the development of new clinical equipment and the conduct of clinical trials where the results of that research are published in the public interest and in order to improve patient care should fall within this exclusion. NHS contracting authorities would however need to avoid the inclusion of clauses in any contract awarded to an outside body in which the public body retains the intellectual property rights in the outcome of the research.

21.31 Even where research is commissioned exclusively for the use of an NHS contracting authority in the conduct of its own affairs, so long as the remuneration for that service is partly paid for by a third party then the exclusion can still apply. However, again recital 35 contains the warning that 'purely symbolic participation in the remuneration of the service provide should not prevent the application of this directive'.

The procurement principles and key duties

21.32 There are a number of key legal rules that apply to any contracting authority when conducting a procurement competition that falls within the scope of the PC Regs 2015. These are summarised below.

21.33 The general rules are set out in section 2 of Part 1 of the PC Regs 2015. Regulation 18 sets out the 'principles of procurement'. It states:

> (1) Contracting authorities shall treat economic operators equally and without discrimination and shall act in a transparent and proportionate manner.
> (2) The design of the procurement shall not be made with the intention of excluding it from the scope of this Part or of artificially narrowing competition.
> (3) For that purpose, competition shall be considered to be artificially narrowed where the design of the procurement is made with the

intention of unduly favouring or disadvantaging certain economic operators.

21.34 Compliance with these general rules is the primary duty on all contracting authorities. Breaches of these general rules is most often relied on by a disappointed bidder challenging a procurement competition.

Confidentiality and conflicts of interest

21.35 In order to operate a fair procurement process, all bidders have to be treated equally within a procurement process. Part of that obligation involves ensuring that bids submitted by individual bidders are kept confidential, or a later bidder would have an advantage over an earlier bidder. The maintenance of strict confidentiality of any bids submitted to a contracting authority is thus a key duty set out at reg 21 of the PC Regs 2015.

21.36 Given the commercially sensitive nature of material included in any bid, difficult issues arise in court proceedings where a disappointed bidder wishes to challenge the award of the contract to a successful bidder. The court endeavours to balance the need for a fair trial with the need to maintain confidentiality by creating defined 'confidentiality rings' to limit who is entitled to see confidential information from a challenged bidder and the scoring of the winning bid. The precise organisation of such arrangements will depend on the individual circumstances of a case but the court is astute to ensure that its proceedings are not used by disappointed bidders as a way of obtaining confidential information from their rivals for future commercial advantage.

21.37 Conflicts of interest are dealt with in reg 24, which requires contracting authorities to take appropriate measures to effectively prevent, identify and remedy any conflicts of interests arising in the conduct of the procurement competition. In the first case to consider an application to lift an automatic standstill under the 2015 PC Regs 2015, the High Court considered that the alleged breach of this Regulation was sufficiently serious to warrant a refusal to lift an automatic suspension in *Counted4 Community Interest Company v Sunderland City Council*.[16] CCG commissioning in which GP practices are potential providers is a particularly high risk area in this respect.[17] NHS England in June 2017 revised its guidance for CCGs on managing conflicts of interest in light of the experience of CCGs since the 2014 reforms in dealing with this issue.[18]

The standard procurement competition procedures: an outline

21.38 Section 3 of Part 2 of the PC Regs 2015 sets out the competitive award procedures that apply to procurement competitions for contracts that fall within the PC Regs 2015. Regulation 21(1) makes it clear that compliance with such

16 [2015] EWHC 3898 (TCC).

17 See chapter 5 on the powers and duties of CCGs' for more detail on the specific provisions governing GPs' involvement in CCG commissioning.

18 See www.england.nhs.uk/wp-content/uploads/2017/06/revised-ccg-coi-guidance-jul-17.pdf.

procedures is mandatory. It states: 'when awarding public contracts, contracting authorities shall apply procedures that conform to this Part'.

Competitive award procedures

21.39 Under the PC Regs 2015 there are five procedures, with particular rules that apply to when and how such procedures can be used by a contracting authority. They are:

a) the open procedure;
b) the restricted procedure;
c) the competitive dialogue procedure;
d) the negotiated procedure; and
e) an innovation partnership.

21.40 Contracting authorities must award contracts that fall within the scope of the PC Regs 2015 using one of these specific competitive award procedures. The following is an outline of the features of the main procedures and when they can be used.[19] Detailed rules applying to the form of the requisite notices, the use of electronic communications to advertise contracts and receive bids, and time limits for the receipt of tenders, are set out in the regulations – but for the purposes of this chapter are not discussed in detail.

The open procedure

21.41 The open procedure is the simplest form of the five procedures. It is generally used for reasonably straightforward competitions for contracts for the supply of goods and services where the contracting authority has a clear idea of its requirements and the identity of the supplier is not critical: its defining feature is that any interested economic operator may submit a tender in response to a contract notice (reg 27(1)).[20] Minimum time limits for the receipt of tenders are specified as 35 days (or, in cases where a Prior Information Notice (PIN) has been issued, 15 days).

The restricted procedure

21.42 The restricted procedure differs from the open procedure in that the contracting authority can limit the number of tenders it will consider, by only inviting tenders from some of those who have expressed an interest and have satisfied objectively justifiable conditions in order to enable the bidder to enter into the competition. Under this procedure, the same general requirement exists to advertise the contract so that all economic operators have an opportunity to be considered. This can either be done by a contract notice, or, in the case of sub-central government authorities, via a PIN.

21.43 The contracting authority can then select from those interested in bidding a limited number whom it then invites to tender. It does so by applying qualification criteria, the choice of which is also governed the PC Regs 2015. The contracting authority is required to use objective and non-discriminatory criteria in making this choice, which have been published in advance. It is also required to specify the minimum number of bidders who will be invited to bid for the contract.

19 Innovation partnerships are not discussed in detail for the purposes of this section.
20 The requirements of a contract notice are discussed further at para 21.53 below.

21.44 An invitation to tender (ITT) is then issued to those that have both qualified and been selected. The ITT will contain the procurement documents including the contract notice, the technical specifications which the authority requires the awarded contract to meet and information regarding the award criteria and their weightings.

The competitive dialogue procedure

21.45 The competitive dialogue procedure was introduced in 2004 via the former Public Sector Directive (the predecessor to the Public Procurement Directive) in order to allow greater flexibility in how contracting authorities could carry out procurement competitions for more complex projects where the contracting authority has not yet finally decided on the particular design. It allows discussions with bidders over their proposed solution. That flexibility is designed to allow for the identification and development of solutions suited to what the contracting authority requires.

The negotiated procedure

21.46 There are two types of negotiated procedure under the 2014 Public Procurement Directive: the 'competitive procedure with negotiation', or the 'negotiated procedure without publication of a contract notice'. Under the latter type, a contracting authority can proceed to negotiate with one or more bidders without any prior advertisement or need to conduct a competition at all. Under the directive and the PC Regs 2015 it can only be used in very limited circumstances set out below,[21] which essentially operate as derogations from the duty to advertise.

21.47 The grounds for use of the competitive procedure with negotiation are the same as those that apply to the use of the competitive dialogue procedure set out above. This procedure is very similar to the competitive dialogue procedure and indeed some have queried the rationale for retaining both procedures in the 2014 directive.[22]

The duty to advertise: contract notices, PINs and derogations from the duty to advertise

21.48 As referred to above, a fundamental requirement of a contract caught by the PC Regs 2015 is the duty to advertise.

21.49 Pursuant to reg 26(2) of the PC Regs 2015, a contract that falls within the scope of the regulations can only be awarded if preceded by a 'call for competition' (ie an advertisement). This will usually by via the publication of a 'contract notice' to inform potential bidders that the contracting authority is embarking on a procurement competition. In certain circumstances, a call for competition can be achieved via the issue of a PIN. Both types of advertisement are described below.

21.50 However, before those types of advertisement is addressed, a prior question arises, namely whether a derogation applies which removes the duty to advertise altogether.

21 See paras 21.51–21.52 below where the reg 32 derogations are discussed.

22 *Arrowsmith*, fn 11 above, para 9–02.

The regulation 32 derogations

21.51 Regulation 32 of the PC Regs 2015 provides that a negotiated procedure without notice may be used in a number of the following circumstances, the most relevant ones to health services contracts being:

a) *Regulation 32(2)(a):* Where no tenders or no requests to participate (or no suitable tenders or no suitable requests to participate) have been submitted in response to an open procedure or restricted procedure, provided that the initial conditions of the contract are not substantially altered.
b) *Regulation 32(2)(b):* Where the services can be supplied only by a particular economic operator for any of the following reasons:
   i) competition is absent for technical reasons; or
   ii) the protection of exclusive rights, including intellectual property rights.

   These exceptions only apply when no reasonable alternative or substitute exists and the absence of competition is not the result of an artificial narrowing down of the parameters of the procurement. It has been suggested that the exception at point i) could apply, for example, where the facility is owned by an existing provider and the location is specific and it does not make practical sense to expect bidders to provide a new building (for example, A&E and associated trauma and Intensive Care Units).
c) *Regulation 32(2)(c):* Insofar as is strictly necessary where, for reasons of extreme urgency brought about by events unforeseeable by the contracting authority, the time limits for the open or restricted procedures or competitive procedures with negotiation cannot be complied with. The extreme urgency must not be attributable to the contracting authority (reg 32(4)). This is a derogation that is likely to be relied on in the commissioning of healthcare services more than any other sector, for example to deal with a public health issue or where another provider suddenly fails.
d) *Regulation 32(9)–(12):* Where a contracting authority wants to purchase new services which are a repetition of similar services entrusted to the economic operator by way of an original contract, provided that the services are in conformity with a basic project for which the original contract was awarded which was advertised. The basic project must indicate the extent of the possible additional services and the conditions under which they will be awarded.

21.52 It is important to note that the derogations above are likely to be interpreted strictly by the Courts and there is no indication in either EU or domestic case law that a more lenient approach applies specifically to the healthcare sector.

Contract notices

21.53 Contracts awarded by the open procedure must be advertised by means of a 'contract notice'. This is an important document: failure to advertise the contract correctly could potentially result in a declaration of ineffectiveness being granted by the court.[23] Regulation 49 of the PC Regs 2015

23 See further below at para 21.119.

states that contract notices shall contain the information set out in part C of Annex 5 to the Public Procurement Directive and shall be sent for publication in accordance with reg 51. Regulation 51 requires contract notices to be sent to the EU Publications Office for advertisement in the Official Journal of the European Union (OJEU) (hence contract notices are often referred to as OJEU notices).

21.54 Part C of Annex 5 specifies 30 separate items of information that contract notices must contain, including a description of the nature and extent of works, or the nature and quantity or value of supplies, nature and extent of services, and the estimated total order of magnitude of contract(s).

21.55 In addition to the contract notice itself, reg 53 of the PC Regs 2015 requires contracting authorities to provide electronic access to the relevant procurement documents. This is a package of documents that contains a copy of the draft contractual terms. It is described in reg 53 as the following:

> 'procurement document' means any document produced or referred to by the contracting authority to describe or determine elements of the procurement or the procedure, including the contract notice, the prior information notice where it is used as a means of calling for competition, the technical specifications, the descriptive document, proposed conditions of contract, formats for the presentation of documents by candidates and tenderers, information on generally applicable obligations and any additional documents.

Prior Information Notices

21.56 Regulation 26(9) of the PC Regs 2015 states that where the contract is awarded by restricted procedure or competitive procedure with negotiation, sub-central contracting authorities may make the call for competition by means of a PIN in accordance with reg 48(5)–(7). This therefore allows greater flexibility in procurements carried out by NHS commissioners. As discussed below, under the LTR, a contract for healthcare services can be advertised using this method.

21.57 Pre-2015, a PIN was an optional notice giving general advance notice to the market of a contracting authority's intention to hold a procurement competition. It could in certain instances reduce the timescale for certain stages in the contract award procedure. Under the PC Regs 2015, the PIN can now be used as the call for competition itself. The PIN is required to contain the information specified in reg 48 of the PC Regs 2015 (which in turn refers to the information specified at section I of part B of Annex 5 to the Public Procurement Directive). A PIN can remain valid for 12 months (see reg 48(7)).

21.58 Changes are made to the rules about the publication of contract notices/PINs by the LTR. The rules are in reg 75 of the PC Regs 2015, which provides:

> (1) Contracting authorities intending to award a public contract for the services referred to in regulation 74[24] shall make known their intention by any of the following means–

24 Regulation 74 refers to 'Public contracts for social and other specific services listed in Schedule 3', which includes the Common Procurement Vocabulary (CPV) code for health and social care services.

(a) by means of a contract notice, which shall contain the information referred to in part H of Annex V to the Public Procurement Directive; or

(b) by means of a prior information notice, which shall–

(i) be published continuously,

(ii) contain the information set out in part I of Annex V to the Public Procurement Directive,

(iii) refer specifically to the types of services that will be the subject-matter of the contracts to be awarded, and

(iv) indicate that the contracts will be awarded without further publication and invite interested economic operators to express their interest in writing.

(2) Paragraph (1) shall not apply where a negotiated procedure without prior publication could have been used, in accordance with regulation 32, for the award of a public service contract.

(3) Contracting authorities that have awarded a public contract for the services referred to in regulation 74 shall make known the results of the procurement procedure by means of a contract award notice, which shall contain the information referred to in part J of Annex V to the Public Procurement Directive.

(4) Contracting authorities may group contract award notices on a quarterly basis, in which case they shall comply with paragraph (5) by sending the grouped notices within 30 days of the end of each quarter.

(5) Contracting authorities shall send the notices referred to in this regulation for publication in accordance with regulation 51.

21.59 The above rules apply for publication of any contract for NHS clinical services.

Material amendments to public contracts

21.60 A considerable body of ECJ case-law had developed prior to the 2014 Directive as to whether a material amendment to a contract would constitute a fresh contract award requiring re-advertisement which has now been codified in the Article 72 of the Directive. Regulation 72 of the PC Regs 2015 implements this and sets out a series of circumstances in which a contracting authority may make changes to a contract or framework agreement without triggering a fresh procurement.

21.61 Regulation 72 of the PC Regs 2015 applies to health services contracts which fall within the LTR and sets out the circumstances in which a contracting authority may make changes to a contract or framework agreement during its term, triggering a requirement to re-advertise and carry out a fresh procurement.[25] Those circumstances are set out in reg 72(1):

(a) where the modifications, irrespective of their monetary value, have been provided for in the initial procurement documents in clear, precise and unequivocal review clauses, which may include price revision clauses or options, provided that such clauses–

(i) state the scope and nature of possible modifications or options as well as the conditions under which they may be used, and

(ii) do not provide for modifications or options that would alter the overall nature of the contract or the framework agreement;

25 Whether similar material amendments require a fresh procurement competition under the PPCC2 Regs 2013 is more problematic as those Regulations are silent on this issue: see para 21.103 below.

(b) for additional works, services or supplies by the original contractor that have become necessary and were not included in the initial procurement, where a change of contractor–
   (i) cannot be made for economic or technical reasons such as requirements of interchangeability or interoperability with existing equipment, services or installations procured under the initial procurement, and
   (ii) would cause significant inconvenience or substantial duplication of costs for the contracting authority,
   provided that any increase in price does not exceed 50% of the value of the original contract;
(c) where all of the following conditions are fulfilled:–
   (i) the need for modification has been brought about by circumstances which a diligent contracting authority could not have foreseen;
   (ii) the modification does not alter the overall nature of the contract;
   (iii) any increase in price does not exceed 50% of the value of the original contract or framework agreement.
(d) where a new contractor replaces the one to which the contracting authority had initially awarded the contract as a consequence of–
   (i) an unequivocal review clause or option in conformity with sub-paragraph (a), or
   (ii) universal or partial succession into the position of the initial contractor, following corporate restructuring, including takeover, merger, acquisition or insolvency, of another economic operator that fulfils the criteria for qualitative selection initially established, provided that this does not entail other substantial modifications to the contract and is not aimed at circumventing the application of this Part;
(e) where the modifications, irrespective of their value, are not substantial within the meaning of paragraph (8); or
(f) where paragraph (5) applies.

Grounds for rejection of bids, exclusion of bidders and selection criteria

21.62 Before evaluating the bids themselves, contracting authorities can (and in certain instances should) reject tenders on certain grounds, including on the basis of the identity of the bidder. There are four main ways that this is permissible under the PC Regs 2015:

a) First, there is a duty to exclude firms on certain mandatory disqualification grounds.
b) Second, under the open and restricted procedures, a contracting authority has a discretion to reject tenders from certain economic operators on specified grounds set out in the Directive relating to those firms' suitability, including in particular their economic and financial standing, professional or technical ability, professional honesty, solvency and reliability.
c) Third, authorities can (and in certain instances should) exclude tenders that fail the mandatory requirements laid down in the procurement document.
d) Fourth, contracting authorities should exclude all bids that are abnormally low.

21.63 Regulation 57 sets out a number of mandatory grounds for exclusion of a tender from a particular bidder. These include where a bidder has been convicted of certain criminal offences, primarily bribery, corruption, terrorism and money laundering offences; and where a bidder has been held liable for breaching its tax or social security obligations by an administrative tribunal or a court.

21.64 Regulation 57(8) sets out the discretionary grounds on which a contracting authority may decide to reject a bid from a particular tenderer. The situations in which it can do so include where a company is bankrupt or in administration and persistent deficiencies in the performance of a prior contract.

21.65 Contracting authorities are also under a duty to investigate abnormally low tenders and have a discretion to reject tenders for which there is no satisfactory explanation for the low level of price offered (reg 69). However, there is no express duty to reject abnormally low tenders (in contrast to where there is non-compliance with certain social and environmental legislation).[26]

21.66 Regulation 58 enables contracting authorities to impose selection criteria for economic operators to participate in a procurement competition. These criteria may relate to a) the suitability to pursue a professional activity; b) economic and financial standing; and c) technical and professional ability.

Bid evaluation and application of award criteria

21.67 Following the submission of bids, in both the open and restricted procedures, the contracting authorities proceed directly to make their choices in accordance with objective evaluation criteria set out in the procurement documents.

21.68 Criteria can be set either on a pass/fail basis or a scored basis. In the case of the former, contracting authorities should be careful not to impose these criteria unless absolutely critical, given the lack of discretion to waive mandatory pass/fail criteria once bids have been submitted: in Case T-40/01 *Scan Office Design SA v European Commission*[27] the European Court made it clear that there is no discretion for the contracting authority to disregard such a failure. It said:

> However, even if the contracting authority has a certain margin of discretion in the context of a negotiated procedure, it is always bound to ensure observance of the terms and conditions of the tender specifications, which they have freely chosen to make mandatory.

21.69 The basic principle governing the award of a contract is that the contract must be awarded to the 'most economically advantageous tender': Article 67(2) of the Public Procurement Directive. Regulation 67 of the PC Regs 2015 reflects this. It clarifies that the most economically advantageous tender can be identified on the basis of price/cost and/or a price-quality ratio.

26 See *Arrowsmith*, fn 11 above, para 7-268 for a fuller discussion as to the uncertainty as to whether there is a duty to reject abnormally low tenders.

27 [2002] ECR II-5046.

(1) Contracting authorities shall base the award of public contracts on the most economically advantageous tender assessed from the point of view of the contracting authority.

(2) That tender shall be identified on the basis of the price or cost, using a cost-effectiveness approach, such as life-cycle costing in accordance with regulation 68, and may include the best price-quality ratio, which shall be assessed on the basis of criteria, such as qualitative, environmental and/or social aspects, linked to the subject-matter of the public contract in question.

21.70 It is expressly required by reg 67(9) of the PC Regs 2015 (and in any event is required to comply with the general principle of transparency) that contracting authorities disclose in the procurement documents the weightings to be given to the evaluation criteria.

21.71 It is a corollary of the requirement of transparency that award criteria must be clear, precise and unequivocal, so that a reasonably well informed and diligent tenderer can understand their exact significance and interpret them in the same way,[28] and, second, the contracting authority is able to ascertain whether the tenders submitted satisfy that criteria applying to the relevant contact: *Commission v the Netherlands*,[29] referred to by Coulson J in a succinct summary of the key principles in *Woods Building Services v Milton Keynes Council*.[30]

21.72 Problems can arise in the use of sub-criteria and their weightings. There is no obligation on a contracting authority to use sub-criteria. Nor, where a contracting authority does use sub-criteria, it seems is there any express requirement for weightings to be ascribed to those sub-criteria.[31] However, where an authority uses sub-criteria and weightings for those sub-criteria, even when there is no obligation to do so, both the sub-criteria and weightings ought to be disclosed when issuing the procurement documents: see the CJEU's judgment in *Emm.G.Lianakis v Dimos Alexandroupolis*.[32]

21.73 Further problems arise where contracting authorities seek to change the award criteria after bids have been received. While changes to criteria after bids have been opened is prohibited, subject to compliance with the principles of equal treatment and transparency, there is nothing to prevent changes prior to that stage. However, if the changes are material, a contracting authority may have to revert to an earlier stage in the process by allowing an opportunity for any other bidders to participate, if the changes are such that might lead a bidder to submit a bid in circumstances where previously it would not have wished to do so based on the published evaluation criteria.

21.74 The 2014 Public Procurement Directive sought to clarify some of the previous issues encountered with the 2004 Public Sector Directive regarding the use of performance criteria as award criteria (rather than as selection criteria deployed at the qualification stage). The CJEU in *Lianakis* had

28 What is often referred to as the RWIND test: see, for example, *EnergySolutions EU Ltd v Nuclear Decommissioning Authority (No 2)* [2016] EWHC 1988 (TCC) at [151].

29 [2013] All ER (EC) 804.

30 [2015] EWHC 2011 (TCC) at [5]–[12].

31 This is the view also taken in *Arrowsmith*, fn 11 above, para 7-208.

32 Case C-532/06, [2008] ECR I-251, at para 38. This was applied by the High Court in *Letting International v Newham LBC* [2008] EWHC 1583 (QB).

held that qualification and experience of staff were matters that could not be taken into account at the award stage (as opposed to the qualification stage). Article 67(2) of the 2014 Directive expressly provides that organisation, qualification and experience of staff can be relevant in applying award criteria.[33]

21.75 When applying award criteria, the CJEU has stated that the court should only interfere if there has been a serious and manifest error in the assessment. This was set out by Morgan J in *Lion Apparel Systems v Firebuy*[34] (and most recently applied in *EnergySolutions EU Limited v Nuclear Decommissioning Authority*[35]) in the following terms:

> In relation to matters of judgment or assessment, the authority does have a margin of appreciation, so that the court should only disturb the authority's decision where it has committed a manifest error. When referring to manifest error, the word manifest does not require any exaggerated description of obviousness. A case of manifest error is a case where an error has clearly been made (at [37]–[38]).

The contract award decision and the standstill period

21.76 Following the application of the criteria and selection of the winning bidder, in all four procedures the next stage is the contract award decision and the publication of a notice about the award. This is an important document, as its purpose is to explain to disappointed bidders the reasons why they were unsuccessful. It is also an important document as its service triggers what is known as the standstill period – ie a specified period in which the awarded contract cannot be entered into (ie signed). That in turn is significant because once a contract is entered into, the number of remedies open to an aggrieved bidder is limited. A contract award notice must contain the elements set out in reg 86 of the PC Regs 2015, which sets out the mandatory contents of such notices including the reasons that the successful bidder was appointed.

21.77 Although only limited amounts of information need to be provided, failure to include these mandatory elements could result in a contract being concluded in a breach of the standstill period, with serious consequences for the contracting parties since a breach of the standstill period can result in a declaration of ineffectiveness. This remedy, and the others available to aggrieved bidders, is discussed further at para 21.112 below.

The Light Touch Regime for health services contracts

21.78 The procurement of health, social and certain other services is regulated by the so-called LTR under Articles 74–76 of the Public Procurement Directive 2014, which are implemented into domestic law by regs 74–77 of

33 See *Arrowsmith*, fn 11 above, paras 7-191–7-194 for a discussion on the general relationship between qualification/selection and award criteria.

34 [2007] EWHC 2179 (Ch).

35 [2016] EWHC 1988 (TCC).

the PC Regs 2015. The Crown Commercial Service has published statutory guidance on the new LTR (last updated in October 2016) ('the CCS guidance').[36]

21.79 The LTR regulates the award of contracts with an estimated value in excess of the relevant financial threshold (€750,000). With effect from 1 January 2016, the sterling equivalent for the purposes of the threshold is £589,148. The main obligations that arise under the LTR are set out in the subsections below.

Discretion to advertise by either a contract notice or PIN

21.80 The key obligation under the LTR is the duty to advertise the intention to award the contract in question, but a discretion is afforded as to the means of advertisement. Regulation 75 requires contracting authorities intending to award a public contract subject to the LTR to advertise in the Supplement to the OJEU, either by means of a contract notice or a PIN as a call for competition. That discretion to choose the means by which advertising is to take place is one of the key differences between the LTR and the standard procurement procedures in the PC Regs 2015 (the existence of that discretion may affect the availability of the remedy of a declaration of ineffectiveness – this is discussed below).

21.81 By virtue of reg 105 of the PC Regs 2015 there is no duty to publish an advertisement on Contracts Finder for healthcare services (although such a duty nonetheless arises under reg 4(2) of the PPCC2 Regs 2013 in any event).

Principles for awarding contracts subject to the LTR

21.82 Regulation 76 of the PC Regs 2015 contains a measure of flexibility for NHS contractors to take wider considerations into account when making contract awards for services where the LTR applies. In particular, by virtue of reg 76(7) contracting authorities are not obliged to follow any of the standard procedures that apply to fully regulated procurement competitions (described above). However, whatever procedure adopted, contracting authorities must comply at a minimum with EU principles of transparency and equal treatment (reg 76(2)).[37]

21.83 Regulation 76 provides:

(1) Contracting authorities shall determine the procedures that are to be applied in connection with the award of contracts subject to this Section, and may take into account the specificities of the services in question.

(2) Those procedures shall be at least sufficient to ensure compliance with the principles of transparency and equal treatment of economic operators.

36 See www.gov.uk/government/uploads/system/uploads/attachment_data/file/560272/Guidance_on_Light_Touch_Regime_-_Oct_16.pdf.

37 As noted in the PLA Working Paper at para 29, there is considerable case-law on the EU principles of transparency and equal treatment and this case-law continues to apply to procurements which are subject to the LTR. Contracting authorities should continue to have regard to the Commission's interpretative communication on the Community law applicable to contract awards not or not fully subject to the provisions of the Public Procurement Directives.

(3) In particular, where, in accordance with regulation 75, a contract notice or prior information notice has been published in relation to a given procurement, the contracting authority shall, except in the circumstances mentioned in paragraph (4), conduct the procurement, and award any resulting contract, in conformity with the information contained in the notice about–
  (a) conditions for participation,
  (b) time limits for contacting the contracting authority, and
  (c) the award procedure to be applied.

(4) The contracting authority may, however, conduct the procurement, and award any resulting contract, in a way which is not in conformity with that information, but only if all the following conditions are met:–
  (a) the failure to conform does not, in the particular circumstances, amount to a breach of the principles of transparency and equal treatment of economic operators;
  (b) the contracting authority has, before proceeding in reliance on sub-paragraph (a)–
    (i) given due consideration to the matter,
    (ii) concluded that sub-paragraph (a) is applicable,
    (iii) documented that conclusion and the reasons for it in accordance with regulation 84(7) and (8), and
    (iv) informed the participants of the respects in which the contracting authority intends to proceed in a way which is not in conformity with the information contained in the notice.

(5) In paragraph (4)(b)(iv), 'participants' means any economic operators which have responded to the notice and have not been informed by the contracting authority that they are no longer under consideration for the award of a contract within the scope of the procurement concerned.

(6) All time limits imposed on economic operators for the purposes of this regulation, whether for responding to a contract notice or taking any other steps in the relevant procedure, shall be reasonable and proportionate.

(7) Without prejudice to the generality of paragraph (1), and subject to the other requirements of this Chapter, contracting authorities may apply procedures for the purposes of this regulation which correspond (with or without variations) to procedures, techniques or other features provided for in Chapter 2, as well as procedures which do not.

(8) In relation to the award of contracts subject to this Section, contracting authorities may take into account any relevant considerations, including–
  (a) the need to ensure quality, continuity, accessibility, affordability, availability and comprehensiveness of the services;
  (b) the specific needs of different categories of users, including disadvantaged and vulnerable groups;
  (c) the involvement and empowerment of users; and
  (d) innovation.

21.84 There is no reported case-law on the workings of the LTR. The CCS guidance is short on specific examples as to how an NHS commissioner could use the 'flexibilities' set out at reg 76(4) to run a lawful procurement process which nonetheless departs from the rules of the competition originally set out in the contract notice or PIN provided it has not breached the principles of transparency and/or equal treatment.

21.85 Regulation 76 appears to require NHS commissioners to design a procurement process which complies with the principles of transparency and equal treatment, but then permits the NHS commissioner to award the contract in a way that departs from its own advertised process if it is considered appropriate to do so having regard to the factors set out in reg 76(8), namely:

a) the need to ensure quality, continuity, accessibility, affordability, availability and comprehensiveness of the services;
b) the specific needs of different categories of users, including disadvantaged and vulnerable groups;
c) the involvement and empowerment of users; and
d) innovation.

21.86 Before changing the rules of the competition, the NHS commissioner has to have given due consideration to the fact that the rules are being changed, decided that the NHS commissioner will still comply with the principles of transparency and equal treatment despite a change in the rules, documented that decision and informed the bidders and anyone else who responded to a contract notice that the rules are being changed.

21.87 While this process provides a theoretical opportunity for NHS commissioners to make adaptions to the contract award procedures after the publication of the initial procurement process, it is far from straightforward and opens up an NHS commissioner to the possibility of a challenge. Accordingly, any NHS commissioner who was considering using these 'flexibilities' would be well advised to get expert legal assistance to guide the NHS commissioner through the amended process.

Standstill obligations under the LTR

21.88 Regulation 86(5) of the PC Regs 2015 exempts contracting authorities from the 'standard' standstill obligation (that applies to fully regulated procurements by virtue of reg 86 (and described above)) where the contract can be awarded without prior publication of a contract notice. Some commentators consider that since LTR contracts can be advertised by a PIN rather than a contract notice, there is no obligation to adhere to a standstill period. The CCS guidance holds that view and states that a standstill period may not strictly be required. The CCS guidance states that:

> The legal position is less clear under the new rules for the Light-Touch Regime (LTR). A standstill period may not strictly be required ... But in the light of uncertainty, CCS suggests that contracting authorities will usually wish to send a standstill notice and observe the standstill period.

21.89 However, the general view of procurement practitioners (which the author of this chapter shares) is that contracting authorities are nonetheless best advised to stand still before awarding contracts under the LTR and would expose themselves to a considerable risk of ineffectiveness claims and other legal challenges if they fail to do so.[38]

38 The Procurement Law Association Working Paper at para 2.16 notes that ECJ case-law in the *Alcatel* and *Commission v Austria* decisions which required a standstill period was based on provisions of the Remedies Directive (89/665/EEC), which clearly apply to LTR procurements.

The PPCC2 Regs 2013 – scope and key duties

Introduction

21.90 As set out above, the LTR in the PC Regs 2015 applies to health services contracts above €750,000. An additional set of regulations also apply to the procurement of all healthcare services for the purposes of the NHS,[39] regardless of value: the PPCC2 Regs 2013. These apply to all 'relevant bodies' which are defined in reg 1 as CCGs and the National Health Service Commissioning Board (ie NHS England).

21.91 The PPCC2 Regs 2013 govern the 'procuring' of healthcare services for the purposes of the NHS. Procuring services from an NHS Trust is certainly caught by the regulations.[40] However, 'procuring' is not defined in the regulations, and no express provision is made for 'in-house' procurement. The extent to which it captures 'in-house' commissioning by CCGs (that would otherwise be permissible under the PC Regs 2015 under the *Teckal*/in-house exemption discussed above) is therefore unclear. In practice, this is only likely to be an issue were CCGs to make extensive use of their circumscribed powers under section 223 of the HSCA 2012 to form companies, and that does not seem to be the case to date.

The procurement objectives

21.92 Regulation 2 of the PPCC2 Regs 2013 sets out the objectives of an NHS procurement process. It states that:

> When procuring health care services for the purposes of the NHS (including taking a decision referred to in Regulation 7(2), a relevant body must act with a view to–
> (a) Securing the needs of the people who use the services,
> (b) Improving the quality of the services, and
> (c) Improving efficiency in the provision of the services,
> Including through the services being provided in an integrated way (including with other health care services, health-related services, or social care services).

21.93 Regulation 3 of the PPCC2 Regs 2013 sets out further duties. Regulation 3(2) of the PPCC2 Regs 2013 requires the relevant body to act in a transparent and proportionate way, and to 'treat providers equally and in a non-discriminatory way, including by not treating a provider, or type of provider, more favourably than any other provider, in particular on the basis of ownership'. These principles are (at least on the face of it) the same as the general duties that apply under EU law to any contracting authority.

21.94 However, subsection (3) adds a new duty regarding the selection of a provider that goes beyond the duty to select the most economically

39 This includes NHS Contracts under section 9 of the NHS Act 2006.

40 This is arguably one of the biggest changes from the situation prior to the 2012 NHS reforms, when all intra-NHS procurement may have fallen within the *Teckal* exemption. For a more detailed discussion of this see the Procurement Law Association Working Paper at section 4.

advantageous tender under the PC Regs 2015. Regulation 3(3) of the PPCC2 Regs 2013 states that:

> The relevant body must procure the services from one or more providers that–
> (1) Are the most capable of delivering the objective referred to in regulation 2 in relation to the services, and
> (2) Provide best value for money in doing so.

21.95 Regulation 3(4) of the PPCC2 Regs 2013 refers back to the procurement objective in reg 2 to improve the quality of the services and efficiency in their provision. It states:

> (4) In acting with a view to improving quality and efficiency in the provision of the services the relevant body must consider appropriate means of making such improvements, including through–
> (a) the services being provided in a more integrated way (including with other health care services, health-related services, or social care services),
> (b) enabling providers to compete to provide the services, and
> (c) allowing patients a choice of provider of the services.

The need to conduct a procurement competition via a contract notice

21.96 The position is clear that for any procurements for healthcare services over €750,000, a full, OJEU-advertised competition for health services has to be carried out under the PC Regs 2015.[41] It is therefore moot as to whether under the PPCC2 Regs 2013 a competition has to be carried out for those types of procurements.

21.97 However, the position is less clear for those contracts which fall below that PC Regs 2015 threshold but are nonetheless caught by the PPCC2 Regs 2013. This is because there is no express requirement in the PPCC2 Regs 2013 for a competition to be carried out in all circumstances. Regulation 5 of the PPCC2 Regs 2013 introduces the confusion, because at least on its face it provides that the only situation in which a commissioner is entitled to dispense with a competition is where the services is capable of being delivered by just one provider. It states:

> (1) A relevant body may award a new contract for the provision of health care services for the purposes of the NHS to a single provider without advertising an intention to seek offers from providers in relation to that contract where the relevant body is satisfied that the services to which the contract relates are capable of being provided only by that provider.

21.98 The position of the government and of Monitor is that there is no absolute requirement to carry out a competition.

21.99 Monitor's guidance accompanying the PPCC2 Regs 2013 expressly refers to the absence of any requirement on NHS commissioners to run a competition, with the emphasis instead being repeatedly placed on the requirement to commission services in a manner which represents the

41 Whether via a PIN or contract notice: see above at para 21.80 regarding the discretionary advertisement options under the PCR for LTR contracts.

best interests of patients (as set out in reg 2 of the PPCC2 Regs 2013).[42] Monitor also refers to the fact that it has no power under the regulations to force the running of any competition. It also suggests that the decision as to whether or not to publish a contract notice is a matter for commissioners having regard to the various objectives set out in reg 3. It suggests there at least three circumstances in which it would be appropriate to procure without running a competition (in contrast to the single exception referred to in reg 5):

- Where there is only one provider that is capable of providing the services in question. In these circumstances, the Procurement, Patient Choice and Competition Regulations make it clear that a commissioner can award a contract to a single provider without publishing a contract notice.
- Where a commissioner carries out a detailed review of the provision of particular services in its local area in order to understand how those services can be improved and, as part of that review, identifies the most capable provider or providers of those services.
- Where the benefits of publishing a contract notice would be outweighed by the costs of doing so.

21.100 The government has hitherto shared this interpretation of reg 5. In response to a published opinion by one of the authors of this book on the (then draft) 2013 regulations the government stated that 'the regulations do not impose compulsory competitive tendering requirements on commissioners and expressly preclude Monitor from directing a commissioner to hold a competitive tender'.[43] Its view was that the 2013 regulations were not intended to change the position under the antecedents to the PPCC2 Regs 2013, the procurement guidance entitled *Principles and rules for cooperation and competition* (PRCC). This view also manifested itself again in the explanatory note to the PPCC2 Regs 2013 which was issued by the Department of Health.[44] The difficulty with this position is that the PRCC contained no provision similar to reg 5.

21.101 It remains arguable that reg 5 should be read as specifying the only circumstance where a competition is not required.[45] This is consistent with reg 4 of the PPCC2 Regs 2013 which requires relevant bodies to

42 Monitor's *Substantive guidance on the Procurement, Patient Choice and Competition Regulations* (September 2013), p38. The persuasive force of that Guidance has not been determined by the Courts. However, some commentators suggest that it would be afforded significant weight by the Court (by analogy with the approach the court took in *R (QSRC) v NHS Commissioning Board and another* [2015] EWHC 3752 (Admin)). See the Procurement Law Association's Working Paper on NHS Procurement p24 for a fuller discussion of this particular issue.

43 The two opinions by David Lock QC and the single opinion of Ligia Osepciu were provided to the campaign group 38 degrees and are publicly available, as is the government response dated March 2013.

44 'In Regulation 5, we have removed the words that inadvertently created the impression that there were only very narrow circumstances in which commissioners could award a contract without competition. Monitor's guidance on the Regulations will make clear that we are continuing the same approach as now under the Principles and Rules for Co-operation and Competition.'

45 There is a very useful and detailed analysis of both views by the Procurement Law Association in section 3 of its Working Paper.

publish contract notices on the NHS procurement website.[46] It states 'where advertising an intention to seek offers from providers in relation to a new contract for the provision of healthcare services for the purposes of the NHS, a relevant body must publish a contract notice on the website maintained by the Board under paragraph (1)'. Such a reading is also consistent with the general position under EU procurement law, whose principles manifest themselves in (even if not directly incorporated by) reg 3(2) of the PPCC2 Regs 2013.[47]

21.102 Whatever the correct legal position (which has yet to be considered by the courts), the course of action which contains the least risk seems to be for a CCG or NHS England, when carrying out procurements for health services contracts, to publish a contract notice on both the NHS website and, where the services are above the LTR threshold set out in the PC Regs 2015, in the OJEU (via the European Commission Publishing Agency).

Modification of health services contracts during their term

21.103 The question as to whether amendments to contracts not caught by the LTR regime are permissible absent a fresh procurement competition is unclear. The PPCC2 Regs 2013 make no reference to the circumstances in reg 72 of the PC Regs 2015, under which material amendments are permissible under that regime. Regulation 5(2) of the PPCC2 Regs 2013 states that:

> (2) For the purposes of paragraph (1), a relevant body is not to be treated as having awarded a new contract–
> (a) where the rights and liabilities under a contract have been transferred to the relevant body from the Secretary of State, a Strategic Health Authority or a Primary Care Trust; or
> (b) where there is a change in the terms and conditions of a contract as a result of–
> (i) a change in the terms and conditions drafted by the Board under regulation 17 of the 2012 Regulations (terms and conditions to be drafted by the Board for inclusion in commissioning contracts), or
> (ii) new terms and conditions drafted by the Board under that regulation.

Criteria to determine any qualified provider lists

21.104 Further complexities arise in the case of competitions for inclusion on any qualified provider (AQP) lists. Chapter 10 on acute care contracting explains that any provider holding an NHS Standard Contract is required to accept a clinically appropriate referral from any NHS commissioner, even if that provider does not have a contract with that commissioner. Accordingly, any provider which holds an NHS Standard Contract is entitled to treat NHS patients and to be paid for treating such patients, without setting up a network of contracts with different NHS commissioners.

46 See www.supplying2nhs.org/.

47 See the Procurement Law Association Working Paper for a fuller analysis as to the significance of the use of EU terminology in the domestic PPCC2 Regs 2013.

21.105 Regulation 7 of the PPCC2 Regs 2013 sets up rules for the application of transparent, proportionate and non-discriminatory criteria to determine which providers should qualify to be included on a list from which a patient is offered a choice of provider. There is a key distinction drawn in reg 7(2) between lists of providers in respect of first outpatient appointments with a consultant (or member of a consultant's team), and other providers. Under this regulation, in respect of the former type of list, a relevant body has to include a provider on a list if that provider meets the criteria established by the relevant body. In respect of other lists, reg 7(4) appears to afford a discretion not to include a provider where that would mean exceeding a limit set by the relevant body on the number of providers to be included on the list. A similar discretion applies when determining which providers to enter a framework agreement with and selecting providers to bid for potential future contracts to provide healthcare services for the purposes of the NHS (reg 7(5) and (6)).

21.106 Regulation 7 is arguably inconsistent with the operation of reg 39 of the National Health Service Commissioning Board and Clinical Commissioning Groups (Responsibilities and Standing Rules) Regulations 2012[48] insofar as it suggests that NHS commissioners have the right to limit the types of provider to which an NHS patient can be referred for a first outpatient appointment. There is no such limitation in reg 39. Accordingly, pursuant to that regulation, the choice of 'clinically appropriate health service provider' is a matter for the referring GP and not an NHS commissioner. The only criteria is that the provider must have a commissioning contract with an NHS commissioner (although this does not have to be an NHS Standard Contract). The inconsistency between the two sets of regulations has yet to be considered by the courts.

Anti-competitive behaviour

21.107 Various other more minor duties are also imposed by the rest of the regulations, including in relation to the maintenance of a record of contracts awarded (reg 3(5) and reg 9). However, a more significant duty appears at reg 10, which provides:

> (1) When commissioning health care services for the purposes of the NHS, a relevant body must not engage in anti-competitive behaviour, unless to do so is in the interests of people who use health care services for the purposes of the NHS which may include–
> (a) by the services being provided in an integrated way (including with other health care services, health-related services, or social care services); or
> (b) by co-operation between the persons who provide the services in order to improve the quality of the services.
>
> (2) An arrangement for the provision of health care services for the purposes of the NHS must not include any term or condition restricting competition which is not necessary for the attainment of–
> (a) intended outcomes which are beneficial for people who use such services; or
> (b) the objective referred to in regulation 2.

48 SI No 2996.

21.108 The purpose of this regulation appears to be to permit an NHS commissioner to engage in contracting behaviour which, objectively considered, is 'anti-competitive' if the behaviour is focussed on providing health and social care services in a joined up way or in promoting co-operation between people who provide health and/or social care services in order to improve the quality of the services.

21.109 Anti-competitive was defined in section 64(2) of the HSCA 2012 as follows: 'anti-competitive behaviour' means behaviour which would (or would be likely to prevent, restrict or distort competition'. Section 62(3) of the HSCA 2012 provides that 'Monitor must exercise its functions with a view to preventing anti-competitive behaviour in the provision of healthcare services for the purposes of the NHS which is against the interests of people who use such services'. The extent to which the permissive approach to anti-competitive behaviour as set out in reg 10 is intra vires the HSCA 2012 has not been tested in the courts.

Patient choice

21.110 Regulation 11 of the PPCC2 Regs 2013 requires the Board not to restrict the ability of a person to apply for inclusion in the list of patients of a practice providing primary medical services, or to express a preference to receive such services from a particular medical practitioner or class of medical practitioner.

21.111 Regulation 12 of the PPCC2 Regs 2013 places a requirement on relevant bodies to offer a choice of alternative provider in accordance with reg 48(4) of the National Health Service Commissioning Board and Clinical Commissioning Groups (Responsibilities and Standing Rules) Regulations 2012, in the circumstances laid down in reg 47 of the 2012 regulations. These rules apply where NHS patients have not been treated during the maximum waiting times prescribed under Part 9 of those regulations. Such patients have a right to choose an alternative provider who will be able to provide them with treatment within a reasonable time.

Remedies and challenging an NHS procurement decision

21.112 This section is divided into three main parts. It first considers the main substantive remedies under the PC Regs 2015 and the PPCC2 Regs 2013 respectively (in particular declarations of ineffectiveness, damages and complaints to Monitor). It then considers the automatic suspension (in itself a type of remedy) and gives an outline of the main principles that the courts apply when asked to lift such a suspension.

Remedies under the PC Regs 2015

21.113 The remedies available under the PC Regs 2015 differ, depending on whether or not the contract has been entered into. The remedies outlined below only apply to above threshold procurements. Unless there is a sufficient cross-border interest, there are no remedies for below threshold procurements.[49]

21.114 If the contract has not been entered into, reg 97(2) of the PC Regs 2015 states that the court may:

(a) order the setting aside of the decision or action concerned;
(b) order the contracting authority to amend any document;
(c) award damages to an economic operator which has suffered loss or damage as a consequence of the breach.

21.115 Where a contract has already been entered into, pursuant to reg 98(2) the court:

(a) must, if it is satisfied that any of the grounds for ineffectiveness applies, make a declaration of ineffectiveness in respect of the contract unless regulation 100 requires the Court not to do so;
(b) must, where required by regulation 102, impose penalties in accordance with that regulation;
(c) may award damages to an economic operator which has suffered loss or damage as a consequence of the breach, regardless of whether the Court also acts as described in subparagraphs (a) and (b);
(d) must not order any other remedies.

21.116 The remedy of damages is a significant tool for an aggrieved bidder and one that can present a serious risk to contracting authorities. The Supreme Court has confirmed for an award of damages to be met, the breach has to be sufficiently serious and there must be a direct causal link between the breach of the obligation and the damage sustained by the injured party:[50] *Nuclear Decommissioning Authority v Energysolutions EU Ltd* (now called ATK Energy EU Ltd).[51]

21.117 The penalties that can accompany a declaration of ineffectiveness are set out at reg 102, which provides that where a court makes a declaration of ineffectiveness, the court must also order that the contracting authority pay a civil financial penalty of the amount specified in the order.

21.118 Where it does not make a declaration of ineffectiveness in the exercise of its discretion, or where there has been a breach of the standstill period or contract advertising requirements but no declaration has been sought, the court is under a duty to order at least one, and may order both, of the following penalties: a) that the duration of the contract be shortened to the extent specified in the order; b) that the contracting authority pay a civil financial penalty of the amount specified in the order (reg 102(2) and (3)). When the court is considering what order to make under para (1) or (3),

49 See *Mansfield DC v Secretary of State for Communities and Local Government* [2014] EWHC 2617 for the approach the court takes in the event of a failure to consider whether there is a potential cross-border interest for below threshold procurements and whether that amounts to a breach of general TFEU principles. A challenge based on such principles would in principle be actionable by way of judicial review, Article 358 infraction proceedings and/or possibly a tortious claim for breach of statutory duty under the European Communities Act 1978, with a six-year limitation period: see *A G Quidnet Hounslow LLP v Hounslow LBC* [2012] EWHC 2639 (TCC).

50 Ie the so-called *Francovich* conditions deriving from the European Court of Justice's decisions in *Francovich v Italian Republic* (Joined Cases C-6/90 and C-9/90) [1991] ECR I-5357.

51 [2017] UKSC 34 at [39].

the overriding consideration is that the 'penalties must be effective, proportionate and dissuasive'.

21.119 The grounds of ineffectiveness are set out in reg 99, and in summary are as follows:

a) where there has been a failure to advertise the contract via a contract notice (unless a voluntary transparency notice has been served);
b) a breach of the standstill period or an automatic suspension; or
c) in the case of a framework agreement, a failure to carry out any call-off competition in accordance with the terms of the framework agreement.

21.120 It is important to note that it is arguable that the remedy of a declaration of ineffectiveness is unlikely to apply to procurements for healthcare services, because by virtue of falling with the LTR there is no obligation to advertise the contract via a contract notice (there is a choice as to whether to do so or via a PIN). Nor is there an obligation to adhere to a standstill period. Nonetheless, the CCS guidance on the LTR and the standstill period suggests that it is advisable for standstills to be run. Failure to carry out such a standstill would give rise to potential breaches of equal treatment and transparency, and any decision not to do would have to be carefully reasoned and documented.

Remedies under the PPCC2 Regs 2013

21.121 Unlike the PC Regs 2015 which can only be enforced by the court, Monitor (now NHS Improvement) is also given enforcement powers under the PPCC2 Regs 2013. In addition to its investigative powers under reg 13, Monitor has the power to declare an arrangement for the provision of heath care services for the purposes of the NHS ineffective, where it is satisfied that a breach of the primary duties outlined above has occurred.[52] It also has to be satisfied that the breach is 'sufficiently serious' (reg 14(2)). Monitor also has powers to direct a relevant body to put in place measures in order to prevent failures to comply with the regulations and to mitigate the effect of such failures. It also a power to vary or withdraw an invitation to tender for the provision of healthcare services (reg 15(1)).

21.122 The second part of the 2013 guidance issued by Monitor pursuant to section 78 of the HSCA 2012 deals with its approach to enforcement. The guidance states that Monitor expects to follow the interpretation of the regulations set out in the guidance when exercising its enforcement powers under the regulations (although acknowledging that the regulations and the HSCA 2012 ultimately are the statement of law and not the guidance).

Investigations by Monitor

21.123 According to its website, Monitor to date has only commenced five investigations into complaints alleging a breach of the PPCC2 Regs 2013. The timetables issued by Monitor suggest generally an anticipated timeframe of less than 18 months to publish decisions following complaints, although

52 Specifically, regs 2, 3(1)–(4), 4(2) and (3), 5–8 or 10(1).

as the guidance notes there is no specified timeframe for investigations into complaints to be concluded. Of the five investigations commenced, two were closed without any formal findings, one held that there were no breach of the regulations, and two of the investigations were concluded upon the acceptance of undertakings from the commissioners concerned. Therefore there is no example yet of Monitor having to make any declaration of ineffectiveness.

Parallel proceedings

21.124 Part of the reason why Monitor has commenced relatively few investigations may be the reluctance of those outside the NHS to trust one NHS body to adjudicate (and possibly award damages against) another NHS body. Section 76(7) of the HSCA 2012 provides:

> A failure to comply with a requirement imposed by regulations under section 75 which causes loss or damage is actionable, except in so far as the regulations restrict the right to bring such an action.

21.125 Regulation 17 of the PPCC2 Regs 2013 provides that a person who brings an action under the PCR for loss or damage cannot bring a parallel legal action under section 76(7) of the HSCA 2012. However, there are no other restrictions in the PPCC2 Regs 2013 which limit the right of claimants to sue NHS commissioners for breaches of the duties set out in the PPCC2 Regs 2013. Accordingly, a bidder who is wrongly denied a contract to which the PPCC2 Regs 2013 applies has the right to sue the NHS commissioner for damages in the High Court. A bidder would also have the right to bring a challenge by way of judicial review for a breach of the PC Regs 2015. It is doubtful that a complaint to Monitor is a sufficient alternative remedy which would preclude a High Court entertaining a claim for judicial review, not least given the discretion by Monitor as to which investigations it considers appropriate to investigate and indeed the time taken for such investigations to conclude.

Lifting an automatic suspension

21.126 Where a contract has not yet been entered into, the issue of a claim form has the effect of automatically suspending the power of the contracting authority to enter into that contract. In such instances, if the contracting authority wishes to proceed to conclude the contract, it has to apply to lift the suspension.

21.127 When considering whether or not to lift the suspension, the court applies the *American Cyanamid*[53] tests that apply to standard interim injunctions, namely:

a) Is there a serious issue to be tried?
b) If there is, are damages nonetheless an adequate remedy?
c) If damages are not an adequate remedy, where does the balance of convenience lie?

53 [1975] UKHL 1.

21.128 The application of those tests is very fact dependent. However, the cases to date suggest that where the contract in issue is designed to improve patient services and would save an NHS body a considerable amount in financial terms, in practice it will be hard to argue successfully that an automatic suspension should continue. This is because the court, when assessing where the public interest lies, is likely to take into account and attach significant weight to 'the public interest in the NHS providing the best possible service to the public without disruption and with minimal risk to its patients' (per Coulson J in *Sysmex (UK) Ltd v Imperial College Healthcare NHS Trust*[54]).

21.129 Some detailed observations as to how the High Court has applied the three tests generally and in an NHS context are considered below.

Serious issue to be tried

21.130 In considering the first of three tests set out above, once it is accepted that there is a serious issue to be tried then (save in exceptional circumstances where one side has some kind of simple 'knock-out point') it is not appropriate as a matter of principle to invite the court to conduct a mini-trial or to ask the court to endeavour to reach any conclusions as to the strength or weakness of one or both sides' case: *Sysmex (UK) Limited v Imperial College Healthcare NHS Trust*,[55] applying *Kent Community Health NHS Foundation Trust v NHS Swale Clinical Commissioning Group and another*.[56]

Adequacy of damages

21.131 When considering whether damages are an adequate remedy, the following two general principles identified in *Covanta Energy Ltd v Merseyside Waste Disposal Authority*[57] apply:

a) if damages are an adequate remedy, that will normally be sufficient to defeat an application for an interim injunction, but that will not always be so;
b) the simple concept of the adequacy of damages has been modified at least to a certain extent, so that the court must assess whether it is just, in all the circumstances, that the claimant be confined to his remedy in damages.

21.132 Again, the outcome of the application of this test is highly fact dependent. For example, the loss of a particularly prestigious contract or the potential for damage to the unsuccessful tenderer's reputation has in certain cases been identified by the courts as being incapable of compensation in damages (see, for example, *NATS (Services) Ltd v Gatwick Airport Ltd and another*[58]). The assessment of the risk of damage to reputation is a particularly fact sensitive

54 [2017] EWHC 1824 (TCC) at [98]. However, where an NHS Trust is the incumbent provider, a different approach may well be taken; see *Lancashire Care NHS Foundation Trust v Lancashire CC* [2018] EWHC 200 (TCC).

55 [2017] EWHC 1824 (TCC) at [21]. Sysmex (UK) Limited was challenging the award of a managed services contract in respect of pathology services, and was ultimately unsuccessful in arguing that the automatic suspension should be continued.

56 [2016] EWHC 1393 (TCC).

57 [2013] EWHC 2922 (TCC).

58 [2014] EWHC 3133 (TCC) at [72].

question and depends on the strength of the evidence adduced to establish that risk. Further complexity has been introduced with the test of 'sufficiently serious breach' by the Supreme Court. [59]

21.133 Some NHS bodies who have brought proceedings as the claimants in a procurement challenge have sought to argue that the mere fact that the NHS body is a not-for-profit organisation or is a public body which exists solely to provide patient services means that damages would be an inadequate remedy. This argument was dismissed by the High Court in the *Kent Community* case referred to above. The court rejected the submission that damages should be regarded as an inadequate remedy simply because the claimant, whether as a not-for-profit organisation or for other reasons, has not suffered and will not suffer substantial financial loss.[60] The court also observed that the mere fact that the claimant was a public body that exists for the sole purpose of providing NHS healthcare services to its patients in itself was not determinative of the question, as to hold otherwise would undermine the purpose of the procurement and commissioning regime within the NHS, namely to allow procurement of services from private bodies. The court said:

> As the organisational structures of the NHS and the existence of the regime which permits procurement of services from other types of body or organisation makes clear, this cannot and does not give the Trust a monopoly or the right to primacy or priority in the context of NHS procurement. Nor does it determine whether or not damages would be an adequate remedy.[61]

Balance of convenience and the public interest

21.134 The public interest in the lawful conduct of public procurement competitions has been acknowledged by the courts as a relevant factor when considering the third test (the balance of convenience). However, a counterbalance to that public interest is the delay before a case reaches trial, where, for example, upholding an automatic suspension would prevent the efficient and timely introduction of arrangements which CCGs consider to be in the best interest of people within the CCGs' area: *Kent Community Health NHS Foundation Trust v NHS Swale Clinical Commissioning Group and another*.[62] Where a challenge is brought by an NHS body against a procurement decision taken by a CCG, and both parties take diametrically different views on what is in the public interest, the court is unlikely to take public interest arguments into account as a significant weight on one side or another.[63]

21.135 The impact of continuing the suspension on the quality of care is a highly material factor in assessing where the balance of convenience lies, and in practice will mean that in most cases where the purpose of the

59 See para 21.116 above. This issue was raised (but not answered) by the High Court in *Lancashire Care NHS Foundation Trust v Lancashire CC* [2018] EWHC 200 (TCC).

60 At [17].

61 At [19(i)].

62 [2016] EWHC 1393 (TCC) at [26].

63 [2016] EWHC 1393 (TCC) at [26]. Although see the ground taken in the *Lancashire Care* case referred to at para 21.132.

contract being tendered is to improve health services, it is likely that an automatic suspension will be lifted. The court in *Sysmex* said:

> ... where there is credible evidence that patient care will suffer if the suspension is not lifted, it will usually be the case that the least risk of injustice will favour the lifting of the suspension.[64]

21.136 It also held that the costs savings that could be made, if those can be shown to have an effect on a trust's ability to meet its financial targets (and therefore risk an NHS intervention in the trust), also are a material factor.

Time limits to bring an NHS procurement challenge

21.137 Different considerations apply depending on whether or not what is pursued is a claim for a breach of the PC Regs 2015 (normally heard in the Technology and Construction Court), and/or a claim for breach of the PPCC2 Regs 2013, or a claim by way of judicial review (heard in the Administrative Court).

21.138 Situations can arise where a challenge is brought both to a commissioning decision under the HSCA 2012 and a procurement decision under the PC Regs 2015. In such instances, a claim for judicial review may well be the most appropriate mechanism to bring such a challenge. However, in such instances, care must be taken to ensure that the much shorter time periods for filing such a claim (compared to the standard deadline for filing a judicial review) set out in the specific rule under CPR 54.5(6) are observed.[65]

21.139 In certain cases, a claim can also be brought by a person who is not an economic operator as a third party by way of judicial review against procurement decisions. The circumstances in which they would have standing are limited, but in an NHS context such challenges may be easier to bring particular if a breach of the PPCC2 Regs 2013 is alleged.[66]

Breach of the PC Regs 2015

21.140 A breach of the obligations under the PC Regs 2015 by virtue of reg 91 is actionable by any economic operator which, in consequence, suffers, or risks suffering, loss or damage.

21.141 Proceedings have to be commenced in the High Court (reg 92). The Technology and Construction Court hears claims brought under the PC Regs 2015 (although not necessarily judicial reviews in which procurement issues form some or all of the grounds of claim, which should still be filed in the Administrative Court).

21.142 Strict time limits apply, which in turn depend on the remedy sought and grounds alleged:

64 At [72].

65 This is discussed further at para 21.145 below.

66 The High Court considered the standing of third parties to bring procurement challenges in *R (Wylde and others) v Waverley BC* [2017] EWHC 466 (Admin).

a) *Where a declaration of ineffectiveness is not sought.* Pursuant to reg 92 of the PC Regs 2015, proceedings must be started within 'within 30 days beginning with the date when the economic operator first knew or ought to have known that grounds for starting the proceedings had arisen'. The court has a discretion to extend time up to a maximum of three months. If, having filed a claim, a claimant identifies fresh grounds of challenge, the court can allow an extension of time to amend a pre-existing claim, although the better and safer course of action would be to file a fresh claim within 30 days and have them consolidated: see, for instance, the approach the court took in *Perinatal Institute v Healthcare Quality Improvement Partnership.*[67] The court noted in that case that the regulations do not in terms impose a particularly onerous test to grant an extension of time and that the test was framed in terms of 'good reason' not exceptional circumstances.

b) *Where a declaration of ineffectiveness is sought.* A claim must be filed within 30 days of the contract award notice or notification that a contract has been concluded, or, in cases where no such notice or notification has been made, within six months.

21.143 Particular care needs to be taken in respect of potential breaches of PC Regs 2015 identified by a claimant during a public procurement competition. If there is a challenge to the legality of the tender documents, then the challenger must commence proceedings within 30 days of the issue of those documents. The challenger's cause of action accrues when the defective tender documentation is published, not when a contract is awarded on the basis of that unlawful documentation: see *Jobsin Co UK plc v Department of Health.*[68] The safest course of action if grounds for claim have been identified in the course of a competition would be to file proceedings before any contract award decision has been made, seeking either expedition of the hearing or a stay of the proceedings until after the contract award decision. The High Court in *Joseph Gleave and Son Limited v Secretary of State of Defence*[69] confirmed that there is no presumption of an expedited trial if a claim is made during a competition (rather than after the contract award decision).

Breach of the PPCC2 Regs 2013

21.144 There is no time limit specified in the PPCC2 Regs 2013 to make a complaint to Monitor or to commence an action for damages in the High Court. Damages could be claimed for breach of a statutory duty and the primary time limit of six years in section 9 of the Limitation Act 1980 appears to apply to such a claim. A claim for judicial review is also possible, for instance seeking a declaration or to quash a decision to award a contract.

21.145 The usual rule under CPR Part 54 is that such a claim must be brought promptly and in any event within three months. However, care must be

67 [2017] EWHC 1867 (TCC).

68 [2001] EWCA Civ 1241.

69 [2017] EWHC 238 (TCC).

taken to ascertain whether or not the decision is also 'governed by' the PC Regs 2015, because if so a much shorter time period (potentially as short as 30 days) may apply. This is because CPR 54.5(6) imposes a similar deadline to a claim brought for a breach PCR. That rule states that:

> . . . where the application for judicial review relates to a decision governed by the Public Contracts Regulations 2015, the claim form must be filed within the time within which an economic operator would have been required by regulation 92(2) of those Regulations (and disregarding the rest of that regulation) to start any proceedings under those Regulations in respect of that decision.

21.146 Regulation 92(2) specifies a 30-day time limit. The test is whether the decision is 'governed by' the PC Regs 2015, not whether the grounds alleged are for a breach of those regulations. Nor is it sufficient to show that the decision may be affected by the PC Regs 2015: see *R (QSRC Ltd) v NHS Commissioning Board (NHS England)*[70] (in this particular case the court held that the decision was not governed by the PC Regs 2015).[71]

70 [2015] EWHC 3752 (Admin).
71 At [115].

Index